A HISTORY OF WORLD CIVILIZATIONS

A HISTORY OF WORLD CIVILIZATIONS

General Editor

EDWARD R. TANNENBAUM

Contributing Authors

GUILFORD A. DUDLEY
JOHN E. FAGG
C. WARREN HOLLISTER
CARTER JEFFERSON
THOMAS R. METCALF
EDWARD R. TANNENBAUM
ROBERT L. TIGNOR
IRWIN UNGER
FREDERIC WAKEMAN, Jr.

JOHN WILEY & SONS, Inc.
New York · London · Sydney · Toronto

Cover: Terence Spencer/Black Star

Library of Congress Cataloging in Publication Data
Main entry under title:

A History of world civilizations.

    Includes bibliographies.
      1. Civilization—History. I. Tannenbaum, Edward
R., ed. II. Dudley, Guilford, 1932–

CB59.H5   901.9   72-2438
ISBN 0-471-84480-2

Printed in the United States of America

10 9 8 7 6 5 4 3 2 1

This book treats the history of the world in its full diversity instead of as an adjunct of European civilization. It assumes that, during the past 100 years and for the foreseeable future, modernization is the dominant force in the world. Hence, modernization is the major theme of the second half of this book, both in the Western countries in which it originated and everywhere else since then. Before that time the traditional societies of Europe, Asia, Africa, and Precolumbian America held sway, and they are described as comprehensively as possible in a textbook of this length. The ancient Greeks and Romans still rate an important place in world history, not only because of their own achievements but also because of their influence on other civilizations far beyond the Mediterranean world. The ancient Sumerians, Egyptians, Indians, and Chinese created impressive and enduring civilizations and speculated imaginatively about the mysteries of life and the universe. Their modern successors, however, are being forced to abandon traditional ways almost overnight, and their modernization is occurring quite differently from that of Europe and North America. This book helps the reader to understand this transformation in its own terms.

In addition to its novel emphasis, this book is based on the most recent scholarship and is written with today's students and instructors in mind. It is organized so that an instructor can assign parts of chapters or leave out whole chapters without losing the overall continuity. Academic jargon has been avoided, and the language used is simple without sacrificing the basic ideas around which historians weave their narrative. Some recurring ideas—social structure, feudalism, imperialism, nationalism, and the like—are defined in boxed essays throughout the book to guide the student in grasping relevant comparisons between diverse societies in different ages. This book gives the student many images of cultural diversity while also reminding him that all men and women have had similar longings, fears, and joys since prehistoric times. In an age of increasingly fragmented and specialized training it allows each individual to sense the full potential of his humanity.

Guilford A. Dudley wrote the material on the civilizations of the ancient Near East and Asia to A.D. 1600 in Chapters 1, 2, 3, and 7. John E. Fagg wrote Chapters 17 and 27 plus the section on Precolumbian America in Chapter 2. C. Warren Hollister wrote Chapters 4, 5, 6, 8, and 9. Carter Jefferson wrote Chapters 14, 15, 21, 22, 23, and 25. Thomas R. Metcalf and Frederic Wakeman wrote Chapters 18, 19, 24, and 28. Edward R. Tannenbaum wrote Chapters 10, 11, 12, 13, and 26 plus the Prehistory section of Chapter 1. Robert L. Tignor wrote Chapters 20 and 29. Irwin Unger wrote Chapter 16.

The authors acknowledge the helpful comments of the following teachers and scholars who read this book at various stages of its composition:

Arthur D. Thomas, Jr., Henry Ford Community College; Professor William J. Prout, Air Force Academy; Professor Phyllis Yuhas, Ball State University; Professor Eugene Boardman, University of Wisconsin—Madison; Professor Gene A. Brucker, University of California—Berkeley; Professor William Church, Brown University; Professor Jill Claster, New York University; Professor Robert Collins, University of California—Berkeley; Professor Don E. Fehrenbacher, Stanford University; Professor Frank Frost, University of California—Santa Barbara; Professor Gordon M. Jensen, The University of Maryland; Professor Tom B. Jones, University of Minnesota; Professor Orest Ranum, The Johns Hopkins University; Professor Steven Ross, University of Texas; Professor Jeffery Russell, University of California—Riverside.

The authors deeply regret the untimely death of Guilford A. Dudley during the production of this book.

June 1, 1972   Edward R. Tannenbaum

CONTENTS

*Boxed essays

*Boxed essays

     *Boxed essays

ix   *Contents*

*Boxed essays

*Boxed essays

*Boxed essays

LIST OF MAPS

Maps by Wesley B. McKeown

A HISTORY OF WORLD CIVILIZATIONS

Introduction

History is the changing patterns of events that happen to communities of persons. A community consists of three ingredients: (1) persons, (2) their artifacts (nonhuman material objects interacting with persons—from the bow and arrow to the most complicated electronic equipment), and (3) patterns among both persons and artifacts; these patterns are the community's culture. The history of such communities is concerned with how they come into existence and gradually establish their cultural patterns among their people and artifacts, how these patterns modify human needs into human desires, and how they are constantly modified by internal pressures to satisfy desires and by external pressures from other communities. Sometimes communities thrive and flourish; sometimes they dwindle and perish. It used to be said that a happy community—or nation—had no history; what was meant was that its political leaders led uneventful lives and that neither their own subjects nor outsiders challenged their power. Today we know that history has to do with other matters as well. Population changes, a new religion or ideology, or even the introduction of a road, a school, or television, can change the life of a community more than the doings of kings and generals.

Since men first began to organize themselves into communities 100,000 years ago there have been hundreds of thousands of small, weak, and short-lived communities. Most of these have been parasitic; they have lived from hunting, fishing, or merely gleaning, thus decreasing rather than increasing the amount of wealth in the world. Since the discovery of techniques of farming and domesticating animals less than ten thousand years ago men have been able to become producers, thus increasing the amount of wealth in the world. Even since then there have been more parasitic communities (like the Sioux and the Eskimos) than producing communities (like the Zuñi and the Chinese). And there have been only about 24 true civilizations.

World history centers on the experiences of civilizations, the highest type of community. The usual distinction between an ordinary producing community and a civilization is that the latter has writing and city life. This definition is inadequate because it describes rather than explains the basis of civilization and because it is not completely true. In the

1

year A.D. 1000 the emerging Western civilization had almost no city life; in the fifteenth century Andean civilization, even under the Inca Empire, had no writing. A better, if not perfect, definition of a civilization is a producing community "with an instrument of expansion." "The three essential parts of an instrument of expansion are incentive to invent, accumulation of surplus, and application of this surplus to the new inventions."[*]

Civilizations have varied in the degree to which they had each of these three factors, upon which every kind of material progress and many kinds of nonmaterial progress depend. Mesopotamian civilization before 2700 B.C., early Chinese civilization before A.D. 1200, and Western civilization during much of its history were organized in ways that encouraged and rewarded inventiveness. On the other hand, civilizations based on slavery—like those of the ancient Greeks and Romans or the southern states of the United States before 1860—were notoriously uninventive. Accumulation of surplus has been carried out by various types of organization: a priesthood to whom everyone paid tribute, a state collecting taxes, a slaveowning class claiming most of the production of another class. In the early days of Western civilization the military organization of feudalism allowed the lords to collect economic goods from the mass of peasants in return for political protection. Later on the economic organization known as capitalism permitted businessmen to accumulate profits. Until the late nineteenth century only Western capitalists systematically applied a major part of their surplus to new inventions. In all other civilizations the social groups controlling the surplus soon ceased to apply it to new ways of doing things because they had no desire to change the community in which they were supreme. Instead, they applied the surplus to nonproductive forms of display—palaces, monuments, elaborate forms of entertainment, competition for social honors or prestige—and to imperialist wars.

The modern period in world history is distinguished from all past periods by the fact of sustained economic growth. This characteristic first appeared in the eighteenth century in Western Europe and especially in North America. During the nineteenth and twentieth centuries a gradually increasing number of communities (usually nations) began to use the surplus of their economic activity to generate the momentum of its future expansion, often borrowing the inventions and organizational techniques of the West. The modernization of these communities brought about an economic and social transformation: their predominantly rural and agricultural societies and economies became predominantly urban and industrial. In the process their cultural patterns were also transformed.

But the process of modernization involves more than economic growth and urbanization through division of labor and industrialization. Today it is relatively easy for developing nations to borrow new knowledge and techniques from abroad and to produce leaders willing to force these on their tradition-oriented countrymen. Originally, however, the accumulation of new knowledge and techniques and the rise of modernizing leaders developed slowly in Western Europe between the thirteenth and the eighteenth centuries. These first two stages in the process of modernization had to come before the third stage—the economic and social transformation—could begin. The fourth stage—the integration of all individuals, social groups, and geographical regions into a national society—also began first in the West.

Since modernization is now a fact in many parts of the world and a goal almost everywhere else, it will be the major theme from Part III onward of this book. And since it first developed in and spread from Western civilization, this civilization and its offshoots will be treated more fully than the others until the past hundred years or so, that is, in half of Part II and in Parts III and IV. Part I and half of Part II deal with the other major civilizations in the world up to about A.D. 1500. Parts V, VI, and VII carry the story of Western civilization and its impact on the rest of the world up to the present but give major emphasis to the transformation of old civilizations and the emergence of new ones in the Soviet

[*] Carroll Quigley, *The Evolution of Civilizations* (New York: The Macmillan Company, 1961), p. 70.

Union, China, Japan, Southeast Asia, the Middle East, and Africa.

Of the twenty-four or so civilizations in the history of the world, eight thrived and all but one—the Chinese—disappeared before A.D. 500.

Mesopotamian civilization in its various transformations flourished from about 4000 B.C. to around 300 B.C., when the ancient Persian Empire was conquered by Alexander the Great and taken over by the Greeks. Egyptian civilization flourished during much of this same period and suffered the same fate. Indic (early Indian) civilization, comprising a group of cities in the Indus Valley, flourished from the third millenium B.C. until it was overrun by the Aryans around 1500 B.C. Cretan (Minoan) civilization lasted for well over one thousand years until it was destroyed by Dorian Greeks around 1100 B.C. Early Chinese (Sinic) civilization culminated in the Han Empire and around A.D. 400, was disrupted by the Huns. Hittite civilization, in Asia Minor, lasted from 1900 to 1000 B.C. Canaanite civilization, which originated in Palestine and Syria and was spread to the Western Mediterranean by the Phoenicians, persisted from about 2000 to 100 B.C., when the Romans conquered the Carthaginian (Punic) Empire. Classical civilization lasted from the emergence of the Greeks around 900 B.C. to the fall of the Roman Empire in the West, around A.D. 500.

Other civilizations rose and fell between the millenium before Christ and the sixteenth century A.D. These include Mesoamerican civilization culminating in the Aztec Empire, Andean civilization culminating in the Inca Empire, and eight or more civilizations that existed at various times in Ethiopia, Cambodia, Indonesia, Tibet, and West Africa.

Finally, in addition to Western civilization, five others have lasted into the twentieth century: Chinese, Hindu (from 900 B.C.), Islamic (A.D. 600), Japanese (A.D. 400), Orthodox (Russian) (A.D. 600).* But modernization has already created new civilizations in the Soviet Union and Japan and has transformed beyond recognition the traditional civilizations of China, India, and parts of the Islamic world, particularly Turkey.

* Byzantine culture, from which Russia was converted to Orthodox Christianity, is difficult to classify. It hardly produced a wholly new civilization, since it retained many features of Classical culture. On the other hand, except for religion and an alphabet, it gave too little to Russian civilization to be considered an earlier phase of that civilization.

PART I | *Ancient Civilizations*

The early civilizations of Asia, North Africa, and Europe were all traditional in the sense that, once a certain level of economic and cultural expansion had been achieved, their rulers resisted further changes of any kind; moreover, they justified the existing order and existing ways of doing things as traditions founded by some god or hero in the remote past. This justification by tradition applied not only to the political and social orders but also to the whole culture, from pottery and farming techniques to religion and art. In our own age, when the justifications for practically everything are being called into question, it is particularly difficult to grasp the force of tradition in making people accept their lot without a second thought in earlier times. The difference between the modern and traditional outlooks is more than a matter of life-styles or attitudes toward authority; it involves a basic contrast in the way the past is viewed. In a traditional society the past is almost always viewed as an inescapable framework — including the gifts of the gods and the sins of the fathers — within which everyone must acknowledge his own destiny. In a modern society the past is usually viewed as a mere prologue to better things to come, or, in extreme cases, as an intolerable burden. Although the civilizations of ancient Egypt and China have perhaps been unjustly singled out for the stultifying effects of their traditions and the inflexibility of their rulers, all ancient civilizations shared these traits to a great extent. The early Greeks and Romans developed a less authoritarian and more questioning outlook, but their "modern" phases — the Hellenistic period and the late Empire — were marked by confusion, retrenchment, and decadence, rather than the confidence, expansion, and progress which we normally associate with the modern outlook.

Yet the ancient civilizations described in this section invented many of the things — both good and bad — that have influenced all later civilizations. Their artifacts and techniques included the use of bronze and iron, the domestication of the horse, and irrigation. Certain staple foods developed in ancient times have remained so down to the present: the Mediterranean diet, which put relatively little pressure on soil fertility, was based on olive oil, grape wine, and wheat; it originated with the ancient Cretans and spread throughout most of the area controlled by the Greeks and Romans; examples elsewhere include rice, which originated in Southeast Asia, and corn from the Andes, in South America. Indeed, cooking was one of the earliest civilized arts. Other inheritances from ancient times are slavery and the segregation of women.

By A.D. 500 Buddhism and Christianity were already the most widely

6

and diversely practiced religions in the world. For modern Europe and America the influence of early Christianity and Roman law is obvious. The ancient Chinese invented printing, paper, gunpowder, and the compass; the ancient Hindus developed religions that are practiced throughout Asia and that periodically appeal to disenchanted Westerners. The phonetic alphabet originated with the Canaanites, a Semitic people, and modified versions eventually spread to most other peoples. The early Indo-European languages, whose offshoots are now spoken throughout Europe and America and in much of India, developed categories of gender, sharp distinctions of person and number, and a great emphasis on chronological tense. These elements came into Greek culture from the Indo-European heritage and contributed to Greek rationalism. The ancient Hebrews, Semites like the Canaanites, also contributed to modern intellectual processes by moving from a mythological to a logical view of the universe, with rigid distinctions between God and man, past and future, life and death, male and female (especially regarding deity), man and nature, individual and group, righteous and unrighteous. Other ancient peoples before the Greeks did not make these logical distinctions; their "logics" were of a different sort and, in the case of India, remained so until very recently.

CHAPTER 1

Prehistory and the Civilizations of the Ancient Near and Middle East

Until recently most historians assumed that "history" began with the first written records and that everything that had happened earlier to the species *Homo sapiens*—intelligent man—was "prehistory." And since the first written records appeared in ancient Mesopotamia and Egypt about 5000 years ago, "history" was said to have begun in those two lands and the area between them, called collectively the Near East—as opposed to the Far East, which included China, Japan, and Southeast Asia. Today we refer to the ancient Near East, together with the rest of North Africa and Iran, as the Middle East, a term no more logical than the earlier one and leaving India equally unlocated except as a part of Asia. For ancient times, therefore, the old term Near East will be kept, with Middle East being used when Persia (modern Iran) is also involved. Although the earliest civilizations appeared in that part of the world, the history of mankind can now be traced much further back than 5000 years, thanks to the discoveries of archaeology: bones, tools, pottery, remains of buildings, art objects, and the like. Furthermore, the findings of paleontol-ogy have made it possible to trace the predecessors of the modern races of man back through the first known race of the species *Homo sapiens,* the Neanderthal, and earlier species of the broad genus man (*Homo*) to his manlike antecedents in the last great Glacial epoch, called the Pleistocene, which lasted from 3,000,000 to 10,000 years ago.

PREHISTORY

Experts presently think that human types evolved during the last great Glacial epoch, from 3,000,000 to 10,000 years ago. They seem to have appeared first in Africa, then, beginning around 300,000 years ago, in Europe and Asia. About 20,000 years ago, before the melting ice sheets raised the ocean level, the ancestors of the American Indians entered the New World from Asia via the land bridge across what is now the Bering Strait. This entire period of prehistory is called the Paleolithic (Old Stone) Age because the only surviving tools created by the predecessors of modern man were made of stone. The first stone tools date back two and one-half mil-

Neanderthal encampment. Reconstruction by Z. Burian.

lion years and were fashioned by manlike creatures in southern and eastern Africa. About half a million years ago the first specimen of the genus man, *Homo erectus,* appeared; the sites frequented by him show that he led a communal life and knew the use of fire. Among the extinct races of the species *Homo sapiens* the most familiar was Neanderthal man, who ranged throughout Europe and the Mediterranean between 110,000 and 35,000 years ago. Less primitive-looking types of similar ancestry in North Africa and Asia were beginning to evolve into the races of modern man nearly 40,000 years ago. The Neanderthalers were skilled hunters and toolmakers. They buried their own dead, and they probably felt the first primitive stirrings of religion in the form of a cave bear cult involving ceremonial sacrifices of captive bears and the preservation of their skulls and leg bones. The first known race of modern man, Cro-Magnon, replaced the Neanderthalers in Western Europe rather abruptly around 35,000 B.C., and remained there until about 10,000 B.C. Although the Cro-Magnons apparently did not mingle with the European Neanderthalers, they do seem to have diversified in many populations in other parts of the world. We still know very little about the rest of the world at the end of the ice age, but much of it was already occupied: Africa was partially inhabited by the

ancestors of today's Bushmen, but the modern black African was not there, and where he came from remains to be discovered; so does the ancestry of the Mongoloid peoples who inhabit most of eastern Asia.

Although human beings certainly look different from apes, it is their culture more than their looks which distinguishes them from all other creatures. As used here culture refers to patterns of behavior and values learned in a specific society rather than inherited from a genetic group. Apes, birds, and even bees learn certain elementary patterns of behavior in communal situations, to be sure, but man's apparently unlimited capacity for transmitting and changing his cultural traditions is unique. At first his only cultural advantage over apes was his ability to fashion tools. This ability, made possible by a larger brain, showed foresight and planning for which there is no evidence even today among captive chimpanzees manipulating sticks or strings in order to bring food or other visible objects within immediate reach. Improvement in the techniques of toolmaking, in turn, influenced a broad field of culture, from hunting and warfare to dwellings, clothing, and transport. Culture allowed men to begin to master diverse physical environments and to make conscious choices unknown to other living beings.

The principal medium for ordering human experience and transmitting culture is language or, more precisely, articulate speech. It is now estimated that articulate speech, in contrast to noises, gestures, and postures, may have first come into use 100,000 years ago, as the human brain grew in size and as tools became more skillfully made and standardized. Verbal (and, later, mathematical) symbols gave men and women mental tools as valuable in their struggle with nature as the material ones that so far have provided the main basis for the reconstruction of prehistory. Language expanded men's memories, not only as individuals but also as part of consciously defined groups (families, clans, tribes, villages, peoples). Indeed, language became the basis for almost all nonmaterial aspects of culture, from the simplest forms of naming and storytelling to the most elaborate levels of abstraction in philosophy and science. Even the Neanderthalers seem to have

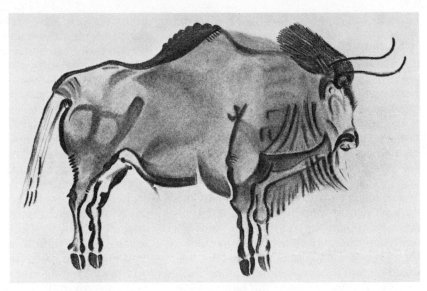

A masterpiece of prehistoric painting: a bison from the caves of Altamira in Spain, c. 10,000 B.C.

spoken a crude, infantlike language and recognized their individual mortality, as evidenced in their careful attention to burial. As they and later primitive men ruminated about the existence of hidden powers on which their own well-being depended, they began to try to deal with these powers through magic and religion, two of the most pervasive characteristics of human society.

In primitive societies no clear distinction was drawn between rituals associated with magic and religion on the one hand and practical activities on the other; this mingling can be seen in the extraordinary artistic achievements of Cro-Magnon men. In certain caves in France and Spain, today's tourist can still see the paintings that these men made of the animals they hunted. Although these paintings and other cave art were apparently turned to magical use—as means of gaining power over the animals portrayed, ensuring their fertility, and making them vulnerable to the hunters' spears—they probably did not originate as mere aids in the eternal quest for food. Some scholars insist that Cro-Magnon cave art was particularly significant because it began as a disinterested, leisure-time, activity, a means of attuning people to their surroundings through

the projection of symbols. In addition, however, this art probably formed part of a religious ritual involving dance and mime, as suggested by the symbolically masked figures of dancing men who seem to be identifying themselves with the animals they sought to kill. Another religious aspect of Cro-Magnon and other late Paleolithic art was the small carvings and statuettes of women, which seem to have been objects of veneration and whose voluptuous contours may have been associated with fertility rites.

Whereas both their innate capacity and their culture distinguished Paleolithic men from apes, the gap that separates them from us is primarily economic and cultural. It is doubtful that we would do any better than they did knowing nothing of metals, agriculture, domestic animals, or written language—the four principal assets on which most civilized societies are based. Societies based on hunting strictly limit the options open to men and women, regardless of their innate capacities. As the anthropologist Margaret Mead says: "You don't chase elephants with a baby on your hip." By analogy with allegedly primitive hunting societies that have survived into the twentieth century, it is difficult not to speculate that the peoples of Paleolithic times also lived in groups seldom exceeding 50 individuals, that the basic unit was the natural family, and that food-sharing, men's sexual possessiveness, and women's functions of child care and homemaking all developed more or less together.

Moreover, the most highly civilized men remain biologically and emotionally equipped for life as primitive hunters, and the strain is showing. For example, their bodies continue to produce substances such as adrenalin and cholesterol to help them through periods of peril or stress but, unlike their Paleolithic ancestors, their sedentary existence does not allow them to burn off these substances. Under our layers of civilized culture there is still a bit of the savage in all of us. According to the biologist René Dubos: "Even when man has become an urbane city dweller, the paleolithic bull which survives in his inner self still paws the earth whenever a threatening gesture is made on the social scene."

Ecological change between about 10,000 and 8000 B.C. disrupted many Paleolithic hunting societies and fostered the beginnings of agriculture and the domestication of animals in the Old World. As the ice sheets retreated and the climate of Europe and Asia grew warmer, the open landscape where reindeer, horses, and bisons had grazed gave way to forests. The hunters of this transitional period had to adapt themselves to new types of game by using bows and arrows and dogs. While the domestication of the dog temporarily increased the efficiency of the economy, this animal's capabilities in rounding up a herd of sheep or goats was eventually to make hunting economies and societies obsolete as animals and plants suitable for early attempts at a farming economy developed in the postglacial period in the hill country of Palestine, Syria, and Iraq. Plant cultivation and animal husbandry as supplements to hunting first appeared in these areas in the ninth millennium B.C. Archaeological evidence from Jericho presents a picture of continuous development between 8000 and 7000 B.C., from hunting site to village to the first known walled town with an economy that supported several thousand inhabitants. By 5000 B.C. much of southwestern Asia,

from Turkey to Iran, was dotted with permanent agricultural villages, and there are indications of irrigation in a few places. These villages were still in the Neolithic (New Stone) Age, but their technology now included pottery, and their craftsmen were beginning to learn to work with copper.

The techniques of herding and farming spread to other societies over an increasingly large area to the east and west of the original center. In eastern Europe Neolithic agricultural communities were established by the sixth millennium and had spread to the western Mediterranean and up the Danube and down the Rhine by the end of the fifth, and to Britain by the late fourth millennium B.C. Farming economies in Central Asia and northwestern India probably go back at least to the fourth millennium. The beginnings of agriculture in China could have resulted either from importation from outside or independent invention, but it is impossible to date them from existing evidence; the situation is similar for most of Africa. In the New World agriculture was necessarily the result of independent invention; the cultivation of plants began in the seventh millennium B.C., the growing of corn in the middle of the third. But the lack of animal domestication made the civilizations that were to develop in the Americas noticeably different from those of the Old World. The failure of the most advanced American Indians to develop the wheel was probably related to the absence of domesticated draught animals to pull carts or wagons.

Animal domestication and plant cultivation reflected a broadening of prehistoric mental outlooks. One example was the realization that castrating a bull could produce a docile draught animal of great strength. This realization also opened the way to a better understanding of breeding through the use of a few selected bulls to serve the cows and the transformation of the others into oxen. Understanding the relatively slow breeding cycle of animals and plants helped Neolithic farmers develop concepts of permanency and a time perspective beyond the life-span of a single natural family. This long-term view was evident in the highly developed complex of ideas concerning succession and heritable property in the earliest agricultural societies we know of from written documents; it also showed up in the raising of surplus crops to trade for pottery, copper, and other goods produced by local craftsmen. By the fourth millennium B.C. in Iraq and Palestine temple architecture on a monumental scale indicated not only a desire for buildings that would last beyond a single life-span but also religious ceremonies and traditions and priestly classes similarly conceived as permanent.

The nonliterate peasant communities of the Old World formed the bases on which literate civilizations were to be built in Mesopotamia (Iraq), Egypt, Asia Minor, India, and China. Most of these budding civilizations seem to have gone through similar stages of economic, social, and technological development involving specialization, division of labor, urbanization, and the use of bronze and iron. Nevertheless, their essential and distinguishing characteristics varied so much that these must have already existed in simpler form in the preliterate cultures out of which these civilizations grew. It has been argued that self-sufficient, culturally distinct peasant societies represented the normal pattern of existence and that the civilizations that sporadically developed out of a few of them were exceptions, each the product of innovating circumstance, often created by individuals as well as by an impersonal challenge from the environment. For example, in the third millennium B.C. the form of civilization which emerged in Egypt was different from that of contemporary Mesopotamia, even though the development of writing and monumental art was similar in both areas. In Mesopotamia the first civilization was politically organized around autonomous city-states with their assemblies, elders, and priests, along with independent temple organizations. This pattern was typical of most of western Asia. In Egypt, on the other hand, from the beginning of civilization there was one king, and he was a god. This pattern may have been an outgrowth of the African world of little tribal rainmaking god-kings. We may speculate that the ancient civilizations of Mexico and the Andes, as well as those of India and China, also grew out of quite distinct folk cultures.

Civilization, then, is an arbitrary term used to denote large settled societies with complex governments usually associated with the skill of writing to supplement memory as a means of maintaining and transmitting the essential records and knowledge of a whole people. But the term is often self-serving, and its proponents, from the ancient Egyptians and Chinese down to the present, have used it to distinguish themselves from less sophisticated peoples who did not share their "advanced" religion, technology, and art or, more cruelly, from simpler folk whom they have been able to conquer or enslave. "Civilized" peoples usually make a distinction between these "barbarians" and more primitive savages, but in the case of settled peasant communities the better term is folk—a people with a common culture who have not yet become organized into a large, independent political unit.

Just as we have our biological inheritance from Paleolithic hunters, so our cultural heritage has many remnants from the folk cultures of preliterate peasant societies. Until full-scale industrialization replaced them beginning around 100 years ago, such societies remained the dominant influences in the lives of the rural masses in many parts of Europe and Asia; they are being uprooted today in many parts of Latin America and Africa. In Europe itself, the cradle of our present civilization, many pre-Roman and pre-Christian customs have survived—from mistletoe and Easter rabbits to special foods and beverages to all kinds of folklore. These peasant customs were often overlaid with elements from the literate culture of the upper classes while remaining basically "barbarian." Some young people today, reacting against their own civilization, have tried to revive elements of preliterate cultures, particularly in music, insofar as these can be recreated among late descendants of European peasants and African slaves.

Before turning to recorded history, from the first true civilizations down to the present, it should be noted that the increase in the world's population has taken place in a series of surges, reflecting the three most basic cultural innovations of man. The first innovation was the slow development of tools, which allowed man's antecedents to move out of the trees into new environments

Oldest known writing is contained on the two sides of this limestone tablet from Kish, c. 3500 B.C.

and to exploit these more intensively, supplementing the plant food they gathered with hunted game. Three hundred thousand years ago the human population had probably reached a million; 25,000 years ago, during the heyday of the Cro-Magnon peoples in Europe and the Middle East, it had grown to more than 3 million. The second innovation, the double discovery of how to domesticate animals and how to grow crops, came earliest in western Asia, a little over 10,000 years ago. Within 2000 years (around 6000 B.C.) the effects of these discoveries allowed the world's population to jump from some 5 million to an estimated 86 million. Thereafter civilizations, with their divisions of labor and large-scale organization, facilitated a further jump to over 700,000,000 in A.D. 1750. The third innovation, industrialization, began then and has made possible a population of close to 4 billion in the early 1970s. More than 3 percent of all the human beings who have ever lived inhabit our shrinking planet right now.

ANCIENT MESOPOTAMIA

It was no accident that the four most ancient civilizations arose in the basins of flood rivers: the Tigris and Euphrates rivers of Mesopotamia (Land between Two Rivers),

the Nile River of Egypt, the Indus River of India, and the Yellow River of China. In each case the challenge of these flood rivers called forth the organization of society on a larger scale than the world had yet seen.

The Rise of Sumerian Civilization

The first of these civilizations developed in the swampy lower reaches of the Tigris and Euphrates rivers where they entered the Persian Gulf about 150 miles north of the present coastline. For some 1500 years primitive peoples had been living a hand-to-mouth existence on the fish and fowl of the area. Then, about 4000 B.C., a new people took the first steps toward civilization in the delta creating the 'Ubaid culture. The wide dispersion of their wheel-turned pottery testifies to their influence among outsiders and their pursuit of trade. Indeed, the occasional use of copper, unavailable in the valley, presumes trade. The most significant contribution, however, was in the field of religion as represented by the temple architecture, a preview of the more monumental works of their successors. The 'Ubaid culture, which preceded the birth of civilization, reflected the beginning of an urban, materialistic outlook, indicated in expanding trade, and a religiously sanctioned political

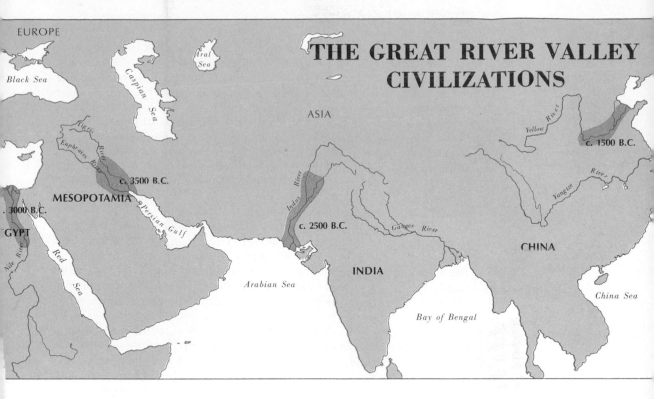

authority symbolized by temples as the only important buildings.

The emergence of civilization coincided with the appearance in Mesopotamia of another people, the Sumerians, who differed in language from the existing population. These vigorous people mixed with the inhabitants and built their civilization on the foundations that had already been laid. The earliest example of writing is a limestone tablet dated about 3500 B.C. with pictographs (simplified pictures) on both sides which are clearly related to the cuneiform writing evolved in the next several centuries. Cuneiform utilized standardized symbols impressed by a stylus on a clay tablet that was often hardened by baking. Each simplified symbol might represent a single word, or related words of different sounds, as well as a syllabic sound. Such multiple use reduced the number of symbols that had to be learned. To avoid confusion, prefixed or suffixed signs frequently indicated the meaning intended. The Sumerian writing system survived the death of the language and was adapted to the writing of the languages of succeeding Se-

mitic and Indo-European peoples until replaced by alphabetic scripts.

The era of Sumerian dominance, which lasted more than 1000 years, may be divided into an Early Sumerian Era (c. 3500–2900 B.C.) and an Early Dynastic Era (c. 2900–2340 B.C.) that was followed by several centuries of alien domination before a short-lived but brilliant Sumerian revival (c. 2135–2027 B.C.). Unfortunately, information about both early eras is limited principally to the physical remains uncovered by the painstaking excavations of archeologists. Although several hundred tablets dating from the Early Sumerian Era have been found, their pictographic writing is difficult to decipher and in any case was limited to economic memoranda. The following Early Dynastic Era is represented by thousands of cuneiform tablets, but again they are for the most part economic records. Apparently the Sumerians were not historically minded, preferring to entrust their fate to the gods, or perhaps the archeologists have been thus far unlucky. Almost all the Sumerian literature discovered to date is in versions compiled

MYTH

A myth is an explanation of how things came to be what they are; more specifically, it tells the people in a religious society who they are and where they came from. The Book of Genesis in the Bible is an obvious example of a myth in this sense. Every creation myth shows how some reality came into existence, be it the cosmos or only a fragment of it, such as an island, a species of plant, or a human institution. In telling how a thing was born, a myth reveals a violent invasion of the sacred — the ultimate cause of all real existence — into the mundane world. Along with rituals and sacred laws, myths define and support the social and cultural norms of a given society as part of that society's total religious "package." Their unique quality, however, is the way they point to the primordial generative powers underlying human life. These powers, even when personified as gods and goddesses, act in mysterious ways that transcend rather than transgress the norms of human society — such as taboos against murdering or sleeping with members of one's immediate family. Nearly every religious society has initiation rites related to a myth which bring the young people into the community. The community as a whole "lives" its mythology through other rites on sacred occasions celebrating the birth and resurrection of its savior, at significant points in the seasonal cycle, or at times of life-crises or natural catastrophes. By putting the individual temporarily into close rapport with the mysterious generative powers of the cosmos, this myth and these rites give meaning to his life and that of his community in the face of the apparent senselessness of ordinary existence.

The reality of a myth is inaccessible on the level of normal scientific or logical discourse; it can be revealed only in analogies of mythic or ritual symbolism. Many ancient myths conceive of time as a mathematically structured ever-returning cycle and evil or disruptive forces as dragons; some Greek and Indian myths unite religious and sexual experiences. The symbolic language of myth resembles in some ways that of poetry, or music, or dreams; for this reason it is rejected as "primitive" by people who believe that the human mind has evolved to higher levels of understanding. However, a growing number of anthropologists has substituted "archaic" for "primitive" in describing a level of thought that was different from rather than inferior to modern scientific and logical thought. The mathematical ability of the ancient Babylonians or the Maya was different from ours but impressive in its own way; even the thinking of surviving "primitive" peoples today is more complex than was formerly supposed. In a sense, the kind of thinking that once produced myths seems to be at work again in a new form of scientific and logical thinking called general systems analysis. In both kinds of thinking the goal is to find a form of expression that reveals similar patterns in a wide variety of phenomena: the physical universe, culture, social relations, economics, politics, and the like. Indeed, the form of expression most favored by today's systems analysts is mathematics — a different mathematics from that of the ancient Babylonians, or Pythagoras, or the Maya, but based on an apparently similar quest for all-embracing explanations of life, the world, and the interrelations between the known and the unknown.

ANCIENT MESOPOTAMIA

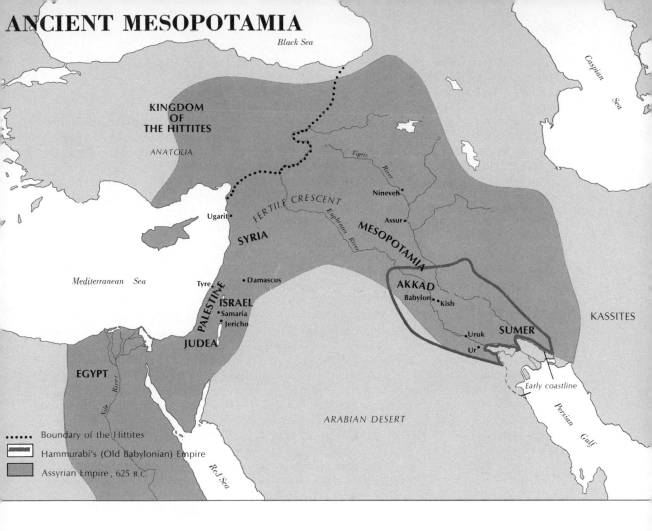

and edited in the second and first millenia after they had been overwhelmed by Semitic successors. Some of their epic heroes, such as Gilgamesh, have, however, been identified with actual rulers of the Early Dynastic Era given in a Sumerian king list. Thus a fragile historical link with this second period of Sumerian development has been established.

Early Sumerian Era (c. 3500–2900 B.C.)

Within a few centuries after their arrival in Mesopotamia the Sumerians developed city-states on old sites into populous and prosperous centers by exploiting the plentiful virgin land to be brought under the plow by irrigation canals, dikes, and drainage ditches. These city-states reached their peak around 3100 B.C. Each city had its patron deities, and the most impressive buildings were their temples, built and rebuilt on the same base in more and more monumental proportions. The most famous examples of this period are the White Temple and Pillar Temple of the city of Uruk. The Pillar Temple provides a rare instance of limestone being used in the high bases, as much as 40 feet high, on which the temples were built overlooking the city and the plain below. Since stone was not locally available and had to be imported, its use suggests the importance attached to the deities and the wealth that could support such an expenditure. The Pillar Temple was also characterized by massive columns as much as eight and a half feet in diameter. The temples were decorated with mosaics of clay cones of different colors embedded in the mud bricks; the effect must have been brilliant.

The gods and goddesses to whom these temples were consecrated were viewed not only as protectors of the cities but also as owners of the land. Their priesthoods apparently organized and directed all the people in the work of reclamation, maintained the dikes and ditches, and collected the gods' shares of the produce. In other words, the priesthoods controlled the development of this earliest civilization on behalf of the patron deities of the respective city-states. The chief priests, especially if they became hereditary, were in a position to enhance their authority and assume what amounted to a combination of kingship and chief priesthood supported by religious sanction and economic control.

Wheat was a major crop, but sheep raising was then and later an equally important source of income. The importance of sheep is illustrated by a myth about the shepherd-god Dumuzi who defeats the farmer-god in a contest for the hand of Innana, goddess of love and queen of heaven. Ultimately, Dumuzi dies and becomes a god of the underworld so that his wife may be released to return to her role in the world above. In this religious myth the importance of the pastoral aspect of the Sumerian economy is confirmed. Indeed, peaceful interaction and exchange with nomadic sheep-raising tribes on the periphery of Sumer must have been normal with the Sumerians. Such contacts provided the tribesmen with fodder and water as well as their other products in exchange for sheep, labor, and military service.

The pictographic tablets also contain frequent references to barley and to cattle and dairy products as staples. Barley later became the dominant crop as excessive irrigation and inadequate drainage raised the salt content of the soil. Fish were common in the diet, and the date palm and the vine are mentioned as well as the goat and pig. Lion, wild sheep, and deer were hunted. The priests, at least, enjoyed a daily ration of beer.

Copper, which had to be imported, is frequently mentioned, and seed-plows, nails, and a wide variety of household utensils were in daily use. Pottery turned on a fast wheel was plainer and less colorful than formerly as artistic talent was redirected to metal products. Weapons included the bent bow, the socketed axe, the spear, and the dagger. Boats and both two- and four-wheel wagons facilitated transport. Wagons drawn by donkeys (the horse and the camel were not introduced till the second millenium) may have provided some mobility in military campaigns. But the major Sumerian contribution to military tactics was a disciplined infantry in place of the mad melee of individual combats which had characterized more primitive tribal warfare.

Division of labor was evident in the development of specialized occupations such as carpenters, blacksmiths, shepherds and, of course, scribes and priests. Such a complex civilization called forth scientific investigation based on the development of mathematics employing both a decimal system and a sexagesimal system. This latter system uses a unit of 60 and is especially flexible; its influence is still apparent in our 360-degree circle and our divisions of the hour. These early mathematicians also understood and used fractions. Recent excavations have revealed that the Semitic heirs of the Sumerians mastered the fundamental laws of mathematics not long after 2000 B.C., if not earlier. Most striking is the recovery of a clay tablet giving a full and clear exposition of what has been known as the "Pythagorean" theorem, after the Greek philosopher and mathematician of the fifth century B.C.

Outside the temple area, tablets of economic memoranda have been found which suggest that the priests did not have a monopoly of either literacy or trade. Whether merchants operated as individuals or as agents of the temples, an extensive trade was conducted with the upland area of Iran to the east and the Fertile Crescent and Anatolian Plateau to the northwest to obtain the stone, metals, and timber that Sumer lacked. Artistically sculptured stone cylinder seals of this period as well as other evidence

Proto-Sumerian cylinder seal, c. 3000 B.C.

of Sumerian influence have even been discovered in southern Egypt. In addition to temple architecture and the depictions on cylinder seals, Sumerian artists of this era produced sophisticated and realistic sculptures and reliefs in stone and metals.

Early Dynastic Era
(c. 2900–2340 B.C.)

Increasing strife between city-states over boundaries and control of trade called for strong governments under effective military leaders. As a result, what probably started as a temporary delegation of dictatorial power to a commander in an emergency evolved into kingship that became hereditary. Kings allied with the priesthoods in fighting to assert their power over neighboring city-states. The priests contributed religious sanction for their authority and economic resources for their campaigns. In theory the warrior-kings, like the priests and the citizens, were servants of the patron deities of the cities, but military success tended to raise the kings' real status. In time royal palaces, separated from the temple areas, reflected the wealth and power of the rulers. Increased economic opportunities and the enlarged tasks of gov-

ernment under successful dynasties probably encouraged the growth of a middle class of merchants and bureaucrats which was later to undermine the economic dominance of the priesthoods. As more and more land as well as economic activities came under private ownership and control, a more stratified society developed. Despite these changes, however, the traditional religious and cultural dominance of the temples and their attendants endured.

Amid the warfare among city-states and the rise and fall of dynasties and local "empires," the unity of Sumerian civilization was maintained by the practice of each new ruler obtaining religious confirmation of his authority in return for gifts carried to the city-state of Nippur, sacred to Enlil, the chief Sumerian god. Since religion played such an important role in the organization and control of Sumerian life, we must try to understand the often ambiguous interpretation the priests gave of the universe and man's position in it. Moreover, such an understanding must rely on later myths that may have been altered.

Originally, all that had existed was a boundless primeval sea, which was pictured as still surrounding the universe.

In some manner, heaven, earth, and the constantly moving and changing atmosphere in between were created out of the sea. The earth was conceived as a flat disk separated from a dome-shaped heaven by the atmosphere. Later on, the moon, sun, and stars were created, followed by plant, animal, and human life.

For religious purposes and to explain the operation of the universe, each of its components was associated with an immortal being conceived in human form and instilled with human interests and appetites. According to the cosmic plan, each deity was responsible for the proper functioning of its part. Thus there was a whole hierarchy of gods and goddesses of whom the most important were the three who controlled heaven, air, earth, and freshwater. These were the creating deities, and the creative technique often attributed to them was the power of the divine word; they uttered the command and it was. Thereafter, this doctrine was generally followed in religious thought in the Near East. Of course, earthbound Sumerian poets often provided a more human explanation of creation.

The three chief deities were the heaven god An, the air god Enlil, the earth and fresh water god Enki. At one time the patriarchal An was probably the most important, but in the early dynastic period Enlil, whose Sumerian home was the sacred city of Nippur, had become supreme perhaps because he was credited with the creation and control of the productive features of life on earth through a host of lesser deities. He gave kings their crowns and determined whether or not their works would prosper.

Sumerian writers never ceased reiterating their conviction that immortality was only for the gods and goddesses, not for mortal man. Moreover, the very existence of man depended upon the favor of the gods. The best way to retain their goodwill was to serve them faithfully and observe rigorously the divinely established rites and laws. But the most faithful service provided no guarantees. Since life for the mortal servants of the gods was considered uncertain and insecure, they acquired a pessimistic and fatalistic outlook. While a major deity might heed the supplications of a ruler, he would obviously be too busy to listen to an ordinary man. Each commoner therefore took a minor deity to plead his case with the major gods.

These views are illustrated by the *Gilgamesh Epic,* the best-known myth about this heroic age. It relates the ordeals of Gilgamesh, fifth ruler of the first dynasty of Uruk (c. 2800 B.C.), who was defeated in his quest for immortality; it also gives an early account of the flood story. Man had been created and given cities as religious centers in which to worship according to divine rites and laws. After a long debate in an assembly of the gods a reluctant decision was made to destroy man by flood, presumably for failing to maintain the rites and laws. Obviously the decision was not unanimous, and some of the deities lamented the loss of their human servants. The Sumerian Noah, a king, was warned of the impending doom in a dream and then advised to build a giant boat. The flood and storms tossed the boat for seven days and seven nights before it subsided.

When the seventh day arrived,
The flood (-carrying) south-storm
subsided in the battle,
Which it had fought like an army.
The sea grew quiet, the tempest was still, the
flood ceased.
I looked at the weather: stillness had set in,
And all of mankind had returned to clay.
The landscape was as level as a flat roof.
I opened a hatch, and light fell upon my
face. . . .
The raven went forth and, seeing that the
waters had diminished,
He eats, circles, caws, and turns not round.
Then I let out (all) to the four winds
And offered a sacrifice.
I poured out a libation on the top of the
*mountain.**

Another interesting poem tells of the reaction of Gilgamesh to an ultimatum from the king of Kish which suggests that his authority was something less than absolute. First, he

* Selections from "Akkadian Myths and Epics," translated by E. A. Speiser in James B. Pritchard, *Ancient Near Eastern Texts Relating to the Old Testament,* 3rd. ed., with Supplement (copyright © 1969 by Princeton University Press), pp. 94–95. Reprinted by permission of Princeton University Press.

consulted the elders, who recommended submission rather than face the possibility of destruction. Dissatisfied with this advice, he then turned to an assembly of the men of the city, who declared themselves ready to fight to the finish for their independence. These references to assemblies suggest the existence of institutions that needed to be consulted, at least in a crisis; in another poem, however, Gilgamesh himself is pictured as an oppressive tyrant. In any case, the trend of the times was in the direction of authoritarianism with the development of an administrative bureaucracy demonstrating the customary arrogance and corruption.

Since the gods were believed to have created all things, the Sumerians with eminent logic concluded that they had created evil as well as good, immorality as well as morality. Generally, however, the gods were represented as favoring those values most esteemed by Sumerian civilization: goodness and truth, law and order, justice and freedom, righteousness and sincerity, mercy and compassion. And rulers always claimed to uphold these virtues. Indeed, it was a common ideal of traditional "oriental" despotism in the Near East and elsewhere in Asia that it should be tempered with benevolence and that the care and protection of the poor, the weak, the widow, and the orphan were the moral responsibility of the ruler.

The need of temples and rulers for trained clerks and officials generated formal education, and reading, writing, and arithmetic established that inevitable association of teacher and pupil with the endless exercises essential to mastery of these civilized disciplines. Many tablets obviously represent student exercises by the range of writing competence they demonstrate. Although education was for the wealthy few, several homely stories show that the relationships of parents, pupils, and teachers have changed little through the ages. Discipline was rigorous and Sumerian pedagogy did not believe in sparing the rod. One story relates a typical student's day in which he made his recitation, ate a lunch of two rolls his mother had given him, and did more written and oral work in the afternoon. In the evening his father praised his written work and his recitation. But the next day the monitor said he

was tardy and with a quaking heart he entered the classroom and bowed to the teacher. Despite this demonstration of respect, however, he had a bad day, and that evening he persuaded his father that his schoolwork might improve if the teacher were invited to dinner and given gifts. The teacher accepted and after dinner and gifts rhapsodized on the promise and diligence of his student. Apparently, teachers were inadequately paid and welcomed gratuities.

Another story about the problem of an indulgent parent and a delinquent child is as old as civilization. After upbraiding his son for truancy the father told him how to behave in school and then required him to repeat these instructions. The father proceeded to berate his son for his ingratitude, pointing out that he never made him work as the sons of other fathers did. And how did his son repay his kindness? He neglected school and wasted his time wandering in the streets and searching out pleasures. Instead, he should emulate his brothers or even his closest friend and win the respect of his kinsmen. Finally, like fathers throughout the ages, he asserted that dutiful sons should follow in their fathers' footsteps, adding that the scribal art was the most honored of professions.

Mesopotamian Imperialism

As frequently happened in history, unification in Mesopotamia was accomplished by a frontier state that was militarily more vigorous than the heartland of the civilization it defended. Sargon, ruler of the Semitic* city-state of Akkad, upriver from Sumer proper, was the founder of the Akkadian Empire (c. 2340–2150 B.C.). Moreover, he was credited with conquests as far as the Mediterranean to the northwest and Elam to the southeast of Sumer, but his expeditions in these directions probably gained no more than a temporary supremacy. His city-state had fully adopted Sumerian culture, and he acknowledged Sumerian civilization by ob-

---

* Semitic was one of the major language groups of the Middle East; another one, in Egypt and much of North Africa, was Hamitic. Semitic languages included Assyrian, Hebrew, Aramaic, and Arabic.

An Akkadian king, possibly Sargon of Agade.

which improved upon the imperial techniques of the Akkadian Empire. Thanks to a more complex administration fuller records have been found than for any of its predecessors illustrating political centralization and a planned economy directed by an elaborate bureaucracy. The growth of independent influence and power was checked by the frequent transfer of governors and the appointment of garrison commanders who reported directly to the ruler. The wealth of the regime was demonstrated by the numerous works of art and by the construction of the great stepped temple (*ziggurat*) of Ur on a massive base approached by three long staircases. At its greatest extent, imperial authority incorporated parts of Assyria to the north and Iran to the east.

Again, internal difficulties combined with external raids to produce a breakdown of the empire into smaller successor realms until Hammurabi, ruler of the strategically located Semitic city of Babylon, restored unity to the Mesopotamian area and founded the Babylonian Empire (*c.* 1792–1530 B.C.). Like Sargon, he was a supporter of Sumerian civilization, but he elevated the god of Babylon, Marduk, as his benefactor to a dominant position in the religious hierarchy. Hammurabi is best known for his law code, based on previous codes, which gives a picture of human relationships and social stratification in ancient Mesopotamia.

Hammurabi's Code

Hammurabi is depicted on a stone slab as receiving the code from the god of justice, and the decisions of the courts, held at the temples, were believed to carry the endorsement and sanction of the gods. By modern standards the penalties appear harsh. The death penalty in various forms was obviously prescribed as a deterrent. The ancient doctrine of "an eye for an eye" was moderated in some instances by the substitution of set fines. The differences in penalties according to social class illustrate the stratified nature of society. The emphasis throughout the code on property and property rights demonstrates the materialistic orientation of this society. Many fields and orchards were owned by church or state and granted to individuals in

taining confirmation of his authority in the traditional fashion from the sacred city of Nippur. A centralized regime appointed Semitic governors for the subject cities supported by contingents of troops. Trade under the protection of the rulers flourished and increased the prosperity of the enlarged area of Sumerian civilization. Less capable successors proved unable to protect the empire, and it gradually disintegrated as each city negotiated its own arrangement with the intruders. Despite the loss of unity, however, the far-flung trading activities continued to develop because they were mutually beneficial to all parties.

After several decades of disunity a brilliant Sumerian revival was engineered by the Third Dynasty of Ur (*c.* 2135–2027 B.C.),

SOCIAL STRUCTURE

Every society has a structure—a theoretical model or framework—within which social relations take place. In many "primitive" societies kinship and marriage systems provide such a structure. In more advanced traditional societies the social structure is often embodied in a system of hereditary castes. Sometimes these castes reflect a situation in which one group has conquered and/or enslaved another religious, ethnic, or racial group; sometimes, as in India, the castes originally represented specific social roles: priests, warriors, merchants, and peasants. In India those people who did not belong to any caste were literally "outcasts"; in Europe until the nineteenth century Jews were considered outcasts by most Christians; in the United States until less than a generation ago most whites treated most blacks as members of an inferior caste. Another type of traditional social structure comprises estates or orders conceived as corporate bodies, like the mandarin scholar-bureaucrats in Old China or the medieval European guilds, clergy, nobility, and universities. In very recent years some labor unions and ethnic minorities seem to be reviving a corporate conception of their place in the social structures of today's materially advanced countries. But in most modern societies the structure still divides its members into social classes. There are many possible class divisions, the broadest being between upper, middle, and lower classes. (In Europe the upper-middle class is often called the bourgeoisie.) Although class status is not legally hereditary, mobility from one class to another has been very difficult in most societies.

In many societies the upper class is a ruling class; this term, like social structure, is a model or ideal type that helps us understand political as well as social and economic relations. Where there has been such a class it has usually attained its power through property ownership and inheritance. In most cases, however, it has ruled indirectly through elites—the top people in administration, the military, the law, religion, and education—who have represented particular aspects of its interests. Where there is no ruling class there is often a political elite that founds its power on the control of administration—as in the Soviet Union and other Communist countries—or on military force—as in certain Latin American and Islamic countries. In a period of rapid change like our own, some highly advanced societies have developed a multiplicity of elites among which it is impossible to identify an enduring group of powerful individuals or families. But no society in the past has endured without some kind of structure, and new elites and new classes are already struggling to establish a new one with themselves on top.

return for service or rent, but a substantial amount of land was privately owned and salable. Apparently, all who held church or state lands owed military service, but all others were free from conscription.

The most important laws came first in the code, and the rest followed in a descending order of significance. The first four laws were procedural, assessing the penalty of the crime for false accusations or false testimony.

As one would expect, the first positive law concerned the church and state and prescribed the death penalty for theft of either one's property. The paternal authority of the father was upheld as the sole custodian of family property. Other provisions with a modern ring to them, however, protected the rights of wives and children. On the other hand, wayward wives and undutiful sons were subject to severe penalties.

The great ziggurrat of Ur.

Marriage was arranged by the parents, the groom's father providing a marriage price and the bride's father a dowry. No marriage was valid without a written contract. Either party could obtain a divorce for various reasons. The wife, as a mother, gained the management and use of her deceased husband's estate in trust for his sons. A daughter was only entitled to support and a dowry. Both physicians and veterinarians practiced surgery under a scale of fixed fees for successful operations, but the penalties for failure, such as cutting off the surgeon's hand, made the former profession hazardous. The establishments of women wine sellers—the saloons of the day—were places of such ill-repute that special laws were required for their regulation. The woman wine seller was apparently a common cheat and her shop the customary hangout of criminals and other undesirable elements. Any woman connected with a temple who even opened the door of a wineshop was to be burned to death.

On the accumulated experience of the past Hammurabi built a well-ordered empire in which the state and its adjunct, the church, played a large role. Yet, despite state regulation, most men were free to pursue their destinies within reasonable limits. A few men were wealthy and could pass their wealth on to their sons in equal shares. A substantial middle class provided the backbone of the urban economy. The abundance of correspondence suggests that literacy was relatively widespread. The labors of a large number of poorer freemen and a perhaps even larger number of slaves supported this literate civilization. Meanwhile, commercial and imperial expansion widely diffused the features of Mesopotamian civilization, both material and spiritual, and stimulated by example the advancement of both old and new peoples throughout the Near East.

In the thousand years after the fall of the Babylonian Empire (c. 1530 B.C.) a confusing array of states arose and sought control of the trade routes. Methods of government varied from ruthlessness to toleration, but the most significant feature was the overall trend toward the creation of a larger, all-encompassing entity. The Sumerians had blazed the trail of civilization which others have followed with variations of their own.

Like other traditional civilizations, Sumerian civilization was based on the production of an agricultural surplus to support a growing population of nonfarmers, such as craftsmen, merchants, scribes, and priests, in their specialized, civilizing endeavors that in turn generated greater wealth and a standard of living above mere survival for more and more people. Major Sumerian discoveries that contributed to the subsequent development of civilization include the wheel, the plow, and a host of other tools, water control and management, writing and literature, mathematics, astronomy, astrology, and the calendar. The Sumerians also developed sculpture in the round and relief and the column, the arch, and the vault in architecture. They invented bookkeeping, banking, credit, and contracts essential to economic organization and trade, and perhaps most important of all, the city as an administrative, economic, and cultural center. In addition, their rulers during the Early Dynastic Era struggled to create a larger unity for the Land of Sumer, but it was left to their Semitic successors to develop imperial techniques for the creation of larger entities. Foreign trade, so essential to filling the Sumerian need for metals, timber, and stone, diffused their material goods and culture far and wide, even reaching southern Egypt before 3000 B.C. In the realm of religion, their myths and practices exercised a profound influence on succeeding religious development in the Near East and some of them were even transmitted to Western Christianity. Such an abbreviated list of achievements is impressive, and their value cannot be underestimated. But the most important Sumerian contribution was

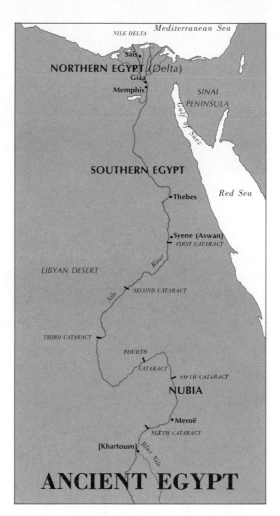

the very advancement of human society and social organization to that stage known as civilization.

ANCIENT EGYPT

A second distinctive civilization benefiting from Sumerian example and influence emerged not long after in the valley of another flood-river, the Nile. Like Sumer, Egypt has been styled as the "gift" of its river. This "greatest single stream on earth" rises at the equator, where daily tropical rains maintain a constant volume of water, and meanders approximately 4000 miles before ending in the Mediterranean Sea. At Khartoum, the White Nile, as the main stream is called, is joined by the Blue Nile, which rises in the mountains of Ethiopia. The Ethiopian rainy season supplied the floodwaters on which Egyptian agriculture relied until modern dams checked the flooding. At the first cataract, where the waters tumbled over a granite ridge, Egypt began. For over 500 miles a narrow ribbon of cultivated land, seldom more than seven miles wide, was irrigated and fertilized by the silt-laden waters of the Nile. On either side of this continous oasis desert conditions prevailed. Then for the last 100 miles the river divided to produce the rich alluvial fan of the delta.

While the annual flood that began every July made possible the intensive cultivation essential to the support of an agricultural civilization, the river also served as a year-round highway, thanks to a reliable wind blowing upstream from the Mediterranean most of the year. At an early date Egyptians learned to use the sail to take advantage of this natural blessing, facilitating communications and thus early unification. In contrast with Mesopotamia, Egypt was also blessed with a plentiful supply of building stone that could be rafted to construction sites during the flood. Copper and turquoise were mined in the nearby Sinai Peninsula. Only a shortage of timber drew Egyptian traders abroad to fill the need with the famed cedars of Lebanon.

In comparison with Mesopotamia, the regularity of the Nile and the relative isolation and self-sufficiency of Egypt contributed to greater cultural stability and a more optimistic outlook, but nature was by no means wholly benign. The volume of the annual flood fluctuated widely with sometimes devastating results. Other natural catastrophes, such as a plague of locusts, could also contribute to the uncertainty and insecurity of life from year to year. In addition, Egypt has never enjoyed complete isolation, even if such a condition were desirable. In predynastic times new peoples frequently migrated into the Nile valley, and in dynastic times any complacency that might develop was shaken by invasions by land and by sea. Conversely, defense and trade encouraged the rulers to engage in imperialistic adventures abroad from the beginning. The term "Empire" only designates a period

of relatively greater imperial activity. Therefore, Egyptian attitudes cannot be entirely attributed either to nature's bounty or to the relative isolation of Egyptian civilization.

In Egypt, civilization and unification arose at the same time. Since it seldom lost its unity for long, its history has been organized according to the successive dynasties of rulers into three major periods: the Old Kingdom (c. 3000–2180 B.C.)* followed by a period of breakdown (c. 2180–2080 B.C.), the Middle Kingdom (c. 2080–1700 B.C.) followed by another breakdown and alien domination (c. 1700–1570 B.C.), and the New Kingdom or Empire (c. 1570–1075 B.C.) after which the realm was weak and divided until a brief but brilliant renaissance under the Saite Dynasty (c. 650–525 B.C.). Unlike Sumer, Egypt did not experience the rise of city-states and their conflicts for supremacy. Indeed, cities did not develop in Egypt except as administrative centers for the rulers, perhaps because of the ease of communications on the Nile. Instead, the countryside was characterized by strings of villages situated on land unsuitable for cultivation and interspersed with occasional market and temple towns. In the predynastic era primitive agriculture was introduced sometime before 4000 B.C., probably by immigrants from Palestine. After 3600 B.C. more advanced agricultural technology involving diking, drainage, and irrigation coincided with a new wave of immigrants from the Syria-Palestine area. Shortly before unification, indirect Sumerian influences appeared in the form of Sumerian-type sun-dried bricks and buildings, cylinder seals, artistic motifs, and writing. But these borrowings were rapidly adapted to the distinctive needs and character of Egyptian civilization.

The process of unification is obscure. Southern Egypt from the first cataract to the delta was unified into one state, while one or more states controlled the delta. For some information on the process we are indebted to a stone palette commemorating the victory

* The first two dynasties are often separately labeled the Archaic Period (c. 3000–2686 B.C.), followed by the Old Kingdom (c. 2686–2180 B.C.), because the former is not as well documented.

The two sides of King Narmer's palette.

of King Narmer of southern Egypt over the delta. On one side the larger than lifesize ruler is depicted wearing the high white crown of southern Egypt and on the other side the red crown of northern Egypt. Despite the permanence of unification this conception of two Egypts was preserved in annual rites as a symbol of the idea of balance and harmony that permeated the Egyptian view of the universe. Narmer is also represented as the falcon-god Horus, son of Osiris, and the mighty bull, son of the sky-goddess (depicted as a cow). Thus the divinity of the ruler is proclaimed from the beginning, which stands in contrast to the Sumerian belief in human mortality.

Egyptian Religions

Although many similarities may be found in the Sumerian and Egyptian interpretations of the universe and its creation, a basic dif-

ference in outlook and emphasis can be identified. Both imagined an original formless chaos, described as the primordial waters, out of which form and substance issued. The components of the universe were visualized similarly with the dome of the sky separated by the atmosphere from the flat disk of the earth. But here came an important difference: the Egyptian insistence on harmony and symmetry demanded a counter-sky below to balance the sky above.

Both agreed that there was a divine order in the universe with each deity responsible for the proper functioning of its component. But to the Sumerians this divine order was generally interpreted as beyond the understanding and control of mere mortals. What impressed them most was the fact of unpredictable change, which they illustrated by elevating Enlil—the god of the atmosphere, of the storm, of constant change—to the position of primacy among the gods. On the contrary, what impressed the Egyptians most was the regularity, the harmony, and the symmetry that they could observe in nature.

This contrast in the interpretation of observed natural phenomena as translated into religious terms has usually been explained as reflecting the different physical environments of Mesopotamia and Egypt, and certainly these arguments are validly based on the relatively more regular and dependable nature of the Egyptian environment. Perhaps as important, however, was the simultaneous development of civilization and unity in Egypt. Absolute rulers of a unified dominion desired emphasis on cohesion and stability. Advocacy of change was not in their interest. Therefore, they encouraged a unification and stabilization of predynastic religious views that probably differed considerably from one end of the Nile to the other. There are hints of a number of previous clanlike organizations with totemic animal symbols. Whatever the prior religious views may have been, certain views demonstrating regularity were singled out and integrated by absorbing differing myths as manifestations of the same underlying concept. And these were concentrated in the living god, the ruler, who comprehended all deities at one and the same time.

Two natural phenomena were obvious examples of regularity: the Nile with its annual flood and the sun with its daily recurrence. Surprisingly, the Nile never received the attention the sun did, perhaps because it was not so dependable. In any case, the sun-god *Ra* soon became the chief deity, and the pharaoh* was his son. Each day the sun died in the west (to the Egyptians darkness was like death), passed through the primordial waters under the earth, and was reborn daily from this source of all creation bringing light and life-giving warmth to man and crops. At the same time the sun was the son of the sky-goddess, represented as a great cow, and as such was pictured as a mighty bull born each day. The many manifestations of the sun-god seem confusing and illogical to us, but they were entirely complementary in the Egyptian view of nature. All things, including gods and goddesses, were created, and therefore all partook of the same nature which was freely transferable. Thus there was nothing contradictory to Egyptians in the conception of being ruled by a living god and this ruler incorporating a number of manifestations at the same time. In one instance the pharaoh was entitled the sun, a star, a bull, a crocodile, a lion, a falcon, a jackal, and the two guardian gods of Egypt, each being merely different aspects of his godhead. Being divine, the king was in fellowship with the gods and could exercise the function of any one of them—indeed actually *be* any one of them—in promoting the welfare of Egypt.

This conception of a god-king contributed to another aspect of Egyptian religious thought. As a living god, the ruler at death would join his fellow gods in immortality. At first he was thought to take with him those who had served him well. Thus during the early dynasties, high officials and nobles built their tombs around the pharaoh's. But if the king and a select few could gain immortality, why could not all good Egyptians join them? Later this idea was fully developed in the cult of Osiris. The belief in the essential unity of nature and, consequently, the divine spark in every man stand in sharp contrast to Sumerian doctrine, which never tired of proclaiming the mortality of men as servants of the gods.

In addition to regularity, Egyptian religion also sought balance and harmony. For each god there was created a goddess who according to the Egyptian conception was both sister and wife. The first couple, air and moisture, produced earth and sky which, in turn, created two couples, Osiris and Isis and Set and Nephthys, who were concerned with the creatures of the earth, animate and inanimate, human and divine. This pairing of deities was applied also to the things of this world in order to achieve balance and harmony, such as the two lands of Egypt with its two crowns and two guardian gods.

* This title for the ruler of Egypt, which only came into use during the New Kingdom, was derived via Hebrew from the name of the palace, "Great House," and reflects the belief that the living god could not be referred to directly by name. Similar indirect usages without such august connotations are common today, such as "the White House," "10 Downing Street," or "the Kremlin."

Another aspect of the emphasis on divine harmony was the god-king's responsibility to maintain *ma'at* — usually translated as "justice" — in his earthly realm. But *ma'at* meant something more than justice; it meant the application of the principles of divine harmony in administering Egyptian affairs and thus included the ideas of truth and righteousness. The ruler and those who acted in his name were required to keep in mind the need for harmony and to go beyond simple justice in evaluating in each case what truth, righteousness, and the welfare of Egypt demanded. Therefore, the living gods of the early dynasties at least were encouraged and empowered to exercise initiative in dealing with the problems and needs of the people and the country, utilizing their divine insight to implement harmony on earth. Under these circumstances the absence of written law codes is not surprising. Here again despotism is justified by the demand that it be ethical and benevolent, as well as balanced by concern for the consequences.

According to the Osirian myth, Osiris was the original god-king who taught the people agriculture and the arts of civilization. His wicked brother Set, representing the forces of destruction, slew him, cut him to pieces, and scattered the remains. Osiris' sister and wife, Isis, found the pieces, put them together, and restored him to life. The resurrected god-king ruled again for a time and then became judge of the dead, his posthumous son Horus taking his place as god-king. This story is another familiar account of death and resurrection explaining the regeneration of plant and animal life. As utilized by the pharaohs to support their authority, each new king was a reincarnation of the god Horus and on death was joined with his father Osiris as judge of the dead. In the later development of the Osirian myth as a salvation cult, each Egyptian after death was judged on his conduct in this life. As in most religions, this procedure became ritualized under the control and for the benefit of the priesthood.

The Old Kingdom (c. 3000–2180 B.C.)

The unimpressive mud-brick and timber tombs of the first two dynasties have suffered so much from deterioration and plundering that little evidence remains on which to reconstruct a picture of the times. The only literary works thought to have been composed in this period are a precocious effort at religious integration known as the Memphite Theology and a surgical treatise with a surprisingly experimental approach that suggests the questing spirit of a daring young society on the move.

A type of writing paper made from the pith of papyrus reeds was invented at least as early as the first dynasty. A simplified cursive script for writing hieroglyphs (derived from pictographs) was also devised to ease the task of record-keeping. Nevertheless, throughout ancient Egyptian history, tradition and religion demanded the continued use of hieroglyphic writing for tomb inscriptions because of their sacred character.

For practical purposes the study of mathematics and astronomy was fostered. Mathematical development was needed for accurate measurement in a land where the annual flood often wiped out boundaries, for engineering irrigation works and tombs, and for assessment in a complex system of taxation. Knowledge about the sun, the moon, and the stars was needed for accurate directional orientation of tombs and temples and for reliable calendars to forecast the flood season and to determine the correct time for religious rites.

The scanty remains of arts and crafts demonstrate not only sharply improved skills but also bold experiments and innovations that substantiate the vitality of this young civilization. The picture of society is one of a vigorous, confident, and industrious people taking the fullest possible advantage of the opportunities for improvement offered by unification. The god-kings were proving their ability to advance the earthly welfare of the people, and for the moment the people were chiefly concerned with the opportunities for the good life here and not much concerned about the hereafter. Even the kings, who theoretically owned the whole land of Egypt, shared and, indeed, inspired this enthusiasm. They did so by plowing back their wealth into productive public works that further increased their income, which was derived from taxes taking an average of one-fifth of production.

The momentum and exuberance generated in the first two dynasties carried over into the third, but it was becoming harder to find constructive investments for the vastly increased revenue pouring into the royal coffers. Expansion of the material base of Egyptian civilization continued, but the pace slowed down. Sufficient surpluses existed for the construction of Djoser's Step Pyramid (c. 2650 B.C.) the first "house of eternity" constructed entirely of stone. In six steps it arose to 204 feet overlooking a complex of dummy buildings in imitation of the wood and brick structures in which the living ruler performed his duties. False doors concealing solid rubble interiors emphasize the unreal and magical purpose of this "city of the dead." The whole area was surrounded by a massive stone wall more than one mile in circumference with 14 gates only one of which was real. The purpose of the whole complex seems to have been to guarantee by imitative magic the permanence, stability, and harmony of the united realm of the two lands of Egypt. The pyramid form, which was to be repeated on a grander scale in the great pyramids of the Fourth Dynasty, appears to recognize the primacy of the sun-god in the Egyptian religious hierarchy.

The architect of this vast work, Imhotep, is the first example of a universal genius whose reality as a human being has not been lost in legend. In addition to his genius as an architect, preserved for all time in the Step Pyramid, this chief minister of Djoser was renowned as an astronomer, priest, writer, sage, and physician. His reputed skill as a physician was so great that he was later deified as the god of medicine.

With such a servant, Djoser's reign must have prospered exceedingly. His successors were apparently not so fortunate. Several tried to emulate his tomb-building effort but were unable to complete their undertakings. Not until the Fourth dynasty was a succession of rulers able to marshal the resources and skills to repeat this feat on a more grandiose scale in the famous pyramids at Giza, the tombs of the Pharaohs Khufu, Khafre, and Menkaure.

Whether or not, as some authorities have suggested, those pyramids were vast public works designed to ameliorate an unemployment problem, the scale of these enterprises clearly indicates that the pharaohs had reached a pinnacle of power and wealth. The possibility that the diversion of resources to such nonproductive works may have contributed to subsequent decline does not alter this conclusion. In any case, the decline was gradual, reflecting a slow shift of power and influence from the pharaoh to a self-assertive nobility.

The largest of the pyramids, that of Khufu, was erected on a square base of 13 acres and rose to a point 481 feet high. More than two million huge blocks of limestone, averaging two and one-half tons each, were carefully fitted to form the core, which was then faced with finer limestone blocks. The seams of the facing stones were cut to a precision of one ten-thousandth of an inch. The engineering achievement was magnificent, and modern scholars have tried to reconstruct the technique used in view of Old Kingdom technology. Perhaps their most significant conclusion is that large numbers of workers were employed only when the blocks were floated to the site during the annual flood. At that time farmers were in any case idle.

In the arts and crafts, as in architecture, the greatest efforts were devoted to productions in enduring materials, especially stone, whether the products were stone vessels and ornaments or sculptures and reliefs. Despite the adoption of similar pictorial conventions, the Egyptians' sense of oneness with nature inspired a restrained naturalism in contrast with the more abstract and symbolic style of the Sumerians.

The people, both nobles and commoners, enjoyed a lively, materialistic, this-worldly set of values. When they thought of the next life, they expected it to be just as happy, well-equipped, and vigorous as this life. This point of view is confirmed by inscriptions and reliefs in tombs. One nobleman who lived about 2400 B.C. is pictured engaging fully in an active, constructive life of hunting, fishing, farming, herding, and building with both humor and humanity as common themes. This outlook contrasts sharply with the almost morbid concern with death and the next life that characterizes the tomb inscriptions of the later New Kingdom.

The general trend, at least among the

nobles, was a progressive development of self-confidence and individualism. The early desire to be buried near the pharaoh in order to share in his immortality was abandoned as nobles became hereditary officials in the later Fourth dynasty. The self-assured governor who ruled his domain like a petty pharaoh confidently built his tomb near his residence. As the grip of the pharaoh over the affairs of the realm weakened, the corruption and self-seeking of local nobles created conditions of oppression that belied the continued claims of benevolent justice. The resources and power of the pharaohs were sapped by alienation of property and income to support temples and greedy nobles. Before long, ruthless competition produced the decentralization and anarchy that undermined and overthrew the ideals of regularity, balance, harmony, and unity that had characterized the government, religion, and way of life of the Old Kingdom.

The collapse of central authority ushered in a century (c. 2180–2080 B.C.) of social upheaval and internal turmoil, complicated by foreign intrusions, which many contemporaries bewailed in personal accounts that probably exaggerated their discomfort. One such account observed that servants had abandoned their posts to go forth and seize the property of the rich, while noble lords and their ladies were forced to labor in the fields and workhouses. Farmers neglected their chores because they had no idea what the morrow might bring. The ruler himself had been carried off by poor men. Sons even turned their hands against their fathers, and virtuous men threw themselves to the crocodiles in despair. To cap this tale of woe whose worst effects were apparently limited to the delta, invaders joined in the pillaging, turning fertile fields into deserts. Overwhelmed by this disaster, the author exclaimed: "Ah, would that it were the end of men, no conception, no birth!"*

The Middle Kingdom (c. 2080–1700 B.C.)

Eventually, unity was restored and the boundaries regained by the rulers of Thebes,

* James B. Pritchard, ed., *Ancient Near Eastern Texts*, pp. 441–43.

some 450 miles south of the delta. Again, as so frequently recurs in history, unity was achieved by vigorous leaders from a frontier area of Egyptian civilization.

The form of social and political organization had been set by the Old Kingdom. The Middle Kingdom followed this form, but the disorders and difficulties of the last days of the Old Kingdom and succeeding breakdown contributed to a change in the substance of royal authority and in the essence of social values and practices. The extent of this alteration may be debated, but the reality of, at least, a shift in emphasis is generally agreed on.

The nobles were too well established in their own areas for elimination. They were disciplined into acceptance of subordination to the crown but retained sufficient local influence to check the assertion of absolute power by the pharaohs. On the other hand, the pharaohs, to gain greater independence of action, opened the bureaucracy to all qualified applicants and subsidized education in order that able commoners might qualify for appointment. In this way the rulers sought to minimize the effects of social stratification by opening avenues of advancement to all their subjects.

During the Middle Kingdom, the doctrine of *ma'at* received special emphasis in terms of securing social justice. Officials were regularly admonished to give special attention to the welfare of society's unfortunates: the poor, the widow, and the orphan. Yet the repeated appeals suggest the continued abuse of power. Indeed, the general view was expressed that all subjects had rights as well as duties. As the shepherd of his people, the pharaoh had the duty to see to it that his deputies protected these rights in addition to obtaining compliance with the duties. Many writings emphasized that the gods were more impressed with righteous conduct than with material works dedicated to them.

A change in religious outlook reciprocally supported the emphasis on ethical conduct. The belief developed that every person by proper conduct could prepare for individual salvation. The deceased person would appear before a tribunal of gods which would weigh his good deeds against his bad deeds to determine his fate. And this fate was dependent on the individual's behavior, not on the benevolence of the pharaoh. Texts were written inside coffins for the guidance and protection of the deceased. Thus the gods came to be viewed as concerned for all mankind, not just their earthly agent.

These changes only represent a shift of emphasis in values, modifying the approach to life and death which was still characterized by a materialistic, individualistic, this-worldly attitude. The worldly attitude was simply tempered by a greater recognition of ethical restraints on human relations. In a sense the value system had not been changed at all. The values implicit at the outset of Egyptian civilization were only given a fuller, more refined expression. The original Egyptian conception of balance, harmony, and justice was merely extended and more fully implemented.

The refinement of Egyptian civilization in this period was reflected in the large literary output, suggesting a broadening of the base of education and literacy. It was also reflected in the growth of foreign trade, mostly under the auspices of the pharaohs. Egyptian trading connections spread far and wide, especially with Minoan Crete. The remarkable skill of Egyptian craftsmen created a foreign demand for their products, and knowledge of Egyptian wealth naturally aroused the envy of less prosperous peoples.

Near the end of the Middle Kingdom, pottery inscribed with curses of foes, both foreign and domestic, was purposely smashed in an attempt to exorcise by magic the growing threats at home and abroad. The internal weakness of the dynasty invited the invasion of Egypt by a mixed horde under the leadership of the Hyksos, a people of uncertain origin. They enjoyed the military advantage of horse-drawn chariots, an innovation probably learned from Indo-Europeans.

For many centuries peoples outside the centers of civilization had been moving about and interacting peacefully or forcefully with their civilized neighbors. Before 2000 B.C. peoples speaking Indo-European languages from beyond the Caucasus Mountains and the Caspian Sea began to press into Anatolia, Iran, and the mountainous terrain in between, conquering or pushing before them the residents of those areas. The Indo-Europeans appear to have been the first to utilize the horse to draw light, spoked-wheel war chariots, but this practice could be and was rapidly transmitted to those with whom they came into contact.

The New Kingdom or Empire (c. 1570–1075 B.C.)

The Hyksos, who were described by an Egyptian writer as "a blast of God" who ruled "in ignorance of Ra" (probably another exaggerated exercise of literary license), exploited northern Egypt for more than a century (c. 1700–1570 B.C.) before being expelled by a resurgent Egypt again led by Theban princes from the south. The long domination by aliens was a traumatic experience to the hitherto self-confident Egyptian spirit, and it left its scars. Either the gods had failed Egypt, or the Egyptians had failed their gods and suffered punishment.

One result was a fanatical pursuit of the Hyksos using horse-drawn chariots into Palestine, Syria, and even beyond the Euphrates to forestall any revival of the threat to Egypt. These campaigns involved the New Kingdom in imperialistic adventures that have given the next several centuries the additional label of Empire. The military forces concentrated in the hands of the pharaohs for campaign after campaign gave them greater absolute power than ever before. Plunder and tribute from control of all major east-west trade routes filled the royal coffers.

A more important result was the gradual development of extreme religiosity. Rulers gave thanks to the gods for their victories by having monumental temples constructed and supporting them with lavish endowments of land and people. Eventually, the temples are estimated to have owned one-third of the land, while serfs and slaves laboring in temple factories produced one-half or more of the manufactured goods. Naturally, in return for royal favors, the priesthood supported the absolute power of the pharaohs until they came to rely more on the priests than the priests did on them.

The growing concern of the people about the next life was also cultivated by the priests, especially those of the cult of Osiris, who fully defined their doctrine during this period. With magic formulas, which indeed stressed high moral standards, they stood ready to ease the passage of the worst sinner — for a fee. The long list of sins made every man a sinner dependent on divine mercy. The ethical standards were beyond human accomplishment. The former balancing of good against bad deeds at the final judgment was replaced by weighing the heart against a feather. Conformity and submission in this life were advocated in the hope of a better life after death. The old lust for life and spirit of individualism, although still depicted in tombs, were subordinated to the demand for conformity to the needs of the group and the state. Intellectually and emotionally individuals yearned for the freedom and independence of the past.

A generalized and unorganized dissatisfaction with the religious state of affairs may have encouraged the pharaoh, Akhnaton (c. 1370–1353 B.C.), to attempt a religious revolution, but other factors provided additional incentives. Religious development, despite royal assertions to the contrary, had weakened the religious sanction of the god-king. He was no longer viewed as the single, or even the most important, source of salvation. Moreover, the religious establishments had gained control of such a large proportion of Egypt's economic resources that they could deal on equal terms with the living god. Therefore, there was ample political justification for religious reform. If Akhnaton had succeeded, the power of the priesthood would have been broken and all sources of authority, both spiritual and secular, would have been concentrated in the pharaoh.

Akhnaton replaced the whole religious hierarchy with the worship of the sun, Aton, conceived abstractly and not in human form. In a new city dedicated to Aton, the deity was represented by a sun disk whose rays ended in hands holding the hieroglyph for "life." Before this symbol stood the surprisingly realistic figure of Akhnaton as the sole intermediary between this universal deity and all mankind. Indeed, one of the by-products of this short-lived reform was the temporary release from traditional conventions of Egyptian artists who demonstrated their innate talent in naturalistic artistic works. Such an abstract universal monotheism was too radical for the times and died

Akhnaton and his wife worshipping the Aton.

with its creator. It was too abstract for popular comprehension and, for obvious reasons, was solidly opposed by the priesthood. The mere fact of its implementation during Akhnaton's reign, however, illustrates how much power the pharaoh still wielded.

Around 1200 B.C., Egypt repelled two invasions in search of plunder by the Sea Peoples, probably Indo-Europeans and others from the Aegean and Asia Minor, but the Empire lost its last footholds in Syria and Palestine. One group of the Sea Peoples founded the Philistine state in Palestine which became the principal opponent of the Hebrews. Egyptian unity was precariously maintained for another century followed by four centuries of weakness and division before the brilliant revival of the Saite Dynasty (652–525 B.C.).

THE HITTITES

The principal challenge to the continued Egyptian efforts to maintain control of Palestine and Syria came in the fourteenth and thirteenth centuries B.C. from the Hittites, an Indo-European people who had established a kingdom in the Anatolian Plateau as early as the seventeenth century B.C. The ancient trade between Anatolia and Mesopotamia introduced them to Mesopotamian culture, and they adopted cuneiform writing for their records. In the sixteenth century a Hittite king led a plundering raid into Mesopotamia and met almost no opposition. Before he realized what he was accomplishing, he had entered the imperial capital, Babylon, and had slain the last of Hammurabi's successors. But he was unprepared to consolidate his success, and the destruction of the Babylonian dynasty only opened the way for domination of Mesopotamia by the Kassites from the neighboring Iranian highlands. These Kassites were a mixed people with Indo-European rulers who merely preserved Babylonian civilization.

By the fourteenth century B.C. the Hittites had secured their flanks and were prepared to challenge Egyptian ascendancy in Syria. The ensuing clash of imperialisms was the largest and longest struggle the world had yet seen. Vast hosts marched back and forth and clashed in mighty battles. Siege and countersiege promoted the arts of war and fortification. The end result was stalemate, proclaimed by a series of treaties in the thirteenth century. These treaties divided Syria, provided for mutual extradition of fugitives, stipulated a defensive and offensive alliance, and declared in good diplomatic parlance "peace and brotherhood between the contending parties forever." Egyptian monopoly of the major trade routes had been broken, but both powers were exhausted by the struggle.

The same fresh wave of Indo-European migration that brought the Sea Peoples to Egypt overwhelmed the Hittite homeland before 1200 B.C. The collapse of the two major powers of the Near East left a power vacuum for four centuries during which lesser states were able to form and prosper in the Syria-Palestine buffer region, such as the Phoenician, Aramean, and Hebrew states. During this period, trade continued to grow despite political disunity. The Phoenicians were the successors of Minoans and Myceneans in the domination of maritime trade in the Mediterranean and also developed an alphabet that gradually supplanted the cuneiform symbols as the system of writing throughout the area.

The alphabet was a major legacy of the ancient Near East to Western civilization.

The Arameans specialized in the overland trade between the Persian Gulf and the Phoenician ports. The camel facilitated the development of new routes across the hitherto forbidding desert. Damascus under the Arameans became an important distribution center. For a time the unified Hebrew state benefited from control of caravan routes from Arabia which bypassed Egypt. As might be expected in such a crossroads area, the cultures of the Semitic peoples of Syria-Palestine were a selective adaptation of influences from abroad and demonstrated little originality, with one notable exception. The Hebrews' outstanding contribution was in the field of religion, which will be described presently. Finally, a new imperial power arose that created a larger empire than any of its predecessors and set in motion the development toward an even larger unity.

THE ASSYRIANS

As early as 3000 B.C. a Semitic people known as Assyrians after their chief city, Assur, had settled down to a predominantly pastoral life in the foothills along the upper Tigris River. During the subsequent millennia they adopted Mesopotamian culture and may be designated a fringe area of Mesopotamian civilization. They were assailed constantly by other peoples whose movement toward Mesopotamia they checked and with whom they mixed, creating an ethnic amalgam. Their military function promoted the centralization of political authority, although throughout their history the support of a military aristocracy had to be recognized and rewarded by the rulers.

Late in the twelfth century B.C., Assyria made its first attempt at imperialism, hoping to take advantage of the political fragmentation in Syria, but the effort was premature. Not until the ninth century did a series of able rulers begin to build a new type of empire by taking advantage of improved means of transportation and communication to exercise a more direct control over conquered territories. The Assyrian Empire reached its greatest extent just prior to its sudden and fatal end late in the seventh century B.C., incorporating all the civilized and economically valuable areas of the Near East, including Mesopotamia and Egypt.

Thanks in large part to the biblical record and their own boastful accounts, the Assyrians have come down in history as the epitome of ruthlessness and barbarity. Moralists have never tired of pointing out the object lesson of their sudden destruction by enraged subjects. Such an interpretation does violence to the facts.

In the first place, ruthlessness was nothing new in Near Eastern warfare. Slaughter and mass enslavement, in which human beings were classified along with other plunder, were commonplace before institutional and communication advances made possible direct control over distant conquered areas. As examples, both Hittite and Egyptian records boast of slaughter and human loot. In fact, for the first century and a half Assyrian practice appears generally to have been more humane in this respect. Seeking acknowledgement of their supremacy and tribute from defeated rulers, they had not yet tried to establish the direct rule that characterized the last century and a half of their empire. Therefore, the Assyrians did their best to promote trade, although they left the trading activities to the more experienced Phoenicians and Arameans.

The Egyptians, however, never having accepted their loss of control of the major trade routes, fomented rebellions among Assyria's tributary states in the Syria-Palestine region. In reaction, the Assyrian ruler Tiglath-Pileser III (745–727 B.C.) instituted the policies of terror, mass deportation, and direct rule. The last step ushered in a new stage in imperial development. Some local lords were allowed to stay in power, subject to an Assyrian governor, but other vital areas and cities, such as Damascus, were placed under Assyrian administrators. Imperial policy was still flexible and experimental.

In 720 B.C., Samaria, the capital of Israel, was taken after a three-year siege and a mass deportation terminated its independence. Sennacherib (705–681 B.C.), the most ruthless of Assyrian rulers, reduced the Phoenician cities (which Egypt had encouraged to revolt), ravaged Judea, and razed Babylon to punish rebellion. His successor tried a different approach by rebuilding Babylon and giving it a local ruler. The effort to mollify the Mesopotamians ultimately failed when they joined the Medes of Iran in destroying Assyria. Meanwhile, the principal thorn in Assyria's side, Egypt, was conquered, temporarily uniting the two major civilizations of the Near East.

The success of the later campaigns was aided by the development of a new military arm, a cavalry of mounted warriors, which greatly increased mobility and impact. Mounted messengers had been used for some time to speed communications and to facilitate imperial administration. Royal post roads tied together the chief administrative cities of the empire. Indeed, without this improvement the effective rule of such a large realm would be difficult to conceive. In addition, the use of iron for weapons and plowshares had spread after 1200 B.C., ushering in the Iron Age.

Ashurbanipal (668–626 B.C.), the ruler who completed the conquest of Egypt, is also renowned for building up and beautifying the imperial capital, Nineveh. His most valuable contribution to later ages was the collection of the literary works of all his subjects in a great library. The site, accursed and undisturbed since Assyria's overthrow, has furnished scholars with a treasure trove for the recovery of the past.

At its zenith, when Assyria had apparently reduced all its foes and instituted an efficient imperial administration, its military strength rapidly evaporated. The Assyrian people had been bled in centuries of incessant campaigns, and the remaining forces were dispersed in far-flung garrisons. Mercenaries proved unreliable. The successful revolt of Egypt demonstrated the inherent weakness of the empire and encouraged rebellious intrigue in every province. The death blows

An Assyrian lion hunt.

were delivered by the joint forces of the Medes of western Iran and the Mesopotamians. Notably, both of these tributary areas were ruled by native princes and were not subjected to imperial governors. In 612 Nineveh was razed, and six years later the allies destroyed the last Assyrian army. As a people, the Assyrians disappeared from the pages of history, but the trail they had blazed in military and imperial development was not forgotten and was immediately followed with appropriate modifications by their successors. Through their efforts ancient imperialism had come of age (see essay on Imperialism, Chapter 19).

With tribute pouring into the royal coffers, the later Assyrian rulers were able to dedicate large sums to religion and the arts. Not only Nineveh, but Mesopotamian cities as well were benefited by the royal bounty. In art, literature, religion and, indeed, in all aspects of culture the Assyrians were the heirs, preservers, and promoters of Mesopotamian civilization, which was to be continued on an even grander scale by the short-lived Neo-Babylonian Empire.

THE NEO-BABYLONIAN EMPIRE (612–539 B.C.)

After the destruction of Nineveh the Babylonian ruler took as his share of the spoils the more civilized heartland of the Assyrian Empire with the major trade routes, while the Medean king inherited the less tamed areas to the east and north of the Tigris. But the new Babylonian ruler, Nebuchadrezzar II (605–562 B.C.) was not unopposed in his claims. Saite Egypt, fearful of allied success, had announced its intention of contesting the Babylonian claim by fighting on the Assyrian side in the last decisive battle. Consideration of the international balance of power dictated that the Egyptians support their recent oppressors.

Like the Assyrian rulers, Nebuchadrezzar had to deal with Egypt's effort to reassert its influence in Syria-Palestine. Although his forces regularly defeated the Egyptians in the field, the struggle was long and hard, not being concluded until the fall of the Phoenician city of Tyre in 572 B.C. after a thirteen-year siege. One result of this contest, which looms large in the Old Testament, was the reduction of Judea after repeated rebellions, the capture of Jerusalem, and the carrying off in 586 B.C. of the Hebrew elite to what is called the "Babylonian Captivity."

Nebuchadrezzar was much less proud of his military exploits than of his public works, such as irrigation canals, caravan roads, temples, and palaces. After almost a millenium, Babylon was once more an imperial capital and the chief seat of civilization in the Near East. National pride in this rebirth generated an artistic and cultural renaissance, as

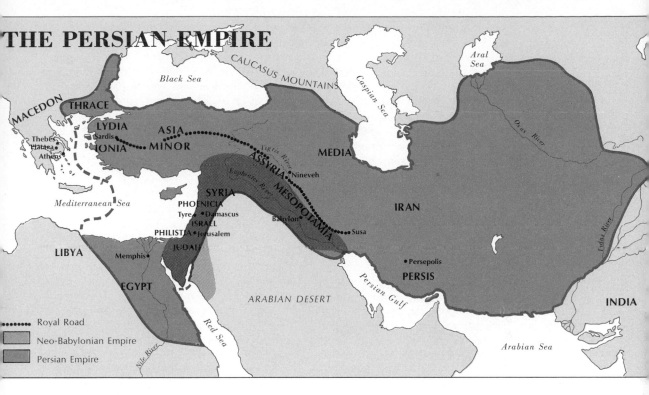

THE PERSIAN EMPIRE

Royal Road
Neo-Babylonian Empire
Persian Empire

in Saite Egypt, drawing heavily on tradition. This was the city of the famous "hanging gardens," one of the seven wonders of the world selected by the Greeks. This was the city harboring every vice and depravity that tortured the puritanical consciences of the Hebrew religious leaders.

The ancient Mesopotamian religious doctrine, which reduced men to mere servants of the gods, received renewed emphasis and stimulated study of the stars to discover one's destiny. As a result of the accent on astrology, the heavenly bodies were charted and catalogued with greater accuracy than ever before, laying a foundation for the later development of astronomy. Religiously, astrology made the individual dependent on experts whose calculations were beyond ordinary comprehension; no longer could the individual rely simply on supplications and sacrifices to his personal patron deity. Moreover, there were no guarantees. A man's fate still rested on the whim of the gods.

THE PERSIAN EMPIRE

While the Neo-Babylonian Empire was luxuriating in its revived power and achieving a new peak of prosperity, its end and absorption into a far larger empire were being prepared by poorly understood events transpiring among the Indo-European speaking peoples who had settled in western Iran. A subordinate chieftain, Cyrus of Persia, supplanted his Medean overlord in 550 B.C. and led the united peoples in a series of amazingly rapid conquests. The rulers of the major states (Nabonidus of Babylonia, Amasis of Egypt, and Croesus of Lydia) were not unaware of the coming storm and tried in vain to coordinate a common defense. Cyrus the Great and his successor were able to conquer them one by one starting with the weakest, the fabled Croesus of Lydia (in western Asia Minor), which had created the first coinage of a gold and silver alloy called electrum and grown rich through trade with the Greeks. Croesus consulted the Greek oracle at Delphi which advised him that if he went to war with Cyrus a great empire would be destroyed. He never dreamed it would be his own. In any case, his only choice was to fight or submit. In 546 B. C. the conquest of Lydia gave Cyrus control of the whole of Asia Minor. For a few years he campaigned in the east to forestall nomadic raids and then took advantage of the Babylonian priesthood's discontent with Nabonidus. After routing the Babylonian army, Cyrus took the capital city without a struggle in 539 B.C. The balance of his reign was occupied with the consolidation of these conquests. Then his son, Cambyses (530–525 B.C.), added Egypt to the Persian empire.

Cyrus had wisely adopted a moderate and tolerant policy toward the conquered territories, allowing them to retain their religions while he, as their new king, performed their religious ceremonies and subsidized their temples and priests. All exiles, such as the Hebrews, were permitted to return to their homelands and even assisted in rebuilding their temples. But the Persian conquerors carried in their cultural baggage a vigorous religion infused with a high ethical content and a sense of mission.

Zoroastrianism

We do not know exactly when Zoroaster (Zarathustra) preached his new revelation and just what his original teachings were, but he probably lived not long before the creation of the empire, about 600 B.C. The Zend-Avesta, which purports to represent his teachings, was not compiled in its present form until the Christian era. To what extent the priests, called *magi*, altered his message cannot be determined. The major point in dispute is whether he taught a monotheistic faith in Ahura-Mazda, the god of light, or a dualistic doctrine in which Ahriman, the god of darkness, is locked in continuing conflict with Ahura-Mazda. In fact, the earliest evidence indicates that Ahura-Mazda was viewed as the supreme, if not the sole, god who would ultimately prevail. Darius I (521–485 B.C.), who gained the throne in the strife following the premature death of Cambyses, clearly declared his debt to Ahura-

Mazda and established his worship as the state religion. Perhaps the death of Cambyses and the succeeding turmoil were instigated by priests who were discontented with the imperial policy of religious toleration. Whether a result of royal patronage or the tired and uninspired condition of other religions, Zoroastrianism spread rapidly. Certainly, on its merits alone, it had a strong appeal.

Zoroastrianism reformed the ritual-ridden and priest-dominated religion of the Iranian folk. A central feature had been the sacred fire. While preserving the idea of a sacred fire, however, Ahura-Mazda's revelation to Zoroaster created a wholly new and dynamic religion in which the forces of the universe were in conflict preparing the world and man for the ultimate day of judgment.

As taught, this was a universal religion. All men were invited to support the forces of good, commanded by Ahura-Mazda, against the forces of evil, led by Ahriman. The active participation demanded of each individual preserved freedom of choice, and the prescribed course of action required virtuous conduct involving positive acts of will and self-denial on the part of the believer. Practical virtues included hard work, the honoring of contracts, obedience to superiors, tilling of the soil, and begetting many children to enlarge the ranks of the army of good. More abstract injunctions enjoined honesty, brotherly love, hospitality, and care for the poor. The broad categories of sin included selfish pride, gluttony, laziness, covetousness, lust, anger, slander, and waste. Specific sins included adultery, abortion, and usury. With its stress on the active life, Zoroastrianism forbade ascetic practices, such as self-punishment, fasting, and excessive grief, as essentially selfish and contrary to the communal virtues as well as to the obligations to produce food and children.

Zoroastrianism was the first religion to set a definite timetable when Ahura-Mazda would finally prevail and establish an eternal paradise. In 9000 years Zoroaster would come again as a promise of ultimate redemption. He would be followed by the miraculous birth of a messiah who would make the final preparations for the conclusion of the struggle at the end of 12,000 years. At that

The King of Kings, Darius I, with Xerxes behind him.

date would occur the resurrection of the dead and the day of judgment. The righteous would cross the bridge to paradise, while the sinners would join Ahriman in the fiery abyss. According to the weight of their sins, however, the wicked would be sentenced to a longer or shorter period of suffering. Ultimately, all, saints and sinners, would enjoy eternal life in paradise. The appeal of this religion and its influence on its successors are self-evident and need no elaboration.

Like other universal religions, Zoroastrianism in time lost its purity. The organized priesthood reintroduced ritualistic magic based on old superstitions. Moreover, as the religion spread, it picked up alien elements from the older religions it sought to replace. Two influential variants developed later: Mithraism and Manicheism (see pp. 136, 183–184). Today Zoroastrianism continues to be practiced by the Parsees in India.

Although Darius I declared Ahura-Mazda to be his patron, there is no indication that he added religious to territorial imperialism. He no longer gave active support to local religions, laws, and customs but toleration remained the imperial policy. On the other hand, the many insurrections he had to suppress to secure his succession made Darius well aware of the need for a more efficient system of imperial administration, a chore neglected by the busy conquerors, Cyrus and Cambyses. Not that Darius neglected imperialism; he extended the frontiers in the west into Thrace in Europe and in the

east into the Indus valley. But his most important contributions were in the field of imperial government.

Persian Imperial Administration

First, the status of the "Great King" was raised from that of a simple warrior to that of an all-powerful despot whose word was law and whose person could be approached only through a maze of intermediaries amid much pomp and ceremony. This creation of an "oriental" court not only protected the ruler against assassination but also instilled a deeper respect for his person and power among the many different subject peoples within the Persian realm.

Second, Darius divided the empire into more than twenty provinces (satrapies). While he retained direct rule over the two centers of civilization, Mesopotamia and Egypt, the other provinces were assigned to civil governors (satraps) who were either royal relatives or trustworthy nobles. Associated with the satrap was a separate military commander. Each had to cooperate with the other and was required to report directly to the king on the other's activities. As an additional check, a provincial secretary was appointed by the king to inspect the mails. A further precaution was a system of traveling inspectors known as "the eyes and ears of the king." By this division of authority and additional safeguards Darius sought to minimize the possibilities of his provincial rulers building up power bases against him.

The satrap collected the taxes to be forwarded to the royal treasuries, and the fixed assessment was usually lower than in the past. But the extra exactions of Persian officials, their monopoly of higher offices, military conscription, and frequent disdain for subject peoples combined to generate discontent that often resulted in abortive rebellions.

Communications have always governed the size and method of administration of empires. Darius sought to solve this problem for his vast realm by the construction of post roads. Best known was the 1500-mile road between the chief imperial capital, Susa, and Sardis, the capital of Lydia, over which royal messages carried night and day by mounted relays could be delivered in ten days. These roads also promoted a huge growth of trade within the largest political entity created until that time. The Aramean merchants expanded the range of their commerce carrying with them their language and alphabet. Cuneiform was replaced by an alphabet of 39 letters, based on the Aramean, for writing Persian.

The army illustrates the problem of a loosely-organized, tolerant empire unable to institute a centralized administration and to enforce a measure of cultural conformity. It relied, as the Assyrian army had, on native Persians and Medes and an elite corps of "10,000 Immortals" to provide a reliable core. This small body was supplemented by contingents from the subject peoples with their customary arms. A vast and colorful host of this nature might overawe a foe, but in combat it was unwieldy and uninspired by any deep loyalty. The first reverse could precipitate a general rout.

Nevertheless, this decentralized empire, tolerant of its diverse components, managed to suppress the frequent rebellions and maintain its frontiers for two centuries. The system of imperial organization and administration drew on Assyrian precedents with modifications; it served as a model for succeeding empires in the Middle East.

The empire's greatest weakness has not yet been noted. This was the Great King himself. Effective government depended on the ability and conscientiousness of this single figure with unlimited power. No device could be found to assure his efficiency or to provide for the removal of an inefficient ruler. Thus the key to this system of checks and balances was unchecked himself.

The Persians utilized the skills and talents of their more advanced subjects to build and beautify the imperial capitals. While these artists and architects naturally introduced their own motifs in their works, the columnar style of architecture was derived from the Persian tradition of columned porticoes made of wood, not from Greek or Egyptian precedents as has sometimes been supposed. In the other amenities of civilization the Persians borrowed freely from their more cultured subjects and added nothing of their own except an inborn sense of esthetic appreciation which has always characterized the people of Iran and their products. The pedestrian products of mass production that satisfied Mesopotamians and Egyptians held no appeal for them, with one exception. Mass-produced coinage was of such obvious utility that it was borrowed from Lydia and carried throughout the realm and abroad by trade.

THE HEBREWS

A minor people known as the Hebrews were responsible for a major contribution to what has been singled out as the most influential contribution of the Middle East—religion. In addition, they produced the first substantial historical work in the Old Testament. This was no mere chronicle of events, but a conscious selection compiled to illustrate and explain what they considered the most important aspect of their history—the course of their religious development. Since we are chiefly concerned with the Hebrews' religious contribution, scant attention will be paid to other aspects of their history.

The early books of the Old Testament can only be deemed legendary, drawing on a variety of ancient myths and current tales; we should also view with skepticism the account of the Hebrews prior to the Exodus and their migration into the hills of Palestine between the Jordan River and the coastal plain late in the thirteenth century. Tribes of pastoral nomads, eventually known as Hebrews, may have migrated into Syria-Palestine, already occupied by another Semitic people of the same language group, about 1800 B.C. The Old Testament suggests that their religion at this time was a typical amalgam of worship of the forces of nature and magical practices. Contact with the culturally more advanced Canaanites introduced them to polytheistic beliefs, particularly the prevalent fertility cults. Several centuries later, famine may have driven some tribes to seek refuge in Egypt. The Exodus under Moses' leadership presumably occurred around 1250 B.C. While passing through the Sinai peninsula, Moses persuaded his followers to accept Yahweh, who may have been the deity of a Hebrew tribe in the area. Through the common acceptance and worship of Yahweh the various clans and tribes were brought together in a loose confederation to accomplish the gradual conquest and unification of Palestine over the next several centuries. It will be recalled that after the overthrow of the Hittites and the breakdown of imperial Egypt about 1200 B.C. the peoples of the Syria-Palestine crossroads were free to work out their own destinies until the rise of Assyria. The principal Hebrew foe became the Philistines, a remnant of the Sea Peoples, who dominated Palestine from fortified cities on the southern coastal plain. Many battles were also fought by the pastoral Hebrews with Canaanites living in fortified towns.

During this period, Yahweh was conceived in human form as the folk god and champion of his chosen people who acted in an arbitrary and unpredictable fashion and had to be appeased by ritual sacrifices. He was not a universal god—only the god of the Hebrews—and not much of a promoter of spiritual or ethical conduct—only a dispenser of rewards and punishments for loyalty or disloyalty. His chief function, then, was to unify and lead his people to victory in their struggles with other peoples and other gods, and in this role he suffered setbacks and defeats. He was the supreme lawgiver, but the purpose of his laws was to induce political cooperation and social order. Any promotion of ethical behavior was an ac-

cidental result. Old Testament scholars generally doubt that the Ten Commandments, in their present form, are older than the eighth century B.C.

Shortly before 1000 B.C. the Judge, Samuel, recommended that Saul be elected the first king of the united Hebrew tribes, but his reign ended in suicide after a defeat in which he lost his son. The hero David (c. 1000–961 B.C.) was the founder of the short-lived Kingdom of Israel. He drove the Philistines back, reduced the Canaanite cities, and extended his realm across the Jordan to the east and to Damascus in the north, gaining control of the overland trade routes. In these conquests he was aided by an alliance with the Phoenicians, who dominated the overseas trade routes. Jerusalem, an old city with natural defenses, was chosen as the political and religious capital because it represented neutral ground between the two halves of the Hebrew kingdom, Judea and Israel. Solomon, the builder (961–922 B.C.), succeeded his father David, the warrior. He brought great wealth to the realm through fostering trade, although he lost some outlying areas such as Damascus to the Arameans. He is famed for his luxurious "oriental" palace harboring 700 wives and 300 concubines (who as foreign brides reflected his diplomatic vigor), and for constructing a great temple to house the Hebrew Covenant with Yahweh. This era also saw a blossoming of literature. But the people were unhappy with the rapid transition from tribal life to a bureaucratic state needing heavy taxation to support it, and on Solomon's death the tribes of Israel rebelled bringing to an end the glory of a united realm. The remainder of Hebrew political history may be considered an epilogue until the recreation of Israel after World War II. The greatest religious achievement, however, was yet to come.

The settling down into an agricultural and urban way of life and the mixing with other peoples undermined the dedication to Yahweh and encouraged the worship of other gods. This wayward condition inspired religious reformers, first, to drive out the alien gods, and second, to initiate the era of the prophets (eighth and seventh centuries B.C.) who revolutionized the conception of Yahweh and his worship. The teachings of these inspired men, which carried Hebrew thought to its zenith, cannot be done justice in a brief summary. They should be directly consulted in the Old Testament.

First, Yahweh came to be viewed by the prophets as the sole god of the universe, not just the god of the Hebrews. There was no other god beside him. This was the first assertion of pure and unalloyed monotheism. Furthermore, Yahweh was a god of goodness, justice, and mercy who used his power to guide men back to the path of righteousness. Possibly, these ideas stemmed from the need to explain the reverses the Hebrews suffered during these centuries. A god of all mankind directed the actions of Assyrians as well as Hebrews. Thus he used the Assyrians to punish the Hebrews for their sins or destroyed the invincible host of Sennacherib by means of a plague as an act of mercy toward his Hebrew people.

Finally, sin was not merely the violation of a law of the Book, but included any unjust act, or even thought. In this way the conception of sin was expanded from a legalistic to a humanistic doctrine. Obedience to the letter of the law was not enough; observance of the spirit of the law was just as necessary. Men were urged to look inside themselves and honestly assess and reform their actions and attitudes toward their fellow men. On this basis the all-knowing Yahweh would judge them, and punish, reward, or show mercy toward them. The poetic instruction of the Prophet Micah sums up this attitude clearly.

Wherewith shall I come before the Lord,
*   And bow myself before the high God?*
Shall I come before him with burnt offerings,
*   With calves of a year old?*
Will the Lord be pleased with thousands of
*   rams,*
*   Or with ten thousands of rivers of oil?*
Shall I give my firstborn for my
*   transgression,*
*   The fruit of my body for the sin of my*
*   soul?*
He hath showed thee, O man, what is good;
*   And what doth the Lord require of thee,*
But to do justly, and to love mercy,
*   And to walk humbly with thy god.*
*   (Micah 6: 6–8)*

The command to social justice reflected the growth of inequities in Hebrew society. Under the circumstances that had already seen the extinction of Israel by the Assyrians, one can understand utopian visions of a future time when a "Prince of Peace" would cause wolves to lie down with lambs and when complete justice would prevail. This dream poetically expressed by the Hebrew prophets is still the dream of mankind today. The deliverance the prophets envisioned was an earthly salvation. No Hebrew thinker as yet entertained any idea of an afterlife.

During the "Babylonian Captivity" the intellectual elite was exposed to the full force of their captors' pessimism and fatalism, as well as the fleshpots of the ancient world's most notorious city. In reaction, the priests tried to maintain discipline by placing a heavier emphasis on the law and ritual practices than had ever existed before. Also, unable to justify their misfortunes in any other way, they redefined Yahweh as a deity beyond human comprehension. Man had no choice but to submit without question to whatever was His will. Yahweh alone understood His own divine purpose.

Upon their return from exile the priests gradually asserted their religious supremacy. They were reinforced by the law—which was given the sanctity of revelation—and supported by the Persians. The rigidity of their outlook, however, as well as the influence of Zoroastrian ideas, stimulated the development of splinter movements. Some transferred the source of evil from man to Satan. Some looked for salvation from the woes of the world in an afterlife. These conceptions were supplemented by ideas of a spiritual messiah, resurrection of the dead, and a last judgment. Although most of these doctrines did not become part of the orthodox faith, they fertilized the ground for further expressions of spiritual vitality culminating in the teachings of Jesus of Nazareth.

In this initial chapter the story of man has been surveyed from his long evolution in small groups as a hunter and food-gatherer, largely at the mercy of his environment, through the domestication of plants and animals about 10,000 years ago which supported larger, more self-sufficient, and permanent settlements, to the creation of the first agricultural civilizations in the flood-river basins of Mesopotamia and Egypt. Organization and direction of manpower in the communal tasks of diking, drainage, and irrigation brought forth from the rich soil agricultural surpluses for the support of growing populations and the nonfarming specialists who produced the works of civilization. By around 2000 B.C. Mesopotamia and Egypt with irrigated areas of about 10,000 square miles each fed populations of about one million each. Although the conditions under which the two civilizations developed were comparable, each evolved a distinctive culture reflected in its institutions and ideological formulations.

In both civilizations the intimate relationship between religion and political authority, is evident, even though it took distinctively different forms. This relationship, conceived as early as 4000 B.C., has reappeared in almost every succeeding regime in the area to the present day. In Mesopotamia, kingship arose to meet the needs of defense and foreign relations, but the kings, like the priests and the people, were viewed as servants of the gods to whom they owed their crowns. In less threatened Egypt the god-kings, although challenged by the nobility, maintained their supremacy as living gods.

Foreign trade became especially important in the Mesopotamian economy because of the region's deficiency in metals, stone, and timber, and it diffused its culture far and wide throughout this crossroads area. Comparatively self-sufficient Egypt had less need of trade, which remained largely a royal monopoly. Military action in support of trade

and in defense of the Mesopotamian heartland led to imperialism and to development of the techniques of imperial administration, starting with Sargon of Akkad and culminating in the Assyrian and Persian empires which brought the two great civilizations of the ancient Near East under one rule. Egypt also engaged in imperialism, particularly after the pursuit of the Hyksos resulted in the conquest of Palestine and Syria. This conquest gave Egypt a virtual monopoly of trade with the east, filling the coffers of the New Kingdom, until it was challenged by the Hittites.

The Sumerians as the creators of the first civilization made many vital discoveries and contributions to subsequent civilizations — from writing and the wheel to mathematics and religion. Greek visitors were also tremendously "impressed with Egyptian antiquity and religiosity," and Greek artists were significantly influenced by Egyptian art. But less prominent peoples also made major contributions to European development. The Phoenicians, whose merchants and colonists opened up the whole Mediterranean region, carried with them their version of the alphabet as a major legacy as well as a rich cargo of other ideas and products of Near Eastern origin. Undoubtedly the most influential contribution to Europe, however, was the ethical monotheism evolved by the Hebrews which in its Christian form eventually overcame its Near Eastern competitors.

With the overthrow of the Persian Empire by Alexander the Great in 330 B.C. the history of the ancient Near East became part of the history of Greece and Rome until the rise of Islam.

SUGGESTED READINGS

Howell, F. Clark, *Early Man*. New York: Time-Life Books, 1970.

Clark, Grahame and Stuart Piggott, *Prehistoric Societies*. Baltimore, Md.: Penguin Books, 1970. Paperback.

Childe, V. Gordon, *What Happened in History*. Baltimore, Md.: Penguin Books, 1964. Paperback.
   A stimulating and perceptive analysis and interpretation that assesses developments from prehistoric times through the fall of the Roman Empire.

Piggott, Stuart, ed., *The Dawn of Civilization*. New York: McGraw-Hill, 1961.
   The chapters on prehistoric times, Mesopotamia, and Egypt by acknowl-

edged authorities are well done and the illustrations, while sometimes imaginative, are excellent.

Kramer, Samuel Noah, *History Begins at Sumer.* Garden City, N.Y.: Doubleday & Co., 1959. Paperback.
Fascinating essays on a number of Sumerian "firsts" in history.

Roux, Georges, *Ancient Iraq.* Baltimore, Md.: Penguin Books, 1964. Paperback.
An excellent up-to-date account.

Wilson, John A., *The Culture of Egypt.* Chicago: University of Chicago Press, 1956. Paperback.
This monograph adds depth to the picture of Egyptian civilization.

Frankfort, Henri et al., *Before Philosophy.* Baltimore, Md.: Penguin Books, 1951. Paperback.
A penetrating analysis of Mesopotamian and Egyptian religions and values by leading scholars.

Pritchard, James B., ed., *Ancient Near Eastern Texts.* 3rd ed.; Princeton, N.J.: Princeton University Press, 1969.
The best way to get the "feel" of a civilization is by reading its own writings, even in translation.

Gurney, Oliver R., *The Hittites.* Baltimore, Md.: Penguin Books, 1952. Paperback.

Zaehner, Robert C., *The Dawn and Twilight of Zoroastrianism.* New York: G. P. Putnam's Sons, 1961.

Moscati, Sabatino, *The Face of the Ancient Orient.* New York: Doubleday & Co., 1962. Paperback.
An interpretive account.

CHAPTER **2**

The Earliest Civilizations of India, China, and the Americas

This chapter continues the story of the earliest civilizations with accounts of ancient India, ancient China, and pre-Colombian America. Like Mesopotamia and Egypt, the civilizations of India and China developed in the basins of flood rivers calling for the mobilization of manpower at least to check the ravages of annual flooding, even if greater rainfall reduced the dependence on irrigation works for agriculture. Each of these civilizations developed its own distinctive outlooks and values. In India, religion and religious thought became predominant, whereas in China the secular and rational views of the scholar class came to prevail in society and the state. The creators of the first Indian civilization may have known and been influenced by its Sumerian predecessor, but Chinese civilization appears to have been a native development receiving possibly a few products from abroad, such as seeds and metallurgy. The civilizations of Middle America and South America apparently developed in total isolation from Eurasian influences and even without significant contacts with each other.

ANCIENT INDIA TO *c.* 500 B.C.

The Indus Civilization (*c.* 2500–1500 B.C.)

Although the Ancient Near East was unique in producing two distinctive civilizations, the Indian subcontinent was distinguished by having two successive civilizations separated by a dark age of six or more centuries. Tantalizing hints suggest that the religion, ideals, and values of the first civilization were somehow transmitted to become vital ingredients of the later Indo-Aryan civilization. But we can only guess about such a connection without decipherable written records to throw more light on the archeological evidence.

Like its predecessors, this civilization arose on a flood river, the Indus and its tributaries in the Punjab (Land of Five Rivers). Of the early civilizations, it was the most extensive, covering with a uniform culture an area of almost 500,000 square miles, or roughly the region of present-day Pakistan. In addition, it

45

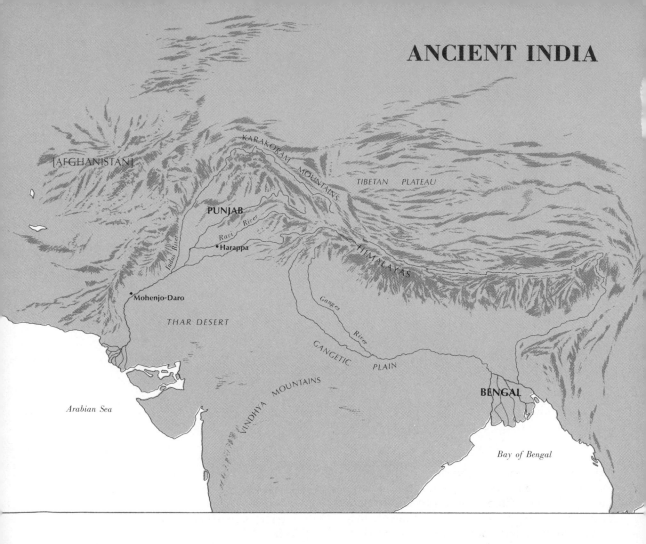

possessed the two largest urban centers yet known for this period, Mohenjo-daro, some 250 miles north of the present mouth of the Indus River, and Harappa, nearly 400 miles farther north and east on the Ravi tributary of the Indus. A further feature was the amazing continuity and conservatism of style and technology which characterized this civilization from beginning to end, an attitude shared by later Indian civilization. Although the cities had to be rebuilt a number of times after devastating floods, the builders adhered to the original city plans, which were almost identical. They were the earliest planned cities laid out in blocks approximately 200 by 400 yards with wide, straight streets. (Hammurabi's Babylon was the first planned city in the Near East.) Moreover, they were equipped with a sewage system. Each home had a bath area hooked up to the bricklined

municipal sewer line. The homes, all substantial, varied in size, suggesting a prosperous middle-class society with some individual opportunity for improvement. The unwalled cities were each more than three miles around and flanked on the west by a fortified citadel on an artificial mound 40 to 50 feet above the plain. At both cities large public granaries with ventilation ducts under the floors provide further evidence of municipal organization and supervision. Nearby barracks may have housed workers or soldiers.

Whatever may have been the form of government, the citadel occupied by some large buildings was certainly its headquarters. At Mohenjo-daro a large pool, similar to the ritual tanks of later India, may have served a ritual purpose for purification. If this interpretation is correct, political and religious authority may have been joined together, but no monumental temples have been identified to support such a view.

The Indus civilization suddenly emerged about 2500 B.C. with signs of only a brief pioneering period by settlers from villages to the west. The distinctiveness of its culture precludes the possibility of direct colonization from Mesopotamia, though knowledge of that civilization probably inspired the effort. The most reasonable hypothesis is that, following a few small-scale attempts at settlement, a major effort was undertaken by these people who had a knowledge of bronze, ceramics, and agriculture. Because of the need for manpower they mixed freely with primitive people previously living a hand-to-mouth existence in the valley and thus established an apparently open society from the beginning. After initial success they spread rapidly up and down the river highways in search of raw materials. Before long, trade led them to take to the sea and build coastal outposts 300 to 400 miles east and west of the mouth of the Indus. By about 2350 B.C. trade with Mesopotamia is attested by Indus products found there. In short, success followed success so swiftly that this civilization developed and spread in only a few generations. Perhaps the penalty for such initial success was the determination to preserve it by avoiding all innovation.

The Indus people did, however, make some important contributions: domestication of the chicken, cotton and cotton cloth, and the invention of a saw with offset teeth. But more impressive was the exceptional conservatism of their craftsmen. Even though their technology was in no way inferior and samples of improved products were occasionally imported, they clung doggedly to the old forms. For example, the shafthole axe had been adopted throughout western Asia, yet the Indus smiths continued to produce the flat axe to which the shaft had to be bound. Likewise, although the strengthening of knives and spearheads with midribs was common elsewhere, weaker flat blades persisted to the end of the Indus civilization. Such conservatism will also be found to characterize later Indian civilization.

For the most part, the artistic expression of this rather materialistic society was personal

Stone sculpture, probably representing a priest, from Mohenjo-daro.

and religious, involving small, but often finely modeled, objects. Most abundant are the flat seals or amulets carved from soft stone that was hardened by baking. Many animals which must have been familiar are realistically pictured on these seals: elephants, rhinoceros, tigers, antelopes, crocodiles, and most common of all, the humped bull native to India. The fact that the bull also accounts for three-quarters of the terracotta animal figurines strongly suggests his probable association with religion. The seals commonly include writing in as yet undeciphered symbols. Of course, these brief accounts can be no more than names, titles, or religious invocations. Although the Indus people were literate, they apparently used perishable material for lengthier accounts.

Composite depictions combining human and animal parts are suggestive of later Indian religious art. Especially interesting are examples of what appears to be a prototype of the Hindu god Shiva provided with horns and seated in the typical Indian position of meditation with associated phallic sym-

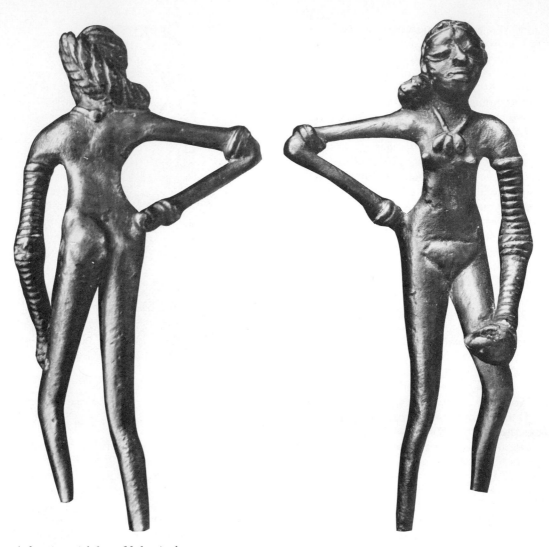

A dancing girl from Mohenjo-daro.

bolism. Numerous representations of the mother goddess, whose cult was common throughout the ancient world, have also been found. The religion of the Indus civilization apparently concerned nature and especially the issue of fertility and reproduction.

In a lighter vein, a charming human touch is given by terracotta and occasionally metal toys which include comic figures and solid-wheeled carts identical with those still used to haul goods today. Several types of dice indicate that gambling was as common an amusement then as later.

This flourishing civilization appears to have been destroyed by a combination of internal deterioration and external blows. Before 2000 B.C., it will be recalled, primarily pastoral tribes speaking Indo-European dialects were moving into the outlying areas of the Near and Middle East employing horse-drawn war chariots with spoked wheels. Among them was a group of related tribes who came to call themselves Arya (anglicized as Aryan), a generic term meaning "kinsmen," preserved in the names of Iran for modern Persia and Eire for Ireland. They gradually moved eastward from Iran into

Afghanistan before descending into the Indus valley after 1600 B.C.

Meanwhile, signs of difficulties and fear appear in the latest archeological levels of the Indus cities. This essentially open society now admitted refugees who were accommodated by subdividing rooms and allowing shoddy construction to press into the streets, violating the hitherto rigorous city plan. Alien pottery of the type in villages to the west supports the probability that much of the new population consisted of refugees from outside the area of Indus civilization. Within the Indus area the fear of raids may have led farmers to abandon their fields and to seek safety in the cities. Without daily care, agricultural production would suffer with consequent food shortage in the overpopulated cities. In other words, the delicate balance of the Indus economy was upset by one or more of many possibilities, while no defensive measures were taken by this conservative society other than strengthening the citadel, perhaps to ward off attacks by starving city mobs.

The only evidence of a violent end comes from Mohenjo-daro. There, on the last archeological level, skeletons of persons cut down in flight are strewn in contorted positions with plentiful signs of mortal wounds. The Aryans may very well have delivered this final blow. In the *Rigveda* the Aryan war-god is described as the "fort destroyer," and where else in the Indian subcontinent were there forts to destroy? The Indus culture undoubtedly persisted at the village level to influence the rise of Indo-Aryan civilization many centuries later, but the collapse of the cities cut the heart out of the Indus civilization.

The Vedic Age
(c. 1600–900 B.C.)

Historically, the subsequent centuries until well after 1000 B.C. are India's Dark Age. The chief source of information is the *Rigveda*, a collection of heroic poetic accounts describing the activities and religious views of those Aryan tribes that revived civilized life in India in the Ganges basin after 900 B.C. Since the 1028 hymns of the *Rig-veda* were only finally selected and declared at that time a sacred literature to be transmitted orally without alteration by the priestly class of brahmans, we cannot be certain how accurately they portray earlier conditions and events. The other Vedas are useful supplements, particularly the *Atharvaveda* because it reflects popular religious beliefs and practices that included many non-Aryan elements.

The general picture is one of incessant warfare against the natives and among themselves as these primarily pastoral tribes slowly migrated from Afghanistan through the Indus valley into the Ganges basin. Chieftains called *rajas* were selected for their military prowess by assemblies of warriors, although a trend toward hereditary succession is apparent. A noble class went to war in horsedrawn chariots. Free commoners served as foot soldiers. At the bottom of society were the slaves or serfs, mostly non-Aryan captives. Women still enjoyed considerable respect and prestige, although they were clearly subordinated to men in this patriarchal society. A priestly class to perform properly the increasingly complex rituals appears in the later hymns as advisers to the chiefs. Social distinctions were still loose, but four classes emerged that later became the basis for more rigid caste distinctions: priest (brahman), warrior (kshatriya), peasant and merchant (vaishya), and non-Aryan serf or servant (shudra).

The Aryans contemptuously described the natives as short and swarthy demons with thick lips and flat noses who lived luxuriously in fortified places. Most loathsome was their worship of the phallus. Despite a strict taboo against mixing with the natives, the Aryans, already a mixed people, could not be kept from intercourse and interaction. Non-Indo-European words appear even in the *Rigveda*. Much later, non-Indo-European characteristics almost submerged Aryan culture, but here again Indian conservatism preserved the first of the Vedas as the primary sacred text.

The Aryan hierarchy of gods contained obvious parallels to those of other Indo-European peoples. Dyaus-piter, the father of the gods, is clearly derived from the same original form as the Greek Zeus and the

Roman Jupiter. But by Vedic times he was already subordinated to other deities, principally Indra, god of storms and war, whose chief weapon was appropriately the thunderbolt. In their own image the Aryan warriors pictured Indra as a spirited, lusty deity, addicted to feasting and drinking. The inebriating beverage, *soma,* prepared from some unidentified plant, possibly hemp, was sacrificially imbibed by the god and his communicants, inducing hallucinations and visions.

Varuna, second only to Indra, was the master and guardian of the cosmic order and, as such, punished men for sinful acts. Unlike the rowdy Indra, he sat in serene majesty in heaven receiving reports of human misconduct from his spies. Thus, he was an all-knowing god whom mere mortals approached with fear and trembling. Sacrifice alone would not be sure to appease him; the sinner had to do penance. In addition to ritual sin, Varuna abhorred lying, inhospitality, violation of friendship, and immoral acts, especially those induced by anger, alcohol, or gambling.

Several deities were related to the sun. One, who was to play a major role in later Hinduism, was Vishnu, pictured as crossing the earth in three giant strides.

By the end of the Vedic era the brahmans had convinced most, if not all, believers that the very existence of the universe depended on their regular performance of the prescribed sacrifices. Without them chaos would ensue. At the same time, however, there is a fresh spirit of inquiry for answers beyond the gods—who themselves had to conform to the cosmic order—in one of the last hymns of the *Rigveda,* a creation hymn whose conception and uncertain conclusion strike a new note seemingly at odds with the rest of this work. Perhaps it was a late addition.

Nor Aught nor Nought existed; yon bright sky
Was not, nor heaven's broad woof outstretched above.
What covered all? What sheltered? What concealed?
Was it the water's fathomless abyss?

There was not death—yet was there nought immortal;
There was no confine betwixt day and night;
The only One breathed breathless by Itself,
Other than It there nothing since has been.
Darkness there was, and all at first was veiled
In gloom profound—an ocean without light—
The germ that still lay covered in the husk
Burst forth, one nature, from the fervent heat.

Who knows the secret? Who proclaimed it here?
Whence, whence, this manifold creation sprang?
The Gods themselves came later into being—
Who knows from whence this great creation sprang?
He from whom this great creation came,
Whether His will created or was mute,
The Most High Seer that is in highest heaven,
He knows it—or perchance even He knows not.

Certainly this hymn threw wide open the gates for speculation and inspired the search for ultimate answers which characterizes the Aranyakas and Upanishads and, in fact, the bulk of subsequent Indian intellectual activity. Setting the stage for this quest, however, were the political, social, and economic developments after 900 B.C.

The Rise of Indo-Aryan Civilization (*c.* 900–500 B.C.)

Perhaps pushed from behind, the Aryans took up the challenge of the Ganges basin and, under the leadership of increasingly powerful hereditary rulers, pressed forward along the north bank to the edge of the delta in Bengal. The brahmans, in return for royal patronage, cooperated in enhancing the prestige and authority of the rulers. The struggle for supremacy involved bitter wars

* Max Muller, *Chips from a German Workshop* (New York: Charles Scribner's Sons, 1881), I, 76–77.

the vague memories of which are preserved in the heroic epics composed in their final form at a much later date, the *Mahabharata* and the *Ramayana*.

The clearing of the jungle for cultivation also brought about social and economic changes. In order to exploit such terrain, permanent settlements devoting more attention to agriculture were necessary. The transition from a tribal to a territorial society undermined the earlier sense of community and kinship, throwing the individual more on his own, and on the central government. The consequent feeling of insecurity may have encouraged the growing asceticism and pessimism that accompanied the advance toward civilization. As prosperity stimulated the formation of larger political units under autocratic rule, the increased gap between ruler and ruled created a spiritual uneasiness reflected in the speculations of sensitive thinkers.

The dominant characteristic of the new thought was religious individualism. Ritual ministrations of the brahmans no longer provided satisfaction. A quest for mystic knowledge and enlightenment above and beyond the sacrifices to the gods reflected a more sophisticated attitude toward the here and the hereafter. Undoubtedly, non-Aryan doctrines were exercising a greater influence. Among these were the doctrine of *samsara*, the transmigration of souls in rebirth after rebirth, and the associated concept of *karma*, whereby the good and bad acts of this life determined the condition of the next life. Although the source and evolution of these two doctrines are not clear, they had become fully developed and generally accepted by the fifth century B.C. All forms of animal life, and in some sects even plants, were incorporated in this perpetually revolving "wheel of life." Even the gods were included in this process.

For the average man such a conception was not unattractive. It placed the burden for a humble station in this life on the misdeeds of a former life and offered the promise of a better future life to those who behaved well in this one. But some found the prospect of perpetual rebirth appalling. The ascetic was dedicated to the search for the secret that would release him from this endless cycle of birth and death, a goal that the sacrifices of the brahmans could not secure.

The Aranyakas (forest texts) are transitional teachings of ascetics who went to meditate in the forests, a dangerous and uncongenial environment from the Aryan point of view. While recognizing the need for the brahman sacrifices, they sought to explain the symbolic meanings of the ritual, and to them this meaning was more important than the act of sacrifice itself.

The more advanced metaphysical thinkers of the Upanishads also recognized the gods, but sought the larger, more encompassing truth which, they taught, each man possessed within himself—if he could but discover it. This conception was the particular Self, atman, the counterpart in each individual of the universal Reality, Brahman.* As conceived by these mystics, the two are identical and eternal. Those who concentrate on sacrifices and the accumulation of worldly merit fail to understand the higher, universal truth, which is unchanging reality. As a consequence, they are reborn and do not escape this illusory life with all its pains and passions. In contrast, those who go into the forest with a heart full of penitence and faith in Brahman find tranquility and discover their imperishable souls (atman) and oneness with Brahman.

The objective of these mystics was release (*moksha*) from the chain of matter, the wheel of life. Release could only be obtained by penance, study, and meditation leading to the individual realization that the Inner Self and the ultimate Reality were one and the same, now and forever. This realization would end the endless cycle of birth and death by means of a mystical merger of one's Self and the eternal Truth. The tie to everchanging and, therefore, illusory matter would be terminated. The path to this goal prescribed the minimizing of one's dependence on the material things of this life by

* Care should be taken to distinguish between *brahman* (priest), *Brahman* (universal Reality or Truth), and *Lord Brahma* (creator god of the universe who became part of the later Hindu trinity with *Vishnu*, the preserver, and *Shiva*, the destroyer).

living the life of the ascetic in which even life or death was inconsequential. The necessity of reducing the connections with this world to a minimum led in time to the formulation of systematic preparatory exercises called *yoga* (see Chapter 3, p. 84).

Each Upanishad was directly linked to the Vedas, and the total accomplishment was interpreted as the completion or end of the Vedas, the Vedanta. Most of the mystics were brahmans who considered their teachings as a continuation and culmination of the doctrine implicit in the Vedas. This was so even though the Upanishads reflect the intrusion of non-Aryan elements and substantially altered the intellectual outlook and emphasis of the Vedic religion.

The growth of mysticism resulted necessarily in a reorientation of religious values. Formerly the brahmans had made ritual sacrifice so important that its proper and regular performance was equated with the maintenance of the cosmic order. Now it was reduced to its original import as a means of obtaining worldly favors from the gods. Spiritual power and respect was transferred from the sacrifice to the seer who by asceticism had gained transcendental knowledge and wisdom. The popular reverence for such persons was a powerful reinforcement and inducement to the further development of asceticism. In this way the spiritual ground was fertilized for the nourishment of the more radical teachings of Buddhism and Jainism.

This shift in religious outlook was naturally accompanied by an alteration in ethical standards. The old virtues of a tribal society of warriors were transformed by the doctrines of transmigration and *karma* to suit a settled agricultural society living cheek to jowl. The requirement of virtuous conduct disparaged violence in favor of gentleness, kindliness, and cooperativeness—qualities of greater value to an orderly civilization. If one's status in the next life depended on one's deeds in this life, then there was a strong incentive for the practice of high standards of human behavior. These two doctrines also supported the dedicated performance of the duties of one's station in this life, which helped greatly to maintain social and political stability. The channeling of the highest intellectual endeavor into the ascetic's search for transcendental knowledge above and beyond the pains and pleasures of this life also contributed to social and political stability and quietude.

By the end of the sixth century B.C. the Aryan conquerors had collaborated with their non-Aryan subjects in producing a civilization in the Ganges valley with substantial states, cities, and towns supported by intensive, irrigated agriculture. A new crop, rice, had been domesticated and was destined to have an important future throughout Asia. In government, the elected Aryan chief had evolved into the hereditary ruler whose authority was checked mainly by the brahman religious monopoly.

Jainism

Jainism and Buddhism were only the more enduring of many unorthodox teachings of this period of spiritual ferment which rejected the ritualism and exclusivism of orthodox Brahmanism and challenged the doctrine of perpetual rebirth. Mahavira (c. 540–468 B.C.) is believed by Jains to have been the twenty-fourth and last inspired teacher during a long period of decline in the cosmic cycle. Like his contemporary, the Buddha, he was the son of a chieftain of one of the tribal oligarchies north of the lower Ganges which probably were largely non-Aryan in blood and culture.

His philosophy was essentially materialistic and dualistic. He imagined an egg-shaped universe filled with an infinite number of separate and finite souls, called *jiva* (life), which were mixed with matter and floated upward or downward according to their material weight. Eternal bliss was to be gained by eliminating this material burden until the soul floated to the top of the universe and adhered there like a drop of pure water. The soul was burdened by actions (*karma*) that were lighter or darker in hue according to the seriousness of the action. This life was pictured as a fire in which *karma* were constantly being consumed, but fresh *karma* were constantly providing fresh fuel, usually in excess of that burned up. The path to bliss, then, required a regimen of extreme asceticism with fasting, good deeds, and penance to burn up the darker *karma* and to minimize the influx of fresh *karma*. The ultimate form of asceticism would result in death by starvation.

Of all Indian philosophies, Jainism has placed the heaviest emphasis on nonviolence because the soul incurs the darkest stains by the destruction of life. But the darkness of the hue is graded downward from human life through animal and plant life to inanimate "life." This gradation has encouraged vegetarianism as the least damaging means of sustaining life. Moreover, this doctrine has led Jainists to avoid farming and to specialize in commerce as the source of livelihood involving the least destruction of life. Jainist commercial success has been enhanced by the emphasis placed on honesty and austerity. The two million Jainists of India today are especially prominent in the business community. Nonviolence and the other ethical teachings of Jainism lack the attractiveness of those of other religious philosophies because virtuous behavior was dictated for the selfish benefit of the individual Jainist's soul, not because of any consideration or compassion for his fellow man. Indeed, involvement of one's own feelings with others is believed positively to endanger one's own spiritual welfare. Good deeds, charity, nonviolence, all are motivated by the selfish end of individual salvation.

In contrast with other doctrines, Jainism has undergone no fundamental alterations. It divided into two sects over the issue of whether monkish renunciation prescribed nudity or permitted the wearing of a white robe, but there was no basic difference in doctrine. Today the "space-clad" sect avoids offense by wearing garments in public. Theoretically Jainism recognizes no deity, but in practice religious images of Mahavira and his predecessors are revered, and often Hindu gods are given, with typical Indian tolerance, supplementary worship for the temporal blessings they may bestow. None of these deviant practices, however, has changed the doctrine and discipline of Jainism, whose dedicated monks deeply influenced the youthful mind of India's twentieth century leader, Mahatma Gandhi.

Buddhism

Siddhartha Gautama (c. 536–483 B.C.) was the son of the chief of the Shakya tribe. Unlike the teachings of Mahavira, those of Gautama underwent so much change that their original form and content cannot be delineated with certainty except in the broadest terms.

According to tradition, Gautama, appalled at the extent of human suffering, abandoned his life of princely comfort at the age of twenty-nine and for six years pursued a program of extreme asceticism in the hope of discovering the ultimate truth. Finally, realizing that all of his suffering and penance had been in vain, he gave up extremism, regained his health, and then sat down under a pipal (fig) tree, determined to remain there in meditation until he learned the secret of existence. After resisting every type of temptation, he achieved enlightenment and became the Buddha (the Enlightened One).

His fundamental doctrine is set forth in the "Four Noble Truths." The first noble truth is that life is sorrow and suffering. The second noble truth identifies the cause of sorrow as the blind desire of the ego for satisfaction and permanence which can never be gained in this changing and impermanent life. From these two truths the third noble truth logically presents the answer for eliminating sorrow by stopping craving and gaining release from the demands of the ego. This cure, however, is more easily prescribed than achieved; and the fourth noble truth lays down a program, the "Noble Eightfold Path," which will lead to extinguishing the desires of the ego and eliminating the ignorance that prevents men from gaining the ultimate knowledge.

Up to this point the doctrine appears to present a negative renunciation of life. Now a positive program of thought and action is prescribed for disciplining the desires of the ego, recognizing the transitory quality of life and all one's actions by self-examination, and practicing the four cardinal virtues of love, compassion, joy, and serenity. The true disciple loves all creatures, not just humans, and would do nothing to cause any one of them a moment of suffering. At the same time he feels deep compassion for their sorrow

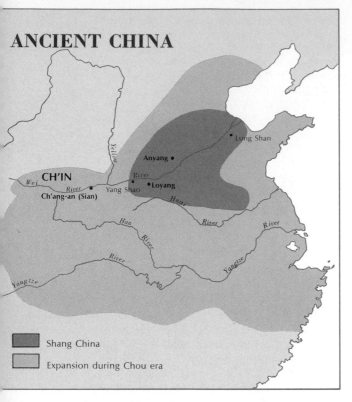

ANCIENT CHINA

CH'IN

Yellow

River

Lung Shan

Anyang

River

Wei

River

Ch'ang-an (Sian)

Yang Shao

Loyang

Huai

Han

River

River

River

River

Yangtze

Yangtze

▓ Shang China

░ Expansion during Chou era

---

ture of all existence and the oneness of the unchanged and unchanging universe. With this knowledge the Buddhist disciple is released from the ignorance that results in clinging to life and individuality. There is, however, no renunciation of life or of the reality of sorrow and suffering, at least, not in early Buddhism. (Later Buddhism is discussed on pp. 79–82.)

THE RISE OF CHINESE CIVILIZATION TO 221 B.C.

Chinese civilization, isolated from its predecessors in the Near East and India, arose after 2000 B.C. in the flood basin of the lower reaches of the Yellow River and expanded later into the Yangtze basin and the other territories farther southward that form the agricultural heartland of China today. As its name implies, the Yellow River picks up a heavy load of rich silt called loess and distributes it across the North China plain through frequent floods and shifts in the river's course. Loess is a fine-grained, easily eroded loam deposited for hundreds of thousands of years by northwest winds. Such soil is so easy to work that it invites the development of farming. On the other hand, the silt continually raises the riverbed. As a result, man's efforts to contain the river have caused it to burst the dikes with catastrophic results. For this reason, the Yellow River is popularly labeled "China's sorrow."

Two Stone Age cultures of uncertain date have been identified in the Yellow River basin: the Yang Shao in the west with painted pottery and the Lung Shan in the east with finer, burnished pottery frequently turned on a fast potter's wheel. Most distinctive, however, are the angular shapes of the finest Lung Shan ware offering a preview of later bronze products. Where the two cultures have been found together, the Lung Shan lasts longer and presumably represents a more advanced culture that moved westward from the vicinity of the Shantung Peninsula and continued into the Bronze Age. Several sites of both cultures are large, covering areas up to 250 acres. Therefore, although the closely concentrated buildings are comparatively primitive, the size of the settlements indicates an advanced degree of social and political organization. The clearest evi-

---

and does all he can to alleviate it. Such actions have the purifying effect of diminishing the novice's concern for himself by diverting it to others in contrast to the self-centered concern for others of the Jainist. After these preparatory steps the novice should be ready for the final step of "Right Contemplation" which could lift the veil of ignorance and lead him to the final, indescribable goal of enlightenment.

Unlike other forms of Indian asceticism, Buddhism emphasized moderation and decried extremism either in asceticism or the pursuit of worldly pleasures because both enhanced rather than diminished egoism. The middle path and the practice of altruism were deemed most conducive to attaining the end of enlightenment.

What enlightenment was, or is, could only be hinted at. To give it a name, such as *Nirvana,* is an error, for no finite term can define that which is not only infinite but beyond description and definition with reference to human experience. As one aspect, enlightenment involves realization of the transient na-

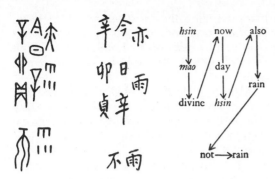

dence of continuity between the Lung Shan culture and the Shang era is the discovery of oracle bones. Although they bear no inscriptions, suggesting that writing had not yet been devised, the technique of heating the bones until cracks appeared, which could then be interpreted, is identical with the Shang procedure.

The unique characteristics of these two prehistoric cultures and the evidence of continuity between them suggest that Chinese civilization was developed independently. Of course, ideas and products probably were received from the outside, but where fashioned by human hands, they were given an entirely Chinese character. Imports possibly included the idea of pottery, bronze, the wheel, grain seeds, and domesticated animals, but no one can be certain that these were not independently discovered and developed.

Chinese mythology, compiled at a comparatively late date, attributes the rise of Chinese civilization to a creator followed by three sequences of brothers, the twelve Heavenly rulers, eleven Earthly rulers, and nine Human rulers. These three groups represent symbolically the three elements of Chinese cosmology—heaven, earth, and man. Then came five personified culture heroes credited with such vital inventions as fire, agriculture, the calendar, and the Chinese system of writing. The last two rulers broke the practice of succession in the family by choosing the most able man to succeed them. (Little credence can now be given to this myth, but Chinese scholars and officials once drew on it in order to buttress their criticisms of the conduct of government.) According to tradition, the next ruler returned to succession within

his family and thus established the Hsia dynasty (c. 1994–1523 B.C.). Although there is no archeological evidence for this dynasty, the reign lengths are reasonable compared to the incredible number of years ascribed to the preceding rulers. (Someday archeology may connect this dynasty with one of the prehistoric cultures.) The last ruler is described as a thoroughly vicious and profligate despot—a convention applied by traditional Chinese historians to the last ruler of each dynasty.

The Shang Dynasty (c. 1523–1027 B.C.)

The Shang dynasty, like its predecessor, practiced succession from brother to brother as well as father to son. This mode of succession suggests a society in which maturity and military ability were at a premium, a state in which the ruler's authority depended on the respect he could command.

For the latter half of the dynasty, archeology has confirmed traditional Chinese history by excavation of the capital at Anyang. Suddenly, it would seem, we are confronted with a literate civilization with an exceptionally advanced bronze metallurgy. The most valuable discovery historically was more than 10,000 oracle bones inscribed with Chinese characters confirming most of the rulers in the traditional Shang king-list. In this first example of the ancestral cult the rulers called on the spirits of their ancestors for advice and guidance.

The questions and their answers as divined ("read") in the oracle bones present a picture of the beliefs, practices, and problems of the times. Apparently, in addition to assuring good crops, the ruler was regularly occupied with warfare in which the loyalty of subordinate lords was by no means certain. The picture of royal life is one of vast activity in which every action required ritual endorsement by the king's ancestors. The concern with appeasing the unseen forces of the spirit world is further illustrated by human as well as animal sacrifices in connection with the construction of major buildings and royal tombs.

The Chinese writing system deserves special notice. More than any other single element it has influenced and shaped Chinese civilization, as well as those neighboring civilizations that developed under Chinese influence. In the method of writing on the oracle bones all the fundamental principles had already evolved suggesting, but not proving, a long period of prior evolution. Some 5000 characters have been identified of which more than 1500 are clearly related to their counterparts today. This direct relationship has fostered an awareness of cultural continuity and a feeling of reverence for the past.

For the most part, the Chinese characters are ideographs compounded from what were originally pictographs. For example, the character meaning "bright" is a compound of the pictographs for "sun" and "moon." The ideographs represent uninflected monosyllables with a general meaning, but the language is not strictly monosyllabic. New words have been created from two or more characters. Since the number of syllables is limited, the formation of multisyllabic words has been essential for clarity in the spoken language, distinguishing and adding to the mysterious quality of the written language. The difficulty of mastering the written language gave a special status to the educated elite that came to be synonymous with the ruling estate. Thus, in the popular mind, literacy enveloped their rulers with an aura of legitimacy in place of the religious sanction that supported political authority in other civilizations.

The writing of the characters with a brush also made calligraphy a highly regarded form of artistic expression. In a sense, every literate Chinese was an artist, and most famous painters were also renowned calligraphers. The relationship of writing and painting made painting the most esteemed art form. Illiterate peasants decorated their homes with prized examples of calligraphy which carried the double mystique of writing and high art.

Without a doubt, however, the most important contribution of the Chinese method of writing has been its promotion of cultural cohesion through its unique ability to overcome differences in dialect and even language. The Chinese character indicates meaning; any syllable or syllables may be associated with it. If the West had such a system of writing, the written form of "no," for example, would be identical whether it was pronounced "non," "nein," or "nyet." In other words, in writing there would be no language barriers nor the cultural barriers they promote. Not only has the Chinese writing system facilitated cultural diffusion and unity, thus helping to create the most populous nation on earth, but it has also promoted a sense of community with those states that borrowed and adapted it to their languages. The common denominator has been, and still is to some degree, the Chinese writing system; not a common religion as is the case in other areas.

A second major contribution of the Shang era was the unparalleled skill and artistry of its bronzesmiths. The advanced stage of metallurgy is illustrated by the varying proportions of copper, tin, and lead employed to produce successfully the intricate designs and decorations. Obviously these masterpieces could have been produced only by specialists who felt free to experiment with their materials.

Drawing on the combined resources supplied by archeology and tradition Shang civilization may be portrayed as a settled agricultural society that retained a strong patriarchal organization based on the family and the clan. As today, the family name came first, followed by the personal name. The society was further divided by a great gulf between commoners and nobles. The contrast between the two is brought out by the continued use of pit dwellings for commoners compared with the large buildings which housed their lords. The nobles maintained their authority and prestige not only by their military function and a monopoly of expensive weapons but also by the magical cult of their ancestors. The strength of the belief in the spiritual powers of the lords was also reinforced by the human sacrifices that continued to be practiced occasionally in the succeeding dynasty.

The direct authority of the ruler probably did not extend any great distance from his capital. Many other kings are mentioned against whom the Shang ruler had to mount frequent military campaigns in order to maintain his supremacy. At best, he was the "first among equals" exacting homage (see essay on Feudalism, p. 210) and some tribute from the other lords throughout the North China plain. He also organized joint expeditions against sheepherding nomads who were constantly intruding into Chinese territory.

A bronze ritual vessel of the Shang dynasty.

The Chou Dynasty
(c. 1027–256 B.C.)

Typically, tradition describes the last Shang ruler as a wholly evil and immoral tyrant reluctantly overthrown by the king of Chou, a frontier agricultural state in the loess basin of the Wei River, which joins the Yellow River at its eastward bend. (This highly strategic region has more than once been the base of operations for the unification of China under a new leader, the latest example being the Communist conquest from its Shensi headquarters.) Protected by mountains from easy incorporation into the Chinese domain, the region could cultivate a parochial sense of independence subject to the limited influence of Chinese culture. Yet the Yellow River encouraged contact and exchange with the North China plain, besides providing a natural thoroughfare for attack. Furthermore, direct contact with nomadic peoples to the north and west stimulated a martial spirit and provided a source of military experience and alien ideas that were often invigorating. Finally, this region was the eastern terminus of the natural trade routes with the West. Such trade not only supplemented the economy but also nourished a more receptive and flexible outlook.

The Chou conquest did not cause any sharp break in the evolution of Chinese civilization. The capital was maintained at the center of the source of Chou strength in the

Wei River valley near modern Sian. The decentralized system of political organization was continued with some modifications in favor of the ruler. Several states in the plain were given to relatives, but in other cases the former rulers, after pledging allegiance, were confirmed as rulers of their territories. Even those ruling families displaced from their former possessions were usually granted lesser estates to support the continuance of their ancestral cults. The customary political and economic unit, as in the past, was the walled city with the neighboring villages and towns dependent on it. The primitive state of communications hindered a greater centralization of power. Therefore, as in the Shang dynasty, the authority of the Chou rulers ultimately rested on military strength, supplemented by the belief in their religious functions as essential to the general welfare.

According to Chinese tradition the Chou rulers took the title of "Son of Heaven" and justified their assumption of power on the doctrine that the mantle of the "Mandate of Heaven" had been transferred to them. The title, "Son of Heaven," illustrates the essential function of the divinely appointed ruler as the intermediary between men and the controlling forces of nature. The chief deity to which the ruler had to make regularly prescribed sacrifices was Heaven.

Sacrifices to other deities, such as Earth and the royal ancestors, continued to be specific responsibilities of the ruler in his capacity as chief priest. (Today two of the most impressive structures in Peking are the square altar to Earth and the round altar to Heaven built during the Ming dynasty.) Further evidence of continuity was the continued use and development of the Chinese system of writing and the continued practice of divination with oracle bones. In addition, magnificent bronze vessels continued to be cast of the same style and technology.

Little can be said with certainty about events during the Western Chou era, the period until the removal of the capital eastward to Loyang in 769 B.C. Generally speaking, political development was characterized by the gradual decline of the rulers' authority, particularly near the close of this era when China was still divided into almost 200 principalities of widely varying extents. Social and political organization was still based on kinship, the chief ministers being drawn from the lord's immediate family. A greater reliance on agriculture than hunting to supply the lord's table suggests the destruction of game and the expanded utilization of arable land. The peasants communally worked the lord's land and supported him with labor and handicrafts, such as silk cloth, in return for protection and aid.

Originally all lords apparently had to travel to the Chou court to be invested with their authority by the ruler. This practice implied royal ownership of all land with the right to dispose of it as the ruler saw fit. The ceremony also involved a pledge of loyalty that strengthened the real authority of the ruler. By the eighth century the general neglect of the investiture ceremony and the lack of court attendance for any reason underlined the decline in royal authority and prestige.

During the Eastern Chou period (769–256 B.C.), when the capital was moved to Loyang, the ruler was reduced to the status of a ceremonial figurehead, while the major states gradually usurped all the attributes of sovereignty, including even the title of king. As time passed, the political picture took on all the characteristics of international relations among a number of independent states,

both large and small. The only semblance of unity was provided by the heritage of a common culture. But in the expanding frontier states, especially in the south, Chinese culture at best was no more than a thin veneer over a more barbarous base.

The "Spring and Autumn" era, named after a classic historical work covering the years 722 to 481 B.C., was characterized by the setting up of leagues of Chinese states under successive regional lords to fill the vacuum left by the demise of the Chou rulers' power. In addition, the conduct of war tended to be restrained by a code of aristocratic honor inspired by reverence for the maintenance of ancestral cults. Peasants and non-Chinese "barbarians" might be slaughtered, but aristocratic warriors were concerned about their mutual survival. Some lords expanded by subordinating neighboring lords, but the most successful ones were those in a position to conquer and incorporate the territories of people not yet deemed to be within the pale of Chinese civilization. Moreover, the regional lords needed a more complex system of administration and taxation in order to gain closer control and to wring the maximum income out of the land.

In spite of the substantial degree of differentiation that had evolved, a general picture of conditions and relationships within a state can be sketched. At the top a hereditary lord with absolute power performed the sacrifices necessary for the welfare of his state. Under him was a hereditary class of aristocratic warriors, who doubled as administrators and tax collectors. These specialists were socially separated by a wide gulf from the peasants who supported them by their manual labor. Although the social separation may not have been so extreme this early, its essence is well illustrated by the later adage: "The ritual does not extend down to the common people; punishments do not extend up to the great officers" (from the *Book of Rites*). Without rights, the peasants were conscripted for public works or war at the lord's will. Without ancestral cults of their own, both the spiritual and worldly welfare of the peasants depended on the lord's beneficence. But the picture should not be overdrawn; the welfare of the lord depended reciprocally on the loyal and devoted service of his subjects. Unreasonable tyranny contrary to custom was not in his interest. The injunctions to virtuous conduct applied equally to the ruler and the lord. He, too, could lose the "Mandate of Heaven." As the lords usurped in practice the prerogatives of the ruler and engaged in contests for power with other lords, this became even more the case.

Almost all moral restraints were lost in the growing tempo of bitter struggle of the succeeding "Warring States" era, starting in the mid-fifth century. Legitimacy no longer commanded the respect that had formerly protected the weaker lords. Not only were states gobbled up but their ruling families were extinguished.

Three significant innovations altered the nature of warfare during the Eastern Chou period. One innovation was the introduction of iron, which not only revolutionized warfare but also farming, with the iron-tipped plow. The second innovation was cavalry, learned undoubtedly from the nomads who with this technique put renewed pressure on the chariot-equipped forces of the northwestern frontier states, such as Ch'in. The third and most important innovation was the mobilization of the manpower of each state to serve as a large and disciplined infantry force. Evidence of nomadic pressure as well as enlarged resources was the construction of substantial walls along the borders to check raids by small mounted bands and to delay and give warning of major nomadic incursions.

Yet Chinese civilization grew and matured at a vastly accelerated pace, despite the political disunity and disorder of the Warring States era and the increasing amount of resources channeled into wasteful and destructive warfare. Social, economic, and even political development took place not only within the heartland but also in the new additions that more than doubled the area of Chinese civilization. In addition to territorial expansion, China also grew greatly in population thanks to advances in both technology and communications. The spread of a money economy beginning in the fifth century facilitated change. A frequent paradox of history is the appearance of rapid growth and development amid increasingly bitter political strife.

On the other hand, the marshaling of talent and the premium placed on productiveness stimulated social and cultural change and development. Heredity carries no assurance of talent and, therefore, for efficiency the hereditary officials had either to be replaced or assisted by educated officials of proven ability. Thus there developed the prospect of a career open to talent, and the barrier of social origin became less absolute. Also the need for education promoted the profession of teaching of which the outstanding example is Confucius, whom we shall discuss presently.

By the fifth century the accelerating social, economic, and political changes generated the rise of the "Hundred Schools of Thought," each seeking solutions to the growing turmoil and tension. The almost total concern with social, economic, and political problems is what one would expect, especially in view of the comparatively underdeveloped state of Chinese religion. In contrast with the Near East and India, Chinese thought was overwhelmingly secular in orientation.

Three schools with their individual variations dominated the amazingly creative thought of the later Chou era: Confucianism, Taoism (pronounced dowism), and Legalism (perhaps, more accurately defined as Statism). All three were predominantly concerned with human relationships, the relationship of man to man and man to the state, and from this point of view may be described as humanistic. Of course, each also sought to find in nature the universal rules that should govern human relations and thus was influenced by the Chinese cosmological triad of heaven, earth, and man. Of these three, however, man was clearly their central concern.

The three schools represented three views of Chinese society. Confucianism looked to the family as the basic social unit whose regulation would produce harmony in both society and the state. Taoism looked to the individual whose proper regulation would produce harmony with nature and thus bring peace to society. Legalism, decrying the innately evil nature of man, looked to the state to regulate human relations by a rigorous code of punishments and rewards which

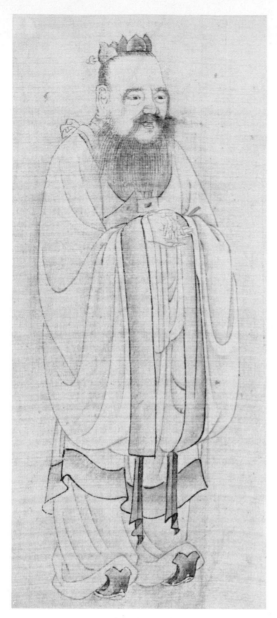

Confucius as imagined by later Chinese.

Confucius (*c.* 551–479 B.C.)

Confucius was the first and, in the long run, the most influential of the Chinese philosophers and teachers. Because he left no writings of his own the most reliable information on his teachings must be derived from the *Analects,* a purported compilation of his sayings as recalled by his immediate disciples.

The primary assumption, from which his other teachings stemmed, was the belief that the troubles of his time were the result of a falling away from the virtuous behavior and observance of the rules of social order which he believed had prevailed in the early Chou period. Therefore, he devoted himself to the study of the past and insisted that he was a transmitter and not an originator, a conservative and not a revolutionary. Moreover, he did not concern himself with metaphysics and would have rejected the title of philosopher. In reaction against the superstition of his times he struck a note that may be described as agnostic: he did not repudiate religion and, indeed, emphasized the importance of proper performance of the traditional rituals, but beyond this he asserted that the ways of heaven were beyond human knowledge and control. According to Confucius, a true scholar should concentrate his attention on the management of worldly affairs.

In spite of his call for a return to an idealized past, Confucius was, in fact, proposing revolutionary solutions. Although he upheld the restoration of the traditional hierarchy, his advocacy of ethics as basic to good government and the good life was an original contribution. Hereditary rulers were called on to employ ministers so educated as to appreciate the paramount virtue of public service, emphasizing both loyalty to the ruler and dedication to the welfare of the people. Such "cultivated gentlemen" would have developed both the inner virtues of upright integrity, righteousness, and conscientiousness and the external virtues stemming from these: loyalty, altruism, and humanheartedness. This emphasis on the employment of "gentlemen" who were cultivated by education accepted implicitly the idea of a bureaucratic state in which hereditary

would mobilize human resources for the mutual benefit of the state and its subjects. Confucianism and Taoism looked to a past golden age as the model for reform. Legalism realistically insisted that present conditions must be met by contemporary solutions. All three schools represent reactions to the rapid change and growing disorder of the Eastern Chou period.

status was limited to the ruler; on the other hand, it rejected the ruthless and disorderly behavior of the lords. Moreover, Confucius explicitly asserted that lowly birth was no bar to becoming a gentleman. As he said, "In education there are no class distinctions." In these two ways—by advocating a civil service of "cultivated gentlemen" and by ignoring class distinctions in the selection of candidates—Confucius actually broke with the past. Nevertheless, he was no egalitarian. He maintained that nature made a few people fit to be trained as rulers and the rest to labor in support of themselves and their rulers. Hence, each one should acknowledge his role and work reciprocally for the benefit of the other. In this sense, Confucius was a traditionalist.

Confucius pictured an ideal society, based on the family, of graded relationships in which recognition of the rules of human relationships would create stability and harmony. He prescribed five basic relationships only one of which was equal, that of friend and friend. The other four were absolute relations of superior and inferior: husband and wife, father and son, elder brother and younger brother, ruler and subject. Although absolute obedience was required of inferiors, the superiors in each case were obligated to protect and look after the welfare of their inferiors.

A cardinal conviction of Confucius was his belief in a government of men, not of laws. This doctrine followed logically from his argument that power should be put in the hands of gentlemen educated in virtue. "Lead the people by laws and regulate them by penalties, and the people will try to keep out of jail, but will have no sense of shame. Lead the people by virtue and restrain them by rules of decorum, and the people will have a sense of shame, and moreover will become good." This conception, so at odds with the modern Western emphasis on law and on the office rather than the man, seems to have remained influential in the People's Republic of China.

In addition to ethical altruistic behavior in dealing with others, Confucius also emphasized the importance of the correct performance of the institutionalized rites of Chinese society as a stabilizing influence and as an expression of respect for the feelings of others. This emphasis on rites, like that on conduct, was inspired by the growing neglect of these forms and by the selfish individualism of his times. In other words, it was another means by which Confucius sought to revitalize the decaying morality in human relations.

Such a philosophy with its moderation and emphasis on duty was ideally suited to the production of able civil servants. For this reason, and not because it sought stability by looking to an idealization of the ancient past for precedents, it was well adapted to the wave of the future in China and ultimately prevailed, although with significant modifications and alterations.

Mo-tzu (*c.* 479–381 B.C.)

The teachings of Confucius were by no means immediately accepted. In fact, they stimulated other thoughtful men to reconsider the overriding problem of human relationships singled out by him. Mo-tzu concentrated his critical attacks against the formalism and coldness he saw in Confucian doctrines and, therefore, his teachings may be deemed a Confucian heresy. Because of the need to refute Confucius he developed a dialectical method of argument adopted by a later school that specialized in dialectics. He condemned Confucius as a defender of an aristocratic order in contrast to his own more egalitarian outlook, yet he, too, wanted virtuous men appointed to office.

Much more important differences with Confucius were Mo-tzu's doctrines of universal love and utilitarianism. Criticizing Confucius' graded love according to the rules of human relationships, Mo-tzu advocated equal love for all men. He argued that the limited and partial love taught by Confucius left room for the hatred that was the cause of disorder and warfare in the world. Therefore, he denounced aggression and devoted a great deal of attention to defense as necessary until his doctrine of love was universally accepted. He realized that an active program of conversion would be necessary and argued that as Heaven guides men by rewards and punishments the state, too, must devise a system of rewards and punishments to guide its subjects.

This break with the Confucian ideal of a government of men rather than laws prepared the ground for the later authoritarian doctrines of the Legalist school (see below, p. 64). In contrast with the openmindedness of Confucius, an evangelical sense of mission led Mo-tzu to demand absolute conformity and discipline from his students. His interest in universal love led him to advocate utilitarian restraints and to denounce all activities that did not contribute to the material welfare of the people, such as militarism, luxury, and ritual expenses. Mo-tzu insisted that all resources should be husbanded to meet the three essential needs of food, clothing, and shelter. Yet, despite his proclaimed equalitarianism and concern for the common man, his support of the authority of the ruler and his officials, backed up by rewards and punishments, left the people with less freedom and provided a precedent for the Legalists.

Taoism

Unlike Confucius, the traditional founder of the second most important school of thought, Lao-tzu, cannot be identified, and the *Tao Te Ching* (*The Way and the Power Classic*) attributed to him is obviously the product of several minds. Essentially it is an anti-intellectual protest against an increasingly complex society and government and an appeal for a return to the simplicity of a mythical past when men followed the Way (*Tao*) of nature without making the futile attempt to control and manipulate man and nature for selfish ends. The second classic work of Taoism, by Chuang-tzu (*c.* 369–286 B.C.), carries a substantially different message. It is even more enigmatic and, instead of trying to reform society, takes as its central purpose the emancipation of the individual.

Popular Taoism, which developed later, drew on ancient superstitions and magic to dupe the people, but its quest for the elixir of life and the changing of common metal into gold (which attracted royal patronage) accounted for most of China's medical and scientific knowledge. All sorts of substances were experimentally tasted and tested resulting in the discovery of anesthetics and a host of useful drugs. Scholarly rejection of scientific inquiry may be partially explained by its association with the superstitious and magical practices of Taoism, but a more basic reason was the Confucian emphasis on humanism and the morality of men and government.

Although the teachings of the *Tao Te Ching* and Chuang-tzu both made important contributions to Chinese civilization, Chuang-tzu's conception of the mystical recluse communing with nature in quest of the eternal truth probably exercised a greater influence. It provided the scholar with the perfect counterpart or complement to the Confucian call to duty. When he lost office or suffered a setback, he could retire to some place of natural beauty for meditation—perhaps, with the aid of a little wine. In other words, Taoism provided the scholar-official with an ideal safety valve to relieve tension. In addition, the Taoist emphasis on the beauty of all creation countered the man-centered humanism of Confucianism and furnished esthetic inspiration for Chinese literature and art.

Like Indian conceptions of the same type, the Way (*Tao*) is essentially indescribable in human terms. It is timeless, eternal, and formless. The means of following the Way, usually translated as "doing nothing," is misleadingly negative and better translated as "doing nothing contrary to nature." In this sense it is a condemnation of bureaucratic meddling with the life of the people. It advocates a minimum of governmental action on the ground that the source of disorder within and between states is selfish striving and ambition. Foreign policy should be gentle and nonassertive. Avoid antagonizing neighbors and give them no cause to covet your land. The path of violence will inevitably lead to a violent end. A Taoist analogy noted that while water was soft, it could wear away the hardest substance.

Whereas the *Tao Te Ching* sought to reform society by advocating selfless nonassertion, Chuang-tzu was almost exclusively concerned with freeing the individual from the bondage of life. Perhaps he believed that the depravity of the society of his day was beyond the possibility of reform. In his view of the transient and relative nature of all material things, including man, he approached closely Buddhist and Vedantist philosophy.

All life, he wrote, is involved in continous change and "passes by like a galloping horse," taking its own course despite any efforts to alter it. The ever-changing phenomena of the external world are essentially unreal; what is real and natural comes from within, where true virtue abides. The true sage will seek to comprehend this inner virtue, which is the only path to knowledge of the Way. When he realizes the oneness of all nature, he will rise above the bondage of life and death. Meditation and intuition, rather than the study of transient things, are the only way to gain the ultimate truth: knowledge of the *Tao*. It may readily be appreciated how this aspect of Taoism prepared Chinese scholars for the reception of Buddhism later on (see p. 96).

Mencius (c. 372–289 B.C.)

Mencius was the most important interpreter of Confucianism. Although he, too, looked to the past for precedents, he was far more concerned than Confucius with the present, material foundations of society. Indeed, he asserted that virtuous conduct and government would be of small avail if the material prosperity of the people had not been adequately provided for; in this connection he advocated a land-reform program.

With his special concern for the people, Mencius is noted for his elaboration of the doctrine of the Mandate of Heaven, which became an integral part of Confucianism. In support of this doctrine he quoted from the *Book of History:* "Heaven sees as the people see; Heaven hears as the people hear." Thus successful rebellion was given divine sanction. Where Confucius had upheld the hereditary right of rulers, Mencius, perhaps influenced by Mo-tzu's teaching, reduced them to replaceable servants of the people whose tenure depended on just and effective administration.

Mencius is best known, however, for his thesis that man is by nature good but subject to infinite corruptibility in the same way that the ancient perfection of the social and political order had become corrupted. The innate goodness in man must be cultivated by education and virtuous government. Those who have become evil have neglected the development of their innate virtue.

Mencius' position might have been forgotten if it had not been challenged by the more radical and somewhat heretical Confucianist, Hsün-tzu.

Hsün-tzu (*fl.* 298–238 B.C.)

By the time of Hsün-tzu the old order had entered its deaththroes, and any hope for its reestablishment appeared futile. To his way of thinking the time had come for a realistic and rational reappraisal of Confucianism in the light of contemporary conditions.

Looking about him, he was appalled at the dependence on diviners to predict the course of events. Although he did not deny the operation of Heaven in human affairs, he insisted that it was beyond prediction and control by such charlatans. Instead, the rulers should concentrate on those affairs subject to human manipulation and control. In fact, he was an advocate of progress, arguing that man can improve his environment and livelihood by positive, rational efforts.

From this overriding humanistic emphasis Hsün-tzu was led to a consideration of the fundamental factors governing human nature and concluded that man is by nature evil and that under the influence of his passions he is filled with selfishness, envy, and hatred. Goodness is acquired as a result of the rules of society, the laws of the state, and the discipline of education, both formal and informal. Although innately evil, man and society are infinitely perfectible.

Later Confucianists were repelled by Hsün-tzu's analysis of human nature as evil and failed to appreciate the progressive vista opened up by his doctrine of perfectibility. His emphasis on the need to regulate, guide, and control man to overcome his evil propensities provided a philosophical foundation for the stress on laws in Legalism, as expounded by two of his students. Thus, Hsün-tzu, or more accurately his pupils, shifted subtly away from the Confucian emphasis on a government of morally trained men to a government of laws administered by men.

The Yin-Yang School

What should be apparent by now is that, as in other civilizations, the "Hundred Schools of Thought" in China were interacting on and borrowing from each other in preparation for a later synthesis. One of the more important of these schools was one which, drawing on an ancient belief, sought to explain systematically the working of nature on the two opposed, but complementary, principles of Yin and Yang. The attributes of Yin are female, dark, cold, and negative; the attributes of Yang are male, light, hot, and positive. Unlike Western dualism, these two principles are not separate and distinct, but essentially united in a shifting relationship in which one prevails for a while and then the other. This conception contributes to the basic optimism of the Chinese people because it supports the belief that the worse things become the nearer they are to shifting for the better. The Yin-Yang doctrine combined with the complex combinations of the "five elements" of wood, metal, fire, water, and earth and their cosmic correlatives has been an important factor in philosophical as well as popular thought throughout Chinese history.

Legalism and the State of Ch'in

Meanwhile, during the later Chou period, the larger states, locked in a fight to the finish, had already stressed the centralization of power in the hands of the ruler and the development of government by laws rather than men. The looser, personalized relationship of the small states of former times was no longer feasible. More than any other, the state of Ch'in epitomized this development and, therefore, it is not surprising that the two chief exponents of Legalism found employment there.

Both Han-fei-tzu (*d.* 233 B.C.) and Li Ssu (*d.* 208 B.C.) as students of Hsün-tzu were deeply influenced by his rationalism and his belief in the need for specific rewards and punishments. But they were also influenced by Mo-tzu's authoritarianism and utilitarianism and even more by the Taoist disdain for conventional morality and scholarship. Indeed, in their well-ordered state, once the law code had been fully elaborated, the ruler, like the Taoist ideal, would do everything by doing nothing.

Han-fei-tzu ridiculed the other philosophers for their failure to examine and deal with things as they are. Moreover, he criticized the patronage extended to these men of learning who not only were unable to solve current problems but were also constantly at odds with each other and more concerned with the welfare of the people than with that of their patron. He asserted that the people in their ignorant shortsightedness were bound to object to those measures that were best for them in the long run. Regardless of their complaints, the ruler should conscript labor to expand the arable area, fill his granaries and treasuries by taxation in preparation for famine and war, exact harsh penalties to eliminate the unruly, and require universal military training and service without favoritism.

Even before Legalist doctrines had been set forth systematically they were implemented in a practical way in the state of Ch'in, which seized the Chou symbols of authority in 256 B.C. and completed the conquest of all the Chinese states in 221 B.C. The hereditary aristocracy supported by landholdings was eliminated, and all land was reclaimed and granted directly to its tillers by the ruler. All officers, both civil and military, were appointed and paid by the ruler. A code of rewards and punishments and standard weights and measures were prescribed. Large water control projects expanded agricultural production and facilitated communication. All aspects of the economy were put under state control and regulation. In sum, then, the interests of individuals and families were wholly subordinated to those of the state, and all power was concentrated in the ruler and his select group of Legalist advisers.

AMERICAN INDIAN CIVILIZATIONS

Although the American Indian civilizations flourished more than a thousand years after the first civilizations in India and China, they are treated here for two reasons. First, they were of a comparable level. Second, they were the earliest civilizations in the New World and they developed out of folk cultures almost as old as those of East Asia.

When Columbus landed in the Bahamas in 1492, he thought he was in the Indies and therefore called the natives "Indians," a name that has lasted to this day. Most of the aboriginal inhabitants of the New World were, indeed, related to the Asians, for their ancestors had migrated across Siberia into Alaska at the end of the last Ice Age, when a land bridge existed, and even afterward by means of boats. It is barely possible that humankind in the Americas had survived the Ice Age, since remains show that the species existed. Moreover, theories of continental drift lead some geologists to believe that North and South America were once connected with Africa and Eurasia, and human beings in the Western Hemisphere might have been isolated. And there are many suggestions that small groups of people might have reached the New World by boat from Africa, Asia, and the islands of the South Pacific. We know that Vikings came to North America for a time around A.D. 1000, and legends of white gods or supermen in Mexico and South America at the time of the Spanish conquest promote speculation that other Europeans might have sailed to those areas. Yet all we are sure of is that migrations over several millennia occurred from Siberia into Alaska and southward.

The natives of the New World were so varied in appearance, language, and culture that we can establish only in a few cases that the inhabitants of one region had contacts with those of other regions. In the lands overrun by the Spaniards there were several cultures of considerable advancement: the Pueblos of the present-day American Southwest, a variety of nations in Mexico and Central America, a small society in Colombia, and a series of civilizations in the central Andes. On the fringes of those areas and in Brazil and the Caribbean the natives seemed primitive. As for their number, the early Spaniards reckoned many millions. Their later estimates greatly reduced the figure, and modern students seldom place the number at more than 25,000,000 for the entire New World. Recent demographic studies, however, have revised these guesses upward, suggesting that half as many people lived in Mexico or Peru at the time of the conquest as live there today. The principal reason for this change is that we now realize that a shocking decline in population occurred in the first generation or so of contact with the Europeans, the result mainly of

diseases but also of warfare and the disorganization of the pre-Columbian economy.

Mexico

From 800 B.C. on, Mexico was the home of people with fixed abodes and an economy centered about the cultivation of corn (maize). Huge buildings, including pyramids and temples, attest to their advancement, as do statues, carvings, and jewelry. Perhaps the Olmecs were the first civilized people of this area. There were others: Zapotecs, Mixtecs, Totonacs, and Toltecs. When the Spanish arrived under Cortés in 1519 an upstart nation, the Aztec, had established dominion over the others and had absorbed much of their culture. Based on Tenochtitlán, a city constructed on islands in a large lake (since drained and now the site of Mexico City), the Aztecs had conquered their neighbors in the fifteenth century. Other great cities, such as Tula, Cholula, Teotihuacán, Mitla, and Monte Alban—now attractions for vast numbers of tourists—had been largely abandoned. Little was known of the people who had built them.

Imperialism in its most primitive form prevailed. Once the Aztecs subdued another nation, they disarmed their victims and forced them to pay regular tribute in gold, silver, jade, turquoise, food, cotton, clothing, and human beings. The human tribute in some cases became slaves or concubines, but mostly they were desired for sacrifice in spectacular ceremonies held about every three weeks to propitiate the gods, notably Huitzilopochtli, an idol shaped like a potbellied hummingbird. So bitterly were the Aztecs hated by the dependent peoples that the Spaniards found ready allies.

If the ideological basis of Aztec militarism was the cult of war gods, its economic base was the exploitation of other peoples and the occupation of the best farmlands in the high, sunny central valley. Here, the most fertile areas were parceled out to Aztec tribes which, in turn, were subdivided into clans. The clans distributed land on a rotating basis to families and maintained communal areas. The clans also ruled the people in most matters of immediate importance, but were directed by the tribal rulers. They, in turn,

THE HIGH CIVILIZATIONS of the AMERICAS

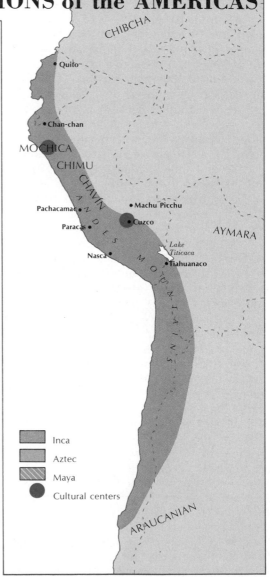

answered to a council for the entire Aztec nation which elected a monarch from a large imperial family. Montezuma II reigned at the time the Spaniards arrived. Believing a legend that a benevolent god, white and bearded, named Quetzalcoatl had promised to return to Mexico, Montezuma allowed Cortés to enter Tenochtitlán peacefully. Actually, the Aztec ruler had a large and hitherto victorious army, one composed of citizen-soldiers equipped with javelins, hatchets, arrows, and spears.

The Aztec clergy were large and privileged. Their power was visible notably during the sacrificial ceremonies, when they threw the victims on their backs and tore out their hearts, perhaps killing thousands in a single ceremony while the population, drugged and drunken, danced and chanted during the spectacle. The clergy were also healers and advisers; they probably drew most of the colorful pictographs (resembling comic strips without words) that perpetuated the kind of history the ruling groups wished to have remembered. They taught that the human race lived precariously, having been destroyed several times in the past by floods, fire, or earthquakes, and that its lease on life was subject to renewal every 52 years. The arrival of the Spaniards coincided with the end of one of these periods.

The Spaniards were astonished by the size and splendor of the city of Tenochtitlán. Recent estimates by Mexican authorities place its population at half a million, making it larger than any city in Europe of the time. Connected by three causeways to the mainland, it could be easily defended and supplied. There were pyramids, gigantic temples, and elaborate palaces and gardens for the rulers. On the various islands and "floating gardens" were comfortable, often beautified, homes. The people participated in athletic events and dancing. Their use of drugs and cactus alcohol was restricted to sacrificial days, when the whole city apparently plunged into an orgy of both worship and sadism. Dress was often colorful and ornamented highly. There seemed to be abundant food: corn, peppers, beans, fruits, and game. Acceptance of a stratified society and a fatalistic belief in the will of the gods, together with a productive economy and national pride, perhaps made life agreeable for the average Aztec.

The Maya

The Mexicans had considerable contact with the Maya of Yucatán, perhaps beginning with the supposed expulsion of Quetzalcoatl about A.D. 1000 from Mexico and his arrival in Maya country. Scholars differ as to whether the parent culture of Middle America was Maya or Mexican, but the two came together in Yucatán. It seems certain that an older Maya civilization, perhaps the most brilliant in ancient America, had flourished farther south in Guatemala and Honduras from about the time of Christ to A.D. 800. Although the area is not particularly fertile, the climate is enervating, and the jungle constantly threatening to take over if man is negligent for a few seasons, the Maya had a productive economy based on corn and many centers or cities. Of these, Palenque, Tikal, Copán, and Calakmul are the best known to us. Their pyramids, amphitheaters, temples, palaces, and ballcourts were built with extraordinary engineering skill. With their graceful construction, painting, and sculpture, they are also extremely beautiful. Apparently these cities lived in comparative peace, since there is little evidence of fortifications or arsenals.

Instead, one beholds a cult of beauty that reached into the humblest classes, as their dress, ornamentation, and pottery attest. The

A Maya noble offers a sacrifice of birds.

Maya were the only ancient Americans to have writing, which appears on manuscripts or stone monuments. So far, we have been unable to decipher most of it, although scholars are working on the problem with computers. The Maya also had a calendar more exact than the one used by Europeans at the time. Their mathematicians performed prodigious calculations and had discovered the zero before the Europeans learned of it from the Arabs and Hindus. And although the Maya apparently had no glass for telescopes, and the climate often limits visibility, they had an advanced knowledge of astronomy. They had not discovered the true arch, but they understood acoustics better than modern builders. Their religion was also sophisticated, with legends of previous creations and falls of the human race, the belief in a complicated system of heavens and hells, and so many symbols and practices resembling Christianity that the Spaniards

The Temple of Quetzalcoatl at Teotihuacán.

long insisted that Europeans must have taught them. Underlying Maya religion was the conviction that pain and death were necessary to achieve salvation. Yet human sacrifice was rare, usually a matter of an occasional willing victim plunging into a well in order to assure benefits for others.

During the ninth century A.D., the great city-states were abandoned, some in haste, with important construction lying uncompleted. We do not know why. Speculation centers around famines, epidemics, revolution against the ruling class, invasion by human foes, drug addiction, and moral collapse. In Yucatán the Maya created another civilization, which flourished from about A.D. 900 to 1200. It then fell into such decline that the Maya encountered by the Spaniards seemed to know little about their glorious past. The new cities, Chichen Itza, Mayapán, Uxmal, and others, were constructed similarly to the older Maya centers

in the south, but they also made use of such Mexican symbols as the feathered serpent and were walled. The Yucatán or post-Classic period was one in which warfare was conspicuous. Perhaps militarism or drugs explained the stagnation and virtual collapse of Maya civilization by A.D. 1500.

The Inca

In the nations that we now know as Peru and Bolivia sedentary agricultural societies can be traced back about 5000 years. Little is known about their exact nature, however, for the Spaniards found no written records and had to depend on oral accounts. Modern archaeology has provided much information, since the climate is such that ruins are unusually well preserved. Yet fundamental mysteries remain. In the Andean highlands or *altiplano* are enormous megalithic structures of a culture known as Tiahuanaco. On the desert coasts are partially buried cities we call Chan-Chan, Pachacamac, Nasca, Mochica, and Paracas. Between the coasts and the highest of the Andes are spectacular ruins such as Cuzco, Chavín, Sacsahuaman, Pisac, Machu Picchu, and others. From the architecture, carvings, metalwork, pottery, and textiles of these various centers we can infer that there was a relationship, but there is little hope of establishing a satisfactory history prior to the rise of the Inca nation about A.D. 1200. It is reasonable to assume that the Andean civilizations had some contacts with those of Central America or even the South Pacific islands. It may be that trans-Pacific migrants brought influences from Asia or, indirectly, from the Ancient Near East. Thus far no positive proof has been found to support such surmises, fascinating as they are.

The Inca society overthrown by the Spaniards in 1532 was based on various ancient cultures. Probably, the Inca, like the Aztecs, overran a large area rather suddenly in the fifteenth century. To a far greater degree than the Aztecs, however, the Inca succeeded in obliterating the language, civilization, and historical knowledge of their victims. They had a taut control that integrated religious, political, and economic life and glorified the sun, which they worshipped. Claiming divinity and descent from the sun, their monarch, who was selected by his father as successor, was absolute. From Cuzco he exerted authority through viceroys and officials in an astonishingly complex bureaucracy. He had a loyal professional army and an efficient spy system. Even nobles and formerly independent rulers of conquered nations were completely at his mercy. No one had rights or freedom. The monarch ruled the economy, transplanting populations and dictating what the various towns or fertile areas should produce. He knew what was going on because of oral records kept by a professional class of memory experts. In the interest of assuring high labor productivity, he restricted the use of corn alcohol, drugs, tobacco, and leisure time. So as to maintain a high birth rate to supply future laborers, he saw to it that young people who had not married voluntarily were paired off and mated.

Much as Inca civilization has been criticized for its harshness and the comprehensiveness of its tyranny, it has admirers. The part of South America where it prevailed has probably never provided more food, clothing, housing, medical attention, and psychological satisfaction to its inhabitants than it did in Inca times. The work ethic related labor to social and spiritual values so that a person was supposed to know and accept his place in the system, and was not to seek to change it or to improve his position. In the farming regions the people toiled communally. Produce was divided so that all shared, and food—white potatoes, corn, beans, and grain—was stored for consumption during bad seasons. Inca skills in terracing, irrigation, and fertilizing surpassed those of the Europeans. Yet there were no animals that could be domesticated except for the llama, which would consent to carry only light burdens, but whose wool and meat were available for the upper classes. The Inca economy produced necessities for all, but it offered a drab and utilitarian life. Clothing was simple. Houses were mere shelters, austere and not beautiful or comfortable. Even dances and athletics were colorless when compared to those of the Aztecs or Maya, although they had a haunting quality.

The architecture of the ancient Andeans baffles modern men. Fortresses, palaces, and temples were plain, even ugly, but they were cleverly put together without mortar so as to withstand earthquakes. This required cutting stones without metal instruments and transporting enormous pieces over some of the most rugged terrain on earth. It is clear from this construction that Inca engineering was highly advanced. Inca roads also excite wonderment. Fanning out from Cuzco, absolutely straight regardless of obstacles, they had rope bridges for the numerous chasms of the Andes, and footholds and ladders for steep places. Storehouses along the way provided refreshment for the royal messengers, parcel carriers, and armies. Rebellious colonists being removed to other sections and laborers on their way to projects for the state also used the roads, but free travel by the population was not allowed. Medicine was advanced, with cocaine, quinine, bonesetting techniques and, as we know from surviving skulls, brain surgery. The more examples of ancient Andean painting, sculpture, and textiles that come to light, the more resentment modern people have for the Spaniards who so abruptly destroyed the Inca civilization—and for the Inca themselves, who must have blotted out much of the knowledge developed by previous cultures.

Other Indians

The Aymará of Bolivia shared Inca civilization, as did the Quito of Ecuador. In Chile the Araucanians were able to maintain their independence against Inca, Spaniard, and Chilean alike until about a century ago, thanks to their own heroism and a terrain of mountains and forested islands that provided defense. The Guaraní of Paraguay have survived, always passive before domestic oppressors but fierce warriors against foreigners. The natives of Argentina and Uruguay were nomadic and primitive, unable to stand long against the Spaniards. In Brazil the Tupi-Guaraní and the Ge were mostly nomadic. Their skills in hunting, their cannibalism, and the refusal of the men to work made them a trial to the Portuguese Jesuits who eventually dominated many of them. Also in Brazil were Caribs, respected warriors and feared cannibals who long deterred Portuguese colonization in some areas. They also lived on the coasts of Venezuela and Colombia, where they put up a protracted resistance against the Spaniards. The Caribs were in the process of pushing out of northern South America a large linguistic group known as Arawaks, a generally gentle folk who had moved into the Caribbean islands at the time of the Conquest. They were the ones whom Columbus encountered when he first landed. His initial impression that they were noble savages did much to influence European attitudes toward Indians both during his time and later.

Summary

Columbus himself and most of the early Iberian settlers soon came to disparage the Indians, especially those of the Caribbean islands and Brazil. These natives often went naked and painted their bodies; their sexual practices were apparently loose and, so it often seemed to the Europeans, perverted; they labored little in their tropical lands and had scant sense of personal property; and some engaged in cannibalism and human sacrifice. When the Spaniards overran the large Indian civilizations of the mainland, they were impressed with the physical grandeur of the cities and the artistic clothing and jewelry. But they recoiled from the mass slaughter of the Aztec ceremonies and the harshness of the Inca system. They realized that no Indians used the wheel. Nor was iron utilized, even in weapons and implements, and very little bronze. Except for small dogs and the llama, there were no domesticated animals, and no fowl but the turkey. The Indians had no compass or gunpowder. There was no writing other than the Maya, itself almost forgotten. It seemed that all societies, whether nomadic or urban, tribal or national, had rigid class stratification. Moreover, the Indians warred with each other and permitted their rulers to oppress and exploit them. Most of the Indians then and later struck the Europeans as passive, dissimulating, and fatalistic in the way of peoples long accustomed to tyranny and cruelty. There seemed to be scant notion of progress, or little feeling that a static society could or should be improved.

These attitudes, of course, did not do justice to the Indians. Whether they were primitive or civilized, they seemed to integrate their religion with social-political-economic realities in ways that probably afforded some psychological satisfaction. The Indian seldom warred with nature. Instead, he adapted to it. Our present-day concern with ecology causes us to respect the Indians all the more for this attitude. By linking work with worship, by sharing labor and produce, and by largely doing without money, the Indians enjoyed an economy more just and productive than the one the Iberians later forced on them, or even the one that the Latin Americans have today. In astronomy, mathematics, and engineering, the most advanced Indians equaled the Europeans. In healing, they probably surpassed their conquerors. Their restraint in the use of drugs and alcohol, at least at the time of the Conquest, compared favorably to other peoples. Indian music, dances, athletics, and ceremonies attest to a high esthetic sense, a mixture of joy in living with spiritual expression. Only in recent times have the artistic works of the Indians come to command admiration for the use of color, design, and abstract conceptions.

The Indians have given much to the rest of the human family. The white potato alone has become a major item of food in the world. Corn, beans, tomatoes, squash, chocolate, tapioca, vanilla, turkeys, and manioc have greatly enriched the food supply of the planet. Rubber and tobacco have become items of almost universal use. Lost, however, were the secrets of the Maya astronomers and the Inca builders as well as many medicinal practices. Much as later generations have lamented the destruction of Tenochtitlán and the degradation of Cuzco, perhaps the greatest casualty has been the Indian attitude toward life and the universe. The restless and insatiable people of modern times tend to regard that philosophy with nostalgia and romance.

In this chapter the Indus civilization and the emergence of its successor, the Indo-Aryan civilization, after a dark age of many centuries, have been examined with particular attention to those features of enduring significance. The Indus civilization is fascinating because it covered the largest area and possessed the largest, planned urban centers at such an early date, but any account of it and its probable contributions to Indo-Aryan civilization must be tentative because of our dependence on the archeological record alone. Aryan culture was severely altered, if not totally submerged, by local influences that may very well reflect the persistence of Indus culture. In Indo-Aryan civilization religion played a particularly important role, and the brahman priests cooperatively supported the rulers for their mutual benefit, but their self-imposed separation as a privileged, hereditary class diminished their concern as a group for the fate of dynasties. On the other hand, the challenges from within and outside their fold encouraged the brahmans to develop a tolerant and comprehensive attitude toward divergent religious views and philosophies, such as Jainism and Buddhism.

In Chinese civilization, religion remained underdeveloped and a priesthood never evolved, unless the despised diviners and exploiters of popular beliefs are so regarded. The ruler as Son of Heaven was in a sense the chief priest held responsible for maintaining harmony between Heaven, Earth, and Man on pain of losing the Mandate of Heaven, but this doctrine was something less than a highly developed religious conception. On the contrary, Chinese institutional and ideological development was distinguished by its secularism, rationalism, and pragmatic concern for good government.

Like the Indus civilization, reliable knowledge about the early civilizations in Guatemala, Mexico, and the Yucatán Peninsula of Middle America and the Andean region of South America is limited to the archeological record partly because of suppression of the past by the latest Indian civilizations and partly because of the destruction by unappreciative Spanish conquerors. Nevertheless, evidence of impressive achievements in monumental architecture and the arts of healing, astronomy, mathematics, and engineering has been uncovered which commands respect and regret for the loss of this knowledge. In addition, many Indian foods became important contributions to the rest of the world, particularly potatoes, corn, and tomatoes. Finally, the way in which all the traditional agricultural civilizations learned to live with and adapt to their natural environments is only beginning to be appreciated as a consequence of the growing concern about environmental pollution and destruction.

Meanwhile, the peasants and workers whose labors supported these traditional civilizations have gone largely unnoticed and unchanged through the ages until modern times. Disciplined and subordinated by the literate religious and secular elites, they lived, died, and did their duty with few recorded complaints.

SUGGESTED READINGS

Wheeler, Sir Mortimer, *The Indus Civilization.* Cambridge, England: Cambridge University Press, 1968. Paperback.
  A readable account by a leading authority.

Allchin, Bridget and Raymond, *The Birth of Indian Civilization.* Baltimore, Md.: Penguin Books, 1968. Paperback.
  A more detailed summary and analysis of the Indus civilization.

Basham, A. L., *The Wonder That Was India.* New York: Grove Press, 1954. Paperback.
  An excellent general study of pre-Muslim India.

Kosambi, D. D., *Ancient India.* New York: Meridian Books, 1969. Paperback.
  A good study, more limited in scope.

Zimmer, Heinrich, *Philosophies of India.* New York: Meridian Books, 1956. Paperback.
  A stimulating, but difficult and challengeable, analysis and interpretation.

DeBary, Wm. Theodore, et al., *Sources of Indian Tradition*. New York: Columbia University Press, 1958. Paperback.
A careful selection of readings with particularly good introductions.

Li Chi, *The Beginnings of Chinese Civilization*. Seattle: University of Washington Press, 1968. Paperback.

Gernet, Jacques, *Ancient China*. Berkeley and Los Angeles: University of California Press, 1968.
A well-written interpretive study.

Hsu, Cho-yun, *Ancient China in Transition: An Analysis of Social Mobility, 722–222 B.C.* Stanford: Stanford University Press, 1965. Paperback.

Watson, William, *Early Civilization in China*. New York: Frederick Ungar, 1966. Paperback.
Profusely illustrated study by an art historian.

DeBary, Wm. Theodore, et al., *Sources of Chinese Tradition*. New York: Columbia University Press, 1960. Paperback.
Another excellent selection, like that on India, to supplement this and subsequent chapters on China. Of course, the Analects *of Confucius and other classics are available in a variety of inexpensive paperback editions.*

Wauchope, Robert, ed., *The Indian Background of Latin American History*. New York: Alfred A. Knopf, 1970. Paperback.

Thompson, J. Eric S., *The Rise and Fall of Maya Civilization*. Norman: University of Oklahoma Press, 1966.

Vaillant, George C., *Aztecs of Mexico: Origin, Rise, and Fall of the Aztec Nation*. Revised. Garden City, N.Y.: Doubleday & Co., 1962.

Von Hagen, Victor W., *Realm of the Incas*. New York: The New American Library, 1957. Paperback.

CHAPTER **3**

India, China, and Japan
to c. A.D. 600

In this chapter the story of Indo-Aryan civilization is continued through its peak of cultural development under the Guptas. Under the impact of challenges from Buddhism, Jainism, and internal criticisms, ritualistic Brahmanism evolved into Hinduism, whose tolerance and flexibility found room for a broad spectrum of practices extending from primitive religious beliefs to sophisticated philosophical doctrines. Buddhism, too, was transformed, dividing into two major schools, and, before declining and disappearing in its homeland, diffused its teachings to Southeast and East Asia.

Chinese civilization experienced its first great imperial era before suffering its most extended political breakdown of more than three and one-half centuries, which was made worse by nomadic conquest of the northern homeland and the alien challenge of Buddhism. Nevertheless, China was destined to be reunified by a series of vigorous dynasties and was carried to its highest level of achievement under Confucian leadership.

Finally, the foundations of a distinctive Japanese civilization were laid during the period covered by this chapter.

INDO-ARYAN CIVILIZATION

Indian political development produced only two native empires—the Maurya and the Gupta—that incorporated major portions of the subcontinent and endured for more than a century. Normally this vast and varied land was divided into a great number of competing kingdoms and principalities. Indo-Aryan civilization is better known for its cultural accomplishments in the arts, literature, and especially philosophy and religion, which commanded the energies of the best minds and talents. For a people who believed they were living in the *Kali-yuga*, the final age of decline in a vast cosmic eon, and whose primary concern was preparation for a future rebirth, this present life and government were secondary considerations to be endured and survived in the best way possible. Therefore, most people did their duty according to their status in life but seldom felt any strong sense of attachment to their rulers. As a consequence, popular rebellions, on the one hand, and personal loyalty beyond the range of a ruler's kinsmen, on the other hand, were both rare in Indian history. Unity on a

73

large scale could only be based on thorough-going autocracy, not participation. Nevertheless, Indian thought also included the idea of a semidivine Universal Emperor (*Chakravartin*) who was well-meaning and dedicated to the welfare of the people. Of course, divinity in India was cheap; every brahman was also semidivine and brahman saints then as now commanded far more popular veneration than any ruler.

Chandragupta Maurya

The techniques of imperial administration appear to have been borrowed from Persia, particularly after the conquest of northwestern India by Darius I, but their application in the creation of an empire including all of northern India was the work of Chandragupta Maurya (*c.* 322–298 B.C.). Chandragupta was a contemporary of Alexander the Great, who had conquered the Persian Empire and spread Greek influence throughout the Middle East. (See pp. 132–134.) A Greek account suggests that he failed to persuade Alexander to assist him in overthrowing the principal kingdom in the Ganges basin. Nevertheless, within a few years Chandragupta carried out the task himself and proceeded to build the Maurya Empire. About 305 B.C. he defeated Alexander's successor, Seleucus, and acquired the Indus basin and part of present-day Afghanistan. An alliance with Seleucus was sealed by the gift of 500 Indian war elephants in return for a Greek bride.

The ruthless Chandragupta was aided in the consolidation of his realm by an exceptionally able and equally cold-blooded brahman minister, Kautilya, who was a determined advocate of a centralized, bureaucratic regime. Moreover, with cynical realism, he distrusted everyone and established a complex system of spies to maintain administrative efficiency and forestall subversion from any quarter. Under the influence of Kautilya, the reputed author of the Indian classic on statecraft, the *Arthashastra,* northern India was organized into a prosperous realm directly administered by salaried officials.

However, the power of Indian rulers was strictly limited by customs, taboos, and traditional norms for behavior. Officials tended to

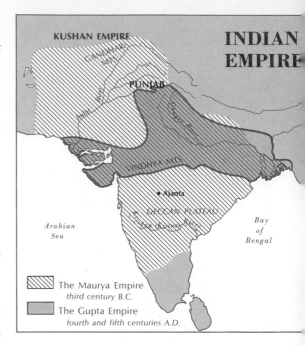

INDIAN EMPIRE

KUSHAN EMPIRE

PUNJAB

Arabian Sea

Bay of Bengal

VINDHYA MTS.

DECCAN PLATEAU

Ajanta

▨ The Maurya Empire
  third century B.C.

▧ The Gupta Empire
  fourth and fifth centuries A.D.

become hereditary, and the fact that they were paid in the form of land grants led to imperial decentralization and disintegration. The liquidation of ruling and noble families went against Indian norms for behavior. In addition, the power of the rulers was checked by brahman prestige. Rulers were accepted primarily as the leading champions of order and the status quo in an age of anarchy, an age that all observers regarded as one of decay and decline. Thus Indian civilization proved notably deficient in fostering enduring political unification, particularly when compared to Chinese civilization. As a consequence, generally inconclusive interstate warfare was to ravage India throughout most of its history, punctuated by alien invasions from the northwest. But the conventions of Indian warfare generally excluded excessive cruelty and barbarity.

Ashoka and Buddhism

Chandragupta's little known son, Bindusara, marshaled the resources of northern India, marched over the Vindhya Mountains, and conquered the Deccan, the vast plateau of central India. His son, the renowned Ashoka (*c.* 269–232 B.C.), rounded out the Maurya Empire, which extended some 1500 miles from below the Kistna (Krishna) River in the south to Afghanistan in the north. Ashoka's bloody conquest in the southeast cost 100,000 lives in battle and an even great toll among noncombatants. After that he was overcome with remorse and turned to Buddhism, abandoning expansion by warfare in favor of what he called "victories of righteousness." He was shrewd enough, however, to tolerate and patronize the competing faiths that had arisen during the past two centuries of religious ferment.

Ashoka's beliefs and government program are uniquely documented in proclamations he had inscribed on rocks and pillars throughout his vast realm. One of these describes his deep and abiding grief at the loss of life in his last conquest. Henceforth, he asserted, forgiveness, so far as possible, would be the guideline of his government. He even sought to tame the wild forest tribesmen by reasoning with them. At the same time, however, he warned them and all would-be rebels to beware of testing his compassion too far for fear of being slain. Thus Ashoka's pacifism and idealism were pragmatically limited by his view of the welfare of the state and his subjects. His interest in security, self-control, justice, and happiness led him to recognize the need for enforcing law and order. Finally, this inscription expressed his conviction that "the greatest of all victories is the victory of Righteousness." But he never thought of relinquishing any conquered territory to its former ruler. Moreover, there is no record of any reduction in the size of the army.

Nevertheless, as much of a political realist as he was, Ashoka did represent the Indian *chakravartin*, the benevolent universal emperor, extolled in all the religions and philosophies of India. He set an example of enlightened, humanitarian government, relaxing the sterner justice of the past. Judicial torture and capital punishment were retained, but the condemned were granted a three-day stay of execution to prepare themselves for death. The former secret police were converted into "officers of righteousness" who censured provincial administrations and fostered more humane relations between man and man. Ashoka considered himself the gentle father of his people and

frequently reproved local officials for failing to maintain this principle in their governmental actions. He encouraged the doctrine of nonviolence (*ahimsa*), which was becoming general in all Indian religions and philosophies, by prohibiting animal sacrifices, regulating animal slaughter for food, substituting royal pilgrimages for the grand hunts that had been the traditional sport of kings, and greatly reducing the eating of meat in the royal household. Although royal approval perhaps accelerated the development of vegetarianism, Ashoka mainly capitalized on a trend that was already well under way.

As a patron of public works, Ashoka displayed tolerance and political wisdom by supporting the construction of non-Buddhist as well as Buddhist shrines. Roads were extended and improved by planting fruit trees for food and shade, digging wells, and building inns. The ruler set up medical clinics for both men and animals and sponsored the cultivation of medicinal plants to be given to them free of charge. Finally, he supported Buddhist missionary activity abroad. Despite the claims in the inscriptions, the only important spiritual conquest was the island kingdom of Ceylon, which became the principal base for the spread of Buddhism to Southeast Asia.

The net effect of Ashoka's reforms, then, may be said to have enhanced paternalism and the centralization of imperial authority, regardless of Buddhist influences. Indeed, it could be argued that Ashoka used Buddhism to advance his own ends as a ruler.

Although he was clearly a Buddhist, Ashoka's understanding of Buddhism was shallow and superficial and probably reflected the popular knowledge and appreciation of this doctrine at a time when it was only one, and not the largest, of the creeds competing for public acceptance. Certainly, the emperor was in a better position to learn its precepts than the ordinary layman. Yet his inscriptions indicate that it meant to him mainly a system of morality and altruistic behavior helpful in promoting peace and goodwill on earth and entrance into heaven after death. Moreover, he believed that the improvement in morals inspired by his reforms had attracted the traditional gods into active support of him and his program to

Capital of column built by the Buddhist emperor, Ashoka. The figure is the symbol of the Republic of India today.

promote the public welfare. The frequency of his references to heaven suggest that Buddhism was already developing the idea of individual salvation.

Whatever benefits the Indian people and Ashoka may have gained from his support of Buddhism were rapidly dissipated after his death when the provincial governors drawn primarily from the royal family asserted their independence. Buddhist altruism disappeared from government which reverted to the Indian "law of the fishes" according to which the little fish is the natural prey of the big fish. But, while Ashoka lived, India enjoyed greater peace and prosperity over a larger area than under any successor until British rule in the nineteenth century. The use of the capital of an Ashokan pillar as the central feature on the seal of the Republic of India is only an appropriate recognition of India's greatest ruler.

Disunited India: North and South

The breakup of the Maurya Empire was followed by a succession of alien incursions from the northwest; first came Bactrian Greeks in the second century B.C., then nomadic Scythians known as Shakas in India, then the Turkish-speaking Yueh-Chih who had been pushed westward from the Chinese frontier. Some invaders patronized one religion, some another. Some created fairly large, but short-lived, empires. Politically these empires were no more than loose overlordships that generally began to dissolve on the deaths of the able leaders who had founded them. The centralized, bureaucratic empire of the Maurya type was not easily recreated. Many of these conquerors eventually settled down on grants of land as forebears of the later Rajput warrior class.

Sometime in the last half of the first or the first half of the second century A.D., the Yueh-Chih under Kanishka created an empire known as the Kushan, which included northwestern India and much of Central Asia. This empire and its ruler are important for the patronage and transmission of Mahayana Buddhism to China over the major overland trade routes under Kushan control.* The Kushan period is also notable for the promotion of the Gandhara school of Buddhist art which transmitted Greek artistic influences to China. Paradoxically, a Turkish and not a Greek Indian dynasty carried out this achievement, employing some Greek-style sculptors attracted to India by the growth of East-West trade.

In southernmost India and Ceylon, non-Aryan peoples built prosperous kingdoms that developed a flourishing overseas trade with Southeast Asia and the West. In Southeast Asia their merchants purchased Chinese as well as local products that were then sold along with Indian goods to Western merchants. Since the days of imperial Rome, Asian silks, jewels, and spices have found a ready market in the West, paid for mostly

* For discussion, see *Buddhism: The Two Vehicles* below.

with gold, although Roman-trained mercenaries serving in Indian armies may have helped the balance of payments. To Southeast Asia Indian merchants exported their culture, particularly Hinduism and Buddhism, as well as their products, principally cotton cloth. Two monuments illustrating Indian influence are the huge Buddhist shrine of Borobudur, carved out of solid rock by an eighth-century Javan state, and the ruins of Angkor Wat in Cambodia, built by the Khmer Empire of the ninth to thirteenth centuries A.D.

The Gupta Empire

After five centuries of political division and alien intrusions another Chandragupta, unrelated to the founder of the Maurya Empire, gained prominence in the former Gangetic center of power and founded the Gupta dynasty (c. A.D. 320–550), which restored the glory of empire on a lesser scale and the prosperity necessary to carry Indian culture to a new peak of achievement. The Guptas attempted to eliminate rival rulers and to establish a centralized government on the Maurya model, but most of the rival states were too well developed to make this goal an easy task. Outside the Ganges basin the Guptas generally had to settle for tribute from rulers who were otherwise independent.

Although the Guptas extended no special patronage to Buddhism and, in fact, favored the brahmans, Buddhism was in a flourishing condition as attested in the record of a six-year sojourn in India by the Chinese Buddhist pilgrim, Fa-hsien. The few non-Buddhist references in this account present the picture of a humane society, thanks to the moderating influence of Jainist and Buddhist ethics. All but the lowest strata of society were by now vegetarians. Administration was mild and crime was rare. Fa-hsien was able to travel safely throughout the country without a passport. Hinduism had evolved out of sacrificial Brahmanism, incorporating or adapting much of the ethical and other teachings of the unorthodox creeds.

Fa-hsien's visit fell in the reign of Chandragupta II (c. 376–415), which is considered the greatest era of Indo-Aryan civilization. The zenith of Indian art is represented in

The Buddha as imagined by an artist of the Gandhara school, third–fourth century A.D.

sculpture by the spiritually impressive Buddhas of Sarnath and in painting by the gorgeous murals in the cave temples of Ajanta. Although original and creative works of art continued to be produced for several centuries, they subsequently became increasingly stilted and stylized. In literature, where there are many great writers and great works to choose from, one figure stands out, the poet and dramatist Kalidasa, whose role has been appropriately compared to that of Shakespeare in English literature. The play, *Shakuntala*, is considered his masterpiece. Indian mathematicians and scientists learned a great deal from translations of Greek texts, but they invented decimal notation and the concept of zero, which were ultimately transmitted via the Arabs to the West where they facilitated the growth of modern science. Although astronomy was handicapped by the lack of the telescope and a great interest in astrology, exceptionally accurate measurements were made in large, well-

View of Borobudur, monumental Buddhist temple carved out of solid rock in Java, eighth to ninth century A.D.

equipped observatories. The renowned astronomer Aryabhata understood the rotation of the earth and suggested a heliocentric or sun-centered theory for the solar system as early as the fifth century, but for the purposes of measurement and tabulation the geocentric (earth-centered) theory was assumed. As in the arts, creative vigor in literature and the sciences tapered off and was undistinguished after the eighth century.

After the disintegration of the Gupta Empire, northern India once more gained a brief period of unity under the brilliant ruler, Harsha (c. 606–647), but his empire was even less centralized and more under the control of great landowners than the Gupta Empire had been. Again, we are indebted to a Chinese pilgrim, Hsuan Tsang, for a picture of this era. He was more observant of secular affairs than Fa-hsien, and his chronicle tells about the ruler as well as social conditions. He admired Harsha, who admitted him to a place of honor in his court. In fact, in his later years the ruler appears to have come under strong Buddhist influence. The pilgrim's account indicates, however, that Buddhism was in decline and that influences from southern India were infecting both Buddhism and Hinduism with a more emotional and devotional outlook. Travel was no longer

View of Angkor Wat Temple, Cambodia, twelfth century A.D.

safe. Hsuan Tsang was twice robbed and once almost sacrificed to the goddess Durga by river pirates in the heart of the empire.

Buddhism: The Two Vehicles

It will be recalled that the Buddha taught that life is sorrow—stemming from the ignorant and futile desire of the ego for satisfaction and permanence in this world of constant change—and that sorrow can only be eliminated by suppressing the ego. To do this one must learn that what is real and true is unchanging, eternal, and universal whereas what is perceived by the ordinary senses is unreal, transient, and particular. Attainment of such knowledge is not to be gained by asceticism but by following the middle path of moderation recognizing the sorrow and transitory qualities of life with heart-filled compassion for the suffering of all living things.

Such a discipline will lead to enlightenment, that indescribable and ineffable state of transcendent knowledge. In short, the Buddha taught the *method of mental preparation* for the attainment of ultimate knowledge, as the various schools of Yoga did in Hinduism. But the ultimate knowledge itself was beyond ordinary rational thought and could only be gained through intuitive enlightenment.

Thanks to Ashoka's patronage, Buddhism gained widespread acceptance and increasing popularity through the third century A.D., after which it underwent a gradual decline. During this time the message of the Buddha was transformed from a nontheistic philosophy into a theistic religion by his followers, who elaborated their views in volumes of scriptures. Even the Buddha himself came to be worshipped in idols by the first century A.D. Despite the convening of several great

The Descent of the Ganges. Monumental Indian relief, seventh century A.D.

councils to determine the orthodox doctrine, a major schism developed between the Lesser and Greater Vehicles, Hinayana and Mahayana.

A common way of expressing some sense of the quality of enlightenment and its remoteness from human understanding was to compare the doctrine with a vehicle (*yana*), specifically a ferryboat. In a land of great rivers without many bridges it seemed natural to use the comparison with a fording place in Jainism and a ferryboat in Buddhism.

In the Buddhist parable the river is pictured as so wide that the far bank can scarcely be perceived. The near shore, on which one is standing, represents life, filled with desire, suffering, and death—all due to ignorance. Entering on the Noble Eightfold Path of the Buddhist discipline is like boarding the ferryboat without any idea of what will be found at the end of the voyage. As the ferryboat reaches midstream, both banks, the bank of life and the bank of enlightenment, have become indistinct in detail. All that has genuine substance is the ferryboat, the fellow-passengers, and the swirling waters that must be overcome. Finally, the far shore is reached, the shore of life is lost in the distance, and the passengers disembark. The ferryboat is left and forgotten because it, like the Buddhist discipline, is a mere vehicle no longer of use to those who have gained enlightenment. The discipline is for seekers; it is of no use except as a tool to teach others how to find the way. Each individual must use it and, having achieved the goal, discard it. Thus, the parable concludes with a paradox; for those who have reached the far shore there is no shore, neither near nor far; there is no river, no crossing, no ferryboat, because there can be no duality in perfection. There is no rebirth and no enlightenment. All such perceptions are illusions of life. This is the great awakening, the achievement of perfect knowledge. Essentially, then, the teachings of the Buddha stress psychological and moral self-discipline and are not theological or even metaphysical.

The Hinayana* prevails today with local variations in Ceylon, Burma, Thailand, Laos, and Cambodia. It claims to stick more closely to the teachings of the Buddha by maintaining that enlightenment can be achieved only by arduous individual effort via the Noble Eightfold Path in emulation of venerated *arhants* (perfect beings or saints) who set examples for others to follow.

The Mahayana school is represented by a number of sects that gained the greatest followings in China, Korea, Japan, and Vietnam, incorporating a variety of local beliefs. The Mahayanists, perhaps influenced by Middle Eastern religious ideas that were brought to India by invaders and refugees after the third century B.C., decried the limited opportunity of enlightenment offered by the Hinayanists only to the minority that was capable of following the Noble Eightfold Path. Instead they taught that no small ferryboat but rather a superliner was ready and waiting to transport all the faithful. This ship was manned by Bodhisattvas, those who had reached the edge of *nirvana* but out of over-

whelming compassion for suffering mankind would forego the final step until all had been saved. Stopovers in heaven were provided for the faithful, where final preparation for enlightenment would take place. In one sect a mere declaration of faith in one's dying breath guaranteed a passport to heaven. Thus the transition from a philosophy leading to enlightenment to a theistic religion with a host of deities was achieved. In some sects the nature of heaven as merely a way station en route to enlightenment was lost sight of in the popular mind and became the ultimate goal to be reached by worship and simple declarations of faith.

The foregoing statement by no means does justice to the philosophical development that led to this religious conclusion, and only a few sects went this far. Mahayana Buddhism represents rather the natural development of an emphasis on brotherly love that filled the teachings of the Buddha, especially the four cardinal virtues of love, compassion, joy, and serenity. How could one unselfishly and genuinely observe with love and compassion the sufferings of mankind and yet remain serenely detached in pursuit of one's own enlightenment? Moreover, had not the Buddha (more likely his successors) taught that all that separated man from enlightenment was ignorance, a simple absence of realization? Small wonder, then, that the individual discipline prescribed by the Noble Eightfold Path was subordinated in importance to a consideration of the ultimate goal of release for all living beings from the sorrow and suffering of the "wheel of life" with its perpetual round of rebirths.

Buddhism had never rejected the gods; it had only reduced them to the realm of this ever-changing universe, subject like everything else to dissolution and rebirth. Since the Buddha had passed into that transcendent, ineffable condition that could not be described as existence or nonexistence, he surpassed the gods. But theoretically he could not be adored in a statue or other image because he was beyond form. His memory and teachings, however, were venerated from an early date in symbols, such as the Wheel of the Law, his footprints, a vacant throne, or the trident-shaped symbol representing the early Buddhist declaration of faith

---

* This is the derogatory name coined by opponents of this school; adherents of this doctrine call it Theravada Buddhism.

called the Three Jewels: "I take refuge in the Buddha, I take refuge in the Doctrine, I take refuge in the Order." By the first century A.D. the final step had been taken of worshipping statues of the Buddha in human form. Indeed, in Mahayana Buddhism past and future incarnations of the Buddha with special attributes were added to what became an increasingly complex hierarchy of Buddhas and Bodhisattvas along with artistic depictions of heavens and hells.

By the end of the first century A.D. Mahayana Buddhism had reached full vigor and flourished in India for several centuries while spreading its doctrines abroad. Mahayanists, Hinayanists, and even brahmans were still able to coexist, even in the same monastery, but their views had completely diverged in emphasis. In later centuries Hinduism, which absorbed and adapted many of the popular features of Buddhism, undermined its position in its homeland. In addition, both Buddhism and Hinduism became subject to the influence of a sect that stressed magic and female deities as the active counterparts of passive male mates. Tantric Buddhism (see pp. 86–87), which became most popular in Bengal, subsequently influenced Lamaism, the religion of Tibet and Mongolia, after its destruction in India by Muslim conquerors of the twelfth century.

Introduction to Hinduism

What is called Hinduism evolved after 500 B.C. out of Brahmanism under the influence of internal criticism and under the challenge of the non-Vedic teachings, such as Jainism and Buddhism. As it evolved, the complex and imperfectly understood interplay, adaptation, and exchange of conceptions produced a number of philosophies, religions, and deities united only by the common acceptance of the Vedas as sacred revelation and of the class and caste system (see p. 88) as the device supposedly prescribed in the Vedas for the organization and integration of the social hierarchy from the brahman class downward. The general sacred law (dharma), which the top brahman castes were supposed to observe in full, was modified according to the conditions of each class and caste so that each one had its own set of rules and regulations. In particular, the

ruler was integrated into this system by the obligation to enforce dharma, a power and function symbolized by the white umbrella carried over his head. Thus Hinduism encompassed more than religion and philosophy, providing a whole way of life which has demonstrated remarkable flexibility and adaptability during the past 2000 years.

New doctrines and cults have been incorporated and given a place alongside older practices and beliefs by means of the tolerant and perhaps condescending doctrine that there are innumerable valid and appropriate levels of truth from primitive worship of the forces of nature to the most intellectual philosophies. Every deity and religious practice are believed to represent at least some part of the ultimate truth, and each one with its rites is believed to be helpful in guiding men along the path to truth. This tolerant and comprehensive attitude has supplied a measure of social and cultural unity amid the political, linguistic, racial, and even doctrinal diversity of India. Only Islam and Christianity were able to resist assimilation by Hinduism.

In addition to class and caste, secular and religious life was regulated by two fourfold systems of classification which were developed to order and regulate all aspects of life. The first prescribed the four stages (ashrama) of life from youth to death, setting appropriate periods in a Hindu's life for fulfilling earthly and spiritual obligations.

The first stage was devoted to the study and memorization of substantial portions of the Vedas under the strict discipline of a guru (teacher). One entered this apprenticeship between the ages of eight and twelve—when a boy of the upper three classes was initiated as "twice-born"—and continued normally until twenty. The student fully subordinated himself to his teacher, faithfully carried out all assignments, and accepted without question all knowledge communicated to him. The extent to which this stage was observed outside the brahman class cannot be determined; for most Indian youths it probably involved mastering their trade and the rules and regulations of their caste.

In the second stage of life the male Hindu married, raised a family, and dedicated himself to the promotion of its welfare within the rules of his caste. When this stage was completed, he was then free to turn over family affairs to his sons and retire, with or without his wife, to pursue a life of meditation and self-denial as a hermit in quest of the ultimate truth. It is impossible to determine how many Indians entered this third stage, but the desire of sons to take over their inheritances and the management of family affairs probably propelled more fathers into it than spiritual considerations alone might have induced. The fourth stage involved complete separation from dependence on the family by taking up the life of a wandering beggar as a final renunciation in preparation for death.

This system of the four stages of life put religion into its own compartment so that it would not interfere with the normal and necessary functions of society. By prescribing a time and place for both secular and religious duties it provided a proper balance and moderation, giving appropriate weight and importance to secular obligations.

Also supporting moderation and complementing the four stages of life was the fourfold classification of the ends of man. First, was the sacred law (*dharma*), covering man's religious, social, and moral obligations. This category included the four stages of life which were thus integrated with the ends of man. Therefore, the sacred law differs according to age as well as class and caste. Indeed, in the broadest sense this law regulates all aspects of human relationships, but in practice three other ends of man became differentiated: *artha* (material gain), *kama* (pleasure and love), and *moksha* (release from rebirth which was the goal of the last two stages of life).

Kama: Pleasure and Love

Although the word *kama* embraces every aspect of human pleasure, in India, as elsewhere, its sexual connotation received the greatest attention. In its connection with the second stage of life, which many literary references deemed the most important of the four stages, *kama* as love was invested with more than secular significance; it was a sacred duty essential to the perpetuation of the wheel of life. Hindu literature and art are filled with sexual symbols and often outright eroticism. Later forms of worship made of

sexual union a sort of sacrament illustrating the unity that transcends duality, thus exaggerating the religious obligation attached to producing a family.

The *Kamasutra* (Treatise on Love and Pleasure), compiled in the early centuries of the Christian era, is the best known of a number of works providing detailed guidance for cultured members of the upper classes, not only on human love but also on the social graces and the esthetic appreciation of art forms. In dealing with love, it reveals exceptional sensitivity for the feelings of the female partner, in part inspired by the fact that with marriages arranged by their families newlyweds were frequently complete strangers, and in part reflecting the refined level of taste and culture achieved by Indian civilization. In other words, lovemaking had been developed into a high art whose end was the achievement of maximum pleasure for both partners. The means to this end called for the mastery of complex skills.

Indian custom classified all women as minors under the protection of some man. Wives were instructed to devote themselves entirely to their homes and husbands whom, regardless of any shortcomings, they should worship as gods. On the other hand, the husband was admonished to honor and treasure his wife as his better half from whom all the benefits of companionship, comfort, encouragement, love, and happiness flowed.

Although the treatises on *kama* devoted the most space to the relationship of man and woman, the esthetic appreciation of art, drama, and music also received substantial attention. While the themes of the various art forms were almost wholly drawn from religion, religion and life were very closely integrated in Indian thought. Sensual pleasure was not sharply separated from religious feeling, as has frequently been the case in the West, with consequent inhibitions. To the Indian mind there was nothing unsuitable in the voluptuous proportions of the female deities enshrined in the temples. In short, nature in all its manifestations was deemed a divine work of art, and an artist sought to distill in his work the divine essence in the natural event or story through which he delivered his religious message. In esthetic appreciation of a work of art, then, the object, character, or story was considered only incidental. The most important factor in the esthetic process was that the observer's own sensitivity and emotion enabled him to appreciate the aspect of ultimate truth the artist meant to convey. Thus esthetic appreciation involved spiritual appreciation, at least for the cultured individual with an "attuned heart" and sense of taste. Indian art forms were thus able to accomplish a happy union of religion and nature because the Indian outlook saw in them no contradiction, but rather an essential unity.

Moksha (Release) and Yoga

With the acceptance of the doctrine of rebirth, the fourth end of man, the quest for release (*moksha*) from the wheel of life, became and has remained a fundamental part of Indian religious and philosophical thought, both heterodox and orthodox. This quest for permanence amid the impermanence of existence, for ultimate truth amid the delusions of this world, has already been observed in the Upanishads, Jainism, and Buddhism. In the development of Hinduism the quest has produced answers in the form of religion, theistic philosophy, and nontheistic philosophy—the path of religion emphasizing devotion and the path of philosophy emphasizing knowledge.

Yoga was originally a separate sect, but in its broad meaning of "spiritual discipline" it came to apply to the preparatory exercises of all Hindu sects. Like the Buddhist Eightfold Path, Yoga prescribed a means of achieving the goal of realization of the eternal and inactive "soul" and thus release (*moksha*) from worldly bondage. Although the techniques varied from sect to sect, the following steps were generally deemed essential. Selfless moral conduct abjuring violence, theft, dishonesty, lust, and greed would cleanse the mind and prepare it for meditation. Sitting in difficult postures, notably the familiar Lotus posture with the feet on the opposite thighs, was believed necessary for meditation. Deep, prolonged, and rhythmic breathing was part of disciplining the body with the aim of training the senses to disregard their perceptions. The mind was disciplined by concentrating on a single object, such as the navel, until it filled the mind to the exclusion of everything else. The final goal was temporary dissolution of the personality of the yogi in a deep trance. Subsequently, variant techniques were devised some of which yield results yet to be explained by modern science.

Bhagavad Gita

The apparent renunciation of the value and reality of this life involved in early doctrines, both orthodox and unorthodox, was in time overcome by the most revered work of Hinduism after the Vedas, the *Bhagavad Gita* (Song of the Lord), which was part of the world's longest epic poem, the *Mahabharata*. The setting for the doctrine, which reconciled action with knowledge and devotion and *dharma* with *moksha,* was the period before a great battle when the warrior Arjuna was overcome with remorse at the prospect of slaying his relatives in the ranks of the foe. His charioteer, Krishna, the god incarnate, then explained at great length why Arjuna must do his duty as a warrior.

The warrior who believes he is a killer and that his victim has been killed is still in ignorance of the real truth. He is confusing the material body, which is born, grows, changes, and dies, with the eternal soul, which is unborn, unchangeable, and indestructible. For everything that is born, death is certain and for everything that dies, rebirth is certain. Therefore, the warrior should not grieve about his role in what is inevitable. Indeed, the *dharma* of the warrior commands him to fight and to kill, and if he should fail to do his duty, he would commit a sin.

Having explained the noncontradictory nature of the demands of *dharma*, Krishna then went on to explain that in this life action of some sort cannot be avoided. What is important is not the action but one's attitude toward it. The proper attitude is one of selfless detachment from the result of the action.

To live means to act, even if this action should be limited to the normal needs of the body. But beyond these simple actions, essential to individual survival, a man whose mind controls his body is obligated to fulfill his prescribed role in society, particularly if he wishes to achieve his spiritual goal. To give himself up to mere physical pleasures and to ignore his tasks in rotating the wheel of life would be to lead a sinful life, and indeed, to live in vain. Therefore, by doing his prescribed tasks without attachment to the results of his actions, a man will attain his highest goal. Moreover, as a leader, he is under the additional obligation to set an example of superior conduct because, as he leads, people will follow. Krishna pointed out that even he as a god must continue to act without weariness or else "these worlds would fall into ruin," and then he would be a creator of chaos, a destroyer and not a creator.

The *Gita* was a work of synthesis and reinterpretation of current doctrines carried out by brahmans over a long period of time. Therefore, it is not surprising to find incorporated and integrated into its teachings the class system promoted by the brahman class and both the nontheistic philosophy of knowledge and the devotional theism which was gaining strength in the upper classes. Moreover, the *Gita* also incorporates Indian pantheism, whereby every god is but a manifestation of the Supreme One and worship of the least of them is worship of Him. In fact the poem asserts that all things in this world are pervaded by Him in His nonmanifest form. "All beings abide in Me, but I do not abide in them." Furthermore, even the lowliest — women and members of the lowest class who are not twice-born — are eligible for salvation through worship of Him, no matter how indirectly or improperly this worship is performed. This doctrine countered Jainist and Buddhist criticism of the exclusiveness of Vedic religion. Indeed, one of the reasons for the high regard in which this work is held is that every school and cult can find support for its position in it.

Advaita Vedanta

Subsequent Hindu thinkers worked out variations on the foregoing themes, stressing one aspect or another, but only one of them, the revered Shankara (c. 788–820), warrants our attention as the expounder of the Hindu philosophy that still commands the allegiance of most educated Indians. As interpreted by this brilliant South Indian brahman, the only reality, the ultimate truth was Brahman, the impersonal Universal Soul of the Upanishads, with which the individual soul, *atman*, was

identical. Everything else — the world, the universe, the gods — was illusion (*maya*) and unreal. This is strict monism,* and Shankara's followers distinguished themselves from other Vedantists (followers of Hindu philosophy) by the label *advaita* (allowing no second).

In developing his ideas, however, Shankara had to reconcile certain inconsistencies appearing in the Upanishads and in the Vedas with his monistic philosophy. To do this he utilized the old Indian device of differing levels of truth. On a lower level of relative truth the god Brahma (see footnote, p. 51) was recognized as the creator of the world of experience, or reality. Indeed, Shankara himself worshipped the god Shiva as an aid in purifying and preparing his mind for higher thought. But the ultimate and absolute truth, he insisted, transcended deity and form. As his opponents were quick to point out, his conception of Brahman, the universal Reality, did not differ in essence from the ultimate truth of Buddhism, and he was accused of being a crypto-Buddhist.

Regardless of criticism, however, his philosophy has proved most convincing to educated Hindus. In Vedanta, release can be obtained only by introspective meditation leading to the intuitive realization of the oneness of the self and the universal Reality. But religious devotion to a particular deity can help in preparing and purifying the mind for the attainment of liberation. And in a condescending fashion Vedantists concede that any worshipper has at least put his foot on the bottom rung of the ladder to ultimate truth.

The Indian Gods

The frequency of references to the worship of deities has probably already suggested the growing influence on the educated classes of the way of devotion (*bhakti*) to salvation as distinguished from the way of knowledge emphasized by the various schools of philosophy. As has been observed, even the philosophers acknowledged the gods and had to find a place for them in their teachings. Although there is little literary evidence, it

* Philosophy asserting a single substance or principle, as contrasted with dualism.

The god Shiva, Lord of the Dance.

may be reasonably assumed that the worship of gods and goddesses and impressive aspects of nature prevailed among the lower classes from the beginning and gradually penetrated the upper classes who refined it and after the Gupta era gave it a philosophical foundation. By the time there is substantial literary evidence, worship had replaced sacrifice and various levels of worship had already evolved. We know this first from the two epic poems, the *Mahabharata* and the *Ramayana,* and then from the many Puranas that describe the missions performed in the many incarnations of the gods.

The most common practice appears to be the simple adoration and service of the statue in which the god was believed to dwell. The image was fed, bathed, given flowers, and even put to bed with his wife. This devotion may be said to be characterized by respect and awe. But the more advanced worshipper already regarded the idol as merely a symbol to remind him of the godhead who loved men and could be loved in return. Of course, it followed that the devotee demonstrated his love of god by love of his fellowmen who were also subjects of god's love.

The personalized love between man and the idol in which the deity was believed to reside received its earliest and most fervent expression in the south, whence it spread to the north. Indeed, the darker-hued southerners, drawing inspiration from their own distinctive heritage, contributed the bulk of new creative vigor after the opening of the Christian era. Southern India had only been brought within the orbit of Aryan civilization by the Maurya conquests, and it undoubtedly contributed its own religious attitudes and practices as well as new deities to the development of Vedic religion.

Fuller elaboration of the doctrine of love led to the concept of the goal of union in which the personality of the worshipper is submerged and absorbed into that of the deity and, thus, is released from worldly bondage. By the Christian era, if not earlier, two supreme gods, Vishnu and Shiva, whose incarnations accounted for a number of other gods, had become generally recognized by the educated class. Vishnu is viewed as wholly benevolent. He has incarnated himself in one form or another on many occasions because of his concern for the welfare of the world. The character of Shiva is less clear-cut. He is fierce as well as paternal and will in time destroy all things. In this latter aspect he is frequently depicted engaged in the "dance of death" which will end a cosmic cycle. He also incorporates the pre-Aryan fertility cult and is frequently worshipped in the form of phallic symbols.

Hinduism is fundamentally tolerant. The followers of Vishnu or Shiva accept the reality of the other; each merely relegates the other god to a secondary position as an emanation of their god. This kind of tolerance has made possible a large amount of assimilation in the course of Indian religious history. Indeed, there has been no serious antagonism to those of alien religions which have resisted assimilation, such as Christians, Zoroastrians (called Parsees), Jews, and even Muslims.

Tantrism

A final, ecstatic stage in the development of Hinduism and Buddhism also originated in the south and is known as Tantrism after its scriptures, called Tantras. It involved the worship of the female counterparts of the gods, called *shakti*, who were believed to represent the active energy of their passive partners. Although Tantrism was associated in practice with the quest for magical power by means of symbols and formulas, its underlying doctrine was that release was attainable in this life for the initiate through a realization that release and bondage were identical. Indeed, for the tantrist the two terms were meaningless — a distinction without any difference in their mystical way of seeing things. While accepting the monism of Advaita Vedanta, Tantrism shifted the emphasis to the world as the dynamic manifestation of the divine truth to be approached through love of the goddess (*shakti*) as the dynamic aspect of divinity.

Not only were bondage and release conceived as one and the same by the tantrist, but when engaged in worship, all ritual restrictions and taboos were eliminated as also meaningless. Without restraint, therefore, the participant in tantrist rituals experienced all aspects of this world normally prohibited, such as alcohol, meat, fish, and sexual intercourse. At the same time, all distinctions of class and caste were set aside for the initiates. Such overstepping of the bounds of the moral and social order prescribed by *dharma* was permitted only during tantric worship and only after a long period of spiritual training and under the guidance of a spiritual teacher (*guru*). *Dharma* still applied when the celebrants returned to the world of ego-consciousness and left the world of purity and perfection.

These rites have been decried as decadent by critics, especially Westerners, but they represent a world-affirming outlook in contrast with the world-negating outlook of ascetic renunciation. Ascetic renunciation had been brought into balance with the demands of society by the four stages of life. Now a more positive, world-affirming viewpoint was developed in the tantric doctrine that release was to be gained by the full appreciation of nature, rather than by rejecting it or setting it aside. In this way every natural act is only part of the dynamic aspect of divinity and becomes not a mere animal act but a religious rite.

The emphasis on the worship of the wife of the god as his dynamic aspect revived the ancient conception of the mother goddess. Each female deity was considered a manifestation of the mother goddess responsible for the functioning of this world regardless of their different names, such as Devi, Durga, Kali, and so on. Even a worshipful approach to one's wife as a symbol of *shakti* was encouraged. The emphasis on sexual intercourse as symbolizing the identity, the oneness in duality, of god and goddess may have inspired the erotic statuary that has so often shocked or charmed Western observers.

Social and Economic Life

Information on the social and economic life of the Indian people is scanty, but a general picture can be drawn, recognizing that there were wide variations from place to place just as India remains diversified today. No population figures exist, although intensive cultivation must have supported tens of millions in Ashoka's time. Although the kings and lords theoretically owned the lands they ruled, most of the peasants were free landholding farmers whose surpluses were the foundation of this traditional agricultural civilization. Landless laborers worked the fields directly farmed by lords and supplied a labor force for state-owned mines and textile operations. The cities were principally administrative and religious centers but also contained a population of workers, craftsmen, and merchants. The renowned temples had grown wealthy from donations and controlled vast estates. Foresighted rulers maintained state granaries in case of famine and invested in public works, such as irrigation, to increase productivity and, hence, their revenues. The ruling classes enjoyed special privileges and looked down on the lower classes in this very class-conscious society. At an early date some people were considered outside the system of four classes, generally, because of their abhorrent or uncleanly occupations. They grew into the 50 million Untouchables of the twentieth century. Nevertheless, frequent complaints about "the confusion of classes" suggest that social mobility between classes was fairly common until post-Gupta times when class and caste distinctions became more rigid and exclusive.

Caste may have developed later and should not be confused with class. The four classes have remained basically unchanged, while castes were continuously being formed or dissolved on many bases including occupation, religion, race, and locality. In the post-Gupta era the castes multiplied and became more prominent, a tendency that accelerated under alien rule. Every class, including the brahman, was subdivided into castes which totaled in the thousands, but caste was far more influential and important among the lower than the higher classes. This difference in emphasis suggests the probable origin of castes as protective groupings of less secure elements in a complex society. Castes were ruled by committees of elders, usually hereditary, that could enforce caste rules by ostracism. There was no worse punishment in Indian society than to become an outcaste. In other words, castes were self-governing units that protected the interests of the group against outside forces and absorbed the loyalty directed in other countries toward the community and the state. Under alien rulers they were vital factors in preserving Indian culture and its diversity. Despite the efforts of the present government to eliminate castes as a barrier to modernization, they persist as an important feature of the traditional social and economic structure in the countryside.

As in other agricultural civilizations, the basic unit of Indian society was, and still is, the extended family including brothers, uncles, and cousins with their families sometimes living under the same roof. The family jointly owned the immovable property under the administration and control of the senior father. The father's authority, although limited by custom, was reinforced by the ancestral rites over which he presided. Three generations of the dead were linked to their living descendants in these rites. From youth the individual was trained to subordinate himself and find his security in the family. Marriage was arranged for the benefit of the family, and according to the Hindu ideal, the groom should be three times the age of the bride, for example, 24 and 8 years of age, respectively. By the post-Gupta era when

social regulations were hardening, widows could not remarry, at least in the higher classes, out of respect to the deceased husbands to whom they had been irrevocably joined. It was customary to invest the family's surplus wealth in gold and jeweled adornments for the wives. The wife with her bracelets, necklaces, and other ornaments was thus a walking treasury and testimonial to her husband's success.

Hemmed in by class, caste, and family restrictions that were upheld by religious sanctions and taboos, the ordinary Indian led a closely circumscribed life, but he also enjoyed the security that membership in these groupings provided. In turn, his industriousness supported the exceptionally luxurious and sophisticated life of his rulers.

IMPERIAL CHINA: 221 B.C. TO A.D. 589

As Chinese civilization presents an exceptional record of cultural continuity, so the Chinese Empire persisted as a political institution for a remarkably long time, from its establishment by the short-lived Ch'in dynasty in 221 B.C. to the overthrow of the Manchus in A.D. 1912. Indeed, this institutional persistence largely resulted from the gradual assertion of cultural and political domination by the tradition-bound Confucian scholar-elite with its stress on the moral role of government. Each new dynasty required the services of these educated men to administer such a vast realm, and they, in turn, enforced the Confucian prescription for government on the rulers. The large majority of Confucian scholars who did not gain government appointments served the state unofficially by inculcating Confucian doctrines among the people. In the period covered by this chapter, however, Confucianism was being formulated and tested; it did not become dominant until the succeeding era. First, it had to meet the challenge of the other schools in working out a synthesis adapted to a unified empire. Then it was confronted with the ideological challenge of Buddhism. Despite a political breakdown of nearly four centuries and conquest of the north by non-Chinese nomads, which tended to discredit

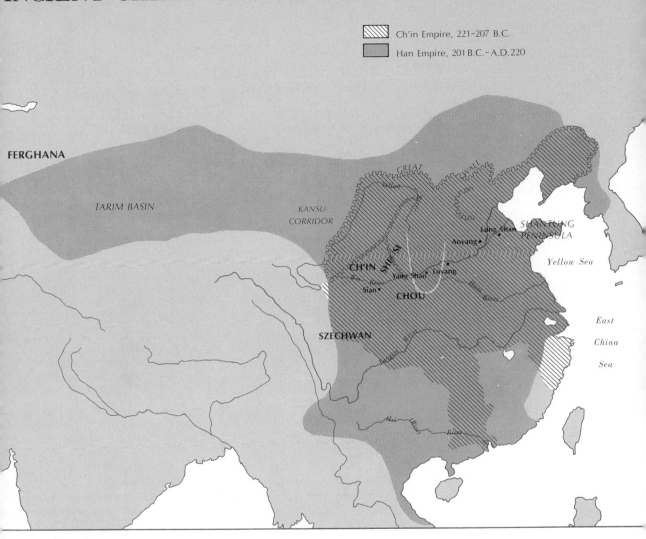

⟨hatched⟩ Ch'in Empire, 221–207 B.C.

⟨shaded⟩ Han Empire, 201 B.C.–A.D. 220

FERGHANA

TARIM BASIN

KANSU CORRIDOR

GREAT WALL

Yellow

Long Shan

SHANTUNG PENINSULA

Anyang

Yellow Sea

CH'IN

SHE-SU

Yang Shao

Loyang

River

Sian

CHOU

Huan River

East China Sea

SZECHWAN

Yangtze River

Hsi River

it, Confucianism was able to reassert its governmental role in the reunified China of the Sui, T'ang, and Sung dynasties. Moreover, the idea of a unified state under one culture was too well established to be lost in China, as it was in Europe during the same period. The cultural uniformity instilled by a single written language and the tradition of Confucian scholarship presupposed an ultimate reunification of the Chinese people.

The Ch'in Dynasty (221–207 B.C.)

The forceful unification of China by the short-lived Ch'in dynasty under the banner of Legalism accomplished a revolution. The division of the cultural area of China among competing hereditary lords was ended by the first Emperor, Shih Huang Ti, and his Legalist prime minister, Li Ssu. Aristocratic families, reportedly numbering 120,000 persons, were separated from their estates and placed in what amounted to a concentration camp near the imperial capital. Their lands were redistributed to the peasants, who were urged to increase production for the support of the state. The country was divided into administrative units ruled by appointed and salaried officials. A vast road-building program, utilizing conscripted labor, was undertaken to improve communications and enable the army to move rapidly to any threatened area.

89 *India, China, and Japan to c. A.D. 600*

The Great Wall of China.

The armies of the old states were disarmed and disbanded, releasing large numbers of soldiers who found it difficult to adapt to civilian life. Many former soldiers and other dissidents could not keep out of trouble and were condemned to hard labor, especially on the building of the Great Wall, which reputedly cost one million lives. In order to overcome local patriotism and for purposes of defense, large masses of people were moved to newly acquired frontier areas. As this policy implies, the emperor engaged in almost continuous campaigns to expand the empire.

Legalist doctrine prescribed uniformity of all instruments of nationwide use and ideological conformity. Weights and measures, axle widths, and the written language were standardized. On ideological conformity a great debate ensued, but the hard line of Li Ssu prevailed. Scholars of other schools had to conform or face punishment. The most

outspoken were executed or condemned to labor gangs. The most notorious Legalist measure to eradicate opposing doctrines was the "Burning of the Books." All works of other schools, all histories of other states and, indeed, all works of a nonpractical nature were ordered to be burned. Furthermore, anyone who referred to the past as a way of criticizing the present was to be executed along with all members of his family.

Such oppression and the burdens of public works and wars alienated all elements of society, even the peasantry who had initially benefited from land redistribution. Heavy taxes and forced labor drove many to abandon their lands and take to banditry under leaders from their own ranks or surviving aristocrats. In 210 B.C. Shih Huang Ti died and in 207 B.C. his survivors were violently overthrown, less than 15 years after the triumphant establishment of the Ch'in dynasty.

The Han Dynasties
(202 B.C.–A.D. 9, A.D. 25–220)

Out of the struggle for power a wily peasant, Liu Pang, emerged victorious and established the Han dynasty. Perhaps because of his peasant distrust of scholar-officials, as well as the need to reward his followers and to relax the rigorous centralization of the Ch'in, he divided much of the land of China into new principalities. In view of the vast extent of the empire, primitive communications, and the limited income that could reasonably be extracted from an agricultural economy, the only alternative appeared to be a large bureaucracy supported by heavy taxes on the peasantry. The ruler soon spent the balance of his life eliminating the seven "kings" who were not members of the imperial family. At the same time, he initiated the policy of transferring actual power in these new domains to imperial officials. His successors spent the next 50 years reducing the remaining lords to impotence. In spite of this limited revival of political decentralization, which at least reduced the cost of the central government and transferred peasant hatred concerning exploitation to the lords, Liu Pang and his successors retained in a modified form the machinery of imperial government developed by the Ch'in dynasty.

Liu Pang (202–195 B.C.) developed a limited bureaucracy which thereafter increasingly drew on the supply of Confucian scholars. Even so, the institutionalized Confucianism of the Han era had to be modified to fit the requirements of an empire, and it absorbed many elements from other schools. Before considering Han Confucianism, however, two other recurring problems require brief attention.

Although Liu Pang's court was exceptionally frugal, providing a respite for internal recovery, he and his successors were confronted by the external threat of the nomadic Hsiung-nu (known later in Europe as the Huns), a strong tribal confederation whose raids had caused the Ch'in ruler to build the Great Wall. Desperately needing peace to deal with internal problems, Liu Pang placated the leader of the Hsiung-nu by means of the flattering gift of an imperial princess along with a supply of silk and other Chinese products in exchange for horses to mount his cavalry. But this characteristic stratagem did not eliminate the nomadic menace that waxed and waned according to the changes in weather and the accidents of tribal leadership. Another technique that was employed involved supporting one chieftain against another to encourage tribal strife. Only as a last resort was costly military conquest attempted, and, even when it was successful, the gains seldom lasted very long.

Another recurring problem concerned the succession to the throne. The founder of a dynasty was naturally a vigorous individual with first-hand knowledge of imperial problems, but his successors tended to be raised by the women of the imperial harem and had little or no contact with the outside world. If at their accessions they were minors, their mothers as empress dowagers wielded great, and often decisive, power, and under the pressure of family loyalty frequently utilized their influence to place their relatives in control of the government. The first notable example of this problem was Liu Pang's widow, the ruthless Empress Dowager Lu Hou, who did such a thorough job that she almost succeeded in displacing her husband's family altogether. At her death those loyal to Liu Pang rose and wiped out her family, restoring one of his sons to the throne. But the problem of court intrigue and the cloistered life of the rulers was never solved throughout the history of the empire.

Han Confucianism

Brief as it was, the oppression of the Ch'in dynasty threw the various schools of thought into a disarray from which recovery was a slow and prolonged process. Although the reaction to Ch'in oppression discredited Legalism as a recognized school, it was so intimately related to the concept of empire that many facets of its doctrines and much of its machinery of government had to be continued in practice. Only gradually was Confucianism able to rise and gain recognition as the orthodox doctrine of state and society. The complete success of Confucianism, which was not achieved until the era of the Later Han dynasty (A.D. 25–220), was only possible because of the way in which it adapted and adopted many features of the other schools, including the Legalist, Taoist, and Yin-Yang. In this synthesis, however, Confucian doctrines furnished the predominant elements and, therefore, the title of Confucianism is appropriate.

During the rule of Liu Pang's widow, the Ch'in prohibition against philosophical and historical works was lifted, and the reconstitution and study of classic texts began. Eventually, five classics were singled out as essential to the education of a Confucian scholar: the *Classic of Songs*, the *Classic of Documents*, the *Classic of Changes*, the *Spring and Autumn Annals*, and the *Book of Rites*. Although these works were endowed with the sanctity of scripture, extensive, and often fanciful, commentaries were required because of their terseness, which made their meaning obscure, and the need to adapt their messages to the very different circumstances of a unified state.

The world of man organized into a single central state under an absolute ruler called forth an interpretation of the universe in terms of the traditional triad of heaven, earth, and man. In the process of fashioning this view much Taoist and Yin-Yang theory was drawn on, in contrast with Confucius' more limited concern with the regulation of human affairs on an ethical basis. Although subsequently modified, especially by Buddhist influence, the general formulation during the Han era of what was labeled Confucianism provided, until recent times, the intellectual and cultural foundation not only for China but also to a substantial degree for its neighbors: Korea, Vietnam, and Japan.

According to this formulation, the empire had always existed under an absolute ruler responsible for the orderly relationship of man with earth and heaven; it had also undergone cyclical ups and downs according to Yin-Yang theory and the proper exercise of responsibilities by the rulers. One function of the ruler was to perform the rites essential to maintaining harmony with earth and heaven and to keep a weather eye out for omens and portents that might indicate malfunctioning. This view of the ruler's role encouraged observation and analysis of natural phenomena for the purpose of discovering the laws governing natural relationships. These practices were intended to be "scientific" but, in fact, became little more than superstitious determinations. By default, investigation in the field of natural science fell to the Taoists whose substantial accomplishments, particularly in the field of medicine, have recently gained recognition by Western investigators. A second function of the ruler was the protection of the realm through the maintenance of an adequate military force. Finally, the ruler was responsible for the material and particularly the moral welfare of the people, but with a minimum of meddling in their affairs. This responsibility included the construction and maintenance of public works and the delegation of his authority to appointed scholar-officials who from Wu Ti's reign (141–87 B.C.) were increasingly selected on the basis of examinations that emphasized proficiency in Confucian studies.

The inability of an agricultural economy to support a large bureaucracy, reinforced by the Taoist emphasis on laissez-faire, inspired the doctrine that the people were expected to manage their own affairs with a minimum of recourse to the state. In fact, however, vigorous emperors like Wu Ti, while supporting the new Confucianism, actually intervened extensively in the economic life of the people to secure the revenues needed for military expansion and other activities. Such activist policies were decried by Confucianists for sapping the economic strength of the state. Naturally, the scholar-officials preferred an inactive emperor who left the management of affairs to them.

In short, the emperor as head of the human hierarchy was held responsible for maintaining order and well-being among men and harmony between man, earth, and heaven; yet he was supposed to accomplish this task with a minimum of active intervention, laws, and expense. If things went well, he enjoyed the mandate of heaven. If things went badly, he—and not the scholar-officials who only exercised delegated authority—was solely to blame and in danger of losing his mandate. Because no government could administer China without the services of the Confucian scholar-officials, each new dynasty tended to be a replica of its predecessor with only minor alterations. Thus Confucianism supported the institution of hereditary rulers as long as the rulers supported Confucianism. This reciprocal relationship could be destroyed only by external force or internal rebellion caused by excessive economic oppression and natural calamities. The Confucian social hierarchy placed the scholar class at the top with privileged status. Second in esteem was the peasantry whose labor provided its prime support. In third place came the craftsmen, who filled a useful and productive function, while the merchants were despised as parasites who profited from the labors of their countrymen. Since the beginning of the Warring States era, scholars of various schools had complained about the plague of merchants and moneylenders that reflected the growth of commerce and cities in an increasingly complex economy.

Emperor Wu Ti (141–87 B.C.)

By the time of the accession of this energetic ruler, China had enjoyed 60 years of mild government and relative peace in which to recover from Ch'in oppression and the ravages of rebellion. The growth in both population and wealth resulted in a need for land reform, which was attempted with little success. Wu Ti followed Legalist policies by ruling as well as reigning. Costly campaigns, undertaken almost yearly, resulted in the conquest of North Vietnam, North Korea, and the Kansu corridor and Tarim basin vital to the control of trade with the West. In 104 B.C. one daring general led armies across the high Pamirs and subdued the region of Ferghana in present-day Russian Turkestan. These military expeditions extending more than 2000 miles from the capital across desert wastes represent a spectacular, but expensive, achievement.

To pay for them, Wu Ti initiated extensive state intervention into domestic economic affairs. Vast irrigation, canal, and road-building programs were carried out by means of conscripted labor in addition to heavier taxes exacted from the people. To maintain conquered territory approximately 700,000 people were resettled in the arid Kansu corridor. Colonization, however, may have also eased the pressure of overpopulation. Further measures included the es-

tablishment of state monopolies for vital products, such as iron, salt, liquor, and coinage. In addition, the government directly entered commercial affairs through a bureau of "Equalization and Standardization" that set up marketing offices to purchase products in oversupply for storage and resale where they were in short supply. The latter practice and the establishment of monopolies were justified by the state as protection against private exploitation and as a means of stabilizing prices and supplies. Although these aims may have been sincerely undertaken, the price record suggests that profit for the government was an added motive.

During Wu Ti's reign Ssu-ma Ch'ien, whose public disgrace for defending an unsuccessful general included castration, composed a monumental history of China from its legendary origins to his own time. This study was not only the outstanding literary contribution of the Early Han dynasty but it also set the high standards of historical scholarship and objectivity that all subsequent Chinese historians sought to emulate. Such a contribution to a culture that looked to the past as a guide to present action cannot be overestimated.

Wang Mang and The Later Han Emperors

For the balance of the Early Han Dynasty (202 B.C.–A.D. 9), the character of the government fluctuated between strong, assertive rulers and weak rulers dominated by the bureaucracies. None, however, had the ability or the will to cope effectively with the mounting internal problems, particularly the growth of large, virtually untaxed estates. Finally, an exceptionally able scholar-official succeeded in obtaining control of the government.

Wang Mang was one of two radical reformers who made major efforts to enhance the authority of the central government and to check the tendency toward decentralization. Both failed because they could not win the support of the scholar-official class, which had a vested interest in the status quo. Both were exponents of Confucianism, but their similar programs demonstrate the continuing influence of Legalist views. Wang

Mang has been condemned by Confucian historians as a usurper. The later reformer, Wang An-shih (1021–1086), although he sought to carry out his program under imperial auspices, has been denounced as a heretic who would have subverted the Confucian philosophy and practice of government.

Although Wang Mang was already renowned as a Confucian scholar and gentlemen, he was brought to power by his aunt who as empress dowager filled the important ministries with her relatives. After loyally serving several child emperors, he finally seized power and proclaimed the Hsin (New) dynasty (A.D. 9–23) to facilitate his reform program.

One of his first edicts ordered the confiscation of large estates for redistribution to taxpaying peasant farmers; another decreed the abolition of slavery. Unable to overcome opposition, Wang Mang had to withdraw both decrees within three years, although he did place a prohibitive tax on slaveholding. In other efforts to aid the peasants and increase imperial revenues, he revived Wu Ti's program of state purchase and storage of surpluses to maintain fair prices, which alienated the merchants. State loans without interest for Confucian family rites and at low interest rates for productive activities would have undermined lucrative private moneylending. In order to shift the burden of taxation from the peasants, Wang Mang tried to introduce an income tax. For the most part, these reforms were subverted by unsympathetic officials and failed to produce the anticipated revenues. Wang Mang attempted to solve this problem by subsidizing thousands of young scholars. In desperation, he resorted to currency debasement, causing severe inflation, and added new state monopolies. None of these expedients succeeded, however, and faced by alien incursions and peasant rebellions, Wang Mang was killed by his own troops, bringing an end to his dynasty.

Every dynasty in its last stage has been weakened, if not overthrown, by peasant rebellions. A feature of Chinese peasant rebellions was their organization under the leadership of secret societies inspired by popular religious beliefs, in this case the Taoist Red Eyebrows. In times of economic oppression and distress, brought on, in part, by overpopulation and neglect of public works, peasants were forced to abandon their fields and take to banditry. A growth of banditry compounded the woes of the government and the farmers and increased the general distress. Risings under religiously inspired leaders claiming magical powers would sweep across the land, developing into rebellions covering one or more provinces which government forces often proved incapable of suppressing. The government was then further weakened by the loss of revenues from the rebel-dominated region and faced the loss of the Mandate of Heaven. Although the rebels sometimes succeeded in overthrowing a dynasty, their efforts to establish a new regime always failed. Successful administration in China always required the services of the educated elite, which would not openly support peasant rebels.

A census in A.D. 2 counted a population of almost 60 million, which helps to explain the economic difficulties of Wang Mang's time. A comparatively small bureaucracy recruited mainly from wealthy landholding families attempted to rule this vast realm with the landed families serving as a link between their local areas of influence and the central government. Efforts such as Wang Mang's to break down the tax-exempt landed families never succeeded during the period covered by this chapter, but these families also did not enjoy much security, seldom lasting more than three or four generations. Below this bureaucratic-landholding elite was the vast sea of the peasantry whose taxes and rents supported the landholders and the government. Most of the peasants were either taxpaying landowners or rentpaying tenants, but as Wang Mang's edicts suggest, slavery also existed. The peasants were left to govern themselves in their villages. The selection of a village headman by the family elders was usually confirmed by the local official. The headman's principal function from the government's point of view was the collection of taxes and the settlement of disputes without resort to the local official. Village life was enlivened by frequent festivals, the visits of storytellers and jugglers, and the festivities accompanying funerals, marriages, and births, and was interrupted by calls for conscript labor and military service. But only too often the farmer fell into the clutches of the moneylender, which could lead to his reduction to tenant status. According to the Confucian code of family relations, women were subordinated to men, but in peasant families the senior mother could be a petty tyrant toward her daughters-in-law and, in practice, sometimes ruled her husband and the entire family.

After Wang Mang's death two more years of chaos ensued before a member of the Han dynasty was restored to the throne. The civil strife eliminated enough of the wealthy families to allow the revival of prosperity and the regaining of lost conquests under able rulers of the Later Han dynasty (A.D. 25–220). But the basic problems that Wang Mang had sought to solve were never squarely faced and corrected. Chinese control was not only reasserted over the Kansu corridor and the Tarim basin but extended to the whole region between the Pamirs and the Caspian Sea, the result of the genius and determination of one general, Pan Ch'ao (A.D. 32–102), the military representative of an outstanding family. His father, Pan Piao, began a dynastic history of the Early Han dynasty which was mostly written by his brother, Pan Ku, and completed by his sister, Pan Chao, China's first and still foremost female scholar. This monumental work, which served as a model for its numerous successors, incorporated the Confucian cyclical theory of history in terms of the rise and fall of dynasties.

The chief device developed by the Later Han emperors to offset the monopoly of power held by the Confucian bureaucracy was a reliance on eunuchs as advisers and ministers. This cure, however, proved worse than the disease. The playing off of eunuchs against bureaucrats and clique against clique merely resulted in bloodbaths at court which undermined what little Confucian virtue remained. The ultimate beneficiaries of this breakdown of government morale were the generals of large landed families who maintained private professional armies after the collapse of the system of conscription. Although the Han empire officially lasted until A.D. 220, the central government was

Example of Chinese statuette of caparisoned horse, sixth century A.D.

powerless after the outbreak in A.D. 184 of the Taoist Yellow Turban rebellion, which was suppressed with great difficulty by semiautonomous generals.

The Three Kingdoms and Six Dynasties Era (A.D. 220–589)

This longest period of disunity in Chinese imperial history severely tested the validity and, indeed, the soul of Chinese civilization. Initially, China was divided into three successor regimes which carried on bitter and ruthless warfare for the mantle of the Han. In this struggle the northern state of Wei was finally victorious and temporarily reunified China. Although the rulers of these regimes tried to assert centralized control and reestablish imperial administration, each was, in fact, dependent on the uncertain allegiance of lords and generals commanding their own armies. Bargaining and treachery were the order of the day, but more than a thousand years later, idealized, legendary accounts of this epoch relating deeds of chivalry were compiled in a classic of Chinese literature, *The Romance of the Three Kingdoms.*

Early in the fourth century the Chinese in the north proved unable to repel attacks by nomads from the northwest, who were attracted by the opportunities for plunder. The invaders who already had employed Chinese advisers and adopted many aspects of Chinese civilization soon intermarried with the Chinese and set up short-lived regimes on the Chinese model. They also precipitated a southward migration of great landowning families with their hosts of retainers, who soon carved out new domains. As a consequence, the south grew rapidly in population and wealth. But far more important than these political vicissitudes were the vital challenges met and overcome by Chinese civilization.

Confucianism was already being subverted during the Later Han era by the growth of great landowning families and corruption at the court. The failure of Confucianism as a political doctrine persuaded many scholars to turn to philosophical Taoism and disregard the widespread political chaos. But the bankruptcy of Confucianism should not be exaggerated. Every dynasty at least avowed its dedication to Confucianism and the reunification of the empire. In fact, the multiplication of courts may have increased employment opportunities for scholars, even if they had a smaller voice in the conduct of affairs. As in Western Europe after the Fall of Rome, barbarian conquerors also posed a serious challenge to Chinese civilization. This civilization, however, held onto its southern base and enjoyed greater success than the West in civilizing its conquerors in the north. The greatest challenge came not from physical invasion but from an alien spiritual invasion, Mahayana Buddhism, which carried with it a set of values largely at odds with those of China.

Buddhism

By the last years of the Later Han era, when the disorders of the times were contributing to a revival of Taoism, Buddhism became a significant influence among some scholars who were searching for new answers. At first, this alien faith was accepted as a variant form of Taoism and, indeed, for the purposes of translation from the Indian languages, borrowed Taoist terminology. In the period of its greatest influence, from the fourth to the ninth centuries, Buddhism was approached selectively and adapted to fit the conditions of Chinese civilization. The antisocial and otherworldly aspects of Buddhism were resisted, if not rejected, and emphasis was placed on those features and values that could ease the sufferings of this life and could make a positive contribution to society. Even if Buddhism had not arrived, the political failure of Confucianism would have diminished its influence, and those Buddhist features that gained widest acceptance might, in any case, have been sponsored by Taoism. Therefore, the alien character and impact of Buddhism should not be overemphasized. China altered Buddhism more than Buddhism altered China.

But Buddhism did make some important contributions. Monasticism, although modified, was a permanent addition to Chinese culture. The growth of monasticism, which in turn meant the growth of vast tax-free estates, compelled the government later to limit and regulate it. New Yogic exercises and meditative disciplines were welcome supplements to techniques already evolved by Taoism. New magical practices were also seized on as additions to the Taoist stock of magical lore. Many new deities that were furnished with characteristic Chinese attributes added variety to and stimulated popular religion. The Indian ideas of transmigration, *karma,* and *nirvana* proved too abstruse for ordinary people, but the idea of an afterlife in paradise gained great popularity. Vegetarianism, however, had little impact on Chinese dietary habits. Chinese art had previously been stimulated by the influence of nomadic art in the direction of less stylized and more realistic representations. The Greek-influenced Gandhara style of northwest India was transmitted to China, while Buddhist statues stimulated the development of sculpture. Indeed, Buddhism provided a host of new subjects and themes to fire the imagination of Chinese artists. The Chinese, with their ingrained respect for scholarship, were impressed by the sheer volume of Buddhist literature, although their devotion

Colossal Buddha (height: 45 feet) from the great cave temples at Yun-Kang, Shansi. Second half of fifth century A.D. Notice the trace of the "Greek smile."

to synthesis left them puzzled by the diverse and contradictory nature of the various works. With characteristic industriousness Chinese Buddhist scholars selected, classified, and sought to reconcile divergent doctrines. For this purpose they welcomed the Indian conception of relative levels of truth. Concerned with obtaining accurate editions of Buddhist works, a large number of Chinese pilgrims traveled to India beginning with Fa-hsien who left China in A.D. 399 and returned in 414 (see p. 77). Fa-hsien and a number of successors kept diaries that are invaluable for Indian chronology and for their pictures of Indian life. Finally, the Buddhist challenge later led to a more sophisticated reformulation of Confucian cosmology known as Neo-Confucianism, as we shall see in Chapter 7.

The more enduring and popular Chinese Buddhist sects, which also gained large followings in Japan, included the T'ien-t'ai (Japanese, Tendai), which drew together the elements of Buddhist thought that were most ap-

pealing to Chinese scholars. In a typical act of Chinese synthesis the Confucian scholar's love of ritual, study, and moral discipline was wedded to the Buddhist stress on meditation, concentration, and intuition. The first steps were deemed essential preparation for the last. The T'ien-t'ai sect's advocacy of the *Lotus Sutra* aided in its establishment as the most popular scripture of East Asian Buddhism. Numerically largest was the Pure Land sect, which stressed the devotional aspect of Mahayana Buddhism, requiring only a sincere declaration of faith to gain admission to paradise. The later True Word sect gained popularity through its use of magic, incantations, and ceremonies—especially its masses for the dead.

The last to develop was the almost exclusively Chinese Ch'an (Japanese, Zen) sect, drawing its major inspiration from the Taoist love of nature and simplicity. In addition, the formation of this sect represented a reaction against the complex ritual and intellectualism of the other Buddhist sects. Although

JAPAN

HOKKAIDO

Sea of Japan

HONSHU

KOREA

TSUSHIMA

KYUSHU

SHIKOKU

Mt. Fuji

Ise

YAMATO PLAIN

Pacific Ocean

artistic and poetic expression—the approach whereby the artist sought to present in each work the particularized essence of universal and eternal truth. This attitude encouraged a simplistic, impressionistic style of representation.

JAPAN TO A.D. 700

In neighboring areas suited to settled agriculture, the Chinese cultural impact was so overwhelming that it all but wiped out indigenous cultures. To the south, where most of this expansion took place, it penetrated North Vietnam. To the north and west, climate and terrain limited the possibilities of settled agriculture and, thus, the extension of Chinese civilization. To the northeast, Chinese expansion introduced settled agriculture to southern Manchuria on an unstable basis. Nevertheless, this shallow foothold provided a route for the penetration of Chinese influence into Korea and its ultimate transmission to the islands of Japan, where a unique civilization evolved under the stimulus of Chinese forms.

The chief factor enabling the Japanese to adopt and adapt selectively those aspects of Chinese civilization best suited to Japanese culture was geography. Like the British isles, the islands of Japan are protected, but not isolated, from continental influence by a salt water "moat." But this "moat" is 100 miles wide for Japan, whereas the straits of Dover are narrow enough to allow one to see the opposite shore on a clear day. Until World War II, two Mongol invasion attempts were the only external challenges to Japan. Therefore, change came only from internal and indigenous pressures, and foreign borrowings could be deliberate and easily identified. This condition gave the Japanese a greater sense of continuity than other peoples and helps to explain the unique retention of outmoded institutions along with often contradictory innovations. Indeed, their freedom from external pressure may have encouraged them to be culturally progressive and conservative at the same time, a quality they still retain.

In addition to isolation, other geographical factors help to explain the uniqueness of Japanese civilization. The rugged terrain of

derived from Taoism, by sheer accident its stress on meditation and intuitive realization of the Buddha-nature within oneself approached closely the original teaching of Gautama. The antiintellectual emphasis of Ch'an relegated good works, asceticism, ritual, and study to the world of the senses; they could be of little use in achieving intuitive enlightenment. Personal realization could only come by a rigorous course that would relieve the mind of dependence on ordinary logic and sense perceptions. In place of the study of texts, the Ch'an technique relied on oral instruction by a master. Because of this procedure, several techniques were developed by different masters, but the most usual was the posing of problems meaningless in common-sense terms to break the pupil's reliance on customary reasoning. This regimen, emphasizing self-discipline and self-reliance, was to have a special appeal to the military class in Japan. On the other hand, the aim of finding the universal in the particular inspired the approach to nature that so deeply influenced

these volcanic islands possesses great natural beauty, stimulating esthetic development but restricting the possibilities of settled agriculture to less than one-fifth of the land. Moreover, the land is divided into a large number of relatively isolated valleys traversed by short, swift streams that tumble from the mountains to the sea. This division into islands and valleys encouraged the Japanese to utilize the sea—particularly the protected Inland Sea—as a highway. The sea also dominates the climate. A warm ocean current bathes the southern coast, providing the warm and wet weather essential to intensive rice farming. The production of two rice crops a year in one field is practiced as far north as the Kanto Plain at the base of which is located today's largest metropolitan center, Tokyo. Nature, however, is not always kind, and the same warm current brings destructive typhoons during the late summer and fall. In addition, frequent earthquakes make the Japanese well aware of the awesome power of nature as well as its bounty. The northern half of Japan comes under the influence of a cold ocean current from the north, but only Hokkaido, the northernmost major island and last refuge of the disappearing Ainu people, has resisted the development of settled agriculture. The mixing of warm and cold currents has made the seas off Japan extremely rich in sea-life. Since prehistoric times the Japanese have exploited this natural resource for their chief supply of protein. Buddhism's prohibition of meat-eating was never extended to seafood and, in fact, intensified attention to fishing and seafaring.

Japanese Origins

The Japanese people are an uncertain mixture of more advanced Mongoloid immigrants from the mainland with the indigenous population of fair-skinned, hairy Ainu, who worshipped bears. Whatever the origins of the Japanese may have been, the first reference in a Chinese history of the first century A.D. describes an agricultural people divided into approximately 100 political units residing in southern Korea and Kyushu. The people ate with their fingers, went about barefooted, and daubed their bodies with paint. Besides borrowed Chinese practices, such as divination by baking bones, they already practiced ritual purification by bathing and announced themselves at a shrine by clapping their hands. The social structure was already stratified with hereditary rulers, frequently women who were believed to possess magical powers. These practices, are recognizable as traditionally Japanese along with those described in later Chinese accounts, such as their reverence for the sun, the sea, and the mountains.

By the later third century large earthen tombs reflect a growth in the wealth and power of the rulers. This tomb culture is closely related to that in Korea and illustrates Korea's importance as a bridge for the transmission of cultural influences. Until 562, the Japanese maintained a foothold in Korea. Moreover, Koreans, often deeply imbued with Chinese culture, were invited to settle in Japan because of their skills, such as writing in Chinese. They often achieved aristocratic status. Tomb figurines show that the aristocrats were already mounted and armored warriors with iron weapons. As in many other places, the high cost of a warrior's equipment was the principal foundation of the aristocracy.

At an uncertain date one militant group sailed up the Inland Sea from Kyushu to central Honshu and drove the Ainu from the Yamato Plain. The ruling clan (*uji*) claimed priority over other clans on the ground of descent from the grandson of the sungoddess and by the mid-fifth century had gained recognition from a majority of them. Even though Yamato supremacy was recognized, local authority resided in ruling clans, each claiming descent from a common ancestor and worshipping its own deity. Yamato power seems to have been based on subordinating a number of clans, giving them specialized hereditary functions of a military or religious nature and supplementing this strength by grants of land. At this stage of Japanese development, and for many centuries to come, political power was measured in terms of manpower instead of territory. Another means of extending Yamato power was to gain control of local cults and organize them into a hierarchy headed by the sungoddess, whose chief shrine was located at

Ise on a point of land facing the rising sun. Later, this agglomeration of cults dedicated to striking aspects of nature and legendary ancestors was given the Chinese-derived title of Shinto (the Way of the Gods). It remained a simple, cheerful form of worship with the chief emphasis on ritual cleanliness. After ritual purification the worshipper claps his hands to announce his presence, bows, and makes an offering at the shrine. The annual shrine festivals are gay affairs at which everyone, including the god or goddess, has a good time. This simple and straightforward religion with shrines in impressive natural settings still possesses an almost universal appeal for the Japanese people.

The Chinese Impact

From earliest times Chinese influences had filtered into Japan via Korea. As the Yamato state grew in strength and authority during the fifth century, an influx of skilled Korean immigrants stimulated the rate and extent of cultural borrowing. At the same time, economic and political development was preparing the Japanese for reception of the more sophisticated aspects of Chinese civilization which were already established in Korea. As a result, borrowing shifted from unconscious acquisitions to a conscious quest for suitable innovations.

The first conscious borrowing was Buddhism as part of a power struggle between major clans at the court. If such a religion were successfully introduced, subsidized, and controlled by the central government, it could greatly enhance the spiritual authority of Yamato by undermining that of the local Shinto cults under clan control. After several earlier attempts to introduce Buddhism failed, the Soga military clan triumphed over the opposition of rival clans that championed Shinto. A Soga victory on the battlefield confirmed the spiritual efficacy of Buddhism.

In order to insure their position in a family-structured hierarchy, the Sogas had intermarried with the Yamato imperial family. The half-Soga Crown Prince Shotoku in a typical Japanese maneuver abstained from the succession and, as regent (A.D. 592–622), actually ruled Japan as the power behind the throne. He was reputedly a great Buddhist scholar and patronized the spread of Bud-

dhism, but even more importantly, he appreciated the advantages of the Confucian conception of government and in A.D. 604 issued a "Seventeen Article Constitution," stressing those features that he believed to be most essential to a reform program.

Only the second article concerned Buddhism. In true Confucian style all but two of the rest were general ethical admonitions calling for harmony, obedience to imperial orders, decorum in the relations of superior and inferior, selfless devotion to duty, appointments on the basis of merit, and other Confucian virtues. They were all obviously directed against the characteristic self-seeking of hereditary clansmen and intended to enhance the authority of the central government. Of the two remaining articles, one forbade the levying of taxes by clan leaders—a function reserved to imperially appointed officials. The other article borrowed the Chinese system of conscripted labor with which Shotoku built roads to improve overland communications. The final article appears to represent an early statement of the traditional Japanese preference for joint responsibility and rule by committees rather than individuals. It prescribed joint consultation on weighty affairs. In this article a Japanese modification of a borrowed doctrine may be detected.

As a way of implementing the Confucian idea of an institutionalized bureaucracy based on merit, Shotoku set up a hierarchy of 12 graded ranks. From the beginning, however, this program was subverted by the necessity of giving imperial appointments to influential and powerful clan leaders. A more important step for the future was the sending of embassies to China accompanied by students of both Buddhism and government. The impact of these Chinese studies is underlined by the important role that returned students played in the more radical Taika (Great Change) Reforms (A.D. 646).

The Soga clan had become overbearing and threatened to usurp the throne. Ironically a leader of the clan that had most adamantly opposed the introduction of Buddhism engineered the coup d'etat that overthrew the Sogas. For his services he was awarded the surname of Fujiwara. His descendants, sometimes all-powerful, sometimes powerless, maintained their position as the senior noble family until World War II.

Thanks to the pioneer work of Shotoku, the new leaders, particularly the returned students, were able to propose a more sweeping and specific program. First, government appointees took a census of the people and the cultivated land. On the basis of the census an imperial edict of 646, in effect, nationalized and redistributed the land to the peasants who farmed it. Only appointed officials were to be granted the income of specified lands for their support. The rest of the taxes were supposed to accrue to the central government, although they might be largely expended on local projects. Taxes on the peasants were assessed not only in kind but also in goods and labor service. A subsequent edict followed the logic of its predecessor by ordering the abolition of all hereditary units whose members should henceforth be loyal subjects of the state, gaining rank only by appointment.

As the wording of the edicts illustrates, these reforms were considered a long-range program whose full implementation applied immediately only to the provinces in the neighborhood of Yamato. Over the next 60 years a succession of able administrators extended and enforced them over a larger area. During the eighth century, when these reforms achieved their widest application, detailed land and population registers were maintained, and the opulence of the court established at the first capital city of Nara testifies to the collection of a large income. But the very foundation of the Confucian state, the examination system for the selection of officials on the basis of merit, was never adopted, and the great clans, although accepting nominal subordination to the emperor, continued in fact to control the countryside.

In this chapter the story of Indo-Aryan civilization has been carried through its cultural zenith. Although the Indians were less talented than others in empire-building, the Maurya Empire of Ashoka directly ruled most of the subcontinent and can be compared to the other great empires of Asia. The Gupta realm was politically much less impressive, directly controlling little more than northern India. Subsequently, India was to fall under the political domination of invaders, first the Muslims and then the British.

Chinese civilization has been traced through its first imperial era and the early development of Confucianism as the dominant philosophy of state and society followed by its most severe and prolonged political breakdown, when Confucianism and Chinese values were challenged by the intrusion of Buddhism. China survived and was reunified, as we shall see in the next chapter on Asia, by successive dynasties that carried Chinese civilization to its peak. Finally, the beginnings of Japan's unique civilization have been examined through the initial efforts at political centralization.

SUGGESTED READINGS

Rawlinson, H. G., *India*. New York: Frederick A. Praeger, 1952. Paperback.
   A good supplement to Basham.

Thapar, Romila, *A History of India*. Baltimore, Md.: Penguin Books, 1966. Paperback.
   Another good supplement to Basham.

Conze, Edward, *Buddhism: Its Essence and Development*. New York: Harper & Row, 1959. Paperback.
   The interpretation of a leading authority.

Conze, Edward, *Buddhist Thought in India*. Ann Arbor: University of Michigan Press, 1967. Paperback.

Zaehner, Robert C., *Hinduism*. London: Oxford University Press, 1966. Paperback.

Radhakrishnan, Sarvepalli, *The Hindu View of Life*. New York: Macmillan, 1939. Paperback.
  Stimulating account by one of India's leading scholars.

Nikhilananda, Swami, *The Upanishads*. New York: Harper & Row, 1968. Paperback.

Egerton, Frank, *Bhagavad Gita*. New York: Harper & Row, 1968. Paperback.

Hutton, J. H., *Caste in India*. London: Oxford University Press, 1961. Paperback.
  The classic study of India's basic institution.

Grousset, René, *The Rise and Splendour of the Chinese Empire*. Berkeley and Los Angeles: University of California Press, 1953. Paperback.
  A colorful and readable general account.

Lattimore, Owen, *Inner Asian Frontiers of China*. Boston: Beacon Press, 1962. Paperback.
  Unique and invaluable study of the frontier throughout Chinese history.

Wright, Arthur F., *Buddhism in Chinese History*. New York: Atheneum, 1965. Paperback.

Sansom, George, *A History of Japan to 1334*. Stanford: Stanford University Press, 1969. Paperback.
  First of three volumes on premodern Japan.

CHAPTER 4

The Ancient Greeks

In this chapter's discussion we return to the Near East to study the contributions of the ancient Greeks to the civilizations of that area and to Europe. Like the Aryans in India, the Greeks were an Indo-European people who borrowed much of their culture from the more settled, sophisticated peoples they conquered. Like the Chinese, their civilization was more secular than religious. But the Greeks were unique in their openness to new ideas, in their political freedoms, and in their cultural imperialism. Not until the past 400 years or so has any people managed to impose its cultural patterns on so many others in so many parts of the world. By the time of Christ the educated classes throughout the Near East and the Mediterranean world—including Rome—spoke Greek as a second language and affected Greek ways. And in philosophy, drama, and the arts Greek culture continues to fascinate some Europeans and Americans even today.

THE AEGEAN AND GREEK WORLDS TO THE SIXTH CENTURY B.C.

A century ago the Homeric epics were seen merely as inspired fancy and the Trojan War was taken no more seriously than the legends of Atlantis; the picture that emerges from Homer's poems of a highly-developed civilization in the Peloponnesus, dominated by King Agamemnon of Mycenae, was thought to be a folk myth and nothing more. But during the 1870s and 1880s Heinrich Schliemann, a retired businessman and amateur archaeologist, confounded the scholarly world by excavating Troy, Mycenae, and other Homeric sites, thereby giving reality to a supposedly imaginary civilization that had flourished some eight centuries prior to the golden age of Athens. Early in the present century Sir Arthur Evans excavated at Cnossus on the island of Crete and found evidence of a civilization resembling that of Mycenae on the Greek mainland, but even older and more splendid. In 1952 Michael Ventris deciphered the *Linear B* script used at several mainland Greek sites and, for a time, at Cnossus itself. The work of Schliemann, Evans, Ventris, and other students of the early Aegean period has literally opened a new world to us, but the study of this first European civilization remains intensely fluid and exciting, with old theories constantly being upset by new discoveries.

Minoan Civilization

The civilization of ancient Crete has been called "Minoan" after the half-legendary King Minos of Cnossus.* It was this civilization that gave rise to many of the legends of the classical Greeks and that underlay much of their culture. The Minoans themselves drew from still earlier sources, developing the technology and art of Egypt, Mesopotamia, and western Anatolia in highly original ways. As early as the third millennium Minoans had begun to trade with the Near East. Shortly after 2000 B.C. the great Minoan palaces were built. During the next six centuries these palaces were destroyed time and again by earthquakes but always rebuilt on a grander scale than before. The "palace period," between about 1800 and 1400 B.C., marks the apex of Minoan civilization. The greatest monument of the age was the Palace of Cnossus, a magnificent rambling structure of several stories surrounding a central court. The palace contained storage rooms where tall jars of olive oil and wine were kept, a remarkable plumbing system which made possible flush toilets and baths in the beautifully decorated royal apartments, and a pillared throne room of great splendor. Minoan Crete had several smaller palaces as well as numerous luxurious private town houses and country mansions. Surprisingly, the palaces and towns of the Minoan golden age had no appreciable fortifications. Some have concluded that the whole island was united under the kings at Cnossus and that the Minoan fleet provided sufficient protection against enemies from without.

The Minoans owed their success to their isolation and their ships. Isolation gave Crete a feeling of security, optimism, and light-heartedness, and the lure of the sea resulted in cultural dynamism. Long before the Phoenicians ventured into the Mediterranean, Minoan seafarers were trading with Anatolia, Syria, North Africa, the Aegean Islands, and even Spain. They imported tin and copper for the superb Minoan bronze ware that in turn became a chief item of export along with del-

* The name "Minos" is suspiciously similar to the names of other legendary founder-kings: Menes of Egypt, Mannus of Germany, Manu of India, and so on.

icate polychrome pottery fashioned by Minoan craftsmen with consummate skill and taste. Minoan art is light and flowing; plants, animals, and marine life are portrayed with arresting naturalism. The artists produced no monumental works of sculpture but excelled at making tiny, exquisite statuettes. The Minoan style is characterized by elegance and grace rather than grandeur.

Minoan agriculture was devoted chiefly to the production of grain, wine, and olive oil—the so-called Mediterranean triad—which were also the chief agricultural commodities of classical Greece. The Minoan economy was exceptionally prosperous during the golden age of Crete, enabling the aristocracy to live luxuriously. Women enjoyed a relatively high status in society and are depicted in the statuettes and frescoes of the age dressed elaborately in hooped skirts with wasp waists, tight-fitting bodices that left the breasts exposed, and marvelously complex hairdos. A French archaeologist was so charmed by a statuette of one of these elegant Minoan ladies that he named her *La Petite Parisienne*.

The lively spirit of the Minoans is nowhere better illustrated than in their love of games. Minoan art has left us scenes of boxing matches, acrobatics, and bull-leaping. The latter, which probably had a religious significance, involved both male and female athletes grasping a bull by the horns and leaping over his body. A group of curious scholars went to the length of asking an American cowboy how this might have been done, and were told flatly that it could not be done at all. Yet bull-leaping scenes abound in Minoan art, and we can only conclude that somehow it *was* done—perhaps through the joint efforts of superbly trained athletes and an unusually obliging bull.

Minoan religion centered on the worship of a female deity—the Earth Mother. This goddess of fertility was widely known in the Near East. She was known to the Sumerians as Inanna, to the Babylonians as Ishtar, to the Egyptians as Isis, and she would later be worshiped in classical Greece as Demeter. She is depicted by Minoan sculptors in typical court dress with hoop skirt and bare breasts, sometimes with snakes in her hands.

Like the later Greeks, the Minoans put little emphasis on the priesthoods. Indeed, there are no Minoan temples whatever; the gods were worshiped in the palaces, at sanctuaries in private homes, at outdoor shrines, and in caves. However important religion may have been to the individual Minoan, the formal religious organization of this gay and aristocratic society was inconspicuous to a degree unknown in the ancient Near East.

The Mycenaean Greeks

Sometime after 2000 B.C. the first Greek-speaking peoples arrived in southern Greece.* Their coming is associated with the first great Indo-European migration into southern Europe and the Near East. From about 1580 onward the Greek settlements increasingly came under the cultural influence of Minoan civilization although they seem to have retained their political independence. Great fortress towns such as Mycenae, Tiryns, and Pylos in the Peloponnesus dominated the surrounding country. These early Greeks were divided into tribes which themselves were subdivided into clans; each clan consisted of a number of related families which had their own distinctive cult and held their lands and wealth in common. The Mycenaean Greeks learned much from the Minoans; their culture differed from that of Crete chiefly by its emphasis on weapons and fortifications. They adapted the Minoan script (Linear A) to their own different language; the result was Linear B which used a modified Minoan syllabary to express Greek words. Their art, architecture, and customs were all strongly influenced by the Minoans; they even took up bull-leaping, and their women began adopting Minoan dress, hairdos, and cosmetics. (The painted face is traditionally a mark of primitivism in men; of sophistication in women.)

Before long Mycenaean sailors were challenging the Cretan supremacy in the

Gold death mask of a Mycenaean king.

Aegean. In about 1475 a band of Greeks may have come to power in Cnossus itself. In about 1400 Minoan civilization was shaken severely when a devastating invasion of the island left the towns, villas, and palaces in ruins. The great palaces were never rebuilt on their previous scale, although there is evidence that Cnossus was inhabited for several generations thereafter. With the disintegration of the Minoan state, the Mycenaean Greeks became the masters of the Aegean World. Between about 1400 and 1200 they grew rich on their commerce and flourished exceedingly. It is at the end of this period, perhaps around 1200, that King Agamemnon of Mycenae led the Greeks against Troy. But even at the time of the Trojan War the political stability of Mycenaean Greece was being disturbed by the initial attacks and migrations of the Dorian Greeks and other tribes that were largely untouched by the civilizing effects of Minoan-Mycenaean culture. In about 1120 B.C. the Dorian invasion of the Peloponnesus began in earnest. The Linear B tablets found in Mycenaean cities of this era disclose frantic but vain preparations for defense. One after another, the Mycenaean cities were sacked and burned, and the civilization that had begun in Crete and later spread to the mainland came to an end at last.

* Professor Carl W. Blegen is followed by most scholars in dating their arrival at 1800 B.C. plus or minus a century: *The Mycenaean Age* (Cincinnati, 1962), p. 30. Another distinguished specialist, Leonard Palmer, argues vigorously in behalf of a later date: c. 1580 B.C.: *Mycenaeans and Minoans* (New York: Knopf, 1962).

The Greek Dark Age (*c.* 1120–800 B.C.)

The Dorian invasions were associated with the second great wave of Indo-European migrations between about 1200 and 900. The destruction of Mycenaean culture was approximately concurrent with the collapse of the Hittite state and the end of the Egyptian Empire. The far-flung maritime activities of the Phoenicians in the following epoch were made possible by the Dorian disruption. Between Mycenaean and classical Greece lies a gap of several centuries known as the "dark age" of Hellenic history. The Greeks lapsed into illiteracy, and when they began to write once again it was not in the old Minoan syllabary but in an alphabet adapted from the Phoenicians. The Mycenaean Greeks were violently displaced by the invasions. Most of the Peloponnesus became Dorian, and in time the leadership of that area, once exercised by Mycenae, passed to the new Dorian city of Sparta. Athens, as yet an unimportant town, held out against the invaders and became a haven for refugees. A group of mainland Greeks known as Ionians fled across the Aegean and settled along the western coast of Anatolia and on the islands offshore. Thenceforth, that region was known as Ionia and became an integral part of Greek civilization (see the map on p. 110). Throughout most of dark-age Greece, political conditions were chaotic, and sovereignty descended to the level of the village and the clan.

Homer

With the appearance of the Homeric epics in eighth-century Ionia the darkness began to lift. Both the *Iliad* and the *Odyssey* are the products of a long oral tradition carried on by the minstrels of Mycenaean and post-Mycenaean times who recited their songs of heroic deeds at the banquets of the nobility. Whether the epics in their final form were the work of one man or several is in dispute. In any case, both are filled with vivid accounts of battle and adventure, but at heart both are concerned with ultimate problems of human life. The *Iliad,* for example, depicts the tragic consequences of the quarrel between two sensitive and passionate Greek leaders, Agamemnon and Achilles, toward the end of the Trojan War:

Divine Muse, sing of the ruinous wrath of Achilles, Peleus' son, which brought ten thousand sorrows to the Greeks, sent the souls of many brave heroes down to the world of the dead, and left their bodies to be eaten by dogs and birds: and the will of Zeus was fulfilled. Begin where they first quarrelled, Agamemnon the King of Men, and great Achilles.*

Despite Homer's allusion to the will of Zeus, his characters are by no means puppets of the gods, even though divine intervention occurs repeatedly in his narrative. Rather they are intensely—sometimes violently—human, and they are doomed to suffer the consequences of their own deeds. In this respect, as in many others, Homer foreshadows the great Greek tragic dramatists of the fifth century.

Achilles' dazzling career with its harvest of ten thousand sorrows prefigures the career of Greece itself. The gods were said to have offered Achilles the alternatives of a long but mediocre life or glory and an early death. His choice symbolizes the tragic, meteoric course of Hellenic history.

Homer was the first European poet known to us and he has never been surpassed. The *Iliad* and the *Odyssey* were the Old and New Testament of ancient Greece, studied by every Greek schoolboy and cherished by Greek writers and artists as an inexhaustible source of inspiration. The epics were typically Greek in their rigorous and economical organization around a single great theme, their lucidity, their moments of tenderness that never slip into sentimentality—in short, their brilliantly successful synthesis of intellectualism and humanity.

The Homeric Gods

The gods of Mt. Olympus, who play such a significant role in the Homeric poems, had a great variety of individual backgrounds. Poseidon, the sea god, was Minoan; Zeus, the hurler of thunderbolts and ruler of Olympus, was a Dorian god; Aphrodite, the goddess of

---

* Translated by H. D. F. Kitto in *The Greeks* (rev. ed., Penguin, 1957), p. 45.

love, was an astral deity from Babylonia; Apollo was Anatolian; and a number of other gods were local deities long before they entered the divine assemblage of Olympus. By Homer's time these diverse gods had been arranged into a coherent hierarchy of related deities common to all Greeks. The Olympic gods were anthropomorphic; that is, they were human in form and personality, capable of rage, lust, jealousy, and all the other traits of the warrior-hero. But they also possessed immortality and various other superhuman attributes. The universality of the Olympic cult served as an important unifying force that compensated in part for the localism that always characterized Greek politics. Yet each clan and each district also honored its own special gods, many of whom, like Athena the patron goddess of Athens, were represented in the Olymic pantheon. The worship of these local gods was associated with feelings of family devotion or regional and civic pride. The gods were concerned chiefly with the well-being of social groups rather than the prosperity or salvation of the individual, and their worship was therefore almost indistinguishable from patriotism. (See essay on *Myth,* p. 16.)

Among the lower classes ancient fertility deities remained immensely popular. Demeter, the goddess of grain, and Dionysus, the god of wine, were almost ignored in the Homeric epics but seem to have been far more important to the Greek peasantry than were the proud, aristocratic deities of Olympus. Eleusis, a small town near Athens, became the chief religious center for the worship of Demeter, and the rites celebrated there, the Eleusinian Mysteries, dramatized the ancient myth of death and resurrection. The worship of Dionysus was characterized by wild orgies during which female worshipers would dance and scream through the night.(In time these rites became more sedate and respectable.) Both Demeter and Dionysus offered their followers the hope of personal salvation and immortality that was so lacking in the Olympic religion. At the bottom of the social order animism persisted in all its bewildering and exotic forms: the world of the Greek peasant, like that of his Near-Eastern contemporaries, was literally crawling with gods.

THE RISE OF CLASSICAL GREECE

The Polis

By Homer's time, Greek culture was developing throughout the area surrounding the Aegean Sea—in Ionia along the Anatolian coast, on the Aegean islands, in Athens and its surrounding district of Attica, in the Peloponnesus, and in other regions of mainland Greece. (See the map on p. 110). The roughness of the Ionian Coast, the obvious insularity of the islands, and the mountains and inlets that divided Greece itself into a number of semi-isolated districts discouraged the development of a unified pan-Hellenic state, but the existence of the myriad city-states of classical Greece cannot be explained entirely by the environment. There are numerous examples of small independent states separated by no geographical barriers whatever—of several autonomous districts, for example, on a single island. Perhaps the Greeks lived in city-states simply as a matter of choice. Whatever the reason, classical Greek culture without the independent city-state is inconceivable.

We have used the term "city-state" to describe what the Greeks knew as the "polis." Actually, "polis" is untranslatable, and "city-state" fails to convey its full meaning. In classical times the word was packed with emotional and intellectual content. Each polis had its own distinctive customs and its own gods and was an object of intense religious-patriotic devotion. More than a mere region, it was a community of citizens—the inhabitants of both town and surrounding district who enjoyed political rights and played a role in government. Words such as "political," "politics," and "polity" come from the Greek "polis"; to the Greeks, politics without the polis would be impossible. Aristotle is often quoted as saying that man is a political animal; what he really said was that man was a creature who belonged in a polis. In a vast empire like that of Persia, so the Greeks believed, slaves could live—barbarians could live—but not free and civilized men. The polis was the Greeks' answer to the perennial conflict between man and the state, and perhaps no other human institution has succeeded in reconciling these two concepts so satisfactorily. The Greek expressed his intense individualism *through* the polis, not in spite of it. The polis was sufficiently small that its members could behave as individuals rather than mass men; the chief political virtue was participation, not obedience. Accordingly, the polis became the vessel of Greek creativity and the matrix of the Greek spirit. A unified pan-Hellenic state might perhaps have eliminated the intercity warfare that was endemic in classical Greece. It might have brought peace, stability, and power, but at the sacrifice of the very institution that made classical Greece what it was.

Still, the system of independent warring "city-states" was a remarkably inefficient basis for Greek political organization. They were able to evolve and flourish only because they developed in a political vacuum. The Minoans were only a memory, and Macedonian and Roman imperialism lay in the future. During the formative period of the polis system in the ninth, eighth, and seventh centuries the Assyrians were concerned primarily with maintaining their land empire, and the seafaring Phoenicians were not a dangerous military power. The chief threat to the Greek of the dark age was the violence of his own people. As a matter of security the inhabitants of a small district would often erect a citadel on some central hill which they called an acropolis (high town). The acropolis was the natural assembly place of the district in time of war and its chief religious center. As local commerce developed, an agora or market place usually arose at the foot of the acropolis, and many of the farmers whose fields were nearby built houses around the market, for reasons of sociability and defense.

The Social Orders

At about the time that the polis was emerging, descendants of the original tribal elders were evolving into a hereditary aristocracy. An occasional polis might be ruled by a king (*basileus*) but, generally speaking, monarchy died out with Mycenae or was reduced to a ceremonial office. By about 700 B.C., or shortly thereafter, virtually every Greek king had been overthrown or shorn of all but his religious functions, leaving the aristocracy in full control. The aristocrats had meanwhile appropriated to themselves the lion's share of the lands that the clan members had formerly held in common. Slowly the polis was replacing the clan as the object of primary allegiance and the focus of political activity, but the aristocracy rode out the waves of change, growing in wealth and power.

Below the aristocracy was a class of small farmers who had managed to acquire fragments of the old clan common lands or who had developed new farms on virgin soil. These Greek farmers had no genuine voice in political affairs, and their economic situation was always hazardous. The Greek soil is the most barren in Europe, and while the large scale cultivation of vine and olive usually brought a profit to the aristocrat, the small farmer tended to sink gradually into debt. His deplorable condition was portrayed vividly by the eighth-century poet Hesiod, a peasant himself, who wrote in a powerful, down-to-earth style. In his *Works and Days* Hesiod describes a world that had declined from a primitive golden age to the present "age of iron," characterized by a corrupt nobility and a downtrodden peasantry. For the common farmer, life was "bad in winter, cruel in summer—never good." Yet Hesiod insists that righteousness will triumph in the end. In the meantime the peasant must work all the harder: "In the sweat of your face shall you eat bread." Out of an age in which the peasant's lot seemed hopeless indeed, Hesiod proclaimed his faith in the ultimate victory of social justice and the dignity of toil.

Colonization (750–550 B.C.)

Even as Hesiod was writing his *Works and Days*, a movement was beginning that would bring a degree of relief to the small farmer and the still lower classes of the landless and dispossessed. By 750 B.C. the Greeks had once again taken to the sea—as pirates in search of booty or as merchants in search of copper and iron (rare in Greece) and the profits of trade. In this adventurous age a single crew of Greek seamen might raid and plunder one port and sell the loot as peaceful merchants in the next. During the course of their voyaging they found many fertile districts ripe for colonization, and during the two centuries between about 750 and 550 B.C. a vast movement of colonial expansion occurred that was to transform not only Greece itself but the whole Mediterranean world. Most of the more important Greek polises sent bands of colonists across the seas to found new communities on distant shores, and in time some of these colonies sent out colonists of their own to establish still more settlements. The typical colonial polis, although bound to its mother city by ties of kinship, sentiment, and commerce and a common patriotic cult, was politically independent. We cannot speak of colonial empires in this period; even the word "colony" is a little misleading.

The motives behind the colonial movement are to be found in the economic and social troubles afflicting the Greek homeland. Colonization meant new opportunities for the landless freeman and the struggling peasant. It provided the aristocracy with a useful safety valve against the revolutionary pressures of rising population and accumulating discontent. And there were always a few disaffected aristocrats to lead the enterprise. In the rigorous environment of the pioneer colony hard work was much more likely to bring its reward than in the Greece of Hesiod. Here were all the opportunities for rapid social and economic advancement commonly associated with a frontier society.

Accordingly, in the course of two centuries or so, the Greek polis spread from the Aegean region far and wide along the coasts of the Mediterranean and the Black Sea. The great Ionian polis of Miletus alone founded some 80 colonies. So many Greek settlements were established in southern Italy and Sicily that the whole area became known as *Magna Graecia*—Great Greece. The small colonial polis of Byzantium, dominating the trade route between the Black Sea and the Mediterranean, became, a millennium later, the capital of the East Roman Empire (under the name of Constantinople) and remained throughout the Middle Ages one of the greatest cities in the world. The Greek colony of Neopolis (New Polis) in southern Italy became the modern Napoli or Naples; Ni-

kaia on the Riviera became the modern Nice; Massilia became Marseilles; Syracuse in Sicily remains to this day one of the island's chief cities. Through the polises of *Magna Graecia* Greek culture and the Greek alphabet were transmitted to the Romans, but this was merely one important episode in a process that saw the diffusion of Greek civilization all along the shores of Southern Europe, North Africa, and Western Asia.

The colonial experience was profoundly significant in the evolution of the Greek way of life. The flourishing commerce that developed between the far-flung Hellenic settlements brought renewed prosperity to Greece itself. The homeland became an important source of wine, olive oil, and manufactured goods for the colonies. The needs of the new settlements stimulated the growth of industrial and commercial classes: smiths and potters, stevedores and sailors, transformed many polises from quiet agrarian communities into bustling mercantile centers. A new elite of merchants and manufacturers began to rival the old landed aristocrats in wealth and to challenge their traditional monopoly of political power. During the seventh and sixth centuries many of these wealthy upstarts forced their way into the councils of government alongside the old noble families.

The Tyrants

The century from about 650 to 550 was an age of fundamental economic and political change: the introduction of coinage from Lydia was a boon to the mercantile elite, but tended to sharpen and amplify differences in wealth. It was in this age that the Ionian poet Pythermus wrote the golden line that alone of all his works has survived: "There's nothing else that matters—only money." The ever-increasing abundance of metal brought the heavy armor necessary in the warfare of the day within the financial reach of the middle class, and the mounted aristocratic army of earlier times began to give way in the early seventh century to a citizens' army of well-drilled, mailed infantrymen called hoplites. It was not long before the classes who fought for the polis began to demand a voice in its affairs. Finally, the colonial movement was beginning to wane. The best colonial sites were gradually preempted, and the rise

CLASSICAL GREECE

of new powers like Carthage in the west and Lydia and Persia in the east prevented further expansion. As the safety valve slowly closed, the old pressures of economic and social discontent asserted themselves with renewed fury. One after another the polises of Greece and Ionia were torn by bloody civil strife as the middle and lower classes rose against the wealthy and privileged. In many instances these conflicts resulted in the overthrow of aristocratic control by "tyrants" who, like many of their modern counterparts, claimed to govern in the interests of the common people.

To the Greeks a tyrant was not necessarily an evil man but simply a ruler who rose to power without hereditary or legal claim. Typically, the tyrants did not smash the machinery of government but merely controlled it. They were new men, attuned to the currents of their age, who used the new coined money to hire armies of mercenaries and manipulated social discontent to their own advantage. Since they owed their power to the masses they sought to retain their support by canceling or scaling down debts, sponsoring impressive public works projects, redistributing the lands of aristocrats, and reforming taxation. But in most Greek communities tyranny did not last long. Some tyrants were overthrown by the older privileged classes; others, by the middle and lower classes who, as they became increasingly self-confident, sought to assume direct control of political affairs. By the opening of the fifth century the Greek political structure displayed every imaginable configuration of upper, lower, and middle class rule.

Sparta

Sparta and Athens, the two dominant "city-states" of the fifth century, stood at opposite ends of the Greek political spectrum. Neither played an important role in the colonization movement, for both adopted the alternative course of territorial expansion in their own districts. But while Athens evolved through the traditional stages of monarchy, aristocracy, tyranny, and democracy, Sparta acquired a peculiar mixed political system that discouraged commerce, cultural inventiveness and the amenities of life for the sake of iron discipline and military efficiency.

During the eighth and seventh centuries Sparta underwent the same political and social processes as other Greek states and played a vigorous role in the development of Greek culture. Yet from the beginning the Spartan spirit was singularly sober and masculine, and military concerns were always central to Spartan life. The stern severity of its art and its Dorian architecture contrasted sharply with the charming elegance of Ionia and the cultural dynamism of Attica. Politically, Sparta had always been conservative. When the aristocracy rose to power, the monarchy was not abolished but merely weakened. With the rise of the commoners certain democratic features were incorporated into the Spartan constitution yet the monarchy and aristocracy endured. Sparta could adapt cautiously to new conditions but found it terribly difficult to abandon anything from its past.

Toward the end of the eighth century, when other Greek states were beginning to relieve their social unrest and land hunger by colonization, Sparta conquered the fertile neighboring district of Messenia, appropriating large portions of the conquered land for its own citizens and reducing many Messenians to slavery. These unfortunate people, described by a Spartan poet as "asses worn by loads intolerable," were Greeks themselves and were much too proud to accept their enslavement with resignation. In the late seventh century the Spartans crushed a Messenian revolt only after a desperate struggle. It now became clear that the Messenians could be held down only by strong military force and constant watchfulness. It was at this point that Sparta transformed herself into a garrison state whose citizens became a standing army. Culture declined to the level of the barracks; the good life became the life of basic training.

Sparta became a tense, humorless society dedicated to the perpetuation, by force, of the status quo. Fear of Messenian rebellion grew into a collective paranoia as some 8000 Spartan citizens assumed the task of keeping 200,000 restless slaves in a state of permanent repression. Between the citizens and the slaves was a group of freemen without political rights who engaged in commercial activities (forbidden to the citizens themselves). The state slaves themselves — the helots — included not only Messenians but other Greek families as well, some of whom had been enslaved during the original Dorian conquests. The Spartan state divided its lands into numerous lots, one for each citizen, and the helots who worked these lots relieved the citizens of all economic responsibility, freeing them for a life of military training and service to the state.

The Constitution of "Lycurgus"

The writers of antiquity ascribed the Spartan constitution to a legendary lawgiver named Lycurgus, and despite its evolutionary elements it operated with such rigorous logical consistency as to suggest the hand of a single author. Sparta had two kings whose powers had been greatly reduced by the sixth century. One or the other of them served as supreme commander on every military campaign, but at home their authority was overshadowed by that of three other bodies: (1) an aristocratic council of elders, (2) an executive board of five *ephors* elected from the whole citizenry, and (3) an assembly that included every Spartan citizen over thirty. Thus, if one counts only her handful of citizens, Sparta was a democracy, although a limited one. The assembly had the function of approving or disapproving all important questions of state, but it did so by acclamation rather than ballot, and its members were not permitted to debate the issues. Accordingly, this democratic assembly was by no means an arena of rough and tumble political conflict. It was characterized rather by the same dreary conformity that overhung all Spartan life.

The lives of Sparta's citizens were tended and guided by the state from cradle to grave, always for the purpose of producing strong, courageous, highly disciplined soldiers. The introduction of styles, luxuries, and ideas from without was rigorously controlled. At a time when coinage was stimulating economic life elsewhere Sparta used simple iron bars as her medium of exchange. Spartan citizens seldom left their homeland except on campaigns, and outsiders were discouraged from visiting Sparta. Spartan infants were abandoned to die of exposure if they were puny or malformed. At the age of seven the Spartan boy was turned over to the state and spent his next thirteen years in a program of education in military skills, physical training, the endurance of hardships, and unquestioning devotion to the polis. The typical product of this system was patriotic, strong, and courageous, but incurious. At twenty he entered the citizen army and lived his next ten years in a barracks. He might marry, but he could visit his wife only if he was sufficiently resourceful to elude the barracks guards (this seems to have been regarded as a test of skill). At thirty he became a full-fledged citizen. He could now live at home, but he ate his meals at a public mess to which he was obliged to contribute the products of his assigned fields. The fare at these public messes was Spartan in the extreme. One visitor, after eating a typical meal, remarked, "Now I understand why the Spartans do not fear death."

The Spartan citizen had almost no individual existence; his life was dedicated to the state. If the helot's life was hard, so was the citizen's. Life in Sparta would seem to be a violent negation of Greek individualism, yet many Greeks were unashamed admirers of the Spartan regime. To them, Sparta represented the ultimate in self-denial and commitment to a logical idea. The Greeks admired the ordered life, and nowhere was life more ordered than in Sparta. To the Greek, there was a crucial difference between the helot and the Spartan citizen: the helot endured hardships because he had to; the citizen, because he *chose* to. And the Spartans always remembered that the object of their heroic efforts was the maintenance of the status quo — not aggressive imperialism. They were the best warriors in Greece, yet they employed their military advantage with restraint. To the accusation of artistic sterility a Spartan might reply that his state was artistic in the most basic sense of the word — that Sparta, with all its institutions directed uncompromisingly toward a single ideal, was itself a work of art.

Athens

Athens dates from the Mycenaean Age, but not until much later did it become prominent in Greek politics and culture. By about 700 B.C. the earlier monarchy had been deprived of political power by the aristocracy, and the entire district of Attica had been united into a single state whose political and commercial center was Athens itself. But the free inhabitants of Attica became Athenian citizens, not Athenian slaves, and the district was held together by bonds of mutual allegiance rather than military might. To be an Attican was to be an Athenian.

The unification of Attica meant that the polis of Athens comprised a singularly extensive area, and consequently the Athenians suffered less severely from land hunger than many of their neighbors. Athens therefore sent out no colonists, yet as a town only four miles from the coast it was influenced by the revival of Greek commerce. Very slowly, new mercantile classes were developing. Athenian political institutions were gradually modified, first to extend political power to the lesser landed gentry, next to include the merchants and manufacturers, and finally to accommodate the increasing demands of the common citizens.

Solon and Pisistratus

In the 590s a wise and moderate aristocratic poet-statesman named Solon was given extraordinary powers to reform the laws of

Athens. His reforms left the preponderance of political power in the hands of the wealthy but nevertheless moved significantly in the direction of democracy. Solon's laws abolished enslavement for default of debts and freed all debtors who had previously been enslaved. More important, the lowest classes of free Athenians were now admitted into the popular assembly (whose powers were yet distinctly limited), and a system of popular courts was established. For the Athenian, selection by lot was simply a means of putting the choice into the hands of the gods. Its consequence was to raise to important offices men who were their own masters and owed nothing to wealthy and influential political backers. Of course the system also produced a predictable quota of asses and nincompoops, but recent history attests that the elective principle is by no means immune to that fault. On the whole, selection by lot worked well in Athens and gradually became a characteristic feature of Athenian democracy.

Solon's laws were seen by many among the privileged classes as dangerously radical, but the lower classes demanded still more reforms. The consequence of this continued popular unrest was the rise of tyranny in Athens. Between 561 and 527 a colorful tyrant named Pisistratus dominated the Athenian government. Twice he was expelled by angry aristocrats; twice he returned with the support of the commoners. At length he achieved the elusive goal of all despots: he died in power and in bed. Pisistratus was the best of all possible tyrants: he sponsored a magnificent building program, patronized the arts, revolutionized agriculture by confiscating vast estates of recalcitrant noblemen and redistributing them among the small farmers, and established Athenian commercial outposts in the Dardanelles, thereby taking the first crucial steps along the road to empire. He gave Athens peace, prosperity, and a degree of social and economic harmony that it had long needed.

The Constitution of Cleisthenes

Pisistratus' two sons and successors proved incompetent and oppressive. One was assassinated; the other was driven from power by exiled nobles who returned with Spartan military support. But many of the aristocrats had grown wise in exile and were willing to accept popular rule. Under the leadership of a statesmanlike aristocrat named Cleisthenes a new and thoroughly democratic constitution was established in the closing decade of the sixth century which became the political basis of Athens' most glorious age. Cleisthenes administered the final blow to the aristocratic leaders of the old tribes and clans. Until the time of his reforms loyalty to clan and tribe had remained strong. Now, Cleisthenes abolished these ancient groups, replacing them with ten new "tribes" whose membership was no longer based on kinship. Each of the ten tribes was made up of numerous small territorial districts scattered throughout Attica. Consequently, members of every class—commercial, industrial, rural, and aristocratic—were about evenly divided among the ten tribes.

Cleisthenes may also have been responsible for introducing the principle of ostracism, which provided a further safeguard against the evils of violent factionalism. In any case, its first recorded use was in 488. Each year thereafter the Athenians decided by vote whether or not they would ostracize one of their number. If they decided affirmatively, then any citizen might propose the name of a person whom he considered a threat to the well-being of the polis. Whichever candidate received the most votes in the Assembly was banished from Athens for ten years. He kept his citizenship and his property but was no longer in a position to interfere with the operation of the polis.

All matters of public policy were decided by the Assembly whose membership included all Athenian citizens from landless laborers to great aristocrats. Citizenship was given to every Athenian freeman of eighteen years or over, and in the mid-fifth century the total citizenry has been estimated at about 50,000 men. There were also, exclusive of women and children, about 25,000 resident aliens called "metics" who were free but without political rights, and perhaps some 55,000 adult male slaves. When we speak of Athenian democracy we must always remember that a considerable group of Athens' inhabitants were enslaved and had no voice in politics whatever. Nevertheless, citizenship was far less exclusive than in Sparta, and with respect to the citizenry itself Athens was more thoroughly democratic than any modern state. The citizens did not elect the legislators; they *were* the legislators.

For the transaction of day-to-day business, Cleisthenes provided a smaller body—a Council of Five Hundred—for which every Athenian citizen over thirty was eligible. The Council was made up of 50 men from each tribe chosen annually by lot from a list of tribal nominees. Each of these 50-man tribal groups served for one-tenth of the year. Their order of rotation was determined by a crude machine that archaeologists have recently discovered. It worked much like our modern bubble gum machines: a stone for each of the ten tribes was put in the machine, and each month one stone was released, thus preventing any tribe except the last from knowing in advance when its term would begin.

Random selection pervaded the Athenian constitution. Every day a different chairman for the 50-man panel was chosen by lot. Most of the various magistrates and civil servants also came to be selected by lot for limited terms and were strictly responsible to the Council of Five Hundred and the Assembly. This was a citizens' government in every sense of the word—a government of amateurs rather than professional bureaucrats.

But neither Council nor Assembly could provide the long range personal leadership so essential to the well-being of the state. The Assembly was too unwieldy, the Council too circumscribed by rotation and lot. Consequently, the chief executive power in Athens came to be exercised by a group of ten generals (*strategoi*), one from each tribe, who were elected annually by the Assembly and were eligible for indefinite reelection. Even the most zealous democrat could scarcely wish to see his generals chosen by lot or rotated every year. These were offices for which special talent was essential, and the Athenians wisely tended to choose as their *strategoi* men from the aristocracy who had behind them a long tradition of military and political experience. The greatest Athenian *strategos* of the fifth century, Pericles, was precisely such a man, and his extended tenure in office illustrates the remarkable equilibrium achieved in the golden age between aristocratic leadership and popular sovereignty. Even Pericles was subject to the Assembly on which he depended for support and reelection. He could exercise his authority only by persuasion or political manipulation—never by force.

THE ZENITH AND DECLINE OF CLASSICAL GREECE

During the sixth century, while Solon, Pisistratus, and Cleisthenes were transforming Athens into a prosperous democracy, the cultural center of the Hellenic world was Ionia. Here on the shores of Anatolia the Greeks came into direct contact with the ancient Near East. The results of this contact were fruitful indeed, for the Ionian Greeks adapted Near Eastern art, architecture, literature, and learning to their own different outlook creating, as we shall see, a brilliant, elegant culture, far more gracious and luxurious than any that existed in Greece itself. It was in this setting that Greek philosophy, science, and lyric poetry were born. Ionian polises underwent much the same political and economic developments as those of Greece, and by the sixth century the lower classes were attempting to overthrow the control of the aristocrats. In Miletus the aristocrats and commoners went to the extreme of burning one another alive.

These internal social struggles were affected drastically by the intervention of outside powers. During the 560s and 550s the coastal cities of Ionia fell one by one under the control of the Lydians, and when Lydia was conquered by Cyrus the Great in 546 they passed under Persian control. In 499 there occurred a general Ionian rebellion against Persian rule during which the Athenians were persuaded to send 20 ships to aid their desperate kinsmen. But the Athenian aid proved insufficient and by 494 the Persians had crushed the insurrection, punctuating their victory by sacking Miletus. Ionia's gamble for independence had failed and, even more important, Darius the Great of Persia was now bent on revenge against Athens. The Persian Wars, the Greek historian Herodotus observes, were precipitated by the sending of 20 ships.

The Persian Wars (490–479 B.C.)

In 490 Darius led an army across the Aegean to teach the Greeks a lesson in respect. As was so often the case, the Greeks, even in the face of this calamity, found it impossible to unite. The Spartans held aloof in the Peloponnesus, claiming that they could not send their army until the moon's phase was auspicious, and other states preferred to await further developments. Consequently Athens was obliged to face the Persians almost alone. At Marathon in Attica the two armies met, and the Athenian hoplites, fighting shoulder to shoulder for the preservation of their homes and their polis, won a brilliant victory that not only postponed the Persian threat but also engendered in Athens a powerful sense of pride and self-confidence. The sovereign of the world's greatest empire had been defeated by a small army of free Athenian citizens. For such men as these, so it seemed, nothing was impossible.

The buoyant optimism that filled Athens in the wake of Marathon was tempered by the sobering thought that the Persians were likely to return in far greater numbers. Darius spent his last years planning a devastating attack against Greece, but when the new invasion came in 480 it was led by Darius' successor, Xerxes. A Persian army of about 180,000 fighting men, stupendous by the standards of the age, moved by land around the northern Aegean shore accompanied by a powerful armada. Xerxes had paved his way into Greece by alliances with a number of opportunistic Greek cities such as Argos and Thebes. In the meantime Athens had been preparing for the onslaught under the enterprising leadership of Themistocles, a statesman of great strategic imagination, who saw clearly that Athens' one hope was to build a strong fleet and seize control of the Aegean from the Persian Empire. By the time Xerxes led his forces into Greece, Themistocles' fleet was ready.

Sparta had by now awakened to the danger of a Persian conquest and was equally alarmed at the possibility of Athens winning additional prestige from another miraculous single-handed victory. As Xerxes moved southward through northern Greece a small army of Spartans and other Greeks led by the Spartan King Leonidas placed itself across the Persian path at Thermopylae, a narrow pass between sea and mountains through which Xerxes' host had to move before breaking into the south. When the two armies met, the Persians found that their immense numerical superiority was of little use on so restricted a battlefield and that man for man they were no match for the Greeks. But at length a Greek turncoat led a contingent of the Persian army along a poorly defended path through the mountains to the rear of the Greek position. Now completely surrounded, the Greeks continued to fight and died to the last man in defense of the field. Although the battle of Thermopylae was a defeat for the Spartans, it was also a symbol of their dedication. The inscription that was later placed over their graves is a model of Spartan brevity and understatement:

Tell them the news in Sparta, passer by,
That here, obedient to their words, we lie.

Much delayed, Xerxes' army now moved against Athens. The Athenians, at Themistocles' bidding, evacuated Attica and took refuge elsewhere, some in the Peloponnesus, others on the island of Salamis just off the Attic coast. The refugees on the island had to look on helplessly as the Persians plundered Athens and burned the temples on the Acropolis, but Themistocles' strategy was vindicated when the Greek and Persian fleets fought a decisive naval engagement in the Bay of Salamis. The bay provided insufficient room for the huge Persian armada to maneuver, and the lighter, faster Greek fleet, with the new Athenian navy as its core, won an overwhelming victory. Persia's navy was decimated before the eyes of Xerxes, who witnessed the disaster from a rocky headland. Commanding his army to withdraw to northern Greece for the winter, Xerxes himself departed for Asia never to return. In the following spring (479) the Persian army was routed at Plataea on the northern frontier of Attica by a Pan-Hellenic army under Spartan command, and the Greeks won a final victory over the tattered remnants of the Persian army and fleet at Cape Mycale in Ionia.

Now, one after another, the Ionian cities were able to break loose from Persian control. Hellas had preserved its independence and was free to work out its own destiny. As an ironic postscript to the momentous struggle, Themistocles, the key figure in Athens' triumph at Salamis, fell from power shortly thereafter, was exiled, and ended his days in the service of the king of Persia.

The Athenian Empire

To some historians the moment of truth for classical Greece was not Marathon, Salamis, or Plataea but, instead, the brief period immediately afterward when the possibility of establishing the Spartan-led Pan-Hellenic League on a permanent basis was allowed to slip by. Yet as more recent history attests, it is far easier to unite against a common foe than to maintain a wartime confederation in the absence of military necessity. Common fear is a stronger cement than common hope, and the creation of a Pan-Hellenic state from the Greek alliance of 480 to 479 was of the same order of difficulty as the creation of a viable world state from the United Nations of World War II. Considering the intense involvement of the typical Greek in his polis, it seems doubtful that Greek federalism was ever a genuine option.

Nevertheless, the Greek world in 479 could not be certain that the Persian invasions were truly over. Sparta, always fearful of a helot revolt at home, withdrew from the league to concentrate on its own affairs, and Sparta's Peloponnesian confederates withdrew also. Athens, however, was unwilling to lower its guard. A large fleet had to be kept in readiness, and such a fleet could not be maintained by Athens alone. Consequently a new alliance was formed under Athenian leadership which included most of the maritime polises on the coasts and islands of the Aegean from Attica to Ionia. The alliance was known as the Delian League because its headquarters and treasury were on the island of Delos, an ancient Ionian religious center. Athens and a few other cities contributed ships to the Delian fleet; the remaining members contributed money. All were entitled to a voice in the affairs of the Delian League, but Athens, with its superior wealth and power, gradually assumed a dominant position. Slowly the Delian League evolved into an Athenian Empire. In 454 the league treasury was transferred from Delos to Athens, where its funds were diverted to the welfare and adornment of Athens itself. The Athenians justified this extraordinary policy of financial juggling by the argument that their fleet remained always vigilant and ready to protect league members from Persian aggression, but their explanation was received unsympathetically in some quarters. An Ionian visiting Athens might well admire the magnificent new temples being erected on the Acropolis. But his admiration would be chilled by the reflection that his own polis was contributing financially toward their construction. Certain members decided to withdraw from the league only to find that Athens regarded secession as illegal and was ready to enforce the continued membership of disillusioned polises by military action. With the development of this policy in the 460s the transformation from Delian League to Athenian Empire was complete.

The half century (480 to 431) between Salamis and the beginning of the showdown with Sparta was the Athenian Golden Age. The empire rose and flourished, bringing Athens unimagined wealth, not merely from imperial assessments but also from the splendid commercial opportunities offered by Athenian domination of the Aegean. Athens was now the commercial capital of the Mediterranean world and the great power in Greece. Sparta and her Peloponnesian allies held aloof, yet Athenian statesmen such as Pericles hoped that one day they too would be brought by force under Athens' sway.

The Golden Age

The economic and imperialistic foundations of Athens' Golden Age are interesting to us chiefly as a backdrop for the momentous cultural explosion that has echoed through the centuries of Mediterranean and European civilizations. Through a rare and elusive conjunction of circumstances a group of some 50,000 politically conscious Athenian citizens created in the decades after Salamis a unique, many-sided culture of superb taste and unsurpassed excellence. The culture of the Golden Age was anticipated in the sixth and even earlier centuries, and the period of creativity continued, especially in the intellectual sphere, into the fourth. But the zenith of Greek culture was reached in imperial Athens during the administration of Pericles in the middle decades of the fifth century. We will examine this achievement more closely later. For now, suffice it to say that fifth century Athens showed what the human spirit at its best is capable of attaining.

The Athenian achievement is so glittering that one is in danger of viewing the Golden Age as mythical. In reality the architecture and sculpture of the Acropolis, the tragic dramas, the probing philosophical speculation, were produced against a background of large-scale slavery, petty politics, commercial greed, and growing imperial arrogance. Pericles, who remained in power almost continuously from shortly after 460 to his death in 429, provided much-needed direction to democratic Athens, but he maintained the support of the commercial classes by advocating an ever-expanding empire. His policy of extending Athenian imperialism to dominate the entire Greek world aroused the fear and hostility of Sparta and its Peloponnesian League. Corinth, the second greatest city in the league and Athens' chief commercial rival, was especially apprehensive of Pericles' imperialism. In 431 these accumulating tensions resulted in a war between the Peloponnesian League and the Athenian Empire—a protracted, agonizing struggle that ultimately destroyed the Athenian Empire and shook the Greek political structure to its foundations. The fifth century saw the polis system at its best and at its worst: on the one hand, the culture of Periclean Athens; on the other, the Peloponnesian War.

The Peloponnesian War

The war ran from 431 to 404. Athens dreamed of bringing all Hellas under its sway, and Sparta and its allies were determined to end the threat of Athenian imperialism. Athens was coming to be regarded as a tyrant among the states of its own empire, but so long as Athenian ships patrolled the Aegean, rebellion was minimized. Ironically,

Pericles the Athenian statesman.

the mother of democracies was driven to ever more despotic expedients to hold its empire together.

In 430 and 429 Athens, crowded with refugees, was struck by a plague that carried off perhaps a quarter of its population, including Pericles himself. The loss of this far-sighted statesman, combined with the terrible shock of the plague, led to a rapid deterioration in the quality of Athenian government. Leadership passed into the hands of extremists, and the democracy acquired many of the worst characteristics of mob rule. A general who, through no fault of his own, failed to win some battle might be sent into exile. (Such was the experience of Thucydides, Athens' greatest historian.) When the Athenians captured the island of Melos, an innocent neutral in the struggle, all its men were slaughtered and its women and children sold as slaves.

Pericles had observed on the eve of the war that he was more afraid of Athens' mistakes than of Sparta's designs. His fear was well founded, for as the war progressed

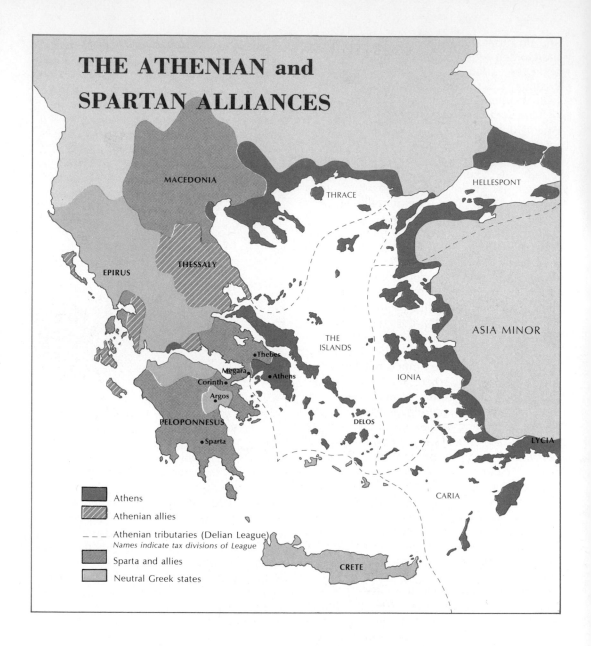

THE ATHENIAN and SPARTAN ALLIANCES

MACEDONIA

HELLESPONT

THRACE

EPIRUS

THESSALY

ASIA MINOR

THE
ISLANDS

•Thebes

Megara•

Corinth•   •Athens

IONIA

Argos

PELOPONNESUS

DELOS

•Sparta

LYCIA

CARIA

Athens

Athenian allies

Athenian tributaries (Delian League)
Names indicate tax divisions of League

Sparta and allies

Neutral Greek states

CRETE

along its dreary course Athenian strategy became increasingly reckless. The better part of the Athenian fleet was lost when two ill-planned expeditions against distant Syracuse ended in complete disaster. As Athens' grip on the Aegean loosened, its subject cities began to rebel, and at length a Peloponnesian fleet, financed in part by Persian gold, destroyed what was left of Athens' navy. In 404 Athens surrendered—its wealth lost, its spirit broken, and its empire in ruins.

Long thereafter it remained the intellectual and cultural center of the Greek world—it was even able to make something of an economic and political recovery—but its years of imperial supremacy were gone forever.

The Fourth Century

The period between the end of the Peloponnesian War in 404 and the Macedonian conquest of Greece in 338 was an age of chaos and anticlimax during which the polis system was drained of its creative force by incessant intercity warfare and a disastrous decline in social responsibility. The immediate result of Athens' surrender was Spartan power over the Greek world. The victorious Spartan fleet had been built with Persian money, and Sparta paid its debt by allowing Persia to reoccupy Ionia. The Spartans were much too conservative to be successful imperialists, and although for a time they followed a policy of establishing oligarchic regimes in the polises of Athens' former empire—indeed, in Athens itself—they quickly proved incapable of giving coherence and direction to Hellas. In Athens and in many other states the oligarchies were soon overthrown, and Greece passed into a bewildering period of military strife and shifting centers of power. For a brief period Thebes rose to supremacy. Athens itself began to form a new Aegean league only to be frustrated by Persian intervention. In the middle decades of the fourth century power tended to shift between Sparta, Athens, and Thebes, while the Greek colony of Syracuse dominated Sicily and southern Italy. Envoys from Persia, always well supplied with money, saw to it that no one state became too powerful. A Greece divided and decimated by incessant warfare could be no threat to the Persian Empire.

Ironically, Persia's diplomacy paved the way for an event its rulers had been determined at all costs to avoid: the unification of Greece. The debilitating intercity wars left Greece unprepared for the intervention of a new power on its northern frontier. Macedon was a semi-backward mountain kingdom whose inhabitants, although distantly related to the Greeks, knew almost nothing of Hellenic culture. In 359 a talented opportunist named Philip became king of Macedon. He tamed and unified the wild Macedonian tribes, secured his northern frontiers, and then began a patient and artful campaign to bring Greece under his control. Having spent three years of his boyhood as a hostage in Thebes he had acquired a full appreciation of both Greek culture and Greek political instability. He hired the philosopher Aristotle as tutor for his son Alexander, and he exploited the ever-increasing Greek distaste for war by bluffing and cajoling his way into the south.

His conquests of Greek towns were accompanied by declarations of his peaceful intentions, and when at last Athens and Thebes resolved their ancient rivalry and joined forces against him it was much too late. At Chaeronea in 338 Philip won the decisive battle and Greece lay at his feet.

Philip allowed the Greek states to run their own internal affairs but he organized them into a league whose policies he controlled. With the subordination of Greek freedom to the will of King Philip the classical age of Greek history came to an end. With the accession of Philip's illustrious son, Alexander the Great, two years later, a new age began which would see the spread of Greek culture throughout the Near East and the transformation of Greek life into something drastically different from what it had been before.

The Decline of the Polis

Classical Greece was a product of the polis, and when the polis lost its meaning classical Greece came to an end. The essence of the polis was participation in the political and cultural life of the community. The citizen was expected to take care of his private business and at the same time attend the assembly, participate in decisions of state, serve in the administration, and fight in the army or navy whenever necessary. Statesmen such as Pericles were at once administrators, orators, and generals. The polis at its best was a community of well-rounded men—men who had many interests and capabilities—in short, amateurs. In the sixth and early fifth centuries, when Greek life had been comparatively simple, it was possible for one man to play many roles. But as the fifth century progressed the advantages of specialization grew. Military tactics became more complex. Administrative procedures became increasingly refined. Oratory became the subject of specialized study. As the various intellectual disciplines progressed it became more and more difficult to master them. The age of the amateur gradually gave way to the age of the professional. The polis of the fourth century was filled with professional administrators, orators, scholars, bankers, sailors, and businessmen whose demanding careers left them time for little else. Citizens were becoming absorbed in their private affairs, and political life, once the very embodiment of the Greek spirit, was losing its fascination. Citizen-soldiers gave way increasingly to mercenaries, partly because civic patriotism was running dry but also because fighting was now a full-time career. The precarious equilibrium achieved in the Golden Age between competence and versatility—between individual and community—could only be momentary, for the intense creativity of the fifth century led inevitably to the specialization of the fourth. It has been said that "Progress broke the Polis,"* yet progress was a fundamental ingredient of the way of life that the polis created.

THOUGHT, LITERATURE, AND THE ARTS IN THE CLASSICAL AGE

The civilizations of the ancient Near East did significant pioneer work in mathematics, engineering, and practical science; the Hebrews developed a profound ethical system based on divine revelation; but it was the Greeks who first took the step of examining man and his universe from a rational standpoint. It was they who transcended the mythical and poetic approach to cosmology and began to look at the universe as a natural rather than a supernatural phenomenon, based on discoverable principles of cause and effect rather than on divine will. It was they who first attempted to base morality and the good life on reason rather than revelation. Accordingly, the Greeks were the first philosophers—the first logicians—the first theoretical scientists. The Babylonians had studied the stars to prophesy; the Egyptians had mastered geometry to build tombs, and chemistry to create mummies; the Greeks had much to learn from their predecessors, but they turned their knowledge and their investigation toward a new end: a rational understanding of man and the universe. Their achievement has been described as "the discovery of the mind."

This is not to say that the Greeks were irreligious. Their dramas, their civic festivals, their Olympic Games were all religious cele-

brations; their art and architecture were devoted largely to honoring the gods; their generals sometimes altered their strategy on the basis of some divine portent. But the Greek philosophers succeeded by and large in holding their gods at bay and untangling the natural from the supernatural. Like the Jews, they rejected the "I-thou" relationship of man and nature, but unlike the Jews they were not intensely involved in the worship of a single, omnipotent deity. The Greeks had no powerful official priesthood to enforce correct doctrine. To them as to other ancient peoples the cosmos was awesome, but they possessed the open-mindedness and the audacity to probe it with their intellects.

Ionia: the Lyric Poets

Open-mindedness and audacity—so alien to the depotisms of the Middle East—were nourished by the free and turbulent atmosphere of the polis. Greek rationalism was a product of Greek individualism, and among the first manifestations of this new spirit of self-awareness and irreverence for tradition was the development of lyric poetry in seventh and sixth century Ionia. Greek lyric poetry was a notable literary achievement, but its importance transcends the realm of letters. The works of lyric poets such as Archilochus in the seventh century and Sappho of Lesbos in the sixth disclose self-consciousness and intensity of experience far exceeding anything before. At a time when Spartan mothers were sending their sons to war with the stern admonition, "Return with your shield—or on it," the Ionian Archilochus was expressing a far more individualistic viewpoint:

> Some lucky Thracian has my shield,
>   For, being somewhat flurried,
> I dropped it by a wayside bush,
>   As from the field I hurried;
> Thank God, I made it clear away,
>   To blazes with the shield!
> I'll get another just as good
>   When next I take the field.

With such lines as these Archilochus ceases to be a mere name and emerges as a vivid, engaging personality. He is history's first articulate coward.

The most intensely personal of the lyric

* Kitto, *The Greeks*, p. 161.

poets was Sappho, an aristocratic lady of sixth-century Lesbos, who became the directress of a school for young girls—apparently a combination finishing school and religious guild dedicated to Aphrodite, the goddess of Love. Her passionate love lyrics to her students used to raise eyebrows and have given enduring meaning to the word "lesbian," but the people of antiquity saw Sappho as the equal of Homer. Never before had human feelings been expressed with such perception and sensitivity:

Love has unbound my limbs and set me
   shaking
*A monster bitter-sweet and my unmaking.**

The Ionian Philosophers

The same surge of individualism that produced lyric poetry gave rise to mankind's first effort to understand rationally the physical universe. So far as we know the first philosopher and theoretical scientist in human history was the sixth-century Ionian, Thales of Miletus, who set forth the proposition that water was the primal element of the universe. This hypothesis, although crude by present standards, constitutes a significant effort to impose a principle of intellectual unity on the diversity of experience. The world was to be understood as a single physical substance. Presumably solid objects were made of compressed water and air of rarefied water. Empty space was perhaps composed of dehydrated water. Thales' hypothesis did not commend itself to his successors, but the crucial point is that Thales had successors—that other men, following his example, would continue the effort to explain the universe through natural rather than supernatural principles. Intellectual history had taken a bold new turn and was headed into a fruitful, uncharted land.

The Ionian philosophers after Thales continued to speculate about the primal substance of the universe. One suggested that air was the basic element, another, fire. The Ionian Anaximander set forth a primitive theory of evolution and declared that men were descended from fish. But these intellec-

tual pioneers, their originality notwithstanding, disclose a basic weakness that characterized Greek thought throughout the classical age: an all-too-human tendency to rush into sweeping generalizations on the basis of a grossly inadequate factual foundation. Beguiled by the potentialities of rational inquiry they failed to appreciate how painfully difficult it is to arrive at sound conclusions. Consequently, the hypotheses of the Ionians are of the nature of inspired guesses. Anaximander's theory of evolution, for example, was quickly forgotten because, unlike Darwin's, it had no significant supporting data.

The Pythagorean School

Pythagoras (c. 582–507 B.C.) represents a different intellectual trend. A native of Ionia, he migrated to southern Italy where he founded a curious brotherhood, half scientific, half mystical. He drew heavily from the mystery cults of Dionysus and Demeter. He was influenced especially by Orphism, a salvation cult that was becoming popular in the sixth century. The cult of Orpheus stressed guilt and atonement, a variety of ascetic practices, and an afterlife of suffering or bliss depending on the purity of one's soul. This and similar cults appealed to those who found inadequate solace in the heroic but worldly gods of Olympus. Following the basic structure of Orphic dogma, Pythagoras and his followers advocated the doctrine of transmigration of souls and the concept of a quasi-monastic communal life. Entangled in all this was their profoundly significant notion that the basic element in nature was neither water, air, nor fire, but *number*. The Pythagoreans studied the intervals between musical tones and worked out basic laws of harmony. Having demonstrated the relationship between music and mathematics, they next applied these principles to the whole universe, asserting that the cosmos obeyed the laws of harmony and, indeed, that the planets in their courses produced musical tones that combined into a cosmic rhapsody: the music of the spheres. Implicit in this bewildering mixture of insight and fancy is the pregnant concept that nature is best understood mathematically.

The mathematical thought of the Py-

* *Greek Literature in Translation*, ed. Oates and Murphy, p. 972.

thagoreans included a mystical reverence for the number ten, which they saw as magical. But despite their number mysticism, which modern science rejects, they played a crucial role in the development of mathematics and mathematical science. They produced the Pythagorean theorem and the multiplication table, and their notions contributed to the development of modern science in the sixteenth and seventeenth centuries. The Greeks were at their best in mathematics, for here they could reason deductively — from self-evident concepts — and their distaste for the slow, patient accumulation of data was no hindrance.

The Fifth Century

In the course of the fifth century a great many of the central problems that have occupied philosophers ever since were raised and explored: whether the universe is in a state of constant flux or eternally changeless; whether it is composed of one substance or many; whether or not the nature of the universe can be grasped by the reasoning mind. Democritus set forth a doctrine of materialism that anticipated several of the views of modern science. He maintained that the universe consists of countless atoms in random configurations — that it has no center and no periphery but is much the same one place as another. In short, the universe is infinite and the earth is in no way unique. Like Anaximander's theory of evolution, Democritus' atomism was essentially a philosophical assertion rather than a scientific hypothesis based on empirical evidence, and since infinity was not a concept congenial to the Greek mind, atomism long remained a minority view. But in early modern times Democritus' notion of an infinite universe contributed significantly to the development of a new philosophical outlook and to the rise of modern astronomy.

It was in medicine and history rather than in cosmology that the Greeks of the fifth century were able to resist the lure of the spectacular generalization and concentrate on the humble but essential task of accumulating verified facts. In the field of medicine, Hippocrates and his followers recorded case histories with scrupulous care and avoided the facile and hasty conclusion.

Their painstaking clinical studies and their rejection of supernatural causation started medicine upon its modern career.

A similar reverence for the verifiable fact was demonstrated by the Greek historians of the period. History, in the modern sense, begins with Herodotus, a man of boundless curiosity who, in the course of his extensive travels, gathered a vast accumulation of data for his brilliant and entertaining history of the Persian Wars. Herodotus made a serious effort to separate fact from fable, but he was far surpassed in this regard by Thucydides, a disgraced Athenian general who wrote his masterly account of the Peloponnesian War with unprecedented objectivity and an acute sense of historical criticism. "Of the events of the war," writes Thucydides, " . . . I have described nothing but what I either saw myself or learned from others whom I questioned most carefully and specifically. The task was laborious, because eyewitnesses of the same events gave different accounts of them, as they remembered or were interested in the actions of one side or the other." To Thucydides, the polis was a fascinating arena where diverse political views contended, and since he was inclined to view political issues as the central problems of existence, he ascribed to the polis a dominant role in the dynamics of history.

The Sophists

In philosophy, history, and science, reason was winning its victories at the expense of the supernatural. The anthropomorphic gods of Olympus were especially susceptible to rational criticism, for few people who were acquainted with Ionian philosophy or the new traditions of scientific history and medicine could seriously believe that Zeus hurled thunderbolts or that Poseidon caused earthquakes. Some philosophical spirits came to see Zeus as a transcendent god of the universe; others rejected him altogether. But if one doubts that Zeus tosses thunderbolts one is also likely to doubt that Athena protects Athens, and the rejection of Athena and other civic deities was bound to be subversive to the traditional spirit of the polis. Religious skepticism was gradually undermining civic patriotism, and as skepticism advanced, patriotism receded. Once again

A Greek classroom.

we are brought face to face with the dynamic and paradoxical nature of the Greek experience: the polis produced the inquiring mind, but in time the inquiring mind eroded the most fundamental traditions of the polis.

The arch skeptics of fifth-century Athens were the Sophists, a heterogeneous group of professional teachers drawn from every corner of the Greek world by the wealth of the great city. Much of our information about the Sophists comes from the writings of Plato, who disliked them heartily and portrayed them as intellectual prostitutes and tricksters. In reality most of them were dedicated to the life of reason and the sound argument. Unlike the Ionian philosophers, they were chiefly interested in man rather than the cosmos. They investigated ethics, politics, history, and psychology and have been called the first social scientists. In applying reason to these areas and teaching their students to do the same they aroused the wrath of the conservatives and doubtless encouraged an irreverent attitude toward tradi-

tion. Of course, the Greeks were not nearly so tradition-bound as their predecessors and contemporaries, but there is a limit to the amount of skepticism and change that any social system can absorb. Many of the Sophists taught their pupils techniques of debating and getting ahead, while questioning the traditional doctrines of religion, patriotism, and dedication to the welfare of the community. One of them is described by Plato as advocating the maxim that might makes right. In other words, the Sophists as a whole stimulated an attitude of iconoclasm, relativism, and ambitious individualism, thereby contributing to the dissolution of the polis spirit.

Socrates (469–399 B.C.)

Socrates, the patron saint of intellectuals, was at once a part of this movement and an opponent of it. During the troubled years of the Peloponnesian war he wandered the streets of Athens teaching his followers to test their beliefs and preconceptions with the tool of reason. "An uncriticized life," he observed, "is scarcely worth living." Like the Sophists Socrates was interested in human rather than cosmic matters, but unlike many of them he was dissatisfied merely with tearing down traditional beliefs. He cleared the ground by posing seemingly innocent questions to his listeners which invariably entangled them in a hopeless maze of contradictions; but having devastated their opinions he substituted closely-reasoned conclusions of his own on the subject of ethics and the good life. Knowledge, he taught, was synonymous with virtue, for a person who knew the truth would act righteously. Impelled by this optimistic conviction he continued to attack cherished beliefs — to play the role of "gadfly" as he put it.

Gadflies have seldom been popular. The Athenians, put on edge by their defeat at Sparta's hands (which was hastened by the treachery of one of Socrates' pupils) could at last bear him no longer. In 399 he was brought to trial for denying the gods and corrupting youth and was condemned by a close vote. In accordance with Athenian law, he was given the opportunity to propose his own punishment. He suggested that the Athenians punish him by giving him free meals at public expense for the rest of his life. By refusing to take his condemnation seriously he was in effect condemning himself to death. Declining an opportunity to escape into exile, he was executed by poison and expired with the cheerful observation that at last he had the opportunity of discovering for himself the truth about the afterlife.

Plato (427–347 B.C.)

Socrates would not have made good on an American university faculty, for although he was a splendid teacher, he did not publish. We know of his teachings largely through the works of his student Plato, one of history's towering intellects and a prolific and graceful writer. In his *Republic*, Plato outlined the perfect polis — the first utopia in literary history. Here, ironically, the philosopher rejected the democracy that he knew and described an ideal state far more Spartan than Athenian. The farmers, workers, and merchants were without political rights; a warrior class was trained with Spartan rigor to defend the state; and an intellectual elite, schooled in mathematics and philosophy, constituted a ruling class. At the top of the political pyramid was a philosopher-king, the wisest and most virtuous product of a state-training program that consumed the better part of his life. Culture was not encouraged in the Republic; dangerous and novel ideas were banned, poets were banished, all music was prohibited except the martial, patriotic type.

What are we to make of a utopia that would encourage Sousa but ban Brahms — a polis that could never have produced a Plato? We must remember that democratic Athens was in decline when Plato wrote. He could not love the polis that had executed his master, nor was he blind to the selfish individualism and civic irresponsibility that characterized fourth-century Greece. Plato had the wit to recognize that through the intensity of its cultural creativity and the freedom and breadth of its intellectual curiosity the polis was burning itself out. Achilles had chosen a short but glorious life; Plato preferred long mediocrity, and stability was therefore the keynote of his Republic. There would be no Sophists to erode civic virtue, no poets to exalt the individual over the community (or abandon their shields as they fled from battle). Plato's cavalier treatment of the mercantile classes represents a deliberate rejection of the lures of empire. Like a figure on a Grecian urn his ideal polis would be frozen and rigid — and enduring.

There remains the paradox that this intellectually static commonwealth was to be ruled by philosophers. We tend to think of philosophy as a singularly disputatious subject, but Plato viewed truth as absolute and unchanging and assumed that all true philosophers would be in essential agreement — that future thinkers would simply affirm Plato's own doctrines. This assumption has proven to be resoundingly false, yet Plato's conception of reality has nevertheless exerted an enormous influence on the development of thought. His purpose was to reconcile his belief in a perfect, unchanging universe with the kaleidoscopic diversity and impermanence of the visible world. He stated that the objects that we perceive through our senses are merely pale, imperfect reflections of ideal models or archetypes that exist in a world invisible to man. For example, we observe numerous individual cats, some black, some yellow, some fat, some skinny. All are imperfect particularizations of an ideal cat existing in the Platonic heaven. Again, we find in the world of the senses many examples of duality: twins, lovers, pairs of jackasses, and so forth, but they merely exemplify more or less inadequately the idea of "two" which, in its pure state, is invisible and intangible. We cannot see "two." We can only see two *things*. But—and this is all important—we can *conceive* of "twoness" or abstract duality. Likewise, with sufficient effort, we can conceive of "catness," "dogness" and "rabbitness"—of the archetypal cat, dog or rabbit. If we could not, so Plato believes, we would have no basis for grouping individual cats into a single category. In short, the world of phenomena is not the *real* world. The phenomenal world is variegated and dynamic; the real world—the world of archetypes—is clear-cut and static. We can discover this real world through introspection, for knowledge of the archetypes is present in our minds from birth, dimly remembered from a previous existence. (Plato believed in a beforelife as well as in an afterlife.) So the philosopher studies reality not by *observing* but by *thinking*.

Plato illustrates this doctrine with a vivid metaphor. Imagine, he says, a cave whose inhabitants are chained in such a position that they can never turn toward the sunlit opening but can only see shadows projected against an interior wall. Imagine further that one of the inhabitants (the philosopher) breaks his chains, emerges from the cave, and sees the real world for the first time. He will have no wish to return to his former shadow world, but he will do so nevertheless out of a sense of obligation to enlighten the others. Similarly, the philosopher-king rules the Republic unwillingly through a sense of duty. He would prefer to contemplate reality undisturbed. Yet he alone can rule wisely, for he alone has seen the truth.

Plato's doctrine of ideas has always been alluring to people who seek order and unity, stability and virtue, in a universe that appears fickle and chaotic. Plato declared that the greatest of the archetypes is the idea of the Good, and this notion has had great appeal

to men of religious temperament ever since. His theory of knowledge, emphasizing contemplation over observation, is obviously hostile to the method of experimental science, yet his archetypal world is perfectly compatible with the world of the mathematician—the world of pure numbers. Plato drew heavily from the Pythagorean tradition—"God is a geometer," he once observed—and Platonic thought, like Pythagorean thought, has contributed profoundly to the development of mathematical science. As for philosophy, in Europe at least, it developed for almost the next two thousand years in the shadow of two giants. One of them is Plato; the other, Aristotle, Plato's greatest pupil.

Aristotle (384–322 B.C.)

Plato founded a school in Athens called the Academy (from which arises our word, *academic*). To this school came the young Aristotle, the son of a Thracian physician in the service of the king of Macedon. Aristotle remained at the Academy for nearly two decades. Then, after serving at the Macedonian court as tutor to Alexander the Great, he returned to Athens, founded a school of his own (the Lyceum), and wrote most of his books. At length he was condemned by the Athenians for impiety, fled into exile, and died shortly thereafter in 322, one year after the death of Alexander. Thus Aristotle's life corresponds to the final phase of Classical Greece.

Aristotle was nearly a universal scholar. He wrote definitively on a great variety of topics including biology, politics, literature, ethics, logic, physics, and metaphysics. He brought Plato's theory of ideas down to earth by asserting that the archetype exists in the particular—that one can best study the archetypal cat by observing and classifying individual cats. Thus observation of things in this world takes its place alongside contemplation as a valid avenue to knowledge. Like Hippocrates and Thucydides, but on a much broader scale, Aristotle advocated the painstaking collection and analysis of data, thereby placing himself at odds with the main body of Greek thought. Although his political studies included the designing of an ideal commonwealth, he also investigated and classified the political systems of many existing polises and demonstrated that several different types were conducive to the good life. His splendid biological studies followed the same method of observation and classification, and he set forth the concepts of genus and species which, with modifications, are still used. His work on physics has been less durable since it was based on an erroneous concept of motion, a fundamental belief in *purpose* as the organizing factor in the material universe, and an emphasis on qualitative rather than quantitative differences (for example, that the heavenly bodies were more perfect than objects on the earth.) Mathematics had no genuine role in his system; in general, early modern science was to draw its experimental method from the Aristotelian tradition and its mathematical analysis from the Pythagorean-Platonic tradition.

Aristotle's physics and metaphysics were based on the concept of a single God who was the motive power behind the universe—the unmoved mover and the uncaused cause to which all motion and all causation must ultimately be referred. Hence, Aristotelian thought was able to serve as a philosophical framework for later Islamic and Christian thought. Aristotle's immense significance in intellectual history arises from his having done some of the best thinking up to his time in so many significant realms of thought. It was he who first set forth a systematic logic, who first (so far as we know) produced a rigorous, detailed physics, who literally founded biology. A pioneer in observational method, he has been criticized for basing conclusions on insufficient evidence. Even Aristotle was not immune to the tendency toward premature conclusions, yet he collected data as no Greek before him had done. His achievement, considered in its totality, is without parallel in the history of thought.

Plato and Aristotle represent the apex of Greek philosophy. Both were religious men—both, in fact, were monotheists at heart. But both were dedicated also to the life of reason, and, building on a rational heritage that had only begun in the sixth century, both produced philosophical systems of un-

paralleled sophistication and depth. Their thought climaxed and completed the intellectual revolution that brought such glory and such turmoil to Greece.

Periclean Culture and Life

History has never seen anything like the intense cultural creativity of fifth-century Athens. It has been said that the Athenians of the Golden Age were incapable of producing anything ugly or vulgar; everything from the greatest temple to the simplest ornament was created with unerring taste and assurance. Emotions ran strong and deep, but they were controlled by a sure sense of form that never permitted ostentation yet never degenerated into formalism. The art of the period was an incarnation of the Greek maxim: "nothing in excess"—a perfect embodiment of the taut balance and controlled excitement that we call "the classical spirit."

It is not difficult to understand how Greek citizens, whose freedom far exceeded that of any previous civilized people, produced such a dynamic culture. It is less easy to explain the harmony and restraint of Greek classicism, for no people had ever before lived with such intensity and fervor. Herodotus tells us that even the barbaric Scythians lamented the Greek impulse toward frenzy, and a speaker in Thucydides observes that the Athenians "were born into the world to take no rest themselves and to give none to others." The Greek ideal was moderation and restraint precisely because these were the qualities most needed by an immoderate and unrestrained people. A degree of cooperation and self-control was essential to the communal life of the polis, and civic devotion acted as a brake on rampant individualism. During its greatest years the polis stimulated individual creativity but directed it toward the welfare of the community. Individualism and civic responsibility achieved a momentary and precarious balance.

The achievement of this equilibrium in the fifth century was a precious but fleeting episode in the evolution of the polis from the aristocratic conservatism of the previous age to the irresponsible individualism of the fourth century and thereafter, hastened by the growth of religious doubt and the tendency toward specialization. This process is illustrated clearly in the evolution of Greek art from the delicate, static elegance of the "archaic style" through the serious, balanced classical style of the fifth century to the increasing individualism, naturalism and particularism of the late-classical fourth century. In sculpture, for example, one observes a development from aristocratic stiffness to a harmonious serenity that gradually displays signs of increasing tension and individualization. The works of the fifth-century sculptors were idealized men — we might almost say Platonic archetypes. The fourth-century sculptors tended to abandon the archetype for the specific and the concrete. In short, as Greek life was evolving from civic allegiance to individualism, from traditionalism to originality and self-expression, from aristocracy to democracy, there was a moment when these opposites were balanced — and the moment was frozen and immortalized in some of the most superb works of architecture, sculpture, and dramatic literature the world has known.

In Periclean Athens individualism was still strongly oriented toward the polis. One of the most basic differences between the daily life of the fifth-century Athenian citizen and that of the modern American is the Athenian's emphasis on public over private affairs. The private life of even the most affluent Athenian was rigorously simple: his clothing was plain, his home was humble, his furniture was rudimentary. With the intensification of individualism in the fourth century, private homes became much more elaborate, but during the Golden Age the Athenian's private life was, by our standards, almost as Spartan as the Spartan's. The plainness of private life was counterbalanced, however, by the brilliant diversity of public life. Under Pericles, imperial Athens lavished its wealth and its genius on its own adornment. The great works of art and architecture were dedicated to the polis and its gods. Life was enriched by the pageantry of civic religious festivals, by spirited conversation in the marketplace (the agora), by exercise in elaborate civic gymnasiums complete with baths and dressing rooms, and of course by participation in political affairs. The Greeks socialized the amenities of life; the pursuit of excellence in body and mind, so typical of Greek culture, was carried on in a communal atmosphere. The good life was not the life of the individual but the life of the citizen.

Only a minority of the inhabitants of Athens were actually citizens. As we have seen, slaves, metics (resident aliens), children, and women were all excluded from the privileges of citizenship. Although many metics prospered in business, many slaves were well-treated, and many women had loving husbands, only the citizens could participate fully in the life of the polis. Aristotle sought to give rational sanction to this state of affairs by proving (to his own satisfaction) that slaves and women were naturally inferior beings. The citizen's wife in Periclean Athens remained in the home. She had heavy domestic duties but few social responsibilities, was legally under her husband's control, and since her education was confined to the level of "home economics," her husband was not likely to find her especially interesting. At the parties and festive gatherings of the citizens the only ladies present were foreigners, often Ionians, who were more notable for their charm and wit than for their virtue. Typical of these ladies was Pericles' mistress, Aspasia, a sophisticated, well-educated Ionian whose name, appropriately enough, means "welcome." The wives of Athens were denied the rich public life of the Golden Age, and their lot is expressed eloquently in one of the tragedies of Euripides: "For a man may go, when home life palls, to join with friends and raise his spirits in companionship. But for us poor wives it is solitary communion with the one same soul forever."

Drama

The magnificent civic culture of the Golden Age achieved its most notable triumphs in drama, architecture, and sculpture. All three illustrate the public orientation of Greek cultural life. Greek tragedy arose out of the worship of Dionysus, as the songs and dances of the worshipers gradually evolved into a formalized drama with actors and a chorus. The sixth-century Athenian tyrant Pisistratus gave vigorous support to the Dionysian drama, and by the fifth century it had become a great civic institution. Wealthy citizens were expected to finance the productions, and each year a body of civic judges would award prizes to the three best tragedies. By modern standards the performances were far from elaborate. The most important of them took place in an outdoor "Theater of Dionysus" on the southern slope of the Acropolis. The chorus sang and danced to a simple musical accompaniment and commented at intervals on the action of the drama. Behind the chorus were low, broad steps on which the actors performed. There were never more than three actors on the stage at one time, and the sets behind them were simple in the extreme. The dramas themselves were based on mythological or historical themes, often dealing with semilegendary royal families of early Greece, but the playwrights went beyond the realm of historical narrative to probe deeply some of the fundamental problems of morality and religion. The immense popularity of these stark, profound, and uncompromising productions testifies to the remarkable cultural elevation of fifth-century Athens. The citizens who flocked to the Theater of Dionysus constituted a critical and sophisticated audience. Many had themselves participated in the numerous dramas that were constantly being performed both in the city and in the surrounding Attican countryside. It has been estimated that each year some 3000 citizens had the experience of performing in a dramatic chorus, and thousands more had been trained, as a part of the normal Athenian curriculum, in singing, dancing, declamation, and acting. The drama was a central and meaningful element in the life of the polis and serves as an added illustration of the many-sidedness of human experience in the Golden Age.

The three great tragedians of fifth-century Athens were Aeschylus, who wrote during the first half of the century; Sophocles, whose productive period covered the middle and later decades of the century; and Euripides, a younger contemporary of Sophocles. All three exemplify the seriousness, the order, the controlled tension that we identify as "classical," yet they also illustrate the changes the classical spirit was undergoing. Aeschylus, the first of the three, tended to emphasize traditional values. Deeply devoted to the polis and the Greek religious heritage, he probed with majestic dignity the fundamental relationships of man and his gods, the problem of injustice in a righteous universe, and the terrible consequences of overweening pride. Sophocles was less intellectually rigorous, less traditional than Aeschylus, but he was a supreme dramatic artist with an unerring sense of plot structure and characterization. His plays treat the most violent and agonizing emotional situations with restraint and sobriety. In Sophocles the perfect classical equilibrium is fully achieved. Never have passions been so intense yet under such masterly control. The younger dramatist Euripides displays the logic, the skepticism, and the hard-headed rationalism of the Sophists who were then the rage of Athens. One of his characters makes the audacious statement, "There are no gods in heaven; no, not one!" and Euripides, far more than his predecessors, demonstrated a deep, sympathetic understanding for the hopes and fears, the unpredictability and irrationality, the *individuality* of human nature. Aeschylus' characters were chiefly types rather than individuals; in Sophocles the individual emerges with much greater clarity; but Euripides portrays his characters with profound insight and psychological realism. With the tragedies of Euripides the new age of skepticism and acute individualism has dawned.

The depth and power of fifth-century tragedy is exemplified in Sophocles' *Antigone* which deals with the perennial problem of individual conscience and state authority. Antigone's brother has betrayed his country and has been killed. Her uncle, the king of Thebes, refuses to permit her brother's burial even though burial was regarded as mandatory in the Greek religious tradition. Torn by the conflict between the royal decree and her sense of religious obligation, Antigone defies the king, buries her brother, and is condemned to death. She addresses the king in these words:

I did not think that thy decrees were of such force as to override the unwritten and unfailing laws of heaven. For their duration is not of today or yesterday, but from eternity, and no man knows when they were first put forth. And though men rage I must obey those laws. Die I must, for death must come to all. But if I am to die before my time, I'll do

The Parthenon, the Temple of Athena at Athens.

it gladly; for when one lives as I do, surrounded by evils, death can only be a gain. So death for me is but a trifling grief, far better than to let my mother's son lie an unburied corpse.

The lighter side of the fifth-century theater is represented by the great comic playwright Aristophanes who, taking advantage of the freedom of the Athenian theater, subjected his fellow citizens great and small to merciless ridicule as he exposed the pretensions and follies of imperial Athens during the Peloponnesian War. A product of the age of Socrates and the Sophists, Aristophanes expressed his deep-rooted conservatism by lampooning them. Socrates appears in a comedy called *The Clouds* hanging from a basket suspended in the air so that he could contemplate the heavens at closer range, while his students below studied geology, their noses in the earth and their posteriors upraised toward the sky. Aristophanes was an ardent pacifist who condemned Athenian participation in the Peloponnesian War and

mocked the war leaders with a frankness that would seldom be tolerated by a modern democracy during wartime. The audacity of his criticism illustrates the degree of intellectual freedom that existed in fifth-century Athens, yet his plays betray a yearning for the dignity and traditionalism of former years and a disturbing conviction that all was not well.

Architecture and Sculpture

Every aspect of fifth-century culture displays the classical spirit of restrained excitement. We find it in Athenian drama where the most violent deeds and passions are presented in an ordered and unified framework. We find it in the history of Thucydides, who treats with penetrating and dispassionate analysis the impetuous and often childish excesses of the Peloponnesian War. And we find it in the architecture and the art of fifth-century Athens: deeply moving yet perfectly balanced and controlled. When Xerxes burned the Acropolis he left the next generation of

Athenians with a challenge and an opportunity: to rebuild the temples in the new, classical style—to crown the polis with structures of such majesty and perfection as the world had never seen. Athenian imperialism provided the money with which to rebuild, and Pericles, against the opposition of a conservative minority, pursued a lavish policy of civic beautification as a part of his effort to make Athens the cultural center of Hellas. The age of Pericles was therefore a period of feverish public building; its supreme architectural monument was the central temple on the reconstructed Acropolis—the Parthenon. This superb structure, dedicated to the patron goddess Athena, is the ultimate expression of the classical ideal. It creates its effect not from a sense of fluidity and upward-reaching as in the much later Gothic cathedral, but from an almost godlike harmony of proportions. Here indeed was "nothing in excess."

The genius of the architects was matched by that of the sculptors who decorated the temples and created the great statues that were placed inside them. The most distinguished of the fifth-century sculptors was Phidias, the master sculptor of the Parthenon, who was responsible either directly or through his helpers for its splendid reliefs. Phidias made a majestic statue of Athena in ivory and gold for the interior of the Parthenon and a still larger statue of the same goddess which was placed in the open and could be seen by ships several miles at sea. The work of Phidias and his contemporaries comes at the great moment of classical balance. Their works portray man as a type, without individual problems or cares, vigorous yet serene, ideally proportioned, and often in a state of controlled tension.

The architecture and sculpture of the Parthenon and its surrounding temples exemplify perfectly the synthesis of religious feeling, patriotic dedication, artistic genius, and intellectual freedom that characterized the age of Pericles. It would be pleasant to think of the Athenians of this period enjoying the beauty of these temples that so wonderfully express the mood of the age. But such was not the case. The Parthenon, the first of the Acropolis structures to be completed,

The Charioteer of Delphi.

was not finished until 432, a scant year before the outbreak of the Peloponnesian War that ultimately brought Athens to her knees. By 432 the old civic-religious enthusiasm was already waning. For centuries after, Greek art would be a living, creative thing; indeed, some of its most illustrious masterpieces were products of these later centuries. But the balanced, confident spirit of Periclean Athens—the spirit that informed the works of Sophocles and Phidias and inspired the Parthenon—could never quite be recovered.

The god Zeus or Poseidon.

THE HELLENISTIC AGE

Alexander The Great
(336–323 B.C.)

The decline of the polis in the fourth century culminated, as we have seen, in the triumphs of King Philip and the subordination of Greece to the power of Macedon. In 336 B.C., barely two years after his climactic victory over Athens and Thebes at Chaeronea, Philip of Macedon was murdered as a consequence of a petty palace intrigue and was succeeded by his son, Alexander, later to be called "the Great." In his final months Philip had been preparing a large-scale attack against the Persian Empire, hoping to transform the grudging obedience of the Greek city-states into enthusiastic sup-

port by leading a great Pan-Hellenic crusade against the traditional enemy of Hellas. Alexander, during a dazzling reign of thirteen years, exceeded his father's most fantastic dreams, leading his all-conquering armies from Greece to India and changing dramatically the course of the ancient world.

Although he was only twenty when he inherited the throne, Alexander possessed in the fullest measure that combination of physical attractiveness, athletic prowess, and intellectual distinction which had always been the Greek ideal. He had a godly countenance, the physique of an Olympic athlete, and a penetrating, imaginative mind. He was a magnetic leader who inspired intense loyalty and admiration among his followers, a brilliant general who adapted his tactics and strategy to the most varied circumstances

Hermes with infant Dionysus; a masterpiece by Praxiteles.

age. Alexander's turn of mind is symbolized by the two objects that he always kept beneath his pillow: the *Iliad* and a dagger.

At first the Greek city-states were restive under Alexander's rule. He quelled their revolts with merciless efficiency, destroying rebellious Thebes and frightening the rest into submission. But there was real enthusiasm for his campaign against the Persian Empire, and in time, as one victory followed another, Alexander came to be regarded as a national hero—the champion of Greece against the barbarian. In the spring of 334 B.C. he led a Greco-Macedonian army of some 40,000 men across the Dardanelles into Asia Minor. During the next three and one-half years he won a series of stunning victories over the aged and ramshackle Persian Empire, freeing the Ionian cities from Persian control and conquering the imperial provinces of Syria and Egypt. Then, striking deep into the heart of the empire, Alexander won a decisive victory over the unwieldy Persian army near Arbela on the Tigris in 331 which enabled him to seize the vast imperial treasure, ascend the imperial throne, and bring an end to the dynasty of ancient Persia.

This was a glorious moment for the Greeks. The foe that had so long troubled Hellas was conquered. More than that, the ancient Near East was now under Greek control, open to the bracing influence of Greek enterprise, Greek culture and Greek rationalism. Alexander's conquest of Persia set the stage for a new epoch—a period known as the *Hellenistic Age* as distinct from the previous *Classical Age*. The Greeks were now the masters of the ancient world, and under their rule a great cosmopolitan culture developed, distinctly Greek in tradition yet transmuted by the influence of the subject oriental civilizations and by the spacious new environment in which the Greeks now lived.

The Hellenization of the Near East was stimulated by Alexander's policy of founding cities in the wake of his conquests and filling them with Greek settlers. These communities, although intended chiefly as military and commercial bases, became islands of Greek culture which were often able to exert

and won for himself a reputation of invincibility, and an ardent champion of Hellenic culture and the Greek way of life. He was the product of two great teachers: Aristotle, the master philosopher and universal intellect, and King Philip himself, the greatest general and most adroit political opportunist of the

a powerful influence on the surrounding area. Most of them were named, immodestly, after their founder. The greatest of them by far was Alexandria in Egypt which Alexander founded near the mouth of the Nile. Alexandria quickly outstripped the cities of Greece itself to become the great commercial center of the Hellenistic world, and before long it had developed a cultural and intellectual life that put contemporary Athens to shame.

No sooner had he ascended the throne of Persia than Alexander began preparations for further campaigns. The final seven years of his life were occupied in conquering the easternmost provinces of Persia and pushing on into India, impelled by an insatiable thirst for conquest and by the lure of undiscovered lands. His spirit and ingenuity were taxed to the utmost by the variety of difficulties that he encountered: the rugged mountains of Afghanistan, the hostile stretches of the Indus Valley, fierce armies equipped with hundreds of elephants. At length his own army, its endurance exhausted, refused to go further. Alexander returned to central Persia in 323 where, in the midst of organizing his immense empire, he fell ill and died, perhaps of malaria, at the age of thirty-two.

The empire of Alexander was the greatest that the world had ever seen—more extensive even than the Persian Empire. Wherever he went Alexander adapted himself to the customs of the land. He ruled Egypt as a divine pharaoh and Persia as an oriental despot, demanding that his subjects prostrate themselves in his presence. (His Greek followers objected vigorously to this.) He married the daughter of the last Persian emperor and urged his countrymen to follow his example by taking wives from among the Persian aristocracy. His goal was nothing less than a homogeneous Greco-Oriental empire—a fusion of east and west. To what extent this policy was the product of deliberate calculation, to what extent a consequence of his intoxication with the splendors of the ancient Orient will never be known. But the project was scarcely underway when Alexander died, leaving behind him an overwhelming sense of loss and bewilderment and a vast state that nobody but a second Alexander could have held together.

Alexander the Great.

The Successor States

The empire was divided among the able and ambitious generals of Alexander's staff who founded a series of Macedonian dynasties that ruled Greece and most of the ancient Near East until the Roman conquests of the second and first centuries B.C. There was great conflict over the division of the spoils, and for several decades after Alexander's death the political situation remained fluid. But in broad outline the succession went as follows: Ptolemy, one of Alexander's ablest generals, ruled Egypt, establishing the Ptolemaic dynasty that lasted until a Roman army deposed Cleopatra, the last of the Ptolemies, in 30 B.C. From Alexandria, their magnificent capital, the Ptolemies ruled with all the pomp and severity of the most powerful pharaohs, enriching themselves by merciless exploitation of the peasantry and suppressing all political activities, even among the multitudes of Greeks in Alexandria. The great metropolitan capital, with its imposing public buildings, its superb library and museum, its far flung commerce, and its million inhabi-

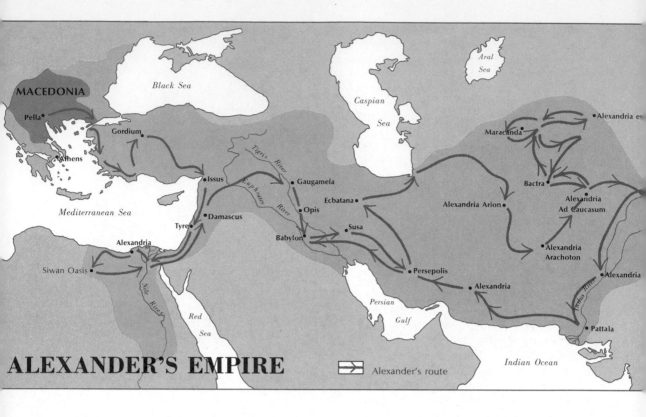

MACEDONIA
Pella

Black Sea

Caspian Sea

Aral Sea

Gordium

Athens

Issus

Tigris River
Euphrates River

Gaugamela

Ecbatana

Opis

Maracanda

Alexandria es

Bactra

Alexandria Arion

Alexandria Ad Caucasum

Mediterranean Sea

Tyre
Damascus

Susa

Babylon

Alexandria

Alexandria
Arachoton

Siwan Oasis

Nile River

Red Sea

Persian Gulf

Persepolis

Alexandria

Tigris River

Alexandria

Pattala

ALEXANDER'S EMPIRE

➡ Alexander's route

Indian Ocean

tants was the wonder of the age, but elsewhere Egypt remained essentially unchanged except for a growing hostility toward the uncompromising authoritarianism of the Greek regime.

Northern Syria and most of the remaining provinces of the old Persian Empire fell to another of Alexander's generals, Seleucus, who founded the Seleucid dynasty. The kingdom of the Seleucids was far more heterogeneous and loosely organized than that of the Ptolemies, and as time went on certain of the more self-conscious Near Eastern peoples began to rebel against the Seleucid policy of Hellenization. This was particularly true of the Persians and Jews who had each produced powerful transcendental religions and resented bitterly the influx of Greek religious thought. Farther to the east, the more remote provinces of the Persian Empire gradually fell away from Seleucid control. The center of Seleucid power was the great city of Antioch in northern Syria which was second only to Alexandria in population, wealth, and opulence.

The third important successor state, Macedon, passed into the hands or a dynasty known as the Antigonids whose authority over the Greek cities to the south was never very firm and whose power was usually inferior to that of the Ptolemies and Seleucids. A number of smaller states also developed out of the wreckage of Alexander's empire, but the three dominant successor kingdoms were Antigonid Greece, Seleucid Asia, and Ptolemaic Egypt.

The Change in Mood

These huge political agglomerations now replaced the small city-states as the typical units of the Greek world. The new environment provided vast opportunities and encouraged a sense of cosmopolitanism that contrasts with the provincialism of the polis. This was a prosperous age, an age of vigorous and profitable business activity and successful careers in commerce and banking. The good life was reserved, however, to the

An old market woman, an example of Hellenistic realism.

political affairs or in the intense life of a free community, the overseas Greek found himself adrift in a wide and bewildering world over which he had no control. The cosmopolitanism of the Hellenistic age was accompanied by a sense of estrangement and alienation, of uncertainty, loneliness, and impotence. The trend toward extreme individualism, professionalism, and specialization which we have already observed in the fourth century was enormously accelerated. The impulse toward greater realism and individualism in sculpture was pushed to its limits, and many Hellenistic sculptors turned to portraying the bizarre and the grotesque—ugliness, deformity, agony, and old age—sometimes with exceedingly effective results. The civic consciousness of the comic playwright Aristophanes in the fifth century gave way to the highly individualized and superficial realism of the Hellenistic drawing-room comedy and bedroom farce. The Hellenistic Age produced superb works of art, but they lacked the serenity and balance of the earlier period. Whether this fact detracts from their artistic merit or adds to it is a matter of taste, but they are obviously products of a radically different society—still brilliant, still intensely creative, but anchorless.

Religion and Ethics

Hellenic religion with its traditional civic orientation was all but transformed in this new, kaleidoscopic age. Old bonds and old loyalties were broken as many adventurous Greeks were uprooted from their home cities and thrown on their own. The result was a mood of intense individualism which found expression in a variety of religious and ethical ideas stressing personal fulfillment or personal salvation rather than involvement in the community. Individualism and cosmopolitanism went hand in hand, for as the Greek abdicated spiritually from the polis and retired into himself, he came to regard all humanity as a multitude of individuals—a universal brotherhood in which intelligent Persians, Egyptians, and Jews were no worse than intelligent Greeks. The traditional contrast between Greek and barbarian faded, for it had been the free spirit of the polis that had

fortunate few. Slavery continued, even increased, and the peasants and urban commoners were kept at an economic level of bare subsistence. The typical agrarian unit was no longer the small or middle-sized farm but the large plantation worked by slaves.

The polises in Greece itself retained throughout the new age a portion of their earlier autonomy. Old civic institutions continued to function, and citizens still had a voice in domestic politics. But the Greek peninsula was now an economic backwater, and cities like Athens and Thebes were overshadowed by the new superstates. Ambitious Greeks were lured by opportunity far from their homeland, as they had once been lured to imperial Athens. No longer involved in

set the Greek apart, and the polis, in its traditional sense, was now becoming an anachronism. Yet the concept of cosmopolis, the idea of human brotherhood, was too abstract to provide the sense of involvement and orientation that the polis had formerly given. The rootless Greek tended to turn away from his old Olympic gods and seek solace in more personal and potent religious concepts. Hellenistic religion is characterized by a withdrawal from active social participation—a search for sanctuary in a restless and uncertain world.

The Hellenistic age saw a vigorous revival of mystery and salvation cults such as Orphism and the worship of Dionysus and Demeter which had always lurked behind the Olympic foreground. And various Near Eastern mystery religions now became popular among the Greeks. Almost all of these were centered on the death and resurrection of a god and the promise of personal salvation. From Egypt came the cult of Osiris who died, was reborn, and now sat in judgment of the dead. From Asia Minor came a version of the ancient and widespread fertility cult of the Great Mother. From Persia, somewhat later, came the cult of Mithras, a variation of Zoroastrianism, which added to the traditional concept of a cosmic moral struggle between good and evil the idea of a savior-hero who redeemed mankind. Alongside these and other oriental cults came a revival of neo-Babylonian astrology, of magic, witchcraft, and sorcery. Many ambitious men of the upper class were devoted to the goddess of Fortune who rewarded talent and ambition and brought her worshipers material well-being. The Hellenistic world became a huge religious melting pot in which a single individual might be a devotee of a number of cults. Many thoughtful people adopted the idea of "syncretism," that is, the notion that the gods of different peoples are actually various manifestations of the same god—that Zeus, Osiris, even Yahweh, all symbolize a single divine spirit. (The more orthodox among the Jews found this doctrine abominable.) Religious beliefs and religious attitudes throughout the Hellenistic world were tending to become homogenized, thereby preparing the soil for the later triumph of Christianity.

Skeptics, Cynics, Stoics and Epicureans

Many Greeks of the post-Classical age turned neither to the old Orphic and Dionysian cults nor to the salvation cults of the Orient but sought to adapt elements of the Hellenic intellectual tradition to the new conditions. One group, the Skeptics, intensified the relativism of the Sophists by denying the possibility of any knowledge whatever, either of gods, man or nature. The human mind, they maintained, is incapable of apprehending reality (if, indeed, there is any such thing as "reality"), and all beliefs and statements of fact are equally unverifiable. In doubting everything they carried rationalism to its ultimate, self-destructive limit and reflected the profound uncertainty of the new age.

Another group, the Cynics, demonstrated in various forms of eccentric behavior their contempt for conventional piety and patriotism and their rebellion against the hypocrisy that they detected in the lives and attitudes of their contemporaries. Diogenes, the most famous of the Cynics, was something of a fourth-century hippie who sought integrity in a world of phonies. He rejected all official and traditional religions, all participation in civic life, marriage, the public games, and the theater. He ridiculed the prestige that was associated with wealth, power, and reputation and honored instead the simple life of courage, reason and honesty—a life of virtue—which could best be attained by a rejection of civilization and a return to nature. The man of integrity, the wise and honest man, should live like a dog, without pretensions and uncluttered by worldly possessions. Indeed, the very word *cynic* originally meant *canine* or "doglike." So Diogenes wandered the streets begging for his food, a homeless but free man. His bedchamber was a gigantic pitcher outside a temple of the Great Mother; his latrine was the public street. He obeyed no laws, recognized no polis, and became, next to Alexander, the most illustrious man of his age. He was a colorful symbol of the great Hellenistic withdrawal from the polis into the individual soul.

The same withdrawal is evident in the two religio-ethical systems that emerged in the fourth century and influenced human thought and conduct for centuries thereafter: Stoicism and Epicureanism. Both were philosophies of resignation that taught men to fortify their souls against the harshness of life. Zeno, the founder of the Stoic School, stressed, as the Cynics did, the vanity of worldly things and the supreme importance of individual virtue. Every man, whether statesman, artist, or peasant, should pursue his calling honestly and seriously. The significant thing, however, was not individual accomplishment but individual effort; such things as politics, art, and husbandry were ultimately valueless, yet in pursuing them as best he could the individual manifested his virtue. Since virtue was all-important, the good Stoic was immune to the vicissitudes of life. He might lose his property; he might even be imprisoned and tortured, but except by his own will he could not be deprived of his virtue which was his only really precious possession. By rejecting the world the Stoic created an impenetrable citadel within his own soul. Out of this doctrine there emerged a sense not only of individualism but of cosmopolitanism; the idea of the polis faded before the wider concept of a brotherhood of men.

Ultimately the Stoic emphasis on virtue was rooted in a lofty cosmic vision based on the Greek conception of a rational, orderly, purposeful universe. The harmonious movements of the stars and planets, the growth of complex plants from simple seeds, all pointed to the existence of a divine plan which was both intelligent and good. We humans were incapable of perceiving the details of the plan as it worked in our own lives, yet by living virtuously and doing our best we could cooperate with it. The God of the universe cared about mankind, and the stern nobility of Stoic ethics was tempered and humanized by this optimistic assurance.

Epicurus, whose school was Stoicism's great rival, differed from Zeno both in his concept of human ethics and in his vision of the universe. He taught that man should seek happiness rather than virtue. Yet happiness to the Epicureans was not the pursuit of sex, liquor, and euphoria, but rather a quiet, balanced life. The life of the drunkard is saddened by countless hangovers, the life of the philanderer by countless complications. Happiness was best achieved not by chasing pleasures but by living simply and unobtrusively, being kind and affectionate to one's friends, learning to endure pain when it comes, and avoiding needless fears. In short, good Epicureans did not differ noticeably from good Stoics in actual behavior, for virtue was the pathway to happiness. But the Epicureans rejected the optimistic Stoic doctrine of divine purpose. Epicurus followed the teachings of the atomists in viewing the universe not as a great hierarchy of cosmic spheres centering on the earth, but as a vast multiplicity of atoms much the same one place as another. Our world is not the handiwork of God, but a chance configuration. The gods, if they exist, care nothing for us, and we ought to draw from this fact the comforting conclusion that we need not fear them.

Epicureanism even more than Stoicism was a philosophy of withdrawal. It was a wise, compassionate teaching that sought to banish fear, curb passions, and dispel illusions, but its doctrine of happiness was too limited and too bland to stir the millions and convert empires. Yet through the lofty epic poetry of the Roman writer Lucretius (98–53 B.C.), it made its impact on the intellectual life of Rome. Although never as popular as Stoicism, it gave solace and direction, during the remaining centuries of antiquity, to an influential minority of wise and sensitive men.

Hellenistic Science

In the Hellenistic age, Greek science reached maturity. The naive generalizations of the earlier period gave way to a rigorous and highly creative professionalism. Aristotle's salutary example was followed and improved on by the Hellenistic scientists who collected and sifted data with great thoroughness before framing their hypotheses.

Alexandria was the center of scientific thought in this age. Here the Ptolemies built and subsidized a great research center—the Museum of Alexandria—and collected a library of unprecedented size and diversity containing some half-million papyrus rolls. At Alexandria and elsewhere science and mathematics made rapid strides as Greek rationalism encountered the rich, amorphous heritage of Near Eastern astrology, medical lore, and practical mathematics. The fruitful medical investigations of Hippocrates' school were carried on and expanded by Hellenistic physicians, particularly in Alexandria. Their pioneer work in the dissection of human bodies enabled them to discover the nervous system, to learn a great deal about the brain, heart, and arteries, and to perform successful surgical operations. In mathematics, Euclid organized plane and solid geometry into a systematic, integrated body of knowledge. Archimedes of Syracuse did brilliant original work in both pure and applied mathematics, discovering specific gravity, experimenting successfully with levers and pulleys to lift tremendous weights, and coming very close to the invention of calculus.

The wide-ranging military campaigns of Alexander and the subsequent cultural interchange between large areas of the world led to a vast increase in Greek geographical knowledge. Eratosthenes, the head of the Alexandrian Library in the later third century, produced the most accurate and thorough world maps that had yet been made, complete with lines of longitude and latitude and climatic zones. He recognized that the earth was a sphere and was even able to determine its circumference with an error of less than 1 percent. He did this by measuring the altitude of the sun at different latitudes, calculating from this data the length of one degree of latitude on the earth's surface, and multiplying the result by 360 (degrees).

The same painstaking accuracy and dazzling ingenuity is evident in the work of the Hellenistic astronomers. Aristarchus of Samos suggested that the earth rotated daily on its axis and revolved yearly around the sun. This heliocentric hypothesis is a startling anticipation of modern astronomical conclusions, but Aristarchus' erroneous assumption that the earth's motion around the sun was uniform and circular rendered his system inaccurate. Its failure to explain the precise astronomical observations then being made at Alexandria and its violation of the hallowed doctrine of an earth-centered universe prevented its wide acceptance. Later the great Hellenistic astronomer Hipparchus developed a complex system of circles and

subcircles centered on the earth which accounted exceedingly well for the observed motions of the heavenly bodies. Hipparchus' ingenious system, perfected by the Alexandrian astronomer Ptolemy in the second century A.D., represents antiquity's final word on the subject—a comprehensive geometrical model of the universe; it was fundamentally wrong yet it corresponded satisfactorily to the best observations of the day. And it should be remembered that a scientific hypothesis must be judged not by some objective standard of rightness or wrongness but by its success in accounting for and predicting observed phenomena. By this criterion the Ptolemaic system stands as one of the impressive triumphs of Hellenistic thought.

Within the 400 years between the time of Homer and of Aristotle, the ancient Greeks created one of the most remarkable civilizations in history. In both its Spartan and Athenian forms the polis stimulated a civic culture with an unprecedented degree of citizen concern and participation. Greek philosophers and scientists asked questions that were unheard of in traditional societies; Greek dramatists probed the depths of human feeling and interpersonal conflict; Greek artists invented the classical style, with its emphasis on detachment, harmony, and balance. The Greeks were among the world's most passionate people, yet they sublimated much of their passion in their literature and art, including the art of rhetoric which, for better or worse, is still with us, not only in politics and law but also in advertising and social relations. Too independent to form a unified nation, the Greeks experimented with almost every form of government until they finally lost their independence to the Macedonian dynasty and moved into the Hellenistic age.

Greek culture exerted a fundamental influence on the Roman Empire, the Byzantine and Muslim civilizations and medieval Western Europe, but it did so largely in its Hellenistic form. The conclusions of the Hellenistic philosophers and scholars tended to be accepted by the best minds of later ages, but the Hellenistic spirit of free inquiry and intellectual daring was not matched until the sixteenth and seventeenth centuries. There is something remarkably modern about the Hellenistic world with its confident scientists, its cosmopolitanism, its materialism, its religious diversity, its trend toward increasing specialization, its large-scale business activity, and its sense of drift and disorientation. But the Hellenistic social conscience remained dormant and Hellenistic economic organization, regardless of superficial similarities, was vastly different from ours. Based on human slavery rather than machines, it provided only a tiny fraction of the population with the benefits of its commercial prosperity. The great majority remained servile and illiterate. Still, the upper classes throughout the Mediterranean world and the Near East were exposed to Greek culture and the Greek language, and the Greeks themselves were deeply influenced by Oriental thought. From Syria, Asia Minor, and the Nile Valley to Magna Graecia in the West a common culture was developing with common ideas and common gods. The way was being paved for the political unification of the Mediterranean world under the authority of Rome, and its spiritual unification under the Christian Church. Alexander's dream of a homogeneous Greco-Oriental world was gradually coming into being, but if Alexander had foreseen the consequences of his handiwork — the conquest of Hellas by an Italian city and an oriental faith — he might have chosen to spend his days in seclusion.

SUGGESTED READINGS

Cottrell, Leonard, *The Bull of Minos*. New York: Grosset and Dunlap, 1958. Paperback.
An entertaining account of Minoan-Mycenean archaeology.

Higgins, R., *Minoan and Mycenaen Art*. New York: Praeger, 1967. Paperback.

MacKendrick, P., *The Greek Stones Speak*. New York: Mentor, 1962. Paperback.

Rose, H. J., *Handbook of Greek Mythology*. New York: Dutton, 1958. Paperback.
The best scholarly treatment of the subject.

Bury, J. B., *A History of Greece*. New York: Macmillan, 3rd ed., rev. by R. Meiggs, 1951.
The best political survey, covers Greek history in detail to the death of Alexander.

Finley, M. I., *The Ancient Greeks*. New York: Viking, 1963. Paperback.
An excellent recent survey of Greek life and thought, brief but authoritative.

Finley, M. I., ed. and trans., *Greek Historians*. New York: Viking, 1959. Paperback.
Contains much of Herodotus, Thucydides, Zenophon, and Polybius.

Kitto, H. D. F., *The Greeks*. Baltimore, Md.: Penguin Books, 1957. Paperback.
An illuminating and provocative interpretation of Greek history to Alexander written by an enthusiastic Phil-Hellene who finds little to criticize in ancient Hellas.

Frost, F. J., *Democracy and the Athenians*. New York: Wiley, 1969. Paperback.

Thucydides, *The History of the Peloponnesian War*, trans. by Richard Crawley. New York: Modern Library, 1961. Paperback.

Auden, W. H., ed., *The Portable Greek Reader*. New York: Viking, 1948. Paperback.
Perhaps the best of many available anthologies.

Buchanan, Scott, ed., trans. by B. Jowett, *The Portable Plato*. New York: Viking, 1948. Paperback.

Cornford, F. M., *From Religion to Philosophy*. New York: Harper, 1957. Paperback.

Richter, G. M., *Handbook of Greek Art*. New York: Phaidon, 1960. Paperback.

Rose, H. J., *Handbook of Greek Literature*. New York: Dutton, 1964. Paperback.
The most satisfactory survey of this rich subject.

Snell, Bruno, *The Discovery of the Mind*. New York: Harper, 1953. Paperback.
A provocative interpretive study tracing the rise of self-awareness in philosophy, literature, and the arts.

Cary, Max, *A History of the Greek World from 323 to 146 B.C.* London: Methuen, 2nd ed., 1951.
An excellent, balanced account of Hellenistic history—political, economic, military, intellectual, and cultural.

Farrington, Benjamin, *Greek Science*. Baltimore, Md.: Penguin Books, 1961. Paperback.
A thorough and comprehensive study running from the Ionians to Ptolemy and Galen in the second century A.D.

Tarn, W. W., *Hellenistic Civilisation,* rev. by Tarn and G. T. Griffith. Cleveland: Meridian, 1952. Paperback.
The classical account of the post-Classical age.

Wilcken, Ulrich, *Alexander the Great*. New York: Norton, 1967. Paperback.

CHAPTER 5

The Roman World

The rise of Rome from an inconsequential central-Italian village to the mastery of the ancient Mediterranean world is perhaps history's supreme success story. The process was slow as compared with the dazzling imperialistic careers of Persia and Macedon, but it was far more lasting. There was nothing meteoric about the serious, hard-headed Romans—they built slowly and well. Their great military virtue was not tactical brilliance but stubborn endurance; they lost many battles but from their beginnings to the great days of the Empire they never lost a war. Since it was they who ultimately provided the ancient world with a viable and all-encompassing political framework, students of history have always been fascinated by the development of Roman political institutions. Rome's greatest contributions were in the realm of law, government, and imperial organization. In her grasp of political realities lay the secret of her triumphant career.

REPUBLICAN ROME

Had Alexander lived to middle age instead of dying at thirty-two he might well have led his conquering armies westward into Italy, Sicily and North Africa. Here he would have encountered three vigorous cultures: Carthage, the city-states of Magna Graecia, and the rapidly-expanding republic of Rome. Carthage was originally a Phoenician commercial colony but its strategic location on the North African coast, just south of Sicily, gave it a stranglehold on the western Mediterranean. It soon developed an extensive commercial empire of its own and far outstripped the Phoenician homeland in power and wealth. Carthage established a number of commercial bases in western Sicily which brought her face-to-face with the Greek city-states that dominated the eastern sections of the island.

The Greek polises of Sicily and southern Italy, known collectively as Magna Graecia, were products of the age of Greek colonization in the eighth and seventh centuries. Their political evolution ran parallel to that of the city-states in Greece; they experienced the same violent struggles between aristocratic, oligarchic, and democratic factions and the same intense cultural creativity. And like Old Greece, Magna Graecia was tormented by incessant intercity warfare. By Alexander's time the Sicilian polis of Syracuse had long been the leading power of the

141

A Chimera, a fine Etruscan bronze.

area, but the smaller polises guarded their independence jealously, and real unification was delayed until the Roman conquests of the third century brought these Greek cities under the sway of a common master.

Early Rome

The beginnings of Roman history are obscure. It seems likely that by about 750 B.C. settlers were living in huts on the Palatine Hill near the Tiber River. Gradually, several neighboring hills became inhabited, and around 600 these various settlements joined together to form the city-state of Rome. The strategic position of this cluster of hills, 15 miles inland on one of Italy's few navigable rivers, was of enormous importance to Rome's future growth. Ancient ocean-going ships could sail up the Tiber to Rome but no farther, and Rome was the lowest point at which the river could be bridged easily. Hence Rome was a key river-crossing and road junction and also, at least potentially, a seaport. It was at the northern limit of a fertile agricultural district known as Latium whose rustic inhabitants, the Latins, gave their name to the Latin language. Immediately north of Rome lay the district of Etruria (the modern Tuscany) whose highly civilized inhabitants, the Etruscans, shaped the culture of the earliest Romans.

The Etruscan ruling class may have migrated to Etruria from Asia Minor around 800 B.C. bringing with it into central Italy important elements of the rich cultural heritage of the eastern Mediterranean and the Near East. The Etruscans borrowed heavily from the Greeks. Their art, their city-state political structure, and their alphabet, were all Hellenic in inspiration, but they adapted these cultural ingredients to their own needs and created out of them a vivacious, pleasure-loving civilization of considerable originality. It was in Etruscan form that Greek civilization made its first impact on Rome. The Romans adopted the Greek alphabet in its Etruscan version and perhaps through Etruscan inspiration they organized themselves into a city-state, thereby gaining an inestimable advantage over the numerous half-civilized tribes in the region between Etruria and Magna Graecia. During much of the sixth century, Rome was ruled by kings of Etruscan background whose talented and aggressive leadership made the Romans an important power among the peoples of Latium. The community grew in strength and wealth, and an impressive temple to the Roman god Jupiter was built in Etruscan style atop one of the hills. Rome was becoming a city in fact as well as in name.

About 509 B.C. the Roman aristocracy succeeded in overthrowing its Etruscan king, transforming Rome from a monarchy into an aristocratic republic. The king was replaced by two magistrates known as consuls who were elected annually by an aristocratic Senate and who governed with its advice. The consuls exercised their authority in the name of the Roman people but in the interests of the upper classes. The governing elite was composed of wealthy landowners known as patricians who defended their prerogatives with great zeal against the encroachments of the common people—the plebeians or plebs. Plebeian-patrician intermarriage was strickly prohibited, and for a time the plebeians were almost entirely without political rights.

But step by step the plebeians improved their condition and came to play a significant role in the government. They began by organizing themselves into a deliberative body that later took the form of an important political organ known as the Tribal Assembly. They elected representatives called tribunes to be their spokesmen and represent their interests before the patrician-controlled city government. The tribunes acquired the remarkable power of vetoing anti-plebeian measures issuing from any organ of government, and anyone violating the sanctity of a tribune's person was to be punished by death. Under the leadership of their tribunes the plebeians were able to act as a unit and to make their strength felt. On at least one occasion they seceded as a body from the Roman state, leaving the patrician governors with nobody to govern and the patrician army officers with no troops to lead.

In about 450 B.C. the Romans took the important step of committing their legal customs to writing. The result was Rome's first law code—the Twelve Tablets. By later standards these laws were harsh (defaulting debtors, for example, suffered capital punishment or were delivered up for sale abroad), but they had the effect of protecting individual plebeians from the capricious authority of the patrician consuls. The Twelve Tables are exceedingly significant in Roman constitutional development, constituting as they do the first great monument in the evolution of Roman law.

Having gained a measure of legal protection, the plebeians turned to the problem of land distribution and forced the government to grant them additional farms out of its own estates and from the territories of newly-conquered peoples. Gradually the Tribal Assembly of the plebeians acquired the power to initiate legislation and thereby came to play an important part in Roman government. Intermarriage was now allowed between the two classes, and a law of 367 B.C. opened the consulship itself to the plebeians. At the same time, or shortly afterward, it was stipulated that at least one of the two consuls be a plebeian. In the years that followed, plebeians became eligible for all offices of state. Collectively, these measures went far toward transforming Rome into a nominal democracy. This transformation was completed in 287 B.C. when legislation issuing from the Tribal Assembly acquired the force of law without the necessity of being ratified by the aristocratic Senate.

The law was now, at least theoretically, in the hands of the people.

In the interest of simplicity and brevity we have not been able to do justice to the extreme complexity of Roman republican government. It included numerous magistrates with various functions and, at one time or another, several different assemblies. The Tribal Assembly, for example, shared power with another public body of great importance: the Centuriate Assembly. Both were made up of the total Roman citizenry, plebeian and patrician alike, but each had its own specific power and function. Moreover, these two Assemblies differed significantly in organization. The Tribal Assembly, the more democratic of the two, was based on tribal or residential districts known as wards. Each ward had one vote, and the poorer rural wards outnumbered the urban ones. But since the patrician wards had the privilege of voting first, most matters had been decided by the time the plebeian wards cast their votes. By this means the patricians were able to limit plebeian political power within the nominally democratic framework.

The Centuriate Assembly, patterned on the organization of the Roman army, was divided into groups known as "centuries." The number of centuries allotted to each class depended on the number of men that class supplied to the army, and since wealth was the basis of Roman military service, the Centuriate Assembly was dominated by the wealthy. Empowered to elect Rome's chief magistrates and to vote on questions of war and peace, the Centuriate Assembly remained powerful throughout the later years of the Republic. With its wealth-based organization, it further compromised the so-called "democratic" regime that was established in 287.

Roman democracy after 287 was more apparent than real. The domination of the patricians was fading, but it was giving way to a more subtle domination by a wealthy oligarchy of leading plebeian and patrician families. For during the fifth and fourth centuries a number of plebeians had accumulated extensive estates, and many of them now rivaled the patricians in wealth. By being elected to magistracies, many wealthy plebeians gained admission into the Senate which, by the third century, had ceased to be a patrician preserve. Indeed, by 287 the old division between patrician and plebeian was becoming anachronistic. It was replaced by a new division between the poor and the wealthy. Since more and more wealthy plebeians were gaining admission into the Senate, it is conventional among historians to term the wealthy landholders of the later Republic the "senatorial aristocracy."

The complex machinery of Roman republican government offered many opportunities for the new oligarchy to retain in practice the control that in theory belonged to the people. By means of political manipulation and patronage, the wealthy made their influence felt in the Tribal Assembly; they had a preponderant voice in the Centuriate Assembly, and they dominated the Senate—which lacked direct legislative power but retained enormous influence and prestige. In short, Rome in 287 was only a paper democracy. In reality, it was a plutocracy—a government of the wealthy—whose policies were controlled by the senatorial aristocracy.

Nevertheless the political realism of the Romans is well illustrated by the fact that the sweeping constitutional changes that took place between the fall of the Etruscan monarchy in 509 B.C. and the legislative supremacy of the Tribal Assembly in 287 B.C. occurred without major insurrections or excessive bloodshed. During these years much Roman blood was spilled on the battlefield but comparatively little on the city's streets. The willingness to settle internal conflicts by compromise—the ability of the patricians to bend before the winds of social change—preserved in Rome a sense of cohesiveness and a spirit of civic commitment without which its conquests would have been inconceivable.

The Career of Conquest

Civic commitment was a hallmark of the early Roman. Devoted to the numerous gods of city, field, and hearth, he was hard working, respectful of tradition, obedient to civil and military authority, and dedicated to the welfare of the state. The backbone of Old Rome was the small, independent farmer who worked long and hard to raise crops from his fields and remained always vigilant against raids by tribesmen from the surrounding hills. To men such as these life was intensely serious. Their stern sobriety and rustic virtues were exaggerated by Roman moralists looking back nostalgicly from a later and more luxurious age, but there can be little doubt that the tenacious spirit and astonishing military success of early republican Rome owed much to the discipline and steadfastness of these citizen-farmers. As triumph followed triumph, as the booty of war flowed into Rome from far and wide, the character of her citizenry inevitably suffered; one of the great tragic themes of Roman history is the gradual erosion of social morality by wealth and power—and by the gradual expansion of huge slave-operated estates at the expense of the small farmer. But long before this process was complete the empire had been won.

The expulsion of the last Etruscan king in 509 B.C. was followed by a period of retrenchment during which the Romans fought for their lives against the predatory attacks of neighboring tribes. In time an alliance was formed between Rome and the communities of Latium in which Rome gradually assumed the role of senior partner. Hostile tribes were subdued after long and agonizing effort, and shortly after 400 B.C. the Etruscan cities began to fall, one by one, under Roman control. The Romans were usually generous with the Italian peoples whom they conquered, allowing them a good measure of internal self-government, and were therefore generally successful in retaining their allegiance. In time, if a conquered people proved loyal, they might hope to be granted Roman citizenship. In this generous fashion Rome was able to construct an empire far more cohesive and durable than that of Periclean Athens. (Neither Pericles nor any of his contemporaries could have conceived of granting citizenship to non-Atticans.) Gradually the Roman conquests gained momentum. Battles were often lost—Rome itself was sacked in 387 B.C. by an army of Gauls from the north—but the Romans brushed off their defeats and pressed on. By 265 B.C. all Italy south of the Po Valley was under their control. Etruscan power had collapsed, and even the Italian cities of Magna Graecia acknowledged Roman supremacy. Now, midway through the third century, Rome took its place alongside Carthage and the three great Hellenistic successor states as one of the leading powers of the Mediterranean world.

Carthage and Rome stood face to face, and in 264 B.C. these two great western powers became locked in the first of three savage conflicts known as the Punic Wars (after *Poenus*, the Latin word for Phoenican or Carthaginian). Rome was now forced to build a navy and take to the sea. The wars, especially the first two, were long and bitter. Rome lost numerous battles, scores of ships, and warriors and seamen by the hundreds of thousands. During the Second Punic War (218 to 201 B.C.) the armies of the masterly Carthaginian general Hannibal swept back and forth across Italy winning victory after victory, and only the dogged determination of the Romans and the loyalty of their subject-allies saved the state from extinction. But the Romans hung on, suffering many defeats but always managing to win the last battle. At the conclusion of the Third Punic War in 146 B.C. Carthage was in ruins and its far-flung territories in Africa, Sicily, and Spain were in Roman hands.

Two Italian warriors carrying a dead comrade.

In the meantime Rome was drawn almost inadvertently into the rivalries among the Hellenistic kingdoms of the eastern Mediterranean. Ptolemaic Egypt, Seleucid Asia, Antigonid Macedon, and the several smaller Greek states had long been at one another's throats; Rome's victories over Carthage increased its power to the point where it was stronger than any one of them. Greek states frequently sought Roman aid against their enemies, and more often than not the Romans gave the requested support in order to maintain the balance of power in the east and to prevent any one Greek kingdom from becoming dangerously strong. Rome entered the Greek world more as a pacifier than as a conqueror, but eventually it tired of its endless task as referee and remained to rule. During the second century almost all the Hellenistic world fell either directly or indirectly under Roman control. Rome won a decisive victory over the Seleucids in 189 B.C.; it conquered Macedon in 168 B.C.; in 146 it demolished the ancient Peloponnesian city of Corinth and transformed Greece into a Roman province under the direct authority of a governor appointed by the Roman state. The remaining Hellenistic kingdoms were now completely overshadowed and had no choice but to bow to Rome's leadership. Gradually they too became provinces.

Rome followed no blueprint for conquest—indeed many of its leaders were isolationists who would have preferred to remain aloof from the Greek east—but the political conditions of the Hellenistic states exerted a magnetic attraction that was irresistible. As the second century drew toward its close, Rome was the master of the Mediterranean world. There now arose the baffling problem of adapting a government designed to rule a city-state to the needs of an empire.

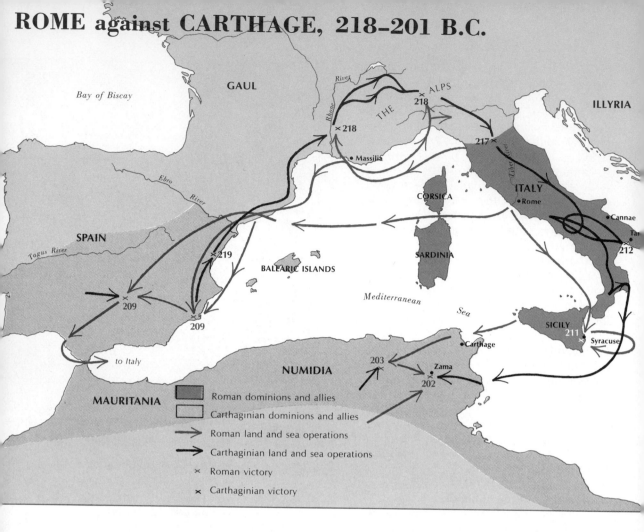

ROME against CARTHAGE, 218–201 B.C.

GAUL

Bay of Biscay

ILLYRIA

River

THE ALPS

218

×218

Massilia

217×

Rhone

Tiber River

ITALY

Rome

CORSICA

Cannae

SPAIN

Ebro River

Tagus River

×219

Tar

212

209

209

BALEARIC ISLANDS

SARDINIA

Mediterranean

Sea

SICILY

211

Syracuse

Carthage

to Italy

203×

Zama

202

NUMIDIA

MAURITANIA

Roman dominions and allies
Carthaginian dominions and allies
Roman land and sea operations
Carthaginian land and sea operations
× Roman victory
× Carthaginian victory

Social and Political Changes (264–146 B.C.)

The years of the three Punic Wars witnessed a transformation in the structure and spirit of Rome itself. These changes can be attributed partly to the intoxicating effect of un-imagined wealth and military success that gradually undermined the old civic virtue and encouraged a mood of arrogance and materialism. More specifically, as Rome was conquering the Greek world, it was falling increasingly under the influence of Hellenistic culture. Later Roman writers such as Cato and Sallust lamented that Roman soldiers were corrupted by the luxuries of eastern Mediterranean lands. Ultimately, Greece was perhaps the victor after all. The full tide of Hellenistic skepticism and individualism, which had earlier done so much to dissolve the Greek polis, now began its corrosive

work on Roman conservatism and civic dedication. As in Greece, the effects of this process were both good and bad. What Rome lost in civic virtue it gained in cultural and intellectual depth, for prior to its Helleniza-tion, Rome was almost totally lacking in high culture. The Stoic notion of universal brotherhood was a singularly appropriate philosophy for a great empire, and it was a fortunate thing for the conquered peoples that in later years so many Roman statesmen became Stoics. But with Greek art, literature, and learning came the disquieting Helle-nistic feeling of drift and alienation, aggra-vated by the importation of Hellenistic agri-cultural techniques.

The great Hellenistic successor states had emphasized the large plantation over the small independent farm, and now, as the conquests brought vast wealth and hordes of slaves into the hands of the Roman upper classes, most of central and southern Italy was converted into huge farms known as *latifundia*, worked by slaves and operated according to the latest Hellenistic techniques of large-scale scientific farming. Where the small farms had produced grain, the *latifundia* concentrated on the more lucrative production of wine and olive oil or the raising of sheep. The small farmers, whose energy and devotion had built the Roman Empire, were subjected to such heavy military demands that they found it increasingly difficult to maintain their farms. Many sold out to the *latifundia* owners and flocked into the cities, especially Rome itself, where they were joined by masses of penniless immigrants from the provinces and transformed into a chronically unemployed, irresponsible mob. In later years their riots terrorized the government; their hunger and boredom eventually gave rise to the custom of subsidized food and free entertainment of an increasingly sadistic sort—"bread and circuses."

While Rome was engaged in its struggle with Carthage, important changes were occurring in the social structure of the Roman ruling elite. With the acceleration of commerce, a new class of businessmen and public contractors was developing that in time acquired such wealth as to rival the landed senatorial aristocracy. This new class came to be known as the equestrian order because the wealth of its members enabled them to serve in the Roman army as cavalry rather than infantry. The equestrian class was effectively excluded from the Senate. Fundamentally apolitical except in instances when its own interests were at stake, it was content to share with the senatorial aristocracy the rising living standards that were coming into Rome with military triumphs and increased contact with the Hellenistic world. As the equestrians and landed nobility came to live in increasing luxury, the gap between rich and poor steadily widened, and the pressures of social unrest began to threaten the traditional stability of Roman civilization.

Meanwhile the Roman government, which had earlier acted with restraint toward its subject allies in Italy, was proving itself incapable of governing justly its newly ac-

The Capitoline wolf symbol of Rome.

quired overseas territories. Most of Rome's non-Italian holdings were organized as provinces ruled by aristocratic Roman governors and exploited by Roman tax gatherers. Infected with the selfishness and greed of Hellenistic individualism at its worst, governor and tax gatherer often worked in partnership to bleed the provinces for personal advantage. The grossest kinds of official corruption were tolerated by the Roman courts of law whose aristocratic judges hesitated to condemn dishonest officials of their own class for the sake of oppressed but alien provincials. Indeed, some provincial governors made it a practice to set aside a portion of their booty to bribe the courts.

Violence and Revolutions: The Last Century of the Republic

The deep-seated problems that afflicted Rome brought about a century-long period of violence and unrest, between 133 and 30 B.C., which resulted ultimately in the downfall of the Republic and the advent of a new imperial government. The first steps toward revolution were taken by two aristocratic reformers, the brothers Tiberius and Gaius Gracchus, who advocated a series of popular reform measures and thereby built up a powerful faction among the Roman commoners who were struggling against the entrenched aristocracy of wealth. Tiberius Gracchus served as tribune in 133 B.C., and Gaius held the same office a decade later. The two Gracchi were deeply concerned with the ominous course of the Republic. Both recognized that the decline in able recruits for the Roman army and the deterioration of morale among the citizenry were caused by the virtual elimination of the small farm from central Italy. Their solution was to create out of the vast public lands owned by the Roman state a large number of new farms for the dispossessed. This was a courageous and compassionate program, but the virtuous Roman farmer of yesteryear could not be conjured back into existence at this late moment. As it happened, most of the public lands had long before fallen under the effective control of powerful members of the senatorial aristocracy. These wealthy men, long accustomed to farming state lands for their own profit, reacted frigidly to the proposal that they should now give up portions of these lands so that the state might create small farms for the impoverished. In the political holocaust that followed, both Gracchi were murdered—Tiberius in 133, Gaius in 121. The senatorial aristocracy demonstrated that, despite past concessions, it was still in control. But it also betrayed its political and moral bankruptcy. Violence had been introduced into Roman political affairs, and the whirlwind now unleashed was to buffet the Republic for a century and finally demolish it.

For a generation the lower classes continued to press for the Gracchan reforms, and the senatorial aristocracy found itself pitted not only against the masses but sometimes against the equestrian order as well. But the great political fact of the last republican century was the rise of individual adventurers who sought to use successful military careers as springboards to political power. During the decade of the eighties, two able military commanders, Marius and Sulla, contended against one another for political supremacy. Marius drew much of his support from the lesser classes, whereas Sulla tended to ally with the wealthier and more established, but both were motivated strongly by personal ambition. In 106 B.C. Marius had taken the portentous step of abolishing the property qualification for military service and re-

cruiting volunteers from the poorest classes. Prior to Marius' reform, the resources of Roman military manpower had been declining alarmingly, but now the jobless masses thronged into the legions. Military service became, for many, the avenue to economic security, since soldiers of a successful and politically influential general could often expect to receive on retirement a gift of land from the Senate. The army began to acquire a more professional outlook than before, and soldiers came to identify themselves with their commanders rather than with the state. The opportunities for a ruthless and ambitious general with a loyal army at his back were limitless. But Marius was unwilling to go so far as to seize and overthrow the government. The more ruthless Sulla had no such scruples. In 83 B.C. he marched on Rome with his own devoted legions and, in the following year, made himself dictator. Once in power, he purged his enemies and proscribed a number of wealthy citizens, enriching himself from their confiscated fortunes. But Sulla had no intention of holding power indefinitely. A conservative at heart, he employed his dictatorial prerogatives to establish a series of laws that confirmed and strengthened the power of the inept Senate, then retired to affluent private life on his country estate in Campania, leaving the Republic to stagger on.

In the decade of the sixties, the great senatorial orator Cicero strove desperately to unite senators and equestrians against the growing threat of the generals and the riotous urban masses. Cicero's consummate mastery of Latin style, both in his orations and in his writings, earned him a lofty position in the field of Roman literature, but his political talents proved inadequate to the task of saving the Republic. His dream of reconciling the interests of senators and equestrians was shattered by the selfishness of each, and his efforts to perpetuate the traditional supremacy of the Senate were doomed by the Senate's own incapacity, by the smoldering unrest of the city mobs, and by the ambition of the military commanders. It was Cicero's misfortune to be a conservative in an epoch of revolutionary turbulence—a statesman in an age of generals.

Caesar the Dictator.

long era of peace and stability to the Mediterranean world, was chiefly the handiwork of two men: Julius Caesar and his grand-nephew, Octavian, later called Augustus. Julius Caesar was a man of many talents—a superb general, a brilliant and realistic politician, an inspiring leader, and a distinguished man of letters whose lucid and forthright *Commentaries on the Gallic Wars* was a significant contribution to the great literary surge of the late Republic. Above all, Caesar was a man of reason who could probe to the heart of any problem, work out a logical, practical solution, and then carry his plan to realization.

Julius Caesar and Augustus

Caesar managed to ride the whirlwind of violence and ruthless ambition that was shattering Roman society during the mid-first century B.C. His political intuition and unswerving faith in himself and his star catapulted him to increasingly important political and military offices during the turbulent sixties. Opposed and distrusted by the conservative Senate led by the great orator Cicero, he allied himself with Pompey, a talented, disgruntled general, and Crassus, an ambitious millionaire. These three formed an extralegal coalition of political bosses, known to later historians as the "First Triumvirate," which succeeded in dominating the Roman state.

Leaving Italy in the hands of his two colleagues, Caesar spent most of the following decade (58–50 B.C.) in Gaul leading his army on a spectacular series of campaigns that resulted in the conquest of what is now France and Belgium and established his reputation as one of history's consummate military scientists. Caesar's conquest of Gaul pushed the influence of Rome far northward from the Mediterranean into the heartland of western Europe. The historical consequences of his victories were immense, for in the centuries that followed, Gaul was thoroughly Romanized. The Roman influence survived the later barbarian invasions to give medieval and modern France a romance tongue and to provide western Europe with an enduring Greco-Roman cultural heritage.

While Caesar was winning his triumphs in Gaul his interests in Italy were suffering. His

The Republic was now approaching its final days in an atmosphere of chaos and naked force. The dominant political figures of Cicero's generation were military commanders such as Pompey and Julius Caesar, who bid against one another for the backing of the lower classes, seeking to convert mob support into political supremacy. Characteristically, the three great men of their age, Pompey, Cicero, and Caesar, all met violent deaths. The utter failure of republican government was now manifest, and the entire imperial structure seemed on the verge of collapse. As it turned out, however, Rome was to emerge from her crisis transformed and strengthened, and her empire was to endure for another 500 years.

IMPERIAL ROME

The new order, which saved Rome from the agonies of the late Republic and brought a

advocacy of land redistribution and of other policies dear to the hearts of the lower classes earned him the hostility of the Senate, and his spectacular military success threatened to thwart Pompey's own ambition to be first among Romans. Out of their common fear of Caesar, Pompey and the Senate now joined forces, and in 49 B.C. Caesar was declared a public enemy. His career at stake, Caesar defied the Roman constitution by leading his own loyal army into Italy. In a series of dazzling campaigns during 49 and 48 B.C., he defeated Pompey and the hostile members of the Senate. Pompey fled to Egypt and was murdered there, and the Senate had no choice but to come to terms with the man who now towered unchallenged over Rome.

Caesar was a magnanimous victor. He restored his senatorial opponents to their former positions and ordered the execution of Pompey's murderer. He could afford to be generous for he was now the unquestioned master of the state. The Republic had traditionally, in time of grave crisis, concentrated all power in the hands of a dictator who was permitted to exercise his virtually unlimited jurisdiction for six months only. Caesar assumed the office of dictator and held it year after year. Ultimately he forced the Senate to grant him the dictatorship for life. He also acquired the personal inviolability of the tribune and assumed several other key republican offices. Besides all these, he retained the title of *pontifex maximus* (supreme pontiff or chief priest of the civic religion), which he had held for some years. In 44 B.C. he was more-or-less deified: a temple was dedicated to his genius—the spirit of his family or clan—and the month of July was named in his honor. Most of the political institutions of the Republic survived but they were now under his thumb. He controlled the appointment of magistrates, manipulated the assemblies, and overawed the Senate. The whole Roman electorate had become his clients.

Caesar used his power to reform the Republic along logical, realistic lines. The magnitude of his reforms defies description. He introduced a radically new calendar that, with one minor adjustment, is in almost universal use today. He organized numerous distant colonies that drained off a consider-able number of Rome's unemployed masses, and halved the Roman bread dole. He did much to reform and rationalize Italian and provincial government and to purge the republican administration of its abuses. In short, he was the model of what would much later be called an "enlightened despot." Some historians have supposed that Caesar was aiming at a monarchy along Hellenistic lines, but it is more accurate to view him as a supremely talented Roman applying his intellect to the rational solution of Roman problems.

Caesar's remarkable success attests to the creative power of the human mind; his ultimate failure, however, suggests that in human affairs reason is not always enough —that the ingrained historical traditions of a people will resist the surgery of even the most skillful rationalist reformer. Caesar's reforms were immensely beneficial to the people of the Empire, but he went too far too fast. His disregard for republican institutions was too cavalier, and his assumption of the dictatorship for life alarmed powerful elements in the Senate. On the Ides of March (March 15), 44 B.C., he was stabbed to death at a Senate meeting by a group of conservative senatorial conspirators led by Brutus and Cassius. As they rushed from the Senate the assassins shouted, "Tyranny is dead!" They were wrong: it was the Republic that was dead, and Rome now had only the choice between one-man rule and anarchy. By killing Caesar, they had given up the former for the latter.

Caesar's assassination resulted in fourteen more years of civil strife during which the conservative party of Brutus and Cassius struggled against would-be heirs to Caesar's power while the heirs struggled against one another. In the complex maneuvers of this civil war some of the most famous figures in ancient history played out their roles. Mark Antony, Caesar's trusted lieutenant, defeated Brutus and Cassius in battle, and both committed suicide. The golden tongued Cicero, Rome's supreme literary craftsman, was murdered for his hostility to Antony. And when the fortunes of war turned against them, Antony and his exotic wife, Queen Cleopatra of Egypt, took their own lives. The ultimate victor in these struggles was a young man who had been almost unknown at the time of Caesar's death. Octavian, the later Augustus, Caesar's grandnephew and adopted son, had woven his way through the era of strife with matchless skill. A young man of eighteen when Caesar died, Octavian proved to the world that he was in truth Caesar's heir. For although inferior to Caesar in generalship and perhaps also in sheer intellectual strength, Octavian was Caesar's superior as a realistic, practical politician. During his long, illustrious reign Octavian completed the transformation of the Roman state from republic to empire. But his reforms were more traditionalist in spirit than Caesar's, and he succeeded — where Caesar had failed — in winning the Senate's respect. He reformed the Romans and made them like it.

The Augustan Age

In 31 B.C. Octavian's forces crushed those of Antony and Cleopatra at Actium. A year later Octavian entered Alexandria as master of the Mediterranean world. He was then the same age as Alexander at the time of his death, and it might be supposed that the two world-conquerors, both young, brilliant, and handsome, had much in common. But Octavian refused to visit Alexander's tomb in Alexandria, observing, so it was said, that true greatness lies not in conquest but in reconstruction. It is appropriate, therefore, that Octavian's immense historical reputation lies not in his military victories — which were won by his generals rather than himself — but in his accomplishments as peacemaker and architect of the Roman Empire.

The reformation of Rome, completed by Octavian, gave the Mediterranean world two centuries of almost uninterrupted peace and prosperity during which classical culture developed and spread to the outermost reaches of the Empire. This unprecedented achievement caused men, in the turbulent centuries that followed, to look back longingly at the almost legendary epoch of the "Roman Peace." Octavian accomplished the seemingly impossible task of reconciling the need for one-man rule with the republican traditions of Old Rome. He preserved the Senate; indeed, increased its prestige. He retained the elected republican magistracies.

The Emperor Augustus.

He made no attempt to revive the office of dictator, for he preferred to manipulate the government in more subtle ways. He controlled the army and, like Caesar, he concentrated various key republican offices and powers in his own person — *pontifex maximus,* consul, the authority of the tribunes, and others. In 27 B.C. he was given the novel name of Augustus, a term that carried with it no specific power, but had a connotation of reverence — almost holiness. And like Caesar he was honored by having a month (August) named in his honor. It is characteristic of his philosophy of government, however, that Augustus preferred the relatively modest title of *princeps* or "first citizen." He was the leading Roman — nothing

Augustan art and propaganda, a detail from the Altar of Peace, symbolizing the fertility of Italy.

more. He lived relatively modestly, associated freely with his fellow citizens, revered the dignity of the Senate, and dressed and ate simply. But if the Principate (the government of the *princeps*) was at heart a monarchy, it was by no means an arbitrary one. Augustus ruled with a keen sensitivity toward popular and senatorial opinion and a respect for traditions.

Still, Augustus was the true master of Rome; the nature of the Empire was such that the liberty of the old Republic simply could not be preserved. The Roman electorate was incapable of governing the Empire, and a democratic empire with universal suffrage was inconceivable. Roman liberty was the single great casualty of the Principate, but its loss was rendered almost painless by the political deftness of the first *princeps*. In its place Augustus provided peace, security, prosperity, and justice. The administration of the provinces was now closely regulated by the *princeps,* and the gross corruption and exploitation of the late Republic were reduced. In Rome itself an efficient imperial bureaucracy developed which was responsible to the *princeps* alone. Although class distinction remained strong, it was now possible for an able man from one of the lower classes to rise in the government service, and men

with literary and artistic gifts were sought out and supported by Augustus as a matter of policy.

The stable new regime, the promise of enduring peace, the policy of "careers open to talent," and the leadership of Augustus himself combined to evoke a surge of optimism, patriotism, and creative originality. In the field of arts and letters the "Augustan Age" is the climax of Roman creative genius, surpassing even the literary brilliance of the troubled late Republic of which Cicero stands as the supreme example. Under Augustus, Roman artists and poets achieved a powerful synthesis of Greek and Roman elements. Roman architecture was obviously modeled on the Greek, but it just as obviously expressed a distinctively Roman spirit. Roman temples rose higher than those of classical Greece and conveyed a feeling that was less serene—more imposing and dynamic; less horizontal—more vertical. Augustan poetry—the urbane and faultless lyrics of Horace, the worldly, erotic verses of Ovid, the majestic cadences of Virgil—employed Greek models and ideas in original and characteristically Roman ways. Rome's supreme poem, Virgil's *Aeneid*, was cast in the epic form of Homer and dealt, as Homer's *Odyssey* did, with the voyage of an important figure in the Trojan War. But Aeneas, Virgil's hero, was also the legendary founder of Rome, and the poem is shot through with patriotic prophecies regarding the great destiny of the state which Aeneas was to found. Indeed, some readers have seen in Aeneas a symbol of Augustus himself. The *Aeneid* also contains a compassionate humanitarian strain lacking in Homer but evident in the enlightened policies of Augustus and his successors — especially the emperors of the second century. Above all, there is the feeling of hope that the Roman people — founded by Aeneas, and now led by the great peacemaker Augustus — have at last fulfilled their mission to bring enduring concord and justice to the long-tormented world:

But Rome! 'tis thine alone, with awful sway,
To rule mankind, and make the world obey,
Disposing peace and war thine own majestic
  way;
To tame the proud, the fetter'd slave to free:
*These are imperial arts, and worthy thee.**

Imperial Leadership after Augustus

Augustus died at the age of 76 in A.D. 14. During the decades following his death, the Principate grew steadily more centralized and more efficient. The imperial bureaucracy expanded, the provinces were reasonably well governed, taxes were relatively light and intelligently assessed, the law became increasingly humane, and the far-flung inhabitants of the Empire enjoyed unprecedented peace and prosperity. It is a tribute to Augustus's wisdom that the system that he created was sturdy enough to endure and flourish despite the relative incapacity of many of his imperial successors. The abilities of the first-century emperors ranged from uninspired competence to downright madness, descending on occasion to the vainglorious absurdity of a Nero or the grotesque lunacy of a Caligula, who wallowed in the pleasure of watching his prisoners being tortured to death. Caligula is reported to have allowed his favorite horse to dine at the imperial table during formal state dinners,

The Emperor Hadrian.

consuming the finest food and wines from jeweled dishes and goblets. At Caligula's death he was on the point of raising the beast to the office of consul. Caligula and Nero were autocrats of the worst type, and both were removed violently from power. On the whole, however, the emperors of the early Principate retained the traditional "constitutional" attitudes exemplified by Augustus himself.

The second century A.D. witnessed a dramatic improvement in the quality of imperial leadership. Rome's rulers between A.D. 96 and 180 have been called the "five good emperors." One nineteenth-century historian described them in these words: "For eighty-four years a series of sovereigns, the best, the wisest and the most statesmanlike that the world has ever seen — Nerva, Trajan, Hadrian, Antoninus, Marcus Aurelius — sat upon the throne of the world."* And although more recent historians would look askance at such sweeping praise, there can be no question but that the "five good emperors" were sovereigns of rare ability.

The high level of imperial leadership that characterized this era can be attributed

* *Aeneid,* Book VI (tr. John Dryden).

* Thomas Hodgkin, *The Dynasty of Theodosius* (Oxford, 1889), p. 18.

North Sea
Atlantic
Ocean
BRITANNIA
Londinium
GERMANIA
Rhine River
GAUL
PYRENEES
Po River
SPAIN
ITALY
Rome
Pompeii
Carthage
AFRICA
Danube River
DACIA
Black Sea
Byzantium
Pergamum
Athens
Mediterranean Sea
CAUCASUS MTS.
Caspian Sea
PARTHI
Antioch
Euphrates River
Damascus
Jerusalem
Alexandria
EGYPT
Nile River

Extent of the Empire, A.D.

Conquered by Trajan,
abandoned by Hadrian

THE ROMAN EMPIRE, A.D. 117

largely to the temporary solving of one of the knottiest dilemmas in the whole imperial system—the problem of succession. In theory the Senate chose the *princeps,* but in fact the succession usually fell to a close relative of the previous emperor and was often arranged by the emperor in advance. Too often this hereditary principle allowed the Empire to fall into the hands of an unworthy ruler; occasionally a disputed succession was settled by violence and even civil war. But none of the great second-century emperors—Trajan, Hadrian, Antoninus Pius, or Marcus Aurelius—came to power by normal hereditary succession. In each case, the previous emperor *adopted* as his son and successor a younger man of outstanding ability. The policy of adoption worked well for a time, but it did not represent a deliberate rejection of the hereditary succession princi-

ple. It was simply a consequence of the fact that none of the "five good emperors" had a son except Marcus Aurelius—the last of them. Marcus followed the hereditary principle—which had never consciously been abandoned—and chose his own son, the incompetent Commodus, as his heir. With the disastrous reign of Commodus (A.D. 180–192) the great age of imperial rule came to an end. It was followed by a century of military despotism, assassinations, economic and administrative breakdown, cultural decay, and civil strife which almost brought an end to the Roman state.

The Empire under the Principate

Before moving into the troubled third century, let us look briefly at the condition of the

Empire at its height. During the two centuries from the rise of Augustus to the death of Marcus Aurelius (31 B.C.–A.D. 180), the Empire expanded gradually to include a vast area from the Euphrates to the Atlantic — from the Sahara to the Danube, the Rhine, and the Cheviot Hills of northern Britain. A considerable amount of territory was added to the Empire under Augustus, and several later emperors, notably Trajan, made impressive conquests. But most of the emperors were content to guard the frontiers and preserve what had earlier been won.

The burden of defending the far-flung frontiers rested on an army of some 300,000 to 500,000 men, organized on principles laid down by Augustus. Infantry legions manned by Roman citizens on long-term enlistments were supplemented by auxiliary forces, both infantry and light cavalry, made up of non-Romans who were granted citizenship at the end of their extended terms of service. The army was concentrated along the frontiers except for the small, privileged praetorian guard that served the emperor in Rome itself. A high degree of mobility was insured by the superb system of roads which connected the city of Rome with its most remote provinces. Paved with stones fitted closely together, these roads were nearly as eternal as the city they served. They eased the flow of commerce as well as the movement of troops and remained in use many centuries after the Roman Peace was shattered by anarchy and barbarian invasions.

The Empire's greatest commercial artery was not built of stone; it was the Mediterranean, completely surrounded by imperial territory and referred to affectionately by the Romans as *Mare Nostrum* — "our sea." Strong Roman fleets patrolled the Mediterranean and kept it free of pirates for the first time in antiquity so that peaceful shipping could move unimpeded between the many ports of the Empire. Now as never before the immense territories encompassed by the Roman frontiers were well governed, well policed, and bound together by roads and protected seaways.

Under the aegis of the Roman Peace, commercial prosperity, Roman institutions, and classical culture spread far and wide across the Empire. As distant provinces became increasingly Romanized the meaning of the words "Rome" and "Roman" gradually changed. By the time of Augustus these terms were no longer confined to the imperial city and its inhabitants but had come to embrace the greater part of Italy. Now, as the decades of the Roman Peace followed one another, citizenship was progressively extended to more and more provincials until finally, in A.D. 212, every free inhabitant of the Empire was made a citizen. Emperors themselves now tended, as often as not, to be provincials: the great second-century emperor Trajan, for example, was a native of Spain. In time the terms "Rome" and "Roman" acquired a universal connotation: a Greek monarch in Constantinople, a Frankish monarch at Aachen, a Saxon monarch in Germany, a Hapsburg in Vienna could, in later centuries, all refer to themselves as "Roman emperors."

The most conspicuous effect of Romanization was the urbanization of the entire Empire. The city-state, the characteristic political phenomenon of the Greco-Roman world, now spread through the outer provinces — into Gaul, Spain, the lands along the Rhine and Danube, even remote Britain. The city still retained much local self-government and normally controlled the rural territories in its vicinity. In other words, the city was the key unit of local administration — the government of the Roman state remained fundamentally urban. Paradoxically, the cities of the Empire, especially in the west, were of relatively minor importance as commercial and manufacturing centers. Rome experienced no industrial expansion and, although small-scale urban industry often flourished, chiefly in the east, the economy of the Empire remained fundamentally agrarian. Many of the western cities — especially Rome itself — consumed far more than they produced and acted as parasites on the imperial economy. Basically they were administrative and military centers whose mercantile significance was secondary. During the first two centuries of the Empire the economy was prosperous enough to support them, but this would not always be the case. In time the cities would decline, and with them the whole political structure of the Greco-Roman world.

In the early Empire, as in the late Republic, slaves played a crucial role in the economy, especially in agriculture. But as the frontiers gradually ceased to expand and the flow of war captives diminished, the chief source of slaves was cut off. Large landholders now began to lease major portions of their estates to free sharecroppers called *coloni* who tended to fall more and more under the control of their landlords and sank slowly to a semiservile status akin to that of the medieval serfs. The *coloni,* like the impoverished masses who continued to crowd the larger cities, enjoyed little of the buoyant prosperity of the Principate. The age of the "five good emperors" was, by ancient standards, an epoch of material well-being, but it would be absurd to compare it to the abundance of the advanced industrial states of today. Roman society always included, beneath its veneer, a vast, wretched substratum of half-starved peasants and paupers.

The condition of the lower classes would have been still worse but for the humane policies of the imperial government. It was especially among the great second-century emperors that Stoic attitudes of human brotherhood, compassion, and social and political responsibility took hold. Unlike Caligula and Nero, who used their power to indulge their bizarre whims, emperors such as Hadrian and Marcus Aurelius viewed their authority as a trust, a responsibility to govern in the interests of the people whether rich or poor. The Empire of the second century is ornamented by its social conscience no less than by its leadership in military and administrative affairs.

The Silver Age

The cultural epoch from approximately the death of Augustus to the death of Marcus Aurelius is known as the Silver Age. Less illustrious than the golden Augustan Age, it nevertheless produced literary, intellectual, and artistic accomplishments of the first order. Some observers have seen in Silver Age writers such as the Stoic playwright Seneca, the satirist Lucian, and the biographer Plutarch, a decline in creative genius. They have stressed the stale conformity of second-century Roman art and literature re-

sulting from the absence of genuine freedom, the "homogenization" of culture, and the dullness of peace and security. Such judgments are necessarily relative, and many sensitive spirits through the centuries have viewed writers of the Silver Age with enormous admiration. Whatever one may think of the originality and excellence of Silver Age literature, there can be no question but that culture and learning spread outward and downward. Remote provincial cities built temples and baths, theaters and triumphal arches in the Roman style. Libraries and schools were scattered abundantly across the Empire, and the extent of urban literacy is demonstrated by the many irreverent and obscene scribblings and campaign slogans discovered by modern excavators on the buildings of Pompeii, buried and preserved by the eruption of Vesuvius in A.D. 79.

Alexandria, the Hellenistic metropolis, retained its commercial and intellectual importance throughout the age of the Principate, producing some of the most brilliant early Christian theologians as well as several distinguished scientists who developed and synthesized the achievements of earlier Hellenistic science. Greek and Hellenistic astronomical thought, for example, was developed into a sophisticated and comprehensive model of the universe by Ptolemy of Alexandria (*d.* about A.D. 180) who expanded the work of his predecessors into a geocentric world-system that accounted, with remarkable precision, for the observed motions of the sun, moon, and planets among the stars. Ptolemy also wrote the most complete geography of antiquity, and Galen (A.D. 131–201), a great medical scientist from Hellenistic Pergamum, produced a series of works on biology and medicine that dominated these fields for more than a thousand years. The *Meditations* of Marcus Aurelius, the last of the "five good emperors," is a moving expression of the Stoic philosophy that deepened and humanized so much of the best thought of the era. In literature and art, science and philosophy, the Silver Age produced an effortless synthesis of Greek and Roman traditions. The rich legacies of Greece, Rome, and the ancient Orient were summarized and fused into a coherent whole.

Roman Law

Of all the achievements of this epoch perhaps the most far-reaching—certainly the most distinctively Roman—was the development of imperial law. The rigid code of the Twelve Tables was gradually broadened and humanized by the magistrates of the later Republic and early Empire, by the great legists of the second and third centuries A.D., and by the enlightened intervention of the emperors themselves. As the Romans became acquainted with more and more peoples, each with its unique set of laws and customs, they gradually emancipated themselves from the peculiarities of their own law and strove to replace it by a body of fundamental principles drawn from the laws of all people. The *Jus Gentium* or "law of peoples" slowly transformed the Roman code into a legal system suitable to a vast, heterogeneous empire.

The evolution of Roman law into a universal system of jurisprudence owed something also to the Greek concept of the *Jus Naturale*—the "law of nature"—which has played a prominent role in the history of Western thought. More abstract than the *Jus Gentium,* the "law of nature" or "natural law" is based on the belief that in a divinely ordered world there are certain universal norms of human behavior which all people tend to follow, regardless of their own individual customs and traditions. These norms, based on lofty considerations of political and social justice, served to rationalize and humanize the law of the Empire and to provide it with a sturdy philosophical foundation. Accordingly, Roman law, a product of the Latin practical political genius influenced by Greek speculative thought, gave substance to the Augustan ideal of justice. Codified at enormous effort by the sixth-century emperor Justinian, it has become a crucial part of the Western heritage—the basis of many legal systems to this day in Europe and its former colonies.

THE MYSTERY RELIGIONS AND CHRISTIANITY

Roman Religion

Roman religion is immensely complex, for the Romans not only recognized many gods but had numerous separate cults. Like the Greek city-states, Rome had its official civic deities—Jupiter and Juno, Minerva and Mars, and many others, who by the later Republic had become identified with parallel gods of the Greek Olympic religion. The Roman Jupiter was the Greek Zeus, the Roman Minerva was the Greek Athena, and so on. Besides these Roman state deities there were the innumerable local gods of the myriad cities and districts of the Empire. And in Rome itself as well as throughout the Empire there were countless unofficial cults that normally enjoyed the toleration of the Roman state. None of these pagan cults was exclusive; none claimed a monopoly on truth, and a single individual might without compromise associate himself with several of them.

With the coming of the Principate an important new element was added to the state religion: the cult of the emperor. Augustus, like Julius Caesar, had been honored by the deification and worship of his "Genius," and both Augustus and his successors (with a few notorious exceptions) were deified by the Senate after their deaths. In those provinces where god-kings were traditional the *princeps* was viewed as a deity while still alive, and it soon became customary for Romans and provincials alike to participate in formal religious observances to the deified emperors as well as to the major deities of the city of Rome. These observances were at heart more patriotic than religious. They were useful in encouraging the allegiance of diverse peoples and, in accordance with religious attitudes of the day, few objected to the addition of a handful of new deities to the divine crowd that they already worshiped. To the Jews, and later the Christians, these religio-patriotic observances were another matter, for the jealous God of the Jews permitted the worship of no other. But Rome recognized the Jews as a people apart and usually excused them from participation in the official cults. The Christians, on the other hand, suffered gravely from their refusal to worship the emperors and gods of Rome. To the Romans such intransigence savored of both atheism and treason. It is no accident that Christianity alone of all the religions of the Empire was the object of serious Roman persecution.

The god Mithras sacrifices the heavenly bull.

The Mystery Cults

The centuries after Augustus witnessed a slow but fundamental shift in Roman religious attitudes, from the veneration of the traditional gods of household, clan, and city to the worship of transcendental deities imported from the Near East. The gods of Old Rome, like those of the Greek Olympus, had safeguarded the welfare of social and political groups; the new gods cared little for such things but offered instead the hope of individual redemption, salvation, and eternal life. As the Roman imperial age progressed, the allegiance of the people slowly shifted from Jupiter and Minerva to the Egyptian Isis, the Persian Mithras, the Phrygian Great Mother, the Syrian Sun god, and other exotic deities who offered solace and eternal joy to people for whom the world was not enough — even the world of the Roman Peace.

This surge of mysticism was actually a continuation and expansion of a trend we have already observed among the Hellenistic Greeks. The same forces that had encouraged the widespread rootlessness and disorientation of the Hellenistic world were now at work throughout the Roman Empire: cosmopolitanism, gradually increasing autocracy and, among the underprivileged masses, grinding poverty and loss of hope. The shift from civic god to savior god, from this world to the next, constitutes a profound transformation in mood — a repudiation of traditional Greco-Roman humanism. As the peace of the second century gave way to the anarchy of the third, the high hopes of classical humanism — the dream of a rational universe, an ideal republic, a good life — were beginning to seem like cruel illusions, and the movement toward the mystery cults gained enormous momentum.

The Emergence of Christianity

Two fundamental trends characterized religious development in the Roman Empire: the growing impluse toward mysticism that we have just examined, and the interpenetration and fusion of doctrines and practices between one cult and another — a process known as *syncretism*. The syncretic quality of Christianity itself has often been observed, for in numerous instances its beliefs and rituals were similar to those of earlier religions.

Obviously, Christianity drew heavily from Judaism—nearly all the earliest Christians were Jews—but it was also anticipated in various particulars by Zoroastrianism, Mithraism, the Isis-Osiris cult, the Greek mysteries of Dionysus and Demeter, and even Stoicism. Many Christian doctrines had long pre-Christian histories: the concept of death and resurrection, the sacramental meal, baptism, personal salvation, and the brotherhood of man under the fatherhood of God, to name but a few. Yet Christianity was far more than a new configuration of old ideas, and it would be misleading to think of it as merely another of the oriental mystery religions. It differed from them above all in two basic ways: (1) its god was the jealous God of the Hebrews, unique in all antiquity in his claims to exclusiveness and omnipotence, and now released by Christianity from his association with a specific chosen people and universalized as the God of all mankind; (2) Christianity's founder and Savior was a vivid historic personality, Jesus, beside whom such mythical idealizations as Mithras or Isis must have seemed tepid and diffuse.

Jesus, a younger contemporary of Augustus, was a figure in the Hebrew prophetic tradition whose life and teachings show little if any Greek influence. He is depicted in the Gospels as a warm, attractive, magnetic leader who miraculously healed the sick, raised the dead, and stilled the winds. His miracles were seen as credentials of the divine authority with which he claimed to speak. His ministry was chiefly to the poor and outcast, and in Christianity's early decades it was these classes that accepted the faith most readily. He preached a doctrine of love, compassion, and humility; like the prophets he scorned empty formalism in religion and stressed the sober, unprepossessing life of generosity toward both friend and enemy and devotion to God. He does not seem to have objected to ritual as such, but only to ritual infected with pride and complacency and divorced from charity and upright conduct. His severe criticism of the moral shortcomings of the established Jewish priesthoods, combined apparently with his claims to speak with divine authority, resulted in his crucifixion as a subversive.

According to the Gospels, Jesus's greatest miracle was his resurrection—his return to life three days after he died on the Cross. He is said to have remained on earth for a short period thereafter, giving solace and inspiration to his disciples, and then to have "ascended" into heaven with the promise that he would return in glory to judge all souls and bring the world to an end. The first generations of Christians expected this second coming to occur quickly, and it is perhaps for that reason among others that formal organization was not stressed in the primitive church.

The early Christians not only accepted Christ's ethical precepts but worshiped Christ himself as the divine incarnation of the omnipotent God. The Christ of the Gospels distinguishes repeatedly between himself—"the Son of Man"—and God—"the Father"—but he also makes the statement, "I and the Father are One," and he enjoins his disciples to baptize all persons "in the Name of the Father and the Son and the Holy Spirit." Hence, Christianity became committed to the difficult and sophisticated notion of a triune Godhead with Christ as the "Son" or "Second Person" in a Trinity that was nevertheless one God. The doctrine of the Trinity gave Christianity the unique advantage of a single, infinite, philosophically respectable god who could be worshiped and adored in the person of the charismatic, lovable, tragic Jesus. The Christian deity was both transcendent and concrete.

The Early Church

The first generation of Christianity witnessed the beginning of a deeply significant development whereby the Judeo-Christian heritage was modified and enriched through contact with the main currents of Greco-Roman culture. Christ's own apostles were no more influenced by Hellenism than their Master, and some of them sought to keep Christianity strictly within the ritualistic framework of Judaism. But St. Paul, a Hellenized Jew and early convert, succeeded in orienting the church according to his own vision of a universal brotherhood, free of the strict Jewish dietary laws and the requirement of circumcision (which were bound to discourage the conversion of non-Jews), open to all people everywhere who would accept Jesus as God and Savior—and open also to the bracing winds of Hellenistic thought. St. Paul traveled far and wide across the Empire preaching the message of Christ as he interpreted it, winning converts, and establishing Christian communities in many towns and cities of the Mediterranean world. Other Christian missionaries, among them St. Peter and his fellow apostles who had been Christ's immediate followers, devoted their lives as St. Paul did to traveling, preaching and organizing—often at the cost of ridicule and persecution. Tradition has it that St. Paul and all the apostles died as martyrs. Their work was tremendously fruitful, for by the end of the apostolic generation Christianity had become a ponderable force among the underprivileged masses of Italy and the east. Within another century the new religion had spread throughout the greater part of the Empire.

From the first, the Christians regularly engaged in a sacramental meal which came to be called the "eucharist" or "holy communion" and was viewed as an indispensable avenue of divine grace through which the Christian was infused with the spirit of Christ. By means of another important sacrament, baptism, the postulant was initiated into the brotherhood of the church, had his sins forgiven, and received the grace of the Holy Spirit. A person could be baptized only once, and baptized persons alone could consider themselves true Christians, but in the early church baptism was frequently delayed until adulthood and, therefore, many unbaptized persons were associated with the Christian communities without being Christians in the full sense of the word.

As Christian historical documents become more common, in the second and third centuries A.D., the organization of the church begins to emerge more sharply than before. The documents of this period disclose an important distinction between the clergy, who govern the church and administer the sacraments, and the laymen, who play a more passive role. The clergy itself was divided into several ranks, the most important of which were the bishops, who served as rulers and pastors over the various urban communities, and the priests, who led the services and administered the sacraments under the jurisdiction of the bishops. And the bishops themselves were of various degrees of eminence. Above the common bishops were the metropolitans or archbishops who resided in cities of special importance and exercised control over an extensive surrounding area. At the top of the hierarchy were the bishops of the three or four greatest cities of the Empire—Rome, Alexandria, Antioch, and later Constantinople—who were known as patriarchs and who enjoyed a spiritual hegemony (often more theoretical than real) over vast areas of the Mediterranean world.* As time went on, the bishop of Rome—the pope—came to be regarded more and more as the highest of the patriarchs, but the actual establishment of papal authority over even the Western church was to require the efforts of many centuries.

Christianity and Hellenism

Medieval and modern Christian theology is a product of both the Hebrew and the Greek traditions. The synthesis of these two intellectual worlds began not among the Christians but among the Jews themselves, especially those who had migrated in large numbers to Alexandria. Here Jewish scholars—in particular a religious philosopher of the early first century A.D. named Philo Judaeus—worked toward the reconciliation of Jewish revelation and Greek philosophy, drawing heavily from Aristotle, the Stoics, and particularly Plato, and developing a symbolic interpretation of the Old Testament that was to influence Christian thought enormously over the centuries.

Following many of the fruitful leads of Philo, Christian theologians strove to demonstrate that their religion was more than merely an immensely appealing myth—that it could hold its own in the highest intellectual circles. The Savior Christ, for example, as true God and true man, constituted a unique synthesis of the material and spiritual worlds. In Greek terms, Christ reconciled Plato's dualism, for Christ was at once a particular person and an archetype. Christianity differed from most of the Near Eastern mys-

* For a time there was a patriarch of Jerusalem.

tery religions—especially those emanating from Persia—in its refusal to reject the material world. Matter could not be evil of itself, for it was the handiwork of God; the human body could not be wholly corrupt, for Christ himself was a human in the fullest sense. Christianity was therefore not so radically at odds with Greek humanism as, say, Mithraism—although its concept of sin and its doctrine of the fall of man through the disobedience of Adam were obviously far removed from the traditional humanistic point of view of the Greeks.

The fusion of matter and spirit, so fundamental to orthodox Christianity, did not escape challenge among the early Christians. Once the expectation of an immediate second coming began to fade, many Christians started to examine their faith more philosophically than before and to raise difficult questions about the nature of Christ and the Trinity. A diversity of opinions emerged, some of which seemed so inconsistent with the majority view that they were condemned as heresies. As questions were raised and orthodox solutions agreed on, the Christian faith became increasingly precise and increasingly elaborate. The early heresies sought to simplify the nature of Christ and the Trinity. One group, known as the Gnostics, interpreted Christ in the light of the Persian notion that matter was evil. They insisted that Christ was not really human—only a divine phantom—that a good God could not assume a physical body. Others maintained that Christ was not fully divine—not an equal member of the triune Godhead. The latter position was taken up by the fourth-century Arians, whom we shall meet in the next section. The orthodox position lay midway between these two views: Christ was fully human and fully divine—a coequal member of the Holy Trinity who had always existed and always would, but who was incarnate in human form at a particular moment in time, and who walked the earth, taught, suffered, and died, as the man Jesus. Thus the synthesis of matter and spirit was strictly preserved, and Christ remained the bridge between the two worlds.

The Christian apologists—the defenders of orthodoxy against pagan attacks from with-

Christ as a young Roman.

out and heterodox attacks from within—played a crucial role in formulating and elaborating Christian doctrine, coping with problems that had not even occurred to the apostolic generation. It is of the highest significance that a great many serious Christian thinkers worked within the framework of the Greek philosophical tradition. This is especially true of the greatest of them, the Alexandrian theologian Origen (*d.* 254) who created a coherent, all-inclusive Christian philosophical system on Platonic foundations. Origen was one of the foremost thinkers of his age and is widely regarded as one of the supreme minds in the entire history of the church. His religious system did not win over the pagan intellectual world at a blow—indeed, several of his conclusions were rejected by later Christian orthodoxy—but he and other Christian theologians succeeded in making Christianity meaningful and intellectually attractive to men whose thinking was cast in the Greco-Roman philosophical mold. The greatest of the Greek philosophers, so these Christian writers said, had been led toward truth by the inspiration of the Christian God.

Christianity and the Empire

At the very time that Christian theology was being Hellenized, pagan thought itself was shifting increasingly toward otherworldliness. Origen's greatest pagan contemporary was the Neo-Platonist Plotinus. Indeed, the two had even been schoolmates for a time. One of the deepest and subtlest minds of the age, Plotinus, popularized the doctrine of a single god, infinite and beyond reasoning, unknowable and unapproachable except through an ecstatic trance. Plotinus taught that God was the source of reality and existence. All being, both physical and spiritual, radiated outward from him like concentric ripples in a pool. The Neoplatonists taught that the gods of the pagan cults were all symbols of the one unknowable god and that each pagan cult therefore had validity.

The growth of a transcendental outlook throughout the ancient world created an atmosphere highly nourishing to a salvation religion such as Christianity. The Christian viewpoint was becoming increasingly in tune with the times; it appealed to an age hungry for a profound and consoling doctrine of personal redemption. Yet its triumph was by no means assured, for it faced other salvation religions such as Mithraism and

the Isis cult—and traditional Greco-Roman paganism in its new, otherworldly, Neoplatonic guise. Against these rivals Christianity could offer the immense appeal of the historic Jesus, the every-increasing profundity of its theology, the infinite majesty of its God, and the compassion and universalism of its message preserved and dramatized in its canonical books—the Old and New Testaments. Few social groups were immune to its attraction. The poor, humble, and underprivileged made up the bulk of its early converts, and it was to them that Jesus directed much of his message. Thoughtful men were drawn by its Hellenized theology, men of feeling were captivated by its mysticism, and men of affairs were attracted by the ever-increasing effectiveness of its administrative hierarchy. For in administration no less than in theology the church was learning from the Greco-Roman world.

Before the collapse of the Roman Empire in the West, Christianity had absorbed and turned to its own purposes much of Rome's heritage in political organization and law, carrying on the Roman administrative and legal tradition into the medieval and modern world. Roman civil law was paralleled by the canon law of the church. The secular leadership of the Roman Empire gave way to the spiritual leadership of the Roman pope, who assumed the old republican and imperial title of *pontifex maximus*—supreme pontiff—and preserved much of the imperial ceremonial of the later Empire. As imperial governors and local officials gradually disappeared in the west, their traditions were carried on, in a new spiritual dimension, by metropolitans and bishops. Indeed, the *diocese*, the traditional unit of a bishop's jurisdiction, was originally an imperial administrative district. In this organizational sense, the medieval church has been described as a ghost of the Roman Empire. Yet it was far more than that, for the church reached its people as Rome never had, giving the impoverished masses a sense of participation and involvement that the Empire had failed to provide.

From the beginning the Christians of the Empire were a people apart, convinced that they alone possessed the truth and that the truth would one day triumph, eager to win new converts to their faith, uncompromising in their rejection of all other religions, willing to learn from the pagan world but unwilling ever to submit to it. Their stark seriousness of purpose, their cohesiveness (which doubtless appeared to their enemies as conspiratorial), their sense of destiny, and their refusal to worship the state gods proved exceedingly aggravating to their pagan contemporaries. Consequently, the Christians were often objects of suspicion, hatred, and persecution. The emperors themselves followed a rather inconsistent policy toward them. Violent persecutions, such as those under Nero and Marcus Aurelius, alternated with long periods of inaction. On the whole, the church throve on the blood of its martyrs; the persecutions were neither sufficiently ruthless nor sufficiently lengthy to come near wiping out the entire Christian community.

Most of the emperors, if they persecuted Christians at all, did so reluctantly. The "good emperor" Trajan instructed a provincial governor neither to seek Christians out nor to heed anonymous accusations. (Such a procedure, Trajan observed, is inconsistent with "the spirit of the age.") Only if a man should be denounced as a Christian, tried and found guilty, and then should persist in his refusal to worship the imperial gods, was he to be punished. One can admire the Christian who would face death rather than worship false gods, but one can also sympathize with emperors such as Trajan who hesitated to apply their traditional policy of religious toleration to a people who seemed bent on subverting the Empire.

The persecutions of the first and second centuries, although occasionally severe, tended to be limited in scope to specific local areas. The great empire-wide persecutions of the third and early fourth centuries were products of the crisis that Roman civilization was then undergoing. The greatest imperial persecution—and the last—occurred at the opening of the fourth century under the Emperor Diocletian. By then Christianity was too strong to be destroyed, and the failure of Diocletian's persecution must have made it evident that the Empire had no choice but to accommodate itself to the church. A decade after the outbreak of this last persecution, Constantine, the first Christian emperor, undertook a dramatic reversal of religious pol-

icy. Thereafter the Empire endorsed Christianity rather than fighting it, and by the close of the fourth century the majority of the urban inhabitants of the Empire had been brought into the Christian fold. Rome and Jerusalem had come to terms at last.

THE LATE EMPIRE AND ITS FALL

The Third Century

The turbulent third century—the era of Origen and Plotinus—brought catastrophic changes to the Roman Empire. The age of the "five good emperors" (A.D. 96–180) was followed by a hundred troubled years during which anarchy alternated with military despotism. The army, now fully conscious of its strength, made and unmade emperors. One military group fought against another for control of the imperial title—a man might be a general one day, emperor the next, and dead soon thereafter. No less than 19 emperors reigned during the calamitous half-century between 235 and 285, not to mention innumerable usurpers and pretenders whose plots and machinations contributed to the general chaos. In this 50-year period every emperor save one died violently—either by assassination or in battle. The Silver Age had given way to what one contemporary historian describes as an age "of iron and rust."

A crucial factor in the chaos of the third century was the problem of the imperial succession. All too often, a competent emperor would be followed by an incompetent son. As the power of the army increased and military rebellions became commonplace, the imperial succession came more and more to depend on the whim of the troops. Perhaps the most successful emperor of the period, Septimius Severus (193–211), maintained his power by expanding and pampering the army, opening its highest offices to every class, and broadening its recruitment. A military career was now the logical avenue to high civil office, and the bureaucracy began to display an increasingly military cast of mind. The old ideals of Republic and Principate were less and less meaningful to the new governing class, many of whom rose from the dregs of society through successful army careers to positions of high political responsibility. These new administrators were often men of strength and ability, but they were not the sort who could be expected to cherish the old Roman political traditions. Septimius Severus increased imperial taxes to fatten his treasury and appease his troops. Soldiers prospered at the expense of an increasingly impoverished civilian population as the Empire drifted more and more toward military absolutism. Septimius' dying words to his sons are characteristic of his reign and his times: "Enrich the soldiers and scorn the world."

But Rome's troubles in the third century cannot be ascribed entirely to the problem of imperial succession. As early as the reign of Marcus Aurelius (161–180) the Empire had been struck by a devastating plague that lingered on for a generation and by an ominous irruption of Germanic barbarians who spilled across the Rhine-Danube frontier as far as Italy itself. Marcus Aurelius, the philosopher-emperor, was obliged to spend the greater part of his reign campaigning against the invaders, and it was only at enormous effort that he was able to drive them out of the Empire. During the third century the Germans attacked with renewed fury, penetrating the frontiers time and again, forcing the cities of the Empire to erect protective walls, and threatening for a time to submerge the state under a barbarian flood. And the Germanic onslaught was accompanied by furious attacks from the east by the recently reconstituted Persian Empire led by the able kings of its new Sassanid dynasty (226-651 A.D.).

Rome's crucial problems, however, were internal ones. During the third century, political disintegration was accompanied by social and economic breakdown. The ever-rising fiscal demands of the mushrooming bureaucracy and the insatiable army placed an intolerable burden on the inhabitants of town and country alike. Peasants fled from their fields to escape the much hated tax collector, and the urban middle classes became shrunken and demoralized. The self-governing town, the bedrock of imperial administration and, indeed, of Greco-Roman civilization itself, was beginning to experience serious financial difficulties, and as one

city after another turned to the emperor for financial aid, civic autonomy declined. These problems arose partly from the parasitical nature of many of the Roman cities, partly from rising imperial taxes, and partly from the economic stagnation that was slowly gripping the Empire. Long before the death of Marcus Aurelius, Rome had abandoned its career of conquest in favor of a defensive policy of consolidation. The flow of booty from conquered lands had ceased, and the Empire as a whole was thrown back on its own resources and forced to become economically self-sufficient. For a while all seemed well, but as administrative and military expenses mounted without a corresponding growth in commerce and industry, the imperial economy began to suffer. The army, once a source of riches from conquered lands, was now an unproductive encumbrance.

By the third century, if not before, the Roman economy was shrinking. Plagues, hunger, and a sense of hopelessness resulted in a gradual decline in population. At the very time when imperial expenses and imperial taxes were rising, the tax base was contracting. Prosperity gave way to depression and desperation, and the flight of peasants from their farms was accompanied by the flight of the savagely-taxed middle classes from their cities. The Empire was now clogged with beggars and bandits, and those who remained at their jobs were taxed all the more heavily. It was the western half of the Empire that suffered most. What industry there was had always been centered in the East, and money was gradually flowing eastward to productive centers in Syria and Asia Minor and beyond, to pay for luxury goods, some of which came from outside the Empire altogether—from Persia, India, and China. In short, the Empire as a whole, and the western Empire especially, suffered from an unfavorable balance of trade that resulted in a steady reduction in Rome's supply of precious metals.

The increasingly desperate financial circumstances of the third-century Empire forced the emperors to experiment in the devaluation of coinage—adulterating the precious metals in their coins with baser metals. This policy provided only temporary relief. In the long run, it resulted in runaway inflation that further undermined the economy. Between A.D. 256 and 280 the cost of living rose 1000 percent.

The third-century anarchy reached its climax during the 260s. By then the Roman economy was virtually in ruins. Barbarian armies were rampaging across the frontiers. Gaul and Britain in the west and a large district in the east had broken loose from imperial control and were pursuing independent courses. The population was speedily shrinking, and countless cities were in an advanced state of decay. Rome's demise seemed imminent. As it turned out, however, the Empire was saved by the tremendous efforts of a series of stern leaders who rose to power in the later third century. The Roman state survived in the west for another two centuries and in the east for more than a millennium. But the agonies of the third century left an indelible mark on the reformed Empire. The new imperial structure that brought order out of chaos was profoundly different from the government of the Principate: it was a naked autocracy of the most thorough-going sort.

The Reforms of Diocletian

Even at the height of the anarchy there were emperors who strove desperately to defend the Roman state. After A.D. 268 a series of able, rough-hewn emperor-generals from the Danubian provinces managed to turn the tide, restoring the frontiers, smashing the invading armies of Germanic barbarians and Persians and recovering the alienated provinces in Gaul and the East. At the same time measures were undertaken to arrest the social and economic decay that was debilitating the Empire. These policies were expanded and brought to fruition by Diocletian (284–305) and Constantine (306–337) to whom belongs the credit—and responsibility—for reconstituting the Empire along authoritarian lines. No longer merely a *princeps*, the emperor was now *dominus et deus*— lord and god—and it is appropriate that the new despotic regime that replaced the Principate should be called the "Dominate."

In the days of Augustus it had been necessary, so as not to offend republican sensibilities, to disguise the power of the emperor. In Diocletian's day the imperial title had for so long been dishonored and abused that it was necessary to exalt it. Diocletian and his successors glorified the office in every way imaginable. The emperor became a lofty, remote, unapproachable figure clothed in magnificent garments, a diadem on his head. An elaborate court ceremonial was introduced, somewhat similar to that of Persia, which included the custom of prostration in the emperor's sacred presence.

Diocletian's most immediate task was to bring to a close the turbulent era of short-lived "barracks emperors" and military usurpers. In order to stabilize the succession and share the ever-growing burden of governing the Empire, he decreed that there would thenceforth be two emperors—one in the east, the other in the west—who would work together harmoniously for the welfare and defense of the state. Each of the two would be known by the title *Augustus,* and each would adopt a younger colleague—with the title *Caesar*—to share his rule and ultimately to succeed him. The Empire was now divided into four parts, each supervised by an Augustus or a Caesar. Well aware of the increasing importance of the eastern over the western half of the Empire, Diocletian made his capital in the east and did not set foot in Rome until the close of his reign. A usurper would now, presumably, be faced with the perplexing task of overcoming four widely-scattered personages instead of one. The chances of military usurpation were further reduced by Diocletian's rigorous separation of civil and military authority. The army was considerably enlarged, chiefly by the incorporation of barbarian forces who now assumed much of the burden of guarding the frontiers, but it was organized in such a way that the emperor (or emperors) could control it far more effectively than before.

Imperial control was the keynote of this new, centralized regime. The Senate was now merely ornamental, and the emperor ruled through his obedient and ever-expanding bureaucracy—issuing edict after edict to regulate, systematize, and regiment the state. The shortage of money was circumvented by a new land tax to be collected in kind (that is, goods), and the widespread flight from productive labor was reduced by new laws freezing peasants, craftsmen, and businessmen to their jobs. A system of hereditary social orders quickly developed; sons were required by law to take up the careers and tax burdens of their fathers. Peasants were bound to the land, city dwellers to their urban professions. Workers in the mines and quarries were literally branded. The system was more theoretical than real, for these measures were difficult to enforce, and a degree on social mobility remained. Nevertheless, the Dominate was a relatively regimented society. Economic collapse was temporarily averted, but at the cost of social petrification and loss of hope. The once-autonomous cities now lay under the iron hand of the imperial government, and commitment to the Empire was rapidly waning among the tax-ridden middle classes who had formerly been among its most enthusiastic supporters. To many citizens the cure must have seemed worse than the disease.

But it was Diocletian's mission to save the Empire whatever the cost, and it may well be that authoritarian measures were the only ones possible under the circumstances. For every problem Diocletian offered a solution—often autocratic and heavy-handed, but a solution nevertheless. A thoroughgoing currency reform had retarded inflation but had not stopped it altogether, so Diocletian issued an edict fixing the prices of most commodities by law. To the growing challenge of Christianity, Diocletian responded, regretfully, by inaugurating a persecution of unprecedented severity. As it turned out, neither the imperial price controls nor the imperial persecution achieved their purposes, but the very fact that they were attempted illustrates the lengths to which the Emperor would go in his effort to preserve by force the unity and stability of the state.

The division of the empire among the two Augustuses and the two adopted Caesars worked satisfactorily only so long as Diocletian himself was in power. Once his hand was removed, a struggle for power brought renewed civil strife. The principle of adoption, which the sonless Diocletian had revived without serious difficulty, was challenged by the sons of his successors. The era of chaos ran from the end of Diocletian's reign in 305 to the victory of Constantine over the last of his rivals in 312 at the battle of the Milvian Bridge near Rome.

The Reign of Constantine (A.D. 306–337)

Constantine's triumph at the Milvian Bridge marked the return of political stability and the consummation of Diocletian's economic and political reforms. Diocletian's policy of freezing occupations and making them hereditary was tightened by Constantine in an edict of A.D. 332. Imperial ceremonial was further elaborated, and authoritarianism grew. In certain respects, however, Constantine's policies took radical new directions. In place of the abortive principle of adoption, Constantine founded an imperial dynasty of his own. For a time he shared his authority with an imperial colleague (his brother-in-law), but in 324 he conquered him and thereafter ruled alone. Nevertheless, the joint rule of an eastern and a western emperor became common in the years after Constantine's death, and he himself contributed to the division of the Empire by building the magnificent eastern capital of Constantinople on the site of the ancient Greek colony of Byzantium.

Constantinople was a second Rome. It had its own senate, its own imposing temples, palaces, and public buildings, and its own hungry proletariat fed by the bread dole and diverted by chariot races in its enormous Hippodrome. A few decades after its foundation it even acquired its own Christian patriarch. Constantine plundered the Greco-Roman world of its artistic treasures to adorn his new city and lavished his vast resources on its construction. Founded in A.D. 330, Constantinople was to remain the capital of the Eastern Empire for well over a thousand years, impregnable behind its great walls, protected on three sides by the sea, perpetually renewing itself through its control of the rich commerce flowing between the Black Sea and the Mediterranean. The age-long survival of the Eastern Empire owes much to the superb strategic location of its capital, which dominated the straits between these two seas.

Even more momentous than the building

of Constantinople was Constantine's conversion to Christianity and his reversal of imperial policy toward the church. Although he put off baptism until his dying moments Constantine had been committed to Christianity ever since his triumph in 312. From that time onward he issued a continuous series of pro-Christian edicts insuring full toleration, legalizing bequests to the church (which accumulated prodigiously over the subsequent centuries), and granting a variety of other privileges. Christianity was now an official religion of the Empire. It was not yet *the* official religion, but it would become so before the fourth century was ended.

Several explanations have been offered for Constantine's conversion. He has been portrayed as an irreligious political schemer bent on harnessing the vitality of the church to the failing state. But there seems no reason to doubt that, in fact, his conversion was sincere if somewhat superficial. Strictly speaking, there were no irreligious men in the fourth century.

The Christian Empire

The respite gained by Diocletian's reforms and the subsequent conversion of Constantine made it possible for the church to develop rapidly under the benevolent protection of the Empire. The years between Constantine's victory at the Milvian Bridge in 312 and the final suppression of the Western Empire in 476 were momentous ones in the evolution of Christianity. For one thing, the fourth century witnessed mass conversions to the Christian fold. Perhaps 10 percent of the inhabitants of the Western Empire were Christians in 312 (in the east the figure would be considerably higher) whereas by the century's end the now respectable Christians were in the majority. But, as is so often the case, triumph evoked internal dissension, and the fourth century witnessed a violent struggle between orthodoxy and heresy. Here, too, the Christian emperors played a determining role, and it was with strong imperial support that the greatest of the fourth-century heresies, Arianism, was at length suppressed within the Empire.

The Arians maintained that the purity of Christian monotheism was compromised by the orthodox doctrine of the Trinity. Their

The Emperor Constantine, a fragment of the colossal statue.

solution to this conflict was the doctrine that God the Father was the only true god—that Christ the Son was not fully divine. The orthodox Trinitarians regarded this doctrine as subversive to one of their most fundamental beliefs: the equality and codivinity of Father, Son, and Holy Spirit. Constantine sought to heal the Arian-Trinitarian dispute by summoning an ecumenical (universal) council of Christian bishops at Nicaea in A.D. 325. He had no strong convictions himself, but the advocates of the Trinitarian position managed to win his support. With imperial backing, a strongly anti-Arian creed was adopted almost unanimously. The three divine Persons of the Trinity were declared equal: Jesus Christ was "of one substance with the Father."

But Constantine was no theologian. In after years he vacillated, sometimes favoring Arians, sometimes condemning them, and the same ambiguity characterized imperial policy throughout the greater part of the fourth century. Indeed, one of Constantine's fourth-century successors, Julian "the Apostate" reverted to paganism. At length, however, the uncompromisingly orthodox Theodosius I came to the throne (378–395) and broke the power of the Arians by condemning and proscribing them. It was under Theodosius and his successors that Christianity became the one legal religion of the Empire. Paganism itself was now banned and persecuted and quickly disappeared as an organized force.

Orthodox Christianity now dominated the Empire, but its triumph, won with the aid of political force, was far from complete. For one thing, the mass conversions of the fourth century tended to be superficial—even nominal. Conversion to Christianity was the path of least resistance, and the new converts were on the whole a far cry from the earlier society of saints and martyrs. It was at this time that many ardent Christians, discontented with mere membership in a respectable, work-a-day church, began taking to the desert as hermits or flocking into monastic communities.

Moreover, the imperial program of enforced orthodoxy proved difficult to carry out. Old heresies lingered on and vigorous new ones arose in the fifth century and thereafter. Even Arianism survived, not among the citizens of the Empire, but among the Germanic barbarians. For during the mid-fourth century, at a time when Arianism was still strong in the Empire, large numbers of barbarians had been converted to Christianity in its Arian form, and the Trinitarian policies of Theodosius I had no effect on them whatever. Accordingly, when the barbarians ultimately formed their kingdoms on the ruins of the Western Empire, most of them were separated from their Old-Roman subjects not only by language and custom but by a deep religious chasm as well.

Finally, by accepting imperial support against paganism and heresy, the church sacrificed much of its earlier independence. The Christians of Constantine's day were so overwhelmed by the emperor's conversion that they tended to glorify him excessively. As a Christian, Constantine could no longer claim divinity, but contemporary Christian writers such as the historian Eusebius allowed him a status that was almost quasi-divine. To Eusebius and his contemporaries, Constantine was the thirteenth apostle; his office was commissioned by God; he was above the church. His commanding position in ecclesiastical affairs is illustrated by his domination of the Council of Nicaea, and the ups and downs of Arianism in the following decades depended largely on the whims of his successors. In the east, this glorification of the imperial office ripened into the doctrine known as *caesaropapism*—that the emperor is the real master of both church and state, that he is both caesar and pope—and caesaropapism remained a dominant theme in the Eastern or Byzantine Empire throughout its long history. Church and state tended to merge under the sacred authority of the emperor. Indeed, the Christianization and sanctification of the imperial office were potent forces in winning for the eastern emperors the allegiance and commitment of the masses of their Christian subjects. Religious loyalty to the Christian emperor provided indispensable nourishment to the East Roman state over the ensuing centuries. Conversely, widespread hostility toward imperial orthodoxy in districts dominated by heretical groups resulted in the alienation and eventual loss to the Byzantine Empire of several of its fairest provinces.

Caesaropapism was far less influential in the west, for as the fifth century dawned the Western Empire was visibly failing. Western churchmen were beginning to realize that Christian civilization was not irrevocably bound to the fortunes of Rome. Gradually the Western church began to assert its independence of state control—with the result that church and state in medieval Western Europe were never fused and were often at odds with one another.

The Doctors of the Latin Church

During the later fourth and early fifth centuries, at a time when the Christianization of the Roman state was far advanced but before the Western Empire had lost all its vitality, the long-developing synthesis of Judeo-Christian and Greco-Roman culture reached its climax in the west with the work of three gifted scholar-saints: Ambrose, Jerome, and Augustine. These men are justly regarded as "Doctors of the Latin Church," for their writings dominated medieval thought. Each of the three was thoroughly trained in the Greco-Roman intellectual tradition; each devoted his learning and his life to the service of Christianity; each was at once a philosopher and a man of affairs.

Ambrose (c. 340–397) was bishop of Milan, which by the later fourth century had replaced Rome as the western imperial capital. He was famed for his eloquence and administrative skill, for his vigor in defending Trinitarian orthodoxy against Arianism, and for the ease and mastery with which he adapted the literary traditions of Cicero and Virgil and the philosophy of Plato to his own Christian purposes. Above all, he was the first churchman to assert that in the realm of morality the emperor himself is accountable to the Christian priesthood. When the powerful Emperor Theodosius I massacred the inhabitants of rebellious Thessalonica, Ambrose barred him from the Church of Milan until he had formally and publicly repented. Ambrose's bold stand and Theodosius' submission constituted a stunning setback for the principle of caesaropapism and a prelude to the long struggle between church and state in the Christian west.

Jerome (c. 340–420) was a masterly scholar and a restless, inquisitive reformer with a touch of acid in his personality. He once remarked to an opponent, "You have the will to lie, good sir, but not the skill to lie." Wandering far and wide through the Empire, he founded a monastery in Bethlehem where he set his monks to work copying manuscripts, thereby instituting a custom that throughout the middle ages preserved the tradition of Latin letters and transmitted it to the modern world. Like other Christian thinkers he feared that his love of pagan literature might dilute his Christian fervor, and he tells of a dream in which Jesus banished him from heaven with the words, "Thou art a Ciceronian, not a Christian." But in the end

he managed to reconcile pagan culture and Christian faith by using the former only in the service of the latter. His greatest contribution to Christian thought was in the field of biblical translation and commentary — above all, in his scholarly translation of the Scriptures from Hebrew and Greek into Latin. Jerome's Latin Vulgate Bible has been used ever since by Roman Catholics and has served as the basis of innumerable translations into modern languages. (English-speaking Catholics use the Douay translation of Jerome's Vulgate). It was an achievement of incalculable significance.

The most profound of the Latin Doctors was Augustine (354–430) who spent his final 40 years as bishop of the North African city of Hippo. Like Jerome, Augustine worried about the dangers of pagan culture to the Christian soul, finally concluding, much as Jerome did, that Greco-Roman learning, although not to be enjoyed for its own sake, might properly be used to elucidate the Faith. Augustine was the chief architect of medieval theology. Even more than his contemporaries he succeeded in fusing Christian doctrine with Greek thought — especially the philosophy of Plato and the Neoplatonists. It has been said that Augustine baptized Plato. As a Platonist he stressed the importance of ideas or archetypes over tangible things, but instead of locating his archetypes in the abstract Platonic "heaven" he placed them in the mind of God. The human mind had access to the archetypes through an act of God which Augustine called "divine illumination."

As a bishop, Augustine was occupied with the day-to-day cares of his diocese and his flock. His contribution to religious thought arises not from the dispassionate working-out of an abstract system of theology but rather from his responses to the burning issues of the moment. His thought is a fascinating mixture of profundity and immediacy — of the abstract and the human. His *Confessions*, the first psychologically sensitive autobiography ever written, tells of his own spiritual journey through various pagan and heretical cults to Christian orthodoxy. Implicit in this book is the hope that others as misguided as he once was might also be led by God's grace to the truth in Christ.

Against the several heretical doctrines that threatened Christian orthodoxy in his day Augustine wrote clearly and persuasively on the nature of the Trinity, the problem of evil in a world created by God, the special character of the Christian priesthood, and the nature of free will and predestination. His most influential work, the *City of God,* was prompted by a barbarian sack of Rome in A.D. 410, which the pagans ascribed to Rome's desertion of her old gods. Augustine responded by developing a Christian theory of history which interpreted human development not in political or economic terms but in moral terms. As the first Christian philosopher of history, Augustine drew heavily on the historical insights of the ancient Hebrews. Like the Hebrew prophets of old, he asserted that kingdoms and empires rose and fell according to a divine plan, but he insisted that this plan lay forever beyond human comprehension. Augustine rejected the theory, common in antiquity, that history was an endless series of cycles, arguing on the contrary that history was moving toward a divinely appointed goal. This linear view of history set something of a precedent for the modern secular concept of historical progress. Augustine also rejected the Hebrew notion of tribal salvation, putting in its place the Christian notion of *individual* salvation. The ultimate units of history were not tribes and empires but individual immortal souls.

The salvation of souls, Augustine stated, depends not on the fortunes of Rome but on the grace of God. Christ is not dependent on Caesar. And if we look at history from the moral standpoint—from the standpoint of souls—we see not the clash of armies or the rivalry of states but a far more fundamental struggle between good and evil which has raged through history and which rages even now within each soul. Humanity is divided into two classes: those who live in God's grace and those who do not. The former belong to what Augustine called the "City of God," the latter to the "City of Evil." The members of the two cities are hopelessly intermixed in this world, but they will be separated at death by eternal salvation or damnation. It is from this transcendental standpoint, Augustine believed, that the Christian must view history. Only God could know what effect Rome's decline would have on the City of God. Perhaps the effect would be beneficial, perhaps even irrelevant.

Augustine is one of the two or three seminal minds in Christian history. His Christian Platonism governed medieval theology down into the twelfth century and remains influential in Christian thought today. His emphasis on the special sacramental power inherent in the priestly office remains a keystone of Catholic theology. His emphasis on divine grace and predestination, although softened considerably by the medieval church, reemerged in the sixteenth century to dominate early Protestant doctrine. And his theory of the two cities, although often in simplified form, had an enormous influence on Western historical and political thought over the next millennium.

Ambrose, Jerome, and Augustine were at once synthesizers and innovators. The last great minds of the Western Empire, they operated at a level of intellectual sophistication that the Christian West would not reach again for 700 years. The strength of the classical tradition that underlies medieval Christianity and Western civilization owes much to the fact that these men, and others like them, found it possible to be both Christians and Ciceronians.

"DECLINE AND FALL"

The catastrophe of Rome's decline and fall has always fascinated historians, for it involves not only the collapse of mankind's most impressive and enduring universal state but also the demise of Greco-Roman civilization itself. The reasons are far too complex to be explained satisfactorily by any single cause: Christianity, disease, slavery, soil-exhaustion, or any of the other "masterkeys" that have been proposed from time to time. One must always bear in mind that the Roman Empire "fell" only in the west. It endured in the east, although there, too, Greco-Roman civilization was significantly changed. The civilization of the Eastern Empire during the medieval centuries is normally described not as "Roman" or even "Greco-Roman" but as "Byzantine," and the change in name betokens a profound alteration in mood. In other words, Greco-Roman culture was gradually transformed in both east and west, but its transformation in the west was accompanied by the dismemberment of the Roman state whereas its transformation in the east occurred despite an underlying political continuity in which emperor followed emperor in more-or-less unbroken succession.

In the west, then, we are faced with two separate phenomena—political breakdown and cultural transformation. The political collapse culminated in the deposition of the last western emperor in A.D. 476, but the true period of crisis was the chaotic third century. The recovery under Diocletian and Constantine was only partial and temporary: the impending death of the body politic was delayed, but the disease remained uncured. The impoverished masses in town and countryside had never participated meaningfully in Roman civilization, and the third-century anarchy resulted in the spiritual disengagement of the middle classes as well. Initiative and commitment ebbed in the atmosphere of economic and political upheaval and were stifled by the autocracy that followed. Fourth-century Rome was an authoritarian, highly centralized state that robbed its subjects of their independence and watched over them through a vast network of informers and secret agents. The collapse of such a state cannot be regarded as an unmitigated disaster; to many it must have seemed a blessing.

The west had always been poorer and less urbanized than the east, and its economy, badly shaken by the political chaos of the third century, began to break down under the growing burden of imperial government and the defense of hard-pressed frontiers. Perhaps the fatal flaw in the western economy was its inability to compensate for the cessation of imperial expansion by more intensive internal development. There was no large-scale industry, no mass production; the majority of the population was far too poor to provide a mass market. Industrial production was inefficient, and technology progressed at a snail's pace. The economy remained fundamentally agrarian, and farming techniques advanced little during the centuries of the Empire. The Roman plow was rudimentary and inefficient; windmills were unknown and water mills exceptional. The horse could not be used as a draught animal because the Roman harness crossed the horse's windpipe and tended to strangle him under a heavy load. Consequently, Roman agriculture was based on the less efficient oxen and on the muscles of slaves and *coloni*.

Economic exhaustion brought with it the twin evils of population decline and growing poverty. At the same time that the manpower shortage was becoming acute and impoverishment was paralyzing the middle classes the army and bureaucracy were expanding to unprecedented size and the expenses of government were soaring. One result of these processes was the deurbanization of the west. By the fifth century the once vigorous cities were becoming ghosts of their former selves, drained of their wealth and much of their population. Only the small class of great landowners managed to prosper in the economic atmosphere of the late Western Empire, and these men now abandoned their town houses, withdrew from civic affairs, and retired to their estates where they often assembled sizable private armies and defied the tax collector. The aristocracy, having now fled the city, would remain an agrarian class for the next thousand years. The rural nobility of the middle ages had come into being.

The decline of the city was fatal to the urbanized administrative structure of the Western Empire. More than that, it brought an end to the urban-oriented culture of Greco-Roman antiquity. The civilization of Athens, Alexandria, and Rome could not survive in the fields. It is in the decay of urban society that we find the crucial connecting link between political collapse and cultural transformation. In a very real sense Greco-Roman culture was dead long before the final demise of the Western Empire, and the deposition of the last emperor in 476 was merely the faint postscript to a process that had been completed long before. By then the cities were moribund; the rational, humanist outlook had given way completely to transcendentalism and mysticism; the army and even the civil government had become barbarized as the desperate emperors, faced with a growing shortage of manpower and resources, turned more and more to Germanic peoples to defend their frontiers and preserve order in their state. In the end, barbarians abounded in the army, entire tribes were hired to defend the frontiers, and Germanic military leaders came to hold positions of high authority in the Western Empire. Survival had come to depend on the success of half-hearted Germanic defenders against plunder-hungry Germanic invaders.

Despite the deurbanization, the mysticism, and the barbarism of the late Empire, it is nevertheless true that in a certain sense the Greco-Roman tradition never died in the west. It exerted a profound influence, as we have seen, on the Doctors of the Latin Church and, through them, on the mind of the middle ages. It was the basis of repeated cultural revivals, great and small, down through the centuries. And if in one sense the Roman state was dead long before the line of western emperors ended in 476, in another sense it survived long thereafter — in the ecclesiastical organization of the Roman Catholic Church and in the medieval Holy Roman Empire. Roman law endured to inspire Western jurisprudence; the Latin tongue remained the language of educated Europeans for more than a millennium while evolving in the lower levels of society into the Romance languages: Italian, French, Spanish, Portugese, and Rumanian. In countless forms the rich legacy of classical antiquity was passed on.

The Barbarian Invasions

The Germanic peoples had long been a threat to the Empire. They had defeated a Roman army in the reign of Augustus; they had probed deeply into the Empire under Marcus Aurelius and again in the mid-third century. But until the later fourth century the Romans had always managed eventually to drive the invaders out or settle them under Roman rule. Beginning in the mid-370s, however, an exhausted Empire was confronted by renewed barbarian pressures of an unprecedented magnitude. Lured by the relative wealth, the good soil, and the sunny climate of the Mediterranean world, the barbarians tended to regard the Empire not as something to destroy but as something to enjoy. Their age-long yearning for the fair lands across the Roman frontier was sud-denly transformed into an urgent need by the westward thrust of a tribe of Asian nomads known as the Huns. These fierce horsemen conquered one Germanic tribe after another and turned them into satellites. The Ostrogoths fell before their might and became a subject people. The other great Gothic tribe, the Visigoths, sought to avoid a similar fate by appealing for sanctuary behind the Roman Danube frontier. The Eastern Emperor Valens, a fervent Arian, sympathized with the Arian Visigoths, and in 376 they all crossed peacefully into the Empire.

There was trouble almost immediately. Corrupt imperial officials cheated and abused the Visigoths, and the hot-tempered tribesmen retaliated by going on a rampage. At length Emperor Valens himself took the field against them, but the Emperor's military incapacity cost him his army and his life at the battle of Adrianople in 378. Adrianople was a military debacle of the first order. Valens' successor, the able Theodosius I, managed to pacify the Visigoths but he could not expel them. When Theodosius died in 395 the Roman Empire was split between his two incompetent sons, and, as it happened, the eastern and western halves were never again rejoined. A vigorous new Visigothic leader named Alaric now led his people on a second campaign of pillage and destruction that threatened Italy itself. In 406 the desperate Western Empire recalled most of its troops from the Rhine frontier to block Alaric's advance, with the disastrous consequence that the Vandals and a number of other tribes swept across the unguarded Rhine into Gaul. Shortly thereafter the Roman legions abandoned distant Britain and the defenseless island was gradually overrun by Angles, Saxons, and Jutes. In 408 the only able general in the west was executed by the frantic, incompetent Emperor Honorius who then took refuge behind the marshes of Ravenna. The Visigoths entered Rome unopposed in 410 and Alaric permitted them to plunder the city for three days.

The sack of Rome had a devastating impact on imperial morale, but in historical perspective it appears as a mere incident in the disintegration of the Western Empire. The Visigoths soon left the city to its feeble emperor and turned northward into southern Gaul and Spain where they established a kingdom that endured until the Muslim conquests of the eighth century. Meanwhile other tribes were carving out kingdoms of their own. The Vandals swept through Gaul and Spain and across the Straits of Gibraltar into Africa. In 430, the very year of St. Augustine's death, they took his city of Hippo. A new Vandal kingdom arose in North Africa, centering on ancient Carthage. Almost immediately the Vandals began taking to the sea as buccaneers, devastating Mediterranean shipping and sacking one coastal city after another. Vandal piracy shattered the age-long peace of the Mediterranean and dealt a crippling blow to the waning commerce of the Western Empire.

Midway through the fifth century the Huns themselves moved against the west, led by their pitiless leader Attila, the "Scourge of God." Defeated by a Roman-Visigothic army in Gaul in 451, they returned the following year, hurling themselves toward Rome and leaving a path of devastation behind them. The western emperor abandoned Rome to Attila's mercies, but the Roman bishop, Pope Leo I, traveled northward from the city to negotiate with the Huns on the wild chance that they might be persuaded to turn back. Oddly enough, Pope Leo succeeded in his mission. Perhaps because the health of the Hunnish army was adversely affected by the Italian climate, perhaps because the majestic Pope Leo was able to overawe the superstitious Attila, the Huns retired from Italy. Shortly afterward Attila died, the Hunnish empire collapsed, and the Huns themselves vanished from history. They were not mourned.

In its final years the Western Empire, whose jurisdiction now scarcely extended beyond Italy, fell under the control of hardbitten military adventurers of Germanic birth. The emperors continued to reign for a time but their Germanic generals were the powers behind the throne. In 476 the barbarian general Odovacar, who saw no point in perpetuating the farce, deposed the last emperor, sent the imperial trappings to Constantinople, and asserted his sovereignty over Italy by confiscating a good deal of farmland for the use of his Germanic troops. Odovacar

claimed to rule as an agent of the Eastern Empire but, in fact, he was on his own. A few years later the Ostrogoths, now free of Hunnish control and led by a skillful king named Theodoric, advanced into Italy, conquered Odovacar, and established a strong state of their own.

Theodoric ruled Italy from 493 to 526. More than any other barbarian king he appreciated and respected Roman culture, and in his kingdom the Arian Ostrogoths and the Orthodox Romans lived and worked together in relative harmony, repairing aqueducts, erecting impressive new buildings, and bringing a degree of prosperity to the long-troubled peninsula. The improved political and economic climate gave rise to a minor intellectual revival that contributed to the transmission of Greco-Roman culture into the middle ages. The philosopher Boethius, a high official in Theodoric's regime, produced philosophical works and translations which served as fundamental texts in western schools for the next 500 years. His *Consolation of Philosophy*, an interesting mixture of Platonism and Stoicism, was immensely popular throughout the middle ages. Theodoric's own secretary, Cassiodorus, was another scholar of considerable distinction. Cassiodorus spent his later years as abbot of a monastery and set his monks to the invaluable task of copying and preserving the great literary works of antiquity, both Christian and pagan.

During the years of Theodoric's beneficent rule in Ostrogothic Italy, another famous barbarian king, Clovis (481–511), was creating a Frankish kingdom in Gaul. Clovis was far less Romanized, far less enlightened, far crueler than Theodoric, but his kingdom proved to be the most enduring of all the barbarian successor states. The Franks were good farmers as well as good soldiers and they established deep roots in the soil of Gaul. Moreover, the Frankish regime was buttressed by the enthusiastic support of the Roman Catholic church. For Clovis, who had been untouched by Arianism, was converted directly from heathenism to Catholic Christianity. He remained a brutal barbarian to the end, yet the church came to regard him as another Constantine—a defender of orthodoxy in a sea of Arianism. As the centuries went by, the royal name "Clovis" was softened to "Louis" and the "Franks" became the "French." And the friendship between the Frankish monarchy and the church developed into one of the great determining elements in European politics.

Papal Rome

At the very time that the Germanic kingdoms were establishing themselves in the west the Roman papacy was beginning to play an important, independent role in European society. We have seen how the great mid-fifth century pope, Leo I (440–461), assumed the task of protecting the city of Rome from the Huns, winning for himself the moral leadership of the west. Leo and his successors declared that the papacy was the highest authority in the church and, following the example of St. Ambrose, they insisted on the supremacy of church over state in spiritual matters. In proclaiming its doctrines of papal supremacy in the church and ecclesiastical independence from state control, the papacy was hurling a direct challenge at Byzantine caesaropapism. In the fifth century these papal doctrines remained little more than words, but they were to result in an ever-widening gulf between the Eastern and Western church. More than that, they constituted the opening phase of the prolonged medieval struggle between the rival claims of church and state. The mighty papacy of the high middle ages was yet many centuries away, but it was already foreshadowed in the bold independence of Leo I. The Western Empire was dead, but eternal Rome still claimed the allegiance of the Mediterranean world.

This chapter has covered the thousand years of Roman history, from the foundation of the Republic in central Italy to the collapse of the Empire in the west. The Romans were among the most successful conquerors and administrators in the world. Their system of law allowed them to deal justly with ethnic groups as diverse as Egyptians and Britons; their concept of citizenship eventually included 50 million people in the Mediterranean world, Western Europe, and the Near East. Caesar, Cicero, and Augustus remained political models into modern times, and the Roman Catholic Church preserved Roman administrative know-how and the Latin language. The Empire continued in the east for another thousand years, but Greco-Roman (Classical) civilization was already being transformed by alien forces in the fourth and fifth centuries. The most important of these forces was not the Germanic barbarians nor the peoples of the Near East but Christianity itself. Despite its Hellenistic intellectual overtones and Roman political organization, Christianity was essentially a spiritual phenomenon; though nominally Romans, men like St. Paul and St. Augustine were worlds apart from Aristotle and Cicero.

SUGGESTED READINGS

Grant, Michael, *The World of Rome*. New York: Mentor, 1960. Paperback.

Lewis, N. and M. Reinhold, *Roman Civilization*. 2 vols. New York: Harper, 1955. Paperback.

Rostovtzeff, M., *Rome*. New York: Oxford Galaxy, 1928. Paperback.
   A scholarly masterpiece that stresses social history and perhaps overestimates class antagonisms.

Africa, T. W., *Rome of the Caesars*. New York: Wiley, 1965. Paperback.

Mattingly, H., *Roman Imperial Civilization*. Garden City: Anchor, 1923. Paperback.
   A perceptive and significant study.

Mommsen, Theodor, *The History of Rome*. New York: Meridian, 1963. Paperback.
   The great classical account of the Roman Republic, written originally in the 1850s, and drastically abridged in this new edition by D. A. Saunders and J. H. Collins.

Scullard, H. H., *From the Gracchi to Nero*. New York: Praeger, 1959. Paperback.

Sume, Ronald, *The Roman Revolution*. Fair Lawn: Oxford, 1959. Paperback.
This stimulating study stresses the political significance of the great families of the late Republic.

Bultmann, R., *Primitive Christianity in its Contemporary Setting*. New York: Meridian, 1956. Paperback.
Readable and authoritative.

Cochrane, C. N., *Christianity and Classical Culture*. Fair Lawn: Oxford, 1944. Paperback.
An interpretive tour de force, sympathetic to the rise of the mystical viewpoint.

Cumont, F., *Oriental Religions in Roman Paganism*. New York: Dover, 1956. Paperback.
Outdated in details but still useful.

Gough, Michael, *The Early Christians*. New York: Praeger, 1961.
A good popular account with fine illustrations.

Latourette, K. S., *A History of Christianity*. New York: Harper, 1953.
One of the best short histories of the Christian Church.

Taylor, H. O., *The Emergence of Christian Culture in the West*. New York: Harper, 1958. Paperback.
An ageless study by one of the masters of medieval intellectual history.

Bury, J. B., *History of the Later Roman Empire*. 2 Vols. New York: Dover, 1928. Paperback.
The standard account, full and authoritative, by one of the distinguished historians of this century.

Davenport, B., ed., *The Portable Roman Reader*. New York: Viking, 1951. Paperback.
One of several good anthologies now available in paperback.

Dill, Samuel, *Roman Society in the Last Century of the Western Empire*. New York: Meridian, 1899. Paperback.
A brilliant older work.

Gibbon, Edward, *The Triumph of Christendom in the Roman Empire*. New York: Harper, 1932. Paperback.
Chapters XV to XX from Gibbon's masterpiece, The Decline and Fall of the Roman Empire. *The entire work is available in a three-volume Modern Library edition.*

Gregory of Tours, *History of the Franks,* trans. by E. Brehaut. New York: Norton, 1969. Paperback.

Jones, A. H. M., *The Later Roman Empire*. 3 vols. Oxford: Blackwell's, 1964.
An extremely important recent work that will probably become a classic in the field.

Lot, F., *The End of the Ancient World and the Beginnings of the Middle Ages*. New York: Harper, 1931. Paperback.
A masterly study which places stress on the economic factors in the decline. A valuable introduction by Glanville Downey summarizes recent scholarship on the problem of "decline and fall."

PART II

The Civilizations of Europe and Asia to A.D. 1500

Between A.D. 500 and 1500—give or take a hundred years depending on the area in question—a number of traditional civilizations reached their peak and then began to decline. Despite long periods of domination by Mongols, China changed little after the T'ang and Sung eras. The Muslim conquest of India changed the religious complexion in the north, but Hindu culture and society remained predominant in much of that subcontinent. By the end of this period Muslim conquerors had extended their religion and political rule from Morocco on the Atlantic to Indonesia in the southwest Pacific; in much of the Middle East they had imposed the Arabic language as well on the local peoples. In the Balkans and Asia Minor, Byzantine civilization coincided almost exactly with the thousand years covered in this section; so did the medieval phase of Western civilization. In the Americas, as we have already seen, Maya civilization was flourishing before A.D. 800; the early 1500s marked the ruthless destruction of the civilizations of Mexico and Peru by a handful of Spanish conquistadors, although Indian folk culture persisted in many places. Other civilizations existed at various times during this millennium in Ethiopia, Cambodia, Indonesia, Tibet, and West Africa, and during the same period traditional Japanese civilization took shape.

In the earlier part of this period religion still had an overriding importance in giving a sense of meaning and purpose to the lives of the peoples in all these civilizations. In many of them religion was the guiding force in artistic culture and philosophy; it also gave sanction to the political order and, especially in India, to the social and economic structures. Buddhism, Hinduism, and most other major religions of India and East Asia were pacifistic and oriented toward the individual, but elsewhere religion often served as both a motive and a justification for imperialist wars. This was particularly so for Islam but also for Christianity. Peasant religion operated on a more concrete and practical level than the religion of the elite. In popular Buddhism, for example, The Way was shown to peasants in verses, tales, and sayings associated with the life of the Buddha. Buddhist ethical ideas were also expressed in ritual formulas recited daily before a household altar, a pagoda, or an image of the Buddha. Yet the peasants honored the monks and gave them gifts because they were closer to the sacred teachings. These differences also prevailed among all Christians. But, in times of crisis, when communication between priests or monks and peasants grew weak, peasants sometimes adopted a new, simplified faith in reaction to the overelaborate official version. One example was the popular Taoist reaction to Buddhism and Confucianism in

China; others were the various millenarian and heretical sects in medieval Europe and purifying movements in Islam.

For the future, the civilization that was developing in Western Europe was the most important, even though no non-European living between 500 and 1500 could have foreseen this. More than anyone except the Arab Muslims the Europeans borrowed from other peoples' cultures—Muslim Spain, the Byzantine Empire and, in the late middle ages, even China. They were also exceptional in the extent to which they cleared and colonized new lands, particularly in Northern and Central Europe. (Most of the lands taken by the Muslims were more advanced than their conquerors.) Medieval European civilization reached its height in the thirteenth century and then, like many others, went into a decline. Yet, as we shall see in Part III, there was much continuity between medieval and modern times. Despite the dead weight of tradition, which was as heavy in medieval Europe as anywhere else, and much of which endured well into modern times, Europeans were to show greater resourcefulness than other peoples in adapting their traditions to new needs and in inventing new ways of doing things. Already in the late thirteenth century a few Europeans were preparing the way for modern capitalism and modern science. By the last half of the fifteenth century they were beginning to see the possibilities of printing and gunpowder, Chinese inventions that were to make the Europeans more powerful than any other people in history. Still, in 1500 European civilization was less refined than that of China and was to remain so for at least another two centuries.

CHAPTER 6

The Middle East and Europe
to c. A.D. 1000

MEDIEVAL WESTERN EURASIA: A GENERAL VIEW

In A.D. 500 the western portion of the Eurasian land mass contained two great civilized powers: the Eastern Roman or "Byzantine" Empire centered on Constantinople and, to its east, the Persian Empire under the rule of the Sassanid dynasty. During the centuries that followed, two other civilizations arose —Western Christendom and Islam. In the seventh century Islam conquered and absorbed Sassanid Persia, and the Eastern Roman Empire had to fight for its life against this explosive new threat from the Arabian Desert. But the Eastern Roman Empire stood its ground against the full force of youthful, militant Islam. Important Byzantine provinces were lost permanently to the Arabs, but Byzantium survived as an empire and a civilization for another 800 years. And as Islam and Byzantium struggled with one another, the civilization of Western Christendom was gradually, painfully arising among the former western provinces of the Roman Empire. In

800 the Frankish monarch Charlemagne was crowned Roman Emperor in the West, thereby endowing this new civilization with the dignity and prestige of the ancient imperium. By 800 the three great civilizations of medieval Western Eurasia—Islam, Byzantium, and Western Christendom—were firmly rooted. For the remainder of the middle ages these three would continue to dominate Europe and the Middle East.

It was not until the eleventh century, however, that Western Christendom began to achieve sufficient political stability, economic well-being, and creative power to rival Byzantium and Islam. During the 550 years covered by this chapter, from A.D. 500 to about 1050, Western Christendom was an underdeveloped society struggling for its survival against invaders—and against its own poverty and ignorance. It was in no sense comparable to the civilizations of the Byzantines and Arabs. It commands our attention less for its military, political, intellectual, and artistic achievements than for its success in creating the beginnings of certain institutions and habits of mind that contributed to the

181

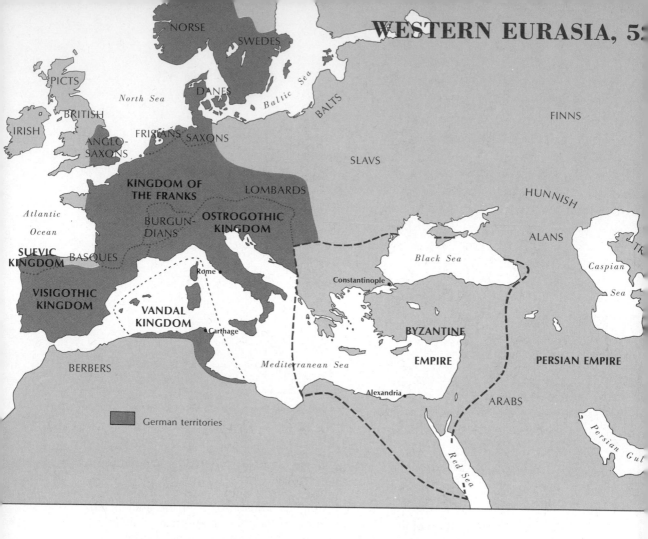

German territories

rise of a great civilization in twelfth- and thirteenth-century Western Europe—a civilization that, later on, extended its power, techniques, styles, and ideologies across the globe.

The peoples of the three civilizations fought not only among themselves and between each other, but also against external nomadic or seafaring "barbarians." Germanic, Viking, Berber, and Slavic tribes were an incessant threat, and even more dangerous were the Altaic invaders from Central Asia who came westward in recurring waves for nearly a millennium. The Huns, who had preyed on the faltering Roman Empire of the fifth century, were followed westward in subsequent centuries by kindred Altaic peoples: Bulgars, Avars, Magyars (Hungarians), Turks, and finally, in the twelfth and thirteenth centuries, the dreaded Mongols.

These Asian invaders possessed ruthlessly efficient military organizations based on light cavalry. Their nomadism made them difficult to attack, and their remarkable military mobility posed a grave threat to the sedentary civilizations that they assailed. Some of these Altaic peoples were eventually absorbed into the religious and cultural frameworks of the defending civilizations. The Bulgars adopted Eastern Orthodox Christianity and submitted to the patriarch and the emperor in Constantinople; the Magyars eventually were converted to Roman Catholicism, and their king became a papal vassal; the Avars were ultimately annihilated as a political force; and the Huns faded back into the east; after 1050 the Seljuk Turks (and the Ottoman Turks four centuries later) were to assume political control of much of Islam and become militant Muslims. But whether

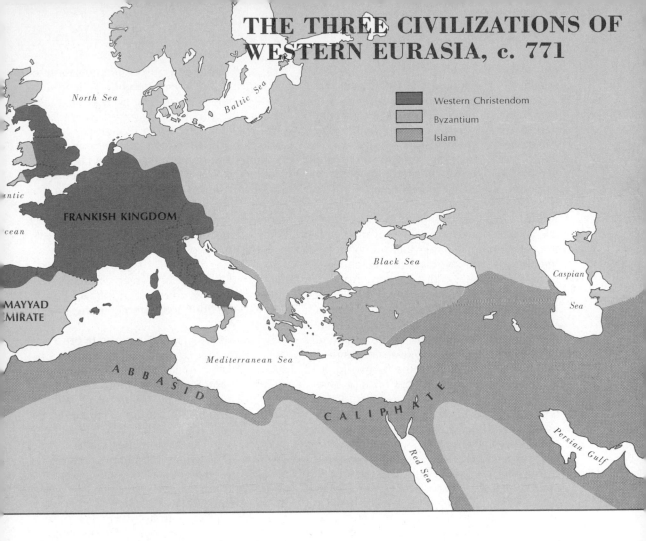

Western Christendom
Byzantium
Islam

North Sea

Baltic Sea

FRANKISH KINGDOM

Atlantic Ocean

UMAYYAD EMIRATE

Black Sea

Caspian Sea

ABBASID

CALIPHATE

Mediterranean Sea

Red Sea

Persian Gulf

repelled, assimilated, or destroyed, these Altaic peoples were for centuries a source of turbulence and terror, and on occasion they threatened the very survival of the civilizations of Europe and Asia.

The cultural sources of Byzantium, Islam, and Western Christendom were by no means limited to the classical and Hebrew traditions. Western Christendom was a fusion of classical, Christian, and Germanic culture; Islam was at least as oriental as it was Greco-Roman, and the culture of Baghdad owed much to the traditions of ancient Persia; Byzantium drew inspiration not only from its Greco-Roman past but also from the Ancient-Near-Eastern heritage, which had permeated the Greek world long before, in Hellenistic times. The solemn and magnificent court ceremonial of ancient Persia, which was borrowed in part by the Roman

emperors of the late third and fourth centuries, influenced both the imperial rites of Constantinople over the next millennium and the rituals of the Roman papacy that continue to the present day.

Again, late-Roman religious thought was influenced by the concepts of Persian Zoroastrianism. The universal conflict between the Zoroastrian god of good, Ahuramazda, and the evil demon, Ahriman, was projected into the world as a series of dualisms: good versus evil, light versus darkness, truth versus falsehood, spirit versus matter. Spirit-matter dualism is to be found in the religious traditions of the Hebrews and even of the Greeks, but it was manifested most clearly and powerfully in Persian thought. Dualism became the dominant note in three great religious movements of the Roman Empire—Gnosticism, Mithraism, and Manichaeism—and through these movements it affected Christianity itself. There were many influential Christian Gnostics in the early history of the church; St. Augustine of Hippo had been a Manichaean before he was a Christian; and Mithraism was one of Christianity's chief rivals among the mystery cults of the third century. Christian orthodoxy consistently resisted the more extreme implications of dualism. Yet Christianity's distinctive vision of a universal synthesis between spirit and matter, soul and body, was modified in the early church, under dualistic influences, into an attitude of renunciation and withdrawal from the world. God had created the earth as well as heaven; God had dignified the human body by assuming it unto himself in the incarnate Christ; yet early Christians, living in a religious atmosphere profoundly affected by the dualistic viewpoint, tended to renounce the body and flee the world. And the dualistic influence on Christian heresy was far stronger. The Christian Gnostics set the pattern early, and their path was followed in later centuries by such sects as the Monophysites of Egypt and Syria, the Bogomiles of the medieval Balkans, and the Albigensians of twelfth- and thirteenth-century southern France. All these Christian heresies looked with grave suspicion on the human body and the physical universe. All reflected, to a greater or lesser degree, the religious mood of ancient Persia.

BYZANTIUM

By about A.D. 500 the former western provinces of the Roman Empire had become a cluster of political fragments ruled by Germanic tribes, but the Eastern Roman emperors, with their capital at Constantinople, retained control of an immense, crescent-shaped empire girdling the eastern Mediterranean from the Balkans through Asia Minor, Syria, and Palestine, to Egypt. The last western emperor was deposed in 476, and the western provinces had by then been lost, but since the reign of Diocletian (284–305) the political power of the Roman Empire had been concentrated in the east. During the fourth and fifth centuries the empire changed internally and contracted geographically, yet it survived as an apparently indestructible

state and, centered on Constantine's eastern capital, it lived on for another millennium.

Nevertheless, the culture of classical antiquity was gradually transformed in the east, just as in the west, even though the line of Eastern emperors continued without significant interruption from the time of Diocletian to 1453. Historians recognize this cultural transformation by giving a new name to the Eastern Roman Empire from about the sixth century onward. It is called the Byzantine Empire, after the ancient Greek town of Byzantium on whose site Constantinople was built. But the cultural change was exceedingly gradual, and one might equally well argue that the era of most significant transition was the third and fourth centuries rather than the sixth.

Byzantine civilization was built on a fusion of three ingredients: Roman government, Christian religion, and Greco-Oriental culture. From Rome, and most particularly from the authoritarian empire of Diocletian and Constantine, Byzantium inherited its administrative system and its law. Byzantine autocracy was based on the political concepts of Diocletian; Byzantine caesaropapism (see p. 168) was a product of Constantine's Christian empire. And the prevailing Byzantine mood, like the mood of the fourth- and fifth-century empire, was one of defense—of self-preservation. To the Byzantines, their state was the ark of civilization in an ocean of barbarism—the political embodiment of the Christian faith—and as such it had to be preserved at all costs. The virtues appropriate to such a state were entrenchment, not conquest; caution, not daring.

The Age of Justinian

The first and greatest exception to these typical Byzantine virtues was the creative surge that occurred during the reign of Justinian (527–565). In some respects, Justinian stands as the last of the old Roman emperors; in others, he was Byzantine. He spoke Latin and dreamed of reviving Rome's ancient dominion over the entire Mediterranean by reconquering the west. It was at his bidding that the rich heritage of the Roman law was assembled into one coherent body. In these respects he was a Roman emperor in the old tradition. But his reign also witnessed a golden age of Byzantine art and the climax of the imperial autocracy and caesaropapism that typified Byzantine culture to the end. One product of his extensive building program in Constantinople was the immense church of Sancta Sophia—Byzantium's greatest work of art. Gold, silver, ivory, and dazzling mosaics adorned its interior, and a vast dome seemed almost to float on air above it. Justinian himself exclaimed on its completion, "O Solomon, I have outdone thee!"

Justinian set a group of talented lawyers at the task of assembling the huge mass of legal precedents, judicial opinions, and imperial edicts that constituted the legacy of Roman law. These materials were arranged into a huge, systematic collection known as the *Corpus Juris Civilis*—the "body of civil law." Justinian's *Corpus* not only became the basis of all future Byzantine jurisprudence but also served as the vehicle in which Roman law returned to Western Europe in the twelfth century to challenge the age-long dominion of Germanic legal custom. The appearance of the *Corpus Juris Civilis* in the medieval west was of incalculable importance to the development of rational legal systems in the European states, and its effect is still evident in the legal codes of modern nations.

Justinian, with his keen sense of the Roman imperial tradition, could not rest until he had made one all-out effort to recover the empire's lost western provinces and to reestablish imperial authority in the city of Rome. His armies, small but brilliantly led, conquered the decaying Vandal Kingdom of North Africa with ease in 533 to 534 and then undertook a bitter, 20-year struggle to wrest Italy from the Ostrogoths. The Ostrogothic regime collapsed at last in 555, but the Italian peninsula was desolated in the process and Rome itself was left in ruins.

During the final decade of his reign Justinian ruled almost the entire Mediterranean coastline. Sardinia, Corsica, the Balearic Islands, and the southern coast of Visigothic Spain all fell into his power. But his bloated empire was impoverished and his treasury empty. A devastating plague struck the empire in 541 and recurred over the succeeding decades, taking a fearful toll of lives and crippling the Byzantine economy. Even

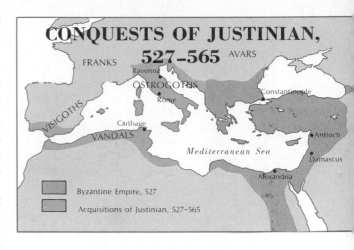

without the plague, Byzantium would have found it difficult to hold its newly conquered territories. With his military attention focused westward, Justinian was powerless to prevent a great flood of Slavic peoples and Altaic Bulgars from ravaging the Balkans. When, in 561, the Avars settled on the Danube shore and proceeded to subjugate the Slavs and Bulgars, Byzantium found itself living in the shadow of a hostile and dangerous barbarian state. Justinian's greatest shortcoming was his inability to match ambitions to resources, and the huge empire that he bequeathed to his successors was bankrupt, exhausted, and dangerously vulnerable.

Retrenchment and Consolidation: Byzantine Government, Religion, and Culture

In 568, three years after Justinian's death, a savage Germanic tribe known as the Lombards (Langobards or Long Beards) burst into Italy, further devastating that troubled land and carving out an extensive kingdom in northern Italy centering on the Po Valley. Byzantium retained much of southern Italy and maintained control of Ravenna and other cities along the Adriatic coast, but its hold on Italy was badly shaken. Shortly thereafter, the Visigoths reconquered the Byzantine territories in southern Spain; and eventually, in the 690s, Byzantine North Africa—the former Vandal state—fell to the Muslims. In 751 the Lombards took Ravenna, and Byzantine power in Italy was reduced still further.

Hence, Justinian's conquests were not lasting; his successors were forced to abandon his ambitious policies and face the hard realities of survival, turning their backs on the west to face more immediate threats from hostile peoples to the north and east. The Persian Empire pressed dangerously against Byzantium's eastern frontier, and the Avars, with their Bulgar and Slavic subjects, won control of most of the Balkans. In the 630s Muslim armies exploded out of Arabia to wrest Syria, Palestine, and Egypt from the empire and put Constantinople once again in grave danger. The Muslims besieged the city on several occasions, most notably in the great investment of 717–718, at which time the dogged Byzantine defense may well have saved not only the empire but much of Eastern and Central Europe from being absorbed into the Arab world. The empire withstood the powerful northwestward thrust of Islam, retaining Constantinople, Anatolia, and an unsteady overlordship in the Balkan peninsula. The Christian kingdoms of the west were able to develop behind this eastern screen.

The defensive, conservative mood of Byzantium is evident in both its bureaucracy and its army. The bureaucracy, huge and precedent-bound, seldom took risks. Resisting the policies of Byzantium's few vigorous and imaginative emperors, it gave cohesion to the state during the reigns of incompetents and thereby contributed significantly to the empire's survival. The army, small and highly trained, also clung to a policy of few risks. Its generals, often men of remarkable skill, tended to pursue policies of cunning and caution. They knew only too well that the preservation of the empire depended on the survival of their armies.

The Byzantine emperors drew invaluable strength from the loyalty of their tax-ridden but fervently Christian subjects. The orthodox Christians within the empire regarded their ruler as more than a secular sovereign. He was God's viceroy, the protector of the Holy Church, and he therefore merited their unquestioned allegiance. Accordingly, Byzantine armies fought not merely for the empire but for God. The Byzantine warrior was no mere soldier; he was a crusader. Christianity was a potent stimulus to patriotism, and the Byzantine emperors received popular support to a degree unknown in pagan Rome.

But the emperor's central position in Byzantine Christianity was also a source of weakness. Religious controversy was an imperial concern, and heresy became a grave threat to the state. The fifth and sixth centuries particularly were plagued by doctrinal disputes, and they cost the empire dearly. The most widespread heresy of the age was Monophysitism, a doctrine that arose in Egypt and spread quickly into Syria and Palestine, encouraging hostility toward the orthodox emperors. The controversy between the orthodox and the Monophysites turned on the question of whether Christ's humanity and divinity constituted two separate natures (as the orthodox said), or were fused together into one nature (Monophysitism). Monophysitism was at once a theological doctrine and a nucleus of political protest. It was upheld in districts that had been civilized long before the days of Roman rule, by peoples whose devotion to Greco-Roman culture was compromised by their commitment to their own far older cultures. Even without Monophysitism, the inhabitants of Egypt and Syria might well have been expected to show separatist tendencies against embattled Byzantium, and Monophysitism, although far more than a mere excuse for rebellion, was nevertheless a serviceable vehicle for the antagonisms of Near Eastern peoples against a millennium of Greco-Roman domination.

The orthodox-Monophysite quarrel raged long and bitterly and constituted a dangerous threat to the unity of the Byzantine Empire until the seventh century, when the rich Monophysite provinces were lost permanently to the expanding Islamic world.

Like its religion, Byzantium's Greco-Oriental culture was molded by the intellectual and cultural currents of the third, fourth, and fifth centuries. The mood of otherworldliness that was growing steadily resulted in a gradual transformation of the classical spirit. There had always been a potent spiritual-mystical element in Greco-Roman culture, coexisting with the traditional classical con-

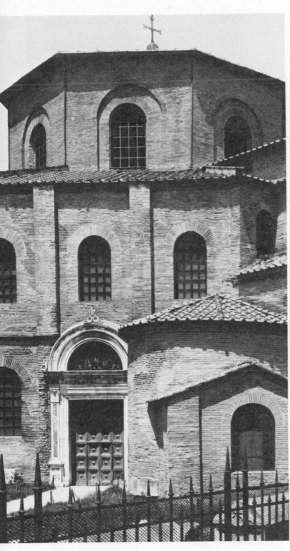

San Vitale, Ravenna, sixth century:
Exterior (above), *interior* (right).

cern with the earthly and the concrete. Now the mystical element grew stronger. More and more of the better minds turned to religious symbolism, spiritual fulfillment, and individual salvation. Artists were less interested in portraying physical perfection, more interested in portraying sanctity. A new Christian art arose that produced slender, heavily-robed mosaic figures with solemn faces and deep eyes. Techniques of perspective, which the artists of antiquity had developed to a fine degree, mattered less to the artists of the late empire. Deemphasizing physical realism, they adorned their works with dazzling colors that evoked a feeling of heavenly radiance and deep religious solemnity.

The artistic tradition that Byzantium inherited conformed so perfectly to the Byzantine spirit that the artists of the Eastern Empire were able to produce enduring masterpieces

Justinian and attendants: Mosaic from San Vitale, Ravenna, sixth century.

that seldom departed from its basic aesthetic canons. Majestic churches arose in Byzantine cities — churches such as Sancta Sophia in Constantinople, St. Vitale in Ravenna, and St. Mark's in Venice — whose interiors shone with glistening mosaics portraying saints and statesmen, Christ and the Virgin, on backgrounds of gold. Here was an art vastly different from that of Greek antiquity, with different techniques and different purposes, yet in its own way just as valid, just as successful, as the art of the Athenian golden age.

In the religious environment of Byzantium, Greek culture was significantly altered, yet Byzantine civilization remained Greek nonetheless. Greek was the language of most of its inhabitants and, despite their deep commitment to the Christian faith, they never forgot their Greek heritage. Indeed, the transition from late Roman to Byzantine civilization is marked by an increasing dissociation from the Latin-Roman past and a heightened emphasis on the legacy of Hellenism. As

time went on, Byzantine scholars forgot their Latin; Greek became the language of the imperial court. The Byzantine Church all but lost contact with the Roman pope. Greek philosophy and letters were studied continuously by educated men who cherished their ties with the Hellenic past.

The irony of the Byzantine Empire was that it aspired to be Roman — Mediterranean — yet it became Balkan and Near Eastern. Syria with its vital commercial life, Egypt with its abundant crops, and above all Anatolia (Asia Minor) with its crucial reservoir of military manpower and imperial tax revenues — these were the heartlands of the early Byzantine Empire. And even when Syria and Egypt were lost in the seventh century to Islam, Byzantium clung to Anatolia and survived. With the rich material and human resources of Anatolia to draw on, Constantinople held fast against all her enemies. Dominating the passage between the Black Sea and the Mediterranean, secure behind its massive landward and seaward walls, it was the greatest city in medieval Europe and the economic and political heart of the Byzantine Empire.

The Macedonian Age: Russia's Conversion to Christianity

After several generations of retrenchment and consolidation, Byzantium began to expand once again under the dynasty of "Macedonian" emperors (867–1056) who established their authority over the Balkan Slavs and Bulgars. Their territorial conquests were accompanied by a rich literary and artistic revival and by a great surge of evangelism. Missionaries such as Cyril and Methodius, "the Apostles to the Slavs," evangelized tirelessly, and their successors drew the south Slavs and Russians into the orbit of Byzantine Christianity and culture. In the second half of the ninth century Byzantine missionaries invented the first Slavonic alphabet and employed it in the creation of a Slavic vernacular Bible and liturgy. Thus the Slavonic written language and the Slavonic Christian Church simultaneously came into being. Ultimately, the evangelism of the Macedonian age brought the Balkans and Russia into the Orthodox Church and into the sphere of Byzantine culture.

The age of the Macedonian emperors was concurrent with the rise of Russia—far beyond the political boundaries of the empire. Byzantium had always had economic and political interests on the northern shore of the Black Sea. In the ninth and tenth centuries trade flourished between the Black Sea and the Baltic, a trade that linked the Byzantine Empire with the vigorous commerce of the Viking world. Numerous Byzantine coin hoards dating from this era have been unearthed in Scandinavia, and Norsemen were widely employed as Byzantine mercenaries. Swedish Vikings probed deep into Russia in the ninth century, and a Swedish dynasty established itself in the Russian trading center of Novgorod, ruling over the native Slavic population and later intermarrying with it. In the tenth century a ruler of Novgorod captured the strategic Russian commercial town of Kiev, which became the nucleus of the first Russian state. Deeply influenced by the indigenous culture, the Kievan dynasty became far more Slavic than Scandinavian.

The Macedonian emperors at Constantinople took pains to maintain warm diplomatic relations with Kievan Russia. Basil II (976–1025), the "Bulgar-slayer," received crucial military aid from Prince Vladimir of Kiev and promised in return to give Vladimir his own sister in marriage. Vladimir's own conversion initiated the conversion of his subjects—and ultimately the rest of Russia—to Orthodox Christianity. Kiev never submitted politically to the Byzantine emperors, but its people became spiritual subjects of the patriarch of Constantinople and were deeply influenced by Byzantine culture. During the eleventh century Kievan Russia disintegrated politically, and in the thirteenth century it was brought under the yoke of the Mongols. But the Byzantine cultural impact survived these disasters, and most Russians remained Orthodox Christians. Centuries later, when the Byzantine Empire was demolished by the Ottoman Turks, the Christian princes of Moscow themselves assumed the imperial title (Caesar—Czar). As Constantinople had been the "Second Rome" they intended Moscow to become the "Third Rome," and sought to exert their dominion over both church and state in a manner resembling that of their imperial predecessors at Constantinople.

The Byzantine Heritage

The Macedonian dynasty ended in 1056, and Byzantium, in the four centuries remaining to it, carried on a prolonged, losing struggle for survival. But its intellectual and artistic life remained vital to the end, and its religion and culture long outlasted the fall of Constantinople in 1453. Byzantium's lasting significance in world history lies above all in its conversion of Russia and the Balkans. There remains today in Eastern Europe a distinct culture, with Byzantine roots, based on the allegiance of millions of people to Eastern (Greek) Orthodox Christianity. Their religion is similar in basic doctrine to the traditional religions of Western Europe, yet it differs in numerous important details. The historic traditions of Russia and the Balkans are varied and complex, but the tradition of Byzantium is not the least among them.

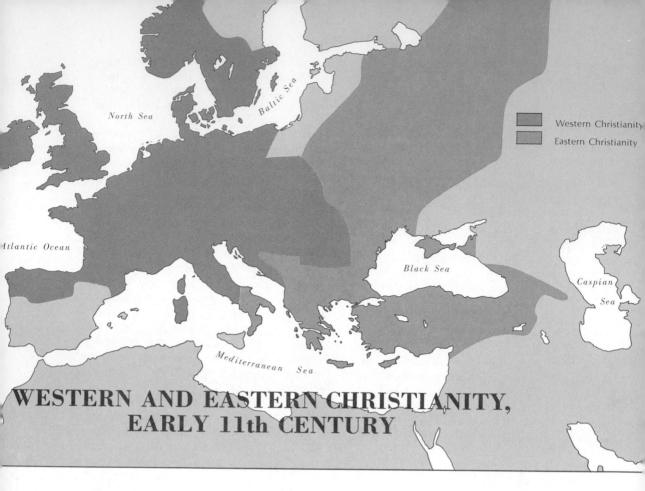

North Sea

Baltic Sea

Atlantic Ocean

Black Sea

Caspian Sea

Mediterranean Sea

■ Western Christianity

■ Eastern Christianity

WESTERN AND EASTERN CHRISTIANITY, EARLY 11th CENTURY

ISLAM

Each of Rome's three "heirs" — Byzantium, Islam, and Western Christendom — has affected world history down to the present-day. The impact of Western Christendom on today's world is readily apparent. Byzantium shaped the future of Russia and the Balkans. Islam remains a distinctive culture and a living religion spreading across an immense area in south Asia, the Middle East, and North Africa — from the East Indies to Pakistan to the Arab world of southwest Asia and Mediterranean Africa. This vast Islamic belt was created by a militant, compelling religion that burst into the world in seventh-century Arabia and spread outward with remarkable speed. In the first hundred years

of its existence it shattered the Christian domination of the Mediterranean, destroyed the Persian Empire, seized Byzantium's richest provinces, absorbed Spain, pressed deeply into France, and expanded far into the heart of southern Asia.

For countless centuries prior to the time of the prophet Mohammed (571–632) fierce nomadic tribes from the Arabian peninsula had repeatedly invaded the rich, civilized districts of Palestine, Syria, and Mesopotamia to the north. Many Semitic invaders of the ancient Near East seem to have come originally from the Arabian Desert — the Amorites, the Chaldeans, the Canaanites, even the Hebrews. These peoples quickly assimilated the ancient civilization of the Fertile Crescent and developed it in new, creative ways. But their kinsmen who stayed in Arabia remained primitive and disorganized.

In the age of Mohammed most Arabians still adhered to their nomadic ways and to their ancient polytheistic religion, but new civilizing influences were beginning to make themselves felt. A great caravan route running northward from southern Arabia served as an important link in a far-flung commercial network between the Far East and the Byzantine and Persian empires. Along this route cities developed to serve the caravans, and with city life came a degree of civilization. The greatest of these trading cities, Mecca, became a bustling commercial center that sent its own caravans northward and southward and grew wealthy on its middleman profits. At Mecca and other caravan cities, tribal life was beginning to give way to commercial life, and new, foreign ideas were starting to challenge old ways and old viewpoints. It was in Mecca that the prophet Mohammed was born.

Mohammed the Prophet

The future architect of one of the world's great religions was born of a poor branch of Mecca's leading clan. With little education behind him, he became a caravan trader, and his travels brought him into close contact with Judaism, Christianity, and Persian Zoroastrianism. An intense, sensitive man with a magnetic personality, Mohammed underwent a mystical experience while in his late thirties and began to set forth his new faith through preaching and writing. He won little support in Mecca, apart from his wife and relatives and a few converts from the underprivileged classes. The ruling businessmen of Mecca were largely immune to the teaching of what they regarded as a low-born upstart. Among other things, they appear to have feared that his new religion would discredit the chief Meccan temple, the Kaaba, which housed a sacred meteoritic stone and was a profitable center of pilgrimages. Their belief that Mohammed's faith would ruin Mecca's pilgrim business was an ironic miscalculation, but their hostility toward the new teaching forced Mohammed to flee Mecca in 622 and settle in the town of Medina, 280 miles northward on the caravan route.

The flight to Medina, known among the Muslims as the Hegira (He-jī'-ra), was a definitive turning point in the development of Islam and marks the beginning date of the Muslim calendar. Mohammed quickly won the inhabitants of Medina to his faith and became the city's political chief as well as its religious leader. Indeed, under Mohammed's direction the religious and civil authority were fused; the sacred community was at once a state and a church. In this respect, Mohammed's community at Medina foreshadowed the great Islamic state of later years.

The Medinans made war on Mecca, raiding its caravans and blockading its trade. In the year 630 Medina conquered Mecca and incorporated it into the sacred community. During the two remaining years of his life, Mohammed, now an almost legendary figure in Arabia, received the voluntary submission of many tribes in the peninsula. By the time of his death in 632 he had united the Arabians into a well-organized political-religious group who were inspired by a powerful new monotheistic religion. The violent energies of these desert peoples were now channeled toward a single goal: the conquest and conversion of the world.

The Religion of Islam

Faith was the cement with which Mohammed united Arabia. The new faith was called *Islam*—the Arabic word for "surrender." Mohammed taught that man must surrender to the will of Allah, the single, almighty God of the universe. Allah's attributes of love and mercy were overshadowed by those of power and majesty. Mohammed did not claim divinity; rather, he saw himself as the last and greatest of a long line of prophets of whom he was the "seal." Among his predecessors were Moses, the Old Testament prophets, and Jesus.

Islam respected the Old and New Testaments and was relatively tolerant toward Jews and Christians—the "people of the book." But the Muslims had a book of their own, the Koran, which superseded its predecessors and was believed to contain the pure essence of divine revelation. The Koran is the comprehensive body of Mohammed's writings, the bedrock of the Islamic faith: "All men and jinn in collaboration," so it was said, "could not produce its like." Muslims regarded it as the word of Allah dictated to Mohammed by the angel Gabriel from an original "uncreated" book located in heaven. Accordingly, its divine inspiration and authority extend not only to its precepts, but also to its every letter (of which there are 323,621). Thus it loses its authority when translated into another language. Every good Muslim must read the Koran in its original Arabic, and as Islam spread, the Arabic language necessarily spread with it.

The Koran is perhaps the most widely read book ever written. More than a manual of worship, it was the text from which the non-Arabian Muslim learned his Arabic. And since it was the supreme authority not only in religion but also in law, science, and the humanities, it became the standard text in Muslim schools for every imaginable subject. Mohammed's genius is vividly illustrated by his success in adapting a primitive language such as seventh-century Arabic to the sophisticated religious, legal, and ethical concepts of his sacred book.

Mohammed offered his followers the assurance of eternal salvation if they led upright, sober lives and followed the precepts of Islam. Above all, they were bound to a simple confession of faith: "There is no god but Allah and Mohammed is his prophet." The good Muslim was also obliged to engage in prayers and fasting, to journey as a pilgrim to Mecca at least once in his lifetime, and to work devotedly toward the welfare and expansion of the sacred community. Holy war was the supremely meritorious activity, for service to the faith was indistinguishable from service to the state. Islamic military campaigns, like those of Byzantium, took on the nature of crusades, but whereas the usual goal of Byzantine armies was defensive—to preserve the "ark of Christ"—the Muslims dreamed of conquest. They divided the world's lands into two categories: the lands already subject to Islam and those yet to be incorporated into the sacred community.

Public law in Islamic lands had a religious basis, and the fusion of religion and politics that Mohammed created at Medina remained a fundamental characteristic of Islamic society. There was no Muslim priesthood, no Muslim "church" apart from the state; Mohammed's political successors, the caliphs, were defenders of the faith and guardians of the faithful. The creative tension between church and state which proved such a stimulus to medieval Western Europe was unknown in the Muslim world.

The Arab Conquest of the Near and Middle East

In the years immediately following Mohammed's death, the explosive energy of the Arabs, harnessed at last by the teachings of the Prophet, broke upon the world. The spectacular conquests that followed resulted in part from the youthful vigor of Islam, in part from the weakness and exhaustion of its enemies. Both Byzantium and Persia were enfeebled by protracted wars, and the Monophysites of Syria and Egypt remained deeply hostile to their orthodox Byzantine masters.

The Arabs entered these tired, embittered lands afire with religious zeal, lured by the wealth and luxuries of the civilized world. They had no master plan of conquest—most of their campaigns began as plundering expeditions—but momentum grew with each unexpected victory. Moving into Syria they annihilated a large Byzantine army in 636, captured Damascus and Jerusalem, and by 640 had occupied the entire land, wresting it permanently from Byzantine control. In 637 they inflicted an overwhelming defeat on the imperial army of Persia and entered the Persian capital of Ctesiphon, gazing in disbelief at its opulence and wealth. Within another decade they had subdued all Persia and arrived at the borders of India. In later centuries, as we have seen, they were to penetrate deeply into the Indian subcontinent and to lay the religious foundations of the modern Muslim state of Pakistan. The Persians gradually adopted the Islamic faith and learned the Arab language, thus preparing themselves for the great role that they would later play in Islamic politics and culture.

At the same time the Muslims were pushing westward into Egypt. They captured Alexandria in the 640s, thus absorbing into their expanding cultural sphere the great metropolis that had been a center of Greek culture ever since the Hellenistic age. With Egypt and Syria in their hands they took to the sea, challenging the long-established Byzantine domination of the eastern Mediterranean. They captured the island of Cyprus, raided ancient Rhodes, and in 655 won a major victory over the Byzantine fleet in the Battle of the Masts.

The Umayyads and the Conquest of North Africa and Spain

In the year 655 Islamic expansion ceased momentarily as the new empire became locked in a savage dynastic struggle. The succession to the caliphate was contested between the Umayyads, a leading family in the old Meccan commercial oligarchy — late to join the Islamic bandwagon but ambitious nonetheless — and Ali, the son-in-law of Mohammed. Ali, the Prophet's cousin, had married Mohammed's daughter, Fatima, his sole surviving offspring. The Umayyad interests rallied behind Muawiya, the dynamic Umayyad governor of Syria, who was responsible for the recent buildup of Muslim seapower. Ali headed a faction that was to become exceedingly powerful in later centuries; his followers insisted that the caliph be a direct descendant of the Prophet.

In 661 the Umayyad forces vanquished the legitimists in battle, and Muawiya became the undisputed caliph of Islam. Moving the Islamic capital to Damascus, in Syria, he initiated an Umayyad dynasty of caliphs that held power for nearly a century. But the legitimist faction that had once supported Ali persisted as a troublesome, dedicated minority, throwing its support behind various of the numerous descendants of Ali and Fatima. In time the political movement evolved into a heresy known as *Shi'ism* which held that the *true* caliphs — the descendants of Mohammed through Fatima and Ali — were sinless, infallible, and possessed of secret knowledge not contained in the Koran. Shi'ism became an occult, underground doctrine that occasionally rose to the surface in the form of civil insurrection. In the tenth century, Shi'ites gained control of Egypt and established a "Fatimid" dynasty of caliphs in Cairo. It inspired a band of Muslim desperados known as the "Assassins," who employed hashish as a means of divine illumination. And it survives to this day in the Ismaili sect led by the Aga Khan.

The intermission in the Muslim expansion ended with the Umayyad victory over Ali in 661. And even though the Islamic capital was now Damascus, the old Arabian aristocracy remained in firm control. Constantinople became the chief military goal, but the great city repulsed a series of powerful Muslim attacks between the years 670 and 718. Byzantium survived for another seven centuries, and the Muslims were effectively barred from southeastern Europe for the remainder of the middle ages.

Meanwhile, however, Muslim armies were enjoying spectacular success in the west. From Egypt they moved westward along the North African coast into the old Vandal kingdom, now ruled by distant Byzantium. In 698 the Muslims took Carthage. In 711 they crossed the Straits of Gibraltar into Spain and crushed the tottering Visigothic kingdom, driving the Christian princes into the fastness of the Pyrenees Mountains. Next the Muslims moved into southern Gaul and threatened the Kingdom of the Franks. In 732, exactly a century after the Prophet's death, they were halted at last on a field between Tours and Poitiers by a determined Christian army led by the able Frankish warrior, Charles Martel.

Both armies at Tours were small and makeshift, yet the battle was decisive; Islam's great surge of Mediterranean expansion was stopped in central France as it had been stopped earlier at Constantinople. The remainder of the middle ages witnessed continued Christian-Islamic warfare and some territorial change — most of Spain, for example, reverted to Christian control in the twelfth and thirteenth centuries. But Islam, Byzantium, and Western Christendom had achieved a relative equilibrium by the mid-eighth century and remained in balance for the next several hundred years.

The Golden Age of the Abbasids

In 750, eighteen years after the battle of Tours, the Umayyads were overthrown by a new dynasty, the Abbasids, Arabian in family background but with a program of greater political participation for the highly civilized conquered peoples, now converting in large numbers to Islam. Above all it was the Islam-

North Sea

Atlantic Ocean

KINGDOM
OF THE
FRANKS

Tours•

Poitiers•
Furthest Islamic
penetration

K. OF THE
LOMBARDS

AVARS

•Toledo

CORSICA

•Rome

•Cordova

Naples•

Constantinople

SARDINIA

BYZANTINE EM

Gibraltar•

MOROCCO

Carthage•
Tunis•

SICILY

CRETE

AFRICA

Mediterranean Sea

The Empire at Mohammed's death

Conquests under the first three Caliphs

Conquests under the Omayyads

The Byzantine Empire

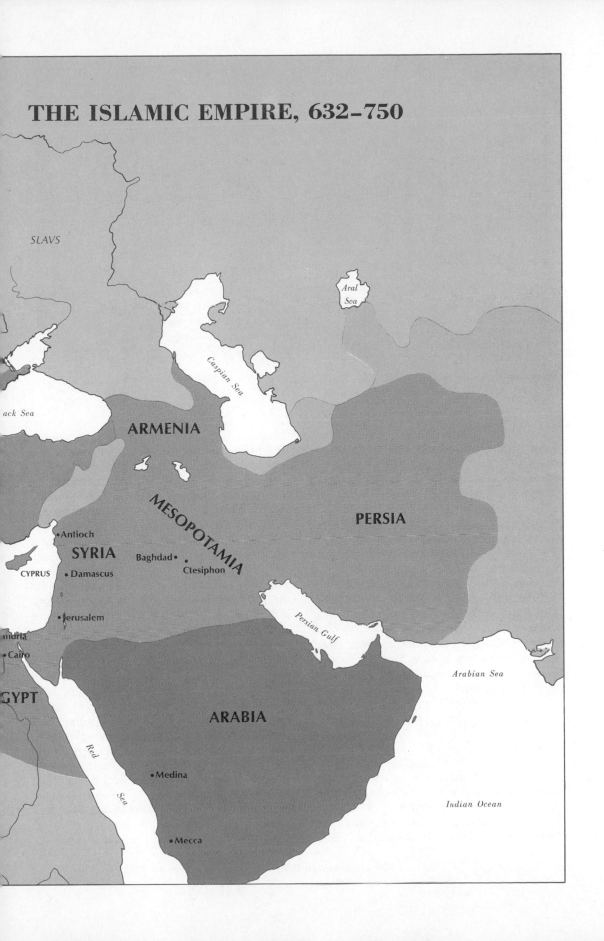

THE ISLAMIC EMPIRE, 632–750

SLAVS

Aral
Sea

Caspian Sea

ack Sea

ARMENIA

MESOPOTAMIA

PERSIA

•Antioch

SYRIA

Baghdad•

CYPRUS

•Damascus

•Ctesiphon

•Jerusalem

Persian Gulf

ndria

•Cairo

Arabian Sea

GYPT

ARABIA

Red

•Medina

Sea

Indian Ocean

•Mecca

Miniature painting of the city of Baghdad.

ized Persian aristocracy that the Abbasids represented, and shortly after the victory of the new dynasty, the capital was moved from Damascus to Baghdad on the Tigris, deep within the old Persian Empire and a short way from the ruins of ancient Babylon.

Baghdad, under the early Abbasids, became one of the world's great cities. It was the center of a vast commercial network spreading across the Islamic world and far beyond. Silks, spices, and fragrant woods flowed into its wharves from India, China, and the East Indies; furs, honey, and slaves were imported from Scandinavia; and gold, slaves, and ivory from tropical Africa. Baghdad was the nexus of a far-flung banking system with branches in other cities across the Islamic world.

The wealth and culture of Baghdad reached their climax under the Abbasid caliph, Harun-al-Rashid (786–809), whose opulence and power quickly became legendary. His reign was marked by vigorous intellectual activity in which the learned traditions of Greece and Rome, Persia, and India, were absorbed and synthesized. In Baghdad Harun's son, the Caliph Mamun, founded the House of Wisdom—which was at once a

library, a university, and a translation center. In this great Abbasid institute Islamic scholars pushed their civilization far beyond the level it had reached under the Umayyads in Damascus. Drawing from various ancient traditions, Islamic culture had come of age with remarkable speed.

The rise of the Abbasids marked the breakdown of the Arabian aristocracy's monopoly of political power. Now the government was run by a medley of races and peoples, often of humble origin. As one disgruntled aristocrat observed, "Sons of concubines have become so numerous amongst us; Lead me to a land, O God, where I shall see no bastards." The Abbasid state drew heavily on the administrative techniques of Byzantium and Persia. A sophisticated, complex bureaucracy ran the affairs of state from the capital at Baghdad and kept in touch with the provinces through a multitude of tax-gatherers, judges, couriers, and spies. The regime undertook extensive irrigation works, drained swamps, and thereby increased the amount of land under cultivation. But the status of the peasant and unskilled laborer was kept low by the competition of vast numbers of slaves. The brilliance of Abbasid culture had little effect on the underprivileged masses who, aside from their fervent Islamic faith, lived much as they had for the last two millennia.

The Breakup of the Abbasid Empire

Nor were the Abbasids able to maintain their power throughout the vast reaches of the Islamic empire. Communications were limited by the speed of sailing vessels and camels, and governors of remote provinces required sufficient independence and military strength to defend themselves from infidel attacks. Such local independence could easily ripen into full autonomy. The Abbasid revolution of 750 was followed by a long process of political disintegration as one province after another broke free of the control of the Baghdad caliphs. Even in the palmy days of Harun-al-Rashid the extreme western provinces — Spain, Morocco, and Tunisia — were ruled by independent local dynasties. And by the later ninth century the trend toward disintegration was gaining strong momentum as Egypt, Syria, and eastern Persia (Iran) broke free of Abbasid control.

Head of a Seljuk Turkish prince: Iran, twelfth or early thirteenth century.

By then the Abbasids were slowly losing their grip on their own government in Baghdad. Ambitious army commanders gradually usurped power, establishing control over the tax machinery and the other organs of government. In the later tenth and eleventh centuries the Fatimid caliphate of Cairo rose to power, extending its authority to Syria and briefly occupying Baghdad itself (1056–1057). Furthermore, since about the mid-tenth century the Abbasid caliphs of Baghdad had been controlled by members of a local Persian aristocratic dynasty who took the title of "sultan" and ruled what was left of the Abbasid state. A century later, in 1055, the chief of the Seljuk Turks conquered Baghdad, assumed the title of "Grand Sultan," and then turned his forces against Byzantium with devastating effect. The Abbasid dynasty survived until 1258 but never regained its power.

The general unrest of the ninth, tenth, and eleventh centuries encouraged waves of popular protest, both socioeconomic and religious. The Ismaili sect, an outgrowth of the earlier legitimist faction, turned to widespread terrorism and revolution. Also, a mystical movement known as Sufism became immensely popular throughout the Islamic world. For centuries the Sufi movement, although never tightly coordinated, had provided the chief impetus to missionary work among the infidel. These Sufi mystics, often illiterate but always fervent, had achieved the conversion of millions of people in Africa, India, Indonesia, Central Asia, and China. It was they, instead of the orthodox religious scholars and lawyers, who could bring hope to the Muslim masses in times of trouble. Drawing from the Neoplatonic notion that reality rests in God alone, the Sufis sought mystical unity with the divine and stressed God's love as against the orthodox emphasis on God's authority. The orthodox Islamic scholars contended vigorously against this mystical trend, but by the tenth century Sufism was the most powerful religious force among the people of Islam. It affects Islamic personal devotion to this day.

Interior of the mosque at Cordova.

Islamic Culture

Throughout the epoch of political disintegration the Muslim world remained united by a common tongue, a common culture, and a common faith. It continued to struggle with Byzantium for control of the Mediterranean and managed, at various times between the ninth and eleventh centuries, to occupy the key islands of Crete, Sicily, Sardinia, and Corsica. As early as the reign of Harun-al-Rashid, virtually all the inhabitants of Syria, Egypt, and North Africa had converted to Islam, even though these lands had once supported enthusiastic and well-organized Christian churches.

The brilliant intellectual awakening of Harun-al-Rashid's day continued unabated for another four centuries. The untutored Arab from the desert became the cultural heir of Greece, Rome, Persia, and India, and within less than two centuries of the Prophet's death Islamic culture had reached the level of a mature, sophisticated civilization. Its rise was a consequence of the Arabs' success in absorbing the great civilized traditions of their conquered peoples and em-

ploying these traditions in a cultural synthesis both new and unique. Islam borrowed, but never without digesting. What it drew from other civilizations it transmuted and made its own.

The political disintegration of the ninth and tenth centuries was accompanied by a diffusion of cultural activity throughout the Muslim world. During the tenth century, for example, Cordova, the capital of Islamic Spain, acquired prodigious wealth and became the center of a brilliant cultural flowering. With a population of half a million or more, Cordova was another Baghdad. No other city in Western Europe could even remotely approach it in population, wealth, or municipal organization. Its magnificent mansions, mosques, aqueducts, and baths, its bustling markets and shops, its efficient police force and sanitation service, its street lights and, above all, its splendid, sprawling palace, flashing with brightly colored tiles and surrounded by graceful minarets and sparkling fountains, made Cordova the wonder of the age.

All across the Islamic world, from Cordova

Mausoleum of the Sassinids, Bukhasa, Central Asia, tenth century.

The Islamic Achievement

The Arab conquests during the century after Mohammed changed the historical course of North Africa and Southwest Asia decisively and permanently. The Arabs conquered their vast territories thrice over: with their armies, their faith, and their language. In the end, the term "Arab" applied to every Muslim from Morocco to Iraq, regardless of his ethnic background. Within its all-encompassing religious and linguistic framework, Arab culture provided a new stimulus and a new orientation to the long-civilized peoples of former empires. With its manifold ingredients, the rich Islamic heritage would one day provide invaluable nourishment to the voracious mind of the twelfth and thirteenth-century west. Later, Islamic armies would bring Byzantium to an end and make Constantinople a Muslim city. Later still, in the sixteenth and seventeenth centuries, they would be at the gates of Vienna. Only in the nineteenth century did Islam become clearly subordinate to the West militarily and politically. And today there are clear signs that this subordination is ending.

WESTERN CHRISTENDOM

During the half millennium following A.D. 500, while Byzantium struggled to preserve its territory and culture, and while Islamic civilization rose and flowered, Western Europe underwent an agonizing process of decline and rebirth. Classical civilization collapsed almost totally, and on its ruins there arose, slowly, the new civilization of Western Christendom.

Medieval civilization owed much to its Greco-Roman heritage, but it drew also from the Judaeo-Christian and the Germanic cultural traditions. The fusion of Greco-Roman and Christian culture had been going on ever since the days of the early Christian apologists, and by the time of Ambrose (340–397), Jerome (340–420), and Augustine (354–430), it was far advanced. During the fifth century the synthesis of these two traditions was progressing rapidly, but their integration with Germanic culture had only begun. Throughout the turbulent centuries of the early middle ages the Greco-Roman-

to Baghdad and far to the East, Muslim scholars and artists were developing the legacies of past civilizations. Architects were molding Greco-Roman forms into a brilliant, distinctive new style. Philosophers were studying and elaborating the writings of Plato and Aristotle despite the hostility of narrowly orthodox Islamic theologians. Physicians were expanding the ancient medical doctrines of Galen and his Greek predecessors, describing new symptoms and identifying new curative drugs. Astronomers were tightening the geocentric system of Ptolemy, preparing accurate tables of planetary motions, and giving Arabic names to the stars—names such as Altair, Deneb, and Aldebaran—which are still used. The renowned astronomer poet of eleventh-century Persia, Omar Khayyam, devised a calendar of singular accuracy. Muslim mathematicians borrowed creatively from both Greece and India. From the Greeks they learned geometry and trigonometry, and from the Hindus they appropriated the so-called Arabic numerals, the zero, and algebra, which were ultimately passed on to the West to revolutionize European mathematics.

Christian tradition was preserved by the church, while the Germanic tradition dominated the political and military organization of the barbarian states that established themselves on the carcass of the Roman Empire in the west. The Germanic invaders soon became at least nominal Christians, but for centuries a cultural gulf remained between the church, with its classical-Christian heritage, and the Germanic kingdoms with their primitive, war-oriented culture. It is true that the early medieval church was only able to preserve ancient culture in a simplified and debased form; as time went on ecclesiastical leaders and aristocratic laymen came more and more to be drawn from the same social background. Still, it remained the great task of the early medieval church to civilize and Christianize the Germanic peoples. In the end the Classical-Christian-Germanic amalgam was achieved, and a new Western European civilization came into being.

Western Europe in the Sixth and Seventh Centuries

Although many towns survived as the headquarters of important bishops and the sites of cathedral churches,* they played a drastically reduced role in the economy of the barbarian states. The important economic centers of the age were the monastery, the peasant village, and the great farm or villa owned by some wealthy Roman or Germanic aristocrat and divided into small plots worked by semifree tenant farmers. A small-scale international luxury trade persisted, but by and large the sixth and seventh centuries were characterized by economic localism. Small agrarian communities produced most of their own needs and were very nearly self-sufficient.

Except in Britain and the western Rhineland, the Germanic invaders were gradually absorbed by the more numerous native populations. Among the Franks, Visigoths, Burgundians, and Lombards, the free farmers often sank to the level of semi-servile *coloni* within a few generations. The Germanic warrior nobility was to retain its separate identity much longer, especially in Italy, where the Lombards held sway from the late sixth to the late eighth century. Even after the old and new upper classes became fused through intermarriage, the aggressive, rough-and-ready values of the Germanic aristocracy prevailed.

The barbarian kings, with the exception of the Ostrogoth, Theodoric, in Italy (493–526), proved incapable of carrying on the Roman administrative traditions they inherited. The Roman tax system broke down almost completely, the privilege of minting coins fell into private hands, and the power and wealth of the government declined accordingly, not because the kings were generous but because they were ignorant. They lacked any conception of responsible government and regarded their kingdoms as private estates to be exploited or alienated according to their whims. They made reckless gifts of land and political authority to the nobility and the church and used what was left for their own personal enrichment. They managed to combine the worst features of anarchy and tyranny.

* Technically, the term *cathedral* denotes the seat of a bishopric—literally, the bishop's throne. A church, whether large or small, is a "cathedral" if it serves as a bishop's headquarters.

Since the Germanic kings were doing nothing to enhance the economy or ameliorate the general impoverishment, the church strove to fill the vacuum. It dispensed charity; it offered eternal salvation to the poor and glamorized the virtue of resignation. But even the church was ill-equipped to cope with the chaos of the barbarian west. The Roman popes claimed leadership over the church yet seldom asserted real power beyond central Italy. Elsewhere ecclesiastical organization was confined largely to the almost deserted towns and the walled monasteries. Only gradually were rural parishes organized to meet the needs of the countryside, and not until the eighth century did they become common. Until then a peasant was fortunate if he saw a priest once a year. The monarchy and the church, the two greatest landholders in the barbarian kingdoms, were better known among the peasantry as acquisitive landlords than as fountains of justice and divine grace. The countryside was politically and spiritually adrift, and peasant life was harsh, brutish, and short.

Monasticism and Early Medieval Culture

What little high culture there was in the early middle ages was centered in the monasteries. Ireland had been won for Christianity by St. Patrick in the fifth century, and, by about 600, Irish monasteries had developed a richly creative Celtic-Christian culture. Irish scholars were studying both Greek and Latin literature at a time when Greek was unknown elsewhere in the west. Irish artists were producing superb sculptured crosses and illuminated manuscripts in the flowing, curvilinear Celtic style. Irish Christianity, isolated from the continental church by the pagan Anglo-Saxon kingdoms, developed its own distinctive organization and spirit, centered on the monastery rather than the diocese. Irish monks were famous for their learning, the austere severity of their lives, and the vast scope of their missionary activities. They converted large portions of Scotland to their own form of Christianity and by the early 600s were doing missionary work on the continent itself.

Meanwhile a very different kind of monastic order, spreading northward from Italy, was making a deep impact on the life of dark-age Europe. This movement was organized in the early sixth century by St. Benedict of Nursia (c. 480–c. 544), a contemporary of Justinian. St. Benedict founded the great monastery of Monte Cassino, between Rome and Naples, and framed a rule of monastic life that inspired and energized the medieval church. Pope Gregory the Great (590–604) described the Benedictine Rule as "conspicuous for its discretion." Rejecting the harsh asceticism of earlier Christian monasticism, it provided for a busy, closely regulated life, simple but not austere. Benedictine monks were decently clothed, adequately fed, and seldom left to their own devices. Theirs was a life dedicated to God and to the quest for personal sanctity, guided by the obligations of chastity, poverty, and obedience to the abbot. Yet it was also a life that was available to any dedicated Christian, not merely to the spiritual hero. Its ideals were service and moderation under wise, compassionate leadership.

In the two centuries after St. Benedict's death his order spread throughout Western Christendom. The result was not a vast, hierarchical monastic organization, but rather hundreds of individual, autonomous monasteries sharing a single rule and way of life. Benedict had pictured his monasteries as spiritual sanctuaries into which pious men might withdraw from the world, but the chaotic, illiterate society of the barbarian west, desperately in need of the discipline and learning of the Benedictines, could not permit them to renounce secular affairs.

The Benedictines had an enormous impact on the world they had sought to abandon. Their schools produced the majority of literate Europeans during the early middle ages. They served as a vital cultural link with the classical past, transcribing and preserving the writings of Latin antiquity. They spearheaded the penetration of Christianity into pagan England at the end of the sixth century, into Germany two centuries later, and, in the tenth century, into Scandinavia, Poland, and Hungary. They served as scribes and advisers to kings and were drafted into high ecclesiastical offices. As recipients of gifts of land from pious donors over many generations, they held and managed vast estates that became models of intelligent agricultural management and technological innovation. As islands of peace, security, and learning in an ocean of barbarism, the Benedictine monasteries became the spiritual and intellectual centers of the developing Classical-Christian-Germanic synthesis that underlay European civilization. In short, Benedictine monasticism was the supreme civilizing influence in the barbarian west.

The Carolingian Age

Just as the new Europe was aroused spiritually by the wide-ranging Benedictines, it was united politically by the new Carolingian dynasty of Frankish monarchs. The original Frankish dynasty—the Merovingians—had declined over the centuries from bloodthirsty autocrats to crowned fools. Their policy of dividing royal authority and crown lands among all the sons of a deceased king further weakened Merovingian authority, and by the later 600s all real power had passed to the aristocracy. The greatest Frankish aristocratic family at this time, the Carolingians, had risen to power in northeastern Frankland and had established a firm grip on the chief viceregal office in the kingdom. The Carolingians became hereditary "mayors of the palace" of the Merovingian kings. In reality they were, by the late 600s, the military and political masters of Frankland, leading their own armed retainers against internal rivals and commanding the Frankish host against foreign enemies. So it was that Charles Martel (714–741), a masterful and ruthless Carolingian mayor of the palace, led the Franks to victory over the Muslims at Tours in 732. Charles Martel's son, Pepin the Short, won for his family the Frankish crown itself, and Pepin's son, Charlemagne, won an empire.

The Carolingians followed the very policy of divided succession that had so weakened the Merovingians. But the Carolingians enjoyed the good fortune of having, over several crucial generations, only one long-surviving male heir. Frankish unity was maintained in the Carolingian age not by policy but by luck.

Charlemagne was a phenomenally successful military commander, a statesman of rare skill, a friend of learning, and a monarch possessed of a deep sense of responsibility for the welfare of his society. Like all successful monarchs of his time, he was a warrior-king. He led his armies on yearly campaigns as a matter of course; the decision to be made each year was not whether to fight but whom to fight. Only gradually did Charlemagne develop a notion of Christian mission and a program of unifying and systematically expanding the Christian west. At the behest of the papacy, he conquered Lombard Italy in 774 and incorporated it into his growing empire. He carved out at Muslim expense a "Spanish March" on the Iberian side of the Pyrenees, centered in Barcelona. He conquered and absorbed Bavaria, organizing its easternmost district into a forward defensive barrier against the Slavs. This East March or *Ostmark* became the nucleus of a new state later to be called Austria. Most important of all, he campaigned intermittently for more than 30 years in northern Germany against the pagan Saxons (772–804). By the early ninth century the Frankish control of Saxony was assured, and in subsequent decades, through the tireless work of Benedictine monks, the Saxons were thoroughly Christianized. A century and a half later, Christian Saxons were governing the most powerful and enlightened state in Europe.

Charlemagne's armies, by incorporating central Germany into the new civilization, had succeeded where the Roman emperors had failed. By 800, Charlemagne was the master of Western Christendom; only a few small Christian kingdoms in the British Isles and northwestern Spain remained outside his jurisdiction. On Christmas Day, 800, his accomplishment was given formal recognition when the pope placed the imperial crown on his head and acclaimed him "Emperor of the Romans." From the standpoint of legal theory, this coronation reconstituted the Roman Empire in the west after an interregnum of 324 years.

But Carolingian Europe differed radically from the Western Roman Empire of old. It was a land without large cities, thoroughly agrarian in economic organization, with its culture centered on the monastery and cathedral rather than the forum. Although

Contemporary bronze figure of Charlemagne.

Charlemagne extended his authority into Italy, Spain, and Germany, his capital and his heart remained in northern Frankland. Thus, Carolingian Europe no longer faced the Mediterranean; its axis had shifted northward. And this northward shift shaped Europe's development far into the future.

The relative brightness of Charlemagne's age resulted from creative processes that had been at work during the preceding darker centuries. One of the most interesting of these processes was the development of a new agrarian technology that eventually increased the productivity of northern European farmlands well beyond the level of the old Roman Empire.

By the opening of the eighth century, the ineffective scratch plow of Roman times had

Charlemagne's Palace church, Aachen, based on San Vitale, Ravenna (see page 187); the chandelier was added in the twelfth century.

been replaced in the northern districts of Western Europe by a heavy compound plow with wheels, colter, plowshare, and moldboard, which cut deeply into the soil, pulverized it, and turned it aside into ridges and furrows. This heavy plow—which may have been introduced from the Slavic lands to the east—could be used in vast areas of rich, heavy soil where the Roman scratch plow was ineffective. It also accentuated the ten-

dency toward dividing fields into long strips cultivated by the eight-ox teams the heavy plow required. Peasants now pooled their oxen and their labor in order to exploit the heavy plow, and in doing so they laid the foundation for the cooperative agricultural communities of medieval Europe, with their strong village councils regulating the division of labor and resources.

The coming of the heavy plow resulted in

a significant change in the method of crop rotation. By the Carolingian age, much of northern Europe was beginning to adopt the three-field system in place of the two-field system characteristic of Roman times. Formerly, a typical farm had been divided into two fields, each of which, in turn, was planted one year and left fallow the next. This pattern continued in southern Europe throughout the middle ages. But the rich northern soils, newly opened by the heavy plow, did not require a full year's rest between crops. They were often divided now into three fields, each of which underwent a three-year cycle system of autumn planting, spring planting, and fallow. The three-field system increased food production significantly and brought unprecedented prosperity to northern Europe, perhaps contributing to the northward shift of the Carolingian era.

Meanwhile the water mill, which was used only occasionally in antiquity for grinding grain, had come into fairly widespread use on Carolingian farms. During the centuries following Charlemagne's death the water mill was put to new uses—to power the rising textile industry of the eleventh century and to drive trip hammers in forges. Thus, technological progress continued over the medieval centuries. By A.D. 1000 the coming of the horseshoe and a new, efficient horse collar—both apparently imported from Siberia or Central Asia—made possible the very gradual substitution of the horse for the less efficient ox on the richer north European farms. And in the twelfth century the windmill made its debut in the European countryside. These post-Carolingian advances resulted in the greater productivity underlying the vital civilization of the twelfth and thirteenth centuries. Carolingian Europe profited from the earlier phase of this steady advance in agrarian technology.

The significant intellectual revival known as the "Carolingian Renaissance" was largely a product of Charlemagne's concern for the welfare of the church and the perpetuation of Classical-Christian culture. Charlemagne assembled scholars from all over Europe; under the leadership of the Englishman Alcuin of York they set about to rescue continental culture from the pit of ignorance into which it was sinking. Alcuin

St. Peter giving symbols of authority to Pope Leo III and Charlemagne—the pallium to Leo III, the imperial standard to Charlemagne. Mosaic in St. John's Lateran, Rome.

prepared an accurate new edition of the Bible, purged of the scribal errors that had crept into it over the centuries, thereby saving Western Christian culture from the confusion arising from the corruption of its fundamental text. Carolingian scholars also purified the church liturgy and encouraged

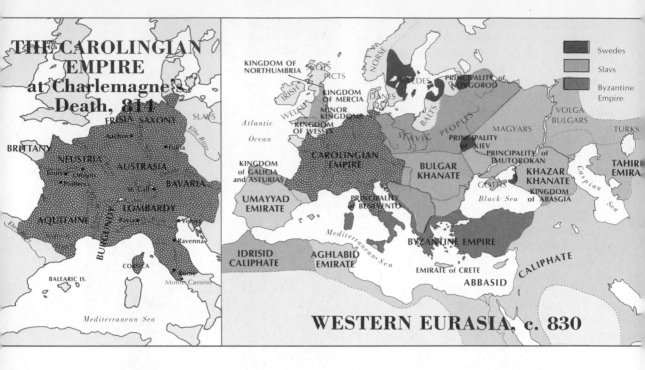

THE CAROLINGIAN EMPIRE
at Charlemagne's Death, 814

WESTERN EURASIA, c. 830

the preaching of sermons. They carried further the monastic reforms begun in Frankland by earlier Benedictines and saw to it that every major monastery had a school. They developed a new, standardized script —the Carolingian minuscule—to replace the varied and sometimes illegible scripts previously employed. And throughout the realm, monks set about copying manuscripts on an unprecedented scale.

With the gradual disintegration of Western European unity after Charlemagne's death in 814, the momentary fusion of political and spiritual energies slowly dissolved, yet the intellectual revival continued. In ninth- and tenth-century monasteries and cathedrals (particularly those of the recently conquered German districts), documents continued to be copied and schools continued to function. By the eleventh century, Europe was ready to build soaring and original intellectual edifices on its sturdy Carolingian foundations.

The Second Age of Invasions and the Western Recovery

The economic and cultural revival under Charlemagne was reversed after his death by an internal political breakdown and new invasions from without. During the ninth and tenth centuries Europe struggled grimly against the attacks of Hungarians (Magyars) from Central Asia, Saracens (Muslims) from North Africa, and Vikings from Scandinavia. In addition to these external pressures, the empire suffered an internal breakdown under Charlemagne's immediate successors. In the Treaty of Verdun (843) the empire was divided among his three grandsons, and the division became permanent. The East Frankish realm became the nucleus of modern Germany; the West Frankish realm evolved directly into the kingdom of France. The Middle Kingdom stretched northward from Italy through Burgundy, Alsace, Lorraine, and the Netherlands and included considerable parts of what are now western Germany and eastern France; its territories soon became fragmented and were to be the source of disputes between France and Germany over the next millennium.

The Saracens of the ninth and tenth centuries, unlike their Muslim predecessors in the seventh and eighth, came as brigands rather than conquerors and settlers. From their pirate nests in Africa, Spain, and the Mediterranean islands they attacked shipping, plundered coastal cities, and sailed up rivers to carry their devastation far inland. In 846 Saracen brigands raided Rome itself, and as late as 982 King Otto II of Germany was severely defeated by Saracens in southern Italy. But by then the raids were tapering off. Southern Europe, now bristling with fortifications, had learned to defend itself and was beginning to challenge Saracen dominion of the western Mediterranean.

The Hungarians (Magyars), fierce Altaic mounted nomads from the Asiatic steppes, settled in Hungary and, between the late 800s and 955, terrorized Germany and northern Italy. Hungarian raiding parties ranged far and wide, seeking defenseless settlements to plunder, avoiding fortified towns, and out-riding and outmaneuvering the armies sent against them. But in time they became more sedentary, gave more attention to their farms, and lost much of their nomadic savagery. In 955, King Otto I of Germany crushed a large Hungarian army at the Battle of Lechfeld in southern Germany and brought the raids to an end at last. Within another half century the Hungarians had adopted Christianity and were becoming integrated into the community of Christian Europe.

The Vikings, or Norsemen, were the most fearsome invaders of all. These redoubtable warrior-seafarers came from Scandinavia, the very land that had, centuries before, disgorged many of the Germanic barbarians into Europe. But to the ninth-century European—the product of countless Germanic-Celtic-Roman intermarriages, warlike still, but civilized by the church and by centuries of settled life—the pagan Vikings seemed a savage and alien people.

Then, as now, the Scandinavians were divided roughly into Swedes, Danes, and Norwegians, and each group had its own area of enterprise. The Danes concentrated on Northern France and England, the Norwegians on Scotland, Ireland, and the North Atlantic, and the Swedes on the Baltic shores and Russia. Yet the three Norse peoples were much alike, and one can regard their raids, explorations, and commercial activities as a single great international movement.

The invasions of the ninth and tenth centuries wrought notable changes in the political and social organization of Western

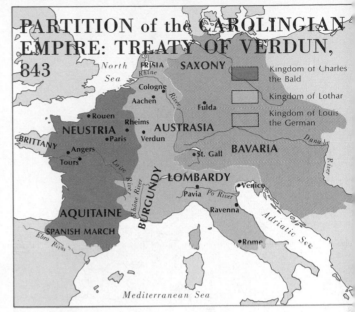

PARTITION of the CAROLINGIAN EMPIRE: TREATY OF VERDUN, 843

Europe. Generally speaking, political authority tended to crumble into small, local units as cumbersome royal armies proved incapable of coping with the lightning raids. This was decidedly true in France, but less true in Germany where the monarchy, after a period of relative weakness, recovered spectacularly in the tenth century. In England, paradoxically, the hammer blows of the Danes ultimately led to the union of several Anglo-Saxon states into a single English kingdom.

In the late eighth century, on the eve of the Viking invasions, England was politically fragmented, as it had been ever since the Anglo-Saxon conquests. Its conversion to Christianity in the sixth and seventh centuries had produced a degree of ecclesiastical centralization but no political unity. Over the centuries, however, the smaller kingdoms had gradually been passing under the control of three larger ones—Northumbria in the north, Mercia in the midlands, and Wessex in the south. The Danish attacks of the ninth century destroyed the power of Wessex's rivals, clearing the field for the Wessex monarchy and thereby hastening the trend toward consolidation that was already underway.

INVASIONS OF EUROPE, 9th & 10th CENTURIES

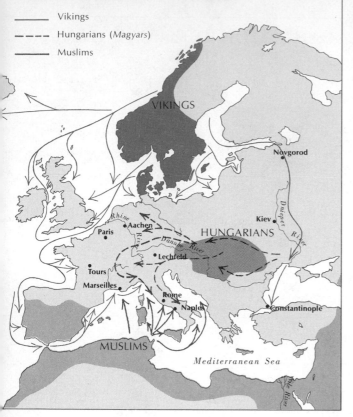

——— Vikings
– – – Hungarians (*Magyars*)
——— Muslims

The Danes might well have conquered Wessex itself had it not been that at the moment of crisis a remarkable leader rose to the Wessex throne. Alfred the Great (871–899) did everything in his power to save his kingdom from the Vikings, fighting them, bribing them, constructing fortress-sanctuaries throughout the land, directing the building of an English fleet. And in the end, Wessex not only endured but expanded significantly under Alfred's leadership. In the 880s a peace treaty between Alfred and the Danes gave Wessex most of southern and western England. The remainder of England—the "Danelaw"—remained hostile, but all non-Danish England was now united under King Alfred.

Like all successful leaders of the age, Alfred was an able warrior. More than that, he was a skilled administrator, lawgiver, organizer, and scholar. Alfred gathered scholars from far and wide—from England, Wales, and the continent—and set them to

work teaching Latin and translating Latin classics into the Anglo-Saxon language. Indeed, Alfred himself participated in this work of translation.

The task of reconquest was carried on by Alfred's successors during the first half of the tenth century. By 954 all England was in their hands, and the kings of Wessex had become kings of England. But numerous Danish settlers remained in northern and eastern England; the fusion of Danish and English customs was to require many generations.

France: The Rise of Feudalism

The Viking attacks brought centralized monarchy to England but feudal particularism to France which, unlike England, was too large for the Vikings to conquer. One group of Vikings was given the right to settle at the mouth of the Seine; they adopted Christianity, and their chieftain became a French royal vassal. Their settlement became the duchy of Normandy, and over the next two centuries the Normans—adopting the French culture, religion, and tongue—became the most energetic warriors in Christendom.

Although many Vikings settled in Normandy, the chief Norse threat to France came in the form of plundering expeditions rather than conquering armies. Distances were too great, communications too primitive, and the royal army too unwieldy for the king to take the lead in defending the realm. Military responsibility and political power descended to local lords who alone could hope to protect the countryside from the swift and terrible Viking assaults. And when the local lords were not fighting Vikings they fought one another. The French Carolingians became increasingly powerless until finally, in 987, the crown passed to one of these lords, Hugh Capet. The new Capetian dynasty would one day produce illustrious kings, but at first it was as powerless as the late Carolingians.

The Viking age witnessed the birth of feudalism in France. In a very real sense feudalism was a product of France's response to the invasions, yet the historical roots of feudalism ran deep. One root was the honorable bond of fidelity and service of a warrior to his lord, the bond that characterized the lord-vassal relationship of earlier Frankish times and the still earlier relationship of the Germanic war leader and his following. Another root was the late-Roman and early-medieval concept of the *benefice*—the estate granted to a tenant in return for service. In Carolingian times vassalage and benefice were joined—the warrior-vassal was granted an estate in return for his legal subordination and military service to his lord. The military benefice thus created was called a *feudum* (hence, "feudalism"), or *fief*.

Two of the chief reasons for the creations of fiefs were (1) the general shortage of money, necessitating payment for services in land tenure rather than wages, and (2) a change in Frankish military tactics in which mounted knights became more important than foot soldiers. The knight was more expensive to equip and maintain than the foot soldier and was commonly given a sizable estate in order that he might properly support himself. The new knights gradually became a landed aristocracy, warriors par excellence, owing their services to local dukes, counts, margraves, or lesser barons, and living off the labor of the peasants who farmed their lands.

The process of carving out fiefs was accelerated by the violence and chaos of the Viking age. This was a period of political disintegration in which the dukes, counts, and margraves, once Charlemagne's trusted local officials, now became virtually independent. Backed by their own vassals, they tended increasingly to usurp royal rights, revenues, and prerogatives. They administered justice and collected taxes without regard for the royal will. In time, they built castles and assumed all responsibility for the defense of their districts. Although they remained technically crown vassals, these feudal magnates did much as they pleased. Their power was limited chiefly by the independence of their own vassals, who began giving fiefs to subvassals and sub-subvassals of their own until there was scarcely a vassal who was not the lord of some still lower vassal. Each vassal held his estate—his fief—from his immediate lord, owing that lord service in his military contingent, obe-

ENGLAND, c. 885

dience to the judgments of his feudal court, and a miscellaneous and widely varying group of dues and obligations.

Born in northern France in the Viking age, feudalism took on many forms as it spread across Europe. Even in northern France it varied widely from region to region. It never encompassed all the land, for even at its height there remained many landowners without feudal obligations or ties. The system has been termed "feudal anarchy" and perhaps, to a point, it was. But given the instability of the old Carolingian Empire and the harsh realities of the Viking era, feudalism emerges as a realistic accommodation to a violent age when local defense was all-important.

FEUDALISM

Feudalism has been variously defined. Many Western scholars have used it loosely to mean any form of political decentralization in which warrior-nobles rule local populations while the king or emperor reigns as a mere figurehead. This definition has been applied to often dissimilar situations in the history of Egypt, India, China, Byzantium, and other non-European societies. Marxist scholarship, on the other hand, defines feudalism imprecisely as any society with a large peasantry that is neither landowning nor enslaved—a "dependent peasantry" that owes the landlord labor-service and is subject to his taxes, his judicial authority and, sometimes, his personal whims. This kind of "feudalism" is seen as an intermediate stage between the personal slavery of ancient times and the wage-slavery of the industrial age. Most non-Marxist medievalists call Marxist "feudalism" "manorialism," distinguishing between the manorial relationship between serf and landlord and the feudal relationship between two members of the warrior-nobility: the lord and the vassal. If we define feudalism in this way—namely, as a system of reciprocal rights and obligations between lords and vassals based, in each case, on a land grant in the form of a *fief* (medieval Latin: *feudum*)—it can be found only in medieval Europe and, to a degree, in the early history of Japan.

Beginning in the eleventh century, Japanese imperial power and commercial activity were slackening and political authority was fragmenting, much as in late-Carolingian Europe. In Japan, as in Europe, ties of personal dependence—chains of vassalage—developed among members of a warrior elite. The emperor survived, as did the monarchs of Europe, but in Japan the feudal chain stopped short of the emperor himself. Still more important, the European notion of a *contractual* relationship between lord and vassal, based on mutual rights and obligations, was largely absent in Japan where "lord-vassal" ties were based more rigorously on submission and subordination than on reciprocity, resulting in a strict hierarchy of sociopolitical levels within the Japanese warrior class.

Even as a singularly European phenomenon, feudalism was not without global significance. In view of Europe's spectacular impact on the world during the past 500 years, it is perhaps more illuminating to discover in feudalism a source of Europe's momentous breakthrough rather than a special case of a common human experience.

The social order of contractual privileges and widely-apportioned sovereignty collapsed in Europe with the revolutionary winds of the seventeenth, eighteenth, and nineteenth centuries. Its successor was the all-sovereign modern state with a citizenry equal before the law. But before the older contractual system had passed, Europe's career of world domination was well advanced. And one cannot help remarking that the only nonwestern country to westernize and industrialize relatively quickly and painlessly was Japan—the one nonwestern country with a quasi-feudal experience of its own.

The feudal chaos of the ninth and tenth centuries, with its extreme fragmentation of sovereignty and its incessant private wars, gradually yielded to a more orderly regime as dukes and counts consolidated their authority over large districts such as Anjou, Normandy, and Flanders. In the eleventh and twelfth centuries royal governments grew stronger, yet the feudal aristocracy remained powerful, drawing its strength from its fiefs; its prerogatives and its contractual relationship with the monarchy were based on the lord-vassal principle of reciprocal rights and obligations. Often, the feudal aristocracy cooperated with the monarchy in governing society, but at times it acted, in its own interest, to curb the autocratic impulses of an ambitious king. Like the church, the feudal aristocracy helped to shield medieval Western Europe from the royal absolutism common to most civilizations. The politics of high-medieval Christendom were marked not by the unchallenged rule of priest-kings but by the ever-changing power relationships and creative tensions between monarchy, landed artistocracy, and international church.

Germany: The Decline and Revival of the Monarchy

East Frankland—which evolved directly into the kingdom of Germany—was attacked first by the Vikings and later by Hungarian horsemen of the east. The late-Carolingian kings of Germany—the successors of Louis the German who had gained East Frankland at the Treaty of Verdun—proved incapable of coping with the Hungarian raids. As in France, real authority descended to the great magnates of the realm. Since much of Germany had been only recently incorporated into Western Christendom, the tribal consciousness of Saxons, Bavarians, and Swabians was still strong, and when the kings faltered, it was the dukes of these "tribal duchies" who seized power.

The German Carolingian line ended in 911, and within a few years the dukes of Saxony had established a new royal dynasty. It was under the Saxon dynasty, and particularly under its greatest representative, Otto I, that the particularistic trend was reversed and the king won supremacy.

THE HOLY ROMAN EMPIRE, 962

The Holy Roman Empire

The Five Stem Duchies

Venice

Otto I—"the Great" (936–973)—based his power on three significant achievements. First, he defended Germany against the Hungarians and crushed them militarily at the Battle of Lechfeld (955), thus opening Germany's eastern frontier to gradual eastward penetration by German-Christian culture. Second, he established royal supremacy over the other tribal duchies, putting down rebellions and recovering royal rights and revenues. And third, he extended German royal control into the crumbling, unstable Middle Kingdom. The dukes of Swabia and Bavaria had notions of seizing the Burgundian and Italian portions of this defunct state. Otto the Great, anxious to forestall them, led his own armies into Italy and, in 962, was crowned Roman emperor by the pope.

The Ottonian Crown, tenth century.

It is the coronation of Otto I in 962, rather than the coronation of Charlemagne in 800, that marks the true genesis of the medieval Holy Roman Empire. Otto's empire differed from Charlemagne's chiefly in the fact that it was a German, or German-Italian, empire—not a universal empire as Charlemagne's pretended to be. Otto and his imperial successors exercised no jurisdiction over France nor the remainder of Western Christendom. The medieval Holy Roman Empire had its roots deep in the soil of Germany, and most of the emperors subordinated imperial interests to those of the German monarchy.

Otto and his heirs were never very successful in ruling Italy, but in Germany the emperor was supreme. The great magnates were, for the most part, his obedient vassals. The church was in his power, and he controlled the important ecclesiastical appointments, handpicking his great bishops and abbots and using them as his trusted lieutenants in the royal administration. After 962 the German monarchy was even moderately successful in appointing popes. The emperor was regarded as *rex et sacerdos*, king and priest, sanctified by the holy anointing at his coronation. He was the vicar of God, the living symbol of Christ the King, the "natural" leader of the imperial church. There would

come a time when the church, under papal leadership, would rebel against this imperial system and ideology, but in Otto the Great's age the time was still far-off.

Otto's remarkable reign gave rise to an intellectual revival that flowered under his two successors, Otto II (973–983) and Otto III (983–1002). This "Ottonian Renaissance" produced talented artists and a group of able administrators and scholars, the most brilliant of whom was Gerbert of Aurillac—later Pope Sylvester II (*d.* 1003). Gerbert visited Spain and returned with a good grasp of Islamic science. The Arab intellectual legacy was beginning to filter into Western Christendom at last. A master of classical literature, logic, mathematics, and science, Gerbert astonished his age by teaching the Greco-Arab doctrine that the earth was spherical. Rumors circulated that he was a wizard in league with the devil, but the rumors were dampened by his elevation to the papacy. Gerbert was no wizard; instead, he was a herald of the intellectual awakening that Europe was about to undergo—a harbinger of the high middle ages.

By 1050 both England and Germany were relatively stable, well-organized kingdoms. The French monarchy remained weak, but its hour was approaching, and meanwhile French feudal principalities such as Normandy, Champagne, and Anjou were achieving political cohesion. Warfare was still endemic, but it was beginning to lessen as Europe advanced toward political stability. Above all, the invasions were over— the siege had ended—and Western Europe would remain untroubled by outside invaders for the next millennium. Hungary and the Scandinavian world were being absorbed into Christendom, and Islam was by now on the defensive.

Throughout Western Christendom, food production continued to rise with the gradual improvements in agricultural technology and the slowly increasing pacification of the countryside. Beneath the level of the ecclesiastical, political, and military aristocracy, 80 to 90 percent of the population continued to labor on the land. Agrarian organization was diverse: medieval agricultural units ranged from small independent farms to large manors divided between the peasants' fields and the lord's demesne fields.* The peasants themselves varied from slaves to freemen, although slaves were sharply declining in number between the ninth and eleventh centuries and the majority of peasants — the serfs or villains — were neither completely free nor completely enslaved. Like the old Roman *coloni*, they were bound to their land. They owed their manorial lord various dues, chiefly in crops, and were normally expected to labor for a certain number of days per week on their lord's fields. But they were not slaves — they could neither be sold nor be deprived of their hereditary fields. After paying manorial dues, they could keep the remaining produce of their lands, and an efficient serf with good land might hope to prosper. Although hardly affluent, they appear to have been distinctly better off than the peasantry of ancient Rome or of Byzantium and Islam.

By the mid-eleventh century Western Christendom was beginning to draw abreast of its two neighboring civilizations in political power and in intellectual and cultural vitality. Byzantium and Islam, having dominated Western Eurasia and North Africa during the early middle ages, were both entering periods of political turbulence and decline. But in Western Europe food production was increasing, the population was expanding, commerce was quickening, political cohesion was growing, great Romanesque churches were rising, minds were awakening. In the church a new impulse toward renewal was galvanizing the spiritual life of the west. Reform monasteries were spreading across the land, and the papacy was about to emerge from its long passivity to challenge the traditional secular dominion over the church. Western Christendom was on the threshold of an immense creative surge.

* Manorialism, which regulated the peasants lives and their relations with their lords, should not be confused with feudalism, which regulated the relations of the nobles with their king and among themselves.

SUGGESTED READINGS

Barker, John W., *Justinian and the Later Roman Empire*. Madison, Wisc.: University of Wisconsin Press, 1966.

Hussey, J. M., *The Byzantine World*. New York: Harper and Row, 1961. Paperback.

Ostrogorsky, G., *History of the Byzantine State*. New Brunswick, N.J.: Rutgers University Press, rev. ed., 1969.
This is the best single-volume history of Byzantium.

Arberry, A. J., ed., *Aspects of Islamic Civilization*. Ann Arbor, Mich.: Ann Arbor Paperbacks, 1967. Paperback.
An anthology of Islamic literature.

Dawood, N. J., trans. *The Thousand and One Nights*. Baltimore, Md.: Penguin Books, 1954. Paperback.

Gibb, H. A. R., *Mohammedanism: An Historical Survey*. New York: Oxford University Press, 2nd ed., 1953. Paperback.

von Grunebaum, Gustave E., *Medieval Islam*. Chicago, Ill.: Phoenix Books, 2nd ed., 1961. Paperback.
A learned and original work, the best on the subject.

Hitti, P. K., *History of the Arabs*. New York: St. Martin's Press, 6th ed., 1958. Paperback.
Broad yet full; a monumental work.

Bloch, Marc, *Feudal Society*, trans. by L. A. Manyon. Chicago, Ill.: University of Chicago Press, 1961. 2 Vols. Paperback.

A masterly work, challengingly written and boldly original in its conclusions.

Bloch, Marc, *French Rural History,* trans. by J. Sondheimer. Berkeley and Los Angeles: University of California Press, 1966.

Boussard, Jacques, *The Civilization of Charlemagne,* trans. by Frances Partridge. New York: World University Library, 1968. Paperback.

Dawson, Christopher, *The Making of Europe.* New York: Meridian, 1946. Paperback.
A brilliant analysis of early medieval culture by a distinguished Catholic scholar.

Einhard, *Life of Charlemagne,* trans. by S. E. Turner. Ann Arbor, Mich.: Ann Arbor Paperbacks, 1960. Paperback.
A short, reasonably trustworthy biography by Charlemagne's secretary.

Ganshof, F. L., *Feudalism,* trans. by P. Grierson. New York: Harper and Row, 2nd ed., 1961. Paperback.
A short, authoritative and rather technical survey of medieval feudal institutions.

Laistner, M. L. W., *Thought and Letters in Western Europe, A.D. 500–900.* London: Methuen, 2nd ed., 1955. Paperback.
The best intellectual history of the period.

Latouche, Robert, *The Birth of Western Economy,* trans. by E. M. Wilkinson. New York: Barnes and Noble, 1961. Paperback.
A splendid, up-to-date account of early medieval economic trends.

Loyn, H. R., *Anglo-Saxon England and the Norman Conquest.* New York: St. Martin's Press, 1963.
An authoritative recent work emphasizing economic and social history.

Sawyer, P. H., *The Age of the Vikings.* New York: St. Martin's Press, 1962.
A highly significant reappraisal of the Viking age.

White, Lynn, Jr., *Medieval Technology and Social Change.* New York: Oxford University Press, 1962. Paperback.
An important and provocative pioneering work which defies categorization. Beautifully written and opulently annotated.

CHAPTER 7

India, China, and Japan to c. 1600

Chapter 3 examined the emergence of vast empires among the major civilizations of Asia prior to approximately A.D. 600. Particular attention was paid to the imperial institutions and distinctive values on which each was founded. The present chapter continues the stories of India, China, and Japan to about 1600. Again, diversity rather than any common themes characterizes the way in which these different civilizations met their respective challenges, although traditionalism remained strong in all of them. Both India and China suffered foreign conquests and reacted differently to them, but comparative isolation enabled Japan to follow an independent course of development.

MUSLIM INDIA

The Muslim Conquest

After the death of Harsha (in 647) (see p. 78) northern India was politically fragmented into a continuously shifting assortment of kingdoms and principalities, mostly ruled by Rajput warriors. Most of their income was invested in warfare with each other, but in many cases self-interest dictated investment of a portion of their revenues in irrigation and other public works that would increase their income. Southern India, divided into a few large states, enjoyed a greater degree of political stability. Moreover, cultural vigor and creativity persisted several centuries longer in this region than in the north. Far more important than internal developments for the future of India was the rise of Islam and its expansion into India.

India's wealth served as a magnet for innumerable invasions from the northwest, most of which were migrations of less advanced peoples who were ultimately absorbed by the tolerant and flexible Indian culture. In contrast to these invasions the Muslim and later the British conquests were carried out by professional military forces of limited numbers who were seeking political control primarily for the purpose of material gain. Although both had religious and cultural fanatics in their ranks and although both ultimately had a significant cultural impact, their initial objectives were limited to attaching themselves as parasites to draw sustenance from the vast and prosperous Indian host.

The first Muslim invasion followed at-

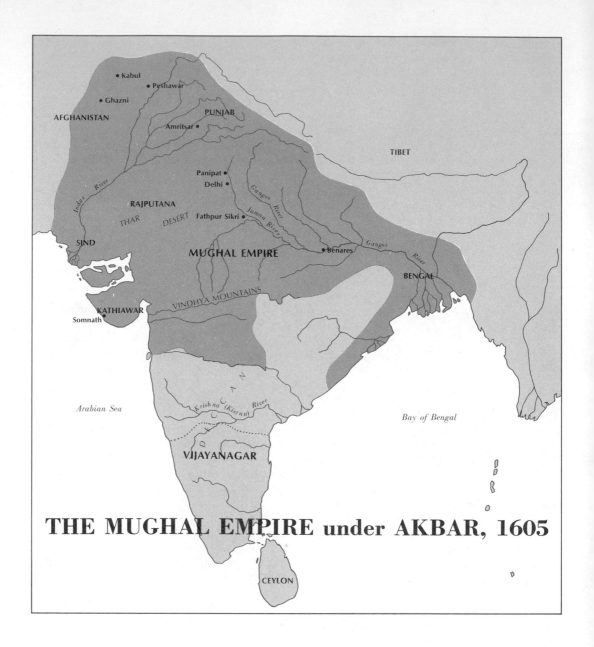

Kabul
Peshawar
Ghazni
AFGHANISTAN
PUNJAB
Amritsar
TIBET
Indus River
Panipat
Delhi
RAJPUTANA
Ganges River
THAR DESERT Fathpur Sikri
Jumna River
SIND
MUGHAL EMPIRE
Bénares
Ganges River
BENGAL
KATHIAWAR
Somnath
VINDHYA MOUNTAINS
Arabian Sea
Krishna (Kistna) River
Bay of Bengal
VIJAYANAGAR
CEYLON

THE MUGHAL EMPIRE under AKBAR, 1605

tacks by Indian pirates on Arab merchant ships. In the year 711 an expeditionary force arrived at the mouth of the Indus and in two years overran most of the Indus Valley. This easy conquest was not pursued because Indian pirates stopped attacking Arab vessels and because Arab forces were fully occupied by campaigns elsewhere. Not Arabs, then, but Turkish-speaking converts from Central Asia were, as military adventurers, to carry the banners of Islam throughout India. For

the most part they were trained professional warriors and not rude nomads seeking a new home. India's wealth attracted their raids, and these raids led to permanent conquest when the advantages of living off this productive land were realized.

In the year 986 a former Turkish slave-soldier, Sabuktegin, made his first raid into the Punjab. With the prestige and booty obtained, he was able to build up a state in present-day Afghanistan with its capital at

Ghazni. But he could maintain his dominion only by repeated raids for fresh resources. In 991 he defeated a Rajput confederacy and captured the city of Peshawar. His son, Mahmud of Ghazni, who succeeded him in 997, made almost annual raids during the winter months, retiring with his loot to the mountains as soon as the weather became uncomfortably hot. The Rajput rulers temporarily overcame their differences and confronted Mahmud's troops with a vast host, but again as in 991, the flexible tactics of the Turks proved superior to those of the large but unwieldy Indian force, which relied on elephants to break the enemy line. While a barricade of wagons bore the brunt of the main Indian assault, maneuverable squadrons of expert cavalry rained arrows on the flanks. Finally, the Rajput commander's elephants panicked, and immediately the rest of the army fled and the slaughter began. In battle after battle, since the time of Alexander the Great, this identical pattern repeated itself. Indian generals, even later Muslim ones, never learned how to deal with a mobile force. Indian military conservatism captured its conquerors.

After a number of years the Punjab had been drained of its resources, and Mahmud had to go farther afield for fresh plunder. He invaded the upper Ganges, where even larger cities with greater loot were taken, and succeeded in 1026 in crossing the great Thar Desert and storming the city of Somnath, sacred to Shiva, on the Kathiawar coast. A dedicated Muslim, Mahmud felt obliged to destroy all idols that fell into his hands. Such idol smashing also provided psychological justification for the depredations of this not uncultured man in a land of infidels.

With the riches gained through plunder, Mahmud beautified his capital city of Ghazni and made it a cultural center, inviting noted scholars and poets to enjoy his patronage. Best known are al-Beruni, who wrote an invaluable study and analysis of all the facets of Indian civilization and its works, and Firdausi, who composed his renowned epic, *Shahnama,* at Mahmud's court. In spite of al-Beruni's expose of the internal weakness of India, Mahmud's successes were not promptly followed up. On the latter's death in 1030, India gained a respite of a 150

years. His successors, less vigorous, were content to live off his accumulated glory and treasure until they lost what was left to the rising Afghan power of Ghur. Meanwhile, new Rajput families had emerged out of their continual war games to replace those destroyed by Mahmud.

In contrast with Mahmud, Muhammed of Ghur was a methodical conqueror, not just a raider. From 1175 to 1190 he consolidated his control over the Punjab, eliminating the last of Mahmud's descendants who had taken refuge there. In 1191 he turned to the east. His first expedition was almost his last. As in Mahmud's time, the Rajput rulers temporarily settled their differences and joined forces to meet the invader in the restricted area through which an army had to pass to enter the Ganges Valley. In the ensuing conflict Muhammed was wounded and his disheartened troops broke and fled. The less mobile Rajput forces, however, were unable to capitalize on their victory by pursuing the enemy, and Muhammed returned the next year to the same field of battle determined to avenge his defeat. The Rajputs were routed and destroyed, and the whole Ganges was opened to conquest, which was carried out mainly by Muhammed's generals. Idolsmashers like their Muslim predecessors, Muhammed and his generals destroyed Hindu idols and temples and all but exterminated the Buddhists in their last centers of strength in the eastern Ganges. The survivors took refuge in Tibet. In 1206 Muhammed was assassinated; he was succeeded by his chief general and former slave, Kutb-ud-din Aibak, the First ruler of the Slave Dynasty of Delhi (1206–1292).

The Delhi Sultanate

The peculiarities of the sultans (rulers) and the details of political intrigue and civil strife among the generals which accompanied every succession need not detain us. More important was the relationship that evolved between the rulers and the ruled. The conquerors were confronted with the major problem of maintaining their identity and vitality as a ruling minority in a wholly alien environment. They were aided in this task by the almost total rejection of Islam by the

Hindus, who retreated into the protective isolation of the caste system, "rendered unto Caesar" the tribute demanded, and sought only to coexist in peace. This negative attitude toward government had been ingrained in most Hindus, and the arrival of Islam merely reinforced a traditional pattern. The defeat of the Rajputs may in large part be attributed to the general Hindu indifference to the fate of their rulers. The compartmentalized hierarchy of caste represented a system of social, economic, and political decentralization that permitted the Muslims to confiscate the property of wealthy individuals without fear of stirring up a general insurrection. In addition, the essentially self-governing castes facilitated the task of administration. Only one group needed to be treated with a measure of respect because of its spiritual influence—the brahman class. Generally the brahmans were exempted from the poll tax levied on nonbelievers and, in return, they cooperated with the new rulers.

This cultural isolation of the Muslims by the Hindus aided the ruling class in maintaining its identity and encouraged it to turn to Persia for cultural tutelage. In any case, the Muslims had to look to external sources for fresh recruits to maintain their military vitality, which tended to be sapped by the debilitating factors of climate and luxury. The influx of Persian culture and Persianized Turkish soldiers was further stimulated by the ravaging Mongol armies that harassed India; for almost a century after Genghis Khan (see p. 230) sent a column in pursuit of the crown prince of Khwaresm as far as Peshawar, India was a place of refuge. The introduction of the dome, the arch, and the minaret clearly shows that art and architecture followed Persian models. The use of Hindu temples as a plentiful source of building material and the employment of Hindu artisans produced a blending of styles in which Muslim features were dominant. The Hindu influence is evident in the luxuriant decoration, which contrasts with the comparatively more austere Persian style. Unlike art, the literature that flourished with the influx of refugees was purely Persian, although gradually a new language called Urdu evolved as a mixture of western Hindi with words of Persian and Arabic origin. (Urdu is the language of Pakistan today.)

In the religious realm the need to maintain Islam's identity and distinction from the many forms of Hinduism encouraged a watchful conservatism in which theologians were relied on to maintain orthodox doctrine. Ultimately, however, a common mystical ground was found in Hindu devotional practices and Persian Sufism (see p. 197). Both shared the urge for personal union with the divine, and Persian Sufis found it difficult not to cross the narrow line to pantheism of the Indian variety. But this movement did not blossom until the sixteenth century. Under the Delhi Sultanate the corruption of the faith was not yet a problem and was carefully guarded against. Among the precautions taken was the distinction between first-class immigrant Muslims and second-class Indian converts.

Thus, aided by Hindu passivity and Persian refugees from the Mongols, the Muslim conquerors had little difficulty in securing their dominion in northern India. As long as they recognized the rules of coexistence and did not seek the enforced conversion of all Hindus, their political authority was acceptable. As long as they merely collected the customary taxes and left the caste authorities free to govern their members without interference, they had little to fear from the Indian people. A gradual blending of Perso-Muslim and Indian cultures did take place, but it, too, did not reach significant proportions until the seventeenth century.

By the end of the thirteenth century the Muslims were ready to expand into southern India. The Deccan, south of the Vindhya Mountains, was invaded, and by 1327 virtually all of India had been politically subjected. Among Hindus there was so little sense of unity and common interest that some rulers collaborated with the Muslims against their traditional Hindu foes. But this first unification of India under the Muslims could not last. The Indian subcontinent was so vast and communications so poor that governors had to be granted virtual autonomy. No matter how able the sultans were—and some were not—or how efficient an administration was developed, decentralization followed its natural course. Meanwhile, a vigorous and prosperous Hindu state, Vijayanagar gained control of the southern portion of the peninsula in 1336 and carried on a continuous struggle with the Muslim states of the Deccan for more than 200 years thereafter. Early Portuguese prosperity was based on trade with this Hindu state.

Meanwhile, at the end of the fourteenth century, internal strife in the north attracted the plundering horde of Tamerlane from Central Asia. In 1398 he invaded India and sacked Delhi after a victory facilitated by the Indian army's traditional reliance on lumbering war elephants. The superiority of mobile cavalry tactics was once again demonstrated. Like earlier raiders, Tamerlane retired before the onset of hot weather, but in his path he permitted greater destruction and slaughter than India had ever seen. His successors exploited India until 1451, when a short-lived but able dynasty filled the gap before another adventurer of Turkish-Mongol descent, Babur, intervened to establish the Mughal (Mongol) dynasty. Once more the old cavalry tactics made it possible for a numerically inferior force to gain a decisive victory at the historic field of Panipat in the narrow passage between the Indus and Ganges basins. This time, however, a new ingredient was introduced: muskets and a stand of artillery manned by Ottoman Turks.

Islam brought written history to India. Some of the written histories are little more than annals, and many others are fulsome accounts intended to win the patronage of the ruler, but a few, like that of the renowned traveler, Ibn Batuta, who visited India in the fourteenth century, are impartial and enlightening analyses. The sensitive and intellectual Babur, however, added a new and invaluable dimension with his informative *Memoirs*. In this work the adventures, hardships, and character of an exceptionally talented man are intimately revealed during his rise to power.

The Mughal Dynasty (1526–1857)

In 1494 at the age of twelve Babur succeeded his father as ruler of the central Asian principality of Ferghana, whose center was situated in a small, but esthetically stimulating, mountain valley west of the Pamir Mountains. After overcoming the efforts of three uncles to unseat him, he set out at the age of fifteen to win his fortune as the heir of Tamerlane, and in 1497, he gained control of Tamerlane's capital, Samarkand. As his *Memoirs* relate, he was overwhelmed by the beauty and perfection of the buildings and gardens of "silken Samarkand." But his fortune was not to be so easily made. When he fell ill and was reported to have died, rebellions broke out and, deserted by most of his men, he wandered as a fugitive undergoing all kinds of hardships. This hardening experience is reminiscent of the travails of Genghis Khan in his youth, and for both men it provided invaluable training in character and leadership. Both gained a deep insight in judging men but, while Genghis learned the need for ruthlessness, Babur's natural humaneness was reinforced. His refusal to permit his troops to engage in rapine and slaughter was unique among Asian military leaders.

After capturing Kabul in 1504 with a force of less than 300 loyal followers, he consolidated his control of Afghanistan before launching probing attacks into India itself in 1519. To the Indian people he proclaimed: "Our eye is on this land and on this people; raid and rapine shall not be." At the critical battle of Panipat in 1526 Babur commanded less than 12,000 seasoned warriors against an Indian levy of 100,000 men and 1000 elephants. Immediately after this victory he occupied the major cities and declared himself sultan, but with his mountaineer background he found both the climate and the customs distasteful and only accepted his role as a command of Allah.

In his *Memoirs,* Babur described the Indian people as unhandsome, unfriendly, unkind, impolite, dull-witted, and without any genius or skill in mechanics or architecture. Moreover, India lacked all the good things with which he was familiar, such as good horses, good meat, good bread, ice water, gardens, baths, and even candles. During the wet season moisture ruined bows, coats of mail, books, clothes, and furniture. During the dry season the north winds filled the air with choking dust. India's only

View of part of Fathpur Sikri built by the Mughal ruler, Akbar; sixteenth century.

redeeming features were its vast size and wealth.

Physically exhausted by his strenuous life of adventure and hardship, this truly great man fell victim to the Indian climate in 1530 at the age of forty-seven, before he had consolidated his conquests, but his *Memoirs* remain as a perpetual memorial to his character and qualities. His son, Humayun, enjoyed initial successes before suffering a decisive defeat and being forced to flee to Persia. He regained full control of his lost realm only a year before his death. His unorthodox and inquisitive son, the great Akbar, who was only thirteen at his accession, also faced a major challenge. His guardian, a Persian Shi'ite, secured his succession in another hard-fought battle at Panipat.

Akbar (1556–1605)

This vigorous and sensitive grandson of Babur recognized that his primary responsibility was the consolidation of Mughal control and the elaboration of an efficient, centralized system of administration. Akbar fulfilled both these aims, bringing the Mughal dynasty to its zenith of power and prosperity. Yet the personality of this obviously able ruler has rightly baffled his biographers.

As a boy, Akbar had little interest in his studies and even refused to learn how to read and write, but he possessed exceptional intellectual curiosity aided by a fantastic memory. He also inherited his family's strong sense of beauty, especially of the beauties of nature that he sought to recreate in his gemlike capital of Fathpur Sikri, subsequently abandoned when the water supply failed. He was interested in science and mathematics. His deepest interest, however, was reserved for his quest for the Truth, chiefly by the investigation of all the philosophies and religions that came within his purview, including Roman Catholicism. His inclination was toward mysticism, both of the Sufi and Hindu varieties. Dissatisfied with all the formal religions investigated, he devised his own eclectic religion, *Din Illahi* (Divine Faith), supposedly combining the best features of all, but it was limited to the court circle and died with him. Whether his religious toleration came from conviction or the desire to unite the diverse spiritual forces within his realm cannot be clearly determined. At any rate, he eliminated the poll tax on non-Muslims and filled a large proportion of administrative posts, even the highest, with Hindus. Perhaps his own explanation best illustrates his attitude.

Men fancy that outward profession to the mere letter of Islam, without a heartfelt conviction, can profit them. I have forced many Hindus by fear of my power to adopt the religion of my ancestors, but now that my mind has been enlightened by beams of *truth, I have become convinced that in this distressful place of contrarieties where the dark clouds of conceit and the mists of self-opinion have gathered round you, not a step can be made without the torch of proof. That belief can only be beneficial which we select with clear judgment. To repeat the words of the Creed, to perform circumcision, or to lie prostrate on the ground from dread of kingly power is not seeking God.**

Naturally Akbar's views alarmed the Muslim theologians, who did not fare well in debates with the representatives of other religions, and a conservative reaction developed in search of a ruler who would uphold the letter of Islam.

Finally, it should be noted that spiritual sensitivity was no check on Akbar's warlike propensities. No Mughal was a more vigorous warrior or gloried more in being in the forefront of battle. There was nothing effete about Akbar. Moreover, he did not shrink from ruthlessness and slaughter. On the other hand, those Hindu princes who submitted were left to administer their territories. After reducing the last pockets of resistance in northern India, he initiated the conquest of the Muslim states of the Deccan, a policy that was ultimately to prove fatal to the Mughals. But, as his intimate companion and biographer reported, Akbar believed a ruler must "ever be intent on conquest, otherwise his enemies rise in arms against him." † As an administrative policy he paid high salaries to his officials and opposed hereditary grants of land as contrary to the maintenance of centralized authority.

Under Akbar's successors, Jahangir (1605–1627) and Shah Jahan (1628–1658), the Mughal regime continued to flourish, thanks mainly to the momentum given it by him. Jahangir shared to a degree his father's tolerance, and Shah Jahan's orthodoxy was not oppressive. But the completely intolerant orthodoxy, the tremendously costly campaigns, and the administrative deterioration under the last renowned Mughal ruler, Aurangzeb (1659–1707), were to impoverish

the empire and undermine the respect for Muslim rule built up by the policies of the earlier Mughals, particularly Akbar.

Mughal Art and Literature

Although the Mughal rulers spent little on internal improvements such as irrigation and roads, they lavished patronage on the arts, which reflect increasing sophistication and technical skill and—with the exception of Akbar's reign—the growing domination of Persian style. As proof of his expressed disdain for India and its arts, Babur imported artists from the whole Islamic world to make his new home habitable. He and his successors were especially interested in the construction of gardens and pools in which they could escape the drab monotony of the north Indian countryside.

The uniqueness of Akbar's synthesizing attitude is illustrated by his city of Fathpur Sikri. The Taj Mahal, the magnificent tomb of Shah Jahan's beloved wife, stands out as the most impressive example of Mughal architecture, but a number of other works can match its beauty on a smaller scale. Its coordinated gardens and reflecting pools typify the Mughal integration of architecture and landscaping. The Taj Mahal has been described as purely Persian, but a closer examination reveals extensive Indian influence in the decorative details. In painting, greater blending is apparent, perhaps because of a reliance on Indian artists. Painting reached its peak under Akbar's indolent but esthetically inclined son, Jahangir, in a blend of Persian and Indian styles.

Literature of every variety composed in Persian flourished, especially under Akbar's patronage when it enjoyed its greatest freedom. Notable are the translations of Indian classics, which made these works available to open-minded Muslim seekers of truth, and the voluminous *Deeds of Akbar*, by his liberal companion and adviser, Abdul Fazl. In addition to an account of Akbar's life, this work includes a history of his predecessors and a detailed description of all aspects of contemporary Indian life and administration.

Sikhism

Although the major religious developments in India have already been sketched, one im-

---

* Quoted in H. G. Rawlinson, *India.* (New York: Frederick A. Praeger, 1952), pp. 311–312. By permission of Cresset Press and the author.
† *Ibid.,* p. 304.

Taj Mahal, Agra, India; seventeenth century.

portant development, an effort to synthesize Islam and Hinduism, warrants separate attention because it produced Sikhism, which still can count more than 6 million dedicated believers. The initial inspiration for this effort at synthesis came from a low-caste weaver of Benares, Kabir (1440–1518), whose devotional verse reflects Sufi influence. Essentially he was an iconoclast, denying the need for temples, idols, or prophets. God, he taught, is everywhere, only awaiting recognition and devotion. Kabir's influence on Sikhism is evident from the number of his verses included in the Sikh "bible," but the real founder of Sikhism was a Punjabi Hindu, Nanak (1469–1538).

Nanak's spiritual discontent led him to take up the wandering life of a Sufi in search of Truth, traveling throughout India to Buddhist Ceylon and even to Mecca. He finally returned to devote the last 15 years of his life to teaching his beliefs. His central doctrine was the unalloyed worship of God, the creator and disposer of all things. Islamic influ-

ence is also apparent in his cardinal declaration: "There is but one God whose name is true, the Creator." Like Kabir, Nanak rejected formalistic worship and rites and denied that knowledge of God was the exclusive possession of any religion. Virtuous conduct and humility are the only true paths to God and his mercy. Love, sincerity, justice, modesty, courtesy, truth, and charity in every thought and action are more important than any form of worship.

The *gurus* (teachers) who followed Nanak built on this foundation the unique practices and attitudes that came to distinguish Sikhism clearly from both Islam and Hinduism. Sikhism evolved its own system of writing, its own ritual and scripture, and its own center at Amritsar, which is named after the Sikh temple there. Communal life was encouraged by a common meal to which all contributed and by congregational worship. As the order grew, the predominance of Hindu converts led to the incorporation of Hindu customs and an increasing alienation from Islam. The fourth *guru* after Nanak was executed for participation in an unsuccessful rebellion and thus became Sikhism's first martyr.

The following two *gurus* were military as well as spiritual leaders and converted Sikhism into a military organization to combat Aurangzeb's persecution. In 1699 the sworn brotherhood of fighting Sikhs was founded with an initiation and communion ceremony. As in Islam, those Sikhs who died in battle were assured of entry into paradise. Thus the corporate sense of the Sikhs was given a more clearly institutionalized expression. They were now a self-perpetuating community of militant saints who held themselves aloof from both Hindus and Muslims. Ironically then, Sikhism, which was pioneered as an effort to find common ground between Islam and Hinduism by drawing on both, became a separate and exclusive community within already divided India.

The Muslim Impact

Although the Muslim conquest failed to break the spiritual hold of Hinduism on the mass of the Indian people, it was not without a deeply significant impact; this is most obvious in the present political division of the subcontinent. Furthermore, some Muslim customs did spread in the Hindu community, such as the veiling of women, which had the effect of lowering their status. In spite of Islam's equalitarian appeal to the downtrodden members of India's caste-ridden social hierarchy, it never secured the conversion of as much as one-quarter of the population. Islam's failure in India stands in contrast to its enduring success throughout the Middle East and North Africa.

The basic incompatibility of prophetic Islam and mystic Hinduism, despite the synthesizing efforts of a Nanak or an Akbar, encouraged the further development of the established caste system and reinforced the Hindu sense of spiritual superiority with its consequent rejection without serious investigation of everything alien. Both of these features represent an introverted attitude adopted as a defensive mechanism for cultural self-preservation. So long as the Muslims, and later the British, accepted the role of a ruling caste and stayed within the limits of the unwritten rule of coexistence, the Hindus put up with them. The caste system had evolved as a substitute for and a buffer against centralized political authority and effectively performed most of the functions normally associated with the state. Governments, whether Hindu or Muslim, were tolerated and taxes were dutifully paid so long as they did not interfere with local caste government, but there was no deep loyalty to these political entities. States and princes might come and go, but the caste-organized society continued and evolved with little or no reference to them.

Although the Muslims introduced Persian culture, which strongly influenced the arts patronized by the ruling class, they did little to improve the social and economic life of India, being content to inherit the established and accepted system of exploiting the peasantry. Where their Rajput predecessors had at least invested a portion of their revenues in the building of productive public works, the Muslims could show little to justify their tax collections other than a large number of magnificent mosques, palaces, fortifications, and tombs. A few of the wiser Delhi sultans had maintained state granaries to supply food at reasonable prices whenever nature turned against the peasants, but most of the Muslim rulers neglected even this elementary precaution. Famines struck one part of India or another almost annually, carrying off untold numbers who, after meeting the demands of the government, had no surpluses to fall back on. But the fertility of India's people proved more reliable than that of her soil, and the human losses were soon recouped. Muslim fatalism, reinforced by the religious barrier, combined to prevent the Muslim rulers from developing much humanitarian concern for their Hindu subjects. On the other hand, Hindu landlords and tax collectors were generally more ravenous and oppressive than Muslim ones. The small social security that the Hindu possessed was to be found within his family and his caste. This condition of general poverty was partially relieved by the growth of trade created by the increasing prosperity of the West, but again, the profit went mainly into the treasure chests of wealthy merchants; the craftsman remained as impoverished as the peasant. Through industriousness and by sheer numbers, the peasants and craftsmen collectively bore the burden of India on their individually weak backs.

IMPERIAL CHINA TO 1644

The Sui Dynasty (A.D. 589–618)

After more than two and one-half centuries of division during which the barbarian conquerors of the north had become thoroughly transformed by Chinese culture, China was reunified by a general of mixed ancestry who established a short-lived but vigorous dynasty, in many ways analogous to the Ch'in. Like the Ch'in, the Sui dynasty established a strong and severe centralized government, although the great families were too well established to be eliminated. The Great Wall was rebuilt, and the various regions of China were linked by canals and roads built by means of vast teams of conscript labor. A major canal carried the rice surpluses of the Yangtze basin to the Yellow River valley, with a later branch delivering supplies to the vicinity of Peking for defense of the frontier. The development of the south during the intervening centuries since the collapse of the Han dynasty had brought about its replacement of the north as the principal granary of China, while the most menacing frontiers remained in the north, necessitating a canal as the only economical means of bulk transport. The Sui dynasty also engaged in extensive and costly military campaigns. As in the case of the Ch'in, this full mobilization and exploitation of human resources, which laid the foundation for the succeeding dynasty's prosperity, alienated all elements of Chinese society and, at the first sign of weakness, inspired rebellions.

The T'ang Dynasty (A.D. 618–907)

Li Shih-min, the able, ambitious, and ruthless second son of a frontier official, also of mixed ancestry, goaded his father into rebellion and placed him on the throne as the founder of the T'ang dynasty, the most vigorous, militant, and cosmopolitan of Chinese dynasties. Unlike the early rulers of the Han dynasty, the first T'ang rulers gave the Chinese people little rest.

After liquidating his brothers, Li Shih-min (626–649) persuaded his father to abdicate in his favor. This restless ruler then turned to an intensive program of internal improvements and external conquests. Both the public works of the Sui and Li's additions, by improving productivity and distribution, provided the surplus resources for such an active program. In spite of occasional setbacks China under this ruler and his more able successors achieved a new peak of power and wealth. With more than 50 million inhabitants it was the most populous state in the world, a distinction it may have achieved as early as the Han era and has retained ever since.

Direct control over the Tarim basin was regained, and military campaigns secured recognition of Chinese supremacy in Tibet, the Trans-Pamir region, and even the upper reaches of the Indus River in modern Afghanistan. A Chinese ambassador to north India who was mistreated recruited Tibetan and Nepalese troops, captured the offending king, and delivered him as a prisoner to the imperial capital at Ch'ang-an. To the south, North Vietnam was reconquered, and to the northeast, the king of the Korean kingdom of Silla, aided by Chinese troops, defeated the other Korean states, including their Japanese allies. Thereafter, a unified Korea remained a faithful subordinate of the T'ang dynasty. In 751, after earlier successes, the decisive defeat of a Chinese army under a Korean general in the Trans-Pamir region by a Muslim army signaled the decline, but by no means the overthrow, of T'ang military strength. At the same time the government was severely shaken by a rebellion led by another non-Chinese general who had won favor at the court. As these events indicate, many aliens, including Syrians and Arabs, were employed by the confident and cosmopolitan T'ang regime. Middle Eastern religions — Islam, Manicheism, and Nestorian Christianity — were welcomed, and both Buddhism and Taoism won the patronage of various emperors.

Much more important in the long run than these inroads, which were merely a continuation of the previous alien impact, was the

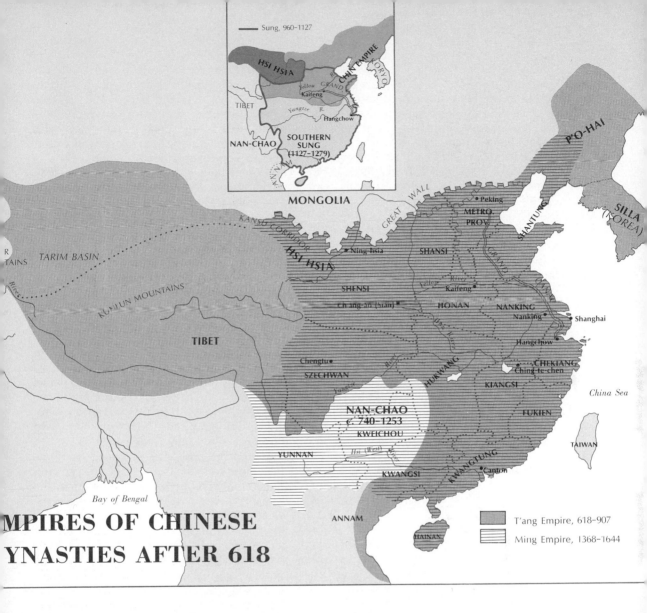

Sung, 960–1127

HSI HSIA

CHIN EMPIRE

TIBET

Yellow R. GRAND

Kaifeng

Yangtze R.

Hangchow

NAN-CHAO

SOUTHERN
SUNG
(1127–1279)

MONGOLIA

TARIM BASIN

KUNLUN MOUNTAINS

TIBET

KANSU CORRIDOR

HSI HSIA

Ning-hsia

SHENSI

Ch'ang-an (Sian)

Chengtu

SZECHWAN

YUNNAN

NAN-CHAO
c. 740–1253

KWEICHOU

Hsi (West)

KWANGSI

Bay of Bengal

GREAT WALL

Peking

METRO.
PROV.

SHANSI

Yellow River

Kaifeng

HONAN

NANKING

Nanking

Shanghai

GRAND CANAL

SHANTUNG

P'O-HAI

SILLA
(KOREA)

Hangchow

CHEKIANG

Ching-te-chen

HUKWANG

KIANGSI

FUKIEN

China Sea

TAIWAN

KWANGTUNG

Canton

ANNAM

HAINAN

China Sea

T'ang Empire, 618–907

Ming Empire, 1368–1644

**MPIRES OF CHINESE
YNASTIES AFTER 618**

gradual reduction of great landed estates and the reassertion of Confucianist supremacy. Neither the Sui nor early T'ang rulers were able to eliminate the aristocracy of great landed families, but the turmoil preceding and following the Sui dynasty did reduce the number and influence of these almost autonomous units. Every effort was made to develop and maintain a free, tax-paying peasantry but, for the most part, this was achieved by opening new lands to agriculture and reclaiming abandoned lands. Moreover, in recognition of the need for trained administrators, both regimes reinstituted the Confucian-oriented civil service examina-

tions in a much more thoroughgoing fashion, providing generous support for advanced education in the provinces and at the imperial capital. As more and more posts in the bureaucracy came to be filled by successful contestants in the examinations, a scholar-gentry order of comparatively small landholders gradually grew up to offset the local domination of large landlords, permanently altering the socioeconomic structure of China.

Also contributing to this basic change was a major tax reform. By the eighth century the T'ang regime was faced with the traditional dilemma of growing costs of government at a time of declining revenues as a result of the reduction of free, taxpaying peasants to tenant status. Until this time, the direct levy of taxes in grain, labor, and military service on free peasant producers had been the major source of governmental income, supplemented by a small land tax, state monopolies, and sundry levies on wealth and commerce. Now the government gradually abandoned the direct levy on free peasants and greatly increased the land tax, which was theoretically assessed on all land according to productivity and regardless of ownership. In practice, however, the prestige and privilege of scholar-gentry landlords permitted them to discover ways of partially evading their obligation. Nevertheless, this new tax system did aid in accelerating the decline of the great families.

The revival of Confucianism was further demonstrated by successive attacks on Buddhism and the general decline of Buddhist and Taoist influence in the latter half of the T'ang dynasty. In the most severe round of state persecution (841–845) Manicheism and Nestorian Christianity were extinguished and Buddhism was severely crippled. These persecutions reflected the growth of a Confucian and Chinese rejection of aliens and alien ideas which came to characterize the succeeding Sung dynasty.

Meanwhile, the fiscal reform did no more than check the declining phase the T'ang regime had entered. Indeed, the growing dependence on foreign mercenaries alienated the Chinese people, especially when they had to be used to suppress popular rebellions. In 907 the T'ang dynasty was overthrown, and, during a 50-year interregnum, China was fragmented into contesting states. Finally, in the north, a Chinese general seized power and by exceptionally diplomatic and generous treatment of friend and foe gained control of most of China.

The Sung Dynasty (A.D. 960–1279)

The founder of the Sung dynasty conformed in every way to the Confucian ideal of the virtuous ruler and thus won widespread support. The Sung emperors' acceptance of Confucianist doctrines made them the least aggressive of Chinese dynasties. In any case,

the great growth of trade by sea since the eighth century meant that control of the northwest and the overland trade routes was no longer essential, and the abandonment of reliance on a conscript peasant army discouraged militancy. The payment of tribute to non-Chinese neighbors seemed a cheaper expedient than recourse to war with all its uncertainties. Moreover, careful fiscal administration produced an income three times that of the T'ang at its height; the increase was drawn principally from the rapidly developing south.

In time, however, the inevitable problems of an excess of expenditures over income caught up with the Sung dynasty. A great increase in the size of the army—which because of the hostility toward aliens was primarily recruited from Chinese paupers—came to absorb 80 percent of the government's income in what amounted to a massive welfare program of little military value. In an effort to overcome these problems, Wang An-shih (1021–1086) got an opportunity to introduce drastic reforms, similar to those of Wang Mang (see pp. 93–95).

Among the proposals instituted by imperial decree were measures to aid the peasants in regaining economic independence and "soak the rich" measures to recapture the wealth that was increasingly being diverted into the coffers of the Confucian scholar-gentry class. Prices were stabilized by a revival of a government marketing program for surpluses. State loans to peasants at lower than prevailing interest rates and government pawnshops were instituted. A revaluation of all land in terms of productivity provided the basis for revised land-tax assessments. The remaining conscript labor obligations were abolished and replaced by a graduated tax that fell more heavily on the wealthy. Movable as well as immovable wealth was included in assessing a graduated tax. In contrast to the abolition of the peasant's labor obligation, his military obligation was revived, requiring each family with more than one son to provide one for military training and service. In addition, to overcome the traditional Chinese weakness in cavalry, peasants in suitable areas were required to care for horses; both the horses and fodder were supplied by the government. To support the program with properly trained civil servants, government schools were multiplied and the examinations were revised to place emphasis on the selection of men versed in contemporary problems. This shift reflected Wang An-shih's position that so-called natural disasters were not heaven-sent but were, instead, the result of human errors and natural causes that could and should be avoided by able administrators.

Many outstanding scholar-officials, including the historians (who gave him a "bad press"), vigorously denounced Wang An-shih's reforms as subversive to Confucianism. But perhaps it is significant that even the hostile historians record no revolts when his reforms were operative. In this respect he fared better than Wang Mang. Nevertheless, his reforms like Wang Mang's were never in force long enough or implemented sincerely enough by the bureaucracy to have a permanent effect.

Sung rule of all of China was lost when non-Chinese warriors who had taken the name of Chin (Golden) overran northern China after quarreling with their Sung allies over the spoils from a border state to which the Chinese had been paying tribute. As a result, the remainder of the Sung Dynasty, which is known as the Southern Sung (1127–1279), was forced to accept a boundary just north of the Yangtze River and the status of a tributary of the Chin Regime.

In spite of the loss of northern China, the greater attention given to the south resulted in such tremendous economic growth that this smaller state became actually wealthier than its larger predecessor. In addition to rural development, the Southern Sung era saw rapid urban expansion supported by the growth of trade. Despite the continued Confucian disdain for the merchant class, the government was not reluctant to tax trade, which came to yield a larger revenue than the land tax.

The development of the south had been accelerating for several centuries. Between the eighth and twelfth centuries its population probably tripled, reflecting investment in water-control projects, the introduction of improved seeds, crop diversification, and more intensive cultivation of all arable land. Although the prosperity of the south was built on agricultural development, a more important source of wealth was the huge growth of trade, particularly overseas trade, based on the demand for improved Chinese products. Technical advances increased the quality and quantity of silk, lacquer, and porcelain production. Muslim ships had initiated the trade, but by the twelfth century large Chinese vessels carrying up to 200 passengers became major participants, thanks in part to the Chinese development of the compass. The use of gunpowder in explosive weapons, although not a factor in trade, illustrates the technological vigor of this era. The growth of commercial quarters in the cities, the development of transport operations, and the multiplication of trade guilds are yardsticks of the greater volume and specialization of commerce. Another index of economic growth are tax returns measured in strings of 1000 copper coins, although they may also reflect greater governmental efficiency in cash collections. At the height of the T'ang dynasty in 749 only two million strings were collected compared with 37 million strings in 1065 under the Sung. Indeed, the use of money multiplied rapidly as illustrated by the minting of 200,000 to 300,000 strings a year by the T'ang, compared to more than one million strings a year by the Sung. Even then the demand for cash exceeded the supply, and both the government and private bankers issued paper money drafts and certificates of deposit to get around the need of transporting bulky coinage from one place to another. In 1024 the government took over the issue of certificates of 200 to 1000 cash each: these certificates were the first real paper money.

In the face of such economic change the great landed families gradually faded away and were replaced in influence by Confucian scholar-landlords. These "gentry," with smaller and often fragmented landholdings, vied for public office. Many of their families had probably made their money in trade, a fact that they conveniently forgot. Attracted by the sophisticated pleasures of the cities, they tended to live there much of the time in a community of scholars, and the higher culture reflected urban tastes. During the Sung the introduction of foot-binding for upper class women perhaps reflects a decline in their usefulness in an urban as opposed to a rural environment. The peasant wife and mother, however, continued to play an important role in family affairs, dominating her daughters-in-law and sometimes even her husband along with the entire family.

T'ang and Sung Culture

An increasingly wealthy urban society demanded and financed a greater cultural sophistication than China had yet enjoyed. Art and literature, which flourished under T'ang and Sung patronage, achieved a peak of refinement esthetically unsurpassed since that time. Both T'ang and Sung art have their respective champions, but all agree that in vigor, variety, sensitivity, and creativity this combined period is unexcelled for its architecture, sculpture, painting, and porcelain. Taoist and Buddhist influence is apparent in all these art forms.

The T'ang period produced China's greatest lyric poets. Li Po (701–762), a Taoist individualist, was inspired by the desire to live life to the fullest extent, employing the pleasures of wine, women, and song. His friend, Tu Fu (712–770), was a conscientious Confucian moralist deeply moved by human suffering and injustice. Po Chu-i (772–846) is noted for breaking the literary conventions and composing his poems in a simpler, more popular style. These three are only the most renowned of thousands of recognized poets of this era alone.

The T'ang-Sung period also produced a tremendous volume of prose works, particularly under Sung patronage. The accumulated wisdom of Chinese civilization was collected and classified for easy reference in vast encyclopedic works. Such monumental efforts were encouraged by the development of printing, both wood-block and movable type, which greatly expanded readership. The invention of paper and printing, two vital foundations of modern civilization, by the traditional civilization with the largest literature should be understood as major contributions. The Sung era is renowned for its historians of whom the most famous was Ssu-ma Kuang (1018–1087). He wrote the first comprehensive history since the Han historian, Ssu-ma Ch'ien, covering the period from 403 B.C. to A.D. 959 under

the appropriate Confucian title, *The Comprehensive Mirror for Aid in Government*. In his work and that of his contemporaries the greater attention to institutional development reflects the greater concern for the functions of a bureaucratized government in which the individual had presumably become less important than the office. Even though Ssu-ma Kuang was a leading opponent of Wang An-shih, he would have agreed that a well-trained official could and should forestall natural disasters through the full knowledge of his responsibilities and conscientious performance of his duties.

Neo-Confucianism

The pinnacle of Sung intellectual achievement was the reworking of Confucianism, which has been labeled Neo-Confucianism. The outstanding scholar who completed this work of synthesis was Chu Hsi (1120–1200), also noted for his abridgement of Ssu-ma Kuang's history to emphasize the moral lessons of Chinese history. Although Chu Hsi's synthesis gained the final stamp of approval as the orthodox doctrine of Confucianism, the altered milieu since Han times, particularly this vibrant Sung era of intellectual reassessment and reformulation, inspired other interpretations as well. As good Confucianists, all schools accepted the validity of the Classics as the basis of Confucianism. In fact, the standard canonization of the Classics and the Four Books (Confucius' *Analects*, the *Mencius*, the *Great Learning*, and the *Doctrine of the Mean*) was drawn up in this era. But vital new elements had been added since Han times to the stock of Chinese intellectual material — Buddhism and the Buddhist-influenced development of Taoism. Merely to reject Buddhist and Taoist doctrines was no longer enough; a convincing Confucian answer to their intellectual as well as their spiritual challenge needed to be worked out that would confirm the this-worldly, nontheistic outlook of Confucianism.

The metaphysics of Chu Hsi accepted the eternal and infinite "Supreme Ultimate" of the non-Confucian *Classic of Changes* as the underlying principle of all existence and change and went on to assert that everything has its fundamental principle of form(*li*),

A stylish lady of the T'ang court, a ceramic figurine.

regardless of whether it materially exists or not at any particular moment. Incidentally, this principle of eternal "forms" or "laws" was the basis for a reinterpretation in support of Mencius' doctrine of man's innate goodness that might become perverted or perfected in a man's actual existence. Complementing the principle of "forms", Chu Hsi postulated *ch'i*, which may be freely translated as "matter," by a combination of which the "form" takes material shape in the phenomenal world. Thus his metaphysics constitutes an inseparable dualism of *li* and *ch'i* (form and matter) which, although appearing to change continuously, represented the eternal unity of the "Supreme Ultimate." With *li* were associated Confucian ethics, always latent, but requiring cultivation by education, study, and "enlightenment," reminiscent of Ch'an Buddhism, to gain full realization of the potentiality for perfection. In other words, man's physical existence is a rough replica of his ideal form and requires extensive polishing to achieve its innate potentiality for perfection.

In the long run, Neo-Confucianist metaphysics did not receive much attention from most Confucianists, who generally accepted it without question or much study and concentrated on the Confucian classics, ethics, and their application to government. Neo-Confucian ethics reaffirmed the family-oriented precept of superior and inferior as the guide to proper human relations. The family conception was applied to the government of the empire over which the ruler exercised the autocratic authority of a father according to the family ideal of benevolent paternalism. But, as the father was to be aided and courteously criticized for any shortcomings, by the same token the ruler was to be aided and guided in government by a bureaucracy of officials whose moral excellence and knowledge of the principles of good government had been proved by successful passage through the examination system. The bureaucratic ideal, equalitarian in principle, in fact favored those scholar-gentry families that could afford the needed education. Moreover, a substantial proportion of appointees had not passed through the examination system. Thus, as in every civilization and institution, Chinese practice fell short of full compliance with its expressed ideal.

Neo-Confucianism, as synthesized by Chu Hsi, in time became firmly established as the orthodox doctrine enshrined in the examination questions. Even Chu Hsi's stress on the "investigation of things" was interpreted to mean the study of the classics and history according to his commentaries on them, an interpretation that effectively stifled any creative thought, let alone scientific investigation. An appreciation of the character and sacrosanct nature of Neo-Confucianism is necessary for an understanding of later stubborn official resistance to new ideas from the West. The expansive creativity and open-minded curiosity about aliens and alien ideas of the T'ang had been submerged by the introverted scholarship and pedantry of the Sung. To the Confucianist mind the Middle Kingdom, as China was called by the Chinese, was the source and center of civilization surrounded by barbarians. The barbarians might overrun the realm, but only by adopting Chinese civilization could they gain even grudging acceptance from the Confucian scholar-elite.

The Mongols in China

Although the conquest of China was the Mongol's most impressive achievement, they operated on a far larger stage, affecting directly or indirectly all of Asia, and even penetrating and creating alarm in Europe. The Mongol population totaled no more than two and one-half million, but the rugged nomadic life of herding, hunting, and tribal warfare produced the world's finest cavalry. These expert horsemen, trained and hardened by a lifetime in the saddle, could stand in their stirrups and discharge from powerful compound bows arrows that could pierce armor with devastating accuracy at ranges up to 600 feet. The ruthless life of survival on the steppes did not cultivate humaneness toward foes; their liquidation of captives, particularly after a difficult and costly siege, was a natural Mongol reaction that spread terror before them. In any case, the nomadic economy could not afford to support unproductive prisoners, even as slaves. It should be noted, however, that the mobilizer of the Mongols, Genghis Khan, was shrewd and tolerant enough to spare and employ in his service the most talented persons among conquered peoples.

His father, a Mongol chieftain, died while he was still a boy, too young and inexperienced to take command. Escaping and eluding those who sought to liquidate him, he demonstrated over the years an ability to survive that attracted followers who were willing to obey his iron discipline and join their fortunes to his. The mere fact of this ordeal, in combination with his personality, built up a determination to conquer or die that led him from conquest to conquest. Even if he had been content with regaining his tribal territory, fear of vengeance inspired his old foes and despoilers to combine and intrigue against him. Once he had eliminated them and united the Mongols, his only path was further conquest to reward his warriors.

In the year 1206, "the conqueror" received the title of Genghis Khan from a grand assembly of chieftains and then broke the power of the Tibetan Tangut regime of Hsi Hsia, centered in the Kansu corridor on his southern flank, before leading his horsemen against the Chin regime of northern China. In campaigns from 1211 to 1215, his forces defeated all Chin armies in the field, ravaged the countryside at will, but had little success against fortified cities. Leaving a smaller force to complete the conquest of the Chin domain, he directed his main forces to conquests in the west. After his death in 1227 his far-flung empire was divided among the sons of his principal wife according to tribal custom, and they completed the conquest of northern China, extinguishing the Chin dynasty in 1234. The Sung rulers had repeated their previous mistake by allying with the Mongols in the destruction of the Chin state. Again, the Sung ruler complained that the Chinese share of the spoils was too small, thus inviting a Mongol assault. The conquest of Sung China was delayed by succession and other problems elsewhere in the Mongol Empire, and even after it began in 1251 the attacks were intermittent. The well-fortified cities of Sung China proved very difficult to capture, even with the aid of experts in siege warfare drawn from the entire Mongol realm, and the last embers of Sung resistance were not extinguished until 1279. The conquest was completed under the leadership of Genghis Khan's talented grandson, Khubilai, who had become Great Khan in 1260 and proclaimed the Yuan dynasty (1271–1368).

Still fired by the Mongol drive for military expansion, this vigorous ruler sent forth expedition after expedition, by land and by sea, but without enduring results. Two unsuccessful assaults were launched in 1274 and 1281 against Japan. Other naval expeditions brought back envoys and exacted tribute from a number of states in Southeast Asia and both coasts of India. Repeated overland expeditions into Vietnam and Burma made the Yuan imperial presence felt, but these campaigns tended to bog down in the unfamiliar and difficult terrain and climate.

In China, Mongol garrisons were maintained at major cities to discourage rebellions and were regularly replaced before they became soft from city living. Recognizing the need to keep in touch with the real source of Mongol strength, the steppes of Mongolia, Khubilai built a new capital at Peking, in the north, and erected a summer capital in eastern Mongolia. Then, in order to facilitate the transport of the grain tax to the new center, two and one-half million laborers dug the Grand Canal, linking Peking with the Yangtze basin; the entire length of the canal was bordered by a paved post road for speedy communications.

As Great Khan, as well as Emperor of China, Khubilai possessed a far broader outlook than his Sung predecessors. After all, China was only the richest portion of his vast domain. Large numbers of non-Chinese staffed his Chinese civil service, especially the top echelon. The embittered hostility of the Confucian scholar class of southern China encouraged a stratification of the bureaucracy: Mongols occupied key posts with other non-Chinese at the next level, northern Chinese who had served the Chin were below them, and southern Chinese were at the bottom, filling no more than 25 percent of the positions regardless of their qualifications. As a result of the subordination of the Confucian scholar-official in his own land, seditious sentiments were widespread and rebellion was an ever-present menace.

During Mongol rule, unemployed but talented Chinese scholars developed two additions to Chinese literature, the drama and the novel, which had already begun to take shape as early as T'ang times. Previously, these two literary forms, which employed the spoken language in order to appeal to a wider audience, had been shunned by Confucian scholars trained in the classical written language. The Mongol reliance on non-Chinese officials, untrained in the classical language, encouraged the employment of a more popular style even in government documents. The drama evolved for the entertainment of urban and court audiences, while the novel developed from the tales told to the peasants by storytellers who traveled from market to market. This contrast between the two literary forms is apparent in their themes, style, and language. The drama is a more sophisticated, stylized art form that draws on romantic and military adventures of the ruling class and frequently reflects the clash between individual desires and Confucian social precepts. The novel, while also dealing with heroic adventures, uses more earthy language and humor and more often concerns peasants and their problems. (Both forms have been sifted under Communist auspices to discover suitable presentations of class struggle, with more fruitful results in the case of the novel.)

Meanwhile, by the mid-fourteenth century the descendants of Khubilai Khan were so absorbed by intrafamily struggles for power that they neglected the maintenance of their authority in central and southern China. In any case, they had never gained acceptance because of their failure to become fully integrated into Confucian society. Although they were religiously tolerant and revived state support of the Confucian cult, they continued to look abroad and gave heavy patronage to Lamaistic Buddhism from Tibet. As a result, rebel movements arose and grew in strength, especially in the Yangtze Valley. At the same time extensive graft and corruption as well as famine and destruction caused by an abnormal sequence of droughts and floods in the north undermined the regime psychologically and economically. The rebel leaders, many of whom were of humble origin, sought patriotic support by advocating the expulsion of aliens and the establishment of a native dynasty that would restore the antiforeign outlook of the Sung. Some even claimed descent from the Sung. As usual, secret societies, religious prophesies, and superstitious appeals were drawn on to reinforce and broaden the base of a leader's support.

The Ming Dynasty (A.D. 1368–1644)

Out of the struggle for power among these rebel warlords, Chu Yuan-chang (1328–1398), an orphaned peasant who had learned to read and write as a novice in a Buddhist monastery, emerged victorious and founded the Ming (Brilliant) dynasty. Most decisive in his rise to power was the capture of the city of Nanking in 1356, which served as a centrally located base of operations. After 12 years spent in consolidating his control over central and southern China, he advanced against the feuding Mongols and captured Peking. The Mongols were expelled from China, but their power was not broken, and they remained a major menace. In recognition of this fact a succeeding Ming emperor moved his capital from Nanking to Peking, rebuilding the Great Wall and constructing what remains today one of the most impressive capital cities in the world.

The Ming dynasty's emphasis on a conservative restoration meant few innovations. Under the emperor the three-way division of administrative functions between the civil service, the military hierarchy, and the board of censors, which kept the other two arms under critical observation, was continued as it had evolved since T'ang times. The long-term tendency of concentrating more authority in the hands of the ruler and exercising more direct control over the provinces was perpetuated and enhanced by the founder's abolition of the post of prime minister, leaving all initiative to the emperor. But the relatively small size of the bureaucracy, which probably never numbered more than 20,000 imperial appointees, plus clerks and servants, belied these autocratic pretensions, particularly in view of its responsibility for governing a growing population of well over 100 million subjects. As before, the effectiveness of the central government at the local level depended on the voluntary and unpaid cooperation and services of the scholar-gentry class in return for the privileged status it enjoyed. At most there were one-half million degree holders of all ranks who, with their families, totaled less than 2 percent of the population, but they set the tone and maintained the stability of Chinese society. At court the contest for appointments encouraged factionalism as well as corruption, and the Ming emperors employed eunuchs to offset the influence of Confucian scholar-officials from the south.

One unique phenomenon sponsored by the second vigorous Ming ruler deserves notice. Following the maritime interests of the Southern Sung and Khubilai Khan, seven major naval expeditions were dispatched between 1405 and 1433 under the command of the Muslim eunuch Cheng Ho for the political purpose of impressing the states along the maritime trade routes with China's might and to secure recognition of Chinese suzerainty. These were no small-scale explorations but mighty flotillas of ships up to 400 feet long that transported as many as

Temple of Heaven, Peking, Ming dynasty.

28,000 men across the vast distances of the south Asian seas. In comparison, the ill-fated Spanish Armada more than a century and a half later carried fewer men on a much shorter voyage. We can well imagine the impression made on local rulers by the sight of this fleet moving into a harbor, dropping anchor, and discharging 20,000 troops in full battle array. These voyages reached as far as the entrances to the Persian Gulf and Red Sea, as well as various points on the African coast, carrying back to the Ming court envoys and tribute from some 50 states, in addition to exotic items such as zebras and giraffes.

Although these feats of seamanship clearly demonstrated the Chinese capability for overseas imperialism, they were abruptly and permanently terminated, primarily because they had served their purpose and because all imperial resources were needed to construct the magnificent new capital at Peking and to meet the revived Mongol menace. As a consequence, the Western intruders, when they appeared in the sixteenth century in their puny ships, went unchallenged and before long arrived at Chinese ports with gunports open. Meanwhile, the despised Chinese merchants continued at their own risk to expand the maritime trade and to establish overseas colonies

Hall of Supreme Harmony in Peking, China, Ming dynasty.

in Southeast Asia which had been initially developed on a large scale during the Southern Sung era. The antitrade attitude of the Ming era is illustrated by its failure to exploit, as the Southern Sung had done, this potential source of tax revenue. But from the government's point of view overseas trade was of negligible importance because China had little need of imports. Moreover, even at the time of Cheng Ho's exploits, China had been unable to suppress Japanese and Chinese piracy on the coast, and when Western traders appeared in their armed vessels, they were initially looked on as no more than a more barbaric breed of pirates. On the other hand, the well-educated Jesuit missionaries, like the patient and tolerant Matteo Ricci who labored initially for influence and conversions at court, made a favorable impression at the Ming court. They aided Chinese astronomers in calendar reform and also helped to cast improved cannon.

In the arts, no civilization that could create such a masterpiece of architectural and landscape design as the capital city of Peking can be considered esthetically moribund. In other media, however, although many individual works of genius can be singled out, Chinese creative talents can be considered to have passed their zenith. The emphasis on seeking models of perfection in the past tended to stifle originality, although technological advances led to a more liberal use of color. The porcelain produced at the imperial kilns was technologically more advanced, but the multicolored decoration did not possess the esthetic appeal of the austere monochromes of the Sung.

In literature and philosophy, the same backward-looking emphasis on past perfection produced massive compilations and commentaries but discouraged striking out on new paths. The government frowned on deviation and supported conformity. In terms of volume alone, this age of analysis probably surpassed the total production of the previous 2000 years. The one influential development in philosophy, the promotion of Confucianist "Idealism" by Wang Yangming (1472–1529) against the orthodox "Rationalism" of Chu Hsi was significantly little more than a restatement of the position of a contemporary opponent of Chu Hsi.

Wang opposed Chu Hsi's stress on dualism

JAPAN, 700–1600

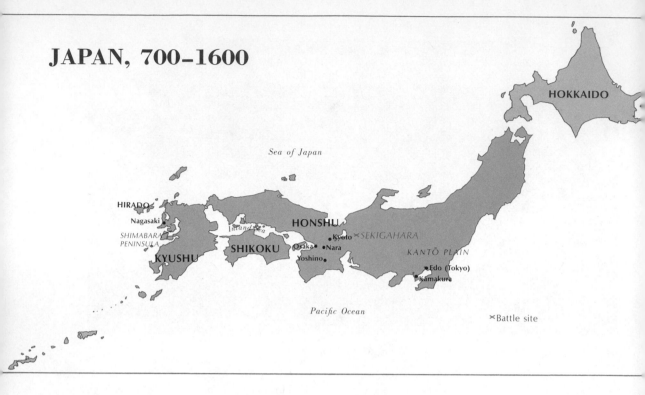

in favor of emphasis on the unity of reality. Even limited truth, he asserted, could not be found by external examination, but only by inductive introversion. In support of this view he made much of Mencius' statement: "All things are complete within me." Wang's greater stress on meditation and intuition narrowed the gap between his school of Confucianism and Buddhism, particularly the Ch'an form. Although his impact in China—where Buddhism had long since passed its prime—could not overcome the established orthodoxy of Chu Hsi's school, his views gained a wide acceptance in Japan, where Zen Buddhism was enjoying a vigorous development.

In due course, the familiar factors of dynastic decline came into play again, leading to increasing decentralization at a time of growing pressure on the frontiers. Imperial revenues were temporarily improved by a reform simplifying the tax structure and providing for direct collection, but military expenses plus corruption soon proved too great for the regime to bear. In the year 1644 a rebel leader captured Peking and overthrew

the Ming dynasty, while the major Chinese army was immobilized by defense of the frontier against the Manchus, tribesmen whose able leaders had for several generations been building a Chinese-type state with the aid of Chinese scholar-officials and generals. Rather than come to terms with a Chinese rebel, the young commander of the frontier army, Wu San-kuei, preferred to serve the Manchus in the establishment of a new dynasty. Allied with the Manchus, he easily destroyed the rebel force and subsequently served the Manchus well in completing their conquest of China.

JAPAN TO 1600

The Nara Era (A.D. 710–784)

Despite the imposing facade of imperial government under the Taika Reforms, Japan was still economically far behind China, and even Korea, in development. Nara was not only the first fixed capital but, even in its stunted development, the first center large enough to warrant the title of city. Ambitiously planned as a smaller replica of the T'ang capital, occupying an area two and two thirds by three miles, it was never constructed as proposed. It did, however accommodate a population in the tens of thousands. In this urban atmosphere students returning from study in China stimulated the rapid adoption of the more refined elements of Chinese civilization. Great Buddhist monasteries arose on the hills around the city, and Buddhist influence in government grew. Chinese art, literature, and music were faithfully imitated. To enhance its prestige, the government sponsored the foundation of branch monasteries and convents supported by grants of land in every province. In 749 an immense bronze Buddha, 53 feet high, was completed and housed in a great wooden hall, which was originally 152 feet high and remains the largest wooden structure in the world. While continuing to patronize Shinto, the state also "domesticated" Buddhism by incorporating Shinto deities into the Buddhist hierarchy of gods and goddesses. In 749 a significant step in this direction was taken when Hachiman, the Shinto god of war, was ceremoniously installed as a bodhisattva.

The Chinese system of writing was extremely ill-suited for the writing of inflected languages, such as Japanese and Korean. Various makeshift techniques were evolved for writing Japanese, but the difficulties encouraged writing in the Chinese language as the simpler course. Naturally the study and use of Chinese greatly aided the dissemination of Chinese culture and ways of thought.

Japanese traits soon modified the political as well as the cultural borrowings from China. After the initial era of reform, governmental positions again came to be filled according to hereditary rank, with scarcely any opportunity for advancement. Thus the very foundation of the Chinese system of government was never established in Japan. As a result the apparent similarity was from the beginning little more than a surface one.

An interesting by-product of the retention of hereditary status in government was the diversion of men of natural talent into Buddhist monasteries. The accumulation of brainpower and wealth by the great monasteries near the capital allowed them to exercise political influence. In fact, the decision to

Face of the Great Bronze Buddha of Nara, Japan, completed in A.D. 749.

relocate the capital was partly a consequence of a Buddhist attempt to usurp the throne.

The Heian Era (A.D. 794–1185)

After the abandonment of Nara, a new capital was laid out on an even grander scale at Heian (Kyoto), where the imperial residence was maintained until 1867. For the first 50 years of the Heian era, the tide of Chinese cultural influence still flowed strongly, marked by the introduction of two more popular sects of Buddhism, Tendai (Chinese T'ien-T'ai) and Shingon (True Word), which stimulated the spread of Buddhism among the people. Subsequently, official relations with China were ended, and the court reexamined and reinterpreted its acquisitions from a Japanese point of view. One result was the development of a more and more sophisticated and effete way of life at the capital which came to be increasingly out of touch with the vigorous development of militant estate-building taking place in the countryside.

Art and literature also turned away from Chinese models to find native inspiration, but with typical Japanese conservatism the Chinese forms continued to be produced and to influence the new styles. The Japanese rarely, if ever, have totally rejected past traditions and practices, preferring to preserve, modify, and blend the old and the new, no matter how logically inconsistent they might appear to be.

Whereas T'ang music can only be studied as preserved in Japan, T'ang architecture was modified to produce the distinctively light and airy structures blending with natural settings which characterize Japanese architecture. The most striking departure from Chinese models took place in secular painting. A simpler style of line drawing with flat, colored surfaces, known as *Yamato-e* (Yamato pictures), was ideally suited to the popular device of pictorial storytelling on a scroll. A characteristic development of this era was the application of the hereditary principle to schools of art. If an artist's son lacked talent, a more talented young man was adopted to perpetuate the style of art in the artist's family. Indeed, the hereditary principle came to be applied to a wide variety of new occupations.

In literature, the desire to compose poetry and prose in Japanese led to the development in the ninth century of two sets of simplified symbols for the syllables of the Japanese language, called *hiragana* and *katakana*. In the early eleventh century these syllabaries made possible an unprecedented and remarkable blossoming of prose compositions by the highly cultivated ladies of the court. Most famous is the novel by Lady Murasaki, *The Tale of Genji,* which remains Japan's greatest literary work. The sensitivity and psychological discernment with which she fathomed and delineated the character of her hero in the course of his amorous exploits set a standard against which all later Japanese novelists have had to measure their work. By her own definition, the novel should deal with life as it is, its virtues and vices, its wisdom and follies, and not create a fairyland beyond reality. Incidentally, her picture of the sophisticated and uninhibited life of the court contrasts with the stern, military virtues of later Japan which were then evolving outside the court. A characteristic common to this and subsequent Japanese culture is the all-pervading sensitivity to beauty in nature and man.

While the culture of the court was attaining a high level of refinement, more prosaic, but enduring, developments were taking place in the countryside. At best, the centralization of national power and resources envisioned in the Taika Reforms had been only partially realized. The authority of the government had been asserted over the whole of Kyushu only in the eighth century and over northern Honshu in the ninth century. State ownership of the land, even where implemented, was limited to cultivated fields. Moreover, tax-free estates had been granted to aristocrats and monasteries, and their influence at court made it possible for them to obtain tax-free status for new acquisitions or donations. Meanwhile, population growth required the development of new lands. Intensive agriculture* utilizing irrigation could only be promoted by those lords with the necessary resources and manpower. A series of edicts culminated in 772 in the removal of all restrictions on the incorporation of wasteland into tax-free estates. The fertility of these virgin lands, improved irrigation, and lower rent persuaded peasants to move to the newly developed estates, abandoning their taxable lands. In time, court aristocrats and monasteries succeeded in having the abandoned lands declared waste and opened to redevelopment as tax-free estates. In other instances local lords achieved the same result by manipulating the land registers. Local lords also found it to their advantage to commend themselves and their estates to monasteries or court aristocrats in return for tax-exemption and legal protection.

The cumulative effects of these various means of evading taxation was a progressive drying up of imperial revenues and the building of large estates by the ablest local lords who maintained a subordinate relationship with great monasteries or court aristocrats as patrons. At the same time, financial pressure forced the emperors to disinherit their younger sons and send them out to make their fortunes under the new family names of Minamoto and Taira. Thanks to paternal sup-

* This is the heavy investment of labor, fertilizers, irrigation, and so on, to gain maximum productivity from a small plot. It applies particularly to rice cultivation throughout Asia.

port and the prestige of these descendants of the imperial line, most of them succeeded in carving out estates and gaining local influence.

Meanwhile, at court, the Fujiwara family by the late ninth century had reduced the emperors to puppets. Minors born of royal fathers and Fujiwara mothers were enthroned under Fujiwara regents. When the emperor came of age, he frequently was persuaded to abdicate and retire to a monastery. In the late eleventh century some vigorous retired emperors challenged the Fujiwara power, drawing upon monastic intellectual and military resources. But the fact that by this time all real power was situated outside the court was evident in the military forces the monasteries could muster to attack each other or dictate to Kyoto. In the countryside the leading lords were engaged in struggles for power, and it was only a matter of time before they would be invited to participate in the struggles at court. Although the central government had become powerless, the imperial tradition was too well entrenched for any power-seeker to attempt usurping the throne. In any case, the Fujiwara had established the tradition of wielding power by delegation — a tradition that was to be greatly expanded in the next period.

As the authority of the central government deteriorated, a rural military aristocracy arose as the only source of law and order. The mounted and armored warrior supported by the income from an estate is a figure similar to the medieval knight in Europe. Successful military lords attracted these warriors, called samurai (servants), and rewarded them with lands. Although the relationship of lord and samurai was based on reciprocal protection and assistance, the material bond was subordinated to an ethical code of honor and loyalty. As in feudal Europe (see essay on Feudalism, p. 210), however, the ties of honor and loyalty were frequently violated in practice, and the outcome of battles was sometimes determined by prearranged desertions.

The Kamakura Shogunate

In 1156 the inevitable occurred; during a power struggle at court, both sides mustered all the support they could get from the countryside. The victor, a leader of the Taira family, retained control of the court instead of dutifully retiring to his estates. The opponents that he could capture were ruthlessly exterminated, and his supporters were rewarded with confiscated estates.

Minamoto Yoritomo, the son of an eliminated foe, was spared because of his youth and entrusted as a ward to a supposedly loyal retainer, Hojo Tokimasa. But this ambitious lord married his daughter to Yoritomo, and in a rebellion that began in 1180 ably advised him in gaining final control. Yoritomo's chief strength lay in the Kanto Plain, the largest in Japan. Henceforth, control of this agricultural unit, which supported the largest number of samurai, became the main key to political power. As Yoritomo's arms swept to victory, samurai rushed to swear allegiance to him. Not only did he liquidate the Taira, but prior to his death in 1199 he had also eliminated all close adult relatives.

Yoritomo resisted the attractions of Kyoto and set up a separate regime at Kamakura in the Kanto. This government, called the Bakufu (tent government), was a relatively simple system of rewarding and punishing the retainers through whom the military control of Japan was maintained. In 1192 his authority was officially confirmed by the imperial grant of the title of shogun (generalissimo), a title previously granted only temporarily to supreme commanders in the field. The assertion of direct control at the local level over most of Japan was gradually accomplished by appointing a loyal retainer for each estate who as steward managed the interests of those with a share in its income and collected the small levy of one-fiftieth of the yield as a symbol of Kamakura's authority. At the provincial level protectors were appointed to supervise affairs in peacetime and to command the provincial contingents of samurai in war. In time both stewards and protectors became hereditary lords whose interests shifted from Kamakura to the local enhancement of their power.

In 1219 the last of Yoritomo's sons and relatives was eliminated and the Hojo family became regents for puppet shoguns. Since the regent usually accepted control by a policy-making committee of Hojo elders, the unique Japanese technique of delegating power without abolishing any traditional positions presents the following picture of progression from the source to the actual location of power: Emperor, Fujiwara Regent, Retired Emperor, Shogun, Hojo Regent, Hojo Family Committee. Only the Japanese with their exceptional reverence for tradition and hereditary status could have devised such a system of government and, what is more, made it function effectively.

Kamakura Culture

In contrast to the effete, "hothouse" culture of Kyoto, Kamakura culture reflected the rugged martial ideals of lords and samurai and was diffused throughout the country, creating a national culture. In literature and the arts, scholars and artists adapted to the demands of their new patrons by producing colorful stories and paintings dealing with deeds of valor. The military code of conduct, labeled *Bushido* (The Way of the Warrior) at a much later date, placed the highest value on loyalty to the lord even to the sacrifice of oneself and one's family. The warrior preferred death to dishonor, and in the late twelfth century suicide by disembowelment (*seppuku*), vulgarly called *harakiri* (belly-slitting), became a ritual.

During the twelfth century, trade with China on a private basis was revived and introduced new Chinese influences, particularly Buddhist sects modified to meet Japanese interests. Inspired preachers of the equalitarian Pure Land and even more radical True Pure Land sects evangelized the peasantry by promising individual salvation in the Western Paradise for all who called on the Buddha Amida with true faith. According to them, rituals, temples, monasteries, or scriptures were not necessary to attain salvation. The nobility was sufficiently disturbed by the implications of the Pure Land doctrines to exile the leader and behead some of his followers.

The even more ardent evangelist, Nichiren (1222–1282), in un-Buddhistic fashion, damned the teachings of other sects as false doctrines and condemned the government for not suppressing these "heresies," predicting calamities for Japan, such as the Mongol invasions. His miraculous escape from execution and his prediction of the Mongol invasion attempts, as well as his impassioned and fearless preaching, gained a large popular following. The Japanese have always admired selfless courage. Furthermore, Nichiren appealed to innate national feeling by asserting that, in this age of worldwide degeneration, Japan could become the home of the one true Buddhist faith. The missionary and militant fervor of Nichiren and the Pure Land sects also led to the formation of fanatical, church-led communities that defended themselves against suppression by the feudal aristocracy. The vigor, singlemindedness, intolerance, militancy, and even the doctrines of the Buddhist evangelicals remind one of certain Protestant sects in Europe in a later age.

Zen (Ch'an) Buddhism, which also took root in Japan at this time, shared with the other new sects the appealing tendencies toward simplicity, anti-intellectualism, and emphasis on the individual, but its stress on this worldly self-realization through rigorous self-discipline stood in sharp contrast to the other sects' simple call for otherworldly faith. Although it gained some adherents among the lower classes, Zen Buddhism found an especially receptive audience among the feudal aristocracy whose martial ideals were complementary to the self-reliance, self-discipline, and superiority of moral to intellectual attainments of Zen doctrine.

Although numerically smaller than the "faith" sects, Zen's influence extended far beyond its immediate adherents and significantly shaped the ideals and values of Japanese civilization. The feature of Zen philosophy that exerted the single greatest influence on other areas of Japanese culture was its stress on finding the ultimate truth within oneself, on discovering the universal within the particular. From this it followed that if the self can contain the whole truth of the universe, any part of nature can contain the whole. As applied, this attitude may be described as the cultivation of the small, the simple, and the natural in preference to the large, the complex, and the artificial. The full elaboration of this outlook was to take place in the Ashikaga period, which has been dubbed the age of Zen culture.

One ritualized expression of Zen culture was the tea ceremony, in which the small group, the austere setting close to nature, the slow, graceful, and prescribed motions of serving, and the simple, even coarse pottery were intended to induce a mental state of tranquillity in contrast to the hurly-burly activities of daily life. Another example was landscape painting in which the artist sought to convey the essence of his subject by bold brush strokes, ignoring details. Often the artist selected some small part, such as a branch in bloom, as the epitome of the whole. Similarly, Zen influence cultivated a preference for natural and gnarled timbers rather than milled lumber. Another art that developed under Zen influence was landscape gardening in which each garden was designed to represent the essence of nature. Zen esthetics also inspired the arts of growing dwarfed trees and creating miniature landscapes planted in bowls. Finally although the Noh drama drew its subjects from popular Buddhism rather than Zen, the form of the drama and the sensitive treatment of the subjects reflect the influence of Zen esthetics.

The Overthrow of Kamakura

Although the Mongol invasions of 1274 and 1281 put a severe strain on Japanese resources, particularly in the southwest, without any compensating rewards for the warriors in loot or land, other internal problems were primarily responsible for the deterioration of the Kamakura shogunate. The hereditary position of protectors and stewards allowed them to become virtually independent, while prolonged peace permitted samurai families to multiply without an equivalent increase in income. As yet no system of limiting inheritances to conserve estates had been devised, and sons and daughters shared an inheritance. The growing ranks of impoverished and indebted samurai were ready for any adventure that might improve their fortunes.

The Kamakura shogunate was overthrown when its general, Ashikaga Takauji, defected with his army to a rebel force led by the emperor he had been sent to suppress. This realistic commander, however, would settle for nothing less than a new shogunate in his family. In 1336 he captured the imperial capital, and the emperor escaped to the moun-

Winter landscape by Sesshu, Japan, fifteenth century.

tains where he and his successors maintained a rival court until 1392.

The Ashikaga Shogunate (A.D. 1338–1573)

Although the Ashikagas operated a regime with headquarters at the imperial capital, Kyoto, almost identical in form to that of Kamakura, they never exercised authority over the whole land. The basic problem that they were unable to overcome was the loss of direct control over the samurai. Japanese feudal development had reached a stage where local lords, later called *daimyo* (great names), commanded the loyalty of the samurai under their protection, and the more samurai they commanded the greater the power they wielded. What power the Ashikaga shoguns possessed depended on the uncertain support of ambitious lords who can be described as little more than allies of doubtful allegiance. After all, Takauji had demonstrated how profitable treason could be. In addition, the shoguns tried to maintain their position as the strongest lords through control of the largest estates. More than their predecessors, they were almost entirely dependent on their own estates for income. Every lord kept for his own use every ounce of income he could extract from his own lands.

Like the "Warring States" era in China, Japan was carved up into a number of territorial domains under autonomous lords intent on expansion. Warfare was endemic and in the last century of the Ashikaga era became increasingly bloody and ruthless. In this era of fierce competition, talent, skill, and luck were what counted. Many noble families disappeared and new lords of humble origins rose to power; indeed, many may have been humbler in origin than their genealogies admit.

As civil strife intensified, the pace of social change and economic growth was accelerated, not checked. Under the direction of lords motivated by enlightened self-interest, the remaining, often scattered, private estates were gradually eliminated, and more absolute rule was established over consolidated administrative units at the village level. Many at the lower levels of privileged status lost their hereditary rights and merged with the peasantry. The consolidation of land encouraged investment in improvements that doubled or even tripled agricultural productivity. Consolidated territories also promoted an increase in industry and trade reflecting a higher standard of living and the growth of a money economy. Professional moneylenders, pawnshop keepers, and bankers arose to meet the needs of the time, and popular rebellions demanding cancellation of debts indicate their impact.

In such unstable times, craftsmen and merchants needed protection. Markets and towns developed under the patronage of lords, temples, and monasteries; merchant and occupational guilds were formed to bargain for privileges and protection. Towns grew up under the protection of castles for the mutual benefit of lords and townsmen. The lord used his influence to lower or eliminate the toll barriers of neighboring lords.

Other towns grew up as commercial centers rather than political capitals, and a few, such as the future port city of Osaka, became essentially autonomous, self-governing entities. Overseas trade flourished as never before, and Japanese sailors, who doubled as swordsmen, did not hesitate to resort to piracy when ports were closed to them. In the China trade, the principal exports were the highly-prized Japanese swords and lances, and the principal imports were Chinese copper coinage and Chinese silks.

In the last century of the Ashikaga era, enterprising lords took a military step with great social and political potentialities. Confronted with a conquer-or-die situation, they formed large bodies of peasant infantry armed with pikes and commanded by mounted samurai. The highly-trained professional warrior was being supplanted by masses of conscripted peasants, and warfare came to require the full utilization of all the material and human resources of the daimyo's domain. The hereditary monopoly of the samurai appeared broken and its check on social mobility removed as able peasants became generals. The common man's new military role gave him an increased importance that the daimyo could not ignore.

This was the Japan the Portuguese discovered in 1543: a land divided into principalities ruled by lords dedicated to the military ideal. This was a land whose political and social structure was far more understandable than China's to sixteenth-century Europeans. In contrast to the Chinese, the Japanese were in a stage of dynamic growth and development similar to that in the West and welcomed new ideas, such as Christianity, and new implements, such as firearms. Naturally, Europeans found this open-minded attitude much more congenial—and profitable. Beginning with the Jesuit St. Francis Xavier (1506–1552), Roman Catholic missionaries found Japan a fertile field for proselytizing, and Western merchants found a lucrative market for their wares. This "open door" to Japan lasted for almost a century before it was slammed shut.

The War Lords

Although the Portuguese observers, who found so many features in Japanese life familiar, expected the political divisions to persist as in Europe, the greater cultural uniformity throughout Japan precluded such a result. As it turned out, Japan was on the eve of reunification at the hands of three great leaders of differing, but complementary, talents: Oda Nobunaga and his lieutenants, Toyotomi Hideyoshi, and Tokugawa Ieyasu.

Oda Nobunaga (1534–1582), a scion of a new family that had recently gained a small territory, began his career of conquest with the decisive defeat in 1560 of the leading daimyo in his area. In Japan, as elsewhere, nothing succeeds like success, and this and subsequent victories brought him a flood of new supporters, notably Tokugawa Ieyasu. In 1568 Nobunaga captured Kyoto and a few years later brought an end to the Ashikaga shogunate. Since militant Buddhist monasteries and communities opposed him, he ordered the destruction of their power over the objections of his advisers. A by-product of his hostility toward Buddhists was a friendly attitude toward Christian missionaries, facilitating conversions to Christianity and the accquisition of firearms. In 1582, Nobunaga was treacherously assassinated and succeeded by Hideyoshi after a struggle for power of more than two years.

Toyotomi Hideyoshi (1536–1598), whose father had given up farming for a military career, followed in his father's footsteps at twenty-two and demonstrated such exceptional ability that he soon became Nobunaga's most trusted general and chief adviser. His rise is the outstanding example of the social mobility of these turbulent times. After winning recognition in 1585, he completed the reunification of Japan in less than six years and then faced the problem of stabilizing Japanese society with its surplus of warriors. Although he had risen from the peasantry himself, he turned back the clock by making all professions hereditary, disarming the peasants, and limiting swordbearing to the samurai. He also cast a suspicious eye on the potentially subversive spread of Christianity and in 1587 ordered missionaries to leave Japan within 20 days on pain of death. But too many of his supporters were converts for immediate enforcement, and no executions were carried out until 1596. One way of employing surplus warriors would be in the conquest of China,

which he had dreamed of as early as 1578. When the Korean king refused free passage through the Korean peninsula for Hideyoshi's troops, the Japanese landed on May 25, 1592, and swept through Korea, capturing Seoul and P'yongyang, in six weeks. But the problem of supply in a hostile country could not be overcome, and when Hideyoshi died, the troops were recalled.

While Hideyoshi was engaged in this futile overseas adventure, Tokugawa Ieyasu (1542–1616) was busy consolidating his control of the great Kanto Plain, situating his headquarters in a great castle he built at Edo (modern Tokyo). Although he was a redoubtable warrior renowned for his terrifying war cry, he always recognized that a feudal lord's power depended on the size of his estate and the resources he could command. At Hideyoshi's death in 1598, Ieyasu's estate was the largest in Japan, even larger than that which Hideyoshi left to his five-year-old son. At the decisive battle of Sekigahara (October 21, 1600), Ieyasu's cautious diplomacy induced desertions from his enemy at critical junctures in the fighting and insured his victory. In 1603 his supremacy was confirmed by the title of shogun.

Heeding the lesson of his predecessors' failure to pass on their power to their sons, he abdicated in 1605 as shogun in favor of his chosen heir while continuing to run the government until his death in 1616. A greater danger, however, was the existence of Hideyoshi's heir, whose headquarters were in Japan's leading commercial city, Osaka. Cautiously, Ieyasu bided his time and then as a final act wiped out this threat by a treacherous assault in 1615.

The Closing of Japan

Among the supporters of Hideyoshi's son were many Christians, and a petty plot was even uncovered among Ieyasu's Christian retainers. Not only were Christians proving difficult to discipline, but also the damaging effects of an adverse balance of trade were coming to be appreciated. The chief attraction of the Japanese trade for Western merchants was the opportunity to sell Western and Asian goods for cash which could be used to purchase Chinese silks and other Asian products.

In 1606 Ieyasu issued his first anti-Christian edict and in 1612 he began to enforce these edicts. In 1614 all missionaries who could be discovered were expelled, but none was executed while he lived. The first executions of missionaries since Hideyoshi's time took place in 1617, but not until 1622 did Ieyasu's successor commit the shogunate to a policy of thorough eradication of Christianity.

In 1636 an edict terminated all Japanese trading overseas, and all foreign merchants were restricted to Nagasaki and Hirado under strict shogunal control. The door that was being gradually closed was slammed shut when a rebellion in 1637 developed into a Christian last stand. Approximately 20,000 warriors with their families held out in an old castle on the Shimabara Peninsula in Kyushu against an army said to number 100,000 and the firepower of a Dutch ship until the spring of 1638; then they were all killed. In 1641 the cooperative Dutch were removed to Nagasaki, where they and the Chinese conducted a closely controlled trade.

Thus within a century Japan shifted from the one extreme of open hospitality to the other extreme of almost complete isolation. Isolationist policy provided the stability that made possible more than two centuries of internal peace, but it also removed alien stimuli and ideas that might have kept Japanese development abreast of the West's.

In this chapter we have seen how Indo-Aryan civilization, past its zenith, was politically subjected to Muslim conquest yet able to maintain its traditional culture by isolating the Muslim conquerors as a ruling elite. In turn, the Muslims as a minority had to cling to their faith and their Persian culture to fend off the threat of absorption. As a result, the two communities arrived at a generally accepted accommodation, whereby the Hindus tolerated Muslim rule as long as the Muslims did not interfere too forcefully with the Hindu way of life.

Chinese civilization reached its peak of political and cultural achievement under the T'ang and Sung dynasties, during which Confucianism became established as the undisputed philosophy of state and society. The great landholding families were gradually displaced by the Confucian scholar-gentry class of small landholders from whose ranks the relatively small bureaucracy of imperial appointees was selected by competitive examinations. For almost a century, China was a part of the Mongol Empire before it regained its independence under the Ming dynasty, which generally sought to restore the glories of the past.

During these centuries, Japan developed its own civilization in relative isolation, digesting and adapting Chinese contributions to fit its needs. With traditional conservatism the imperial institution was preserved, although real power was exercised by others, first the Fujiwara regents and then the Kamakura and Ashikaga shogunates. In the mid-sixteenth century when European traders arrived, they thought Japan was permanently divided into competing principalities that they called "kingdoms." But, in fact, it was on the verge of reunification under the Tokugawa shogunate, which returned to a policy of isolation and checked the rapid social change of the preceding century.

By the end of the sixteenth century all of the traditional civilizations of India, China, Japan, and the Americas began to feel the impact of European adventurers. As we learned in Chapter 3, the Indian empires of the Americas were destroyed by Spanish conquerors, though, as we shall see in Chapter 16, Indian culture among the people resisted extinction. In this chapter we have examined how the Japanese, after an initial warm reception, became aware of the subversive effects of the West and effectively closed their doors for several centuries. China, as it had previously done with other alien overseas traders, attempted to keep the Europeans at arm's length by limiting their contact to designated port cities. The divided and diverse Indian subcontinent was destined in several centuries to see its Muslim and native rulers replaced by British rulers.

SUGGESTED READINGS

Ahmad, Aziz, *Studies in Islamic Culture in the Indian Environment*. Oxford: Clarendon Press, 1966.
   An excellent and penetrating study.

Moreland, W. H., *India at the Death of Akbar*. Delhi: Atma Ram, 1962.

Nehru, Jawaharlal, *The Discovery of India*. New York: Doubleday & Co., 1959. Paperback.
   Valuable as a renowned Indian leader's view of his country's past, although historically unreliable.

Balazs, Etienne, *Chinese Civilization and Bureaucracy*. New Haven: Yale University Press, 1964. Paperback.
   Essays in depth on a variety of problems by a leading French scholar.

Wang Gung-wu, *The Structure of Power in North China during the Five Dynasties*. Stanford: Stanford University Press, 1967. Paperback.
   A specialized study of the critical period between the T'ang and Sung dynasties.

Reischauer, Edwin O., *Ennin's Travels in T'ang China*. New York: Ronald Press, 1955.
   China seen through the eyes of a Japanese monk.

Gernet, Jacques, *Daily Life in China on the Eve of the Mongol Invasions, 1250–1276*. Stanford: Stanford University Press, 1970. Paperback.

Wright, Arthur F., ed., *Confucianism and Chinese Civilization*. New York: Atheneum, 1964. Paperback.
   Essays by leading authorities.

Wright, Arthur F., ed., *The Confucian Persuasion*. Stanford: Stanford University Press, 1960. Paperback.
   More essays by prominent scholars.

Liu, James T. C. and Wei-ming Tu, eds., *Traditional China*. Englewood Cliffs, N.J.: Prentice-Hall (Spectrum Book), 1970. Paperback.
   Another collection of essays by recognized authorities covering a variety of problems.

Rugoff, Milton (trans.), *The Travels of Marco Polo*. New York: The New American Library (Mentor Book), 1961. Paperback.
   An inexpensive translation.

Chang, Carson, *Wang Yang-ming: Idealist Philosopher of Sixteenth Century China*. New York: St. John's University Press, 1962. Paperback.
   Study of prominent Neo-Confucian philosopher by a participant in the intellectual upheaval of modern China.

CHAPTER 8

European Middle Ages, 1000–1300

In Europe and the Near East the period covered in the preceding chapter is called the middle ages, which reached its height in the twelfth and thirteenth centuries. In politics, bold experiments in papal and imperial rule in Italy and Germany were finally overshadowed by the centralized monarchies of England and France. Meanwhile Christian Spanish kings reconquered most of the Iberian Peninsula from the Moors, who had displaced the Arabs there, as the Turks overcame the Arabs in the Near East. Mongol control isolated Russia from the rest of Europe for 200 years beginning in the 1240s. In Western and Central Europe the growth of towns and commerce promoted the new institution of the university and the revival of legal studies. Religion and religious leaders dominated the arts and learning, but the search for a final synthesis of secular and spiritual values was never to be achieved. What was achieved was an amalgam of Greek-Muslim-Christian learning and a potentiality for intellectual growth that was eventually to make Western civilization modern.

THE ECONOMIC EXPANSION OF WESTERN CHRISTENDOM

The high middle ages did not dawn everywhere in Western Christendom at a single moment. Their coming was gradual and uneven. Ever since the ebbing of the Viking, Hungarian, and Saracen invasions, many decades prior to 1050, Western Europe had been pulsing with new creative energy. But, broadly speaking, the scope and intensity of the revival did not become evident until the later eleventh century. By the century's end, Europe's lively commerce and bustling towns, her intellectual vigor and growing political cohesion, her military expansion and her heightened religious enthusiasm left no doubt that potent new forces were at work—that Western Christendom had at last become a mature civilization.

The causes of an immense culture awakening such as occurred in the high middle ages are varied and obscure. One essential element was the ending of the invasions and the increasing political stability that followed. We know that in the eleventh century Europe's population was beginning to rise sharply and that its food production was growing. Whether increased productivity led to increased population or vice versa is difficult to say, but productivity could not have risen as it did without the improvements in agrarian technology that had occurred during the preceding centuries.

The Growth of Towns

The growth in productivity and population was accompanied by a significant commercial revival and a general reawakening of urban life. And the new towns, in turn, became the centers of a reinvigorated culture. The frequent human contacts arising from town life stimulated thought and art. The cathedral and the university, two of the supreme achievements of high-medieval culture, were both urban phenomena; the Franciscan order, the most dynamic religious institution of the age, devoted itself primarily to urban evangelism. Yet the towns were also, and above all, centers of commercial and industrial enterprise. The high-medieval economy remained fundamentally agrarian, but the towns were the great economic and cultural catalysts of the era.

The new towns, unlike the administrative-military towns of the Western Roman Empire or the episcopal towns of the early middle ages, were economically self-supporting. Instead of depending on the labor and taxes of the countryside, the towns lived off the fruits of their own merchant and industrial activities. Small, foul, disease-ridden, and often torn by internal conflict, they were Western Europe's first cities in the modern sense. The growth of the towns corresponded to the general upsurge of commerce. Sometimes the towns originated as suburbs of older cathedral towns, sometimes as trading posts outside the walls of castles. By 1100 they were springing up all over Europe, but they were most concentrated in Flanders and northern Italy, where the opportunities of international commerce were first exploited. The greatest Italian city of the age was Venice, long a Byzantine dependency but by this time an independent commercial republic that carried on a lucrative trade with Constantinople and the east. Other Italian coastal towns — Genoa, Pisa, and Amalfi — soon followed Venice into the profitable markets of the eastern Mediterranean, and their commerce brought vigorous new life to inland towns such as Florence and Milan. The Muslims were all but driven from the seas, and Italian merchants dominated the Mediterranean.

The Flemish towns grew rich from the commerce of the north, trading with northern France and the British Isles, the Rhineland, and the Baltic coast. Both they and the northern Italian towns became manufacturing as well as commercial centers, producing woolen cloth in large quantities. Textile production developed into the major manufacturing enterprise of the age. As the twelfth and thirteenth centuries progressed, towns were rising and prospering in England, France, and Germany. While the Germans were pushing eastward along the Baltic shore, the thriving towns of old Germany were sending out numerous commercial colonies into the new territories — colonies which themselves became important towns. The North German towns, working collectively, came in time to dominate the Baltic trade and developed far-flung commercial links that stretched from Western Europe into Russia. Eventually, these towns formed themselves into an interurban confederation known as the Hanseatic League, establishing commercial colonies in such western cities as Bruges and London. Even before the advent of the German Hanseatic League, the towns of northern Italy had organized for mutual protection into a Lombard League.

This tendency toward confederation illustrates the townsmen's need to combine forces against the repression of the old order. The Lombard League struggled for independence from the Holy Roman Empire. And, on a smaller scale, a great many towns had to fight for their autonomy against the monarchs, bishops, or feudal lords on whose lands the town had risen. Only by collective action could the town merchants win the privileges essential to their new vocation: personal freedom from serfdom or servile status, freedom of movement, freedom from inordinate tolls at every bridge or feudal boundary; the right to own property in the town, to be judged by the town court, to execute commercial contracts, and to buy and sell freely. Collective action expressed itself through tightly regulated merchant guilds, and during the twelfth and thirteenth centuries a number of lords, either through farsightedness or through coercion—or for a price—were issuing town charters that guaranteed many of these rights. Indeed, some lords began founding and chartering new towns on their own initiative.

The charters tended to transform the towns into semiautonomous political and legal entities, each with its own government, its own court, its own tax-collecting agencies, and its own laws. Taxes continued to be paid to the lords in most cases, but they were paid collectively rather than individually.

Within the towns themselves, class distinctions were sharpening. The guilds, composed of merchants who engaged in long-distance trade, tended to dominate, and the craftsmen were, at least at first, in a subordinate status. Before long, however, craftsmen were making their weight felt by combining into various craft guilds. As time progressed, an urban working class grew increasingly numerous; and as conflicts between townsmen and their external lords gradually eased, class conflicts among townsmen grew increasingly severe.

Yet throughout the greater part of the high middle ages the towns were avenues to personal freedom and commercial success, astir with new life and bursting with energy. The wealth that they produced was beginning to transform the European economy. Feudalism changed as kings and lords acquired the wealth necessary to replace landed knights with mercenaries in their armies and to replace feudal magnates with professional judges and bureaucrats in their courts and administration. The feudal aristocracy remained strong, but the traditional feudal concept of service in return for land tenure was fast dissolving.

Agrarian life, too, was changing. Capital and labor were now available to carve out extensive new farm sites from forest and marsh. The great primeval forests of northern Europe were reduced to scattered woods, swamps and marshes were drained, and vast new territories were opened to cultivation. Agricultural surpluses could now be sold to townsmen and thereby converted into cash. Slavery all but vanished, and serfs were freed on a large scale. With the opening of new lands, a competition developed for peasant settlers, and peasant communities were often granted the status and privileges of chartered communes. High-medieval Europe was a buoyant, prosperous society—a society in process of change and growth, which expanded inwardly through the clearing of forest and swamp, and outwardly through the conquest and settlement of vast new territories.

TERRITORIAL EXPANSION OF WESTERN CHRISTENDOM

The open, expanding frontier is one of the most characteristic aspects of Europe in the high middle ages. Considerable areas of the Arab, Byzantine, and Slavic worlds were incorporated within the ballooning boundaries of Western Christendom, intensifying Europe's spirit of enterprise and adding wealth to its flourishing economy.

Western Christendom had been expanding ever since 732, and since about 1000 it had pushed far to the north and east through the conversion of regions such as Scandinavia, Hungary, Bohemia, and Poland. North of the Balkans and west of Russia, most Slavic peoples accepted Catholic Christianity rather than Byzantine Orthodoxy. Indeed, Hungary, Bohemia, and Poland, at one time or another, all acknowledged the political lordship of the pope. During the high middle ages, the population boom produced multitudes of landless aristocratic younger sons who sought land and glory on Christendom's frontiers. The church, always eager for new converts, supported them. The townsmen, seeking ever larger fields for commercial enterprise, encouraged and sometimes financed them. And the proliferating peasantry served as a potential labor force for the newly conquered lands.

Reconquest of Spain and Southern Italy

Thus it was that knightly adventurers from all over Christendom—and particularly from feudal France—streamed southward into

Spain in the eleventh century to aid the Iberian Christian kingdoms in their struggle with Islam. The great Muslim caliphate of Cordova had disintegrated after 1002 into small, warring fragments, and the Christians seized the opportunity. Often the reconquest was delayed by wars among the Christian kingdoms themselves. But at length, in 1085, Christian Castile captured the great Muslim city of Toledo, which thenceforth became a crucial contact point between Islamic and Christian culture. Here, numerous Arabic scientific and philosophical works were translated into Latin and then disseminated throughout Europe to challenge and invigorate the Western mind.

Early in the twelfth century the Christian Kingdom of Aragon, contesting Castile's supremacy, took the offensive against the Moors.* In 1140 Aragon strengthened itself by uniting with Catalonia—the wealthy state around Barcelona which had once been Charlemagne's Spanish March. But further inter-Christian warfare delayed the reconquest until 1212, when Pope Innocent III proclaimed a crusade against the Moors. Advancing from Toledo with a pan-Iberian army, the king of Castile won a decisive victory at Las Navas de Tolosa, permanently crippling Moorish power. Cordova fell to Castile in 1236, and by the 1260s the Moors were confined to the small southern Kingdom of Granada, where they remained until 1492. Castile now dominated central Spain, and Christian peasants were imported en masse to resettle the conquered lands. Aragon, meanwhile, occupied the Muslim islands of the western Mediterranean and won a powerful maritime empire. Thus, the high middle ages witnessed the Christianization of nearly all the Iberian Peninsula and its division into two strong Christian kingdoms and several weaker ones.

Probably the most vigorous and militant force in Europe's eleventh-century awakening was the warrior-aristocracy of Normandy—largely Viking in ancestry but now thoroughly adapted to French culture. These Norman knights—French in tongue, Christian in faith, feudal in social organization—plied their arms across the length and breadth of Europe in the reconquest of Spain, on the Crusades to the Holy Land, on the battlefields of England and France, and in southern Italy and Sicily. Normandy itself was growing in prosperity and political centralization, and an ever-increasing population pressure drove the greedy and adventurous Norman warriors far and wide on distant enterprises.

During the course of the eleventh century the Normans became masters of southern Italy and Sicily. They came first as mercenaries to serve in the chaotic south-Italian political struggles between Byzantine coastal cities, Lombard principalities, and rising seaport republics such as Naples and Amalfi, and ultimately overthrew their paymasters. By the close of the eleventh century they had won southern Italy for themselves and had conquered Muslim Sicily. And in 1130, the Norman leader Roger the Great (d. 1154) fused Sicily and southern Italy into a single kingdom and became its first king.

Roger the Great and his successors ruled firmly but tolerantly over this Kingdom of Sicily and southern Italy, with its variety of peoples, faiths, customs, and tongues. Here, a synthesis was achieved of Byzantine, Islamic, Lombard, and northern French cultural traditions, and a highly effective political structure was created out of the Byzantine and Islamic administrative machinery that the Normans had inherited. The Sicilian capital of Palermo, with its superb harbor and bustling international commerce, its impressive palace and luxurious villas, was known as the city of the threefold tongue. Islamic, Byzantine, and Western scholars worked under royal patronage, providing Western Christendom with Latin translations of Arabic and Greek texts, and doing important original work of their own. East and west met in Roger the Great's glittering, sun-drenched realm.

The Crusades

The Crusades to the Holy Land were the most self-conscious acts of Western Christian expansionism in the high middle ages, although not the most lasting. They arose in

---

* By then most of Muslim Spain was ruled by North African Berbers who, having also conquered Morocco, were called Moors in Europe.

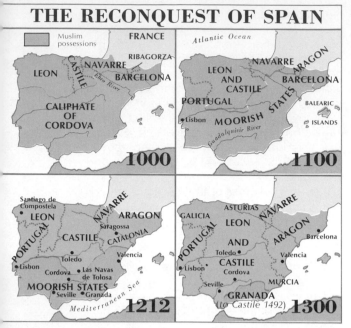

THE RECONQUEST OF SPAIN

Muslim possessions

1000
FRANCE
Atlantic Ocean
LEON
CASTILE
NAVARRE
RIBAGORZA
BARCELONA
Ebro River
CALIPHATE OF CORDOVA

1100
LEON AND CASTILE
NAVARRE
ARAGON
BARCELONA
PORTUGAL
Lisbon
MOORISH STATES
BALEARIC ISLANDS
Guadalquivir River

1212
Santiago de Compostela
LEON
NAVARRE
ARAGON
Saragossa
PORTUGAL
CASTILE
CATALONIA
Lisbon
Toledo
Valencia
Cordova
Las Navas de Tolosa
MOORISH STATES
Seville
Granada
Mediterranean Sea

1300
ASTURIAS
GALICIA
LEON AND
NAVARRE
ARAGON
Barcelona
PORTUGAL
Toledo
Valencia
Lisbon
CASTILE
Cordova
MURCIA
Seville
GRANADA
(to Castile 1492)

great international army—with a large contingent of knights from France, Normandy, and Norman Sicily—poured into Syria and, in 1099, captured Jerusalem. A long strip of territory along the eastern Mediterranean, previously under Islamic rule, was now divided into four Crusader States, the chief of which was the Kingdom of Jerusalem. The king of Jerusalem was the theoretical feudal overlord of the four states, but he had trouble enforcing his authority outside his own realm. Indeed, the knightly settlers in the Holy Land were far too proud and independent for their own good, and from the beginning the Crusader States were torn by internal dissension.

Gradually, the Muslims recovered their strength and began the reconquest of their lost lands. Jerusalem fell to them in 1187, and though in later years such illustrious Christian monarchs as Richard the Lion-Hearted, Emperor Frederick Barbarossa, and St. Louis took up the Cross, the Crusader States continued to crumble. In 1291 they came to an end with the fall of Acre, the last Christian bridgehead on the Syrian coast.

For a time during the Crusading era Constantinople itself was ruled by westerners. The Fourth Crusade (1202–1204) was diverted from Jerusalem to Constantinople by the greed of its Venetian financial backers. The Crusaders took the city by siege in 1204, succeeding where so many before them had failed, and a dynasty of western emperors ruled Constantinople for half a century, until a Greek dynasty replaced them in 1261.

The Crusades were more than merely a colorful failure. For nearly two centuries Christians ruled portions of the Holy Land. There, and in Constantinople, they broadened their perspectives by contacts with other cultures. Western merchants established footholds in Syria, vastly enlarging their role in international commerce and bringing wealth and vitality to the Italian cities. And when the Crusades withdrew at last from the Holy Land, the Italian merchants remained.

Germanic Expansion in Eastern Europe

The high middle ages also witnessed the incorporation of vast areas of Eastern Europe into the civilization of Western Christendom.

response to the conquests in the Near East of the recently Islamized Seljuk Turks and, in particular, a great Turkish victory over Byzantium at Manzikert (1071), which gave the Turks control of Anatolia. When Constantinople appealed to the west for help, Western Christendom, under the leadership of a reinvigorated papacy, responded emphatically.

The Crusades represented a fusion of three characteristic impulses of medieval man: sanctity, pugnacity, and greed. All three were essential. Without Christian idealism the Crusades would have been inconceivable, yet the pious dream of liberating Jerusalem from the infidel was mightily reinforced by the lure of adventure, new lands, and riches. And to the Italian towns, which financed and provided transportation for many of the Crusades, the Near East offered alluring commercial opportunities.

Accordingly, when in 1095 Pope Urban II urged the European nobility to take up the Cross,* the response was overwhelming. A

* Cross is *croix* in French, and crusade is the English version of *croisade*. Since the middle ages, the word has been used loosely to describe any campaign with a religious or moral justification.

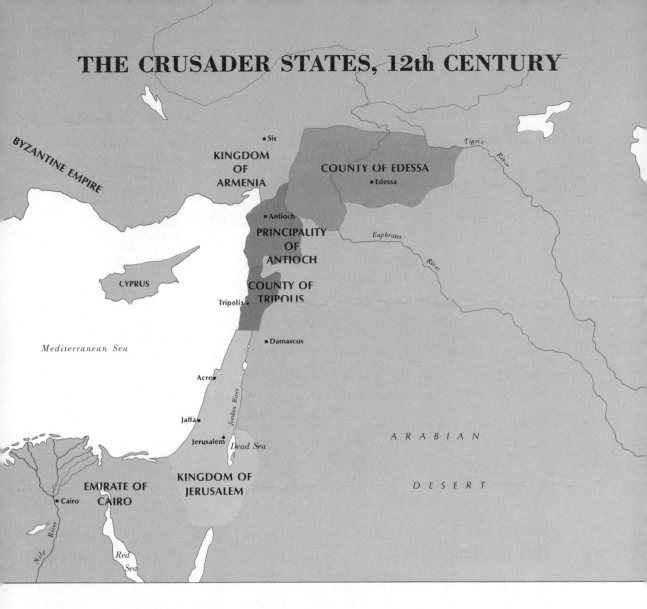

THE CRUSADER STATES, 12th CENTURY

BYZANTINE EMPIRE

KINGDOM OF ARMENIA

• Sis

COUNTY OF EDESSA

• Edessa

Tigris

River

• Antioch

PRINCIPALITY OF ANTIOCH

Euphrates

River

CYPRUS

COUNTY OF TRIPOLIS

Tripolis •

Mediterranean Sea

• Damascus

Acre •

Jaffa •

Jerusalem

Jordan River

Dead Sea

ARABIAN

KINGDOM OF JERUSALEM

DESERT

EMIRATE OF CAIRO

• Cairo

Nile River

Red Sea

The Slavic peoples of the Balkans and Russia passed into the sphere of Byzantine Orthodox Christianity, but those north of the Balkans and west of Russia became Roman Catholics. The process of converting these peoples began in the tenth century when Otto the Great (936–973) defeated the Hungarians at Lechfeld and established his supremacy over the Slavic lands between the Elbe and Oder rivers. For a time thereafter, the dual processes of Christianization and Germanization went hand in hand. But by the year 1000 the Slavs and Hungarians, while accepting Catholic Christianity, were vigorously resisting German colonization

and political suzerainty. Hungary, under its illustrious king, St. Stephen (997–1038), adopted Christianity and turned from nomadism to a settled agrarian society of the western type. But St. Stephen and his successors rejected German influences, submitting instead to a tenuous papal overlordship.

Poland and Bohemia had accepted the overlordship of Otto the Great, and during the later 900s the Christianization of these lands proceeded steadily. But Poland, like Hungary, soon rejected German authority. Under her first king, Boleslav the Great (992–1025), Catholic Christianity became the official religion, but the Polish church freed itself from its former missionary dependence on German bishops and became an independent organization subject to the pope alone. Boleslav I not only freed Poland from German suzerainty but also won extensive new territories for his kingdom, subjugating neighboring Bohemia and expanding his frontiers in every direction.

In the long run, however, Poland proved to be politically unstable. In 1139 the kingdom was partitioned among rival princes, and it remained divided and relatively impotent for the next two centuries. Bohemia broke free of Polish control and accepted the overlordship of the Holy Roman Empire. In 1088 its ruler received, by imperial decree, the title of king, and throughout the twelfth and thirteenth centuries the kings of Bohemia, although technically vassals of the German emperor, ruled a state that was far more powerful and centralized than neighboring Poland.

With Poland's decline in the early twelfth century, the challenge of Christianizing the territories of the southeastern Baltic region was seized by Germany, whose princes were now able once again to expand their authority and commerce eastward in partnership with Christian evangelism. This new German eastward push—known as the *Drang nach Osten*—was not a product of active royal policy but, rather, a movement led by enterprising local aristocrats. They succeeded, over a long period running from about 1125 to about 1350, in moving the eastern boundary of Germany from the Elbe River past the Oder to the Vistula at Slavic expense. They consolidated their gains by building innumerable agrarian villages and encouraging a massive eastward migration of German peasants. New towns were established that maintained close commercial ties with the older North German towns and that eventually joined with them in the Hanseatic League. The league itself, with its flourishing outposts to the east, was able to dominate the rich trade between Western Europe and the Baltic and Russia. Thus as the new lands were conquered, they were in large part Christianized and Germanized.

The later phases of the *Drang nach Osten* were spearheaded by the Teutonic Knights, a semimonastic German crusading order which transferred its activities from the Holy Land to northern Germany. The Teutonic Knights penetrated far northward into Lithuania, Latvia, and Estonia and even made an unsuccessful bid to conquer the Russian principality of Novgorod in 1242. Ultimately, the Teutonic order was obliged to forfeit some of its conquests, yet much of the German expansion proved to be permanent.

COUNTER-PRESSURE FROM THE EAST: TURKS AND MONGOLS

By the late thirteenth century the European expansion was drawing to an end. Generally speaking, the northern, western, and southern frontiers remained fluid, sometimes expanding, sometimes contracting. The German *Drang nach Osten* continued to the mid-fourteenth century, yet as early as the 1240s, the Mongols seized most of the Russian principalities and for a brief moment pierced into the heart of Catholic Central Europe.

Byzantium's recovery of Constantinople in 1261 was a relatively slight achievement. The Latin Empire of Constantinople (1204–1261) had from the beginning been rent by feudal particularism, and the Byzantines had retained power in the eastern districts of their temporarily headless empire. And long after Constantinople returned to Byzantium, a sizeable fragment of the Latin Empire endured in southern Greece. Meanwhile, the Serbs and Bulgarians had repudiated Byzantine control in the northern Balkans. A powerful Bulgarian empire dominated the region between Greece and Hungary during most of the thirteenth century, giving ground in the fourteenth to a resurgent Kingdom of Serbia. With most of the Balkans lost and most of Anatolia in Turkish hands, Byzantium after 1261 was a mini-state living on hope and borrowed time.

Islam, like Byzantium, was generally on the defensive during the high middle ages. The Muslims lost Sicily and most of Spain, and for a time they were driven from the Syrian coast. Their Mediterranean commerce declined, and every important Meditrrranean island passed into Christian hands. The Mongols came and went, and in the interim destroyed lives property, and the Abbasid Caliphate, but produced no permanent change in the boundaries of the Arab world.

The victories of the Seljuk Turks had stimulated the First Crusade, and the internal disintegration of the Seljuk state in the 1090s had permitted its success. In 1171, however, the Muslims recovered the initiative when Saladin, a brilliant Kurd, seized control of Egypt. Three years afterward he added Muslim Syria to his domains, and in 1187 he reconquered Jerusalem from the crusaders. Egypt remained, far into the future, a powerful, centralized kingdom—the chief Islamic state in the Near East. Crusading armies of the thirteenth century hurled themselves against it in vain. Midway through the century, political control of Egypt passed to the long-lived Mamluk dynasty of Turkish sultans, who quickly demonstrated their strength by crushing the invading Mongols near Nazareth (1260) and driving them from Syria. In 1291 the Mamluks completed their conquest of the Crusader States with their victory at Acre, and from then until 1517 all Egypt and Syria remained under Mamluk control.

The high middle ages witnessed great changes in Islamic civilization. Commerce, although it flourished to a degree under the Mamluks, had generally declined from its former vigor, and land became increasingly the mark of wealth. The Islamic power center had shifted decisively from Iraq to Egypt—from Baghdad to Mamluk Cairo. The rulers of Islam were no longer Arabs but Turks. The Islamic aristocracy had become largely Turkish, and the Arabs declined into a suppressed proletariat. When the Mamluks themselves fell in the sixteenth century, another Turkish dynasty—the Ottomans— replaced them.

Buffeted by Turkish, Christian, and Mongol invaders, the Arabs of the twelfth and thirteenth centuries turned from their former attitude of intellectual adventurousness to the apparent safety of a narrow, unquestioning orthodoxy. Science and philosophy were being repressed in the Arab world at the very time of their rebirth in Western Christendom, with the consequence that Islamic intellectual history after the twelfth century tends to be tedious and sterile. This cultural retrenchment and failure of nerve did not affect the success of Islamic arms for several centuries, but ultimately it resulted in Islamic civilization's being outstripped and overshadowed by the civilization of Christendom.

Like the Turks, the Mongols (Tatars) were an Altaic people from Central Asia. Under their merciless leader, Genghis Khan (1167–1227), they won an empire far larger and more populous than ancient Rome's—an empire encompassing China, Korea, and the vast stretches of Central and Northern Asia. In 1237 a large Mongol army led by Genghis Khan's son, Batu, descended on Europe. Keiv was sacked, and nearly all of Russia fell under Mongol domination. In the years 1241–1242 Central Europe suffered a two-pronged Mongol assault, the northern force vanquishing the Poles and Teutonic Knights, the southern force routing the Hungarians and reaching the Adriatic. At this point, with resistance seemingly dissolving before them, the Mongols suddenly turned eastward again. The Great Khan had died, and Batu returned to Asia to help choose his successor.

The Mongols never resumed their attack on Central Europe. They struck westward once again in the 1250s, but this time against Islam, destroying Baghdad and the Abbasid Caliphate in 1258 and dooming once-prosperous Iraq to centuries of stagnation and poverty. But Muslim Syria was saved by the decisive Mamluk victory of 1260, and thereafter the Mongol threat abated. By the later thirteenth century the power of the Great Khan was fading, and the Mongol Empire was disintegrating into independent regional Khanates. One of them—the Khanate of the Golden Horde—ruled Russia through local princes for over two centuries.

The principalities of Russia had been struggling with one another ever since the disintegration of the Kievan state in the early twelfth century. Now, with the Mongol invasion, the southern principalities were destroyed, but several northern principalities survived as semi-independent tributary states. The greatest of the northern princes, Alexander Nevsky of Novgorod (1220–63), managed to placate the Golden Horde, while also defeating an invading Swedish army and turning back the eastward thrust of the Teu-

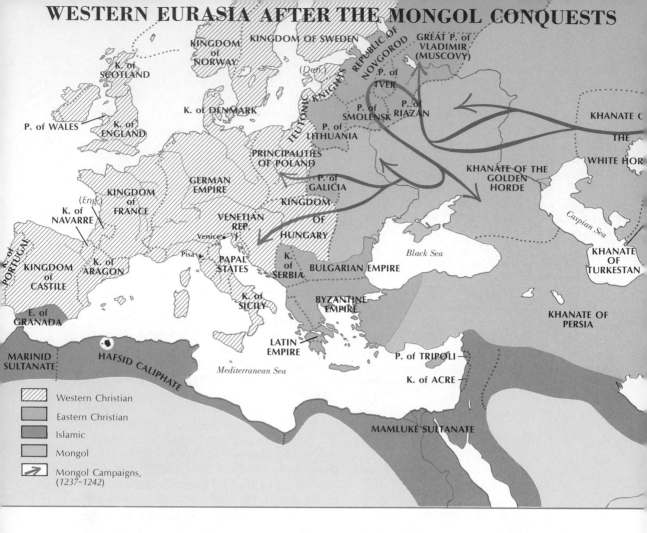

Map labels: KINGDOM of NORWAY; K. of SCOTLAND; KINGDOM OF SWEDEN; KINGDOM of NORWAY; (Den.); REPUBLIC OF NOVGOROD; P. of TVER; GREAT P. of VLADIMIR (MUSCOVY); KHANATE O; THE; WHITE HOR; K. of DENMARK; P. of SMOLENSK; P. of RIAZAN; TEUTONIC KNIGHTS; P. of WALES; K. of ENGLAND; P. of LITHUANIA; PRINCIPALITIES OF POLAND; GERMAN EMPIRE; P. of GALICIA; KHANATE OF THE GOLDEN HORDE; (Eng.); KINGDOM of FRANCE; KINGDOM OF HUNGARY; Caspian Sea; K. of NAVARRE; VENETIAN REP.; Venice; KHANATE OF TURKESTAN; K. of PORTUGAL; KINGDOM of CASTILE; K. of ARAGON; Pisa; PAPAL STATES; K. of SERBIA; BULGARIAN EMPIRE; Black Sea; E. of GRANADA; K. of SICILY; BYZANTINE EMPIRE; KHANATE OF PERSIA; MARINID SULTANATE; HAFSID CALIPHATE; Mediterranean Sea; LATIN EMPIRE; P. of TRIPOLI; K. of ACRE; MAMLUKE SULTANATE

Legend: Western Christian; Eastern Christian; Islamic; Mongol; Mongol Campaigns, (1237–1242)

tonic Knights. Nevsky eventually gained control over the northern princes; these efforts won for him the admiration of all Russia, and canonization by the Russian church. His career illustrates the survival of Russian initiative in the years following the Mongol conquest.

In the early days of the Mongol invasions, Russia suffered severe devastation and economic upheaval; this was followed by two centuries of heavy tribute payments. There was never any appreciable Mongol settlement in northern or central Russia nor, apart from the tribute, was there much interference in local affairs. But Russian princes tended to ape the ruling techniques of the Mongols and some of them married Mongol princesses. The princes of Moscow, who freed Russia from Mongol domination in the late fifteenth century, adapted to their own uses many ele-

ments of the "oriental despotism" that they had overthrown. Because it was cut off for several crucial generations from Byzantium and Western Europe, Russia was set back both economically and culturally.

POLITICAL EVOLUTION IN THE WEST: c. 1050–1300

While the frontiers of Western Christendom were expanding, developments of the greatest historical significance were occuring in the Western European heartland. England and France evolved into centrally governed kingdoms on the road to nationhood. The papacy and the Holy Roman Empire, on the other hand, were locked in struggle. On the eve of their conflict, in 1050, Germany had the mightiest monarchy in Western Christen-

The Holy Roman Emperor with orb and sceptre: manuscript illumination from the Gospel Book of Otto III, A.D. 1000.

dom, and the German king—or Holy Roman emperor—held the papacy in his palm. By 1300 the Holy Roman Empire was reduced to a specter of its former greatness, and the papacy, after 250 years of political prominence, was exhausted, battle-scarred, and on the brink of a prolonged decline.

The Papacy and the Holy Roman Emperors

The second half of the eleventh century was an epoch of religious awakening and reform. The Christianization of the European countryside had been proceeding steadily over the previous centuries, and a powerful wave of religious enthusiasm was now sweeping the new towns. Ever since the early tenth century, monastic reform had been surging through Europe, and a centralized network of reform monasteries known as the Congregation of Cluny had become, by the eleventh century, a potent agent of spiritual regeneration.

Despite papal claims of the spiritual authority of churchmen over laymen and popes over bishops, the papacy had long been weak, and the church of the mid-eleventh century remained under the firm control of the lay* aristocracy. This arrange-

* The term lay means anyone not in holy orders; its opposite is clerical.

ment had become traditional and unquestioningly accepted, but to the bearers of the soaring new piety, a captive church—well-fed, conservative, docile, and mildly corrupt—was unacceptable. Pious Christians such as the monks of Cluny protested against the widespread vices of clerical marriage and simony (the purchasing of church offices). And reformers of a still more radical stance, including many of the later-eleventh-century cardinals and popes, challenged the feudal and princely domination of the social order. They insisted that churchmen must not be appointed by laymen but must be elected by other churchmen in accordance with ecclesiastical law. The aristocracy, long accustomed to governing through loyal ecclesiastical subordinates, fought violently against the new reformers with their notions of church independence. In the face of this lay hostility, the reformers gained control of the Roman Synod of 1059 and issued two ringing decrees that, ultimately, transformed the power structure of medieval Europe.

Striking out in behalf of ecclesiastical independence, the Synod of 1059 declared (1) that thenceforth the pope would not be appointed by emperors or Roman nobles but would be elected by the cardinals, and (2) that laymen would no longer invest new churchmen with the symbols of their offices. For when a layman invested a bishop-elect with the symbolic ring and pastoral staff, the implication was that the bishop owed his office to his lay patron. Henceforth, the church would be its own master.

For nearly 250 years thereafter a powerful, independent papacy strove with considerable success to rule a centralized, hierarchical church—to wrest ecclesiastical appointments from lay control and to subordinate monarchs to its spiritual jurisdiction. Throughout this era the papacy's chief antagonists were the Holy Roman emperors, who struggled to keep control of the imperial church and to extend their political authority deep into Italy. Geographically, papacy and empire were cheek to jowl; ideologically, they were worlds apart.

During the long struggle, the empire employed military power against the papacy, and the papacy replied with potent spiritual sanctions against the emperors—excommunicating them, declaring them deposed, even ordering the suspension of church services (the *interdict*) throughout their domains. There were, oftentimes, imperially supported antipopes and papally supported anti-emperors. The papacy would counter imperial force with the military force of its current allies as, for example, the Sicilian Normans, the particularistic German princes, or the North Italian towns. And, at times, England and France were drawn into the conflict, always on opposite sides.

The first great papal-imperial crisis occurred during the pontificate of the fiery reformer Gregory VII (1073–1085). Pope Gregory reissued the lay-investiture ban, and his act was immediately challenged by the young emperor Henry IV (1056–1106). The crisis deepened as Gregory excommunicated Henry IV's advisers, Henry declared Gregory deposed, and Gregory declared Henry deposed and excommunicated. At this point many restive German princes, irritated by the ever-tightening imperial centralization, rose against their excommunicated sovereign and threatened to choose another monarch unless Henry IV obtained Gregory's forgiveness. So it was that in 1077 Henry crossed the Alps and stood penitent and barefoot in the snow before Gregory at the Tuscan castle of Canossa. This ultimate act of royal humiliation was also an act of political expedience, for at Canossa Henry was forgiven and reinstated. He returned to Germany to rebuild his power, and once his throne was secure he resumed the struggle against papal reform. Amidst the thunder of armed clashes and renewed excommunications and depositions, Gregory VII died. But there were other popes who would fight, as Gregory had, for a papal monarchy over a free international church—for the supremacy of *ecclesia* over *imperium*. And there were other kings and emperors who, like Henry IV, would struggle grimly to retain their prerogatives over both laymen and churchmen within their dominions.

The Investiture Controversy itself was settled by compromise in 1122. The emperor yielded the right to invest churchmen, while retaining a real, if indirect, voice in their appointment. But the core of the church-state struggle remained untouched. The rival

THE HOLY ROMAN EMPIRE, 1190

KINGDOM OF DENMARK

North Sea

Baltic Sea

LITHUANIA

PRUSSIANS

•Lübeck

SAXONY

BRANDENBURG

Elbe River

Oder River

Vistula River

KINGDOM OF POLAND

RUSSIA

Cologne •

Rhine River

LORRAINE

KINGDOM OF FRANCE

Worms •

FRANCONIA

KINGDOM OF GERMANY

BOHEMIA

ALSACE

SWABIA

•Augsburg

Danube River

KINGDOM OF BURGUNDY

Constance •

BAVARIA

KINGDOM OF HUNGARY

Rhine River

LOMBARDY

• Milan

• Venice

KINGDOM OF ITALY

BULGARIANS

Pisa•

TUSCANY

Adriatic Sea

SERBIA

CORSICA

Sutri •

Rome •

• Anagni

BYZANTINE EMPIRE

SARDINIA

KINGDOM OF SICILY

Mediterranean Sea

Palermo •

Holy Roman Empire

claims of monarchs who aspired to fuller sovereignty and of an international church that aspired to power and independence within each state could not be reconciled.

The conflict broke out anew in the reign of the great German emperor, Frederick Barbarossa (1152–1190), who sought to establish firm imperial control in northern Italy and met the fierce opposition of the papacy and the Lombard League of North Italian city-states. The struggle continued during the pontificate of Innocent III (1198–1216), the most powerful of all popes, who directed his astute diplomatic skills not only against recalcitrant emperors but against the kings of England and France as well. He forced King Philip Augustus of France to return to an abandoned first wife; he forced King John of England to accept an archbishop that John had not wanted; and, maneuvering shrewdly through the quicksand of German politics, he enforced his will in a disputed imperial succession.

The final phase of the struggle commenced just after Innocent III's death, when his youthful handpicked emperor, Frederick II (1211–1250), defied the papacy and sought to bring all Italy under his rule. Frederick II was a brilliant anticlerical skeptic, known to his admirers as *stupor mundi* — the Wonder of the World — and suspected by his enemies of being the incarnate antichrist. He inherited the Norman Kingdom of Sicily from his mother and Germany from his father. It took all the skill of the papacy and the unremitting efforts of the North Italian cities to defeat his armies and thwart his ambitions. Shortly after Frederick II's death, the imperial office fell vacant and remained unoccupied for 19 years (1254–1273). At length, it passed to Rudolph of Hapsburg, through election by the German princes and with papal approval.

By now the imperial office had lost its power. Two centuries of conflict had transformed Germany from a strongly governed state into a chaos of independent magnates. The ambitious princes had usurped imperial lands, revenues, and rights, until, by the late thirteenth century, they had become powers unto themselves. The papal policy of promoting internal dissension and of encouraging rival emperors from competing houses had destroyed the hereditary principle in Germany. The emperors were now elected by the chief princes, and a son succeeded his father only if the powerful princely electors approved. Thus, the papal-imperial conflict doomed Germany to centuries of disunity and political impotence in the affairs of Europe.

Italy suffered, too, for it was the chief papal-imperial battleground. Yet the North Italian cities, encouraged and supported by the papacy, won their independence from imperial authority and emerged from the conflict as independent communes. Cities like Milan, Florence, and Siena — once under imperial jurisdiction — were now autonomous city-states in which, by the late thirteenth century, a rich urban culture was brewing.

The papacy emerged victorious over the empire, yet it, too, lost much in the struggle. Pope Gregory VII had ridden the wave of the new popular piety and, by and large, the townsmen and monastic reformers had been with him. Innocent III, on the contrary, was no man of the people but an aristocratic canon lawyer. He and his successors were highly skilled in the fields of law, diplomacy, and administration. They built a superb bureaucracy and they humbled monarchs. But gradually, almost imperceptibly, they lost touch with the religious aspirations of the common people. Basically, the power of the papacy rested on its spiritual prestige, and the flock of Christ would not always give its complete homage to lawyers, tax-gatherers, and politicians. The high-medieval papacy was not a corrupt institution. Rather, it was the victim of its own impulse to enter dynamically into all human affairs. In the beginning it aspired to be a great spiritual force in the world; in the end it became worldly.

As the thirteenth century closed, the papacy was itself humbled, not by the weakened Holy Roman Empire but by the rising monarchies of England and France, whose kings taxed their churchmen against papal wishes and defied the fulminations of Rome. In 1305 French troops seized the proud, intransigent Pope Boniface VIII, and a few years later a French pope, Clement V, abandoned Rome and made his capital at Avignon, in the shadow of the French monarchy. The old medieval powers—papacy and empire—were, by the end of the high middle ages, giving way before the centralized kingdoms that would dominate early modern Europe.

England

England was already a unified monarchy by the mid-eleventh century. In the course of the high middle ages it became far more tightly unified, far more sophisticated in its laws and administration, and far richer and more populous. In 1066 William, Duke of Normandy, won a momentous victory at Hastings and established a new royal dynasty in England. William the Conqueror's new kingdom was unique in its lucrative royal land tax—the danegeld—and in its well-functioning system of local courts. The Conqueror further centralized his power by adding significantly to the royal estates and by granting extensive lands as military fiefs to loyal Norman vassals who usually respected the royal authority. William I's great land survey of 1086, recorded in *Domesday Book*, illustrates both the administrative precocity of his government and its claim to ultimate jurisdiction over all of England's lands and people.

The process of political consolidation gathered momentum under William I's twelfth-century successors, particularly Henry I (1100–1135) and Henry II (1154–1189). Henry I, for example, developed a remarkable royal accounting bureau—the Exchequer—which processed the revenues collected by the royal representatives in the shires—the sheriffs ("shire reeves"). And under Henry II, significant steps were taken toward the development of a common law, under the jurisdiction of royal courts, to supersede the various and complex jurisdictions of local and feudal courts. Generally speaking, legal actions relating to the all-important subject of land tenure passed under royal jurisdiction in Henry II's reign. The political unification of England by the Anglo-Saxon kings beginning in the late ninth century was now being paralleled by a legal unification under the expanding jurisdiction of the twelfth-century royal courts.

The era also witnessed the dynastic fusion of England with portions of northern France.

The effect of William's conquest in 1066 was the formation of an Anglo-Norman state, and, as a result of successive royal marriages, Henry II ruled not only England and Normandy but Anjou, Aquitaine, and other French principalities as well. This immense constellation of territories—known as the "Angevin Empire"—remained intact for half a century (1154–1204), dwarfing the domains of the French crown. At length, King Philip Augustus of France seized the northern French districts of the Angevin Empire from the unlucky King John of England (1199–1216). Thenceforth, for more than a century, English royal jurisdiction was limited mainly to the British Isles. John made important advances in Ireland and, late in the thirteenth century, Edward I (1272–1307) conquered Wales. But not until the 1330s and 1340s, with the opening of the Hundred Years' War, did an English king once again lead his armies into northern France.

During the thirteenth century the English central administration continued to increase in refinement and scope. Royal authority over lands and law, which had been advanced so promisingly under Henry II, reached its climax in Edward I's reign. The central government was now issuing statutes binding on all Englishmen, and the common law was carried everywhere by a powerful system of fixed and itinerant royal courts. Full administrative records were being maintained, and the simple Exchequer of Henry I's day had evolved into a complex and highly efficient machine, drawing large revenues from the prosperous manors and bustling towns of thirteenth-century England.

But the steady growth of the thirteenth-century royal administration gave rise to a concurrent trend toward limiting the powers of the king himself: *Magna Carta* (1215) and the rise of Parliament in the later thirteenth century are the chief monuments in this trend, and both were rooted in the earlier feudal order.

England, like other medieval kingdoms, was a feudal monarchy dominated by the lord-king and his aristocratic vassals. Since the traditional feudal relationship of lord and vassal was a relationship of *mutual* rights and obligations, a monarchy arising out of such a system tended to be limited rather than abso-

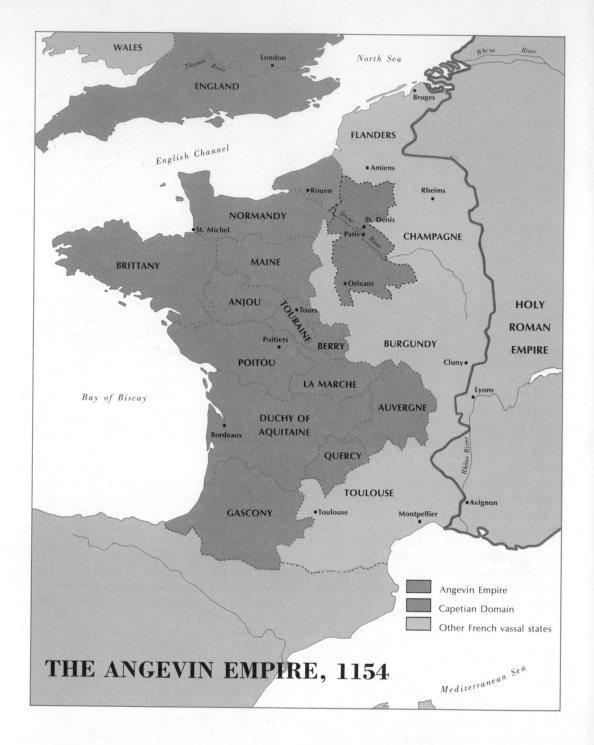

WALES

London

ENGLAND

Thames River

North Sea

Rhine River

Bruges

FLANDERS

English Channel

Amiens

Rouen

Rheims

NORMANDY

St. Michel

St. Denis

Seine

Paris

River

CHAMPAGNE

BRITTANY

MAINE

Orleans

ANJOU

TOURAINE

Tours

HOLY

ROMAN

EMPIRE

Poitiers

BERRY

BURGUNDY

Cluny

POITOU

LA MARCHE

Bay of Biscay

AUVERGNE

Lyons

DUCHY OF
AQUITAINE

Bordeaux

QUERCY

Rhône River

GASCONY

TOULOUSE

Toulouse

Montpellier

Avignon

Angevin Empire

Capetian Domain

Other French vassal states

THE ANGEVIN EMPIRE, 1154

Mediterranean Sea

lute. The king was always bound by customs —feudal, regional, and national—and arbitrary royal taxes or directives were always resisted.

Thus, *Magna Carta* (or the Great Charter), the reputed keystone of England's "government under the law," was a profoundly feudal document which limited royal exploitation of feudal and customary rights in a variety of specific ways. It was, indeed, a product of baronial resistance to the centralizing policies of the monarchy—designed to strengthen and make more specific the traditional safeguards of the lord-vassal relationship against an ambitious king who had exceeded the customary limits of his lordship.

The English baronage undertook several major rebellions during the thirteenth century—not with the purpose of weakening the royal administration but, rather, with the purpose of sharing in its control. The monarchy, forced to recognize these essentially conservative demands of its feudal magnates, gradually transformed the great baronial royal council—the *curia regis*—into Parliament. By the reign of Edward I, late in the century, the power struggle had been largely resolved. When the king issued his statutes, or proclaimed new unprecedented taxes, or made unusual military demands on his subjects, he now did so "in parliament"—with the consent of the great barons of the realm sitting with him in council. Indeed, the soaring prosperity of town and countryside resulted in the inclusion in royal parliaments of representative burgers and members of the rural gentry—the "knights of the shire." The composition of Edward I's parliaments varied, but by the close of the thirteenth century they were coming increasingly to include all three classes—barons, shire knights, and townsmen (with bishops and abbots meeting separately in ecclesiastical "convocations)". In the course of the fourteenth century the burgers and shire gentry split off into a separate House of Commons, which gradually, during the Hundred Years' War, gained control of the royal purse strings.

High-medieval England did not invent constitutional monarchy. Similar constitutional developments were occurring in France, the Spanish kingdoms, the German principalities, and elsewhere. And, as in England, they always evolved out of old Germanic and feudal notions that held custom superior to king and upheld the rights of vassals with respect to their lords. In England alone, however, do we find the evolution from feudalism to constitutionalism occurring as a continuous process down to modern times.

France

The French monarchy began the high middle ages far weaker than its English counterpart and ended far less restricted by national customs and national assemblies. The Capetian dynasty, which had gained the weak French throne in 987, remained, at the time of the Norman Conquest, limited to an uneasy jurisdiction over the dimunitive Ile de France around Paris and Orleans. To realize the immense potential of their royal title, the Capetians had three great tasks before them: (1) to master and pacify their turbulent barons in the Ile de France itself, (2) to expand their political and economic base by bringing additional territories under direct royal authority, and (3) to make their lordship over the feudal duchies and counties of France a reality rather than a mere formality.

During the twelfth and thirteenth centuries a series of remarkable Capetian kings pursued and achieved these goals. Their success was so complete that by the opening of the fourteenth century, the Capetians controlled all France, either directly or through obedient vassals. They had developed by this time a sophisticated royal bureaucracy almost as efficient as England's and far more single-mindedly devoted to the interests of the king. The Capetians followed no set formula. Instead, their success depended on a combination of luck and ingenuity—on their clever exploitation of the powers that, potentially, they had always possessed as kings and feudal overlords. They succeeded in avoiding the family squabbles that had, at times, divided Germany and England. Whereas Germany exhausted herself in struggles with the papacy, and even England was torn at times by church-state conflicts, the Capetians maintained relatively good relations with the church. They had the enormous good fortune of an unbroken sequence of direct male heirs from 987 to 1328. Above all, they seldom overreached themselves. They avoided grandiose schemes, preferring to pursue modest, realistic goals. They extended their power gradually and cautiously by favorable marriages, by confiscating the fiefs of vassals who died without heirs, and by dispossessing vassals who violated their feudal obligations to the monarchy. Yet they

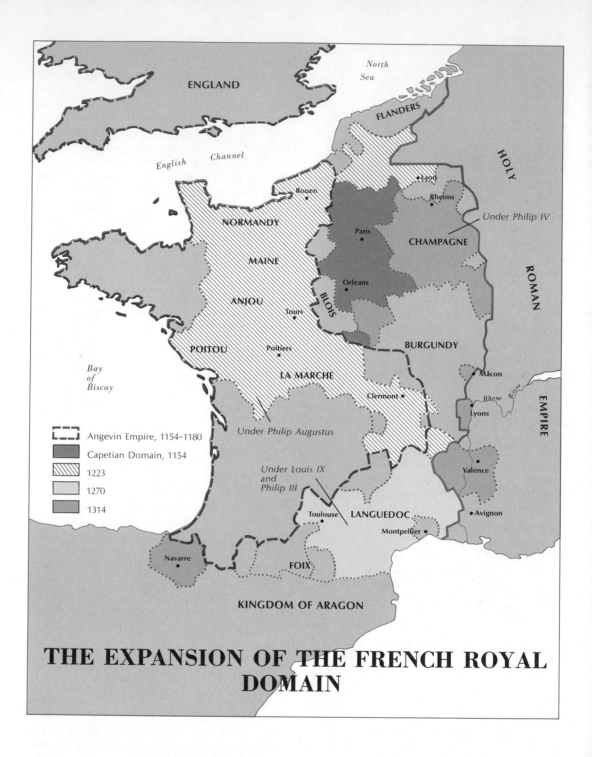

ENGLAND

North Sea

FLANDERS

HOLY

English Channel

Rouen •

• Laon

Rheims •

Under Philip IV

NORMANDY

Paris

CHAMPAGNE

ROMAN

MAINE

Orleans •

ANJOU

BLOIS

Tours •

BURGUNDY

POITOU

Poitiers •

Mâcon •

LA MARCHE

Rhone *River*

Bay of Biscay

Clermont •

Lyons •

EMPIRE

Angevin Empire, 1154–1180
Capetian Domain, 1154
1223
1270
1314

Under Philip Augustus

Valence •

Under Louis IX and Philip III

LANGUEDOC

Toulouse •

• Avignon

Montpellier •

Navarre

FOIX

KINGDOM OF ARAGON

THE EXPANSION OF THE FRENCH ROYAL DOMAIN

had no desire to absorb all the territories of their vassals. Rather they sought to build a kingdom with a substantial core of royal domain lands surrounded by the fiefs of loyal, obedient magnates.

In the period beginning about 1060 and lasting until about 1180, the Capetians succeeded in taming the Ile de France and in bringing some of their powerful vassals into a condition of increased dependency. The years between 1180 and 1314 were dominated by the rule of three great Capetian kings—Philip II "Augustus" (1180–1223), St. Louis IX (1226–1270), and Philip IV "the Fair" (1285–1314)—who built a powerful, encompassing monarchy on their ancestors' foundations. King Philip Augustus, whose Ile de France was dwarfed by the vast French dominions of the Angevin kings of England, worked shrewdly and tirelessly to shatter the Angevin Empire. His success came, at last, during King John's reign. Philip Augustus, utilizing his position as supreme feudal lord over John's French lands, summoned John to his feudal court in Paris to be tried for a relatively minor act of malfeasance. John refused to submit to the trial, and Philip, accordingly, declared John's French fiefs forfeited. In the role of the just lord, Philip sent armies against Normandy and Anjou. John fought ineffectively for a time, then fled to England, and his immense dominions in northern France passed into the French royal domain (1204). In one stroke, Philip Augustus had won the extensive territorial base essential for Capetian control over France.

The golden age of the Capetian monarchy occurred in the reign of Philip Augustus' grandson, Louis IX (1226–1270), later made a saint. Louis was a strong, pious king who ruled France wisely and firmly, winning invaluable prestige for the crown through his crusades and charities while his devoted royal officials worked unremittingly to extend the king's power. Capetian officials, unlike their English counterparts, were drawn largely from among ambitious townsmen and university graduates—men lacking strong local roots, utterly devoted to the royal interest. The fusion of local and royal interests, evident in the English administration in general, and the English Parliament in particular, failed to develop in France. Rebellion became the chief instrument of the French nobility for curbing royal power. Thus the potentialities for both royal absolutism and anarchy were present in thirteenth-century France, although neither threat materialized until after the close of the high middle ages.

Medieval culture reached its climax in St. Louis' France. Town life flourished, and in the towns superb Gothic cathedrals, with

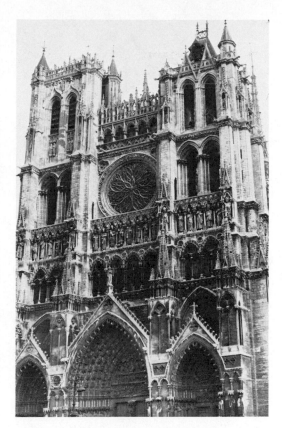

Gothic architecture: west facade of Amiens Cathedral, France, thirteenth century.

newly realistic sculpture, were being erected. This was the great age of the medieval universities, and the most distinguished university of the age, the University of Paris, enjoyed the favor and protection of the French crown. The universities produced brilliant and subtle theologians; they also produced learned, ambitious lawyers—men of a more secular cast who devoted their talents to the king and took over the royal bureaucracy. The Capetian government became steadily more complex, more efficient, and from the aristocracy's standpoint, more oppressive.

These trends reached their culmination under St. Louis' ruthless grandson, Philip IV, "the Fair" or the "the Handsome" (1285–1314)—a mysterious, silent figure whose reign was marked by unceasing royal aggression against neighboring lands, against the papacy, and against the nobility. Philip the Fair sought to bypass the feudal hierarchy

Gothic sculpture: (above) Apostle's head, from the Cathedral of Sens, France, c. 1190–1200; (right) Head of the Virgin Mary, from the west facade of Rheims cathedral, France, first half of the thirteenth century.

by demanding the direct allegiance of all Frenchmen. Royalist doctrine, anticipating the goals of later French monarchs, proclaimed the king supreme in France and France supreme in Europe. And in Philip the Fair's reign the doctrine came close to realization. The papacy was humbled, the wealthy crusading order of Knights Templars was looted and destroyed, and France began to expand eastward at the expense of the weakened Holy Roman Empire. In 1302 the French Estates General was summoned for the first time, for reasons akin to those that prompted the development of the English Parliament. But, owing in part to the chasm between king and nobility, in part to the ingrained localism of rural France, the medieval Estates General lacked Parliament's potential for creative development as a vital organ of the central government. The Capetians had made the king supreme in France

and, in so doing, had taken the initial steps along the road from feudal monarchy to absolutism.

RELIGION AND CULTURE

To many restless modern souls, the society of the high-medieval world appears to be admirably secure and cohesive—a society in repose, confident of its values and its cosmology, and equally confident of its means of expressing these values in its art, thought, and institutions. Yet, in reality, high-medieval culture was always on the move—changing, dynamic, often struggling to reconcile seemingly irreconcilable opposites. One should not merely admire the success of the high Gothic cathedral builders, or the thirteenth-century philosophers, in synthesizing faith and logic. One should also see that the synthesis achieved in St. Thomas

Aquinas' *Summa Theologica* or Amiens cathedral was a brilliant, passing response to the challenges of a transitory historical moment. Amiens cathedral should be appreciated both as a superb expression of the thirteenth-century spirit and as the unique product of a single instant in the evolution of medieval architecture, differing significantly from the cathedrals of a generation earlier or later.

High-medieval culture is so richly various as to defy generalization. Yet one may say—with all appropriate reservations and exceptions—that most creative men of the high middle ages were working, consciously or unconsciously, in the daring hope of creating a Christian civilization, of building an earthly City of God, of reconciling the worlds of matter, intellect, and spirit. Pious men of the early middle ages had sought to flee the world, retiring to the desert or the walled monastery. But men such as Pope Gregory VII (1073–1085) turned their faces outward and strove to Christianize all society. Likewise, many of the new religious orders of the high middle ages rejected the traditional Benedictine goal of withdrawal from the world and performed their work in secular society. The great twelfth-century order of Cistercian monks was cloistered and austere, but their greatest representative, St. Bernard (1091–1153), became embroiled in high politics, preaching the Second Crusade, chiding the papacy itself, and generally playing the role of peacemaker among Christian princes. By St. Bernard's time other new religious orders—the Austin canons, for example—were devoting themselves collectively to work in the world. The Crusades gave rise to military-religious orders such as the Knights Templars, Knights Hospitallers, and Teutonic Knights, all of whom lived under monastic rules yet worked to further the military expansion of Europe. Finally, and most important, the thirteenth-century mendicant (begging) orders—the Dominicans and Franciscans—epitomized the high-medieval ideal by preaching and serving among the townsmen and heretics while also binding themselves to lives of chastity, obedience, and personal and corporate poverty.

St. Francis of Assisi (c. 1182–1226) repre-sents in his life and work a supreme expression of the high-medieval ideal and a reconciliation and synthesis of previous religious movements. He was a joyous, loving man, devoted to God, determined to lead a life in imitation of Christ's, working in the world among the poor and diseased. In him, as in a number of his contemporaries, the old Persian dualism of good versus evil, soul versus body, spirit versus matter was reconciled and made one. The material world was God's creation, and St. Francis loved it and sang its praises:

Praise to thee, my Lord, for our sister,
  Mother Earth,
Who sustains and directs us,
And brings forth varied fruits, and plants and
  flowers bright . . .

If the high-medieval dream of a Christian world could be expressed so beautifully in St. Francis and the Franciscan movement, it could also give rise to brutality and repression. In an age of faith, concerned with reconciling world and spirit, heresy could not be tolerated. Yet in an atmosphere of intense popular piety and intellectual adventurousness, heresy was bound to arise. It was particularly widespread in the towns of twelfth-century southern Europe, where protest movements against the un-Christlike wealth of affluent churchmen sometimes evolved into outright rejection of church authority. Groups such as the Waldensians—devoted to apostolic poverty—and the Albigengians—reviving the "antimatter" doctrines of Persian dualism—presented grave threats to an established church that dreamed of a City of God on earth, united in faith. In 1208 Pope Innocent III summoned a crusade against the Albigensian heretics of southern France, and for a generation Christian armies slaughtered Albigensians, devastated the rich culture of the region, and ultimately destroyed the heresy. In 1210 just two years after the calling of the Albigensian Crusade, the same Pope Innocent III gave his formal sanction to St. Francis and his followers. And in 1223, three years prior to St. Francis' death, the papacy established the Inquisition. This centralized tribunal was designed to coordinate the work of suppressing

St. Francis of Assisi: late thirteenth-century fresco, attributed to the artist Cimabue, in the lower church of S. Francesco, Assisi.

heresy, a task that had long been under local episcopal jurisdiction. Paradoxical as these papal actions might seem, they all arose from the same motive: to bring about a truly unified Christian society. And in the thirteenth century the inspiration of the Franciscans proved more effective to that end than the savagery of the Albigensian crusaders or the repressive legal proceedings of the Inquisition.

The dynamic urge toward the synthesis of opposites emerges clearly in the evolution of high-medieval literature from epic to romance. The eleventh-century *Song of Roland* was immensely popular among the northern French and English nobility. It was characteristic of many similar long heroic poems of its time known as *chansons de geste* (songs of great deeds). These *chansons* were martial epics that stressed the virtues of knightly prowess, brotherhood in arms, and lord-vassal loyalty. Roland was unflinchingly loyal to his lord, Charlemagne, and Roland's

vassals were generally just as loyal to Roland. A breach of faith between lord and vassal was, in Roland's world, the ultimate sin.

During the era of *Roland's* greatest popularity in northern Europe—the late eleventh and twelfth centuries—a radically different literary tradition was flowering in southern France, where a sophisticated aristocracy preferred songs of love to songs of war. Here was born the romantic-love tradition of Western civilization, with its idealization of women and its emphasis on gallantry, courtesy, and the consuming, bittersweet madness of being in love. And here the troubadors produced lyric poems of remarkable sensitivity and enduring value—sometimes passionate, sometimes witty, sometimes agonizing, always short. The great moral imperative of the southern romantic-love tradition was the priority of love over all else. Fidelity to one's beloved was absolutely obligatory, even if it meant—as it usually did—infidelity to one's spouse. In this age of arranged political marriages, the maxim arose that romantic love between husband and wife was impossible.

By the mid-twelfth century the northern and southern traditions began to interpenetrate, creating a tension between opposites that demanded resolution. From *Roland* came the words:

Men must face great privation for their lord,
Must suffer cold for him, and searing heat,
And must endure sharp wounds and loss of
  blood.

But from the southern French lyric poetess Beatriz de Dia (c. 1160) came sentiments of a radically different sort:

My heart is filled with passion's fire.
My well-loved knight, I grant thee grace,
To hold me in my husband's place,
And do the things I so desire.

Out of this confrontation of moral and stylistic opposites, came the northern *romance* which, like the *chanson de geste,* was a long narrative poem but which, like the southern lyric, was sensitive and romantic. The character of *Tristan*—in the romance *Tristan and*

Dante holding his **Divine Comedy,** *the cathedral of Florence to the right, the mountain of Purgatory to the left.*

Iseult—and the character of Lancelot in the Arthurian romances both embody the profound tension between loyalty to lord and devotion to one's beloved. Both Tristan and Lancelot respected their lords yet loved their lords' wives. Both heroes put the demand of love above the demand of feudal loyalty, and both love affairs ended in disaster. The opposites could not be reconciled.

Yet reconciliation and synthesis were achieved on another level in the romances of the Holy Grail, whose heroes—knights such as Percival and Galahad—directed their love toward God. As brave and resourceful as Roland, as sensitive as Tristan, Percival quested not for his lady but for the Grail of the Last Supper. In the great *Parzival* romance (c. 1220) of the German poet Wolfram von Eschenbach, the hero synthesizes and transcends the values of epic, lyric, and romance.

At the end of the high middle ages the Florentine Dante Alighieri, in his spiritualized love lyrics and in his *Divine Comedy,* carried the synthesis to its loftiest level. Dante is himself the questing hero, traversing all dimen-

Romanesque architecture (above) *the western apse of the Cathedral of Worms, Germany, eleventh century.* (Right) *Interior of Saint Savin-sur-Gartempe, France, near Poitiers, showing twelfth-century frescoes on the barrel vaulting.*

sions of the medieval world—earth, hell, purgatory, and heaven. His beloved Beatrice plays the role not of temptress but of his guide upward through heaven. At last, Dante is led to his ultimate goal—not the symbolic Grail but the naked presence of God himself:

Here power failed to the high fantasy,
But my desire and will were turned—as
  one—
And as a wheel that turneth evenly,
By Holy Love, that moves the stars and sun.

The evolution from Roland to Dante embodies a constant widening of the human psyche—a steady multiplication of ideal attributes from the prowess and loyalty of Roland to the heightened sensitivity of the equally intrepid Tristan to the mysticism of Percival to the inquisitive many-sidedness of Dante. The ever-increasing emphasis on emotionalism and religious sensitivity embodied in this development is equally evi-

dent in other modes of expression. High-medieval piety, for example, evolved from the awe and mystery characteristic of earlier Christianity to a new emotional dynamism. The figure of the divine Christ sitting in judgment gave way to the tragic figure of the human Christ suffering on the Cross for man's sins. And the Virgin Mary became the cosmic symbol of feminine tenderness and mercy—the compassionate intercessor for hopelessly lost souls. In sculpture the imaginative distortion and fantasy of the Romanesque style gave way, in the later twelfth century, to the assured, naturalism of the Gothic. And in architecture the shift from the stolid, earthbound Romanesque to the tense, upward-reaching Gothic, expresses this same change of mood.

One might well regard the cultural evolution of the high middle ages as a progression from justice toward mercy, from traditional norms toward emotionalism, from epic toward romance, from masculinity toward

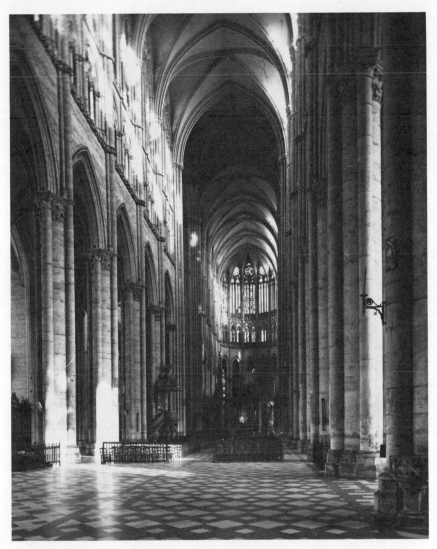

Gothic architecture: Amiens Cathedral, France thirteenth century.

femininity. Yet to describe the thirteenth-century culture simply as emotional, romantic, and feminine would be to distort it out of recognition. Rather, it was a culture in a state of taut equilibrium between emotion and logic, faith and reason, mercy and justice, femininity and masculinity.

The soaring French cathedrals of the high Gothic age, although magnificent symbols of religious aspiration, were also products of a rigorous logic. Every unit—every bay and chapel—of a Gothic cathedral was structurally and aesthetically related to every other unit in a balanced and tightly-reasoned whole. The cathedral's great west portals indicated, by their size and position, the spatial organization of the interior into nave and aisles. The interior illusion of stone vaulting springing from glass walls was explained and logically clarified to all beholders by the external flying buttresses that supported the cathedral's skeleton structure and made possible its walls of luminous glass. These flying buttresses are at once aesthetically beautiful, structurally essential, and logically satisfying. At Rheims cathedral they are decorated with great angels that beautify them while making them all the more conspicuous. The architect intended them to be conspicuous, so that the logical organization of his structure might be obvious to all. The angel buttresses of Rheims, like Rheims cathedral itself, and like all the cathedrals of its era, symbolize the fusion of heart and mind—faith and reason—to which the thirteenth century aspired. And the fulfillment of this aspiration—for a golden, unrecoverable moment in the early-and mid-thirteenth century is exemplified in the superb Gothic sculpture of the Rheims west facade: naturalistic, noble, and utterly assured—superbly competent in its depiction of the human face and body, preferring serene and beautiful idealizations to the portrayal of individual wrinkles leers, warts, and squints. That would come, but for the moment the culture of Europe was in equipoise.

And one cannot help but be reminded, in the Rheims sculpture, of a kindred equipoise achieved by Periclean Athens. Both cultures had arrived at the point of unquestioned competence and sophistication but had not yet become thoroughly professionalized, individualized, or disillusioned. In both cultures the faith and hope of youth overlapped for a moment the skill and unclouded intelligence of maturity, producing a synthesis that lies beyond the grasp of most ages.

The thirteenth-century synthesis is nowhere more evident than in the field of philosophy. Medieval scholars were obliged to cope with many pairs of opposites and, indeed, the formal reconciliation of these opposites became the keystone of the medieval philosophical method. The brilliant philosopher Peter Abelard (1079–1142), whose immense popularity helped transform the schools of Paris into a great university, risked the anger of the church by producing his influential *Sic et Non* (Yes and No). Here Abelard collected opinions from the Bible, the Latin Fathers, and papal and conciliar degrees on a great variety of theological issues, demonstrating that these hallowed authorities frequently disagreed on important religious matters. Abelard's *Sic et Non* method was developed and perfected by philosophers over the next several generations. And the civil and canon lawyers, whose commentaries on Justinian's recently recovered *Corpus Juris Civilis* and whose compilations of ecclesiastical law were raising legal studies to the level of a science, adopted this same method of analyzing conflicting opinions. But Abelard's successors, in both philosophy and law, took the further step of reconciling the contradictions and proposing conclusions.

The twelfth century was an age of high adventure—the era of crusades and rising kingdoms, of bold experiments in the radically new Gothic style, of Tristan torn between loyalty and love, and of Percival who reconciled the two and offered them both to God. In the rising towns the university was born, and in the universities men were intoxicated by the newly found tool of logic. They sensed its immense potential and did not yet know its limitations. The logical method of Abelard made many converts, but there were others who feared its impact on the faith. St. Bernard, austered mystic and arbiter of Europe, hounded Abelard across France and secured official condemnation of his views. Later in the twelfth century when Aristotle's complete writings became available to western Christendom through translations from the Arabic, the dualism of faith and reason seemed all the more irreconcilable. Aristotle had taught that the world had always existed; Christianity taught that it was divinely created. Aristotle denied personal immortality; Christianity affirmed it. As the thirteenth century dawned, many of Europe's finest minds were convinced of both the truth of Christianity and the intellectual supremacy of Aristotelian logic. Some advocated the concurrent acceptance of two antagonistic systems of truth, the one doctrinal, the other rational. But others—particularly a group of Dominican scholars working in mid-thirteenth-century France—endeavored to reconcile faith and reason in one overarching synthesis.

This fusion was achieved in the works of the Dominican St. Thomas Aquinas (1225–1274), whose immense *Summa Theologica*, organized according to a highly elaborated *Sic et Non* method, was a majestic endeavor to embrace all significant problems of theology and metaphysics. In its very comprehensiveness it exemplifies the thir-

A fresco of St. Thomas Aquinas showing his intellectual relationship to Jesus, the Church Fathers, Aristotle, Plato, and Averroes.

teenth-century shift from intellectual exploration to mature, encompassing synthesis. St. Thomas was always careful to distinguish between reason and revelations yet, argument by argument, step by step, he demonstrated that they were harmonious—two paths to one truth. Not every doctrine was susceptible to logical proof, for if this were true, then divine revelation would be redundant. But no Christian doctrine could be disproved, for truth is one, and logic and revelation are both infallible guides to it. Using these two guides together, carefully, rigorously, the great philosophical questions

Two later-medieval depictions of St. Thomas Aquinas.

can all be answered—the existence and nature of God, the nature and destiny of man, and the significance of God's created world and man's institutions. In his day, St. Thomas Aquinas represented, for many, the perfect union of intellect and belief—of mind and soul. His *Summa Theologica* takes its place alongside the high-Gothic cathedral, Dante's *Divine Comedy,* and the piety of St. Francis, as a supreme and mature expression of medieval Europe's dynamic resurgence.

Yet there were many, both in St. Thomas' own time and in later generations, who doubted the validity of his achievement. While St. Thomas was baptizing Aristotle, some of his contemporaries, particularly those in the Franciscan order, remained faithful to the earlier Christian intellectual tradition of Plato as interpreted by St. Augustine. The Englishman Robert Grosseteste, Bishop of Lincoln (*d.* 1253), undertook a synthesis all his own—between the mathematical orientation of Plato and the experimentalism of Aristotle—and produced from these two previously separate traditions a precociously modern scientific methodology. Grosseteste's experimental-mathematical approach proved capable of prodigious future development; St. Thomas' philosophy, on

the contrary, was so comprehensive as to be virtually self-contained. It was not a mere methodology but a superlatively finished product; it could be accepted, modified, or rejected, but little improved.

The leading philosophers after St. Thomas tended first to modify, then to reject the assured synthesis of the *Summa Theologica.* Many remained Thomists; some still do. But the most original of the fourteenth-century philosophers devoted themselves to tearing down the intellectual bridge between faith and reason, insisting that the two cannot communicate. Likewise, the taut aesthetic-logical synthesis of high Gothic eroded gradually into the highly-decorated fantasy of the Flamboyant Gothic style. Sculpture lost its confident serenity and became sentimentalized and individualized. The high medieval romance lost its tension and its inspiration and became tedious; creative writers turned to stark realism or, as in Italy, to ancient classical modes. At the same time the age of economic prosperity and geographical expansion was passing. In 1291 the last Christian outpost in the Holy Land fell to the Muslims. In the early fourteenth century England was ravaged by famine. Commerce and agriculture began to contract all over Europe.

Midway through the fourteenth century the Black Death struck, and the Ottoman Turks began flooding into the Balkans. Optimism and hope gave way to cynicism, peasants' rebellions, religious frenzy, mass mysticism, and witchcraft. The high middle ages had passed.

The agonies and disorientations of the fourteenth and fifteenth centuries have been variously interpreted, perhaps with equal justification, as the death pangs of the middle ages and the birth pangs of modern Europe. Yet the medieval and modern epochs, different as they may seem, were bound together by a tough web of traditions, institutions, and attitudes. Modern Europe inherited medieval Europe's boundless, restless dynamism, and many modern reformers and revolutionaries have dreamed their own versions of the medieval City of God on earth. Parliament, the university, technological inventiveness, scientific methodology, devotion to logic, the common law, the sweet pains of love, and the commercial city—all of them have played determining roles in modern Western civilization. All of them flourished in the high middle ages, and some of them were born there.

SUGGESTED READINGS

Southern, R. W., *The Making of the Middle Ages*. New Haven: Yale University Press, 1953.
   A brilliant, sympathetic interpretation of the eleventh and twelfth centuries.

Pirenne, Henri, *Economic and Social History of Medieval Europe*. New York: Harvest, 1956. Paperback.
   A compact, richly interpretive survey by a great scholar.

Runciman, Steven, *A History of the Crusades*. 3 Vols. New York: Harper and Row, 1951–1954. Paperback.
   Comprehensive and authoritative.

Tellenbach, Gerd, *Church, State and Christian Society at the Time of the Investiture Contest*. Oxford: Basil Blackwell, 1940.
   The finest analysis of the Investiture Controversy in English.

Barraclough, Geoffrey, *The Medieval Papacy*. New York: Harcourt, Brace, Jovanovich, 1968. Paperback.

Kantorowicz, Ernst, *Frederick II*. New York: Unger, 1957.
   An excellent biography.

Douglas, David, *William the Conqueror*. Berkeley, University of California Press, 1964. Paperback.

Hollister, C. W., *The Making of England, 55 B.C.—A.D. 1399*. Boston: D. C. Heath, 1966. Paperback.

Fawtier, Robert, *The Capetian Kings of France*. New York: St. Martin's Press, 1960. Paperback.
   A short, masterful treatment, highly recommended.

Knowles, David, *The Evolution of Medieval Thought*. New York: Vintage, 1964. Paperback.

Leclercq, Jean, *The Love of Learning and the Desire for God*. New York: Mentor, 1962. Paperback.
   A short study of monasticism.

Leff, Gordon, *Medieval Thought*. Baltimore, Md.: Penguin, 1958. Paperback.
A survey that emphasizes the development of metaphysics.

Lewis, C. S., *The Allegory of Love: A Study in Medieval Tradition*. New York: Oxford University Press, 1958. Paperback.

Haskins, C. H., *The Rise of the Universities*. Ithaca, N.Y.: Cornell University Press, 1957. Paperback.
Short and highly competent; a pleasure to read.

Haskins, C. H., *The Renaissance of the Twelfth Century*. New York: Meridian Books, 1957. Paperback.
An epoch-making book, particularly strong in the area of Latin literature.

Hollister, C. W., *The Twelfth-Century Renaissance*. New York: Wiley, 1969. Paperback.

Panofsky, Erwin, *Gothic Architecture and Scholasticism*. New York: Meridian Books, 1957. Paperback.
A challenging study which endeavors to demonstrate lines of connection between these two great medieval enterprises.

McIlwain, C. H., *The Growth of Political Thought in the West*. New York: Macmillan, 1932.
The preferred one-volume account of medieval political theory.

Ullmann, Walter, *A History of Political Thought: The Middle Ages*. Baltimore, Md.: Penguin, 1965. Paperback.
A short, provocative summary by a leading modern authority on medieval political theory.

De Villehardouin and De Joinville, *Memoirs of the Crusades,* trans. by Sir Frank Marzials. London: Everyman, 1908.
Excellent contemporary accounts of the Fourth Crusade and the crusading adventures of St. Louis.

CHAPTER 9

European Middle Ages, 1300–1500

THE DECLINE OF THE HIGH-MEDIEVAL SYNTHESIS

Like most eras of transition, the fourteenth and fifteenth centuries were violent and unsettled, marked by a gradual ebbing of the self-confidence on which the high-medieval synthesis had rested. Prosperity gave way to sporadic depression, optimism to disillusionment, and the thirteenth-century dream of fusing the worlds of matter and spirit came to an end. Social behavior ran to extremes—to rebellion, sensualism, flagellation, cynicism, and witchcraft. Powerful creative forces were at work in these centuries, but they were less evident to most contemporary observers than the forces of disintegration and decay. The shrinking of Europe's economy, population, and territorial frontiers was accompanied by a mood of pessimism and claustrophobia, exploding periodically into frenzied enthusiasm or blind rage. The literature and art of the period express a preoccupation with fantasy, eccentricity, and death. England and France were torn by war, and both were ruled for a time by madmen. The Black Death struck Europe in the mid-fourteenth century and returned periodically to darken men's spirits and disrupt society.

These varied symptoms of social neurosis were associated with a gradual shift in Western Europe's political orientation—from a Christian commonwealth to a constellation of territorial states. The Roman Catholic church fared badly during the late middle ages. The western kingdoms were racked by civil and external war and, at times, by a near-breakdown of royal government. Yet during the final half-century of the period (c. 1450–1500) strong monarchies emerged in England, France, and Spain. These three states were destined to dominate Western European politics far into the future. By 1500 the monarchy was beginning to replace the church as the object of men's highest allegiance. The pope had become mired in local Italian politics, and medieval Christian internationalism was breaking up into sovereign fragments.

CHURCH AND STATE IN THE LATE MIDDLE AGES

The late-medieval evolution from Christendom toward nationhood was not so much a transformation as a shift in balance. Even during the high middle ages the ideal of a Christian commonwealth, guided by pope

273

and clergy, had never been fulfilled. At best, popes could win momentary political victories over kings and could achieve an uneasy equilibrium between royal and clerical authority within the European kingdoms. And by the end of the thirteenth century the balance was already tipping in favor of monarchs such as Edward I of England and Philip the Fair of France. Two centuries later, in 1500, the papacy was far weaker as an international force and the monarchies stronger, but "nationhood," by any strict definition, had not yet come. Still, papal authority over the churches within the various kingdoms, which had been a significant reality in the high middle ages, was becoming tenuous by 1500. The princely electors of Germany had long before denied the papacy any role in imperial elections or coronations, and papal influence in the appointment of French, English, and Spanish prelates had ebbed. More important still, the late middle ages witnessed a collapse of papal spiritual prestige and a widening chasm between Christian piety and the organized church.

Christianity did not decline noticeably during this period; it merely became less ecclesiastical. The powerful movement of lay piety, which had been drifting away from papal leadership all through the high middle ages, now became increasingly hostile to ecclesiastical wealth and privilege, increasingly individualistic, and increasingly mystical. The wave of mysticism that swept across late-medieval Europe was not, for the most part, openly heretical. But by stressing the spiritual relationship between the individual and God the mystics tended to deemphasize the role of the ordained clergy and the sacraments as channels of divine grace. The mystic, although he believed in the efficacy of the Holy Eucharist, devoted himself chiefly to the direct mystical apprehension of God, for which no clerical hierarchy, no popes, and no sacraments were needed.

Mystics and Reformers

Mysticism had always been an element in Christian devotional life, and it was well known to the high middle ages. But with the breakdown of the high-medieval synthesis, and with the growth of complacency and corruption within the church, mysticism became, for the first time, a large-scale movement among the laity. Early in the fourteenth century, the great Dominican mystic, Meister Eckhart (d. 1327), taught that man's true goal is utter separation from the world of the senses and absorption into the Divine Unknown. Eckhart had many followers, and as the century progressed, several large mystical brotherhoods took form. The greatest of them, the Brethren of the Common Life, was founded about 1375 by the Flemish lay preacher Gerard Groot, a student of one of Eckhart's disciples. The Brethren of the Common Life devoted themselves to simple lives of preaching, teaching, and charitable works. Their popularity in fifteenth-century Northern Europe approached that of the Franciscans two centuries before, but the Brethren, unlike the Franciscans, took no lifetime vows. Their schools were among the finest in Europe and produced some of the leading mystics, humanists, and reformers of the fifteenth and sixteenth centuries. Erasmus and Luther were both products of the Brethren's schools, as was Thomas à Kempis (d. 1471) whose *Imitation of Christ* stands as the supreme literary expression of late-medieval mysticism.* The *Imitation of Christ* typifies the mystical outlook in its emphasis on adoration over speculation, inner spiritual purity over external "good works," and direct experience of God over the sacramental avenues to divine grace. The *Imitation* remained well within the bounds of Catholic orthodoxy, yet it contained ideas that had great appeal to the sixteenth-century Protestant reformers. The emphasis on individual piety, common to all the mystics, tended to erode the medieval Christian commonwealth by transforming the Catholic church into a multitude of individual souls, each groping his way toward salvation alone.

This element of Christian individualism was carried at times to the point of outright heresy. John Wycliffe (d. 1384), a professor at Oxford, anticipated the later Protestants by placing the authority of Scriptures over the pronouncements of popes and councils. Extending the implications of contemporary mysticism to their limit, Wycliffe stressed the

---

* Although most scholars attribute The Imitation of Christ to Thomas à Kempis, the attribution is not certain.

individual's inner spiritual journey toward God, questioned the real presence of Christ in the Holy Eucharist, deemphasized the entire sacramental system, and spoke out strongly against ecclesiastical wealth. This last protest had been implicit in the thirteenth-century Franciscan movement, although St. Francis had shown his devotion to apostolic poverty by living it rather than forcing it on others. The compromises of later Franciscanism on the matter of property had given rise to a zealous splinter group—the "Spiritual Franciscans—whose insistence on universal ecclesiastical poverty had made them anticlerical and antipapal. John XXII (1316–1334), the shrewd Avignonese "financier pope," had been obliged in 1323 to denounce the doctrine of apostolic poverty as heretical. And Wycliffe, more than one-half century later, was stripped of his professorship and convicted of heresy. Owing to his powerful friends at court, and to the unpopularity of the papacy in fourteenth-century England, he was permitted to die peacefully, but his followers, the Lollards, were less fortunate. Their fate is suggested by the title of a parliamentary act of 1401: "The Statute on the Burning of Heretics." There were to be no Lollards in England to celebrate King Henry VIII's break with Rome in the 1530s.

English Lollardy represented an extreme expression of a growing discontent with the official Church. Wycliffe's doctrines spread to faraway Bohemia where they were taken up by the reformer John Hus. The Hussites used Wycliffe's anticlericalism as a weapon in the struggle for Czech independence from German political and cultural influence. John Hus was burned at the stake at the Council of Constance in 1415, but his followers survived into the Reformation era as a dissident national group. Both Wycliffe and Hus represented, in their opposition to the organized international church, a reconciliation of personal religious faith with the idea of national sovereignty. If Christianity was to be an individual affair, then the political claims of popes and prelates were meritless, and secular rulers might govern without ecclesiastical interference. Thus the radical thrust of late-medieval Christianity, by its very anticlericalism, tended to support the growing concept of secular sovereignty. Ardent religious spirits such as John Hus— and Joan of Arc, burned as a heretic in 1431—could fuse Christian mysticism with the beginnings of patriotism.

Crisis of the Papacy: The Schism and the Conciliar Movement

The mystics and reformers, implicitly or explicitly, rejected the pope as the mediator between God and the Christian community. Actually, the late-medieval papacy did little to merit the awesome responsibility of mediator. Under pressure from King Philip the Fair the papacy had moved to Avignon, on the Rhône River, officially outside the domains of France yet always in their shadow. There a series of French popes ruled from 1309 to 1376. The Avignon popes were subservient to the French crown only to a degree. They were capable of independent action, particularly when France had weak rulers, but their very location suggested to non-Frenchmen that they were no longer an impartial international force. Until 1376 attempts to return the papacy to Rome were foiled by the insecurity and violent factionalism of the holy city. Meanwhile the Avignon popes carried the thirteenth-century trend toward administrative and fiscal efficiency to its ultimate degree. Englishmen and Germans resented paying high taxes to an apparent tool of the French crown. And the immense, bureaucracy of papal Avignon could hardly be expected to inspire mystics and reformers. As the material wealth of the papacy grew, its spiritual capital declined.

In 1376, Pope Gregory XI finally moved the Holy See from Avignon back to Rome. Chagrined by the turbulent conditions he encountered there, he made plans to return to France, but died in 1378 before he could carry them out. Urged on by a Roman mob, the cardinals—most of whom were homesick Frenchmen—grudgingly elected an Italian to the papal throne. The new pope, Urban VI, had previously been a colorless functionary in the ecclesiastical establishment. Now to everyone's surprise, he became a zealous reformer and began taking steps to reduce the cardinals' revenues and influence. The French cardinals fled Rome, canceled their previous election on the grounds of mob intimidation, and elected a French pope who returned with them to Avignon. Back in Rome, Urban VI appointed new cardinals, and for the next 37 years the Universal Church was torn by schism. When the rival popes died, their cardinals elected rival successors. Excommunications were hurled to-and-fro between Rome and Avignon, and the states of Europe chose their sides according to their interests. France and its allies supported Avignon, England and the Holy Roman Empire backed Rome, and the Italian states shifted from one side to the other as it suited their purposes. Papal prestige was falling in ruin, yet in the face of agelong papal claims to absolute spiritual authority, there seemed no power on earth that could claim to arbitrate between two rival popes. The church was at an impasse.

As the schism dragged on, increasing numbers of Christians became convinced that the only solution was the convening of a general church council. Both popes argued that councils were inferior to them and could not judge them, and Christians were perplexed as to who, if not the popes, had the authority to summon a council. At length the cardinals themselves, in both camps, called a council to meet in Pisa. There, in 1409, a group of 500 prelates deposed both popes and elected a new one. Since neither pope recognized the conciliar depositions, the effect of the Council of Pisa was to transform a two-way schism into a three-way schism. The situation was not only scandalous but ludicrous. Finally the Holy Roman emperor, drawing on the ancient precedent of the Emperor Constantine, summoned the prelates of Europe to the Council of Constance (1415–1418). Here, at last, the depositions of all three popes were voted and enforced, and the schism was healed by the election of a conciliar pope, Martin V (1417–1431).

To many thoughtful Christians the healing of the schism was not enough. The papacy stood discredited, and it was argued that future popes should be guided by general councils meeting regularly and automatically. The role of councils and assemblies was familiar enough to contemporary secular governments. Why should not the church, too, be governed "constitutionally"?

Such views were being urged by political philosophers such as Marsilius of Padua in the fourteenth century and Nicolas of Cusa in the fifteenth, and they were widely accepted among the prelates at Constance. That these delegates were essentially conservative is suggested by their decision to burn John Hus, who came to Constance with an imperial promise of safe conduct. Yet the Council of Constance made a genuine effort to reform the constitution of the church along conciliar lines. The delegates affirmed, against papal objection, the ultimate authority of councils in matters of doctrine and reform, and they decreed that thenceforth general councils would convene at regular intervals.

These broad principles, together with a number of specific reforms voted by the Council of Constance, met with firm opposition from Pope Martin V and his successors, who insisted on absolute papal supremacy. The popes reluctantly summoned a council in 1423 and another in 1431, but worked to make them ineffective. The last of the important medieval councils, the Council of Basel (1431–1449), drifted gradually into open schism with the recalcitrant papacy and petered out ingloriously in 1449. By then Europe's enthusiasm for conciliarism was waning; the conciliar movement died, and a single pope ruled unopposed once more in Rome.

The men who sat on the papal throne between the dissolution of Basel (1449) and the beginning of the Protestant Reformation (1517) were radically different from their high-medieval predecessors. Abandoning much of their former jurisdiction over the international church, they devoted themselves to the beguiling culture and bitter local politics of Renaissance Italy. By now the popes were mostly Italian, and so they would remain on into the future. Struggling to strengthen their hold on the Papal States, maneuvering through the shifting sands of Italian diplomacy, they conceded to northern monarchs an extensive degree of control over church and clergy in return for a formal recognition of papal authority and an agreed division of church revenues between pope and king.

The shift in emphasis from international Catholicism toward secular sovereignty occurring in the late-medieval period was ably and forcefully expressed in Marsilius of Padua's important treatise, the *Defensor Pacis* (1324). Here the dilemma of conflicting sovereign jurisdictions, secular and ecclesiastical, was resolved uncompromisingly in favor of the state. The church, Marsilius argued, should be stripped of political authority, and the state should wield sovereign power over all its subjects, lay and clerical alike. Thus the church, united in faith, would be divided politically into dozens of state churches obedient to their secular rulers and not to the pope. In its glorification of the sovereign state, the *Defensor Pacis* foreshadowed the evolution of late-medieval and early-modern politics.

It was only after 1450, however, that the western monarchies were able to assert their authority with any consistency over the particularistic nobility. During the period from the early-fourteenth to the mid-fifteenth century, the high-medieval trend toward royal centralization seemed to have reversed itself. The major Iberian powers—Aragon, Castile, and Portugal—were tormented by sporadic internal upheavals and made no progress toward reducing Granada, the remaining Islamic enclave in the peninsula. For most of the period, England and France, were involved in the Hundred Years' War (1337–1453), which drove England to the brink of bankruptcy and ravaged the French countryside and population.

England: The Growth of Parliament and the Hundred Years' War

Nevertheless, the unwritten English constitution developed significantly during these years. In the course of the fourteenth century, Parliament changed from a body that met occasionally to a permanent institution and split into Lords and Commons. The House of Commons, consisting of representative townsmen and shire knights, bargained with a monarchy hard pressed by the expenses of the Hundred Years' War. Commons traded its fiscal support for important political concessions, and by the century's end it had gained the privilege of approving or disapproving all taxation not sanctioned by custom. With control of the royal purse

strings secured, Commons then won the power to legislate. Adopting the motto, "redress before supply," it refused to pass financial grants until the king had approved its petitions, and in the end, Commons petitions acquired the force of law.

Without belittling these constitutional advances, one must recognize that the late-medieval Commons was largely controlled by the force or manipulation of powerful aristocrats. Elections could be rigged; representatives could be bribed or overawed. And although Parliament deposed two English kings in the fourteenth century—Edward II in 1327 and Richard II in 1399—in both instances it was simply ratifying the results of aristocratic power struggles. It is significant that such parliamentary ratification should seem necessary to the nobility, but one must not conclude that Parliament had yet become an independent agent. Symbolically, it represented the will of the English community; actually it remained sensitive to aristocratic force and tended to affirm decisions already made in castles or on battlefields.

The Hundred Years' War, which proved such a stimulus to the growth of parliamentary privileges, also constituted a serious drain on English wealth and lives. Beginning in 1337, the war dragged on fitfully for 116 years with periods of savage warfare alternating with prolonged periods of truce. Broadly speaking, the conflict was a continuation of the Anglo-French rivalry that dated from the Norman Conquest. Since 1066 England and France had battled on numerous occasions. In 1204 the Capetian crown had won the extensive northern French territories of the Angevin Empire. Normandy, Anjou, and surrounding lands had fallen more-or-less permanently into French royal hands, but the English kings retained a tenuous lordship over Gascony in the southwest. The English Gascon claim, cemented by a brisk commerce in Bordeaux wine and English cloth, gave rise to an expensive but inconclusive war (1294–1303) between Philip the Fair of France and Edward I of England. Competing English and French claims to jurisdiction in Gascony constituted one of several causes for the resumption of hostilities in 1337.

Another cause of the Hundred Years' War was the Anglo-French diplomatic struggle for

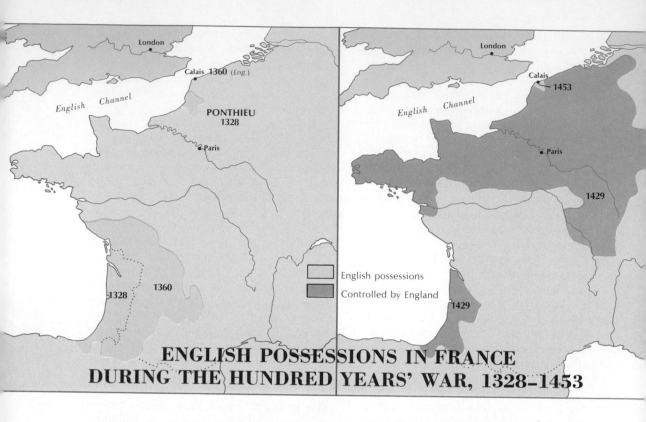

ENGLISH POSSESSIONS IN FRANCE
DURING THE HUNDRED YEARS' WAR, 1328–1453

control of Flanders, which France needed to round out its territories and which England needed to secure its profitable wool trade. Tension mounted in 1328 when, on the death of the last French Capetian, King Edward III of England (1327–1377) laid claim to the throne of France. Edward III's mother was a daughter of Philip the Fair, but the French nobility, refusing to be governed by an English monarch, revived the ancient custom that the succession could not pass through a female. Accordingly, they chose Philip V (1328–1350), the first king of the long-lived Valois dynasty. Edward III accepted the decision at first, but in 1337, when other reasons prompted him to take up arms, he revived his claim and titled himself king of France and England.

None of these causes can be considered decisive, and war might yet have been avoided had Edward III and Philip V not been chivalric, high-spirited romantics longing for heroic clashes of arms. The same spirit infected the nobility on both sides, although the French knights lost their ardor when English longbowmen won smashing victories

at Crecy (1346) and Poitiers (1356). The English revered Edward III so long as English arms were victorious, but they deposed his successor, Richard II (1377–1399), who showed no interest in fighting Frenchmen. Henry V (1413–1422) revived hostilities and gained the adulation of his subjects by winning a momentous victory over the French at Agincourt in 1415. But Henry V's early death, and the subsequent career of Joan of Arc (see p. 280), turned the tide of war against the English. By 1453, when the long struggle ended at last, England had lost all of France except the port of Calais. The centuries-long process of Anglo-French disentanglement was completed, and Joan of Arc's vision was realized: her dauphin (crown prince) ruled France unopposed as King Charles VII.

The Hundred Years' War had been over for scarcely two years when England entered an era of civil strife between the rival houses of York and Lancaster. The Wars of the Roses, which raged off and on between the years 1455 and 1485, were the medieval English nobility's last orgy of violence.

English commoners were tired of endless bloodshed and longed for firm royal governance. They achieved it, to a degree, in the reign of the Yorkist Edward IV (1461–1483). And after a final burst of warfare, strong monarchy came permanently to England with the accession of the first Tudor king, Henry VII (1485–1509). Both Edward IV and Henry VII sought peace, a full treasury, and effective government, and by the late fifteenth century these goals were coming within reach. The economy was reviving, many of the more troublesome nobles had perished in the Wars of the Roses, and most Englishmen were willing to exchange violent independence for obedience and peace. All that was needed now was strong royal leadership, which was supplied in full measure by the willful, determined Tudors.

France

The Hundred Years' War was a far greater trial to France than to England. All the fighting took place on French soil, and numerous mercenary companies, even when they were not engaged in actual warfare, continually pillaged the French countryside. King John the Good (1350–1364)—a very bad king indeed—was powerless to cope with the English or bring order to a demoralized, plague-ridden land. In 1356, a decade after the French military debacle at Crecy and eight years after the onset of the Black Death (see p. 286), France was stunned by a crushing defeat at Poitiers. French nobles fell in great numbers, and King John himself was taken prisoner by the English.

The Estates General, meeting in Paris under the leadership of a dynamic Parisian cloth merchant, Etienne Marcel, momentarily assumed the reins of government. In 1357 they forced King John's son, the young Dauphin Charles, to issue a radical constitutional statute known as the "Great Ordinance." This statute embodied the demands of the bourgeois-dominated Estates General to join with the monarchy in the governance of France. The Estates General were thenceforth to meet on regular occasions and to supervise the royal finances, courts, and administration through a small standing committee. The Dauphin Charles, deeply hostile to this infringement of royal authority, submitted for a time, then fled Paris to gather royalist support in the countryside.

By 1358 the horrors of plague, depression, and mercenary marauders had goaded the French peasantry into open revolt. The Jacquerie—as the rebellious peasants were called—lacked coherent goals and effective leaders, but they managed for a time to terrorize rural France. On one occasion they are reported to have forced an aristocratic wife to eat her roasted husband, after which they raped and murdered her. But within a few months the aristocracy and urban elites succeeded in crushing the Jacquerie with a savagery worthy of the rebels themselves. The peasants' rebellion of 1358 evoked a widespread longing for law and order and a return to the ways of old. This conservative backlash resulted in a surge of royalism which doomed Etienne Marcel's constitutional movement in Paris. Marcel himself was murdered in midsummer, 1358, and the Dauphin Charles returned to the city in triumph.

The Great Ordinance of 1357 became a dead letter after Marcel's fall, and in later centuries the Estates General met less and less frequently. The Dauphin Charles, who became the able King Charles V (1364–1380), instituted new tax measures that largely freed the monarchy from its financial dependence on assemblies and made it potentially the richest in Europe. The Estates General, unlike the English Parliament, failed to become an integral part of the government, and French kings reverted more and more to their high-medieval practice of dealing with their subjects through local assemblies. There were "Parlements" in France—outgrowths of the central and regional courts—but their functions remained strictly judicial; they did not deliberate on the granting of taxes, and they did not legislate. French national cohesion continued to lag behind that of England primarily because France was a much larger, more populous, and culturally diverse country. During the late middle ages its great dukes still ruled whole provinces with little interference from Paris. In the absence of an articulate national parliament the only voice that could claim to speak for all the French people was the voice of their king.

Charles V succeeded in turning the tide of war by avoiding pitched battles. His armies harassed the English unceasingly and forced them, little by little, to draw back. By Charles's death the French monarchy was recovering, and the English, reduced to small outposts around Bordeaux and Calais, virtually abandoned the war for a generation. But Charles V was succeeded by the incompetent Charles VI (1380–1422) — "Charles the Mad" — who grew from a weak child into an insane adult. His reign was marked by a bloody rivalry between the houses of Burgundy and Orleans. The Duke of Orleans was Charles the Mad's brother, the Duke of Burgundy his uncle. In Capetian times, such powerful fief-holding members of the royal family had usually cooperated with the king, but now, with a madman on the throne, Burgundy and Orleans struggled for control of the kingdom. In the course of the fifteenth century, the Orleanist faction became identified with the cause of the Valois monarchy, and Burgundy evolved into a powerful independent state between France and Germany. But at the time of Charles the Mad all was uncertain. With France ravaged once again by murder and civil strife, King Henry V of England resumed the Hundred Years' War and, in 1415, won his overwhelming victory at Agincourt. The Burgundians then joined the English, and Charles the Mad was forced to make Henry V his heir. But both kings died in 1422, and while Charles the Mad's son, Charles VII (1422–1461), carried on a halfhearted resistance, the Burgundians and English divided northern France between them and prepared to crush the remaining power of the Valois monarchy.

At the nadir of his fortunes, Charles VII, as yet uncrowned, accepted in desperation the military services of the peasant visionary, Joan of Arc. Joan's victory at Orleans, her insistence on Charles' coronation in Rheims, and her capture and death at the stake in 1431 have become legendary. The spirit that she kindled raised French hopes, and in the two decades following her death Charles VII's armies went from victory to victory. The conquest of France had always been beyond English resources, and English successes in the Hundred Years' War had been mainly a product of wretched French leadership and

paralyzing internal division. Now, as the war drew at last to a successful close, Charles VII could devote himself to the rebuilding of the royal government. He was supported in his task by secure tax revenues, a standing army, and the steady development of effective administrative institutions.

As with the English, the French in the later fifteenth century longed for strong monarchy and effective government. And Charles VII and his Valois successors, like the Tudors, were prepared to govern firmly. By 1500 the French monarchy was ruling through a central administration of middle-class professional bureaucrats. The nobility was pampered but apparently tamed, the towns were flourishing, and new royal armies were carrying the dynastic claims of the Valois kings into foreign lands.

Spain

The course of Spanish history in the late middle ages runs parallel to that of England and France, with generations of internal turmoil giving way in the later fifteenth century to political coherence and royal consolidation. As the high-medieval *Reconquista* came to a halt around 1270, the Iberian Peninsula contained two strong Christian kingdoms — Castile and Aragon — the weaker Christian Kingdom of Portugal along the western coast, and Muslim Granada in the extreme south. Aragon, smaller than Castile, was more highly urbanized and far more imperialistic. During the thirteenth and fourteenth centuries its kings conquered the Mediterranean islands of Majorca, Minorca, Sardinia, and Sicily. The old Norman kingdom of Sicily (including southern Italy) had passed, after the death of Emperor Frederic II, to a junior member of the French Capetian house. The Sicilians, rebelling against French control in 1282, invited King Peter III of Aragon to be their monarch, and after a savage twenty-year struggle — the War of the Sicilian Vespers — the kingdom was divided in two. Aragon thenceforth ruled the island of Sicily while, on the Italian mainland, a "Kingdom of Naples" remained under the control of the French dynasty. The two kingdoms, Sicily and Naples, were reunited in 1435 under an Aragonese king, but for long years thereafter southern Italy and

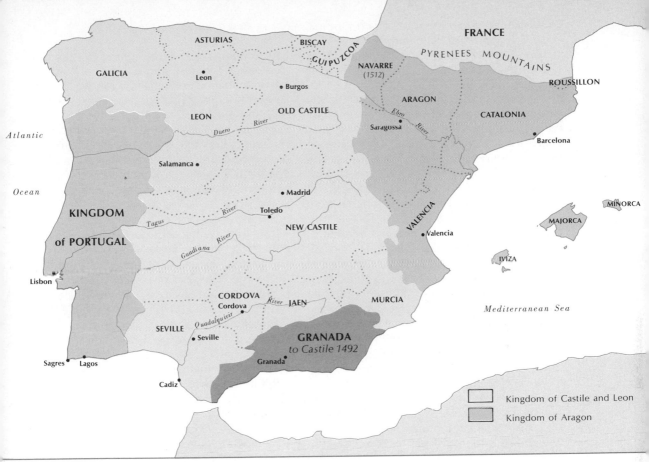

Sicily remained a source of antagonism between Spain and France.

Aragon and Castile were both plagued by civil turbulence during the late middle ages. Aragonese kings strove with only limited success to placate the nobility and townsmen by granting significant concessions to the Cortes, the regional representative assemblies. A prolonged revolt by the mercantile class in the Aragonese province of Catalonia was put down in 1472 only with the greatest difficulty. Castile, in the meantime, was torn by constant aristocratic uprisings and disputed royal successions. Peace and strong government came within reach at last when Ferdinand of Aragon married Isabella of Castile in 1469. Isabella inherited her throne in 1474; Ferdinand inherited his in 1479. And thereafter, despite the continuation of regional Cortes, tribunals, and customs, an efficient central administration

governed the two realms and eventually transformed them into the Kingdom of Spain.

In 1492 the new kingdom completed the long-delayed *Reconquista* by conquering Muslim Granada. Working tirelessly to enforce obedience, unity, and orthodoxy, the Spanish monarchy presented its Muslim and Jewish subjects with the choice of conversion or banishment, and the consequent Jewish exodus drained the kingdom of valuable mercantile and intellectual talent. The Catholic Inquisition became a tool of the state and, as an instrument of both political and doctrinal conformity, it brought the crown not only religious unity but lucrative revenues as well. The nobility was persuaded that its best interests lay in supporting the monarchy rather than in opposing it, and regional separation was curbed. With unity established and with the immense wealth of the New World soon to be pouring in, Spain in

1500 was entering a period of rich cultural expression and international power.

The wealth of Spain and Portugal in the sixteenth century was to result from their strategic location at the extreme west of Europe, facing the Atlantic. The first Atlantic explorations, however, were pioneered by Italian seamen who could draw on their experience in Mediterranean commerce. In the early fourteenth century, Venetian galley fleets were making yearly expeditions through the Straits of Gibraltar to England and Flanders, and Genoese merchants were trading with the Canary Islands. By the mid-fifteenth century the Canaries, Madeiras, Azores, and Cape Verde Islands had all passed into Spanish or Portuguese hands, but the ships of the Iberian monarchies continued to depend often on the skill of Italian captains and crews. It was the Genoese captain, Columbus, who brought the Spanish monarchy its claim to the New World.

Missionary zeal, curiosity, and greed were the mixed motives of these explorations. In the long run, greed was the primary consideration of both the sponsoring monarchies and the captains and private merchants who could make their fortunes from successful voyages. But the great patron of Portuguese West-African exploration, Prince Henry the Navigator (1394–1460), seems to have been driven in large measure by the hope of Christian evangelism and the longing to discover unknown lands. From his court at Sagres, ships were sent westward to the Atlantic islands and southward down the African coast, and at Sagres itself Prince Henry collected an invaluable store of geographical and navigational data for the instruction of his captains. The Portuguese West-African voyages continued intermittently after Prince Henry's death and reached their climax in 1479–1499 when Vasco da Gama rounded the Cape of Good Hope and reached India. The 6000 percent profit realized by da Gama's voyage demonstrated emphatically the commercial potentialities of this new, direct route to the Orient. The old trade routes were short-circuited, and the Ottoman Empire and Renaissance Italy both underwent a gradual commercial decline. The future lay with the rising Atlantic monarchies.

Germany and Italy

Late medieval Germany and Italy suffered from much the same sort of regional particularism that afflicted England, France, and the Iberian Peninsula, but the late fifteenth century brought no corresponding trend toward centralization. Both lands passed into the modern era divided internally and incapable of competing with the western monarchies. The weak elective Holy Roman Empire that emerged in Germany from the papal-imperial struggles of the high middle ages was given formal sanction in the Golden Bull of 1356. The Bull made no mention of any papal role in the imperial appointment or coronation, leaving the choice of succession to the majority vote of seven great German princes. These "electors" included the archbishops of Mainz, Trier, and Cologne, the Count Palatine of the Rhine, the Duke of Saxony, the Margrave of Brandenburg, and the King of Bohemia. The electoral states themselves remained relatively stable, as did other large German principalities such as the Hapsburg duchy of Austria, but the empire itself became powerless. Germany in 1500 was a conglomeration of more than 100 principalities—fiefs, ecclesiastical city-states, free cities, counties, and duchies—their boundaries shifting periodically through war, marriage, and inheritance. Imperial authority in Italian politics was as dead as papal authority in imperial elections. Germany and Italy were disengaged at last, but both continued to suffer the prolonged consequences of their former entanglement.

Through the domination of small states by larger ones during the fifteenth century, late-medieval Italy evolved into a delicate power balance between five strong political units: the Kingdom of Naples, the Papal States, and the three northern city-states of Florence, Milan, and Venice. Naples was ruled first by a French dynasty, and later by Aragon. Rome remained subject to a tenuous papal control, compromised by the particularism of local aristocrats and the political turbulence of Rome itself. Milan, and later Florence, ceased to be republics and fell under the rule of self-made despots. Throughout this period, Venice remained a republic dominated by a narrow commercial oligarchy.

The despots, ruling without the sanction of anointment or legitimate succession which a royal title confers, governed by their wits and by the realities of power, uninhibited by traditions or customs. They have often been regarded as symbols of the "new Renaissance man," but in fact their opportunism was a quality well known to the northern monarchs, and their ruthlessness would have surprised neither William the Conqueror nor Philip the Fair. Yet the very insecurity of their positions and the fragile equilibrium of the five major Italian powers gave rise to a considerable refinement of traditional diplomatic practices. Ambassadors, skilled at compliments and espionage, were exchanged on a regular basis, and emerging from the tendency of two or three weaker states to combine against a stronger one came the shifting alliances known as the "balance of power" principle.

The Italian power balance was upset in 1494 when a powerful French army invaded the peninsula. For generations thereafter Italy was a battleground for French-Spanish rivalries, and the techniques and concepts of Italian Renaissance diplomacy passed across the Alps to affect the relations of the northern kingdoms. The modern tendency to ignore moral limitations and ecclesiastical mediation — to base diplomacy on a calculated balance of force — was growing throughout late-medieval Europe, but it reached fruition first in Renaissance Italy.

Eastern Europe

Eastern Europe was, in general, no more successful than Germany and Italy in achieving political cohesion. Poland, Lithuania, and Hungary (as well as the Scandinavian states to the north) were all afflicted by aristocratic turbulence and dynastic quarrels. The Teutonic Knights were humbled by Slavic armies and internal rebellions, and the kingdoms of Serbia and Bulgaria were overwhelmed by the Ottoman Turks. Only the Russians and Ottomans were able to build strong states, and both, by 1500, were uncompromisingly autocratic.

Beginning in 1386, Poland united for a time with rapidly expanding Lithuania, and the Polish-Lithuanian state became the largest political unit in Europe. It was also, very possibly, the worst governed. Under the Lithuanian warrior-prince Jagiello (1377–1434), who converted to Catholicism when he accepted the Polish crown, the dual state humbled the Teutonic Knights at the decisive battle of Tannenberg (1410). But even under Jagiello, Poland-Lithuania had no real central government; its nobles would cooperate with their ruler only against the hated Germans, and even then only momentarily. Stretching all the way from the Black Sea to the Baltic, incorporating many of the former lands of the Teutonic Order and most of the old state of Kievan Russia, Poland-Lithuania lacked the skilled administrators and political institutions necessary to govern its vast territories. Its nobles were virtually all-powerful, and its peasantry was slipping toward serfdom. Its political impotence guaranteed that no strong state would emerge between Germany and Russia during Europe's early modern centuries.

Modern Russia evolved gradually out of the Muscovite Principality that had managed to survive and expand during the centuries of Tatar domination. The Grand Princes of Moscow extended their influence in northern Russia by collaborating with their Tatar Khans and winning the support of the Orthodox church. They were appointed sole collectors of the Tatar tribute, and on occasion they helped the Tatars crush the rebellions of other Russian princes. Moscow became the headquarters of Russian Orthodox Christianity, and when the Turks took Constantinople in 1453, Moscow, the "Third Rome," claimed spiritual sovereignty over the Orthodox Slavic world. At first the Muscovite princes strengthened their position with the full backing of the Tatar Khans, but toward the end of the fourteenth century Moscow began taking the lead in anti-Tatar resistance. At last, in 1480, Ivan III, the Great, Grand Prince of Moscow and Czar of the Russians, repudiated Tatar authority altogether and abolished the tribute.

The Muscovite princes enjoyed a certain measure of popular support in their struggle against the Tatars and in their battles against the Roman Catholic Lithuanians, but their rule was autocratic to a degree worthy of Genghis Khan himself. Nascent republicanism in city-states such as Novgorod was crushed with the expansion of Muscovite authority. The grand princes were despots, inspired politically by Central Asia rather than by the West. Their state had no local nor national assemblies and no articulate middle class. Russia was eventually to acquire the material and organizational attributes of a great power, but the centuries during which it had been isolated from the rest of Europe could not be made up overnight.

The great outside threat to Eastern Europe came from the southeast, where the Ottoman Turks pressed into the Balkans from Asia Minor. These Altaic tribesmen, driven from their Central Asian homeland by the Tatars, came into Asia Minor first as mercenaries, then as conquerors. Adopting the Islamic faith, the Ottomans subjected the greater part of Asia Minor to their rule and intermarried with the local population. In 1354, bypassing the diminutive Byzantine Empire, they invaded Europe. During the latter half of the fourteenth century they crushed Serbia and Bulgaria and extended their dominion over most of the Balkan Peninsula.

By the year 1400, Constantinople was surrounded and apparently doomed, but the remains of the Eastern Roman Empire were given another half century of independence by virtue of an unexpected onslaught of Central Asian invaders under the conqueror Tamerlane (see p. 218). Sweeping into Asia-Minor, he won a tremendous victory over the Ottomans in 1402 at the battle of Ankara. Immediately thereafter he turned eastward toward China. On his death in 1405 his loose-knit empire collapsed, and after some delay the Ottomans returned to their Balkan aggressions. At the decisive battle of Varna, in 1444, they decimated an anti-Turkish crusading army and consolidated their hold on southeastern Europe. After the great Ottoman victory at Varna, the storming of Constantinople in 1453 was little more than a postscript. Yet all Europe recognized that the Sultan Mohammed II, in conquering the unconquerable city, had ended an era.

The Ottoman Empire endured until the twentieth century; as the Republic of Turkey it endures still. Like the Muscovite princes, the Ottoman sultans were autocrats. Slaves served in their administration and fought in their armies alongside mounted noblemen of

Saint Basil's Cathedral, Moscow, sixteenth century.

the Ottoman landed aristocracy. And while the sultans were living in splendor on the Golden Horn, overlooking the Bosporus, their government was insulating southeastern Europe from the civilization of the west.

ECONOMIC CHANGE AND SOCIAL UNREST

The shift from boom to depression came gradually and unevenly to Western Europe in the years around 1300. From the early fourteenth century through much of the fifteenth, a number of related trends—shrinking population, contracting markets, an end to the long process of land reclamation, and a creeping mood of pessimism and retrenchment—resulted in a general economic slump and a deepening of social antagonisms. These trends were far from universal. They were less marked in northern Italy than elsewhere, and various localities north of the Alps, by profiting from favorable commercial situations or technological advances,

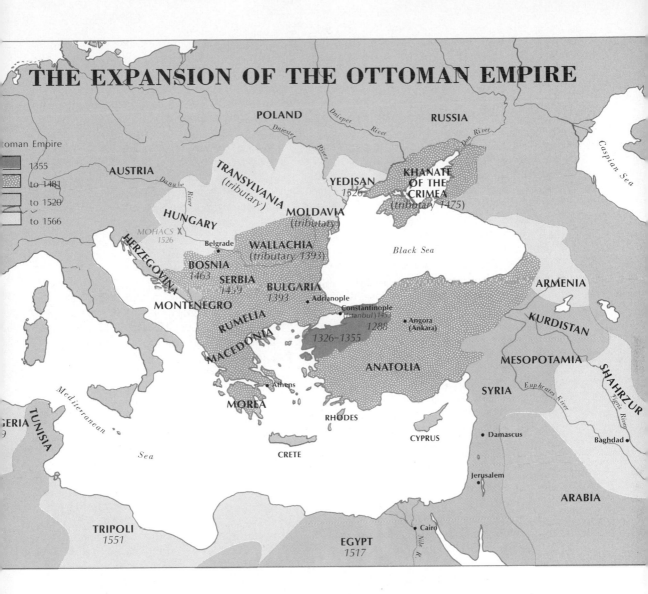

THE EXPANSION OF THE OTTOMAN EMPIRE

Ottoman Empire

1355

to 1481

to 1520

to 1566

POLAND

RUSSIA

AUSTRIA

TRANSYLVANIA
(tributary)

YEDISAN
1526

KHANATE
OF THE
CRIMEA
(tributary 1475)

Caspian Sea

HUNGARY

MOLDAVIA
(tributary)

Dnieper River

Dniester River

Don River

HERZEGOVINA

MOHACS X
1526

Belgrade

WALLACHIA
(tributary, 1393)

Black Sea

BOSNIA
1463

SERBIA
1459

BULGARIA
1393

Adrianople

ARMENIA

MONTENEGRO

RUMELIA

Constantinople
(Istanbul) 1453
1288

Angora
(Ankara)

KURDISTAN

MACEDONIA

1326-1355

MESOPOTAMIA

SHAHRZUR

ANATOLIA

SYRIA

Euphrates River

Tigris River

Danube River

Mediterranean

Athens

MOREA

RHODES

CYPRUS

Damascus

Baghdad

ALGERIA

TUNISIA

Sea

CRETE

Jerusalem

ARABIA

TRIPOLI
1551

EGYPT
1517

Cairo

Nile R.

---

became more prosperous than before. At a time when many English towns were declining, Coventry and certain others grew wealthy from the rise of woolen-cloth production. The Flemish town of Bruges remained throughout most of the late middle ages a bustling center of commerce on the northern seas. Florence, with its large textile industry and its international banking, was to become the focal point of Italian Renaissance culture. In Florence and elsewhere, enterprising individuals and families grew wealthy from the profits of international commerce and banking. The Bardi, Peruzzi, and Medici were the great Florentine

banking families, and they had their counterparts north of the Alps in such figures as Jacques Coeur of Bourges—financier of the fifteenth-century French monarchy—and the Fuggers of Augsburg. But such great financiers as these were exceedingly insecure in the turbulent years of the late middle ages. The Bardi and Peruzzi houses collapsed in the mid-fourteenth century, and Jacques Coeur was ruined by his royal debtor, King Charles VII. Even though some fortunes continued to grow, the total assets of late-medieval bankers fell considerably below those of their thirteenth-century predecessors. The success of families such as the

Medicis and Fuggers illustrates the late-medieval tendency toward an increasingly unequal distribution of wealth. The other side of the picture is to be seen in intensified urban strife and peasants' rebellions.

The late-medieval depression began well before the coming of the Black Death (1348–1349). The fundamental trends of demographic and economic decline were not initiated by the plague, but they were enormously aggravated by it. Carried by fleas that infested black rats, the bubonic plague entered Europe along the trade routes from the East and spread with frightening speed. The death toll cannot be determined with any precision. The best estimate would probably be one-fourth to one-third of Europe's population. In many crowded towns the mortality rate may well have exceeded 50 percent, whereas isolated rural areas tended to be spared. Consequently, the most progressive, most enterprising, and best-trained Europeans were hit the hardest. Few urban families can have been spared altogether. Survivors of the terrible years 1348 to 1349 were subjected to periodic recurrences of the plague and, in fact, Europeans for the next three centuries experienced recurring bouts of the dread disease. Fourteenth-century medical science was at a loss to explain the process of infection, while lack of sanitation in the towns encouraged its spread. Some fled their cities, some gave way to religious frenzy or debauchery, and some remained faithfully at their posts, hoping for divine protection against the pestilence. But none emerged from the ordeal unaffected.

The towns of late-medieval Europe, confronted with shrinking markets and decreasing opportunities, lost their earlier social mobility and buoyancy. Privileged classes closed their ranks, the guilds guarded their monopolies, and heredity became the chief avenue to the status of guild master. In their grim efforts to retain their share of declining markets, guilds struggled with one another, with the district nobility, and with the increasingly desperate urban proletariat, its class consciousness growing as its upward mobility was choked off. Few towns of late-medieval Europe escaped being torn by class violence. In 1378 Florence experienced the most severe workers' rebellion of the period.

In general the rich businessmen retained their privileged economic status in the face of lower-class pressure by sharing their political authority with great magnates or kings or, in Italy, by abdicating it to despots. The wealthy merchants and bankers were usually able, through political control or manipulation, to keep down wages despite the plague-induced labor shortage and to smash the resulting lower-class uprisings.

The rural nobility of Western Europe, like the urban upper class, managed to survive the turbulent socioeconomic changes of the late middle ages. Faced with a gradual shift from a barter to a money economy, the nobles were able, with some exceptions, to hold their extensive lands and preserve much of their wealth. They responded to the decline in grain prices by accelerating the high-medieval processes of leasing their own lands to peasants and commuting customary peasant services to fixed money payments. In this way, aristocratic incomes were protected against deflation so long as peasants could manage the agreed payments. The peasantry continued to rise in legal status from land-bound serfs to free tenant farmers until, by 1500, serfdom had almost disappeared from Western Europe. But the passing of serfdom was by no means accompanied by increased peasant prosperity. On the contrary, the declining population and the contracting grain market resulted in abandoned fields and a growing class of landless paupers. Some rural noblemen retained direct control of their land, hiring workers to farm it or converting it from grain crops to the more profitable wool growing.

In general, then, the peasant lost much of his earlier servile status by commuting his manorial obligations of payments in goods and labor services into cash; by 1500 he tended to be a rent-paying tenant or a landless wage earner. And the nobleman dealt in receipts and expenditures rather than in the exploitation of customary services. These changes had begun in the high middle ages and were largely completed by 1500. At times of drastic population decline, as in the decades following the Black Death, the resulting labor shortage tended to force up wages, and the nobility fought this tendency either through collective conspiracy or through legislation. In England, for example, the Statutes of Laborers of 1351 and thereafter were aimed at freezing wages in the wake of the plague. They succeeded only to a point, and at a price of creating a deep sense of grievance among the peasantry, a feeling that contributed to the abortive English Peasants' Revolt of 1381. This confused and bloody uprising was merely one of a considerable number that terrorized late-medieval Europe. Like the Jacquerie rebellion in France, and like many similar peasant insurrections of the period, it bore witness to an unbalanced society in which classes struggled bitterly for their share of a declining wealth.

In Eastern Europe the peasant's lot was even worse than in the west, for the eastern nobility was reducing its peasantry to serfdom at the very time that western peasants were achieving legal freedom. The late-medieval landed nobility of both Eastern and Western Europe jealously guarded its privileges against peasantry and monarchy, and for a time, in both east and west, this nobility seemed to be reversing the high medieval trend toward stronger royal government. With the exception of Russia, eastern monarchies made no real progress against their nobles, but by the later fifteenth century, western monarchies were beginning to curb the fractious independence of the landed aristocracy. The new Tudor monarchy in England tended to favor the mercantile class, but in Spain and France the nobility was rewarded for its political submissiveness by economic favoritism and privileged positions in the royal administration, the army, and the church.

Thus, the western nobles were evolving from robber barons into silk-clad courtiers. The traditional role of mounted knight in the feudal host was a thing of the past, for monarchs were now fighting with mercenaries, and footsoldiers were winning most of the major battles. Moreover, the increasing use of gunpowder was making knightly armor and knightly castles highly vulnerable. But while the feudal knight was vanishing from European armies, he was becoming ever more prominent in art, literature, and court ceremonial. The fifteenth century was an age of elaborate shining armor, fairy-tale castles,

coats of arms, and extravagant tournaments. Knighthood, driven from the battlefield, took refuge in fantasy, and an age of ruthless political cynicism saw the full flowering of a romantic code of chivalric ethics. Behind this fanciful façade, the landed aristocracy retained its privileged position atop the social order.

The consolidation of royal authority in late-fifteenth-century Western Europe coincided with a general economic upsurge following a long recession. Europe's population in 1500 may well have been lower than in 1300, but it was increasing again. Commerce was quickening and towns were growing. Technological progress had never ceased, and now water-driven fulling mills were increasing wool production, while water-driven pumps were draining mines. With advances in mining technology, Europe was increasing its supply of silver and the various metals essential to its rising industries: iron, copper, alum, and tin. The development of artillery and movable-type printing depended not merely on the inventive idea but also on many generations of progress in the metallurgical arts. Furthermore, advances in ship design and navigation lay behind the Atlantic voyages that would soon bring a torrent of wealth into Western Europe. By 1500 the long economic crisis had passed; Europe had entered on an era of economic growth and world expansion that would far outstrip her earlier surge in the high middle ages.

INTELLECTUAL AND CULTURAL EVOLUTION

Printing and gunpowder were the two most spectacular technological innovations of the late middle ages. Gunpowder came first, and by the fifteenth century it was being used with some effect in the Hundred Years' War, the Turkish conquests and, indeed, most of the military engagements of Europe. Printing from movable type was developed midway through the fifteenth century, and although its effect on European culture was immense, the full impact was not felt until after 1500. Even among the "new men" of the Italian Renaissance, printed books were regarded as vulgar imitations of handwritten originals.

This fact should warn us against viewing late-medieval Europe—and even Renaissance Italy—exclusively in terms of new beginnings. There was, to be sure, a strong sense of the new and "modern" among many creative Europeans of the period, but there was also a perpetuation of medieval ways, styles, and habits of thought. Often one encounters a sense of loss over the fading of medieval ideals and institutions, a conviction that civilization was declining. The Renaissance humanist Aeneas Sylvius—later Pope Pius II (d. 1464)—could look at the Turkish threat and the strife among Christian states and conclude that there was nothing good in prospect. The generation living after 1500, aware of the voyages of exploration and of the growing prosperity and political consolidation, might well be hopeful of the future, but between 1300 and 1500 a gloom hung over much of Europe. The rise of modern civilization was less apparent than the decay of the middle ages.

Beneath the gloom one finds a sense of nervous unrest, a violent emotionalism that gives dramatic intensity to late-medieval works of art but robs them of the balanced serenity characteristic of the best thirteenth-century creations. Society was in a state of crisis. The practice of self-flagellation acquired wide popularity, and the Dance of Death became a favorite artistic theme. In an era of depression, plague, and disorder, the high-medieval synthesis could no longer hold together. Unity was giving way to diversity.

The breakdown of hierarchy and order expressed itself in a hundred ways—in the intensifying conflict between class and class, in the architectural shift from organic unity to flamboyant decoration, in the divorce between knightly function and chivalric fantasy, in the evolution from Christian commonwealth to territorial states, and in the disintegration of St. Thomas Aquinas's fusion of faith and reason. The medieval dream of a City of God on earth had achieved its supreme intellectual embodiment in Aquinas's hierarchical ordering and reconciliation of matter and spirit, body and soul, logic and revelation. The fading of that dream is nowhere more evident than in the attacks of fourteenth-century philosophers on the Thomist system.

St. Thomas' *Summa Theologica*, like the cathedral of Chartres, unifies religious aspiration and logical order on the basis of an omnipotent God who is both loving and rational. The fourteenth-century attack on this reconciliation was founded on two related propositions. (1) To ascribe rationality to God is to limit his omnipotence by the finite rules of human logic. Thus, the Thomist God of reason gave way to a God of will, and the high-medieval notion of a logical divine order was eroded. (2) Human reason, therefore, can tell us nothing of God; logic and Christian belief inhabit two separate, sealed worlds.

The first steps toward this concept of a willful, incomprehensible God were taken by the Oxford Franciscan, Duns Scotus (d. 1308), who produced a detailed critique of St. Thomas's theory of knowledge. Duns Scotus did not reject the possibility of elucidating revealed truth through reason, but he was more cautious in his use of logic than Aquinas had been. Whereas St. Thomas is called "The Angelic Doctor," Duns Scotus is called "The Subtle Doctor," and the extreme complexity of his thought prompted men in subsequent generations to describe anyone who bothered to follow Duns' arguments as a "dunce." The sobriquet is unfair, for Duns Scotus is an important and original figure in the development of late scholasticism, as the method of reasoning of these scholars came to be called. Yet one is tempted to draw a parallel between the intricacies of his intellectual system and the decorative elaborations of late-Gothic churches. A Christian rationalist of the most subtle kind, he nevertheless made the first move toward dismantling the Thomist synthesis and withdrawing reason from the realm of theology.

Another Oxford Franciscan, William of Ockham (d. 1349), attacked the Thomist synthesis on all fronts. Ockham argued that God and Christian doctrine, utterly undemonstrable, must be accepted on faith alone, and that human reason must be limited to the realm of observable phenomena. In this unpredictable world of an unpredictable Creator, one can reason only about things that one can see or directly experience. With this radical empiricism Ockham ruled out all metaphysical speculations, all rational arguments from an observable diversity of things to an underlying unity of things. And out of this great separation of reason and faith came two characteristic expressions of late-medieval thought: the scientific manipulation of material facts, and pietistic mysticism unsullied by logic. In Ockham and many of his followers, one finds empiricism and mysticism side by side. For since the two worlds never touched, they were in no way contradictory. An intelligent Christian could keep one foot in each of them.

The Ockhamist philosophy served as an appropriate foundation for both late-medieval mysticism and late-medieval science. Some mystics, indeed, regarded themselves as empiricists. For the empiricist is a person who accepts only those things that he experiences, and the mystic, abandoning the effort to *understand* God, strove to *experience* him. Science, on the other hand, was now freed of its theological underpinnings and could proceed on its own. Nicholas Oresme, a teacher at the University of Paris in the fourteenth-century, attacked the Aristotelian theory of motion and proposed a rotating earth as a possible explanation for the apparent daily movement of the sun and stars across the sky. Oresme's theories probably owed more to thirteenth-century scientists such as Robert Grosseteste than to Ockham, but his willingness to tinker with the traditional explanations of the physical structure of God's universe is characteristic of an age in which scientific speculation was being severed from revealed truth.

Many late-medieval philosophers rejected Ockham's criticism and remained Thomists, but owing to the very comprehensiveness of the achievement of St. Thomas Aquinas, his successors were reduced to detailed elaboration or minor repair work. Faced with a choice between the tedious niggling of late Thomism and the drastic limitations imposed by Ockham on the scope of philosophical inquiry, many of Europe's finest minds shunned philosophy altogether for the more exciting fields of science, mathematics, and classical learning.* When the philosopher John Gerson (*d.* 1429), chancellor of the Uni-

versity of Paris, spoke out in his lectures against "vain curiosity in the matter of faith," the collapse of the faith-reason synthesis was all but complete.

The fifteenth century witnessed a revival of Platonism and Neo-Platonism, in Renaissance Italy and in the north as well. The two leading philosophers of the Italian Renaissance, Marsilio Ficino (*d.* 1499) and Pico della Mirandola (*d.* 1494), were both Platonists. They were able to draw from an extensive body of Plato's writings that had been unknown to the high-medieval west, yet neither Ficino nor Pico was a first-echelon figure in the history of western thought. Neither possessed the acumen of the best high-medieval philosophers, and neither approached the profoundity of their great contemporary north of the Alps, Nicholas of Cusa (*d.* 1464).

Educated by the mystical Brethren of the Common Life, Nicolas of Cusa became first a conciliarist and later an ardent papist. He agreed, up to a point, with Ockham's view that human reason is limited to the disconnected phenomena of the physical universe. But he insisted that the contradictions and diversity of the material world were reconciled and unified in an unknowable God. Nicolas of Cusa regarded God as beyond rational apprehension—approachable only through a mystical process which he termed "learned ignorance." Like Aquinas, he believed that any such order could be grasped by human reason. Yet his concept of an unknowable God was derived from a tradition far older than Ockhamism. It was rooted in the late-Roman Neo-Platonism of the pagan Plotinus (see p. 162) and his Christian followers, a tradition that had been an undercurrent through the entire middle ages. Like the older Neo-Platonists, Nicholas of Cusa conceived of the universe as a ceaseless creative unfolding of the infinite God. But, going far beyond his Neo-Platonic predecessors, he reasoned that a universe emanating from an infinite deity cannot be limited by human concepts of space and time. In short, God's created universe was potentially infinite. And since a universe without bounds is a universe without a physical center, Nicholas of Cusa concluded that neither the earth nor the sun occupied any special position in it.

* The revival of classicism in the Italian Renaissance will be discussed in the next chapter.

(Left) *Flamboyant Gothic exterior: Saint-Maclou, Rouen.* (Below left) *Perpendicular Gothic interior: Chapel of Henry VII, Westminster Abbey, London.* (Below right) *Choir of Saint-Etienne at Beauvais, begun 1506, showing the absence of capitals, the uninterrupted upward thrust of the columns, and the elaborate vaulting.*

(Above) *High-Gothic sculpture: Christ, "Le Beau Dieu," west front, Amiens Cathedral, thirteenth century.* (Above right) *Late-medieval sculpture: "Three-Mourners," from the tomb of Philip the Bold of Burgundy, by Claus Sluter and Claus de Werve.* (Below) *The Pulpit, Siena cathedral.*

The earth was not at the center, nor was it stationary, since in an infinite universe position and motion are entirely relative. God was at the center, Christ was at the center, but only in the sense of metaphysical priority, not in the sense of physical location.

In his emphasis on mysticism and the limitation of human reason, Nicholas of Cusa was in tune with his age. In his synthetic vision of an ordered cosmos he echoed the thirteenth century. And in his bold conception of an infinite universe he anticipated modern philosophy and astronomy.

The change from high-medieval synthesis to late-medieval diversity is clearly evident in the field of art. The high-Gothic balance between upward aspiration and harmonic proportion—between the vertical and the horizontal—was shifting in the cathedrals of the later thirteenth century toward an ever-greater emphasis on verticality. Formerly, elaborate capitals and horizontal decorative lines had balanced the soaring piers and pointed arches of the Gothic cathedrals, creating a sense of tense equilibrium between heaven and earth. But during the late middle ages, capitals disappeared and horizontal lines became discontinuous, leaving little to relieve the dramatic upward thrust from floor to vaulting. Late medieval churches achieved a fluid, uncompromising verticality, a sense of heavenly aspiration that bordered on the mystical.

By about the mid-thirteenth century, the basic structural potentialities of the Gothic style had been fully exploited. Windows were as large as they could possibly be, vaultings could be raised no higher without structural disaster, and flying buttresses were used with maximum efficiency. The fundamental Gothic idea of a skeletal stone framework with walls of colored glass had been embodied in cathedrals of incomparable nobility and beauty. During the late middle ages, cathedrals changed in appearance as tastes changed, but the originality of post-thirteenth-century Gothic architects was inhibited by their devotion to a style that had already achieved complete structural development. Accordingly, the innovations of late-Gothic architecture consisted chiefly of new and more elaborate decoration, with the result that a number of late-medieval churches are, to some modern tastes, overdecorated.

Unrestrained verticality and unrestrained decorative elaboration were the architectural hallmarks of the age, and both reflected a shift away from rational unity and balance. Like Ockham's universe, the fourteenth- and fifteenth-century church became a fascinating miscellany of separate elements. Thus the "flamboyant Gothic" style emerged in late-medieval France, while English churches were evolving from the "decorated Gothic" of the fourteenth century to the "perpendicular Gothic" of the fifteenth and sixteenth centuries, with its lacelike fan vaulting, its sculptural profusion, and its sweeping vertical lines.

Sculpture and painting, like architecture and thought, evolved during the late middle ages toward multiformity. The serene, idealized humanism of thirteenth-century sculpture gave way to heightened emotionalism and to an emphasis on individual peculiarities. Painting north of the Alps reached its peak in the mirrorlike realism of the Flemish school. Painters such as Jan van Eyck (d. 1440), pioneering in the use of oil paints, excelled in reproducing the natural world with a devotion to detail that was all but photographic. Critics of the style have observed that detail seems to compromise the unity of the total composition, but in a world viewed through Ockham's eyes this is to be expected.

The decay of high-medieval forms of expression is vividly demonstrated in the late-medieval romance, which had once served as a vital literary form but now became sentimentalized, formalized, and drained of inspiration. Late-medieval writers could achieve vitality only by turning from warmed-over chivalry to graphic realism. Geoffrey Chaucer (d. 1400), in his *Canterbury Tales,* combines rare psychological insight with a skill in descriptive characterization worthy of the Flemish painters or the late-Gothic stone carvers. And François Villon (d. 1463), a

Flemish School: "The Annunciation," by Rogier van der Weyden.

Flemish School: "The Banker and his Wife," by Quentin Metsys.

brawling Parisian vagabond, expressed in his poems an anguished, sometimes brutal realism that captures the late-medieval mood of insecurity and death.

In the Europe of 1500, commerce was thriving again and the population was growing. New inventions—gunpowder, the three-masted caravel, the windmill, the water pump, the printing press—were changing the ways men lived. The papacy had degenerated into a local principality, but England, France, and Spain had achieved stable, centralized governments, and were on the road toward nationhood. European ships had reached America and India, and the first cargo direct from the Orient had arrived in Portugal. The late-medieval gloom was lifting and the world lay open to European enterprise.

Late-Medieval painting: "King John the Good,"
French school of the fourteenth century.

SUGGESTED READINGS

Aston, Margaret, *The Fifteenth Century*. New York: Harcourt, Brace, Jovanovich, 1968. Paperback.

Calmette, Joseph, *The Golden Age of Burgundy*. New York: Norton, 1963.

Cheyney, E. P., *The Dawn of a New Era: 1250–1453*. New York: Harper and Row, 1962. Paperback.

Fennell, John, *The Emergence of Moscow: 1304–1359*. Berkeley: University of California Press, 1968.

Ferguson, Wallace K., *Europe in Transition: 1300–1520*. Boston: Houghton Mifflin, 1962.
An excellent textbook; the best one-volume general account.

Gilmore, Myron P., *The World of Humanism: 1453–1519*. New York: Harper and Row, 1962. Paperback.

Hexter, J. H., *Reappraisals in History*. New York: Harper and Row, 1961. Paperback.

Holmes, George, *The Later Middle Ages: 1272–1485*. New York: Norton History of England, 1966. Paperback.

Huizinga, Johan, *The Waning of the Middle Ages*. Garden City, N.Y.: Doubleday Anchor, 1954. Paperback.
Concentrating on France and the Netherlands, this masterpiece of cultural history captures superbly the late-medieval mood.

Jacob, E. F., *Essays in the Conciliar Epoch*. Manchester, England, 1953.

Langland, William, *Piers the Ploughman*, trans. by J. F. Goodridge. Baltimore, Md., Penguin, 1959. Paperback.
A profound allegorical poem of late fourteenth-century England.

Lewis, P. W., *Later Medieval France: The Polity*. New York: St. Martin's Press, 1968.

Mariejol, J. H., *The Spain of Ferdinand and Isabella*. New Brunswick, N.J.: Rutgers University Press, 1961.
Written originally in French in the nineteenth century, this valuable work has been edited and updated by B. Keen.

Mollat, G., *The Popes at Avignon: 1305–1378*. New York: Harper and Row, 1965. Paperback.
An older account written originally in French, treating the Avignon papacy thoroughly and skillfully.

Morrison, T., ed., *The Portable Chaucer*. New York: Viking, 1949. Paperback.

Perroy, Edouard, *The Hundred Years War*, trans. by W. B. Wells. New York: Capricorn Books, 1965. Paperback.
A comprehensive account, particularly illuminating on the history of late-medieval France.

Pirenne, Henri, *Early Democracies in the Low Countries*. New York: Harper and Row, 1963. Paperback.
A provocative examination of urban politics, institutions, and class struggles.

de Roover, Raymond, *The Rise and Fall of the Medici Bank*. New York: Norton, 1963. Paperback.

An authoritative study which elucidates the policies and methods of this great financial institution in the context of both Florentine local politics and the fifteenth-century European economy.

Tierney, Brian, *Foundations of the Conciliar Theory.* Cambridge, England: Cambridge University Press, 1955.
An excellent modern work by a gifted American historian of the medieval Church.

Vernadsky, G., *The Mongols and Russia.* New Haven, Conn.: Yale University Press, 1953.
An excellent, detailed treatment.

PART III | *European Civilization, 1500–1815*

During the sixteenth century Western civilization gained a new lease on life and developed and expanded with increasing confidence thereafter. The Renaissance replaced medieval modes of thought and art with those of Classical civilization and paved the way for the triumph of reason and national cultures. The Protestant and Catholic Reformations restored many people's faith in themselves and in the world around them, although religious zeal sometimes led to civil war. The exuberance and dynamism of the age was vividly expressed in the writings of Shakespeare, Cervantes, and Rabelais as well as in the actions of explorers and conquistadors. Although the cultural impact of overseas "discoveries" was slow until the eighteenth century, the gold and silver of Latin America gave an almost immediate stimulus to European economic life. Money and capitalism grew together and fostered a secular, individualist ethic that was to dominate Western civilization well into the twentieth century. Also, as the size and power of states grew, the struggle to control them became increasingly intense.

Only by the late seventeenth century did the centralizing dynastic monarchies of continental Europe manage to get the nobles and churches to accept their dominance in a new traditional society called the Old Regime. In a sense, the Old Regime had developed first and disappeared first in England—roughly from the time of Henry VIII to Charles I, whose beheading in 1649 marked its end there, just as it was beginning in earnest in France and Spain. By the early eighteenth century, Austria, Prussia, and Russia had also adopted the basic features of the Old Regime and, indeed, these were to last in those countries longer than in the west. The hallmarks of the Old Regime—epitomized in the France of Louis XIV and Descartes—were authority, order, and reason. The educated classes came to believe that everything was capable of being understood and domesticated. Even the uneducated masses stopped fearing witches by the end of the seventeenth century in most places, although their economic poverty and social segregation gave them no hope for a better life in this world. Under conditions of extreme hardship a few of Europe's poor migrated to the New World, but most remained in their traditional villages, still immune from the new wealth and new modes of thought of the eighteenth century, when the Old Regime reached its peak.

The first steps toward the modern world as we know it were the accumulation of new kinds of knowledge and the rise to power of leaders willing to use this knowledge to replace the Old Regime with one open to changes in the organization of property, power, and status. Although the roots of modern science can be found in the late middle ages, it was in the seventeenth century that the true scientific revolution took place. Culminating in Newton, this revolution eventually made the physical universe and its laws the model for economic and social thought and allowed men to make nature work for them. Already in the late seventeenth century the philosopher John Locke was urging the institution of natural laws and natural *rights,* particularly the rights of private property, in an England that was acquiring its first modernizing leaders as a result of the revolution that beheaded Charles I. Locke's political ideas also had a strong influence on the new government installed by the American Revolution. But the greatest changes affecting the largest number of people were initiated by the French Revolution in 1789. Nowhere else was the Old Regime so systematically and dramatically overthrown by leaders dedicated to the ideals of reason and justice. And because the new order captured the allegiance of the masses—for the first time in history anywhere on such a scale—France was able to spread the ideas and institutions of its revolution to other parts of Europe. By the early nineteenth century the first two steps toward modernization were well under way in Western Europe and North America, and the days of the Old Regime were numbered elsewhere.

CHAPTER 10

Innovation and Crisis in the Early Modern Period, 1500–1648

Although most people in Western and Central Europe from 1500 to 1648 tried to cling to their medieval ways, a small number of pioneers brought about changes in several fields. In culture and politics Italian innovators had been developing the new outlook known as the Renaissance as early as the late fourteenth century, although it did not spread northward until after 1500. The Protestant Reformations of the sixteenth century changed religion not only by rejecting the authority of the pope and much Roman Catholic doctrine but also by redefining the relationships between the individual and the clergy and between the church and the state. The rudimentary economic techniques of medieval capitalism expanded into vast new areas as a result of the geographical explorations of the early modern period. Technological developments such as gunpowder and improved seamanship made possible the creation of overseas commercial empires, while printing spread new ways of thinking among the growing minority of people who could read and write.

But the transition of European civilization from medieval to modern form was slow and uneven. Most of the masses and some important elites resisted every change in their medieval way of life. Eighty to ninety percent of all Europeans were still peasants, some serfs and some legally free; their traditional village society was hardly touched by the innovations of the early modern period. The nobles of England, France, and Spain resisted both the centralizing policies of the kings and the rise of the capitalist bourgeoisie. Economic expansion and rising prices brought a degree of social mobility—both upward and downward—but status and privilege remained strongly entrenched. The Greek Orthodox Russian and Balkan lands, although occasionally touched by developments in the west, were little affected by them.

THE RENAISSANCE

The Italian Renaissance began as a revival of the secular humanism of ancient Rome, in opposition to medieval culture. Secular

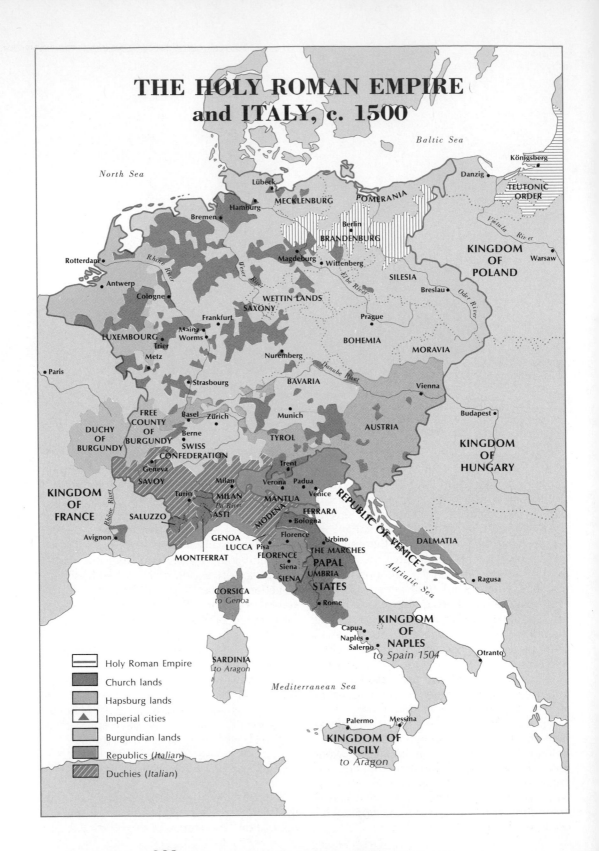

THE HOLY ROMAN EMPIRE
and ITALY, c. 1500

Baltic Sea

Königsberg

North Sea

Danzig

TEUTONIC ORDER

Lübeck

Hamburg

MECKLENBURG

POMERANIA

Bremen

Berlin

BRANDENBURG

Vistula River

Rotterdam

Rhine River

Magdeburg

Wittenberg

KINGDOM OF POLAND

Warsaw

Antwerp

Weser River

SILESIA

Elbe River

Breslau

Oder River

Cologne

WETTIN LANDS

SAXONY

Prague

LUXEMBOURG

Frankfurt

Mainz

Worms

Trier

Metz

Nuremberg

BOHEMIA

MORAVIA

Paris

Strasbourg

Danube River

BAVARIA

Vienna

FREE COUNTY OF BURGUNDY

Basel

Zürich

Munich

AUSTRIA

Budapest

DUCHY OF BURGUNDY

Berne

SWISS CONFEDERATION

TYROL

KINGDOM OF HUNGARY

Geneva

SAVOY

Trent

Verona

Padua

KINGDOM OF FRANCE

Rhône River

Turin

Po River

MILAN

Milan

MANTUA

Venice

REPUBLIC OF VENICE

SALUZZO

ASTI

MODENA

FERRARA

Bologna

DALMATIA

Avignon

GENOA

LUCCA

Pisa

Florence

Urbino

Adriatic Sea

MONTFERRAT

FLORENCE

THE MARCHES

Siena

PAPAL STATES

UMBRIA

Ragusa

CORSICA
to Genoa

SIENA

Rome

KINGDOM OF NAPLES

Capua

Naples

Salerno

to Spain 1504

Otranto

SARDINIA
to Aragon

Mediterranean Sea

Palermo

Messina

KINGDOM OF SICILY
to Aragon

	Holy Roman Empire
	Church lands
	Hapsburg lands
▲	Imperial cities
	Burgundian lands
	Republics (*Italian*)
	Duchies (*Italian*)

means earthly, concerning this world, as opposed to the medieval concern with the "other world," the "hereafter." Humanism means the study of the pagan classics, rhetoric, poetry, and history in conjunction with moral philosophy. The Italian environment in which the Renaissance took root was already more secular than the rest of Europe in the late middle ages. Urban civilization and Roman law had survived in some form even during the dark ages and were in full flower again by the thirteenth century. Moreover, medieval Italy produced merchants and bankers who were less restricted in their activities by guilds, great lords, and kings than their counterparts in Northern Europe. Finally, in the fifteenth century, the typical ruler in the Italian states was the son or grandson of a commoner, often a soldier of fortune, who came to prefer the title of prince to that of despot. To bolster their power and prestige, these princes eagerly adopted humanist rhetoric and built imposing palaces. Many of these innovations originated in Florence, but the Renaissance reached its peak in Rome under two great Italian princes—Pope Julius II and, later, Pope Leo X. The worldliness of these popes was to be one of the major factors that sparked the Lutheran Revolt, as we shall see.

The first humanist was the Florentine poet and scholar Francesco Petrarca (1304–1374), better known as Petrarch. He reestablished moral philosophy as a secular study and insisted on the value of literature—especially classical Latin literature—as a means of self-improvement and improvement in society. Petrarch's enthusiasm for classical antiquity was made popular among Florentines who could read Latin by Giovanni Boccaccio (1313–1375) in his *Genealogy of the Gods,* a handbook for the appreciation of ancient poetry. In the medieval view, reality was abstract, universal, and hierarchical; to the humanist reality was temporal, finite, specific, and unique—qualities emphasizing the human experience.

Petrarch's greatest contribution to the development of the humanist outlook in public affairs was his discovery (1345) of some hitherto unknown letters of Cicero to his friend Atticus. These letters reveal Cicero as an active Roman citizen trying to save the

Republic from the despotism of Julius Caesar and from civil war. This attitude was taken over for political purposes by Coluccio Salutati, the patriotic chancellor of Florence from 1375 to 1406. The main political problem that Salutati had to deal with was the aggressive designs of the despots of Milan on the Republic of Florence. He and his associates wrote letters and polemics in defense of Florentine liberty and on the duties of the patriotic citizen. One of his main arguments was that Florence had inherited the liberty of Republican Rome and that it therefore had all the virtue necessary to resist the Caesarian ambitions of the current Milanese despot. This kind of propaganda had a strong appeal to the civic pride of the Florentines and was an effective weapon in their relations with other states.

Civic humanism in Florence quickly became the basis for a new secular outlook based on ancient literature and philosophy. Humanist scholars uncovered unknown Latin works and studied Greek texts brought in by Byzantine scholars. Many Florentines scorned their efforts to imitate the style of classical Latin in their own writings. But the humanists' tendency to stress accommodation to the here-below, as opposed to the next world, was in tune with the spirit of the age. One humanist, quoting Cicero, said, "The whole glory of man lies in activity." Another, paraphrasing Aristotle, said, "The possession of external goods affords an opportunity for the exercise of virtue." By the mid-fifteenth century the ascetic monk no longer had a monopoly on virtue in Italy. The professional soldier, the civil servant, the poet, and the family man could be virtuous too.

As humanist scholars formulated new moral values, humanist teachers made them the basis of a new kind of education. In Florence and in other parts of Italy young men from well-to-do families went to newly founded boarding schools featuring a curriculum of classical studies and physical exercises. As the active life replaced the religious ideal of earlier education, the goal was to mold citizens and balanced personalities through the humanities. Poets, orators, historians, and essayists were studied as examples; once they were mastered, discourse

Brunelleschi, Florence cathedral.

on all subjects became possible. The power of expression, especially in an elegant literary style, was declared essential to the educated layman in all fields. This educational program was well described by Battista Guarino (1374–1460), head of a famous academy at Ferrara. In *De Ordine Docendi et Studendi* (1459), Guarino says:

"In Ovid's words 'the more we drink, the more we thirst.' For when the mind has begun to enjoy the pleasures of learning, the passion for fuller and deeper knowledge will grow from day to day. But there can be no proficiency in studies unless there be first the desire to excel. Wherefore let a young man set forward eagerly in quest of those true, honorable, and enduring treasures of the mind which neither disease nor death has power to destroy. Riches, which adventurers seek by land and sea, too often win men to pleasure rather than to learning; for self-indulgence is a snare from whose enticements it is the bounded duty of parents to ween their children, by kind words, or by severity if need arise. Perchance then in later years the

echo of a father's wise advice may linger and may avail in the hour of temptation. . . . "*

The secularization found in wisdom, politics, and education also appeared in Florentine art during the early fifteenth century in the works of Masaccio (1401–c. 1428), Donatello (c. 1396–1466), and Filippo Brunelleschi (1377–1446). The detailed realism of late Gothic painters gave way to a simpler realism that set the style not only for Italian Renaissance painting but for all European art until the late nineteenth century. Masaccio mastered the technical problems of perspective, of light and shadow, and of giving the appearance of roundness and depth to his figures and scenes. He replaced the late Gothic concern for decoration with a "Classical" conception of unity in composition. Donatello began the practice of measuring human figures to produce the ideally proportioned figure in sculpture. His equestrian

* Cited in William Harrison Woodward, *Vittorino da Feltre and Other Humanist Educators* (Cambridge University Press, 1905), p. 161.

Raphael, "Sistine Madonna."

statue of Gattemalata, a soldier of fortune, is completely secular and classical in feeling; Gattemalata looks like a Roman general. This statue became a landmark in the history of art, as did the superb dome with which Brunelleschi crowned the Florence cathedral. Brunelleschi measured Roman ruins to produce this combination of the most perfect forms and harmonious proportions in architecture. But he was no mere imitator, and his buildings had a striking originality of their own.

In the middle of the fifteenth century the Renaissance spread from Florence and a few other centers to the rest of Italy and reached its peak in Rome. Popes Julius II and Leo X could spend more money than anyone else, and each became the patron of the outstanding artists of his age. Raphael (1483–1520) covered the walls of the popes' private apartments with murals, and Michelangelo (1475–1564) spent four years on his back painting the ceiling of the Sistine Chapel. Pope Julius II sponsored the construction of the biggest, most impressive church in the world over the grave of St. Peter. This building, austere, monumental, and crowned with a mighty hemisphere of a dome, brought the grand manner of Renaissance architecture to a climax.

The artists themselves created works that transcended the interests of these worldly popes and of the despots and bankers of northern Italy. When dealing with religious subjects, they created a sublime vision of God become man, as in Raphael's late Madonnas, Leonardo da Vinci's "Last Supper," and Michelangelo's frescoes on the ceiling of the Sistine Chapel. Their secular subjects expressed a spiritual ideal of refined humanity, as in Leonardo's "Mona Lisa" and Raphael's "School of Athens," or a conquering heroism, as in Michelangelo's statue of David. Whereas medieval art sometimes was commissioned by and catered to the tastes of private patrons, it was during the Renaissance that patrons, now setting themselves up as exclusive connoisseurs, became the rule. These Renaissance patrons gave free reign to the genius—another new concept—and versatility of the individual artist, who, in turn, produced works of increasing grandeur and subtlety.

By the beginning of the sixteenth century the versatility of the artist came to be considered the ideal for all cultivated men. The humanist credo now was: I am a man, and nothing human can be strange to me. The ideal Renaissance man believed in the fullest expression of all the potentialities of the mind, the heart, the body, and the spirit. Everything was permitted, as long as one carried it through with style and grace, whether one was composing a poem or a diplomatic dispatch, discussing philosophy, or poisoning an enemy. Such an outlook was obviously restricted to a small elite with enough money, talent, and leisure to pursue life to the fullest. In his guidebook, *The Courtier,* Baldassare di Castiglione turned this outlook into a formula for the behavior of aristocratic gentlemen.

The Renaissance was not all gracious living and artistic virtuosity; it opened up new fields of scholarship which were soon developed in Northern Europe as well as Italy. The humanists made available the entire body of ancient Greek learning for later use by professional scientists and philosophers. Artists and engineers made discoveries in optics, perspective, archaeology, and building construction, which were also taken over by professional scientists after the middle of the sixteenth century. Historical writing was purged of mythical and religious influences and given a straight narrative form. Renaissance historians showed a new seriousness in the treatment of sources; they also clearly marked off one historical era from another. Lorenzo Valla (*d.* 1457) founded the disciplines of classical philology and textual criticism. His *Notes on the New Testament* in its original Greek version had an enormous effect on Biblical studies and on the development of vernacular literature. For only after the vernacular languages had absorbed the achievements of humanism in style, vocabulary, grammar, and subject matter were they able to replace Latin in every area of expression.

The most innovative development of the Italian Renaissance was the behavior of its political leaders. Niccolò Machiavelli (1459–1527), who had served Florence as a diplomat, analyzed their behavior for his contemporaries and for posterity in *The Prince.* This book was mainly concerned with the need of Italians for strong, secular government to keep order among the many Italian states and to protect them from French and Spanish invaders. But it has greater significance as the foundation of modern political theory. Machiavelli detached politics from religion and moral philosophy; he described its "effective reality" as an unholy and unscrupulous struggle for power over the lives of men through control of the state, as in the following quotation. "The chief foundations of all states, new as well as old or composite, are good laws and good arms; and as there cannot be good laws where the state is not well armed, it follows that where they are well armed they have good laws" (*The Prince,* Chapter 12). He noted that private life is different from public life and that the rules of the one have no relevance for the other. Politics is a struggle for power and must be conceived and practiced according to its own rules, aims, and motives. In defining politics this way, Machiavelli was

An English classroom in the sixteenth century.

merely recording the experiences of many princes of Europe. His originality lay in his insistence that the only way to understand their behavior was to study it from the point of view of a scientist.

Yet despite their secular and scientific approach to certain questions, many men of the Renaissance still clung to medieval beliefs about miracles, witchcraft, astrology, and the necessity for preparing for the next world, to which God or the stars would call them at some fixed time. No matter how much they admired pagan antiquity, many of them never abandoned their belief in a divine Providence or in the virtues of the contemplative life. Their belief in a revival of an earlier golden age also placed them closer to the middle ages than to modern times. *Progress*, the most characteristic idea of the modern world, meant little to them. This idea seems to be closely linked to economic growth and scientific and technological advances, all of which came after the Renaissance was over.

The innovations of the Italian Renaissance began to move north by the sixteenth century. Castiglione's *The Courtier* taught the squires and courtiers of England and France a reasoned code of service, a taste for expensive leisure, and the rewards of an active life. The northern kings made use of professional diplomats and generals to gain advantages over one another, as the Italian city-states had. Humanist scholarship and educational practices gave a new course to European culture for the next 200 years. "Classical" forms and themes survived in the fine arts and in vernacular literature and drama. The works of Rabelais, Shakespeare, Rembrandt, and Bach were based on the achievements of the Renaissance. At the same time an international community of scholars continued to thrive and to communicate freely with one another in humanist Latin.

Printing

The spread of these ideas was hastened by the development of printing. But the development of printing was important in itself because this, the first mass medium gradually changed the modes of thought and imagination of literate people, thus making it pos-

An early printing press.

ify and transmit every kind of learning. Thus printing initiated a technological breakthrough whereby experience could be processed through linear thinking.

As Europeans moved in the direction of visualized measurement and quantification of life, they gained a great advantage over all the other civilized peoples of the world: the power to act without reaction or involvement. Many artists and writers resisted this change, lamenting its effects in numbing the other senses, in downgrading religious and aesthetic experience as "irrational," and in divorcing science from art; as the French philosopher Blaise Pascal said: "We know the truth not only by reason but also by the heart." Nevertheless, this specialization by dissociation was the basis of the power and efficiency of Western man. Only by dissociating their actions from feeling and emotion could people say: "Damn the torpedoes. Full steam ahead!"

The new modes of thought and feeling conditioned by printing affected all the developments of the early modern period, as suggested by the following quotations from Marshall McLuhan's *The Gutenberg Galazy.* "Renaissance Italy became a kind of Hollywood collection of sets of antiquity, and the new visual antiquarianism of the Renaissance provided an avenue to power for men of any class" (p. 119). During the Reformations ". . . The new homogeneity of the printed page seemed to inspire a subliminal faith in the validity of the printed Bible as bypassing the traditional oral authority of the Church. . . . It was as if print, uniform and repeatable commodity that it was, had the power of creating a new hypnotic superstition of the book as independent of and uncontaminated by human agency" (p. 145). "The Machiavellian mind and the merchant mind are at one in their simple faith in the power of segmental division to rule all—in the dichotomy of power and morals and of money and morals" (p. 174). "Print, in turning the vernaculars into mass media, or closed systems, created the uniform, centralizing forces of modern nationalism" (p. 199).

Modern nationalism did not develop fully until the nineteenth century, but it had its origins in the budding national literary cul-

sible for Europe to become modern before any other part of the world. Printing from movable type, which was first brought to Europe from China in the middle of the fifteenth century, emphasized the visual over the other senses. The repetitive, linear patterns of the printed page conditioned people to view all kinds of problems in ways that could be expressed in such patterns. "Linear thinking" emphasized quantification and repeatability, which were essential to all the changes that were to make European civilization modern: price systems and markets, mass production, science and technology, large-scale bureaucratic forms of organization, nationalism.

As with movable type, the breaking up and rearranging of actions, functions, and roles could be applied wherever desired. Scientists in the late middle ages had already discovered the principle of translating nonvisual concepts like motion and energy into visual terms. Printing applied this principle to writing and language, making it possible to cod-

tures of the early modern period. Although Germany remained politically disunited, Luther's translation of the Bible provided the basis for the language of modern German literature. The national literary language of Spain was launched by Miguel de Cervantes Saavedra (1547–1616) in his novel *Don Quixote*, that of France by François Rabelais (c. 1490–1553) and Michel de Montaigne (1533–1592); in 1635 the French Academy was founded for the purpose of disciplining the vocabulary and grammar of the national language. The language of Shakespeare and of the King James Bible were milestones in the development of modern English literature.

THE REFORMATIONS

By 1500 medieval culture, society, and politics were losing their relevance to the way men were thinking and behaving, as was the medieval Christian church. In earlier times the church had been able to reform itself, put down heresies, and resist the secular princes while maintaining its doctrine intact. But in the first half of the sixteenth century it faced a fundamental religious controversy that soon gained enough support to end the unity of Western Christendom. The Protestant reformers held a pessimistic view of the human condition and doubted the ability of the existing church to save men's souls. Their decision to break with Rome was based on institutional as well as personal and internal differences. Where the civil authorities favored a break with Rome, the Protestant Reformation triumphed; where they decided to suppress it, the Reformation rarely survived.

In the middle of the sixteenth century the Roman church did succeed in reforming itself without altering its doctrine. By then, however, the religious unity of the west had been broken. It was replaced by uniformity within each local church, for the Protestant Reformation was not a movement toward religious liberty. Nevertheless, it began as a movement of the spirit with a new religious message. Luther's main contribution was his conception of the relationship between God and man as direct and personal. The Protestant Reformation replaced the authority of

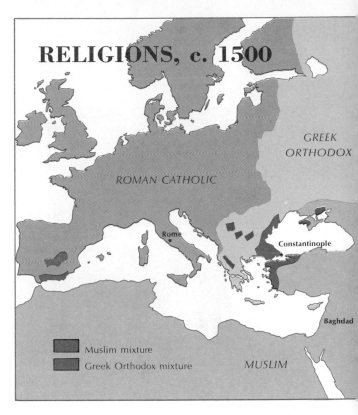

the popes with the authority of the Bible, as interpreted by the local church.

The Lutheran Revolt

The Protestant Reformation triumphed first in Germany for several reasons. First, Germany consisted of small states whose princes were too weak to mitigate the abuses of the church, as the kings of Spain, France, and England had done. Second, monks and priests who lived up to the ideals they proclaimed still exercised an enormous authority among the pious Germans who criticized the church's abuses. Then, too, at the beginning of the sixteenth century most of Germany did not yet feel the secularization of existence and the fading of medieval ascetic ideals. Since Germans from all sections of society also resented the unique hold the papacy had on their weak and divided land, they were especially receptive to the message of a reformer like Martin Luther (1483–1546), who was both a monk and a priest.

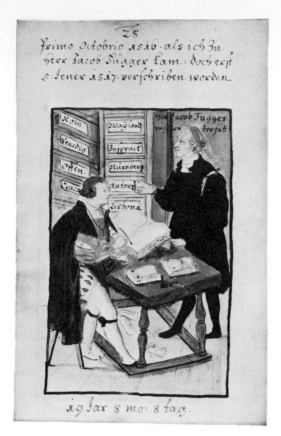

A Protestant view of the "sale" of indulgences by churchmen (engraving by Hans Holbein the Younger).

Luther came from a family of middle-class conformists. He was reared in an atmosphere of Catholic piety and given the traditional medieval tools of learning. To please his parents he enrolled in the law school at the University of Erfurt in 1505, although he would have preferred to devote himself to religion. Within a few months, however, fearful that his sins would prevent his salvation, he decided to enter the local monastery of the Augustinian Order of Hermits. He said later: "Not freely or desirously did I become a monk . . . but walled around with the terror and agony of sudden death, I vowed a constrained and necessary vow."

Between 1507 and 1517 Luther spent most of his time trying to cleanse himself of sin through fastings, scourgings, and prayer beyond the rule of his monastic order. But while preparing his lectures on the Bible for the new University of Wittenberg, he found the solution to his torment in one of St. Paul's letters to the Romans: Man could become righteous (just) only by confessing his innate sinfulness, throwing himself on God's mercy, and accepting His grace. Here was the essence of Luther's doctrine of justification by faith alone. Luther did not immediately see how it conflicted with church doctrine. Only his involvement in the indulgence controversy and the later attacks of his enemies made him realize the full implications of his personal religious discovery.

The indulgence controversy arose in 1517 when Pope Leo X allowed the agents of Archbishop Albert to "sell" indulgences* in towns near Wittenberg. Luther was outraged by the way Germans were being misled into believing that they had bought pardons for their dead relatives in purgatory and absolution for their own future sins. In protest he wrote out 95 theses, along with a covering letter to Archbishop Albert, and posted them on the door of the Wittenberg castle church on All Saints' Day, 1517. Most of these propositions were not revolutionary; only those were that said the pope had no jurisdiction over purgatory and that he could not transfer the "surplus" of good works accumulated by past saints to the "credits" of present sinners through his indulgences. According to Luther, "the true treasure of the Church is the holy gospel of the glory and grace of God."

Luther had written his 95 theses in Latin for disputation with other theologians, but within two weeks they were translated into German and then widely circulated in print. What might normally have been a "squabble among monks," as Pope Leo X called it when he first heard of it, became a public issue. By 1520 Luther had taken an increasingly revolutionary position in public debate. He had denied the divine origin of the papacy and

* According to *The Catholic Encyclopedia* (New York: Appleton, 1910, VII, 783), "an indulgence is the extra-sacramental remission of the temporal punishment due, in God's justice, to sin that has been forgiven, which remission is granted by the Church in the exercise of the power of the keys [to the Kingdom of Heaven], through the application of the superabundant merits of Christ and the saints, and for some just and reasonable motive."

praised John Hus, whom the Council of Constance had condemned as a heretic just over 100 years earlier. In June 1520 Pope Leo X finally issued the bull *Exsurge Domine,* proclaiming that if Luther did not recant all he had said, he too would be condemned as a heretic.

By the end of 1520 Luther had completed his break with Rome and appealed directly to the public for support in a series of printed tracts and pamphlets. His *Address to the Christian Nobility of the German Nation* invited the princes to take over church property and found reformed state churches themselves. *The Babylonian Captivity,* addressed to the clergy and the learned world, argued that the Roman Church had "captured" the sacraments of the true church and had falsely claimed that its priests had the sole power to make them "work." Luther abandoned all but three of the sacraments—baptism, penance, and the Eucharist—and altered their meaning. Priests, whom Luther now called ministers, should still preach the Gospel and administer the sacraments, but they had no miraculous powers. By denying the clergy any special powers or status Luther rejected not only the pope but the whole religious establishment. He said that priests could marry and he released monks and nuns from their vows. In December 1520 Luther publicly burned the papal bull, thus making death at the stake seem the only possible outcome of his revolt.

Luther was saved from this fate by Elector Frederick of Saxony. Although Frederick himself never broke with the church, he suggested to the newly elected Holy Roman Emperor, Charles V, that Luther's case be heard at the imperial diet, which was to meet in the town of Worms in April, 1521. There Luther, in his simple monk's garb, told the impressive assembly of ecclesiastical and secular princes:

Unless I am convicted by Scripture and plain reason—I do not accept the authority of popes and councils, for they have contradicted each other—my conscience is captive to the Word of God. I cannot and will not recant anything, for to go against my conscience is neither right nor safe. God help me. Amen.

Charles V, who had given Luther a safe conduct to the diet, told him to go home and placed him under the Ban of Empire. Elector Frederick then hid him in his castle at Wartburg. In this place of exile Luther set about translating the New Testament into German. Since man could be saved only through God's Word, he should be able to read it in his native language. Luther's German Bible, along with the hymns he wrote later, not only served as an inspired spiritual guide but also transformed the German vernacular into a literary language.

Although Luther preached "Christian Liberty" for the spirit, he became disturbed at the way other people were using his doctrine for their own ends. A group of poor German knights wanted to make war on the Catholic bishops and increase their power in the Holy Roman Empire at ecclesiastical expense. Luther refused to sanction the use of the sword on priests, and the rebels were defeated. Then, in 1524–1525, the peasants of southwestern Germany tried to use his name in a mass uprising against their feudal lords. Luther was horrified by what he called these "murdering, thieving hordes of peasants," and he urged the civil authorities to destroy them. By the mid-1520s he had abandoned his early efforts to convert individual Germans. During the next 20 years Lutheranism became the religion of the small, economically backward territorial states of northern Germany through the decision of the princes, not through mass conversions. Luther increasingly favored a religion of the inner life and a church under princely control.

Despite Luther's denunciations of the use of force, the Lutheran princes formed the Schmalkaldic League and were ready to fight the emperor himself, if he should try to make them abjure their faith and give up the church property they had seized. They refrained from open warfare until 1547, partly out of deference to Luther, who died in 1546, but mainly because Charles V was too busy fighting the Turks to force the issue in Germany before then. During the next few years, however, the Lutheran princes fought the emperor's forces, gaining military support from Catholic France in return for the transfer of three imperial archbishoprics in the western Rhineland to the French crown. Their victory was sealed in September 1555 by the Peace of Augsburg.

This settlement formally recognized the right of each German prince to choose the Lutheran or Roman Catholic faith as his own (no other sects were recognized) and to impose it on all his subjects. The principle involved was *cuius regio, eius religio* — the religion of the ruler must be that of the realm. Dissenters would not be tolerated and had to move to a state where their faith was the official one. Germany was now about equally divided between Lutheran and Catholic states, and the Reformation there was over.

Meanwhile, Lutheranism had spread to other parts of Northern and Central Europe. It was able to exist as the faith of a minority under the loose political structure of Poland, Bohemia, and Hungary. But the kingdoms of Denmark-Norway and Sweden-Finland and the Baltic lands of the Teutonic order set up national Lutheran churches. Thus in much of Europe, Lutheranism either was established as an act of state — with the secular ruler as the head of the church — or was tolerated as a minority religion.

The Reformation in England

Nowhere was the Reformation more exclusively an act of state than in England. The issue that sparked it was King Henry VIII's desire to divorce his wife, Catherine of Aragon. For five years, beginning in 1527, Henry tried to force papal compliance by numerous threats and appeals. Then, in 1532, he allowed himself to be convinced by his able adviser, Thomas Cromwell, that the divorce did not need the sanction of the pope and that Parliament could settle the matter. Between 1532 and 1534 Parliament, guided by Cromwell, passed a series of acts that created the independent Church of England. These acts transferred all papal powers to the crown and made the king the head of the Church of England. The new Archbishop of Canterbury, Thomas Cranmer, used his power as the highest ecclesiastical judge in the land to declare Henry's first marriage void and to marry him publicly to the pregnant Anne Boleyn. Henry gave expropriated monastic properties to the gentry in order to strengthen their support of the crown, but he did not alter the doctrine and worship of the English church, which remained as Catholic as Rome itself until he died. The only change was the introduction of an English translation of the Bible into the services.

England became a legally Protestant (Anglican) country under Henry VIII's successors. By the early 1550s clergymen could marry and were considered simply ministers of the word. Archbishop Cranmer produced his *Book of Common Prayer* and revised the doctrine and ceremonies of the Church of England along the lines of the continental Reformed churches* in his Forty-Two Articles (1553). Protestantism received a temporary setback during the reign of Mary (1553–1558), Henry and Catherine of Aragon's Catholic daughter. But Elizabeth I, Henry's daughter by Anne Boleyn, could rule England only as a Protestant, since she was an illegitimate child in Catholic eyes. In 1562 she approved as the prescribed faith the Thirty-Nine Articles, which were deliberately vague so as to satisfy as many people as possible, yet this settlement did not end the religious controversy. A sizable minority of English Catholics, as well as the Irish, who were ruled by the English crown, resisted the forced imposition of the Anglican church on them and clung to their Catholicism. Before the end of Elizabeth's reign, the English Puritans also began to challenge Anglicanism. The Puritans, who were Calvinists, were outstanding examples of the newer, more radical forms of Protestantism which spread rapidly after 1555.

Calvinism

John Calvin, the founder of Calvinism, was born in 1509 in northern France. His father, a local lawyer and civil administrator, sent him to the best schools, and until his mid-twenties Calvin thought of himself primarily as a man of letters. Then he experienced a sudden conversion, which transformed him into a seeker of knowledge of God and his Law through the Bible. He fled France in 1534 and lived in Basel, Switzerland, and several Italian cities before taking up resi-

---

* Particularly those following the ideas of the Swiss Protestant, Ulrich Zwingli (1484–1531).

dence in the French-speaking Swiss city of Geneva in 1536. It was during this period that he published the first edition of his most important work, the *Institutes of the Christian Religion*.

The *Institutes* was the clearest and most authoritative statement of Protestant theology to come out of the Reformation, and it had more widespread appeal than any other. Here was a convincing and logical demonstration of how man should live in close communion with his Creator. Calvin showed people that the experience of living according to high ideals made a mockery of materialistic pleasure-seeking. The main goal of the true Christian was to know God. According to Calvin, God predestined some men to eternal life and others to eternal damnation. Yet, He was a merciful Savior as well as a stern Father. Those men whom He had selected for salvation could not see into His mind, but they could learn, through His Word, to know the meaning of Christ's sacrifice as overcoming the taint of sin. This knowledge would lead to faith in God's mercy and justice and overcome individual worry about fate. Thus Calvin's doctrine of predestination gave people confidence and hope.

Unlike Luther, Calvin wanted to make religion a dynamic social force; he was particularly concerned that the community of the elect be one in which the religious and civil authorities were equal in power. Within 20 years of his first visit to Geneva he had reshaped that city into his ideal Christian community. All legislative, judicial, and administrative functions were divided between the municipal council and a church consistory of pastors, teachers, elders, and deacons. Twice a year a commission of pastors and elders inspected every house in town to see that there were no superstitious pictures on the walls and that all residents were diligently attending the five weekly sermons and receiving the Lord's Supper regularly. The council punished such ungodly offenses as card- and dice-playing, light songs, and dancing. It even regulated the way people dressed, thus initiating the simple Puritan style that was to appear for over a century wherever Calvinism took root. In addition to the regularly constituted authorities, Calvin insisted that each citizen was his brother's keeper and should spy on his neighbor.

Although attempts to create the Kingdom of God on earth went against the trend of an emerging society of secular states, Calvinism spread to many parts of Northwestern and Central Europe after the mid-sixteenth century. Calvin had created a doctrine, a catechism, and a program of church discipline with great potential appeal. In 1559 he also founded an academy in Geneva for the instruction and training of ministers. Hundreds of Protestant leaders from other countries studied there and then brought his teachings back to their native lands, modified to suit local conditions. Thus the Elector of the Palatinate, in western Germany, insisted on strong governmental control of doctrine and discipline, a modification later adopted by some Calvinists in England and Scotland. The English Calvinists under Elizabeth were particularly concerned about "purifying" — hence the name Puritans — the Anglican church of "popish" elements in the ritual, such as elaborate vestments, instrumental music, and incense. In 1560 John Knox, who had studied in Geneva, persuaded the Scottish Parliament to accept a modified version of Calvinism and to organize a state church, which was called Presbyterian. Elsewhere, the Calvinists became a persecuted minority and emphasized the right to revolt against governments that interfered with the establishment of God's kingdom on earth. This was especially so in France, where Calvinists were known as Huguenots, and in the Netherlands, as well as in England. Refugees from these three countries also spread Calvinism to Germany, Poland, Bohemia, Hungary, and, by the early seventeenth century, to the New World.

Anabaptists

Most sixteenth-century Protestants were no more tolerant than Catholics of more extremist sects like the Anabaptists. The Anabaptists, who were the most radical sect of the time, wanted to imitate the early Christians, who had accepted adult baptism as a sign of their conversion and who had refused to serve the state as soldiers and magistrates. Although they lived in various parts of Europe and differed on certain issues, particularly pacifism, the Anabaptists shared three basic principles: (1) the church is a voluntary association; (2) church and state should be separate; (3) religious liberty should prevail. This program threatened all the existing churches, both Protestant and Catholic. By the mid-sixteenth century the Catholic and Protestant authorities had executed tens of thousands of Anabaptists in Northwestern and Central Europe. Those who managed to escape this blood bath fled to Bohemia and Poland, where they survived as the Brethren, Hutterites, and Mennonites. The Mennonites were to filter back into Germany, and eventually to North America, in the more tolerant eighteenth century.

The Catholic Reformation

By the mid-sixteenth century the Catholic Reformation had begun both as a movement for reform *within* Church and as a campaign against Protestantism. In the campaign against Protestantism, called the *Counter-Reformation,* the Jesuits, the Inquisition, and the Hapsburg rulers of Spain and Austria tried to win Protestants and Catholic backsliders back to the Roman faith. These efforts, which will be discussed later, were sparked by a resurgence of religious feeling among Catholics and by the reforming work of the Council of Trent.

During the first half of the sixteenth century a number of new religious orders in Italy and Spain helped revive Catholic piety and charitable activities; the most influential was the Jesuit order founded by St. Ignatius Loyola (1491–1557). Loyola came from a knightly Basque family and until his thirtieth year was a soldier and courtier. Then, while convalescing from a severe war wound, he spent his time reading about the lives of Christ and the saints. He renounced his former habits, distributed his worldly goods to the poor, and spent eight months at Manresa, Spain, as a beggar and a self-punishing penitent. In Manresa Loyola underwent a series of religious experiences and illuminations which formed the basis for his future career and which he incorporated into his *Spiritual Exercises.*

These widely disseminated *Spiritual Exercises* stressed the practice of "methodical prayer." They required many hours of concentration and reflection on one's own sins and on steeling oneself as a soldier of Christ. Here was a Christian discipline that made religion intensely emotional and personal. Only a minority of Catholics practiced it, but this minority helped revive the Catholic faith in the sixteenth century.

Meanwhile Loyola had decided to teach others the way to God as he had discovered it himself at Manresa; he did this by acquiring a scholarly education and then, with six of his followers, founding the Society of Jesus—popularly known as the Jesuits. In 1540 the pope gave them their charter, and thereafter those in the top grade of the new order took a special vow directly to the pope and went on foreign missions. Unlike the monastic orders, the Jesuits led active rather than contemplative lives. They were priests rather than monks, although they lived according to a strict rule. The Jesuits received an advanced education in the humanities, philosophy, and theology, using Loyola's life as their model. By the time of his death their activities included not only missionary work (mainly in Asia—especially through St. Francis Xavier—and in Africa) and education but also the struggle against Protestantism in Europe.

The Jesuits spearheaded the Counter-Reformation through their teaching and their pastoral activities. In order to save Catholicism they founded schools to train a new generation of priests and laymen in a more positive and confident kind of faith. The Jesuits also developed a talent for handling confessions; they convinced the sinner that he had not really sinned at all unless he had fully intended to do so. This talent, plus their educational and missionary skills, ingratiated them with the rulers of Bavaria, Austria, and Poland, with whose help they were to stamp out Protestantism in these lands by 1590. The Jesuits championed a personal and emotional religion, combining the rigors of "methodical prayer" with a vivid and dramatic style of church art, including lifelike wax statues, painted angels that seemed to fly down from the ceiling, and sumptuous church buildings. Finally, the Jesuits played an important role in reaffirming official Catholic theology at the Council of Trent.

This council, summoned by Pope Paul III, met intermittently from 1545 until 1563. Only a small proportion of the eligible members of the international Catholic hierarchy attended the meetings, yet its work completed the reform within the Roman Catholic church and became the basis for modern Catholicism. The Council of Trent reaffirmed the official Catholic doctrine: man's nature is tainted by original sin, but not irredeemably compromised; God offers His grace to everyone. The core of Catholicism is redemption through Christ: each man can earn this gift of grace through love of God, demonstrated in faith and good works. Each man chooses to accept God's grace or reject it of his own free will. The church alone is his guide in interpreting Christ's teachings, which include the Holy Scriptures and the writings of the Doctors of the early church. It alone administers the seven sacraments, clarified at Trent, which are the visible signs of God's grace. All Catholics are compelled to accept this doctrine on pain of excommunication.

The main reform of the Council of Trent was elimination of abuses within the clergy. To raise the educational level of the parish priests, the council required every diocese to have a seminary to train them. It strengthened the authority of the bishops, forbade them to hold more than one benefice, and required them to reside in their dioceses. The council assigned the following tasks to the Holy See: (1) publication of an *Index* of books Catholics would be forbidden to read, (2) compilation of a catechism for the use of parish priests, (3) revision of the breviary, (4) revision of the missal.

The next two popes completed the reform within the church and then took up the work of the Counter-Reformation in earnest. The "Holy Office" of the General Roman Inquisition, founded in 1542, tried an increasing number of suspected heretics. Spain's territorial conquests in Italy extended Jesuit influence and led to the repression of controversial Italian thought. Outside of Italy, Spain introduced its own Inquisition into most of its far-flung possessions. The Spanish Inquisition was also to become the chief nonmilitary instrument of Philip II's anti-Protestant crusade.

GEOGRAPHICAL AND ECONOMIC EXPANSION

Western Europe's second wave of expansion* covered the years 1450 to 1650. The overseas areas into which it expanded at that time—the Western Hemisphere and the coastal areas of Africa, India, and Southeast Asia—were politically weak and inferior in military organization and technology. Moreover, the dynamism of the Renaissance and the Protestant and Catholic Reformations inspired men like Christopher Columbus, Hernando Cortez, Saint Francis Xavier, Sir Walter Raleigh, Henry Hudson, Samuel de Champlain, and the traders and settlers who followed them. Their self-confidence, discipline, and rational planning, often combined with religious zeal, made possible a great wave of expansion.

But in the early modern period, Europe's greatest advantage lay less in the innovations of the Renaissance and the Reformations than in its ships and their voyages, which linked together the uncharted ocean routes of the world for the first time. Other civilizations have experienced cultural and religious revivals, created complex and durable political institutions, made notable contributions to the arts of diplomacy and war, and then have stagnated, fallen apart, or been conquered by barbarian invaders. Early modern European civilization might well have faltered on a new plateau and then declined like the others if it had not broken out of its geographical and economic confines.

The world's oceans posed many problems to their first explorers. For example, the equator was believed to be a zone of boiling waters with magnetic rocks that pulled ships to the bottom of the sea and with fantastic marine monsters that attacked men and ships. These terrors declined with experience, but real dangers—storms, tidal waves at the Cape of Good Hope, and the risk of famine on crossings of uncertain duration in sailing ships whose captains lost their bearings—remained. Diseases such as scurvy, smallpox, and typhus took a heavy toll. Rarely did a week pass without one or two

* On Western Europe's first period of expansion, roughly the eleventh to the late thirteenth century, see pp. 244–250.

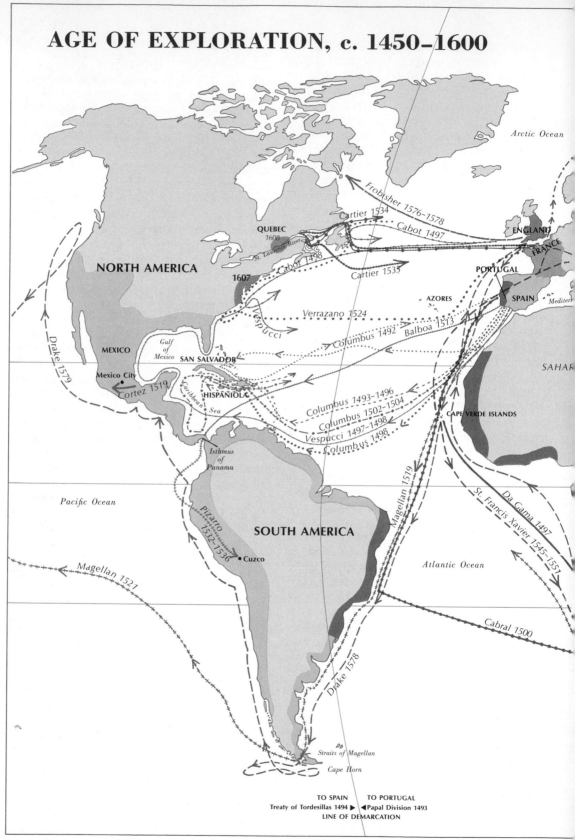

AGE OF EXPLORATION, c. 1450–1600

Arctic Ocean

Frobisher 1576–1578

Cartier 1534

Cabot 1497

ENGLAND

FRANCE

QUEBEC
1608

Cabot 1498

St. Lawrence River

NORTH AMERICA

Cartier 1535

PORTUGAL

1607

AZORES

SPAIN

Mediter

Verrazano 1524

Vespucci

Columbus 1492   Balboa 1513

SAHAR

Gulf of Mexico

MEXICO

SAN SALVADOR

Drake 1579

Mexico City

Cortez 1519

Caribbean Sea

HISPANIOLA

Columbus 1493–1496

Columbus 1502–1504

Vespucci 1497–1498

Columbus 1498

CAPE VERDE ISLANDS

Isthmus of Panama

Da Gama 1497

St. Francis Xavier 1545–1551

Pacific Ocean

Pizarro 1532–1536

• **Cuzco**

SOUTH AMERICA

Magellan 1519

Atlantic Ocean

Magellan 1521

Cabral 1500

Drake 1578

Straits of Magellan

Cape Horn

TO SPAIN   TO PORTUGAL
Treaty of Tordesillas 1494 ▶ ◀ Papal Division 1493
LINE OF DEMARCATION

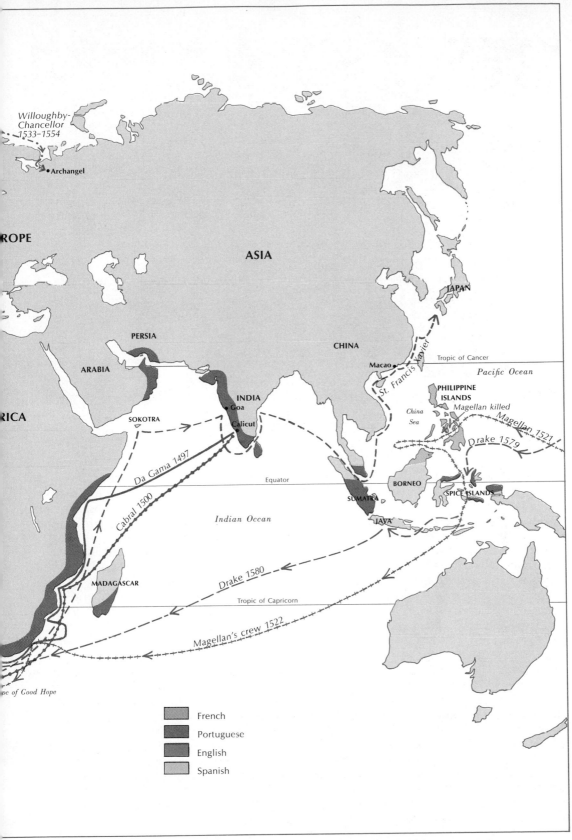

Willoughby-
Chancellor
1533–1554

• Archangel

ROPE

ASIA

PERSIA

ARABIA

INDIA
• Goa

SOKOTRA

Calicut

AFRICA

Da Gama 1497

Cabral 1500

Equator

Indian Ocean

MADAGASCAR

Drake 1580

Tropic of Capricorn

Magellan's crew 1522

pe of Good Hope

CHINA

Macao •

St. Francis Xavier

JAPAN

Tropic of Cancer

Pacific Ocean

PHILIPPINE
ISLANDS

Magellan killed

Magellan 1521

Drake 1579

China
Sea

SUMATRA

BORNEO

SPICE ISLANDS

JAVA

	French
	Portuguese
	English
	Spanish

The flagship, built by Sir Walter Raleigh, of the English fleet that defeated the Armada.

burials at sea. Yet a peculiar restlessness drove the explorers ever onward in the face of all these hardships.

While the Portuguese explorers were probing their way southward down the coast of Africa, a Genoese sea captain, Christopher Columbus, asked King John II of Portugal to sponsor him on a voyage to the west. King John turned him down, and it was Queen Isabella of Castile who finally subsidized Columbus's four westward voyages in search of "the Indies" between 1492 and 1502. Columbus mistook Cuba for Cathay—home of the Great Khan—and Haiti for Japan. Until his death in 1506 he continued to insist that he had discovered the *true* (East) Indies and that somewhere down the coast of South America, which he believed was part of the Malay Peninsula, there was a strait leading into the Indian Ocean. During the first half of the sixteenth century, the Spaniards continued to view the American continent as a bothersome land mass that barred their way to an all-water route to the East Indies. The

only Spanish colony in the East Indies was the Philippines, which Magellan had discovered in 1521. Spain's actual conquest and colonization of these islands began in 1565 from bases in the New World.

The Portuguese were the first to find the shortest all-water route to the Far East. Their initial territorial foothold grew into an "empire": a series of isolated trading posts, fortresses, and naval bases along the coasts of Africa, the Persian Gulf, India, and the islands of Southeast Asia. Only in sparsely populated areas like Angola and Mozambique (and Brazil) did small Portuguese settlements eventually take root in the hinterland. Trade with "the Indies" was Portugal's central concern. But the royal government's share of the Asian trade did little more than pay the expenses of war and government overseas and contribute to the embellishment of Lisbon. By the late sixteenth century the king of Portugal's "empire" in the Indies had somehow turned into an all-but-bankrupt grocery business.

Spain's New World Empire

The Spaniards concentrated on the New World: there they destroyed three civilizations and many cultures, and transformed the lives of all the Indians (see pp. 512–516). The conquistadors divided the conquered lands into vast feudal estates and paid only nominal allegiance to the king of Spain. They substituted themselves for the native aristocracy and exercised seignorial rights over the Indians. Although the Spanish government had passed antifeudal and pro-Indian legislation, it was no longer enforced by the 1570s. The government of the colonies became increasingly decentralized.

Ignoring the Spanish government's policy of assimilation, the conquistadors maintained themselves as a superior race and tried consciously to give the natives a feeling of inferiority. There were many mixed marriages in Mexico and some in South America, but the growing number of half-breeds (*mestizos*) were treated as second-class Spaniards by the dominant whites. Since the landowners faced a perennial shortage of labor, they overworked their own Indians and reduced conquered tribes to virtual slavery. Lack of immunity to European diseases reduced the Indian population of Mexico alone from, perhaps, 25 million in 1519 to one-tenth that figure by 1600. With the agricultural labor force declining everywhere the Spanish settlers turned to the more lucrative economic activities of mining and ranching. (In Mexico the number of cattle rose from 0 in 1550 to over 100,000 by 1620.) Both types of enterprise were carried on by private capitalists, and the government in Madrid had to be content with its royal fifth from the silver mines and with other forms of taxation.

Yet, despite its abuses and shortcomings, the Spanish colonial empire succeeded in spreading European power and influence to a large part of the Western Hemisphere. Missionary activity was widespread, and the majority of the Indians became at least nominal Christians. Moreover, many Indians in the towns adopted the language and culture of Spain. A slow but steady immigration from the mother country and a large number of *mestizos* assured the permanence of Hispanic civilization in the New World. Universities and printing presses were established in Mexico City and Lima in the mid-sixteenth century. The subjugation of the natives and the destruction of their leaders, their institutions, and much of their culture removed the possibility of organized rebellion against European rule. The colonists gradually developed their own way of life, and it was they, not the Indians, who ultimately broke their political ties with Spain (see pp. 519–522).

The Impact of Overseas Expansion in Europe

The discovery and exploitation of new lands and seaways eventually affected all of Europe. During most of the sixteenth century Mediterranean commerce remained more important than that of the Atlantic and Indian oceans. Barcelona, Marseilles, Genoa, and Venice continued to send the products of Southern Europe to the north and to trade with the Near East, despite the Barbary pirates, the often hostile Turks, and the Portuguese water route to the East Indies. But by the end of the century the prosperity of the Mediterranean world was over. Not only Italy, but Germany, too, declined economically, as Atlantic ports replaced the Rhineland and southern German cities as commercial and banking centers. Even remote Russia was inadvertently "discovered" in the 1550s by English explorers searching for the Northwest Passage through the White Sea.

While the Atlantic powers drew on international scientific and navigational skills, they organized and financed exploratory and trading expeditions in an intensely national way. European concepts of trade and diplomacy changed radically as new ambitions and new rivalries developed over colonies, transoceanic trade, and the newly found stores of precious metals. Spain was receiving huge quantities of silver from the New World—60 million pounds from Potosì, Bolivia alone—in the late sixteenth and early seventeenth centuries. The reserves of the other countries seemed inadequate in comparison, and the scramble for bullion became a major goal of the diplomatic machinations of that period. Not only did the English and the French dispute the wealth of the New World with the Spaniards but they also

The Augsburg office of the international Fugger banking house.

subsidized privateers like Francis Drake, John Hawkins, and Jean Fleury to steal Spanish silver on the high seas.

The wealth of the New World allowed Spain to live beyond its resources and helped the economic development of other Atlantic states more than its own. Spain could not supply its colonists with all the goods and laborers they needed. The rigidity of the Spanish economy, shorn of its enterprising Jews and Moors, made it impossible for industry and agriculture to respond to these increasing demands. In fact, Spain used much of its newly acquired metals to buy foreign goods and services for domestic consumption and to finance its abortive attempts to dominate Western Europe by force of arms (see pp. 327–330). Moreover, who can say how many men of courage and ability went to the colonies to seek their fortunes, and thus were lost to Spain?

Early Capitalism

Capitalism is a term introduced in the nineteenth century to describe an economic system dominated by capitalists. A capitalist is a businessman who furnishes capital to other people to produce goods and perform services that create income, a share of which they return to him. Capital is that portion of income that is invested for these purposes, rather than spent or hoarded. Each time a businessman makes a profit he has more capital to invest. As more businessmen make more profits that they can invest, the total amount of capital in a given society increases. When there is enough to finance a significant proportion of a society's economic activities, we can speak of the rise of capitalism.

The accumulation of capital had begun in the thirteenth century, when large-scale trade with the Orient and Northern Europe brought substantial profits to merchants in the cities of Italy and the Low Countries. These profits were reinvested in trade and commerce and, by the mid-fourteenth century, in manufacturing—especially woolen textiles—and in loans to popes and princes. Another source of late medieval capital accumulation was income from urban property. By the mid-fifteenth century mining and mortgages for urban building construction became additional sources of investment capital.

In addition to accumulating capital, medieval businessmen developed new techniques and practices. Since the transfer of large sums of money over long distances was cumbersome and dangerous, they devised the "bill of exchange"—a written order to pay a certain sum of money to a person or his account—as a means of paying their debts. Bills of exchange could also be used as security to raise funds or they could be sold to banks, which charged a fee later known as a discount, for cash. Mortgages became the first kind of negotiable security in Italy in the fifteenth century and in France in the early sixteenth century. The first temporary part-

CAPITALISM

There are many definitions of capitalism, but the most useful one for a student of world history is: an economic and political system based on private property in which surpluses not consumed are used for the rational organization of resources and formally free labor in order to bring profits to private investors. In its full, industrial, form capitalism first developed in England in the late eighteenth century. During the nineteenth century it spread over Europe, North America, and the British Dominions and, together with its colonial extensions, it came to dominate the world. Wherever it held sway the political and legal structures were organized to protect and support it, especially by sanctifying private property. In the ancient Near East and Mediterranean worlds there had been various kinds of commercial capitalism in which accumulated surpluses were invested for profit, and this limited form of "early" capitalism reappeared in Italy in the thirteenth century and in the Low Countries a century later. But it used slave labor in ancient times and was restricted by feudal entail and the guild system in the middle ages. Only in the sixteenth century and after did this commercial form of capitalism develop beyond its traditional bounds and begin to change into industrial capitalism.

Although capitalism was supposed by theory to operate under complete laissez-faire and perfect competition, these conditions almost never prevailed and have virtually disappeared in the twentieth century. In the most advanced countries large corporations and groups of corporations acting together have all but eliminated effective competition, while governments have abandoned laissez-faire in their efforts to tax and regulate private business and to control the business cycle. Furthermore, this "modified capitalism" has taken on elements formerly associated with socialism: a continuing redistribution of income through legislative measures; social security and welfare programs; institutions for joint economic planning by government officials, union leaders, and corporate management. But as long as ownership, investment, and profits remain largely in private hands, today's "modified capitalism" should not be confused with socialism. Socialism is an economic and political system in which ownership, investment, and profits are under public control.

nerships were formed to float large loans or finance a trading voyage. The invention of double-entry bookkeeping in fifteenth-century Italy allowed businessmen to balance their credits and debits on two sides of the ledger.

The diffusion of American bullion stimulated the growth of capital and the spirit of enterprise among merchants, bankers, and manufacturers in Northwestern Europe. These capitalists not only perfected their techniques and expanded the scale of their operations, but they also exhibited a degree of free choice unmatched in other fields of endeavor. With their "mobile wealth" (various forms of money, as opposed to "immobile wealth," land) they could invest alternately or even simultaneously in commerce, manufacturing, mortgages, government loans, and usury. These early modern capitalists were the source and the symbol of all major material progress and of the most excessive forms of exploitation of their fellow men. In an age when almost everyone else—from the humblest peasant to the most privileged aristocrat—was bound by traditional ways of doing things, they had the greatest privilege of all, the privilege of *choosing*. Freedom of choice, however restricted by governments and monopolies, made possible the development of modern society.

A distinctive businessman's psychology grew over the years. It was eminently rational, based on the calculation of profits and margins of risk. For the businessman the main purpose of money was to make more money. He extended credit mainly to move goods, with the expectation of being paid back in a short period of time. The church condemned the lending of money at interest as usury, but businessmen could profit without pangs of conscience from the concealed loans in bills of exchange, mortgages, and other commercial and banking instruments. Kings might repudiate their debts, but businessmen dealt with one another on terms of mutual trust. They became masters at predicting and manipulating other people's behavior. But once they agreed on a transaction, they considered it "signed, sealed, and delivered."

Economic Expansion and its Consequences

Economic growth means an increase in the amount of goods and services per capita of population. It requires the presence of capital, and it requires instruments for creating credit, for making investments, and for combining the savings of many persons. We have seen how Europe developed these instruments and how the influx of precious metals from the New World filled Europe's need for more money. These two factors helped to stimulate commercial expansion, but economic growth also depends on improvements in the utilization of natural resources and labor.

In the early modern period population growth was far more significant than technological progress in fostering such improvements. Population expansion after 1450 was made possible partly by the cultivation of lands abandoned during the century of population depletion following the Black Death. As more food was produced, more people could live in cities and work in manufacturing and commerce. In the sixteenth century, at least, 20 European cities had more than 50,000 inhabitants; Venice, Naples, and London had more than 100,000; Paris had 300,000; and Istanbul (Constantinople)

had 700,000. The resulting increases in the total work force, the division of labor, and the number of consumers all stimulated economic growth.

By the mid-seventeenth century, this economic growth could not keep pace with the increase in population. By then the total population of Europe (including Russia to the Urals) had reached 100 million, a very large population with respect to the economic and technological level of the time. Indeed, France, with 20 million, was prematurely overpopulated. Soon there was little good land left to bring under new cultivation. Agricultural techniques remained backward and crop yields low, so that by the seventeenth century Europe was beginning to have difficulty feeding itself. Furthermore, as more human beings competed on the labor market, real wages declined, thus limiting the amount of goods the poor could buy. This factor was partially offset by the growing number of middle-class people with money to spend. However, technological backwardness remained a hindrance to economic growth.

The only permanent way to increase the amount of goods and services for a whole society is improved productivity; output must be raised in relation to input. In the early modern period, Europeans made only modest advances in this direction. Their major achievement was an increased reliance on water transportation. It takes only one thirty-fifth as much power to move a given weight over water as it does over land. The nations on the Atlantic coast benefited most from this fact. England could import forest products and furs from Russia via the White Sea. The Dutch could import grain from Prussia and Poland via the Baltic. Cannon, textiles, ships' riggings, and other manufactured goods could be brought from England, the Low Countries, and France to Cadiz and then shipped to Spanish colonists in the New World. Spices, silks, dyestuffs, cotton, coffee, tea, cocoa, tobacco, and sugar could be shipped from Asia and America to Europe. Although the masses of Europeans continued to consume only local products, the opening up of the world's sea routes provided a notable increase in the amount of goods available to those people who could afford them.

Productivity improved in manufacturing more than in agriculture, but it was still inadequate. Since the middle ages the guilds had tried to monopolize the production of consumer goods, especially textiles, and had resisted technological innovations. Machinery was introduced in the newer "industries": printing, mining, metallurgy, and armaments. But this machinery was manipulated mainly by human power, and it brought only a modest increase in productivity.

The most notable advance in sixteenth-century manufacturing was organizational rather than technological. Manufacturing was now done by the *domestic system*, or cottage industry, where the work was done in rural homes rather than in urban shops. This system was most often used in the textile industry. The guilds, which had controlled industry in the middle ages, retained their local markets in the growing cities, but their restrictive regulations prevented them from meeting the general demand for textiles. Hence enterprising merchants organized the manufacture of cloth in the countryside. A new type of businessman had come into being, the entrepreneur. He supplied individual villagers with raw materials, tools, and models. One group of workers specialized in spinning the yarn. After the entrepreneur collected the yarn and paid these workers, he gave it to others who wove or knitted it into cloth. In the late sixteenth century he was able to provide his knitting workers with a new machine, the stocking frame, with which they could make many times more stitches per day than they had formerly done by hand. The entrepreneur finally took the cloth to still other workers who dyed and finished it.

The entrepreneur of the textile industry became a lasting feature of all industry. The word *entrepreneur* means someone who undertakes an enterprise. In some cases he solicited capital investments from other people and paid a commission to still other people to sell his merchandise. He was essentially an organizer, a promoter. The entrepreneur controlled the means of production, paid the workers, and undertook to find markets for their products. The entrepreneurial spirit, which was soon to spread to other kinds of economic activity, was the most important stimulus to the rise of early modern capitalism.

The economic expansion of early modern times produced its own crises. Trade and commerce played a dynamic role in allowing specialization and better use of available resources by the mid-seventeenth century, but the material gain barely supported the accompanying increase in population. There was a limit to what new techniques of organization and exchange could accomplish in a preindustrial civilization. Instead of raising the overall level of living they created a few more rich people and a great many more poor people. Rising prices reflected not only new supplies of precious metals but also a growing disparity between the number of people and the amount of goods available to them. Economic expansion and rising prices lessened the distinctions between rich bourgeois and nobles, increased the separation between these two classes and the poor masses, and divided all three into subgroups. The resulting strains in the social order were aggravated by the growth of selfish individualism.

THE BIRTHPANGS OF THE MODERN STATE

While the economic expansion of the early modern period created strains and tensions, attacks on medieval political and religious institutions produced new kinds of civil strife and international warfare. The modern state began to emerge from these two kinds of violence. By 1648 France, Spain, the Dutch Republic, and Sweden were well on their way toward modern statehood. In that year, England was in the midst of the constitutional and religious struggle that was to make it the most modern state of all. On the other hand, Italy and Germany were further from unity and independence than they had been in 1500. During the first half of the sixteenth century the Italian states were overrun by French and Spanish armies, and some of them became permanently occupied by Spain. During the first half of the seventeenth century the Holy Roman Empire was ravaged by both civil war and foreign invasions. Thus the homelands of the Renaissance and the

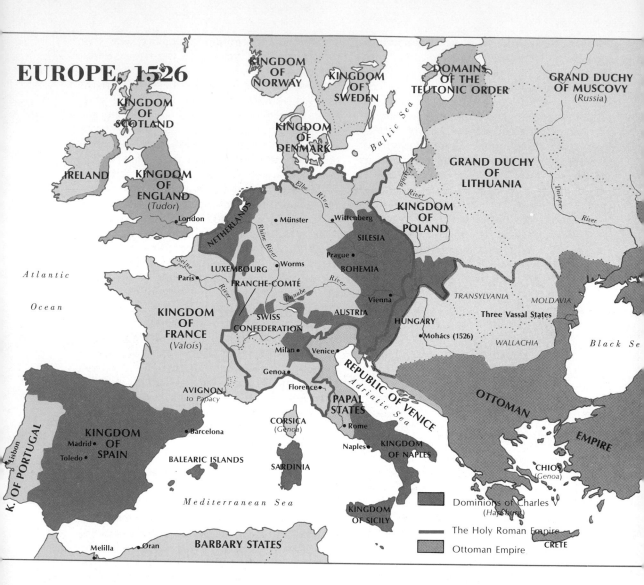

EUROPE, 1526

KINGDOM OF SCOTLAND

IRELAND

KINGDOM OF ENGLAND (Tudor)
• London

Atlantic

Ocean

NETHERLANDS

• Münster

• Wittenberg

SILESIA

LUXEMBOURG
• Worms
Paris •
FRANCHE-COMTÉ

Prague •
BOHEMIA

KINGDOM OF FRANCE (Valois)

SWISS CONFEDERATION

Vienna •
AUSTRIA

HUNGARY
• Mohács (1526)

Milan •   Venice •
Genoa •

REPUBLIC OF VENICE

AVIGNON
to Papacy

Florence •

Adriatic Sea

PAPAL STATES

OTTOMAN

CORSICA (Genoa)

• Rome

KINGDOM OF SPAIN
Madrid •
Toledo •
• Barcelona

BALEARIC ISLANDS

SARDINIA

Naples •
KINGDOM OF NAPLES

EMPIRE

CHIOS (Genoa)

K. OF PORTUGAL
Lisbon

Mediterranean Sea

KINGDOM OF SICILY

CRETE

Melilla •   • Oran

BARBARY STATES

KINGDOM OF NORWAY

KINGDOM OF SWEDEN

DOMAINS OF THE TEUTONIC ORDER

GRAND DUCHY OF MUSCOVY (Russia)

KINGDOM OF DENMARK

Baltic Sea

GRAND DUCHY OF LITHUANIA

KINGDOM OF POLAND

Elbe River

Rhine River

Seine River

Danube River

TRANSYLVANIA   MOLDAVIA

Three Vassal States

WALLACHIA

Black Sea

Dnieper River

Dominions of Charles V (Hapsburg)

The Holy Roman Empire

Ottoman Empire

Reformation became the chief victims of the new kinds of thought and behavior they had introduced.

In the early modern period the most powerful state on the European scene was the Ottoman Empire. (See pp. 603–606.) By the mid-sixteenth century it comprised all the Balkan Peninsula and most of Hungary and present-day Rumania, as well as the bulk of the Arab world, from Algeria to Iraq. In the late seventeenth century the Turks were at the very gates of Vienna. Yet, despite its wealth and strength, the Ottoman Empire did not develop the self-sustaining institutions of a modern European state. The Ottoman state

was the sultan, his advisers, and his administrators. When the sultan was weak, the empire was weak. Another long-term weakness of the Ottoman Empire was its cultural, intellectual, and technological stagnation. Much of its culture remained bound by traditional forms. The Turks imported European arms and technicians, but they never developed their own technicians, and many Turks persisted in viewing science as the work of the devil.

The New Monarchies

Every state has a constitution. Whether written or merely implied in the traditions,

Infantry armed with harquebuses at the battle of Pavia, 1525.

customs, and institutions of the society concerned, it defines the relationships between the rulers and the ruled: the constitution of a state *is* its form of government. Beginning in the late fifteenth century the kings of France, England, and Spain consciously tried to change the constitutions of their realms in order to increase their powers. These "New Monarchs" gave new functions to medieval traditions, customs, and institutions, and they created new agencies of strong, central government. Their progress was aided by a desire among many of their subjects for a strong leader as the sole alternative to the widespread disorders and insecurities of the fourteenth and fifteenth centuries. The king thus acquired the aura of a hero. But in most places there was strong resistance to the change from the medieval to the modern form of monarchy. Furthermore, although kings sought to limit the power of the nobles, they also needed and used nobles to fight in their armies and to administer their kingdoms.

The political power of the New Monarchs at home and their conquests in Italy and the Holy Roman Empire rested on their monopolization of new techniques of warfare. Artillery made it possible to end the private power of overmighty dukes and princes by shattering the walls of their castle fortresses. In sixteenth-century France, England, and Spain the possession of artillery and fortified castles gradually became restricted to kings. The struggle between France and Spain for control of Italy showed that henceforth only large states with extensive resources could carry on sustained wars. And only those large states whose constitutions assured the uninterrupted power of the monarchy could carry on such wars without risking military rebellion from great lords at home. The Holy Roman Empire, Poland, Russia, and even the imposing Ottoman Empire all suffered the consequences of ignoring this maxim.

Francis I (1515–1547), an ambitious, capable, and popular ruler, was the first of the

New Monarchs in France. In 1516 he gained a large degree of control over the Catholic church in France through the Concordat of Bologna, which he negotiated with Pope Leo X. He won the gratitude of the growing merchant class by not overtaxing it and by maintaining order. Although some of his officials tried to upset existing forms in order to augment their own power, Francis himself was careful to show respect for the privileges of various provinces, towns, and social classes. While retaining their loyalty in this way, he gained an increasing proportion of his revenue from the sale of offices and from the one-tenth of the church's income to which he was entitled. Francis patronized the arts and built a sumptuous Renaissance court at Fontainebleau, about 40 miles southwest of Paris. This new court, reflecting the image of a powerful monarchy, attracted a new class of royal servants—especially lawyers—to whom Francis sold or gave offices, honors, privileges, and noble titles. He consolidated his own power by keeping the different privileged groups in constant rivalry and making them all dependent on him.

Still, the power of the French king had its practical limits. Although he usually could make his will prevail through personal intervention, he could not intervene everywhere for he commanded only a small number of officials—one for every 1250 inhabitants in the early sixteenth century compared with one for every 70 inhabitants 300 years later—and the transportation systems and communication were inadequate to allow a ruler unlimited scope. Local authorities preserved a good deal of initiative in the provinces, which still maintained their political and cultural diversity. Medieval traditions of local loyalty, privilege, and group solidarity died hard. Furthermore, the power of the king was limited by the very officials he created. Once they had bought their offices, they held them as property rights and could not be legally deprived of them. With this kind of security they began to act like a new privileged class. They enriched themselves at the expense of the royal treasury and furthered their own interests, which were not always those of the king.

Like his contemporary Francis, Henry VIII of England (1509–1547) strengthened the monarchy considerably. The Tudor dynasty consistently sought the support of the lesser gentry and middle classes. In this tradition, Henry enabled the new peers his father had created to enrich themselves with the lands of the dissolved monasteries. Most of the country gentry served as the king's unpaid justices of the peace, as the local administrators of all decrees of the central government, and as its tax collectors. The merchants did not challenge the political power of the gentry and the crown as long as they were permitted to make more money in commerce and in organizing domestic manufacturing. Under Henry VIII, middle-class lawyers like Thomas Cromwell rose to the highest ranks in the royal government.

With the great nobles outnumbered by the new peers and with the gentry and middle classes for support, Henry was able to go further than any other monarch of his day in asserting the complete sovereignty of the state. England already had the most uniform and centralized judicial system in Europe (see p. 257; Henry's ministers now transformed the Court of the Star Chamber into a major instrument for strengthening royal power. Henry had to share his sovereignty with Parliament, since it alone could change the law of the land and grant new taxes; however, Henry—and Elizabeth I later on—managed to get Parliament to do his bidding. We have already noted how he forced it to make him the head of the Church of England, thus giving the English monarchy the biggest single addition to its powers since the time of William the Conqueror.

The development of the modern Spanish monarchy began with Ferdinand of Aragon (1479–1516) and his wife, Isabella of Castile (1474–1504), and became permanent under their heirs. As in France and England, the monarchs in Spain set themselves the task of taking power away from the nobles and concentrating it in the royal government. Ferdinand and Isabella rallied the church and the common people to the crown by playing on their hatred for Jews and Moors. These non-Christian peoples had come into Spain during the Muslim conquest beginning in the eighth century and were the most economically active elements in the country. Over the centuries many Christian Spaniards had

Philip II's soldiers.

intermarried with them and converted to their faiths. But the *Reconquista* (see p. 247) of the Muslim territories in the middle ages had made the Spaniards intensely conscious of their Catholicism and intolerant toward non-Catholics, and some Spanish Jews "reconverted" to Catholicism. In 1480 Ferdinand and Isabella established the Inquisition to investigate the Christian orthodoxy of converted Jews. They forced the Jews to leave Spain in 1492 and expelled the Muslims ten years later. They continued to use the Inquisition to rally support, and soon it became the most effective institution the Spanish monarchy had for strengthening its own political power, for it created a reign of terror against all potential opponents of the royal authority.

Under Philip II (1556–1598) Spain was the strongest, most unified Christian state in Europe. In addition to the Iberian Peninsula (Portugal was forced into a dynastic union with Spain between 1580 and 1640) Philip ruled the Netherlands, Franche-Comté, over half of Italy, and a vast empire overseas. He had the best soldiers, sailors, and diplomats in the world as well as tons of precious

metals pouring in from his American colonies. But the price Spain paid for its political, religious, and ethnic unity was the loss of the most dynamic people in its economy: the Jews, the Moors and, after 1609, the Moriscos (converted Moors). The forced fanaticism of the Inquisition did not forge deep social ties among its people, and Spain wasted its wealth and manpower in a "glorious" but fruitless crusade against Protestant Europe.

Philip's Crusade against the Netherlands, England, and France

Philip II was a reluctant crusader. He did not openly declare war on England until 1588 or on France until 1589. His main concern was to keep his dynastic empire intact. He also wanted to keep it completely Catholic, but he was not willing to force Catholicism on "heretics" elsewhere unless they threatened his own possessions. For almost three decades he had been giving surreptitious support to English and Scottish Catholics against their Anglican and Presbyterian rulers and to the ultra-Catholic party in France against the

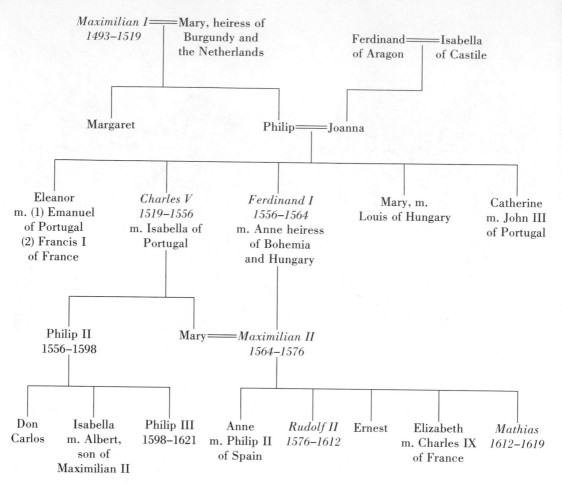

The House of Hapsburg in the sixteenth century. Names and dates of Holy Roman Emperors are given in italics.

Huguenots and the crown. Still, it was the revolt in the Netherlands, which directly threatened his sovereignty there, that finally prompted him to agree with his more avid advisers that he had better control England, Scotland, and France as well.

The Netherlands revolt involved both dynastic and religious issues. Philip had inherited the Netherlands from his great-grandmother, Mary, and all his predecessors had allowed the Netherlanders to go about their own business and manage their local affairs as long as they paid their taxes and acknowledged the formal sovereignty of the Hapsburg dynasty. The provinces that comprised the Netherlands felt no sense of national unity: the northern provinces spoke Dutch,

the middle provinces Flemish, the southern province the Walloon dialect of French. Their constitution was medieval, with a large degree of local "liberties." To Philip, however, the Netherlands were Spanish and should submit to royal authority and Catholic orthodoxy as enforced by the Inquisition. But many Walloons, Flemings, and Dutch had become Calvinists and had achieved religious solidarity by adopting the Belgic Confession in 1566; these Netherlanders were doubly determined to resist Philip's pressure.

Their resistance turned into the first revolution for national independence in modern history. It began in 1566, and both sides practiced terrorism and economic warfare. Under the leadership of William the Silent of

Orange, the Dutch Calvinists preyed on Spanish shipping and raided Spanish-held ports. In late 1576 the Spanish garrison at Antwerp mutinied and sacked the city. In 1581 the Dutch provinces, along with the Flemish cities of Antwerp and Ghent, proclaimed their independence from Spain, thus becoming the first state in modern history to dissociate the idea of the nation from that of loyalty to a dynastic monarch. But in 1584 the Dutch suffered serious setbacks, and Queen Elizabeth I of England came to their aid.

Elizabeth's open aid to the Dutch soon transformed the civil war in the Netherlands into an international war between England and Spain. Elizabeth overcame her dislike for helping rebels against a legitimate sovereign in order to forestall Spanish intervention in English affairs, since she feared Philip would aid English Catholics seeking her throne. Her rival for the throne was Mary Stuart, a descendant of Elizabeth's grandfather and a Catholic. Mary had been deposed as Queen of Scotland by John Knox and his Presbyterian followers in 1568 and had fled to England, where Elizabeth kept her under house arrest for almost 20 years. As long as Mary was alive, Philip had resisted pressure from English and continental Catholics to invade England and put her on the English throne, despite Elizabeth's aid to the Dutch rebels. But fear of such an invasion made English patriots of all sects rally around their queen; it also prompted Elizabeth to build a fleet of ships that were faster and more adaptable to the wind than any others in the world. In 1588, when Elizabeth's execution of Mary gave Philip his excuse for an invasion, the English navy was ready for it.

Philip's plan was that a fleet assembled in Spain would sail to the Netherlands and escort a Spanish army across the Dover Straits to the English coast. The Spanish Armada was the most formidable concentration of naval power the world had ever seen. In the 10 days between its appearance off the coast of Plymouth and its passage through the Dover Straits it fought four separate battles with the English fleet, ushering in a new era in naval warfare. Each side had to change its prearranged tactics, and each made mistakes and suffered heavy losses. The main reason for the Spanish failure was that its invasion barges, blockaded by a Dutch fleet, could not get out of Dunkirk harbor to meet the Armada's deep-draught ships. The livelier English ships dealt a major blow to the Armada in the narrow Dover Straits, forcing the Armada to move northward around the coast of the British Isles and back to Spain — defeated.

The defeat of the Spanish Armada had immense long-range effects. Spain was to remain at war with France until 1598, England until 1604, and the Dutch until 1609, and its preponderance on the continent was to last for more than a generation. But after 1588 the emerging national states of northwestern Europe felt increasingly free to develop in their own way without conforming to any externally imposed creed.

The failure of the Armada brought Philip into the religious and constitutional struggle that had been tearing France apart for almost two decades. Despite official persecution, the number of Huguenots had grown steadily in many provincial cities in the 1550s. Then almost half of the nobility adopted Calvinism in the 1560s and 1570s. These nobles refused to be persecuted for their faith, like ordinary townsmen. The temporary weakness of the French monarchy spurred them to open revolt, since between 1559 and 1589 neither the Queen mother, Catherine de Medici, nor her weak sons could command the kind of loyalty that Elizabeth had in England. Three religious factions fought each other for political power in France. Catherine and the moderate Catholic nobles sometimes joined forces with the ultra-Catholic House of Lorraine and Guise against the Huguenots in the name of religious unity, but the effort of the Guises to take over control of the state prevented these alliances from lasting very long. Some Huguenots, in turn, tried to convert the religious struggle into a constitutional issue. While the nobles rebelled in the name of their lost feudal "liberties," Calvinist political theorists published printed tracts justifying rebellion in the name of religious liberty.

Terrorism and counter-terrorism rose as the wars continued with no end in sight. The worst atrocity was the Massacre of Saint Bartholomew's Day, in 1572, when several thousand Huguenots were dragged from their

The Massacre of St. Bartholomew's Day.

beds and slaughtered. Catherine de Medici, prompted by the Guises, had ordered this action as a means of eliminating the Huguenot leaders who had assembled in Paris for the marriage of her daughter to King Henry of Navarre, a descendant of Louis IX and head of the Bourbon dynasty. Then the Parisian masses, unleashed by their fanatical priests, went on a rampage of cruelty toward everyone suspected of being a heretic—Henry of Navarre himself escaped with his life only by temporarily becoming a Catholic. Soon afterward the Huguenot masses in southwestern France also got out of hand in their passion for revenge.

The situation came to a head in 1589 when Henry of Navarre, a Huguenot, succeeded the last of Catherine de Medici's sons as king of France, and Philip II joined the ultra-Catholics in an all-out effort to depose him. Except for the Catholic extremists, however, most Frenchmen did not want their country to become a Spanish satellite. Thus in France, as in England, patriotism foiled Philip's plan. Yet Henry IV, the nominal leader of the Protestant minority, had

to be made acceptable to the Catholic majority. Henry solved the problem by agreeing to guarantee religious liberty to the Huguenots and to adopt the faith of the majority of Frenchmen himself. He was then able to defeat the Spanish and Guise armies and march triumphantly into Paris in 1594.

The rallying of the French people to their own Catholic king was in some ways a more decisive blow to Philip's crusade than the defeat of the Armada. The religious and constitutional struggle in France ended in 1598 when Philip renounced all claims on French territory. He died a few weeks later, a broken man.

In 1598 Henry IV opened a new era in French and European history by recognizing the legal existence of two religions in the same state. This he did with the *Edict of Nantes*. Protestantism was excluded from all episcopal cities and from any place within 20 miles of Paris, but the Huguenots were to have access to all public offices and the same civil rights as Catholic Frenchmen. In addition, they obtained some fortified towns in southwestern France and were recognized,

Roman Catholic
Lutheran
Anglican
Calvinist
Roman Catholic and Protestant mixture
Greek Orthodox and Muslim mixture

Presbyterian

Presbyterian and Anglican mixture

North Sea

Baltic Sea

Puritan

Dutch Reformed

Mennonite

•Amsterdam

•London

Hutterite

Paris•

Vienna•

Atlantic Ocean

Huguenot

Geneva•

Swiss Reformed

Adriatic Sea

Greek Orthodox

•Rome

Muslim

Madrid•

Mediterranean Sea

to a certain extent, as an armed political party. Later rulers were to limit the rights of the Huguenots, but the Edict of Nantes was of momentous significance in introducing the principle of religious toleration to the European world.

The Thirty Years' War and the Beginnings of Modern International Relations

Whereas Philip II's attempt to conquer England, France, and the Dutch Netherlands stimulated these countries to resist and strengthened their patriotism, the Thirty Years' War (1618–1648) delayed Germany's

emergence as a strong and independent national state for more than 200 years. This devastating war began as a struggle between the Bohemian and Austrian estates and the Hapsburg dynasty, but it soon became a German civil war, a conflict between Catholicism and Protestantism, and an international power struggle. On one side were Ferdinand II (who was the dynastic ruler of Austria, Bohemia, and Hungary and the Holy Roman Emperor from 1619 to 1637), the Spanish Hapsburgs and, until 1638, most of the Catholic German princes. On the other side were the Protestant princes of the Empire, princes who were eventually joined by Sweden and

EUROPE, 1648

	Holy Roman Empi
	Spanish Hapsburgs
	Austrian Hapsburg
	Hohenzollerns
	Kingdom of Swede
	Republic of Venice

by France, which placed its rivalry with the Hapsburgs above its Catholicism.

The loss of lives and property during the Thirty Years' War was even greater than in France and the Netherlands a half century earlier. As the war dragged on, native and foreign armies ravaged Germany without achieving decisive victories. Sometimes famine drove troops out of territories they had just invaded. In such cases, they destroyed everything they could not take with them: houses, vines, grain fields, and livestock. Some towns became almost deserted, and many peasants temporarily fled to the forests where they were reduced to eating grass,

bark, and wild fruit. By the mid-1640s Emperor Ferdinand III and Elector Maximilian of Bavaria could no longer hold out against the French and the Swedes. They began peace negotiations in 1643, but continued fighting in the hope of gaining better terms. The Peace of Westphalia was not signed until 1648.

The Peace of Westphalia ended the religious wars in the Holy Roman Empire and permanently divided it into an approximately equal number of Protestant and Catholic states. Thus the Austrian Hapsburgs were no more successful in their efforts to stamp out Protestantism in Germany than the Spanish

Hapsburgs had been in the Netherlands, England, and France. The Peace of Westphalia also confirmed the political disintegration of the Empire into a hodgepodge of small sovereign states. This development had been well under way for some time; the peace settlement merely made it legal. Two states, the Swiss Confederation and the Dutch Republic, severed all ties with the Empire and gained complete independence. Except for Bohemia and some French-speaking territories west of the Rhine, the Empire was now completely German. Yet never was it more disunited. In the name of religion and their medieval "liberties" the German princes had successfully resisted the centralizing efforts of Emperor Ferdinand II. Each prince was now completely sovereign and had the right to conduct his own foreign as well as domestic affairs. France and Sweden made themselves the guarantors of this new "constitution," which was the negation of everything a constitution was supposed to be since, henceforth, the Empire's "government" — its electors, its diet, its supreme court — had no real power.

The Thirty Years' War and the Peace of Westphalia also set a new course for international relations. Diplomacy came into its own with first-rate ministers from France, Spain, and Sweden. Hundreds of diplomats at the peace conference represented almost every state, large and small, in Central and Western Europe. Out of their deliberations there emerged two basic notions: (1) individual sovereign states were the central forces of political life; and (2) relations between sovereign states were subject to mutually accepted rules. International relations were now frankly secularized; thus the frequent wars among sovereign states could no longer be considered religious crusades.

By 1648 the main trends of early modern European history had clearly emerged. The shift from religious to secular values was well under way in politics, the arts, and thought.

Capitalism and the entrepreneurial spirit had fostered a major economic expansion, and Europe's population had doubled in two centuries. Overseas explorations had begun to give some people a new outlook toward the physical world, an outlook that, as we shall see later, was also influenced by new scientific theories. But none of these trends had triumphed completely in 1648. The first wave of Europe's economic expansion ended without providing the means to feed a growing population. Although religion ceased to be a factor in international politics, it remained a critical issue in the internal affairs of England and France. Many sensitive individuals everywhere strove anxiously to reconcile their religious yearnings with the new secularism.

Each major innovation produced its own crisis. This has always been true, for most men and institutions have always been basically conservative. But in the early modern period something unprecedented began to occur; with the introduction of printing Europe entered an era of great technological progress, when an increasing number of people gradually became accustomed to change itself as a fact of life.

By 1648 national states and national cultures were emerging in Western Europe. The nation-state was to become the typical framework within which modern society developed; national governments, national economies, and national armies and navies were to be the main forces of modern times. The English and the French were to persecute their religious minorities again in the name of political unity, but no foreign power was ever able to make them forget that they were Englishmen and Frenchmen first, Catholics and Protestants second. Later wars and revolutions were to reinforce people's loyalty to king and country, and the growth of mass education and mass communication was eventually to make the nation-state the main focus of loyalty for all sections of the population.

SUGGESTED READINGS

Rice, Eugene F., Jr., *The Foundations of Early Modern Europe.* New York: W. W. Norton, 1970. Paperback.

Cassirer, Ernst, Paul O. Kristeller, and John H. Randall, eds. *The Renaissance Philosophy of Man.* Chicago: University of Chicago Press, 1955. Paperback.
Selections from six representative thinkers of the Renaissance, with critical introductions.

Elton, Geoffrey R., *Reformation Europe, 1517–1559.* New York: Harper-Row, 1966. Paperback.
A fine, up-to-date interpretation.

Bainton, Roland H., *Here I Stand: A Life of Martin Luther.* Nashville, Tenn.: Abingdon Press, 1959. Apex Books. Paperback.
The authoritative biography—sympathetic and thorough. Stresses religious aspects of the Reformation.

Hughes, Philip. *A Popular History of the Reformation.* Garden City, N.Y.: Doubleday and Co., 1957. Paperback.
By an eminent Catholic scholar. Especially good on the Catholic Reformation.

Bainton, Roland H., *The Age of the Reformation.* Princeton, N.J.: D. Van Nostrand, 1956. An Anvil original. Paperback.
A comprehensive selection of the writings of the great reformers.

Nef, John U., *Western Civilization Since the Renaissance.* New York: Harper and Row, 1963. Torchbook. Paperback.
Even though this thoughtful and learned work is not always convincing in its effort to disprove any positive correlation between war and technological advances, the chapters on early modern economic and military development are excellent.

Parry, J. H., *The Establishment of European Hegemony: Trade and Expansion in the Renaissance,* New York: Harper-Row, 1966. Paperback.

Cipolla, Carlo M., *Guns, Sails, and Empires: Technological Innovation and the Early Phases of European Expansion.* New York: Funk and Wagnalls, 1968. Paperback.

Neale, John E., *Queen Elizabeth I.* Garden City, N.Y.: Doubleday and Co., 1957. Anchor. Paperback.
The standard biography.

Mattingly, Garrett, *The Armada.* Boston: Houghton Mifflin Co., 1959. Paperback.

CHAPTER 11

Society, Politics, and War under the Old Regime, 1648–1789

Despite economic and social differences between Eastern and Western Europe, the political systems of most of the major states were more similar from 1648 to 1789 than in any other period. Under these systems—called collectively the Old Regime—the monarch was sovereign, but the hereditary aristocracy retained its social and cultural dominance. Indeed, as long as land remained the major form of wealth, the great landowners of the nobility were able to pressure the royal governments to strengthen their own political influence in many places. France and the Austrian monarchy were the two most typical examples of the Old Regime. Not until the French Revolution in the 1790s were the political and social bases of the Old Regime destroyed in France and its Western European satellites. Not until the abolition of serfdom and the beginnings of industrialization after the mid-nineteenth century was the Old Regime undermined in the great empires of Central and Eastern Europe.

In the eighteenth century Europe increasingly influenced other parts of the world.

Overseas the Anglo-French struggle for wealth and empire led to the exploitation of the Caribbean islands with African slaves, the growth of the North American colonies, and the subjugation of India. The rising powers of Central and Eastern Europe also felt the influence of the more advanced countries. As Austria, Prussia, and Russia became part of the European state system, their rulers adapted the military and bureaucratic institutions of the west to their own needs. Their aristocracies also copied the social and cultural models of the west, and especially of France. Although Eastern European society, with its mass of serfs and its insignificant bourgeoisie, remained backward, Austria, Prussia, and Russia joined Great Britain, and France to constitute the "Big Five" in international relations until the early twentieth century.

FRANCE AND EUROPE IN THE AGE OF LOUIS XIV

In France the centralizing policies of the royal government had been challenged

335

His Royal Majesty King Louis XIV.

frequently during the half century preceding Louis XIV's assumption of personal power in 1661. Louis XIII (1610–1643) had greatly increased the use of the *lettre de cachet,* a letter bearing the royal seal, to notify personally a disobedient subject or official of his arrest, imprisonment, or exile. His brilliant first minister, Cardinal Richelieu, gave wider powers to the office of *intendant,* a traveling official who made the king's authority felt through the realm. But the Huguenots, the princes of the blood, and the great nobles rebelled against all efforts to limit their pretensions to independence. Peasants and urban workers attacked royal revenue agents in protest against increased taxes, especially the one on salt. Since the Bourbons did not call the Estates General (the French equivalent of the medieval English Parliament) after 1614, they had no trouble from that quarter. But the Parlements (royal law courts) tried to take over the role of the Estates General as a legislative body.

In 1648 the Parlements, along with the princes of the blood, launched a series of rebellions, called collectively the Fronde. Louis XIV was only ten years old at the time,

and the government was in the hands of the first minister, Cardinal Mazarin, who had succeeded Richelieu in 1642. Not until 1653 was Mazarin able to suppress the disorder and violence of the Fronde. When the majority of French people recognized the essentially partisan ambitions of the insurgents, they accepted the authoritarian government that would maintain order and tranquility in the kingdom. Meanwhile, Mazarin was initiating the young Louis XIV into the ways of statecraft; when Mazarin died in 1661, Louis resolved to be his own first minister, so that only he would understand the totality of affairs and thus be indispensable.

Partly out of vanity and partly in order to live up to his exalted conception of his role as a king by divine right, Louis made himself a dazzling and awe-inspiring public figure. From the time His Majesty arose in the morning until the time he retired at night his every action demanded a ceremony with elaborate rules of protocol. Princes of the blood vied with one another for the honor of helping him put on his shirt. His meals were artistic productions of many courses. A typical evening's entertainment "at home" might include a troupe of ballet dancers, a masked ball, and an extravagant display of fireworks. Everyone around His Majesty bowed, curtsied, and catered to his every wish. His courtiers compared him to the sun, and his emblem said that no one was his equal. Louis XIV made a cult of majesty.

Louis also made himself the source of law and justice. He silenced the Parlements—which had claimed equal power in these matters during the Fronde—by ordering them to confirm his authority to tax and to register his edicts immediately and without change. Anyone might be accused of the crime of lese majesty—an affront to His Majesty—and find himself in the Bastille. Like the *lettre de cachet,* this converted fortress on the east side of Paris became a symbol of political oppression and the absence of civil rights.

Louis sought to utilize the old sentiment of vassalage to bind his officials to their sovereign through a personal tie. Through this tie and in the exercise of personal power he concentrated the state in himself; in doing so, Louis prepared Frenchmen to advance eventually to the concept of the impersonal modern state. One's service to the sovereign, the embodiment of the state, became most important in determining one's social rank. In the highest offices of the realm Louis gradually replaced hereditary nobles—nobility of the sword—with men of bourgeois origin, most notably his minister of commerce and finance, Jean-Baptiste Colbert, the son of a textile merchant. Louis also conferred hereditary titles of nobility on his highest bourgeois officals, making them a nobility of the robe—so called for the robes worn by French magistrates.

Louis also had to mollify the nobles of the sword. He continued to appoint them as governors and to reserve most of the higher ranks of the army and the church for them and their sons. His wars provided them with employment and opportunities for achieving glory and enhancing their prestige. Also, the king insured their servility with pensions, dowries, and ecclesiastical benefices. His most spectacular means of domesticating the nobility of the sword was to keep its higher members busy fawning over the Sun King in an unending series of courtly ceremonies and festivals. In order to create a proper setting for his court, Louis XIV built the palace of Versailles 10 miles outside of Paris. The Duke de Saint Simon commented on Louis' policies and their purposes as follows:

"The frequent fêtes, the private promenades at Versailles, the journeys, were means on which the King seized in order to distinguish or mortify the courtiers, and thus render them more assiduous in pleasing him. He felt that of real favors he had enough to bestow; in order to keep up the spirit of devotion, he therefore unceasingly invented all sorts of ideal ones, little preferences and petty distinctions which served his purpose as well." *

Versailles not only served as a gilded cage for all who counted among the French nobility but it also became a symbol of Louis XIV's power in France and in all of Europe. It was a

* From Louis de Rouvroy, Duc de Saint-Simon, *The Memoirs of the Duke of Saint-Simon on the Reign of Louis XIV and the Regency*, tr. Bayle St. John (London, 1926), II, 364.

world in itself, with scores of bedrooms, vast reception halls, acres of formal gardens, a chapel, a theater, and government offices. Only the richest king in Europe could have built such a palace; it cost 100 million dollars. Louis XIV became the model absolute monarch. Long after his death the kings and princes of Europe constructed smaller versions of Versailles and tried to emulate his "cult of majesty."

In addition to building up the royal bureaucracy and surrounding himself with devoted ministers and officials, Louis XIV was determined to enforce religious uniformity on all his 20 million subjects. His ideal was "one faith, one law, one king." When he assumed personal power there were still about one million Huguenots in France, and although they had come to accept the royal authority as unquestioningly as the Catholics, they did not meet Louis' ideal of "one faith." Thus he put increasing pressure on the Huguenots to convert to the official religion of the state. First he sent Catholic missionaries into their midst; then he deprived them of their remaining legal privileges. When these measures proved to be too slow, Louis began quartering troops in Huguenot homes. Finally, in 1685, he revoked the Edict of Nantes, making the "so-called Reformed religion" illegal in France. Tens of thousands of Huguenots emigrated to England, Holland, Germany, and America. Those who remained in France and kept their Calvinist faith suffered as a persecuted minority.

With the church disciplining people's private thoughts and feelings, the government also tried to regiment the arts and letters for the glory of the state. It controlled the printing and sale of most books and periodicals; it censored all theatrical productions. Not since ancient Rome had a European ruler gone as far as Louis XIV in using artistic display for his own glorification. He had his military victories celebrated in triumphal arches, in heroic statues of himself in public squares, and in paintings and tapestries in his palaces. Like the great nobles at Versailles, the members of the French Academy came to view themselves as lesser gods in the service of the Sun King. France's greatest playwright, Jean Racine (1639–1699), once said: "All the words of the language, all the syllables seem precious to us because we regard them as so many tools with which to serve the glory of our Illustrious Patron.''

Louis XIV's overriding concern was to develop his country's military and economic resources in order to strengthen the state at home and in its relations with the outside world. The needs of war played a great part in strengthening the state. The organization and maintenance of a large standing army and a regular navy added to the functions of the bureaucracy and prompted the government to foster economic growth so that it would have more wealth to tax. Here, too, Louis XIV provided models for the other rulers of Europe.

Yet even the great Colbert could not solve all of France's financial and fiscal problems, especially in the face of the severe and prolonged depression the country experienced after 1650. French manufactured goods brought in considerable profits from abroad and new sources of taxable income at home. The government collected more taxes than ever before, but it still did not tax the wealth of the privileged classes, particularly the landed nobility. This weakness in the nation's tax structure was to plague French governments throughout the eighteenth century. As a result of Colbert's efforts to promote and control the economy, Louis XIV had more wealth at his disposal than his predecessors had ever dreamed of. But Louis wasted much of his economic power in costly wars, and his successors were to go increasingly into debt.

In the late seventeenth century "reasons of state" came to determine how wars were fought as well as why they were fought. As bureaucrats took the place of nobles of the sword in making government policy, they introduced an element of caution and economy into the conduct of their countries' wars. The function of bureaucrats has always been to serve the state. They were suspicious of soldiers who wanted to risk the whole army in a single battle. Well-trained professional troops were becoming too valuable to be wasted in this way. Thus land warfare became an affair of maneuvers and sieges, and naval warfare mainly a matter of blockades and raids on commercial shipping. This was the way Louis XIV's first three

wars were fought: the War of Devolution (1667–1668) against the Spanish Netherlands: the Dutch War (1672–1678); and the War of the League of Augsburg (1688–1697), which involved a French invasion of the Rhineland, a trade war against the English and the Dutch, and minor skirmishes with the English in North America. (Simultaneously, Austria, Venice, Russia, and Poland were fighting the Ottoman Empire in Eastern Europe.)

When the stakes were really high, daring rulers relieved cautious bureaucrats of much of their power. In the War of the Spanish Succession (1701–1713) the stakes were the highest anyone could imagine. A world empire was "up for grabs." Just before he died, Charles II, the last of the Spanish Hapsburgs, had willed this empire to Louis XIV's grandson (Louis's wife was a Spanish princess), who became Philip V of Spain. Although Emperor Leopold, the head of the Austrian branch of the Hapsburg family, prepared for war, the English and the Dutch were willing to accept this arrangement as long as the French and Spanish crowns remained separated. Louis not only rejected this separation but he also insisted that French merchants receive preferential treatment in all Spanish markets at the expense of their English and Dutch rivals. In addition, he closed down the Dutch garrisons along the southern border of the Spanish Netherlands, which they had gained the right to control at the end of an earlier war. The response in London and The Hague was the emergence of war parties. By 1701 all the rulers of Western and Central Europe were ready to go to war, while their bureaucrats and ministers shook their heads. For more than a decade thereafter Louis XIV fought alliances of the other European powers to preserve his gains, but in the end he lost the war.

The Treaties of Utrecht and Rastadt (1713–1714) divided the lands of the Spanish Hapsburgs as follows: Louis XIV's grandson, Philip V, retained Spain, the Spanish overseas empire, and part of Italy; the Austrian Hapsburgs received the Spanish Netherlands and part of Italy; Great Britain gained Gibraltar and the slave-trading concession in Spain's American colonies. In North America England took over Nova

Scotia and Newfoundland from France. The Dutch regained the right to garrison border fortifications in the now Austrian Netherlands. Finally, the French agreed that France and Spain would remain permanently separated.

The peacemakers sought to make the new *balance of power* the permanent basis of European international relations; they could not insure permanent peace, but they did create a system in which each state could defend its independence against foreign aggression. During the eighteenth century, Prussia and Russia joined France, Great Britain, and Austria in the "club" of great powers, while other powers—the Dutch Republic, Spain, Sweden, Poland, and Turkey—declined. Europe as a whole had developed a complex pattern of international relations that allowed culturally diverse states to develop independently and to form alliances for mutual protection against any state that threatened to upset the balance of power.

After Louis XIV died in 1715, the Old Regime in France failed to adapt itself to the economic and social changes of the eighteenth century. The royal government remained dedicated to the public good, but it lacked a Louis XIV to make it work as it was organized to work. Although the privileged orders were unable to control the royal government, they were determined to prevent it from doing anything that threatened their rights and status. If the royal government had been stronger, it might have made the institutional changes necessary to meet the new conditions created by the expansion of trade, the growing importance of colonial empires, and the enrichment of the middle and upper classes. But the entrenched traditions of divine-right monarchy, the weakness of Louis XV (1715–1774), and the resistance of the privileged orders forbade such a solution. The hereditary nobles refused to pay taxes, the wealthy commoners were reluctant to lend money to a government that did not represent them, and the Parlements reasserted their right to block royal efforts to raise new forms of revenue.

The Old Regime in France fostered deep-seated resentment among newly wealthy Frenchmen by not accommodating them.

Although a few French statesmen wanted to use the ideas of the Enlightenment* to make the Old Regime more liberal and humane, the weak French monarchy only continued to encourage the privileged few to become more exclusive. A stronger government might have kept the aristocracy more "open," thus strengthening the social basis for its authority. But in authoritarian France, the wealthy bourgeoisie, barred from both power and privilege, eventually saw that it could only improve its status by open rebellion.

THE ANGLO-FRENCH STRUGGLE FOR WEALTH AND EMPIRE

In the mid-eighteenth century international relations were conducted by professional diplomats and professional soldiers who could commit their governments to wars and then abandon them with ease. Wars were now fought by professional armies and had little effect on civilians. The Central European wars of this period were largely self-contained; the wars between Great Britain and France were fought in North America and India for control of colonies.

The colonial wars between Great Britain and France were consciously tied to economic motives. Imperialism and economic growth were dependent on each other. By the mid-eighteenth century the plantation system in the New World colonies was not only adding to the wealth of English and French entrepreneurs from the trade in sugar, rum, and slaves, but new American foods, especially the potato, were also helping to sustain a new wave of population growth in Europe. The standing armies and navies maintained by the major powers to protect their national interests constituted a new and important market for goods and services. For example, the manufacture of uniforms for the 160,000-man French army and the 100,000-man British navy provided work for countless people, and profits for a significant number of private merchants and investors. The governments themselves subsidized the manufacturers of ships, cannon, and muskets. All the money earned from equipping

* See pp. 378–388.

Impressment of seamen into the British navy.

and servicing the military forces gave rise to further demand for other people's goods and services, both at home and abroad.

Mercantilism and Colonies

During the seventeenth and eighteenth centuries Europe's rulers tried to make the most of the material and human resources at their disposal through a policy called *mercantilism,* which was an early form of economic nationalism. In the sixteenth century, Spain had been the strongest state in Europe, and had had the largest supply of precious metals. Mercantilist theorists, therefore, equated national power with large reserves of bullion. According to them, the states that lacked bullion had to acquire it by selling goods and services to foreigners. The Dutch concentrated on selling services: commerce, shipping, and banking. England and France gave more emphasis to the export of manufactured goods.

Mercantilism—or the mercantile system—required government supervision of all these kinds of economic activity in the interest of state power. As foreign trade brought growing prosperity, governments tried to strengthen their control over trade for the good of the state. This meant subsidizing the home export industries, supporting a national merchant marine, and limiting imports to those that were essential, that did not compete with native products, and that could be paid for with exportable goods rather than cash. Governments encouraged investment in trading companies by giving them monopolies in various parts of the world. They tried to regulate standards of workmanship to preserve the reputation of their country's exports. They undertook—not too successfully—to protect native producers by preventing the smuggling in of cheaper, or better, foreign products. Finally, again following the example of Spain, the English, Dutch, and French governments sought to acquire colonies as cheap sources of raw materials and as protected markets for manufactured goods.

The first Europeans had come to the New World in search of treasure and an all-water route to the Orient. In the sixteenth century the Spaniards had claimed and partially occupied the Americas from California and Florida south (except for Portuguese Brazil). In the seventeenth century Swedes and Dutchmen established small colonies in Delaware, New Jersey, and eastern New York. But from the late seventeenth century on, the British and the French became the sole contenders for control of most of North America and the West Indies. The original English settlers in Massachusetts (Puritans), Maryland (Catholics), and Pennsylvania (Quakers) had come to America to escape religious discrimination at home, and some French Huguenots had settled in the English coastal colonies after the Revocation of the Edict of Nantes. Nevertheless, the majority of Englishmen and Frenchmen who migrated to the New World came for economic reasons.

By 1715 the French and British had established empires in North America. The French had extended their holdings from their original settlement in Quebec (1608) north to the mouth of the St. Lawrence and south to the mouth of the Mississippi. In the Treaty of Utrecht they had lost Newfoundland, Nova Scotia, and the Hudson Bay Territory to the British, but they controlled all of eastern Canada, the Great Lakes region, and the Ohio, Mississippi, and Missouri valleys. The main French settlement was in the St. Lawrence Valley, where there were about 20,000 French settlers in 1715 and about 65,000 by 1763, an increase resulting mainly from natural reproduction rather than further immigration. The rest of the French Empire in North America was a vast, sparsely populated forestland. There were about 400,000 Indians, a handful of Jesuit missionaries who tried to convert and "civilize" them, and a few thousand fur trappers who intermarried with them.

The British colonies along the Atlantic seaboard resembled the French in their separation into distinct groups and in their autonomous spirit, but they had a larger population and a higher level of production and commerce; and they were overwhelmingly Protestant. Their population had increased from 255,000 in 1700 to 1,640,000 in 1763, mainly through voluntary immigration by Scotch, Irish, Germans, and forced "immigration" by Africans. In the south, plantation farming of rice, tobacco, and indigo predominated; the plantation owners controlled local affairs and became an untitled landed aristocracy. Most New Englanders were small farmers, although fishing and shipping became increasingly important. In the Middle Atlantic colonies agriculture was diversified, and commerce thrived in cities like Philadelphia and New York. Unlike the French Catholics, the English Protestants made few efforts to convert the Indians. They merely pushed them off the land and annihilated those who fought back.

Mercantilist theory held that the main function of the colonies was to bolster the economy of the mother country. British and French colonies generally had been founded and controlled by trading companies licensed in London or Paris. By the eighteenth century the colonists themselves managed most of their local affairs, while the royal governors saw to it that they obeyed the laws of the home government, especially in matters of foreign trade. But as the British colonists in North American began to pursue their own economic interests, friction arose. In 1732, Parliament prohibited the importation of hats from the colonies and restricted their manufacture. A year later, under pressure from British planters in the West Indies, it passed the Molasses Act. This act placed prohibitive duties on the sugar and molasses the colonists were importing from the French Antilles, where prices were 40 percent cheaper than in the British islands. And to prevent competition with British products, the British government in 1750 forbade the manufacture of iron products in New Jersey. It said, "If America should take it into its head to manufacture so much as a nail, England will make it feel the full weight of her power."

Plantation scene in the West Indies.

In the eighteenth century the British and French islands in the West Indies were ideal colonies. They furnished goods completely lacking in the mother country, and they produced almost nothing that the mother country produced. They bought their manufactured goods in England and France and their slaves from English and French entrepreneurs operating along the coast of West Africa. The population of the Antilles, which by 1763 was 90 percent African, equaled that of the whole of British and French North America. A few rich European planters exploited the mass of slaves and lived in fantastic luxury. Indeed, their wealth and commercial importance made the home government cater to them more than to the North American colonists, as proved by the Molasses Act.

Nevertheless, the activities and interests of the colonists themselves limited the effectiveness of mercantilism. Despite the efforts of the colonial powers to regulate trade and manufacturing in the colonies, smuggling was rampant. In peacetime illegal trade was probably greater than legal trade between the British and French colonies in North America and the West Indies. In the Ohio Valley and other parts of the hinterland, the British and French settlers engaged in local wars over the fur trade. By the 1740s the colonists forced their home governments to go to war to further their own economic and political interests, rather than those of the European motherlands.

The geography and economy of the New World plus intimate contact with Indians and transplanted Africans, made the European settlers increasingly different from their countrymen back home. From Virginia to Brazil, slavery gave plantation owners a racist outlook unknown in Europe; and fur trappers in Canada, western Pennsylvania, and Virginia had little in common with the peasants of France or northern Ireland. The "nations" of America were acquiring their distinct cultural characteristics even before the wars of the second half of the eighteenth century aided the independence movement among the European colonists. Both the English- and Spanish-speaking colonists began to call themselves "Americans," the Portuguese-speaking colonists "Brazilians,"

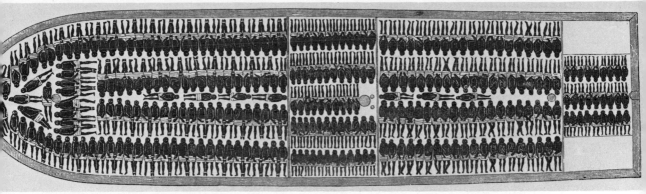

The loading plan of a slave ship.

the French-speaking settlers in Quebec "Canadians."

Yet the growing cultural differences between the colonists and their compatriots "back home" did not alter the fact that the New World was part of a global economy operating primarily for the benefit of Western Europe. We shall see later how, in the nineteenth century, trade between Europe and America continued to grow and how European capital began to pour in on an increasing scale, even after many of the colonies had become independent. Meanwhile, the British, French, and Dutch intensified their competition for the trade of the Far East, and the British and French began to clash in their commercial dealings with India. Directly or indirectly, the rest of the world was working increasingly for Europe and was enriching the European middle and upper classes.

The Struggle for Supremacy in North America

The Anglo-French war that began in 1744 expressed the bitter rivalry between these two countries' sugar colonies, but it ended inconclusively in 1748; it was while their home governments were technically at peace (1748–1756) that the colonists in North America intensified their struggle for the control of that continent. In 1749 a group of Virginians organized the Ohio Company to develop the land west of the Appalachians through both settlement and trade. Since both the French and the Indians claimed the territory that the Ohio Company wanted to develop, they began to work together to resist Anglo-Saxon penetration. But as long as their home governments remained at peace, no showdown was possible.

Nevertheless, by the end of 1755, the French and their Indian allies were pushing the British colonists back beyond the mountains to their seaboard bases. In the face of this kind of setback, the British government finally decided that it had to drive the French out of North America. At this point the struggle for North America merged with a new general war between Great Britain and France and their continental allies in Europe.* France devoted a greater part of its efforts to the continental war than Great Britain did and thus lost the struggle overseas — in the French and Indian War in North America and in the war for control of India.

The first step in Great Britain's conquest of France's North American empire was the capture of Louisbourg, at the mouth of the St. Lawrence, in the summer of 1758. A few months later the British destroyed French ascendancy in the Ohio Valley by taking the site of Fort Duquesne, now abandoned by the French; it was later named Pittsburgh. They also threatened French communications between the St. Lawrence and the Great Lakes by capturing Fort Frontenac on Lake Ontario. Most ominous for the French was the ability of the British to prevent naval reinforcements and supply ships from reaching Canada. The Governor-General, the Marquis of Montcalm, not only

* We shall discuss the new system of alliances and the outcome of the Seven Year's War later (see pp. 358–360).

Fighting between American colonists and Indians.

had to rely increasingly on his own meager military forces but he also began to lose the allegiance of his Indian allies, since he had no more European goods to trade with them.

In 1759 the British began their all-out assault on the St. Lawrence Valley from their newly won bases; the crucial campaign was General James Wolfe's attack on Quebec. Starting from the mouth of the St. Lawrence, Wolfe moved his amphibious force slowly upstream toward the capital of New France. It was a hazardous operation in every respect: hostile Indian fighters attacked the British whenever they moved too close to the shores; in midstream the waters of the St. Lawrence were treacherous and required expert seamanship. Wolfe also faced frequent opposition from his junior officers, who questioned his judgment and resented his stern, aloof manner. When the expedition finally reached Quebec, it had to scale the high cliffs on which the citadel stood. Montcalm was now isolated, and his food supplies were running low. At last he sent his troops out of the fortress to do battle with the British

on the famous Plains of Abraham. Quebec surrendered five days later (September 18, 1759), after both Wolfe and Montcalm had lost their lives. With the surrender of Montreal in September 1760, the British had won the struggle for North America.

In 1763, in the Treaty of Paris, France retained its West Indian islands, and Great Britain kept Canada and all of North America west to the Mississippi. Many Englishmen would have preferred to have kept the former, which were richer, and to relinquish the latter, but strategic considerations won out over economic ones. The British understood that they had to eliminate the French threat to the expansion of their mainland colonies. They also eliminated the Spanish threat by forcing Spain to give up Florida and compensating her with all former French holdings west of the Mississippi, called the Louisiana Territory.

By 1774 the British effectively controlled all territory east of the Mississippi. They practically eliminated lingering Indian resistance to their colonists' westward expansion, but

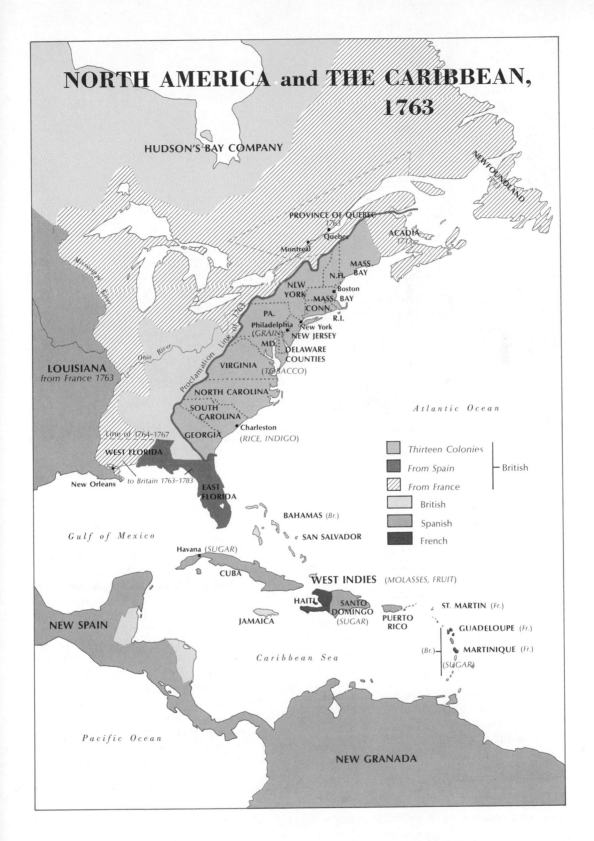

NORTH AMERICA and THE CARIBBEAN, 1763

HUDSON'S BAY COMPANY

NEWFOUNDLAND

Mississippi River

PROVINCE OF QUEBEC
1763

ACADIA
1713

Quebec

Montreal

MASS.
BAY

N.H.

NEW
YORK

Boston

MASS. BAY

CONN.

R.I.

PA.

Philadelphia
(GRAIN)

New York

NEW JERSEY

Ohio River

MD.

DELAWARE
COUNTIES

LOUISIANA
from France 1763

VIRGINIA
(TOBACCO)

Proclamation Line of 1763

NORTH CAROLINA

SOUTH
CAROLINA

Atlantic Ocean

Line of 1764-1767

GEORGIA

Charleston
(RICE, INDIGO)

WEST FLORIDA

New Orleans

to Britain 1763-1783

EAST
FLORIDA

Gulf of Mexico

BAHAMAS (Br.)

SAN SALVADOR

Havana (SUGAR)

CUBA

WEST INDIES (MOLASSES, FRUIT)

NEW SPAIN

HAITI

SANTO
DOMINGO
(SUGAR)

PUERTO
RICO

ST. MARTIN (Fr.)

JAMAICA

GUADELOUPE (Fr.)

(Br.)

MARTINIQUE (Fr.)

Caribbean Sea

(SUGAR)

Pacific Ocean

NEW GRANADA

	Thirteen Colonies	
	From Spain	British
	From France	
	British	
	Spanish	
	French	

The Library on Fifth Street, Philadelphia, in the eighteenth century.

they made two mistakes that were soon to incite the colonists to revolt against them. First they increased the colonists' taxes and continued to put mercantilist restrictions on their trade and manufacturing. Second, they tried to limit their expansion north of the Ohio by extending the boundary of Quebec Province to that river. The Quebec Act (1774) proved a satisfactory way of incorporating the 65,000 French settlers into the British empire but, ironically, it antagonized the British colonists in whose interests the mother country had defeated both the French and the Indians.

In 1776 the revolt of the colonists was to negate most of Great Britain's gains in North America. The British were to find that the permanent foundations of their world empire lay in an entirely different setting.

The Struggle for India

The British Empire in India was the most important single example in modern times of European supremacy overseas. Founded in the mid-eighteenth century, it remained Great Britain's prime possession until 1947. Moreover, its founding set a pattern for expansion against other old but declining civilizations in Asia and North Africa, an expansion that required new techniques and new types of men.

In the 1740s, when British and French adventurers sought to extend their power in India, that vast subcontinent was politically disunited. The remnants of the Mughal Empire (see pp. 543–544) consisted of a medium-size state around Delhi in the north and the southern state of Hyderabad, ruled by a semi-independent viceroy. Independent Muslim princes also ruled most of the eastern coast; the two main states there were Carnatic in the south and Bengal in the north. Elsewhere Hindu rulers predominated. English and French trading companies had established footholds along the coasts of India, acknowledging the control of the local princes but avoiding open conflicts with one another. Then, soon after war broke out between England and France in 1744, the East India companies of these countries became involved in a life-and-death struggle for power in eastern India. The two principal leaders in this struggle were the Marquis Joseph François Dupleix (1697–1763) and Robert Clive (1725–1774).

Dupleix was the first of the imperialists in India. Although born a nobleman, he became a renegade to his class and an adventurer. As governor-general of the French East India Company (1741-1754), his intervention in Indian political affairs was for commercial reasons and private gain. Gradually his fertile imagination and boundless ambition planted in him the idea of a French empire in India. First he tried to get his own candidates recognized as the rulers of Hyderabad and Carnatic. He wanted to make these puppet rulers grant him part of the revenues of their states because his company's resources were inadequate for his purposes, and he asked for no money from the government in Paris. Since France could spare him only a handful of officers, Dupleix supplemented his military forces with *sepoys*, European-trained Indian troops. With these techniques he extended his control over southeastern India. But the English opposed him in the early 1750s, even though they were officially at peace with France. The French government forced Dupleix to come home in 1754, and he died in poverty and disgrace nine years later.

The English, not the French, were to build an empire in India, and England's first empire-builder was also an adventurer. Robert Clive was a soldier and an officer in the British East India Company. Dazzled by Dupleix's successes, Clive tried to follow his example. He won several native rulers away from the French with bigger and better promises, threats, and intrigues. But he received more military and naval support from his home government than did Dupleix.

Clive founded the British Empire in India by taking over the rich and populous state of Bengal. The ruler of that territory was bitterly anti-British, and in 1756 he sent a large army against the English settlement in Calcutta. Many of the Europeans escaped before the attack, but 146 of them were packed into a prison cell called "The Black Hole." Only 23

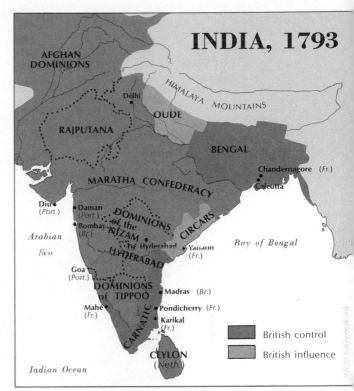

of them survived until the next morning; the rest died from suffocation. Outraged by this atrocity, Clive resolved to capture Calcutta and did so. Next, at the Battle of Plassey (1757), he and his forces won an easy military victory over the ruler of Bengal, who was then replaced by a British puppet.

The Battle of Plassey was of supreme importance in the growth of British power in India (see pp. 549–552). It was the first major European victory over an oriental potentate on his own soil. Not only did it establish British supremacy in northeastern India, it virtually settled the outcome of the struggle with the French. For it was from his secure base in Bengal that Clive launched his attack on the French holdings along the southeast coast. The Treaty of Paris (1763) allowed the French to keep a few of these trading posts, but they soon lost their importance. In India, as in North America, the British had won a decisive victory in their bid for world supremacy.

In their struggle for wealth and empire, the British and the French had an enormous superiority over non-Europeans in the eigh-

Robert Clive at the Battle of Plassey.

teenth century. This superiority was not only in material supplies and military tactics, but also in discipline and training, which seemed to make the European a type apart, cool-headed, energetic, tenacious, brave—although also quite ruthless. In India, where the bravest fighters were subject to disastrous panics because of lack of discipline, one native potentate said to an English general: "What soldiers you have! Their line is like a brick wall. And when one falls another fills the breach. That's the kind of troops I would like to command!" This superiority earned the Europeans not only victories and subjects, but also allies and friends. It was one of the principal means by which they penetrated and began to control many parts of the world.

THE OLD REGIME IN EAST CENTRAL AND EASTERN EUROPE

In the late seventeenth and eighteenth centuries the line running from the southern

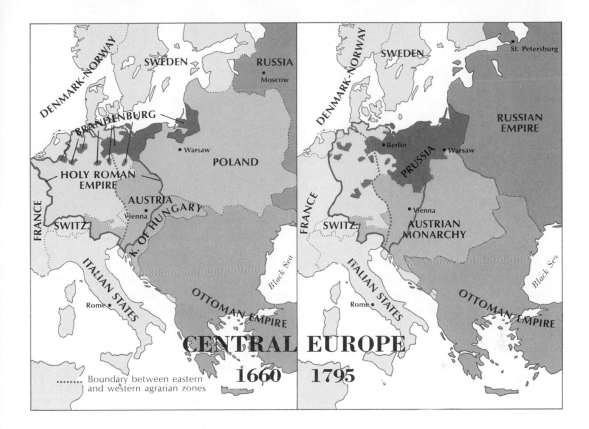

CENTRAL EUROPE
1660   1795

Boundary between eastern
and western agrarian zones

boundary of Denmark to the northwestern boundary of present-day Yugoslavia (see map above) had no checkpoints or border guards, and it did not represent the conscious effort of any state to isolate itself from its neighbors. It most resembled the kind of line that separates a rich district from a poor one in a large modern city. Even though it is invisible, one knows when one has crossed it by the way people on the other side live and work and by their relations with one another and with the authorities. Running through the center of the moribund Holy Roman Empire of the German Nation, this invisible line marked the division between the societies of Western and Eastern Europe.

During most of the eighteenth century the German states west of the invisible line— along with Denmark, Norway, Sweden, Switzerland, Italy, Spain, and Portugal— were the backwaters of Western Europe. Their ruling families provided marriage partners for European royalty everywhere; their writers, composers, and scholars produced many notable works. They stagnated polit-

ically but, at least, they were ruled by kings and aristocrats who spoke the native language. In east Central and Eastern Europe the opposite situation prevailed, and political frontiers had little to do with national cultures.

Socially, west Central Europe tended to resemble France and east Central Europe tended to resemble Russia in the eighteenth century. East of the line, the mass of peasants had sunk into a kind of serfdom in which they had to do forced labor for their lords on large estates. West of the line most peasants owed little or no forced labor and tilled small plots of land as tenants, sharecroppers or, in some cases, as independent proprietors. Class barriers were more rigid in the east than in the west. There were the nobles at the top, the serfs at the bottom, and not much in the middle. The bourgeoisie, which was growing in size and influence in the west, became increasingly insignificant the further east one went.

The social backwardness of east Central and Eastern Europe reflected the economic and political backwardness of these areas. Those wealthy landowners who wanted luxuries had to exchange their agricultural and forest products for the luxury goods and services of Western Europe. Because the productivity of their unfree peasants was low, there was little economic growth at home. Cities like Vienna, Budapest, Warsaw, and St. Petersburg were mainly administrative capitals rather than commercial centers. There were some merchants, but they lacked the dynamism and the rational techniques of organization shown by their more numerous counterparts in the west. Even as Prussia and Austria began to build up professional bureaucracies, there were few bourgeois lawyers, magistrates, or statesmen to challenge the political authority of the big landowners.

Although landowning aristocracies remained dominant in almost all of eighteenth-century Europe, there were important differences between those in the east and those in the west. The aristocrats of England and Sweden leased most of their lands to tenant farmers over whom they had relatively little direct economic control, whereas Polish and Hungarian squires still personally supervised the running of their estates. Even the landlord's local political power in England was not as absolute and unchallengeable as in Hungary and Poland. The service nobilities created by the sovereigns of Russia and Prussia had little in common with the aristocracies of the west. And the pashas and hospodars who ruled the Balkan provinces of the Ottoman Empire behaved more like oriental despots than European feudal lords.

A final difference between Western and Eastern Europe was that the major powers in the west, Great Britain and France, achieved their most important military successes overseas, whereas Austria, Prussia, and Russia gained successes of this kind at the expense of their weaker neighbors in Europe. The two maps on page 349 show the political boundaries of east Central and Eastern Europe in 1660 and 1795—before and after the developments described here. The most striking feature of the later map is the complete disappearance of Poland, whose territories had been divided among three of its stronger neighbors. In addition, Sweden had lost its holdings in the eastern Baltic to Russia, and Turkey had lost considerable territory to both Russia and Austria.

The Austrian Monarchy

In his role as Holy Roman Emperor (a title the reigning Hapsburgs held almost without interruption from 1438 to 1806) the head of the Austrian Monarchy controlled the formal institutions of the Empire—the Diet, the Imperial Chamber, and the Aulic Council—but these institutions had no real political power. In practice the princes and free cities of the Empire had their own independent governments, controlling both their foreign and domestic policies; the head of the Monarchy had no control over them.

Until the end of the seventeenth century the Austrian Monarchy itself comprised the dynastic lands of the Hapsburgs in Central Europe: the crown lands of Austria, the Kingdom of Bohemia, and the Kingdom of Hungary—most of which was occupied by the Ottoman Turks between 1526 and 1699. It remained a workable dynastic state by seventeenth-century standards, but it lacked a common army, common taxes and economic policies, and a unifying legal structure.

The man responsible for the military successes that transformed this loosely consolidated, multinational dynastic state into a great power was a non-Austrian, Prince Eugene of Savoy (1666–1736), an international aristocrat of French background. He won spectacular victories over Austria's traditional enemies: France and the Ottoman Empire. In the Treaty of Karlowitz (1699) the Turks permanently abandoned almost all of the vast medieval Kingdom of Hungary, which Emperor Leopold I (1658–1705) proceeded to incorporate into his hereditary lands. In the Treaty of Rastadt (1714) the Austrian Monarchy received Spain's Italian possessions and the Spanish Netherlands, both of which Louis XIV had fought for, long and hard. Prince Eugene not only added considerable territory to the Austrian Monarchy, he also reformed the supply, equipment, training, and command of its standing army. He made "Austria" a great military empire of 20 million people. Freed permanently from the Ottoman Turkish threat, it could now concentrate on consolidating its power in Central Europe.

The Austrian Monarchy still faced the problem of how to keep its many dynastic lands under one ruler. The problem took on a particular urgency when it became clear that Emperor Charles VI (1711–1740) would have no male heir. To make certain that his daughter Maria Theresa would be recognized as ruler of all the Hapsburg holdings, Charles VI issued the Pragmatic Sanction in 1713. Gradually the diets of the Hapsburg lands and most of the rulers of Europe signed this document, in which they promised to respect the territorial integrity of the Austrian Monarchy. But before the twenty-three-year old Maria Theresa (1740–1780) had collected all the crowns she was supposed to inherit, the War of the Austrian Succession began (see p. 358 for further discussion). This war was one factor that helped bring about the consolidation of the Austrian state.

Under Maria Theresa and her advisers the Old Regime in Austria slowly and haphazardly acquired a bureaucracy and a trained professional standing army staffed by aristocratic officers from all over the realm. Along with the Hapsburg dynasty itself, these institutions held the Austrian-Bohemian lands together under Maria Theresa and afterward. Although administratively separate, Hungary remained loyal to the House of Hapsburg as long as her landowning nobles were given a free hand with their serfs and exemption from taxation. In Austria and Bohemia, professional bureaucrats strengthened the authority of the central government in Vienna and gradually acquired an esprit de corps of their own. For the first time in their history, these lands were given a unified judicial system, with judges trained in Roman law. The officers in the Austrian army also acquired an organizational and psychological unity that was remarkable in view of their different national origins.

The Roman Catholic church also served as a unifying force in the Austrian Monarchy. More than 80 percent of the people in the realm belonged to it, and the Hapsburgs were notoriously devoted to its interests. The Jesuits had long since rooted out Protestantism in the Austrian crown lands, and in the eighteenth century they were finishing the job in Bohemia.

Maria Theresa herself set an example of piety and family devotion for all her subjects; with her numerous children and her devoted husband, she seemed to personify Mother Austria. She set a high standard of respectability at her court and took a sober interest in religious and political affairs. She also did more than any ruler of her time to protect the serfs in her domains (except Hungary) from the arbitrary exactions of their landlords.

Although the territorial princes and nobles opposed Hapsburg centralization, the high court nobility favored it. After all, they had the privilege of serving the most exalted dynasty in Europe. Moreover, all the highest offices of the state, the church, and the army went to them. Whether they were Italian, Czech, Hungarian, Croatian, or Polish, they learned to speak German and became devoted to the crown.

Viennese culture was at once local and cosmopolitan. The atmosphere of Vienna attracted intellectuals and artists from many European cities. Half the repertoire of Vienna's great new theater consisted of Italian opera, the other half of broad popular farces in the Viennese dialect. Maria Theresa had her new Schönbrunn palace built according to a French plan with Spanish and Italian embellishments, and this baroque style was copied in other buildings of the day. The music of Mozart epitomized the aristocratic, cosmopolitan high culture of eighteenth-century Vienna.

The Growth of Prussia

At the beginning of the eighteenth century Prussia resembled the Austrian Monarchy in several ways. It was essentially a collection of diverse lands (see map, p. 352) held together by obedience to a ruling dynasty—the House of Hohenzollern. It had a rigid social and economic structure dominated by large landowners and sustained by the inefficient labor of unfree peasants. The part of Prussia inside the Holy Roman Empire had suffered the debilitating effects of the Thirty Years' War. The part outside the empire (East Prussia) had only been freed from the overlordship of Poland in 1660—just as the bulk of Hungary was reconquered from Turkey in 1699.

There were also several important differences between Prussia and Austria in

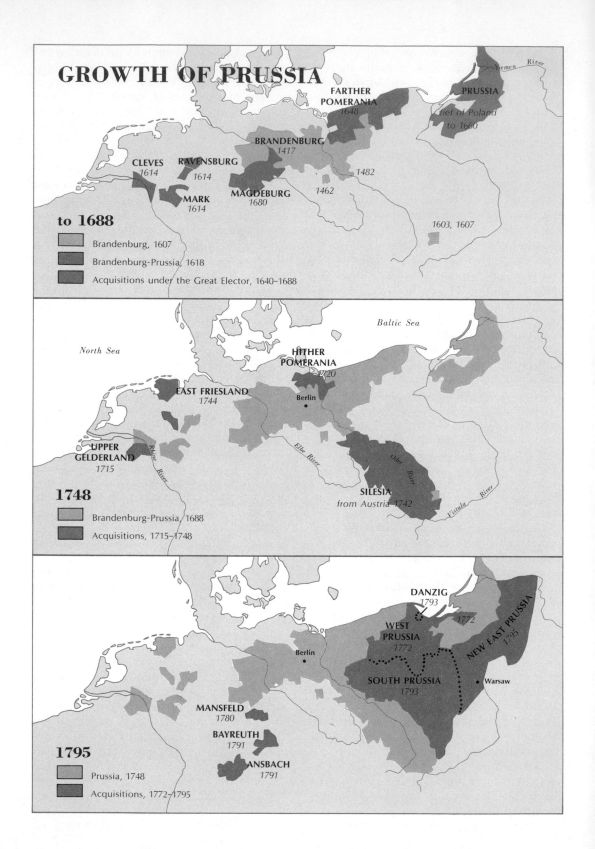

GROWTH OF PRUSSIA

to 1688

FARTHER POMERANIA
1648

PRUSSIA
fief of Poland to 1660

Niemen *River*

BRANDENBURG
1417

CLEVES
1614

RAVENSBURG
1614

1482

MARK
1614

MAGDEBURG
1680

1462

1603, 1607

- Brandenburg, 1607
- Brandenburg-Prussia, 1618
- Acquisitions under the Great Elector, 1640–1688

1748

Baltic Sea

North Sea

HITHER POMERANIA
1720

EAST FRIESLAND
1744

Berlin

UPPER GELDERLAND
1715

Rhine River

Elbe River

Oder River

SILESIA
from Austria 1742

Vistula River

- Brandenburg-Prussia, 1688
- Acquisitions, 1715–1748

1795

DANZIG
1793

1772

WEST PRUSSIA
1772

NEW EAST PRUSSIA
1795

Berlin

SOUTH PRUSSIA
1793

Warsaw

MANSFELD
1780

BAYREUTH
1791

ANSBACH
1791

- Prussia, 1748
- Acquisitions, 1772–1795

1713. Prussia was much smaller in size and population, almost exclusively Protestant, and almost completely German in language and culture. But the most important difference was that the Hohenzollerns had gone considerably further than the Hapsburgs in transforming their dynastic lands into a modern state when King Frederick William I (1713–1740) came to the throne at the end of the wars of Louis XIV.

Frederick William I's grandfather, the Great Elector, Frederick William (1640–1688) had decided that the only way to maintain the interests of the Hohenzollern dynasty was to have a standing army and a central bureaucracy to serve him in his scattered provinces without interference from their noble-dominated estates. With his personal revenue he created a small army, used it to browbeat the recalcitrant provincial estates into voting a permanent tax to support it, and then sold its services to various foreign powers. Although he used this additional income to strengthen his army and to increase his independence from the nobles, he also made significant concessions to them. Like Louis XIV, he reduced their political influence over the central government, but unlike Louis, he cemented a working alliance with its members, who were called *Junkers* in Prussia. The Great Elector confirmed their absolute authority over their serfs and their political preponderance over the towns; he also encouraged the Junkers to serve as army officers. He made no effort to coordinate the activities of his nascent bureaucracy, and competing jurisdictions survived until the beginning of the nineteenth century. Yet he had made an important start in giving his bureaucrats a sense of loyalty to the state.

Just as the Great Elector had sold the services of his army to the King of Poland in return for the recognition of his sovereignty over ducal Prussia in 1660, his son, Elector Frederick III (1688–1713), sold them to the Hapsburg Emperor for the title of King in Prussia in 1701 By the time that Elector Frederick III died, the Kingdom of Prussia meant all of the Hohenzollern lands, both inside and outside the empire. But it remained for Frederick William I to give this small, backward kingdom its character as a garrison state bent on becoming a great power.

Under Frederick William I the officer class of the Prussian army acquired a strong corporate spirit. At first many nobles opposed their forced militarization, but the king overcame their opposition by establishing a corps of cadets for the education of the Junkers, by making military service a criterion of social distinction, and by setting a personal example of devotion to the army and the state. Unlike France, where only a small minority of the 50,000 adult nobles habitually served as officers, in less populous Prussia nearly all the noble families had at least one son in the army. The Prussian officer's code stressed service, duty, and sacrifice as the supreme human virtues. An officer was promoted on the basis of merit; he could not buy his rank with money or family influence. His fellow officers saw to it that he obeyed the code and never shirked his duties.

Frederick William I also strengthened the corporate spirit of his bureaucrats and used them to enforce his mercantilist policies. Like his grandfather, he tried to foster new business enterprises in order to avoid buying manufactured products abroad. He also forbade the importation of foreign grains and the exportation of raw wool. Private enterprise increased, although always under bureaucratic supervision, and the working man was controlled in a more impersonal way by the state than he had ever been in the old guilds. Like the Great Elector, who had "imported" 20,000 enterprising French Huguenots, Frederick William I encouraged immigration from abroad to strengthen his manpower resources. During his reign, hundreds of thousands of soldiers, craftsmen, and peasants came to Prussia from other countries and settled there permanently.

When Frederick William I died in 1740, he had made Prussia the most militaristic state in Europe and had raised its population from one-and-a-half to almost two-and-a-half millions: Berlin was now a city of 100,000. He had also increased the government's revenue to about 7 million thalers a year—with a surplus of nearly 8 million thalers packed away in casks in the cellars of the royal palace. He had transformed the bulk of the nobility into a dedicated military caste, brought the workers under state supervision, and forced the peasants to provide recruits for his army and to pay about 40 percent of their income in state taxes. He had instilled habits of discipline and obedience into his subjects and had made the state into an armed camp. Finally, with the small population and still backward economy at his disposal, he had built up the fourth largest and the best-trained army in Europe. This was the army with which his son defied the great powers during the wars of the mid-eighteenth century.

Frederick II (1740–1786) became one of the most impressive kings of modern times. He knew he was brilliant, and he believed that any task he set himself would turn out better than if left to a subordinate. Despite all the new agencies he created, he tried to run the state almost by himself: like Louis XIV, he set a model of kingship that few could follow successfully. He earned the title "the Great" as a result of his military and political achievements.

Frederick the Great's wars weakened Prussia economically only temporarily. In the long run, the conquest of the Austrian province of Silesia in the early 1740s more than paid for itself, adding almost 2 million people and rich natural resources to the national economy. Frederick did little to improve the lot of Prussia's peasants, but he forced them to grow—and eat—new crops like the potato and the sugar beet; in the early 1770s there would have been a danger of famine without the potato. Frederick encouraged the domestic system of manufacturing under private entrepreneurs and started Berlin on the path toward industrialization in the production of silk and woolen textiles. As under his father, nearly two-thirds of the state revenue went to the support of the army. But under Frederick the improved national economy was able to sustain a peacetime army of almost 200,000 men, nearly 4 percent of the population.

The one area of Prussian life in which Frederick made a pioneer effort was the administration of justice. In 1746, with the help of the Prussian chief justice, Samuel von Cocceji, he set out to establish a single centralized judicial system, to weed out incompetent lawyers and judges, and to codify the law for the whole realm. Although the legal code was not completed until 1795, the first two goals were achieved within five years. The ordinary citizen now had greatly increased security in his civil rights, and especially in his property rights. Frederick's judicial reforms thus encouraged capitalistic development as well as consolidating the power of the state.

Under the Old Regime no state was a true national community, but Prussia remained more divided socially and culturally than France or even Spain. As in these countries, social barriers remained rigid, and people of different classes and estates were taxed and rewarded in unequal ways. In Prussia, however, the Junkers served the state as an exclusive military caste and prevented the king from abolishing the forced labor of their unfree peasants. Prussia's business and professional classes lacked initiative and did little to further the intellectual life of the country. The leading lights at Frederick the Great's court and at the Berlin Academy were mostly foreigners. Although the ancestral Hohenzollern lands were overwhelmingly Protestant, Frederick added at least 2 million Silesian and Polish Catholics to his realm, and he himself was a Deist. Thus neither religion nor a native high culture gave Prussia a community spirit; the power of the state alone provided its unifying superstructure.

The Emergence of Russia

Like the Hohenzollerns in Prussia and the Hapsburgs in Austria, the Romanov dynasty, which came to the Russian throne in 1613, created an Old Regime that was to last until World War I. In the eighteenth century the two outstanding Russian rulers who tried to transform their backward country into a great power along Western lines were Peter the Great (1682–1725) and Catherine the Great (1762–1796).

Seventeenth-century life in Muscovite Russia was a mixture of Byzantine and Tatar forms grafted onto old Russian customs. At the court in Moscow the tsar and his noblemen all wore long beards and dressed in long flowing robes with wide sleeves. The court nobles were superstitious and preoccupied with protocol. The service nobles (*dvoriane*) wielded administrative, military, judicial, and police power throughout the country and became the absolute masters over the peasants on their estates. The small group of merchants and craftsmen in the towns remained as custom-bound and unenterprising as the rest of the population, except for the German colony in a suburb of the capital. The Russian Orthodox church dominated the intellectual and artistic life of the country, so that Russia, in contrast to the countries of Western Europe, had no national secular culture. Millions of people still observed the formal church ritual, but it had lost much of its spiritual force.

Russia thus remained backward and poor. Its peasants lived at a near-subsistence level constantly threatened by famines. Consumption of alcoholic beverages was directly related to the people's misery, and the Russian masses were to hold the record in Europe well into the twentieth century. Impoverished by their low productivity, Russia's peasants sank increasingly to the level of serfs, as they could not meet their obligation of labor and cash to their landlords and the additional taxes to the tsar's government. Hence many of them became serfs voluntarily—in effect, the private property of their masters—because serfs did not have to pay taxes.

The discontented masses, especially those in Russia's southern borderlands, did not always accept their lot without protest. Groups of fighting frontiersmen known as Cossacks defied the central government and tried to lead an independent existence in the vast plains of the Ukraine from the Dnieper to the Volga rivers. In 1670 a Don Cossack named Stenka Razin led a revolt that assumed the proportion of a national uprising. Peasants began killing their landlords as far north as Moscow itself. The government put down Razin's revolt, but similar uprisings were to be regular occurrences in later centuries.

This was the Russia that Peter the Great tried to "westernize" and organize into a European power. His primary reason for westernizing was the need to modernize his army in order to defeat the powerful, modern army of the Swedes and to gain a short water route to Europe and Baltic bases for his navy. The second motive was to create an efficient, loyal bureaucracy that would make his political power absolute. What Peter wanted from the west was the *techniques* that would give him a strong army and a strong government.

Peter himself was an impressive person. He was well over six feet tall and physically attractive, despite a slight nervous twitch. His energy was enormous, and his mind inquisitive. In many respects, however, he was the opposite of his older contemporary Louis XIV of France. He wore simple clothes, beat his courtiers with a club, and used foul language. Shortly after becoming tsar, he made a tour of Western Europe. To the Western Europeans, Peter seemed like an Asiatic potentate who had discovered technology and who tried to force his superstitious and benighted subjects to become engineers and mechanics overnight, for he had been impressed by the shipbuilding techniques of the Dutch and the English and tried to copy them.

In 1700 Peter's first attack against Sweden's East Baltic territories was a disaster, despite the fact that it was launched in alliance with Denmark and Poland. Luckily for Peter, however, the Swedish king, Charles XII, directed his attention against Poland instead of following up his victory over the Russians. During the next few years Peter had time to remodel his army and build up his navy with the help of technicians and generals imported from Western Europe.

The war with Sweden was resumed in 1709 and dragged on until 1721, when Russia finally emerged victorious. It received all of the Swedish lands on the Baltic Sea from southern Finland to Poland (see map, p. 357), all inhabited by non-Russians. Spectacular celebrations attended by representatives of many European countries marked the final achievement of the long-sought and hard-earned victory. Peter had already begun the construction of a new capital, called St. Petersburg, near the Baltic coast, his new "Window on the West," and changed his title from "Tsar of all the Russias" to "Emperor of all the Russias."

Like most of Peter's celebrated reforms, the new town and the change of title were direct or indirect outgrowths of military needs. Because Peter's wars consumed tremendous amounts of money, he instituted tax reforms to increase the government's income. In order to levy and collect taxes more ef-

A seventeenth-century image of a fierce Cossack.

ficiently he took a census; peasants and serfs formed one category in this census, in effect, degrading the peasants to serfdom. Peter also had to improve and enlarge his bureaucracy to carry out his tax reforms and to make educational reforms that would provide a supply of trained administrators. One reform led to another with no long-range planning; most of them were hastily improvised under wartime pressures, and many of them did not last beyond Peter's death.

The only governing principle behind Peter's reforms was his conviction that every one of his subjects, from the lowest serf to the highest noble, should pay taxes and serve the state in some capacity. The census of 1718 created more male serfs and made them all liable for the new poll (head) tax. State peasants—those who worked the lands owned by the crown—were technically free, but their lives differed little from those of the serfs. Unattached free men were conscripted into the army, assigned to the estate of some landlord, or put into forced labor in state-owned forests and mines. Peter, a good mercantilist, organized the urban craftsmen into associations and guilds and encouraged the wealthier merchants to found new industries. But he forced them to pay heavier taxes than ever and to submit to close government supervision.

All nobles were required to enlist in the service of the state for life. Peter abolished the remaining titles and privileges of the old hereditary nobility. He tried to establish the principle that everyone, noble or commoner, should earn his rank by working up to it in some agency of the state. Hating these obligations, the nobles tried to evade them whenever possible. Nevertheless, Peter's Table of Ranks (1722) was his most lasting reform. It created an official class that kept the masses in check and served the state until the twentieth century.

The church did not escape Peter's attention either. He felt that whatever influence it still had over the masses should be placed directly in the service of the state. He abolished the office of patriarch and put a layman in charge of the newly created Holy Synod for Church Affairs. There was opposition to this plan, but this reform also lasted until the twentieth century.

In his later years Peter placed a new emphasis on Western cultural models, at least, for his court nobles. His first step was to issue a translation of a German handbook on gentlemanly behavior (1717). Gentlemen would henceforth not pick their noses or clean their teeth with a knife, they would spit to one side and not in the midst of a group, they would doff their hats to acquaintances at three paces distance. Peter forced the noblemen to shave off their beards and to don wigs and Western-style clothing, and he even succeeded in forcing the noble ladies out of their accustomed seclusion and onto the dance floor.

Peter's emphasis on Western culture affected only a thin upper crust of Russian society. Only gradually during the eighteenth century did the court and higher nobles adopt the behavior and thought patterns of the west. But instead of providing the dynamic leadership that Peter had intended,

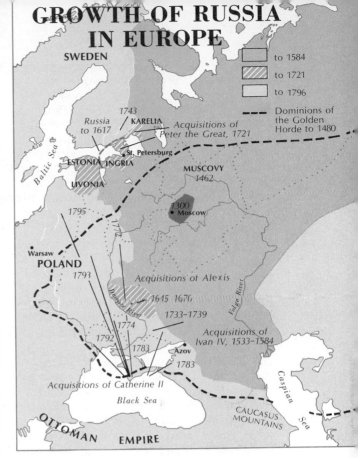

they devoted their energies and imagination to outdoing their aristocratic Western European teachers in extravagant and irresponsible living. They spoke French (the international language of the cosmopolitan eighteenth-century aristocracy); they built lavish palaces in St. Petersburg; they had as little contact as possible with their estates and the miserable wretches whose forced labor provided them with their income. Despite the new names Peter gave things, Russia's social structure, political institutions, and economic practices remained basically unchanged. Still, like Frederick William I of Prussia, Peter did succeed in giving his realm a militaristic stamp. And, like Frederick the Great, he made his country a great power.

Perhaps Peter's greatest failure was his inability to provide for an orderly and peaceful succession to the throne. Catherine the Great, a German princess, came to power in 1762 in the last of the palace revolutions that became a standard after Peter's death. During the intervening years the emperors and empresses of Russia had needed the support of the noble palace guards against rival claimants to the throne, and in order to get it they considerably reduced the nobles' obligations for state service. Then Peter III, Catherine's husband, dramatically released them from these obligations altogether.

Catherine was an intelligent and forceful woman. Determined to rule alone, she won the backing of the palace guards and with it overthrew the unfortunate Peter, whom her zealous backers then killed. She corresponded with the most brilliant writers of Western Europe, had many lovers, and tried to project the image of an enlightened despot (see pp. 402–403). But in the early 1770s the greatest peasant uprising in Russia's history, led by the Volga Cossack Emilian Pugachev, forced her to restore the historic link between the landlord and his serfs and the power of the ruler over all his subjects. This Catherine did in the Charter of the Nobility in 1785, which confirmed the nobles' freedom from state service and reduced the serfs to the status of chattel slaves who could be bought and sold at will. Thus, aside from further enslaving the masses, Catherine changed Russia even less than Peter the Great had done. Her main achievements were her foreign conquests.

THE POWER STRUGGLE IN CENTRAL AND EASTERN EUROPE, 1740–1795

Although Frederick the Great "started" the War of the Austrian Succession in 1740, a number of other rulers quickly joined him in trying to despoil Maria Theresa of territories whose integrity they had agreed to respect in the Pragmatic Sanction. Two months after Frederick's quick conquest of Silesia in April 1741, France signed an alliance with Prussia; Bavaria and Saxony soon joined this alliance. Spain, too, entered the conflict in the hope of conquering Hapsburg possessions in Italy.

The War of the Austrian Succession was a typical example of eighteenth-century international relations. Like the War of the Spanish Succession, 40 years earlier, it involved dynastic claims, "reasons of state," sheer aggression, and the maintenance of the balance of power. As always, Great Britain

aided the enemies of France; in the 1740s this meant mainly Austria. But as each belligerent pursued its own goals, the alliance against Austria gradually disintegrated. In the peace settlement of 1748, Maria Theresa recovered all her possessions except Silesia and some small Italian territories. This peace treaty, however, did not settle the future of Central Europe any more than it laid to rest the conflict between Great Britain and France.

Between the end of the War of the Austrian Succession and the outbreak of the Seven Years' War, a "diplomatic revolution" took shape; it was instigated by Prince Wenceslas Anton von Kaunitz (1711–1794), Maria Theresa's shrewd state chancellor. He wanted to bring France and Russia into a grand alliance that would leave Prussia isolated. Then Austria could destroy her, reannex Silesia, and reestablish traditional Hapsburg leadership in Germany. But Kaunitz did not get his French alliance until the other three powers played into his hands.

Great Britain took the first step by signing a convention with Russia in September 1755. In return for a subsidy, Empress Elizabeth (1741–1762) promised to attack Frederick II from the rear if he should join France in an attack on Hanover (the English king's homeland). Frederick now faced the threat of a combined onslaught by Great Britain, Austria, and Russia. In January 1756 he escaped from this threat by signing his own convention with the English. This convention made Prussia, rather than Russia, the guarantor of Hanover; in return, the German States would not enter the Anglo-French war that had already broken out in North America.

The Anglo-Prussian convention at last persuaded the French that Kaunitz was right, that Austria and France should forget their ancient rivalry and work together against their now common enemies. The French reaction was based on a wish to punish Frederick for his scarcely concealed contempt for them. If not for this, the neutralization of Germany would have allowed France to concentrate its energies on the colonial struggle with Great Britain, thus serving its real interests. Although still unwilling to contemplate offensive action against Prussia, the French signed a defen-

Frederick the Great before the Battle of Leuthen.

sive alliance with Austria in May 1756. To seal the bargain, Maria Theresa gave her daughter Marie Antoinette in marriage to the heir-apparent to the French throne, the future Louis XVI. Kaunitz's "diplomatic revolution" was completed when Russia, also resentful of Frederick's convention with Great Britain, finally joined the Franco-Austrian alliance at the end of the year.

Frederick the Great's fortunes rose and fell several times during the Seven Years' War (1756–1763). In November 1757 he won his greatest victory at Rossbach over Franco-Austrian forces twice the size of his own.

Nevertheless, in the years 1758 to 1761 Prussia's military position steadily worsened. Frederick's salvation came in early 1762 as a result of the defection of Russia. Empress Elizabeth, in some ways an even more inveterate enemy than Maria Theresa, died in January. Peter III, her unstable successor, was a fanatical admirer of Frederick and he ordered an immediate armistice. With Russia out of the war and the British victory over the French almost complete, Maria Theresa could no longer hope to recover Silesia.

The Central European phase of the Seven Years' War ended in February 1763 with signing of the Treaty of Hubertusburg. The relative positions of Prussia and Austria in Germany had not really changed since 1742. But a great deal else had changed. Great Britain and France had reversed their alliances with the German powers. The Treaty of Paris, which ended the Anglo-French phase of the Seven Years' War, gave Great Britain complete mastery in North America and India. And British concessions to defeated France in the West Indies gained Prussia more favorable terms than it could have expected on the basis of its own performance.

Ironically, the real victor of the Seven Years' War was Russia; in 1763 it was a stronger force than ever in European international relations. When Peter III's wife Catherine became empress she withdrew from the war entirely. For the moment she concentrated on consolidating her power at home; then she was ready to embark on her own program of expansion in Eastern Europe. Neither Prussia nor Austria had really won the Seven Years' War. Whereas they had to be satisfied with the status quo of the 1740s in Germany until almost the end of the century, Russia took the lead in partitioning the vast territories of Poland and the Ottoman Empire.

Between 1772 and 1795 Catherine's armies added hundreds of thousands of square miles and several million non-Russian people to the Russian Empire at the expense of Poland and Turkey. Since each act of Russian imperialism against these two countries threatened the balance of power in Eastern Europe, the other great powers became involved, either to preserve the balance or to gain "compensation." France, Austria, and ultimately Great Britain supported the Turks against the Russians. On the other hand, Poland's neighbors, Prussia and Austria, joined Russia in gobbling up that country completely.

Russia's first war with Turkey began in 1768. Despite brilliant Russian victories in the Black Sea and the Balkans, the domestic difficulties that led to the Pugachev revolt forced Catherine to accept a compromise peace in 1774. According to the Treaty of Kuchuk Kainardji, Russia acquired the northern shore of the Black Sea and detached the Crimea from Turkish control, but it had to give up its conquests in the Danube Valley. The bulk of the Ottoman Empire still stood, but its territorial integrity was threatened by a provision in the treaty authorizing Russia to protect certain Orthodox churches within its borders.

This provision of the Treaty of Kuchuk Kainardji thus opened a new era in European politics. Russia was to use it again and again as an excuse to interfere in Turkish affairs, taking another slice of territory each time. Although Austria had taken its share of Turkish land, it was soon to join France and Great Britain in defending the Ottoman Empire against Russian aggression. This happened after Catherine's second war against the Turks (1787–1792), in which Russia pushed its boundary westward to the Dniester River.

Meanwhile eighteenth-century Poland could not defend itself against its more powerful neighbors. Like Hungary, Poland was a multinational landlord state dominated by nobles who jealously guarded their medieval liberties. But unlike Hungary, which was part of the Austrian Monarchy, Poland was not attached to a great power. The Polish "state" was still medieval; it had no large standing army, no bureaucracy, no national law courts, and no national taxation system. In its diet any nobleman could stop any positive action by the king by casting a negative vote—a *liberum veto*. When Catherine's army forced King Stanislas to grant his Orthodox subjects equal rights with Catholics, the Polish nobles formed the Confederation of Bar (1768) and fought Stanislas and the Russians for four years. Fearing a Russian victory, Austria and Prussia seriously considered entering the conflict. To avoid a military confrontation, Frederick the Great took the diplomatic initiative and organized the First Partition of Poland in 1772. (See maps, pp. 249, 252, 257.)

This land grab illustrated perfectly the cynicism and hypocrisy of eighteenth-century rulers. "In the name of the Holy Trinity . . . and out of fear of the total disintegration of the Polish state" Maria Theresa annexed the province of Galicia, with its two-and-one-half million inhabitants. She cried, but she considered Galicia just "compensation" for the loss of Silesia. Frederick

Turkish cavalry in the late seventeenth century.

took most of West Prussia with over half a million inhabitants, thereby filling in the gap between East Prussia and the main part of his kingdom. Catherine, preoccupied with the Turks, had to be content with a slice of eastern Lithuania, with 1,700,000 inhabitants.

In 1793 and 1795 neither the efforts of Polish patriots to revitalize their kingdom nor the preoccupation of the three "interested" powers with the wars of the French Revolution prevented the Second and Third Partitions of Poland. In the name of "compensation Poland had been completely destroyed, and contempt for the rights of states and peoples had been transformed into a system.

By the late eighteenth century the modern European state system was fully developed. There were five great powers, each with a strong central government, a sizable military establishment, and a sophisticated diplomacy. The declining states on the periphery of Western Europe — Spain, Portugal, the Dutch Republic, Denmark, Sweden — managed to carry on an independent existence. But Poland disappeared from the map, and the smaller states of Germany were the pawns of the great powers. For power alone decided the relations between states in eighteenth-century Europe.

The three eastern powers were catching up with Great Britain and France in political and military organization and in their techniques of foreign policy, but they remained backward in other ways. In Western Europe commercial capitalism was successfully exploiting the labor and resources of America, Asia, and Africa with the most advanced techniques of the preindustrial era. This spirit of initiative — leaving aside the injustices it perpetrated — was lacking in Eastern Europe. With a few notable exceptions, most of the scientific and intellectual innovators of the eighteenth century were Western Europeans, as we shall see in the next chapter. The lower classes deferred to the aristocracy everywhere but, except in parts of Prussia and Austria, the Eastern European middle class was small, barely tolerated, and often foreign (Jewish or German in Russia and Poland, Greek in the Ottoman Empire).

The extent of Russia's backwardness was dramatized by the effect of its newly conquered territories on its internal development. The bulk of these territories were to the west, and usually more advanced than Russia itself. All three of the new great powers of Eastern Europe became multinational empires as a result of their annexations, but the Russian Empire had the most trouble in assimilating its conquered minorities. Its Baltic provinces were almost entirely non-Russian; except for the immediate vicinity of the new capital of St. Petersburg, they were inhabited by Estonians, Latvians, Lithuanians, and Germans. The Russian government generally allowed the German landlords to rule the Baltic area as they had done for centuries, at the same time using their superior military and administrative abilities for national purposes. It had greater difficulty absorbing the millions of Belorussians, Ukrainians, Lithuanians, Poles, and Jews it had taken from the old Kingdom of Poland. These troublesome minorities — especially the Poles and Jews* — were to make Russian governments increasingly intolerant and reactionary.

At the end of the eighteenth century the Old Regime in Prussia and Austria also became reactionary in many respects. Austria had created the beginnings of a modern bureaucracy and judicial system, but the noble princes in Hungary and Galicia still ruled the local populations like semifeudal lords. Prussia was the most tightly organized of the three eastern powers, but its annexation of Poland caused problems and it was becoming complacent at home. The social structures of Russia, Austria, and Prussia remained rigid, and serfdom still prevailed. Neither the ideas of the Enlightenment nor the French Revolution were able to persuade the reactionary rulers of Eastern Europe to abolish this most backward and pernicious institution of their Old Regime.

* By 1795 the bulk of Europe's Jews lived in the Russian Empire.

SUGGESTED READINGS

Friedrich, Carl J. and Charles Blitzer, *The Age of Power,* Ithaca, N.Y.: Cornell University Press, 1957. Paperback.
  A short survey covering the period 1685–1715. Excellent.

Lewis, W. H., *The Splendid Century: Life in the France of Louis XIV.* Garden City, N.Y.: Doubleday and Co., 1957. Paperback.
  Lively and rich in detail.

Anderson, Matthew S., *The Eighteenth Century, 1718–1783,* New York: Oxford University Press, 1964. Paperback.
A very good survey in comparative history.

Laslett, Peter, *The World We Have Lost.* New York: Scribner, n.d. Paperback.
Good on demographic, economic, and social patterns of preindustrial England.

Wright, L. B., *The Atlantic Frontier: Colonial American Civilization, 1607–1763.* Volume III of the New American Nation Series, ed. Richard B. Morris and Henry S. Commager, Ithaca, N.Y.: Cornell University Press, 1963. Paperback.
An authoritative survey.

Gooch, George P., *Maria Theresa and Other Studies.* London and New York: Longmans, Green, 1951.
See especially the suggestive appraisal of Maria Theresa.

Lindsay, J. O., ed., *The Old Regime, 1713–1763.* Volume VII of *The New Cambridge Modern History,* Cambridge, Eng.: Cambridge University Press, 1957.
The chapter by David B. Horn on the diplomatic revolution is outstanding.

Sumner, B. H., *Peter the Great and the Emergence of Russia.* New York: The Macmillan Co., 1962. Collier Books. Paperback.
The best study in English.

Soloveytchik, George, Potemkin: *A Picture of Catherine's Russia.* London: T. Butterworths, 1938.
Delivers what the title promises.

Gershoy, Leo, *From Despotism to Revolution, 1763–1789.* New York: Harper and Row, 1963. Torchbook. Paperback.
Another excellent volume in the Rise of Modern Europe series. The best general account of Enlightened Despotism.

CHAPTER **12**

Civilization under the Old Regime, 1648–1789

The principles of authority, reason, and order were used by Europe's rulers from Louis XIV onward to end the religious and constitutional struggles of the early modern period, but the intellectual and cultural life of Europe was not so easily tamed. During the seventeenth century many educated Europeans experienced a crisis of thought and feeling which was vividly expressed by Pascal, Milton, and Rembrandt and, into the first half of the eighteenth century, by Bach. In an era increasingly dominated by rational, "linear" modes of thought, architecture was the first art-form to abandon the intense and agitated style of the baroque for classicism, and music was the last. Although the scientific revolution of the seventeenth century did not resolve the European crisis in thought and feeling, during the eighteenth century it gave the men of the Enlightenment their qualified belief in progress.

The new knowledge combined with the belief that it could be applied in ways that would improve the world proved the necessary first step in the process of modernization. The second step, the consolidation of

modernizing leadership, began with the English, American, and French Revolutions.* The third step—economic and social transformation through industrialization and urbanization—and the fourth step—the integration of all sections of the population into a single national society—were taking place in bourgeois democracies in the late nineteenth and twentieth centuries. But in the late nineteenth century, authoritarian leaders in Germany and Japan were able to modernize from above without liberal and democratic forms. And in the twentieth century Communist leaders, after completing the overthrow of the Old Regime begun by Russian and Chinese liberals, forced modernization on their subjects with unprecedented ruthlessness.

European civilization in the eighteenth century in many respects was no more modern than other great civilizations of the past, from Rome to China. Not until 1757, at the Battle of Plassey, did a European power gain its first major military victory over an oriental

* To be discussed in Chapter 13.

364

potentate on his own soil. Not until 1763 did James Watt begin his experiments with the steam engine. The first successful democratic revolution did not get under-way until 1776, and this was in an area where there was virtually no privileged aristocracy or established church. In England the traditional peasantry and landlords had been removed as obstacles to the consolidation of modernizing leadership (see p. 394), yet this consolidation was far from complete at the end of the eighteenth century. The one thing that eighteenth-century European civilization had more of than all the others was knowledge.

GROWTH OF APPLIED KNOWLEDGE

Until the last century the history of technology was a slow, haphazard evolution of tricks of the trade drawn from the experience of anonymous craftsmen. During the seventeenth and eighteenth centuries science was in its formative stage, preoccupied with its own foundations rather than with the practical applications of its theories, although there were some exceptions. Printing from movable type was an excellent example of applied knowledge, rather than new knowledge. Before printing, manuscripts were written and reproduced by hand. Typography mechanized the handicraft of the scribe by visually arresting and splitting up the act of writing. Other examples of mechanization through applied knowledge, from the wheel onward, include levers, pulleys, gears, couplings, and wind- and water mills.

Other civilizations made noteworthy inventions, but it was the Europeans, conditioned to linear thinking through print, who eventually separated the functions inherent in industry and applied knowledge. The Chinese pioneered in the invention of paper, printing, gunpowder, and the compass. Yet they did not develop the modern scientific approach and industrialization because, for one thing, "the purpose of printing for them was not the creation of uniform repeatable products for a market and a price system. Print was an alternative to their prayer-wheels and was a visual means of multiplying incantatory spells, much like advertising

in our age" (McLuhan, *The Gutenberg Galaxy,* p. 34).

Even in Europe the habit of using applied knowledge in new ways came slowly. The distinguished American historian Samuel Eliot Morison has expressed his bewilderment over the fact that Columbus' starving sailors were unable to catch fish when their ships were grounded near the shores of the New World. The reason was that in 1492 people had not yet acquired the ability to translate one kind of experience into new patterns. The first great literary tribute to applied knowledge was Daniel Defoe's *Robinson Crusoe* (1720), whose hero exemplified the adaptability and resourcefulness of the new, modern man.

The capitalist entrepreneur was another type of new, modern man. The entrepreneur found that certain inventions were profitable when organized into large-scale businesses. The European book trade is a good example: between the 1440s (when the first printed books were published) and the year 1500, 20 million books were sold; between 1500 and 1600, 140 to 200 million; for the eighteenth century the figure was more than half a billion. Another example of a major advance in applied knowledge organized on a capitalist basis was commercial navigation on the high seas: in 1600 Europe had, perhaps, 600,000 to 700,000 tons of merchant shipping; by the 1780s, it had almost three and one-half million tons.

Another major technological advance of the early modern period—gunpowder—was organized and promoted by governments. Primitive muskets and cannon came into general use at the end of the fifteenth century and were improved gradually thereafter. In the eighteenth century the most striking improvement was in land artillery. A French artillery officer named Jean-Baptiste Vaquette de Gribeauval made all parts of any type of cannon interchangeable, so that repairs would be possible near the battlefield. In order to make his lighter cannon more mobile (the heavier ones he reserved for sieges), he improved the harness with which the horses pulled them. The cannon could now be drawn into battle at a trot over rough terrain. Finally, he improved the accuracy and range of his cannon with sights and

Eighteenth-century merchants and craftsmen peddling their wares.

elevating mechanisms. Thus, through specialization and improved techniques, the smoothbore cannon became a deadly weapon in the service of the infantry.

Between the mid-fifteenth and mid-eighteenth centuries a slow growth in applied knowledge had created the necessary base for the Industrial Revolution, which came only with the large-scale use of steam power in the nineteenth century. Some historians call the accumulation of mechanical techniques during those centuries a pre-industrial revolution. Complicated machines were used in mining, metallurgy, and textile manufacturing, with cranks, lifting jacks, connecting rods, gear systems, and transmission

Illustration of a pin factory, from Diderot's Encyclopedia.

chains regulated by flywheels. During the second half of the eighteenth century lathes, drills, and reamers, all of which had been known for a long time, were adapted for industrial use. Those were also the years in which the spinning jenny and flying shuttle were first used to mechanize the textile industry. But these and other new machines were limited by existing forms of energy: water power and wind power were hopelessly inadequate. Until the advent of steam power, Europe's main sources of energy were beasts of burden and burning wood. Nevertheless, the advent of steam power had been prepared and made possible by the extension of applied knowledge in the preceding centuries.

The first important break in traditional methods of farming also occurred in eighteenth-century England. By careful experimentation, Jethro Tull discovered that dropping seeds into rows of holes produced higher crop yields than the traditional method of simply throwing seeds on the surface of the ground. Lord (Turnip) Townsend discovered that crop rotation preserved the nutritive elements in a given plot of land better than letting it lie fallow periodically. Furthermore, the turnips and clover that he rotated with wheat provided forage for livestock.

Improvements in agriculture made possible a new wave of population growth in the eighteenth century. Selective breeding produced better meat and heavier cattle, sheep, and hogs to feed an ever-growing urban population of well-to-do citizens. The greatest growth came among the rural poor. Here the lowly potato was particularly important. Introduced into Ireland in the early eighteenth century, it allowed the population of that country to double in less than 100 years. Its effect in preventing famine in Prussia in the 1770s has already been mentioned. By the end of the eighteenth century the potato had become the staple food for millions of European peasants, including those in Russia.

Before the Industrial Revolution the most effective use of applied knowledge was made by businessmen in mobilizing labor and capital for ever-increasing profits. The mobilization of labor in the domestic system of manufacturing in Europe was mentioned previously (see p. 323). In the early seventeenth century the English and Dutch East India Companies introduced a new form of business organization, the joint-stock company, which was later extended to banking and mining. Its main advantage was that it could mobilize large amounts of capital for long periods of time, since it was a permanent partnership of shareholders who received periodic profits on their investments. By 1715 there were 140 joint-stock companies in England alone. Stock exchanges facilitated the sale of stocks to the public in Amsterdam and London by the late seventeenth century and in Paris after 1724.

Paper money also came into wide use in the early eighteenth century. The Bank of England and the Bank of Amsterdam received large stocks of precious metals for safekeeping in their vaults and issued bank notes that were promises to pay a given amount of gold or silver to the bearer on demand. Experience showed that all the bearers of these notes did not demand such payment at the same time. Consequently, the banks issued more paper money than their reserves of precious metals could cover. This paper currency added greatly to the total amount of money available for business transactions and new investments. Along with later forms of paper credit, paper money was one of the most original examples of applied knowledge perfected by Europeans.

THE SCIENTIFIC REVOLUTION

In the long run new scientific knowledge had more profound effects than applied knowledge, since it changed men's thinking as well as their behavior. Educated Europeans from the eleventh to the seventeenth century had borrowed heavily from the civilization of the ancient Mediterranean world in thought and letters; in the thirteenth century, Greek achievements in science and mathematics also began to be known through Latin translations from Arabic, and authentic Greek texts were known during the Renaissance. By the mid-sixteenth century the whole body of Greek scientific knowledge was readily available in printed books.

The Greeks had produced Archimedes and other scientists, yet only in the seventeenth century did the *method* of Archimedes gradually replace that of Aristotle as the accepted source of knowledge about the natural world. That is, the scientific method displaced philosophy: where philosophy sought knowledge through speculation and logic, science seeks it through experimentally controlled theories. Until this happened, the study of nature was more philosophical than scientific.

Galileo and Kepler

The first modern physicists and astronomers were as eager as earlier philosophers to find the divine plan of the world. What made them revolutionary was their insistence on controlling their new theories with repeatable visual proof. Galileo described the new attitude in this passage:

It is the followers of Aristotle who have crowned him with authority, not he who has usurped or appropriated it to himself. And since it is handier to conceal oneself under the cloak of another than to show one's face in open court, they dare not in their timidity get a single step away from him, and rather than put any alterations in the heavens of Aristotle, they want to deny out of hand those that they see in nature's heaven.

As a precursor of modern science the Pole Nicholas Copernicus (1473–1543) is more significant for having invented a mathematical planetary *system* than for having postulated a moving earth and a stationary sun. He opened the way for a new type of thinking, which was to explain the movement of bodies in the heavens and on earth in terms of mathematically expressed natural laws. In mathematics the value of most symbols is a *function* of something else. It now remained for the notion of functionality to triumph in the laws of the natural world.

The Italian Galileo Galilei (1564–1642) was the first modern scientist to support mathematical theories about the physical world with observations and experiments. He directed the mind toward problems that could be handled through measurement and calculation. According to him, the scientist should seek to examine shape, size, quantity, and motion rather than commonsense phenomena and the ordinary appearances of bodies, which all his predecessors had primarily dealt with.

Galileo destroyed the classical astronomy of Ptolemy with his telescopic observations. Borrowing the techniques of a Dutch lensmaker, he constructed his own telescope in 1609 and turned it toward the heavens. Men had been gazing at the stars for thousands of years, but no one had ever seen what Galileo saw. He saw four of the satellites of Jupiter and regarded them as a visible model of the whole solar system. By observing that Venus had phases like the moon he deduced that this planet revolved around the sun.

Galileo's observations supported Coper-

* From Galileo Galilei, *Dialogue Concerning the Two Chief World Systems—Ptolemaic and Copernican,* tr. Stillman Drake (Berkeley: University of Calif. Press, 1953), p. 111.

nicus arguments against Ptolemy, and they dealt a crushing blow to Aristotle. For Galileo could *demonstrate* to anyone who would look through his telescope that the universe was a physical structure containing two types of physical bodies, stars and planets. Contrary to Aristotle's thesis, the heavens were not perfect, invariable, and essentially different from earthly things. The earth was a planet. It was composed of the same kind of physical matter as Venus, Mars, Mercury, and Jupiter and, contrary to Ptolemy's thesis, all these planets revolved around the sun.

Some university professors refused to look through Galileo's telescope; all astrologers went on talking about the supposed influences of the stars on human behavior; and in 1633 the Roman Inquisition compelled Galileo to "abjure, curse, and detest" the Copernican doctrine as a heresy. But Galileo's real convictions were clear: the new natural philosophy that he helped to found had to view the universe as governed by laws of motion.

Galileo's greatest achievement was in the mathematical analysis of motion. Through numerous and complex physical and mental experiments and mathematical calculations he discovered the principle of inertia. Here, too, he completed the refutation of Aristotle, whose theory of motion had already been under attack for 200 years. According to Aristotle, the "purpose" of a moving body was to seek a resting place, and it required a continuously acting force to remain in motion. To Galileo, a body in motion along a straight line would not only go on moving indefinitely without any continuously acting force, it would also require some other force to stop it. From this single discovery Galileo was able to build up a whole theory of mechanics. This great achievement showed a rapid evolution in thought requiring clarity of definition, a systematic elaboration of mathematical expression, the rethinking of the nature of motion, and an ingenious recognition of functions that made quantitative calculations possible.

Galileo never compared the motion of a projectile with that of a planet; it was his German contemporary Johannes Kepler (1571–1630) who first described the laws of planetary motion. The two men referred favorably to each other's work and corresponded regularly for many years, but they followed independent paths in their studies. The synthesis of their two distinct points of view was not to come until a generation after both had died.

These two founders of modern science were utterly different kinds of men. Despite his mathematical ingenuity and his interest in astronomy, Galileo was "down to earth" both temperamentally and in his main scientific concerns. He became a conscious propagandist for the new natural philosophy and wrote many of his books in Italian so that others besides scholars could read them. His *Dialogue Concerning the Two Chief World Systems* was a truly popular book. Kepler, on the other hand, was the prototype of the Central European mathematical genius—retiring, eccentric, and incapable of communicating his thoughts in ordinary language. He was "up in the clouds" both temperamentally and in his main scientific concerns. His books, which were written in abstruse Latin and permeated with number-mysticism, show the kind of man he was: two good examples are the *Cosmographic Mystery* (1597) and *The Harmonies of the World* (1619).

Yet part of Kepler's genius lay in his ability to overcome his superstitions about the mystical meanings of numbers and perfect geometrical forms in the interest of quantitative accuracy. He would have liked the true orbits of the five known planets of his day to have been perfect circles and to have corresponded to the five regular solids. But this fantastic scheme did not fit the set of *quantitative* observations that he had acquired from his patron and friend, the Danish astronomer, Tycho Brahe (1546–1601). As a true scientist, therefore, Kepler revised his theory to fit the best set of facts available to him. The result was that he discovered the first two laws of planetary motion: (1) the planets move on elliptical, not circular orbits, with the sun at one focus; (2) the line joining the sun and a planet sweeps out equal areas in equal times (see diagram). With the aid of the improved trigonometry of his day and the invention of logarithms by the Englishman John Napier (1550–1617),

Tycho Brahe in his planetarium.

Kepler discovered his third law of planetary motion: the squares of the period of the orbit are proportional to the cubes of their mean distance from the sun.

Kepler not only discovered the new descriptive laws of planetary motion, he also showed the possibility of a new physical theory of the universe. Galileo had gone part of the way in giving Copernicus' mathematical model a physical explanation. Kepler went further. It was he who first conceived of the universe as a *system* of bodies whose arrangement and motions could be explained by universal generalizations demonstrable from qualitative observations and checked by accurate quantitative measurements. This was the true significance of the scientific revolution.

Neither Galileo nor Kepler saw that the same mechanical laws might apply on earth and in the heavens. Descartes suggested that a Universal Mathematics was needed to describe the universal laws of motion. But not until Newton combined mathematics with new experiments was the synthesis of Galileo's earthly mechanics and Kepler's celestial mechanics fully achieved.

Descartes and Newton

The Frenchman René Descartes (1596–1650) came closer than anyone else to making himself the Aristotle of the new science and the new philosophy. Like Aristotle, he was a philosopher first. Like Aristotle, he established an apparently foolproof method of acquiring knowledge. Unlike Aristotle, however, Descartes made significant contributions to the science of physics and was one of the world's great mathematicians.

Descartes not only provided an explanation of the behavior of matter in motion, he also thought it explained everything in the natural world. He provided the explanation by *defining* matter and motion to include everything else—except God and the human soul. According to Descartes' definition, matter is that which occupies space. In other words, it is extension. All other qualities of matter—weight, color, texture, and the like—can be reduced to combinations of its extensive or spatial qualities. Motion is the displacement of matter. That was all there was to it! Descartes said: "Give me motion and extension, and I will construct a world." The world Descartes constructed consisted entirely of particles of matter hitting one another in fixed mechanical patterns.

Descartes made a famous philosophical assumption—the autonomy of the human mind—that hampered his work as a scientist. When he was in his early twenties he experienced a psychological crisis. He wanted to know reality as it really was, and he began to doubt and finally rejected all the traditional sources of this knowledge: Scholastic reasoning, in which he was well-trained, holy scripture, the senses—everything. There was only one thing that he could not throw out: the fact of his doubting. Here was the basic certainty: "I think, therefore, I exist" (*cogito ergo sum*). From this indubitable starting point he could advance afresh with full confidence in the knowledge that his thinking would reveal. As we have stated, Descartes came to explain all natural phenomena, in-

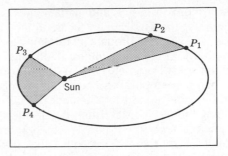

Kepler's First Two Laws of planetary motion.

cluding the human body, as matter in motion. He continued to view the human mind as something different, a kind of ghost, or soul, in the machine. This notion was inconsistent with his own mechanistic view of nature.

Although Descartes was too optimistic in hoping that the mind could duplicate the mechanics of the universe in the abstract symbols of a universal mathematics, his most permanent contribution to modern science was his method of abstract model-building. Today's scientists no longer view their models as ultimate explanations, but they have fully vindicated their use as the best way to make some sense out of what happens in the infinite and infinitesimal "worlds" we cannot see.

Descartes also invented an important mathematical tool, analytical geometry. Since he believed that the more abstract a concept was, the truer it was, he decided to improve the traditional geometry of his day. He eliminated the "accidental" visual aspects of geometrical figures by expressing lines and curves in numerical symbols and their relations in equations. In addition, he introduced the idea of movement, which was lacking in Greek geometry. He determined the position of a point on a graph by its distance from the sides of the graph and thus invented the plotting of a curve. In doing so, Descartes coordinated the geometrical idea of representation with the algebraic idea of two variables in an equation having an indefinite number of simultaneous values. In this way he strengthened the seventeenth-century scientists' habit of viewing everything as a function of everything else.

By the late seventeenth century a number of thinkers had advanced man's knowledge of astronomy, physics, and mathematics considerably; the Englishman Sir Isaac Newton (1642–1727) then brought all this knowledge together into a grand synthesis. Although he did not see all problems in ways unimagined by his contemporaries, Newton exercised greater ability and mathematical skill in solving them. He established the developing physical sciences at a new level where they remained until the nineteenth century was well advanced. Newton brought those branches of physical science that were studied in the seventeenth century to a peak of achievement. He made optics a branch of physics by demonstrating that the theory of light and the theory of matter complemented each other. He gave the principles of dynamics their explicit form and formulated general laws of motion from which Galileo's principle of inertia and Kepler's three laws of planetary motion all followed as necessary consequences. For example, he showed that the Moon's motion, given its distance from the Earth, conformed to the same law as that of freely falling bodies at the Earth's surface. In this and other ways he advanced the idea of a universal gravitational force acting between all particles of matter with an intensity inversely proportional to the squares of their mutual distances. The gravitational force emanating from the sun is sufficient to keep the planets in their orbits, while such a force emanating from a planet keeps its satellites in their orbits.

Like most great scientists, Newton had to invent new techniques for solving problems that the old ones could not handle. The most pressing problem of this type was the mathematical analysis of continuous changes. Now that practically everything was conceived as being in motion, the old kinds of measurements no longer worked. To carry through his mathematical deductions, Newton invented infinitesimal, or fluxionary, calculus,*

---

* The German mathematician-philosopher Gottfried Wilhelm Leibniz (1646–1716) developed a similar calculus with a superior notation independently a few years later. The charges and countercharges of plagiarism between the two men illustrated a new type of problem in scientific research and had the unfortunate result of cutting England off from continental discoveries in pure and applied mathematics until the early nineteenth century.

which was analogous to partial differentiation and partial integration. With this tool he was able to calculate the infinitesimal decrease in the force of gravity at increasing distances from the Earth.

Newton shared Descartes' philosophy of nature as a mechanistic order. He tied this order together with the principle of gravity, but he was unable to explain the *cause* of gravity. His most famous book was *The Mathematical Principles of Natural Philosophy (Philosophiae Naturalis Principia Mathematica)*, first published in 1678 and amended in a second edition in 1713. In this book—usually referred to simply as the *Principia*—he developed a theory that accounted for all matter in motion "as if" it were regulated by gravity. This explanation "worked" better than Descartes' notion of impact. Still, Newton's world was a dull affair, soundless, scentless, colorless. It consisted merely of particles of matter hurrying endlessly and meaninglessly, but in an ordered way capable of being expressed in mathematical formulas. The disciples of Descartes and Newton believed in the same new philosophy. Their main quarrel concerned the proper method of the new science.

The Scientific Method

In the seventeenth century the method of the physical sciences, excluding chemistry, tended to be abstract and mathematical; that of the biological sciences tended to be concrete and descriptive. Despite this variety, the question of the proper method of science became a major issue in the seventeenth century. Some thinkers favored the *empirical* approach, which stressed observation and experiment; others advocated the *rationalistic* or *analytical* approach, which emphasized general ideas.

The first modern prophet of pure empiricism was the English philosopher-statesman Francis Bacon (1561–1626). Like Descartes, Bacon "rang the bell and called the wits together" in the assault on traditional ideas, prejudices, and preconceptions. In his *New Organon*—which was to replace Aristotle's collection of logical treaties of the same name—Bacon insisted on the organizing and recording of experiments as the only sure method of acquiring new knowl-

Louis XIV visiting the French Royal Academy of Sciences.

edge. Unlike Descartes, Bacon performed no experiments himself, but his manifesto inspired a number of seventeenth-century British scientists to do so. By the mid-eighteenth century, French scientists were also to favor the empirical approach and to glorify Bacon out of proportion to his actual importance. For, by harping on the virtues of inductive reasoning, Bacon missed the point that the new physics and the new astronomy were inconceivable without mathematics, which is the most abstract form of deductive reasoning.

In his *Discourse on Method* (1635) Descartes gave the classic presentation of the rationalist, or analytical, method, which is sometimes called the *Cartesian* method. First, one must be sure that one's basic ideas are clear, distinct, and true. Second, one must break down a complex issue into its simplest separate components; this is the process of analysis. Third, one must build up an ordered arrangement of these components into a logical whole; this is the process of synthesis. Fourth, one must be meticulously complete in detecting all the relevant items that belong in the final synthesis. Descartes and his many admirers believed that by applying this method, they could explain everything there was to know by reasoning.

Thus empiricism gives priority to knowledge gained through the senses, whereas rationalism begins with abstract ideas. In practice, however, Galileo, Newton, and even Descartes—when he was being a scientist rather than a philosopher—combined both approaches.

Newton fused the empirical and analytical methods in his own work and established this combination as the model for scientific investigation in all fields. His method operated as follows. First, by inductive reasoning, he discovered the fundamental principles embodied in phenomena. For example, by observing that a number of apples fell to the ground he could have reasoned that all apples fall to the ground. Second, he generalized these principles by abstracting them from any real objects—in this case apples—and then expressed them mathematically. In this form the principles would apply in all cases of falling objects. Finally, he showed the physical validity of these mathematical generalizations by appealing to observation and experiment. (What do you mean, all objects don't fall? Look!)

CULTURE AND THOUGHT IN THE SEVENTEENTH CENTURY

The scientific revolution did not resolve the European crisis in thought and feeling. Some people thought that science should usurp the place of philosophy, supersede religion, and supply the answers to all the longings of the human heart. Others reasserted the primacy of faith and feeling. A few became skeptical about all forms of truth.

The Baroque Age

By the early seventeenth century the national expressions of Renaissance exuberance had given way to a more intense and agitated style that reflected and aggravated the crises of that troubled age. The *baroque* style conveys feelings of strain and tension, of conflicts between opposing forces, and of great human effort to contain all these strains, tensions, and conflicts in some kind

of dynamic equilibrium. It uses words, sounds, colors, and shapes in overelaborate and often distorted ways. The form of this style always seems dangerously close to dissolving into some inner or cosmic chaos. It points up the fact that the crises of the seventeenth century were not merely clashes between armies, governments, religious and political factions, and social classes; man felt a psychological rupture within himself and a fear of losing contact with the eternal and the universal, in other words, with God. That was why baroque painters like El Greco and Rembrandt and sculptors like Bernini made their religious figures appear so intensely human. Similarly, baroque composers from Monteverdi to Bach invented complicated effects to give vital import to the impersonal cosmos.

In literature and drama the baroque expressed itself more as a special type of heroic character than as a formal style. An extreme example is the character of Satan in *Paradise Lost* (1667), by John Milton (1608–1674).

. . . . *aspiring*
To set himself in Glory above his Peers,
He trusted to have equalled the most High,
If he oppos'd; and with ambitious aim
Against the Throne and Monarchy of God,
Rais'd impious War in Heav'n and Battle
  proud,
With vain attempt.

The legendary figure of Don Juan was a more typical model of the seventeenth-century hero than Satan. He appeared in plays by Tirso de Molina (1571–1648) and Molière (1622–1673) not only as a seducer of other men's wives, but as a man who assumed many guises in an everlasting search for personal fulfillment. In Molière's play, Don Juan ends up in the same place as the fallen archangel, and for the same sin: pride.

In the baroque age many educated men felt that an inner experience of God was more important than any ritual. They believed that man is basically bad, a slave to his passions and appetites. Without God's gift of grace he is utterly doomed. Yet he cannot enter into the necessary mystical communion with God unless he renounces all personal pride and worldly vanities. This pessimistic view of man and religion has cropped up many times in history. Perhaps it asserted itself so strongly in the seventeenth century because pride and worldly vanities were so rampant in that baroque age. It permeated many sects, but we shall examine only two of them: the French Jansenists and the English Puritans.

Taking its name from the teachings of the Flemish scholar and bishop Cornelius Jansen (1585–1638), Jansenism spread to France in the 1640s and troubled sincere Catholics there throughout the reign of Louis XIV. Its headquarters (until Louis destroyed it in 1713) was the convent of Port Royal, on the western edge of Paris. The pious scholars who settled there were seeking the quiet and seclusion they felt that they needed in order to discover God. Their denial of man's freedom to choose or reject God's grace and their doctrine that Christ had died for a small elite smacked of predestination and were therefore heretical. Their radically ascetic attitude particularly irritated the Jesuits, who were becoming increasingly worldly and rationalistic. The Jansenists might have been quietly crushed if they had not had as their champion one of the foremost thinkers of the time, Blaise Pascal (1623–1662). Pascal's *Letters to a Provincial Friend* (1656–1657) attacked the moral laxity of the Jesuits and defended the Jansenist way of life. These *Letters* were widely read and they caused many French Catholics to doubt the effectiveness of routine piety in bringing salvation.

Pascal, an eminent scientist, mathematician, philosopher, and prose stylist, was truly a baroque thinker. On the one hand, he could invent a calculating machine and discover the principles of barometric pressure; on the other hand, he could totter on the brink of despair until he finally felt a mystical contact with an intensely personal God. This sense of mystery gave Pascal and the Jansenists an exalted quality that troubled and exasperated their more rational contemporaries. They could be unjust, as when Pascal accused Descartes of being a Deist, but they could be disarmingly human, too.

The English Puritans also burned with the "inner light" of revealed religion, although they were less docile than the Jansenists. They waged war on their rightful king, beheaded him, and tried to impose their straitlaced morals on English life under Cromwell's rule (see p. 392). Their perseverance in carving a commonwealth out of the wilderness in America is known to every schoolchild, as is their bigotry and intolerance. The very word Puritan has come to mean a narrow-minded conception of morality, a hostility to pleasure, and a self-righteous assurance of doing God's will on earth. But just as the Jansenist Pascal championed reason and free inquiry in the case of Galileo, so the Puritan Milton fought passionately for freedom of speech in England. And the author of the awe-inspiring *Paradise Lost* could also be warmly human in his lyrical poems and in his private life.

Political Thought: Hobbes and Locke

Freedom versus authority, natural law versus divine law—these were the issues in the great debate over what was the best form of society in the seventeenth century. The theoretical arguments on these issues reflected the real political crisis of the time, the clash between science and religion, and the overriding interest in Nature. The main focus was on the state as a political body. What was the true basis of its power? What had society been like before the state came into existence?

In his *Leviathan* (1651) the Englishman Thomas Hobbes (1588–1679) set forth the doctrine that the ruling prince should have absolute power. Unlike continental theorists, however, Hobbes based his doctrine on natural law as discovered through reason, rather than on divine right. For Hobbes, the state was a gigantic artificial man, a monstrous machine that governed men by treating them as instruments, as tools. (The name Leviathan is taken from the monster described in the Book of Job.)

From his experience during the English Civil War,* Hobbes formulated what life would be like in a "state of nature." This

* The political thought of Hobbes and Locke obviously reflects the events of the English Civil War of the mid-seventeenth century and the Glorious Revolution of 1688. These events will be discussed at the beginning of Chapter 13 as the first example of the rise of modernizing leadership. But the student should consult that material now as background for Hobbes and Locke.

Frontispiece to Hobbes' Leviathan *(1651).*

would be anarchy: all public services would cease to function, armed bands would loot and rape at will, there would be no law courts, no policemen, and no regular supplies of food and water. More specifically, the Civil War convinced Hobbes that the efforts of opposing groups to impose their value-systems on each other could be wholly destructive of the values each group was trying to pursue. It was this insight that prompted him to look for a political system that would curb violent confrontations and restore order and security to his country.

Furthermore, Hobbes was a pessimist. He had a very poor opinion of his fellowmen. If left to themselves, they would tear each other to pieces, as they seemed to be doing in the wars of his day and as he presumed that they did in the original state of nature—before men became reasonable enough to create the political state in order to secure peace and safeguard their lives and property from one another's predatory instincts. In the an-

archy of the state of nature, men were free, but their freedom was constantly threatened by the war of all against all. They therefore decided to give up their freedom in exchange for safety.

Since men gave up their natural freedom for life and security, it was only natural that they should make the guardian of their lives and security—the state—as strong as possible. According to Hobbes, sovereign power was indivisible, inalienable, and unlimited. Because men could never agree among themselves about what was right or wrong, they had to leave these decisions to the state. Its authority, wrote Hobbes "is to trump in cardplaying, save that in the matter of government, when nothing else is turned up, clubs are trumps." Any form of coercion was justified to maintain civil order. To insist that a subject possessed inalienable rights would be to destroy all authority. Any effort to separate the powers of the executive, legislative, and judicial branches of the government would undermine the whole basis of the state.

Hobbes' younger contemporary John Locke (1632–1704) held a quite different view. He maintained that the powers of government were limited, that the sole basis of its authority was the "tacit consent" of the people, that it had to operate within the framework of a rule of law, that the different branches of government should act as checks and balances against each other, and that an unjust and unlawful sovereign might be lawfully resisted. This theory of government formed the basis for the *liberal* political tradition from Locke's time down to the present.

Like Hobbes, Locke based his political doctrine on natural law as discovered by reason. He, too, conjured up a picture of an imaginary state of nature as the starting point for showing the source of state power. And although Locke was basically optimistic about his fellowmen, his state of nature was as anarchic as that of Hobbes. The law of nature tells men that "no one ought to harm another in his life, health, liberty, or possessions." But in the state of nature there are no effective means of enforcing this law, hence, the need to set up a government. In contrast to Hobbes, however, Locke believed that when men set up a government they did not forfeit their natural rights of life, liberty, and property.

Natural rights was a new concept in the history of mankind. How do we discover them? The same way we discover natural law: through reason. Yet Hobbes found no such "rights" through reason, and they certainly cannot be discovered scientifically. It is comforting to think that Locke's "natural rights"—called the "inalienable rights of life, liberty, and the pursuit of happiness" in the American Declaration of Independence—are real. Nevertheless, Locke the empiricist was resorting to Cartesian "innate ideas" on this point.

Locke said that the duty of a government was to protect and guarantee the rights of its citizens. This was why they had set it up in the first place. The natural law applies to sovereigns as much as to individuals in a state of nature. If a sovereign infringes on it, he can be overthrown. For government by rule of law is the essence of political liberty.

But Locke was no democrat. He wanted only property owners to have a voice in the affairs of government, which was exactly what happened as a result of the Revolution of 1688. His "natural rights" were *civil* rights. *Political* rights—the right to vote and to hold office—he reserved for the wealthy. Locke's liberalism lay, instead, in his desire to limit the power of the state. He believed that in setting up a government men agreed to surrender only as much of their natural liberty as they thought necessary for the assurance of an ordered society. But he agreed with Hobbes that the state was necessary to any society and that, in order to serve the public good, it must be strong.

The Triumph of Classicism

The strongest state in the late seventeenth century was France under Louis XIV. Not only did Louis XIV use his artists and writers to glorify him as the personification of the state, he also wanted them to impose a sense of order and unity on the world. They obliged him by developing a new aesthetic style, classicism. Their notable achievements and the prestige of France spread French cultural influence to many parts of Europe.

The essence of classicism is that reason controls artistic expression. It justifies the rules of each art form and keeps the imagination from going astray. Reason is permanent and universal, the same at all times and in all places. It dictates the canons of good taste and gives the arts their moral functions of purifying the emotions and of setting standards of what is beautiful and what is appropriate. It prescribes the rules for portraying nature and human behavior without imperfection and confusion. The artist or writer must not mix serious and frivolous elements, he must not make his characters behave in ways unsuitable to their social status, he must avoid the crude, the bizarre, or the strange. A play must not present events that last for more than one day or that occur in more than one place. A painting must have a central focus with everything around it arranged to form a complete and self-contained whole. Inspired by reason and a desire for order, classicism is an aesthetic of unity.

Although it was widespread, classicism did not completely succeed in resolving the crisis in thought and feeling. Baroque tendencies persisted in both art and behavior. Italian opera—"that insult to human reason"—conquered all of Europe from Vienna to London. People began to weep unashamedly, on the stage and in private. Some writers began challenging Louis XIV's authoritarian conception of government as well as classicism in the arts. Nevertheless, classicism and absolutism retained their appeal as ways of imposing order on the world. They continued to be imitated in France and in most of Europe under the Old Regime. France had created what seemed to be a new kind of culture. It was artificial, it lacked warmth and spontaneity, and it stifled freedom of thought and expression. Yet it had an elegance and a predictability that endeared it to most European aristocrats throughout the eighteenth century.

THE AGE OF ENLIGHTENMENT

In the eighteenth century many educated Europeans thought of themselves as the most civilized people the world had ever known. In the preceding two centuries Europeans had conquered America and learned much from the older civilizations of the east; now they believed that they surpassed even the ancient Greeks and Romans in artistic and intellectual creativeness. Never before had war been so tame, manners so polite. Never before had so many people lived so comfortably and enjoyed so much leisure. The more civilized these educated Europeans thought they were, the more concerned they became with what was still uncivilized in the Old Regime. This concern was the guiding force of the intellectual and cultural movement known as the Enlightenment.

The Enlightenment was above all a search for new, secular ideas about the nature of man and his place in society. Its leaders believed that the "light" of the scientific method, which they called Reason, would make ignorant beliefs and smug intolerance disappear and help informed and unselfish minds find the best ways for improving man's lot. The Enlightenment could not completely accomplish these goals, but it did give the intellectual climate and social policies of the second half of the eighteenth century a new

direction. It also fostered values that are still relevant today: reason, toleration, humanitarianism, social usefulness, and a liberalism that believed in allowing each individual to realize his greatest possible potential.

The Social and Cultural Setting

The ideas of the Enlightenment were rooted in the environment of the age. Unlike earlier intellectual movements, the Enlightenment sought to reach all educated people, not only specialists. Its function was as much to *spread* new ideas through high-level popularizations as it was to solve the world's problems.

European culture acquired a broader social base in the eighteenth century. Although the middle classes did not seriously challenge the institutions of the monarchy, the established church, or the aristocracy, their growing wealth and education made them increasingly eager to participate in the cultural life of the age. Hence, culture no longer catered exclusively to closed groups like the clergy, the king's courtiers, and the higher nobility. The growth of the urban middle classes provided an educated public with new cultural demands. Some members of the upper bourgeoisie wanted nothing better than to follow the artistic and literary tastes of the aristocracy. But the bulk of the commercial and professional people developed distinctive tastes of their own, tastes that fostered the triumph of new public forms of expression such as the novel, the symphony, and the newspaper.

To be sure, the bulk of the European population was still composed of socially and culturally isolated peasants. Their inability to read barred them from the literary and intellectual culture of the age; they knew only their traditional folk cultures. Even in the towns and cities the lower classes were mostly illiterate and socially segregated. Eighteenth-century culture was restricted to the middle and upper ranks of urban society—perhaps 3 or 4 percent of the total population in England and France and considerably less as one moved eastward. Nevertheless, this cultivated minority constituted a larger public than had ever existed.

As comparatively wide sections of society acquired a taste for serious literature, both

"Gin Lane," by Hogarth.

books and periodicals adapted their style and tone to the new reading public. Their language became less precious and less ornate, their ideas became simplified and more closely related to daily life. Novels like Henry Fielding's *Tom Jones* (1748) and Johann Wolfgang von Goethe's *Sorrows of Young Werther* (1774) were intensely personal descriptions of contemporary behavior. By the 1770s even the theater offered satire, as in Richard Sheridan's *The Rivals,* and social criticism, as in Pierre Beaumarchais' *The Barber of Seville,* as well as the conventional classical tragedies in Greek or Roman settings. Finally, the French *Encyclopedia* was the most successful and enduring medium of high-level popularization in all fields.

Public interest in literature, science, and social philosophy fostered other new media for diffusing new ideas. Aristocratic ladies organized cultural and intellectual evenings in the salons of their town houses. There noted writers conversed with the ladies and gentlemen of high society eager to learn the latest ideas—along with the latest gossip, of course. More important than the salon was the *cafe,* or coffeehouse. In this typically urban, middle-class institution, men gathered periodically to talk and to read the many journals and newspapers to which it subscribed. Meanwhile, the lending library made it possible for people to read more books than they could afford to buy. The number of learned academies increased rapidly; in France alone, fourteen provincial academies were founded in the first half of

"The salon of Madame Geoffrin"; among those present are Diderot, D'Alembert, and Rousseau.

the eighteenth century. Even more characteristic of the educated amateurs' longing for "enlightenment" were the private clubs that were formed to discuss current books and articles and reports on the members' own "research." These clubs included nobles and bourgeois, professional men and priests—another sign of the broader social base of culture.

Freemasonry, another important medium for spreading the ideas of the Enlightenment, got its start in England in the early eighteenth century. At that time, a group of educated Englishmen took over the guilds of mason-builders which had survived from medieval times. They preserved many of the symbols and secret rites of these guilds but replaced the old professional masonry with a "philosophical" masonry. Lodges of Freemasons appeared in France by 1725 and spread all over the continent by mid-century. Everywhere members dedicated themselves to renovating the moral and social order with the ideas of liberty and brotherhood. They were Deists who worshipped Newton's "Great Builder of the Universe." Despite repeated condemnations by the papacy, the movement continued to attract followers from all social classes in Catholic as well as Protestant countries.

The Philosophes

Although the writers who spread the ideas of the Enlightenment called themselves *philosophes*, a number of them were neither French nor professional philosophers. The Enlightenment was centered in France, but it was shaped by men of many nations. Even the two most typical French *philosophes* —Voltaire and Diderot—were not philosophers in the way that the Scotsman David Hume and the German Immanuel Kant were. They were philosophizing publicists whose main purpose was to convince the general reader to adopt their way of thinking.

The *philosophes* flourished between the 1730s and the 1780s, but their outlook had its origins in the late 1600s. By then the Cartesian method of logical analysis, shorn of Descartes' "innate ideas," had become generally accepted. Locke's *Essay Concerning Human Understanding* (1690) furnished an empirical theory of knowledge with the senses as the *source* of ideas, and Newton had shown what the combination of Cartesian rationalism and Lockian empiricism could achieve. His laws of motion and his orderly "clock universe" became the basis of eighteenth-century discussions of religion and ethics as well as science. The *philosophes* also learned how to focus the empirical-analytical attack on tradition from the skeptic Pierre Bayle, whose *Historical and Critical Dictionary* (1697) insisted that every belief must be doubted until justified by history and logic. Hence the *philosophes* were the prototypes of the modern intellectual, alienated, at least in part, from his own society and searching for a better one.

The *philosophe* Denis Diderot (1713–1784) epitomized the modern intellectual not only in his modest origin (his father was a prosperous craftsman), but also in his lively curiosity and in his sophisticated knowledge in so many fields. He was best known in his own time for his work in organizing and editing the French *Encyclopedia,* his

interest in science and technology, and his reputation as a freethinker. The *Encyclopedia* was the *philosophes'* most effective propaganda medium, and many of them wrote articles for it. Diderot said that the program of all the contributors was "to assemble the knowledge scattered over the face of the earth; to explain its general plan" to their contemporaries and to future generations who, by becoming better informed, would be "happier and more virtuous." According to Diderot's co-editor, the mathematician Jean le Rond d'Alembert (1717–1783): "The truth is simple and can always be made accessible to everyone."

Diderot's best works on drama and art criticism, his novels, and his philosophical writings were not published until after his death. In his *Rameau's Nephew,* an imaginary dialogue between the author and a depraved youth, Diderot pilloried all the chief enemies of the *philosophes* and attacked the abuses of a social organization that forced talented but needy men to cater to the whims of haughty and often unworthy patrons. Diderot went even further and asked if the disintegrating society of late eighteenth-century France could ever be reformed effectively unless some way were found to curb the inherent baseness of human nature itself.

Since many of the *philosophes* challenged the existing authorities, they had to find ways of getting around the censors. In the *Encyclopedia* Diderot cleverly used footnotes, cross-references, and even definitions, for this purpose. For example, he concluded his definition of *Anarchy* with the sentence: "We can assert that every government tends toward despotism or *anarchy.*" The reader could hardly miss the warning. Other writers put their indictment of European political institutions, irrational religious beliefs, and barbarous customs into the mouths of exotic foreigners. Charles de Secondat, Baron de la Brède et de Montesquieu (1689–1755), did this in his *Persian Letters* (1721), which has been called the first book of the *philosophe* movement. Voltaire sometimes wove his criticism into apparently innocuous novels like *Candide* (1759).

François Marie Arouet, better known as Voltaire (1694–1778), is the most famous example of the new type of writer in the eight-

Voltaire reading at his desk.

century society as intolerance, superstition, and legalized cruelty, Voltaire was no democrat. According to him, the mass of ordinary people had to be kept in line by the traditional forces of order.

Ideas of the Philosophes

The *philosophes'* combination of analysis, empiricism, and skepticism gave the Enlightenment its unique character. It limited the kinds of questions they asked to those that could be answered by an appeal to reason and experience. "True nature" was comprehensible to "right reason." Everything else was "supernatural" or "unnatural" and, hence, not worth talking about, except to be exposed as a fraud. The *philosophes* assumed that, although the world was imperfect, men could improve it by making certain choices; many evils could be eliminated, many institutions could be reformed, and many superstitions could be argued out of existence.

Their specific reasoning gave the *philosophes* two basic standards for making value judgments: *humanity* and *social utility*. Whatever helps man to achieve personal happiness is good; whatever hinders him from doing so is bad. Each *philosophe* had his own moral arithmetic for measuring the goodness of any act or idea for society, but they all accepted social utility as the basic standard.

One final assumption of the *philosophes* needs to be stressed. In addition to "right reason," "true nature," humanity, and social utility, they all believed in *change*. The world was obviously different from what it had been 50, 100, or 1000 years earlier. (Whether or not it was *better* was a more complicated matter.) The *philosophes'* celebrated belief in progress was limited by their underlying pessimism about man and history.

Whatever improvements the *philosophes* hoped to make in society, most of them accepted human nature—with its passions as well as its reason—as something one could not change. It was simply there, like any other fact of nature. The triumphs of the human mind in astronomy and mathematics showed what human nature was capable of

eenth century. He had established a reputation as a poet and playwright in his native Paris while in his thirties. After visiting England he returned to France in 1734 to become a publicist for British empiricism and liberalism. In addition to his novels and moral essays, his *Century of Louis XIV* became a model for a new cultural approach to the study of history—an approach that emphasized how people lived and expressed themselves as well as describing kings and battles. In all his writings Voltaire sought to maintain a high literary standard while expressing what he had to say as clearly as possible. Here was the modern professional writer in his full glory: clever, testy, vain, independent and, above all, civilized.

Voltaire wrote for all educated people, not just kings (although he spent three years at the court of Frederick the Great) and aristocrats (although he had many friends among them). Of bourgeois origin himself Voltaire firmly believed that the ruling classes had no monopoly on intelligence and creativeness. Indeed, he often ridiculed the stupidity of princes, judges, and priests. Although he called on a new enlightened elite to eliminate such uncivilized features of eighteenth-

as it was. Reason could perhaps direct the education of future generations and so achieve a comparable degree of progress in other fields. But no man could be educated beyond his natural capacity.

Most *philosophes* did not believe that the history of mankind proved the inevitability of progress. Some said that history moved in cycles; according to this view each civilization repeated the same life pattern of birth, growth, old age, and death—the same development from barbarism, to primitive organization, to higher organization, to disintegration. Other *philosophes* said that history moved in an aimless way dictated largely by chance—as in Voltaire's use of Pascal's famous observation that the whole face of the earth might have been different if Cleopatra's nose had been a fraction of an inch shorter. Hardly any of the *philosophes* believed in inevitable decline, but those who preached an unqualified doctrine of the perfectibility of man and civilization were exceptional. Indeed, the crowning work of eighteenth-century historical writing, Edward Gibbon's *Decline and Fall of the Roman Empire* (1776–1787), tried to show how Christianity had undermined the confidence and sapped the strength of the most impressive civilization within the ken of Western man.

The *philosophes* condemned organized Christianity as the main obstacle to the advance of their civilization. To them the intolerance of the established churches was the greatest evil of the time. Voltaire launched the battle cry, *écrasez l'infâme* ("crush the infamous thing") in his effort to clear the memory of Jean Calas, a Protestant put to death on the charge—based on mere rumor—of murdering his son to prevent his conversion to Catholicism. If people still wanted to believe in the "superstitions" of organized Christianity, that was their business. But Voltaire insisted that the churches should be denied all influence in public life: education, censorship, politics, and the regulation of public morals. Thus Voltaire became the champion of *toleration* and *anticlericalism* as essential policies in a civilized society. Both the friends and the enemies of the Enlightenment have viewed

Voltaire in this guise as its main symbol ever since.

Montesquieu's *Spirit of the Laws* (1748) was the most ambitious investigation of the organization of society as a whole to use the approach of the *philosophes*. Despite frequent appeals to "natural relations" and common sense, Montesquieu did not propose to discover a universal set of laws for all societies. Instead, he tried to show how differing social customs, historical traditions, and geographical environments gave a different spirit to the laws of each society. Thus the vast empires of the ancient Mediterranean world and of Asia tended to be despotisms supported by the spirit of fear. Small city-states like Athens, Venice, and Geneva were usually republics supported by the spirit of civic virtue, an active participation in community affairs, and, when necessary for the public welfare, a certain self-effacement. Finally, large monarchies were supported by the spirit of honor, that is, by their noblemen's consciousness of the privileges and obligations of rank (*noblesse oblige*). Montesquieu obviously favored what he called free monarchy, but he insisted that the specific laws of any type of state should provide the maximum liberty and humaneness possible within its constitutional limits.

Although Montesquieu was a liberal in his insistence on personal liberty and the rule of law, he was a conservative in defending the French aristocracy against encroachments by the royal administration. As a member of the nobility of the robe it was understandable that Montesquieu should take this position. But in the second half of the eighteenth century the conservatism of the Parlements and the resurgence of the "feudal" nobility led most French *philosophes* to feel that the nobles of the sword and of the robe were holding back social progress in order to preserve their own selfish interests.

Although on political matters most *philosophes* put their faith in enlightened kings rather than in noblemen, an important group of them stressed freedom from government interference in *economic* matters. They criticized the mercantilist policies of eighteenth-century governments as being contrary to the laws of nature. In fact, the French

A Parisian water-carrier in the eighteenth century.

opponents of mercantilism called themselves *physiocrats,** that is, advocates of the government of nature. According to the physiocrats, economic phenomena constituted an order of facts that obeyed certain laws derived from the nature of things. The natural role of the individual was to pursue his own economic interest. The natural role of government was to let him do this with as little interference as possible: *laissez faire, laissez passer* (let it be done, let it get on). Then people would be able to produce more goods, thus enriching the community and providing more revenue for the state, as well as increasing their own profits.

This economic philosophy with its emphasis on free enterprise (*laissez faire*) and private property was to become the gospel of bourgeois capitalism for the next 150 years.

* Pierre-Samuel Dupont de Nemours (1739–1817)—whose son later established what was to become the world's largest chemical corporation in the United States—invented the name physiocracy. Louis XVI's sometime finance minister Anne Robert Jacques Turgot (1727–1781) invented the phrase, *laissez faire, laissez passer.*

But the French physiocrats spoke for the landowning class, which was still largely noble in the eighteenth century. According to them, this was the most essential class in any society. Next came the farmers who worked the land. Last came the bourgeoisie, the "sterile class," which produced nothing new. The true founder of economic liberalism from the bourgeois capitalist point of view was the Scottish moral philosopher Adam Smith (1723–1790).

Like the physiocrats, Adam Smith tried to prove that free enterprise and private property benefited the community as well as the individual, as indicated by the title of his classic work, *An Inquiry into the Nature and Causes of the Wealth of Nations* (1776). Unlike the physiocrats, however, Smith argued that the person who transformed raw materials into manufactured goods did increase their value and, hence, the total wealth of the community.

Smith used the idea of division of labor as the key to the wealth of nations to justify a revolutionary new policy: *free trade.* According to him, reason dictates that whole nations, as well as individual men, should concentrate their labor on the forms of production for which they are best suited: "What is prudence in the conduct of every private family can scarce be folly in that of a great kingdom. If a foreign country can supply us with a commodity cheaper than we ourselves can make it, better buy it of them with some part of the produce of our own industry employed in a way in which we have some advantage." It is foolish to buy inferior goods at high prices in one's own country when comparable goods of better quality can be bought more cheaply abroad and paid for by exporting goods that can be produced most efficiently at home. Each nation of the world and each region should use its comparative advantages of climate, materials, and skills. But free trade should not apply in cases where it would aid potential enemies. Nor did Smith believe that division of labor required a nation to abandon its own production of the minimum needs of war.

Although a staunch moralist, Smith refused to see the implications of unfettered free enterprise for the workingman. He justified the morality of his economic philosophy with the familiar values of the *philosophes:* reason, individual liberty, natural law, social usefulness. His economic man was both rational and acquisitive. If allowed complete freedom to pursue his self-interest, he would know how to make the most out of his capital and his skill. A whole society of such free economic men would produce more wealth than any other kind of society. The natural laws of supply and demand would eliminate the inefficient producers, thus giving the consumers the best products at the lowest prices. As the nation's wealth increased, some of it would eventually filter down to the workers themselves. As a political economist Smith was content that he had described the best, that is, natural, functioning of a nation's economy. As a moralist he felt impelled to add an "invisible hand" that made this system a just one. Later British political economists in the Adam Smith tradition were to drop the "invisible hand."

French *philosophes* like Montesquieu, Diderot, and Voltaire typified the Enlightenment, but the movement was international. It had its exponents in men like Benjamin Franklin in the American colonies and in the isolated genius Michael Lomonosov in Russia. The most influential appeal for the reform of criminal law was written by the Italian jurist Cesare Bonesana, Marchese di Beccaria (1735–1794). In his *On Crimes and Punishments* (1764) Beccaria expounded the revolutionary idea that society should concentrate on preventing crime, not just on punishing it. In addition to Adam Smith, Scotland produced the philosopher David Hume (1711–1776), whose rigorous skepticism was ultimately to lead to twentieth-century notions of relativity and probability. According to Hume, all inferences derived from experience—even the idea of cause and effect—are merely the result of custom or habit. It was this view in Hume's *Treatise on Human Nature* (1740) that aroused the last and greatest philosopher of the Enlightenment, the German Immanuel Kant (1724–1804), to his own work on the nature of human understanding. The other major thinker who influenced Kant was Jean-Jacques Rousseau (1712–1778), who lived mostly in France but who never lost the puritanical outlook of his native Geneva.

RESISTANCE AND COUNTERACTION

The strongest reactions against the dominant rationalism and materialism of the Enlightenment came first from the established churches and next from individuals and groups that stressed the primacy of the heart, the spirit, and personal fulfillment. They included revivalist religious sects like the Methodists and Baptists in England and the Pietists in Germany, Rousseau's pleas for new departures in politics and education, and Kant's effort to establish a new basis for knowledge and morality.

Rousseau

Rousseau was the great rebel against eighteenth-century civilization, especially as he viewed it in France. He thought it artificial, its manners too elaborate, its taste too sophisticated, its people of refinement too hypocritical and frivolous, its religion too formal, and its unbelief too glib. For Rousseau all this went against nature, by which, in his later writing, he meant man's nature. Going "back to nature" did not mean "going around on all fours," as Voltaire charged. Rousseau pleaded for a civilization that would allow the strong emotional side of man's nature to develop in a harmonious way. His main complaint against the *philosophes* and the aristocratic culture of his time was that they neglected man's emotions.

Rousseau's greatest longing was to be free to be himself. As he approached the age of forty he decided that this was impossible in the civilization of his day. He began his personal "reform" by giving up the outward symbols of civilized living. In his *Confessions* he says: "I gave up gold lace and white stockings, took to wearing a round wig, and put aside my sword." Henceforth Rousseau devoted his writings to describing the possible ways of reforming civilization so that other men could be free to be themselves.

Rousseau passionately believed that man was born free and inclined toward moral good. Man was not responsible for the emotional ingredients in his nature. It was up to society to help him realize his full capacity for self-determination, through good laws and institutions and through the right kind of

The back-to-nature fad: Queen Marie Antoinette playing the shepherdess.

education and religion. This "philosophy of the heart" was a major challenge to the whole civilization of the Enlightenment.

Rousseau's idea that governments had no authority apart from the individuals over whom it was exercised was truly revolutionary in the eighteenth century. In his *Social Contract* (1762) he says: "The depositories of executive power are not the masters of the people but its officers. . . . The people may establish or remove them as it pleases." Like Locke, Rousseau believed that the people in a "state of nature" formed a government through a mutual agreement, a social contract. But unlike Locke, Rousseau did not grant even a limited degree of sovereignty to a government thus formed. According to Locke, the governed accept the sovereignty of their government as long as it protects their civil rights. According to Rousseau, "each person gives himself to *all,* but not to any *individual.*" Rousseau calls the will of this "all" the "general will."

Rousseau tried to use his idea of the general will to reconcile his concern for individual liberty with his recognition of the need for organized government. In the *Social Contract* he defines liberty as obedience to a law that we prescribe to ourselves by our own individual wills. Then he argues that the general will is an expression of the better side of each individual will. There is a moral law that each person discovers within himself and that is the same for everybody in a given community. A government that expresses the general will has the right to force its citizens to obey this law, since people form governments only to guarantee their individual liberty. Those who violate the general will not only jeopardize the liberty of others but also harm the better side of themselves. Rousseau says that they must therefore be "forced to be free."

Another revolutionary idea of Rousseau's was that all men are equal. On this point, too, Rousseau blamed civilization as it had evolved to his time for destroying the natural equality of men. For as society had become more civilized it had created forms of wealth and power with which some people exploited others. Rousseau did not believe that everyone should necessarily have the same degree of wealth and power. He simply wanted the law to limit each person's share to the point where it could not suppress the liberty, self-respect, and self-determination of another individual. "It is precisely because the force of things always tends to destroy equality that the force of legislation should always tend to maintain it." Thus the law should force men to be equal as well as free.

Later critics of Rousseau charged him with favoring the tyranny of the masses, but Rousseau himself did not believe that a government based on the sovereignty of the people — that is, a democracy — could be achieved in a large state. It could only work in a small city-state like Geneva, and only then if all the citizens participated in it directly. In fact, when Rousseau later suggested reforms for the constitution of Poland, he recommended the preservation of the elective monarchy, the privileges of the nobles, and even serfdom until the serfs had been taught responsibility.

Rousseau is best understood in terms of his own time. In the eighteenth century dominant minorities imposed their will on powerless majorities everywhere. To Rousseau this arrangement was morally wrong. He believed that he had found the true moral basis of society, law, and government in man's natural equality and capacity for goodness. All of the *philosophes* were somewhat naive in thinking there was one way to know how society could best be organized. Adam Smith's belief that the sum of individual acts of economic self-interest naturally produced the greatest public good, Montesquieu's belief that men of privilege naturally feel more obligations toward their fellow men than ordinary people, Locke's belief, incorporated into the American Declaration of Independence, that all men are born with certain natural rights are all somewhat naive. Rousseau differed from the others mainly in seeking knowledge through the heart rather than through reason.

Kant

Just as Rousseau's "philosophy of the heart" — with its emphasis on feeling and individual fulfillment — was to find its fullest expression in nineteenth-century romanticism, Kant's doctrine that the ultimate reality lies in the world of ideas and the spirit rather than in sense experience launched a second major nineteenth-century movement — *idealism*.

In his *Critique of Pure Reason* (1781) Kant conducted a series of mental "experiments" concerning the "facts" of human reason, that is, the kinds of propositions with which reason operates. Then he found the laws that tied these facts together. Finally he discovered the principle on which these laws depended. Most philosophers in the past had started with objects in the natural world and asked how they "came into the mind." Kant started with the mind and asked how it knew objects in the world outside itself. He granted that these objects were real, but he denied that the mind could know them as they truly were. It knows them only as *forms* (phenomena), not as things in themselves.

According to Kant, we experience the world in terms of certain basic assumptions that already exist in our minds: space, time, cause, quantity, quality, means, relation, and the like. These assumptions, or categories, exist a priori — that is, prior to our experience — and they transcend (go beyond) what is given by experience. It is these a priori, transcendental categories alone that dictate the forms by which we know the objects of the natural world. The principle on which these categories — which Kant thought comparable to Newton's laws — depend is the existence of the mind as a living reality, prior to and transcending the senses.

Paralleling his categories of pure reason, Kant's "categorical imperative" for morality is an absolute idea, independent of all individual examples and circumstances. Kant based his view of morality on his stern demand that man take full personal responsibility for respecting the dignity and rights of other men. Like Rousseau, Kant believed that man's natural feelings impelled him toward good will, but Kant emphasized reason as the guide to man's judgment. And reason told the individual that whatever the circumstances, a true act of good will had to follow a rule that he would not hesitate to see become a universal law. "Do unto others as you would have them do unto you." This was Kant's "categorical imperative."

Kant shared the growing demand of the late eighteenth century for a higher morality and a greater autonomy for the individual personality. In 1784 he proclaimed that "Enlightenment is man's release from his inability to make use of his understanding without direction from another." Like Rousseau and Diderot, he challenged the mechanistic assumptions of Newtonian physical science as arrogant and inhuman. All three attacked conformity to external customs of the society of their time as inimical to man's personal and cultural expression.

The men of the Enlightenment believed that humanitarianism and social usefulness were the basic values of a civilized society, but neither they nor anyone since has found the formula for realizing both values completely at the same time. Even Rousseau said that in order to achieve the best society, some individuals would have to be *forced* to be free and equal. Voltaire championed humanitarianism for individuals, but his definition of civilized humanity excluded the masses as born losers. As we shall see in the next chapter, when the leaders of the American and French revolutions tried to put the basic values of the Enlightenment into practice, there were many losers too: in both revolutions the defenders of the old order lost their privileges and sometimes their property and their lives; the American Declaration of Independence said that all men are born free and equal but neglected to mention the slaves.

Still, no other civilization had ever raised so many fundamental questions about itself in the name of science and reason. Everywhere else tradition and custom prevailed. It was men like Galileo, Descartes, and Adam Smith who laid the intellectual groundwork for modern civilization. And in the late eighteenth century new leaders began to give this civilization its political base.

SUGGESTED READINGS

Boas, Marie, *Scientific Renaissance, 1450–1630*. New York: Harper and Row, n.d. Paperback.
See especially on applied knowledge.

Hall, A. Rupert, *From Galileo to Newton*. New York: Harper and Row, n.d. Paperback.
An excellent, readable account.

Cohen, I. Bernard, *The Birth of a New Physics*. New York: Doubleday-Anchor, 1960.

Butterfield, Herbert, *Origins of Modern Science, 1300–1800*. Rev. ed. New York: The Macmillan Co., 1961. Collier Books. Paperback.
This brilliant survey stresses the difficulties in placing science on a firm foundation.

Santillana, Giorgio de, *The Crime of Galileo.* Chicago: University of Chicago Press, 1955.
  Brilliant, controversial study of Galileo's life and trial.

Hazard, Paul, *The European Mind, 1680–1715,* Cleveland: World Publishing Co., 1963. Meridian. Paperback.

Hazard, Paul, *European Thought in the Eighteenth Century: From Montesquieu to Lessing,* New Haven: Yale University Press, 1954.
  A very good survey.

Havens, George R., *The Age of Ideas: From Reaction to Revolution in Eighteenth Century France,* New York: Holt, Rinehart and Winston, 1955. Paperback.
  A very readable and accurate survey; particularly good on Diderot.

Brinton, Crane, ed., *The Portable Age of Reason Reader.* New York: Viking, 1956.
  A good selection of the writings of the Enlightenment.

Hauser, Arnold, *The Social History of Art.* 4 vols: New York: Random House, 1960. Vintage. Paperback.
  The first five chapters of Volume III give a provocative though not always convincing interpretation of the relationship between artistic and social trends in the eighteenth century.

Hampson, Norman, *The Enlightenment.* Volume IV of the *Pelican History of European Thought.* Baltimore: Penguin, 1971. Paperback.
  Excellent on cultural history.

CHAPTER 13

The English, American, and French Revolutions

In the late eighteenth century enlightened liberals' criticism of the Old Regime grew into attacks and, in some places, revolution by democratic radicals. In North America, July 4, 1776 and in France, July 14, 1789 ushered in an era of revolution and war that was to last until Napoleon's final defeat at Waterloo on June 18, 1815. By then the radicals had been driven underground, and the liberals were on the defensive; only in the newly created United States of America did the accomplishments of the revolution survive intact. Yet in many places where governments and legal systems had been restructured along rational lines, the reforms remained, despite the reemergence of reactionary princes and politicians. The wars of the revolutionary and Napoleonic eras demonstrated the necessity of this restructuring not only in France and the countries it annexed to its empire but also among its enemies, most notably Prussia.

In England the political order had been rationalized in the seventeenth century to protect the unrestricted use of private property for personal enrichment. Much of this

English political and legal heritage, epitomized in the ideas of John Locke, was incorporated into the new American constitution and, somewhat later, in the constitutions of Canada, Australia, and New Zealand.

Thus it may be said that consolidation of modernizing political leadership began in England in 1640, in the United States in 1776, in France in 1789, and in certain other areas of Western and Central Europe before the end of the Napoleonic period.

THE ENGLISH REVOLUTION

Although the civil and religious wars in seventeenth-century England resembled those in France and Germany in many ways, their outcome was quite different for several reasons. Unlike France and Germany, England had tamed its princes and great nobles militarily in the sixteenth century. Henry VIII and Elizabeth I had favored the gentry and university-trained laymen, utilizing them as loyal servants of the crown. England was also freer from the influence of the clergy than most European countries. The abolition of the monasteries by Henry VIII and the redistribution of their lands to the gentry had given members of this class the incentive to engage in capitalist agriculture and sheep-raising. The Renaissance had glorified the active life in France as well as in England, but French aristocrats were active primarily in warfare, whereas English aristocrats had acquired more of the acquisitive outlook of capitalism. They began to question the form of government when the Stuart kings, who ruled after the death of Elizabeth, mismanaged the country's foreign affairs and threatened to bolster their absolutism by restoring clerical influence at home.

The burning question was: Who embodied the supreme authority of the state, the Stuart kings or Parliament? The struggle over this constitutional question raged intermittently from the time James I (1603–1625) came to the throne until the time James II was deposed in 1688. In the 1640s and 1650s it was complicated by religious and social conflicts within the parliamentary faction and by the ascendancy of a strong military leader, Oliver Cromwell. Although the religious issue also complicated the final stage of the constitutional conflict in 1688, the basic question was whether England should be ruled by an absolute monarch or by a Parliament representing the aristocracy.

The aristocracy of the time consisted primarily of the landowning nobility and gentry, but it had long since abandoned its feudal opposition to a strong centralized state. By the 1640s it promoted the first modern example of a strong state ruled by a corporate elite, instead of by an absolute monarch or a federation of aristocrats. Indeed, during the Civil War the English aristocracy—also for the first time—gave a large number of commoners a role in public affairs, if only temporarily.

Background of the Civil War

Through intermarriage and cooperation in business, the landowning gentry and the city merchants had developed common interests; they now wanted to translate their wealth, which exceeded that of some great nobles, into political power. Yet the gentry and the great nobles shared a common education in Latin grammar schools, where they acquired the rhetoric and ideals of the aristocratic Roman Republic. Their representatives in Parliament were clever politicians and debaters who knew how to appeal to public opinion, how to use their university learning to discover legal arguments for their demands, and how to develop an effective committee system in the House of Commons for organizing their attacks on Stuart policies. Every time the Stuarts asked Parliament for more money, it demanded that they give up some of their authority. Finally, Charles I (1625–1649) dissolved Parliament in 1629 and governed without calling it again for 11 years.

The Stuarts' religious policies also aroused increasing opposition both inside and outside of Parliament. The main opponents of the Stuarts were the Puritans. Although a handful of them fled to Holland and thence to Massachusetts, the majority wanted to take over the Church of England and "purify" it of its "popish" ritual and organization. They provided the most dynamic leadership in Parliament against the king, and the printed sermons of their preachers were the "best sellers" of the day.

Charles I might have weathered the attacks of the English Puritans and avoided a civil war but, instead, he got himself into serious trouble by trying to impose Anglicanism on Scotland. Charles was the king of Scotland and Ireland as well as England, and he was determined to assert his absolutism wherever he ruled. But Scotland had its own Presbyterian state church, its own parliament, and the ability to raise a regular army. Thus, when Charles ordered the Anglican liturgy to be read in Edinburgh, the Scots formed a national league to resist any changes in their religion and openly prepared for war. In trouble in Scotland and financially distressed in England, Charles *had* to call a new session of Parliament in 1640 and to make major concessions to its champions. Then, in 1641, a major rebellion broke out in Ireland because the Irish feared that Protestant England would use their Catholic religion as an excuse for seizing their lands. Conflict between Charles and Parliament over command of the army to suppress the Irish rebellion led to an irreparable breach in the summer of 1642.

Parliament appointed a committee of public safety in London, and the king raised the royal standard at Nottingham.

The Civil War and the Puritan Revolution, 1642–1660

Six years of intermittent fighting transformed the English Civil War into a real revolution. The Cavaliers, led by the great Anglican and Catholic lords and the conservative Anglican gentry, fought for the king, still hoping to bring him around to their view of government. The Anglican clergy and most of the peasants were also royalists. The supporters of Parliament, whom the royalists contemptuously called Roundheads because they did not wear wigs, included the majority of the urban middle classes and the Puritan and Presbyterian gentry. But as the war dragged on, this apparent division along social and religious lines blurred. Soon members of the same family were fighting on opposite sides. The parliamentary side eventually became divided within itself: the more radical Puritans demanded a republic and religious freedom, while the Presbyterians still hoped to preserve the monarchy and a state church for the whole of the British Isles. Some of the common soldiers demanded a government in which everybody would have a say; as country squires, Cromwell and his generals opposed this kind of political and social leveling. In the end, the Puritan army dictated the most revolutionary changes that any European country had yet experienced. In late 1648 it "purged" the 96 Presbyterian members of Parliament. Since the Anglican and Catholic members had joined the royalist side in 1642, only a "Rump" of Puritans remained.

In 1649 the Puritans consummated their revolution. The "Rump Parliament" tried and executed the king and abolished the monarchy and the House of Lords. The Puritans made England a Commonwealth, retaining the legislative power for Parliament and giving the executive power to a Council of State. Ultimate sanction for the Commonwealth rested with the army and its leader, Cromwell.

The Puritan revolution fought the king in the name of constitutionalism and the rule of law only to succumb, ironically, to rule by a small faction and then to a personal dictatorship—a pattern that was to repeat itself in the French and Russian revolutions later. Cromwell was a reluctant dictator, but dictator he was. Not only did he have to crush the extreme democrats, he also had to subdue the Scots and the Irish by armed force, and by 1652 he was also fighting the Dutch. The army was therefore never demobilized and, indeed, became the main political force in England. In 1653 Cromwell dissolved the "Rump Parliament" and made himself "Lord Protector of the Commonwealth of England, Scotland, and Ireland." But Cromwell's regime, having abolished the House of Lords, was unable to gain any backing from the great aristocrats. The Lord Protector could not establish himself as an acceptable legitimate monarch. In addition, Puritan rule was too strict and bigoted for most Englishmen.

The Commonwealth did not survive Cromwell's death in 1658. A few months later the generals overthrew his son Richard and began quarreling among themselves. One of them, George Monk, threw in his lot with the civilians who viewed a return to the monarchy as the only solution to the impending anarchy. A new Parliament was elected, and it invited the son of the beheaded Charles to return from his exile in France. In May 1660 the new king returned to London as Charles II. The crowds cheered him, but he knew that it was freedom from Puritan "tyranny" rather than his own popularity that made them cheer.

The Restoration and the Glorious Revolution, 1660–1689

In many ways the second two Stuarts—Charles II (1660–1685) and James II (1685–1688)—seemed to echo the first two. The monarchy and the House of Lords were restored, a new House of Commons took office, and once again royal absolutism battled against parliamentary supremacy and the rule of law. But the two major sides had been chastened by their recent defeats and tried to avoid going to extremes. The struggle

The House of Commons, shown on the reverse side of "The Great Seal of England," 1651.

between them became almost exclusively *political*. Moreover, foreign help played a larger role after 1660 than it had played before.

Charles II tried to enhance the authority of the crown at the expense of Parliament and, as far as possible, to imitate the form of government established by Louis XIV in France. Charles' admiration for Louis led him to conclude an alliance with him, and Louis gave Charles a regular subsidy. At home, Charles bought the support of about 100 Anglican Cavalier members of Parliament, who came to be known as Tories (literally, Irish robbers). The opposition group, called Whigs (literally, Scottish cattle thieves), included many sons of Roundheads. Neither faction was a real party yet, although they were gradually to acquire more cohesion during the eighteenth century. The Tories tended to represent the interests of the conservative country gentry, whereas the Whigs tended to represent the modern capitalist landlords and the wealthy middle classes in the towns.

Disagreeing on most issues, the Whigs and Tories both opposed Catholicism and royal absolutism. Charles II had kept his Catholic sympathies to himself and had increased his personal power by devious means; his brother James II was less circumspect. Hence under James II the danger of a Catholic monarchy with absolutist pretensions and pro-French leanings temporarily united the Whigs and Tories, and together they made the "Glorious Revolution" in 1688. They invited William of Orange, a Dutch prince, grandson of Charles I, and husband of James' Protestant daughter Mary, to come to England with an army and make James II abandon his pro-Catholic policies. When James' own army melted away, he fled to France, whose kings continued to support Stuart pretensions to the English throne until the mid-eighteenth century.

The Revolution of 1688 was thus a bloodless one. William of Orange, now William III, and his wife Mary* took an oath to preserve the limitations that the new Parliament imposed on the English monarchy. These limitations were then incorporated into the Bill of Rights, whose most important provisions were: (1) the making or suspending of any law without the consent of Parliament is illegal; (2) the levying of taxes without the consent of Parliament is illegal, (3) maintaining a standing army without the consent of Parliament is illegal; (4) the elections of members of Parliament must be free; (5) there must be freedom of debate in Parliament; (6) Parliament should meet frequently; (7) Englishmen have the right to petition the sovereign; (8) Englishmen have the right to keep arms; (9) Englishmen have the right to trial by a jury; (10) excessive bail should never be demanded.

Consequences of the English Revolution

The English Revolution put the state in the hands of the wealthy classes. Satisfied with their control over it through Parliament, they were willing to place more money at the state's disposal than any continental monarch could muster. Increased revenue from taxes and loans permitted the state to grow stronger than ever. The Bill of Rights and the separation of powers among the executive, legislative, and judicial branches of government guaranteed rule by law and property rights. Privilege and discrimination remained, to be sure, but social and economic relations lost many of their traditional restraints. The main victims of the English Revolution were peasants who were unable to resist the encroachments of the landed

* Queen Anne, Mary's sister, reigned from 1702 to 1714 and died childless. Since her brother James was a Catholic, her only acceptable Protestant successor was a German prince who was a great-grandson of James I. Thus Elector George of Hanover became King George I of England, Scotland, and Ireland in 1714, adopted the Anglican faith, and established the Hanoverian dynasty.

upper classes and those unenterprising members of the gentry who were unable to improve their economic situation either on the land or in commerce or government service. The main winners were the capitalist-oriented upper classes. The fact that most of them were capitalist-oriented and that traditional peasant society was virtually destroyed meant that there was to be no important reactionary opposition to the later growth of commercial and industrial capitalism. The aristocrats' attitude toward government was expressed by John Locke:

*The reason why men enter into society is the preservation of their property; and the end why they choose and authorize a legislative is that there may be laws made, and rules set, as guards and fences to the properties of all the society, to limit the power and moderate the dominion of every part and member of the society.**

Thus the English Revolution was the first to clear the way for a modernizing political leadership, although its consolidation was to come slowly. During the eighteenth century the aristocracy ran British affairs in its own interests. Aristocratic rule was often corrupt, it neglected the lower classes, but it got things done. It won an empire in Canada and India but lost the allegiance of the English-speaking colonists through its own selfishness. Despite political differences among themselves, the Whigs and Tories closed ranks against the democratic revolution that threatened them at home and in all of Western Europe after 1789. They represented two different outlooks among the wealthy classes, not two different classes. Not until the 1830s were they to become willing to share political power with the rising urban industrialists. Only when this happened was the consolidation of modernizing leadership, begun in 1649, completed.

THE AMERICAN REVOLUTION AND THE FORGING OF A NEW NATION

Revolutionary wars tend to simplify issues: one must be either for the revolution or against it, a patriot or a traitor. All other

* From *Two Treatises on Government*, Chapter IX.

The Boston Massacre, March 5, 1770.

issues that formerly divided the insurgents must be temporarily submerged in the struggle against the common enemy. When this enemy begins to be viewed as a foreign power, the struggle molds the previously divided insurgents into a national community. If the insurgents have certain common traditions, this community coheres after its victory over the enemy, especially if the majority of the "traitors" has permanently left the scene. The revolt of the Thirteen American Colonies against British rule was the first successful example of this pattern of events. As such, it had an immediate impact on Europe and became a model for later revolutions in Latin America.

In the decade leading up to 1776 the Thirteen American Colonies were different from Europe, but they had a king, and they had an untitled aristocracy, although its influence was weaker than in Europe. They also had traditions of liberty and equality stronger than those in Europe. The oldest colonies had been founded with a large degree of in-dependence from Great Britain. By the eighteenth century, most colonies had royal governors, but they also had their own assemblies elected by a wider suffrage than any in Europe: 80 percent of adult white males in Massachusetts, just over one-half in New Jersey, and a little under one-half in Virginia. These assemblies exercised a considerable degree of self-rule. In addition to sharing these traditions of political equality and political liberty, the white population enjoyed all the civil liberties of Englishmen. The distribution of wealth in colonial America was far less uneven than in the Old World, but the rich and the poor were far enough apart to cause trouble.

Despite their internal differences most Americans disapproved of Great Britain's efforts to strengthen its control over the Thirteen Colonies in the decade before the revolution. These measures, particularly increased taxes and limitations on westward expansion (Quebec Act, 1774), were mainly products of the French and Indian War. The

A Society of Patriotic Ladies vows to drink no more tea until the duty on it is repealed.

Stamp Act of 1765—which placed a tax on newspapers, playing cards, and legal documents—had united almost all the colonists against the British for the first time. But when Parliament repealed it a year later, the momentary unity of the colonists disappeared. Then new efforts to make the colonists serve British interests provoked mounting resistance. New import duties in the late 1760s provoked riots, and when the British decided to station a military force in Boston radical patriots called Sons of Liberty stoned the soldiers. In one incident the soldiers fired on the crowd, killing five people; the citizens were especially enraged when the commanding officer was acquitted at his trial.

In 1773 a group of citizens disguised as Indians dumped a shipload of tea into Boston harbor. They did this in protest against the Tea Act, which deprived American shippers and retailers of the profits of the tea trade by giving the British East India Company a monopoly over it. In 1774, to punish Massachusetts for the "Boston Tea Party," Parliament passed the "Intolerable Acts." These acts closed the port of Boston, forbade town meetings, and compelled the province of Massachusetts to provide food and lodging for British soldiers sent there to enforce these disciplinary measures.

In September 1774 the isolated acts of protest in the American Colonies became an organized revolution. A Continental Congress representing all the colonies except Georgia met in Philadelphia. At first the purpose of the delegates was to recover their "just rights and liberties" and to restore "union and harmony between Great Britain and the colonies." But the Tory-dominated British Parliament refused to back down. The incident that brought the conflict past the point of compromise was open fighting between the people of Massachusetts and the king's troops at Lexington and Concord in April 1775. Violence spread, and local militias were formed to maintain law and order. In May 1775 a second Continental Congress organized these militias into a "Continental Army" under the command of General George Washington. The demand for complete separation from Great Britain increased when the British government placed the insurgent colonists outside the protection of the British crown in December 1775.

Thomas Paine's widely circulated pamphlet, *Common Sense* (January 1776), helped to spread the argument for independence among the general public. Paine, a former British exciseman and new arrival in America, gave the classic democratic argument against the "remains of aristocratical tyranny in the House of Lords" and the "remains of Monarchical tyranny in the person of the King." General Washington called Paine's arguments for independence in the name of democracy "sound doctrine and unanswerable reason" and even William Pitt, Earl of Chatham, in a speech on November 18, 1777, said: "If I were an American, as I am an Englishman, while a foreign troop was landed in my country I never would lay down my arms,—never! never! never!"

The formal Declaration of Independence on July 4, 1776 was based on practical considerations as well as ideals. If the British crown refused to maintain law and order in the colonies, the colonists would have to form their own government to do so. If financial aid was to be sought from France, the French would have to be convinced that it was for the purpose of breaking up the British Empire and undoing the British victory of 1763. Thus a little more than a year after the Battle of Lexington, the Continental Congress announced the arrival of the United States of America as an independent state "among the powers of the earth."

America won its independence from Great Britain after five years of hard fighting and with considerable outside help. At first the Continental Army made little headway against the superior British forces, even though the French had been giving money and supplies to the insurgents since the start of the rebellion. Then in 1778 the French formed a military alliance with the colonies. This alliance was crucial not only because of the French soldiers and naval forces it brought to America but also because of its diplomatic effect on Great Britain. It reopened the struggle for colonial supremacy with France and with Spain and Holland, who joined France in its war against the British. The rest of Europe created a League of Armed Neutrality in 1780 to resist British searches of their ships bound for America.

Britain now paid the price for having antagonized practically every power on the continent in 1763. Furthermore, it was divided at home. Some Whigs were ready to recognize American independence so that they could blame the Tories for ruining the empire and thereby turn them out of office. Ireland was also restive, and British troops were sent to maintain order. For all these reasons, Great Britain made a separate peace with the United States after Cornwallis's defeat at Yorktown in October 1781.

Whereas the final *military* victory of the American colonists owed much to outside factors, the emergence of the United States as the modern world's first democracy was a purely American achievement. A prominent minority of the colonists opposed a complete break with Great Britain; these loyalists came from all classes, but a high proportion of them identified themselves with the values of the British governing class. By the end of the war more than 60,000 loyalists out of a total population of 2,500,000 (including 500,000 slaves) had permanently emigrated to

The "Sons of Freedom" pulling down the statue of King George III in New York City's Bowling Green, July 9, 1776.

Canada. This loyalist emigration was extremely important in removing a potential reactionary force from American society. Those untitled aristocrats who became patriots accepted the principle of equality during the war and incorporated it into the Constitution of 1787.

The ratification of the Constitution by the states brought an end to the "Critical Period" of American history, the years 1783 to 1789. During the revolutionary war the Articles of Confederation had provided for a Congress to carry out military and foreign policy but with no power to enact laws or levy taxes. This system worked adequately during the urgency of united action in wartime, but after the 1783 peace, Congress's recommendations received little attention either inside or outside the United States. The states, increasingly concerned with their own power, became divided among themselves, and some of them continued to pour forth a flood of paper money that defrauded creditors. Discontented debtors also threatened property rights. During the winter of 1786 to 1787 an uprising of 2000 poor farmers led by

Daniel Shays was put down by the loyal militia of Massachusetts. But Shays' Rebellion made many property owners fear that the nation was teetering on the edge of anarchy. It was this fear that prompted the states to seek a national government that could maintain law and order, while still preserving states rights and individual freedom.

In a sense, the Constitution of the United States reaffirmed the traditions of liberty and equality of colonial times, but it was truly revolutionary in explicitly stating that all public power came from the people. The people had exercised their sovereignty in framing the Constitution, in giving themselves alone the power to change it, and in agreeing to live under the restraints imposed by it. Their elected legislators could pass other laws, but they could not change the organization of public power — the law of the land. It was this example of liberty, equality, and rule of law that immediately captured the imagination of so many Europeans.

It took a generation to develop the national institutions envisioned by the Constitution.

From 1789—when most states ratified this document—to December 1814—when the Treaty of Ghent ended the War of 1812—the supporters and opponents of a strong federal government tried to shape the new regime according to their own outlooks. Thomas Jefferson and the Republicans championed states rights and a society of small farmers; Alexander Hamilton, James Madison, and the other Federalists stressed nationalism and economic expansion. As in Great Britain and France, the needs of war and business, rather than political rhetoric, gave the national development of the United States the second direction during this period and thereafter. In addition, the need to consolidate vast territorial acquisitions west of the Appalachians required federal control over conflicting private interests.

As the first President of the United States, George Washington set the pattern for a strong executive. He was determined to make his own executive decisions. He also insisted, as did Madison later, that the members of his cabinet be responsible to him alone, rather than to Congress. Secretary of the Treasury Hamilton strongly influenced the President on foreign policy and dictated domestic policy to Congress. While new federal courts upheld the Constitution, new treasury officials busied themselves with raising new taxes and putting the nation's finances in order.

Hamilton, the architect of the national economy, was one of America's first modernizing leaders. He believed that a large-scale expansion of industry and commerce was essential to the nation's future. The growth of manufacturing had been stimulated by the suspension of imports from England during the revolutionary war. To promote further growth, large quantities of capital and men willing to invest it were needed. Hamilton helped to fill this need by issuing interest-bearing bonds to fund the national debt and to assume the debts of the individual states. This funded debt would, in turn, become the basis for industrial and commercial investment, since it would be used as the capital for a federally chartered bank. The Bank of the United States would accept both the new federal bonds and coin for its stock; against this it would issue paper money that could be lent to manufacturers, merchants, shippers, and other entrepreneurs. Aside from future interest, huge profits could be made from the purchase of temporarily depreciated national and state securities. Hamilton assumed that as industry and commerce grew, so would the national government, supported by entrepreneurs who wanted to protect their investments in it.

The incorporation of new territories transformed the original group of seaboard states into a continental power. In the Land Ordinance of 1785, Congress laid down the general principles by which land would be transferred from public to private hands. In 1787 the Northwest Ordinance organized all the territories between the Ohio and Mississippi rivers and established the precedents followed thereafter for admitting new states to the Union. Kentucky became a state in 1792, Tennessee in 1796, Ohio in 1803. In 1803 the Louisiana Purchase added all of the continent to the Rocky Mountains except Texas, and Louisiana itself became a state in 1812. The westward movement of settlers required the opening up of roads—and eventually canals—to link the various sections of the new nation. Understandably, the westerners were especially interested in further territorial gains. President Jefferson hoped to "assimilate" the Indians, but the westerners forced them to cede their territories and move on. In 1811, under the leadership of Tecumseh, the Indians decided to fight back, and a savage Indian war followed. In this war the westerners hoped to annex Upper Canada.

The War of 1812 did not produce the results intended by the War Hawks. Its origins lay not only in alleged British aid to the Indians but also in British interference with America's neutral rights in trading with Europe during the Napoleonic wars. Eastern merchants and shipowners were willing to risk British seizures of their vessels and impressments of their seamen; the profits far outweighed these inconveniences. But the western and southern War Hawks (who wanted to annex Florida, held by Britain's ally Spain) prevailed. When war was declared, the United States was ill-prepared. During Jefferson's two terms as President (1801–1809) Republican policies had been

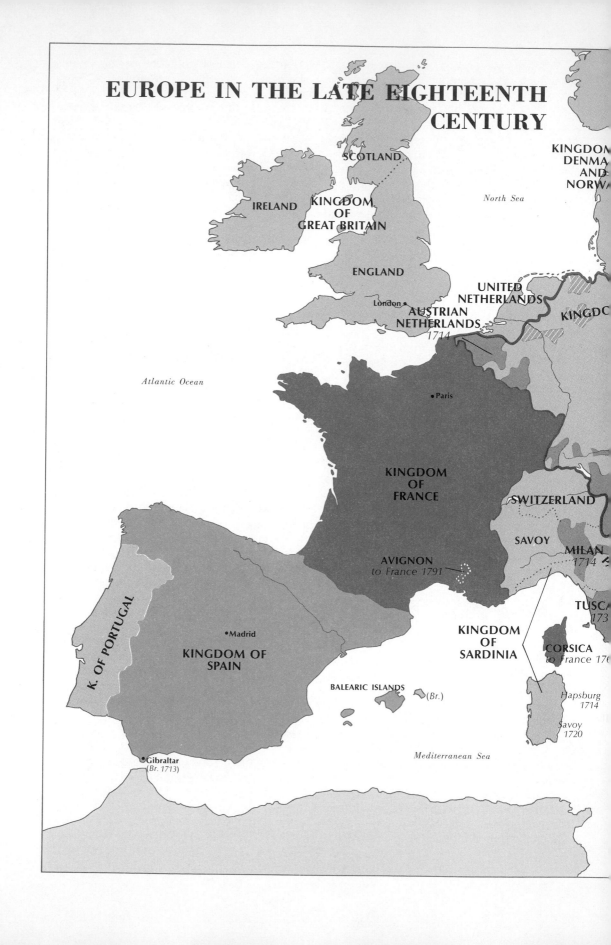

EUROPE IN THE LATE EIGHTEENTH CENTURY

SCOTLAND

IRELAND

KINGDOM
OF
GREAT BRITAIN

ENGLAND

London •

KINGDOM OF
DENMARK
AND
NORWAY

North Sea

UNITED
NETHERLANDS

AUSTRIAN
NETHERLANDS
1714

KINGDOM

Atlantic Ocean

• Paris

KINGDOM
OF
FRANCE

SWITZERLAND

SAVOY

MILAN
1714

AVIGNON
to France 1791

TUSCA
173

K. OF PORTUGAL

• Madrid

KINGDOM OF
SPAIN

KINGDOM
OF
SARDINIA

CORSICA
to France 176

BALEARIC ISLANDS   *(Br.)*

*Hapsburg
1714*

*Savoy
1720*

•Gibraltar
(Br. 1713)

Mediterranean Sea

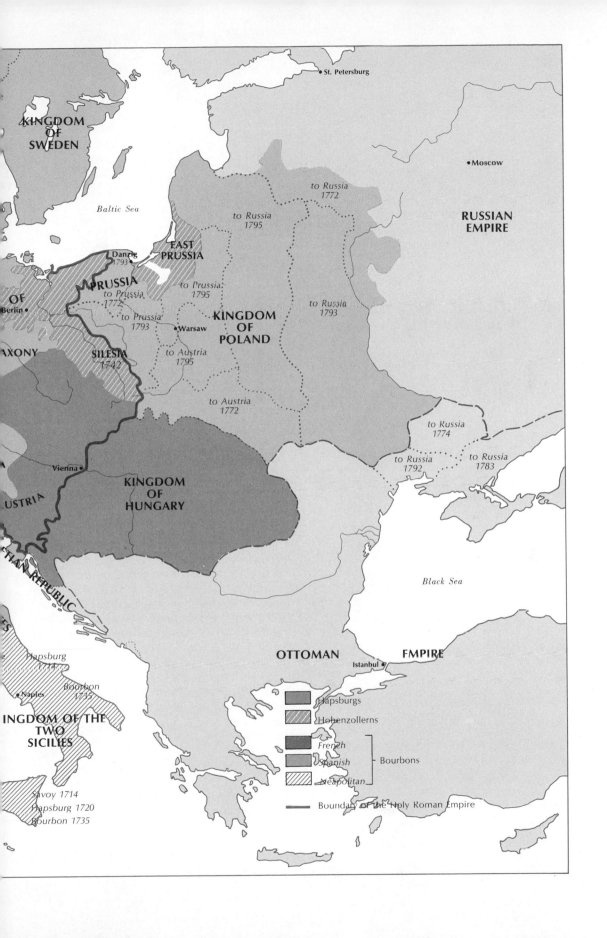

KINGDOM
OF
SWEDEN

Baltic Sea

• St. Petersburg

• Moscow

RUSSIAN
EMPIRE

to Russia
1772

to Russia
1795

EAST
PRUSSIA

Danzig
1793

PRUSSIA

OF

Berlin •

to Prussia
1772

to Prussia
1793

SAXONY

SILESIA
1742

to Prussia
1795

• Warsaw

KINGDOM
OF
POLAND

to Austria
1795

to Russia
1793

to Austria
1772

to Russia
1774

Vienna •

AUSTRIA

KINGDOM
OF
HUNGARY

to Russia
1792

to Russia
1783

Black Sea

TIAN REPUBLIC

Hapsburg
1714

Naples •

Bourbon
1735

KINGDOM OF THE
TWO
SICILIES

OTTOMAN   EMPIRE

Istanbul •

Hapsburgs

Hohenzollerns

French

Spanish   Bourbons

Neapolitan

Savoy 1714
Hapsburg 1720
Bourbon 1735

Boundary of the Holy Roman Empire

designed for a peaceful, agrarian nation. Under President Madison, the War Hawks wanted to continue to limit taxes and naval expenditures. Eventually they took the measures necessary to avoid a military disaster, but they did not win an acre of new territory. Ironically, New England, which had opposed the war, gained the most from it. With British imports suspended, hundreds of thousands of new cotton spindles began whirling in eastern factories. Hamilton, although he died in 1804 and his national bank was allowed to lapse in 1811, had triumphed over Jefferson as the prophet of America's future development.

THE COMING OF THE FRENCH REVOLUTION

There was widespread political unrest on both sides of the Atlantic during the last third of the eighteenth century; in Europe this unrest exploded in the French Revolution of 1789. Protests against privilege and inequality had begun earlier in the British Isles and in some of the smaller countries of Northwestern Europe. Inspired by the American Revolution, many European radicals demanded governments representative of and responsible to the people; most of them still limited "the people" to taxpayers, but their goal represented an early version of modern political democracy. In direct opposition to them was an aristocracy that was trying to reassert or extend its own privileges and powers. Caught between these two contending forces, many of Europe's monarchs sought to preserve their authority by reforming society from above—a policy known as enlightened despotism. This policy failed partly because of aristocratic resistance before 1789 and partly because the French Revolution, which championed social as well as political democracy, prompted a conservative reaction throughout Europe.

The Failure of Enlightened Despotism

Many reforms of the enlightened despots were based on the practical need to increase revenues and manpower resources for their wars. Others, however, reflected a desire to justify authoritarian rule in the cold light of reason and social usefulness. As we saw in the last chapter, the publicists of the Enlightenment championed modern values and institutional reforms. Although some of the enlightened despots—or, at least, their ministers—drew on the ideas of the Enlightenment, their efforts to make their rule more modern failed because they would not or could not repudiate the privileges of the traditional aristocracy.

Enlightened despotism was the most successful in France, Sweden, and the Austrian Monarchy in the decades preceding the American Revolution. The monarchs of these countries initiated administrative reforms and reduced the powers of the aristocracy. In Sweden, King Gustav III (1771–1792) also abolished torture, improved the poor laws, and proclaimed religious toleration and freedom of the press. The example of the Austrian Monarchy is especially instructive for the period after 1776 because its ruler, Joseph II (1765–1790), tried harder than any other ruler to make enlightened despotism work.

Joseph II's outlook and policies earned him the title "the revolutionary Emperor." A staunch anticlerical, he suppressed most of the monastic houses, legalized civil marriage, had the state take over the church's responsibility for poor relief and care of the sick, and proclaimed the legal toleration of Protestants and Jews. Having no respect for the nobility, he made the nobles subject to the same criminal procedures as everyone else and made them pay taxes; he also enlisted commoners in his civil service. Joseph's most revolutionary policy was his grant of legal freedom to the serfs in his realm; those who wished to could now leave the estates of their landlords, marry without permission, and take up new trades. But those peasants who remained as agricultural workers on the estates owed the same obedience and labor service as before. Consequently, the main effect of Joseph II's legal abolition of serfdom was to increase the peasants' hostility to the nobles and the nobles' hostility to him. Under Leopold II (1790–1792) the aristocratically controlled provincial diets forced the repeal of most of Joseph's reforms, so that the "revolution from above" failed in the end.

The legally constituted privileged orders triumphed in Russia and Prussia as they did in the Austria of Leopold II. In 1785, Catherine the Great's Charter of the Nobility (see p. 358) completed the development of the Russian nobility into a legally privileged and irresponsible aristocracy better able to dominate the Russian serfs. Her reputation as an enlightened despot rested mainly on the carefully cultivated image that she conveyed to her *philosophe* friends in the West. In the Prussia of Frederick the Great (see p. 354) enlightened despotism was not the pure sham that it was in Russia, but there, too, the monarchy had to make concessions to a resurgent aristocracy. Thus, in Austria, Russia, and Prussia, enlightened despotism gave way to a new understanding between the monarchy and the privileged aristocracy. The new arrangement was to survive the French Revolution, and, in general, to last until the beginning of the twentieth century in most of Eastern Europe.

In France the situation was quite different; there the monarchy antagonized both the commoners and the privileged orders. When Louis XVI came to the throne in 1774 he wanted to be a good king. Although no dullard, he had neither the glamor nor the shrewdness of a Frederick the Great, a Catherine the Great, or a Joseph II, and he lacked the will to carry through a consistent policy of reform. Moreover he did not know how to gain support from any section of society for the individual reforms his ministers proposed, reforms that might have gained the allegiance of the middle classes. Furthermore, government efforts to infringe on the traditional "liberties" of the parlements, the nobles, and the church hierarchy lost Louis their allegiance. In the 1780s the French aristocracy intensified its effort to increase its privileges and powers—an effort it had launched once before in the early part of the century but which had been partially thwarted by Louis XV. This aristocratic resurgence reached its peak on the eve of the French Revolution.

Enlightened despotism failed everywhere. Its reforms were always incomplete, since it could not eliminate overlapping jurisdictions, traditional privileges, and the sanctity of the crown. The combination of an aristo-cratic resurgence and a democratic movement—both using claims of constitutional liberties and natural rights—ruined any chance of its ever working.

Causes of the Revolution in France

Until a unique combination of circumstances prompted the king to call the Estates General for the first time in 175 years, hardly anyone expected to see the Old Regime overthrown by force. Many people knew that something was wrong. There was an economic crisis aggravated by population pressure; the aristocratic resurgence exasperated sections of the bourgeoisie and the peasantry; enlightened political ideas were raising constitutional issues, and enlightened despotism was not working very well. Many Frenchmen were losing confidence in the justice and reasonableness of the existing government and its laws. As their old loyalties faded, they felt their obligations as impositions and their forced respect for their superiors as a form of humiliation. Existing sources of prestige and hitherto-accepted forms of income and wealth seemed undeserved. Frenchmen lost their sense of community. In this situation the former bonds between social classes were broken by jealousy and frustration. This widespread dissatisfaction with the existing order was the first cause of the French Revolution.

The second cause of the French Revolution was the rallying of the most dynamic and effective leadership to the side of change. Neither the king nor his ministers could control the events they set into motion. They appealed to public opinion and then lost the leadership of this opinion to the revolutionaries in the Estates General, in the streets, and in the press.

The third cause of the French Revolution was the weakness of the government of the Old Regime. In the second half of the eighteenth century, the machinery of the royal government was gradually falling apart. Neither the king's ministers nor the *intendants* who ran much of provincial France could stay this process under the ineffective leadership of Louis XV and Louis XVI. Only a determined monarch could have abolished France's overlapping administrative jurisdictions, reformed the tax system, and eliminated the obsolete, medieval, survivals in the law. The courts, too, needed a thorough overhaul to make them serve the needs of all the king's subjects. At the end of his reign, Louis XV had canceled the privileges of the Parlement of Paris when the judges of that court thwarted his minister's program for fiscal reform. But one of the first moves taken by Louis XVI was to restore its full authority. Like so many high officials, the judges bought or inherited their posts, which they continued to regard as a means of private enrichment instead of as a public trust. Under the Old Regime, France lacked the delicate amateurs who ran the civil service and local affairs in England and, unlike Prussia and Austria, it had not yet begun to use trained professional bureaucrats.

Like the machinery of the royal government, the social and economic structure of the Old Regime was crumbling. The First and Second estates—that is, the higher clergy and the nobility—no longer performed many of the functions that had formerly justified their wealth and privileges. These ecclesiastical and social elites might have been able to retain their ascendancy over the Third Estate—the bourgeoisie—had they not hopelessly antagonized the rising elite of wealth and talent in this estate. The eighteenth-century French bourgeoisie consisted of the well-to-do commercial and professional classes. Although these people had diverse interests and aspirations, they all came to hate the snobbery and privileges of the first two estates, especially their exemption from taxation. They also resented the success of the resurgent aristocracy in acquiring a virtual monopoly over the better posts in the government, the church, and the army.

Although members of the bourgeois elite were to lead the revolution, the urban and rural masses provided indispensable backing. Ordinarily the lower classes had little in common with the bourgeoisie, and during the course of the revolution the interests of these two heterogeneous groups were to clash repeatedly. What brought them together in 1789 was their common hostility to the Old Regime in a time of economic crisis.

This economic crisis resulted partly from rising prices and partly from a greatly increased population. In 1789 France had 26 million people, an increase of almost 40 percent in two generations. (One European out of seven was a Frenchman.) Civil peace and improved means of transporting food to areas of famine were allowing greater numbers of people to survive, particularly among the poor. Still, many of the poor could not find enough work, and even those who could saw their wages lagging behind rising prices, which were driven up by new supplies of gold and silver from Brazil and Mexico. By 1789 there was much unemployment, both among the town workers and among the peasants who earned part of their living in domestic manufacturing.

Population growth and rising prices also aggravated the problem of hunger in the face of a severe bread shortage. Bread was the principal food for the lower classes, and the grain harvest of 1788 had been disastrously bad. Because of the shortage, the price of bread was higher than at any time in the preceding 100 years. Hordes of landless workers flocked to the cities or roamed the countryside in search of work and food. These "brigands" frightened the small peasant proprietors and urban craftsmen as well as the rich, as we shall see presently.

Millions of peasants were bitter about France's outmoded and unjust system of land tenure. Since the twelfth and thirteenth centuries many peasant tenants had acquired hereditary rights to the land for which they still paid fixed quitrents. In early modern times, inflation had reduced the value of these rents to a pittance. Then, in the eighteenth century, the nobles began finding ways to increase these payments to boost their revenues in order to meet the rising prices. This "feudal reaction," which corresponded to the aristocratic resurgence in political matters, brought the discontent of the small peasant landowners to a fever pitch, especially since they also resented the heavy taxes of the government and the tithes of the church during the economic depression.

In 1789 the grievances of the small landowners combined with those of the urban craftsmen, who were very different from factory workers. Those who were "in business for themselves" resented the guilds for their restrictive practices and the First and Second estates for their tax exemptions. Those who did piecework or who were paid in wages blamed the merchant-entrepreneurs for the decline in their real income, but the government made a better target. The mass of small producers and nonpropertied classes of the towns and the countryside did not wear *culottes* (knee breeches) like the bourgeoisie and the nobility. Indeed, in the revolutionary fervor of the years 1789 to 1794 they were to glory in their status as *sans-culottes*. But they carefully distinguished themselves as "the people" from the mob of jobless "brigands."

The hopes and grievances of all sections of French society coalesced when the king promised to summon the Estates General for the first time in 175 years in May 1789. He made this move only after all his other efforts to gain new taxes to stave off the mounting financial crisis failed. Heavy expenditures during the American Revolution had worsened the chronic financial difficulties of the government, and by 1787 it was on the verge of bankruptcy. In that year, Louis XVI tried to persuade the nobles, the church, and the parlements to grant him new taxes; when they refused, he stripped the parlements of most of their powers. This reversion to "despotism" also antagonized the leaders of bourgeois opinion, who at first sided with the privileged orders in their demands for constitutional government, taxation by consent, freedom from arbitrary arrest, and freedom to express legitimate grievances. It was this combined opposition that forced Louis XVI not only to convene the Estates General but also to have the delegates elected by nearly universal manhood suffrage, to request Petitions of Grievances (*cahiers de doléances*) from the Third Estate, and to give this estate twice as many delegates as the First or Second estates.

All Louis XVI had wanted was new taxes but, within less than two months of its opening session, the Estates General transformed itself into a National Assembly ready to make a revolution. The leaders of the Third Estate, backed by a few liberal noblemen and churchmen, brought about this transformation. The key issue was whether the delegates would vote together by head or separately by estate. Only a vote by head

could have given the Third Estate—with its representation doubled plus a small number of allies in the other two—a majority. The king knew this and used all kinds of pressure to make the three estates meet separately. But the leaders of the Third Estate and their noble and clerical allies responded with ever greater resistance, arguing that they were the true representatives of the people and swearing "never to separate . . . until the Constitution of the kingdom was established and affirmed on a sound basis." In the pamphlet *What is the Third Estate?*, the liberal Abbé Sieyès in early 1789 wrote:

(1) *What is the Third Estate? Everything.*
(2) *What has it been in the political order up to the present? Nothing.*
(3) *What does it demand? To become something. . . .*

REVOLUTIONARY FRANCE

The mass uprising of the summer of 1789 propelled France into a series of revolutionary experiences unprecedented in history. During the next six years the country went through three constitutions, rebellions by the extreme right and the extreme left, a totalitarian dictatorship, and an international war in which modern ideological issues played a crucial role. The French Revolution not only overthrew the Old Regime and brought class antagonisms into the open; it also forged a nation. Millions of Frenchmen suddenly began to think of the revolutionary government as their own. Their opinions of how it should be constituted and what its policies should be differed, but they agreed in their desire to defend it against its enemies at home and abroad.

Through all these upheavals, however, the new, modern order based on the "principles of 1789" remained. It abolished all forms of privilege and gave every citizen individual liberty and equality of rights. It rid the institution of private property of feudal entail and began to replace laws based on status with laws based on contractual agreements. It did away with the guilds, internal tariff barriers, and other hindrances to the freedom to hire labor, the freedom to produce, and the freedom to buy and sell. It expropriated the wealth of the church and refashioned this

The storming of the Bastille, July 14, 1789.

The Revolt of the Masses and the Overthrow of the Old Regime

institution into an agency directly dependent on the state. Finally, it gave France rational administrative and judicial systems that lasted until our own time.

In early July 1789, the beginning of the alliance between the revolutionary bourgeoisie and "the people" was marked by the formation of a militia—soon to be called the National Guard—and the installation of a revolutionary government at the Paris City Hall. Although they feared the urban masses, the bourgeois spokesmen for the Third Estate feared a royal or aristocratic reaction more. Hence under their leadership and with the help of dissident troops in the city, the people of Paris vented their accumulated rage on the Bastille, the fortress-prison in the eastern part of the city.

The storming of the Bastille on July 14, 1789 had a decisive effect on the political situation. Tens of thousands of Parisians took part in it, and 150 of the attackers were killed or wounded. The victorious crowd slaughtered the handful of defending troops, impaling their heads on pikes. Almost everyone interpreted the intoxicating news that the Bastille had fallen as a major defeat for "despotism"; the victors not only freed the seven political prisoners inside but they also tore it down stone by stone. At Versailles the news frightened the king so much that he sent away his troops.

The news of the fall of the Bastille and of the fleeing "*aristos*," led by the king's brother, also unleashed the mass upheaval in the countryside. In the last weeks of July the peasants became convinced that the "aristos" were inciting the "brigands" to attack them. As the Great Fear mounted in intensity, the peasants, armed against nonexistent brigands, turned their weapons against the hated *seigneurs* and their bailiffs. They stormed the chateaux and government offices where the records of their "feudal" obligations were kept and burned them. Neither the police nor the government officials did anything to stop them, and the law courts were suspended. This anarchy in the countryside forced the Constituent Assembly (as the National Assembly called itself by September) to go beyond its goal of political reform to more radical changes in France's social structure.

By August 5 the deputies at Versailles had abolished the vestiges of feudalism, and on August 26 they recognized the civil equality of all Frenchmen in the Declaration of the Rights of Man and the Citizen. The noblemen renounced their remaining seigneurial rights; the clergy renounced its tithes. Henceforth all land could be bought and sold outright by anyone, and every Frenchman was to be subject to the same rates of taxation and to have equal access to all public offices. The main accent of the Declaration of the Rights of Man and the Citizen was on liberty, "the power to do anything that does not injure others." The first Article declared that "men are born and remain free and equal in rights." Article Two defined man's natural rights as "liberty, property, security, and resistance to oppression." According to Article Three, sovereignty belongs to the nation, not to the king. The Declaration went on to say that only the law could limit the exercise of men's rights, and that the law was the expression of the general will. "All citizens have the right to take part personally or by their representatives in its formation. It must be the same for all, whether it protects or punishes." The law protected all citizens against arbitrary arrest and imprisonment and punished no one for his opinions or the free expression of them in the press.

The king did not approve of the August decrees and the Declaration of Rights, but the people won because they were organized. Never had any nation expressed such a burst of civic spirit as the French in 1789. People from all classes were participating directly in the revolution. Bourgeois patriots met in clubs to discuss reforms, watch over local affairs, and prod the authorities. There were many such political clubs, the most energetic, as we shall learn, being the Jac-

obins. The *sans-culottes* in the towns did the same things in their popular assemblies, which controlled the new communes (democratic municipal governments). Lawyers, merchants, craftsmen, and even a few noblemen joined the National Guard and began organizing it into regional federations. Finally, the press, now freed from censorship, kept the citizens alert.

The revolt of the masses continued when, on October 5, a crowd of women, accompanied by the National Guard, marched to Versailles. The women wanted the king to give them bread and to come to Paris, where they could keep an eye on him. Whether or not Marie Antoinette told her husband "let them eat cake," she was certainly against everything the revolution stood for and opposed leaving Versailles. The Marquis de Lafayette, who had fought with George Washington and who now headed the National Guard, tried to pacify both sides by appearing on the balcony with the queen, kissing her hand, and assuring the crowd that she and her husband would gladly go back to Paris. They were not glad, but they went, accompanied by wagonloads of bread from the royal bakeshop.

The victory of the Parisian masses seemed completed when the Assembly followed the royal family to the capital. Thereafter the king was their prisoner, and the Assembly was constantly subjected to the intimidations of the more aggressive political factions in Paris. For the next two years the Assembly governed France as a sovereign while framing a constitution that the king could no longer reject.

The new constitution reflected the aspirations of the bourgeois leadership more than those of the masses. It emphasized individual liberty, limited monarchy, and weak government; it also limited the right to vote to male citizens over 25 who paid direct taxes equal to the income of three days' work. These citizens voted for electors in local assemblies. There were higher property and income qualifications for electors and for deputies, which only members of the bourgeoisie could meet.

In addition to framing a constitution, which was to endure for less than a year, the Constituent Assembly issued a number of

"Camille Desmoulins calling the people to arms in the garden of the Palais Royal," by Honoré Daumier.

longer lasting decrees in line with the principles of social equality. It abolished all outward signs of social privilege; henceforth, noblemen were forbidden to use their former titles or to display their coats of arms, and every Frenchman was to be addressed simply as Citizen so-and-so. All Frenchmen could now enter any form of employment. Social classes still remained fairly closed, but there were no longer any legal distinctions among them. Money and talent replaced privilege and birth as the main criteria of social status.

The administrative, judicial, and economic reforms of the Constituent Assembly had less profound effects on people's daily lives than its social decrees, but they were actually more radical and longer lasting. In 1789 France was a complicated and illogical mosaic of provinces, bailiwicks, civil and ecclesiastical dioceses, conflicting local administrations and degrees of self-government, military districts, and unequal judicial divisions. The Assembly abolished all of these and reorganized the country into 83 departments (counties) of approximately equal size. The new judicial divisions were provided with a uniform system of courts, and all judges were to be paid by the state. France had to wait until the time of Napoleon for its modern civil code, but the Assembly inaugurated a standard judicial procedure and a uniform penal code based on the enlightened ideas of Beccaria (see p. 385). In accordance with laissez-faire principles, the Assembly abolished the monopolies and privileges of the chambers of commerce, manufacturers' associations, trading companies, and craft guilds. It also abolished all internal tariffs, thus facilitating freedom of trade throughout France and helping the development of banks, financial institutions, and credit. Another aid to economic activity was the institution of a uniform system of weights and measures—the metric system.

The Constituent Assembly temporarily solved the government's need for revenue by nationalizing the property of the church and selling it to the public, but its restructuring of the church itself divided the French people more seriously than any of its other reforms. The Civil Constitution of the Clergy suppressed the monastic orders, made the priests and bishops servants of the state, and required them to take a loyalty oath to the new regime. Pope Pius VI condemned both the Civil Constitution and the revolution itself; thereafter the French clergy and its followers were split between those who took the oath and those who did not—the nonjuring priests.

Within a year after the Constituent Assembly disbanded in September 1792 the political system it created had disappeared. Whereas the American colonists had learned to run their local affairs *before* they obtained their own national government, the French people had to acquire this kind of experience on the spur of the moment. Indeed, the very structure of the new French system handicapped it from the start. The militant leadership at the local level was usually more radical than the national government, and political decentralization widened the gap between the two. Moreover, the executive—that is, the king—and the new Legislative Assembly refused to cooperate most of the time. France had no George Washington to reconcile opposing factions and symbolize national unity. She had, instead, Louis XVI, whose heart was with the forces of counterrevolution.

This system also failed because of continuing opposition from the radical right and the radical left. The radical right, led by the Count of Artois, the king's brother, tried to persuade the monarchs of Central Europe to invade France, crush the revolution, and restore the king and the church to their former status. The radical left, led by Georges Jacques Danton and Maximilien Robespierre, wanted to depose Louis XVI and give all citizens full political rights. In April 1792, France did indeed go to war against Austria, which was joined by Prussia in July. The king supported the war, hoping that the revolutionary government would lose. The bourgeois leaders of the new order launched it hoping that it would rally the disenfranchised to the defense of the nation and spread the benefits of liberty and national self-determination abroad. Instead, the people of Paris made a "second revolution" on August 10, 1792.

The Revolution Fights for its Life

The insurrection of the Paris Commune on August 10, 1792 was the first example in modern history of a successful revolution led by the masses. The insurgents seized the royal palace and tried to arrest the king and queen. While the attackers were slaughtering their Swiss Guards, the royal couple fled next door to the meeting hall of the Legislative Assembly. It, too, had to bow before the conquerors of August 10. After deposing the king and letting the Commune imprison him, it voted itself out of existence. But first it announced the election, by universal suffrage, of a new Constituent Assembly, to be called the Convention.

This Convention immediately abolished the monarchy and decreed that its own acts would be dated from the Year I of the Republic (September 22, 1792).* In December the Convention tried Louis XVI for treason, and on January 21, 1793 the king was guillotined in the great square that is now called the Place de la Concorde. Louis XVI's execution bound the French counterrevolutionaries irrevocably to the European war against the regicides and brought other powers into the war on the side of Austria and Prussia.

* The months were also given new names, usually evoking the appropriate season—thus Brumaire (the foggy month), Thermidor (the hot month), and the like.

Although its main purpose was to frame a new constitution, the Convention also had to consolidate the Revolution, maintain a government, and wage a war against much of the rest of Europe. This task was particularly difficult because the deputies were deeply divided among themselves. The Girondists favored economic freedom and a federal government; they sat on the right. The deputies of the left supported the policies of the Paris Jacobins. Both factions were thoroughly middle class and property-minded, but the Jacobins insisted on economic controls and strong central government, at least for the duration of the war. Then the events of 1793 strengthened the forces of the counterrevolutionary right and the radical left outside the Convention and divided its two main factions into conservative and radical wings.

As in the summer of 1792, the Paris radicals blamed the conservative forces for France's military defeats in the spring of 1793. Despite their parliamentary immunity, 29 Girondist deputies were arrested on June 2, 1793. The rest fled to the provinces. Although many of them continued to think of themselves as patriots, others joined the forces of counterrevolution.

The Revolution was indeed fighting for its life by the summer of 1793. Its armies were being driven back on almost all fronts, and counterrevolutionary uprisings were spreading to the provinces. Incited by nonjuring priests and agents of the *émigrés* (French nobles who had "emigrated" to other countries), the peasants of the western province of Vendée had already begun their rebellion in March. When the Girondists rose up in July, more than two-thirds of the country was in open rebellion against the Convention. Coupled with the foreign menace, this mounting counterrevolutionary violence at home called for extreme measures to maintain the revolution.

The Committee of Public Safety and the Terror

In August 1793 the Convention created the Committee of Public Safety to deal with the wartime emergency; by December, the committee's twelve members were trying to control every aspect of French life. There is no doubt that their military mobilization saved France from invasion. Their levy-in-mass made all bachelors between the ages 18 and 25 subject to call into the army and declared that the entire population—both sexes and all ages—was liable to service of one kind or another. Conscripts and volunteers were merged with the old army of professionals into a mammoth patriotic force of over a million men. The Committee of Public Safety also tried to enforce price controls; although these were frequently violated, they did prevent a spiraling inflation and insured the provisioning of the armed forces.

In September 1793 the Convention gave the Committee of Public Safety authority to organize the Terror as a means of punishing traitors, preventing further counterrevolutionary uprisings, and enforcing the controls of the levy-in-mass. Anyone suspected of any kind of unpatriotic behavior—or even thoughts—was arrested. During the next ten months more than 300,000 Frenchmen were imprisoned. Of these, 16,594 were executed as a result of trials, and over 20,000 were shot without trial or died of disease or other causes while awaiting trial. No one was safe—that was what the Terror meant. It worked because the revolutionary surveillance committees and Jacobin clubs in the provinces often outdid the representatives of the national government in hounding suspected subversives and forcing their fellow citizens into patriotic conformity.

The leading member of the Committee of Public Safety was a leftwing Jacobin named Maximilien Robespierre (1758–1794). Yet even he could not satisfy the *sans-culottes'* demand that every Frenchman be made a small independent producer—which meant redistributing much of the nation's property and income—without terrifying the property-owning bourgeoisie, which formed the base of his government. The Terror provided the *sans-culottes* with the "psychological satisfaction" of seeing the severed heads and gushing blood of thousands of their betters. But their interests were basically opposed to those of the Jacobins, and the alliance between the two groups stood only until the worst threats of foreign invasion and counterrevolution had passed. In the spring of 1794 the open break came when Robespierre arrested and executed several of the most militant radical demagogues. In July, having

Robespierre being brought to the guillotine.

already antagonized the moderates in the Convention by executing some of their leaders, Robespierre was deserted by both the *sans-culottes* and his fellow Jacobins, who wore knee breeches just as he did.

The Thermidorean Reaction

The reaction began on the 9th of Thermidor (July 27, 1794), when Robespierre and several of his colleagues were arrested by more moderate Jacobin leaders. The conspirators of the 9th of Thermidor wanted not to end the Terror but only to get rid of Robespierre. Yet the need for the Terror decreased as the danger of invasion declined with new French military victories, and the Jacobin leaders who overthrew Robespierre fell out of favor themselves. The survivors of the Girondist faction came back to the Convention in December 1794, and the majority of the deputies abolished most of the emergency measures of the Committee of Public Safety.

The Thermidorean Reaction brought a more conservative political regime and reprisals against the Jacobins. The ultra-democratic constitution framed by the Convention had never gone into effect; the Constitution of 1795 resembled that of 1791 in giving the right to vote only to those Frenchmen who paid direct taxes, but it differed in maintaining the Republic and in placing more executive power in the hands of five "directors" than the king had had under the first constitution. Meanwhile, middle- and upper-class youths attacked Jacobin supporters in the streets, and the power of the Jacobins was ruined by crippling restrictions on all organized political activity. After the initial wave of revenge, the new regime, called the Directory, settled down to four years of uninspired rule.

THE NAPOLEONIC WARS AND THE BEGINNINGS OF MODERNIZING LEADERSHIP ON THE CONTINENT

Many historians claim that the French Revolution ended with the Thermidorean Reac-

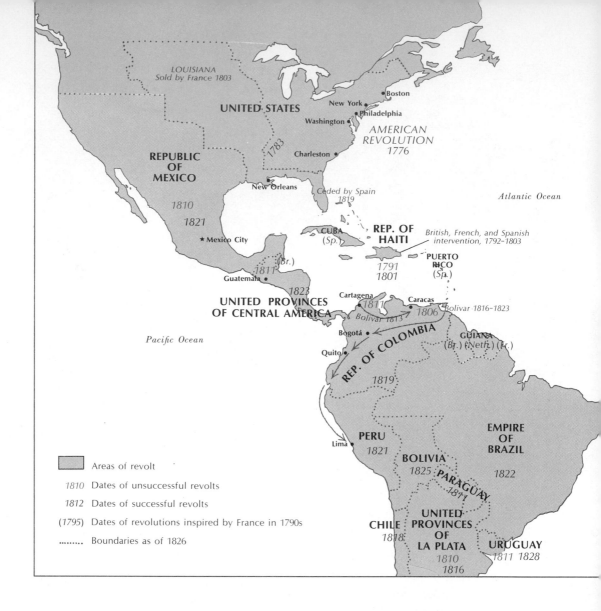

LOUISIANA
Sold by France 1803

UNITED STATES

New York • Boston
Washington • Philadelphia

AMERICAN
REVOLUTION
1776

1783

Charleston •

REPUBLIC
OF
MEXICO

New Orleans

Ceded by Spain
1819

Atlantic Ocean

1810

1821

★ Mexico City

CUBA
(Sp.)

REP. OF
HAITI

British, French, and Spanish
intervention, 1792–1803

PUERTO
RICO
(Sp.)

1811

Guatemala •

(Br.)

1791
1801

1823

UNITED PROVINCES
OF CENTRAL AMERICA

Cartagena
1811

Caracas
1806

Bolivar 1816–1823

Bolivar 1813

Pacific Ocean

Bogotá •

REP. OF COLOMBIA

GUIANA
(Br.) (Neth.) (Fr.)

Quito •

1819

PERU

Lima •

1821

EMPIRE
OF
BRAZIL

BOLIVIA
1825

PARAGUAY
1811

1822

CHILE
1818

UNITED
PROVINCES
OF
LA PLATA

URUGUAY
1811 1828

1810
1816

Areas of revolt

1810 Dates of unsuccessful revolts

1812 Dates of successful revolts

(1795) Dates of revolutions inspired by France in 1790s

········ Boundaries as of 1826

tion and the rise of the Directory in 1795. Napoleon Bonaparte said that it ended when he became First Consul (dictator) in November 1799 and turned the period of innovation and civil strife into a period of consolidation and internal stability. Nevertheless, the Directory had tried to maintain a middle course between leftwing radicalism and counterrevolution; it was its failure to do so that allowed this famous general to take over the job. Whenever the Revolution was *over*, it had not entirely *failed*. Until 1814, and to some extent even afterward, the bourgeois elite managed to safeguard the "principles of 1789"—with the important exceptions of political democracy and rep-

resentative government—as well as unrestricted capitalist enterprise.

The French Revolution and the World

The French Revolution was part of a larger revolutionary movement in the Western world. In the Dutch and Austrian Netherlands and in parts of Switzerland democratic revolts—albeit unsuccessful ones—had occurred before the summer of 1789. There had also been unrest in the British Isles. Like the American revolutionaries, the English and Irish radicals of the 1780's were generally hostile to the aristocratic British Parliament, and although the authorities managed

IRELAND
1798

UNITED
KINGDOM
1798

★London

BATAVIAN
REPUBLIC
(1795)

• Berlin

GERMAN
STATES

BELGIUM
1783

★Paris

FRENCH
REVOLUTION
1789

FRANCE

HELVETIAN
REPUBLIC
(1798)

1821 (1797)
(1798)

(1798)

PORTUGAL

1820

★Lisbon

★Madrid

SPAIN
1812, 1820

ITALIAN
STATES
(1799)
1820

Mediterranean Sea

Moscow •

Decembrist Revolt
1825

RUSSIAN
EMPIRE

Warsaw • Polish Revolutions
1791, 1794

★Vienna

AUSTRIAN EMPIRE

SERBIA
1804

OTTOMAN

EMPIRE

GREECE
★Athens
1821

REVOLUTIONS, 1776–1828

to sidetrack all movements for basic political changes, radical groups reappeared in England in the 1790s. There was also a mutiny in the British navy in 1797 and a violent insurrection in Ireland in 1798. Between 1790 and 1796 there were revolutionary incidents, clubs, and plots in Germany, Italy, Austria, Hungary, and Poland, in which French influence was remote and indirect. The same may be said of the revolutions in Spain's New World colonies between 1810 and 1814.

On the other hand, revolutions followed the arrival of the French armies in many places. In Belgium, Holland, Switzerland, and Italy the French did little more than give assistance to local patriots, but in the Rhine-

land in 1794 and in Malta and Egypt in 1798 they initiated revolution. French military occupation did not, however, automatically bring revolution. In Spain, which the French occupied from 1808 to 1814, the main changes were made by the counterrevolutionary opposition.

Whatever the revolution's origins, however, its opponents blamed the French and fought a series of long and bloody wars against them. These wars involved the traditional struggle for empire and the balance of power as much as the extermination of the revolution. Yet the slogans of counterrevolution as much as anything else bound France's enemies together. They hated Napoleon for

NAPOLEONIC EUROPE, c. 1810

KINGDOM OF DENMARK AND NORWAY

KINGDOM OF SWEDEN

FINLAND
to Russia 1809

St. Petersburg

UNITED KINGDOM OF GREAT BRITAIN AND IRELAND

London

Copenhagen

Tilsit

Königsberg

KINGDOM OF PRUSSIA

Berlin

ADVANCE

Moscow

BORODINO (1812)

RETREAT

Atlantic

Ocean

WATERLOO (1815)

Paris

LEIPZIG (1813)

CONFEDERATION OF THE RHINE

GRAND DUCHY OF WARSAW

RUSSIAN EMPIRE

FRENCH EMPIRE

SWITZERLAND

Vienna

AUSTERLITZ (1805)

AUSTRIAN EMPIRE

BESSARABIA
to Russia 1812

KINGDOM OF SPAIN

Madrid

KINGDOM OF ITALY

Danube River

CORSICA

ELBA

Rome

MONTENEGRO

KINGDOM OF PORTUGAL

KINGDOM OF SARDINIA

KINGDOM OF NAPLES

Istanbul (Constantinople)

TRAFALGAR (1805)

Gibraltar (Br.)

Mediterranean Sea

OTTOMAN EMPIRE

MOROCCO

ALGERIA

TUNIS

KINGDOM OF SICILY

MALTA (Br.)

ABUKIR (Battle of the Nile, 1798)

EGYPT

French Empire

Controlled by Napoleon

Allied with Napoleon

---

his military conquests; they also hated him as a "Jacobin."

The Napoleonic Era

Napoleon Bonaparte (1769–1821) was a modernizing leader, and it was his military ambitions, not his domestic policies, that brought about his final downfall after one of the most sensational careers in modern times. As a member of the rough-and-ready Corsican nobility he had gained a lieutenant's commission in the king's army. Then the Revolution gave him his chance to rise rapidly in rank, since many of the senior officers went over to the counterrevolutionary side. Under the Directory, General Bonaparte piled up one military victory on another and, in November 1799, his troops helped him overthrow the Directory and made him dictator. Thereafter he used his popularity as a military hero and his brilliant mind—steeped in the rationalism of the Enlightenment—to extend the modernizing efforts of the revolution and to secure his own control of the government.

Napoleon consolidated his personal power by rallying the nation behind him in three ways. He invented the plebiscite, a popular referendum based on universal suffrage, and called for plebiscites in 1799 and

"Napoleon and his soldiers at the Battle of Eylau," by Jean-Antoine Gros.

1802 to approve his dictatorship and for another in 1804 to approve his crowning of himself as Emperor of the French. He gave his regime a broad social base by preserving the doctrine of "careers open to talent" while also reconciling some of the *émigrés* with new offices and new titles. In 1801 he ended the ten-year split in the church by signing a mutually acceptable concordat with the pope. This concordat was to last for more than 100 years. It restored some of the pope's powers over the French bishops, but the church's property was not restored, and the state was to remain purely secular, paying the salaries of the priests and of Protestant ministers and Jewish rabbis. By temporarily disarming the counterrevolution, the concordat was Napoleon's most successful tool for promoting conciliation and stability in France.

After stabilizing France, Napoleon began to renovate the nation's institutions; his guiding principles in this endeavor were equality, authority, and efficiency. He gave France the most highly centralized modern bureaucracy in the world, with the Council of State at the top and with thousands of well-paid professional administrators. He maintained the local administrative units created in 1790 but introduced a new representative of the central government—the *prefect*—as the final authority in each department. Napoleon's economic and financial reforms consolidated the gains of the revolution and completed the emancipation of bourgeois capitalism from the restraints and inefficiency of the Old Regime. He established a corps of national tax-collectors and created the Bank of France on the model of the Bank of England. In 1804 the Bank of France issued a new, stable currency, the franc, which was to retain its gold value of 20 cents for over 100 years. Napoleon also created a centralized system of secondary and higher education for training his new elite of talent.

Napoleon's most famous and most enlightened reform was his Civil Code. Not since

"Execution of Spanish guerrillas by the French after the uprising on May 3, 1808," by Francisco de Goya.

the Roman Emperor Justinian had anyone defined all the possible legal relations involving private individuals and their property in such a rational and comprehensive way. There was a statute for everything; nothing was left to custom or chance. The Civil Code incorporated the modern conception of private property from John Locke through the French Revolution. In making contracts rather than status the basis of civil society, it marked the permanent triumph of the bourgeoisie. Most bourgeois Frenchmen were even willing to give up their political liberties in return for this blessing. For Napoleon remained a dictatorial ruler until his downfall.

Napoleonic France, with its modern state apparatus, its superb army, and its patriotic citizenry, was the most formidable force Europe had ever known. With his brilliant strategy and tactics and unprecedented masses of manpower, Napoleon added large parts of Europe to his Empire, which by 1810 totaled 71 million people, including only 27 million French. By then he had decisively defeated Austria and Prussia, reduced the latter to half its size, and made Russia a temporary ally. Only England still fought him unbeaten, mainly because of its supremacy at sea. England was able to withstand Napoleon's efforts to cripple it through his Continental System, a series of economic embargos that denied it access to the European market. But England alone could not beat Napoleon. Not until after his disastrous defeat in Russia in 1812 were the other powers to resume their earlier coalitions against him.

In 1813 the four other great powers — Great Britain, Russia, Austria, and Prussia — were finally able to put more soldiers in the field than France. Moreover, the bulk of Napoleon's own soldiers were now raw, teen-age recruits, and middle age and overwork began to make the emperor lose some of his sure touch. One by one his former allies and dependent rulers turned against him. Finally, in mid-October, the Allies defeated him in the Battle of Leipzig.

The Allies made their victorious entry into Paris on March 31, 1814. Napoleon was then exiled to the island of Elba, off the west coast of Italy. His return to the throne and his defeat at Waterloo the next year were little more than a theatrical epilogue. Napoleon and his empire were finished. The Allies had already restored the Bourbon pretender to the throne of his fathers and his dead brother. Louis XVIII indicated the tone of the whole post-Napoleonic period when an aide brought him the joyous news. "Sire! You are the King of France!" The new sovereign coldly replied, "And when have I been anything else?"

Beginnings of Modernization on the Continent

The triumph of the counterrevolutionary forces did not end all the innovations stimulated by the French conquests. Although the idea of national self-determination was ignored in the peace settlements, the reactionary rulers of Europe had used the anti-French feelings of their subjects to bolster their own war efforts, and nationalism was to reappear in many places after 1815. France had set the example of what an independent national community could do, and it was later to be followed by the Belgians, Greeks, Swiss, Italians, Germans, and other national groups all over the world. Almost everywhere the nation-state was to become the framework in which modernization was to occur.

Europe from Spain to Poland had gotten a taste of modern society during Napoleon's rule. Those territories that had been under French control the longest were the most affected by the new forms of political and social life. Only in Belgium and the Rhineland did the seignorial regime disappear completely and without compensation. East of the Rhine Napoleon had to compromise with the landlord class at the expense of the would-be peasant proprietors. In the Duchy of Warsaw the Polish nobles retained all the land, whereas the serfs received only nominal freedom, and the Jews, who were initially given civil rights, were then denied them in 1809. The principle of "careers open to talent" was less rigorously enforced in the more recently acquired French dependencies. Yet, even there, the nobility lost its legal privileges in taxation, office holding, and military command.

More than any single instrument, the Napoleonic Civil Code permanently modernized the social institutions of every territory where it was applied. It brought the "principles of 1789" — the equality of persons, forms of property, and inheritances; religious toleration; and the secular state — to Belgium, Holland, Rhineland Germany, Italy, and Spain. Although the Civil Code was revoked in 1814 in Spain and Italy, it strongly influenced the new national law codes of these two countries in the late nineteenth century. By then it had also been adopted in modified form in Rumania, Egypt, Haiti, Quebec, Louisiana, and a half dozen Latin American countries.

Even the four great powers, which Napoleon never succeeded in destroying, were not completely immune to the idea of structural changes. In Austria the Old Regime survived intact, and Great Britain made no institutional changes before 1815. But Tsar Alexander I (1801–1825) of Russia toyed with a number of administrative, legal, and financial reforms at first and even appointed a committee to draw up a plan for such reforms; he also launched a program to "assimilate" the several million Jews in the western part of his empire. The Napoleonic invasion ended these schemes, however, and after 1812 Russia became the most reactionary country in Europe.

Prussia changed the most between 1806 and 1813. Having been deprived of half of its territory and most of its standing army by Napoleon, it began this period as a mere shadow of its former self. But it was the only purely German state capable of overthrowing French domination in Central Europe, and displaced German patriots flocked to Prussia to help it rebuild its army and its state. General Gerhard von Scharnhorst and Count Neithardt von Gneisenau rebuilt the army by setting up a system

Appeal of King Frederick William III of Prussia, "To my people" for an all out
war of liberation against the French.

that later developed into what we call universal military training: all young men were to serve a short term in the regular army and then become part of the reserves. Baron Heinrich von Stein and Prince Karl August von Hardenberg tried to make Prussia a real political community. They modernized the state administration by eliminating overlapping jurisdictions. They gave the middle classes a greater voice in municipal affairs and opened the lower officer ranks in the army to them. Stein's "abolition" of serfdom gave legal status and freedom of movement to the mass of the population, but many peasants remained dependent on their landlords as hired laborers, and the Junkers gained one-third of the land of every peasant who wanted to convert the other two-thirds of his tenure into private property. In laying the foundation for a modern state and a modern economy through their legal reforms, Stein and Hardenberg actually strengthened the power of the king and the aristocracy. This result was to give the modernization of Prussia and Germany a different form from that of Britain, France, and the United States.

THE PEACE SETTLEMENTS, 1814–1815

The peace settlements of 1814 to 1815 marked the complete triumph of the balance of power in international affairs. For "reasons of state" the aspirations of mere peoples were simply shelved. Power alone counted. The international ideological war had ceased to be an overriding consideration, and it ended with France's military defeat. In fact, now that France was safely Bourbon again, it was quickly accepted into the "club" of the four other great powers. Lesser powers, dispossessed sovereign princes, and nationalist pressure groups had no influence on the peace settlements; the Big Five reorganized Europe and the colonial world* to suit themselves.

The Congress of Vienna (September 1814 to June 1815) decided the fate of Europe. There was little argument over the settlement in the West. Everyone agreed that there should be a barrier of strong states along France's northern and eastern frontiers. Thus a new Kingdom of the Netherlands was formed, combining the former Dutch Republic and Belgium (former Austrian Netherlands), and Prussia was given almost all of the German left bank of the Rhine. The Kingdom of Piedmont-Sardinia was given the old Republic of Genoa. In compensation for Belgium, Austria got the remainder of northern Italy—to be called the Lombard-Venetian Kingdom. The old ruling families were eventually restored in central and southern Italy as well as in Spain and Portugal. Switzerland was restored as an independent confederation—the only republic in Europe.

---

* Great Britain was the main gainer overseas; it got the former Dutch colonies in Ceylon and South Africa and some French islands in the West Indies and the Indian Ocean. It also confirmed its domination of the Mediterranean by keeping Malta and some islands off the northwest coast of Greece.

It was far more difficult to reestablish the balance of power in Central and Eastern Europe to everyone's satisfaction, and the struggle for the spoils almost broke up the Congress of Vienna. In the end the territory of the Duchy of Warsaw was included in the new state called "Congress Poland," with Tsar Alexander I as its "constitutional" king. Some Poles remained in Prussia and Austria, but Russian influence now extended 250 miles farther west than it had after the third partition of Poland in 1795. (Russia had also acquired Finland and Bessarabia during the Napoleonic period.) Prussia got two-thirds of Saxony. The rest of Saxony and the Napoleonic kingdoms of Bavaria, Württemberg, and Hanover were kept virtually intact. Along with Prussia they formed a part of the loose German Confederation of 39 states, whose borders corresponded pretty much to those of the Holy Roman Empire. But the Empire itself was not restored, and all the other formerly sovereign princes were left with nothing but their empty titles and their memories.

Radical changes swept the Western world between 1789 and 1815. To be sure, many achievements of the past endured. The Newtonian view of the physical world was to persist for almost another century. Sovereign states became stronger and more imperialistic than ever. Economic development proceeded at about the same pace as before (only in England did industrialization change it radically before 1815). Nevertheless, many basic features of European civilization were never to be the same again.

The traditional class structure lost its legal basis in most of Western and Central Europe. Although social classes were to remain an important part of European life long after 1815, never thereafter were noblemen to have the kinds of power and privilege they had enjoyed in the past. The middle classes had come into their own, and the masses had begun to assert themselves.

War changed too. In order to defend their revolution against foreign attack, the French put a million men into the field of battle. In order to defeat them, other states mobilized mass armies as well. The age of gentlemanly wars fought by mercenaries was over. Once the masses became involved, wars acquired an increasingly nationalistic flavor.

The needs of war and the ascendancy of the bourgeoisie also made government more efficient and more rational. Here, too, the French initiated the change, and other nations followed suit. They developed modern civil administrations run by talented commoners. Many countries also adopted the Napoleonic legal code, with its emphasis on logical consistency, equality before the law, and the sanctity of property. The English, American, and French revolutions assured the long-run ascendancy of modernizing leaders who fostered the interests of the entrepreneurial class. The Napoleonic wars and the War of 1812 made the governments of the United States, Great Britain, and France more responsive than ever to the need for economic modernization.

Finally, the ideals of political democracy and national independence became part of the European and American consciousness. By 1815 democratic government survived unscathed only in the new American republic; but the French had given this ideal to their fellow Europeans, and it was to reassert itself in France and elsewhere within a few decades. The French and the Americans gave the ideal of national independence to the people in Latin America as well as in Europe, and although it was thwarted in most places in 1815, it was to reappear shortly thereafter.

The most permanent legacy of the era of the French Revolution and Napoleon was its radicalism. A radical is someone who cherishes values incompatible with those embodied in existing institutions. He is so deeply estranged from these institutions that he refuses to compromise with them in any way. The radical of the left insists on the destruction of the old order and the creation of a new one. The radical of the right insists on the destruction of the new order and the recreation of the old one. Each type of radical had appeared from time to time before 1789. But in that fateful year the conflict between them began an epidemic of revolutions and counterrevolutions continuing in many parts of the world even today.

SUGGESTED READINGS

Hill, Christopher, *Reformation to Industrial Revolution, 1530–1780,* Vol. 1 of *The Making of English Society,* New York: Pantheon, 1959.

Firth, Charles H., *Oliver Cromwell and the Rule of the Puritans in England.* New York: Oxford University Press, 1953.
Best scholarly biography.

Palmer, Robert R., *The Age of the Democratic Revolution.* Vol. I. Princeton, N. J. Princeton University Press, 1959. Paperback.
An impressive attempt to relate democratic movements in all countries from the American colonies to Russia. Challenging comparative history for the advanced reader.

Rossiter, Clinton L., *Seedtime of the Republic: The Origin of the American Tradition of Political Liberty,* New York: Harcourt, Brace and World, 1953.
Stimulating analysis of intellectual currents in the colonies on the eve of the Revolution.

Alden, John Richard, *The American Revolution, 1775–1783.* Vol. IV of The New American Nation Series. New York: Harper and Row, 1951. Torchbook. Paperback.
The best general survey.

Lefebvre, Georges, *The Coming of the French Revolution.* Trans. Robert R. Palmer, New York: Random House, 1961. Paperback.

Rude, George, *The Crowd in the French Revolution*. New York: Oxford University Press, 1965. Paperback.

Reflects recent emphasis on the role of the sans-culottes.

Hampson, Norman, *A Social History of the French Revolution*. Toronto: University of Toronto Press, 1967. Paperback.

Stimulating and novel.

Brunn, Geoffrey, *Europe and the French Imperium, 1799–1814*. New York: Harper and Row, 1963. Torchbook. Paperback.

Markham, Felix, *Napoleon and the Awakening of Europe*. New York: Collier, 1965.

An admirably compact and up-to-date biography.

PART IV

Europe and the Americas to World War I

After 1815 nationalism, industrialization, and democracy quickened the pace of change in Europe and the Americas; indeed, more things changed everywhere during the next 100 years than during the preceding 300—hence, the greater concentration from this date onward in this text. Although national cultures were beginning to develop in North America before 1776 and in parts of Middle and South America before the early 1800s, only afterward did each of the new nations in these areas acquire a history of its own. This was also true for Germany and Italy, whose unifications were completed only in the years 1870 to 1871. In all cases the struggles for national independence and unity involved the middle classes and, occasionally, as in the United States, even the masses in public affairs. This kind of involvement did not necessarily lead to full-scale political democracy, but it did mean that the leaders of most European and American states had to cater to the wishes of their people in one way or another. In the Revolution of 1905, the tsar of still autocratic Russia was forced to see this necessity just as the monarchs of Western and Central Europe had been in the Revolutions of 1848. Aside from their bourgeois leadership, a new element in these revolutions was the urban proletariat that was being created by industrialization.

Industrialization hastened other changes besides political ones. First, it precipitated a completely new form of economic growth, which eventually made possible a higher material standard of living for an ever-larger number of people. Second, it forced the majority of workingmen, women, and children out of agriculture and into manufacturing, mining, transportation, commerce, and a host of service occupations; for example, the introduction of compulsory elementary education toward the end of the nineteenth century required hundreds of thousands of new teachers in each of the major countries. Third, industrialization reinforced the parallel trend of urbanization, so that city people and city ways prevailed increasingly. Finally, all these developments, by destroying old values and uprooting millions of people, brought cultural and social changes that would have been unthinkable in a traditional society. For many reasons—of which the frontier and the "melting pot" are most frequently cited—the United States was the most extreme example of these changes. But by the end of the century new social groups in Europe as well were demanding recognition and behaving in novel ways: highly educated women rode bicycles and fought for equal rights; second-generation city workers forgot their folk culture and kinship ties to become anonymous newspaper readers and spectators in vaudeville

424

houses; business tycoons of humble origin tried to make their material-istic, competitive ethic the dominant one in the whole society; militant labor leaders, joined by some intellectuals, preached revolutionary doc-trines like socialism, syndicalism, and anarchism; other intellectuals denounced the prevailing materialism and faith in science, emphasizing instead hitherto unexamined forms of consciousness and the uncon-scious.

Like industrialization, nationalism and nation-building were not un-mixed blessings. With a few notable exceptions the new nations of Latin America offered little improvement in the lives of their impoverished masses. Mexico, which seemed to offer the most, was also the most serious victim of foreign, particularly United States and French, imperial-ism. The United States itself suffered an agonizing civil war that drama-tized the country's regional and racial divisions, some of which, like the English-French division in Canada, are still with us. Extreme nationalism led to racism in Europe in the form of anti-Semitism at home and discrimi-nation against colored peoples in the rest of the world. This kind of nationalism among the masses was also used to reinforce the new wave of imperialism toward the end of the nineteenth century, and in 1914 it got completely out of hand during the diplomatic crisis that culminated in World War I.

CHAPTER 14

Industrialization and State-Building in Europe, 1815–1870

Most educated Europeans viewed Napoleon's fall as the end of a long nightmare that had begun with the French Revolution in 1789. They hoped that they were awakening not to a new world of change and strife, but to a reconstructed world of stability and peace in which change, if it came, would be imperceptible, and war, if unavoidable, would be limited.

In every area of life the signs of this attitude were apparent. Governments quashed dissent and refused reform at home while their diplomats tried to establish an international system that would stop revolution and conquest. Writers and painters accented the beauties of an idyllic (and mythical) past and concerned themselves with the individual psyche as opposed to the "artificial" structure of society. Workers destroyed new machines, seeking to perpetuate the old economy. Deserted churches found new congregations. Conservatism—a tenacious desire for peace and order—dominated everywhere.

But the two great forces of the nineteenth century, nationalism and industrialization, were already becoming too powerful to be stopped. Few men understood these forces, even partially; those who did came to realize that decades, perhaps centuries, of chaos lay ahead. Two outstanding prophets of the century, Alexis de Tocqueville (1805–1859) and Karl Marx (1818–1883), looked at their own societies and foresaw the struggles to come. De Tocqueville, the conservative, could forecast nothing but disaster and an end to liberty, whereas Marx, the radical, expected the catastrophe but clung to a faith that out of catastrophe would come Utopia—and a greater liberty. Both men have been proved correct in much that they said, but which one was nearer the truth cannot yet be determined, for nationalism and industrialization, the two forces they were concerned with, are still bringing about changes in society.

ROMANTICISM

The political and economic upheavals of the early nineteenth century were reflected in profound changes in the world of intellect and art. Throughout most of the eighteenth century classicists had tried to use reason to impose rules of order and unity on all forms of art and thought. But by the later part of the century the imperfections and confusion that classicism was supposed to avoid became all too clear in real life. Goethe's *Sorrows of Young Werther* (see p. 379) and Rousseau's "philosophy of the heart" (see p. 385), foreshadowed the romantics' rejection of existing injustices. Then the French Revolution, the Napoleonic Wars, and the Industrial Revolution brought all traditional beliefs and institutions into question. The youth of the early nineteenth century believed that it had to build something new or perish. This urge was the essence of the romantic temperament.

The three main tenets of romanticism were individualism, imagination, and feeling. The scientific attitude of the *philosophes,* most of whom had been deeply interested in social organization, economics, and politics, was overwhelmed by a new subjectivity, a pervading belief in the individual, and in unfettered experimentation. Thus, first in Germany and Great Britain, and then in France and other continental countries, classical moderation gave way to its opposite, a delight in extremes. Interest in "noble savages" in exotic lands had already been stimulated by the travel literature of the late eighteenth century. By then there was also a growing interest in the occult and in medieval romances and folklore. The career of Napoleon brought a new fascination with heroes and with the uniqueness of the individual. In their efforts to create new expressive forms, the romantics proclaimed that rules should be ignored and individual feelings valued more than reason or convention. It was during the romantic period that the subjective imagination was first accepted as the mainspring of the arts.

Many romantics of the early nineteenth century, struck by the inhuman suffering caused by revolution, war, and industrialization in their own time, were quite reactionary. William Wordsworth (1770–1850) and the other Lake Poets exalted nature and abhorred crowded cities; Sir Walter Scott (1771–1832) glorified the middle ages, pre-

sumably the period when chivalry ruled the world; François René de Chateaubriand (1768–1848) extolled the grandeur of religion, not for its truth, but for the beauty of its ceremonial. Soon, however, the character of this refusal to accept the modern world changed. By 1830, romanticism was coming to be associated with demands for social progress instead of with reaction.

Romanticism took different forms in different countries. In Germany, romantic poets, critics, and philosophers rejected Kant's separation of spirit and reality in the world (see p. 384) and proclaimed that true understanding depended on the inseparable emotional and rational sides of man, best exemplified in his aesthetic sense; Goethe's *Faust* was the model of their incessant striving for an unattainable human perfection. In England, the goal of personal fulfillment in nature gave way to open rebelliousness against convention; George Gordon, Lord Byron (1788–1824), exhibited in his own life as in his poem *Don Juan* the extreme of this side of romanticism: the restless and aimless hero. The Byronic hero appeared in two outstanding examples of Russian literature: Alexander Pushkin's *Eugene Onegin* (1826) and Michael Lermontov's *A Hero of Our Time* (1840). In France the romantic rebellion against convention inaugurated a bohemian way of life that has reappeared periodically ever since, complete with living in garrets, not washing, letting one's hair grow long, and having no visible means of support.

But romanticism is an artistic style as well as a temperament. This style emphasizes the subjective and emotional possibilities of each artistic medium and neglects its formal and structural aspects. The romantic writer, painter, or composer tries to cut short the road of communication to his audience by eliminating what he believes to be unnecessary formal conventions. The romantic style reached its climax in France around 1830 in the paintings of Eugène Delacroix (1798–1863), the verse plays and novels of Victor Hugo (1802–1885), and the music of Hector Berlioz (1803–1869). Romanticism dominated European music longer than any other art form, from the time of the Hungarian, Franz Liszt (1811–1886), and the

Scene from **Hernani,** *by Victor Hugo; this romantic drama stirred literary passions so much that it caused a riot when it opened in 1830.*

German, Richard Wagner (1813–1883), until well into the early twentieth century.

THE NEW INTERNATIONAL SYSTEM AND THE RISE OF NATIONALISM

Haunted by memories of war and revolution, Europe's leaders came together after Napoleon's fall, determined to put an end to both. The diplomats of the Congress of Vienna (1814–1815) based their efforts primarily on a clear recognition of the old and tried balance of power principle. Despite its many failures, this principle was for centuries the only significant deterrent to constant warfare. It was based on three ideas:

1. No sovereign state can be allowed to become more powerful than all the rest put together.
2. No state's existence or vital interests may be threatened.

3. Communications between states must be good enough to allow every state to become fully aware of any danger to the functioning of the system.

These principles seldom were spelled out, but statesmen time and again acted on them instinctively. They formed the basis on which the settlement was drawn up at Vienna.

The Congress System

A reasonable settlement was not all that the diplomats at the Congress of Vienna sought. To safeguard the newly established peace, some system of dealing with potential aggressors appeared necessary. Even small states had to be protected if general war was to be avoided. The man most consistently associated with the system devised for preserving the new status quo was Prince Clemens von Metternich (1773–1859), Austria's prime minister; this cosmopolitan aristocrat dominated the Congress of Vienna and

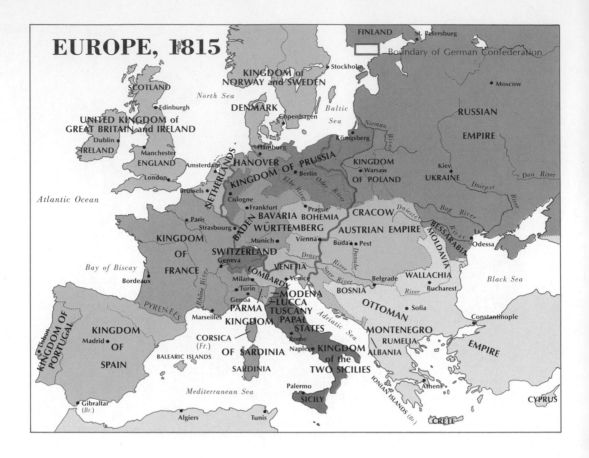

EUROPE, 1815

Boundary of German Confederation

the conservative international order as long as it lasted. At the Congress, Tsar Alexander I suggested the formation of a "Holy Alliance" based on "the sublime truths taught by the eternal religion of God our Saviour." Such an idea was not likely to appeal to the hard-headed politicians ruling Europe, but Prussia and Austria signed the treaty simply to keep the good will of the tsar. Britain refused on the ground that it could agree only to specific actions, not to such vague ideas as those involved in the Holy Alliance. But the British could and did join the Quadruple Alliance, which was established to prevent revolution in France, to prevent French aggression, and to provide for frequent meetings, on the model of the Congress of Vienna, at which the powers could discuss their joint interests and agree on actions they might take to preserve those interests.

The Congress system, as it was called, lasted only a few years; Britain, particularly, preferred to stay out of European affairs un-

less its own specific interests were endangered. Thus in the early 1820s it refused to sanction Austrian intervention to suppress a revolution in Italy and similar French intervention in Spain. The Congress powers were also unable to prevent Spain's Latin American colonies from gaining their national independence. In this case the British supported the United States, which assumed the role of "protector" of its new sister republics to the south. In fact, the United States was too weak to uphold the independence of the Latin American states; British naval power was the force that kept Europeans from intervening in Latin American affairs. Already weakened by Britain's withdrawal, the Congress system expired when, in the late 1820s, the English, French, and Russians aided the Greeks in their struggle for national independence against the Ottoman Empire, a clear violation of the status quo that the system was supposed to preserve. Nevertheless, the idea of cooperation remained strong, and not until the Revolutions of 1848, which led to radical changes in the European balance of power, did the menace of general war return.

Origins of Nationalism

After Napoleon's fall, nationalism was the force that began to affect Europe most intensely. By the late eighteenth century patriots in many areas had come to believe that people of the same ethnic group should be united in one nation, independent and indivisible. National consciousness remained restricted to educated minorities, which alone were aware of the unique history and culture of each nation. The German phi-losopher Johann Gottfried von Herder (1744–1803), an early nationalist, believed that each nation had something distinct to contribute to the development of man. The idea that each nation was unique was at first more important than the idea that one nation might be superior. But war and political strife lessened even educated people's appreciation for the customs of others, and the wars of the French Revolution and Napoleon spread nationalism to almost all levels of society. The Napoleonic wars took millions of men away from their homes and sent them to exotic lands that they recognized to be very different from their own.

NATIONALISM

Nationalism varies in character, depending on social and political circumstances. Its basic meaning, however, has always been devotion to a particular group of people, usually speaking a common language, who occupy a defined territory and share a set of historical experiences. In less than 200 years nationalism has displaced kinship ties, religion, and loyalty to particular persons as the keystone of society. Loyalty and devotion to a nation, independent or not, has become the strongest force promoting cooperation among large numbers of individuals.

Nationalism first appeared in the late eighteenth century in England, France, and the Thirteen Colonies as partiotism—love of the fatherland—combined with the recognition that whole nations shared certain important attributes. Politically, the basis of nationalism has been the desire of persons of similar ethnic or historical backgrounds to govern themselves in their own lands; this is the concept of national self-determination, which may justify any sort of government, provided that it is not subservient to "foreigners." Culturally, nationalism involves a belief in the "spiritual" uniqueness of one's own nation and, often, in its superiority over others. Both these attitudes grew up along with the rise of popular government. Beginning with the American and French revolutions, nationalism has often been revolutionary, for national pride went hand in hand with demands for wider participation in determining the nation's destiny.

Peoples everywhere have been united by nationalism, and quarrels among near neighbors have been ended. Competition with "foreigners" has led to tremendous economic, technological, and artistic achievements. But nationalism has also brought with it growing violence. Peoples who have won their own independence have often sought to dominate others; this has been one of the roots of modern imperialism. Nationalism has become entwined with ethnic and religious exclusiveness, and numerous ethnic minorities in Europe and Asia—Poles, Slovaks, Croatians, Jews, Armenians, and many other groups—have suffered nationalist persecution. Racism, too, has been intermixed with nationalism, leading to the persecution of racial minorities within national boundaries: Jews, blacks, and American Indians are obvious examples, as are various Chinese and Indian communities in Asia and Africa.

Frenchmen revolted in the name of liberty. When they found themselves under attack, they naturally sought to justify their cause by assuming that their enemies, still under the sway of kings, were lesser men. Many believed that France had been chosen by God to carry the gospel of liberty to less fortunate lands. Unfortunately, even soldiers who fought in the name of liberty were still soldiers: they not only killed men who fought them or disagreed with their political ideas, but they also killed and plundered men, women, and children who were innocent of any political ideas at all. The nationalism of the French quickly provoked nationalist reactions among the peoples they defeated. In a series of lectures in French-occupied Berlin, Johann Gottlieb Fichte (1762–1814) clothed nationalism in philosophic terms and preached the superiority of German culture.

Nationalism after 1815

In the period following the Congress of Vienna Europe's rulers viewed nationalism as subversive, since most nationalists followed the French in believing that citizens should participate in their governments. Even in the German states student societies that had fostered patriotism in the wars against Napoleon were now considered so dangerous that, in 1819, Metternich persuaded the leading German monarchs to outlaw them; this was done in the Carlsbad Decrees. Some nationalists then became active revolutionaries, such as those in the Young Italy movement of Giuseppe Mazzini (1805–1872), which was devoted to preparing the way for Italian independence and unity. Others, like the Czech historian František Palacky (1798–1876), devoted themselves to rediscovering the history and culture of subject nationalities that lacked states of their own. The dominant intellectual current, romanticism, easily encompassed the growth of passionate nationalism, particularly since so many nationalists stressed the glorious past in their polemics.

In its early stages nationalism was clearly a revolutionary doctrine. It grew along with the concept of citizenship: a man was a "subject" of his king, but a "citizen" of his country. When subjects began to feel that they were citizens, they also felt that they had a stake in the fortunes of their own na-

tions—and they therefore felt a need to participate in the control of the nation whose destiny they shared. The monarchs of Europe were suspicious of nationalism, which was, after all, a strand in the complex of ideas promoted by the French Revolution, just as were liberalism, democracy, and socialism, the three great political doctrines that became prominent during the nineteenth century. Moreover, most monarchs stood to lose control of parts of their kingdoms if nationalism triumphed, for most of them ruled territories occupied by widely divergent ethnic groups. The Austrian Empire was made up of Czechs, Slovaks, Hungarians, Serbs, and a half dozen other minorities ruled by yet another minority—the Germans. It was the most obvious example of the danger of nationalist fragmentation of states, but most other kingdoms contained at least a few thousand subjects who shared the national languages and customs of other peoples. Thus nationalism would not only undermine the power of princes over subjects of their own national origins but would also promote the breaking up of states based on old dynastic ties.

Nationalist Revolts

The first important nationalist revolution of the nineteenth century was that of the Greeks, who had long existed under the spasmodically oppressive rule of the Turks. Led at first by Alexander Ypsilanti (1792–1828), a Greek prince who had served in the Russian army, they staged a series of revolts throughout Greece beginning in 1821. The great powers were reluctant to aid them, despite the popular support they enjoyed in Europe, but English, French, and Russian attempts to end the fighting worked in favor of the Greeks, who finally won their independence in 1832. The Belgians, Roman Catholic and already building a significant textile industry, had been placed under the rule of the Protestant, preindustrial Dutch in 1815; in 1830 they revolted and won their independence mainly because the great powers, each one afraid that the other might gain in influence, could not agree on a plan for quashing the revolt. Italian and Polish revolts in 1830 and 1831, both inspired by nationalist ideas, were put down by Austrian and Russian troops.

THE RISE OF INDUSTRIAL SOCIETY

Since the invention of agriculture in the neolithic age men had been bound to a cruel cycle of prosperity followed by sudden outbreaks of famine, war, or pestilence, which killed them by the thousands. When the population in a particular area reached the point at which food became scarce, only migration (which usually brought war) or death could right the balance. Gradually, however, population ceilings had been raised. New foods, such as corn and potatoes, made possible the production of far greater nutritional value per unit of farmland. New inventions, such as the moldboard plow, dramatically increased the amount of land available for cultivation and decreased the amount of labor necessary to cultivate it. By the time of the high middle ages, certain individuals began to learn the lesson taught by the plow: technological innovation could radically improve the basis of human existence. This new attitude was implemented first in Great Britain.

The Industrial Revolution in Great Britain

During the prosperous mid-eighteenth century the population of the entire world was growing rapidly. The stage was set for another era of devastation. In Britain, however, the disaster was averted. The island position of Britain turned the people toward the sea, and by this time they had developed trade throughout the world. The profits from that commerce, combined with the gradual improvement in agricultural technology, helped to produce increases in farm production that made British subjects on the average the richest of men by the middle of the eighteenth century. It also made possible, and necessary, the improvement of river and coastal transport. The British had other advantages: a strict system of primogeniture forced innumerable younger sons of the nobility to join the lesser orders in doing productive work, thereby raising the status of that work; a strong central government limited feudal division of the nation; the weakness of the guild system, particularly in textile manufacture, made innovation easier;

and a tradition of encouraging education had produced a population more than half of which was literate. Finally, the British lived on a land rich in deposits of coal and iron.

Several steps are usually required to transform raw material into a finished product, and any innovation that makes one step easier puts pressure on the producer to improve every step in the process. Thus the adoption of John Kay's flying shuttle in the 1750s and 1760s considerably increased the speed of weavers; some new method was needed to produce more yarn to keep them busy. This problem was soon solved by the invention of new spinning devices—carding machines, the jenny, the water frame, and then Samuel Crompton's mule (1779), which combined features of the frame and the jenny. Suddenly the supply of yarn was vastly increased—and the weavers, whose need had prompted these inventions, found themselves with more yarn than they could use. The power loom, invented by Edmund Cartwright in 1787, was the answer; that loom, in turn, encouraged the development of better sources of power. This process, once begun, never stopped, for each invention made obvious the need for others. Consumption of cotton for cloth manufacturing multiplied 12 times between 1770 and 1880.

The large and comparatively wealthy English population was eager to buy cheaper cloth, and hundreds of thousands of overseas customers awaited cheap goods of every kind. Thus demand kept pace for many years with the increasing production that was stimulated by technological innovation.

Profits were high, and English entrepreneurs reinvested their gains in industry to pay for the new machines that were transforming the nature of production. From the coal mines where it had long been in use to pump water out of flooding mine shafts, the steam engine, improved by James Watt (1736–1819), was brought to the production of cloth. Entrepreneurs, harried by the dishonesty of cottage spinners and weavers who habitually (and understandably) augmented their miserable wages by stealing a part of the product of their labors, were delighted to gather their operatives in factories. There, steam power could be made available, and foremen could prevent loss by theft. Virtually

Rolle Canal, near Tarrington, Devonshire: part of England's excellent pre-railway transport network.

overnight new towns, then great cities, grew near the coal mines, where fuel was cheaper.

As soon as Watt's invention had proved its worth, the need for further refinement was obvious, and the machine tool industry was developed to make the needed refinements. Once innovation had really begun in one industry, it spread through the entire economy.

Yet there were problems. Canals, which carried raw materials to factories and goods to markets, were owned by the private companies that built them. As trade increased, the canals realized vast profits. They were monopolies, and their owners took advantage of the situation to raise tolls inordinately. The answer, soon obvious, was the railroad; that is, a mobile steam engine pulling loads of goods. Thus railroads were built, and competition kept both canal and rail transport costs low. The iron industry boomed as the demand for rails and rolling stock grew. Once the major railroads had been constructed, the "first industrial revolution" had run its course, and Britain, in less than a century, had been transformed.

Beginnings of Industrialization on the Continent

No other country had all of Britain's advantages. Germany and Italy were still "geographical expressions," nations divided into collections of large and small states. France was large, but transportation was relatively poor. Moreover, no other country had both coal and iron ore in such proximity as they existed in England. Even their apparent assets hurt Britain's would-be competitors. Because wood was scarce, the British were forced to learn to use coal to fire their blast furnaces, even though coal was, at first, far less efficient. British technicians, therefore, invented blast furnaces that would use coal efficiently. France, on the other hand, had little coal and plenty of wood, so Frenchmen naturally kept to traditional methods, shutting out the necessity for innovation. Nor were Germany and France, still suffering from long and disastrous wars, as rich as Britain. People had less money to spend, hence, demand for new products was relatively low. On the

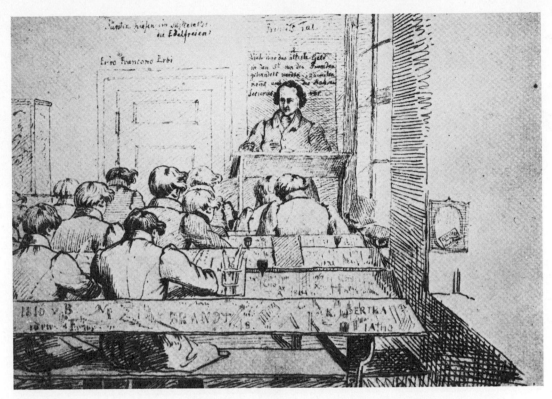

Jacob Grimm, the author, taught in one of Germany's nineteenth-century classrooms.

continent, moreover, class lines were still enormously significant. People who did have money tended to spend it, as they always had, on ostentatious luxuries instead of investing it in industry, which somehow smacked of vulgarity. But governments on the continent, aware of the realities of power, realized that industrialization was no longer a novelty but a national necessity.

German industrialization really began from 1828 to 1834, while the *Zollverein* (customs union) was being built up under Prussian leadership. Reactionary politicians controlled most of the German states, but the flood of cheap British goods forced them to defend their own power by encouraging industrial growth. The *Zollverein* was a union of German states which formed a large free trade area within which demand could be effective; until it was formed, local tariffs had hindered trade. The German governments also encouraged the growth of banks oriented toward industrial development, and,

in 1848, they put an end to serfdom, thus making it possible for much-needed labor to find its way into the factory towns. Once demand could make itself felt and capital became available, industry began to make rapid strides. Railroads were quickly built, and the excellent German educational system, reformed and expanded early in the nineteenth century, was quickly adapted to producing managers and technicians who equaled those of any other nation.

France built its first railroads in the 1830s, but capital was scarce and Frenchmen were slow to discard their traditional manufacturing practices. Factories began to develop in the north during the second quarter of the century, but significant industrialization really got under way only in the 1850s (see p. 444).

Other countries, lacking resources and hindered by social systems that were still essentially medieval, could do little to keep up. Probably the most striking aspect of the first

Making rails at Lecreusot, France's greatest steel works, in 1850.

nations to modernize was the fact that they were already the richest, most politically advanced societies in the world. Industrialization produced great social changes, particularly as it paralleled urbanization, but earlier changes had made industrialization possible. Without "social capital"—effective government, relatively advanced educational systems, and an extensive breakdown of traditional culture—there was little chance for modernization.

The Effects of Industrialization

Even in the most advanced European agricultural societies 80 percent of the population had to work at producing food. Hence the vast majority of Europeans lived in villages, close to the fields they tilled. Because transport was crude, hundreds of small towns served as markets and as centers of administration. Only a few large cities, most of them centers of royal government, could exist. With the advent of industrialization, however, many small towns, bypassed by new,

more efficient methods of transportation, declined. Cities grew ever larger, new cities grew up as centers of economic activity, and some of the small towns grew rapidly into major urban centers. These developments changed the fabric of life for entire populations.

Peasants, many of whom had augmented their incomes by engaging in small manufacturing tasks through the putting-out system, found themselves drawn to the new factory towns, since the factories gradually destroyed cottage industry. On the land, families had worked together at their own pace—planting, cultivating, harvesting, and sometimes weaving or spinning. Their lives were regulated not by clocks but by weather and the seasons. In factory towns, however, men, women and children worked apart, often seeing each other only at night and on holidays. Their work tended to be routine, their hours were long, and overseers set a pace that was controlled ultimately not by nature but by the machines they tended.

They worked in huge, crowded, noisy factories rather than in the fields. Local governments, overwhelmed by the sudden influx of population, did little or nothing to provide for sanitation; houses, built quickly and cheaply, were crowded and flimsy.

Although the new factory workers were not well off, peasant life itself had been anything but pleasant. Moreover, the vast majority of men and women benefited greatly from the increased production that the factories made possible. Factory workers generally made more money, dressed better, and ate better than peasants did, and they were more often literate. Some were driven off the land, but most of them entered the factories as a matter of choice; they could have remained peasants.

Both life-styles, peasant and factory worker, had advantages and disadvantages. Change, however, is itself likely to be upsetting, both psychologically and physically. Family life was strained, and in the factory towns immorality was rife and drunkenness common. Social workers involved with present-day "poverty programs" testify that many men who have been unemployed for long periods have great difficulty adapting themselves to the regular life and tedious work of the factory even today. Yet laziness, drunkenness, and immorality were quite common among peasants as well as factory workers, as many contemporaries reported. Some of the laments for the poor factory worker clearly spring not from careful investigation but from an idealization of peasant life; but they are not entirely unjustified.

If the change from peasant to factory worker was the most striking of the social effects of industrialization, other changes were also significant. For several centuries improvements in military technology and methods of government had been causing the position of aristocrats to deteriorate; the industrial revolution virtually finished them off. Noblesse oblige rapidly gave way to a ruthless ethic of gain. Newly rich entrepreneurs rapidly demanded and won power in governments that had long been at least partly subservient to the nobility. Mass production was eventually to put into the hands of common men products that had been available to only the very rich: well-made clothes, the means of travel, and access to education. Many aristocrats adapted to the new situation by becoming capitalists and industrialists themselves, but many others, unable to bring themselves to make the change, found themselves surpassed in wealth and influence by their former "inferiors."

Skilled artisans also were forced to change their lives. Relentlessly, machines took over the jobs done so well in the past by the cobbler, the miller, the hand-loom weaver, and others like them. They either became entrepreneurs (and many did), learned to work as machinists, or found themselves joining the ranks of the unskilled in factories. Peasants, too, gradually found their world altered as machines invaded the fields and made farms into food factories, with all the changes that this implied for the farm laborer.

Finally, merchants and entrepreneurs, key men in the development of industrialism, themselves had to undergo an important change in attitudes. Medieval ideas of the "just price," the wickedness of usury, the merchant as servant of society, had been dying slowly for several centuries, but with the advent of industrialization they were swept away completely. Many employers could no longer take seriously the idea that they were somehow the "fathers" of their workers. Profit was the key to survival. Prices had to be based not on what was "just," but on what the traffic would bear. Money had to bring its price; when the market declined, men had to be laid off. Only the ruthless could stay in business when times were hard. The sovereignty of profit was, to many men, a disquieting development. That so much was written to justify it by so many thoroughly upright, well-meaning scholars — men like the gentle parson Robert Malthus (1766–1834), whose *Essay on the Principles of Population* (1798) helped to make economics "the dismal science" — shows how great was the load of guilt the entrepreneur had to carry.

Economic growth and associated social change were limited mainly to small areas of Western and Central Europe (and the U.S.A.) before 1870. Only there had the new scientific and technical knowledge that had begun to develop in the late middle ages spread widely throughout the population.

Moreover, modernization required a national leadership that was willing to accept change, and only in Western and parts of Central Europe had the Old Regime been either completely destroyed or, at least, prevented from hindering economic growth and efficiency. Even in the areas in which the climate of opinion and the social structures permitted modernization and the availability of natural resources encouraged it, change came slowly. Nevertheless, it produced not only benefits but inconvenience; it not only created new wealth but also destroyed ancient ideas and traditions. Even slow modernization was certain to produce violent upheavals.

LIBERALISM

Liberalism grew out of a fusion of the Utilitarian philosophy of Jeremy Bentham (1748–1832) and James Mill (1773–1836), the demands for intellectual liberty most clearly formulated by the thinkers of the Enlightenment, and the creed of laissez-faire in economics. English economists, most notably Adam Smith in *The Wealth of Nations* (see p. 384), had formulated a theory that if governments refrained from attempting to control the economic activity of a nation, the "natural law" of the market would produce the most beneficial possible use of the nation's resources. Bentham and Mill found a replacement for the crumbling values of feudal society in their argument that society should operate for "the greatest good of the greatest number." Demands for freedom of thought and expression, heard as far back as Socrates and the Stoics and brilliantly proclaimed by the poet John Milton in the seventeenth century, became part of the basic attitudes of Enlightenment thinkers such as Hume and Voltaire. Succinctly stated, the liberal philosophy held that a maximum of freedom would produce a maximum of wealth, knowledge, and human happiness. Liberals were seldom able to agree on how best to put their ideas into practice, but the basic doctrine was so attractive that it has deeply influenced all subsequent political thought. The classical statement of the liberal creed is generally agreed to be the essay *On Liberty,* written by John Stuart Mill (1806–1873) and published in 1859.

Early in the nineteenth century, however, practical difficulties forced even the strongest supporters of liberalism to recognize that the doctrine would have to be modified, at least in its economic aspects. In England, the first nation to industrialize, it was easy to accept the idea that government should leave economic affairs to private enterprise, since private enterprise had given England new methods of production that allowed her merchants to capture control of the world market in manufactured goods. But to France, Germany, the United States, and any other nation that sought to develop its own industry, this doctrine was hardly convincing. Faced by a flood of English goods, less advanced countries needed not only time in which to build their own industries but also protection from English competition and some kind of effective planning. Scarce resources had to be distributed carefully if they were to be used to promote the nation's growth, and capital had to be accumulated rapidly. England's success so dazzled some foreign economists that they slavishly followed their English colleagues, but others quickly saw that laissez-faire economics gave all the advantages to England and left their own countries in a completely hopeless position. Thus men like the German Friedrich List (1789–1846) quickly demanded that governments establish protective tariffs to shelter fledgling home industries from English competition; others argued that governments should actively encourage the development of banking systems, plan and finance the construction of railroads, subsidize technical education, and otherwise move to hasten development that private enterprise could produce only slowly, if at all. They still insisted, however, that governments leave to private initiative that which private initiative could successfully accomplish. Thus, outside of England, liberal economic ideas led to a kind of limited mercantilism. Not until the 1870s, however, did protection become the rule, even in the most backward areas.

David Ricardo (1772–1823), the leading exponent of laissez-faire doctrines, doubted that any general improvement in the worker's lot was possible. He formulated what came to be called the Iron Law of Wages: if workers' wages were raised above subsistence level, the number of workers (that is, population) would increase enough to bring wages back down to the lowest possible point, whereas if wages went below subsistence level, the number of workers would decrease until wages rose once more. Ricardo himself said that changes in customs might conceivably moderate population increases, thus making possible a permanent rise in the "subsistence" wage—that is, the minimum standard of living might rise. His followers, however, tended to disregard his qualifications and to insist that the workers' misery was simply the effect of a law of nature. Economic liberals argued that labor was a commodity, a kind of raw material like the iron or coal that went into the making of products. Wages, therefore, must be determined by the interaction of supply and demand, just as were the prices of iron and coal. Any attempt at a general increase in wages would simply produce an increase in the cost of all other commodities, leaving workers in the same relative position as before; wages might be higher but they would buy no more than they had previously. Many businessmen sponsored lectures to teach their workers these "truths of political economy" to induce them to resign themselves to long hours of work at very low pay.

SOCIALISM AND EARLY TRADE UNIONISM

The existing conditions were so bad that laborers eventually were forced to rebel, and a few educated men sympathized enough to plead their case. The rebellion took two main paths: one involved attempts to improve the lot of workers within the existing social and economic structure; the other led to demands for revolutionary reconstruction of society, either by peaceful means or by violence. Much of the theory of those movements had been formulated by 1870, but the translation from theory to practice only began later.

Labor unions began as small, local organizations of skilled workers who joined together to limit the numbers of apprentices trained and, thus, to keep laborers in their fields scarce. They also sought to help each other in time of need by pooling their resources. Until 1824, almost all worker organizations were prohibited in England by the Combination Acts, passed in the 1790s. But even when those laws were repealed, unions were harassed by laws against restraint of trade. It was not until 1871, with the passage of the Trade-Union Act, that British unions were guaranteed a legal status. On the continent full legalization came even later.

Many thoughtful men believed that trade unionism would never cure the ills of industrial society, and the word "socialism" was coined in the 1820s to describe a galaxy of suggestions for radical social change. There were three main variants of the new radicalism: (1) new government-controlled reforms like those proposed by Count Claude Henri de Saint-Simon; (2) cooperative plans like those of Robert Owen; and (3) essentially anarchistic schemes like those of Pierre-Joseph Proudhon.

Saint-Simon (1760–1825), a French nobleman who made a fortune in land speculation and then lost it experimenting in industry, was one of the first men to see clearly the central importance of economics in the organization of society. War and waste repelled him equally. He argued, therefore, that the state should be managed by scientists, engineers, and industrialists, the men who efficiently produced the world's goods, rather than by quarrelsome "parasites" like lawyers, bureaucrats, and priests. The church, however, he approved of, at least in principle, because it brought men together despite its imperfections. Hence, he dreamed of a new industrial society bound together by a new Christianity, whose outlines he sketched in his last book. His system was unfinished, but his followers carried on his thought, and many of them, inspired by his works, took leading roles in the industrialization of France.

Robert Owen (1771–1858), a successful English textile manufacturer, built a model community at New Lanark, near Manchester, between the years 1814 and 1824. Visitors praised his experiment, but most of them considered its success entirely due to Owen's personal leadership. His workers appeared to be pious, literate, and industrious, and his factories were showplaces, but Owen managed them all down to the last detail. He seemed to be perpetuating an older, paternalistic system, and other factory owners were unwilling to follow his lead. Moreover, Owen gradually became more and more radical, advocating the creation of new industrial communities run on socialist principles and attacking religious orthodoxy. By 1830 many young workingmen regarded him as a revolutionary leader, and factory owners refused to listen to his plans. Later attempts to create Owenite communities all failed, but many of Owen's suggestions were taken up later by more practical innovators.

Probably the most important of these early revolutionary thinkers was Proudhon (1809–1865), whose assertion that "property is theft" won him wide notoriety. He was the first significant writer to insist that workers control their own factories. Government, he believed, was unnecessary: society should be organized as a federation of factories and farms which would contract with each other to produce the goods that men needed to live. Centralized government, he argued, was tyranny, even when the government was chosen by the people. Many of the members of the Paris Commune of 1871 (see p. 465) were followers of Proudhon, and his works strongly influenced later syndicalists (see p. 460).

MARXISM

The first sign of a new and powerful movement appeared in 1848 with the publication of the *Manifesto of the Communist Party* by Karl Marx (1818–1883) and Friedrich Engels (1820–1895). Marx, the son of a German lawyer, studied philosophy at the University of Berlin and then became a liberal journalist in Cologne. He was soon forced into exile, and in Paris he met Engels, the son of a wealthy German manufacturer and himself a young businessman. When the *Manifesto* appeared in 1848, Marx was nearly thirty, his collaborator twenty-eight. The partnership continued, with the two men writing several important polemical works capped by Marx's masterpiece, *Das Kapital,* the first vol-

ume of which appeared in 1867. Marx spent much of his life in London, working on his books in the reading room of the British Museum. Engels worked until he was forty-nine at one of his father's branch factories in Manchester, supporting Marx and his family as well as himself and writing in his spare time. From this collaboration came the philosophical system known as Marxism and the political movement known as Marxist or "Scientific" socialism. Marxists slightingly referred to earlier socialist thinkers like Owen and Saint-Simon as "Utopian socialists."

Marxism is based on the historical philosophy known as economic determinism (or, as Marx called it, historical materialism) and a logical system Marx and Engels called dialectical materialism. Dialectical logic was invented by the ancient Greeks, but Marx learned it from the works of the Prussian philosopher, Georg W. F. Hegel (1770–1831). Hegel was, in philosophical terms, an Idealist, who regarded matter and events as mere projections of an Absolute Idea, which was the only reality. Historical progress, Hegel argued, came from the unfolding of the Absolute Idea in a continuing conflict: each manifestation of the Idea called forth its own opposite, then both were included in a new synthesis that was still another manifestation of the Idea. Marx accepted the dialectic, but he rejected Idealism and insisted that the dialectic involved matter, not ideas.

The key fact of history, Marx argued, is the struggle for control of the means of production, not some unknowable "Absolute Idea." Progress comes through the dialectical clash of socioeconomic classes: the feudal aristocracy created its opposite in the *bourgeoisie,* or merchant class, which triumphed only to find that it had brought into being its own nemesis, the *proletariat.* The class struggle would end only with the final success of the proletariat, which would bring into existence a "classless society." Marx's evidence for his theory is extremely complex, but essentially he maintained that all ideas, religions, governments, and social organizations reflected the relations between men and the "means of production." Thus states or dominant philosophies or religions were nothing more than weapons of the ruling class against its class opponent. Ideas matter, according to

Marx, but ultimately they depend on economic reality.

Marxism promised its proponents inevitable victory. The capitalist system, Marx argued, continually forced more and more men to become propertyless proletarians. All profit, he said, is the result of the exploitation of labor, for the value of any product is the value of the labor required to make it, and profit can only result when part of the proceeds of a man's labor is taken from him to line the pockets of a capitalist. Proletarians own nothing but their labor, which they must sell to live. Marx argued that ultimately the proletarians would see that they were being robbed, and then they would rise up and destroy the exploitative capitalist system. These arguments seemed to imply that violent revolution was inevitable, although both Marx and Engels occasionally indicated that they thought that the proletarian triumph might come peacefully. This ambiguity split the Marxist movement almost from the start between revisionist or reformist socialists, who believed in a peaceful struggle, and revolutionary socialists, who insisted that only violence would bring them to power. Until 1870, however, Marxism was little more than the cult of a tiny minority, virtually unknown to the vast majority of Europeans. In the west, liberalism, not socialism, was the dominant social philosophy of the middle decades of the nineteenth century.

POLITICAL DEVELOPMENTS IN GREAT BRITAIN AND FRANCE

In all of Europe the period immediately after the defeat of Napoleon was one of unabashed reaction. Everywhere the established order tried to halt the changes that had already begun. England was no exception. Until around 1830, the old system of aristocratic control of the House of Commons through bribery and family connections remained entrenched. Rural gentry forced the passage of a set of Corn Laws (grain tariffs) that guaranteed the profits of farmers and drove the price of bread so high that town workers were reduced to near-starvation. They also were able to maintain a poor law that required paupers to remain in the areas in which they were born, thus guaranteeing themselves a supply of cheap labor, seriously hindering the movement of workers to factory towns, and forcing certain entrepreneurs to pay very high wages. But in England industry was already strong, and these hindrances did not prevent its continued growth. Manufacturers and factory workers, whatever their grievances against each other, were one in demanding reform.

Finally, in 1832, reforms were passed. Boroughs whose population had declined either lost their representation in the Commons or saw it reduced. New factory towns, many of them never before represented, were given seats in Parliament. Property requirements for voters, formerly weighted heavily in favor of landowners, were altered to give well-to-do townsmen the franchise. When the House of Lords tried to prevent passage of the Reform Bill, riots, arson, and actual civil uprisings made the danger of revolution clear, and the prime minister, Lord Charles Grey (1764–1845), forced the Lords to give in.

Even under the new rules only about one-eighth of English male adults could vote, but the locus of power had shifted. The new manufacturing class was gaining control. The old Poor Law, which defied liberal economic doctrine by supplementing wages, was replaced in 1834 by a law that forced the unemployed into miserable workhouses. The poor hated the new law, but the new system pleased the factory owners. In 1835 the Municipal Corporations Act made it possible for the new cities to begin to undertake some of the neglected tasks that might make town life more tolerable. In 1838 laboring men and industrial capitalists formed the new Anti-Corn Law League, and in 1846 they succeeded in destroying the customs duties that were the last defense of the rural landowners. With the adoption of free trade in grain, liberal economics had become the nation's orthodoxy. As a result, England became almost wholly a manufacturing center, dependent on imports for its food.

The landed interests were not completely defeated, however, since they quickly realized that they could combine with the urban workers against the manufacturers. Soon after 1832 laws were passed restricting child labor despite the cries of laissez-faire enthu-

Poorhouse at Cripplegate, England, in 1864, essential part of an economic system that forbade welfare payments or work relief projects.

siasts that the economy would be ruined. In 1847, as a result of shocking reports of Royal Commissions on factory conditions, Parliament passed the Ten Hours Act, which limited the work of women and children in industry to ten hours a day. Because men and women worked in the same factories on interdependent processes, the law tended over later decades to reduce the work of men to ten hours as well. Doctrinaire economic liberals prophesied disaster, but the economy survived. These acts not only lightened the lives of workers, they also gave new hope to the lower classes.

The Chartist movement, embodying demands for universal male suffrage and other parliamentary reforms, represented a dangerous threat to the new industrial oligarchy. The Chartists presented to Parliament petitions carrying more than three million signatures. Just as earlier reforms had been passed without violence, most of the Chartist de-

mands gradually became law. But the revolutionary year of 1848 largely bypassed England, and not until the Reform bill of 1867 was passed by the newly formed Conservative party under the leadership of Benjamin Disraeli (1804–1881) did the urban worker finally win the vote.

The old Whig and Tory parties had been loose coalitions of families and interest groups, but after the extension of the franchise in 1832, new political clubs were formed and began to build modern party machinery. Whigs and Tories fought among themselves during the parliamentary struggles of the mid-century, and by the 1860s the modern Conservative and Liberal parties had come into existence. Perhaps because the English upper classes had learned their lessons earlier, English democracy grew through the nineteenth century without revolution; elsewhere in Europe, rulers were not so fortunate.

Chartists marching to a protest meeting at Kennington, England, April 10, 1848.

In France, the aristocrats who returned after Napoleon's fall were said to have "learned nothing and forgotten nothing." Louis XVIII (1814–1824), whose brother had been executed in 1793, managed to restrain them for a few years, but his successor, Charles X (1824–1830) gave them free rein, and the so-called "ultraroyalists" attempted to undo most of the changes that the revolution had made. The king's counter-revolutionary policies sparked the almost bloodless revolution of July 1830, which put power in the hands of the wealthy bourgeoisie. During the 18 years of the "July Monarchy," presided over by King Louis Philippe, industrialization began, largely in northern France, and the construction of a railroad network was started. But Louis Philippe and his chief minister, François Guizot (1787–1874), made few concessions to the lower middle classes and the growing class of urban workers. When business recession was capped by a bad harvest in 1847, the merchants and artisans of Paris renewed their demands for reforms. Stubborn as ever, the king refused to allow even peaceful protest meetings. His regime collapsed when soldiers fired into a crowd of demonstrators in February 1848.

In France the Revolution of 1848 expressed the idealism of a generation of romantics who longed for democracy and social justice. The provisional government of the Second Republic was dominated by democrats, but they were unwilling to take the radical steps necessary to placate the unemployed and the socialists. The Constituent Assembly elected in May was equally hesitant, since peasant voters had elected a conservative majority out of fear of the Paris "reds." Still desperate for employment and threatened by a conservative reaction, a large mob of workers and artisans rose against the assembly on June 24. Two days later they were crushed by the army, whose cannon easily destroyed their barricades. Ten thousand rebels were killed or wounded, and ten thousand were taken prisoner. The revolution was over.

In December 1848, France showed both its desire for glory and its disdain for democracy by electing as president the nephew of Napoleon I, Louis Napoleon Bonaparte, who ran as an upholder of social stability. Three

Mob taking possession of the Tuilleries Palace throne room, Paris, February 1848.

years later, on December 2, 1851, Louis Napoleon made himself dictator, and his coup was approved by a vast majority of French voters. In 1852 he declared the empire restored.

The Second Empire lasted through a period of major economic expansion. During the 1850s and 1860s, France acquired a national railroad and telegraph network and a modern banking system that was capable of financing the nation's industrialization. More factories were built, and mining and metallurgy developed on a large scale. Napoleon III also sponsored public works that included the rebuilding of Paris and the construction of the Suez Canal. He liked to think of himself as "Saint-Simon on horseback"—that is, as a sponsor of modernization and a champion of the workingman. But his support of business interests prevented him from giving the workers more than token reforms.

Napoleon III received his most consistent support from France's peasants. Many businessmen lost their enthusiasm for his regime when he tried to bring about free trade with England in 1860. Clerical circles applauded his defense of the pope against Roman revolutionaries in 1849 and his encouragement of Catholic influence in French schools, but their ardor cooled as Napoleon III encouraged the Italian unification movement, which threated the papacy. By the late 1860s he had gone a long way toward making the Second Empire a liberal, constitutional monarchy in an attempt to gain bourgeois support. His regime finally fell as a result of his ill-advised foreign adventures, not because of discontent at home. In the mid-1860s his effort to establish a puppet emperor in Mexico ended in a fiasco; his attempt to influence German affairs led to his defeat in 1870 in the Franco-Prussian War and his overthrow by Parisian republicans.

CENTRAL EUROPE: THE UNIFICATION OF GERMANY AND ITALY

In 1815 Germany and Italy were both composed of many quarreling states. By 1871

France's most ambitious imperialist venture in the Western Hemisphere ends with the execution of deposed Emperor Maximillian of Mexico (1867).

newly aroused national feeling had combined with the aggressive expansionism of a brilliant statesman to weld each of them into unified nations. In each case, the momentum for unification began with the near collapse of the Austrian Empire.

The wars of Napoleon I had destroyed what was left of the Holy Roman Empire, but after the Congress of Vienna Austria was still the greatest power in Central Europe, while Prussia and the lesser German states were completely independent. Austria proper was a land of Germans, but they were a minority in an Empire that included Hungary, Bohemia, Moravia, and parts of what are now Italy, Poland, and Yugoslavia. Metternich and his emperor, Francis I (1792–1835), were Europe's leading exponents of the status quo. They made no effort to continue the modernizing efforts of Maria Theresa and Joseph II; instead, they returned to the church some of its lost power, catered to the wishes of the nobility, and generally hindered the development of industry. But despite their efforts, liberalism and nationalism grew throughout the Empire.

The February 1848 revolution in Paris set off uprisings throughout Central Europe. Metternich was driven into exile. Diets in Hungary and Bohemia declared their nations independent, although they still recognized Emperor Ferdinand I (1835–1848) of Austria as their ruler. The kings of Piedmont-Sardinia and the two Sicilies were forced to grant constitutions. Milan and Venice ousted Austrian troops, Tuscany and Venetia became independent republics, and the Romans revolted against the pope. In Berlin, the king of Prussia was also forced to promise to grant a constitution. Other German rulers quickly lost con-

Students at the barricades in Vienna during the Revolution of 1848.

trol. In May an all German congress met in Frankfurt, most of its members fully committed to liberalism and to the unification of Germany, including the German provinces of the Austrian Empire.

But there were several factors blocking unification. Most peasants in Central Europe cared nothing for nationalism once they had rid themselves of the vestiges of serfdom. Industrialization had only begun, the bourgeoisie was weak, and the liberal intellectuals at Frankfurt represented virtually no one but themselves. Once over their fright, the German monarchs reasserted their powers. Austrian generals subdued Prague and for-

cibly took Bohemia and the Austrian possessions in Italy back into the empire. A new revolt in Vienna was put down in October. Ferdinand abdicated, and his successor, Francis Joseph (1848–1916), repudiated his father's liberal pledges. But in 1849 he had to call on Russia to help him regain control in Hungary, and in 1867, after a military defeat by Prussia, he had to accept the creation of a Dual Monarchy, Austria-Hungary, in which Hungary was an equal partner.

In Prussia the Revolution of 1848 also failed. Not long after the king, Frederick William IV (1840–1861), had appointed a Constituent Assembly, he dismissed it and issued a constitution of his own. He also refused to accept the crown of a united Germany from the congress at Frankfurt. The revolutionary wave in Central Europe was spent.

The Italians were the first to rise once more against their Austrian overlords. Count Camillo Benso di Cavour (1810–1861), leading minister in the Kingdom of Piedmont-Sardinia, succeeded in trading Napoleon III the territories of Nice and Savoy for his aid against Austria. In a brief war in 1859, French and Piedmontese troops defeated the Austrians and took over Lombardy. Then Italian nationalists, inspired by Cavour, overthrew the governments of the principalities of the north, which had depended on Austrian support. By March 1860, King Victor Emanuel II of Piedmont-Sardinia (1849–1861) controlled all of northern Italy except Venetia, which remained Austrian. A few months later Giuseppe Garibaldi (1807–1882), a revolutionary general who had played a leading part against Austria in 1848, took Sicily with his band of Red Shirts. By September he had conquered Naples as well for Victor Emanuel II, who was to reign until 1878 as united Italy's first king. Cavour, fearing that Garibaldi would march on to Rome, which was defended by the French, ordered Piedmontese troops into the Papal States and arranged plebiscites that resulted in the foundation of the Kingdom of Italy in March 1861. In 1866, by joining the Prussians in war against Austria, the new kingdom acquired Venetia. Finally, in 1870, it was able to occupy Rome when Napoleon III, at war with Prussia, had to withdraw his troops.

Garibaldi furnished military leadership and Mazzini propaganda to the partisans of a liberal, unified Italy, but the success of their movement depended on Cavour's skills as well. By using diplomacy solely for the aggrandizement of his own monarch, Victor Emanuel II, Cavour procured the foreign aid that was indispensable if Austria was to be forced out of the Italian lands. On the other hand, lack of mass participation in the unification movement made it less democratic than Mazzini and Garibaldi had wished it to be.

Just as the unification of Italy was primarily the achievement of Cavour, a traditional liberal statesman bent on increasing the power

UNIFICATION OF ITALY

of his own monarch, the unification of Germany was carried out by Prince Otto von Bismarck (1815–1898) a traditional conservative statesman with similar aims.

Bismarck, a nobleman and a veteran diplomat, came to power in 1862 when King William I (1861–1888) found his plans for an army reform thwarted by the parliament his predecessor had established after the rebellion of 1848. Bismarck solved the problem by ignoring the parliament and financing the affairs of government by collecting taxes without parliamentary approval. His conduct might have provoked a new rebellion, but his triumphs in war so dazzled the country that his unconstitutional methods were forgiven, and most of the liberals who continued to oppose him lost their seats in parliament to his conservative supporters.

A year after he took office, Bismarck made an alliance with Austria and went to war with Denmark to end a dispute over the possession of the border provinces of Schleswig and Holstein. Because Bismarck had used the taxes he collected illegally to reform the

DENMARK SWEDEN

Baltic Sea

North Sea

SCHLESWIG

(to Oldenburg) RÜGEN

(to Hamburg) HOLSTEIN

EAST PRUSSIA

RUSSIAN

LÜBECK MECKLENBURG

EAST FRIESLAND Hamburg• •LAUENBURG (acquired 1865) MECKLENBURG STRELITZ

WEST PRUSSIA

EMPIRE

OLDEN-BURG •Bremen KINGDOM OF SCHWERIN

Vistula River

Warsaw•

Rhine River

HANOVER BRANDENBURG •Berlin POSEN

NETHERLANDS

POLAND

WESTPHALIA LIPPE BRUNSWICK PRUSSIA ANHALT SAXONY

KINGDOM OF HANOVER

WALDECK

KINGDOM OF SAXONY

SILESIA

BELGIUM

RHINE PROVINCE OF PRUSSIA

HESSE-KASSEL HESSE-DARMSTADT SAXONY DUCHIES REUSS

Cracow• GALICIA

•Ems NASSAU •Frankfurt *Main River*

BOHEMIA •Prague MORAVIA

DARMSTADT

BAVARIAN PALATINATE

•Metz LORRAINE

GRAND DUCHY OF BADEN

AUSTRIAN

Strasbourg•

KINGDOM OF WÜRTTEMBURG

HOHENZOLLERN

KINGDOM OF BAVARIA

Danube River

Vienna•

•Munich EMPIRE

ALSACE

AUSTRIA

SWITZERLAND TYROL

UNIFICATION OF GERMAN

army, the allied forces won easily. When Austria and Prussia disagreed over the disposition of the territory they had taken, Bismarck fought once more, and in June, 1866, his troops defeated the Austrian army. Victorious Prussia annexed considerable territory in northern Germany from Austria's allies there, and even in the southern German states, traditionally dominated by Austria, Prussian influence became paramount. But Bismarck treated the defeated Austrians gently; they were to become his allies once more. Four years later, when Napoleon III attempted to prevent a German prince from accepting the vacant throne of Spain, Bismarck grasped the opportunity to provoke a war with France.

Rulers of the south German states, eager to share in Bismarck's glory, joined Prussia in the war; for this reason and because of

Prussia's vast pool of reservists the German armies were twice as large as those of France. They also had far better staff and supply systems. Making the fullest use of Prussia's excellent railroad system, the Germans quickly broke through the French frontier defenses and defeated the French at Sedan, where Napoleon III was captured. Republicans in Paris toppled the empire on September 4, 1870. Their heroic efforts to continue the war failed, however. Paris, beseiged in September, was starved into submission, after great suffering, in January 1871, and a new French government, elected in February, sued for peace. Hypnotized by Prussian power, the south German states asked William to become emperor of a united Germany. On January 18, 1871, in the Hall of Mirrors at Versailles, the second German Empire was born. German Austria, however, remained outside the union.

The existence of the new empire, industrially advanced and larger in area and population than any western European state, completely altered the the power structure of the continent. Bismarck had achieved far more than even he had expected, and after 1871 he had the power to attempt even greater gains. Moreover, Bismarck's contemptuous treatment of the Prussian parliament profoundly influenced German attitudes toward liberalism and democracy, for the Iron Chancellor had convinced a great many Germans that their greatest chance for glory lay in leaving their fate in the hands of an autocratic government rather than in trying to win control of the state for themselves.

RUSSIA

In 1815 the Russian Empire stretched from Poland to China and from the Arctic Sea to Persia, India, and Turkey; much of the east was inhabited by nomadic tribes, and in the west the vast majority of the population was made up of serfs who were little better off than slaves. The tsars and the nobles, living in constant fear of peasant uprisings — indeed of any change — went to extreme lengths to maintain their power.

Alexander I, who had helped to ruin Napoleon, did little more than talk of reform at home. When he died, in December 1825, a handful of officers, many of them veterans of the Napoleonic wars, led a few confused troops in a rebellion designed to bring changes that most of them hardly understood. They were crushed.

Alexander's successor, Nicholas I (1825–1855), reasserted an old tsarist tradition by instituting reforms on his own authority but mercilessly crushing every attempt to force reforms against his will. He commissioned the publication of a collection of all Russian laws and used it as the basis for the construction of a Code of Laws for the empire in 1832. He also made minor improvements in the status of the serfs and put the chaotic finances of his realm in order. But he also tightened restrictions on the press, instituted strict supervision of the universities, and established a special division of the government to suppress political dissent. The government was a harsh autocracy, and its reforms brought virtually no improvement in the condition of the masses. Industry grew very slowly, without government aid, during his reign.

Not until Alexander II (1855–1881) came to power amid the disasters of the Crimean War (1854–1856) was it recognized that change was inevitable. This first major war since 1815 involved Russia on one side and Turkey, Great Britain, and France on the other. Russia's military defeat not only weakened its international prestige, but also showed how ill-advised had been Nicholas I's efforts to isolate his country from the new technological developments in the west, for within a few weeks new British and French steamships had landed more than 150,000 men in the Crimea. The new tsar ended this isolation soon after the war and launched a series of reforms that were designed to make the Russian state more efficient.

After long consultations with representatives of the reluctant provincial nobility, in 1861 Alexander II issued a law that formally granted freedom to the serfs of the empire. Peasants were allowed to buy the plots of land that they had worked as serfs. The government paid the landowners, and peasants were to repay the government over a period of 49 years. This law might have revolutionized the lives of the peasants, but the repayment of government land-redemption

Tsar Nicholas I orders cannons fired on the Decembrist revolutionaries in Swate Square, St. Petersburg, on December 14, 1825.

loans was made the responsibility of the peasant commune, so most peasants still had to remain in their villages. Moreover, the three-field system of agriculture remained in force in most areas until 1905, and the government made little effort to improve farming methods.

Alexander's decision to free the serfs was based essentially on political rather than economic grounds. During the Crimean War peasant unrest was widespread, and the tsar believed that if he did not sponsor emancipation it would be brought about by the peasants themselves. In 1861, the government showed no sign of wanting to industrialize the nation and, indeed, it feared that the development of factory towns would spread "the cancer of the proletariat." Thus the village commune not only served to assure payment of land redemption dues but also hindered industrialization by preventing labor mobility; government leaders thought that the commune helped to maintain political stability.

Despite the government's lack of interest in industry, strategic considerations, including the desire to prevent famine by facilitating the transport of grain, necessitated the building of railroads. Alexander therefore issued decrees subsidizing private groups that would build railroads, and the construction of a comprehensive rail network was seriously begun toward the end of the 1860s.

Another major innovation came with the reorganization of local government in 1864. Provincial and district councils called *zemstvos* became representative institutions and were made responsible for road-building, health services, and education. Despite the fact that the upper classes were heavily overrepresented in them, the zemstvos immediately began to make vast improvements in schools, hospitals, and roads in Russia's more populated areas.

Thus Alexander II began to build the infrastructure required for modernization even though his government had no intention of abandoning traditional ways. The emancipation reform was a half-measure, and Russia's backwardness in agriculture remained a hindrance, but labor mobility was increased slightly, and the building of railroads, schools, and hospitals made possible the industrial gains that were to come later.

By 1870 the face of Europe had changed. From England and France the trend toward modernization had spread eastward, and men everywhere were trying to cope with problems unlike any that they had encountered before. England had completed the second phase of modernization: well over one-half of the population was urban, a modern party system had come into being, and industry had outstripped agriculture as the nation's major source of income. In France and in the new German Empire, the political and economic structure necessary for modernization had been developed, and industry had begun to grow rapidly. Even in backward Russia the steps had been taken that set the stage for modernization despite the conscious opposition of the ruling classes.

The failure of the revolutions of 1848 and of experimental communities like the ones of the Owenites had seriously weakened romantic ideals of peaceful change, and the way was paved for the spread of ideologies of power and violence. Nationalism, too, had changed. In the wake of the triumphs of Cavour and Bismarck the romantic ideas of Mazzinian radicalism were rapidly giving way to the philosophy of *Realpolitik;* more and more, idealists were becoming convinced that not persuasion, but only "blood and iron," would bring victory for their ideas. Finally, the rise of the German Empire utterly changed the distribution of power in Europe. Most Europeans still believed that progress was inevitable, but thoughtful men, pondering the words of Tocqueville and Marx, had begun to believe that the price of progress might be high.

SUGGESTED READINGS

Landes, David S. *The Unbound Prometheus: Technological Change and Industrial Development in Western Europe from 1750 to the Present.* Cambridge: Cambridge University Press, 1969. Paperback.
The best comprehensive treatment of the subject.

Nicolson, Harold. *Congress of Vienna: A Study in Allied Unity, 1812–1822.* New York: Viking Press, 1946. Compass paperback.

Shafer, Boyd C. *Nationalism: Myth and Reality.* New York: Harcourt, Brace & World, 1955. Harvest paperback.

Wilson, Edmund. *To the Finland Station.* New York: Doubleday, 1940. Anchor paperback.
Part I is bad, but Parts II and III make an excellent introduction to the history of socialism.

Marx, Karl, and Friedrich Engels. *The Communist Manifesto.* New York: Henry Regnery Co. [1848]. Gateway paperback.
The most important political document of the nineteenth century.

Taylor, A. J. P. *The Course of German History.* New York: G. P. Putnam's Sons, 1946. Capricorn paperback.

————. *The Hapsburg Monarchy, 1809–1918.* New York: Harper and Row, 1948. Torchbook paperback.
Two good introductory surveys.

Mack Smith, Denis. *Italy. A Modern History.* Ann Arbor: University of Michigan Press, rev. ed., 1969.

Bury, J. P. T. *France, 1814–1940*. New York: A. S. Barnes, 1962. Perpetua paperback.
The best short survey.

Thomson, David. *England in the Nineteenth Century*. Baltimore: Penguin Books, 1964. Pelican paperback.

Seton-Watson, Hugh. *The Russian Empire, 1801–1917*. Oxford: Oxford University Press, 1967.

Mosse, Werner E. *Alexander Second and the Modernization of Russia*. New York: Macmillan, 1958. Collier paperback.

CHAPTER 15

The New Era of Social Conflict in Europe, 1871–1914

By 1871 the economic and social transformation of England and France had begun and with it came new kinds of social conflict. Although the new society was growing ever more wealthy, that wealth was distributed unevenly. The old aristocracy of birth was being superseded by an aristocracy of wealth, and a miserable peasant class was being superseded by a miserable working class. The new masses of workers concentrated in big cities were far more formidable, however, than the small groups of peasants in isolated villages. Moreover the new technology produced miracles of transportation and communication that guaranteed the speedy dispersion of news and ideas—news of class struggles, and ideas of reform or rebellion.

With modernization came an increase in the tempo of social conflict, and where peasant uprisings and bread riots had punctuated village and preindustrial urban life, the organizations natural to modern society made inevitable the growth of fierce, long-lived battles between the rich and the poor. Modernization seemed to be institutionalizing

rebellion. There were two courses governments could follow to avoid rebellion: they could improve the condition of workers or they could promote nationalistic and imperialistic adventures to take the workers' minds off their poverty. Some leaders consciously took the first course; others, most of them unconsciously, took the second; neither approach was entirely satisfactory. Reforms always seemed inadequate; nationalism produced hatreds that were to result in larger and more destructive wars than Europe had ever known before. From 1871 to 1914 some dedicated leaders produced half-successful reforms, while others stoked the fires of new, more bitter social conflict. Meanwhile, as people gradually came to realize, Europe was drifting slowly toward war.

THE SPREAD OF MODERNIZATION

Modernization proceeded ever more rapidly in Europe after 1871. In England, France, Belgium, Germany, and Italy, governments that welcomed modernization were in power, and even in Russia and Austria, where old elites still ruled, steps that provided the basis for modernization had reluctantly been taken. Only in Spain, the Balkans, and the borderlands of Eastern Europe were old institutions still strong enough to preserve an essentially medieval way of life, and even in those areas the demands for change were beginning to threaten the old structure of society.

Population Growth and Urbanization

Population continued to grow rapidly, but in Northern and Western Europe, which had shown the greatest increase in the first half of the nineteenth century, the rate of growth slowed down; in France growth nearly ceased. In Central and Eastern Europe the growth rate continued to increase. The birth rate was highest in rural areas; consequently, the continuing rapid growth of cities was due mainly to immigration from the countryside. In most cases birth rates fell steadily as modernization increased, while death rates fell even more rapidly. The decline in birth rates seems to have been largely a result of an increasing use of birth control and abortion, both means of limiting family size in order to improve standards of living. Mortality rates began to decline rapidly around 1850, largely because improved public health procedures, particularly sanitation, dramatically reduced the incidence of infectious diseases. Cholera, typhus, typhoid, scarlet fever, and smallpox, which had caused about one-third of all deaths in the eighteenth century, gave way to ailments of old age such as lung and artery diseases and cancer. Thus population grew, and much of the increase ultimately went to swell the size of the cities.

The urbanization of Europe proceeded rapidly in the last half of the nineteenth century. In 1850 only in England did more than 20 percent of the people live in cities of 100,000 or more population, but by 1910 Germany, Holland, and Belgium had reached that level of urbanization; in France, Portugal, Italy, Denmark, and the Austrian and Czech lands in the Dual Monarchy between 10 and 20 percent of the population lived in such large cities.

Economic Transformation

Both urbanization and overall population increase accompanied the spread of industry. The first stage in Britain's transformation into an industrialized country was practically complete by the end of the 1850s. Railroads knit the nation together, and the heavy industry that had been necessary for their construction produced constantly increasing quantities of steel and new machinery. After the 1850s Germany surpassed Britain in her rate of industrial growth. In Britain, improvements in manufacturing processes failed to produce the spectacular profits that they had produced in earlier days. As France, Germany, and the Low Countries entered the market with industrial goods, the British found it more difficult to dispose of their products. Latecomers could take advantage of earlier British experience to save time and capital, skipping steps on the road to industrialization by starting off with well-tried machines and manufacturing techniques. Perhaps equally significant was the British belief in free competition, which left industrialization to eager individuals. Whereas the British banking system simply made capital available, German banking, steered by a powerful government, not only supplied capital but actively encouraged and directed its use.

These contrasting features of the British and German economies became obvious only after the Panic of 1873, a sudden drop in stock prices that marked the onset of a worldwide depression. At that time industry everywhere slowed perceptibly but although Germany's economy recovered almost immediately, Britain's did not hit its old stride until near the end of the century. In Europe, generally, the period from 1873 to 1896 was one of general decline in prices and of increase in competition among national economies. After 1896 a sudden influx of gold from newly discovered South African fields set prices rising once more, and the development of new kinds of industry through discoveries in electricity, organic chemistry, and internal combustion engines provided the power for a new burst of growth that lasted until 1914. Once more unlimited progress seemed attainable, but the effects of the panic still lingered.

The Panic of 1873 also helped destroy the old notion that free trade between nations of unequal industrial development was either desirable or possible. The prestige of English practice had outweighed the complaints of continental businessmen and economists for many years, and free trade was the rule in Europe between about 1845 and 1873. With the coming of hard times, however, most European countries quickly took shelter behind high protective tariffs.

The industrial depression also hastened the growth of big business. Technological progress increasingly raised the capital requirements of industrial firms; for example, the new equipment used in the Bessemer steel process, introduced in Europe in the 1860s, was far too costly for most producers. Thus many marginal firms, already endangered by expensive innovations, could no longer afford to compete with large businesses. Increasingly, giants such as Krupp in Germany and Schneider-Le Creusot in France came to dominate steel production, while in other industries similar innovations produced similar industrial giants. In some cases, a few large companies agreed to merge or to pool their profits. This was the era of cartels and "gentlemen's agreements," when manufacturers made various kinds of agreements to reduce competition by dividing markets among themselves.

With the coming of tariffs, big business, and cartels, the rejection of complete free enterprise was universal. Workers had fought the necessity of selling their labor as a commodity from the first, forming trade unions and striking in order to frustrate the "natural laws" of the market, which threatened them with starvation. Now businessmen, threatened with bankruptcy, followed suit by setting up their own protection against the workings of the market. Limited competition remained popular, but calls for governments to keep hands off economic affairs, no matter how loudly they were voiced, were no longer serious. Unlimited freedom of enterprise had been shown to be a kind of Utopia nobody really wanted.

Mass Education and the New Public Opinion

Until the middle of the nineteenth century most people had little or no interest in conditions outside their own villages or towns, but the economic and political upheavals that came with the beginnings of modernization made it both necessary and possible for entire populations to know about and to influence national and world affairs. The thinkers of the Enlightenment had dreamed of a populace well enough educated to understand the dictates of natural law. Practical politicians—the outstanding example was Napoleon I—established elite educational systems designed to provide administrators for a more complex state. Finally, intelligent industrialists saw the need for workers capable of reading at least the instructions needed for their work. The result of these converging ideas was the development of systems of mass education in all the modernizing nations.

France and Germany took halting steps toward the development of such systems early in the century, but most of their efforts were devoted to the establishment of secondary school systems in which the sons of the middle class could learn the attitudes and capabilities required for social and political leadership. They encouraged the establishment of private elementary schools, as did England, but gave them little direct aid. In England the Education Act of 1870 laid the basis for a national school system, and schooling up to the age of ten was made free and compulsory in 1891. France and Germany instituted free and compulsory schools in the 1880s, and even in Russia primary schools spread rapidly after 1880. Literacy rose in Britain from 66 percent in 1870 to 95 percent in 1900, in France it rose from 60 to 95 percent, in Belgium from 55 to 86 percent. The contrast with nations still in the earliest stages of modernization was striking: in Russia, 80 percent of the population was still illiterate in 1900, as was 67 percent in Spain and 50 percent in Italy and Hungary.

By 1900 school attendance was required in most nations of Western Europe, and secondary education was becoming available

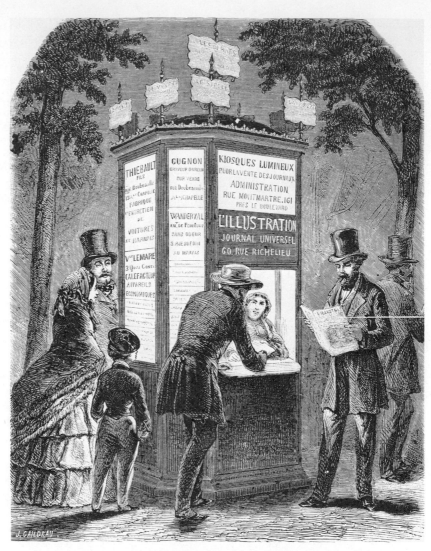

Lighted newspaper kiosks beckoned Parisians eager for news and gossip with the invention of the penny press.

to increasing numbers of their children. Adults were carrying on their studies in such institutions as the British university extension courses and the French "popular universities," both private night schools taught by dedicated intellectuals, usually without pay. Ordinary citizens learned to read and became far better informed than they had ever been before.

These changes in the status and abilities of the masses were paralleled by technological developments, particularly in printing, that made possible the development of the mod-

ern mass-circulation newspaper. Few eighteenth-century newspapers had reached a circulation of more than 20,000 copies sold, and the best known had often sold no more than 5000 or 6000 copies. Generally, they had been expensive, and they had catered to a wealthy clientele. By 1830, however, the steam press had significantly reduced the cost of newspaper production, and in the decade following there appeared in the United States and in France the first "penny newspapers," whose circulations reached 40,000. By 1870, the modern rotary press reduced costs still more, and by 1900 newspapers with a daily circulation of a million had come into being in every industrialized country.

Propaganda was nothing new, but by 1850 it had become a major industry. Newspapers and magazines had to reflect the opinions of their readers in order to survive, but they also molded public opinion. The newspaper that openly "slanted" the news in favor of particular political views became common, as did the paper that sought the largest possible readership by maintaining the appearance of objectivity, stressing sensational news that would attract buyers, and quietly supporting widely held traditional values.

The Intellectuals

This explosion of printed matter called into existence a new "social class" — the intellectuals. Scholars, lawyers, government officials and other learned men had long devoted part of their energies to publicizing their opinions, but with the advent of the mass media — newspapers, magazines, and cheaply printed books — vast numbers of reasonably well educated popularizers were needed. In the past, most authors had been forced to pay the costs of publishing their own writings and, therefore, they usually had depended on the largesse of rich patrons. After about 1850 they lived off not a single patron but a faceless multitude that would pay them well for entertainment or instruction. Far better informed than most of their readers, they used every opportunity to build a phalanx of support behind any cause they favored.

Although every cause, even the most reactionary, found intellectuals to plead its virtues, these men tended to come from relatively modest surroundings; they were usually abreast of the most advanced thought of the day, contemptuous of tradition, and eager for change. Thus every wave of unrest found powerful support among them.

Popularizers seldom created new ideas — that was the business of scholars or politicians, or sometimes the masses themselves — but they could carry to a huge audience ideas that they favored or were paid to support. They could also reinforce already popular attitudes, trading on nationalism, for example, or religion, in order to make a profit.

The new journalism attracted huge numbers of recruits, and its rapid expansion meant that most of the young men who sought fame or fortune as writers could find employment in their chosen field. Most intellectuals tended toward radicalism, but most of them were at least not wholly discontented. Novelists like Emile Zola (1840–1902), whose pleas for the unjustly convicted Captain Dreyfus (see p. 466) led ultimately to this man's vindication, did not demand revolution, but attempted to act as the conscience of society. On the other hand, in countries that were slow to modernize and, thus, lacked the literate audience that could support them, intellectuals often were extremely subversive. Many obscure Russian university students, who might have found well-paid positions as newspaper or magazine writers farther west, used their talents not as writers but as revolutionary agitators. The same pattern exists today in many nations of Asia, Africa, and Latin America.

As a group, the intellectuals became important only a century ago, but their influence has increased with the growth in numbers and distribution of cheap books, newspapers, and newer mass media. Moreover, the institution of mass education and new propaganda techniques permanently increased the potential for widespread social conflict in modernized nations at the same time that it made possible the growth of national cohesion.

MASS MOVEMENTS

Industrialization and urbanization uprooted millions of people both physically and culturally and threatened to make them part of an anonymous mass. The state — especially the nation-state — tried to integrate the masses into the larger society through compulsory primary education, universal military training, and popular suffrage. Cheap daily newspapers also tended to give the urban masses a glimpse of a wider world. But different groups of people viewed the wider world differently and, aided by the intellectuals, they found new ideologies with which to express their group interests in mass movements. Socialism and syndicalism frightened the ruling classes of Europe the most, but these

Election poster showing extreme nationalists' passionate hatred of Jews, whom they called "a different race from us and our enemy."

ideologies were almost eclipsed by the single most important public passion of the nineteenth century: nationalism.

Nationalism

During the first half of the century nationalism in Western Europe had been an ideology of the left. It had sprung into prominence during the French Revolution as part of the pattern of Jacobinism. The monarchs of Europe viewed it as a dangerous doctrine that was closely associated with democratic agitation. After 1848, however, supporters of royalty or of military rule began to use nationalism as a weapon against revolution. The first Napoleon, after all, had traded on nationalism to build his own power. His nephew, Napoleon III, fought the Crimean War partly to win national glory that would buttress his own popularity. And Bismarck, surely no democrat, succeeded in winning the support of his liberal opponents in the

Prussian Diet by appealing to their growing national pride. On the other hand, republicans began to have second thoughts, and socialists loudly insisted that workingmen, exploited everywhere, were men without countries.

During the French Revolution, nationalists in every country began to think that their own nations were not only unique but superior to other nations. The most obvious evidence of superiority was, of course, military power, and thus nationalism became wedded to militarism. But armies not only fought wars; they also were used to put down the Revolutions of 1848 and numerous strikes and riots. Moreover, the character of armies was changing. The most reactionary aristocrats, forced out of government but unwilling to go into business, retained their hold on the army and the church and turned them into bastions of reaction. As a result, republicans, trade unionists, and radicals of the left reacted by coming to hate them both. Around the turn of the century the metamorphosis was almost complete; conservatives and reactionaries, recognizing the value of the army as a weapon against strikes, riots, and rebellions, became militaristic nationalists, while the left became increasingly hostile to the army and to nationalism. The right gained most by this switch in attitudes, for nationalism was a potent force. The antinationalist attitudes of republicans and socialists generally failed to take root among the masses.

The great exceptions to this pattern in development were Austria-Hungary and Russia, empires in which nationalism could only be a threat to the state. Because self-determination was so important to the oppressed peoples, they were bound to remain nationalist; their hatred for the army was a national rather than a class hatred.

Many leftwing intellectuals and political leaders understood that nationalism worked against the aims that they supported, but their conservative opponents won far more support by using the facts of European life to promote militarism. After Bismarck took Alsace and Lorraine and let his victorious troops march into Paris in 1871, how could socialists convince the average Frenchman that capitalism, not Germany, was his real enemy? Conversely, how could Germans, flushed with victory, fail to feel superior to the French? National pride, cultivated for two generations, had become part of the outlook of nearly every semiliterate European; it almost replaced religion as the basis of social cohesion. Poor men, unable to look forward to a better life, clung to the illusion that mere citizenship in what they took to be the world's greatest nation somehow made them better than any foreigner. Nationalism served a deep psychological need; it could be rooted out only if something else could replace it, and no replacement was then available, despite the growth of the labor movement.

Trade Unions, Socialism, and Syndicalism

By 1871 trade unions had begun to develop in all the industrial areas, but only in England were they becoming a serious factor in economic life. During the next three decades they grew tremendously throughout Europe. New ideologies also attracted workers: the two most important were Marxist socialism and revolutionary syndicalism.

Most workers in early industry were too tradition-bound to fight for improvement in their daily lives and, as mentioned previously, governments everywhere forbade trade unions and strikes as illegal restraints on free enterprise. Unions of artisans—bakers, printers, small machine-shop workers, and the like—survived from medieval times or developed early in the industrial era roughly on the pattern of guilds, their aims usually limited to the provision of insurance to their members and the setting of apprenticeship rules. Occasional strikes took place throughout the nineteenth century, but not until the 1860s in Britain and later elsewhere were serious efforts made to include the mass of factory workers in unions. Those efforts, when they came, usually were led by middle-class intellectuals or particularly aggressive leaders of craft unions. Restrictions on union activity were removed in Belgium in 1868, in England in 1874, in Germany in 1881, and in France in 1884.

Massive industrial unions that included unskilled workers first were organized in Britain in the late 1880s, and in France and Germany in the 1890s. They grew rapidly, and after 1890, strikes increased continually in number and significance. The unions never succeeded, however, in persuading even one-half of a nation's workers to join their ranks.

Political action came to attract far more members of the working class than unions did. Marx's *Communist Manifesto* was virtually forgotten after its appearance in 1848, but Marx and Engels continued to work on their doctrine, and *Das Kapital* was published in 1867. Meanwhile, in 1864 Marx and a few revolutionaries from other countries formed the International Workingmen's Association (the First International). Although Marx controlled the organization, it included anarchists as well as Marxists, and internal bickering about goals and tactics prevented its accomplishing anything. It ceased to operate in 1876, but Marxists soon founded new political organizations to take its place. The German Social Democratic party was founded in 1875, and a Belgian Socialist party in 1879. Several competing socialist parties were founded in France in the 1880s, as was the Second International. Far more effective than its predecessor, the Second International served as an information bureau for the socialist movement, and its occasional congresses set socialist policy on a number of issues of general interest. Even so, socialist policy varied from country to country, and the individual parties can best be treated in the context of each nation's politics.

The revolutionary syndicalists rejected Marxism. The ideas of Proudhon, in particular, still attracted them. To these men, Marx's dictatorship of the proletariat was anathema; they distrusted any government, even one that claimed to rule in the name of the working class, and favored a social system in which each factory or office would be essentially independent, contracting with other social units to serve mutual needs. They also tended to demand immediate action against governments, unlike many Marxists, who believed that revolution must wait until the time was ripe.

Revolutionary syndicalists put their faith in the general strike as the weapon that would overturn society, but they were never strong enough to produce any permanent political impact. They tended, in fact, to be most numerous in nations such as France, Spain, and Italy, which were relatively lacking in industry and whose governments willingly used battalions of peasant soldiers to break any serious strike. Even in France, where revolutionary syndicalists controlled the largest federation of unions, in practice they ignored their theory and conducted themselves much as if they were ordinary unionists.

Although revolutionary syndicalism was close to anarchism, the most militant anarchists refused to accept the discipline of any social unit, even the unions through which syndicalists worked. Anarchists were never numerous, but their use of terrorist violence made them notorious. Anarchists assassinated several important statesmen, including Presidents Marie François Sadi Carnot (1837–1894) of France and William McKinley (1843–1901) of the United States. They also bombed cafes and police stations in several countries during the 1890s and the first years of the twentieth century. Their tendency to commit these outrages resulted in their being used as the excuse for the passage of various laws abridging civil liberties. These laws hurt socialists, syndicalists, and even law-abiding liberals more than they hurt the anarchists.

SCIENTIFIC AND INTELLECTUAL TRENDS

Most intellectuals were not concerned with revolutionary ideologies. Some tried, however, to use new scientific theories to explain past and present societies. Others criticized both science and the prevailing materialism of the age as dehumanizing. At the beginning and again at the end of the nineteenth century there were romantic expressions of subjectivism and distrust of the general and the abstract.

Yet scientific studies advanced throughout the century. Physicists continued to refine the work of Newton, producing significant advances in the fields of mechanics and thermodynamics. Chemists, building on the work of Antoine Lavoisier (1743–1794), made more startling advances, particularly with the acceptance of the atomic theory proposed by John Dalton (1766–1844), an English teacher of mathematics and chemistry. The development of organic chemistry, which produced profound effects on industry later in the century, really began in 1860 with the publication by Marcelin Berthelot (1827–1907) of absolute proof that organic compounds can be synthesized. Thus progress in the physical sciences laid the base for the triumphs of the twentieth century.

The Theory of Evolution: Darwinism

It was not physics or chemistry but geology and biology that had the greatest impact on the public, for the single most significant scientific work of the century was *The Origin of Species,* published in 1859 by Charles Darwin (1809–1882).

The idea of evolution had been known for years, but there was one serious barrier to the acceptance of any evolutionary theory: few people thought the world was old enough to have undergone evolution. Widely accepted estimates of the age of the earth, most of them based on biblical statements, went to only a few thousand years, but evolution obviously required tens of thousands. Sir Charles Lyell (1797–1875) proved by studying layers of shells in a volcanic area that the earth was far, far older than most people had thought. His major work was published in 1830. By that time various thinkers, the most important of whom was Robert Malthus, had long been arguing that life was a struggle in which the strongest survived, and Darwin used that idea, which he called "natural selection," to explain how evolution occurred. For more than 20 years he gathered fossil evidence before he published his version of the theory of evolution and startled the world.

Thus Darwin did not originate the idea of evolution, but his evidence made it convincing. Although a fuller explanation of the operation of evolution awaited later work in genetics, Darwin had laid the groundwork for rapid advances in biology. His work also caused consternation in theology and deeply influenced social thought.

The famous French writer Anatole France (1844–1924) remembered late in his life that during his schooldays "Darwin's books were

our Bible." From schoolboys to bearded philosophers, evolution was a marvel that served some private or public purpose. Thomas Henry Huxley (1825–1895), "Darwin's Bulldog," shouted down the many opponents of evolutionary theory everywhere, and believers in the literal truth of the Bible were forced on the defensive. Nationalists—that is, nearly everyone in Europe—quickly decided that "survival of the fittest" justified any successful war and every imperialist venture. Racism was reinforced, since most white men now believed that the power of their race proved them superior to nonwhites. Propagandists like Houston Stewart Chamberlain (1815–1927) insisted that not just the white but the "Aryan" race was the source of the world's progress. Such ideas were spread far and wide in the new cheap newspapers.

Darwin's discoveries also confirmed the popular faith in science, since now science not only had unveiled the secrets that produced ever more rapid progress but it had also shown, many people believed, that progress was inherent in the life of mankind. The novels of Jules Verne (1828–1905) became immensely popular, since he confidently wrote of a world in which men traveled under the sea, flew in the air, transmitted pictures by wireless telegraph, and even traveled in space—and many people confidently believed that his prophecies would be fulfilled. The argument of the materialist philosopher Herbert Spencer (1820–1903) that progress was "not an accident but a necessity" seemed to be confirmed. Religion and idealism seemed no longer necessary: with the aid of science, men would produce heaven on earth.

Waning Confidence in Science

After 1880, however, many members of the upper classes and a great many intellectuals lost at least part of their faith in the glorious future. The source of this remarkable turnabout can be found in science itself. Toward the end of the century, physicists and astronomers began to find discrepancies in the admirable mosaic that science had built. Their discoveries of phenomena unexplained in Newton's system led to the theory of relativity, announced in 1905 by Albert Einstein

(1879–1955), but Einstein's complex description of nature was no help to "materialists" who were learning for the first time that "matter" is only a peculiar collection of electrical charges. This new scientific revolution undoubtedly did upset many of those who understood it, but most laymen remained blissfully unaware that atoms were anything but microscopic billiard balls.

Another possible reason for the loss of confidence was a new revulsion at the condition of humanity. Science was supposed to benefit mankind, but after centuries of so-called progress, the mass of men, even in the most progressive nations, seemed little better off than they had been thousands of years before. Certainly that was true, but the men most vociferous in denouncing the squalor in which their fellows lived, educated socialists, held on to their faith in science. Science, they argued, if properly used, would put an end to misery.

One possible explanation for the new pessimism is that the well-to-do classes lost their faith in a bright future when they saw the socialist parties gaining increasing support from the workingman. The first May Day celebration in Paris took place in 1890; a wave of anarchist terrorism began at about the same time. Socialists began to win seats in the parliaments of Europe. And the danger of a war that might shake society seemed to grow every year. Even Spencer, the great exponent of individualism and optimism, came to believe that the era of individualist triumph would come only after a period of socialism and war. The "loss of faith" was confined mainly to those who had benefited most from the fruits of industrialization, and few of them knew what real scientists were doing or worried much about the fate of the poor. They worried, instead, about themselves.

Popularity suddenly descended on men whose opposition to materialism would have attracted little attention in the past. Friedrich Nietzsche (1844–1900), writing in the 1880s, argued that materialism and the emphasis on reason had sapped the vitality of mankind, that only by returning to a love of life and the irrational universe can man surpass himself. He was ignored until the year he died. Then the "irrationalist" tide

came in, and he was hailed as a prophet. The French philosopher Henri Bergson (1859–1941) filled lecture halls with fashionable crowds who came to hear him praise intuition over reason and spontaneity over scientific thought. He made immensely popular the idea that a "life force," which he called *élan vital,* was the prime mover in the lives of men and the history of mankind.

Doctor Sigmund Freud (1856–1939) of Vienna studied "irrationalism" scientifically. He traced the behavior of human beings to the workings of each man's *unconscious,* a part of the mental structure that serves as a reservoir for the memory of the individual's every experience and where those experiences most painful to remember are repressed. These unpleasant memories, Freud said, force us to react to new experiences in ways that seem irrational—sometimes even self-destructive—because we have not been able to cope effectively with earlier experiences. Only by bringing those memories to consciousness can they be disposed of properly. Freud's discoveries—made in a somewhat prudish, middle-class, male-dominated society—have been significantly modified, but without his original insights huge areas of human experience would still be inexplicable. Although his work is still controversial, few scholars would deny his immense influence. One of the most obvious uses of his work has been, of course, as evidence that man is far from a rational being. Freudian psychology did not become widely known until after World War I, but then it strongly reinforced the antiscientific arguments of the turn of the century.

DOMESTIC POLITICAL DEVELOPMENTS

Living in an era of rapid economic and intellectual change, beset by problems common to all modernizing countries, each nation of Europe reacted in its own distinctive way. For all, however, the major internal problems involved the demands of the poor for a greater share in the nation's wealth.

Great Britain

In England the Reform Bill of 1867 extended the suffrage to all but the poorest male citizens. But the vote meant little as long as positions of political power remained in the hands of the upper classes. In 1870 the philosophical differences between Conservatives (Tories) and Liberals were, in fact, minimal, particularly in matters involving the structure of society: neither party was willing to go very far to alleviate the suffering caused by the long economic slump that began in 1873. Benjamin Disraeli, the Conservative leader, made an impressive record as prime minister in 1875 by securing the passage of public health and housing legislation and by liberalizing the restrictions on trade unions, but useful as that legislation was, it left most workers far from satisfied. Liberals, committed to a policy of laissez-faire, performed even less effectively, and after Disraeli's death "Tory Democracy" was largely forgotten by the Conservatives. Both parties worried more about international affairs than about the nation's internal problems. One obvious solution for the workers, the formation of a party of their own, was years in the making.

The first serious call for a Labour party was sounded in 1893 by the Fabian Society, a group of intellectuals first organized ten years earlier in an effort to convert members of the ruling parties to programs of socialist reform. Its propaganda efforts having failed, the Society called on workers to "abandon Liberalism, to form a Trade Union party of their own." In the same year, Keir Hardie (1856–1915), leader of a Scottish miners' union, organized a federation of unions in an attempt to elect to Parliament candidates who favored socialist reform. Most unions, however, were slow to respond; they preferred to win economic gains through strikes and negotiation. Only in 1900 did representatives of the Fabians, Hardie's Independent Labour party, and the Trades Union Congress finally agree to found the Labour Representation Committee, which soon became the Labour party. A year later, however, a court handed down the Taff Vale decision, forcing a Welsh railroad union to pay damages after a strike. Because all the piecemeal gains of past years seemed in jeopardy, workers at last began to support their own party.

Meanwhile, violent strikes continued to plague the country. A new Liberal govern-ment headed by Herbert Henry Asquith (1852–1928) achieved the passage of an old-age pension bill in 1906, and David Lloyd George (1863–1945), Chancellor of the Exchequer in Asquith's cabinet after 1908, piloted the National Health Insurance Act of 1911 through Parliament against strong opposition. Asquith also succeeded in stripping the House of Lords of its right to a permanent veto over legislation.

But the Liberal government failed to solve the "Irish question." The Catholic Irish, grossly exploited by English landlords since Cromwell's time, were in a state of virtual rebellion. Various "home rule" schemes were wrecked either by the landlords or by Irishmen who refused to accept partition into a Catholic south and Protestant north. The issue reached crisis proportions in 1914, when the outbreak of the World War I temporarily shelved it.

Germany

Bismarck's aim in establishing the new German Empire was to enhance the power of the Prussian king, who became the emperor, and of the Prussian aristocracy. Thus the imperial constitution gave Prussia preponderance, particularly in foreign affairs. The only real power of the popularly elected *Reichstag* lay in its right to vote the budget, but Bismarck easily maintained a majority that would do his bidding. The army remained under the control of Prussia alone.

As soon as the empire was established, Bismarck immediately set out to make it stronger by attacking the privileges of the Catholic church. He began his *Kulturkampf* (struggle for civilization) in 1872. Backed by the majority National Liberal party, he pushed through the *Reichstag* laws that expelled the Jesuit order from Germany, reduced Catholic power in education, and generally cut down Catholic influence in the empire. By 1878, however, the German Social Democratic party was a more serious threat than the Catholic church. Unable to win the support of the National Liberals for a series of repressive anti-Socialist laws, Bismarck dropped his war against the church, turned to the Catholic Center party for support, and got his laws passed. Bismarck next tried to gain popular support by having en-

Emperor Wilhelm I of Germany crowned in the Hall of Mirrors at the Palace of Versailles (1871).

acted a number of significant social welfare laws: sickness and accident insurance legislation was passed in 1883 and 1884, and an old-age insurance act in 1889. He had already won the plaudits of industrialists by turning to protectionism, which became government policy in 1879. That policy also delighted aristocratic Prussian landowners, who were suffering from a drop in wheat prices caused by increasing competition from Russian growers.

Bismarck managed to keep his parliamentary majority, but the anti-Socialist laws failed to destroy the Social Democratic party. Although party meetings and publications were outlawed, socialists could still run for office, and the number of socialist deputies nearly tripled between 1878, when the repressive laws were passed, and 1890, when

they were rescinded two years after a new emperor, William II, came to the throne.

Emperor William II ("Kaiser Wilhelm"), who was bent on asserting personal rule, removed the aging Bismarck from office almost immediately. Succeeding chancellors rarely challenged the emperor's will, and neither the *Reichstag* nor the political parties provided leadership for needed political reforms. Thus, because of its remoteness from the people and their representatives, the imperial government could not mold its subjects into a national community. Nevertheless, between 1895 and 1914 Germany grew economically stronger, and social welfare legislation was extended. Most Germans, pleased with new riches and uninterested in democratic forms that they had never really experienced, seemed satisfied with William's

Execution of Dominican friars by Parisian rebels during the last days of the Commune, May 1871.

leadership, particularly because he continually titillated their national pride by flaunting German power in international affairs. The policy that kept William popular thus led the nation directly into war and defeat.

France

Six years were to elapse after the Franco-Prussian War ended before France's new regime, the Third Republic, was definitively established.

In March 1871, Parisian radicals, exasperated by the government's failure to continue wartime relief measures, revolted and established a commune whose belligerent socialist language frightened the ruling classes of all Europe. Finally, in May, the parliament, meeting at Versailles, sent troops who quashed the rebellion after a week of bloody fighting. For a decade the left in France was paralyzed by its defeat, but the legend of the Paris Commune inspired revolutionaries everywhere for half a century. It also prejudiced conservatives against "leftists" of any sort.

The new parliament elected in February 1871 was dominated by monarchist deputies. Monarchists had campaigned on a peace platform and peace was popular. But the deputies' major interest was social conservatism, and for them limited monarchy was the best means to that end. When the Bourbon pretender said that he would accept the throne only if he could be a ruler, not a mere figurehead, many French monarchists were unwilling to surrender to his demands. The impasse led finally, in 1875, to the constitutional establishment of France's Third Republic—in the words of one of its founders, "the government that divides us least." By 1877 the rural areas that predominated in the country were returning a majority of conservative republicans to the Chamber of Deputies. Monarchists continued to agitate, but their power declined, and by 1890 the continuation of republican government was assured.

The conservative republicans in power were, like the ruling groups in Germany and England, interested primarily in maintaining the social status quo rather than in raising the status of the lower classes. The two great political issues from 1871 to 1905 were the struggle between supporters of the church and their anticlerical opponents—common to all the heavily Roman Catholic nations in Europe—and quarrels over imperialist ventures.

Most devout French Catholics believed implicitly that the Republic was a godless regime because the church was prevented from controlling public education. They were heavily involved in monarchist political movements. Many republicans, on the other hand, sincerely believed that Catholics wished to submit the nation to the domination of the pope, a foreign prince. Moreover, Pope Pius IX (1846–1878), who had been badly frightened by the Roman revolution of 1848, had continually attacked republicanism, liberalism, and socialism. Jules Ferry, a leading republican politician who was twice premier, led the anticlerical attack in the 1880s by pushing through a number of laws that, like those initiated by Bismarck during the *Kulturkampf,* sharply limited Catholic influence in education by restricting the rights of priests to teach. Faced with Ferry's successes, the liberal Pope Leo XIII used his influence to try to break up the old alliance between throne and altar and to "rally" French Catholics to the republic in return for republican generosity toward the church. This *ralliement* was showing modest signs of success when it was destroyed by the outbreak of the Dreyfus affair.

Captain Alfred Dreyfus, the first Jew to serve on the French General Staff, was convicted of selling information to Germany in 1894. By 1898, the efforts of his family to prove his innocence forced a new trial. Militarists, anti-Semites, monarchists, and reactionary Catholics, many sincere and others merely interested in embarrassing the republican government, noisily insisted that Dreyfus was guilty. Anticlericals from diverse political groups fought for his freedom, some sincerely, some merely to embarrass their opponents. At times the judicial aspect of the Dreyfus case was virtually forgotten in the political strife that developed. The Dreyfusards, as Dreyfus' defenders were known, triumphed, then punished their opponents by forcing the separation of church and state in

1905. Since Napoleon's time, the state had paid the salaries of priests; that support was suddenly removed.

Bitterness remained, but the struggle between clericals and anticlericals receded into the background, as it had in Germany two decades earlier, when socialists and others who demanded economic reforms grew strong enough to press their case. In every election between 1902 and 1914 socialist representation in the Chamber of Deputies grew. Socialist deputies fought for tax reform and welfare laws and against military appropriations and imperialism. Their efforts coincided with the strike movement carried on by militant trade unionists. Conservatives kept control, however, and after 1911 the threat of war undermined the strength of social reformers still more. In 1914 France was still a stronghold of laissez-faire.

Russia

One major army reform in the 1870s marked the only significant governmental progress in Russia almost from the time the serfs were freed (see p. 449). Fearing the reaction of landowners to any further attempts to improve the status of the peasants, the government made no serious efforts to introduce new farming techniques or to establish an effective credit system for the poorer peasants. The government of Alexander II did subsidize the building of railroads, however, and, as a result, new centers of textile and metallurgical manufacture were developed. Like other European nations, Russia raised tariffs in the late 1870s and a capable finance minister, Serge Witte (1849–1915) succeeded in strengthening Russian finances and attracting a good deal of foreign capital. Although backward in agriculture, Russia showed signs by 1900 of developing significant industrial power.

But Russia's modernization was hindered by the educational policies of the tsar. Although other European countries slowly built systems that increased the number of competent men available to industry, the Russian government reduced instruction in the sciences in secondary schools, apparently convinced that it provoked opposition to traditional ideals. The education min-

Workers in a textile mill at Ivanovo, part of Russia's rapid industrial development before the revolution.

istry, frightened by outbreaks of student rebellion, sharply curtailed academic freedom in the universities and prohibited student organizations. Numerous intellectuals, increasingly alienated from the government, tended to turn toward revolutionary activity. Failing in their attempts to provoke a great peasant insurrection, many of the more daring radicals adopted political assassination as a revolutionary technique. After several attempts, they killed Tsar Alexander II in 1881. From then until 1905 repression continued to be intensified.

Under Alexander III (1881–1894) what little freedom still existed in Russia was systematically stifled. Censorship was tightened; universities were put under even stricter controls. Alexander's successor, Nicholas II (1894–1917), made no changes in his father's policies. When depression hit in 1899, causing substantial unemployment, and when Russia became involved in a losing war with Japan a few years later, dissatisfaction reached new heights.

Political parties were, of course, illegal, but they nevertheless existed. Three basic groups were established: the Social Revolutionary party, the Russian Social Democratic party, and the Constitutional Democratic party.

The Social Revolutionary party, formally founded in 1901, developed out of the old populist movement, which was based largely on the writings of the philosopher Peter Lavrov (1823–1900). Lavrov argued that educated Russians could bring about socialism by carrying their ideas to the peasants, and despite years of failure, many intellectuals still believed that the peasantry, which made up the great majority of the population, had to be mobilized for revolution.

Unlike the Social Revolutionaries the Social Democrats were Marxists; they put their hopes in the new working class. Hounded out of Russia by the efficient tsarist police, Marxist leaders organized the party in Switzerland and smuggled their propaganda back into their homeland. Their first attempt to hold a national congress failed, but in 1903 the second congress met in Brussels and London. There George Plekhanov (1856–1918) the party's founder, and his supporter Martov (J. O. Tsederbaum, 1873–1923) took the orthodox Marxist position that the Social Democrats must become a mass party of workers and help to bring about a bourgeois democratic revolution, after which they might begin preparations for a new struggle for socialism. Lenin (V. I. Ulyanov, 1870–1924) was more impatient: he and his followers insisted that the party be made up of an elite of professional revolutionaries—a "vanguard of the working class" who would quickly transform the bourgeois revolution into a socialist revolution. Lenin's group had a small majority—hence, they became the Bolshevik, or majority, wing of the party. Martov and Plekhanov thenceforth led the Mensheviks, or minority members. By 1905 the party had members or sympathizers in most significant Russian industries.

Still revolutionary, but much more moderate in their demands, were the Constitutional Democrats (Kadets), who were mostly leading professors and liberal landowners. They, too, formed an illegal party in 1903, but unlike the socialists, they sought for Russia a constitutional government along Western European lines.

Faced with systematic repression, none of these parties could develop, as Western parties had, primarily as spokesmen for interest groups working for immediate piecemeal reforms. They were forced to be revolutionaries because the government simply resisted any change at all. None of them were led by businessmen, practical politicians, or actual workers or peasants; the leaders were, with rare exceptions, intellectuals to whom doctrine was at least as important as practical gains. In the dark years from 1900 to 1905 they found more and more support among the ignorant masses, who knew little of doctrines but were desperate for any improvement in their lot.

Revolution finally came in January 1905. When Father Gapon (a priest who was also a government agent) led a mass of striking workers on a protest march to the Winter Palace in St. Petersburg, troops fired on the demonstrators, killing 70 men and women

and wounding 240. Throughout the year, strikes, riots, and protest meetings continued. In October, a general strike was called; railroads ceased to function, and in the cities electricity and water supplies were cut off; even professional people stopped performing their services. In St. Petersburg, workers established a *soviet* (council) under the guidance of Trotsky (Leo Bronstein, 1879–1940), a leading Menshevik. Faced with complete chaos, his troops still not back from the Siberian front after the defeat by Japan, the tsar finally agreed, on October 30, 1905, to institute a constitution and to establish a representative parliament called the *Duma*. He also agreed to institute freedom of the press. These concessions were enough for the Kadets and most of the strikers, and the strikes came to an end. Within two years, however, the tsarist government had reduced the new Duma to a debating society and, by judicious use of the police, had driven most of the leading revolutionaries underground or into exile.

Nevertheless, Nicholas II had recognized the need for reforms. A new prime minister, P. A. Stolypin, who took office in 1906, began breaking up the backward village communes and introducing agrarian reforms that slowly but surely began to modernize the Russian hinterland. Although Stolypin was assassinated in 1911, his reforms continued, and new efforts were made: local courts were improved and primary education considerably expanded. Still, the tsarist regime was not fully committed to the creation of a modern society in the way that even the autocratic German emperor was. The tsar might eventually have made that commitment, but World War I brought his overthrow by revolution.

Other European States

In the rest of Europe domestic developments were less momentous. The Austro-Hungarian Monarchy, caught between the demands of Czechs and other minorites for autonomy and the refusal of Germans and Magyars to tolerate any such thing, stumbled from crisis to crisis. In Italy, union had brought parliamentary government, but the ruling politicians vied with each other for desirable offices and political plums instead of facing the

Fighting at the barricades in St. Petersburg, January 9, 1905.

problems that beset the country. Spain was in political chaos, still economically so backward that little progress seemed possible. In the north things were better. Belgium moved toward democracy as it industrialized, while Holland, agricultural still, existed placidly under an enlightened monarch. Norway split off from Sweden peaceably in 1905, and both countries developed quietly. Denmark, another primarily agricultural nation, saw the emergence of a reform movement that was to bring about the establishment of a new democratic constitution in 1915.

THE NEW IMPERIALISM

Around 1880 the European nations suddenly began the biggest scramble for empire in history. Within 30 years all but a few thousand square miles of the Eastern Hemisphere had fallen under the sway of European power. Both causes and effects of this immense conquest are still hotly debated.

Colonial conquests were by no means a new phenomenon in the 1880s, but the nature of European expansion had definitely changed. In previous centuries, conquests were generally one of two types. Many conquests had been undertaken by and for emigrants who wished to establish a branch of their own culture in a new area, usually either because they sought new economic opportunities or freedom to practice religious rites not tolerated in their homeland. The other type involved trading stations like those established by Europeans in Senegal, India, Java, and hundreds of other places around the world. Establishments of both types continued through the nineteenth century, but a new kind was added when Europeans, instead of colonizing like the English in North America or merely setting up extensive trading posts like the Dutch in the East Indies, took over the administration of entire countries.

By the end of the nineteenth century the "new imperialism" had become the prevailing mode, and Europeans attempted to take over large areas of Asia and Africa (see maps, pp. 578–579, 623). European administrators ruled either directly or through local princes. European-style constitutions and legal systems were forced on societies to which they were quite alien, and Europeans felt deeply an obligation to "civilize" the inhabitants of their possessions.

This new kind of imperialism could not have come into existence before the Industrial Revolution. Even in 1900 determined Africans and Asians could on occasion defeat European troops; before the advent of modern weapons and inventions like the steamship, the conquest of large populations in reasonably well-organized societies would have been impossible.

Economic needs have frequently been cited as the cause of the new imperialism. J. A. Hobson (1858–1940), an English essayist, argued in 1902 that wealthy men used their influence to bring about the conquest of undeveloped territories so that they would have new areas in which to invest their excess capital. Lenin, writing in 1916, went a step further, arguing that such actions are inevitable: imperialism, he said, is "the highest stage of capitalism." In fact, however, a relatively small amount of capital was invested in the conquered territories. British capitalists, for example, put most of their money into United States enterprises, and the French

put theirs into Russian development. Moreover, nations like Japan and Italy, with little capital to invest, sought colonies with as much enthusiasm as did England and France. Thus the investment theory is no longer widely accepted. Other economic explanations, such as the the need for markets or for areas to which immigrants could go, are subject to similar rebuttals. England and France traded far more with other industrial countries than with their colonies, and most emigrants went not to Africa or Asia but to independent nations in North or South America.

Although earlier economic explanations of the rise of the new imperialism have now been largely discredited, other explanations have not been easy to find. Economic factors, scholars now argue, did play a part, because statesmen believed that colonies would someday, if not immediately, be needed as markets for both capital and industrial products. Moreover, although the nation as a whole might spend far more money on colonial conquest than it would make, some individuals certainly made personal fortunes; one famous example was Cecil Rhodes (1853–1902) with his South African diamond mines. (In addition to a fund for scholarships he had a whole country—Rhodesia—named after him.) The need for raw materials was also significant, particularly for industries based on tropical products such as cocoa, rubber, or scarce minerals.

Imperialism also served Europe as a safety valve. Restless spirits who sought adventure could find it in overseas expansion; idle soldiers could be kept out of mischief at home by sending them to fight colonial wars; and potentially restive workers could be kept quiet by letting them share in national glory won on faraway battlegrounds. Missionaries and intellectuals, convinced that they had a duty to carry their superior religion and culture to those whom Kipling called "lesser breeds without the Law," could be satisfied. Finally, navies powered by steam needed far-flung coaling stations; armies could find new recruits among conquered peoples; and nations could win strategic positions that would strengthen them against potential rivals.

Thus there appears to be no single explanation of the new imperialism, and each case has to be examined to determine which of

A German missionary preaching in a Togoland village. His creed taught him to advocate imperialism as passionately as did soldiers or merchants.

these many factors may have played parts in bringing it about. Nevertheless, one factor stands out: without the passion and pride encompassed in nationalism, the other factors involved would not have been enough to produce imperial conquest. Time after time governments protested that they had no intention of moving into a particular area, then some general, admiral, merchant, or missionary, finding himself in difficulty far from home, demanded succor from his government. The "honor of the flag" was engaged; newspapers would cry for vengeance, politicians would demand action, and a new conquest would be made. Whatever real advantages might accrue to any particular group, nationalist passion provided the final impetus to colonial invasion.

THE COMING OF WORLD WAR I

Bismarck's triumph in 1871 had consolidated the power of militaristic nationalism in German society and brought into existence a new threat to the peace of Europe. Spain and France had, in their days of glory, ruled most of Europe; England ruled an empire and held its position as the richest country in the world. It would have been unusual for the Germans to remain content while their own power continually increased.

Other nations were also restless. Frenchmen dreamed of the "lost provinces" of Alsace-Lorraine, taken by Germany after the War of 1870 to 1871. Italians, finally united, still clamored for their "unredeemed lands," the South Tyrol and the Trieste region, both still ruled by Austria. Russia was busy colonizing its frontiers in Siberia and Central Asia, seeking new warmwater ports on the Pacific, and dreaming of taking the Straits leading into the Mediterranean world. Austria's government not only wanted Turkey's Balkan territory but deeply feared the results of nationalist propaganda within the empire. In all of Europe, only England seemed to have reason to be satisfied with its lot.

Every country had either a grievance to redress or a reason to fear the power of its neighbors. Bismarck believed that Germany could gain most by keeping the peace. Until 1890, when the new emperor removed him from office, Bismarck pursued a complex diplomatic path that successfully damped down Europe's many potential quarrels. With Bismarck gone, the chances of war steadily increased, for the alliance system he helped to develop to keep the peace now became an instrument for turning an obscure incident into a cause for general war.

For nearly a century Balkan nationalism had been growing as Turkish power, sapped by internal corruption, declined. The two powers most directly concerned in the Balkan problem, Austria and Russia, had skirmished in diplomatic conferences for years, each trying to prevent the other from dominating the area. Austria's concern was more immediate, for nationalistic, aggressive Slavic states in the Balkans threatened her very existence by causing unrest among the Slavs under Austrian rule. Russian nationalists, however, asserted that Russia should protect the new states, since it shared ethnic and religious ties with them. Moreover, Russia sought to control Istanbul and the entrance to the Black Sea for purposes of military security. A Russian victory over the Turks in 1878 gave Russia the preponderance it sought; Austria immediately demanded a conference of European leaders to repair the damage. The Congress of Berlin, chaired by Bismarck, settled the question temporarily by considerably reducing the Russian gains. A year later, in 1879, Germany and Austria signed a treaty of defense against possible Russian attack. In 1881, Russian desires for protection against Austrian activity in the Balkans produced the Three Emperors' League, under which Russia, Germany, and Austria each agreed to remain neutral if one of them found itself at war with a fourth power; this league also regulated events in the Balkans. Temporarily, trouble in the Balkans seemed allayed.

Bismarck was still far from secure, however, for the French dreamed of recovering their diplomatic and political primacy in Europe. France at this time was also competing with Italy for African territory. Ger-

many, Italy, and Austria, therefore, established the Triple Alliance to protect themselves against attack by France. Austria's gain was assurance that Italy would not follow up nationalist demands for Austrian territories inhabited by Italians. Thus Bismarck built alliances that protected Germany against almost any eventuality, but once Bismarck was out of power, these alliances were quickly dissolved.

In 1890 the new German emperor, William II, allowed his alliance with Russia to lapse. French diplomats grasped the opportunity to end their isolation, and in 1894 the Franco-Russian Alliance came into being. It was a "natural" alliance, since both France and Russia feared the German Empire, which had become the strongest power on the continent. Bismarck's alliance system was in this sense "unnatural"—by creating a bloc of overwhelming strength in Central Europe, it contravened the balance of power principle.

England, meanwhile, had chosen "splendid isolation." Its interests were largely overseas, not on the continent, and its only interest in European affairs was to prevent any power from dominating the continent and threatening it. It concentrated its efforts in rivalry with France over African territories and with Russia over the Middle East. Near the end of the century, however, the Germans set about building a navy that would rival England's.

The competition between France and England came to a head in 1898 in the Sudan, when English troops moving south along the Nile came on a small French force at Fashoda and claimed prior rights to the territory held by France. Nationalist tempers flared, and war was averted only because the French, fearing Germany more than they hated England, agreed to withdraw. In return, the English eventually agreed not to oppose French expansion in Morocco; Théophile Delcassé, the French foreign minister, successfully attempted to resolve every remaining Franco-British colonial dispute, and in 1904, the Entente Cordiale was born. It was not an alliance but simply an understanding that France and England would work together to preserve the peace of Europe. In both countries large and powerful groups opposed any strengthening of the En-

Fashoda, 1898. Nationalist newspaper comment nearly provoked a war between Britain and France.

tente, but growing German naval power forced the two countries closer together. They informally agreed to concentrate the French navy in the Mediterranean while England's fleets secured the North Sea. A strong informal commitment to mutual aid thus developed.

Friction between Russia and England, although less intense, was strong enough to cause constant difficulties, particularly in Persia, where each country sought influence. But when Russia was defeated by the Japanese in 1905, its rivalry with Austria in the Balkans flared up once again. French diplomats encouraged Russia and England to settle their colonial differences, and Russia became part of the Entente in 1907.

Thus two opposing sets of powers came into being. Germany, Austria, and Italy—the Triple Alliance—were in constant diplomatic conflict with the members of the Triple Entente over the Balkans, Africa, and the high seas. The Triple Alliance was purely defensive, while the Triple Entente was nothing more than a community of interests with no legal obligations. Yet the scenario for a future

Dividing the pie: France, England, and Germany during the Morocco Crisis.

war had been written, for all the great powers felt encouraged to pursue their interests, perhaps with caution, but with all their strength.

The decade before 1914 was remarkable for the settlement of outstanding imperial rivalries. England settled its differences with France and Russia, as we have seen; what is more surprising is that Germany, a great power in Europe with grand overseas ambitions, also managed to patch up the quarrels caused by its adventurous policies. Trouble came twice, in 1905 and 1911, in Morocco, which France had earmarked as its own, but in both cases peace was preserved. German colonial designs in the Middle East clashed with those of Britain but, again, negotiations led to an amicable settlement. Italy won international approval for its acquisition of Libya and succeeded in detaching it from Turkey without seriously upsetting relations among the great powers. Italy also relinquished to France its claims to Tunisia, which had long promoted friction between these two powers.

Thus it seems that imperialism was at most an indirect cause of World War I. Once the

war began, every major participant developed grandiose colonial claims, but before it started they had always been unwilling to fight among themselves for colonial possessions. Almost intuitively, it seems, the leaders of each great power decided that colonial aggrandizement, although highly desirable, was not worth a major war. Imperial rivalries helped to produce the alliance systems and often strained international relations, but the war came as a result of nationalism.

From the end of the middle ages until the beginning of the nineteenth century, Turkey was strong enough to control its Balkan subjects and prevent encroachment from the north. When Turkish power declined, however, its Balkan empire began to disintegrate. Greece broke away in the 1820s. Serbia, Rumania, and Montenegro became partly autonomous later in the century, and their independence was recognized by the Congress of Berlin (1878), as was that of a newly created Bulgaria. Still, the congress left thousands of Serbs, Croats, Bulgarians, and Rumanians subject to Austria, to Turkey, or to one of the rival Balkan states. Nationalist agitation was constant and vociferous, but it had no chance of success until the Asian defeat of 1905 turned Russian interest once more to the Balkans. Two wars among the Balkan states in 1912 and 1913 were settled to the satisfaction of the great powers in a conference at London in 1913, when the new state of Albania was created and boundaries were redrawn. The Balkan states themselves, however, were far from satisfied. Serbia, in particular, noisily demanded that Austria cede to it the control of neighboring Bosnia, inhabited by other Serbs.

On June 28, 1914, Bosnian nationalists assassinated Archduke Francis Ferdinand, heir to the Austrian throne, during a parade in Sarajevo. Austria decided to seize the opportunity to put an end to Serbian nationalist demands. Count Berchtold, the Austrian foreign minister, sought and received from Germany full backing for whatever action he might take. On July 23, Austria sent Serbia an ultimatum that demanded the virtual surrender of Serbian independence. The Serbs gave in on most points, but Austria refused the concessions. On July 28, the Austrian government declared war, convinced

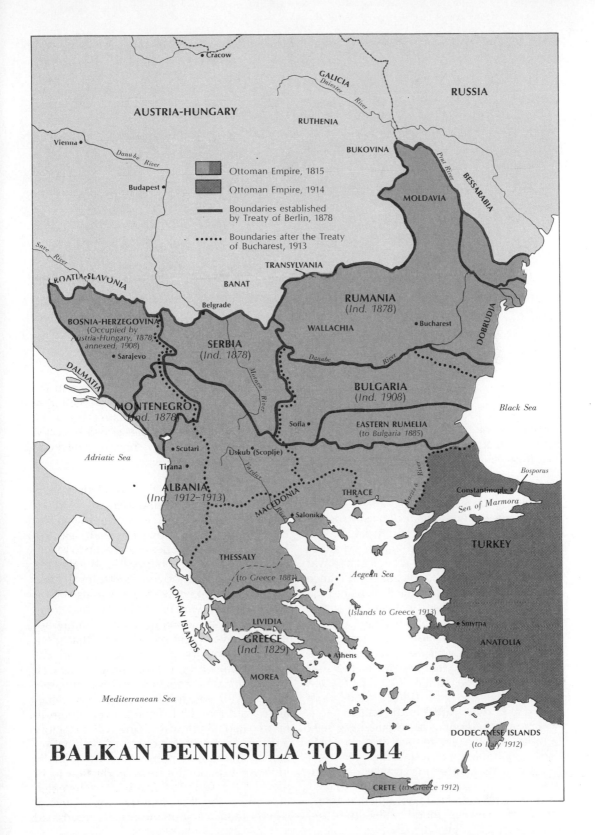

Ottoman Empire, 1815
Ottoman Empire, 1914
Boundaries established by Treaty of Berlin, 1878
Boundaries after the Treaty of Bucharest, 1913

AUSTRIA-HUNGARY

RUSSIA

GALICIA
Dniester River

RUTHENIA

BUKOVINA

Vienna •

Danube River

Prut River

BESSARABIA

MOLDAVIA

Budapest •

Save River

TRANSYLVANIA

CROATIA-SLAVONIA

BANAT

RUMANIA
(Ind. 1878)

Belgrade

BOSNIA-HERZEGOVINA
(Occupied by Austria-Hungary, 1878; annexed, 1908)

WALLACHIA

• Bucharest

DOBRUDJA

• Sarajevo

SERBIA
(Ind. 1878)

DALMATIA

Danube River

MONTENEGRO
(Ind. 1878)

BULGARIA
(Ind. 1908)

Morava River

Black Sea

Adriatic Sea

• Scutari

Sofia •

EASTERN RUMELIA
(to Bulgaria 1885)

Tirana •

Uskub (Scoplje)

Vardar River

Bosporus

ALBANIA
(Ind. 1912–1913)

THRACE

Constantinople •

Maritza River

MACEDONIA

• Salonika

Sea of Marmora

TURKEY

THESSALY

Aegean Sea

(to Greece 1881)

(Islands to Greece 1913)

IONIAN ISLANDS

LIVIDIA

• Smyrna

GREECE
(Ind. 1829)

ANATOLIA

• Athens

MOREA

Mediterranean Sea

DODECANESE ISLANDS
(to Italy 1912)

BALKAN PENINSULA TO 1914

CRETE (to Greece 1912)

Archduke Franz Ferdinand of Austria and his wife in Sarajevo an hour before they were assassinated (July 1914).

that it was a matter of life or death for the empire.

Meanwhile, Russia prepared to back its Serbian client by mobilizing for war. Germany demanded that Russia demobilize —a Russian attack on Austria would bring the Triple Alliance into operation. When Russia refused, Germany declared war, on August 1, 1914. German military leaders had, however, long planned that in case of war with Russia they would knock out Russia's ally, France, before turning to attack their eastern enemy. Thus they declared war on France on August 3. The attack on France did not automatically bring Britain into the war, because the Entente was only an understanding, not a treaty. But when the Germans invaded Belgium in order to enter France from the north, they triggered traditional British fears of foreign domination of the strategic low countries. Britain's cabinet reacted immediately, and soon British troops were sailing to France to join in the battle.

Nationalist emotions led the Serbs to seek to unite all their countrymen under a single flag. The principle that a state has every right to fight for its ultimate survival led the Austrians to try to prevent the disruption of their empire. Finally, the terms of alliance agreements as well as moral obligations led

Russia, Germany, and France to join in the war. Thus it seems likely that every nation or none is to blame. The immediate cause of the war was the inflammable emotion called nationalism, and every nation in Europe shared it in abundance.

By the beginning of the twentieth century modernization was well under way in Western and Central Europe, and even Russia had taken halting steps along this path. Most of Europe's political leaders had come to recognize the need for change. In Britain and France democratic governments, legally and morally bound to move toward goals chosen by the citizens who elected them, had come into being. In Germany, an essentially autocratic government had decided that modernization was the price of power, and was fully committed to material progress as well as to national ascendancy. In Russia the tsars had moved toward modernization reluctantly, but they had moved. Everywhere in Europe agriculture was giving way to factory industry as the basic source of national income, and urban population was rapidly increasing. Important new production techniques—the sort that need to be invented only once and then may be copied everywhere—had been put into use. Railroads had revolutionized transport, and mechanical power was being applied increasingly to tasks once painfully performed by human labor. Moreover, humans were increasing in numbers, living longer, and living more comfortably.

Where once the vast majority of men had lived in isolated peasant villages, national societies had come into existence. Through public education, modern printing presses, and nationalist rituals, governments were welding their citizens into integrated bodies in which interdependence was the rule and, paradoxically, the same process was allowing individuals far more scope for personal development than they had ever had before.

Nevertheless, the process of modernization was proceeding at an uneven pace. Less developed nations envied and feared those that were more progressive, and the strongest nations nursed grievances against each other. Within nations the class struggle that Marx had predicted was in full swing, for the gap between rich and poor was wide and as obvious as the concentration of political power in the interests of the ruling class. Conservatives fought every attempt at a redistribution of power and wealth, while liberals trusted in gradual reforms to bring about a better life for everyone. Others — socialists, syndicalists, and anarchists — wanted radical changes immediately and were prepared to fight for them. The era of social integration had begun, but so had a new era of social and international conflict.

SUGGESTED READINGS

Cipolla, Carlo. *The Economic History of World Population*. Baltimore: Penguin Books, 1962. Pelican paperback.
Excellent introduction to an immensely complex subject.

Hughes, H. Stuart. *Consciousness and Society: The Reorientation of European Social Thought, 1890–1930*. New York: Random House, 1958. Vintage paperback.
A difficult but essential book.

Schumpeter, Joseph A. *Capitalism, Socialism, and Democracy*. New York: Harper and Row, 1942. Torchbook paperback.
Provocative study of sociopolitical change; includes the best short essay on intellectuals yet written.

Polanyi, Karl. *The Great Transformation: Political and Economic Origins of Our Time*. Boston: Beacon Press, 1944. Paperback.
One of the most illuminating books in the field.

Freud, Sigmund. *Psychopathology of Everyday Life*. New York: New American Library, 1951. Mentor paperback.
The best introduction to the flavor of Freudian thought.

Nietzsche, Friedrich. *Beyond Good and Evil*. New York: Random House, 1966.
Authentic Nietzsche, easier to understand than most of his work, in an edition with a good introduction.

Jefferson, Carter. *Anatole France: The Politics of Skepticism*. New Brunswick, N.J.: Rutgers University Press, 1965.
Study of a great writer whose thought was in many ways typical of intellectuals caught in the "crisis of humanism."

Lichtheim, George. *Imperialism*. New York: Praeger, 1971. Paperback.
The best of hundreds of studies.

Johnson, Douglas. *France and the Dreyfus Affair*. New York: Walker, 1967.
A balanced discussion of this famous case.

Tannenbaum, Edward. *The Action Francaise*. New York: John Wiley, 1962.
Study of the most spectacular of France's rightwing movements.

Dangerfield, George. *The Strange Death of Liberal England*. New York: G. P. Putnam's Sons, 1961. Capricorn paperback.
Fascinating study of a crucial period in English history.

Lafore, Laurence. *The Long Fuse: An Interpretation of the Origins of World War I*. Philadelphia: J. B. Lippincott, 1965. Preceptor paperback.
Good introduction to a highly controversial problem.

CHAPTER 16

North America, 1815–1917

THE UNITED STATES IN 1815

The United States in 1815 was a rich country. A nation of barely eight and one-half million citizens, it covered one and one-half million square miles—some billion acres of the finest soil, timber, and minerals on earth. These resources were largely untapped and unexploited, awaiting the hand of man to be converted into unparalleled abundance. Joined with this extraordinary physical endowment was a social and political system attuned to the most egalitarian ideals of the age. The great majority of Americans, about 75 percent, tilled the soil—a proportion not appreciably different from most of the Western world. The distinction is that these husbandmen were overwhelmingly farm proprietors—men who owned substantial parcels of fertile agricultural land. Outside the slave south and a section of the Hudson Valley, the typical unit of production in the new nation was the family-sized farm worked by a single owner with the aid of his wife and sons. Besides farmers, and not always easily distinguishable from them, there was a substantial class of rural and urban artisans and mechanics. Tradesmen, manufacturers, and local merchants formed the next social class; then came traders in foreign commodities, men who ran the export-import businesses of large seaports such as New York, Boston, Philadelphia, Baltimore, and Charleston. Along with the plantation owners in the south and small groups of professional men, especially lawyers, the large port city merchants constituted the nation's social and economic elite.

Clearly the United States in 1815 was not a perfect democracy. Wealth conferred prestige and power. A Perkins of Boston, an Astor of New York, a Lee or Carter of Virginia, and a Pinckney of South Carolina, was deferred to by his inferiors and rewarded with offices and leadership. Just recently, one of the two great national parties, the Federalists, had appealed to American fears of "mobocracy" with occasional success. Yet compared to Europe this was an egalitarian society. Despite the Federalists, it was egalitarian in its values and its rhetoric. As far back as 1776 the Declaration of Independence had declared "all men created equal," and although some Americans refused to accept this radical doctrine, and many more refused

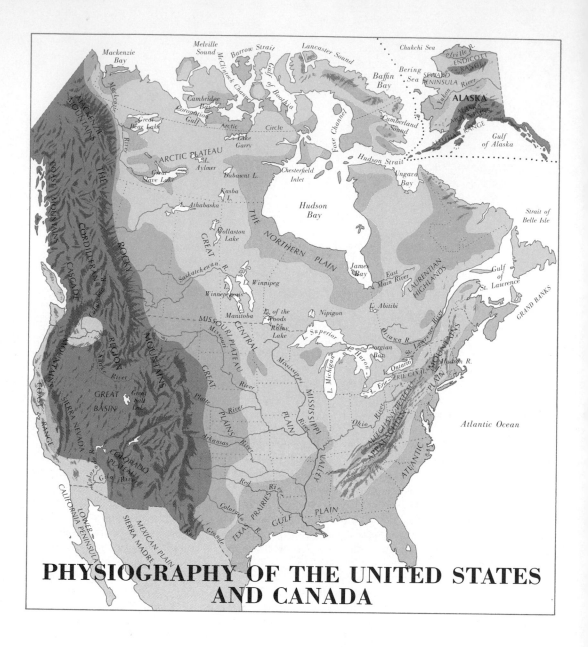

PHYSIOGRAPHY OF THE UNITED STATES AND CANADA

to apply it to blacks, it was becoming increasingly difficult to attack the principle in public.

The country was also relatively egalitarian in its politics. As yet, suffrage for all white men had not been formally achieved, but ever since the eighteenth century a large proportion of white males had voted for local legislative bodies. The farmer and city artisan still did not typically choose men of their own kind for the Burgesses or the General Court. They turned to the local "gentry" for leadership. But with the widest and freest suffrage in the world, America was already on its way to achieving modern representative democracy.

For the majority of free white men, then, the nation was egalitarian and open in its social structure, without a rigid class system. The range of incomes in the United States was smaller than in Europe: there were few millionaires and few paupers. There was no heredity nobility, of course; in fact, even foreign titles of nobility had been forbidden to American citizens by the Constitution. America did have an elite, however. This was a self-made gentry, composed largely of men or the sons of men who had risen to prominence from relatively obscure beginnings. All told, the American experience had already shown that "you couldn't keep a good man down."

The one great blot on the nation's democratic record was the institution of chattel slavery. At its height in the 1770s the egalitarian fervor of the struggle for independence had succeeded in marshaling strong feelings against slavery, and in the states north of the Mason-Dixon Line it had helped either to abolish it outright or to set up machinery for gradual emancipation. But by 1815 the "peculiar institution" was reviving. Plantation agriculture, the economic base of slavery, was also again on the rise. Colonial cultivation of tobacco, rice, and indigo had been hard-hit by the break with Britain, and with the stagnation of the market much of the profit had gone out of the slave system. Then commercial cotton-growing, swept across the lower south. Along with it, on large plantations and small farms, came the slave system of the coastal states. No longer did the remaining scruples of southern planters count for much — not when cotton sold for 20 cents a pound, and when a few acres of Mississippi delta planted in green-seed cotton could bring a lucky man hundreds of dollars in a single successful season.

In a word, the United States in 1815 was a land of economic opportunity for the 80 percent of the population that was white. Even at the bottom of the free labor system the rewards for enterprise were relatively high. It is difficult to estimate precisely the average per capita income of Americans in 1815, but it was probably second only to England and far better distributed than anywhere else. In 1815, ordinary Europeans understood this at least as well as today's economic historians, and they crossed the Atlantic to the New World in vast numbers thereafter.

Abundant resources were supplemented by the highly favorable human environment in America. Economic productivity is as much the result of institutions and values as

of nature's bounty. And the nation's institutions, and its values or *ethic*, were peculiarly congenial to the amassing of wealth. Here were no feudal remains in either agriculture or trade to hinder enterprise. Guild regulations, feudal dues, and restrictions on free movement of labor either had not survived the transplanting of European institutions in the New World or had arrived so enfeebled that they did not last long.

Nor did American religion and ethical values conflict with the pursuit of wealth. These stemmed largely from the Protestantism of Northern Europe, which assumed that man's ultimate purpose was to exalt God and earn salvation. Anglicans, Calvinists, and other Protestants claimed to place things of the spirit above things of this world, and they all professed to hold worldly success in lesser esteem than personal virtue. In practice, however, even God-fearing, churchgoing Americans worried relatively little about salvation and still less about the ultimate meaning of existence. Their religion was often highly practical and social; it taught them to be abstemious, industrious, reliable, and provident. But they believed that the proper stage for the exercise of these virtues was the everyday world of work, family and business, not the monastery or other retreat. Also, as we shall see, American Protestantism, drew from the Old Testament's prophetic strain a sensitivity to social and political injustice that was to nurture a long succession of crusades for public virtue. The faith of Americans did little to hinder the pursuit of material gain and, indeed, by directing men's attention to the things of this world, and by fostering the commercial virtues, probably encouraged it. It is not true that nineteenth-century Americans uniformly identified worldly success with godliness; but neither did they believe that failure was a sure sign of God's grace.

The abundance of cheap land, particularly in the west, made it possible for successive generations of propertyless young men to set themselves up as farm proprietors. Even if few penniless wage earners could afford to begin a western farm right away, wagework in towns, temporary tenantry, or agricultural labor helped in procuring the capital to get started. At the same time the open frontier of new resources buoyed up the nation's economy; it provided a vital impulse to commerce and industry, and by constantly renewing business opportunities, helped strengthen the ever-growing urban middle class.

Mobility contributed to prosperity and economic growth partly by providing incentives to enterprise. Men knew that in America every career was open to talent and imagination. The rewards of success were not confined to an elite but could be garnered by any man, no matter how lowly his origin. Also, mobility, along with the egalitarianism it implied, encouraged an unprecedented volume of investment in "human capital." Machines, factories, and railroads are required to produce goods but so are skills, knowledge, and experience. Hence, education and other investments in human resources are needed to create an alert, literate, innovative, and intelligent population. In republican America, where the public voice was heard and often had to be obeyed, support for education, especially at the elementary level, was relatively generous. And where "getting ahead" was possible for all free men, individual self-investment in the form of school tuition and work years deferred seemed worth the sacrifice. Together this public and private investment helped make early nineteenth-century Americans one of the most literate people in the world.

By 1815, then, the United States, scarcely a half century removed from colonial status, with much of its land still a wilderness, was already among the most "modern" nations in the world. Settled predominantly by people from England—the European nation already furthest advanced toward a modern social structure—and freed from feudal and traditional survivals by the uncongenial nature of the New World environment, America as a community had been "born free." Abundance had reinforced these modernizing tendencies. Where land seemed limitless, tenantry and social dependence were impossible to establish, and wages—where men chose to work for wages—were high. In such an environment egalitarianism and even democracy, already in embryo in the British heritage, took secure root. Initial abundance and freedom prepared the way for further progress. Still primarily agricultural in 1815, the United States was about to embark on an exuberant economic acceleration that by 1865 would transform the young nation into one of the world's great industrial powers.

THE UNITED STATES TO 1865

But grave difficulties would be encountered along the way. In the half century from 1815 to 1865, serious divisive forces worked to tear the community apart. How to overcome these centripetal forces and forge a politically, culturally, and economically indivisible union was the basic problem besetting the nation to 1865.

Beginning of National Consolidation

The Philadelphia Constitutional Convention had taken an enormous step forward in integrating the United States politically. The federal Constitution of 1787 had welded a loose confederation of thirteen sovereign states into a nation. It had created a national government that, within its own broad realm, was sovereign and dealt directly with all the people without the intermediary of the states. It had created a gigantic free trade region within which goods and people could move freely without paying tolls and without fear of arbitrary restraint. The Constitution had authorized a national army and navy, a uniform system of weights and measures, and a uniform currency. It had given to the new national government sole power to conduct foreign affairs and to adjust disputes among the states. It had created a *de facto* national citizenship and had authorized uniform laws of naturalization. It had established a national legislature, a national judiciary and, above all, a national executive.

And yet the Constitution had not ended all controversy about the relative roles and strengths of local and national authority. Although a majority of the American people probably had endorsed the Constitution and national political integration, they did not all agree about the extent to which the states had surrendered their power to achieve that integration. The document was ambiguous on many issues. Frequently unable to compromise opposing positions and fearing that explicitness might only help defeat ratification, the Founding Fathers at Philadelphia had often descended into vagueness. It had, consequently, been possible for men of differing views to accept the new frame of government with the hope that, when specific constitutional issues arose, their own interpretation would prevail.

Through the next 40 years national power was generally augmented. The enactment of the Hamiltonian program* represented a strong centralizing trend. The War of 1812, which at one point threatened to split off New England from the rest of the country, in the end fostered the further growth of federal power. The war clearly demonstrated that the nation was unusually vulnerable to foreign attack and caused many Jeffersonians to abandon their scruples against using federal authority for important public purposes. In the wake of the war a new breed of National Republican, led by such men as Henry Clay and John C. Calhoun, strongly urged the rechartering of the Bank of the United States to provide a sound financial system, a protective tariff to nurture American industry, and a system of roads and canals sponsored by the federal government to tie the country together physically. In the next few years they largely succeeded in enacting this program into law.

Thus, in spite of its ambiguities, the War of 1812 had unexpectedly helped unify the nation. For a few years this consolidating process continued. The decisions of the Supreme Court led by Chief Justice John Marshall enlarged federal powers at the expense of the states. Physical integration proceeded rapidly as well. Endorsed and encouraged by

* Conceived by Alexander Hamilton of New York, the first Secretary of Treasury, the Hamiltonian Program of the 1790s included: (1) funding of both the state and national Revolutionary War debt so as to improve the credit of the United States and attach the public creditor interest to the new national government; (2) establishing of a federally chartered bank to secure a sound currency and to encourage business enterprise; (3) helping the country's infant manufacturing interest by a combination of federal bounties and a protective tariff.

Presidents James Monroe and John Quincy Adams, and subsidized by state governments, private turnpikes began to extend like spokes of a wheel from every major town in the northeast. More important were the new canals, inspired by the immensely successful Erie Canal, which linked New York City with the Great Lakes and the great interior heartland. Completed by New York State in 1825, the Erie assured the supremacy of the port of New York and spurred that city's coastal rivals into a frantic scramble for similar connections to the interior. Meanwhile the new trans-Appalachian states embarked on elaborate programs of state financed connecting canals.

The Erie was probably the only canal project to make money for its sponsors, whether state or private, but the canals proved a great boon to the nation as a whole. Along with the new steamboats, which had begun to appear in great numbers on coastal waters and navigable rivers, the canals, and to a lesser extent the turnpikes, greatly reduced freight and transportation costs. Prices of manufactured goods declined sharply in the west; wheat, beef, flour, and other agricultural products became less expensive in the east. In the 1830s the railroad made its appearance. By 1840 there were almost 3000 miles of track in the United States; in 1850 over 9000; in 1860 more than 30,000. By this last date the total investment in railroads totaled more than $1 billion. The new "iron horse" further reduced cost differentials between sections and greatly increased the speed of passenger travel. By 1860, however, the canals and the paddle-wheelers had already done much of the work of knitting the country together commercially.

The Age of Jackson

At the very time when the new nationalism and the new transportation technology were working to unify the country, other developments were beginning to push in the opposite direction. Some of the political changes making for division in these years grew out of what is generally called Jacksonian Democracy. Actually, Andrew Jackson was more the product of these changes than their creator, but he imprinted on them the force of his personality and won

The Erie Canal at Rochester, New York, 1853.

to the cause of majoritarian democracy thousands who might otherwise have remained indifferent to politics. A self-made man and a national hero who led American troops to victory at New Orleans, Jackson became a symbol of the "natural man," whose untrained instincts would serve as an unfailing guide to good government. The public retained this idealized view of Jackson after 1815 while many of the new forces and new ideas at large in the nation coalesced around him.

These Jacksonian forces and ideas were above all democratic. Before 1815, democracy had not been absent from America, but it had coexisted with a marked amount of political and social deference. Beginning in the 1820s the United States gradually ceased to be a deferential society. No longer would the public accept notions of "higher orders" and "lower orders." Every man now appeared capable of political judgment and, indeed, the natural man, unspoiled by classical learning or the arts of polite society, was now deemed more likely to judge correctly on

public issues than men of established wealth and position. This meant that the new type of politician could no longer afford to remain aloof from his constituents, assuming that they would defer to his superior, informed judgment. The electorate now had to be consulted, flattered, and cultivated as never before, a situation that encouraged the formation of the first modern party machines.

The new democratic spirit also liberalized formal and informal constitutional machinery. In the years between 1815 and 1840 the last vestiges of property qualifications for voting and officeholding were swept away. This period also saw the advent, through state enactment, of the popular choice of presidential electors. The electoral college remained, but it no longer would be an independent body free to vote its own will. Finally, the democratic convention system replaced the oligarchic "King Caucus" for nominating presidential and gubernatorial candidates.

The men behind these changes were a very mixed lot. Not all were Jacksonians, although the Jackson men claimed credit for most of the changes. Even Jackson's supporters were a diverse group. In economic matters the Jacksonians seem to have represented two distinct elements. One was composed of Jeffersonian agrarians who had either reverted to their original suspicion of business and, especially, banks and the money power, or had never abandoned it. Another element represented those men who wished to become part of that very money power and who felt that various privileged business groups, or "monopolies," stood in their way. Finally in the social realm, many Jacksonians were men who were outside the circle of the most respectable classes, whether as Catholics, immigrants, frontiersmen, Protestant evangelicals, or agnostics.

This diverse coalition, after a near miss in 1824, managed to elect Andrew Jackson president four years later. By then the "Era of Good Feelings" that had characterized the years immediately following 1815 had given way to one of bitter partisanship, first over men, and then over principles, as the Jacksonians attacked the Second Bank of the United States, resisted federally sponsored internal improvement, fought tariffs, and voiced a more democratic rhetoric regarding rotation in office.

Opposed to the Jacksonian Democrats was the new Whig party led by such old Jeffersonians as Henry Clay along with old-line Federalists like Daniel Webster. After 1836 the Whigs organized an effective opposition based on resentment of "King Andrew" and on a revived and updated Federalist program combined with the new egalitarian rhetoric. The new Whigs and the new Democrats may not have been carbon copies of the old Federalists and Jeffersonians, but allowing for the overall democratic shift, the resemblances were strong.

For a decade and a half following Jackson's retirement in 1836, Whigs, and Democrats fought on the state and national levels for control, with the Democrats winning all but two presidential contests and generally carrying the south, the west, and the middle states. The election battles were often bitter but, of course, neither party rejected the twin pillars of American society: political democracy and private property.

Meanwhile, a new political issue was injected into American political life, far more divisive and dangerous than the tariff, the Bank, internal improvements, and universal suffrage, although all of them were eventually drawn into its vortex. This was the issue of slavery in its various guises.

The Slavery Issue and Sectional Conflict

Slavery, once nationwide, had become the "peculiar institution" of the south following its abolition in the states north of Maryland and its exclusion from the Northwest Territory by the Ordinance of 1787. On the eve of the Civil War there were approximately four million slaves in the 15 slave states and the District of Columbia who were owned by fewer than 400,000 slaveholding families, about 25 percent of the southern total. Although most white southerners did not own slaves, they were tied to the system through sentiment, ambition, loyalty, ideology, and the sheer inability to conceive of any other relation between blacks and whites.

The institution of slavery was ultimately pernicious for all concerned. In the long run its economic consequences were harmful. The slave was the backbone of the southern labor force and did the hard work in field, home, shop, and even, occasionally, factory. As a labor system, slavery may have been profitable in the sense of providing an adequate return on a slaveholder's investment, but it concentrated wealth in the hands of a few, made white southerners contemptuous of physical labor, and rendered them indifferent to education and other productive "investment" in human beings. After Emancipation the south would come to realize how high a price in social and economic underdevelopment it had paid for its slavery-inspired neglect of human capital.

It was even more clearly disastrous in its social effects. Slavery was a system of strict social control and, as such, was a massive addition to human misery and futility. Although the various southern slave codes did not condone physical brutality, they did not prevent it from occurring. More important the slave system undermined the family. Slave marriages were not legally recognized.

Selling a slave girl at auction, New Orleans, 1831.

Within the slave family authority was lodged with the white master, not the black parents, and parents and children could be separated through sale to slave dealers who plied their trade all over the south. In addition, the system kept millions of men and women in a state of ignorance and dependence for their entire adult lives and squandered an enormous amount of human potential. The wounds that were inflicted on black Americans under slavery left deep and costly scars that are still evident today. That some slaves became autonomous men and women, capable of successfully resisting the system or fleeing from it, is a strong tribute to their unquenchable spirit.

To the institution's further discredit, there was its divisive effect on the nation. Differences over the "peculiar institution" had played a secondary role in the constitutional debates at Philadelphia, and not until 1819 did the slavery question begin to disturb the country seriously. The occasion was Missouri's application for admission to the union as a slave state, a move that threatened to upset the senatorial, and still more important, the symbolic, balance of slave and free states. At this point the issue was solved by Congress' balancing the admission of Missouri with the admission of the new free state of Maine, and dividing the remainder of the Louisiana Purchase into a northern region reserved for future free states (the region north of latitude 36°30') and a southern portion open to slavery. Soon after the Missouri Compromise the battle over slavery intensified and took an ideological and deeply emotional turn that converted it into a highly disruptive issue for the union.

It was abolitionism that made the difference. The antislavery impulse was one of a number of reform movements that ruffled the complacency of the country in the three decades preceding the Civil War. Each of them—temperance, prison reform, world peace, utopian communitarianism, feminism, improving the lot of the insane, as well as abolitionism in its various forms—derived from a fusion of democratic romantic idealism with a Christian perfectionism that held that men could achieve a truly virtuous, holy society in this life. Sparked by religious revivals and the stimulating intrusion of industrialism, these movements swept across the north and west. Most Americans were only slightly affected by them, but they deeply moved and influenced many of the most intelligent, articulate, and vigorous citizens of the Republic.

The south proved resistant not only to abolitionism, but to almost all these movements, holding them to be dangerous and subversive of both religion and society. The social and ideological ferment of the free states in itself differentiated the north from the south in the young nation. But none of these issues was as divisive as abolitionism, which represented a direct attack on the south's immensely valuable and apparently profitable "peculiar institution."

The abolitionists were not always temperate men. Faced with the most backward and inhumane institution still surviving in the modern world, courageous, sensitive men responded with outrage and called down the wrath of an avenging God on those who held slaves and supported slavery. Their candor often provoked violence even in the north, where many men preferred preserving the peace to perfecting society.

The reaction in the south, of course, was even more hostile. Abolitionists were denounced as wild men and monsters; several southern committees offered rewards for the capture and conviction of men like William Lloyd Garrison and Wendell Phillips. The south also mounted a strong counterattack. To match every abolitionist there was a southern "fire-eater," an apologist for slave society who glorified southern institutions and attacked everything northern and free. Eventually, to all but a minority in the south, every northern institution became suspect: free labor, free schools, a free press, liberal religion, all reform movements, and even

northern industrial and commercial enterprise. Native southerners who doubted that their society had attained perfection were ostracized and told to hold their tongues. At the same time southerners were taught to believe that theirs was a benign, gracious, and creative society—a "Greek Democracy"—based on a unique set of noncommercial, nonexploitative human relations. In many ways, by 1860, the south had become almost a distinct society, withdrawn and self-conscious, opposed to the north, and closed to new ideas and new institutions.

Different forms of economic development in the free and slave states reinforced this cultural and psychological divergence. By 1860 the north was well on its way to becoming an industrial society. In New England, Jefferson's Embargo, the War of 1812, and the general decline of American shipping had shifted men's attention and their capital to cotton textiles. In a score of Massachusetts and Rhode Island towns large cotton factories, with hundreds of "operatives," mainly women and children, became the dominant economic institutions. In Pennsylvania and Ohio roaring iron forges and furnaces lit up the landscape. All over the northeast and middle west, machine shops, flour and saw mills, locomotive works, distilleries, tanneries, and other industrial enterprises sprang up, employing a large proportion of the labor force by 1860. Industrially, the south remained far behind. Although a few southerners agitated for commercial and industrial development, the region remained overwhelmingly committed to staple agriculture. In the end, the south not only denounced the north as a cruel and unlovely society, but also opposed northern industrial and commercial interests in the political arena. At various times before 1860 the south and the northeast clashed in Congress over internal improvements, banks, and tariffs. In 1832 the nation was plunged into a serious although transitory constitutional crisis when South Carolina attempted to nullify the tariff measure of that year.

Paralleling the growing north-south division, although considerably milder, were differences between the east and the west. To some extent this tension was implicit in the

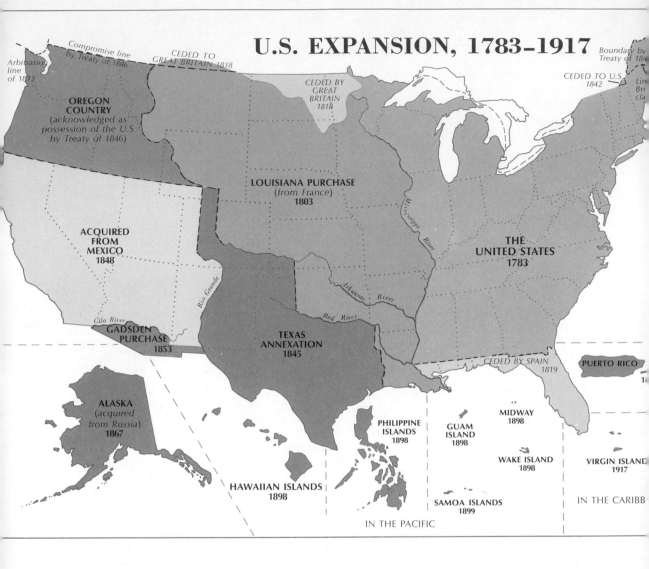

U.S. EXPANSION, 1783–1917

Arbitration line of 1812

Compromise line by Treaty of 1846

CEDED TO GREAT BRITAIN 1818

CEDED BY GREAT BRITAIN 1818

Boundary by Treaty of 184_

CEDED TO U.S. 1842

Lin_ Bri_ cla_

OREGON COUNTRY (acknowledged as possession of the U.S. by Treaty of 1846)

LOUISIANA PURCHASE (from France) **1803**

ACQUIRED FROM MEXICO 1848

THE UNITED STATES 1783

Mississippi River

Arkansas River

Gila River

Rio Grande

Red River

GADSDEN PURCHASE 1853

TEXAS ANNEXATION 1845

CEDED BY SPAIN 1819

PUERTO RICO

ALASKA (acquired from Russia) **1867**

PHILIPPINE ISLANDS 1898

GUAM ISLAND 1898

MIDWAY 1898

WAKE ISLAND 1898

VIRGIN ISLAND 1917

HAWAIIAN ISLANDS 1898

SAMOA ISLANDS 1899

IN THE PACIFIC

IN THE CARIBB_

rise of Jackson to power. Jackson was a westerner, and his victory in 1828 symbolized the political maturing of the trans-Appalachian region. The west tended to be more nationalistic than the east and more given to expansionism and chauvinism. It also tended to endorse federal gold and silver coinage as against bank-issued paper money, generally favored in the east. It supported free homesteads for settlers, while many easterners demanded high prices for public land. These differences were not nearly as threatening to the body politic as slavery, but at times the agricultural west would resound to impassioned denunciations of the commercial-industrial northeast.

The Crises over Slavery Extension

By the end of the 1840s the divisions between north and south began to threaten the very survival of the Union. The first major crisis came over the question of the extension of slavery following the Mexican War. That conflict (1846–1848) had added more than half a million square miles to the southwestern part of the nation. Whether this region, along with the remaining Louisiana

Bleeding Kansas, the mid-1850s.

Purchase Territory, would be open or closed to slavery became the object of sectional conflict for the next decade or more, swamping all other sectional disputes. The south, having given its money and its blood to help acquire these areas, felt entitled to equal consideration in the new territory. This meant that southerners wanted the right to take into the new regions any property, including slaves. Most southerners held that only a state could forbid slave property within its borders. Neither Congress nor a territorial legislature could do so.

Northerners were less united on the issue of slavery extension. A minority agreed with the southern position. A larger group held that people living in the territories had the right to vote slavery in or out. This doctrine was called either "popular sovereignty" or "squatter sovereignty," and as proclaimed by Democrat Stephen Douglas of Illinois, it appealed to American notions of grass-roots democracy. But other northerners, calling themselves "free-soilers," insisted that it was both the right and the duty of Congress, as in the case of both the Northwest Territory and the part of the Louisiana Purchase north of 36°30', to exclude slavery from a region before it attained statehood.

In 1850, Clay, Douglas, and Webster managed to settle a bitter crisis over the admission of California and the other Mexican Cession Territory on the basis of popular sovereignty and a sectional exchange of concessions. Four years later, the Compromise of 1850 was shattered, and the nation plunged into a period of violence and disorder that culminated in a bloody civil war. This crisis was brought on by Douglas's successful attempt in the Kansas-Nebraska Act of 1854 to reopen a portion of the Louisiana Purchase Territory to squatter sovereignty. Even moderate northerners were outraged at what they considered a surrender to the south. They were further angered by the breaches of law and violence that soon erupted in Kansas as each side sought to capture the region for its respective system.

By the late 1850s relations between the sections had deteriorated beyond repair. Northerners in increasing numbers refused to support southern efforts to recover runaway slaves under the Fugitive Slave Act of 1850. In Kansas, one northerner, John Brown, led

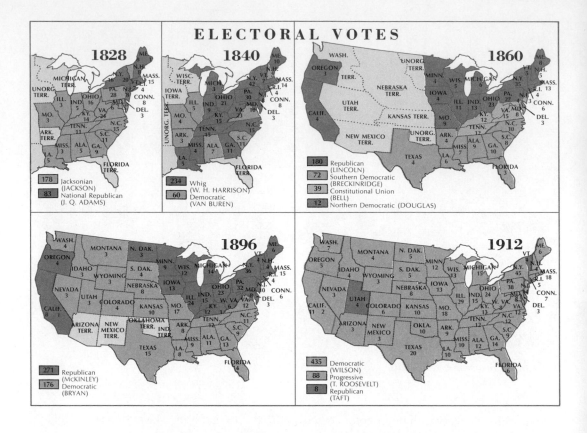

ELECTORAL VOTES

1828

Jacksonian (JACKSON) **178**
National Republican (J. Q. ADAMS) **83**

1840

Whig (W. H. HARRISON) **234**
Democratic (VAN BUREN) **60**

1860

Republican (LINCOLN) **180**
Southern Democratic (BRECKINRIDGE) **72**
Constitutional Union (BELL) **39**
Northern Democratic (DOUGLAS) **12**

1896

Republican (McKINLEY) **271**
Democratic (BRYAN) **176**

1912

Democratic (WILSON) **435**
Progressive (T. ROOSEVELT) **88**
Republican (TAFT) **8**

guerrilla forces that attacked proslavery groups. In 1859 he sought to attack slavery itself in his famous raid on Harper's Ferry, Virginia. Southerners retaliated against the north by denunciation and by acts of individual violence, including the outrageous beating of Charles Sumner, the antislavery senator from Massachusetts, in the hallowed Senate itself. In the wake of the struggle for Kansas a new Republican party appeared. It dedicated itself to restricting the spread of slavery and to defending the economic interests of the industrial classes and the free farmers of the north and west.

The sectional battle came to a head in the presidential election of 1860, the most momentous in American history. The Democrats split between their squatter-sovereignty northern wing, which endorsed Douglas, and a southern group that nominated John C. Breckinridge of Kentucky on a platform of federal protection for slavery in the territories. In addition, a new Constitutional Union party nominated two conservative ex-

Whigs on a purely pro-Union platform. The Republicans chose Abraham Lincoln, a relatively unknown westerner who was considered moderate on the slavery issue and, as a man of Whiggish antecedents, likely to support the Whig program of paternalistic government. Southerners threatened secession if Lincoln won; when he did, seven southern states, led by South Carolina, quickly left the Union.

The Civil War

The agony of the Union was now at hand. As Lincoln was to note at the Gettysburg battlefield three years later (1863), the Civil War would test the validity of the American experiment in continental unity and modern free government. Before it was over both would prove resilient and workable. But at first events seemed to go badly for the forces of cohesion and democracy. Even after Lincoln's firm control replaced lame-duck President James Buchanan's vacillation, the Union's disintegration continued. The firing

CIVIL WAR BATTLES

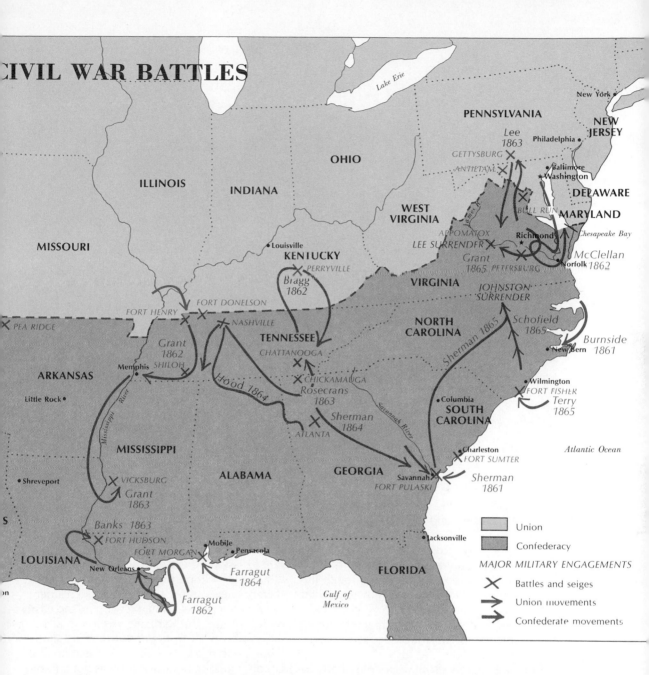

on Fort Sumter in April 1861 and Lincoln's call for troops to suppress insurrection drove four additional slave states to join the Confederacy.

The war itself was full of disappointments and setbacks for the Union. Because so many professional military men were southerners, Lincoln had difficulty finding officers to lead the hundreds of thousands of soldiers who eventually passed through Union ranks.

Only after he hit on the combination of Ulysses S. Grant and William T. Sherman was the President able to make the north's superior manpower effectively felt. In the meantime, superior numbers of invading northern troops were defeated by better-led southerners under Robert E. Lee or Thomas J. ("Stonewall") Jackson. Efforts by the early Union commanders to capture Richmond, the Confederate capital, met repeated defeats

Lincoln visits the Army of the Potomac, 1862.

at the hands of the incomparable Lee. In the west, Grant and Sherman did better, breaking the Confederacy in two along the Mississippi. By 1864 and early 1865, Sherman's foraging army of "bummers" had cut a wide swath of destruction through the lower south. On the sea, a greatly expanded Union navy, using the new iron-clads, blockaded southern ports and helped deprive the Confederacy of much-needed foreign supplies.

On the home front, Lincoln had to face a large number of thorny problems. The war had to be financed, and eventually the government sold billions of dollars of bonds and issued hundreds of millions of paper "greenbacks." Dissension and near-treason were rife in the Union and had to be held in check. At one extreme of the dissenting groups were "Copperheads," who sympathized with the south and believed the war unjust and unnecessary. Some Cop-

perhead newspapers were closed, and a few individuals were imprisoned by military commanders for obstructing recruiting, but Lincoln avoided massive repression. At the other dissenting extreme were the so-called "Radicals"—Republicans of strong anti-slavery views who believed the President too timid in prosecuting the war and too easy on the south. The Radicals wished to attack the south on all fronts and to end its slave-labor system as well as the threat to the Union. Lincoln, although he was not a Radical, eventually accepted much of their war policy. By late 1862 he came to believe that to destroy the Confederacy he would have to destroy slavery. In September 1862 he issued the preliminary Emancipation Proclamation, and on January 1, 1863 all slaves within the jurisdiction of the rebellious states were declared free. Although the Proclamation did not immediately free a single black man, it clearly announced that Union victory would end chattel slavery forever in the United States.

The abolition of slavery was only the most dramatic of a long list of important changes wrought by the war. A national banking system and an internal revenue system were constructed to help finance the war. A great transcontinental railroad network was authorized to be subsidized by means of a large federal land grant. In addition, thousands of men, both in uniform and out, learned new skills and techniques in managing large aggregations of personnel and equipment. These lessons would be useful in the years of national consolidation ahead when these men returned to civilizan pursuits.

In general, the south's secession opened up new opportunities for those groups eager to employ national power for economic ends. With the departure of southern representatives from Congress it became possible to pass "homestead" legislation that distributed free public lands to bona fide settlers. Protective tariffs in 1861 and 1862 reversed the 30 year trend toward free trade. For the first time in a generation substantial appropriations for internal improvements were enacted by a Congress now dominated by the Republicans.

THE UNITED STATES, 1865–1900

The war ended in April 1865 with Lee's surrender and Lincoln's tragic assassination. The next 35 years, are often referred to as the time of "the emergence of modern America." It was in this period that the broad social and economic forces at work in 1860 came to fruition. The forces of industrialism, urbanism, and consolidation were now unhampered by southern agrarians. In every area of American political and economic life, combination, integration, and amalgamation became the normal order of things. Government on all levels grew in power and effectiveness, despite a good deal of corruption. Business units grew in size and complexity as they reached out to encompass national markets. With the completion of the Union Pacific in 1869, the rail system joined the two coasts. Eventually it connected every town and hamlet in the nation. And after

1876 the telephone enormously facilitated the flow of information within and between cities.

Reconstruction

At the end of the Civil War, the American people confronted the painful problems of rejoining the torn and bleeding halves of the nation and of repairing the physical and institutional damage to the south. In the defeated south, the chief issue was race and how the freed slave was to be reintegrated into the region's economy and into its political and social systems. The Emancipation Proclamation, followed by the Thirteenth Amendment, had uprooted some four million, illiterate, unskilled blacks, not prepared by slavery to accept the responsibilities or to face the challenges of a competitive, democratic society. One possible way of handling the situation would have been through a long period of federal tutelage for these new citizens which would have conferred land and education. A few abortive moves were made in this direction, but in the end the former slaves were thrown on the economic and social mercies of the white south. Overwhelmingly they became sharecroppers, often working for their former owners. Their economic and educational status was now little better than it had been under slavery, even though they were legally free to move anywhere and to control other aspects of their personal and private lives.

The only weapon for self-protection that could be conceived of by most of the Radical Republicans—the blacks' special champions within the majority party—was the ballot. Although no doubt necessary for full citizenship, the franchise without a "stake in society" proved ineffectual. But even the ballot proved difficult to ensure. Lincoln's successor, Andrew Johnson, was a member of the nonslaveholding class of the Old South, and like most southern yeomen he disliked the black man. He fought every attempt by the Radicals in Congress to control the Reconstruction process and to extend the franchise to the freedmen. He employed his veto to strike down Radical measures to either aid the blacks or punish their oppressors, although these vetoes were generally overridden by Congress.

The Ku Klux Klan and one of its white victims, 1871.

Anxious to defend the exslaves, fearful of a revived Democratic party that might jeopardize the results of the war, and intent on preserving their own prerogatives, the Radical leaders in 1868 attempted to remove Johnson by impeachment. Although narrowly defeated in this move, Thaddeus Stevens, Charles Sumner, Benjamin F. Wade, and the other Radical leaders in Congress succeeded in wresting control of Reconstruction from the President. The Congressional Reconstruction plan established state governments in the south which accepted the political equality of blacks and, to a lesser extent, their social equality. These state governments were politically progressive, seeking to bring the southern states to the same level as the north in providing important social services. They were also more honest and efficient than the conventional view of Reconstruction suggests. Nor were they dominated by ignorant blacks and northern carpetbag adventurers. The black men who participated in these governments made both intelligent voters and creditable lesser officials. Several blacks went to Congress, and one, Hiram Revels,

took Jefferson Davis' seat as United States Senator from Mississippi. As for the northern carpetbag element, it was undoubtedly important but, at least at the beginning, these Radical governments were supported by substantial groups of southern whites who were willing to experiment with a new society. In the end it was the desertion of this native white, "scalawag" element, often through coercion by terrorist organizations such as the Ku Klux Klan, that returned individual states to conservative rule by the so-called "redeemers."

Meanwhile, many northerners lost patience with the seemingly everlasting problems of the "negro" and the south. Johnson's successor, General Grant, was close to the Radicals, and attempted to lend federal support to the reconstruction state governments. But in 1877, Rutherford B. Hayes, although a Republican, withdrew the last remaining federal troops from the south and surrendered the blacks to the control of the "unreconstructed" whites. The results were not surprising. Bit by bit those few tokens of equality that had been achieved under

Labor troubles during the Gilded Age: The Haymarket Riot of 1886.

Radical rule were withdrawn and were replaced by a system of segregation, a process that was much accelerated in the 1880s and 1890s. The franchise was at first undisturbed, but by 1900 few if any blacks could vote in the south. By this time the south had once more become a highly conservative agricultural society, resting on the backs of several million poor, ignorant, black and white sharecroppers and falling ever further behind the north in wealth and power.

Industrialization and the Growth of Big Business

Following the Civil War, Americans accelerated the process of transforming the continent and unleashing the tremendous forces of modern technology and business organization. As the railroad and telegraph systems were completed, a truly national economy appeared for the first time. Now manufacturers and processors could sell their products all over the country and, indeed, all over the world. These new opportunities stimu-

lated a tremendous growth in size of factories and producing units. Giant corporations, often resulting from the merger of dozens of smaller companies, came to dominate industries such as steel, petroleum, sugar refining, meat packing, copper mining, and aluminum. Other firms brought together under one management many diverse enterprises through the device of the holding company, whereby a parent firm retained a controlling interest in the stock of many others.

The engineers of this spectacular transformation were men who amassed colossal fortunes by the exercise of great managerial skill. Some of them were mere gamblers and financial manipulators who did more wrecking than building. Men such as Jay Gould, Jim Fisk, and Daniel Drew deserve the label "robber baron" that has been attached to the post-Civil War generation of business leaders. But others, like Andrew Carnegie (iron and steel), James J. Hill (railroads), John D. Rockefeller (petroleum refining), Philip D. Armour (meat packing), and J. P. Morgan (banking), although not always fastidious by later standards, increased efficiency, raised output, cut costs and prices and, in general, provided important services to the larger society in return for the wealth that they amassed.

The overall effects of business growth and consolidation were varied. On the one hand, integrated companies provided "economies of scale," including the opportunity to use expensive modern machinery, to utilize by-products, and to engage in extensive industrial research. Clearly, by the twentieth century, Americans were getting better manufactured goods at lower prices than ever before, and were living better as a consequence. By 1900 not only was the United States the greatest industrial power in the world, well ahead of Britain and Germany, its nearest competitors, but individual Americans undoubtedly enjoyed the highest per capita incomes in the world as well.

On the other hand, the advent of "big business" and multimillion-dollar corporations dislocated established American relationships and values and disturbed many citizens of the Republic. To laboring men, the large corporations were a mixed blessing. They contributed to the overall output of the country and to lower prices, but the mammoth firms signaled the end of any direct relationship between employer and employee, and the advent of dreary, repetitious labor. Such corporations meant the large mill towns with their drabness and their subservience to "the company." They meant a loss of autonomy, as wage earners found, or imagined, every aspect of their lives dominated by the "soulless" corporations. They meant insecurity as men experienced the arbitrary actions of boards of directors that were capable of cutting wages or closing down whole plants in order to effect economies or to improve a competitive position. The real wages of American wage earners rose appreciably between 1865 and 1910, but the American workingman, especially the industrial worker, was often restless and discontented.

Labor and Immigration

There seemed to be little the wage earner could do to improve his lot. American labor history in the half century following the Civil War was marked by numerous outbursts of explosive violence. Sometimes these were inspired by imported ideologies such as socialism, anarchism, or syndicalism; more often they merely expressed pent-up anger and frustration. Of the more constructive trade-union activity of Europe, especially Britain, there was surprisingly little. The Knights of Labor in the 1870s and 1880s attempted to organize a wide range of occupational groups into one big union, but its success was modest and temporary. In the late 1880s the American Federation of Labor made headway with the native-born, skilled craftsmen whom it organized into craft unions. The federation categorically rejected socialism and disavowed any purpose other than day-to-day improvement in wages and hours. Within its limited sphere it prospered. But as late as 1917 the great mass of American workingmen remained outside any labor organization, and organized labor as a whole scarcely ranked as a major political or even economic force.

Many factors helped limit the growth and power of the labor movement in the United States. The nation's middle class, large and still growing, was influential in opposing unions. Social mobility allowed *individual* workingmen to ascend the economic and class ladder through hard work, frugality, and ability, thus draining off laborers' discontents. Mobility drew into the middle class some of the most talented and potentially most militant of the wage earners.

The immigrant also helped shape the American labor movement. Immigration to the United States had been relatively light for the first half century following independence. Then in the 1840s and 1850s hundreds of thousands of Irish and Germans, fleeing famine and social dislocation, had poured into the country. North European immigration—German, Irish, Scottish and English, as well as Scandinavian—continued heavy after the Civil War. In the 1880s, however, immigration from southern and eastern Europe—Russia, Poland, Hungary, Italy, and the Balkans—overtook that from the north. These "new immigrants" varied in their characteristics from group to group. Some, like the Russian and Polish Jews, were par-

Immigrants arriving at Ellis Island before World War I.

tially urbanized already; others like the southern Italians were rural laborers. Some like the Czechs were literate; others like the peoples of the Balkans generally could not read nor write. Many, like most of the Jews, came to stay; others, like many Greeks and Italians, hoped to return to Europe as rich men. They were a mixed group but generally they came from the less-developed parts of Europe, were seldom Protestant, seemed to old-stock Americans more alien than previous groups of immigrants; and on the whole they appeared likely to be more difficult to assimilate into national life.

One point of friction between native Americans and the newcomers was the immigrants' lower living standards and their resistance to unionization. Accustomed to a level of living well below the American average, they were able to survive on the wages of unskilled labor and even save money. Accordingly, although they often disliked the intensity of the American labor system, they were willing to tolerate it. In the face of conditions that native Americans

found intolerable, they were acquiescent. They knew nothing of labor unions and collective bargaining: some were used to taking orders from European landlords or their agents; others had been recruited from rural and urban slums where there had been no work at all. In any case, they often saw no more reason to trust the English-speaking labor organizer than the English-speaking foreman or boss. Ancient national animosities, divisive language barriers among themselves, and their difficulties with English, all kept the immigrants from the labor movement, and it is no surprise that the unions as well as many other blue collar Americans sought to close the door to their free admission.

The Farmer's Plight

Labor's fears and grievances following the Civil War were not unique; important segments of the farm population also felt threatened by the transformation of the economy. Agriculture underwent a revolution between

Moro, Oregon c. 1890: a farm community in the wheat country of eastern Oregon.

1865 and 1920. During these years the semi-arid Great Plains developed into an area of large cattle ranches and large wheat farms. Agriculture here entailed risk; for every man who succeeded, at least, one departed, cursing the heat, the wind, and drought, and the grasshoppers. Nevertheless, the total acreage under the plow, the number of farms, the number of agricultural workers, and the total output of crops, all grew enormously. American agriculture, linked to the most advanced technology in the world, was able to support the great growth of domestic urban population and also to provide stupendous surpluses of cotton, wheat, beef, fruits, dairy products, and other commodities for export to industrial Europe.

But in spite of its rapid growth, agriculture's proportion of the annual national output and proportion of the labor force were declining. Representing 53 percent of total value of commodity output in 1870, it had dropped to well under 20 percent by 1920. Moreover, the advent of national and international markets introduced deeply disturbing elements of instability into agriculture. The prices of such important staples as wheat and cotton were increasingly determined by conditions in an international market, where the United States was not the only important producer. Distant developments caused severe price fluctuations that the American farmer could not understand. We have seen that the world slump in prices in the 1870s reflected overproduction and cheaper transport costs via steamship. Wheat, selling for 2 dollars a bushel in 1865, was going for 56 cents in 1894; cotton, at 83 cents a pound in 1865, was down to 7 cents in the mid 1890s. Even during the hard times of the early 1890s farmers probably made money, but it appeared to many staple growers that they had to run very hard, indeed, just to stay in the same place.

One consequence of this severe price deflation was regional readjustment. As staples declined in price, their production moved to those areas with the greatest natural advantages of soil, terrain, and climate. In many European countries this meant painful changes as cheap American wheat forced down world prices. In the earlier-settled parts of the United States a similar conversion occurred. By the end of World War I the northeast had turned to dairying and truck farming, the southeast had taken up fruit and vegetable production, and the old northwest, no longer able to compete with the plains in wheat-growing, turned to corn, livestock, and, around the Great Lakes, to dairying as well.

Successful shifts to the various specialty crops limited farm discontent. In the staple-growing areas, however, discontent was widespread and intense, reflecting the uncertainties of the market and of nature, and the special dependence of farmers far from the coasts on outsiders for financial, marketing, and transportation services. Although the wheat and cotton growers were victims of world market forces, they could not understand these forces and blamed other forces closer to home. Farmers' organizations such as the Grange and the Farmers' Alliance attacked the railroads for squeezing the farmers by means of high and discriminatory rates. At other times land monopolies were blamed for declining farm income. The most acceptable villain, however, was the "money power," a vaguely defined entity, denounced for high interest rates and the deflation of farm prices. By limiting bank credit and, even more, by imposing the gold standard on the nation, the money power had made money dear, prices low, and the burdens of producers and debtors heavy. Its grip could be dislodged only through some device that would smash the monetary logjam, whether by issuing paper "greenbacks," or by "free coinage of silver." Only then, it was said, could control be restored to the people and, at the same time, the vicious, killing deflation reversed.

Politics and Populism

Many of the characteristics of modern "pluralist" pressure politics originated at the end of the Reconstruction in 1877. There were still very large areas of agreement among the politically active citizens of the nation. American government continued to be dominated by the middle-class electorate, with almost everyone supporting democracy and private property. The distinction between Democrats and Republicans was mainly sectional, ethnic, or religious. Party allegiances generally were based on traditional historical allegiances, on the division of spoils, or on issues such as state aid to parochial schools or temperance laws. Organized economic groups petitioned Congress and other public officials and often employed lobbyists to represent their particular demands or to advertise their special cause. But these were invariably narrow bread-and-butter issues that seldom questioned or threatened fundamental social values.

This "consensus," however, was being strained by the new tensions of industrialism and urbanism. The major challenge before 1900 came from the Populist Revolt of the mid-1890s. This movement grew out of agrarian discontent and focused predominantly on the money issue. At times, Populist spokesmen appeared capable of a thorough and incisive critique of American society and an imaginative program of reform. Increasingly, however, they narrowed their aims to the "free coinage" of cheap silver, which they held would end deflation and would break the grip of the "money power."

Limited in its program and vision, Populism was also limited in its appeal. As a separate party with a separate candidate in 1892, the People's Party won only a million votes, confined mainly to the Great Plains, the south, and the silver-mining west. In 1896, after three years of depression, it might have done better, but by that time the Democrats had seized on the silver issue and had nominated for the presidency William Jennings Bryan, whose political stance resembled that of Populism. Rather than divide the free silver vote, the Populists supported Bryan and shared a common defeat at the hands of William McKinley.

When world commodity prices took a sharp upward turn during the next few years, much of the farm discontent evaporated. New domestic social problems soon appeared, or rather old problems returned in a new guise. But first the nation was distracted by a major foreign adventure—the Spanish-American War.

Imperialism

In its relations with its weaker neighbors the United States had, since the Mexican War, exhibited relative restraint, avoiding the race for overseas colonies. Although by the 1880s American investors had begun to export capital to Canada and Latin America, the United States did not, as yet, seek to influence their domestic affairs.

Yet, from one point of view, expansionism and even imperialism had been a constant element in the existence of the United States. From the colonial period onward the great westward migration of Americans had been at the expense of the native Indian tribes. The Indians had been systematically abused, corrupted, coerced, and cheated of their holdings by individuals, states, and even the federal government. For this behavior the nation had been rewarded with a long series of bloody, savage Indian wars. By the end of the nineteenth century the age-old Indian problem was settled by the harsh reservation system which confined the tribes to isolated, inhospitable regions, largely in the arid territories of the Far West. The system destroyed tribal life and broke the Indians' spirit, a tragic consequence that only a few sensitive men of the time bemoaned. By 1890 the Indian tribes were finally pacified, and a long and ugly page in American history was closed.

Still, this westward movement had all been expansion into contiguous territory. Besides, with the notable exception of the Mexican War and the periodic bluster about Canada, it had not been at the expense of westernized powers. The intellectual transformation occurring in the 1890s slowly changed this situation.

The change can best be ascribed to a crisis of confidence. As we have seen, the 1890s was a decade of dissent and political turmoil. Following the financial panic of 1893 it was also a time of economic troubles that frightened many otherwise conservative men. Even those who rejected the monetary explanations and nostrums of the Populists feared

that a serious fundamental social crisis was at hand. Some argued that this crisis had been brought on by the passing of the open frontier. The political and economic troubles, along with the supposed social dangers of a land without the safety valve of unexploited resources, turned men's thoughts to overseas opportunities. Both businessmen and farm spokesmen convinced themselves that, for the first time, American producers needed overseas markets, and perhaps captive markets, for their prosperity. Intellectuals foresaw a vast social upheaval if America failed to find outlets for its surplus capital, energies, and population.

The new mood also reflected the New Imperialism of many European countries. As we have seen, beginning in the 1880s France and Britain, joined in the 1890s by Germany, Italy, Russia, and Japan, sought to carve up the remaining independent portions of the non-European world. It almost appeared as if big-power status and the respect of other nations required the United States to acquire colonies. In addition, doctrines of white racial supremacy now became popular. North Europeans and Americans, observing the ever-expanding material superiority of the west, began to assert the racial and moral superiority of the white race, particularly its Teutonic subdivision.

The new expansionist mood of the United States can be traced back as far as the Reconstruction period, when the nation bought Alaska from Russia and came close to acquiring several Caribbean islands. But not until the surfacing of the new fears and the new attitudes of the 1890s did this impulse become serious. Events were precipitated by the crisis in Cuba, where a revolution against Spanish rule was met with bloody and cruel repression. Americans, stirred up by a sensation-seeking daily press that exaggerated the brutalities of Spanish administration, found it impossible to remain indifferent to the events 90 miles off the Florida coast. The United States finally went to war after months of growing concern and increasing anger toward Spain which were brought to a climax by the unexplained sinking in Havana of the visiting American battleship *Maine*. The conflict was a "splendid little war," ending in total American victory after ten weeks.

By this time the Caribbean islands of Cuba and Puerto Rico had been effectively occupied and a foothold, soon to grow into complete control, had been established in the far-off Philippines.

The United States now faced the problem of what to do with these new possessions. Together with Hawaii and Samoa, both acquired formally after the Spanish-American War although long under American domination, they constituted a small American Empire. But Americans had no experience in handling such noncontiguous, densely settled territories and feared the consequences of their acquisition. It seemed unlikely that these islands could ever become part of the federal Union, and many Americans deplored the effects on national values and traditions of ruling subject peoples. Other Americans disliked the prospect of adding more dark-skinned folk to the nation's ethnic mixture. Still others feared the competition of cheap alien labor. On the other side were considerations of national pride, self-interest, a misguided altruism, and a feeling that full maturity and a proper place within the family of great powers required the United States to retain colonies. Businessmen, moreover, although at first skeptical of the Spanish war, soon perceived the economic advantages of colonies, particularly the Philippines, so close to the supposedly boundless markets of China. Finally, there were those who, in a patronizing way, sincerely subscribed to the notion that Americans had a responsibility to elevate and sustain their "little brown brothers."

In the end the nation accepted the cares and the benefits of a colonial power. Although Puerto Rico was retained, Cuba was accorded its legal freedom, impaired by a protectorate relationship that led to frequent American interference in the island's internal affairs. After crushing a nationalist uprising, American forces expanded the United States' holdings in the Philippines from the region around Manila to the whole of the archipelago. But such direct involvement was not typical of America's imperialist adventures. More common was periodic United States intervention in the affairs of its weaker Latin neighbors for the sake of its investors, or to protect its strategic interests against encroaching European powers that Americans had sought to exclude from the Western Hemisphere ever since the Monroe Doctrine in 1823. Often it seemed that "dollar diplomacy," by which American economic penetration preceded virtual political control, was merely a disguised and inexpensive version of what other nations did more overtly and honestly. United States marines were sent to Nicaragua, Haiti, Santo Domingo, Mexico, and other Latin American countries at various times to enforce order or to make their governments pay their debts.

THE PROGRESSIVE ERA, 1900–1917

Urbanization and Its Problems

War and empire did not bring domestic tranquility: as the twentieth century opened, Americans found themselves beset by difficulties that seemed awesome. In many ways these difficulties resembled earlier agrarian fears of the growth of plutocracy. But now the concerned parties were no longer farmers, but a group much closer to power and influence—the urban middle class.

"Urban" is the key word here. The Progressive movement would not have occurred without the enormous expansion of cities during the generation following the Civil War. The country's urban population had grown rapidly throughout the 1800s, with the greatest increases during the 1860s and 1880s. This explosive growth inevitably increased the power and influence of the nation's cities, but it also brought unprecedented physical, social, and administrative problems. Housing, sanitation, transportation, and effective government all had to be provided for the overgrown villages that were quickly turning into metropolitan centers. The needs were met, but the job was not done well. Housing, sanitation facilities, and rapid transit—the physical side of city growth—were generally supplied by unregulated private enterprise with a resulting waste, ugliness, and disregard of larger collective social needs. Densely packed, cheap dwellings soon deteriorated into slums. Open ground for parks and playgrounds disappeared under blocks of dark tenements

The urban slums: the lower east side of New York, 1900.

with inadequate heat and plumbing. Rapid transit was introduced, but in the form of screeching, dirty "EL" trains, or slow, noisy streetcars. The telephone greatly speeded communication among city residents, but the thousands of telephone poles with their drooping wires defaced every city street. Congestion, dirt, noise, and ugliness seemed to be the price men had to pay to live in New York, Chicago, Philadelphia, or San Francisco in the early twentieth century.

The crux of the problem appeared to be city government, for men often seriously misinterpreted the proper role of city administration in dealing with these urban difficulties. Before about 1900, most middle-class Americans believed, for example, that honest, frugal, middle-class city administrations would do much to improve city life. The urban political machines generally run by rough-hewn, self-made men with the support of the foreign-born and the blue collar classes, seemed utterly inefficient and incompetent. "Turning the rascals out" seemed likely to transform the cities into livable places.

But the middle-class reformers were mistaken. They failed to recognize the important "broker" functions city machines performed in getting things done, and their crucial, although little appreciated work, in providing a rough-and-ready form of social welfare to the urban poor. They were also wrong because their belief in limited, frugal government kept them from seeing that the state was the only agency capable of restraining selfish private interests and of providing capital and guidance for needed social services and public facilities.

The Progressive Program

It was, perhaps, their contact with urban problems that first awakened middle-class city dwellers at the turn of the century to the need for substantial change. But they soon came to recognize the larger difficulties of the nation as a whole. In many ways they borrowed the image of America that the Populists had embraced a decade or so before, although, as befitted the educated, it was an image free of some of the exaggerated fears found in Populism, and free, too, of the simplistic emphasis on monetary solutions. It was a picture of the nation dominated and perverted by large aggregations of private economic power. These "trusts" appeared to be irresponsible, capable of rigging prices, crushing smaller competitors, adulterating their products, mistreating their employees, and corrupting the government. Middle-class Americans were at the mercy of the trusts. As consumers of products now produced in distant places by unscrupulous processors and manufacturers, as small businessmen subject to the overwhelming competition of the chain stores and industrial giants, as once influential citizens forced to see political control slip into the hands of "big business" — in one or even all of these roles, they had reason to fear the contemporary trends in the country. With their perception of developments sharpened by the new exposé journalism called "muckraking," middle-class Americans began to listen to men in both parties who called themselves "Progressives" and who advocated using government either to control or break up big business combinations.

The Progressives operated on all levels of government. In the cities they fought the machines that worked hand-in-glove with the streetcar and utility interests to squeeze valuable franchises from the public for far less than they were worth. Through "settlement houses" and the public school systems they sought to Americanize the immigrants and provide them with skills in order to reduce their dependence on and support of the urban political machines. On the state level the Progressives attempted to control the corporate exploitation of workers through child labor legislation and various laws to reduce the insecurity of the wage earner's life. They also tried to bypass lobby-dominated state legislatures by instruments of direct democracy such as the initiative, the referendum, and the recall. At the national level they gave teeth to previously ineffective antitrust laws of the nineteenth century and sought to regulate business and encourage competition through such new measures as the Hepburn Act, the Federal Trade Commission Act, and the Clayton Anti-Trust Act. They enacted a meat inspection law, a pure food and drug act, and the first substantial reduction in the tariff since the Civil War to protect consumers from grasping and irresponsible manufacturers and processors. They passed conservation measures to protect the nation's resources against predatory mining, lumbering, and ranching interests. They authorized a new central banking structure — the Federal Reserve System — to neutralize the "money power" and remove the weaknesses of an atomized banking system. They provided for popular election of United States senators and presidential primaries to place the federal government beyond the control of "the interests." And, finally, they amended the Constitution to permit the federal government to impose a progressive income tax in order to shift the burden of financing government onto the rich and help redistribute personal income.

Not every American supported the Progressive program, of course, and only the fiercest exertions by the Progressive forces could overcome the resistance of the "old guard" within both parties. At the national level President Theodore Roosevelt publicized the Progressive cause through his pungent words and his flair for drama. Less

The mass processing of meat for the large urban markets of the early twentieth century.

flamboyant, but often more constructive, was a group of Republican senatorial leaders like Albert Beveridge of Indiana, Jonathan Dolliver of Iowa, Hiram Johnson of California, and, most notably, Robert M. LaFollette of Wisconsin. There were also several Progressive state governors and big city mayors who attempted, and often succeeded, in wresting their states and cities from conservative boss control and turning them into laboratories for liberal legislation.

The Progressives achieved some substantial political victories. By 1912, after four disappointing years with Roosevelt's hand-picked successor, William Howard Taft, the nation appeared ready for a Progressive administration that would end once and for all the power of "the interests" and restore the government to "the people." For this purpose a new, more radical Roosevelt leaped into the Presidential contest, and after losing to Taft at the Republican nominating conven-

tion, secured the nomination of the new Progressive, or "Bull Moose," party. The Democrats, turned to the Progressive governor of New Jersey, Woodrow Wilson, a scholar and former president of Princeton University. The aloof, moralistic Wilson was able to clothe the progressive aspirations of the American people in exalted and moving rhetoric and won the contest.

In office, Wilson at first moved slowly. At the outset he emphasized restoring competition rather than regulating big business and promoting social justice. After 1914, however, Wilson was pushed further along the Progressive road by some of his more impassioned supporters and by his desire to win reelection. The last two years of his first administration, accordingly, saw the President forcing through Congress a program to reduce the workday of railway employees, outlaw child-labor in interstate commerce, provide workman's compensation for federal employees, set minimum labor standards for merchant seamen, and provide loans and other aid for farmers.

The Wilsonian program won the President a second term, by a narrow margin, against a Progressive Republican, Charles Evans Hughes. Although further reforms might have been undertaken in Wilson's second administration, World War I soon became his overriding concern. In all probability, however, the Progressive impulse already had achieved as much as it could. It had appeared in response to the social challenge of large-scale corporate enterprise, and it paralleled the beginning of welfare measures at about the same time in Britain; but it had not gone as far as the European "new liberalism" (see p. 463). The United States was both more bourgeois and more prosperous than contemporary Europe, and its experience with an open frontier and the individualism it had engendered had been different. It is unlikely that many Americans wanted to see more drastic reform than had already been achieved.

In any case, by the 1916 Presidential campaign Americans were already being distracted from domestic concerns by World War I, which had begun two years earlier in Europe. Wilson, although personally pro-Entente, had managed to remain publicly neutral and had appeared before the voters in the 1916 Presidential campaign not only as a successful Progressive but also as the man who had "kept us out of war." His victory over Hughes was as much a mandate for neutrality as an endorsement of Progressivism. But neutrality proved impossible in the long run. For the country the fateful issue was the rights of a neutral as threatened by German submarine warfare, although intermixed with it was ethnic pressures, British propaganda, financial commitment to the Entente, and the hope that liberal capitalism might be extended to the whole world and might become the basis for a new international order of peace and prosperity.

In all likelihood the United States could not have escaped entanglement in the war. For over a century it had been its good fortune that the European nations had been able to avoid such a general confrontation. Now that they were once again at each others' throats its participation was hard to avoid. No matter how it struggled, in 1917 as in 1812, membership in the Western community seemed to entail certain commitments, and inevitable involvement.

In one way, then, as Americans once more plunged into a European war, the wheel seemed to have come full circle. But despite the obvious parallel with the past there were enormous differences. In 1812 the United States was as yet a weak, untested community, very much on the fringes of European affairs. Clearly an offspring of western European society, it was nevertheless significantly different. It was culturally inferior but it was superior in almost all the indexes of openness, fluidity, and modernity. The nineteenth century in some ways accentuated these differences. The gap between American and European incomes grew over the years, so that by the twentieth century even the most affluent nations of northern Europe enjoyed a per capita income considerably lower than the American.

But in many ways the differences between Europe and the United States had narrowed. The settlement of the continent by the turn of the new century closed the book for all time on the distinctive American frontier experience. Like Europeans, most Americans would now have to accept their fate as city dwellers. By 1920, for the first time, more than half the American people would be living in urban areas. As the nation set off in 1917 to make the world safe for democracy it still exhibited much of the innocence that had characterized its youth. But now belief corresponded less accurately with reality. Great extremes of wealth and poverty could no longer be hidden. More important, great inequalities of power had developed, and Americans, although reluctantly and half-heartedly, had been forced to suspend their distrust of government in order to avoid plutocracy.

Cultural and intellectual maturing had also brought the two sides of the Atlantic closer together. In 1812 the United States could scarcely be said to have had a literature, a first rate artistic tradition, or a creative scientific establishment. By 1917 many foreigners were reading American novels, using American scientific concepts, and observing with approval and wonder the daring of American skyscrapers. No longer was Europe the producer and America merely the consumer of ideas and cultural products. In later years the gap would narrow still more as American popular culture and life-styles would seize the imagination of Europeans. But already events were pointing to the United States as a senior partner among the advanced nations. In another generation people would be speaking of "The American Century."

CANADA, 1815–1914

North of the United States lay a gigantic land whose history was to take a very different course from that of its neighbor. From the outset the central facts of Canadian existence were the rigors of the northern climate, the cultural divisions between the French and the English, and the presence of a powerful and often threatening neighbor to the south.

Canada has a rugged physical environment. Except for the Ontario peninsula and the Pacific coast, winters are long and cold and summers brief and often hot. Not far north of the American border, in the region west of the Great Lakes, the ground is permanently frozen below the top few inches of soil. In the center of the country is the vast Canadian Shield, a region of extensive and valuable mineral deposits, but also one of shallow soils, bogs, scrub forest, and, in the brief summers, myriads of biting flies and mosquitoes. With vast distances and thin settlement, as well as inhospitable terrain and climate, Canada has presented serious problems to physical movement and communication.

The human environment, in many ways, was also difficult. Settled predominantly by two of the most talented peoples of Europe, the French and the British, the country has had to face the problem of deeply divided loyalties. Frenchmen and Britons in Europe have always differed in their outlook, values, predilections, and talents, and if anything these differences were exaggerated by North American circumstances. Feeling themselves surrounded and dominated by the richer and more powerful British groups, the French clung all the more tenaciously to their institu-

tions of Catholic church, home, and family, and resisted the currents of individualism, aggressive enterprise, and secularism which were becoming increasingly important for success in the nineteenth-century world. On the other hand, the British stock, although Irish, Scottish, and American as much as English, tended to emphasize and even exaggerate its cultural, political, and sentimental ties to Protestantism, to England, and to the empire. To some extent an outgrowth of the French presence, these feelings also reflected the fears of being absorbed culturally and politically by the American giant to the south.

At the opening of the nineteenth century what is today called Canada consisted of seven partially self-governing provinces and a number of more primitive settlements in the west. On the Alantic coast was the old colony of Newfoundland, still a poor, thinly populated collection of fishing communities. The "Maritimes" consisted of the tiny Prince Edward Island and of the larger Nova Scotia and New Brunswick. These were also poor provinces settled largely by people of British ancestry, but including a large element of exiled American loyalists and some French "Acadians." They lived by lumbering, fishing, and farming. Farther west was predominantly French Lower Canada. The economy of this large province, with its cultural capital at Quebec and its financial and commercial capital at Montreal, a city dominated by a small elite of British businessmen, was based on the conservative agriculture of the St. Lawrence Valley, some shipbuilding and raw material processing, and the commerce of the two large towns. West of French Lower Canada was Upper Canada, now Ontario. Here, another group of United Empire Loyalists, joined in increasing numbers by other Americans and large immigrant groups from Britain, occupied a fast-growing string of commercial and agricultural communities in the most temperate and fertile part of Canada. Finally, to the west of the Canadian Shield and on to the Pacific slope were scattered settlements of trappers, Indians, and half-breeds working for the Hudson's Bay Company, which still exercized sovereignty over an immense tract of the north country.

In all this vast stretch of territory there was

little cohesion. The War of 1812, which raised a common enemy in the United States, helped create a limited sense of common nationality among Canadians. But the first step toward actual political unity came only in the 1830s after a bitter fight waged by the French-Canadian Louis Joseph Papineau to guarantee French cultural, economic, and electoral rights and interests. In 1837 Papineau, a talented, democratic, but extravagant and emotional man, led an uprising that was harshly put down by British regulars and British-Canadian volunteers. In the wake of the rebellion the British government appointed a Royal Commission under Lord Durham which, in 1838, published its famous Report recommending the unification of both Canadas under responsible government. The Report, unfortunately, alienated the Canadiens, because it linked unification and a responsible parliamentary regime to an explicit call for French cultural submergence. Thereafter the French felt compelled to continue to resist Canadian unity in the name of French survivance. But despite French recalcitrance the unification recommendations of the Durham Report were eventually enacted into law. In 1841 the two major provinces were united under a legislature that did not, however, enjoy control of the executive as Parliament did in Britain.

The next decade and a half were eventful years for the vast land north of the United States. It was a time of rapid economic and demographic expansion. Between 1820 and 1850 growth in lumbering and agriculture drew hundreds of thousands of immigrants to the Canadian provinces. Along with the exceptionally high rate of natural increase, this migration pushed Canadian population from about 750,000 in 1821 to 2.3 million in 1851. But it was the 1850s that proved to be the most prosperous period for the country during the nineteenth century. By 1861, Canadian population had advanced 37 percent over the preceding decade, with much of the growth in English-speaking Upper Canada.

The process of nation-building and democratization in this period was more uneven. On the credit side, ministerial responsibility on the British model was won from reluctant English governors. On the debit side, the danger of social disintegration was increasing. Following the unification of 1841 all the signs at first pointed to the triumph of centripetal political forces. French Canada East (Lower Canada) and English-speaking Canada West (Upper Canada) did not pull comfortably in tandem. With the population in the west outstripping the east, British-Canadian politicians began to demand representation strictly according to numbers. The French saw this as a threat and began to talk of secession from the dual province.

But then the divisive process was unexpectedly reversed. During the American Civil War and the years immediately following, Canadians felt endangered by truculent annexationist sentiment in the United States. Also, contemporary Britain's receding imperial ambitions promised that the mother country would offer little protection against the American threat. Moreover, Canadian interest in railroads and other expensive public projects was growing, and only a larger union seemed likely to be able to carry the burden. All of these elements crystallized suddenly when, in the early 1860s, the Maritime Provinces began to consider forming a larger union among themselves. The move of the Atlantic Provinces touched off a strong response in the rest of Canada, and in 1867 these events culminated in passage by Parliament of the British North America Act.

This Act, in effect, was the Canadian Constitution, and like its American counterpart, it established a federal union. At first the new Dominion of Canada included only Ontario (Canada West), Quebec (Canada East), New Brunswick, and Nova Scotia. In the early 1870s the Dominion acquired the enormous property of the Hudson's Bay Company in the west and north, although not until it had put down an incipient revolt of the settlers on the Red River led by Louis Riel. These eventually became the provinces of Manitoba, Saskatchewan, and Alberta. British Columbia, with its minerals, its furs, and above all with its vast timber reserves, was admitted into the Dominion in 1871. In 1873 Prince Edward Island reluctantly joined. Only Newfoundland, of the present Canadian union, remained outside.

The next 30 years were full of problems and vicissitudes for the newly formed

Completing the Canadian Pacific Railroad, at Eagle Pass in the Rockies, November 7, 1885.

country. One inducement to unification had been the promise of a government-sponsored transcontinental railroad to knit the nation together. The Canadian Pacific, completed in 1885, fulfilled this promise, but not before financial scandal had touched the prime minister, Sir John MacDonald, or before long delays had goaded British Columbia into threatening to secede. Other difficulties of the period included a long decline in Canadian prosperity coinciding with the worldwide fall in raw material prices from the 1870s to the mid-1890s. Canada, its economy increasingly built on exports of wheat, timber, and minerals to the United States and Europe, was particularly hard hit by the depression. Population growth slowed, with many thousands of the young country's most promising citizens emigrating to the more prosperous United States. In the years 1881 to 1891 alone, more than a million Canadians, both British and French,

left their native land. These setbacks were hard on the young confederation, and at times even a political dissolution of the Dominion seemed possible, with several parts seeking annexation to the United States.

But then, once more, the tide reversed. The world upturn of raw material prices after 1896 brought immense prosperity to Canada, now rapidly filling in the great plains provinces of Manitoba, Saskatchewan, and Alberta with immense wheat farms, many of them run by Americans from across the border. Gold in the Klondike in the late 1890s, new government-sponsored railroads to the north of the Canadian Pacific, enormous new British and American investments in asbestos, pulp mills, nickel mines, and hydroelectric power—all of these were added to the boon of higher world prices to produce another great spurt of growth and affluence. Canadians regained confidence in their nation and in themselves, and the country experienced its first substantial cultural flowering.

Prosperity lasted until the eve of World War I, and during the interval much was done to create a true Canadian nationality. Thousands of immigrants from continental Europe as well as the British Isles and the United States were successfully absorbed into Canadian society. In the country's cultural life the basic division between English and French continued, but both groups ceased to look abroad or below the border for their models. Out of the growing and improving universities came a native educated elite anxious to create a national literature and a cultural tradition.

More important than the cultural maturing, perhaps, was the growing political cohesion. Until the disruptive question of Canadian participation in World War I appeared, much was accomplished to reconcile Canadians of all ethnic backgrounds to the idea of a distinctive Canadian nationality. This trend was abetted by the growing importance of the new western provinces. There the "New Canadians" from the European continent as well as the transplanted easterners were relatively free of the old rivalries and animosities that had divided the Dominion. Under the leadership of the *Canadien* Wilfred Laurier, who served as Prime Minister from 1896 to 1911, the two main ethnic groups increasingly accepted the Dominion as their primary loyalty. The Great War of 1914 to 1918 severely strained the seams of Canadian unity as English-speaking and French-speaking citizens disagreed over the proper role of the Dominion in contributing to the cause of the Entente. Still, much had been accomplished in a century. By 1914, after 250 years of settlement, Canada had finally become a nation.

SUGGESTED READINGS

Taylor, George R., *The Transportation Revolution, 1815–1860*. New York: Rinehart and Company, 1951. Paperback.
The best survey of the pre-Civil War American economy, emphasizing industry, commerce, banking, labor and transportation.

Dangerfield, George, *The Era of Good Feelings*. New York: Harcourt, Brace, 1952. Paperback.
A good survey of American political life between 1814 and 1828.

Stampp, Kenneth, *The Peculiar Institution: Slavery in the Ante-Bellum South*. New York: Alfred A. Knopf, 1956. Paperback.
A good overview of southern slavery in the decade of the 1850s.

Schlesinger, Arthur M., Jr., *The Age of Jackson*. Boston: Little, Brown & Company, 1945. Paperback.
A panoramic view of the political and intellectual life of the period 1828 to 1840. Some of it is controversial, but it is still interesting.

Randall, James G. and Donald, David, *The Civil War and Reconstruction*. Lexington, Massachusetts: D. C. Heath and Company, 1969.
A high-level text that covers the origins, course, and results of the Civil War.

Wiebe, Robert, *The Search for Order, 1877–1920*. New York: Hill and Wang, 1967. Paperback.
An interesting and unusual interpretation of the period from the end of Reconstruction to the end of Progressivism.

Hacker, Louis M., *The World of Andrew Carnegie*. Philadelphia: J. B. Lippincott Company, 1968.
A fine overview of the economy between the Civil War and the twentieth century.

May, Ernest R., *Imperial Democracy: The Emergence of America as a Great Power*. New York: Harcourt, Brace, 1961.

A solid review of America's expansionism in the late nineteenth century.

Pringle, Henry F., *Theodore Roosevelt: A Biography*. New York: Harcourt, Brace, n.d. Paperback.

Still the best one volume biography of the most influential Progressive leader.

Link, Arthur S., *Woodrow Wilson and the Progressive Era, 1910–1917*. Paperback. New York: Harper Torchbooks, 1954.

An excellent analysis of the Wilsonian phase of the Progressive impulse.

Millis, Walter, *Road to War: America, 1914–1917*. Boston: Houghton Mifflin Company, 1935.

An older examination of United States entry into World War I. Skeptical of our involvement, it is still useful and readable.

Whitelaw, William M., *The Maritimes and Canada Before Confederation*. New York: Oxford University Press, n.d. Paperback.

McNaught, Kenneth, *The Pelican History of Canada*. Baltimore: Penguin, n.d. Paperback.

CHAPTER 17

Latin America to the Period of World War I

Spain and Portugal established systems of great endurance in the Western Hemisphere. Fifty years after Columbus's discovery in 1492 most of the area we call Latin America was under Iberian control. Not until well after 1800 was this connection broken. During this period, Spain and Portugal had implanted their language, religion, institutions, and many of their customs and attitudes so firmly that this region is still largely Iberian, although only a minority of its population is of full European ancestry. On the whole, the Spanish and Portuguese must be considered highly successful in the history of overseas colonization.

COLONIAL LATIN AMERICA

Political Controls

The system under which Spain and Portugal ruled much of the two American continents until 1825 was essentially simple. The overseas lands belonged to the monarch of each country; each monarch was regarded as ruling by divine right, as God's vassal on earth. Brazil and the Spanish kingdoms in the Americas were legally equal to the European realms. In fact, however, the monarchs never came to America until the Portuguese reigning queen fled in 1807; the agents who ruled for the sovereigns were nearly always men who had been born in the Iberian Peninsula and who were still rooted there. The conquistadors themselves were usually demoted soon after they won the new lands and were replaced by "peninsulars." In later years the peninsulars continued to be dispatched and recalled by the metropolitan governments, leaving the whites born in the New World, or "creoles," little power in their government and the Indians, blacks, and *mestizos* (mixed-blooded persons) even less. (See p. 319.)

The earliest monarchs, particularly Isabella the Catholic and the Emperor Charles V, concerned themselves with the justice of conquering the newly found peoples, who already had political systems of their own ranging from tribal rule to the Aztec and Inca

Colonial Lima.

monarchies. In general, Iberian sovereigns and their theologians and jurists satisfied themselves with the moral authority of the pope's award of 1493, which divided the recent and prospective discoveries between Spain and Portugal. Their titles were valid, they held, provided that they brought Christianity and European civilization into the overseas pagan territories. Yet there was much dispute over the ethical aspects of imperialism, with the Dominican friar Bartolomé de las Casas leading the anti-imperialist campaign in Spain in the sixteenth century, and the Jesuit Antônio Vieira crusading for the Indians of Brazil against the Portuguese in the seventeenth century. Although many Europeans continued to be disturbed by such issues, the ruling groups' overriding interest in the silver, gold, and other treasures of the New World was a more powerful force than conscience. Even if the Catholic church and the Iberian kings professed from the first that the American Indians were morally equal to the European subjects and that—once converted—they should be so treated, the whites

who lived in the New World usually came to regard the Indians as inferiors. *Mestizos,* scorned by the whites, in turn looked down on Indians. Black peoples forcibly imported from Africa were considered natural slaves, as were their descendants.

Most of the time the king himself did not take a personal interest in the government of the American colonies. The "Indies," as the Spanish American lands were called, were governed by a body known as the Council of Indies; a similar agency administered Brazil from a base in Lisbon. These councils had virtually supreme executive, legislative, and judicial power over the overseas territories. Subject to royal pleasure, they made all major appointments, sent commands to, and inspected the appointed officials. The councils issued decrees in the king's name which had the force of statutes, and they possessed final judicial power. They supervised commercial matters, defense and warfare, fiscal affairs, and ecclesiastical controls. The Americans had no representation whatever.

In the New World, Spain placed viceroys in Mexico City after 1535, in Lima after 1542, in Bogotá after 1739, and in Buenos Aires after 1776. Occasionally, Portugal conferred the title of viceroy on the ranking official in Bahia or Rio de Janeiro, but he was not as strong as his Spanish counterpart. Spanish viceroys, of whom 170 served during the colonial period, personified the majesty of the king, lived in a splendor that modern Latin American rulers have perpetuated, and held themselves aloof from their subjects. They, as well as other officers of the crown, were not supposed to cultivate popularity but, instead, to impress the people with the authority of the government. This tradition, of Roman origin, was combined with the Indian tradition of autocratic monarchs or chieftains. Thus Latin America has always known and expected powerful executives who stressed might more than popularity. Individual liberty was as little known in the colonial empires as it had been in the previous Indian societies.

Lesser officials in charge of frontier districts, provinces, Indian communities, and smaller units were likely to be peninsulars with orders to rule firmly. They were transferred frequently and discouraged from being

SPANISH AND PORTUGUESE EMPIRES IN AMERICA ON THE EVE OF INDEPENDENCE

Disputed

San Francisco

Santa Fe

VICEROYALTY OF NEW SPAIN

El Paso

Los Angeles

Rio Grande

San Antonio

Pensacola

New Orleans

Gulf Stream

Atlantic Ocean

BAHAMA ISLANDS
(Br.)

Havana

CAPTAINCY-GENERAL OF CUBA

Santiago

Santo Domingo

Guadalajara

Veracruz

Belize
(Br.)

JAMAICA
(Br.)

Port-au-Prince
(Fr.)

CAPTAINCY-GENERAL OF SANTO DOMINGO

Mexico City

Acapulco

Guatemala

CAPTAINCY-GENERAL OF GUATEMALA

Caribbean Sea

Coro

Panama

Cartagena

Caracas

CAPTAINCY-GENERAL OF CARACAS

DUTCH GUIANA

FRENCH GUIANA

Magdalena River

Bogotá

VICEROYALTY OF NEW GRANADA

Amazon River

Quito

Guayaquil

VICEROYALTY OF PERU

Pacific Ocean

Recife

BRAZIL

Bahia

Callao

Lima

Cuzco

Arequipa

La Paz

Charcas

Potosí

Paraná River

São Paulo

Rio de Janeiro

VICEROYALTY OF LA PLATA

Asunción

CAPTAINCY-GENERAL OF CHILE

Córdoba

Uruguay R.

Santiago

Mendoza

Concepción

Buenos Aires

Montevideo

Rio de la Plata

Atlantic Ocean

PATAGONIA

Spanish Empire

Portuguese Empire

intimate with the people. Judges of the courts, or *audiencias,* were also peninsulars whose function was to apply the laws of Spain or Portugal and the decrees of the Council of Indies. In time, they built up a body of law (of Roman origin) that is still a potent force in Latin America. Only in the municipal councils, the *cabildos* of the Spanish Indies or the *câmaras* of Brazil, were creoles dominant. Usually composed of white males of property, these bodies handled only local matters and tended to be reverent and unassertive before the might of royal authority.

Comprehensive inspections, or *visitas,* and protracted inquests, or *residencias,* at the end of an official's term, further induced loyalty to the crown. But the great distances involved made it possible for officers to disregard the king's will, and corruption became so pervasive that the entire government often seemed a morass of inefficiency and hypocrisy. Yet the system met the monarch's needs. The Iberian government structure was developed in the sixteenth century by absolute rulers determined to hold the American territories tightly to extract their treasure. It was unlike that of the North American English colonies, which were often fashioned in the seventeenth century by refugees from oppression and which were frequently ignored by the home government, itself subject to revolution. Unsatisfactory as the Iberian governments may have seemed to many, they were not upheld by garrisons but by psychological pressure or inertia.

Church and State

Altar and throne were close allies, the Catholic church supporting the divine right of kings and teaching obedience, and the government guarding the orthodoxy of the people and promoting the growth of the ecclesiastical establishment. Both Spain and Portugal enjoyed the right of patronage, by which the monarchs were practically heads of the church in their respective domains, with power to appoint, assign, and supervise clergymen with little more than token approval from Rome. The church flourished under this arrangement, and devout Catholics believed that it was compensated in Latin America for the losses in Europe to Protestantism. Archbishops, bishops, and priests usually enjoyed great prestige; often they strengthened the political authorities by threats of withholding the sacraments from unruly subjects. They also tended to curb the worst excesses of whites in dealing with Indians or blacks.

The regular clergy—friars, monks, and nuns—performed most of the work of converting the natives and imported blacks to Christianity. Evangelists sometimes baptized thousands of non-Christians in a short time, if necessary countenancing the mixture of Christian practices with pagan. When converts were being sought in isolated areas, the friars went ahead of anyone else. The mission system they developed became the mechanism for settling vast numbers of Indians in villages where the brothers taught not only Christianity but European skills in agriculture and ranching. Much heroism was involved, for some groups resisted the missionaries, and often white settlers tried to force Indians out of the mission villages to make them work their lands. In general, the mission system—managed by the Jesuits, Franciscans, Dominicans, Augustinians, and other orders—imparted the language and skills of Europeans to millions of American Indians. Of particular fame were the Jesuit establishments in Paraguay and Brazil, which excited the admiration of skeptics like Voltaire as agencies of humanitarianism and civilization.

The Holy Office of the Inquisition had courts in Lima, Mexico City, and Cartagena to apprehend heretics, witches, and persons who desecrated churches or committed homosexual offenses. Indians were seldom victimized. In two-and-a-half centuries perhaps 6000 people were arrested, of whom 100 were turned over to the state for public execution, usually by burning. Brazilian offenders were ordinarily sent to Portugal for trial. The Inquisition also censored reading matter and public entertainment, but did so with such ineffectiveness that the colonials often read and discussed a wide variety of forbidden books.

The church performed nearly all of the work in education and welfare that the state does today, and many clergymen preserved Indian culture while they eradicated such

Church of the Jesuits at Cuzco.

practices as human sacrifice and cannibalism. Most of the faculty in colleges and the 15 or so universities of Spanish America (Brazil had none) were clergymen. The work of the regular orders in transmitting European ways to Indians and blacks was rightly respected by the crown. Yet, despite martyrs and saints among the clergy, political authorities and various observers, some of them clergymen themselves, regarded many men of the cloth as immoral, incompetent, and likely to exploit the trust or superstition of the population. The church also came under lay criticism for accumulating so much wealth:

sumptuous religious houses, richly decorated cathedrals, episcopal palaces, comfortable monasteries, and extensive plantations, ranches, and orchards. It was also involved in business, for the church often had fluid capital for investments or loans. In 1800, perhaps half the wealth in some areas, like central Mexico, was owned or controlled by the church. Privileges enjoyed by the clergy, such as immunity from many types of prosecution, became acute issues after the Latin American states gained independence. Yet the church created most of its wealth through labor and good management; it used many of its riches for humane purposes in the absence of state resources. The glorification of God through expensive buildings and works of art was both a comfort and cultural treasure; and more than any other institution, it held Latin America together in comparative peace. Today, more than one-third of the Roman Catholics in the world are Latin Americans.

The Colonial Economy

Spain and Portugal had two purposes in their economic policy toward America. First, they wished to acquire as many riches as possible from their colonies. Second, they sincerely wanted the overseas empires to develop into sturdy societies with European technological advantages and institutions, where Europeans, Indians, Negroes, and persons of mixed blood could live and work according to the values of Western civilization. It was assumed that the mother countries were entitled to monopolize the commerce of the colonies and to regulate economic affairs; this mercantilism was taken for granted in colonial times. The Americas were rich in loose treasure but poor in finished goods. Spain and Portugal, therefore, dictated the exchange of the one for the other whenever they could. In Spain, an effort was made to funnel all goods and persons going to or coming from the Indies through Seville (after 1717, through Cadiz), where a *Casa de Contratación* (House of Trade) served as the agent. The Casa worked closely with the merchant guild at Seville and Cadiz to ship finished products to American ports. A similar institution functioned in Lisbon for Brazil. Once the goods had arrived in the Indies, merchant guilds allied with those of the Iberian peninsula sold them at open fairs to retailers from the various cities. Soon, monopolistic temptations caused these agencies to create shortages, to extort the highest prices possible, and to send as little as they could for as much as the colonists would pay. Naturally, the Americans resented these practices and, all during the colonial period, dealt with smugglers whenever they had the opportunity.

Twice a year for most of the period mammoth fleets sailed from Seville in convoys, one to Veracruz and another to Panama. For the return voyage the two fleets converged in Havana for repairs and sailed as one gigantic convoy between Florida and the Bahamas and, via the Gulf Stream, back to Spain. The eastward voyage was the more dangerous. The galleons were loaded with silver, as well as with passengers, mail, gold, and minor colonial products, and were subject to harassment from pirates or national enemies. Only once, in 1628, was an entire fleet lost. A small fleet also sailed regularly from Acapulco in New Spain (Mexico) to the Philippines, which Spain also owned, taking silver and returning with silk and other Oriental goods. Portugal's fleet system was less rigid than that of Spain. Since Englishmen were among the worst predators, it was helpful that England was Portugal's ally and that English goods made up most of the goods bound for Brazil. Thus Portuguese sailings were relatively safe.

Foreigners were not content to allow the Spanish to monopolize the commerce of the Indies. From the earliest days Spanish ships were captured, and smugglers often crept onto the shore. Sir Francis Drake's spectacular privateering vividly demonstrated the vulnerability of the Spanish colonies during the last third of the sixteenth century. Other English privateers and Dutch corsairs terrorized coastal towns and raided Spanish convoys. Early in the seventeenth century Englishmen, Frenchmen, and Dutchmen occupied islands of the Lesser Antilles and began to raise tobacco. After a generation they converted to the more profitable cultivation of sugar, with the result that Haiti became French, and Jamaica, Barbados, the Virgin Islands, Curaçao, and other islands were lost to Spain. Between 1629 and 1654 the Dutch even occupied a huge portion of northeastern Brazil. Here, as in the Caribbean islands, the various nations brought great numbers of Africans with the effect that these areas have remained populated essentially by blacks. In the last third of the seventeenth century pirates like the notorious Henry Morgan ravaged a number of Caribbean cities. A tradition of violence and lawlessness in the Caribbean has continued.

By 1700 Spain's American empire was restricted to lands actually occupied instead of to those awarded by the pope in 1493.

Portable hand sugar mill in use in Brazil, 1834.

France extended her colonial holdings from Quebec into Louisiana and dreamed of taking Mexico. England had been developing viable colonies since the initial settlement of Jamestown in 1607. Meanwhile Spain's trade monopoly was so damaged by foreigners that only one-tenth of the goods reaching the Indies were of Spanish origin. However, a considerable revival of Spanish strength took place after the Bourbons ascended the throne in Madrid in 1700 (see p. 338), and Spain retained her empire and dominated its economy for another century.

Treasure from the New World enabled the Iberian monarchs to exert far more influence on the world stage than their other resources could have permitted. The initial seizures from the Indians were useful, but the organized extraction of precious metals from the middle of the sixteenth century to the end of the colonial period sometimes amounted to one-fourth of the royal income. Under the Roman law that Spain and Portugal perpetuated, the monarch owned all of the subsoil (as governments of modern Latin American republics now do) but retained a fraction, usually one-fifth, of its wealth in order to encourage private individuals to operate the mines. Silver was by far the most important source of wealth in the Spanish empire: in Zacatecas, Guanajuato, and Taxco in Mexico and Potosí in Upper Peru (modern Bolivia). Gold output from shallow washings in the Caribbean and from mines in Chile and New Granada (modern Colombia) was much smaller. On the other hand, gold and diamonds from Brazil constituted the bulk of the loose treasure that Portugal received. Other sources of royal income were customs duties, sales taxes, tithes, tributes or poll taxes paid by Indians, and sale of offices and "kickbacks" from governmental appointees. There was no land or income tax as such. Although taxes in the Americas were comparatively light, the population resented their imposition, especially when collections were increased markedly late in the eighteenth century.

The vast influx of loose money, often in the form of coins or bars of bullion, caused a great inflation in Europe and spurred the rise of capitalism. Spain and Portugal served mainly as filters, since the treasure that they received tended to pass to Northern Europe in exchange for goods that were later shipped to the Americas; or the money was used to wage wars of no immediate interest to Americans. When the flow ceased, in 1808, Spain and Portugal were found to have "frozen" the gold and silver assets that they already possessed in the construction of royal or private buildings or to have "sanctified" it in churches, cloisters, and works of religious art. There remained no sound basis for economic development. Individuals in those countries and in Latin America often had private fortunes derived from mining, and both the government and the church were extravagantly housed. Yet absentee ownership and an economy based on extractive industries were heritages for the modern nations. Mining had also cost the lives of great numbers of Indians, especially in Peru, and of blacks in Brazil.

In addition to loose treasure the New World provided Europe with the white potato, corn or maize, beans, tomatoes, chocolate, tobacco, and dyewoods and hardwoods. The Europeans disregarded much Indian knowledge of irrigation and terracing, but they transmitted seeds, plants, animals, technology and methods that enriched the Americas. They introduced sugar, coffee, bananas, grapes, rice, wheat, and many kinds of fruits and vegetables—all of which flourished in the New World. Also of vast importance was the importation from Europe of horses, cattle, sheep, oxen, asses, pigs, and chickens. With them went the wheel—and thus wagons, coaches, and roads—and iron implements for plows, axes, and hoes that furthered agriculture and forestry. On the whole, agricultural production was greatly increased and diversified, although often oriented toward export. Cattle raising thrived on the grasslands which, like the sea and the forests, were open. Manufacturing was on a small scale, mostly of products such as clothing, furniture, bells, saddles, glass, candles, and fine work in silver and gold.

Craft guilds upheld high standards but tended to restrict production and to limit skilled workers to white people.

In all, a most fundamental economic transformation occurred through the actions of the Iberians since 1492, with effects on Europe as immeasurable as they were on America. One of the main causes of the independence movement was that a good many creoles believed that further economic progress was possible. But the masses lived in static misery, with no hope of improvement.

Racial Conditions

The demographic transformation was also striking, although it cannot be traced satisfactorily because of the lack of records. Spanish and Portuguese immigration from 1492 to 1825 was never massive, but it was steady. Forced African immigration was both massive and steady in Brazil and the Caribbean islands from about 1550 to 1850, perhaps six or seven million in all, and some Africans went to the mainland Spanish colonies too. Recent scholars have reversed sharply upward previous estimates of the Indian population on the eve of the conquest. Many now hold that the Indians died off so rapidly after the Spanish came that within half a century of contact perhaps only one-tenth survived. European diseases were by far the main cause of this catastrophe, since Indians had little or no immunity to them, but cruelty, wars, overwork, and the disorganization of native societies contributed heavily. By the seventeenth century, the Indians were living on plantations as peons, in church missions as wards, in their own communities subject to white labor drafts and tributes, or wild beyond the pale of white settlement. Mestizos and mulattoes usually comprised the lowest class of free workers and were often migrants. Blacks were nearly always slaves, possibly, as some scholars hold, treated less harshly under Iberian and Catholic laws than under English rule in much of North America. There is no doubt that the whites dominated the Americas: peninsulars as officials of the crown and church, and creoles as landowners, mine operators, shopkeepers, entrepreneurs, and professional men.

THE WINNING OF INDEPENDENCE

By 1825 all the mainland colonies of Spain and Portugal in America had become independent; only the islands of Cuba and Puerto Rico remained under Spain until 1898. The Wars of Independence, as the period 1808 to 1825 is known, destroyed the venerable political machinery that had linked the New World to the Iberian monarchies. They brought to an end economic monopolies and restrictions as well as the Inquisition, although the church as an institution remained strong. After 1825 Britain largely substituted for Spain and Portugal in commerce and as a source of capital and technology. France mainly supplanted the former mother countries in cultural and intellectual matters. The ideas of the Enlightenment and of the French and American Revolutions were accepted by the new class of leaders: progress and liberty, reform and reason, and humanitarianism. The peninsulars who lingered were out of power and unpopular. Creoles had carried through the insurrections and now expected to rule. The fortunes of war enabled many mestizos to improve their status, and some had entered the new governing classes. Indians usually remained in a servile condition, but many had left the mines and missions to settle in towns or as peons on plantations. Most restrictions on them were now lifted, but those who dwelt in Spanish communities were still the lower class and those who lived in their own communities were isolated. Blacks had won control of Haiti and Santo Domingo but were still slaves in other Caribbean islands and in Brazil. Those in the Spanish mainland countries had been officially freed, yet slavery persisted in places. England and the United States had recognized most of the new nations, with the Royal Navy offering genuine protection from European aggression and the Monroe Doctrine of the United States providing moral defense.

The Wars of Independence came as a surprise, since there had been little indication that revolt was likely. Occasional movements for autonomy—as in Paraguay in the 1720s, Venezuela in 1749, Quito in 1765, and New Granada in the 1780s—had not been aimed at royal authority. In the 1780s the Indians of Peru and the present Bolivia were led by Tupac Amaru II, the Inca pretender, in a massive revolt to correct specific abuses. Efforts by the British and the Jesuits (after their expulsion in 1768) to stir up disaffection were insignificant, as were those of more radical revolutionaries like Francisco de Miranda of Venezuela and the Brazilian "Tiradentes" (tooth-puller). Black slaves often escaped to establish free communities in the jungles of Brazil, but the only important settlement, Palmares, was destroyed in 1697. Indian warfare had long been chronic in northern Mexico and in the Andes and Chilean forests; still, these were the unorganized acts of violence of native peoples seeking to protect themselves from white encroachment.

It was the American-born whites, the creoles, who proved susceptible to the doctrines of the French and American revolutions and who, in small numbers, began to plot secession by 1808. Their grievances were chiefly the autocracy, inefficiency, and unresponsiveness of the Spanish political machine, and the arrogance of the peninsular officials who ruled them. Many were truly attracted by liberalism. They also believed that freedom of commerce, especially with Britain, would enrich them. Some craved power and felt the call of nationalism against imperial control. And yet they were not greatly stirred before 1808.

The Iberian empires in America were cut adrift from their mother countries when Napoleon sent armies into Lisbon in 1807 and into Madrid in 1808. The royal Braganzas and their court sailed from Lisbon to Brazil for a sojourn of 13 years. A surge of economic and cultural growth followed the arrival of the royal court. King John VI was compelled to return in 1821 to Portugal, which was then under liberal control. As he left, he advised Crown Prince Pedro, his son, to declare Brazilian independence if radicals in Portugal or revolutionaries in Brazil threatened to destroy the monarchy. This he did in 1822.

In the case of Spain, the new Bourbon king, Ferdinand VII, was forced by Napoleon to abdicate and was interned in France for six years. Because Spain and its empire rejected Napoleon's brother as king, the great imperial machine fell under the direction of fugitive bodies in the peninsula which claimed to exercise the powers of Ferdinand VII. It was an impossible situation. French armies occupied most of Spain. The various agencies had no real authority to rule the overseas lands, even when the Americans were represented on them. And ambitious creoles saw a chance to seize power from peninsular officials in American cities and to rule in the name of the absent Bourbon king. Two years after Ferdinand was liberated, that is, by 1816, his authority had been successfully reasserted everywhere except in the Argentine and isolated parts of Mexico and Venezuela. But the Americans by then had tasted freedom. They were beginning to overcome the Spaniards and local royalists in fringe areas when, in 1820, Spain underwent a liberal revolution that alienated those forces that had been most loyal in America: the church, the landowners, and the militias. Patriot forces won the upper hand and were on their way to victory when, in 1823, Ferdinand VII was restored to absolutist power by the armies of Bourbon France. By then it was too late to woo America. Most of it was free, and the cause of independence had such momentum that it overcame the last, but greatest, royalist forces, those in Peru, by the end of 1824.

New Spain (Mexico), by far the largest of Spain's colonies, is a good example of the pattern that Spanish America followed. When the news of the fall of Ferdinand VII reached Mexico City in 1808, the peninsulars moved rapidly to assure the continuation of imperial rule under whatever authority emanated from Spain. Disappointed creoles, who favored autonomy with themselves ruling in place of the incapacitated king, turned to plotting. On September 16, 1810, their conspiracy was prematurely triggered by an elderly white priest of liberal opinions, Father Miguel Hidalgo. To his surprise his summons to revolt, the ringing of the church bell in the village of Dolores, ignited a fierce race war of Indian against white. Atrocities caused the whites and mestizos to unite. Soon the Indians were beaten by organized

armies and Hidalgo was executed. But his heir, a liberal mestizo priest named José Maria Morelos, continued the rebellion in the mountains of the south and articulated an attractive program for an independent Mexico. He too was captured and killed, and Mexico quieted down. Soon after the Spanish liberal revolution of 1820, however, many conservatives became alienated from Spain. One of them, a royalist officer named Agustín de Iturbide, joined with a remnant of Morelos's forces and declared independence in 1821. A conservative monarchy with a European prince was promised, but in 1822 Iturbide took the crown as emperor himself. His rule lasted less than a year.

Central America, which had long been the captaincy-general of Guatemala under Spanish rule, was quiet during the independence struggles but became free in 1821 when the captain-general himself, Gabino Gainza, joined the patriots. Soon the former captaincy-general united with imperial Mexico for a short time as a state.

Simón Bolívar was primarily responsible for liberating Venezuela, Colombia, Panama, Ecuador, Peru, and Bolivia, and he has remained by far the most admired and influential hero of the Wars of Independence. In addition to being a brilliant military commander, he was eloquent, profound, and sensitive to the ideas of his age and the needs of Latin America. Born in 1783 into one of the richest creole families of Venezuela, he had been educated by radical tutors to be both a skeptic and a republican. Two extensive visits to Europe between 1799 and 1807 had fostered in him a hatred for Spain and an admiration for Napoleonic France and for England which was so strong that he vowed to free South America. His opportunity came in 1810, when Venezuelan creoles ousted peninsular officials and set up a regime in the name of Ferdinand VII. Bolívar went to London to obtain aid. He failed, but he induced the elderly revolutionary Francisco de Miranda to return to Venezuela. The two were instrumental in having Venezuela declared an independent republic in 1811. In a year the republic collapsed, the victim of bickering within the new government, an earthquake that destroyed only the land held by the revolutionaries, and a royalist reaction, whereupon Bolívar turned against Miranda and allowed him to be taken by the Spaniards.

Bolívar rallied Venezuelan patriots in the neighboring state of New Granada (now Colombia), where several revolutionary movements had been in progress since 1810. Invading Venezuela in 1813, he briefly created another republic in Caracas, but it too fell before royalist *llaneros,* or horsemen, and as a result of the news that the restored Ferdinand VII was sending a large expeditionary force. Bolívar fled to New Granada but found it also weakening (it was reconquered in 1816 by Spain). He then went to various Caribbean islands, where he wrote inspirational letters and made amazingly accurate prophecies about the outcome of the struggle and the future of Latin America notably in his so-called Jamaica Letter of 1815, in which he wrote:

The American provinces are fighting for their freedom, and they will ultimately succeed. Some provinces as a matter of course will form federal and some central republics; the larger areas will inevitably establish monarchies, some of which will fare so badly that they will disintegrate in either present or future revolutions.

Finally, the Liberator, as Bolívar liked to be called, joined a group of patriots isolated in the Orinoco delta in Venezuela. There he built up a formidable task force composed partially of British war veterans and supplied by London merchants on credit. He also effected an alliance with the new *llanero* leader, José Antonio Páez, who would long rule Venezuela. And a congress that he called provided the ideological appeal for the liberation and restructuring of America.

Moving up the unpopulated river valleys and across the Andes in 1819, Bolívar descended on New Granada and freed it in one battle. After establishing the bases for a republic to be called Colombia with his lieutenant, Francisco de Paula Santander, in charge at Bogotá, he ousted the Spaniards from Venezuela in 1821. Panama suddenly joined Colombia in that year. In 1822 Ecuador was freed by Antonio José Sucre, Bolívar's favorite aide and intended heir. The Liberator went to Ecuador to meet with José

de San Martín, a ranking Spanish officer who had deserted Spain in 1811 and who had recently brought an army from Argentina to Peru. But the two famous men disagreed, and San Martín withdrew. In 1823 Bolívar went to Peru to organize the final victory over large royalist forces. The battle of Ayacucho at the end of 1824, won by Sucre, accomplished this end, and in 1825 Upper Peru, renamed Bolivia, was freed. The triumphant Liberator proceeded to organize the new republics with himself as president for life. He also called a congress at Panama in 1826 to present a united American front against the monarchies of Europe, which proved unsuccessful.*

Chile had revolted in 1810, when the *cabildo,* or town council, at Santiago set up a state outwardly loyal to Ferdinand VII. Bernardo O'Higgins, son of a recent captain-general of Chile and viceroy of Peru, led the revolt, but his cause collapsed in 1814 when Spanish armies defeated the divided patriots. Returning from Argentina in 1817 with the forces of San Martín, the patriots were victorious and, in 1818, established a free state with O'Higgins as supreme director. San Martín sailed in 1820 to the coast of Peru, naval supremacy having been won by the fiery Scottish adventurer Lord Thomas Cochrane.

Buenos Aires had also ousted the peninsulars in 1810 through the creole *cabildo.* Although the Argentinians prospered considerably from British trade after this, their patriots showed little capacity to agree and govern, which allowed Uruguay and Paraguay to break away. Ignoring the squabbling ideologues, José de San Martín quietly assembled a task force that made an epochal crossing of the Andes from Argentina into Chile in 1817. After his victories there and his landing on the shores of Peru came the disastrous meeting with Bolívar, whereupon San Martín retired to Europe to live out many years in silence and modesty. Only later was he appreciated. Meanwhile, Buenos Aires was free and growing, but even after the congress

---

* Although the Panama congress itself was a failure, it set the precedent for the Pan-American or Inter-American movement, now embodied in the Organization of American States.

Meeting of San Martín and Bolívar at Guayaquil, July 1822.

declared independence in 1816 and attempted to establish a republic in 1825, the Plata area remained disunited.

THE LIBERATORS FAIL AS STATE-BUILDERS

Most of Latin America gained its independence as a by-product of the Napoleonic wars and their aftermath; thus the new countries were ill-prepared to rule themselves. The men who had led the struggles for independence were usually able and idealistic. Yet most of them were overthrown or left in disgust within a few years. Iturbide of Mexico fell from power in less than a year and was

killed when he attempted a comeback. A federal republic that followed him failed because of depression and dissension. After a few months of affiliation with Iturbide's empire, Central America organized a federation. Despite many heroic efforts, the most notable attempted by Francisco Morazán, the federation disintegrated by 1838. Haiti's liberator, Toussaint Louverture, was betrayed by the French. His successor, Jean-Jacques Dessalines, tried to be a black racist emperor and was murdered. A black who followed him, Henry Christophe, made himself king in the north but committed suicide when defeated by rebellious subjects. The mulatto president of the south, Alexandre Pétion, had better luck, and his successor, Jean-Pierre

Toussaint Louverture, requesting English officers to leave the island, 1798.

Boyer, united Haiti and conquered Santo Domingo. After a lackluster rule lasting to 1843, he was overthrown.

The situation was no brighter in South America. In Chile, O'Higgins sought to be a modernizer and conciliator, but he was ousted in 1823 after five years of rule. In Argentina the liberators continued to quarrel. The best of them, Bernardino Rivadavia, enunciated the formula of progress that much later made Argentina great, but he lasted little more than a year as its first president and retired in despondency. Uruguay's founding father, José Artigas, was eventually driven from Uruguay by Brazilian troops.

Not even a genuine royal figure could provide legitimacy or consensus. Brazil's young and popular emperor, Pedro I, antagonized the liberals and alienated patriots by showing concern for Portuguese affairs. After a stormy reign lasting from 1822 to 1831 he quit in disgust. Paraguay isolated itself under a weird dictator, José Gaspar de Francia, who had bested the original liberators.

Most poignant of all, and most fateful, was the failure of Simón Bolívar. Having ruined his health in fighting for national independence under difficult circumstances, he now sought to create large, centralized states under his lifetime presidency and to educate the people slowly in ways of self-government. But by 1830 he was repudiated in all of the lands that he had liberated. In that year, on his way to exile, Bolívar died lamenting that he had wasted his life, that he had plowed the sea. His heir in Bolivia, Sucre, had departed earlier in defeat and disenchantment. The caretaker government he had left in Peru had been quickly overthrown. His old ally, Páez, had withdrawn Venezuela from Bolívar's control, just as Juan José Flores had removed Ecuador. Even Santander, long the acting president of Colombia, had fallen out with the Liberator, who had few supporters anywhere by the time he died.

A basic problem was the absence of legitimacy, the general acceptance of a system as right and natural. The departure of the familiar agents of imperial control had left Spanish America without the public administration and means to finance government. None of the armies could maintain an institutional existence; they all dissolved into irregular forces loyal to any leader who could find means to pay them. The rule of law had departed with the judges and officials of Spain. Economic retrogression was so marked that it took several decades for production to regain the levels of 1800. Mines and plantations had often been deserted. Fighting had ruined many cultivated areas; workers had migrated and livestock had been driven off. Crime and social depravity were general. When the liberators failed to establish authority and restore the economy, people turned on them. They had overthrown Spanish power, but the revolutions they had loosed were unfinished socially, and perhaps unending.

CAUDILLOS AND DICTATORS

The overthrow of the liberators was followed by the age of *caudillos* (chiefs)—the triumph of military leaders and often of reactionary rural forces over the liberal civilians of the cities. During this time, business conditions were usually bad. Foreign commerce, which had started so hopefully with the end of the Spanish monopoly, generally failed to develop. Foreign investors and traders, usually British, more often than not were

defeated by conditions or swindled by Latin American governments. Public education, which most of the liberators had planned to expand, was almost impossible. European immigrants, so craved by the new governments, would not come in significant numbers. During most of the nineteenth century, Latin America lost ground in comparison to Europe and the United States in nearly every respect: politically, economically, socially, and culturally.

Mexico

Mexico's long agony began as a cleavage between liberals and conservatives, but this split quickly degenerated into dictatorship interrupted by periods of anarchy. Antonio López de Santa Anna was responsible for much of this condition until 1855. Elected president in 1832 as a liberal-federalist, he switched sides and strove to be the Napoleon of the west. This strutting peacock had no principles whatever. Shunning work, he abandoned himself for long periods to idle pastimes on his tropical estate near the Gulf while his lieutenants enriched themselves on the republic's sparse revenues. Santa Anna was president eleven times. Despite catastrophic failures, he could gather enough forces to seize the capital, and often he was truly admired by the people for his effrontery. In 1836 he lost an army and was himself captured in an effort to chastise Texas, where American settlers had proclaimed their independence from Mexico. Eventually recovering from this disaster, Santa Anna fought his way to the presidency in the early 1840s and ruled as a conservative despot. After losing out again, he was recalled from exile in 1846 to lead the Mexican army against the United States, this time as a liberal and anticlerical. Despite some signs of honor in this capacity, he sold out to the Americans and again went into exile. Mexico had to acknowledge the loss of Texas and sell to the United States the huge area now known as the Mexican Cession. The liberals were so disgraced by their inability to govern that the conservatives were restored. Seeking to prepare the way for a monarchy, they invited Santa Anna to return in 1853. Instead, he made himself a princeling and again pillaged the country, financing his regime by selling the Mesilla Valley (Gadsden Purchase) to the United States. By 1855 the liberals, who by now had undertaken a serious program to curb the church and the military, gained control, and Santa Anna fled.

Central America and the Caribbean Islands

Rafael Carrera of Guatemala was the first memorable *caudillo* of Central America. He broke up the federation of that area in 1838, and until 1865 he ruled Guatemala, where Indians venerated him and white or mestizo landlords needed him. A staunch conservative, he opposed ideas from abroad and interfered in neighboring republics to suppress liberals. Justo Rufino Barrios, a professedly liberal *caudillo* who ruled from 1873 to 1885, was as oppressive as Carrera, but he was eager to introduce technological advances and started the coffee industry that became so important to his country's economy. Another dictator of his type, Manuel Estrada Cabrera, ruled despotically from 1898 to 1920 and oversaw the creation of a huge banana industry by Americans. His rule was insanely cruel, and it was clear that he, like his predecessors, had no intention of elevating the Indians into citizenship. Guatemala was a paradise for a small elite and for aliens.

El Salvador languished in poverty; its national life consisted mainly of attempts to preserve its independence from Guatemala. Honduras was even more backward and was so subject to strife that no ruler endured for more than an average of a year. Nicaragua was affected by British ambitions to dominate its Caribbean coast and by the many foreigners who crossed it on their way to California. After a short rule in the 1850s by an American adventurer, William Walker, it was ruled by conservatives until 1893. In that year a liberal, José Santos Zelaya, rose to power for a 16-year dictatorship. Some modernity came to Nicaragua because Americans built up a large banana-growing and export business. Costa Rica, a republic composed of whites and with its arable land well divided, has avoided aristocracy and dictatorship for most of its history. Coffee in the 1840s and bananas since the 1890s have brought it prosperity. The latter business was

established by the American, Minor C. Keith, who later started the flourishing United Fruit Company there and in other Central American lands.

Haiti and the Dominican Republic were the only free nations of the Caribbean islands in the nineteenth century. The latter won its independence from Haiti in 1844 but felt so threatened by reconquest that it rejoined the Spanish monarchy for an unsatisfactory four-year period following 1861. Later, its *caudillos* sought to sell the country to the United States. A black dictator, Ulises Heureaux, ruled this overwhelmingly mulatto nation from 1882 until his murder in 1899. Although a tyrant, he stimulated the sugar industry and enticed enough foreign capital to begin the modernization of the republic. Unfortunately, his creditors were unable to collect their debts. Fearing intervention by European powers, President Theodore Roosevelt made an arrangement with the Dominican president which allowed the United States to operate the customhouses in 1905. The debts were paid off, but the Dominican Republic suffered from such disorder that, in 1916, President Wilson sent United States marines to occupy the little nation. They stayed for eight years.

Many of the small nations of Latin America had similar problems in paying their debts and suffered the same fate. Haiti, a rugged and beautiful third of the island of Hispaniola, with an African and French heritage, was indescribably poor, but at least the rural blacks owned individual, tiny patches of land. Haiti wanted nothing to do with the outside world. An elite of mulattoes usually ran the government. In 1847 they elevated a black leader, Faustin Soulouque, to the presidency only to see him transform himself into an emperor two years later and then reign for ten years in as much monarchical splendor as the little country could support. His successor, the mulatto president Fabre Geffrard, restored Haitian ties with Rome, whereupon Catholicism made some inroads on the prevailing *voodoo* cults. Although several rulers made efforts to attract foreign traders and capital, Haiti's unstable government gave it a bad reputation. Yet one modernizing device worked for a time, disastrously. This was the printing of bonds for sale to gullible aliens.

Banana plantation in Costa Rica.

By 1914 so many Europeans had been cheated that intervention by European governments became a serious threat. Soon after World War I began, President Wilson feared that either France or Germany might seize this strategically well-located country. After a series of riotous disorders, in which an ex-president was pulled out of the French legation and torn limb from limb, Wilson set up an American protectorate, which lasted from 1915 to 1930.

Cuba's native *caudillos* had not come into their own, but Spanish rulers prior to 1898 served the cause of autocracy. The island had not rebelled with the other Spanish colonies because it was full of troops and because the white ruling group feared a black uprising like that in Haiti. There was enough discontent, however, to cause the Spanish government in 1825 to impose a permanent state of siege. Spain itself was so misgov-

erned that its rule in Cuba was not efficient, and Cuban creoles at times plotted to join the United States or secure American aid for independence. They were also divided over the issue of slavery in a population that was at least one-third black. Cuba's economy was diversified, with tobacco, coffee, sugar, and livestock supporting it. Yet Spain's political controls and heavy taxes irritated the creoles, many of whom were well informed and in contact with the outside world. From 1868 to 1878 a desultory civil war tore the eastern part of the island during a period when Spain itself was undergoing chaotic changes of regime. A compromise ended the war, but the chief leaders went abroad and continued to plot.

The principal inspiration for *Cuba libre* came from a brilliant writer and orator, José Martí, who raised funds and created sympathy for Cuba in the United States. In 1895 the revolutionists invaded Cuba. The civil war that followed was cruel in the extreme, with Spanish repressive measures offending many Americans. Yet the United States did not intervene until 1898, after its battleship, the *Maine*, was mysteriously blown up in Havana harbor. The Spanish government failed to respond without equivocation to an American ultimatum to free Cuba. The "splendid little war" of 1898 resulted in Spanish surrender and evacuation, whereupon the Cuban patriots found themselves not free but under American military government.

The Bolivarian Nations

Venezuela endured several long ruling *caudillos*, with civil wars during the intervals. The companion of Bolívar, José Antonio Paez, dominated the land most of the time from 1822 to 1846 and from 1861 to 1863. Paez did much to restore and reform the war-torn republic, but by 1864 the liberals had gained in power and finally forced him into exile. The next strong man was Antonio Guzmán Blanco, a fanatical anticlerical and self-styled liberal who maintained a dictatorship from 1870 to 1889, often ruling from Paris through puppets. During this period modern technology appeared in the form of railroads, port facilities, the telegraph, and wagon roads. A sound currency was also achieved, and the dictator lavishly built monuments and buildings to glorify his regime. Following a chaotic interlude after Guzman Blanco's overthrow in 1889, a rustic *caudillo* from the mountainous state of Táchira, the source of all Venezuelan rulers from 1899 to 1945, took over. This rustic, Cipriano Castro, was among the first of Latin American presidents to defy foreign claimants. From 1902 to 1903, Britain, Germany, and Italy blockaded the country, mainly in vain, and Castro was a local hero. In 1908 while in Europe for medical treatment, he was removed by his lieutenant, Juan Vicente Gómez. Gómez realized the importance of foreign commerce and investment and courted the great powers. When vast oil deposits were found in 1914, he acquired a key that would make Venezuela the richest land per capita in Latin America. Yet foreign companies and a few individuals monopolized this income. So did Gómez,

whose regime, although hateful, was so strong that it lasted to 1935.

Caudillos of the classic military type were less prominent in Colombia — or New Granada as it was known from 1830 to 1863 — than in Venezuela. After Bolívar left, his one-time associate, Santander, and succeeding presidents, maintained a semblance of republican rule. The land itself was so divided by the Andes that local units were often able to withstand dictatorship from the capital, Bogotá. Economic life remained very primitive during the nineteenth century except for the beginning of large-scale coffee culture and the introduction of the river steamboat. Intellectual life, however, was fervid, with liberals going far to make the nation a democratic secular state. Their achievements were undone by Rafael Núñez, who ruled from 1880 to 1894. A one-time radical, Núñez became convinced that a centralist, Catholic autocracy was necessary. The pattern of conservatism he created endured to 1930 and is still strong. At the turn of the century, Colombia was suffering from a brutal civil war. The loss of Panama in 1903* jolted its patriots into cooperating under a progressive conservative president, Rafael Reyes, under whom the republic settled into a long period of comparative order and freedom. The national economy improved with the development of the Colombian oil fields, and the new government stability encouraged further economic growth. Early in the twentieth century, Colombia was one of the most stable and modern countries of Latin America notwithstanding its mass poverty.

Ecuador was ruled by a small number of whites divided between conservatives based in Quito, the capital, and liberals in Guayaquil, the major seaport. Juan Jose Flores, its first president, began as Bolivar's supporter and, like the Liberator, became conservative by the time he was ousted, in 1845. Attempting a comeback in 1860, he saw Gabriel García Moreno snatch the presidency from his hands. García Moreno began

---

* After Colombia agreed to sell isthmian canal rights to the United States, it suddenly raised its price, whereupon President Theodore Roosevelt recognized a minor revolt as a Panamanian independence movement and prevented the Colombians from putting it down.

A traditional market in the Andes.

the modernization of Ecuador by fostering education and importing technology, but he was highly reactionary otherwise and a symbol of passionate clericalism in Latin America. Some years after his murder in 1875, the liberals came to power under Eloy Alfaro, who established a quasi-democratic system by the turn of the century. Yet Ecuador remained isolated and poor, most of its inhabitants Indians with no role in national life.

Bolivia was not the model state its creator had hoped for when he gave it his name. The ruling group, living amid only a few thousand whites and a majority of Indians, whose consumption of the drug *coca* and the drink *chicha* kept them in a state of lethargy or stupor, had few contacts with the rest of the world. Bolivia's most ambitious president, Andrés Santa Cruz (1829–1839), sought to establish a great Andean state under his leadership, perhaps as a monarch, since he claimed royal Inca ancestry. Peru, where he had many partisans, fell under his control in 1835, but Chile feared for its independence and shipped an army up the coast to defeat Santa Cruz. There followed a series of short-term presidents, some of them incredibly base and brutal, often supported by gangs of rowdies to whom politics was a form of livelihood. One of these presidents foolishly involved his country in war with Chile in 1879, with the result that Bolivia lost its corridor to the Pacific Ocean, a matter of painful concern to some Bolivians even today. Economic growth was negligible throughout this period; a few mineral exports and subsistence agriculture supported the country and such government as it had.

Peru, long the queen of the Spanish colonies, remained unstable and impoverished throughout the nineteenth century. A few dozen wealthy landowning families and miners preserved the graceful viceregal traditions, but soldiers dominated politics. For some years Peru enjoyed an income from the foreign sale of guano (accumulated bird droppings on the rocky islands off the coast, used as fertilizer). Of far more significance were nitrates scraped up from the deserts of the southern coastland, which were much in demand for use in explosives. This prosperity was enough to finance the government, purchase a navy, and support a regular army as well as introduce luxuries from Europe. Guano soon declined in value, and Peru lost its nitrate lands in a war with Chile (1879–1883) which involved a long occupation of Lima and the cession of three provinces.

Four Americans, however, were responsible for important advances in Peru. Henry Meiggs built railways, largely with Chinese indentured workers, in difficult places; this made mining profitable again. William Wheelwright organized the first steamship line to Peru. And Michael and W. R. Grace funded Peru's manifold debts, thus satisfying foreign creditors while they improved communications and transportation. A rubber boom in the Amazon jungles and new discoveries of copper ore toward the end of the century brought new prosperity to some people. Most of the population was unaffected, especially the Quechua-speaking Indians, who lived in mountainous communities isolated from the whites, and the cholos (mixed bloods), who worked the cotton and sugar plantations on the coasts. Of a long series of presidents and dictators, only Ramón Castilla and Nicolás Piérola stand out during this period. Castilla, who ruled from 1845 to 1851 and from 1855 to 1860, began modernizing the country with the income from guano sales, and he alleviated some of the abuses suffered by the lower classes. Piérola was president from 1895 to 1899 and remained powerful afterward. As a civilian and democrat, he acquainted his aristocratic country with contemporary ideas of progress.

Argentina and Paraguay

Argentina had only one outstanding *caudillo,* Juan Manuel de Rosas, ruler for most of the period from 1829 to 1852 of Buenos Aires Province, which contained half the population. There was, in fact, no Argentine nation. Rather, 14 provinces under rustic gaucho bosses were united by informal ties to Buenos Aires, which controlled the customhouse—the only sure source of revenue. One of the cruelest tyrants in Latin American history, Rosas retarded the Plata area by keeping its contacts with outsiders limited to exchanging hides for a few finished goods. He wanted no European capital or immigrants. Least of all did he desire the culture or ideas of the modern world. Terrorizing the people of his province and intimidating the other gaucho bosses, he inadvertently created a tradition of unity that later proved useful to the Argentine nation. In 1852 Rosas was overthrown by a combination of liberal exiles, gaucho rivals, Brazilians, Uruguayans, and others who had suffered from his dreary despotism.

Paraguay had three notorious, long-ruling dictators in succession. The first was José Gaspar Rodríguez de Francia, an eccentric intellectual who wanted the little nation of Guaraní Indians to be a hermit like himself. From 1814 to his death in 1840 he provided peace by killing off all his opponents and almost achieved his purpose of surviving as the only white man in the country. After Francia's death, the Paraguayans, like bewildered orphans, allowed Carlos Antonio López to become dictator, a position he held until his death in 1862. López opened the land to foreign ships, adventurers, and a few immigrants, but it remained very primitive. His son, Francisco Solano López, inherited the dictatorship and a large army of docile Indians. Planning to build a Platine empire, he enlarged the army and attacked Uruguay, Brazil, and Argentina in a surprise move. A

Argentina gauchos.

war of enormous suffering and barbarity, lasting from 1864 to 1870, resulted in his death and the loss of perhaps nine-tenths of the male population of Paraguay.

SIGNS OF STABILITY AND PROGRESS

The age of *caudillos* terminated in some lands, thus permitting the operation of regular governments which, in turn, permitted the growth of national economies. This growth often derived from Europe and the United States, which benefited greatly from the extraction and export of raw materials and foodstuffs. Most of the technological advances also were supported by outside influences that were interested primarily in profits for themselves. This led to serious problems along with the striking material progress.

Argentina

The rise of Argentina from a near-primitive condition to the most advanced nation in Latin America was stunningly swift. It was made possible by a sound political system created after the overthrow of the gaucho tyrant, Rosas, in 1852 and following nine years of tension between Buenos Aires and the rest of the country. From 1861 on, this republic lived under a constitution similar to that of the United States and enjoyed an orderly succession of able presidents. It was a limited democracy, since voting was restricted and bosses directed the elections. Yet these bosses were, in the main, patriotic and responsible; their corruption was restrained for the times. A high degree of order and liberty prevailed. There was no place for an overbearing army. The dominant groups wanted, and obtained, European capital, culture, immigrants, and machines. Their success transformed Argentina in a short period.

Bartolomé Mitre deserves credit for establishing the stability that opened his country to progress. President from 1862 to 1868, he was followed by Domingo Faustino Sarmiento (1868–1874), foe of the gaucho, whom he regarded as the curse of the land, and founder of a public education system long admired as the finest in the Western Hemisphere. Many subsequent presidents were strong and capable. Few issues divided the political leaders, since they agreed on constitutionalism, mild clericalism, and the promotion of economic growth. The worst contention arose over the position of the province of Buenos Aires, which was so populous and advanced that it dominated the republic. Strife ended after the city of Buenos Aires was made a federal district, leaving the province strong but less likely to intimidate the others.

Argentina had many advantages. Most of it was flat, ideal for railroads. It had a good climate and abundant soil resulting in the finest grasslands and grain farms the world knew. And the population, which became the most European in the New World, was almost unaffected by racial tensions. An average of 5000 Europeans immigrated each year in the 1860s; 30 years later, 200,000 were entering annually, most of them from Italy and Spain.

Once a sound government was operating, Argentina attracted enormous investments by Europeans, who owned at least one-fourth of the country's wealth by 1900. The major cause was the European (mainly English) appetite for beef, which could be satisfied after the introduction of the refrigerated steamship in 1876. Grasslands long unowned were now claimed and fenced, windmills built, slaughterhouses constructed, and new crops of fodder cultivated. An amazing transformation of Argentine herds occurred after fine breeding bulls were imported. What was done for cattle was soon done for sheep, and the export of mutton and wool multiplied almost every decade. Great wheat farms developed so fast that grain exports rivaled those of meat and wool by 1900. Income from this trade enabled Argentines to purchase the best of European finished goods. The land-owning class developed into a true aristocracy, while Buenos Aires became almost as beautiful as Paris and London. With by far the best railway system in Latin America, Argentina was able to open up the provinces of the west and north. Thereafter forestry, mining, sugar cultivation, and viniculture further enriched the nation.

Prosperity was so steady that grave social questions were obscured. The worst problem was that enormous ranches and farms were owned by comparatively few people. Rural labor was debased and often migratory. Immigrants had no homestead acts to benefit them and hence, had to become farm workers or settle in Buenos Aires as proletarians. The middle class grew very slowly. A few Argentines worried about the predominance of foreigners in their country and about their dependence on European markets. A Radical party was slowly constructed by Hipólito Yrigoyen to meet the needs of the urban masses and immigrants. In the face of its pressure, the oligarchy retreated by enacting a universal suffrage law in 1912, opening the way for Yrigoyen to acquire power legally, and he was elected president in 1916.

Uruguay

After many years of war and foreign occupation, Uruguay by 1900 was flourishing for the same reasons operating in Argentina: its wool, wheat, and beef were shipped abroad in great volume while European immigrants and capital came in; it had an excellent public school system and there was a vibrant intellectual life in Montevideo, the capital. Largely because of José Batlle y Ordóñez, its president or principal leader from 1901 to 1929, Uruguay departed from the Argentine pattern. Batlle curbed the monopolistic role of foreign money and nationalized utilities and some industries. He introduced an elaborate system of social welfare, the first in Latin America, which all but eliminated poverty and prevented the growth of a wealthy class. In 1919 he persuaded his countrymen to adopt a multiple executive to replace the single presidency. Thus the little country came as close to social and political democracy as any in the Americas.

Chile

Chile was the first Latin American country to become stable. In 1830 an oligarchy of rural landlords and urban traders established an enduring system of enlightened conservatism. Diego Portales, who framed the system, was murdered in 1837, but an orderly sequence of strong presidents maintained stability until 1891. After that the presidents ceased to be powerful, but the oligarchy continued to rule through Congress. Liberty within order was the slogan, and usually the fact. Even though the Chilean army performed very successfully in two wars with Peru and Bolivia, it was not dominant in government. Nor was the church, respected and favored though it was. The system did not, however, make for social equality. Aristocratic landlords dominated the great Central Valley of this long, narrow land, a very productive agricultural area where peasants and migratory workers lived in a poverty that drove many to alcoholism, Chile's historic vice. Wheat, grapes, and other crops of the temperate zone were the main products. Merchants in the cities and extractors of the poor quality coal of the far south and of copper and nitrates in the north complemented the rural lords. If the rulers were whites, the masses were mestizo, and Indians lived in the forested islands of the south. Chile was attractive to immigrants from Germany and to Basques and Catalans of Spain, but the flow of new citizens was never overwhelming. The ubiquitous Americans, William Wheelwright and Henry Meiggs, were instruments of progress in building railroads and operating steamships.

By the twentieth century, Chile offered an attractive prospect of stable constitutionalism in government, liberty within order, and a sturdy national pride. Nitrates discovered in lands taken from Peru and Bolivia were such lucrative exports that taxes were light, yet public works and a good school system could be financed. Academic culture and publishing flourished. By the end of World War I, it was the poverty of the great majority, the farm workers and miners, that loomed as dangers to the most enduring regime of Latin America.

Brazil

Portuguese America avoided disintegration and caudilloism largely because of its monarchy, which Pedro I had left in 1831 to his five-year-old son, Pedro II. The crown served to maintain unity during a few years of dissension before Pedro II became old enough to master his vast empire, about 1848. He ruled until 1889, and Brazil enjoyed unparalleled internal peace. The emperor himself was the most admired Latin American of his time, since he was democratic in manner and so respectable that he has been called "Queen Victoria in pants." He was not only studious but learned, and as a world traveler he eagerly sought any item of culture or technology that might benefit Brazil. His exercise of power was clever and disguised. He truly ruled, although he did so through a partially elected parliament* and officials who were generally exemplary. Pedro never employed his power of veto, and he deliberately alternated the conservatives and liberals in the hope of developing a two-party system. Constitutional practices, judicial processes, and freedom of speech and press were respected more than elsewhere in Latin America. And the emperor subordinated the military so severely that generals looked with envy on the privileges enjoyed by their counterparts in the Spanish-speaking lands and slowly became disaffected with the monarch.

Black slavery, which had degraded half the population at the time of independence, declined steadily, especially when the African slave trade ceased in 1850 and many Brazilians, among them the emperor, freed their own slaves. A law of 1871 sponsored by Pedro provided for freedom at birth for all. Slaves were often encouraged to escape, and local governments granted emancipation. The place of the blacks was far less lowly in Brazilian society than it was in the United States even after the Civil War. By 1888 there were one-fourth as many slaves as in 1822. In that year, the emperor's daughter, Princess

* The upper house was appointed for life by the emperor from lists submitted by the provinces. The lower house was elected by a complicated but comparatively fair method by literate, tax-paying males.

Isabel, who was serving temporarily as regent, urged parliament to free all slaves. This was done. But the anger of the sugar planters of the northeast and coffee growers in the central coastal area turned on the empire.

This factor, and the defection of important church officials who thought that the empire was restricting their freedom, removed the historic supporters of the monarchy. Moreover, the educated classes were becoming entranced with positivism, a doctrine developed by the French philosopher, Auguste Comte (1798–1857); it rejected many traditional values and glorified scientific progress. Groups in the military were particularly receptive to positivism and some turned to republicanism. After 1880 the army made ever-more stringent demands on the regime for larger budgets and more status. Late in 1889 it sought to force a change in the ministry. As always, Pedro refused to let the army dictate to him. In November 1889 a group of generals isolated him in the palace, forced him to abdicate, and shipped the imperial family to Europe before the populace knew what was happening.

Although there were only a few republicans in Brazil, a federal republic was now proclaimed. Church and state were separated, the army enlarged, the bureaucracy restaffed, and the states allowed more independence. The first president was ousted after he sent troops into Parliament in 1891, and his two successors had to contend with several uprisings, notably a weird backlands rebellion led by a religious fanatic.* By 1900 the republic was secure, and monarchist sentiment died out. The Old Republic, as it is now called, was more militarized and corrupt than the empire, and it governed less effectively. Few Brazilians voted (only literate males had suffrage) and, in any case, state political bosses counted the ballots.

At the time of independence, Brazil apparently was more backward than the Spanish states. By 1900 it was in the first rank economically, technologically, and culturally. The rubber boom had brought life to the Amazon vastness. Coffee exports to the United States were burgeoning, shifting the axis of the economy from the sugar-

Pedro II.

producing northeast to the south central region. Under Pedro II, foreign investment had been encouraged but restricted to prevent monopolies. Immigrants had come in large numbers from Europe after the African slave trade ended. Steamships, a few railroads, cables, telegraphs, banks, streetcars, and public utilities were changing the character of economic life. A few factories or mills made consumer goods. Yet, by World War I, Brazil had weak political institutions that were unresponsive to the growing desires of the masses.

Mexico

After the final flight of Santa Anna in 1855, Mexican liberals attempted to restructure the country as a secular democracy under civilian control in the *Reforma*. Crucial to this program was the ending of special privileges of the army and the church and the division of church lands among independent farmers. Reaction came fast, but the cruel civil war of

---

* This fearsome affair, taking many lives and lasting several years, was immortalized in Brazil's most famous work of literature, *Os Sertões.*

Benito Juárez.

tional feeling against the invaders and aid for the patriots from the United States after its Civil War ended. By 1867 Maximilian had been defeated and executed. Again Juárez resumed the presidency. Entering the capital in a plain black carriage and wearing civilian clothes, he seemed to personify Mexican nationalism and the *Reforma.*

Under the restored republic, Mexico healed some of its wounds but was still in a lamentable condition. General Porfirio Díaz, a mestizo, forced his way to the presidency in 1876 and set up a dictatorship that lasted until 1911. Hypocritically claiming to be an heir of Juárez, he allowed the laws of the *Reforma,* including its constitution of 1857, to continue in name but, in fact, he ruled autocratically through a strong army and a single party that managed all elections and staffed the offices of the supposedly federal republic. An army of rural guards ended banditry; and tough "political chiefs" carried out the dictator's will if local units of government hesitated. Most Mexicans were probably grateful to Díaz for pacifying their long-turbulent country. Abroad, he was showered with praise as a genius who had turned Mexico into a civilized society.

In many respects Díaz was a modernizing leader. For the first time since colonial days Mexico had a sound currency and good credit. Foreign investors learned that they were highly welcome, and capital poured in. Many Europeans bought haciendas, or plantations, that the laws of the *Reforma* had intended to be divided among Mexican farmers. Aliens also established small factories and distribution businesses with official blessings. Americans purchased huge ranches in the north. Mexico's historic mining industry, long in decline, recovered with the introduction of the cyanide process and other techniques provided by foreigners. Great petroleum deposits along the Gulf were sold to British and American companies. With the collusion of the government, foreigners built public utilities and railroads all over Mexico and usually operated them. The growth of commerce and production largely financed abroad seemed to indicate that Mexico was becoming one of the most advanced Latin American nations.

On the other hand, angry forces were gath-

1858 to 1861 ended with victory for the *Reforma* and its leader, now Mexico's greatest hero, Benito Juárez. A full-blooded Indian in a country whose political life had long been dominated by whites, Juárez was small, homely, and awkward as a speaker. He wrote well, however, and his proclamations appealed to the idealism of Mexicans. He was fiercely honest in a country noted for corruption, and he had a strong mystical quality that shamed cynics. After only one year as president in the capital, he faced another threat, this time with the conservatives being supported by Napoleon III and French troops taking advantage of United States preoccupation with the Civil War. Although the French intervention began as an effort to collect debts that Europeans claimed from Mexicans, Napoleon III planned to establish Mexico as a client state that would produce minerals for the benefit of French capitalists. The well-meaning Archduke Maximilian of Austria was induced to become emperor of Mexico. Maximilian had hopes of being a modern, liberal monarch. Thus he alienated his chief supporters, those who opposed the *Reforma.* Of greater importance were the outrage of Mexican naering. Mexican nationalism was offended by the presence of aliens and by their arrogance. Mexico became one of the first countries in modern times to rebel against economic imperialism. By the 1890s it was clear that the Díaz regime regarded mixed-blooded or Indian Mexicans as inferiors who should not be encouraged to improve their social condition or attain an education. Also, anticlericalism increased as Díaz permitted the church secretly to recover much of its ancient position and wealth. Workers in factories and mines were oppressed even more than was common in most of the world around 1900. Díaz plainly opposed their unionization. Worst of all was the need for land reform. Díaz had applied the land division laws of the *Reforma* aimed at the church against Indian tribes as well, with the result that many people were driven from their communal lands by the rural guards or the army and resettled in distant areas. A thousand persons, some foreign, owned nine-tenths of the arable land, while nine million Mexicans owned no land at all. Workers on the haciendas were mere peons, underfed, uneducated, likely to be alcoholic, and forever in debt to the owners. Despite the prosperity and beautification that characterized the face of Mexico, despair seemed eternal.

Díaz was 80 in 1910. Yet he made no plans for a transfer of power. On September 16 he duly celebrated the centennial of Father Hidalgo's cry for independence while guests from all over the world honored him and the populace applauded with its usual reverence. Yet, in May 1911, Díaz was compelled to flee Mexico, his regime having crumbled suddenly before Emiliano Zapata in the southern sugarlands, Pancho Villa in the northern ranches, and Francisco Madero, a onetime beneficiary of the Díaz establishment who now spoke for Mexico's accumulated wrath, leading a revolutionary movement that Mexicans even today regard as continuing. (See pp. 812–815.)

The Latin American economy, severely set back by the Wars of Independence, recovered so slowly that it lost ground relative to the rest of the Western world, particularly the United States. In the Argentine of Rosas, the Mexico of Santa Anna, and other countries ruled by reactionary dictators, there was almost no growth in production and commerce. Development began by the mid-nineteenth century: coffee culture in Brazil and New Granada, guano and nitrate excavation on the Pacific coast, some revival of mining, and a rise of sugar production in the Caribbean area. Late in the century a rubber boom brought prosperity to parts of Brazil and Peru. The cultivation of bananas gave Central America a major export item, as did that of henequen in Mexico. Mining continued to recover, with copper and oil becoming great income earners. Perhaps the most sensational growth was that of the livestock and grain industries in Argentina and Uruguay. Economic development was facilitated by the steamship, railroad, refrigeration, canning, and the use of modern machinery in mining, sugar refining, and textile mills.

Latin America's economy was based largely on the export of raw materials; thus landed wealth was of prime importance. Only big owners could cope with changing business conditions abroad. The disproportionate concentration of land prevalent in colonial times continued or, in the case of Argentina, developed. Only Haiti, Costa Rica, and Uruguay escaped this problem. Elsewhere, great planters, ranchers, and miners controlled most of the wealth while the masses lived in a semiservile state. The bourgeoisie grew very slowly as commerce expanded. Not native capitalists but aliens financed most of the public improvements and economic development and they generally withdrew their profits from Latin America. Many, however, lost their money or were cheated by corrupt governments. The industrial proletariat, centered in areas of mines, railroads, and factories, was small and not yet significant in politics. The surest way to gain an income and property was to be successful in political struggles, but government was the most risky business of all.

Despite the plans of the liberators, public education flourished only in Argentina, Chile, and Uruguay, and even there only after many years of frustration. A few rulers, notably Pedro II of Brazil and Juárez of Mexico, sought to increase schooling, but with disappointing results. Private education benefited only a few. The church provided less schooling than in colonial times. Except in Argentina and Chile, universities also declined until the twentieth century.

Latin America has usually been considered imitative rather than creative in literature, music, and painting. It certainly had an appreciative if small reading public and provided audiences for performers from Europe. Although its own artists, composers, and writers of this period were long neglected, they are now receiving more attention outside of Latin America.

The Roman Catholic church lost ground after the end of the colonial period. Many educated persons then became skeptics or espoused Darwinism (see p. 46) and positivism; the virtual end of censorship facilitated the spread of their ideas. Furthermore, the church lost much of its fluid capital and treasures during revolutions and civil wars. Missions were often ruined, and schools and welfare agencies were closed. The attack on church landed wealth by modernists or political opportunists also was harmful to the institution. The number and quality of clergymen tended to fall as church prestige declined and ties with Rome weakened. Religious toleration came to prevail in most countries, and Protestant missionaries and non-Catholic immigrants broke the monopoly of the church. Everywhere, liberals tended to be anticlerical or even anti-Catholic, while conservatives were likely to support the historic prerogatives of the church.

Latin America's population did not grow rapidly compared to population in other areas during the nineteenth century. The United States alone came to have as many people as all of Latin America. Bleak economic and poor sanitary conditions caused an extremely high rate of mortality and prevented a large natural increase. Black immigration was cut at the time of independence and was entirely stopped by mid-century, when Cuba and Brazil ceased importing slaves. White immigration was not substantial until the last third of the century, when Italians, Spaniards, Portuguese, Germans, and various ethnic groups from Austria-Hungary deluged the southeastern part of South America and arrived in significant numbers elsewhere. Haiti remained black; Costa Rica, Uruguay, and Argentina were almost wholly Caucasian; and Ecuador, Peru, and Bolivia had Indian majorities. In general, the blending of the races continued until most countries were mainly mestizo or mulatto. In pluralistic societies the importance of being white declined. Yet whites dominated the economy and, more often than not, the government. Even so, Latin America was racially tolerant compared to the rest of the world.

Britain's naval supremacy was the chief reason that Latin America was not victimized by European powers seeking colonies as was Africa. Except for the French invasion of Mexico in 1862, Latin America suffered little more than naval blockades or indignities from Europeans, including the British. The United States, however, annexed nearly half of Mexico and made Cuba a protectorate after removing the Spanish army. Other protectorates followed: Panama, the Dominican Republic, Haiti, and Nicaragua. Peaceful commerce between Latin America and the United States grew markedly, and North Americans displaced Europeans as investors by the end of World War I. The Pan-American movement (begun in 1889) and the protestations of successive United States Presidents pointed more to harmonious partnership than to imperialism. But "dollar diplomacy," or the use of armed forces to acquire financial benefits for North Americans, seemed to endanger the freedom of many nations early in the twentieth century, and hostility toward *yanqui* imperialism continued to grow.

SUGGESTED READINGS

Haring, C. H., *The Spanish Empire in America.* Revised edition. New York: Oxford University Press, 1952. Paperpack.
Emphasis on political structure.

Diffie, Bailey W., *Latin-American Civilization: Colonial Period.* Harrisburg: Stackpole & Sons, 1945.
Stresses economic, racial, and social aspects.

Gibson, Charles, *Spain in America.* New York: Harper & Row, 1967. Paperback.
The most modern treatment of institutions.

Madariaga, Salvador de, *The Rise of the Spanish Empire in America* and *The Fall of the Spanish Empire in America.* New York: The Macmillan Company, 1947.
Brilliantly written and spirited defense of Spain's record.

Stein, Stanley J. and Barbara H., *The Colonial Heritage of Latin America.* New York: Oxford University Press, 1970. Paperback.
An essay on the persisting economic dependence of Latin America on the North Atlantic lands.

Parry, J. H., *The Spanish Seaborne Empire.* London: Hutchinson & Co., 1966.
An extensive and provocative account.

Humphreys, R. A. and Lynch, John, eds., *The Origins of the Latin American Revolutions, 1808–1826.* New York: Alfred A. Knopf, 1965. Paperback.
Good selections showing many aspects of the Wars of Independence.

Masur, Gerhard, *Simón Bolívar.* Albuquerque: University of New Mexico Press, 1948.
The soundest treatment of the life and times of the Liberator.

Freyre, Gilberto, *The Masters and the Slaves.* Trans. and abridged. New York: Alfred A. Knopf, 1964. Paperback.
Portuguese, Blacks, and Indians in Brazil.

Boxer, Charles R., *The Golden Age of Brazil.* Berkeley: University of California Press, 1962.
Superb treatment of the later colonial period in Brazil.

PART *Imperialism and War to 1919*

Having already founded and lost great colonial empires in the Americas, the European nations in increasing numbers began exploiting Asia and Africa during the nineteenth century. Except for parts of India, which the British had begun to colonize somewhat earlier, those two continents had been largely free of European influence until then. Yet practically all of Africa was partitioned in just over twenty years, beginning in 1881, and some Africans were driven into forced labor, like those of the New World three centuries earlier. The heavier concentrations of population and more impressive civilizations of the Middle and Far East made the Europeans treat those areas differently; also, partition of the Ottoman and Manchu empires was avoided because it was more likely to lead to war among the major powers. But exploitation short of political domination was common during the nineteenth century, as in the case of British merchants pushing opium on the Chinese people or French bankers pushing high-interest loans on Ottoman and Egyptian monarchs. European enclaves from Shanghai to Casablanca ignored local laws and customs, while Christian missionaries tried to win the very souls of the colonized peoples. Although World War I did stimulate nascent nationalist movements in India, China, and the Arab world, it also brought European colonialism to its peak through the League of Nations Mandates.

The responses of Asian and African leaders to European imperialism varied widely. At one extreme, African chieftains sold their lands, resources, and workers to European entrepreneurs merely for the right to remain as puppet rulers in their traditional societies. At the other extreme, Japanese nobles and businessmen restructured their nation's institutions and habits not only in order to resist Western exploitation but also to become imperialists themselves. Between these two extremes were varying degrees of "defensive modernization" and anti-Western nationalism, all of which proved futile before 1914. By then it was becoming increasingly clear that, if European rule was ever to be thrown off, European methods would have to be used; it was not possible to operate modern military hardware, locomotives, and sewage systems without changing peoples' traditional attitudes and norms for behavior. Sun Yat-sen, the Young Turks, and other "Third World" leaders soon learned this lesson.

Yet the peoples of Asia and Africa were far from completely absorbed in responding to European penetration; they also had their own histories. The most momentous event of the mid-nineteenth century was the Taiping Rebellion, which took the lives of millions of Chinese and nearly destroyed the Manchu dynasty. A few years later the Meiji Restoration in

Japan brought forced modernization more quickly and intensively than anywhere else in the world. Population movements and tribal rivalries continued in Africa under European rule. Arab nationalists were primarily concerned with freeing themselves from Turkish rule until Britain and France took over their territories after World War I. In India the British presence could do nothing to resolve and at times even helped to widen the Hindu-Muslim split. The 1911 revolution in China initiated almost forty years of civil war and false starts until the Communists finally took power after World War II.

The first successful communist revolution occurred in Russia in November 1917 as a direct consequence of World War I. As in the case of China thirty years later, this revolution succeeded partly because of the inability of the existing regime to wage war successfully and partly because the peasant masses, once mobilized, demanded land and bread instead of further military sacrifices. In the more highly modernized nations most people supported their governments until the end of World War I, but even so they insisted that the "democracy of the trenches" be extended into the postwar period. Thus, World War I not only sparked the Russian Revolution but it also opened an age of mass involvement in public affairs on a scale hitherto unknown.

CHAPTER 18

The Initial Impact of the Modern States on Asia

During the early stages of European imperialism each of the three major geographical areas of Asia had different characteristics. Mughal India (1525–1857) was a declining empire, beset by religious tensions between its Islamic rulers and its Hindu subjects. It was in the midst of a process of institutional decentralization as local lords appropriated local power. Ch'ing (Manchu) China (1644–1911) seemed more stable by contrast. Although it, too, had a reigning house ethnically different from its subjects, rulers and ruled shared the same cultural values. The authority of their Confucian tradition rigidly denied modernizing influences. Tokugawa Japan (1603–1868), on the other hand, experienced fundamental social and economic changes that enabled it to develop more rapidly than the others into a modern nation-state.

These three countries reacted to the West in different ways. Although their responses were partly the result of historical stages of Western trade and conquest, they also reflected the particular social and political patterns of each country.

DECLINE OF THE MUGHALS IN INDIA

As we saw in Chapter 7, throughout the seventeenth century all of northern India and much of the Deccan were united under the rule of the Mughal Empire. The great Akbar bequeathed to his immediate successors Jahangir (1605–1627) and Shah Jahan (1627–1658) a legacy of religious toleration and administrative efficiency that they retained while expanding the empire southward and elaborating a court of already lavish magnificence. Beneath this magnificent façade, however, the processes of decay were at work by the laters years of Shah Jahan's reign. Under Shah Jahan's vigorous and forceful successor, Aurangzeb (1658–1707), ominous cracks opened up in the imperial structure.

Islamic Resurgence

A man of austere and puritanical temper, Aurangzeb was unlike any of his predecessors. Whereas they, and especially Akbar,

The Mughal Emperor Aurangzeb (1658–1707).

was the closest the Mughals came to merging Hinduism and Islam.

But the forces of orthodoxy remained strong within the Muslim community, and the Muslims refused to accept this dilution of Islamic doctrine, which they considered a heretical formulation. The orthodox resurgence had begun some fifty years before Aurangzeb's accession with the writings of Shaikh Ahmad Sirhindi (1563–1624). While acknowledging the value of mystical experience, he insisted that such experience must be confined within the bounds of classical Islamic doctrine, that only the revelations of Muhammed and the teachings of the law (*shariat*) could give validity to religious experience. Aurangzeb stood forth as the political champion of this new orthodoxy. He came to power, over the bitter opposition of Dara Shukoh, largely because of the appeal of his religious policy to the Muslim nobility of the empire. He celebrated his triumph in the succession struggle by having his brother executed as a heretic.

The victory of Aurangzeb resolved the religious crisis within Indian Islam. But the domination of Islam separated the rulers from the Hindu masses, causing a political crisis. Aurangzeb passed such measures as the reimposition of the poll tax on unbelievers and the levy of discriminatory tolls on Hindu traders, which produced widespread disaffection among the Hindus. Their resentment helped to trigger brief rebellions among the warlike Rajputs and Sikhs, yet it did not go deep enough to threaten the basic stability of the empire.

Deccan Conflict

A major objective of Mughal policy, as of earlier northern empires, was expansion into the Deccan. Each emperor had pushed the line of Mughal control further south until by 1686 the last of the old Muslim kingdoms of the Deccan had fallen before the Mughal onslaught. At the same time, however, a new Hindu power was emerging in the remote and barren hill country of Maharashtra. A society of sturdy peasants, united by a strong devotional (*bhakti*) faith, the Marathas rose to political prominence in the mid-seventeenth century under the leadership of the dynamic Shivaji (1627–1680). At first only an ambi-

had sought to unite all Indians in devotion to the throne, Aurangzeb subordinated all else to the revival and purification of the Islamic religion in India. This religious zeal emerged from a fear for the future of the Muslim faith in a Hindu land. As the religion of the majority, Hinduism posed a threat to the distinctive features of the alien faith. The tolerant Akbar had pointed the way to a reconciliation of these faiths with his royal cult, the *Din Illahi,* and his patronage of radical *sufi* mysticism. Much of Mughal art and music reflected in their form and subject matter this search for principles common to Hinduism and Islam. The pantheistic philosophy of Aurangzeb's brother, Dara Shukoh, who translated the Hindu Upanishads into Persian and exalted them as the essence of pure monotheism,

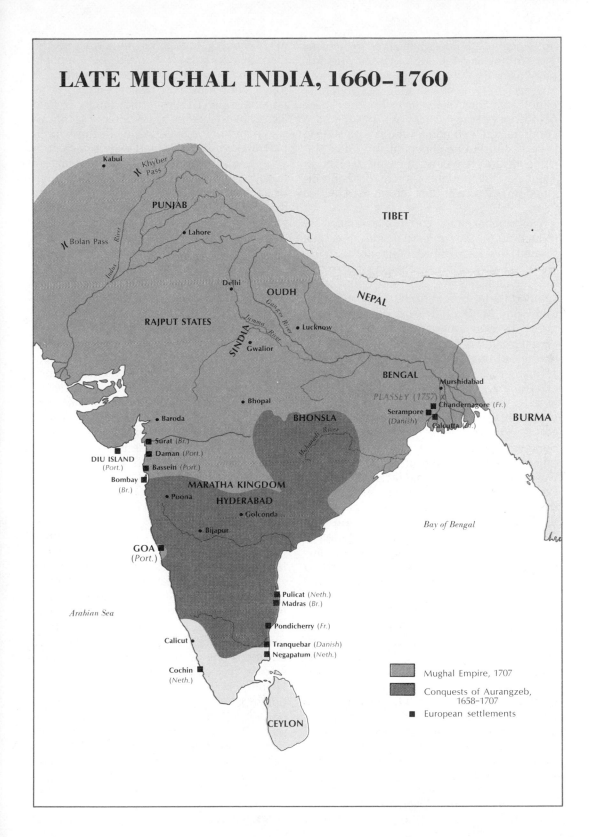

LATE MUGHAL INDIA, 1660–1760

Kabul

Khyber Pass

PUNJAB

Bolan Pass

Indus River

Lahore

TIBET

Delhi

OUDH

NEPAL

RAJPUT STATES

Jumna River

Ganges River

Lucknow

SINDIA

Gwalior

BENGAL

Murshidabad

PLASSEY (1757)

Serampore *(Danish)*

Chandernagore *(Fr.)*

Calcutta *(Br.)*

BURMA

Bhopal

BHONSLA

Mahanadi River

Baroda

Surat *(Br.)*

Daman *(Port.)*

DIU ISLAND *(Port.)*

Bassein *(Port.)*

Bombay *(Br.)*

MARATHA KINGDOM

Poona

HYDERABAD

Golconda

Bijapur

Bay of Bengal

GOA *(Port.)*

Arabian Sea

Pulicat *(Neth.)*

Madras *(Br.)*

Pondicherry *(Fr.)*

Calicut

Tranquebar *(Danish)*

Negapatum *(Neth.)*

Cochin *(Neth.)*

CEYLON

Mughal Empire, 1707

Conquests of Aurangzeb, 1658–1707

■ European settlements

545   *The Initial Impact of the Modern States on Asia*

tious petty fiefholder, Shivaji soon became the symbol and focus of Maratha regional patriotism. By skillfully exploiting these sentiments—to which he added a touch of Hindu religious revivalism—in the space of little more than twenty years Shivaji built a compact and well-administered state, able to keep its Muslim neighbors at bay. After Shivaji's death, however, the full weight of Mughal military might was turned against his kingdom in a war that lasted twenty-five years.

The Mughal strategy in this war called for reduction of the numerous hill forts that formed the base of Maratha power. This approach was ultimately successful in destroying Shivaji's well-knit kingdom, but it strained the resources of the Mughal Empire to the utmost. The newly conquered Deccan territories were ravaged by the march and countermarch of large armies, the north was drained of treasure to finance the incessant campaigning. And, perhaps most serious of all, Aurangzeb's continued presence at the head of the army in the south, where he could not effectively supervise the working of his administration, opened the way to oppression and misgovernment by imperial officials throughout the north. The problem was made worse by the fact that Mughal salaries were customarily paid not in cash but by temporary assignments of cultivated land (*jaghir*) from which officials collected their own pay. Their constant temptation to exploit these lands ruthlessly was normally checked by vigilance from the top and by frequent transfer to new *jaghir* lands. But frequent transfer had disadvantages too, for an official who knew that his tenure of a *jaghir* would be short had an incentive to quickly squeeze all he could out of the peasantry even to the point of leaving the area ruined. The exactions of officials had become severe even before the Maratha wars. François Bernier, a French traveler, noted in the 1660s that cultivators often either "perish in consequence of the bad treatment they receive from the Governor" or "deprived of the means of existence leave the country and take up menial jobs as bearers of burdens, carriers of water, or servants to horsemen."

As imperial control over the official class slackened, the claimants to *jaghir* land grew in number. Throughout the war in the Deccan, Aurangzeb handed out imperial titles on an increasingly lavish scale in a frantic effort to win the Deccani nobles to the imperial side. The resulting scarcity of land forced many nobles to go without *jaghir* assignments for long periods, while those fortunate enough to have land were reluctant to give it up. The later years of Aurangzeb's reign thus witnessed the beginning of an intense struggle for *jaghirs,* accompanied by the growth of factional alignments as various groups among the nobles sought to mobilize power and influence at court.

Disintegration of the Empire

After the firm hand of Aurangzeb was removed, factional strife among the officials combined with the disaffection of the Hindus and the economic dislocation of the peasantry to bring an end to the integrity of the empire. Aurangzeb's successor, Bahadur Shah (1707–1712), a man of good sense and generosity, tried valiantly to arrest the decay, but he was an old man with only a short time to rule, and his conciliatory policies flowed as much from weakness as from good will. He was followed by a series of weak and ineffectual emperors who were little more than the puppets of court factions in Delhi. The most astute of these emperors, Muhammad Shah (1719–1748), managed to survive for thirty years by playing off the various noble factions against each other. But even he had no capacity for effective leadership. As a result, although the empire still possessed a great deal of prestige and still exercised authority over much of north India, it no longer commanded the loyalty of the ruling elite. For them, imperial service was increasingly only a cloak for personal advancement. Even the ablest servants of the empire, despairing of its regeneration, soon abandoned the struggle at Delhi and carved out principalities of their own. The most important of these Muslim successor states were Bengal, Oudh, and Hyderabad, the latter founded, ironically, by one of Aurangzeb's most devoted lieutenants, the incorruptible Nizam-ul-Mulk. The petty *jaghir* holders and Hindu chiefs rapidly followed the example of their superiors, so that by 1750 India was a maze of small regional

The Husainabad Imambara at Lucknow. Built about 1840 by the Nawab of Oudh, it combines debased Mughal and Victorian styles in a way typical of the princes under the British.

and local jurisdictions, all nominally subordinate to Delhi but effectively independent.

As the Mughals' rule weakened, other powers sought to wrest the empire from them. Most likely to supplant them were the Marathas, who had recovered from their defeats by Aurangzeb with renewed strength and self-confidence. By the 1730s and 1740s their mobile cavalry forces were ranging as far north as the suburbs of Delhi and as far east as Orissa and western Bengal. But much in the aims and organization of the Maratha state prevented the realization of any imperial ambition. Even before Aurangzeb destroyed Shivaji's well-knit kingdom, the Marathas had gained much of their revenue by regularly plundering adjacent territories. The income these raids produced, collected methodically every year at a fixed rate, made possible the maintenance of a large military machine in a poor country. Indeed, the Maratha army financed itself. Such a system, however suited it might have been to the Maharashtra region, did not endear the Marathas to their neighbors. The Mughal wars confirmed the Marathas in their plundering habits so that their eighteenth-century revival was accompanied by the collection of tribute over ever-widening areas of the subcontinent. Since the Marathas spared neither Hindu nor Muslim, they could not even claim to embody a national Hindu sentiment. Their vision was too narrow and their aims too selfish to enable them to provide a real alternative to the Mughal Empire.

The Maratha bid for mastery in India was stopped short in 1761 when they were defeated on the battlefield by Afghans under Ahmad Shah Abdali. Invaders from the northwest, like Alexander and Timur (Tamurlane) before them, the Afghans swept down upon the defenseless people of Delhi and the Punjab on several occasions during the 1740s and 1750s. However, rejecting the role of empire-builder, they left India immediately after their victory over the Marathas

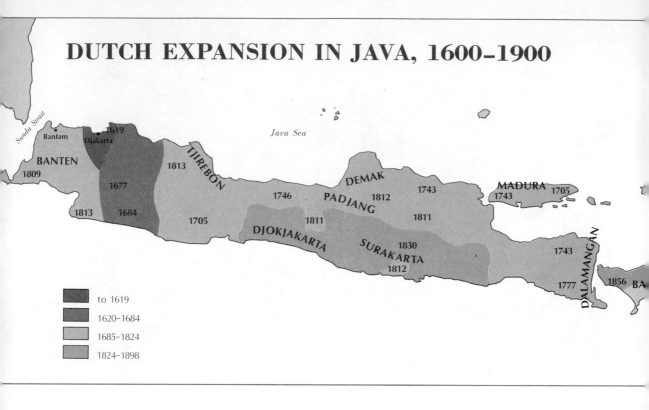

DUTCH EXPANSION IN JAVA, 1600–1900

Sunda Strait

Bantam

Djakarta 1619

Java Sea

BANTEN
1809

TJIREBON

1813

1677

1813   1684

1705

DJOKJAKARTA

1746

PADJANG

DEMAK

1812

SURAKARTA

1811

1830

1812

1743

1811

1743

MADURA
1743

1705

DALAMANGAN

1743

1777

1856 BA

to 1619

1620–1684

1685–1824

1824–1898

and never returned. Thus the Afghan-Maratha conflict meant little in the long run, but it did determine that neither power was to inherit the mantle of the Mughals. The restoration of unity in India had to await the coming of a foreign power with new skills and new ideas.

EARLY EUROPEAN CONTACT: THE CONQUEST OF INDIA AND INDONESIA

Although the first European conquests in Asia were won by the Portuguese, following the successful voyage of Vasco da Gama in 1498, they did not attempt to carve out an extensive land empire for themselves. They preferred instead to control the trade in spices by a network of fortified bases backed by naval superiority in the Indian Ocean. The first steps toward empire in Asia were taken in the eighteenth century by the two northern European powers that had supplanted the Portuguese—Holland and England.

Dutch Spice Trade

Practical businessmen, the Dutch from the outset established themselves at the source of the spice trade in the East Indies. They set up their capital on the island of Java at Batavia (now, as before their arrival, known as Ja-karta) and from there built up a trading network extending from South Africa through Ceylon to Japan. The widespread character of the trade reflected the problem of finding goods to exchange for spices. The people of the Indies had little use for the woolen goods and other staples of northern Europe, while the Dutch and English governments, imbued with mercantilist principles, opposed the drain of gold and silver involved in cash payment. But Indian cotton textiles and other Asian produce were salable in the East Indies. So the Dutch entered into the local carrying trade, using the profits from the sale of cotton cloth and the hiring out of their ships to purchase spices. Many of their outposts were established exclusively to facilitate this trade.

In the East Indies the Dutch trading posts slowly evolved into centers of political dominion. The change came most rapidly on Java, where the Dutch Company at Batavia became embroiled in the wars of the neighboring chieftains, and on the small spice-producing islands, where the Dutch were anxious to control output so as to retain high monopoly profits. By 1800 they controlled the whole of Java, though not the larger, sparsely settled islands of Borneo, Sumatra, and the Celebes. The process of conquest was both speeded and made seemingly painless by the nature of Javanese society. The peasantry, composed of self-sufficient rice growers only loosely tied to society outside the family and the village, readily acquiesced in Dutch overlordship. Moreover, the Dutch were not interested in tampering with the lives and customs of the people. They left local administration in the hands of the old aristocracy, now called Regents, who were given a formal place in the new bureaucracy and subjected only to general supervision by the Dutch.

The Culture System

During the nineteenth century the Dutch continued to value the East Indies primarily for its commercial raw materials and thus concentrated their efforts upon the forcible collection of native produce for shipment to Holland. This tribute-paying relationship was formalized in 1830, after the abolition of the Dutch East India Company, with the introduction of the Culture System under Johannes Van Den Bosch. Under this system, the peasant bound himself to cultivate on one-fifth of his land crops for government export in lieu of paying taxes. This led to the production of new crops — sugar, coffee, and tea, in particular — and to rapid expansion of the area devoted to production for export. The Culture System thus was highly successful in developing the resources of the Indies and in enhancing the wealth of the Netherlands. But its effects upon Indonesian society were less attractive, for the Dutch monopoly of overseas trade destroyed native trading and isolated the subsistence peasant economy from the profitable commercial sector. At the same time, as Dutch peace and order encouraged rapid population growth, more and more people were crowded into a static economy that could sustain them only by elaborate and exhausting efforts at reclamation and irrigation. By the 1870s, as a result, the Javanese peasantry had little to show for almost a century of labor for the Dutch.

The British Enter India

The British first established themselves as traders at a few points on the coast of India and soon followed the Dutch pattern of taking control over ever-increasing areas of the interior. The process of imperial expansion began in Bengal, where the ambitions of the young Clive, the greed of the merchant factors of the East India Company, and the Anglo-French rivalries of the mid-eighteenth century combined to bring about the momentous Battle of Plassey in June 1757. (See pp. 346–347.) As a result of this encounter, the British forced the French out of Bengal and installed the complaisant Mir Jafar as *Nawab* (provincial governor) in place of the contentious Siraj-ud-daulah. The victory at Plassey did not produce the stable puppet regime Clive had hoped for but instead a state of anarchy and confusion unparalleled in Bengal. For almost ten years after Plassey, the British, despite their military predominance, refused all responsibility for government. Instead, excited to feverish greed by stories of the great wealth of the country, they devoted themselves to scarcely concealed plundering, mainly by extorting bribes and abusing their free-trade privileges. Even the East India Company directors at home joined in, for they saw in the revenues of Bengal a source of funds to pay for their export purchases. Mir Jafar was powerless to halt these depradations, and when his successor, Mir Kasim, a vigorous and capable ruler, unexpectedly tried to confine the English to their former role of overseas traders, he was promptly deposed and then defeated at the battle of Baksar (1764).

Responsibility and Reform

After Baksar, the British in Bengal, recognizing at last that there was no other alternative to disorder, slowly began to accept responsibility for the administration of the province, first over revenue, then over judi-

An English officer enjoying Hindu entertainment in the early days of the empire, from Tom Raw, the Griffin, *published in 1824.*

cial affairs. At the same time the Company directors began the arduous process of disciplining their servants in India. Private trade and the receipt of presents were prohibited from the 1770s onward, and in 1805 a special college was set up at Haileybury in England for the training of prospective civil servants. Within a generation the rapacious "nabobs" of Clive's day were transformed into the incorruptible Indian Civil Service, renowned as the "steel frame" of British India.

The East India Company, now gorged with empire, still had to be made responsible to the will of the English people. The first steps in this direction were taken by the Regulating Act of 1773, but decisive measures came only with the Parliamentary inquiries of the 1780s, culminating in the impeachment of Warren Hastings (governor-general 1772–1784). Hastings, basically an honest man and a devoted servant of the Company, was made the scapegoat for the shortcomings of his generation in India. Tried for acts of intimidation and extortion against the princes of Oudh and Benares, which would have gone unnoticed a few years before, he

emerged from the lengthy proceedings—which at times took on the character of a personal vendetta against him—with his reputation cleared but his spirit broken. Nevertheless, the trial helped gain general recognition for the principle that officials in India were accountable in England for their acts and that the Company must exercise its power as a trustee for the benefit of the people over whom it ruled. From the 1780s onward a Board of Control in the British cabinet supervised Indian affairs, while in 1813 the Company was stripped of its trading functions in India and confined to government.

The Extension of Dominion

During the last quarter of the eighteenth century, British Bengal, reorganized and stabilized under Hastings and his successor, General Charles Cornwallis (governor-general 1786–1793), took its place in the system of regional or "country" powers left behind by the collapse of the Mughal Empire. It was allied with some, occasionally at war with others, most notably the Marathas, but not aggressive or expansive, or even noticeably dominant. Yet, in the early years of the nine-

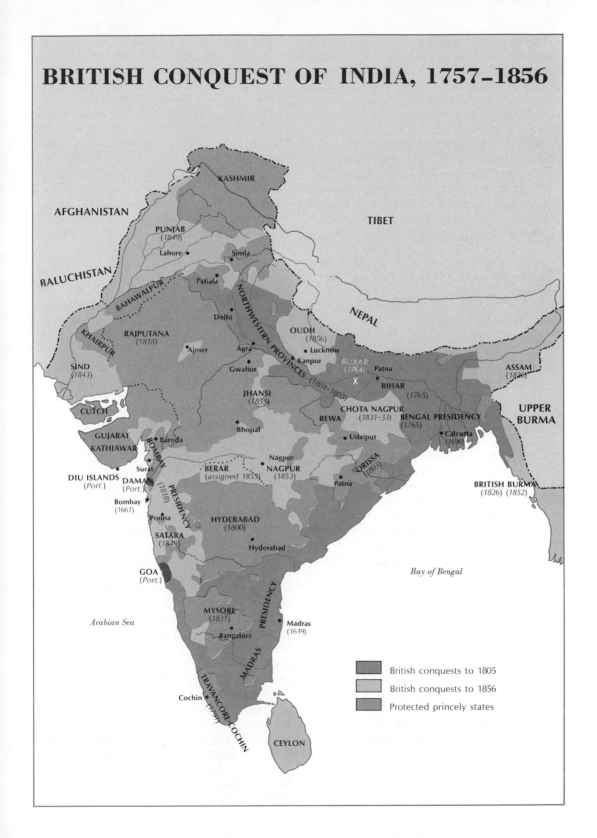

BRITISH CONQUEST OF INDIA, 1757–1856

AFGHANISTAN

KASHMIR

TIBET

PUNJAB
(1849)
Lahore •
• Simla

BALUCHISTAN

BAHAWALPUR

• Patiala

NEPAL

KHAIRPUR

• Delhi

NORTHWESTERN PROVINCES

RAJPUTANA
(1818)

• Ajmer

OUDH
(1856)
• Lucknow
Kanpur
• Agra

ASSAM
(1826)

SIND
(1843)

• Gwalior

BUXAR
(1764)
X

Patna •

BIHAR
(1765)

UPPER
BURMA

CUTCH

JHANSI
(1853)

CHOTA NAGPUR
(1831–33)

REWA

BENGAL PRESIDENCY
(1765)

• Bhopal

• Udaipur

• Calcutta
(1690)

GUJARAT

KATHIAWAR

Baroda •

BOMBAY

Nagpur
•

BERAR
(assigned 1853)

NAGPUR
(1853)

ORISSA
(1803)

DIU ISLANDS
(Port.)

DAMAN
(Port.)

Surat •

• Patna

BRITISH BURMA
(1826) (1852)

Bombay
(1661)

PRESIDENCY
(1818)

• Poona

HYDERABAD
(1800)

Bay of Bengal

SATARA
(1849)

• Hyderabad

GOA
(Port.)

Arabian Sea

MYSORE
(1831)

• Bangalore

MADRAS

PRESIDENCY

Madras
(1639)

Cochin •

TRAVANCORE-COCHIN
(1795)

CEYLON

British conquests to 1805

British conquests to 1856

Protected princely states

teenth century, with extraordinary suddenness, the political scene was transformed; by 1818 Britain ruled all India, directly or indirectly, except the Indus Valley and the Punjab in the northwest. Several forces pushed the British to take complete control. The French threat seemed far more menacing in the time of Napoleon than it had a half-century before. Moreover, the other Indian powers were neither stable nor peaceable in their intentions: Tipu Sultan of Mysore was implacably hostile to the British, while the Marathas, now divided into five major principalities, were constantly at war with one another as well as with the British and were scarcely able even to maintain their own authority. In central India they gave protection to bands of marauders, the Pindari, who raided indiscriminately in every direction.

In the midst of such anarchy and confusion, the British saw their supremacy as the cheapest and most effective way of preserving their position in India and securing satisfactory conditions for trade. By the early nineteenth century, however, the trade in quality Indian handloom goods was declining. In its place was the profitable, if uncertain, trade in opium for the China market and the even more important long-term prospects for the sale of English manufactured goods opened up by the Industrial Revolution. Whereas the East Indies always remained for Holland a source of tropical raw materials, the British increasingly sought markets for Lancashire cotton and Birmingham iron. In a peaceful and united India they saw an almost limitless number of potential customers.

In this era of slow communication the pace of expansion depended largely on the energy and ambition of the officials on the spot. By far the most energetic of these was Lord Wellesley (governor-general 1799–1805). A man of clear imperial vision, he not only defeated Tipu and the Maratha chiefs in battle, annexing much of the territory they had controlled; he also incorporated the weaker and less hostile powers, such as Oudh and Hyderabad, into the British political system. He accomplished this feat by forcing them to sign so-called subsidiary treaties under which the British

guaranteed the native prince against all attacks in return for the payment of a subsidy and the stationing of British troops in his capital. The next major move forward came under Lord Hastings (governor-general 1813–1823; no relation of Warren Hastings). He extinguished Maratha and Rajput power, thus establishing British supremacy in central India, and fought but did not subdue the Gurkhas of Nepal, who henceforth remained a friendly but independent state on India's northern border. The final stage of conquest took place in the 1840s when British control was extended across the Indus to the gates of the Khyber Pass and the Afghan plateau.

Government of India

The early British administrators in Bengal, such as Warren Hastings, believed that the Company should rule in the Mughal tradition, providing a framework of security within which native society could order its own affairs. Sympathetic men interested in preserving Indian customs, they studied the ancient texts of Hinduism and helped revive Oriental scholarship, which found a home in the Asiatic Society of Sir William Jones. But even these men carried with them as Englishmen a belief in private property, individual responsibility before the law, and a court system in which adversaries confronted each other before a judge. These institutions, in their view, underlay a just civil order and could not be denied their Indian subjects. But their sudden introduction into the alien environment of India was highly disruptive. Remote, expensive, and little understood, the law courts, for instance, were often little more than speculative lotteries in which innocent victims were bamboozled by shrewd lawyers and moneylenders, while English judges, bound by strict rules of evidence and procedure, looked on helplessly.

In the Bengal countryside, in similar fashion, the award of private property rights in land elevated the *zamindars,* who had been *rajas* and tax collectors in the later Mughal era, into landlords expected to play the role of English gentry, improving their subjects' lot. Totally unprepared for such a change in their position, the *zamindars* quickly ran afoul of the new English system, which insisted on prompt and full payment of the land tax. Because of their slow ways, many found their estates sold for unpaid taxes to speculators from Calcutta. The greatest sufferers under the new land system, however, were the peasants. In the old days they had possessed hereditary rights of occupancy, and rents had been fixed in accord with customary principles of equity. Now, reduced to the status of tenants, the peasants were wholly dependent on their *zamindari* landlords. As population grew during the early nineteenth century and the *zamindars* became more accustomed to British ways, they began to demand more from the peasantry. The large rentals they obtained financed the brilliant cultural revival of nineteenth-century Bengal, but the *zamindars,* despite continued British prompting, never became improving landlords. Agriculture in Bengal remained backward and the peasantry continued to pay excessive rents until the very end of British rule.

During the first quarter of the nineteenth century the Conservative view of Indian government came under increasing attack as new ideas took root in Great Britain. Advancing industrialism and the rise of the middle class produced the new outlook found in the doctrines of utilitarian liberalism and Christian Evangelicalism. Although the one looked to reason and the other to God for salvation, both movements sought to liberate the individual from the constraints of custom and both had limitless faith in the power of ideas and institutions to mould men's character. Each movement viewed industrial Britain as the high point of modern civilization. India, "bound down to despotism and superstition," stood at the opposite pole. Its only hope lay in complete reformation. To this the reformers, headstrong and optimistic, dedicated themselves.

The missionaries gained entry to India in 1813, although a small and influential group, the Serampore Baptists, had arrived quietly twenty years earlier. The full impact of the reform movement was long delayed by the stubborn opposition of the Company to anything that might unsettle its Indian subjects. In 1828, however, reform at last reached the

highest levels of government with the appointment of Lord William Bentinck as governor-general, backed by the leading philosopher of Utilitarianism, James Mill, as Examiner in the India House at home. The seven years of Bentinck's rule laid the foundations of the modern liberal state in India. Bentinck's first act of reform was the prohibition of *sati,* widow-burning, in 1829. Next came the suppression of *thagi,* the practice of ritual murder and robbery in the name of the goddess Kali. Both acts were justified by an appeal to universal moral principles of decency and humanity, although the values invoked were Western, not Indian. Here, however, positive interference stopped. The government carefully avoided joining the missionaries in further direct attacks on the customs or values of Hindu society. Bentinck and the other reformers in government preferred instead to transform Hindu society through the diffusion of Western education. Their impact on India, though subtle, was deep and far-reaching.

The first Western schools in India were established by the missionaries, who saw in them useful vehicles for the spread of Christian knowledge. Conversions were few, but the mission schools from the earliest days attracted bright young men in search of the secrets of Western superiority. In 1835 a network of secular government schools was set up under Bentinck's direction. Although confined to the major urban centers, these schools produced a new elite, literate in English and destined to spearhead the Indian nationalist movement.

The movement of radical reform reached its height during the rule of Lord Dalhousie (governor-general 1849–1856), who vigorously pushed forward the process of modernization. He introduced the telegraph and railway into India, reorganized and extended the educational system, and set out to eradicate the old aristocratic and princely classes. Regarding these old elite groups as obstacles to progress, the reformers had since the 1820s invariably awarded land rights to the village communities in newly conquered territories and pensioned off the aristocracy. Dalhousie hastened the process by annexing eight of the old princely states,

During the 1857 Mutiny the most common form of punishment for rebellious sepoys was to shoot them from the mouths of guns.

despite their loyalty to the government, on the grounds that British rule would prove a blessing to their inhabitants.

The Revolt of 1857

Dispossession did not destroy the influence of the aristocratic classes, nor did professions of cultural neutrality convince orthodox Hindus that the British did not intend to destroy all they cherished. Dalhousie's bold measures only sharpened their suspicion and widened the circle of the disaffected, so that Dalhousie's departure proved to be the signal for a massive popular uprising on the plains of northern India during 1857. The rising began in the Indian Army when the native soldiers, known as *sepoys*, suspected a plot to deprive them of their religion in the issue of cartridges greased with a mixture of pork and beef fat. The pork fat was defiling to the Muslims, the beef to the Hindus. Rather than accept it men of both faiths murdered their British officers and marched on Delhi,

where they attempted to reestablish the Mughal Empire. Although called the Sepoy Mutiny because of its military origin, the revolt spread widely throughout the country population and brought British administration to a halt over large areas for as long as a year or more.

The British were startled by the suddenness of the outbreak, but they remained secure in their bases in Calcutta and the south; hence, once they had amassed enough troops from home, they suppressed the revolt easily and meted out terrible punishment to all those implicated in it. But Britain's relations with India were never the same again. Until 1857 currents of modernization and strong traditional loyalties had existed side by side. The Sepoy Mutiny was a great protest on the part of traditional India against the colonialism of the West. Its defeat showed the Indian people that the British could not be evicted, that the new ideas had to be assimilated and the new ways learned. The British, in turn, came out of the Sepoy

Mutiny embittered and disillusioned, their optimistic plans for rapid reform irreparably shattered. Henceforth caution replaced zeal, and efficient administration replaced moral reconstruction.

CHINA AND THE MANCHUS

China, like India, was ruled by a foreign elite during the seventeenth and eighteenth centuries. In 1644 tribesmen from what is now Manchuria crossed the Great Wall and established the Ch'ing dynasty (1644–1912) at Peking. Because of an extended native resistance movement, it was not until 1683 that the K'ang hsi Emperor (1662–1722) finally consolidated Manchu rule. Yet within a generation the Ch'ing was accepted as a legitimate Chinese dynasty. There were several reasons for a Sino-Manchu accord in contrast to the Hindu-Muslim antagonism that pervaded India. One was the Manchus' willingness to adopt Chinese culture. Although they did try to preserve their racial identity by forbidding intermarriage with native Chinese and their cultural pride by forcing Chinese to wear the pigtail, the life of the Manchu aristocracy was almost indistinguishable from that of the Chinese gentry. Their sponsorship of Chinese culture proceeded from the new dynasty's realization that it must depend upon the services of Chinese bureaucrats. They had learned from the Mongol example that alien conquerors must trust and use Chinese scholar-officials.

Four centuries earlier, Mongols had entertained the notion of turning North China into grazing land for their herds. Fortunately for the Chinese, though, one aide had pointed out to the Mongol Khan that it was more profitable to tax the peasants than massacre them and turn their grain fields into pastures. As the Mongols then discovered and the Manchus later realized, revenue could not be collected efficiently unless the foreign conquering group inserted itself into the Chinese bureaucratic system. Without the cooperation of thousands of native clerks and magistrates, the new Ch'ing dynasty could not hope to maintain the tax registers, collect rural quotas, and otherwise hold together a country this large.

Manchu Rule

In order for 21,000 Manchu cavalrymen to rule 150,000,000 Chinese the Ch'ing also had to have the passive consent of the peasantry. The conquerors helped secure this by insisting that they had not invaded China. Instead, they claimed to have intervened in China to punish rebels who had toppled the Ming dynasty (1368–1644) and to restore public order in the name of Confucian rule. This was more than propaganda. It was a form of legitimization that ended by converting the Manchus themselves to the highest ideals of Chinese government. Under the K'ang-hsi Emperor, who was the greatest of the early Ch'ing rulers, the court was purged of corrupt eunuchs, taxes were equitably redistributed, the country's flood-control and irrigation devices were repaired, and the government's warehouses were filled with surplus grain. As the number of internal rebellions and famines declined sharply, population increased at an unprecedented pace. By 1800 peace and the use of new crops like potatoes and peanuts had allowed the population to double to 300,000,000 people, making the Chinese the most populous nation in the history of the world and one of the more prosperous ones of that time.

Before 1780 China possessed one of the stablest societies in history. This stability was due mainly to the fact that the men who ran the country were all devoted to a fixed cultural tradition. These men came from the gentry class, which provided the local elite and which was beneath the imperially appointed officials but above the peasantry. The gentry possessed status by virtue of official degrees gained either through examinations in the Confucian philosophic and literary Classics or, in the case of wealthy merchants, through contributions to government funds, by the equivalent of purchase. Only higher degree-holders were eligible for appointment to one of the nine ranks into which the empire's 40,000 civil, military, and educational officials were divided. The ruling elite was neither closed nor hereditary. With careers open to all men of talent or wealth, the system prevented such people from feeling powerless and hence frustrated. On the other hand, recruitment by scholarly

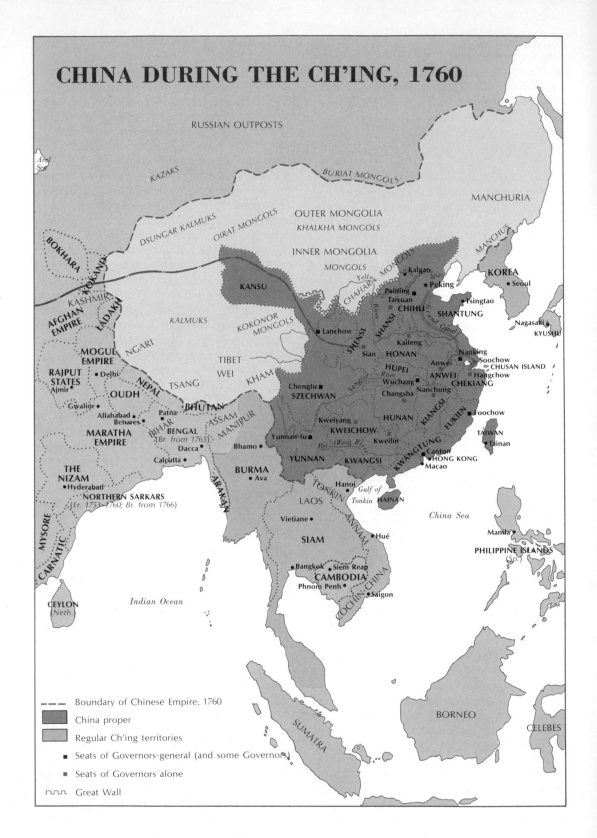

CHINA DURING THE CH'ING, 1760

RUSSIAN OUTPOSTS

Aral Sea

KAZAKS

BURIAT MONGOLS

MANCHURIA

BOKHARA

DSUNGAR KALMUKS

OIRAT MONGOLS

OUTER MONGOLIA

KHALKHA MONGOLS

MANCHUS

KOREA
• Seoul

KOKAND

KASHMIR

KANSU

INNER MONGOLIA

MONGOLS

CHAHAR MONGOLS

Yellow River

• Kalgan

Paoting ■
Taiyuan

★ Peking

CHIHLI

• Tsingtao

SHANTUNG

Nagasaki •
KYUSHU

AFGHAN
EMPIRE

LADAKH

NGARI

KOKONOR
MONGOLS

• Lanchow

SHENSI

SHANSI

Kaifeng ■
Sian ■

HONAN

Nanking

Anwei •

Soochow •

CHUSAN ISLAND

MOGUL
EMPIRE

KALMUKS

TIBET

WEI

KHAM

HUPEI

Wuchang ■

Yangtze River

ANWEI

Hangchow •

CHEKIANG

RAJPUT
STATES

• Delhi

TSANG

Chengtu •

SZECHWAN

Changsha ■

Nanchung •

Ajmir •

NEPAL

BHUTAN

HUNAN

KIANGSI

Gwalior •

OUDH

BIHAR

Patna •

ASSAM

MANIPUR

Kweiyang •

KWEICHOW

Kweilin ■

FUKIEN

Foochow •

Allahabad •
Benares •

BENGAL
(Br. from 1765)

Dacca •

Bhamo •

Yunnan-fu •

Hsi (West) River

TAIWAN

• Tainan

MARATHA
EMPIRE

Calcutta •

YUNNAN

KWANGSI

KWANGTUNG

Canton •
• HONG KONG
Macao •

THE
NIZAM

• Hyderabad

NORTHERN SARKARS
(Fr. 1753–1760; Br. from 1766)

BURMA

• Ava

ARAKAN

Hanoi •

Gulf of Tonkin

HAINAN

China Sea

MYSORE

CARNATIC

LAOS

Vietiane •

China Sea

Manila •

PHILIPPINE ISLANDS
(*Sp.*)

CEYLON
(*Neth.*)

Indian Ocean

SIAM

• Bangkok • Siem Reap

CAMBODIA

Phnom Penh •

Hué •

ANNAM

COCHIN-CHINA

• Saigon

BORNEO

CELEBES

SUMATRA

─ ─ ─ Boundary of Chinese Empire, 1760

▨ China proper

░ Regular Ch'ing territories

■ Seats of Governors-general (and some Governors)

■ Seats of Governors alone

⌐⌐⌐ Great Wall

attainments or loyalty to a fixed cultural tradition meant that China's ruling elite was extremely conservative and resistant to change. The gentry daily defined itself by a unique way of life: mastery of the Chinese Classics, elegant manners, the ability to write refined poetry in beautiful calligraphy, expensive silk robes, and even long fingernails to accentuate the distinction between its members and those who had to work with their hands. Westerners called the scholar-officials of the gentry "mandarins"; the term has since been applied to conservative, educated elites in other countries.

The Ch'ing reached its high point during the reign of the Ch'ien-lung Emperor (1736–1796). Not since the T'ang dynasty (618–907) had Chinese borders encompassed so much: Mongolia, Manchuria, Tibet, and Chinese Turkestan. As Ch'ien-lung's armies pushed deep into Burma and Nepal, other countries like Vietnam and Korea sent tribute to symbolize their acceptance of Chinese supremacy in Asia. Peking was the center of this vast empire. In fact, to Chinese of the time, their country was the source of all civilization, their emperor the Son of Heaven, and their age the most advanced and refined of all eras. While the huge procelain works at Ching-te-chen produced ceramics of delicate hue, poets and painters graced the numerous pavilions of Ch'ien-lung's monumental Summer Palace west of Peking. Hundreds of scholars labored to compile the 36,000 volumes of the "Four Treasuries"—the fullest encyclopedia the world has ever seen. China seemed to encompass everything and thought it needed nothing, even though 16,000 miles away Europe was beginning to enter the Industrial Revolution and to produce machine-made articles to sell to Chinese.

Early European Contact

There were important contacts with Europeans before 1800, but the Chinese were so culturally self-confident that they learned almost nothing from them. Jesuit priests had been employed at court since the late Ming period as astronomers and mathematicians. Some were even trusted advisers of the emperor and dreamed of converting him to Christianity; but to gain acceptance as Con-

fucian courtiers, they allowed Chinese converts to carry on ceremonies venerating their ancestors in the belief that the spirits of their ancestors lived on and could intercede effectively for their descendants. After Dominicans and Franciscans had pointed out to Rome that the Society of Jesus tolerated pagan worship of ancestors among its Chinese converts, a Rites Controversy broke out within the church. In 1707 the Rites Controversy became an issue between the pope and the Ch'ing emperor; Chinese scholars and officials had become jealous of Christian efforts to convert the emperor and feared they would lose their influence at court. The active persecution of Christians by the Yung-cheng Emperor began in 1725. In 1742 the pope prohibited the adulteration of Christian doctrine. Although the priests' influence now declined, they had introduced Chinese scholars to Euclidian geometry, Western geography, and Copernican astronomy. Interest in these new techniques faded rapidly, however, partly because the splendor of the Ch'ien-lung reign made anything not Chinese appear "barbarian" and therefore inferior.

Chinese diplomatic ritual reinforced the feeling of cultural supremacy. Envoys from other countries were not received by the throne unless they presented tribute and beat their heads against the ground nine times ("kowtow"—to strike one's head) as a form of symbolic submission to the ruler of "All under Heaven." Lord Macartney, an English envoy from George III, refused to "kowtow" in 1793 because he believed the gesture self-demeaning and a prop to China's inflated sense of cultural vanity. The Chinese in turn regarded him as a boorish barbarian who was incapable of understanding the proper "rites" of civilized men. Such a lack of mutual understanding made diplomatic exchanges almost impossible between proud Western nations and the Chinese empire.

Chinese Decline

By the 1790s the population of China had begun to outgrow its land. Furthermore, the extravagance of Ch'ien lung's court helped debase officials, who were now frequently involved in bribery. The waterworks fell into disrepair, granaries were emptied, and widespread tax evasion by those with influence increased the burden on the peasants. Soon a series of revolts led by militant Buddhist members of the White Lotus sect broke out all over central China. The rebellion was put down by 1804 after almost a decade of military campaigns that showed how cumbersome and unwieldy the army that had conquered Central Asia forty years earlier had become.

Under Ch'ien-lung, the armies of the realm had consumed as much as 100,000,000 taels (ounces of silver) of government revenue. The cost of maintaining these forces was slowly rising while their military efficiency declined. One reason for this was the padding of the rolls of the 600,000-man Green Standard Army. Another was a lack of discipline among the troops, who looted more ravenously than the rebels. Even the elite Manchu Banner armies, stationed at strategic points to act as a deterrent to military coups by Chinese units, had grown flabby. Although the Manchus had entered China as a militaristic elite, decades of garrison duty had softened them.

China's military weakness was its only similarity with India during the early nineteenth century. It was ruled by a union of Chinese mandarins and Manchu nobles and was therefore much more resistant to foreign conquest than India. Yet this political alliance depended so strongly on a shared commitment to traditional Confucian ideology (which valued the past and abhorred abrupt change) that the prospect of modernization was too unsettling. China lacked flexibility and could not respond to basic social and political changes. Its political and cultural stability—China's greatest strength—proved to be a weakness in the long run.

THE OPENING OF CHINA

Commercial Trade

During the fifteenth century the Chinese had become deeply involved in Far Eastern maritime commerce. Every year thousands of Cantonese and Fukienese junks hauled porcelain ware to Southeast Asia, drugs to India, and raw silk to Japan. When Portuguese galleons first arrived in the South China Sea in the early 1500s, they merely joined in the existing trade. By 1557 they had managed to persuade local Chinese authorities to let them settle at a small fishing village on the west bank of the Canton Estuary.

For almost fifty years the commercial position of this port—which the Portuguese came to call Macao—was marginal to most Chinese trade. In the late sixteenth century, however, Japan attacked China's tributary, Korea, and Peking banned all native trade with Japan. This ban did not diminish the Chinese demand for Japanese copper imports to mint into currency or Japan's craving for fine Chinese silks. Hence the Portuguese quickly presented themselves as neutral brokers in a profitable trade hitherto dominated by Chinese merchants. Macao prospered, quickly expanding into a fortressed port with beautiful townhouses, a large cathedral, and a wealthy middle class, but its commercial heyday was short-lived. The Japanese ruler decided to expel all Portuguese from his country in 1639, and Macao promptly lost its crucial place in Japanese trade to the Dutch at Nagasaki.

In the mid-seventeenth century the factors (trading agents) of the English East India Company, shut out of the East Indies, had also sought access to the coveted goods of China. Early efforts failed—partly because the residents of Macao still jealously guarded their Cantonese monopoly, partly because of civil war in both England and China, and partly because the early Ch'ing wished to seal off the coast to rebellious pirates like Koxinga, who ruled the island of Taiwan after 1662. But when the K'ang-hsi emperor in 1683 finally pacified Taiwan he decided that maritime trade would increase government revenue. Accordingly, several harbors were opened to the English, and a new era of direct multiport trading with the West began, lasting until 1760.

Trade with Europe

The nature of trade between Europe and China changed during the first half of the eighteenth century. Until this time China's major exports were silk and porcelain. Now an enterprising London coffeehouse owner introduced a Chinese medicinal herb called

Canton before the Opium War (1839–1840): Restricted to their trading factories, each bearing a national flag, Western merchants were denied direct access to the Chinese Empire beyond.

tea to the English. This mild stimulant soon became the standard drink of Englishmen of all classes, and the East India Company found itself for the first time monopolizing an item that could be consumed by the urban masses in gigantic quantities. As the Company prospered through the tea trade it became all the more dependent upon its sole supplier, China. Consequently, when the Ch'ien-lung Emperor ordered Europeans in 1760 to confine their trading to the port of Canton, the English had no choice but to acquiesce.

From 1760 until 1842 Canton was the only port open to the English. Trading regulations there became increasingly rigid. All maritime commerce was controlled by an imperial official (the "Hoppo") who licensed Chinese guild merchants (Co-hong) to monopolize foreign trade. A hong merchant had to guarantee or "secure" each vessel that came into Canton. If one of the ship's crew members was involved in a shoreside brawl, the Chinese "security merchant" stood responsible. In practice this meant that Co-hong members were constantly paying ruinous

fines to the Hoppo in order to escape imprisonment. The guild merchants were therefore constantly short of capital. In order to meet their needs, they turned increasingly for loans in the late eighteenth century to the "Agency Houses"—brokerage firms that had grown to dominate private English trade in the Orient.

These Agency Houses primarily banked and invested the funds of East India Company employees. They also made it possible for the British to finance their rule of India. The conquest of that subcontinent had cost a great deal of money so that by the early nineteenth century the East India Company owed the British crown over 28 million pounds sterling, a debt repayable with profits from the tea trade. But what was the Company to use to acquire the tea in the first place? The Chinese were not particularly interested in buying English woolens. Indeed, all that they would take in any quantity was silver. The English, therefore, had to find an Indian product as attractive to the Chinese as tea was to the English. For a time Indian cotton seemed a possibility, but by 1820 it proved

In 1793 Sir George Macartney led an embassy to China. He was treated with the respect due any barbarian envoy. The Chinese described the event: His Majesty, the Emperor, proceeded to the great tent in the Garden of the Ten Thousand Trees where the ambassador of England, Ma-ka-er-ni, entered for an audience. Gifts were bestowed upon him.

inadequate. A substitute was finally found that sold as readily in China as tea in England. This was the addictive drug opium.

The Opium Wars

The East India Company had created its own opium monopoly in India as early as 1773, but the Chinese boom in the traffic of this drug did not occur until after 1819, when lower prices made it accessible to lower-class Chinese. Since more consumption increased addiction, the demand kept increasing, and sales practically doubled from year to year. The East India Company's directors probably felt some embarrassment in their role as drug "pushers." But, on the one hand, profits from opium helped meet the financial needs of their Indian empire, and, on the other, some of the onus could be transferred by having others transport the drug to China. The private Agency Houses were therefore encouraged to buy the opium at the Company's auctions in Calcutta, ship it across the South China Sea in "country ships," and sell it illegally in Canton. As more and more opium flowed into China, the balance of payments reversed, and England soon was taking more than two million pounds sterling of silver out of China every year. The moralists back in England might rave about drug-pushing, but the appeal, "business as usual," overrode other considerations.

Economics was the primary cause of the first Anglo-Chinese War (1839–1842), aptly called the Opium War. However, there were two other major reasons behind the outbreak of hostilities between England and China. First there was China's diplomatic system. The Ch'ing, true to notions of Confucian cultural superiority, insisted that all other nations were "barbarian" and required that they approach China as submissive tributaries. Many Asian monarchs were willing to acquiesce in order to trade with China, but confident European nation-states like England and Russia insisted on diplomatic equality, a concession the Ch'ing court would not allow until forced to. Thus no treaty arrangement of either the opium ques-

From the Western point of view, Macartney was a sincere and noble figure. The Chinese emperor and his court were supposed to be corrupt and obese mandarins. Each side viewed the other with superciliousness.

tion or the frictions of legal trade at Canton could be settled peaceably. In addition, England's increasingly vocal Manchester and Liverpool industrialists were determined to find Asian outlets for their manufactured goods. They believed that an extra inch of cotton cloth added to every "Chinaman's" shirttail would keep England's looms running for years. But the single-port trading system at Canton and the East India Company's monopoly would both have to be abolished. In 1833 the latter was ended just when Chinese agitation over the opium trade was becoming critical.

The Ch'ing had outlawed opium years earlier, but corrupt local policemen continued to let the drug slip into the country. Not only were soldiers and officials becoming addicted, but more and more silver was flowing out of Canton every year. Under China's bimetallic money system, this outflow made rural taxes in silver much heavier for the average peasant than before. The additional tax burden increased the risk of rebellion, and Peking grew alarmed. Some officials argued that opium smoking was so common it could not be stamped out, but the majority felt that China should punish both native smokers and dealers. Consequently, in December 1838, the Tao-kuang Emperor (1820–1850) ordered an imperial commissioner to take all necessary steps to wipe out the trade.

Commissioner Lin Tse-hsü reached Canton from Peking on March 10, 1839 and promptly arrested local officials involved in the opium racket. To get at the source of the drug he blockaded the foreign "factories"

Canton during the heyday of imperialism: Guarded by Sikh servants and carried by Chinese coolies, Westerners now dominated the native landscape.

where European merchants resided and stored their goods. The British Superintendent of Trade quickly handed over all available opium stocks for immediate destruction, but after the English were released as a group to move to their ships, they balked at Lin's order to sign bonds guaranteeing that they would never import the drug again. Commissioner Lin then sought to bring them to terms by closing the seacoast to their vessels. In the fall of 1839 war began with an armed clash between British and Chinese warships at Hong Kong.

During the next three years a series of English expeditions culminated in a slashing attack up the Yangtze River in the summer of 1842. With the empire about to be cut in two by British gunboats, the Chinese emperor had no choice but to agree to the Treaty of Nanking, which declared that five "treaty ports" should be opened to trade, guaran-teed the English a large cash indemnity, accepted consular representation, and ceded the island of Hong Kong to Great Britain. Three other treaties extended similar rights to France and the United States, guaranteed religious toleration for Christians, and declared that foreigners who committed crimes in China had the right to be tried by their own consuls. The last proviso, "the principle of extraterritoriality," became the keystone of foreign domination on Chinese soil. It eventually permitted the great powers to establish "concessions" in cities like Shanghai where westerners developed their own municipal administrations, police forces, and local courts. Thus was modern colonialism born in China.

There were other immediate consequences of the Opium War. First, because of the ease with which the British forces had defeated the Chinese, a few Ch'ing officials became aware of the enormous gap between their own technology and the West's and they hesitantly began a "Self-Strengthening Movement" to create new arsenals and armies. Second, parts of southeastern China were thrown into a period of social disorder. The most severely affected was the province of Kwangtung, which surrounded Canton itself. Local militia, organized to fight the British, degenerated into bandit groups when the war was over, and pirates — always a troublesome presence in these waters — moved inland up the Pearl River system. Moreover, one of the new treaty ports, Shanghai, began to replace Canton as the center of foreign trade, throwing tens of thousands of porters and coolies (unskilled laborers) out of work in Kwangtung. Finally, Christian missions were sanctioned. Through one of these missions a young scholar named Hung Hsiu-ch'üan was exposed to Christian writings. After suffering a severe emotional crisis caused by frustration at failing to pass the official examinations, he decided that he himself was the younger brother of Jesus Christ, destined to recall China to the worship of God. Hung proceeded to recruit others in Kwangtung and especially Kwangsi province into the "Society of God Worshippers." Some of its members had belonged to the Triads, a secret society which declared the Manchus to be racial enemies of the Chinese. Hung Hsiu-ch'üan soon became the leader of a major rebellion.

The Taiping Rebellion

China suffered a disastrous civil war, which raged across the entire country from 1850 to 1865. The immediate causes of the rebellion can be attributed to the first Opium War, but a social crisis had long been in the making. Population growth during the previous century placed a harsh strain on local government. A mere 40,000 officials found it difficult to rule 400 million people effectively. Furthermore, the Chinese agricultural system was incapable of expanding its productivity to feed this huge population. (In the south it already depended on the intensive labor of peasants who arduously harvested two and three crops of rice a year.) Relative scarcity of land increased its cost. Meanwhile the gov-

ernment was reeling from military expenses and costly relief programs for flood damage. It also suffered an inflationary spiral that increased the amount of land taxes without actually supplementing internal revenue. Members of the gentry in turn used their political influence to exempt their lands from these high taxes, thereby increasing the peasants' share of the fiscal burden. Many farmers could not afford to pay their taxes unless they borrowed at high interest rates from village pawnshops or urban usurers. As they sank deeper into debt they had the choice of becoming tenants and paying high rents or fleeing the land altogether. Many moved to the cities, swelling the ranks of the unemployed; others turned to banditry as a way of life, joining secret societies that preyed on travelers and helpless villages. There existed, in short, a national economic and social crisis which the Taiping rebels both reflected and utilized in mounting their civil war against the Ch'ing government.

Hung Hsiu-ch'üan's promises of a Christian utopia, his support for destruction of native temples, and his antiforeign appeals to overthrow the Manchus alarmed and enraged local officials in mountainous Kwangsi province. Government attacks on Hung's followers in 1850 helped transform the Society of God Worshippers into a militant army; it set out on a crusade to eradicate the Manchus and establish a divine kingdom, the *T'ai-p'ing t'ien-kuo* or "Heavenly Kingdom of Great Peace." Marching north out of Kwangsi, the Taiping rebels quickly grew into an army of several hundred thousand. Along the way this army absorbed landless peasants and unemployed coolies into a highly organized civil-military community that shared personal property and through indoctrination convinced its new members of their holy mission. At first their military successes were extravagant, for none of the Ch'ing armies could stand against them. A great tactical error was committed, however, when Hung Hsiu-ch'üan decided in 1853 to establish his capital at Nanking rather than push on to Peking with all his forces. Meanwhile, high-ranking Chinese officials organized local militia into new regional armies that overwhelmed Nanking a decade later.

When the rebellion first developed, the Western powers could not decide which side deserved their support. Some Protestants wanted to believe that Hung, the "Christian emperor," would transform all of China overnight into a Christian kingdom, amenable to the West. But Hung was too convinced of the validity of his visions and too jealous of his religious authority to cooperate. Christianity might be shared with other countries, he argued with missionaries who traveled to Nanking to pay their respects, but he was entitled to be its principal interpreter.

Other Westerners were concerned primarily with obtaining trading privileges, which could be guaranteed only by a stable and reasonably tolerant regime. At first neither the Ch'ing government nor the Taiping rebels seemed to promise much in this regard. The Ch'ing court might be more stable and less fanatic, but it was certainly just as intolerant. While the Hsien-feng Emperor (1851–1861) did all he could to ignore the diplomatic courtesies promised in the Treaty of Nanking, his officials tried their best to revive the tributary diplomacy of pre-Opium War days. Such seeming obstinacy infuriated the English, who seized upon a minor incident to declare war on China once again. This time the French, provoked by the murder of a French Catholic missionary, cooperated. The Second Anglo-Chinese War (1858–1860) resulted in a joint expedition that invaded Peking, forced the emperor to flee, and burned the fabulous Summer Palace. This time the imperial government could no longer ignore the consequences of defeat. Its negotiators agreed to allow Western diplomats to reside in the capital and guaranteed the opening of even more treaty ports without hesitation.

By 1861 the emperor had died in grief, leaving his dynasty in the shaky hands of a group of Manchu regents. Most of China was in the throes of civil war, which is said to have cost the country over twenty million lives, and many thought the dynasty might well fall. Moreover, because the West had humbled the regime, the foreign powers felt that they could deal with it as they wished. They therefore decided the time had come to end neutrality and support the ruling dynasty against the Taipings. Partly because of West-

ern backing (symbolized by the mercenary army of the British officer, Charles George "Chinese" Gordon) but mainly because of the aid of loyal Chinese gentry and scholar-officials, the Ch'ing was able to survive this multiple shock and make a concerted effort to get in step with a world it had only just begun to understand.

JAPAN UNDER THE TOKUGAWA

As we saw in Chapter 7, the "Warring States Period" of the sixteenth century in Japan was characterized by the military rivalries of hundreds of feudal lords (daimyo). No single lord could stabilize the country as long as his own forces remained a loose alliance of independent barons who, in turn, each had his own private army under his own bureaucratic control. One such daimyo, Tokugawa Ieyasu, realized this as early as 1565 and thus was able to defeat his splintered enemies and go on to pacify all Japan. By 1585 he had created an army no longer composed of individual units owing personal allegiance to individual feudal lords, but rather of a larger body of soldiers appointed to serve impersonally under officers appointed by Ieyasu himself. To supply this new army, Ieyasu had to organize official estates or "house lands" controlled by his own stewards (jito), thereby carrying bureaucratization and centralization one step further.

Tokugawa Ieyasu eventually established himself as the nominal deputy (shogun) of the helpless emperor and brought Japan out of civil war into a period of stability and prosperity which lasted from about 1600 until the mid-nineteenth century. The stability of the Tokugawa regime (1603–1868) depended upon a new system of stratification. There was a subtly structured security system that policed both Tokugawa lands and the lords. Without entirely destroying the feudal system, it allowed the Tokugawa shogunate (or bakufu) to rule within a partially feudal and decentralized regime. Japan therefore retained a series of three types of fief. The first were the house lands around Edo (Tokyo) under direct Tokugawa control, which provided tax revenue (reckoned in koku—or bushels — of rice) for the shogunate. The second were those surrounding Tokugawa lands where loyal or "inner" (fudai) vassals were invested as manorial lords. The third were the one hundred powerful "outer" (tozama) fiefs of lords who had originally opposed Tokugawa rule. Their daimyo were recognized as legitimate rulers, but they were kept under constant supervision by the shogunate to prevent revolt. They were allowed to govern their own fiefs much as they pleased, but they could not ally with other powerful lords and they had to spend at least six months of every year in Edo, the new capital, as hostages to the Tokugawa government.

Another security problem facing the Tokugawa shogunate was the disposition of the one million warriors of Japan who had formed the retainer-armies of the sixteenth century. During the civil war period, any farmer of military disposition and training could attain samurai rank. The Tokugawa as well as other fiefs (han) transformed this military class into a hereditary aristocracy comprising 5 percent of the population. It was declared illegal for any single warrior not to belong to the retinue of a higher lord; hence roving bands of uncontrolled warriors were forced to settle down. Over time, this soldier class evolved into a bureaucracy concerned largely with tax collection and civil administration. Since the centers of government were the fiefs' castle towns, the samurai also turned from farming to become urban dwellers. This transformation helped stabilize the power of individual daimyo, because the samurai were too uprooted from rural connections to create local armies on their own. In short, over the course of the seventeenth and eighteenth centuries, the samurai changed from independent warriors into mere retainers, dependent upon their lord for board and keep.

The second measure taken by the Tokugawa to insure stability was the closing of the country to all outside contacts. (See p. 242.) This policy was directed against both foreign influence (whether Christian missionaries or Western guns) and the economic power of the "outer" southwestern fiefs that traded with China and Southeast Asia. A third device of rule was the shogunate's use of imperial authority. The court at Kyoto remained powerless, while Ieyasu and his successors acted in the name of the emperor. Their use of a politically inert but symbolically potent source of legitimacy dates far back in Japanese history. It was now supplemented by a cult of loyalty and service to one's lord sanctioned by hierarchical Chu Hsi Neo-Confucianism imported from China.

All of these elements of Tokugawa rule, essential to the stabilization of government after 1600, paradoxically ended by fostering social conditions that either disrupted the shogun's control of Japan or else set the country on the road to modernization. Therefore, when the Tokugawa finally fell in 1867, contact with the West accelerated trends long in the making. For, in contrast to China, which by 1840 had reached the point of being almost frozen in time, Japanese society had apparently solidified about 1650, but had then begun to undergo social modernization of its own accord due to three elements of Tokugawa rule: the hostage system, the closing of the country, and the emperor.

The Hostage System and Urbanization of the Samurai

Just as each fief's castle town transformed the provincial elite member's way of life by forcing him into an urban existence, so did the hostage system concentrate the nation's leaders in major cities like Edo and Osaka. As hundreds of daimyos with their individual retinues were forced to spend every other year in Edo, the Tokugawa capital grew from a small commercial and military center into a city of one million artisans, merchants, entertainers, and courtesans. To reach Edo, the daimyos had to travel past countless inns up the tokaido (the highway along the eastern sea) from Osaka. Osaka itself had a population of 500,000, for it was to this city that the warrior class brought its rice rations to trade for money or bills of exchange that could be used or banked in Edo. Therefore, the rice brokers who conducted these transactions naturally came to occupy an important place in Tokugawa society. Unlike Chinese monopoly merchants, though, they could not easily earn or buy elite status. Hence they remained a more cohesive class, cultivating capital and entrepreneurial ideals like their

JAPAN UNDER TOKUGAWA, 1600–1868

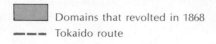
Domains that revolted in 1868
Tokaido route

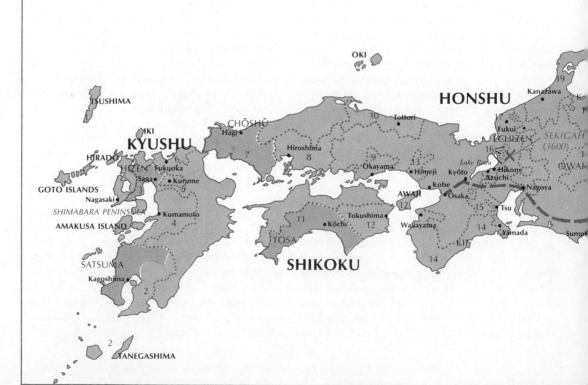

Sea   of   Japan

OKI

HONSHU

TSUSHIMA

CHŌSHŪ
Hagi

KYUSHU

Tottori

Kanazawa

10

19

17
Fukui
ECHIZEN

SEKIGAH
(1600)

Hiroshima

16

Lake Biwa

7

8

9

Okayama

13

Himeji

Kyōto
Azuchi

Hikone

OWA

IKI

HIRADO

6

HIZEN   Fukuoka

Saga

Kurume

3

5

Kobe

Osaka

Tsu

15

Nagoya

GOTO ISLANDS
Nagasaki
SHIMABARA PENINSULA
AMAKUSA ISLAND

Kumamoto

4

AWAII
12

Tokushima

Wakayama

11

Kōchi

12

14

Yamada

KII

Sump

TOSA

14

SATSUMA
Kagoshima

2

SHIKOKU

2   TANEGASHIMA

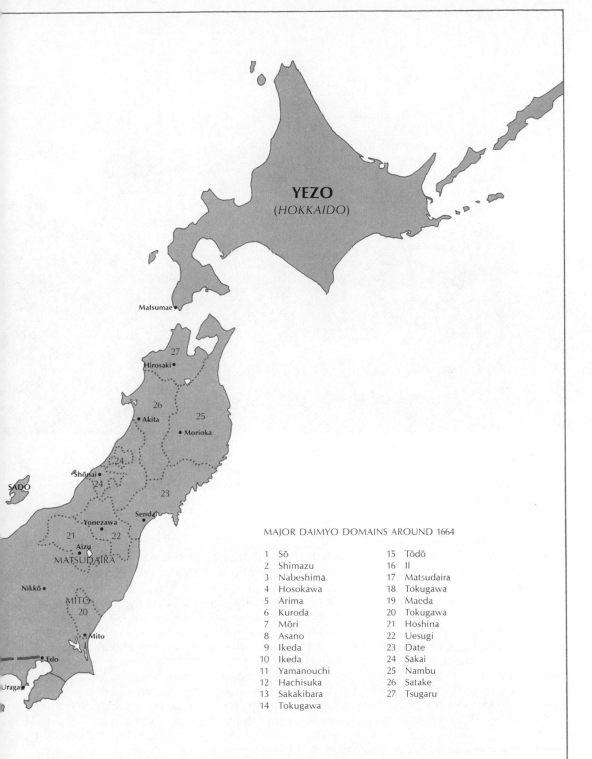

YEZO
(HOKKAIDO)

Matsumae•

27
Hirosaki •

26
•Akita

25
• Morioka

•24•

Shōnai •

SADO

•24

23

Yonezawa •   Sendai•

21   22

Aizu•

MATSUDAIRA

Nikkō •

MITO

20

•Mito

•Edo

Uraga•

MAJOR DAIMYO DOMAINS AROUND 1664

1	Sō	15	Tōdō
2	Shimazu	16	Ii
3	Nabeshima	17	Matsudaira
4	Hosokawa	18	Tokugawa
5	Arima	19	Maeda
6	Kuroda	20	Tokugawa
7	Mōri	21	Hoshina
8	Asano	22	Uesugi
9	Ikeda	23	Date
10	Ikeda	24	Sakai
11	Yamanouchi	25	Nambu
12	Hachisuka	26	Satake
13	Sakakibara	27	Tsugaru
14	Tokugawa		

Pacific   Ocean

Himeji Castle: Surrounded by an outside moat 180 feet wide, enclosing an area of two miles in diameter, the 'White Heron Castle' controlled the western gateway to Osaka. Built by the Ikeda lords, it was expropriated by the Tokugawa in 1616 for its strategic importance.

European counterparts. And, also like Western merchants, they created their own forms of urban culture in Osaka: the gay woodblockprints of the *ukiyo-e,* or "floating world" of big-city geishas, tea houses, and gambling casinos; the dramatic puppet plays of Chikamatsu; the comic genre novels of Ihara Saikaku; the direct and elegant *haiku* poems of Bashō.

The fortunes of the Osaka rice brokers and bankers were built on rice exchange and moneylending; therefore they stood to lose if the hostage system was abolished or government debts cancelled. Another group of merchants, *tonya* or wholesalers who supplied Japan's cities with consumer goods, exhibited some traits of independent capitalist

growth. But they too became tied to the government after 1760 when their monopolies were licensed and defended by the shogun. In fact, the only section of the merchant class that provided a strong impetus for social change was the rural capitalists who invested in sake (rice wine) brewing and interregional trade. After 1800 these men vigorously fought the *tonya* monopoly of urban trade and succeeded in gaining access to city markets. It is estimated that such free traders later supplied about 25 percent of the domestic capital needed for modernization, but before the fall of the Tokugawa they were not powerful enough to challenge the regime. In the last analysis the only group in society that posed a serious threat to the shogunate on the eve of Japan's encounter with the West was the samurai class.

Although many of the samurai found fault with the government for its foreign policy, the causes of their discontent were more profound. Urbanization and commercialization had gravely weakened the supports of an agrarian-based regime. The flamboyant high life of Edo and Osaka captivated most samurai, helping to impoverish them by driving them to Osaka's moneylenders to whom they would pledge rice stipends years in advance in exchange for ready cash. This indebtedness created severe frustrations among the samurai, whose stipends remained fixed during periods of high inflation. By the 1850s, therefore, many had turned into malcontents, restless with their lot and willing to accept extreme political and social change.

One direct effect of the closing of the country was to keep Japan isolated from European imperialism longer than China or India. Yet, because there was a Dutch trading mission at Nagasaki, there was some contact with foreign culture. Perhaps because of the exclusion policy itself, knowledge of the West became a form of forbidden fruit, quite tempting to disaffected samurai. However, the shogunate itself saw great value in learning about Western technology and established a special translation office in 1811 to "investigate barbarian books." By the early nineteenth century there were several famous "Dutch learning" (*rangaku*) experts like Honda Toshiaki and Takano Chōei who helped popularize the study of Western medicine, Western machines, and above all Western weapons long before Perry's black ships arrived in 1853.

The Emperor

Since the Tokugawa shogun ruled in the name of the emperor, loyalty to both figures was deliberately fostered. Indeed, the general ideal of absolute duty to one's superior was infused in all classes of society, especially the samurai. Heroic acts of sacrifice, like the saga of the forty-seven *ronin* (samurai without a master) who avenged the death of their lord and then committed suicide, glorified a sense of subordination to higher

symbols. This attitude was easily converted after 1868 into loyalty to the emperor and a national government. In China, on the other hand, loyalty was diffused and particularist—devoted to one's kin or friends and therefore difficult to direct upward and outward toward universal goals such as the state. There was another, similar contrast between the two countries. In Japan the warriors had become bureaucrats, but they retained a class ethic of military duty (*bushidō*). The Chinese bureaucrat likewise had a professional ethic, which taught him that he must judge the value of any act according to Confucian norms. The samurai official, on the other hand, valued action and duty for their own sake and judged each action on its own without reference to specific universal goals. Therefore, while the Chinese mandarins were unable to transform themselves into modern businessmen or bureaucrats, the samurai could shift more easily into the role of bureaucratic entrepreneur.

The emphasis on loyalty and the Tokugawa's use of imperial legitimization also resulted in a revival of the cult of imperial rule, which eventually provided an alternative to the shogunate. During the eighteenth century certain *kokugaku* (national studies) thinkers began to stress the uniqueness of the Japanese ruler's divine descent from the Sun Goddess. Their ruler embodied, they said, Japan's national essence, just as the Shinto religion (rather than Confucianism) best suited the Japanese spirit. Furthermore, Mito, one of the three collateral houses of the Tokugawa, patronized the compilers of a national history of Japan who used Confucian notions of the state to popularize the belief that the emperor should rule it directly.

Results of Tokugawa Rule

By 1850 Tokugawa Japan was under the sway of a kind of arrested feudalism in which semiautonomous fiefs ruled themselves under loose central supervision. Hence when the shogun's power began to weaken in the 1850s, the rulers of every major fief in the country tried to take the lead in creating a new government. Paradoxically, therefore, this feudalism proved a strength rather than a weakness. Japan thus presents a sharp con-

東海道
九かうさつ
三汰
大津

The Springwater Tea House: One of the many resting places for travelers along the Tokaido, the "Road by the Eastern Sea," along which daimyo *led their retinues on the way to Edo (Tokyo). From a print by Hiroshige, c. 1860.*

trast to both India and China before they experienced Western imperialism. India had been a centralized empire but was well on the way toward disintegration into independent units neither established nor stable enough to compete except on the battlefield; in fact, the warfare between them invited the intervention of rival European powers. China, on the other hand, remained a centralized bureaucracy without any independent units. Unlike Japan, it lacked both an intense focus of national identity and subimperial units that could act collectively when the central government foundered.

The Japanese built a strong nation capable of competing with the West very soon after the fall of the shogunate. By 1867, the following conditions favoring political unification and economic development were clearly in evidence: (1) a high literacy rate (almost 35 percent) because of fief schools; (2) a national network of excellent roads; (3) risk-taking merchants and ample finance capital; (4) a taxable agrarian surplus resulting from high agricultural productivity managed by rural capitalists; and (5) a bureaucratic elite devoted to national strength. The Japanese had a habit of borrowing from other nations that might have helped them adopt Western techniques. They had already borrowed their traditional political institutions, script, and even religion from China. But more important in preparing Japan for rapid social change after 1868 than the ability to borrow was the capacity of its ruling elite to transform traditional ideals of duty and loyalty into two of the most important values for a unified and powerful modern state: public service and common citizenship.

The expansive force of Western imperialism soon made itself felt throughout most of the populous lands of Asia. Initially an affair of monopoly trading companies bent on exploiting the precious goods of the Orient, this expansion by 1860 was dominated by enthusiastic free traders who saw vast markets for their manufactured goods in the thickly settled Eastern countries. Conquest did not, however, automatically follow in the wake of trade, let alone the visions of trade that sustained so many of the new industrialists. Much depended on the strength and resiliency of each society at the time it was first subjected to intensive Western pressure. In India and Indonesia, where medieval empires had already fallen into disarray or collapsed by the early eighteenth century, European imperial expansion from the start took on the shape of colonial subjugation. In China the centralized bureaucracy of the Confucian state, although twice humbled in twenty years by British gunboats, still contrived to fend off some of the demands of the Western powers by reluctant cooperation with treaty-port consuls. In Japan, by contrast, the strong yet flexible social institutions that had grown up under the Tokugawa enabled the country both to keep the Western powers at bay and to lay the foundations of a modern nation-state.

The impact of the West on traditional social organization was everywhere dramatic and disruptive. No society could simply ignore so overwhelming a presence. The convulsions of the 1857 Sepoy Mutiny in India and the messianic Taiping movement in China were but the most striking signs of the currents of change let loose by the new Western contact. Although such movements of violent protest were portents of future revolutionary nationalism, for the moment they were no more than a temporary evasion. The challenge of the West had to be met directly, and it demanded new ideas, new ways, and often a new elite. The discontented samurai of Japan and the English-educated Indians of Calcutta, open and responsive yet still rooted in their own culture, formed the spearhead of the new forces that would, in time, lead Asia back from the depths to which it had fallen.

SUGGESTED READINGS

Totman, Conrad, *The Politics in the Tokugawa Bakufu, 1600–1843*. Cambridge: Harvard University Press. 1967.
Gives an excellent sense of the Tokugawa-heavy balance of power in Japan. Especially good on the founding of the shogunate.

Hall, John Whitney and Marius B. Jansen, *Studies in the Institutional History of Early Modern Japan*. Princeton: Princeton University Press, 1968.
This collection of essays contains some of the very best research to date on Japanese history between 1600 and 1868.

Spence, Jonathan, *Ts'ao Yin and the K'ang-hsi Emperor*. New Haven: Yale University Press, 1967.
The best study available on the early Ch'ing.

Waley, Arthur, *The Opium War through Chinese Eyes*. London: George Allen and Unwin, 1958.
A lively, first-hand account of the war. Highly recommended for pleasure's sake.

Edwardes, S. M. and H. L. O. Garrett, *Mughal Rule in India*. Delhi: S. Chand & Co., 1956.
A comprehensive and readable survey.

Spear, Percival, *The Twilight of the Mughuls*. Cambridge: Cambridge University Press, 1951: paperback reprint, 1971.
Also includes an account of early British rule in Delhi.

Spear, Percival, *The Nabobs*. London: Oxford University Press, 1963. Paperback.
A study of the social life of the English in eighteenth-century India.

Moon, Penderel, *Warren Hastings and British India*. New York: Collier Books, 1962. Paperback.

Woodruff, Philip, *The Men Who Ruled India*. Vol. I, *The Founders*. New York: Schocken Books, 1964. Paperback.
A lively study, somewhat apologetic.

Legge, J. D., *Indonesia*. Englewood Cliffs, N.J.: Prentice-Hall, 1964.
The best short survey incorporating recent scholarship.

CHAPTER 19

The Challenge of the New Imperialism

THE T'UNG-CHIH RESTORATION IN CHINA (1862–1874)

In 1860 the future looked dim for the Ch'ing (Manchu) dynasty. While Taiping rebels occupied the Yangtze valley, other revolts broke out elsewhere: Muslims in the northwest and southwest, tribesmen in the mountainous jungles along the Burmese border, warring clans in the paddy lands of Kwangtung, mounted Nien bandits throughout the Huai Valley. From outside the empire came English and French troops to occupy Peking and force another unequal treaty on China. The Hsien-feng Emperor soon died, leaving factions fighting for control at court. And yet the Ch'ing dynasty continued to rule China for another half-century.

The Self-Strengthening Movement

The T'ung-chih Restoration (1862–1874) was largely the work of Chinese scholar-officials stirred into support of the regime by the social radicalism of the Taiping rebels. Their first concern was self-protection; thus they returned to their home towns and organized peasant militia units to guard family interests. Then, responding to imperial pleas, they amalgamated their village defense forces into larger provincial armies under high-ranking Chinese bureaucrats who were temporarily given permission to form unified regional commands. These regional armies were a major departure from the traditional Manchu policy of separating civil and military hierarchies and from the policy of preventing scholar-officials from serving in their native provinces. But the dynasty had very little choice in the matter; its own central armies were so weak that it had to choose between the lesser risk of military decentralization and the genuine possibility of rebel victory.

Once the Taiping rebels occupied Nanking, the major Ch'ing counterattack was launched from the nearby province of Hunan, where the greatest of the regional commanders, Tseng Kuo-fan, carefully trained an army of "braves." He covered his flanks by persuading other members of the local gentry loyal to him to recruit similar provincial armies to the south and east. After almost a decade of rural pacification, these armies finally recaptured Nanking in 1864 and destroyed the Taiping forces. But this victory did not mean the end of disorder. By the time rebel groups in other parts of China had been defeated, the country had suffered through twenty-three years of civil war, losing over 20 million of its population.

Reconstruction of the shattered system of government control, as well as social welfare policies to relieve the peasants' suffering, were the immediate concerns of most officials. The first task for men like Tseng Kuofan was to restore local leadership to the members of the gentry who had fled the countryside to seek protection in neighboring cities. Their position was bolstered by the reinvigorated Confucianism taught in newly opened local schools and academies. The Chinese Classics were reprinted on a large scale for the literate, while those who could not read were encouraged to attend ceremonial lectures on the Emperor's Sacred Edicts, which exhorted the peasantry to be filial, respectful, and loyal. Nor was the people's livelihood neglected. Farmers were given tax remissions or tools and seed to reclaim abandoned lands. Water works were rebuilt, notoriously corrupt officials were punished, and the examination system was revived.

In short, the leaders of the restoration consciously attempted to return China to its prewar ways by imitating famous statesmen of the past who had managed to inject new life into failing dynasties before the "Mandate" finally changed hands. It seemed as though nothing had happened between China and the outside world to shake the belief that the traditional social system could be restored by means of traditional Confucian methods. Yet the West was not ignored, if only because many high officials recognized that social stability within China depended heavily upon peace without. At first, the West was willing to cooperate: England, France, and Russia did not wish to see China disintegrate, for this might provoke the same kind of struggle among the powers as had the disintegration of the Ottoman Empire. (See pp. 603–606.) Moreover, civil war disrupted trade. The benefits gained from the treaty arrangements of 1860 would be wasted without a Chinese central government to guarantee them. In the eyes of diplomats like the British minister Sir Rutherford Alcock, the Ch'ing dynasty had finally learned its lesson and would now willingly enter the world community of nations. Gunboats should be replaced by solicitous Western advisers who could help China adjust to modern technology and European enlightenment. Indeed, after 1860 foreign consuls and missionaries eagerly encouraged the Chinese to open Western language schools, arsenals, shipyards, and a new bureau (the *Tsungli Yamen*) to conduct foreign relations.

Regionalism and Modernization

One reason for the dynamism of what came to be known as the "Self-Strengthening Movement" was its sponsorship by high Manchu officials like Prince Kung, who shared control of the court after 1861 with two Empress Dowagers. Although one of these—Tz'u-hsi—dismissed Prince Kung in 1884, he had by then provided twenty-three years of support for modernizing impulses that originated in the provinces. These first appeared during the suppression of the Taiping Rebellion when Tseng Kuo-fan and his aide, Li Hung-chang, bought foreign weapons and established China's first modern arsenals. Consequently, modernization measures became more closely associated with the regional commanders or viceroys than with the central government. After all, a scholar-official serving in the Board of Rites was less likely to appreciate the necessity of using modern firearms than men who had employed them in actual warfare. Besides, by sponsoring the creation of new modern armies in the name of national self-defense, a viceroy like Li Hung-chang could create a personal political and military machine. During the last thirty years of the nineteenth century, Li built arsenals, hired foreign technicians, patronized younger and more innovative Chinese who had studied Western learning, opened coal mines, and founded transportation companies. Li Hung-chang's elaborate apparatus both helped defend China and strengthened his own power. Because of his Confucian loyalty to the throne, Li never challenged his monarch. He did, however, pave the way for a later group of professional military officers who lacked this political commitment to the central government and became the regional warlords of the twentieth century.

大清國當今慈禧端佑康頤昭豫莊誠壽恭欽獻崇熙聖母皇太后

Tz-'u-hsi, Empress Dowager of China. This portrait was taken about 1906 after her seventieth birthday when the honorific characters of her name were increased to sixteen. The plaque above her head lists them: "Motherly (Tz'u), auspicious (hsi), orthodox, heaven-blessed, prosperous, all-nourishing, brightly manifest, calm, sedate, perfect, long-lived, respectful, reverent, worshipful, illustrious, and exalted."

Moreover, the intimate association of regionalism with modernization did not contribute to uniform technological development or military strength. The new armies and navies of Li Hung-chang, Tso Tsung-t'ang, Chang Chih-tung, and others were impressive at first sight. However, because there were always three or four regional leaders competing for government appropriations and influence, the military establishment was not unified. Each man jealously guarded his own resources, refusing to cooperate in event of war. Furthermore, no government ministries were founded to take charge of planning and training. Instead, those few "experts" who had studied science in the West were merely appointed as private secretaries in the personal retinues of each regional leader. Even commercial enterprises were created under the patronage of such officials so that any would-be entrepreneurs were dominated by narrow-minded bureaucrats. On the other hand, had men like Li Hung-chang not privately sponsored self-strengthening, no one else would have; most scholar-officials were still opposed to Westernization.

Failure of the Restoration

This paradox of the T'ung-chih Restoration—the desire to halt change with one hand while encouraging it with the other—existed because sponsors of modern weapons and methods believed they were using Western techniques only to preserve traditional Chinese values. The celebrated formula ("let us take Chinese culture as the substance [t'i] and Western learning as the function [yung]") appealed to those who wished to westernize without losing their cultural identity as Chinese. However, the t'i-yung formula soon proved incompatible with either goal. Just as bookish private secretaries stifled entrepreneurship, so did modern technological demands conflict with Confucianism, since an ethic that valued ritualists trained in the Classics could neither appeal to nor provide for specialists trained in gunnery and mathematics. And the eternal validity of Confucius's sayings could not remain unquestioned by those who found technology more important in the modern world.

Only a few of the most sensitive Chinese were beginning to ask these questions of themselves in the last years of the nineteenth century. For the moment, other demands were much more pressing as the era of diplomatic cooperation drew to a close. The Treaties of Tientsin (1858) opened the interior of China to Western missionaries, whose proselytizing led to severe conflicts between Christians and traditional social elements. The power of the local gentry, for example, was threatened by these foreign missionaries, for the missionaries ignored magistrates and zealously protected converts by calling upon foreign gunboats. At the same time, the peasants, alarmed by the presence of the strange new religion, circulated rumors of bizarre ritual practices. It was said that Christians were cannibals who ate children or used their bodies for alchemy. The union of gentry defensiveness and peasant conservatism eventually incited a series of antimissionary riots in the late 1860s. Consequently, missionary pressure groups joined with European traders disappointed by meager profits to demand that more of China be opened up to Western control and exploitation. Therefore, just as authorities in Peking, alarmed by the spread of modernism, began to harden their own stand against the Western presence, the European powers were being pushed by their constituents into an ever more aggressive stance of their own. By 1870, when the French consul and Catholic missionaries were massacred by a Chinese mob at Tientsin, the age of the new imperialism was about to dawn on China.

IMPERIALISM AND NATIONALISM IN INDIA (1858–1914)

Meanwhile, in India the unexpected revolt of 1857, which reduced much of the north to chaos for over a year, came as a profound shock to the British. Yet the rebels were so divided and the outbreak so easily put down that this revolt failed to shake the confidence of the British in their imperial mission. But the uprising did convince them that the administration of the empire had to be overhauled and the policy of speedy Westernization drastically curtailed.

New British Policies

The first casualty of the uprising was the East India Company itself. By 1858, stripped of all commercial functions, it had become an anachronism, and now its governing powers were transferred to a viceroy ruling in the name of Queen Victoria. During the next few years legal procedures were simplified and the executive and legislative councils enlarged and reformed. To make further mutinies impossible, the Bengal army was reorganized, the number of European soldiers was increased, and there was more recruitment from the martial castes of the northwest. The reformed army proved a strong bulwark of the state and remained faithful to the government throughout the upheavals of the nationalist era. More important than army reform, however, was a new policy of friendship with the princes and landed classes. During 1857 the British had seen dispossessed princes heading rebel columns, whereas those still on their thrones, such as the Rajput chieftains and the Hyderabad Nizam, aided the British cause. As a result, after the Mutiny, the viceroy, Lord Canning, guaranteed the remaining princes against annexation and brought them into a new and more personal relationship with the government. The princes responded eagerly to these overtures and soon became a major force for stability in the imperial system.

Similar conciliation was carried out in the provinces of British India. The old landed classes were seen to be, like the princes, a powerful and conservative group, whose influence did not disappear with the loss of their estates. Indeed, in many areas, despite boons given them by the British, the peasants followed their traditional overlords into revolt, while elsewhere the rural population

remained at best passive spectators. Disillusioned with the attempt to enhance the position of the small landholders, the British turned toward the landlords and even restored some to their old estates. Occasional attempts were made to protect the peasantry by the enactment of tenancy legislation providing rights of occupancy and regulation of rents, but the landlords, now in official favor, were usually able to evade these restrictions.

The citadels of religious tradition and custom also were found to be far stronger than had been anticipated by the reformers of the Bentinck era (1828–1835). Thus the British avoided further direct interference in Indian social practices, but they were too deeply committed to the goal of modernization to abandon such activities altogether. They simply redirected their energies. Education benefited to some extent; it was not considered to be social interference since educators did not openly attempt to change Indian institutions. Most of their efforts, however, were directed toward public works. The construction of such works became the credo of most late nineteenth-century English officials

IMPERIALISM

Imperialism in its broadest sense is the policy of empire-building, the bringing of weak countries or peoples under the political rule of strong ones through military conquest. Its most famous practitioners included the ancient Assyrians, Persians, Romans, and Chinese, the Arabs in the seventh and eighth centuries, and the Mughals and Ottoman Turks in the sixteenth century. Thereafter the European powers took the lead, particularly Spain in Latin America and Britain and France in North America. In the late nineteenth century the British defenders of the "white man's burden" proudly used the word "imperialism" to describe both their physical occupation and their economic penetration of large portions of Africa and Asia. But after the Boxer Rebellion in China and the Boer War in South Africa, "imperialism" became a term of abuse along with "colonialism," signifying the exploitation and humiliation of the natives in the colonies by white settlers and administrators.

During the twentieth century, the terms "imperialism" and "colonialism" have become practically interchangeable in the minds of many people. But, though often combined, there can be imperialism without colonialism — as in recent United States military intervention in Southeast Asia. And there can be colonialism — or what is now called "neocolonialism" — without the kinds of military and political control usually associated with imperialism. Noteworthy examples include United States economic and political influence in much of Latin America since the turn of the century and continuing French influence since 1960 in many of those sovereign states of Africa which were formerly French colonies.

577   *The Challenge of the New Imperialism*

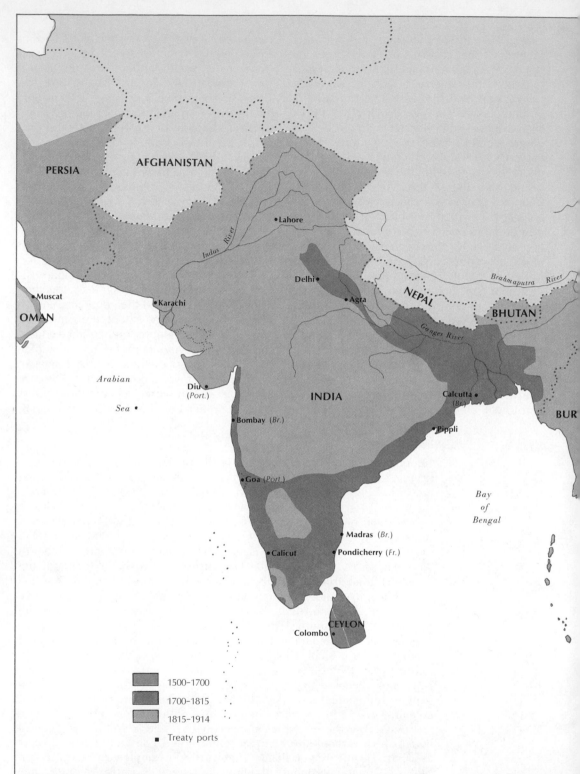

PERSIA

AFGHANISTAN

•Lahore

Indus River

Delhi•

•Agra

NEPAL

Brahmaputra River

•Muscat

•Karachi

OMAN

BHUTAN

Ganges River

Arabian

Diu•
(*Port.*)

INDIA

Calcutta •
(*Br.*)

Sea •

•Bombay (*Br.*)

•Pippli

BUR

•Goa (*Port.*)

*Bay
of
Bengal*

•Madras (*Br.*)

•Calicut

•Pondicherry (*Fr.*)

CEYLON

Colombo •

1500–1700

1700–1815

1815–1914

■ Treaty ports

EXPANSION OF WEST INTO ASIA, 1500–1914

Peking ■

Tientsin ■

Seoul ●

Wei-hai-wei ■

KOREA

Kyoto ●

Yokohama ●

JAPAN

Yellow River

Port Arthur ■

Yellow
Sea

Nagasaki ■

CHINA

Nanking ●

Shanghai ■

Ningpo ■

East
China
Sea

Hankow ■

Yangtze River

Chungking ■

Foochow ■

Tai-pei ●

Mekong River

Amoy ■

TAIWAN

Canton ■
Macao ● Hong Kong ●
(Br.)

Kwangchow ●
(Fr. lease)

Hanoi ●

HAINAN

Manila ●

SIAM
(THAILAND)

FRENCH
INDO-
CHINA

South
China
Sea

PHILIPPINE

Bangkok ●

ISLANDS

Saigon ●

NORTH
BORNEO

Celebes
Sea

BRUNEI

MOLUCCAS

FED. MALAY
STATES

SARAWAK

SUMATRA

Singapore ●
(Br.)

BORNEO

CELEBES

Padang ●

Palembang ●

Java Sea

TIMOR

DUTCH EAST INDIES

Batavia ●

JAVA

in India: roads, bridges, irrigation canals, and railways (the largest rail system in Asia) all took shape under the direction of the government. Industrial development, apart from plantation industries such as tea and jute, was not encouraged, for the British wished to retain India as a market for their own manufactured goods. But neither was indigenous enterprise prohibited, with the result that some local industry did grow up, first in cotton textiles and then, by the early twentieth century, in iron and steel. Its effects, however, did not measurably alter the overwhelmingly agrarian character of the Indian economy.

The British policy of encouraging traditionalism in social relations and modernization only in technological and economic matters bears a striking resemblance to the Confucian restorationism of China at the same time, under the T'ung-chih Emperor. In both cases the goal was to rehabilitate the traditional elite as the leaders of society while equipping them with the tools of the modern world. In India as in China, however, this backward-looking policy, although successful in shoring up the empire in the short run, ultimately proved a source of weakness, for the old elites were incapable of adjusting to the new demands placed on them, while the attempt to placate them made it more difficult for the government to reach any accommodation with the new educated and mercantile elite groups. In India the effects of this policy were further sharpened by the growth of a new colonialist ideology that embittered the relations between Indian and Englishman.

Ever since they had first come to India, the English had remained apart from local society and looked upon it condescendingly. During the early nineteenth century, under the influence of evangelical religion and Victorian morality, this British feeling became more pronounced and was imbued with a tone of contemptuous disdain. But the British liberal still believed in the educability of the Indian people and foresaw a time, distant to be sure, when an India suffused with Western values and institutions could take its place in the family of nations. The Mutiny with its overtones of fear and racial violence dealt a heavy blow to this optimistic vision. A people who had rejected the benefits of European civilization, it was argued, was clearly incapable of appreciating them. During the 1860s and 1870s this view slowly grew into a fullfledged theory of colonialism based on the concept of ineradicable differences between the races and drawing upon an authoritarian strand of liberalism that stressed the rule of law over democracy. This theory, which soon became the creed of most British officials, assumed that the decadent condition of Indian society was a reflection of inherent racial inferiority, that it could not be changed, and that the indefinite extension of beneficent British rule was therefore in India's own best interest. At the same time the assumption that India was a static and changeless land added support to the policy of conciliating the upper classes, who were now regarded as the "natural" leaders of the tradition-bound rural masses.

Liberalism

The new imperial ideology was not altogether unchallenged, for a liberal upsurge in Britain reached India with the viceroyalty of Lord Ripon (1880–1884). A thoughtful and sensitive man, Ripon tried to bring the educated classes into the confidence of government and to widen the scope of their employment. His greatest success was in the field of local self-government where he established elected municipal and district boards free of official domination. However, the Ilbert Bill, his attempt to permit Indian judges to try Europeans in the countryside, only revealed the depth of racial feeling among the British in India. Fearful for their supremacy, they forced Ripon to accept a greatly weakened act.

Ripon in the same way had only limited success in his attempt to infuse Indian foreign policy with the pacific ideals of British liberalism. Conservative viceroys, anxious over recent Russian advances into Central Asia and determined to counter this threat by carving out a British sphere of influence in the mountainous regions beyond the Indus, had twice plunged India into disastrous wars with Afghanistan, in 1839 and again in 1878. Ripon withdrew the Indian army from these exposed forward positions and set Indo-Afghan relations on a firm and friendly basis,

Simla, the summer capital of British India on a ridge 7000 feet up in the Himalayas. Its physical isolation enhanced the distance between ruling Briton and subject Indian.

which continued, with one short interlude, until the end of British rule. He could not, however, halt the process of imperial expansion in the east, where upper Burma was annexed by his successor in response to French moves in Indochina, and in the north, where an expedition was sent across the Himalayas to Tibet in 1904 to counter imagined Russian activity there. At no time did much actual fighting take place, nor were Indian borders ever seriously threatened.

Indian Reformers and Westernization

While the new imperialism was gaining strength among the British official class in India, English education, and with it a new critical spirit, were spreading throughout the country. The new spirit first manifested itself in Bengal, particularly in Calcutta, the capital, for there the British presence was overwhelming and incontestable. It was impossible for the urban Bengali to continue in the traditional patterns of life and thought. In addition, Bengal was a center of missionary activity and the locale of several Western-style schools, most notably the Hindu College, established well before Bentinck's time by wealthy European and Indian patrons. Exposure to new ideas of secular liberalism and rationalism, which were often felt to lie at the base of British success, soon stirred the educated Indian to examine his own culture and to decide whether and how it might need

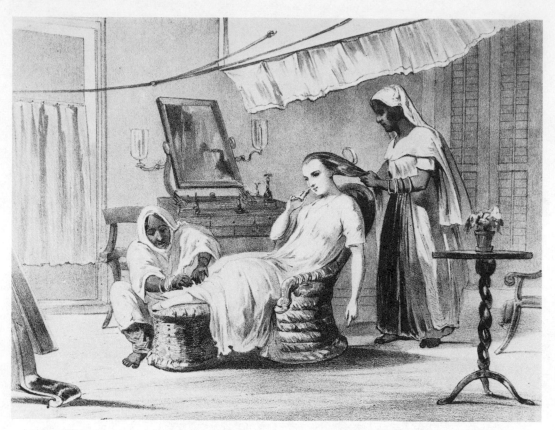

"Our Magistrate's Wife" from the satirical volume Curry and Rice. *The author at the same time depicts and makes fun of the leisurely insulated life of the British in India.*

reform. Few went to the extreme of total acceptance of all things Western, including Christianity, for that involved too great a repudiation of their own heritage to be psychologically acceptable. Apart from a small band of radical enthusiasts in the 1830s, most Indian thinkers tried to cope with the Western impact by incorporating elements of the new culture into a reformed Hinduism.

The first and in some ways the greatest of the reformers was Ram Mohan Roy (1772–1833). Schooled in Persian and Hindu thought as well as Christianity, and intimately associated with the British in Calcutta, Ram Mohan took his stand on the principles of reason and monotheism, which he claimed underlay both Hindu and Western thought and were found particularly in the Hindu *Upanishads*. Thereby freed of any sense of subservience to the West, he pro-

ceeded to mount a full-scale attack upon popular Hinduism, denouncing idolatry, widow-burning, and caste restrictions as irrational and as barriers to progress. Ram Mohan's theistic ideas were upheld after his death by the Brahmo Samaj, a group of his followers led for several decades by Debendranath Tagore, father of the famous poet Rabindranath. Their society always remained too intellectual and eclectic in its views to attract a large popular following, but it was highly influential in shaping the attitudes of the Bengali intelligentsia. The mid-nineteenth century social reform movement, which sought to emancipate the Hindu woman from the constraints of child marriage and polygamy and to overturn the ban on remarriage of widows, owed much to the forceful example set by Ram Mohan and his followers.

By the later nineteenth century, Western ideas, now promoted by a widespread network of government schools, had penetrated to all parts of the country and to groups lower in the social scale and less sophisticated than the educated elite of Calcutta. At the same time, Hindu society was regaining its self-confidence after the stupendous blows of the initial Western encounter. As the failure of the Mutiny showed, it was impossible to restore the past or to ignore the West. But, at the same time, there was increasing reluctance to openly acknowledge dependence on the alien ruler or to apply Western standards of judgment. Reform, as a result, was justified increasingly in terms of indigenous Hindu values. The most striking instance of this can be seen in the Arya Samaj, a society founded by Dayanand Saraswati (1824–1883) which flourished especially in the Punjab. Much like K'ang Yu-wei and the Chinese reformers of the 1890s, who saw in a radically revised Confucianism the basis for a modern China (see p. 597), Dayanand looked to the Vedas, the oldest Hindu scriptures, as the sole basis of authority. In their name he denounced as abuses almost all the practices of contemporary Hinduism, including even the superiority of the Brahmin. The content of his reform program was thus very similar to that of the Brahmo Samaj, but his aim was not so much the assimilation of Western rationalism as the creation of a revitalized Hinduism capable of withstanding the challenge of the West. Its appeal lay in a combination of social reform and education with a stubborn reverence for the archaic past.

Another revivalist movement was that of the holy man Shri Ramakrishna (1836–1886) and his disciple Swami Vivekananda, who gained fame in 1893 at the "Parliament of Religions" at the Chicago International Exposition. Defiantly glorifying the old order, Vivekananda asserted that Hinduism possessed a spiritual depth and solace that compensated for the material superiority of the West. Although Vivekananda left no organized body of disciples behind, his message struck a responsive chord in the hearts of many Indians and helped to relieve the hurt of a century of being treated as culturally inferior.

Ram Mohan Roy (1772–1833), the first great Indian reformer.

The Indian Muslims underwent much the same reexamination and reform of their cultural heritage. In their case, however, the process of adaptation was delayed by several decades, for the Muslims, proud of their own imperial past, did not care to learn the language or master the ways of their British conquerors. Their predominant response during the nineteenth century was one of defensive militancy, a tightening of the bonds uniting the Islamic community under their traditional religious leaders, the *ulama*. One wing of this movement, the Wahabis, for a time even advocated holy war (*jihad*) against the British, while others, particularly after the failure of the 1857 revolt, concentrated on religious purification and education through the medium of the Urdu tongue. The first Islamic modernist was Sayyid Ahmad Khan (1817–1898). A scion of a Mughal court family, Sayyid Ahmad emerged from many years in British government service convinced that Indian Islam must come to terms with the West as well as remain distinct from Hinduism if it was to play a major role in the India of the future. The fruit of this resolution was Aligarh College (founded 1875), which provided a new Muslim professional elite with both Western learning and a sense of Islamic identity.

Growth of Nationalism

The novel ideas the British brought with them to India were not only social and cultural but political as well. Although India was ruled autocratically, in their schools the British taught Shakespeare and Milton, Mill and Mazzini, and from these authors the young Indian came away excited by the ideas of liberty, equality, and democracy. Before the British arrived, India was usually divided into small warring states, and no one conceived of the subcontinent as a nation. While Hinduism provided a basic cultural unity for the majority of the people, it also divided them into castes and sects and thus inhibited the growth of any larger sense of loyalty. There were only local or regional ties, encompassing at most a linguistic area, such as Bengal or Maharashtra. British rule made possible for the first time the growth of a national consciousness in India, not only by providing Western education, but simply by treating the whole country as a single governmental unit. Such measures as the establishment of a nationwide rail and telecommunications network and the execution of all government business in English gave to educated Indians from various regions a common language and a shared experience of ideals and grievances.

The new class that grew up around the Western schools was very small compared with the total population. In 1885 there were only 55,000 persons thinly spread across India who had had any college-level English education, and of these only ten percent had won degrees. These men were restricted almost entirely to urban professional groups such as teachers, lawyers, and subordinate government servants. Concentration in these few occupations was the natural result of a system that emphasized literary education at the expense of scientific, and in which many professions were either closed to Indians, like the army officer corps and politics, or were regarded as degrading, as in the case of agriculture. During the first half of the nineteenth century the English-educated class, like their patron Ram Mohan Roy, extolled the British for bestowing civil liberties and a free press upon India and they remained outspokenly loyal during the disturbances of 1857. Their interests were too closely tied to those of the British for them to support a traditionalist uprising. But they never hesitated to criticize British aloofness, and in the early 1850s they began to form political associations. These societies were usually short-lived and confined to a small section of the educated class. But they accustomed the new middle classes to working together and paved the way for the foundation in 1885 of the first, and still the most important, all-India political organization, the Indian National Congress.

The Congress emerged from the hopes and frustrations of the Ripon era (1880–1884). By promising much but producing little, especially in the debacle of the Ilbert Bill controversy, Ripon convinced educated Indians that they must fight for equal treatment, that only effective organization would produce results. During its first twenty years the Congress was a modest organization with no permanent secretariat and only a few hundred members. It met for only a few days a year to pass resolutions. Moreover, despite the rebuffs and hostility of British officialdom, the Congress remained convinced of the value of the British connection and of the inherent liberalism and sense of fair play of the British people who, they felt, would remedy legitimate grievances fairly presented to the Parliament in London if not in India. But its moderation did not prevent the Congress from forcefully pressing for a variety of political and economic reforms, notably the expansion of the Indian element in the Legislative Councils and the Civil Service and the ending of a colonialist exploitation that drained the country of its wealth with no equivalent return.

However, secure in their imperial splendor, the British made only token gestures toward redress of the nationalists' grievances. Indeed, even respectful criticism was often regarded as sedition. As a result, there grew up within the Congress at the turn of the century an extremist wing disdainful of hat-in-hand petitioning and Western constitutional forms. Led by a fiery Maharashtrian, Bal Gangadhar Tilak (1856–1920), this group sought to strengthen the nationalist cause by invoking sentiments of Hindu revivalism and regional patriotism. Tilak saw a blend of traditional mythology and modern revolutionary tactics as the only way of mobilizing sufficient popular support to wrest concessions from a reluctant British imperial government. To this end he was willing to postpone social reform until after independence and he even promoted religious festivals as a way of enhancing Hindu pride and self-esteem.

Incipient conflict between moderates and radicals was brought to a head and the nationalist movement itself was transformed by the actions of Lord Curzon (viceroy 1898–1905). A forceful and energetic administrator, Curzon overhauled the cumbrous machinery of Indian government, enacted several measures for the benefit of the peasantry and the encouragement of agriculture, and initiated the preservation of ancient monuments. But Curzon never understood or consulted with the educated classes and so blundered into the partition of Bengal, a move that triggered the first mass political agitation in India.

For Curzon the partition was largely a means of improving administrative efficiency in an overgrown province. It was interpreted by the Bengalis, however, as an attack on the integrity of their homeland and an attempt to divide Hindu from Muslim, for the new province of eastern Bengal (now Bangladesh) had a Muslim majority. The British did win substantial Muslim support by the partition but they were overwhelmed by the widespread Hindu protest, felt even in remote rural areas, which took the novel and effective form of boycotting British goods. At the same time the heady excitement of the partition struggle, together with the electrifying news of the Japanese victory over Russia in 1905 (see p. 598), led, particularly among the students, to a glorification of force and the growth of a cult of political assassination in the name of the bloodthirsty goddess Kali. In 1912 the partition had to be undone, but in the meantime the Congress, at first united behind the anti-partition agitation, had split in two over the question of violence. Shocked by terrorist outrages, the moderates under G. K. Gokhale in 1907 expelled the extremists from the organization.

Although stunned by the force of the agitation, the British government, controlled from 1906 by the Liberal party, moved quickly to meet the crisis. Its policy was twofold: first they crushed the extremists by enacting severe repressive legislation and by placing Tilak and other leaders in jail for up to six years; then they tried to win over the moderates by taking some initial steps toward associating Indians with the government. Most important was the Councils Act of 1909, which provided for direct election of a majority of Indians to enlarged legislative bodies. The executive remained in British hands, so that the Act did not give the Indian members any real control. Nevertheless, it clearly pointed in the direction of responsible government and was welcomed by the moderate nationalists for that reason.

The next six years were marked by harmonious cooperation between the government and the Congress, but the calm was only a breathing space. The imprisonment of nationalist leaders could not stem forever the ardent nationalism that lay at the root of extremism, nor could the moderates' taste of power, once whetted, ever be fully satisfied without more reforms. The upheavals and discontents of World War I soon transformed the scene.

THE MEIJI RESTORATION IN JAPAN (1868–1912)

Like China and India, Japan also experienced a "restoration"; but the Japanese version did not revive the traditional social system as a way of ensuring political stability. Instead, it tried to effect rapid social changes through the ancient political ideal of direct imperial rule. This crucial moment in modern Japanese history occurred in 1868 when the feudal daimyo of Japan ceremonially "restored" political power to the young Meiji emperor and ended rule by the Tokugawa shogunate. On the surface, this was a restoration of the traditional form of government. But the young samurai reformers who championed the Meiji emperor's rule then proceeded to use the powerful appeal of his divine legitimacy to destroy the feudal social system and lay the foundations of a modern state.

Reaction to the West

The opening of China after the "Opium War" heightened European desires to bring Japan into "the civilized world," but it was left to the United States of America to realize Western ambitions. After the United States acquired California in 1846-1848, New York financiers began to think of establishing a Pacific steamship run between America's west coast and Shanghai. Japan would be an ideal fueling station. In the fall of 1852, therefore, United States Commodore Matthew Perry set sail with four "black ships" for Tokyo Bay. He reached Japan the next year with a letter to the Japanese emperor from President Millard Fillmore. Remembering China's defeat by Western warships, the Tokugawa shogunate accepted the letter, even though many Japanese believed this would only lead to further concessions. Indeed, when Perry returned in the following spring, Tokugawa negotiators were forced to admit American traders and consuls. Russia and Britain soon followed suit, just as the first United States consul, Townsend Harris, was demanding that more than two ports be opened.

Soon the shogunate found itself caught between Japanese antiforeignism and the inescapable fact that Japan could not win a war against any of the great powers. Whereas most feudal lords realized the risks of yielding to the zealous impulse to reject the West, many of their samurai followers in the outer fiefs joined impatient young imperial nobles at Kyoto in insisting that even death was better than surrender. Almost overnight, Emperor Kōmei became a rallying point for fervid nationalists who shouted "Honor the Emperor" and "Expel the Barbarian" in the same breath. Little known samurai of lesser rank descended in droves upon the emperor's court at Kyoto to join sword-fighting clubs influenced by the passionate Chōshū samurai, Yoshida Shōin. Yoshida argued that the aging ruling elite had lost the right to rule, and that terrorism was justified by the emergency. His eventual execution for an assassination attempt in 1858 only drove the country deeper into turmoil.

These violent younger samurai did more than set heroic examples of patriotism for others. They also helped bring together two of the great "outer" fiefs of southern Japan, Chōshū and Satsuma. Once these fiefs had reconciled their differences, they came to agree that the only solution to the country's problems was the overthrow of the shogunate. During the summer of 1866, civil war finally broke out between the shogun's forces and Chōshū's newly trained armies. Then, on January 3, 1868, Satsuma men seized Kyoto and placed the young Meiji Emperor in charge of the nation. By the end of the year, the Tokugawa were entirely defeated and the Imperial Meiji Restoration an established fact.

Unification and Modernization

The Meiji Restoration was much more than a simple substitution of one ruler for another: it made possible the abolition of the entire feudal system. On March 2, 1869, four of the great daimyo told the emperor:

Now that we are about to establish an entirely new form of government, the National polity and the sovereign authority must not in the slightest degree be yielded to subordinates. The place where your servants live is the emperor's land, and those whom they rule are the emperor's people. How can these be made the property of subjects? Your servants accordingly beg respectfully to surrender their fiefs to your majesty.

This seemingly voluntary surrender of feudal rights to an absolute monarch was actually the work of a new Meiji elite—men like Saigō Takamori, Ōkubo Toshimichi, Kido Kōin, and Iwakura Tomomi, who quickly realized that they would not have a powerful and unified country as long as Japan was divided into competing and autonomous fiefs. Combining judicious threats of force with the powerful appeal of direct imperial rule, they transformed the feudal lords into imperially appointed governors and within another few years appropriated their lands, abolished private armies, and began to erase legal distinctions between samurai and commoners. Aristocratic rank and divided loyalties were replaced by bureaucratic status and national commitment, so that all eyes turned toward the symbolic apex of the country, the emperor himself. In other words, the political ambitions of a new Meiji oligar-

A contemporary Japanese artist portrayed the fife and drum corps of Admiral Perry's second expedition to Japan in 1854. At this time Perry forced the bakufu negotiators to open the country to American consuls.

chy combined with the popular fear of foreign invasion and the universally accepted legitimacy of the emperor to make possible the creation of a modern state.

That state in turn organized an intensive program of modernization without parallel in Asia. Military modernization was the first order of business, and in the name of progress, a conscript army was created along Prussian lines. A modern navy was also trained, with British help, and by 1894 it could boast of fifty-two modern warships, many of which were built in Japanese ship-yards. Indeed, the need for armaments made the government the country's major consumer. Heavy industries (capitalized with one-third of the national budget) were founded by the government, then turned over to private financiers (zaibatsu) who sold back the industry's products to that very same government. The capital was created by devising a national land tax which took a portion of the country's new agricultural surplus, derived from a 30% increase in rice yields during the last quarter of the nineteenth century because of better fertilizers. New income came from a booming foreign trade (by the 1890s silk exports earned Japan $50 million per year), which in turn was facilitated by the government's introduction of modern processing methods. Other innovations accompanied economic progress: a new education system, a Westernized law code, and a banking and currency apparatus. Modernization was the catchword of the age, as translators like Fukuzawa Yukichi popularized English thought and as new literary genres, influenced by the European novel, became the rage.

This stunningly rapid shift in institutions and values was not without its strains. The most obvious conflict was political. Although the feudal domains had been changed into prefectures (ken), sectional identities were far from eradicated. Furthermore, not all samurai were willing to lose their stipends and status. The new government tried to funnel some of their resentment into an avid nationalism by supporting an aggressive foreign policy toward China and Korea, but overseas expansion did not solve the internal social question. Samurai who could not adjust to new conditions clustered around Saigō Takamori, who had retired to his native Satsuma in 1873 after being forced out of the Meiji oligarchy. There, 20,000 diehard samurai became his ardent followers and agitated for a stronger foreign policy and maintenance of their own status. After the samurai were informed in 1876 that they no longer had the unique privilege of wearing swords, Saigō led a Satsuma army against Tokyo. His defeat at Kagoshima in September 1877 by the government's huge conscript army marked the demise of the feudal

warrior class and ended serious military challenges to the oligarchs' rule. Groups from domains like Tosa and Hizen, which opposed the Chōshū clique's monopoly of high government posts, did not rebel but rather tried to make the government more democratic by petitioning in 1874 for the establishment of representative assemblies. By 1881 two major political parties had been formed, the Liberals (Jiyutō) and the Progressives (Kaishintō), both demanding "popular rights" through elections.

For the next eight years, the government (which in 1881 promised a national assembly by 1890) cautiously suppressed the Popular Rights movement while meticulously exploring ways of granting a constitution that would not threaten the oligarchy's power. A peerage, cabinet system, and privy council were established beforehand to ensure control from above; envoys were sent abroad to examine European constitutions. Eventually, an authoritarian German model was chosen; in 1889 the emperor finally granted his subjects a Western style constitution and the right to hold elections to a parliament. During the following decade, the parties experimented with the limited power granted them in the lower house (Diet) of the legislature. Unfortunately, the most important component of parliamentary democracy—ministerial responsibility—was missing. The new government consisted of a cabinet responsible to the emperor, an electorate severely circumscribed by property qualifications, an upper house composed of carefully chosen peers who could be expected to support the regime, and a lower house that could neither initiate legislation nor withhold fiscal appropriations.

The only weapon that the parties possessed was an absolute denial of legislative approval, which usually resulted in the impeachment of the administration's appointed prime minister. When this occurred, the oligarchy dissolved the Diet and demanded new elections. Consequently, by the end of the century party politics had been deeply discredited in the eyes of a public annoyed by constant parliamentary turmoil. Even party leaders came to feel that a direct assault on the ministerial system presided over by oligarchic "Elders" (genrō) like Yamagata

Aritomo and Itō Hirobumi was futile. Cooperation with elements in the government responsive (though never responsible) to the party was more likely to provide cabinet offices and patronage for that party's members.

The failure to allow genuine parliamentary democracy reflected the essential nature of the Meiji state. Meiji leaders believed that the psychological and social tensions of modernization had to be checked by an intense commitment to the emperor, whose very person was an identity symbol for the citizens of their new Japan. Thus they created a system in which every subject viewed himself in a direct, almost mystic relationship with the divine monarch. No room remained for either autonomous ideologies or purely personal identities. The state was not merely a keeper of the public order; rather, each citizen was taught to believe that his moral life was tied to the state. His every act had to harmonize with the needs of the nation. As a result, democratic political movements were suspected of being divisive (hence potentially treacherous) forces diverting the citizen from his obligatory duty toward the public good. Even the Liberal party's leader, Itagaki Taisuke, insisted that

Each individual must cast away selfishness and assume a spirit of unity. The people must become accustomed to banding together by depending on one another. The nation and its government exist so that all the people may pool their strength and guard their rights. Hence, if a man wishes to enjoy liberty through the protection of his government, he must strive to acquire a national liberty.

For the moment the *collective* definition of *individual* goals aided the establishment of a strong central state committed to the common quest for national survival. Later, the same sentiment strengthened ultranationalism and imperialism by promoting the belief that if their emperor was a unique ruler in his divine descent from the Sun Goddess, then the Japanese were likewise a unique people with a sacred mission to guide the rest of Asia along the Imperial Way. Possession of a sense of manifest destiny, however, was not peculiarly Japanese during the later years of the nineteenth century. Other nations saw

their mission in overseas expansion as well. In fact, when Japan began to interfere in Chinese affairs, it was following, not leading, the great powers of Europe in a "new imperialism" that swept over Asia after 1870.

THE NEW IMPERIALISM IN SOUTHEAST ASIA

During the thirty years between 1870 and 1900, the major European powers expanded their influence throughout vast reaches of East and Southeast Asia. Expansion through direct political control and the carving out of spheres of influence marked a new direction in the relations of Western Europe with less developed areas of the world. Known as the new imperialism (see pp. 469–471), these thirty years of exploration and conquest brought under European rule nearly one hundred and fifty million people and marked the first great surge toward empire since the late eighteenth century.

Behind this extraordinary outburst of imperial expansion were numerous motives and impulses. Central to much of it, however, was the advancing industrialization of the major continental European powers, particularly France and Germany. Before 1870 Britain had stood alone as the world's preeminent industrial power. Its control of the seas and a policy of enforced free trade were enough to give it a commanding position in all the markets of the world. During the last quarter of the century, however, the continental nations underwent rapid industrialization, while raising their tariff barriers to protect their fledgling national industries against British competition. But the home markets were rarely large enough to satisfy ambitious entrepreneurs, nor were the basic raw materials of industry always present in ample supply. So they turned their attention overseas to the rich markets and raw materials of Asia and Africa. Since their objective was to develop exclusive preserves for their home industries free from the encroachment of rivals, the continental powers were rapidly driven to conquer and rule the areas they coveted. This, in turn, spurred the British, determined to protect their own lead, into extending formal control over areas they had previously simply traded with and into com-

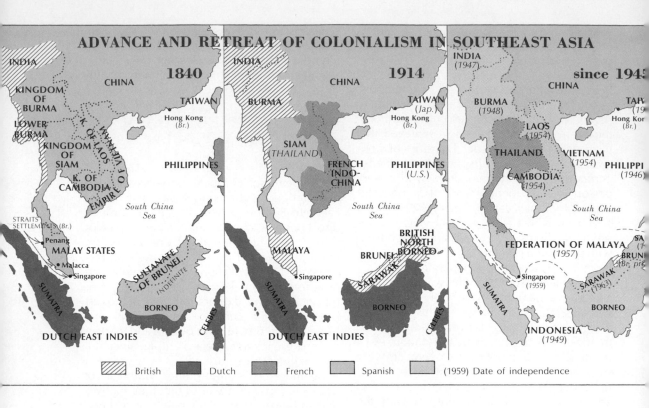

ADVANCE AND RETREAT OF COLONIALISM IN SOUTHEAST ASIA

1840

INDIA
CHINA
KINGDOM OF BURMA
LOWER BURMA
TAIWAN
Hong Kong (Br.)
K. OF VIETNAM
KINGDOM OF SIAM
K. OF CAMBODIA
EMPIRE OF LAOS
PHILIPPINES
South China Sea
STRAITS SETTLEMENTS (Br.)
Penang
MALAY STATES
Malacca
Singapore
SULTANATE OF BRUNEI
INDEFINITE
SUMATRA
CELEBES
BORNEO
DUTCH EAST INDIES

1914

INDIA
CHINA
BURMA
TAIWAN (Jap.)
Hong Kong (Br.)
SIAM (THAILAND)
FRENCH INDO-CHINA
PHILIPPINES (U.S.)
South China Sea
MALAYA
Singapore
BRITISH NORTH BORNEO
BRUNEI
SARAWAK
SUMATRA
CELEBES
BORNEO
DUTCH EAST INDIES

since 194[5]

INDIA (1947)
CHINA
BURMA (1948)
TAIWAN (19[)
Hong Kon (Br.)
LAOS (1954)
THAILAND
VIETNAM (1954)
PHILIPPI (1946)
CAMBODIA (1954)
South China Sea
FEDERATION OF MALAYA (1957)
SA
BRUN (Br. pro
SARAWAK (1963)
Singapore (1959)
SUMATRA
BORNEO
INDONESIA (1949)

British   Dutch   French   Spanish   (1959) Date of independence

peting for unoccupied territories. Often, newly created colonies did not contain very many useful raw materials or developed markets. Indeed, many were for years financial liabilities for their imperial owners. But they were collected anyway in the hope that someday they might be made into profitable commercial enterprises. The spirit was one, in the words of the British liberal imperialist Lord Rosebery, of "pegging out claims for the future."

Dutch in Indonesia

Two of the more successful imperial ventures were the Dutch in the outer islands of Indonesia and the British on the adjacent Malay peninsula. Although long established on Java, the Dutch did not move in force onto the large islands of Sumatra, Borneo, and Celebes until after 1870. By that time private Dutch capital was seeking to enter the economy of the Indies, hitherto monopolized by the government through its forcible collection of native produce for export under the Culture System. (See p. 549.) In 1870 private business pressure secured adoption of a new Agrarian Law that permitted private leasing of uncultivated "waste land." The years following saw a rapid growth of corporate plantations, on both Java and, as they were brought under Dutch control, the outer islands. Although Javanese sugar remained the major export crop of the Indies, by the early twentieth century the outer islands, especially Sumatra, were producing increasing amounts of basic industrial raw materials such as rubber, tin, and oil. In most areas the Dutch continued to monopolize the mercantile opportunities of the new plantations and the profits of the external trade, while domestic petty trade was controlled by a growing class of immigrant Chinese entrepreneurs. The Indonesian peasantry remained confined within the bounds of the old subsistence rice economy. In this manner, the stultifying effects of the "dual economy" lasted throughout the colonial period.

British in Malaya

The initial British involvement in Malaya was a by-product of the China trade. The conquests of Penang in 1786 and of Singapore in 1819 by Sir Stamford Raffles were prompted by the East India Company's desire for bases to protect its ships on the long, arduous journey through the Straits of Malacca and the South China Sea. The impetus for expansion, however, came from private British mercantile houses. Shut out of the Indonesian archipelago by the British government's determination to maintain friendly relations with Holland, the private traders rapidly developed Singapore into a commercial center for the whole of eastern Asia and fought to obtain trade and mining concessions from the various sultans in its peninsular hinterland.

Long reluctant to become involved in the affairs of these chiefs, the British government did not establish protectorates over them until the 1870s. Although justified by the need to suppress piracy and internal disorder, this forward move in fact reflected the competitive imperialism of the new era and brought with it an economic advance even more spectacular than that of the Dutch East Indies. The Malay sultans were left on their thrones, but effective power lay in the hands of British Residents who supervised the administration and smoothed the way for the flow of foreign capital. First to be developed were the Malayan tin mines, which by 1900 supplied half the world's total output. Rubber, brought from Brazil and grown on large plantations, followed in the twentieth century to meet the vast demand created by the automotive industry. Again Malaya soon contributed half the world's total supply.

Native Malays were not excluded from the new commercial economy, as were their Indonesian neighbors, but they remained on the whole indifferent to the new opportunities. As a result, plantation laborers were often recruited in India and impoverished South China, while enterprising Chinese immigrants provided the bulk of the capital for mining and commerce. Similar patterns of migration took place in other Southeast Asian countries as well. In Burma, for instance, Indian merchants and clerks dominated the modern sector of the economy, while on the island of Ceylon indentured Tamil laborers from south India provided the work force for the burgeoning coffee and tea

plantations. Rarely did the process go so far as in Malaya, where Chinese and Indian settlers reduced the Malays to a minority in their homeland, but in almost every Southeast Asian nation racial and ethnic loyalties, often reinforced by separate schools and secret societies, were stronger than territorial ties and inhibited the growth of a sense of cohesion or common purpose. Even the recent growth of nationalism has not been able completely to surmount these divisions.

French in Indochina

National, racial, and monarchical divisions also characterized the lands of Southeast Asia north of Malaya. In fact, it was civil war between the northern and southern halves of Vietnam (Annam) that first invited French penetration of that area. In 1786 Catholic missionaries had urged Louis XVI to back the southern Nguyen claimants to the throne after intense conflict broke out. But by the time the Nguyen won in 1802, the Revolution in France had turned that country away from a royal policy that benefited the Catholic church. Not until Napoleon III's Second Empire in the 1850s did France again seriously pursue colonial expansion in Southeast Asia. Napoleon III's personal enthusiasm for overseas empire and his desire to woo Catholics provoked an expedition to Vietnam in 1858 to avenge the murder of several French missionaries. By 1867 French naval forces had overcome a fervent native resistance movement to acquire Cochin China (the provinces around Saigon) as well as rights over Cambodia.

However, more was at stake in Indochina than Catholic political influence or Napoleonic dreams of empire. After the Third Republic succeeded the Second Empire, a new generation of imperialists avid for colonial grandeur and anxious to turn Frenchmen's eyes away from the touchy Alsace-Lorraine question began to dream of occupying North Vietnam. Furthermore, ambitious young naval officers on the spot, like François Garnier, were willing to risk reprimand from the home government in order to push up the Red River in hopes of unlocking the doorway to the fabled market of South China. By 1874 France was well on the way to gaining control of the area around Hanoi. This provoked the ambitions of another Western power, for Great Britain also hoped to establish a new route into southwestern China through Burma.

Conflict in Southeast Asia

Expansion in India had brought Britain into conflict with neighboring Burma by the early nineteenth century. When the Burmese prepared to invade a disputed frontier region in 1824, the British counterattacked by sea, annexed lower Burma, and forced the imperial court at Ava to permit foreign trade. This was not enough for aggressive British merchants, who continued to complain bitterly about uncooperative trading attitudes, eventually driving their government in 1852 to undertake a second military expedition. By 1862 three Burmese provinces were directly ruled by a British high commissioner and in 1867 the Royal Court (then at Mandalay) signed a treaty granting extraterritoriality and access to the interior.

A second stage then began in the British domination of Burma—one directly influenced by French expansion in Vietnam. By now Great Britain not only wished to gain access to China but had also become extremely possessive of British-held land in Burma. This concern reflected a new and fundamental change in the relationship between events in Asia and in Europe. In 1865 an overland telegraph finally connected India and Great Britain, so that a military defeat at some tiny hill station could be amplified by newspapers in London or Paris to inflame nationalistic popular opinion. Furthermore, the opening of the Suez Canal in 1869 revolutionized trade with the Orient. Burma would never have become an important British colony had merchant steam fleets not been able to exploit its rice crops. Exports quickly doubled, making it possible, in turn, for the Burmese to buy British cottons. As the Burmese economy flourished, Indian moneylenders were encouraged to invest in land and retail shops. Later, the British extracted other products: teak, lead, silver, and oil. By World War II, British and Indians had invested £100,000,000 in Burma.

The higher the economic and political stakes, the greater were English apprehensions aroused by France's expansion in Vietnam. The Burmese king, Thibaw, did little to allay such fears. In 1883 he sent a mission to Paris seeking to use the French to resist further British aggression. Jules Ferry, the French premier, was delighted to increase his country's influence in that part of Southeast Asia and promptly signed a commercial treaty in January, 1884. Thibaw, overestimating France's willingness to support him against Great Britain, then made the mistake of disputing high-handedly with a powerful British teak firm. This action gave the English all the pretext they needed to invade upper Burma. In November 1885, the whole of Burma was brought under British control as an Indian province.

In playing England off against France, Thibaw was consciously emulating Siam (Thailand), which successfully managed to retain a surprising degree of independence just because of European rivalries. But Siamese success at this delicate game was not merely a question of diplomatic agility. King Mongkut had been able to deflate standard justifications for intervention by declaring himself in favor of "Westernization" in 1851. The English soon were allowed to appoint a consul at Bangkok and to secure extraterritorial privileges. In 1868 Mongkut's young successor, Chulalongkorn, carried Westernization further by accepting foreign advisers and abolishing "feudal" institutions like slavery. Eventually, by granting commercial access to France on the east and to England on the west, Siam was allowed to retain its sovereignty. Britain's financial influence expanded rapidly. By 1940, the English had invested £13,000,000 in Siamese shipping, tin, teak, and banking. At the same time, overseas Chinese (active in Siamese affairs since the fifteenth century) gained control of retail enterprises. Siamese political independence was thus maintained at the cost of economic dependence, since 95 percent of industry and commerce was in foreign hands.

France's rivalry with England in Southeast Asia was resolved without open warfare. On the other hand, the challenge France posed to a more traditional imperial power—

Chulalongkorn and his sons. He reigned over Siam as Rama V from 1868 to 1910. At his coronation he began the process of reforming Siam by abolishing his courtiers' custom of prostrating themselves before him.

China—did not end peaceably. China had regarded the Vietnamese as tributaries for centuries. This subordination usually entailed nothing more than Peking's routine recognition of an Annamese monarch's right to rule, but that in turn corroborated China's view of itself as the universal Asian power. And, even after being twice defeated by the West, the Ch'ing court still felt certain responsibilities to the traditional Chinese world order. Self-esteem (as well as realistic strategic concerns) dictated that if a tributary asked for Chinese help against foreign invaders, Peking should oblige. Therefore, when Annam requested Ch'ing aid in 1881 against French encroachments, China boldly reasserted the traditional rights of suzerainty. France promptly challenged that assertion by declaring a protectorate over all of Vietnam in 1883.

The result was an undeclared Sino-French War (1884–1885). Ch'ing forces crossed the Vietnamese border, but neither side at first gained a clear advantage in the mountainous jungle terrain. Eventually the French were able to accomplish a stunning military success elsewhere by conquering Taiwan and destroying the new Foochow naval arsenal. Nonetheless, a minor Chinese victory in Vietnam led to both the downfall of the Ferry cabinet in Paris and the quick ratification of the Treaty of Tientsin (1885). This was minor consolation for China, since the Sino-French War both compromised the "Self-Strengtheners" and exposed China to other imperial ambitions.

On February 14, 1885, French troops take Langson, the headquarters of the Chinese expeditionary forces in Tongking (Northern Vietnam). The Chinese recaptured the town on March 28, a defeat that would cause the parliamentary downfall of the French cabinet and lead to a final peace settlement between the two countries.

THE NEW IMPERIALISM AND CHINA

Japanese Intervention

The most far-reaching event in East Asia in the late nineteenth century was the convergence of the new imperialism on China and its acceleration by the victim-turned-victor, Japan. Once again the aggression began against a traditional Chinese tributary—Korea—now the object of Japanese territorial aims. In 1876, by the treaty of Kanghwa, Japan compelled Korea to open three ports to trade. China first issued a verbal protest, and, when this was rejected, honored its commitment to Korea's king by actually fighting the Japanese at Seoul in 1884. The ensuing negotiations produced a convention that forbade all but bilateral military interventions. Then, less than a decade later, in June 1894, revolt by the Tonghaks

(rebels similar to the Taipings of China) threatened the survival of the ruling Korean dynasty. When Chinese troops moved in to support their vassal king, the Japanese responded in force and refused to leave when the rebellion was under control. By August, the Sino-Japanese War was formally declared, and in a naval engagement off the mouth of the Yalu River, the much-vaunted Ch'ing fleet was ignominiously routed and destroyed, and the Chinese naval bases at Port Arthur and Wei-hai-wei occupied. Within six months the Japanese had occupied the Liaotung Peninsula and had seven divisions ready to march on Peking. The Chinese had no choice but to sign the Treaty of Shimonoseki in April 1895 recognizing the independence of Korea, ceding to Japan the island of Taiwan and the Liaotung Peninsula, and paying Japan a large indemnity.

The Battle of the Yalu River, September 17, 1894: Chinese torpedo boats routed by Japanese vessels. A shore observer reported the fate of the Chinese cruiser, Ch'ao Yung, as it drifted helplessly ashore: "her upper works knocked to pieces; her decks, strewn with mutilated bodies, an indiscriminate mass of wreck and carnage."

The Treaty of Shimonoseki immediately shifted the balance of power in East Asia. Overnight Japan had torn apart the web of arrangements that delicately constrained the conflicting interests of France in South China, Great Britain along the Yangtze, Germany in Shantung, and above all Russia — yearning for a warm-water harbor at Port Arthur in the very part of the Liaotung Peninsula that Japan had just won. On April 23, 1895, therefore, Tsar Nicholas I engineered a Triple Intervention with France and Germany to demand that Japan return Liaotung to the Chinese. This maneuver had two important effects. First, it embittered the Japanese, driving them into a concerted military buildup that culminated in 1905 in the astonishing defeat of Russia's fleet at Tsushima. Second, it accomplished the final transference of the European system of balance of power to China itself.

The European Balance of Power in China

For thirty-five years the great powers had been content to let the Ch'ing rule a united China in exchange for the commercial advantages of the treaty-port system, which supposedly gave no single nation an edge over others. In that way it was believed China would not be partitioned into separate colonial territories. Now, with Japan's sudden intrusion, European statesmen decided that the time had come to stake out spheres of influence. France and Britain demanded and received special rights in South China. Russia demanded and received rights to build the Chinese Eastern Railway across Manchuria to Vladivostok. Then in March 1898, Kaiser William II used the murder of two German missionaries in China to extort a naval base and special economic rights in

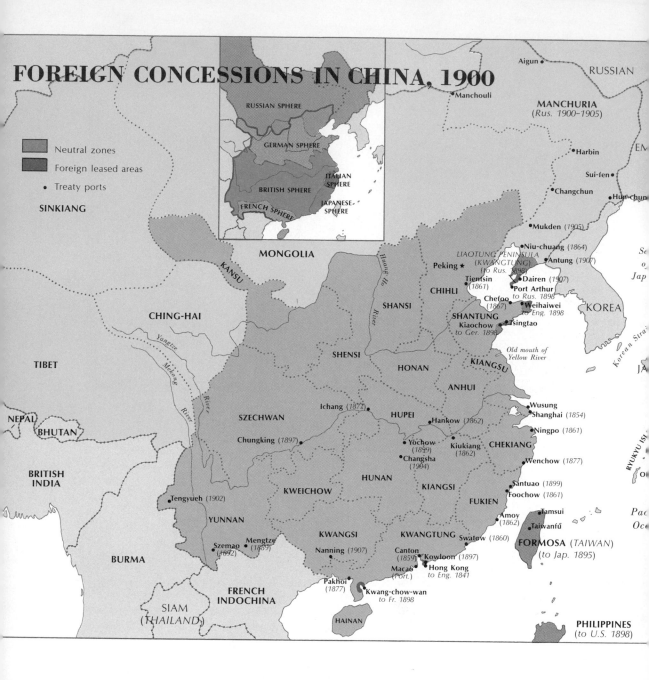

FOREIGN CONCESSIONS IN CHINA, 1900

Neutral zones
Foreign leased areas
• Treaty ports

RUSSIAN SPHERE
GERMAN SPHERE
ITALIAN SPHERE
BRITISH SPHERE
FRENCH SPHERE
JAPANESE SPHERE

SINKIANG

Aigun
• Manchouli
RUSSIAN

MANCHURIA
(Rus. 1900–1905)

• Harbin
• Sui-fen
• Changchun
• Hun-chun

MONGOLIA

KANSU

Huang Ho River

• Mukden (1905)
• Niu-chuang (1864)
• Antung (1907)

LIAOTUNG PENINSULA
(KWANGTUNG)
(to Rus. 1898)

Peking ★
Tientsin (1861)
CHIHLI
Chefoo (1867)
SHANTUNG
Kiaochow
to Ger. 1898

Dairen (1907)
Port Arthur
to Rus. 1898
Weihaiwei
to Eng. 1898
Tsingtao

KOREA

CHING-HAI

SHANSI

SHENSI

HONAN

KIANGSU

Old mouth of
Yellow River

Korean Strait

TIBET

Yangtze River

Mekong River

ANHUI

SZECHWAN

Ichang (1877)

HUPEI
Hankow (1862)

Wusung
Shanghai (1854)
Ningpo (1861)

Chungking (1897)

Yochow (1899)
Changsha (1904)

Kiukiang (1862)

CHEKIANG

Wenchow (1877)

NEPAL
BHUTAN

HUNAN

KIANGSI

Santuao (1899)
Foochow (1861)

BRITISH
INDIA

KWEICHOW

FUKIEN

Amoy (1862)

Tamsui
Taiwanfu

RYUKYU IS

Pac
Oc

Tengyueh (1902)

YUNNAN

KWANGSI

KWANGTUNG

Swatow (1860)

FORMOSA (TAIWAN)
(to Jap. 1895)

Szemao (1892)
Mengtze (1889)

Nanning (1907)

Canton (1859)
Macao (Port.)

Kowloon (1897)
Hong Kong
to Eng. 1841

BURMA

FRENCH
INDOCHINA

Pakhoi (1877)

Kwang-chow-wan
to Fr. 1898

SIAM
(THAILAND)

HAINAN

PHILIPPINES
(to U.S. 1898)

Shantung province. Germany's successful seizure finally precipitated the "scramble for concessions": Russia's leasehold of Port Arthur and Ch'ing recognition of her "special position" in Manchuria, France's base in Kwangtung as well as railway privileges in Yünnan, England's dominance along the Yangtze Valley as well as a port of its own at Wei-hai-wei and the occupation of more ter-ritory (the New Territories) across from Hong Kong. These concessions, added to the treaty-port system, brought major portions of China under thinly disguised colonial control. Foreign policemen, foreign railway zones, foreign businesses, foreign bases, and foreign industries were very much part of the Chinese world.

The United States also took part in the expansion of the Western powers into the Orient. Although by 1899 the United States had annexed Hawaii, Guam, part of Samoa, and all of the Philippines (with Dewey's victory over the Spanish fleet at Manila Bay), it did not benefit from the parceling out of imperialist colonies in China. There the U.S. economic position depended upon commercial access under the earlier treaty-port system, which benefited all foreigners equally. Alarmed at the prospect of being shut out of the new spheres, the United States in 1899 urged an "Open Door Policy" on the various powers, declaring that commercial privileges within each zone should not be withheld from other nations. Although the Open Door Policy was extended in 1900 to "guarantee" Chinese national sovereignty and was highly advertized as an expression of American goodwill toward China, it was really only an affirmation of the treaty-port's "most-favored nation" principle, enacted at the ultimate expense of Chinese independence. That is, the Open Door Policy was designed to permit uninhibited foreign entrance and not Chinese seclusion. Furthermore, it simply signaled a final stage in the history of imperialism in China after 1900, as foreign banking consortiums literally forced loans on Peking in exchange for high interest rates secured by liens on Chinese revenue from the salt monopoly or customs duties.

China's Response

These events had a stunning effect on China. Defeat at the hands of the Japanese (whom the Chinese professed to scorn) forced the government to realize that traditional "self-strengthening" was inadequate. Perhaps more fundamental reforms—like Japan's own Meiji Restoration—were necessary. Anxious young scholar-officials soon found a leader in a utopian Confucian philosopher named K'ang Yu-wei who in 1898 gained the ear of the 27-year-old Kuang-hsu Emperor and initiated a frantic reform movement. A deluge of imperial edicts abolished nonproductive government posts, reformed the examination system, established new schools, and organized a new system of ministerial government. But the edicts of the "Hundred Days of Reform" in the summer of 1898 were never carried out. The conserva-

tive mandarinate and the Manchu aristocracy convinced themselves and the retired Empress Dowager, Tz'u-hsi, that the emperor had fallen into the hands of radical fanatics. Tz'u-hsi organized a military coup; the emperor was imprisoned, his edicts rescinded, and the young reformers either executed or forced to flee abroad.

The combination of domestic reaction and external imperialism deeply affected the national consciousness of the Chinese. Rumors spread among the peasantry that the country was going to be cut up like a melon, that China would cease to exist. Railways, foreign goods, Christians—all were omens and agents of an almost supernatural catastrophe looming ahead. Unless they were rooted out, the world would end. In the northern province of Shantung, popular boxer-magicians fed on the hysteria by preaching that magic spells and secret boxing techniques made their followers invulnerable to bullets. Thousands of desperate and enraged peasants thus joined these boxing clubs and began to attack foreign missionaries and their converts. The movement spread across North China. Some officials insisted the "Boxers" were dangerous fanatics, but others argued that this popular movement should be harnessed by the dynasty to expel the foreigners. The Empress Dowager, already embittered by the reform movement, favored the latter view and authorized the enrollment of the Boxers into official militia.

Government sponsorship caused the Boxer Uprising to spread into Peking itself, where the foreign legations were soon besieged and cut off from the outside world. In Western capitals, visions of a "yellow peril," of hundreds of millions of Chinese hacking all foreigners to death, inflamed the popular imagination; and newspapers clamored for the rescue of the diplomats. On August 4, 1900, 20,000 foreign troops landed at Tientsin and began to fight their way to Peking. Ten days later, they relieved the siege, scattered the Ch'ing garrison, and looted the capital while the Empress Dowager fled deeper inland in the belief that this invasion really might mark the end of Manchu rule over China. But each foreign power was so wary of the other (there were soon 45,000 Japanese, German, Russian, English,

In addition to exacting an indemnity of $333 million, the Boxer Protocol of September 7, 1901, required the Chinese to decapitate ten of their officials who had supported the boxer movement.

French, and American troops in the north) that a restoration of the ruling house seemed a lesser evil than outright occupation. A protocol was signed imposing a $333 million indemnity on China, and the Empress Dowager was allowed to return to the Forbidden City in 1902 and resume control.

The Boxer Uprising represented the Manchu dynasty's last attempt to resist the West without fundamentally altering its own structure. The only alternative after defeat was a new reform movement under the sponsorship of the Empress Dowager herself. Her resolve to modernize the government was strengthened by the example of Japan's victory over Russia.

After the Boxer Uprising, Russia kept its occupation troops in Manchuria, hoping to expand southward into Korea—then a Japanese sphere of influence. Japan, secure on its own flank after signing an alliance with England in 1902, tried to persuade Russia to

withdraw. Six months of fruitless negotiations in St. Petersburg resulted in the outbreak of hostilities between the two nations in February 1904.

The Russo-Japanese War began at sea, where the Japanese navy under Admiral Tōgō bottled up the Russians at Port Arthur and later destroyed the Vladivostok squadron. On land, the Russians were routed at the Yalu River in April 1904 and slowly thrown back to Mukden. There, in the spring of 1905, 310,000 Japanese soldiers attacked an equal number of entrenched Russian troops. In March, after suffering almost 100,000 casualties, the Russian lines broke, to the astonishment of the entire world. Port Arthur had fallen in January. The tsar now had one remaining hope, his Baltic fleet, which was being sailed around the world by Admiral Rodjestvensky. On May 27, 1905, Tōgō's ships encountered Rodjestvensky near the Tsushima Straits. The Japanese navy proceeded to sink all but three of the Russians' 35 vessels.

Japan's victory over Russia in 1905 electrified Asia; a nonwhite nation had defeated one of the "Great Powers." This turnabout inspired nationalist leaders throughout the Far East. It also convinced the Ch'ing dynasty that a monarchy such as Japan's could survive as long as it sponsored major reforms. Sweeping changes were therefore introduced in an effort to modernize China. In 1905 the traditional examination system was abolished, modern schools were founded, and students were sent abroad to study. Chambers of commerce were encouraged, legal codes revised, new ministries created, and conscript armies trained on the German and Japanese models. Above all, the Ch'ing came to believe that imperial power would be enhanced if a close tie—like the Japanese constitutional monarchy—was forged between the throne and the people. Confucianists had emphasized the importance of retaining popular loyalty, of winning "the people's hearts"; but in practice the bureaucracy intervened between the ruler and his subjects. Now the Empress Dowager wished to come to direct terms with the educated populace by encouraging limited political participation. After a constitutional investigating mission was sent abroad in 1905, the imperial court decided to permit the election of local, provincial, and finally national assemblies by a tiny electorate of the wealthy and highly educated.

All of the reforms carried out between 1905 and 1910 seemed necessary for China but proved fatal to the Ch'ing. To abolish the examination system based on mastery of the Classics, for instance, was to admit that Confucianism no longer sufficed as a governing doctrine. Since the Manchus' right to rule had always been expressed in Confucian rather than in national terms, this admission helped destroy the Ch'ing's legitimacy. Similar consequences resulted from the other reform programs. For example, the decision to create assemblies brought together for the first time provincial groupings of merchants, gentry, wealthy landowners, and graduates of the new modern schools. Provided now with a common political aim, these different classes began to form a new elite, proud of its local power and eager for more participation in the nation's affairs. But when a National Assembly convened at Peking in 1910, it was told that it would not be granted legislative power for several years. Disappointment at this delay alienated many from the regime.

Popular enthusiasm for national economic development was similarly thwarted. By 1905 the new provincial elite was coming to believe that China's very existence was threatened unless the nation was mobilized against the foreign powers. Until this time the concept of a *nation* or of national survival was strange to most Chinese. Now, men began to discover a new national, even racial, identity. They were no longer simply "men of Han," or "residents of Hupeh," but rather citizens of China governed by selfish Manchurian nobles who seemed ready to "sell out the country" in order to preserve their ethnically different ruling house. It was up to the people—the new patriots believed—to develop the country's economy, especially its railways, by purchasing shares of public stock. In that way foreign bankers would be kept from controlling China's investments and provincial wealth would be increased. Actually, the government in Peking looked on these provincial railway schemes with favor. But sufficient capital could not be raised by Chinese, and the government had to turn to foreign banking consortiums, which loaned the money but demanded the right to control the building of the railways. Eventually the Ch'ing had to force the provincial elite to give up its plans and turn in the original railway shares— sometimes at a fraction of the original price. Dissatisfaction was widespread, and in Szechwan early in 1911 gentry, students, and merchants even took up arms against the local governor.

The Revolution of 1911

The court's decision to train "New Armies" also weakened the regime. Military academies turned out a new class of professional soldiers who developed private loyalties to leaders like Yüan Shih-k'ai, one of Li Hung-chang's proteges who managed to place his

On February 15, 1912, just after the establishment of the new Chinese republic, Sun Yat-sen leads a procession to the Ming tombs west of Peking to proclaim the triumph of the anti-Manchu crusade. "An earthquake shook the barbarian court of Peking, and it was smitten with a paralysis. Today it has at last restored the Government to the Chinese People."

own followers in military commands throughout the country. Most were garrisoned in Central China, where their control of the nation's arsenals made them a target for recruitment by anti-Manchu revolutionary groups.

The appearance of anti-Manchu conspirators was itself an effect of the government's decision to send students abroad for a modern education. As many as 15 thousand young Chinese were thus brought into contact with Japanese radicals and overseas Chinese nationalists. Their own temporary exile led them to seek companionship in provincial clubs in Tokyo or Paris; these associations in turn founded newspapers, private academies, and political study groups. Through Japanese translations and

the writings of Liang Ch'i-ch'ao, these students feverishly consumed in two or three years the product of centuries of Western political theory: Montesquieu, Rousseau, Mill, Marx, Spencer, Kropotkin. Anarchist and socialist clubs called for revolutionary change, a new world, the end of Manchu tyranny. But there was a great distance between hopes and their realization. Lacking experience in political organization, fund-gathering, and even simple conspiracy, some of the intellectuals believed they needed a leader who could unite the different provincial clubs and political cliques and provide a way of contacting disaffected elements back in China.

The man best suited for this role was a Cantonese Christian named Sun Yat-sen

(1866–1925) who had been educated in Hawaii and Hong Kong to become a physician. Sun had been engaged in revolutionary planning when many of these intellectuals were still in their infancy. In the 1880s he had formed a secret group dedicated to the overthrow of the Manchus and—working through fellow Christians and secret society leaders in Hong Kong—had inspired an abortive revolt in Kwangtung in 1895. He became internationally known when Ch'ing agents captured him in London but were forced to release him after the English press was informed. Sun's enhanced reputation enabled him to travel throughout the world, gathering funds from wealthy Chinese merchants in Honolulu, Singapore, San Francisco, and Batavia. His greatest appeal was his call for direct and immediate action to establish a republic. With the funds he had acquired, his own experience, and his extraordinary oratorical skill, Sun Yat-sen was able to persuade the student revolutionaries in Tokyo in 1905 that he was the leader they had been seeking. Shortly after he issued a call for a united front, a new revolutionary party, the *T'ung-meng hui* (Revolutionary Alliance), was formed. During the next five years, the *T'ung-meng hui* arranged a series of unsuccessful revolts in China that inspired many others to think of revolutionary change.

The "revolution" that finally occurred with an unexpected bomb explosion of October 10, 1911 was not the handiwork of any single group. Provincial leaders, railway stockholders, professional soldiers, secret societies, and student revolutionaries all participated at one time or another. For the Revolution of 1911 was actually a series of provincial secessions from the central government. New Army units began by revolting in Central China. Constitutionalists in other provinces then declared their independence. Elsewhere other militarists persuaded local governors to abandon the regime, while *T'ung-meng hui* revolutionaries seized Kwangtung and vied for power in rival constitutional conventions. During all of this turmoil the most powerful figure in China was not Sun Yat-sen, but rather the one man in control of the military, Yüan Shih-k'ai. Yüan first pretended to help the tottering dynasty in order to be named prime minister; he then secretly ordered a military mutiny against the monarchy, which was panicked into abdication on February 12, 1912. Since the country was then split between a northern regime under Yüan Shih-k'ai and a southern government under Sun Yat-sen, Sun decided for the sake of national unity to let Yuan become provisional president of the new republic. In this way, Sun hoped that a grand alliance of all the elements of the Revolution of 1911 would peacefully draw China together again. His idealism was misplaced, for the overthrow of the Manchus had removed the one enemy that the *T'ung-meng hui*, the provincial leaders, and the new militarists shared. There was no short and easy way to reunite China; for almost another half-century thereafter she remained immersed in civil war and revolutionary struggle against imperialism.

By the outbreak of World War I the new imperialism had made itself felt throughout eastern and southern Asia. In some areas, particularly the peninsular and the island reaches of the southeast, Western rule had been for the first time fastened upon a traditional society. In lands long subjected to foreign rule, such as India, the first stirrings of a new nationalist spirit were to be found underneath the façade of an imperial power that seemed more firmly established than ever. Although not yet threatening to the established order, new ideas of nationalism and the nationalist parties that embodied them were portents of things to come. Farther east, in China, the traditional system lay in ruins by 1914, defeated and discredited by the repeated hammer blows of a half-century and more of imperial pressure. The 1911 Republic was merely a temporary bulwark against growing chaos and disorder.

Japan as usual stood apart. Enterprising and adaptable, the Japanese had quickly sprung back with renewed self-confidence from their first encounter with the West. By the early twentieth century, united under a dynasty committed to rapid modernization, Japan had claimed a place as one of the great powers of the world and was poised to begin its own vast imperial expansion.

SUGGESTED READINGS

Langer, William L., *The Diplomacy of Imperialism: 1890–1902*. New York: Alfred A. Knopf, 1960.
Complex, hard-to-read, this is still the classic study of European diplomacy as it leads to the struggle for concessions in China during the late 1890s.

Gasster, Michael, *Chinese Intellectuals and the Revolution of 1911*. Seattle: University of Washington Press, 1969.
A survey of radical thinkers in China just before the 1911 revolution.

Teng, Ssu-yu and John K. Fairbank, *China's Response to the West: A Documentary Survey, 1839–1923*. New York: Atheneum, 1965.

Wright, Mary C., *The Last Stand of Chinese Conservatism: The T'ung-Chih Restoration, 1862–1874*. Stanford: Stanford University Press, 1957.
A comprehensive description of the Manchu government's restoration of Confucian government after the Taiping Rebellion.

Metcalf, Thomas R., *The Aftermath of Revolt: India 1857–1870*. Princeton, N.J.: Princeton University Press, 1964.
An account of the effects of the Mutiny on British policy and attitudes.

Seal, Anil, *The Emergence of Indian Nationalism*. New York: Cambridge University Press, 1968.
Authoritative account of nineteenth-century developments.

Heimsath, Charles H., *Indian Nationalism and Hindu Social Reform*. Princeton, N.J.: Princeton University Press, 1964.

Wolpert, Stanley, *Tilak and Gokhale: Revolution and Reform in the Making of Modern India*. Berkeley: University of California Press, 1962.
Sympathetic biography of two great early nationalists.

Forster, E. M., *A Passage to India*. New York: Harcourt Brace & Co., 1924. Paperback.
A major novel. Contains a sensitive portrayal of British society in colonial India.

Geertz, Clifford, *Agricultural Involution: The Processes of Ecological Change in Indonesia*. Berkeley: University of California Press, 1966. Paperback.
A penetrating study of the Culture System and its effects on Javanese society.

Craig, Albert, *Chōshū in the Meiji Restoration*. Cambridge: Harvard University Press, 1961.
Arguing that nationalism began as much in the han *as in the country at large, this book traces the origin and development of the Meiji Restoration through the history of one domain.*

CHAPTER 20

The Middle East and Africa to 1914

Since the early nineteenth century the Middle East and Africa have been engaged in a great quest for modernity. By the twentieth century the impact of the West was felt in even the remotest parts of these areas. The Western influence disrupted traditional institutions, and many people felt that Westernization — the imposition of Western ways on non-Western societies — was the only way to modernize. Many African and Middle Eastern intellectuals accepted this view when their traditional, sometimes stone age, cultures were confronted with strong Western technology and impressive Western institutions. But traditional values and institutions were deeply ingrained in most of the people; only a segment of the educated minority renounced most of their ways to adopt Western forms.

For the majority of African and Middle Eastern people, established patterns continued to provide satisfaction. Moreover, a non-Western intellectual elite developed as contact with the West increased, and members of this group soon began to see faults in the Western experience and virtues in their own heritage. They therefore attempted to modernize by blending what they considered valuable in the European tradition with their own tradition. Increasing knowledge of the West sometimes led to assimilation, but sometimes the Africans and Middle Easterners wanted only enough political and economic knowledge to defeat the European attempts at control.

THE OTTOMAN EMPIRE BEFORE 1800

In the Middle East, the Ottoman Empire (the largest Islamic empire since the ninth century) was still powerful in 1800. Its territory stretched from Algeria to the borders of Iran in a west-east axis and from the Balkans to the Arabian peninsula from north to south. The Ottoman Turks had come to power around 1300 under the leadership of Osman (1290–1326), a warrior from Asia Minor. By the late fifteenth century, Sultan Mohammed II (1451–1481) had completed the conquest of most of the Balkans and captured Constantinople (1453). The Ottoman Empire continued to grow until 1566: Selim I (1512–1520) added Syria, western Arabia, Armenia; Suleiman the Magnificent (1520–1566) conquered Hungary, Transylvania, northeastern Rumania, the southwestern part of the Ukraine, and much of North Africa.

The Turks were considered non-European because of their Asian heritage and their Muslim faith, which they had adopted in the ninth and tenth centuries. The Ottoman leaders gloried in their commitment to Islam. They took pride in extending the faith into new areas. Islam united an empire of diverse peoples, tongues, and locations.

The sultan, the supreme ruler of the state, was the central figure in both religion and politics. He was aided by a bureaucracy headed by a grand vizier. In the thirteenth and early fourteenth centuries the army had been recruited on a semifeudal basis. A portion of the tax revenues on arable land was assigned to cavalrymen (Sipahis) who, in turn, made available to the state a certain number of troops on demand. This system was replaced in the early fifteenth century by the devshirme system.

The devshirme system provided recruits for the administration and an expanded army. The state periodically took boys from Christian homes and gave them a general training in the Turkish language and the Muslim way of life. The boys then entered the infantry corps (Janissaries), as they were needed. A select group, however, went directly into the palace service or were distributed to high dignitaries; they could eventually hold powerful positions within the Ottoman bureaucracy. These devshirme recruits — so-called slaves of the Sultan — were not permitted to marry until they reached a certain age and could not bequeath their positions to their children. Because of the immense powers wielded by the government and military, freeborn Muslims were eager to enter the Janissaries and palace service. They eventually succeeded, and by the eighteenth century they had undermined the old rule of noninheritance of offices. Many positions were being monopolized by powerful families.

The vast peasant majority in the Ottoman Empire was the economic base on which governmental and religious institutions rested. Although peasant technology was rudimentary, it provided subsistence and some salable crops. The peasants were heavily taxed, and, except for operation of the devshirme system, there was an unbridgeable gap between the peasantry and the ruling elite. The elite group was literate, urban, wealthy, and orthodox in their religious practices, whereas the peasants were illiterate, rural, poor, and mystical in their practice of Islam.

Between the ruling elite and the peasantry was a large commercial class that grew because the Ottoman Empire possessed a central location in world trade routes. Merchants were organized into guilds and conducted trade as far east as China and as far west as the kingdoms of West Africa. Artisans were also organized into guilds, but neither of these classes developed the autonomous political or economic power of the Western bourgeoisie. They remained subordinate to the government ruling elite and, like the peasantry, were forced to pay heavy taxes.

Many of the merchants and artisans were non-Muslims — primarily Orthodox Christians (especially Greeks) and Jews. The Ottomans had an elaborate framework, known as the millet system, for dealing with their non-Muslim communities. According to Islamic law, people of the Book — Jews and Christians — were to be tolerated because they adhered to a belief in one God and possessed scriptures, but they were to be subordinated to the ruling Muslim community. The Jews and Christians were permitted to organize their own communities through which they administered their religious and civil law, but at the same time their political subordination to the Muslims was made manifest through payment of an extra tax.

At the height of their power, the Ottoman Turks ruled an enormous area, but full Turkish control over the far reaches of the empire was always difficult. Thus the Arab world was administered only loosely by the Turks; their primary concerns were maintaining political stability and collecting taxes on a regular basis. Indeed, when Egypt was first conquered by an Ottoman army in 1517, the sultan permitted many of the old Mamluk rulers to remain in power under Ottoman suzerainty. They were supplanted only when they tried to reassert their autonomy; at this point the Ottomans took complete control. Outlying areas, however, continued to assert their autonomy. Tunis, Algiers, and Tripoli had their own relatively autonomous dynasties. In Syria there were disputes between influential local cliques for control over internal affairs, while Lebanon, mountainous and partially Christian, was usually its own master.

Egypt was one of the wealthiest parts of the Ottoman Empire, and Istanbul had good reason to retain political and fiscal control over it. Yet in the seventeenth and eighteenth centuries Egypt regained much of its former political independence. The Turkish court sent a representative to Cairo as a symbol of sovereignty and still received Egyptian tribute payments, but real political authority lay with a new group of Mamluks. These rulers, like the preceding Mamluk dynasty, were brought as young boys from the Caucasus and given military and political training in Egypt. The Mamluk military tended to divide into factions, struggling with each other for control over the government. The weakness of Ottoman control over Egypt became even clearer in the eighteenth century when Murad and Ibrahim Bey seized power in Cairo, reduced the authority of the Ottoman representative, and cut off regular tribute payments to Istanbul.

By 1800 the Ottoman Empire had declined greatly. The *Sublime Porte,* as the Ottoman court was known, had produced magnificent leaders in the fifteenth and sixteenth centuries, but by the eighteenth century it produced only a series of weak rulers. The sultans increasingly isolated themselves from the people, allowing the grand vizier and other administrators to wield political power. Economic decline was accelerated when European explorers discovered the sea route around Africa and began to trade with East Asia directly rather than through Arab and Turkish middlemen. The redirecting of trade routes came at a time when the Ottoman Empire was already far-flung and its military and administrative institutions quite expensive. The economic resources of the Empire were extended to their limits to support such an elaborate governmental apparatus.

The internal decline of the *Porte* was accompanied by losses of parts of the Empire. After a long period of intermittent warfare with several European powers, the Turks signed the Treaty of Karlowitz (1699), marking the first time Turkey was a defeated power. In accordance with this treaty the Ottomans had to abandon Hungary and other European territory. By 1800 the Ottoman Empire had lost a sizable portion of its European lands and was losing control over its Arab holdings.

NORTH AFRICA

North Africa had been incorporated into the Arab-Islamic world through Arab conquest in the seventh century and then large-scale Arab migrations westward from Egypt in the eleventh century. In the long sweep of its history, North Africa has sometimes been tied politically to the power centers of the Near East, as most of it was during the Ottoman Empire. But North Africa — or the Maghreb as present-day Morocco, Algeria, and Tunisia are often called — has more often been independent and has evolved its own political institutions and varieties of Islam. Also, Arab and Islamic influences have not submerged the earlier traditions. Even today a considerable proportion of the North African population is Berber-speaking; that is, they speak the language of the pre-Islamic period. The Berber and Arab ways of life tend to be dissimilar, although in the nineteenth and twentieth centuries the differences have become less pronounced. The Arabs are Muslims, and the vast majority live in cities or as farmers in the countryside. The Berbers, often non-Muslim, have traditionally made their living from animal husbandry and have retreated from the coast into the hills not controlled by the Arab-dominated government. In North African states, even up to the present time, there has always been tension and conflict between the pastoral and agricultural, the non-Muslim and Muslim, the Berber and Arab, and the outlying areas and the central government.

The history of North Africa dates back many centuries. Its shores were visited by Phoenician merchants who established a mercantile empire around 1100 B.C. One of the trading stations, Carthage, grew into a great empire at the same time as the Greeks and Romans were expanding. Its merchant aristocracy, originally from Phoenicia, put down roots in the North African hinterland and brought under control the area that is today Tunisia. This base supported a far-reaching maritime empire. Eventually Carthage came into conflict with Rome and, despite the leadership of Hannibal, it could not defeat the Romans; the city was finally destroyed in 146 B.C.

Under Roman rule North Africa became one of the principal granaries of Italy. In the third and fourth centuries Christianity spread throughout the area, which became famous for its religious leaders, notably Augustine. (See pp. 169–170.) Yet in the Arab-Islamic conquest of North Africa in the seventh century, Islam supplanted Christianity. During part of the eighth century the Berber peoples revolted against Arab domination, and North Africa became a semi-independent part of the great Abbasid Islamic empire. In the eleventh century an invasion of Arab nomads increased the Arab proportion in the population. At the same time, however, independent Muslim dynasties were being established that helped to fix the identity and autonomy of North Africa as distinct from the rest of the Arab world. Two powerful Moroccan dynasties were the Almoravids (eleventh century) and the Almohads (1147–1269); the former were nomads from the Sahara and Mauretania while the Almohads came from the High Atlas Mountains. In Tunisia a branch of the Almohad dynasty—called the Hafsids—established itself in power in the thirteenth century. Although the Ottomans overran Tripoli, Tunisia, and Algeria in the sixteenth century, they were not able to maintain their control. These areas asserted their traditional autonomy within a century.

The French conquest of the nineteenth and twentieth centuries left more lasting influences in North Africa. Algeria was formally occupied in 1830 although its conquest required at least another 30 years during which the French had to crush a strong resistance movement led by Abdelqader in the 1840s. The French promoted emigration to Algeria and gave lands to European settlers at the expense of Algerians. By 1851, over 150,000 Europeans were resident in the country, and this figure was to grow to one million after World War II. Tunisia was taken over by France in 1881, and after protracted disputes with Germany France successfully laid claim to Morocco just before World War I. In this way, most of North Africa came under French influence. Only Libya remained outside the French orbit because it was occupied by the Italians in 1911. The French language and culture were implanted, in part by the large immigrant population of Morocco, Tunisia, and Algeria.

BLACK AFRICA BEFORE THE EUROPEAN CONQUEST

The history of Africa has been culled from many sources. Arab travelers visited East and West Africa, frequently establishing Muslim settlements, and left written accounts. One of the most famous travelers was the Moroccan Ibn Batuta (1304–1377) whose graphic account of the West African kingdom of Mali is one such important source. He was favorably impressed with "the complete and general safety one enjoys throughout the land" and the way in which the people at court "zealously learn the *Koran* by heart." In the fifteenth century the Arabs were joined by Europeans—Portuguese, Spanish, Dutch, English, French, Germans—who also left written records of their travels. Another important source of historical data is African writing in Arabic. This derives from a class of scholars living in the kingdoms of West Africa. In addition to written data, interpretation of the oral tradition has provided knowledge of the African people.

Anthropologists and historians have discovered that preliterate peoples retain a sense of historical identity through their oral tradition. Many African groups have committed to memory and transmitted through generations the history of their origins, their migrations, their battles, their leaders, and other important historical events. Although these stories sometimes blend historical fact with religious myth, they do contain accurate historical data, and because of their sacred ingredient, they have been spared the kind of embellishment and variation that ordinary folktales suffer over the years.

There are two other sources of historical data. Archeological evidence is yielding information on some of the early African civilizations, as it has for other preliterate so-

A sacrificial vessel carved from wood by a Yoruba artist from West Africa. The Yorubas, along with many other African peoples, were skilled and imaginative artists.

cieties. And the study of linguistics has shown the relationship of African peoples to each other. Similarity of languages used in different parts of the continent indicates that at various stages of development certain groups divided; their subsequent migrations can be traced through the languages currently used. A general picture of Africa before European penetration can be drawn from a combination of all these sources.

The Western view of Africa has not been generous or favorable. Europeans tended to regard the continent as full of savage peoples and wild beasts and without a history worth recording. In the nineteenth century European travelers gave substance to these ideas. In order to magnify their own achievements, they wrote vividly and often inaccurately of the dangers they regularly faced from head hunters and from people with a scant concern for human life. Two famed nineteenth-century explorers of Nigeria thus described a war party: "They were all variously armed with muskets, bows, arrows, knives, cut-

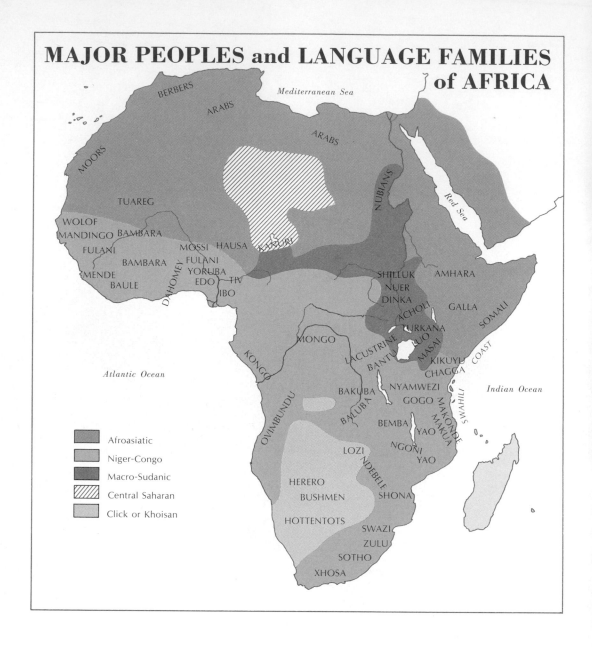

MAJOR PEOPLES and LANGUAGE FAMILIES of AFRICA

Mediterranean Sea

BERBERS

ARABS

ARABS

MOORS

TUAREG

NUBIANS

Red Sea

WOLOF

MANDINGO BAMBARA

FULANI

MOSSI HAUSA

KANURI

BAMBARA

FULANI

MENDE

YORUBA

BAULE

DAHOMEY

EDO

TIV

IBO

SHILLUK

NUER

DINKA

ACHOLI

TURKANA

AMHARA

GALLA

SOMALI

MONGO

LACUSTRINE
BANTU

LUO

MASAI

KIKUYU

CHAGGA

Atlantic Ocean

KONGO

Indian Ocean

SWAHILI COAST

BAKUBA

NYAMWEZI

GOGO

OVIMBUNDU

BALUBA

MAKONDE

MAKUA

BEMBA

YAO

LOZI

NGONI

YAO

NDEBELE

HERERO

BUSHMEN

SHONA

HOTTENTOTS

SWAZI

ZULU

SOTHO

XHOSA

Afroasiatic

Niger-Congo

Macro-Sudanic

Central Saharan

Click or Khoisan

lasses, barbs, long spears, and other instruments of destruction; and as we gazed upon this band of wild men, with their ferocious looks and hostile appearance . . . we wished ourselves safe out of their hands.'' For a long time historians would have agreed with the statement made by a distinguished British historian of Africa that ''Africans had stayed for untold centuries sunk in barbarism, stagnant, neither going forward nor going back.'' The reality of African history is quite different, of course, and, as we have seen, scholars are now realizing that man probably had his beginnings in Africa.

The African continent is inhabited by many different peoples, each with its own history. Even if the histories of all these societies were known (and they are not), it would not be possible to recount them here. Rather it must suffice to describe some of the major institutions and historical themes, using illustrations to give the flavor of Africa.

Camels have crossed the Sahara Desert for centuries and have linked West Africa and North Africa economically and religiously.

Early African technology was rudimentary. Metalworking was known; most societies had ironworkers and blacksmiths and used iron tools and weapons. Wheeled transport, however, was not known in the interior of the continent until the nineteenth century. Camel caravans crisscrossed the Sahara between North Africa and the Sudanic kingdoms of West Africa, but in the tropics goods were carried by men, especially in areas where disease made animal life difficult. Agricultural technology was not highly developed. The typical African farmer used a *machete* for clearing the bush, often after burning off the heavier growth. The only other farm tool in general use was the iron-tipped hoe. Most farmers practiced shifting cultivation, moving to new or fallow land before they had exhausted the soil. Animal fertilizers were successfully employed by these early farmers.

Most African peoples had a deep religious attachment to their land; in the colonial period they greatly resented land seized by or given to settlers, missionaries, and colonial governments. Land was usually held by some corporate group, the domain of an extended family or clan. Religious observances were held on it during planting and harvest seasons. The ancestors were buried there, and the land symbolized an organic and spiritual connection between the dead, the living, and the unborn of a tribe. Traditionally it could not be sold to an outsider without the consent of all interested parties. In Kenya the Kikuyu harbored a sense of injustice against the Europeans for the loss of their land. During land investigations in Kenya in the

The enstoolment of the Asantehene of the Ashanti peoples in present-day Ghana. In precolonial times the Asantehene was the ruler of the Ashanti Confederation, one of the most powerful states in West Africa. This picture was taken during the 1970 enstoolment ceremonies.

1930s, there was one moving moment when Chief Koinange identified his land, previously seized by settlers, by pointing to the place where his ancestors' remains were buried.

Political Institutions

Despite Africa's rudimentary technology, there was considerable diversity in political institutions, social structures, and economic activities. African political units ranged from simple bands of hunters and food-gatherers to complex kingdoms with monarchs and clearly defined bureaucracies and military organizations. A rough distinction has been made between societies where political activities were dealt with by family, clan, and age-grading organizations (the stateless society) and those that possessed political bureaucracies.

One of the best examples of a stateless society was that of the Tiv people presently inhabiting the Benue Valley of Nigeria. The stability of this society was maintained by family and clan ties. Clans were composed of families tracing descent from a common ancestor. When disputes occurred, for example, over land or violent actions, the clans involved met and tried to reach settlements. Once the crises had passed, the individuals broke up into their own relatively autonomous family units. If another people or tribe threatened the Tiv, the entire group united to meet the military crisis, but once it was resolved, the group again reverted to its loose and autonomous structure. The Tiv had no regularly appointed leaders or chiefs, no formal judicial or bureaucratic apparatus, and no specialized military apparatus. These came into existence only on an *ad hoc* basis at moments of need and were as quickly dissolved.

Other institutions for discharging political functions existed in these so-called stateless societies. In East Africa, the Masai and the Kikuyu tribes both lacked powerful chiefs but had an age-grading system by which members of the tribe performed clearly designated political, judicial, military, and economic functions during certain periods of their lives. After circumcision the young male became a warrior, defending his people against their enemies and sometimes leading raids against other tribes for cattle and food. When they reached a certain age, the warriors married, settled down, and became elders, slowly working their way into the tribal councils that made political decisions and resolved disputes within the tribe. Thus, although the Kikuyu and Masai did not have specially designated chiefs, the age-groups were political organizations.

Many African peoples did have chiefs. The Yoruba of southwestern Nigeria and the Ashanti of present-day Ghana had an elaborate hierarchy of chiefs, while in East Africa the Bantu around Lake Victoria—such as the Banyoro, Baganda, and Basoga—had powerful tribal leaders. Ordinarily chiefs came from specially designated royal lineages, but their powers were usually circumscribed. They were chosen by or at least with the assistance of leading commoners in the community. Although they exercised considerable political and military power, they were expected to stay within the bounds of custom and traditional law. Both the Ashanti and the Yoruba had techniques for deposing chiefs who overstepped their authority and violated customary procedures. The chiefs helped to resolve conflicts among their people, had military powers, and enjoyed religious support. They received gifts in the form of food, livestock, and hand-fashioned articles, but they were expected to redistribute much of this largesse to the community. The Ashanti and Yoruba had a hierarchy of chiefs at the

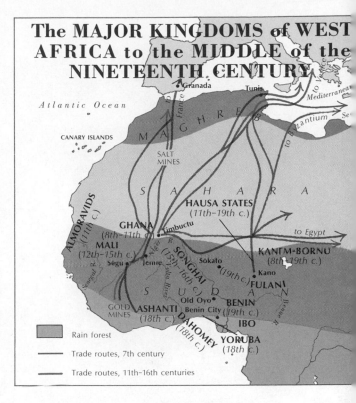

The MAJOR KINGDOMS of WEST AFRICA to the MIDDLE of the NINETEENTH CENTURY

apex of which was the supreme chief of the peoples, the *Asantehene* of the Ashanti and the *Alafin* of the Yoruba.

In the savannah lands of West Africa, the so-called Sudanic belt, inland from the tropical rain forests of the coast and south of the Sahara, there were great kingdoms ruling over extensive geographical areas and diverse peoples. One of the first great West African kingdoms, thriving from about the fourth until the eleventh centuries, was Ghana, located north and west of the present state of Ghana. After the decline of Ghana, other kingdoms arose, the most famous being Mali, Songhai, Bornu, the Hausa states, and the Fulani Empire. These states all controlled the trade in gold, slaves, salt, ivory, and other products between West and North Africa; they all had a monarchical form of government, and they all were influenced by Islam. Islam provided a new basis for political and religious loyalty other than the tribe. It furnished a written language, Arabic, used for education, scholarship and the operation of a more complex administrative system. Islam

*An African market scene along the Congo River. Village markets occur at
fixed times of the week and are important social and economic events.*

also made possible closer ties with the communities of North Africa and even the Middle East.

The political systems of some of the kingdoms were remarkably centralized. Bureaucracies and military organizations were not simply an extension of lineage systems; as the power of rulers developed, they began to recruit men into government service on the basis of their proven ability and loyalty to the system, and not because of their family connections. The tendency toward political centralization was also felt in many non-Muslim communities south of the great West African kingdoms. In Ashanti in the eighteenth century there was a virtual administrative and political revolution during which the *Asantehene* strengthened his office relative to the other chiefs in the Ashanti confederation. He increased his power by developing a bureaucracy and military organization loyal to him alone and used this increased power to bring new territories under his authority.

Economic and Social Life

African societies exhibited a significant degree of economic diversity. Some groups, the Masai and the cattle-Fulani, for example, were nomadic pastoral peoples; they detested farming and preferred to trade with the settled peoples for agricultural products. However, the vast majority of Africans were farmers. Most of them produced for their own clans or tribes, but there was often enough of a surplus for trade, and a West African mercantile class, engaged in short-

and long-distance trading, soon emerged. The long-distance trade across the Sahara was supplemented with a considerable trade in commodities such as kola-nuts within West Africa itself.

Many African societies practiced slavery, but their practice must be distinguished from Western forms. Slaves were usually captured in war or purchased. African slavery has been called domestic slavery because slaves worked in the house and fields doing the same sort of work that the freeborn did, although they often had to do the more distasteful chores, such as fetching firewood and water. In some socially mobile societies slaves were able to rise and gain wealth, political power, and freedom. Along the West African coast in the nineteenth century some of the most powerful rulers were slaveborn. Inland, in Hausa society, slaves were systematically recruited into the state bureaucracy and held positions of great authority.

Population Movement

Over the centuries there has been at least as much population movement in Africa as in Europe and North America. Most tribal histories relate stories of the migration of peoples into their present localities. Ideas, institutions, new agricultural products, and new techniques of cultivation were carried by peoples on the move. Scholars have speculated that the banana and yam were introduced into East Africa from Malaysia and carried across the Sudanic belt to West Africa. There were many reasons why African peoples were moving. African scholars of Islam sought knowledge and religious inspiration in the traditional North African and Near Eastern centers of Muslim learning; merchants traveled widely in quest of wealth; farmers searched for new land.

The Bantu-speaking peoples left their mark on African history through their unceasing movement. Scholars are still speculating on their place of origin, the reasons for their migrations, and the routes they took. Many now think they came from the present-day border area between Nigeria and the Cameroons. From the first century A.D. they began to move in a southern and eastern direction, peopling most of eastern, central,

and southern Africa and mixing with other groups in these areas. One of the fabled states created by African migrant groups was Zimbabwe, which flourished in present-day Rhodesia from the ninth until the sixteenth century. Exactly who these particular migrant peoples were is still not known for certain, although there probably was a Bantu element among them.

Another area of population movement, trade, and interaction was the Nile Valley. In Chapter 1 we saw how in the sixth or early fifth millennium B.C. men began to grow crops in Egypt, thus making it possible to support larger populations at higher material standards; a powerful monarchy and civilization was built on this economic transformation. In the third millennium B.C. Pharaonic Egypt attained preeminence and extended its authority into the Sudan. The people of the Sudan who had been incorporated into the Egyptian Empire learned its political and economic techniques. When Egypt began to decline, the great Sudanic states of Kush and Meroe arose in the first millennium B.C. Kush conquered Egypt in the eighth century B.C.

Population pressure and economic necessity may have been the driving force in many large-scale African population movements. There is evidence to suggest that in southern Africa in the first part of the nineteenth century the *Difaqane* (forced migration) period was brought about by population growth and shortage of land. Between the Drakensburg Mountains and the coast there had grown up a large population, competing for limited land. A veritable political revolution was engineered by Dingiswayo among the northern Nguni peoples. By conscripting all the young men under his control into a standing army and organizing them into regiments of approximately the same age, Dingiswayo increased the power of his people over that of his neighbors. One of his subjects, Shaka of the Zulu people, carried these concepts further. He adopted the military organization of Dingiswayo, armed his forces with a deadly stabbing knife, and instilled enormous loyalty in his army. Relying on this force, estimated at 40,000, he ensured a place for his people in the heavily populated area and drove the weaker groups

A 220-foot-long passage in the Zimbabwe ruins.

in all directions. Other peoples were forced to adopt his military organization and technology, and as they retreated into new territories, they in turn displaced the local inhabitants. The shock waves of Shaka's innovations were felt as far south as the Cape Colony and north to Lake Tanganyika. Many founders of nineteenth-century kingdoms in southern Africa emerged during this era. Moshweshwe, for example, united the southern Sotho into a state that has retained its identity to this day (Lesotho).

Although Africa was the nearest continent to the seafaring Europeans, Europeans did not penetrate the interior until well into the nineteenth century. Most of Africa does not have good natural harbors. The coastal areas were largely inhospitable to the outsider. The tropical rain forests of the coastal regions of West Africa were difficult to traverse and infested with malaria-bearing mosquitos. The Niger, Nile, and Congo, Africa's great rivers, do not give easy access to the continent from the sea. The Niger fans out into innumerable streams in the delta region, and Europeans only discovered the main channel by approaching it from the interior. The Congo, navigable inland for great distances, was not accessible from the sea because of rapids near the coast. The cataracts of the Nile in the Sudan were major obstacles to its navigation. Moreover, the great civilizations of Africa in the precolonial period were inland, turned away from the coast, while the coastal African states were powerful enough to deny European entry into the interior.

Islam in Black Africa

Yet the Sahara was by no means an impenetrable barrier. Indeed, on a few occasions military forces from northwest Africa swept down into West Africa in campaigns of conquest. Not only was there thriving trade across the Sahara, but Arab merchants and nomadic black Africans and Berbers helped to familiarize the Sudanic peoples with the ideas of Islam. The spread of Islam in West Africa owed more, however, to the vigor of a native scholarly class. For a long time Islam was the religion of the ruling classes, not the masses.

The Fulani revolts of the eighteenth and early nineteenth century ushered in a new era of Islam, purified of many of its non-Muslim practices and at the same time accessible to the masses. The Fulani were a people, sometimes pastoral, sometimes sedentary, who had spread throughout the Sudanic belt from Senegal to the Cameroons. Some Fulani were devout Muslims and were incensed at the lax observance of Islam in supposedly Islamic states or its failure to make any headway in other areas. Starting in Futa Jalon in present-day Guinea, various Fulani revolts occurred throughout inland West Africa. The most important of the revolts was that led by Uthman dan Fodio in northern Nigeria at the beginning of the nineteenth century. A man of great Islamic learning and deep devotion, he overthrew the old Hausa states and created a Fulani state, with its capital at Sokoto in northern Nigeria. The Islamic revolts of the eighteenth century sharply accelerated the spread of Islam throughout the Sudanic grassland and Islam continued to make gains in the colonial period.

West Africa was not the only part of tropical Africa to feel the influence of Islam. In southern Africa and along the East African coast, Persian and Arab merchants had set up regular trading colonies as early as the tenth century. In East Africa they established themselves permanently on islands such as Zanzibar and Pemba and in coastal cities. Their mixing with Africans along the coast had resulted in the emergence of Swahili, an Arabized Bantu language. Muslim rulers on the coast were interested primarily in trade in slaves and ivory, not conversions. The rapid spread of both Islam and Swahili into the interior had to await the colonial period, when Swahili began to assume importance as a hybrid common language for much of East Africa.

The European Slave Trade

The influence of Europeans was far from negligible even before they began to penetrate the African interior in the nineteenth century. The slave trade for the plantation economies of the Americas began in the sixteenth century and reached extraordinary proportions in the eighteenth. The figures are difficult to estimate, but according to the most recent estimate by Philip Curtin approximately 9½ million African slaves were landed on the shores of the New World. The horrors of the passage can hardly be exaggerated. Slaves were crowded into the holds of ships, with barely enough food and water for the trip. The slavers usually carried as many people as their ships could possibly hold and expected a high proportion to die. The loss of life was not confined to the famous "middle passage." Large numbers of Africans died while being marched to the coast or while being held captive in stockades on the coast awaiting the arrival of slave ships.

The impulse for abolition of the slave trade came from the nation that had been most energetic in promoting it—England. It arose from religious and humanitarian feelings coupled with a desire on the part of an industrializing society to reorient its economic relationships with Africa. The British abolished slave trading in 1807 and led a campaign among the other European states to follow their lead. Although the European states eventually agreed to end the practice, the nineteenth century still must be counted as one of the ugliest slave trading periods.

Europeans branding slaves on the West African coast prior to the passage across the Atlantic.

European slave raiding encompassed the whole of West and Central Africa from Senegal to Angola. The European slavers were generally confined to the coasts by African states and depended on these states for their supply of slaves, for which the Europeans exchanged firearms, liquor, clothing, and other manufactured goods. The slaves themselves were captured in tribal wars or as outcasts and criminals of society. One of the most ingenious methods of procuring slaves was practiced by the Aro, a subgroup of the Ibo people of present-day southeastern Nigeria. They deceived the Ibos—who consulted the Aro oracle—into allowing individuals judged guilty by the oracle to be sold into slavery instead of being accorded other forms of punishment.

The effects of the slave trade on African societies are hard to evaluate. The most visible effect to Europeans on the coast was that certain African middlemen grew wealthy and politically powerful on this nefarious commerce. What was not so visible was the depopulation of many regions, the continuous and increasingly bloody tribal wars, and the preying of the more powerful on the weak. Europe's willingness to supply firearms to Africans raised the level of violence. Furthermore, slave trading provided no incentives to Africans to embark upon other more rewarding forms of economic activity. It also tended to intensify divisions within African societies, for the ruling elements, especially the powerful political and religious leaders, sold their weaker countrymen into slavery.

South Africa

The one truly notable exception to Europe's confinement along the coast was South Africa. In 1652 the Dutch East India Company established a victualing station at the Cape. In temperate and disease-free South Africa, Europeans could safely grow fruit and vegetables that were effective in preventing shipboard diseases like scurvy. The Company encouraged settlement that quickly took on forms that were to persist in South African history. The settlers were members of the Dutch Reformed Church, which practiced a "primitive Calvinism," emphasizing the Old Testament and predestination. The settlers quickly came to rely on African slave and servant labor; they equated status with color and kept moving the frontier further north in quest of new land. The movement to the north away from the center of political authority was sharply accelerated after the British assumed control over the Cape Colony in 1806. Their new policies, which abolished slavery and reformed laws relating to the legal and civil status of nonwhites, convinced many Boers to seek political freedom. Between 1836 and 1854 the Boers' Great Trek northward resulted in the creation of new political units in Natal, the Orange Free State, and the Transvaal. Natal was brought under British control at the Cape in 1845, but the Transvaal and the Orange Free State were not united with the Cape Colony and Natal until after the Boer War in 1902.

BEGINNING OF MODERNIZATION IN THE MIDDLE EAST

The start of the modern era in the Middle East is usually dated as 1798, when a French army under Napoleon invaded Egypt and defeated the Mamluk forces. Napoleon's forces symbolized the new and modern in Europe: military strength, science and technology, nationalism, and a feeling of cultural superiority. Although the Ottoman Empire had been in contact with Europe, the French invasion of part of the Middle East heartland and their defeat of the once powerful Mamluk military gave convincing proof of Europe's threat to Middle Eastern political security.

The modern era was launched by this confrontation with the West and by a search for those elements in Western civilization that accounted for its vitality. With the invasion of Egypt, the challenge of Europe could no longer be ignored, and Middle Eastern leaders embarked upon sometimes confused, sometimes vigorous efforts to transform their own institutions. Some authorities have called this effort "defensive modernization," since the primary goal was to attain political and military parity with the states of Western Europe.

Egypt

The most dynamic of the early Middle Eastern modernizers was the family of Muhammad Ali in Egypt. The Ottoman sultan had sent Muhammad Ali to Egypt in the wake of the Napoleonic invasion. After the French troops had evacuated the country under combined Egyptian, Ottoman, and English pressure, Muhammad Ali defied the authority of his sovereign, and supplanted both the Mamluk and Ottoman contenders for power. He ruled as viceroy from 1805 to 1848. Although Egypt remained formally a part of the Ottoman Empire, Muhammad Ali was, for all intents and purposes, independent. He had centralized power in his own hands to such an extent that there were no important centers of opposition. Muhammad Ali's successes contrasted with the difficulties experienced in the Ottoman Empire, where Janissaries and religious leaders offered powerful resistance to the sultan's reform programs.

Military considerations dominated the viceroy's modernizing program. As a soldier, Muhammad Ali had seen at first hand the powerful French army, and after Napoleon's downfall he still feared Ottoman designs on Egypt. He generally turned to France for aid,

Egypt's first and most imaginative modernizer, Muhammad Ali, ruler from 1805 to 1848.

and French "advisers" provided most of the important technical assistance. Colonel O. J. A. Seve, later known as Sulayman Pasha, helped to reorganize the Egyptian army along European lines. A French doctor was brought to Egypt to create a modern medical corps. The viceroy also constructed a modern navy, but much of it was destroyed by a European fleet in 1827 during the Greek War of Independence.

Muhammad Ali established modern schools to bring European science to Egypt and to train technicians for the army and government bureaucracy. European teachers were brought to Egypt to staff the new medical, veterinary, and engineering schools. Egyptian students were also sent to Europe, mainly France, to complete their studies. Since Muhammad Ali was interested in assimilating Western scientific knowledge, Egyptian students took technical courses, rarely specializing in the arts and humanities. In order to make Western science more accessible to educated Egyptians, a Translation School was established which published a host of Arabic translations of European scientific treatises. Egyptian students returning from study in Europe were expected to make Arabic translations of books they had used in courses. The leading figure in the translation movement was al-Tahtawi, who had accompanied a student mission to Paris and who throughout his life played an important role in interpreting the meaning of Western civilization to the Islamic world.

Programs of military modernization were expensive, and the Egyptian viceroy, recognizing this fact, sought to transform his economic system by expanding cotton cultivation and export. Only small quantities of cotton had been grown in Egypt before the nineteenth century because in Egypt cotton was a summer crop, and during the summer season—also the low Nile season—there was insufficient water for irrigation. Egypt's engineers solved this problem by constructing deep irrigation canals for drawing off the low Nile waters. In the 1820s Egypt made the first exports of a crop that at its peak later in the century accounted for more than 80 percent of the total value of all Egyptian goods sold abroad.

Not content merely with increased revenues from the new cotton exports, Muhammad Ali devised other means for increasing state revenues; for example, he arbitrarily set up state monopolies over agricultural and industrial products. Any crop or product designated as a state monopoly had to be sold to the state at arbitrarily fixed prices and then was resold by the state at great profit. Most of Egypt's major export and food crops came under state control. The system worked an enormous hardship on the Egyptian peasants, since they were forced to sell cheaply and buy dearly. There are numerous accounts of peasant suffering and even flight from the land during this period. But this harsh and cruel system did in fact enable the viceroy to launch extraordinarily imaginative and expensive reform programs without borrowing European capital, a feat that few modernizing Middle Eastern leaders of the nineteenth century could match.

Muhammad Ali's most ambitious effort was his program of industrialization. He brought European technicians to advise him on his industrial plans and built an iron foundry and numerous textile plants. His infant industries were protected from European manufactures by tariffs. In 1830, at the height of industrial activity, a high percentage of textiles purchased in Egypt had been manufactured at home.

Nevertheless, the Egyptian industries were run inefficiently and at great expense, for machinery had to be imported, and when it broke down it often was not repaired for want of parts or skilled mechanics. Since Egypt had no mineral fuels, many of the machines were run by animal power. But the chief obstacle to Muhammad Ali's plan was opposition from Europeans eager to sell their manufactured products in Egypt. In 1840, the European powers forced Muhammad Ali to sign a treaty by which he abolished his protective tariffs. Deprived of these supports, Egypt's industries were destroyed by cheaper European goods.

The reason Muhammad Ali was forced to give up his protective tariffs was that Great Britain and other European powers had grown alarmed at his efforts to seize Ottoman territory in Syria and Crete in 1839. A year later his armies were ready to attack Is-

tanbul itself and were prevented from doing so only by the diplomatic and military pressure of the European powers. The treaty of 1840 brought an end to both his imperialistic ambitions and his modernizing schemes.

Compelled to reduce the size of his army and to foreswear further territorial conquest, the Egyptian ruler lost interest in reform. Schools were closed; educational missions ceased to be sent to Europe; and European advisers discovered that the Egyptian government was no longer interested in acquiring their talents. Muhammad Ali's successors, Abbas (1848–1854) and Said (1854–1863), allowed his programs to languish, although Said signed the concessions for the construction of the Suez Canal.

Still, despite its shortcomings, Muhammad Ali's foresighted and energetic reign must be regarded as the most striking Middle Eastern example of defensive modernization. He perceived that Egypt's political and economic weakness could be counteracted only through selective borrowing from Europe. He also established the main lines of later Egyptian development: cotton cultivation, hydraulic reform of the Nile and its irrigation canals, and importation of Western education. His accomplishments, however, benefited primarily himself and his family, members of a Turkish ruling elite. Although his reforms indirectly stimulated the growth of Egyptian national consciousness, Muhammad Ali was certainly not an Egyptian nationalist. He exploited the Egyptian people harshly for his personal ambitions.

Ismail, khedive (or ruler) from 1863 to 1879, made the next attempt to modernize Egypt, but by then the ruler was no longer the only locus of power. A half-century of educational reform had created an educated Egyptian elite with their own ideas about the future of their country. During Ismail's reign, this group became strong enough to attack even the khedive. The European mercantile community, which Muhammad Ali had tried to control, also became a powerful, autonomous group in Egyptian politics.

Ismail himself had been educated in France and wanted to see Egypt become more like Western Europe. During his reign the Suez Canal was opened (1869). Verdi's opera *Aida* was specially written to coincide with the opening of the canal, although its performance was delayed until 1871. At the canal opening, the khedive's special guests included Empress Eugenie of France, the Emperor of Austria, the Crown Prince of Prussia, the Crown Prince of the Netherlands, and Prince William of Hesse. On November 17, 1869, the French imperial yacht, the *Aigle,* officially opened the canal. Aboard, Empress Eugenie exclaimed: "Never have I seen so lovely a sight." Later she remarked to a friend that during the whole time on board "she had felt as though a circle of fire was round her head, because every moment she thought she saw the *Aigle* stop short, the honor of the French flag compromised, and the fruit of our labors lost." For Ismail, this great event—the joining of the Red Sea and the Mediterranean —symbolized Egypt's joining European civilization and becoming an outpost of Europe. In many other ways the khedive sought to "Europeanize" his country. He created a Council of Notables imitative of European parliamentary government, although the Council's powers were purely advisory. The wealthier sections of Cairo were embellished with parks and boulevards in imitation of the beautification of Paris. The khedive even permitted a free press to come into existence.

Unlike Muhammad Ali, Ismail resorted to borrowing European capital, with disastrous consequences for his country. At first capital was easily accessible, but as the Egyptian debts mounted, it was provided only at exorbitant rates. By 1879 the Egyptian public debt exceeded £90,000,000, more than ten times Egypt's yearly state revenues. In his efforts to stave off bankruptcy, Ismail pledged a substantial part of state revenues for the payment of the debt, including railway receipts, port dues, and land tax receipts from several provinces. In 1875 he sold Egypt's shares in the Suez Canal Company to the British government—a desperate and ignominious transaction that left Egypt with a small financial return on a vital trade route for which it had conceded land, contributed money, and provided abundant labor during construction. Then, in order to appease his European creditors, Ismail was forced to appoint a British and French adviser over the

two most important government ministries: public works and finance. Ismail's desperate efforts to free himself from the shackles of Anglo-French control only resulted in his being deposed in 1879. Thus, even before the British occupation in 1882 (which will be discussed later), Egypt was falling under the political sway of Europe.

Egyptian indebtedness must be attributed both to Ismail and to rapacious European capitalism. Although the Egyptian government undoubtedly spent some of the money wisely, the khedive's schemes were more ambitious than the resources of Egypt allowed. Moreover, late in his rule, Ismail borrowed to pay off his debts, pledging important Egyptian assets to European creditors. Ismail's extravagances played into the hands of European bankers. Many of those in Egypt were greedy men on the margin of the European financial world. They were interested only in quick profits, and Ismail provided a means to this end. Although the more conservative financial houses in Europe were concerned with sound investment in Egyptian economic development, they, too, were sometimes lured into seeking the quick profits afforded them through loans to the khedive.

Turkey

The first Ottoman sultan to attempt a program of modernization, Selim III (1789–1807), sought to establish a new army but incurred the resentment of the Janissaries, who then forced his deposition; Sultan Mahmud II (1808–1839) moved much more cautiously. He formed a new military corps of his own, based on European models, and then turned it loose against the main garrison of Janissaries in Istanbul in 1826. In the holocaust that followed, 6000 Janissaries lost their lives and another 18,000 were exiled to Asia Minor. Sultan Mahmud II also got rid of most of the semi-independent potentates in the provinces in the 1830s. But the slowness of Ottoman reform is attested by the fact that Muhammad Ali of Egypt would probably have overrun Istanbul in 1840 had foreign powers not interfered to stop him. They did so because they feared the two most likely results of an Egyptian assault on the empire: disintegration with resulting political chaos in the Middle East; or a strengthened state under Muhammad Ali, less responsive to European manipulation.

Until the late nineteenth century Turkish reforming impulses were channeled mainly through the government bureaucracy. The period from about 1839 to 1876 has been called the *Tanzimat,* during which the government issued a number of decrees for the reform of Ottoman institutions. Reforms came as a result of military defeat by Egyptian forces in 1839 and in 1856 after initial losses to Russian forces in the Crimean War. The ostensible goal of the reforms was to secularize the state, promote individual rights and security, extend state operations into the fields of education, public works, and economic development, and introduce the representative principle into local governing organs. The Imperial Edict of Humayun (1856) epitomized these tendencies. It guaranteed every subject of the *Porte* personal liberty, equality before the law, religious freedom, eligibility for civil and military office, and equality of taxation. But, born of defeat, this sweeping edict was soon shelved. The commitment of the ruling elite to these liberalizing changes was always fragile.

In 1876 the Ottoman court granted a constitution providing a Westernized parliamentary government. Some Turkish students of European affairs were convinced that the key to Europe's strength lay in its parliamentary system. Their champion was Midhat Pasha, a high-ranking, reform-minded Ottoman bureaucrat. His energetic reform was short-lived, however, because the new sultan, Abdul-Hamid (1876–1909), preferred absolutism to the reform program and so undermined the experiment and ushered in a long reign of increased political centralization and despotism.

During Abdul-Hamid's reign the impetus for reform came from Turkish nationalists outside the government. The Ottomans themselves began to use Pan-Islamic appeals more effectively than before as a source of imperial unity, but they could not counteract the resentment against the sultan's tyrannical and inefficient methods everywhere in the empire. A group of radical nationalists calling themselves the Young Turks became

alarmed at the sultan's mismanagement of the empire, which had already resulted in significant losses of territory in 1878 at the Congress of Berlin. (See p. 472.) The headquarters of the Young Turks was Paris, but the movement soon began to make inroads at home in the armed forces. In 1908 it inspired the army at Salonika to lead a revolt against Ottoman misrule and revive the 1876 constitution. Although Abdul-Hamid was forced from the throne, the Young Turks retained the sultanate. Their Turkish national consciousness made the new rulers decide against dismantling the Ottoman Empire or significantly decentralizing it. Moreover, the Young Turks governed the non-Turkish speaking parts of the empire almost as autocratically as Abdul-Hamid had. The political subordination of outlying parts of the empire gave a strong impetus to regional nationalisms. In fact, it was during the Young Turk period that Arab nationalism began to be defined and started to demand the separation of Arab territories from Ottoman overlordship.

The Ottoman Empire was first called the "sick man of Europe" in the 1850s. It had been in decline throughout the nineteenth century, and its efforts at reform were often ridiculed by European observers. Yet the empire was not destroyed during the era of the new imperialism (1880–1914). During this period the Ottomans did lose considerable territory: most of the Balkans, to Austria, Russia, and new independent states; Tunisia to France;* Egypt to the British; and Libya to Italy. But the Turkish heartland and the Arab provinces of Syria and Iraq remained intact in 1914. In part, the Ottomans owed their continued existence to the rivalries of the European powers, whose jealousies prevented them from agreeing on a final partition. Still, the "sick man" was not as sick as the Europeans thought. The modernizing efforts did produce some results, and the bonds of Islamic and Ottoman unity were just enough to negate the separatist sentiments within the empire. Its death knell, however, was sounded when the Ottomans entered World War I, placing too great a strain on

---

* Algeria had been conquered by France in the 1830s.

THE NEW IMPERIALISM IN BLACK AFRICA

Africa as a whole suffered the most from Europe's expansion in the late nineteenth century. As late as 1875 Europeans exercised only restricted political authority in Africa. The French had seized Algeria and Senegal, the British had possessions in South Africa and enclaves along the coast of West Africa, and the Portuguese had authority in the coastal areas of Mozambique and Angola, along with rather vague claims in the interior. Yet by 1914 virtually all of Africa had been partitioned among the major powers of Europe. The only independent areas were Ethiopia, which the Italians had been unable to conquer, and Liberia, established as a colony for freed American slaves in 1822.

The largest African empire belonged to the French, but as Lord Salisbury, British Prime Minister in the late nineteenth century cynically remarked: "Anyone who looks at the map and merely measures the degrees will perhaps be of the opinion that France has laid claim to a very considerable stretch of territory. But it is necessary to judge land not only by its extent but also by its value. Much of this land is what agriculturalists would call 'very light land'; that is to say it is the desert of the Sahara." The British, primarily because of their earlier commercial and missionary involvements in Africa, dominated some of the wealthiest regions: Nigeria and the Gold Coast in West Africa, South Africa and the Rhodesias, and Kenya and Uganda in East Africa. Recently unified Germany claimed a large share of African territory with German East Africa, German Southwest Africa, Togo, and the Cameroons. Even some of the smaller and less powerful European nation-states made gains. The Italians seized Libya from the Ottoman Empire, and Portugal, nearly bankrupt yet anxious to fulfill its self-appointed civilizing mission in Africa, rounded out its conquests in Angola and Mozambique. The most bizarre of the experiments was that of Leopold, king of the Belgians. In the 1880s, unable to win support for imperialism from the Belgian populace, he carved out his own domain, the Free State of the Congo, which reverted to the Belgian government only in 1908. The scramble for partition constantly raised the fear of European war, but actual fighting between the competing European states did not occur in Africa during this period.

As we saw in Chapters 15 and 19, the new imperialism involved diverse motives. Before and during the partition of Africa much was written and spoken about its vast economic potential. Many French politicians and publicists thought West Africa could become an El Dorado, and they likened its future to that of British India. Economic gain was certainly important in the British takeover of the Boer Republics in South Africa (1902) where gold had been discovered and had attracted substantial investment. The economic possibilities of Nigeria were recognized by the British and strengthened their determination to control this area. But in many other areas, often those of keen political rivalry, there were no obvious economic assets, and European merchants and investors refused to be interested. In fact, on the whole, the nineteenth century European mercantile and investing class did not redirect its economic attention away from such lucrative areas as the United States, Canada, Australia, Russia, and Eastern Europe to invest in and develop Africa's resources.

Strategic and diplomatic factors loomed very large, especially for the British. The Suez Canal linked India and the Far East closely with Europe. British shipping dominated the canal, which was also valued because it could be used to rush troops and military material to crises in the east. The British could ill afford to have a hostile power in Egypt. In 1881–1882 a nationalist revolt led by Colonel Urabi Pasha, created a politically explosive situation there. The British occupied the country in 1882 primarily to protect their interests in the canal. But Egypt was connected with the Sudan and Uganda through the Nile River, on which Egyptian agriculture depended. Any diversion of water could bring economic ruin to Egypt. So long as these Upper Nile territories were in the hands of African rulers who lacked a knowledge of modern technology, the British need

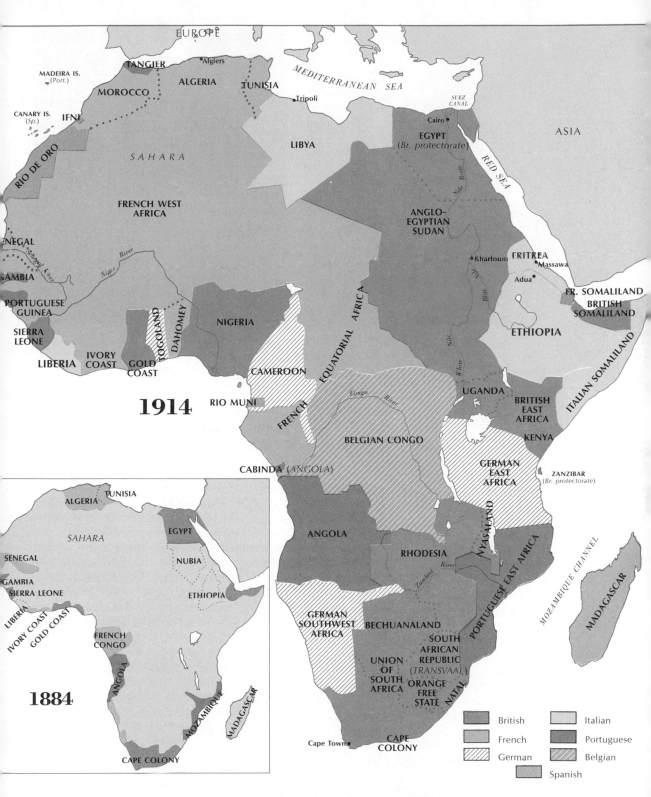

EUROPE

MADEIRA IS.
(Port.)

TANGIER

•Algiers

MEDITERRANEAN SEA

MOROCCO

ALGERIA

TUNISIA

•Tripoli

SUEZ
CANAL

CANARY IS.
(Sp.)

IFNI

RIO DE ORO

SAHARA

LIBYA

Cairo•

EGYPT
(Br. protectorate)

ASIA

RED SEA

FRENCH WEST
AFRICA

ANGLO-
EGYPTIAN
SUDAN

Nile River

ENEGAL

Senegal River

Niger River

Khartoum•

FRITREA

•Massawa

AMBIA

PORTUGUESE
GUINEA

NIGERIA

TOGOLAND

DAHOMEY

Blue Nile

Adua•

FR. SOMALILAND
BRITISH
SOMALILAND

SIERRA
LEONE

IVORY
COAST

GOLD
COAST

CAMEROON

EQUATORIAL AFRICA

White Nile

ETHIOPIA

LIBERIA

1914

RIO MUNI

FRENCH

Congo River

UGANDA

BRITISH
EAST
AFRICA

ITALIAN SOMALILAND

BELGIAN CONGO

KENYA

CABINDA (ANGOLA)

GERMAN
EAST
AFRICA

ZANZIBAR
(Br. protectorate)

ANGOLA

RHODESIA

NYASALAND

Zambesi River

PORTUGUESE EAST AFRICA

MOZAMBIQUE CHANNEL

MADAGASCAR

GERMAN
SOUTHWEST
AFRICA

BECHUANALAND

SOUTH
AFRICAN
REPUBLIC
(TRANSVAAL)

UNION
OF
SOUTH
AFRICA

ORANGE
FREE
STATE

NATAL

Cape Town•

CAPE
COLONY

TUNISIA

ALGERIA

EGYPT

SAHARA

NUBIA

SENEGAL

ETHIOPIA

GAMBIA
SIERRA LEONE

LIBERIA

IVORY COAST

GOLD COAST

FRENCH
CONGO

ANGOLA

MOZAMBIQUE

MADAGASCAR

1884

CAPE COLONY

British   Italian

French   Portuguese

German   Belgian

Spanish

PARTITION OF AFRICA

Two imperialists: Lord Cromer, British consul-general and virtual ruler of Egypt from 1883 to 1907, and King Leopold II of Belgium (1835–1909), founder of his own personal empire in Africa, the Congo Independent State.

not act. But as the European competition for empire grew keener, the British became concerned. Uganda was annexed in 1894 in the face of German and French threats. Then the Sudan, ruled by Sudanese Muslims from 1885 until 1898, became the center of bitter Anglo-French rivalry. Both countries laid claim to it, and in 1898 at Fashoda (now Kodok), on the Upper Nile, an Egyptian force under the haughty British imperialist, Lord Kitchener, halted a French expeditionary group under Jean-Baptiste Marchand. In reality this was a European crisis, not an African one. Marchand's tiny band was no match for Kitcheners troops. Had the French wanted to contest British supremacy on the Upper Nile they would have had to declare a European war. Rather than resort to this, they ordered Marchand's withdrawal, leaving the Nile basin in British hands.

During the partition of Africa a few dynamic and ambitious individuals played extremely influential roles. The German mystic explorer and colonizer, Karl Peters, who believed that the number three was lucky for him and only undertook major activities in years that were divisible by three (1881, 1884, 1887, 1890), disregarded Bismarck's statements that Germany did not want colonies and signed a series of treaties with East African chiefs, thereby laying the foundations of the German empire in East Africa. The most energetic of the British imperialists, Cecil Rhodes, believed that "expansion was everything and that the world's surface being limited, the great object of present humanity should be to take as much of the world as it possibly could." In quest of a British empire stretching from the Cape in South Africa to Cairo, he facilitated British control of Southern and Northern Rhodesia. Undeniably the most ambitious imperialist of all was Leopold of Belgium. As a young man and heir to the throne he had dreamed of empire partially as a means of enhancing Belgium's international standing. Even without the support of the Belgian people and parliament, he created his own state in the Congo, paying for a good deal of the administrative expense from his own fortune.

In his *Man of Destiny* George Bernard Shaw wrote:

As the great champion of freedom and independence, the Englishman conquers half the world and calls it Colonization. When he wants a new market for his adulterated Manchester goods, he sends a missionary to teach the natives the gospel of peace. The natives kill the missionary; he flies to arms in defense of Christianity; fights for it; conquers for it; and takes the market as a reward from heaven.

This cynical view of English hypocrisy and missionary complicity in imperialism cannot be considered completely fair, although the missionaries were an important factor. Missionaries like David Livingstone whetted Europe's curiosity about Africa before the partition and spoke forcefully about Europe's civilizing mission among the less fortunate. Other missionaries had publicized the potential wealth of Africa. During the partition itself British missionaries were influential in bringing Uganda and Nyasaland under British control. The Buganda kingdom in Uganda was torn asunder by a virtual religious war, pitting Protestants, Catholics, and Muslims against each other. The English Church Missionary Society supported the Protestant African group and also exerted pressure on the British government to annex Uganda.

Nor can the African populations simply be regarded as passive throughout the partition years. Some groups, believing that they could benefit from the European presence, encouraged European involvement. On the whole, however, the first African response was resistance. In many cases resistance actually accelerated the pace of imperialism by forcing the hand of the foreign powers and compelling them to make their control more effective. The Egyptian nationalist revolt led by Urabi in 1881–1882 created in the minds of the British such infinite possibilities of political chaos in Egypt that they felt they had to intervene. An uprising in German East Africa in 1890 discredited the merchant company that was ruling and forced the German government to take over the territory.

The rapidity of partition was stimulated by passionate, though mostly ineffective efforts to resist it. Europe had such overwhelming military superiority that Africa had little chance to win, yet there was a great resistance movement. Not all resistance ended in complete and speedy defeat. Ethiopia's King Menelik drove a large Italian army out of his country at the battle of Adowa in 1896. In the Sudan, Muhammed Ahmad announced himself as the Mahdi, the chosen one destined to bring about the final victory of Islam. He gained an enormous following and succeeded in overwhelming Egyptian troops that held the Sudan under Egyptian suzerainty. In 1885 his forces overran the city of Khartum, killing the famous British war hero, General Charles "Chinese" Gordon, whom the British government had sent to the Sudan to effect an evacuation of foreign troops. Despite the Mahdi's death later in 1885, the Sudan remained independent under his successor until an Anglo-Egyptian conquest from 1896 to 1899.

The kingdoms of West Africa also opposed European encroachment, as in the case of Samory Toure, military and political leader of a Malinke empire there. He led a well-armed and disciplined force against the French but realizing that his army was outmatched he divided his forces into three units: an advance column, bringing new areas to the east under control; a second army, occupying an intermediate zone and preparing to move into the area conquered by the first army; and a third army, a rearguard, which laid waste to the territory that had been occupied and that the encroaching army was moving into. In this way, Samory Toure held out for sixteen years (1882–1898) moving his empire eastward from the border of Sierra Leone to north of the Ivory Coast and the Gold Coast. Even the less politically centralized societies provided resistance, although their opposition was more specific and localized.

Although all the revolts were crushed, African resistance did have some success. In certain areas rebellions called attention to colonial injustices and produced a liberalization of colonial policies. The memories of early African rebellions were also important to later nationalists who drew inspiration and pointed with pride to traditions of anti-colonialism.

The Battle of Umdurman, 1898, when Anglo-Egyptian troops defeated the Mahdist forces under the Khalifa and brought the Sudan under foreign control.

EUROPEAN RULE IN AFRICA

Although the European populations took nationalistic pride in the partition of Africa, the day-to-day problems of administration held little fascination. Because of their greater experience with imperial questions, particularly in India, the British generally were more vigorous in ruling their empire than the other European nations. Parliament regularly debated colonial issues, and colonial governors were expected to write annual progress reports on their territories for the consideration of Parliament and the interested public. With the exception of France, the other European states generally left colonial matters in the hands of men on the scene. As long as the colonies were quiescent no one at home asked questions.

Colonial administration was judged largely by the degree of fiscal autonomy and political stability attained. None of the European states wanted empire to be costly. The colonial governors were under unrelenting pressure to balance their budgets and to make no claims on the financial resources of the home governments. Many of the political entities of Africa were created in response to financial pressures. Northern Nigeria was combined with southern Nigeria because the richer southern territories could help finance the administration of the north. The French territories of West Africa were grouped into a loose confederation, partly so that the revenues of the richer coastal territories, like Senegal and the Ivory Coast, could be spent in the poorer hinterland areas. Despite these efforts, many African colonies did not become financially self-sufficient until after World War I. Widespread African resistance to the European colonial system caused a well-justified fear of rebellion. Rebellions proved costly to suppress and seemed contradictory to the European assumption that they were in Africa to help African peoples. Within the limitations imposed by these two goals—fiscal autonomy and prevention of rebellion—European administrators were given latitude to promote economic development, foster social change, and even encourage European settlement.

One of the first experiments for governing Africa cheaply was the chartered company. Both the British and the Germans employed this largely unsatisfactory system. The British had a precedent in the old British East India Company, which was also attractive to Bismarck, who did not want to be bothered by the financial and political problems of an African empire. The best solution apparently was to turn over administration to an interested group of merchants. The most important British examples were the South Africa Company of Rhodes in the Rhodesias, and Goldie's Royal Niger Company in Nigeria. Only Rhodes's company lasted for any length of time. Bismarck was singularly unsuccessful in persuading German businessmen to form such companies. A German Southwest Africa Company collapsed almost overnight for want of funds and interest, and Karl Peters's German East Africa Company proved incapable of handling the sophisticated problems of administering a large and ethnically diverse territory.

The system that best realized the two European goals of fiscal self-sufficiency and prevention of rebellion was developed by the British and became known as indirect rule. Indirect rule meant exercising political control through established rulers and precolonial institutions, as the British had been doing in India. By ruling indirectly, the British kept administration costs relatively inexpensive. Furthermore, they were less likely to create resistance, since the traditional African societies were only slightly disrupted. Europeans ruled indirectly in many areas. In Tunisia, beginning in 1882, the French ruled behind the bey, and in Egypt the British manipulated the khedive as they wished. The system was crystallized and had its most spectacular successes under Lord Lugard and his successors in northern Nigeria, an area ideally suited for a system of ruling indirectly because of its enormous territorial expanse and the existence there of the Fulani Empire. The British would have had difficulty finding either the money or the skilled manpower to govern this whole area directly. Their solution was to employ members of the Fulani ruling elite and their institutions, controlling them from behind the scenes with a small staff of British officials. At the outset then, indirect rule was simply a convenient and inexpensive means for administering large territories.

A more formal and fully rationalized system soon displaced these early expedients. As European administrators, aided by anthropologists, began to understand African societies better, they advanced the argument that these societies could only be changed or "modernized" if the colonial administration understood how the traditional societies had been governed in the past—whether through emirs, chiefs, or tribal councils—and utilized the traditional institutions as a base for gradual change. Lugard himself helped to popularize the evolving ideas in his famous book, *The Dual Mandate in Tropical Africa* (1922). Many observers regarded Donald Cameron as the most skillful practitioner of these ideas. After serving in Nigeria, he became governor of Tanganyika during the 1920s. Tanganyika was the old German East Africa, taken over by the British at the conclusion of World War I when Germany was stripped of its colonies. Here Cameron sought first to understand the nature of East African tribal societies and then to use the traditionally sanctioned rulers and institutions as the basis of his local administration. His goal was not to preserve these structures unchanged but to use them to perform the modern functions of tax collection, political representation, and inculcation of loyalty to the state.

Cameron's program was indirect rule at its best, seeking to adapt old practices to the requirements of a modern polity. In many areas of indirect rule, however, and especially in northern Nigeria, its proponents used these ideas to insulate societies from disruptive modernizing influences. British indirect rulers in Muslim northern Nigeria, like C. L. Temple, had such sympathy for the Fulani way of life that they erected barriers against missionary activity and allowed the north to lag far behind southern Nigeria in education. As an adjunct to their concern for converting Africans to Christianity missionaries established schools and practically monopolized the modern educational system in the first two decades of colonial rule. But the administrators feared a clash between Muslims and Christians in northern Nigeria and were apprehensive that tactless missionary actions might provoke the population into rising against British rule. Consequently, they restricted the missionaries to non-Muslim areas. Because northern Nigeria preserved far more of its traditional way of life than the south, the quest for Nigerian unity was very difficult.

All of the other European powers in Africa sought to incorporate features of indirect rule into their administrative systems to meet the same financial and political problems. Yet each empire preserved its own special characteristics. The major theoretical controversy in the French empire was between assimilation and association. The French had long been proponents of the assimilationist idea: they believed that colonial peoples should be made over in the image of the French, learning the French language, law, and culture. But the French empire had grown so rapidly in the second half of the nineteenth century and had incorporated such diverse peoples that many Frenchmen felt that this goal was beyond French means. Instead, these Frenchmen argued for separate development of colonial peoples along pathways that were more in keeping with precolonial traditions. The exponents of this idea of association wanted to preserve traditional institu-

tions and use indigenous languages for education.

Both ideas were influential in the French colonies. A small segment of the colonial population was given a deep exposure to French education and values, whereas the majority of the population was either given no education or trained in the vernacular in rudimentary subjects. The goal of the assimilationists was the creation of French citizens, citizenship being conferred on colonial peoples who fulfilled the following requirements: (1) proven devotion to France, (2) ability to read and write French, and (3) evidence of financial means and a good character. Yet as late as 1921 the Ivory Coast had only 308 inhabitants with the privileges of French citizens, Dahomey 121, Upper Volta 17, and Niger 9. Senegal, with 22,711 French African citizens in 1921, was an exception, but this was because French legislation in the nineteenth century had ruled that any African born in one of the four communes of Dakar, St. Louis, Gorée, and Rufisque automatically acquired French citizenship.

French rule was arbitrary and sometimes harsh toward the African. A set of decrees, known as the *Indigenat,* gave French administrators the power to imprison for a short period (two weeks) and/or fine individuals without trial for a long list of offenses. By the 1920s and 1930s this list of punishable acts was to include: obstruction of tax collection, refusal to execute works of public order or welfare, omitting to declare a change of domicile, refusal to give information to public officials, aiding agitators or offenders sought by the police, weakening French authority, failure to carry out administrative regulations, illegal wearing of uniforms, troubling public peace, and refusal to receive French money. Terms as vague as "weakening French authority" gave the French administrators enormous arbitrary powers and enabled them to suppress almost all political discontent. The French also made use of forced labor. Most colonial systems permitted some form of forced labor, and the French requirements were lower than the British in many areas. But the French system was deeply resented because it was used on a variety of projects, at times on European-run plantations, whereas the British tried to limit the use of forced labor to projects that brought immediate benefit to the African groups involved. The French also controlled education more tightly than the British. Missionary groups encountered greater difficulties in founding stations and opening schools in the French territories. Much of the educational system was run by the state and catered to a small African clientele. Even though the French schools gave a superior education, their graduates were mostly absorbed into the lower ranks of the colonial bureaucracy.

The French saw their colonies as a reservoir for military recruitment and as a means for redressing their military inferiority vis à vis the Germans. Their conscripted African army was larger than the British African army and even during peacetime served all over the French empire — in Indochina, Syria, and Algeria, as well as West and Equatorial Africa.

Once the enthusiasm of the German people for obtaining African territories declined, they allowed their empire to be run by a small clique of self-interested groups: administrators, the military, settlers, a few commercial firms, and missionaries. These men on the scene, unchecked by the German government at home, exploited their territories so ruthlessly that many of the colonial peoples rose in revolt. In German Southwest Africa the government aided settlers in expropriating land from the Herero and Nama peoples. Although both had small populations, they were driven to revolt in 1904. This revolt was put down with extraordinary brutality, including a so-called extermination order promulgated by General Von Trotha. The Herero population was reduced from an estimated 80,000 to 15,000 while the Nama lost half their population in this revolt.

Almost at the same time German East Africa was torn by a severe revolt known as the Maji-Maji rebellion. Energized by prophetic leaders and spurred on by a belief that magic waters dispensed by religious leaders would confer immunity from German bullets, a large section in the south of German East Africa rose in opposition in 1905. Once again the rebellion was put down with great severity. German colonial administration was probably not more harsh or exploitative than British or French, but the German military suppressed rebellions more violently.

These two major rebellions shocked Germans at home and compelled reforms in the colonial system. Bernhard Dernburg was appointed to head a newly created colonial ministry. He and his successors ushered in a new era of "scientific colonialism," in which the colonies were to be developed for the benefit of all Germans, not just a small clique of men on the scene, and in which the well-being of African populations was given high priority. From 1907 to the outbreak of World War I, Germany spent considerable sums of money on railroad construction, roads, education, and economic development. But this short period of somewhat model colonial administration could not erase the memories of exploitation and rebellion.

In the Congo Leopold's bold experiment in empire-building almost foundered. After expending his own personal fortune he was able to float two large loans from the Belgian Parliament in 1890 and 1896. His goals might well have been thwarted had not the Congo finally found a lucrative export trade in rubber and ivory. By the turn of the century the Congo had become an enormously successful economic enterprise for the Europeans but at the same time a great burden to the African population. Villages were expected to gather a fixed quantity of rubber or ivory or face punishment. Products were transported from Leopoldville to the Atlantic Ocean port of Matadi by means of forced labor. Moreover, Leopold had given immense territorial concessions to European financial companies in order to attract capital and gain support for economic development. A private company undertook to construct a railway from Stanley Pool to Matadi, for which it was rewarded with huge territorial concessions. Since Leopold regarded the Congo as his personal domain, he did not hesitate to grant himself a massive territorial estate, known as the *Domaine de la Couronne*. The profits from the economic activities of this area, which was much larger than Belgium itself, went to Leopold and the royal family and were used for the embellishment of Belgium's leading cities. No more striking example of exploitative imperialism can be found.

By 1900 the Leopoldian system had created its own enemies: humanitarians outraged by the reports of atrocities in the treatment of Africans, missionaries not given a free hand in the Congo, and jealous financial groups squeezed out of the profits of this lucrative trade. In 1904 a Congo Reform Association was established in England and the United States which sought to publicize the repressive nature of Leopold's economic exploitation. The vigorous campaign compelled Leopold to hand over the administration of the Congo to the Belgian state in 1908, and belated efforts were made to put an end to the harsh treatment of the African peoples.

EFFECTS OF COLONIAL RULE IN TWENTIETH-CENTURY AFRICA

The impact of European rule is difficult to gauge. In the long sweep of African history the European colonial era was an interlude of little more than half a century. The Europeans did not have the financial or manpower resources to impinge on the lives of all Africans; many people in independent Africa continue to live as their ancestors had in 1850. Yet colonialism certainly brought important changes. Africa probably gained access to more European capital than it would have attracted if it had remained independent. Capital helped to provide an African economic infrastructure: railways and roads were built for the transport of goods; harbor facilities were constructed. European capital also played a role in the cultivation of new crops, the extraction of mineral resources, and the expansion of trade in general.

There continues to be much resentment against the way in which Europeans drew the political boundaries of Africa. Demarcation lines were generally geometrical and geographical and disregarded ethnic divisions. The political boundaries were often determined in the capitals of Europe by people with only the scantest knowledge of African conditions. Nevertheless, despite many errors, Europe's partition of Africa did endow the continent with new political units from which both nationalism and efforts at nation-building emerged. The European colonial system helped to establish the new bureaucratic organizations, military bodies, and local governing structures around which African efforts at nation-building have been focused.

In other ways European colonialism hindered the modernization of Africa. This fact is most clear in white-settler dominated areas where economic and political changes were sponsored by the European population primarily for its own benefit. The African population in settler areas often lived in reserves, worked as miners and as an agricultural proletariat on European farms, and were denied the political rights exercised by the settlers. In these colonies, Africans could see firsthand the fruits of modernity — high standards of living, schools, modern cities — but were not expected to enjoy them as fully as the dominant European population. Even in the nonsettler areas, colonialism created hindrances that were to be felt most severely when African nations won their independence. Economic development was dominated by European capital and a European financial class. African merchants experienced considerable difficulty in establishing themselves, since they could not compete with the more heavily capitalized European mercantile firms. Usually, the most they could aspire to was small commercial activities as an adjunct of the European firms. Thus, at independence, Africa lacked its own autonomous and vigorous commercial middle class and had to rely on continued European technical and financial support.

The European administrators tended to disparage the Africans' ability to run a complex bureaucracy. Consequently, the Europeans monopolized the top positions in the administration, allowing Africans entry only to the lower ranks. Even in the indirect rule areas, most of the technical positions in the bureaucracy were held by Europeans. After 1945, as Europe began to decolonize, it was to try to give Africans more experience in government, but there was not enough time. Most African states were to enter the era of independence with only a small group of experienced administrators and with insufficient popular allegiance to the new organs of government. Despite their own parliamentary traditions and their glorification of democratic forces of government, the colonial powers provided little stimulus for the growth of democracy in Africa. Most areas were governed autocratically. Parliamentary assemblies were showpieces, consultative bodies throughout most of their history, and elected by a restricted franchise. When, after World War II, it became clear that Africa would soon claim its independence, the frenzied efforts to expand the functions and franchises of elected assemblies were once again too little and too late. Finally, the Europeans showed little inclination to encourage industrialization in Africa, which they regarded as a source of raw materials and a market for European manufactures. Efforts to encourage industries competitive with European manufactured products would have brought a storm of protest from European industrialists.

The impact of Europe cannot be understood entirely from the perspective of the European administrative systems; missionaries, merchants, and settlers were other European agents of change. The missionaries had a radical and at times disruptive impact on Africa. They had a long association with the continent, dating back to the precolonial period. It is difficult to generalize about missionary societies as diverse, for example, as the Anglican Church Missionary Society, the Roman Catholic Holy Ghost Fathers, and the Jehovah's Witnesses. Nevertheless, all wanted to make conversions to Christianity and all tended to interpret Christianity in many ways contrary to traditional African values and practices. Most missionary organizations were opposed to certain fundamental African practices: slavery, polygamy, ancestor worship, female circumcision (excision of the clitoris), ceremonial and tribal dancing that seemed sexually uninhibited to the missionaries, and belief in witchcraft—to mention but a few areas of discord. The missionary groups varied in their methods for undermining these practices; some favored passing laws while others were in favor of moving gradually and by means of education. Nevertheless, their disruptive effect on traditional African societies cannot be denied. Missionary organizations were, for a considerable part of the colonial period, the only source of European education. Most European administrations, pressed as they were to seek financial self-sufficiency, were content to allow the missionaries to play the major educational role. It was only after World War I that colonial governments began to assume a large share of responsibility for African education.

European capital, generally organized into large commercial and mining firms, was another important agency of social change. In areas like Katanga in the Belgian Congo, Northern Rhodesia, and South Africa, firms prospected for minerals and established extensive mining operations. European capital was also active in the West African trade. Cocoa, coffee, peanuts, palm oil, and palm kernels were the major items of export, and finished textiles were the main imports. A few heavily capitalized companies dominated this trade, led by the giant United Africa Company, an amalgam of many other companies that had business in West Africa. Considerable capital was required because of the high risks involved in exporting crops subject to disease and climatic variations, the need to provide loans to small-scale traders and farmers, and the responsibility for creating most of the auxiliary services of the trade, such as warehouses, port facilities, and trading outlets all over West Africa. The astonishing surge in West African trade just before and just after World War I could not have occurred without access to this capital.

Another important element in the commercial sector was the influx of immigrant communites from British India. In East Africa, Indians carried on most of the internal trade and some of the trade outside the continent. In West Africa, although a few Syrian companies emerged to rival the European firms, most of the Syrian traders operated on a smaller scale as intermediaries between the European companies and the rest of the population.

Finally, there were the settlers, located mainly in Kenya, Northern and Southern Rhodesia, and South Africa. They must be distinguished from other European groups because of their intention to make Africa a permanent home. Although they engaged in many occupations, they were, at first, preeminently men of the soil. They experimented with new crops and new agricultural and pastoral techniques. They also tried to make Africa over in their image of Europe and founded and developed modern cities, European schools, and parliamentary assemblies, replete with political parties. They enjoyed a modern standard of living, contrasting markedly with the primitive standard of the African majority.

Although many important aspects of African life did not change as European colonial superstructures were being imposed on the continent, some fundamental transformations are easy to discern. There was a veritable agricultural revolution in many parts of Africa. Crops, either unknown or hardly cultivated, were introduced and became main items of export. Cocoa began to be cultivated in the Gold Coast at the end of the nineteenth century, and before long the Gold Coast was the world's leading cocoa exporter; Nigeria and the Ivory Coast soon followed suit. European settlers introduced sisal, coffee, and tea into the agricultural and export economies of East Africa, while cotton became a staple export commodity in Uganda and the Sudan. The agricultural revolution had enormous implications for Africa. It spread the use of markets and money and tied African economies to the world market. When world prices were high, African and European cultivators prospered, but when the prices declined, hard times and even problems of indebtedness set in.

Urbanization occurred throughout the colonial period, although its greatest advance was to come only after World War II: Leopoldville (Kinshasa) in the Congo (Zaire) and Ibadan in Nigeria were to grow to over a million inhabitants each in the 1950s and 1960s. Africans were attracted to cities because of poverty and overpopulation in the countryside and the bush and by prospects of high wages, and the psychic attractions of city life. Many, of course, were bitterly disillusioned, unable to find steady employment and forced to live in makeshift, unsanitary, overcrowded, rat-infested, slum dwellings. The city environment produced a mixing of African populations from different regions and tribes. In order to adjust to this new world, Africans created organizations, often called voluntary associations, which provided social and emotional supports and new loyalties for their members. These new associations helped to make the Africans politically conscious and contributed to the growth of African nationalism.

Burgeoning African economic activity required African labor and resulted in many pressures for labor recruitment. An African proletariat was needed in the mines of South Africa, Northern Rhodesia, and Katanga, while agricultural workers were required for the plantations and even small farms of the Congo (cotton and palm oil), Kenya (sisal, tea, and coffee), Nigeria, the Gold Coast, and the Ivory Coast (cocoa), and Liberia (rubber). Many Africans were not immediately responsive to wage incentives since they had not yet acquired a taste for European manufactured consumer goods and were not yet familiar with the use of the new currencies. Many societies had a clear division of agricultural duties between men and women; the new work routines challenged these patterns. Various forms of coercion were used to compel African laborers to offer themselves for wage labor. These ranged from outright coercion (such as demanding from the Africans a certain number of working days every year), to the enactment of new taxes, payable only in money, which could be realized mainly through wage labor. Labor recruitment produced large-scale movements of populations; the Thonga peoples of Mozambique, for example, traveling to the mines of South Africa in large numbers, and the Mossi of Upper Volta working as agricultural and industrial laborers in the Ivory Coast and Gold Coast.

European forms of education gained a rapid acceptance among many African peoples. So responsive were the Ibos of southeastern Nigeria and the Bakongo of the Congo, for example, that European missionaries and administrators were not able to keep pace with their demands for schools and teachers. The goals and content of education varied considerably. In certain colonies, like the Congo, the emphasis was on teaching elementary subjects. In order to gain converts some missionary societies oriented their school curriculum to reading and mastering the Bible. Other missionaries had a broader vision of their work and sought to give instruction in secular as well as religious subjects. Although African university education was not established for a long time, a small number of Africans was able to acquire university degrees by studying in Europe and, to a lesser extent, the United States. One basic criticism of African education was that it was not well suited to the African environment. The most prestigious schools tended to be modeled after British or French schools, did not emphasize agricultural and industrial subjects, and tended to disparage the African heritage by excluding it from courses.

Many of the changes during the colonial period were disruptive of traditional life. Labor recruitment deprived societies of a large proportion of their grown men. New economic opportunities and education created a wealthy and educated class, set off, to some extent, from the rest of the population. Missionaries held up the small monogamous family as an ideal. Social and geographical mobility was on the increase, and people with different backgrounds were interacting with each other for the first time. All of these influences tended to reduce the importance of the small, self-sufficient political and economic units that had once been the cement of African society: the family, the village, the age-group, and the clan. Africa was in the cauldron of social change, responsive to new values and loyalties or to a reinterpretation of the old.

Whether organized into empires or tribal states, the societies of Africa and the Middle East had become economically and technologically inferior to industrializing Europe by the nineteenth century. This had not always been the case. Arabs and Persians had dominated the Indian Ocean trade until the Portuguese began to break into this trade in the sixteenth century. The first Portuguese contacts with African peoples in the Congo River basin had been on a basis of equality; the Portuguese sent missionaries and exchanged diplomatic representatives. But the slave trade soon warped these promising European-African contacts. Some of Europe's wealth was clearly based on its control of Africa and East Asian trade. African slaves worked the sugar and cotton plantations of the Americas. No doubt this wealth contributed to European industrialization, which by the mid-1800s gave Europe the technological superiority for territorial domination of Africa and the Middle East.

The societies of Africa and the Middle East were organized around various unifying principles. Some were what we call tribal. Membership was based on speaking a common language, acceptance of common institutions, and belief in a common ancestor. Others were organized on the basis of religion, Islam being the most widespread religion in Africa and the Middle East. The Islamic world was divided among various sects as well as along racial and linguistic lines. The Ottoman rulers spoke Turkish and regarded themselves as distinct from their Arabic-speaking subjects. In most societies there was an ascending order of loyalties. The individual felt allegiance first to his kinship group, then to his local community and various local religious organizations, and finally, to the central institutions of the empire or state to which he belonged.

Between 1880 and 1914 Africa and the Middle East came under the territorial and political domination of Europe. In the long sweep of African and Middle Eastern history the European colonial period (1880–1960) was a short one. Nevertheless it was decisive, not only because of the ways in which it disrupted precolonial societies but also because it brought these societies face to face with the technological, economic, and political power of Europe. No people could ignore this challenge.

Many states had undertaken programs of defensive modernization in order to prevent their absorption by Europe. The partition of Africa showed the futility of their efforts. Muhammad Ali's was the most energetic program, original in conception and implementation. It entailed changes on many fronts: educational, military, agricultural, and even industrial. But it was ultimately thwarted by European opposition. Other states were too weakly organized; some were even ignorant of the European challenge until too late.

SUGGESTED READINGS

Gibb, H. A. R., *Mohammedanism: An Historical Study.* New York: Oxford University Press, 1962. Paperback.

A remarkably succinct introduction to Islamic institutions and history.

Lewis, Bernard, *Arabs in History.* New York: Hutchinson's Universal Library, 1966. Paperback.

The best short history on the Arabs.

Lewis, Bernard, *Arabs in History.* New York: Hutchinson's Universal Library, 1966. Paperback.

An insightful essay on the rise and development of Turkish civilization to the present.

Oliver, Roland and J. D. Fage, *A Short History of Africa.* London: Penguin Books, 1966. Paperback.

This controversial history of Africa still commands a wide following.

Kenyatta, Jomo, *Facing Mt. Kenya.* New York: Secker and Warburg, 1962. Paperback.

Among the numerous good books on African ethnography, this study of the Kikuyu is to be recommended because its author is an African nationalist who rose to be President of independent Kenya.

Oliver, Roland and Mathew Gervase, eds., *History of East Africa,* Vol. I. London: Oxford University Press, 1968. Paperback.

The standard precolonial history of the area.

Wilson, Monica and Leonard Thompson, eds., *South Africa to 1870.* Oxford University Press, 1969.

First volume of the new Oxford history of South Africa.

Fage, J. D., *History of West Africa: An Introductory Survey.* London: Cambridge University Press, 1969. Paperback.

A short and concise summary of this area's history.

Robinson, Ronald and J. Gallagher, *Africa and the Victorians: The Climax of Imperialism.* New York: St. Martin's Press, 1968. Paperback.

This stimulating interpretation of British imperialism in Africa argues that the British occupation of strategically valuable Egypt initiated the scramble for Africa.

Lloyd, P. C., *Africa in Social Change: Changing Traditional Societies in the Modern World.* London: Penguin Books, 1967. Paperback.

A thematic view of the major changes that have been under way in Africa since the colonial era.

CHAPTER 21

World War I and The Russian Revolution

In August 1914, politicians, generals, and ordinary citizens in every belligerent nation expected a quick victory in the war that had just begun. (See p. 474.) Each belligerent hoped to achieve specific ends. Austrian leaders meant to put a stop to the Slavic nationalist agitation that threatened to break up the empire, while Russia sought to exploit Balkan unrest to win free entry into the Mediterranean. Germany and France were both committed to helping their allies, and France had the added objective of winning back Alsace and Lorraine, lost to Germany in 1871. Britain fought to protect its maritime supremacy, believed vital to its very existence, and to prevent Germany from controlling the European continent. Nationalism, Europe's strongest common passion, provided every country with assurance that its cause was just, its victory certain.

Most political foes, swept up in the great wave of nationalist fervor, put aside their struggles and made common cause against the enemy. Every nation saw itself as the victim of wanton aggression, totally innocent of any blame for the coming of the war.

Everywhere, those few who doubted the official line stifled their doubts; any man who openly questioned the justice of his own nation's cause was quickly silenced either by public outcry or by the censor's blue pencil. Governments fed atrocity stories to the newspapers, played up minor successes, and suppressed news of every setback. The illusion that the war would be short died very quickly, but the certainty of ultimate victory remained virtually unquestioned. Not until 1917 did the solidarity induced by nationalism break down. Meanwhile, millions died.

THE BATTLEFIELDS

Europe

German troops fought their way through Belgium in early August 1914, planning to overrun France in a few weeks while Russia was still trying to mobilize its inefficient armies. The invasion plan, drawn up a decade earlier by General Alfred von Schlieffen and constantly brought up to date, called for the army to move past the western flank of

Taxis ready to carry French troops from Paris to the front at a crucial moment in the First Battle of the Marne (September 1914).

the French armies in order to encircle Paris. But Belgian, French, and British troops resisted so strongly that the flanking movement failed; the German commander, Count Helmuth von Moltke, attempted instead to break through the French lines east of Paris. The defenders, aided by reserves brought from Paris, many of them in taxicabs, held firm once more. This Allied victory in what came to be called the First Battle of the Marne put an end to dreams of a short war. When it became clear that the Allies would hold, each side immediately began trying to turn the other's western flank. Neither succeeded, and by November the two armies faced each other along a line from the Swiss border to the Atlantic coast. Both sides dug in, establishing complex networks of trenches protected by barbed wire and machine guns.

Great battles were fought as successive commanders tried to break the deadlock, but the line established in November 1914 changed little through four bloody years. Millions of men were sacrificed in frontal attacks: in 1916, for example, a six-month-long German attempt to capture the French fortresses at Verdun and an Allied offensive on the Somme River together cost both sides a total of more than two million men killed, wounded, or taken prisoner. In April 1915, the Germans launched a highly successful poison gas attack at Ypres, but they had not prepared enough reserves to take advantage of the gap cut in the Allied line. The first successful use of tanks, carried out by the British in November 1917, was not exploited for the same reason.

On the static western front soldiers found

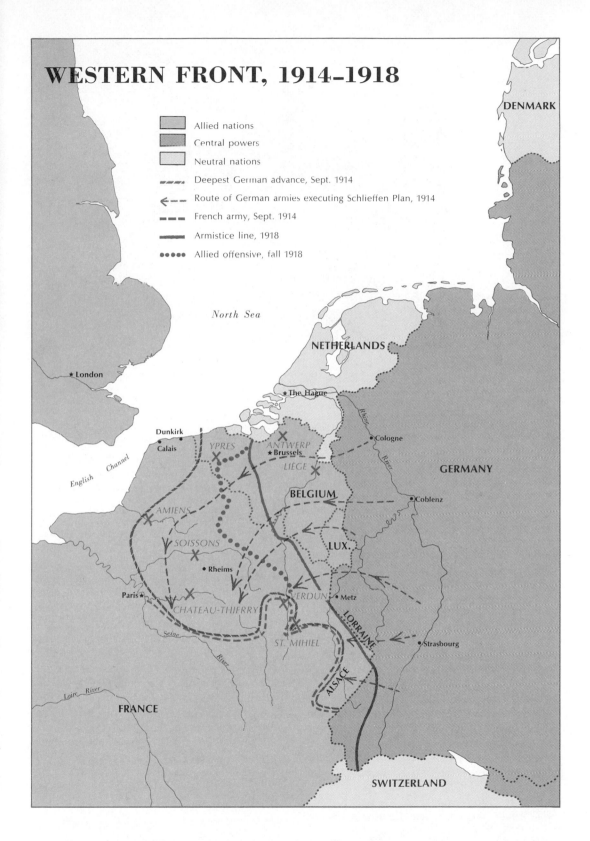

WESTERN FRONT, 1914–1918

	Allied nations
	Central powers
	Neutral nations
-·-·-·	Deepest German advance, Sept. 1914
←--	Route of German armies executing Schlieffen Plan, 1914
---	French army, Sept. 1914
———	Armistice line, 1918
••••••	Allied offensive, fall 1918

DENMARK

North Sea

NETHERLANDS

★London

★The Hague

English Channel

Dunkirk
★Calais

YPRES

ANTWERP
★Brussels
LIÉGE

•Cologne

BELGIUM

GERMANY

•Coblenz

AMIENS

SOISSONS

LUX.

•Rheims

Paris★

VERDUN •Metz

CHATEAU-THIERRY

Seine

ST. MIHIEL

LORRAINE

•Strasbourg

River

ALSACE

Loire River

FRANCE

SWITZERLAND

Trench warfare in Flanders: An observer orders a rifleman to fire.

little room for conventional heroism; callousness was vital, and endurance was the supreme virtue. Attacks were almost always suicidal, because entrenched defenders could endure artillery bombardments and live to kill any enemy who tried to storm their redoubts. As the war wore on, soldiers enlarged their trenches and tried to make them more comfortable, but nothing kept them warm or dry: when the weather was bad they baled out their trenches with buckets and slept on muddy firesteps. Frank Richards, a British private who fought through the entire war without a wound, calmly described the trenches in which he served in 1917:

Some parts of the parapet had been built up with dead men, and here and there arms and legs were protruding. In one bay only the heads of two men could be seen; their teeth were showing so that they seemed to be grinning horribly down on us. Some of our chaps that had survived the attack on the 20th July told me that when they were digging themselves in, the ground being hardened by the sun and difficult to dig away quickly, if a man was killed near them he was used as head cover and earth was thrown over him.

*No doubt in many cases this saved the lives of the men that were digging themselves in.**

In the east, the Russians contributed heavily to the Allied victory at the Marne in 1914 by invading East Prussia several weeks before the Germans expected they would be able to move. But their audacity was costly: they were thrown back with losses of more than 250,000 men in the battles of Tannenberg and the Masurian Lakes. They were more successful against the Austrians, conquering most of Galicia before winter weather brought their advance to a halt. The Serbian armies also won an unexpected victory, throwing back the Austrians before the end of 1914. Austrian morale was so badly shattered by those two defeats that the Germans had to take control of the entire eastern front, organizing new armies in which German and Austrian divisions served together under German command. Even so, the Russians paid highly for their victory, because they could not maintain their strength. In 1915, the Austro-German forces advanced 300

* *Old Soldiers Never Die* (New York: Berkeley, 1966), p. 130.

EASTERN FRONT, 1914–1918

FINLAND
• Helsinki
Petrograd ★

Volga

DEN

holm

Sea

Moscow •

Legend:
- Allied nations
- Central powers
- ⊶⊶⊶ Front in May 1915
- ⊶⊶⊶ Front in Oct. 1915
- ▬▬▬ Front on eve of Russian revolution
- ← Russian offensive, 1914
- ← Brusilov offensive, 1915
- ⟶ German offensive, 1915
- ⟶ German offensive, 1918
- ⊢ Brest-Litovsk boundary

• Riga

Drina

River

Memel •

EAST PRUSSIA

igsberg •

Masurian Lakes

rienburg
nberg •

• Grodna

• Minsk

WARSAW

DZ

• Brest-Litovsk

ow •

• Lublin

• Przemysl

• Lemberg

FARTHEST RUSSIAN ADVANCE

dapest

AUSTRIA-HUNGARY

FARTHEST RUMANIAN ADVANCE, 1916

RUSSIA (U.S.S.R.)

DEEPEST AUSTRO-GERMAN PENETRATION, 1918

Don

River

Kiev •

UKRAINE

Dnieper River

Odessa •

CRIMEA

Sevastopol •

Stavropol •

Black Sea

RBIAN-MONTENEGRAN
DVANCE 1914–1915

• Belgrade

Bucharest ★

RUMANIA

SERBIA

Varna •

ONTENEGRO

★ Sofia

• Adrianople

★ Istanbul (Constantinople)

BULGARIA

ALBANIA

TURKEY

DARDANELLES CAMPAIGN 1915

GALLIPOLI

FARTHEST RUSSIAN ADVANCE

Trooper of the Australia-New Zealand Expeditionary Force carrying a wounded comrade at Gallipoli.

miles, driving the Russians almost completely out of Poland and taking more than 750,000 prisoners before their advance bogged down in September. Russia could no longer menace Germany, even though its own defenses held for two more years.

The Allied commanders on the western front were convinced that the German line must be broken, but in London, Winston S. Churchill (1874–1965), First Lord of the Admiralty, and Lord Kitchener (1850–1916), the British chief of staff, argued for a flank attack in the Balkans. No firm decision was made; half-hearted attempts to capture the Dardanelles or to move up through Greece failed. Thus two years of fighting had produced by 1917 an enormous number of casualties, but neither side was close to victory.

Both sides constantly sought to bring new allies into the fighting. Italy, a member of the Triple Alliance, remained neutral in 1914, since it was not required to aid Austria in an act of aggression against Serbia. The Italian government saw the war, however, as an opportunity to extend its territory and enhance the nation's status as a major power. After lengthy bargaining, the western Allies secretly promised Italy the South Tyrol, Trieste, and part of Turkey in return for help against Austria and Germany. Italy therefore entered the war in May 1915, on the Allied side. Bulgaria, on the other hand, sought Serbian territory. Allied envoys tried to thwart Bulgaria by enlisting Greece and Rumania in their ranks, but the failure of the Dardanelles campaign caused both countries to choose continued neutrality. Bulgaria, apparently having nothing to lose by joining the Central Powers (Germany and Austria), declared war in October 1915, and before the end of the year Bulgarian and Austrian troops finally conquered Serbia. Rumania entered the war in 1916 on the Allied side but was quickly overrun by Germans, Austrians, and Bulgarians.

The War in the Middle East

The Ottoman Empire theoretically controlled most of the Middle East, but in 1914 the sultan's government was involved in revolutionary turmoil. Britain and France hoped Turkey would remain neutral in the war, but Germany sought the Turks as allies, for they were in a position to cut the British route to India. Turkey, threatened by further British expansion from Egypt into Palestine and Syria, and long an enemy of Russia, leaned toward the German side. When the war began, the Liberal government in Britain, traditionally anti-Turkish, commandeered two Turkish warships under construction in British yards. The incensed Turks were delighted to accept the loan of two cruisers offered by the Germans. When the two German ships bombarded Russian ports in the Black Sea in October 1914, Russia, France, and Britain responded by declaring war against Turkey.

Very soon the Allied powers, anticipating victory, were negotiating the partition of the Turkish empire. Russia wanted to annex Istanbul and the Straits; England asserted its right to control of the Suez Canal and the Persian Gulf, the two keys to the route to India. France insisted on control in Syria. In April 1915, France and Britain agreed to Russia's demands for the Straits and surrounding territory in Europe. They then promised Italy the Dodecanese Islands and territory on the southern Anatolian coast as partial repayment for her entry into the war. Next they began a series of negotiations with and about the Arabs; these were to have vast repercussions.

British officials in Egypt agreed in July 1915 with the Amir Hussein ibn Ali (1856–1931), Sharif of Mecca, that the British would recognize Arab independence except in the few areas (mostly in Lebanon) that were largely Christian. Palestine was not mentioned. In April 1916, however, Sir Mark Sykes and M. Georges Picot signed an agreement establishing spheres of influence for France in the area now occupied by Lebanon, Syria, northwestern Iraq, and part of southwestern Turkey, and for England in what are now Iraq and Jordan. Palestine, they agreed, would be placed under international control. Neither of these agreements provided for full Arab independence; moreover, they conflicted (see Chapter 29).

Through the early years of the war the Allies made little headway against Turkey. In mid-1916, however, the Arabs under Hussein revolted against Turkey with British aid. A year later Lloyd George, seeking a way to break the deadlock on the western front, appointed a new commander in the Middle East; by 1918 the British and the Arabs had conquered Palestine, Syria, and the Baghdad area.

Meanwhile, however, the new revolutionary government in Russia published the Sykes-Picot agreement and outraged the Arab world. In November 1917 the British foreign minister, Arthur James Balfour (1848–1930), issued the Balfour Declaration, in which the British government promised to aid in the establishment of a "national home for the Jewish people" in Palestine. Six months later the British also pledged to a group of Arabs that it recognized "the complete and sovereign independence of the Arabs" in areas that were free before the war or were liberated from Turkey by the Arabs during the war. The French concurred. The two governments had promised more than they were prepared to deliver; moreover, a clash between Arabs and Zionists seeking to build a Jewish nation had become inevitable.

THE HOME FRONTS

Nothing had prepared Europe for a war that was to last four years; moreover, this was the first war fought between modern industrial nations, and no one could know what efforts would be demanded. The combatants had stockpiled the arms and ammunition they thought would be required, but by the end of September 1914 they began to suffer from shortages. The vast artillery barrages laid down before every attack ate up ammunition at an enormous rate, and trench warfare consumed men equally rapidly. The British regular army, for example, was virtually wiped out at Ypres in early November 1914. This

British instructors, training Arab troops in Mesopotamia, not only helped defeat the Central Powers but laid a base for later Arab nationalist movements.

"technical surprise" raised the curtain on modern total war.

In such a war whole peoples, rather than small professional armies, had to dedicate all their efforts to victory over the enemy. Once the first flush of patriotic enthusiasm had worn off they were not likely to do so voluntarily. Most of the warring nations soon saw that it was necessary to appoint war production boards with the authority to make contracts, allocate raw materials, and, in most cases, control the use of labor. David Lloyd George (1863–1945) in Britain, Albert Thomas (1878–1932) in France, and Walter Rathenau (1867–1922) in Germany each wielded power over his nation's economy that would have astounded the liberal economists of the nineteenth century. Rationing of scarce goods had to be instituted, and laborers had to work overtime. Because all this required huge sums of money, most of which had to be borrowed, inflation was inevitable. Labor unions agreed not to strike,

and legislators of all parties, including the supposedly antiwar socialists, allowed governments to extend their powers far beyond the limits laid down by written or unwritten constitutions. Military leaders everywhere, once forced to plead for funds, became increasingly powerful as nations recognized their dependence on military might. The concerns of peace were left far behind.

Ordinary Europeans, even those in the most militaristic nations, had never been called upon for such sacrifices, and few of them were willing to make sacrifices simply to change a few boundaries or to add a few thousand acres to their national territories. Governments therefore turned increasingly to propaganda. It was easy to report the atrocities committed by every army, to exaggerate these and to invent others, and to call upon the masses to make a supreme effort for English freedom, the Latin heritage, or German *Kultur*. In less than a year, a war that began as a result of fairly specific quarrels

French women filling shrapnel shells with paraffin.

Wartime Politics

was turned by the nationalist press into a war *jusqu'au bout* — to the death.

Events in most of the major belligerent nations followed a single pattern. At the beginning of the war, with the exception of a few revolutionary socialists like Lenin (see p. 468), members of all parties agreed to cease their opposition in order to help achieve a quick victory. Early attempts to solve wartime problems by creating new subordinate departments designed to mobilize economies were partially successful, but, as the war dragged on, civilian morale deteriorated until a single leader fought his way to the top and made himself a virtual dictator. In conditions of total war the luxury of relative freedom had to be tossed aside in favor of almost military discipline.

Asquith, England's Liberal prime minister, included representatives of the Conservative and Labour parties in his cabinet and created a new ministry of munitions, headed by Lloyd George (see p. 463), in the summer of 1915, but throughout 1916 civilian complaints increased. Irish separatists rebelled on Easter Monday 1916, only to be put down savagely. At about the same time in Scotland, Clydeside factory workers struck because they feared the establishment of military discipline in industry. On May 31 the British fleet suffered a tactical defeat in the battle of Jutland, and shortly afterward the Parliament adopted conscription for the first time in English history. Lloyd George took advantage of the decline in Asquith's popularity to detach a part of the prime minister's Liberal party support, and Asquith resigned.

David Lloyd George, a great orator and a driving leader, was ruthless in politics, but he was equally ruthless in fighting the war: he was obviously what the nation wanted. As soon as he became prime minister, he established a five-man War Cabinet, which directed military operations for the next two years. Under his leadership the government finally became almost all-powerful in the

Mother love in the service of nationalism: a British recruiting poster, 1915.

economy, conscripting men not only into the army but also into the munitions plants, and threatening to draft strikers in order to keep production going full blast.

In France the stabilization of the battle lines was followed by 2½ years of mounting casualties with little to show for them; civilian morale sagged, and the failure of a particularly senseless offensive brought widespread mutiny in the army in the spring of 1917. General Henri-Philippe Pétain (1856–1951), who had held Verdun against a German onslaught despite the loss of 300,000 men the year before, succeeded in alleviating the conditions that had set off the mutinies. But in November 1917, after a series of scandals, the government fell. The new premier, Georges Clemenceau (1841–1929), had been active in politics since 1870; known for his great patriotism, he said his whole program was, "I wage war." He scolded gen-

erals and jailed "defeatists." Somehow he communicated his energy—he was 76—to his weary countrymen and drove them to victory, accumulating almost dictatorial powers in the process.

For Italy, the war went badly from the outset. In October 1917 a combined German and Austrian offensive routed the Italians at Caporetto, and only two months later did the regrouping of the Italian army plus some French reinforcements prevent further disastrous loss of territory. New military leadership and a new prime minister, Vittorio Emanuele Orlando (1860–1952), combined with a new popular spirit in the face of real danger to the nation, stiffened Italian resistance, and the Austrian threat was successfully parried.

With the declaration of war, German politicians in effect abdicated power to the kaiser. For two years the chancellor, Theobald von Bethmann-Hollweg (1856–1921), cooperated with the General Staff, convinced that Germany could make significant territorial gains through a negotiated peace. But the army's failure to defeat the French at Verdun (February–June 1916) led to demands for new, more aggressive leadership. It was provided ostensibly by General Paul von Hindenburg (1847–1934), the national hero who had commanded the victorious German troops at the battle of Tannenberg. The real leader, however, was Hindenburg's quartermaster general, Erich Ludendorff (1865–1937). Ludendorff succeeded in ousting Bethmann and replacing him with a new premier who was a relatively unknown administrator willing to take orders from the high command. In Germany, as well as in France, England, and Italy, power had finally come to those who were determined to do whatever was necessary to win the war. In Germany that meant the military, while among the Western allies civilians took full control. The difference illustrated the contrasting traditions of the various countries.

In Austria the pattern was different. From the start of the war the Dual Monarchy became essentially a German satellite. Most of the subject nationalities supported the war in its early years; only the Czechs sought to evade imperial demands. Croats and Slovenes willingly fought Serbia, and Poles cooperated with the Hapsburgs in the hope that their country could be restored under Hapsburg protection. This cooperation broke down, however, under the pressure of endless war.

On the death of Francis Joseph in November 1916, his successor, Emperor Charles (1916–1918), tried to save his position by compromising with the various nationalities, but his efforts were futile. By 1917 all the minority nationalities were pressing for autonomy, and Charles was forced to open secret negotiations with the Allies, who by then were unwilling to help him save the empire.

THE LAST YEARS OF THE RUSSIAN EMPIRE

Russia was not prepared to fight a long war against a state as technically advanced as Germany. Its army was badly led, lacked field artillery, and was short of ammunition and machine guns. The supply system was chaotic, and Russian industry could not produce war materiel in anything like the necessary quantities. The defeat at Tannenburg late in 1914 was a foregone conclusion. Throughout 1915 the situation grew worse; by the end of that year more than four million Russian soldiers had been killed or wounded.

By the middle of 1915, the Duma was growing restive. The tsar reacted by replacing four incompetent ministers. In August he decided to take personal command of the armies at the front, although he had little military experience. His departure from the capital left the government in the hands of his wife, the Empress Alexandra, a religious mystic who had been for several years almost completely under the influence of an uncouth, debauched, and ignorant "holy man," Gregory Rasputin (1872–1916). In effect, the tsar had turned over his power to Rasputin.

By the beginning of 1917 more than 15 million Russians had been called into the army. Millions of them camped behind the lines, lacking arms that the economy could not provide. Their absence from the farms produced a food shortage, while the immense effort expended in supplying the army made the shortage worse in the cities. The government had to support not only the soldiers but also their families and the 2 million refugees from the battle areas, none of whom were able to pay taxes. Meanwhile, nearly three-quarters of the industrial workers were engaged in the production of arms in government-subsidized factories. Inflation hit hard. As conflict between the empress and the Duma increased, soldiers died, armies were defeated, and the nation became thoroughly demoralized.

Even the conservative politicians in the Duma chafed at the inefficiency of the government. Peasants, nine-tenths of them still untouched by the land reforms begun in 1906, had lost none of their desire for more land. Workers were little better off than English factory labor had been in 1830. Even the nobility was restive. When Rasputin was murdered by several noble officers in De-

Hanged rebels in Middle Asia, 1916. Tsarist authorities burned villages and executed leaders of rebellious minority nationalities.

cember 1916, the entire court was thrown into confusion. The tsar returned to comfort his wife, but he ignored political affairs.

On March 7, 1917, a lockout in Petrograd touched off a general strike.* On March 12, as the strike turned into a massive demonstration, government troops, ordered to fire on the crowds, rebelled and drove off their officers. Meanwhile, mobs killed policemen and opened the jails. On that same night, 250 representatives of factories and military units met and created a Soviet (Council) of Workers' and Soldiers' Deputies, which immediately established a workers' police force and a food commission. Two generals sent troops from the front to attempt to quell the rebellion, but the soldiers fraternized with the rebels when they arrived in the capital. In other cities the government disap-

* Because the Russian calendar was 11 days behind the Gregorian, the events recounted here are remembered as the "February Revolution." The dates used here are those of the Gregorian system. The Soviet government adopted the Gregorian calendar on February 1, 1918.

peared almost without bloodshed; the tsarist government had ceased to function. No organized group of revolutionaries had usurped its power; instead, people of all classes had simply ceased to obey the authorities who had always ruled their lives.

From March to October

On March 14, a Duma committee established a Provisional Government headed by Prince George Lvov (1861–1925) and controlled by Constitutional Democrats. The new cabinet quickly instituted the forms of liberal democracy, proclaiming freedom of speech and press, the right of labor to organize and to strike, and universal, direct, equal, and secret suffrage. The Petrograd Soviet approved the new government, but its decision was of dubious worth, for it immediately began to issue its own proclamations. Most famous of these was "Order No. 1," which not only did away with salutes and titles and called for soldiers' committees to control the actions of officers, but also as-

Soldiers patrolling the streets of Petrograd during the democratic revolution of February 1917.

serted the Soviet's veto power over military orders from the government.

To most Russians, however, the conflict at the heart of the government was insignificant. The end of the old regime produced a holiday atmosphere. Any speaker who praised the revolution, no matter what his politics, was roundly applauded. Army discipline deteriorated rapidly. Workers forced employers to submit their decisions to worker committees and to institute the eighthour day. All over the country soviets—councils of workers and peasants—were formed, and many of them acted as local governments, ignoring commissioners sent by the Provisional Government. Still, the soviets paid lip service to it and made no attempt to overthrow it.

Lenin returned to Russia from Switzerland on April 16, traveling with scores of other socialist exiles whom the kaiser's government permitted to cross Germany into neutral Scandinavia. Upon his arrival in Petrograd* he astonished the committee that

* St. Petersburg; renamed Petrograd in 1914, Leningrad in 1924.

welcomed him by delivering a violent and intransigent speech, the main points of which he outlined in a program known as the "April theses." He demanded an immediate end both to the "imperialist" war and to support for the capitalist Provisional Government; "abolition of the police, the army, the bureaucracy"; nationalization of all private land; and the establishment of a government of soviets. At first even his fellow Bolsheviks rejected his ideas, but by the middle of May his program had become the Bolshevik program and he was once more the undoubted leader of the party. Bolshevik popularity began to grow steadily.

In May the Provisional Government announced its determination to continue the war. The resulting storm of complaint so shook the government that several ministers withdrew. Alexander Kerensky (1881–1970), a rightwing Socialist Revolutionary and the leading figure in the new cabinet, vowed to continue the war and set about restoring discipline in the army.

Meanwhile, strikes continued and grew worse. Government attempts to regulate the economy failed, both because competent ad-

Tsar Nicholas II under guard shortly before he was killed.

ministrators were impossible to find and because workers, free from tsarist regulation at last, would not accept regulation from any government. Production declined; unable to buy manufactured goods, peasants refused to supply the cities with food. Bolshevik influence grew steadily as hunger spread.

Chaotic rioting developed in July. Lenin was convinced that it would not unseat the parliamentary government, but he and the Bolsheviks took over the leadership of the growing strike movement simply in order to maintain their influence among the workers. Kerensky asserted his authority by bringing loyal troops from the front back to Petrograd. He also published documents purporting to show that the Bolshevik leaders were agents

of the German General Staff. In the confusion many workers apparently believed that the charges were true. Lenin fled to Finland to avoid arrest, and the uncoordinated strike movement collapsed.

Kerensky's efforts to restore the armed forces had been reasonably effective. Taking the offensive on July 1, Russian troops broke through on the Austrian front ten days later. German reinforcements, sent in hurriedly, drove them back, however, and by July 24 the Russians were in full retreat, all discipline forgotten. Nevertheless, Kerensky's relative success with the army, plus his effective efforts against the strike movement, gave him new power. On July 21, Prince Lvov resigned, and he became premier.

Lenin arriving at the Finland Station in Petrograd, April 13, 1917.

Kerensky quickly arrested numerous strike leaders, disbanded the most unruly military units, instituted press censorship, and issued a decree forbidding citizens to carry arms. The moderates who feared further revolution breathed more easily.

Reactionaries also took heart. General L. G. Kornilov, hero of the July offensive and newly appointed commander-in-chief, began openly plotting counterrevolution. Hearing news of the plot, Kerensky relieved him of command, but Kornilov rejected the order and directed his troops to march on Petrograd. Railway workers and telegraphers sabotaged the movement and harangued the soldiers, who defected in great numbers. The only effect of the attempted coup was to frighten the masses of Russia, who immediately began to switch their support to parties of the extreme left—most notably to the Bolsheviks.

Lenin, still in Finland, began bombarding the Bolshevik Central Committee with demands that it take advantage of the situation to lead an insurrection. As Bolsheviks began to win major electoral victories—Trotsky became president of the Petrograd Soviet on October 8—the Committee gradually adopted Lenin's views. On October 23, it voted to call for armed rebellion.

News of the Bolshevik decision traveled fast, but Kerensky did not react until the morning of November 6, when the government closed two Bolshevik newspapers. Friendly soldiers reopened the papers within five hours. The next day Bolshevik Red Guards took over the State Bank and the telephone exchange without difficulty. Kerensky left for the front to seek help, but he was too late. On the same night the Bolsheviks captured the Winter Palace, seat of the Provisional Government, after facing only minor resistance, and arrested the cabinet.

Lenin, who had returned in late October to direct the Bolshevik effort, appeared before a regularly scheduled Congress of Soviets on November 8, the day after the coup. An American reporter, John Reed, described his appearance:

A thundering wave of cheers announced the entrance of the presidium, with

Lenin—great Lenin—among them. A short, stocky figure, with a big head set down in his shoulders, bald and bulging. Little eyes, a snubbish nose, wide, generous mouth, and heavy chin; clean-shaven now, but already beginning to bristle with the well-known beard of his past and future. Dressed in shabby clothes, his trousers much too long for him. . . . Now Lenin, gripping the edge of the reading stand, letting his little winking eyes travel over the crowd as he stood there waiting, apparently oblivious to the long-rolling ovation, . which lasted several minutes. When it finished, he said simply, "We shall now proceed to construct the Socialist order!" *

He proposed two resolutions, one demanding peace without annexations, the other abolishing property rights in land. The Congress, dominated by Bolsheviks and leftwing Socialist Revolutionaries, accepted the decrees. That night an all-Bolshevik Council of Peoples' Commissars—a new government—was established with Lenin as chairman.

In Moscow the Bolsheviks won power only after a week's fighting. In the Ukraine, nationalist Mensheviks set up a separatist regime, and in most Cossack lands local authorities maintained their power. Within a month, however, Bolsheviks controlled what was left of the army and the major towns of northern and central Russia and of Siberia. Even where other groups held sway, dissatisfaction was strong and local authorities were weak.

The triumph of the Bolsheviks owed much to Lenin's genius, but the mistakes of the Provisional Government provided the opportunities he exploited. Kerensky refused to make peace, when peace was the overwhelming desire of virtually the entire nation. He refused to institute land reform even when the peasants had demonstrated that they would take the land with or without government permission. Workers and peasants in Russia, accustomed for centuries to living in collectively run villages, had no respect for private property, and the bourgeoisie was far too small in numbers to

* John Reed, *Ten Days that Shook the World* (New York: Vintage Books, 1960), pp. 170–172.

serve as the basis for a liberal, western-style government. By offering peace to the nation, land to the peasants, and freedom from the bourgeoisie to the workers, Lenin quickly undermined the Provisional Government. Just as there existed no organized support for the tsar in February, there was no organized support for the Provisional Government in October. In both cases determined revolutionaries moved into a power vacuum; Lenin's triumph was even easier than that of the Duma in March. Yet his victory was not complete, for he had not yet begun to build the new regime.

LAST YEARS OF THE WAR

Toward the end of 1917 every belligerent was suffering from at least some of the ills that had produced a revolution in Russia. Munitions workers were weary, and inflation was aggravating the effects of war-induced shortages of consumer goods. For the Allies the imminent end of Russian participation in the war was a disaster, because it meant that Germany soon would be able to increase its forces on the western front. Yet one prospect led to optimism: the United States had decided to join the battle.

When the war had begun most Americans, as well as the belligerent governments, were confident that the United States would remain neutral. Almost immediately, however, the strategy of war complicated American relations with the belligerents. England, in control of the sea, blockaded Germany, thereby seriously interfering with American trade. The English government mitigated this difficulty, however, both by handling American ships with the greatest delicacy and by buying almost every shipment of goods that Americans had to offer. Germany retaliated early in the war by using submarines to cut off English supplies. American protests caused Germany to abandon unrestricted submarine warfare for nearly two years, but the English blockade hurt too much. When the German government cast off all restrictions on submarine warfare in February 1917, the United States prepared for retaliation. The discovery of evidence that Germany was trying to attract Mexico to its side in the event that the United States entered the war made it easier for Americans to accept the decision to fight. On April 6, 1917, the United States declared war against the Central Powers.

President Woodrow Wilson (1856–1924) had called in 1916 for a "peace without victory," and he had tried to bring about a negotiated settlement of the war. When the United States entered the struggle he systematically played down American self-interest and insisted that it was fighting for democracy, for the rights of small nations, and for the establishment of a "concert of peoples" that would keep the peace. He also implied that he would refuse to negotiate peace with Germany until its government was replaced by one that better represented the German people.

The President's pronouncements were welcomed by the left in every country. Since the start of the war various groups of liberals and socialists had quietly opposed the expansionist plans embraced by various factions in each of the belligerent nations, but the war governments refused even to specify their war aims. By 1917 these groups had begun to win widespread support as the sacrifices of war became less and less tolerable. The growing movement for a negotiated peace received another windfall in May 1917, when the Petrograd Soviet issued a statement demanding "peace without annexations or indemnities on the basis of the self-determination of peoples." In July 1917, German socialists finally persuaded a Reichstag majority to vote a resolution opposing forced annexations as a result of the war, but the German government, under pressure from Ludendorff, made clear its intention to ignore the Reichstag resolution.

Allied governments, increasingly confident by the summer of 1917 that they would win the war, ignored leftwing demands for conciliatory action. As a result, socialist members of the coalition governments in France and Britain resigned their posts, leaving both countries in the hands of supporters of traditional imperialist policy.

The Bolshevik Revolution quickly changed the military, political, diplomatic, and psychological balance in Europe. On November 8, Lenin's new government issued a Peace Decree proposing the "immediate opening of negotiations for a just and democratic peace." On November 21, it asked the Germans for an immediate armistice, and a few days later it published the secret treaties to which Russia had been a party. The Bolsheviks were asking not for a separate peace that would isolate Russia and cost them huge territories, but for a general conference that would include all the Allies. It was clear, however, that the Bolsheviks would have to make peace, whatever the terms, and on December 3, 1917, they signed an armistice with Germany and Austria-Hungary. Negotiations opened immediately at Brest-Litovsk, on the Russian side of the Russo-Polish border. On December 22, the Russians offered a six-point plan for discussion; it included a pledge to prevent forced annexation of territory, to support self-determination of peoples, to protect the rights of minorities, and to reject reparations. In many ways this Bolshevik plan matched the earlier proposals of Allied socialists and liberals and those of President Wilson. The Austrian foreign minister, Count Ottokar Czernin (1872–1932), implied that the Central Powers would accept the Soviet proposals if all other belligerents would join in the negotiations. This adroit maneuver put tremendous pressure on the Allies to react to the Bolshevik statement.

On January 8, 1918, Wilson accepted the challenge by offering to the world his famous Fourteen Points. Opening with praise for the sincerity of the Russian spokesmen, he concluded that the Allies would not join the Brest-Litovsk talks only because they could not bargain in good faith with Germany's militarist government. The body of his speech listed in simple language his suggestions for the basis of a lasting peace. The Fourteen Points included demands for open diplomacy, that is, an end to secret treaties; freedom of navigation and free trade; disarmament as far as practicable; a series of territorial adjustments in Europe based essentially on self-determination; and the formation of "an association of nations" to guarantee the political independence and territorial integrity of both large and small states.

Wilson's peace platform has been criticized as utopian, but under the circumstances that existed early in 1918 a utopian statement was at least partly justifiable. By defending Russia the American president hoped to persuade the Bolsheviks to hold out a while longer and thus prevent German reinforcements from moving to the west. By attacking the German government, he hoped to bring about revolution in Germany, or at least to strengthen the peace movement there and blunt any new German military effort. His advocacy of self-determination would further weaken Austria if it did not make peace. Finally, his speech was calculated to satisfy the demands of Allied socialists and liberals for a statement of war aims that would repudiate expansionism.

Lloyd George reacted coolly to Wilson's speech, while Clemenceau and Orlando repudiated it. The Bolsheviks were forced by German might to conclude their own negotiations with the common enemy. On March 3, 1918, they accepted the harsh peace terms offered them and signed the Treaty of Brest-Litovsk. Finland, Latvia, Lithuania, Estonia, and the Ukraine became "independent" but were occupied by the German army, Russian Poland passed under Austrian control, and Russia ceded certain Caucasian borderlands to Turkey. Thus the Bolsheviks satisfied the desire for peace that had paved their way to power. They also, however, laid the basis for civil war, because many Russian patriots, incensed when the Bolsheviks accepted such heavy losses, turned to counterrevolution. (See p. 656.)

In Germany, Wilson's words helped to provoke a number of strikes in support of peace, but the revolution he hoped for failed to materialize. The war went on. Ludendorff, gambling on a final offensive that he hoped would break the Allied lines, attacked the British sector of the western front on March 21, 1918. The German offensive at first seemed likely to succeed, but the Allies held firm.

They counterattacked in August, strengthened by fresh American troops, and punctured the German defenses. By October Ludendorff realized that he could fight no longer. The Germans installed a new liberal ministry under the leadership of Prince Max von Baden and sued for peace on the basis of the Fourteen Points. Wilson replied by demanding armistice arrangements that would assure overwhelming Allied military superiority in case the talks broke down, and,

moreover, he demanded assurance that the German government had the backing of the German people. As the negotiations dragged on, riots among German workers, originally provoked by food shortages, turned into demonstrations against the kaiser. When German admirals decided to press a last attack against the English navy, the crews of two battleships revolted. The mutiny spread through the fleet and gave new impetus to disorders among the masses. Socialists led huge demonstrations in the streets of Berlin. Unable to quell the disorders, William II abdicated on November 9, 1918. A new provisional German government signed an armistice with the Allies two days later.

THE PEACE TREATIES

The first two months of the peace conference that opened in greater Paris in January 1919, were occupied with procedural confusion, and when procedures finally were established they were far from perfect. Most objectionable, probably, was the decision to write the treaties without enemy participation, then to hand a treaty to each of the defeated powers as a virtual ultimatum. The later German claim that the Treaty of Versailles was a *Diktat* was not far from the truth.

The Armistice terms amounted to a promise by the Allies that the peace treaties would be based on Wilson's Fourteen Points, with two exceptions: first, the Allies would decide how to interpret the statement on freedom of the seas, and, second, Germany would be expected to pay reparations. The Allies decided early in 1919 that a separate treaty would be made with each of the defeated powers. The treaties finally signed in various Paris suburbs were as follows: with Germany, Versailles, June 28, 1919; with Austria, St. Germain-en-Laye, September 10, 1919; with Bulgaria, Neuilly, November 27, 1919; with Hungary, Trianon, June 4, 1920; with Turkey, Sèvres, August 10, 1920.

From Wilson's point of view the most significant action of the Paris Peace Conference was the creation of the League of Nations. The League Covenant, included in all the peace treaties, provided for the establishment not only of Wilson's "association of nations" but also of an International Court of

GERMANY, 1914 and 1919

Ceded areas
Demilitarized area, 1919
Special status areas
Plebiscite areas

Justice and an International Labor Office. The League itself was to be made up of all the Allied and Associated Powers, which included not only major belligerents such as France, Britain, the United States, Italy, and Japan, but many nations of Latin America and Asia which had either joined the Allies toward the end of the war or had broken off relations with Germany and Austria. Other nations also might be invited to join. In order to win acceptance of the League, Wilson agreed to compromises that he did not like in the various settlements because he believed that once the League was established it would be able to correct inequities in the treaties.

Territorial arrangements were complicated and controversial, for new nations had to be established and boundaries altered in accordance with the principle of self-determination. Germany and Austria lost territory to

allow the reconstruction of Poland. The treaties with Austria and Hungary ratified the destruction of the Dual Monarchy, which took place as the war ended and minority nationalities seceded. Czechoslovakia emerged as a completely new state while Yugoslavia was an expansion of Serbia that combined all the south Slavs. Austria lost Galicia to the new state of Poland and the South Tyrol to Italy. The new states of Austria and Hungary were restricted to ethnic Germans and Magyars, respectively. In the Balkans Rumania seized Transylvania from Hungary, and Bulgaria surrendered land to Rumania, Greece, and Yugoslavia. Turkey's vast territories were divided five ways: Greece received a slice of what remained of European Turkey and part of Anatolia; the Straits were internationalized; Syria and Lebanon went to France as League of Nations mandates; the Arab kingdom of Hejaz became independent; Palestine, Transjordan, and Iraq became British mandates, the last two under puppet Arab kings. Germany lost, beside its old Polish lands, Alsace and Lorraine to France, northern Schleswig to Denmark, and certain small border towns to Belgium.

Some of these territorial changes were obviously desired by the inhabitants of the lands concerned: northern Schleswig, for example, voted to become part of Denmark, and there was little doubt of the desire of Alsatians to return to France. Others were far less satisfactory. Austria, reduced to a very small, homogeneous German-speaking area, wished to be united with Germany, but in this case the Allies preferred to ignore self-determination in order to keep Germany weak. All the other new countries of Eastern Europe included minorities: there were large groups of Germans in Czechoslovakia and Poland; there were also many Hungarians in Rumania, Czechoslovakia, and Yugoslavia. Smaller minorities were also left in all these nations. Yugoslavia and Czechoslovakia not only included minority peoples but were actually made up of ethnically diverse populations that were at best highly suspicious of one another: Croats and Serbs had fought for years, and Czechs and Slovaks shared a deep mutual distrust. Such problems could not be avoided, for many areas contained several ethnic groups, and nothing short of mass forced emigration could have separated them. Minority problems were to plague Europe for many years to come.

Colonial problems were largely untouched by the diplomats. Germany's colonies were confiscated and handed over to Britain, France, and Japan in the guise of League of Nations mandates. These provisions were among those accepted by Wilson in return for the Allies' support of the League.

The Allies sharply limited the armed forces of Germany and Austria in both men and equipment. The restrictions caused little complaint in Austria, but the Germans found them intolerable, particularly since the Allies placed in the treaty a pious declaration of hope that general disarmament would soon follow but showed no serious intention of disarming themselves. The Germans also objected to an Allied requirement that the Rhineland be demilitarized in order to forestall a future attack on France.

The most objectionable feature of the treaties involved reparations. The Allies insisted that Germany agree to pay for both war damages and military pensions, but they left the exact figure of reparations payments to be set by a Reparations Commission. In order to guarantee their right to such payments, the victors forced the Germans to accept a clause specifying that the war had been caused "by the aggression of Germany and her allies." Very few Germans were willing to accept that responsibility; the "war guilt clause" became a powerful weapon for German politicians who sought to upset the treaty.

The new German government (see p. 652) had no choice but to accept the treaty. It had refused to furnish ships to carry relief supplies offered by the victors during a harsh winter, leaving the Germans hungry and cold. Moreover, when it at first refused to sign, the Allied Powers ordered the Allied Commander-in-Chief, Marshal Ferdinand Foch (1851–1929) to prepare to advance beyond the Armistice line into Germany itself. The Germans then capitulated and signed the Treaty of Versailles on June 28, 1919.

In the victorious United States, however, opposition to signing the treaty was more effective. Some senators sincerely viewed membership in the League of Nations as a partial surrender of American sovereignty; others simply saw an opportunity to embarrass Wilson, whom they hoped to defeat in 1920. As a result, in November 1919, the Senate failed to produce the required two-thirds majority to ratify the Treaty of Versailles.

Not only did the Senate's action seriously weaken the projected League of Nations, it also was a major blow to France. Many Frenchmen considered it a betrayal. Wilson, in order to persuade Clemenceau to drop his demand for the creation of a buffer state in the Rhineland, had signed a guarantee to come to the aid of France in case Germany should attack again. Lloyd George had made the same pledge. When the Senate failed to ratify the Treaty of Versailles, it also rejected Wilson's pledge to France. Britain then considered its own pledge void. Not only was France left without American support, but the prewar "cordial understanding" with the English also had been destroyed. This lack of support was to influence French policy and French attitudes toward the United States and Britain from then on. Much of the gratitude Frenchmen felt for American and British aid during the war was wiped out by the apparent treachery of the "Anglo-Saxons."

THE FAR EAST

The first effects of World War I in the Far East came in the form of major benefits to Japan. Brought into the war on the Allied side through the operation of the Anglo-Japanese alliance of 1902, Japan quickly took over the German Pacific islands and the German concessions in China's Shantung province. With the other powers occupied in Europe, Japan had a free hand in its long-term efforts to extend its power and influence in China. In January 1915, the Japanese presented to China's President Yüan Shih-k'ai a set of 21 demands that would have given them almost complete control of the country. Pressure from the Allies forced a reduction in the demands, but Japan won almost complete control in Manchuria and considerable economic power in Shantung and Mongolia.

Yüan Shih-k'ai, chosen president of the new Chinese Republic in 1912, had hoped to follow tradition by establishing himself as founder of a new dynasty. The parliament turned out to be utterly corrupt, as was to be expected in a country totally unused to democratic procedures. Yüan had no difficulty in dissolving it and having his term as president extended to ten years. Then the Japanese, preferring to see China in chaos rather than engaged in reform under a strong new emperor, handed Yüan their 21 demands. Yüan's prestige fell; he had to accept some of the demands, though some he could evade. Yüan's rivals for the throne grasped the opportunity: rebellion broke out in the army, and in March 1916, Yüan cancelled his scheduled coronation. In July he died.

The vice-president, Li Yüan-hung, succeeded to the presidency, and the parliament, disbanded in 1913, returned to Peking. But although the republic had been saved in form, it was dead in fact. The government became the plaything of Japanese-financed warlords, quite incapable of enforcing its decrees. Sun Yat-sen (1866–1925), leader of the republicans, withdrew his support from Peking and established what he called the "provisional government" of China in the Canton area but was unable to win much support. Warlords extorted money from the peasants and fought among themselves. China sank into chaos, while the persecuted peasants attributed their woes to the failures of the weak republican government.

Under pressure from Japan, Britain, and the United States the flimsy government in Peking declared war against the Germans in August 1917. China was in no position to contribute to the fighting, but young Chinese intellectuals persuaded themselves that their country would, as a result of its participation in the war, be freed of the foreign enclaves that dotted the coast. When the peace terms were announced in May 1919, students at Peking University marched to demonstrate their disappointment. A wave of sympathy swept the country, and the May Fourth movement began to symbolize intransigent demands not only for an end to Western power in China, but a new and effective form of government. The Chinese delegation at the Peace Conference had to refuse to sign the Treaty of Versailles. Years passed before unity returned, but many of the leaders of China's successive revolutions received their first political training in the May 4th movement. Thus the war destroyed forever the possibility of installing a new imperial dynasty, completed the destruction of any possible faith in republican government, and gave new impetus to the movement for modernization through revolution.

RUSSIA, 1917–1920

The Bolsheviks, dedicated to their own version of Marxism, began immediately after seizing power to try to build a new society amid economic chaos and civil war. Elections for a Constituent Assembly, scheduled before the revolution, were to be held on November 25, 1917. The new government decided to allow those elections to take place, but to dissolve the Assembly if it endangered Bolshevik control. Approximately 60 percent of the deputies chosen were moderate socialists, while more than 10 percent represented conservative parties. The Bolshevik 25 percent, however, came from the remaining centers of organized power: the front, the Baltic fleet, and the industrial cities. When the majority Socialist Revolutionaries refused during the first session to accept Bolshevik control, the new government informed the delegates that "the guard is tired" and dissolved the Assembly. The nation remained calm, for the politically aware sections of the populace largely supported the Bolsheviks. The new government had passed its first major crisis. Two months later, in March 1918, the Bolsheviks, long a mere faction of a small revolutionary band, marked their new status as a governing party by adopting a new name: they became the Soviet Russian Communist Party.

For nearly three years the Communist government faced civil war and foreign invasion. By the end of 1917 former tsarist officers and other partisans of the old regime, soon backed by patriots unwilling to accept the losses imposed on Russia at Brest-Litovsk, had begun forming a Volunteer Army in the Cossack areas of southwestern Russia. In the spring of 1918, British, American, Japanese, and French troops landed in Vladivostok, Archangel, and the Ukraine, ostensibly to open a new eastern front against the Germans or to protect Allied equipment, but in reality to back up the anti-Bolshevik armies. That summer an autonomous government controlled huge areas of Siberia; it was supported by loyal tsarist officers and about 50,000 Czech war prisoners seeking to reach the western front via the Pacific. The Communist government, hard pressed on every side, met the counterrevolutionary threat by organizing the Red Army. Compulsory military training was instituted in April 1918, and by the end of the year the Communists had some 800,000 troops under arms. Trotsky, the minister of war, crisscrossed the country in his special train directing operations and inspiring soldiers on every front. The "White," or counterrevolutionary, armies gradually deteriorated. The opponents of communism ranged from Socialist Revolutionaries to reactionary mon-

archists; they could never really agree on their aims. Moreover, landlords returned as the White armies advanced, and their attempts to regain their old privileges and powers alienated peasants nearly everywhere that the Whites won control. Lacking coordination and popular support, the Whites buckled under the onslaught of the Red Army. By the end of 1919 Trotsky clearly had won the civil war, even though the last remnant of the White armies was not defeated until the middle of 1920 and Japanese troops remained in Vladivostok until 1922.

The Russian victory was put in jeopardy in May 1920 when the Polish general, Josef Pilsudski (1867–1935), seeking to win Russian territory and to perpetuate an independent Ukraine, sent his own armies into Kiev. Through the summer the battle raged, but the collapse of the White armies gave Trotsky the strength to drive the Poles out of Russian territory and almost to the gates of Warsaw. There the Poles, with aid from France, stopped the Russian advance. When peace was made on October 12, 1920, Russia had recovered most of the territory the Poles had sought to make their own.

While the civil war went on Lenin and his colleagues slowly built up a new state on the ruins of the old. In 1918 Russia was almost completely disorganized. The loss of the Ukraine, a vast grain-producing area, at Brest-Litovsk aggravated the food shortage. Trade was paralyzed by White armies and anarchist bands. Factories closed because there were no raw materials. Soldiers returning from the front found themselves unemployed, and many of them joined bands of looters. Key personnel in industry and government—intellectuals, managers, civil servants—committed sabotage at every opportunity. Yet most workers were loyal to the new government, despite its deficiencies, and the Communists, dedicated to the cause of socialism, were willing to make every sacrifice and commit every crime to achieve their victory. Their state-building was haphazard, but it was effective.

Late in 1917 the government had already begun issuing the decrees that were to revolutionize Russian life. Banks were nationalized; so were those factories not under direct control of their workers. Church and state

Trotsky at the Petrograd Railway Station during the civil war, March 1919.

were separated, and marriage and divorce laws greatly simplified. In February 1918, the laws of the old regime were simply annulled. A decree instituted the Gregorian calendar on February 1, 1918. In July 1918 food requisitioning was begun. In November 1918 all private trade was forbidden, and in February 1920 compulsory labor became a recognized institution. The Cheka, introduced to prevent sabotage, developed into a powerful secret police. When Lenin was wounded in an assassination attempt in August 1918, the government began a "Red Terror" that lasted three months; it has been estimated that about 50,000 Russians perished at the hands of the revolutionary government. ("White terror" in the recaptured areas was equally cruel.) The system, which came to be known as "war communism," was far from complete or coherent, but it served to maintain Communist power and to produce victory in the civil war.

EUROPE IN THE AFTERMATH OF WAR

When the war ended Europeans faced an immense task of political and economic recon-

Women like this one, working in a New England munitions factory in 1918, contributed greatly to the war effort and also helped break down the idea that "woman's place is in the home."

struction. In politically stable countries such as England and France, victorious peoples at first seemed determined to turn back the clock to 1914. Conservative parties won elections and tried to govern as they had before the war, favoring the interests of big industry at the expense of labor and the small businessman. East of the Rhine, however, there could be no turning back, for empires had fallen, new nations had been created overnight, and old economic traditions had been obliterated. Everywhere, east and west, new political forces were ready to make themselves felt. Because wartime shortages of labor had forced governments to cooperate with workers' organizations, unions were stronger than ever. Women, brought out of their homes to work as nurses, machine operators, or clerks, were unwilling to give up the new freedoms they had found.

Combat veterans expected tangible benefits in return for the sacrifices they had made. The prewar world was gone forever, and people everywhere obscurely felt the change. The self-exiled German writer Hermann Hesse (1877–1962), more sensitive than most, expressed that feeling in his tremendously popular novel, *Demian*, published just after the war:

Although the world seemed to be hypnotized by war and heroic deeds, by honor and other old ideals, although the voice of humanity sounded distant and improbable, all that was only on the surface. . . . Deep down something was being born — something that might be a new humanity.*

* *Demian, Die Geschichte von Emil Sinclairs Jugend* (Berlin: Suhkamp Verlag, 1960), p. 210. Translated by Carter Jefferson.

In Russia the Communists confidently believed that their own triumph was only the beginning of a worldwide revolution. Throughout Europe bands of enthusiastic communist sympathizers agreed, while aristocrats, conservatives, and liberal democrats deeply feared they might be right. As the war ended, new soviet republics flashed into existence all over eastern Europe, and large sections of important socialist parties in the West turned to Moscow for leadership. The possibility that Bolshevism could sweep Europe seemed strong. Actually, however, Lenin's government, embroiled in civil war, could do little to help Communists outside Russia, and the conditions that favored the success of communism in Russia did not exist elsewhere. The victorious Allies were quite determined to see that communism did not spread. Moreover, even among the ashes of defeat, nationalism was still the strongest of the emotions that swayed the masses. When the aims of nationalism and revolutionary socialism conflicted, nationalism carried the day. In fact, nationalist attitudes strongly influenced an overwhelming majority of socialists, even though they habitually paid lip service to the idea that the working man had no country. Throughout Europe, socialists provided the bulk of the force that prevailed against attempts to carry out social revolutions.

Only in Germany, Hungary, and Latvia did communist revolts come anywhere near success. German communists organized soviets in Berlin and several other cities in November, 1918, but most German socialists deplored Lenin's tactics and sought to cooperate with businessmen, shopkeepers, and even the army. Germany in 1918 was not like Russia in 1917: the war had already ended, and few Germans saw the state as a remote oppressive organization in which they played no part. They had believed, however, that the old government had to go, for it had led Germany to defeat and the Allies were demanding its overthrow. As we have seen, socialist riots in Berlin had forced Emperor William II to abdicate on November 9. Friedrich Ebert (1871–1925), chairman of the Social Democratic party, had taken power at the head of a provisional government on the following day. He was able to win conditional support from conservative army leaders by avoiding any serious move toward socialism. He introduced equal and secret voting and women's suffrage, freedom of the press, the eight-hour day, and an unemployment program, but left further reforms to a freely elected government.

Anticommunist socialists won three-quarters of the seats in a Congress of Workers' Councils that met in Berlin on December 16. The Congress decided Germany's future: instead of establishing a soviet government, it voted to call elections for a National Constituent Assembly. Such an assembly was sure to organize a standard parliamentary regime.

Leftwing socialists refused to accept the verdict. Members of the Spartacus League, a small organization of revolutionary socialists, led in the formation of a German Communist party on December 30, 1918 just as antigovernment riots broke out once more. The Communists immediately tried to turn the riots into a revolution, but the Socialist Provisional Government used regular army troops and irregular units composed of unemployed veterans—the "Free Corps"—to crush them. Karl Liebknecht (1871–1919) and Rosa Luxemburg (1870–1919), the Communist leaders, were murdered.

The newly elected National Assembly met in January 1919, at Weimar. It drew up a democratic constitution that provided for a parliamentary government, but gave the president power to establish a temporary dictatorship if necessary to restore public order. The constitution was a compromise, but it undoubtedly suited a majority of Germans. When the Assembly was forced by the Allies to ratify the Versailles treaty, however, its prestige was severely damaged. The right, not resigned either to defeat or to democracy, immediately began using the treaty to attack the constitution and the republican government. At the same time, the extreme left sought to discredit the Assembly because it had not established a socialist regime.

A Communist attempt to establish a Bavarian soviet government in Munich ended in a massacre carried out by army and Free Corps forces in May 1919. In Berlin, in March 1920, an attempted rightwing coup led by an obscure official, Dr. Wolfgang Kapp, and backed by elements of the army, failed when German workers reacted to it with a general strike. In the demilitarized Ruhr area an incipient Communist-led rebellion was crushed easily by government forces. By the time the first elections for the new Reichstag were held in June 1920, bitterness had grown to such an extent that the extreme right and left won heavy representation; as a result, the center coalition government that was established lacked a majority and depended for its existence on the grudging support of the Social Democrats. Germany continued to be governed by shaky coalitions until 1933.

Like Hohenzollern Germany, the Hapsburg Monarchy was a casualty of the war, and, just as in Germany, local Communists hoped to dominate in every place where imperial rule had been swept away. Austria-Hungary was turned into a number of new states. The Poles declared their independence at Warsaw on October 7, 1918. The Republic of Czechoslovakia was proclaimed in Prague on October 28. Yugoslavia came into existence on October 29, and on November 2 Hungary repudiated the Dual Monarchy. A state of "German-Austria" was proclaimed on October 30, but Emperor Charles went into exile on November 13, and both Austria and Hungary became republics. The new nations began their existence under tremendous handicaps.

In Hungary, a weak socialist government was ousted peacefully, in March 1919, by a Communist government headed by a journalist, Bela Kun (1885–1937). Although Kun became the bogeyman of European and American conservatives, he could not repeat Lenin's achievements. Because he tried to collectivize the estates of Hungary's nobles rather than simply to distribute the land to the men who worked it, he quickly lost the peasant support he needed to stay in power. He won over some nationalist army officers by trying to prevent the loss of Transylvania to Rumania, but he was unable to resist when Rumanian troops, fighting to keep the disputed territory, invaded Hungary. In November, after the Rumanians had evacuated Budapest, Admiral Nicholas Horthy (1868–1957) took control of the country with army backing. Named regent for the absent emperor by a national assembly, he set up a government frankly dedicated to the maintenance of the privileges of the old landowning class.

Bolsheviks in Russia's Baltic provinces and in Finland set up soviet governments soon after the Russian Revolution, but the German troops that moved in at the end of 1917 helped local conservative forces overthrow them in short order. In 1918, however, new rebellions broke out. The liberal democratic governments of Estonia and Lithuania quickly suppressed the Communists, but in Riga, Latvia, a soviet government held out until May 1919, when it was crushed by a combination of nationalist and German troops. Latvian Communists, unlike those of most other countries, profited from nationalist feelings, for much of the nation's economy was in the hands of a German ethnic minority. Peasants and workers alike looked to Russia for delivery from the German yoke, and the local Communists were assumed to be linked to the Russian government. When the victorious Allies forced German troops to leave the country, however, democratic nationalists took control without difficulty. Their Allied backing was powerful, and Russia could not intervene.

Communists were unsuccessful in the rest of Europe; with rare exceptions, liberal democratic regimes, installed with socialist support, survived easily.

In Vienna, just as in Berlin, the new government was dominated by socialists. In Austria, however, the moderate socialists organized their own militia, thus avoiding the need to cooperate with the army. When Bela Kun's short-lived success in Hungary led Austrian Communists to attempt a coup, the government's militia quickly thwarted them. Vienna, formerly capital of an empire of more than 50 million people, had become capital of a state reduced to only 6 million. It was vaguely socialist, but Austria's rural hinterland was conservative. In 1920 a moderate socialist government was firmly in power, but it was unable to solve the problems of economic dislocation caused by the dismemberment of the empire.

The new Poland suffered particularly because its population had lived for a century under three very different regimes; the nation was not only ethnically mixed but was economically and politically diverse. Russian Poland had been oppressed politically, but its economy had developed enough to assure that its population included a small proletariat; the formerly Prussian area had been exploited ruthlessly in every way; Galicia under Austrian control had remained economically backward but was the center of Polish nationalism and culture. General Pilsudski, a national hero after his defiance of the Germans in the last months of the war, was the leader of a large socialist party, while the urban bourgeoisie, the landowners, and the clergy supported the National Democrats. Pilsudski, no Bolshevik, became the first head of state and consolidated his power by arranging an alliance with the National Democrats. His fruitless attack on Soviet Russia in 1920 simply added to the inflation, which made the economic woes caused by war damage worse. Polish Communists could make no headway, however, for the vast majority of the country's socialists were both anti-Russian and enthusiastically nationalist.

Like the Poles, the Czechs and Slovaks were too pleased with their new independence to embark on political adventures. Communists were unable to make progress in Czechoslovakia, which emerged as a working democracy under the presidency of Thomas Masaryk (1850–1937), its major problem one of trying to assimilate the masses of Germans and other nationalities living within its borders. Rumania, swollen by territorial gains, also had a relatively liberal government; moreover, timely land reforms and the introduction of universal manhood suffrage in 1918 cut the ground from under revolutionaries and solidified the position of the monarchy. Yugoslavia, established by the peacemakers, took years to become a reality. The union of Serbia, Montenegro, and the Croatian lands of the Dual Monarchy was still not official at the end of 1920. Greece, which had finally decided to fight on the side of the victors, was attempting to hold large areas of Anatolia assigned

to it by the Treaty of Sèvres. In Bulgaria struggles between peasants and various socialist factions produced a chronic instability in the government.

Italy had entered the war reluctantly and had come out of it more divided than ever. Nationalists complained that the sacrifices made by the Italians in men and money were not sufficiently appreciated at home or by the Allies, while socialists berated the whole war effort. Furthermore, the country was plagued by mass unemployment and frightening inflation. Leftwing parties, the Socialists and the (Catholic) Popular Party, together won a majority of the seats in the Chamber of Deputies, but their ideological differences prevented them from cooperating in any kind of government. Hence minority governments led by democrats like Francesco Saverio Nitti (1868–1953) and prewar liberals like Giovanni Giolitti (1842–1928) could accomplish nothing constructive. At the end of 1920 the prestige and power of the government were falling rapidly, and both strikers and rightwing gangs were breaking the law with impunity.

Despite appearances, the Russian government had been unable to help much in 1919 in the various attempts made by native Communists in different countries to follow the example set by the Bolsheviks. Lenin hoped, however, to do more than serve as a model. Leaders of the prewar socialist parties had vowed to support a socialist revolution, but most of them had supported the war efforts of their own countries instead. Consequently, after 1914 considerable numbers of socialists came to believe that those leaders had forfeited any claim to respect. The ranks of the embittered swelled as the peace movement grew toward the end of the war. When Lenin declared in 1918 that he intended to found a new, truly revolutionary, international organization, he found supporters in every socialist party.

The first meeting of the new Third, or Communist, International, held in Moscow in March 1919, was attended only by an unrepresentative handful of delegates, for wartime regulations and blockades still hampered travel; the Second Congress of the Comintern, held in 1920, was better attended. In theory all national delegations were equal; the Russians were simply one party among many. In fact, however, most of the foreign delegates were overawed by the Russian achievement and willing to pass whatever resolutions the Russians sponsored. The Second Congress laid down strict rules for admission of parties: they were required to establish illegal underground organizations, to follow the principles of "democratic centralism," and to expel any member who failed to accept strict discipline. This resolution laid the basis for Russian control of the Comintern, since Russians controlled the central organization and could easily compel any party to expel any member who fought against Russian domination.

In France, nearly two-thirds of the membership of the French Socialist party chose in December 1920 to accept the strict Russian conditions; they were able to take over the party's treasury and its publications for the new French Communist party. In Italy, Socialist party leaders were still trying to maintain unity at the end of 1920, while Comintern agents were preparing to oust Italian Socialists who were unwilling to accept Comintern domination. In defeated Germany, the Socialists had split into several factions, and attempts to organize a full-fledged Communist party were leading to increased confusion. Similar struggles were underway among socialists all over the world. In 1920, however, few members of the new Communist parties in countries like Germany and France saw any danger of Russian control: they were confident that they themselves would soon be rulers of proletarian states more powerful than Soviet Russia. They proved overconfident, but there was no doubt that a new threat to capitalist, parliamentary governments had been posed.

World War I — long drawn out, savage in its destruction — shook Europe to its foundations. Trends of the prewar period were vastly accelerated and modernization was hastened. Empires fell to be replaced by national states, most of them committed formally if not in fact to some kind of democratic regime. Economic affairs, once thought to be beyond the province of government interference, had become matters of vital import to every administrator, politician, or political thinker. Necessities of war hastened the growth of government controls over wages, prices, production, job placement, and many other aspects of the daily lives of Europeans. War damage was incalculable: the task of reconstruction was to be enormous.

Perhaps the most difficult form of reconstruction was the rebuilding of human confidence. Men's faith in the future was shaken. Critics of old ideologies had been active for decades, if not centuries, but their efforts had not really affected the masses. The war did. Faith in government as well as in religion was shaken. Moreover, men who had in the past believed that peaceful progress was inevitable as long as democracy existed to permit change were suddenly faced with an alternative. In the most backward of the great powers the Bolsheviks had begun trying to reconstruct society on a new pattern, to modernize a nation by means of a new ideology. It may be that of the myriad transformations produced by the war, the crucial one was the rise of communism in Russia.

SUGGESTED READINGS

Aron, Raymond, *The Century of Total War*. Boston: Beacon Press, 1954. Paperback.
   Particularly good on the "technical surprise."

Liddell-Hart, B. H., *The Real War, 1914–1918*. Boston: Little, Brown, 1930. Paperback.
   Military history by an expert.

Tuchman, Barbara, *The Guns of August*. New York: Dell Publishing, 1962. Paperback.
   Stirring account of the coming of the war.

Horne, Alistair, *The Price of Glory: Verdun, 1916*. New York: Harper and Row, 1962. Colophon Paperback.
   The best narrative history of one of the war's most devastating single battles.

Reynolds, Quentin, *They Fought for the Sky*. New York: Bantam Books, 1957. Pathfinder Paperback.
   Good anecdotal history of the first air war.

Mayer, Arno, *Wilson vs. Lenin: Political Origins of the New Diplomacy, 1917–1918*. New York: World Publishing, 1959. Meridian Paperback.
   On the development of war aims.

Smith, Daniel M., *The Great Departure: The United States and World War I, 1914–1920*. New York: John Wiley, 1965. Paperback.
   Succinct and competent.

Lenin, V. I., *What Is To Be Done?* New York: International Publishers, 1929. Paperback.
   Lenin's blueprint for revolution.

Carmichael, Joel, *A Short History of the Russian Revolution*. New York: Basic Books, 1964.
   Readable and reliable.

Ulam, Adam B., *The Bolsheviks*. New York: Macmillan, 1965. Collier Paperback.
   Analysis of Lenin and his corevolutionaries through 1924.

Seton-Watson, Hugh, *From Lenin to Krushchev: The History of World Communism*. New York: Frederick A. Praeger, 1960. Paperback.
   A good, detailed survey.

PART **VI** *Global Crises to 1949*

The period from 1919 to 1949 was one of unprecedented political, social, and economic upheavals; modernization continued, but the price of change was higher than ever before. Although World War I had been fought primarily in Europe, in many other areas it accelerated changes that had been barely visible before 1914. For one thing, it permanently transformed international relations by giving the United States and Japan decisive roles. The war also hastened the economic development of the British Dominions and parts of Latin America by cutting them off from their European suppliers of goods and services. During the postwar years, Turkey underwent a forced political and social modernization. The "May Fourth Movement" of 1919 marked the beginning of an authentic Chinese revolutionary movement involving students and workers. Indians and Africans who had served in the Allied armies became restive under continuing colonial rule. Arab nationalists, having helped throw off the Turkish yoke, bitterly resented the British, French, and Zionist presence in their lands, though they could do little about it. The peace treaties and the League of Nations were unable to control the forces of nationalism and imperialism which, by the late 1930s, were becoming increasingly rampant in more places than ever.

The war and the economic and social dislocations that followed it brought significant political changes in the most modernized countries. Of the major powers Italy and Germany experienced the most radical changes, and their example made fascism a widely imitated alternative to liberal parliamentary government. But liberalism, with its laissez-faire economic ideals, was also modified in the Scandinavian countries, Australia, New Zealand, and the United States. In one way or another the welfare of the masses had to be attended to, if they were to be integrated into modern national societies — whether the means was called the Corporative State, the Five-Year Plan, or the New Deal. The world depression dramatized the precarious nature of most people's economic and social status in the most advanced countries. In the Soviet Union, which escaped the depression, the consumer needs of the masses were forcibly curtailed in order to provide the capital for industrialization. The example of Soviet Communism inspired a number of Western intellectuals, though it was difficult to explain away Stalin's terrorism at home and his duplicity in dealing with foreign Communists.

Beginning in 1937 in Asia and 1939 in Europe, a series of mammoth conflicts began that changed the world even more than World War I. At first it looked as if Japan were going to rule the whole Far East while Nazi

666

Germany imposed its New Order on all of Europe. Never in history had imperialism brought so many different countries under such intensive exploitation. Modern techniques allowed the Nazis to murder millions of innocent civilians as if they were so many sheep being "processed" in gigantic slaughter houses. But in the end it was the Allies, particularly the Americans and the British, whose technological superiority proved the most destructive militarily. Once they and the Russians liberated Europe from Nazi tyranny their wartime alliance gave way to a new "cold war" and to the appearance of Communist regimes in much of Eastern Europe. In Asia the changes following Japan's defeat were even more decisive. India and Pakistan gained their independence in 1947, Burma in 1948, Indonesia in 1949. By then Mao Tse-tung had driven Chiang Kai-shek's bankrupt regime off the mainland of China and brought the peasant masses into the forefront of world history.

CHAPTER **22**

The Capitalist Democracies to 1939

World War I had been fought with propaganda as well as guns, planes, and submarines. The importance of mass support of every nation's war effort became increasingly clear when war weariness set in, peace movements developed, and governments had to use both threats and promises to keep the flow of recruits and supplies streaming toward the fronts. When the war ended, wealthy men who wielded great influence in every country would have been glad to see the clock turned back and the people they ruled once more submissive. Even in the established democracies, such as the United States, Britain, and France, the huge masses of the poor had lacked the power to bring about major social changes. Domestic policy had been established and carried out by wealthy businessmen and politicians closely associated with them. Foreign policy was set by the same small elite. Because these men controlled major news sources they were able to mold public opinion to conform to their desires.

But modernization was steadily weakening the control of traditional ruling groups everywhere. In most countries the war marked a significant shift in the locus of power. Politicians could no longer ignore the lower economic classes or overawe them with force and threats of force. They could no longer pay heed only to a small ruling group. Millions of soldiers returned from the fronts determined to win a share in the fruits of victory or to revenge themselves on men who had led them to defeat. Factory workers, aware that in a war of machines and material they had been as important as soldiers in combat, sought not only higher wages but political power. Women, for millenia largely confined to household duties, haltingly resolved to make their voices heard. Democracy was no new ideal, but the war had hastened its development immeasurably.

Trade unions, political parties, and pressure groups of every shade were thrown into frenzied activity. Respect for tradition—any tradition—declined precipitously. Gradualism, the idea that a series of small gains would someday produce an ideal society, lost its appeal for millions of people. Whether they had fought to make the world safe for democracy or for German *Kultur*, they demanded results in a hurry.

The war's effects varied from nation to nation. The ruling groups in the victorious

669

countries, with the exception of Italy, were able to maintain a precarious control over their people without a change in forms of government. The losers fared less well: revolution was the order of the day. Governments now reigned on sufferance: as long as life ran smoothly rulers could pretend there had been no change. But the masses were fickle—in case of trouble, they would demand action, and they would oust rulers who would not or could not meet that demand.

The troubles that quickly arose sometimes evoked drastic responses. In Italy the dictatorship of Benito Mussolini (1883–1945) replaced a weak and irresolute parliamentary regime soon after the war. Buffeted by defeat, then by inflation and depression, Germans put their destinies in the hands of Adolf Hitler (1889–1945). In Britain, France, and the United States a relatively quiet decade of readjustment was followed, when depression hit, by frantic efforts to shore up tottering traditional regimes. Then Hitler, bent on avenging Germany's humiliation at Versailles, threatened once more to turn Europe into a battleground. The capitalist democracies, inhabited by millions of people who refused to face the possibility of war, reacted slowly. The two postwar decades turned out to be not the beginning of an era of peace, but only a period of truce in a war that had never ended. Neither were these years the beginning of a new era of domestic cooperation and prosperity; instead they were a period of struggle between the entrenched forces of an old social order and the legions of a new society whose shape could hardly be discerned.

THE POSTWAR ECONOMY AND THE WORLD DEPRESSION

Mass participation in the war led the masses to expect that governments would in the future devote themselves to mass welfare. That assumption clashed dramatically with the laissez-faire economic dogmas still held by ruling groups everywhere except in the Soviet Union. In fact, politicians had to concern themselves with economic developments they could do little to influence. Immediately after the war in most of the victorious nations goods became plentiful but expensive, while the defeated, sunk in political chaos that prevented their economies from operating normally, suffered severe shortages. By 1920, however, the victors, too, were in difficulty. Changes in the conditions of international trade hampered economic growth, but by 1924 the economies of all the modernized nations were once more in fair shape. Then, in 1929, came the worst depression in history. The ebb and flow of the economic tides were reflected immediately in the political affairs of every nation.

Economic Decline

The end of the war created an economic boom in all the victorious nations—in Europe because the privations of war had created a large, unsatisfied demand for material goods, and in the United States because huge wartime government expenditures continued well into 1919. Soon, however, governments cut back their purchases; war plants closed down, thereby seriously reducing employment and the flow of wages to the world's labor force; finally, many returning veterans soon spent their bonuses and joined the ranks of the unemployed. The old basic industries, such as textiles and steel, were particularly hard hit. They had been operating below capacity in 1914, and to fill war orders had merely increased production without improving their operating efficiency. When demand slacked off shortly after the war, industry could either cut prices or cut production. In order to lower prices, owners of older plants would have had to invest capital to build new facilities employing the most recent production techniques. It was much easier, however, to keep prices high, cut back production, and lay off workers. By choosing the latter course, the owners of huge plants made the depression of 1920–1921 inevitable.

Agriculture suffered, too. Just as in industry, wartime demand had stimulated huge increases in production, particularly in North America, Argentina, and Australia. When demand decreased after the war, and peace made possible the resumption of farm production in the battle zones of Europe, prices plummeted. Farmers who had borrowed money to increase production, or who had

Strikers preparing for battle with police at the Standard Oil Company plant in Bayonne, New Jersey, July 1916.

begun farming marginal land, quickly went bankrupt. Farm prices increased as prosperity returned, but they remained low in comparison with the prices of manufactured goods. More than 400,000 American farmers had to leave the land between 1920 and 1929, and ranchers, who had made large fortunes on the plains of the United States and Australia during the war, were hard hit.

Normally, wages would have fallen rapidly as employment declined and prices dropped in the depression of 1920. But unions had grown in numbers and strength during the war, when labor was scarce, and workers were ready to fight to keep wages high. Waves of strikes in the United States, France, and Britain greeted employers' efforts to reduce pay. By and large the strikes failed and wages were cut, for conservative postwar governments were willing to call out troops to help management win its battles. The threat of strikes minimized the pay cuts, however, for employers preferred to avoid strife if they could.

Nineteenth-century economic progress, strong and relatively steady, had depended upon a smooth flow of goods and services in the world market. Most nations were increasing their restrictions on imports even before 1914, however, and the war hastened the end of the old laissez-faire economy. International trade still grew during the 1920s, but its rate of growth was less than a quarter of that of the last half of the previous century. As a result, economic expansion—one of the major ingredients of modernization—lost much of its momentum.

Governments, pressed by their constituents, had begun to interfere increasingly in business before the war, and this trend continued. During the war every belligerent government adopted "temporary" taxes, or "temporary" regulations on prices, wages, and business practices; but many of these became permanent. France and the United States both continued their high tariff policies at the end of the war, the latter instituting new tariffs as well. But the greatest change

Government posters opposing a coal strike, Britain, 1920.

came in Britain, traditionally the strongest advocate of free trade, where wartime tariffs instituted to save shipping space were kept in force when peace came, and new restrictions were established in 1921. In fact, Britain's main competitors had already caught up with her in productivity before the war; free trade was a luxury only the most efficient of producers could afford. Unfortunately, few governments (and few economists) knew how or cared to take action that would offset the damage those tariff increases did to international trade.

The destruction of the multinational Hapsburg empire also hurt world trade. Cities like Vienna and Prague, whose industrial growth had depended on easy access to raw materials produced in rural areas of Eastern Europe, were cut off from their old suppliers by new restrictions. Most of the new nations jealously guarded their own fledgling industries, using high tariffs to protect inefficient

producers. In many cases they prohibited railroad cars from crossing borders, thus forcing costly unloading and reloading. Nations conspicuously unfitted to do so attempted to become self-sufficient rather than depend on potentially or actually hostile neighbors.

The war also ended the monetary stability that had been the foundation on which world trade had rested. Governments spent more money than they had by excessive borrowing and by printing paper currency without the usual gold backing. As the result of the vast increase in the amount of money in circulation—technically known as inflation—some currencies were ruined and all decreased in value during and immediately after the war. Statesmen used all sorts of expedients to restore currency values, because inflation ruined large sections of every population. None of the remedies was entirely successful; France, for example, was still

Passengers on Britain's Grand National train listen to broadcasts in newly fitted out "wireless saloon," March 1923.

fighting inflation in 1926. Because monetary difficulties made complicated regulations on currency exchange necessary, international trade became more difficult and costly. Men with money who might otherwise have put it into international trade used it instead to speculate in currency. Moreover, fears of monetary disaster reinforced protectionist trends.

Monopolies and international agreements in restraint of trade increased. In the United States, where the Republican administrations of the 1920s were strongly influenced by big business, antimonopoly laws went largely unenforced. In Germany and France cartels and monopolies had never been illegal.

Technological Advances

Increases in tariffs, the increase in the number of national boundaries, monetary instability, and a continuing increase in the organization of monopolies all hindered the growth of trade, which, in turn, slowed down economic expansion. Nevertheless, a shaky kind of prosperity returned around 1924 and lasted for about four years. It was based largely on progress in technology.

The modernization of industrial techniques during the interwar years resulted not from radical innovations but from the exploitation of earlier inventions. Wartime demands had widened the use of mass production techniques. Government specifications for many machines required standardization of parts, and the need for rapid production encouraged the use of assembly lines. The high cost of labor in the postwar period hastened the adoption of both these fundamental processes of modern manufacture for civilian production. After the war, manufacturers turned increasingly to electricity for power, and the higher demand made it possible for producers to build more efficient generators and distribution systems. Some 70 percent of American factory production was powered by electricity in 1929, as opposed to 30 percent in 1914; between 1917 and 1927 power production jumped from 25 to 75 billion kilowatts. Transportation also was improved: trucks and tractors began to sup-

An early transport plane and passengers. London-Isle of Wight service, January 5, 1934.

plant horse drawn vehicles, and steam railroad efficiency increased by nearly 75 percent. Mechanical loading devices replaced unskilled labor in many areas, and new machines increased labor productivity in manufacture.

These new techniques contributed to the growth of new kinds of industry; as noted earlier, owners in older industries such as steel and textiles found little incentive to build new plants. But radio, telephone, the automobile, and the airplane, all of immense value to soldiers at the fronts, had developed rapidly during the war, and there was a large demand for these items when it was over. The vacuum tube was generally adopted during the war years and circuit technology greatly advanced. New types of central switching stations were built to handle the rapidly growing volume of telephone messages. Motor cars and aircraft were built to run faster and more reliably. All these wartime improvements provided the bases of

huge new peacetime industries. Radios, telephones, and automobiles became rapid sellers in the early 1920s, although aircraft remained too primitive to become common civilian transport until the 1930s. Chemical production had fewer direct military uses, but it, too, was a relatively new industry in which technological change was rapid.

Largely because of the development of new industries, a development made possible by the exploitation of technological advances, the economies of modernizing nations began to improve once inventories were liquidated and loans repaid or bankruptcy declared. In the defeated nations the return of political order paved the way for economic recovery. Much needed building had been delayed by the war, and in the devastated areas reconstruction was a pressing task. A worldwide building boom stimulated economies everywhere. Yet, though jobs became more plentiful, unemployment levels remained high almost everywhere. Laborers received higher pay in the 1920s than in earlier years, but jobs were less secure, both because there was a large reservoir of unemployed laborers and because the high wages encouraged employers to take advantage of every opportunity to mechanize production. Thus the prosperity of the middle 1920s was unevenly distributed. Even so, it was prosperity of a sort, a prosperity followed by the worst depression in history.

The Depression

By 1928 signs of weakness had begun to appear on the financial scene. The construction boom was over: demand had been fulfilled in the United States, and reconstruction in Europe was complete. Nothing short of a major attempt to raise the living standards of the masses of poor and near-poor people would have enabled those people to buy enough to keep production high, and nowhere did governing elites even consider such an attempt. In the United States, for example, most people who could afford cars at the current price had them; unemployed workers and most farmers could not afford them. But stock prices were still soaring, because speculators did not foresee the approaching fall in demand for goods. Enormous numbers of people borrowed money at high rates to gamble in the market.

In Germany banks had borrowed huge quantities of money from American and English banks to finance the economic boom that followed the stabilization of the mark in 1924. (See p. 712.) When it became more profitable for Americans to lend money to stock market gamblers, they began calling in their loans to the Germans. Then, in October 1929, the U.S. stock market "crashed."

The depression sparked by the "Great Crash" spread through all the modernized nations. American investors, pressed for cash to repay money borrowed for stock operations, called back the remainder of their European loans. In 1931 the Kreditanstalt (the Rothschild bank in Vienna) had to close its doors. German banks, already pressed by the earlier recalls from the United States, were caught in the disaster; many of them could not repay money they had borrowed in England, so English banks were undermined. As factories closed when goods

TABLE 22.1

	REAL PER CAPITA INCOME 1937–1938 AS % OF 1913	MANUFACTURING OUTPUT 1937–1938 AS % OF 1913
United Kingdom	120	139
Germany	114	144
France	110	119
Sweden	169	231
United States	123*	164*

* Base is 1909–1918 instead of 1913.

could not be sold, unemployment skyrocketed. International trade collapsed, and even France, with huge gold reserves, began to suffer, though the banks in England and France survived the crisis far better than those of the United States and Germany. Late in 1931 the depression hit its nadir when the supposedly "safe" British pound was allowed to depreciate in value by 25 percent on the world market. Governments seemed paralyzed, and many men lost faith in the future. Certainly, unrestricted capitalism would no longer be tolerated after a disaster of such magnitude. But efforts to build a new kind of economy were erratic.

Governments everywhere made fumbling efforts to save their people from the ravages of depression. The expedients they used varied greatly from place to place, usually depending on the political system of the nation. But floundering nations badly hurt one another in their attempts to solve their economic problems, and within each nation material hardship led to desperate remedies. None of these remedies really worked. Not until the international friction of the late 1930s led to new arms races did the modernized world begin to recover from the collapse of its economy.

Although the depression made millions miserable and recovery was slow, the economic setback it represented was not as great as is frequently supposed. As Table 22.1 shows, at the end of 1938, when the effects of rearmament had barely begun to show in the statistics, industrial production was still significantly higher than the levels attained

The unemployed, 1933.

just before World War I. The juggernaut of industrialization had been slowed, not stopped.

SOCIAL AND CULTURAL CHANGES

Despite economic disaster, the social trends common to modernizing nations continued with hardly a pause. Population grew; urbanization rarely faltered; styles of life kept on changing.

Along with the population increases, some of which are shown in Table 22.2, came longer life expectancy—in France, for ex-

TABLE 22.2
Population Growth

	(IN MILLIONS)			(IN THOUSANDS)	
	1900	1940		1900	1950
England	32	44	London*	6600	8300
France	39	42	Paris†	3700	5000
Germany	59	70	Berlin	2712	3345
United States	76	132	New York‡	3500	7900

* Greater London.
† Seine Dept.
‡ City only, including suburbs annexed 1900–1950.

"Flappers" leaving the polling station at Southwark, England, after casting their first votes, May 1929.

ample, the average length of life increased from 48.5 to 54.3 years between 1910 and 1930. People grew taller and heavier, though class differences led to significant differences in nutrition, which were reflected in differences in size. In England, for instance, the average young industrial worker of 1938 was nearly four inches shorter than the average middle-class medical student of the same age, even though both were inches taller than their fathers. Disease rates changed: typhus almost disappeared and tuberculosis death rates declined, while diseases of old age increased in incidence.

Conservatives everywhere deplored the "decline of the family," which was marked not only by the increasing tendency of men, women, and children to patronize commercial entertainment but by accelerating changes in the status of women. Before 1914 many women taught school or held menial jobs in business or industry, usually as fac-

tory operatives or typists, and a very small number succeeded as physicians and scientists; in only a few places could they vote. The war brought many millions of women into industry for the first time, and during the following decade all women over 21 won the vote in most modernized nations: in the United States in 1920, Germany in 1919, England in 1928, Sweden in 1923. Government jobs opened to women, and some of them held prominent positions. Alexandra Kollontai, a Russian, became the first woman minister to a foreign country in 1923; Denmark's education minister Nina Bang became the first female cabinet member in a parliamentary government in 1924. In the United States, Frances Perkins, who became secretary of labor in 1933, was the first woman in a president's cabinet. Yet occupation opportunities for the sexes were far from equal. Most careers were still closed to married women, and mothers were rarely encouraged to continue careers. Even in England wives were granted full property rights as individuals only in 1938. The League of Nations began a study of the status of women in 1935, but its commission still had not reported when war ended its deliberations.

The Intellectuals

The British essayist George Orwell (1903–1950) wrote that between 1930 and 1935 Western intellectuals "got out of the twilight of the Gods into a sort of Boy Scout atmosphere of bare knees and community singing." His characterization was apt: during the 1920s the "lost faith" attitudes of the prewar period intensified, but the Great Depression of the 1930s turned the mood of many intellectuals toward a pathetically earnest identification with the poor and downtrodden.

Skepticism and sensualism continued to be the dominant attitudes among intellectuals in the 1920s. The most popular historical work of the decade was *The Decline of the West* by Oswald Spengler (1880–1936), who argued at great length that Western civilization was in its last phase. Writers preached the downfall of culture. Many novelists and poets of the day shared a pessimistic vision: barbarism was about to triumph. Most of them tried to show in their works the uselessness of art or action—indeed, this decade was one of the great periods of modern literature, even though that literature was essentially negative in its outlook. Some intellectuals, like the poet T. S. Eliot (1888–1965), turned to religion, though their relations with the churches were often strained. Others, like the novelist D. H. Lawrence (1885–1930), glorified sensuality. Freud's work, widely interpreted as antirational, reinforced older tendencies to distrust human reason and to deny the possibility of human progress.

Philosophers succumbed to the drift away from belief in any kind of ethic, many of them accepting the arguments of the "Vienna Circle" of logical positivists that ethical statements were nonsense, of no more significance than simple statements of personal likes and dislikes. To philosophers like A. J. Ayer (1910–   ), an Englishman who took the most extreme positivist position, no statement not subject to scientific verification could be said to have any meaning at all. To say "murder is wrong," they argued, is simply to say, "I dislike murder."

But the depression brought a change. If philosophers continued to follow the positivists, many artists and novelists, appalled at the misery around them (and sometimes sharing it), turned in large numbers to a kind of "Marxism of the heart" as the only hope for mankind. Men as different as Arthur Koestler, a Central European Jew, and Granville Hicks, an American of old Anglo-Saxon stock, so hated the bourgeois culture of the day that they saw in Soviet Russia the only hope for the future. For several years in the 1930s many intellectuals in the West adopted as their own the communism that their bourgeois fellow citizens mortally feared. Most of them were only "fellow travelers," unwilling to submit themselves to party discipline, but they were willing propagandists, and some of their books were political tracts of very little literary merit.

Despite both negativism and radicalism, however, the intellectuals of Europe and America remained rooted in the liberal tradition. They still believed deeply in justice and freedom, qualities they found lacking in the hypocritical cultures of which they were part. The purges carried out by the Soviet dictator, Joseph Stalin (see p. 704), disgusted many of them, and Stalin's later collaboration with Hitler killed their sympathies for communism. For most of them, as World War II drew near, only antifascism, not any belief in future justice, could serve as a driving purpose.

Education

Conservatism marked the politics of the democracies after World War I, but in education, as in so many other areas, changes brought on by increasing industrialization could be slowed but not stopped. In all the major modernizing nations older trends continued. The most important of these was the steady increase in the number of young people going to some sort of school and in the number of years they spent there.

In the United States most children of elementary school age were in classrooms by

1914. Elementary schools increased in size and number along with the growth in population in the 1920s; then the number of schools stabilized when the birth rate dropped in the 1930s. Secondary schools increased faster. A widely read report by a Commission on the Reorganization of Secondary Education confirmed the growing belief that all Americans, whether headed for college or not, should attend high schools. Between 1920 and 1940, the number of students in high schools increased from one to seven million; in 1930 more than half of the population from 14 to 17 years of age was still in school. Colleges also grew, but more slowly; the number of college students more than doubled between 1914 and 1940. Vocational education, far less important in the United States than in Europe before the war, spread widely after federal funds were made available by the Smith-Hughes Act of 1917.

Changes in the nature of educational theory also quickened. Educators, particularly during the 1930s, increasingly deemphasized rote learning in favor of closer attention to the social and emotional development of the individual child. Therorists like the philosopher John Dewey (1859–1952), famed as the father of "progressive education," exercised considerable influence, their theories speading among self-styled liberals in the United States and Europe. Yet the practical application of such ideas was slow. Traditionalists vehemently attacked the new ideas, and most teachers and school administrators refused to change their classroom practices. In fact, a real climate of experimentalism in education never came into being—there was much talk, but little action. Probably the most significant alteration in the American system of education in the interwar period was the development of community participation in educational decision making. Before 1914 local school boards were seldom challenged, but after the war the growth of community groups interested in education, most notably the Parent-Teacher Associations, was rapid. The idea of wider community control of schools grew along with increased public participation in politics. Frequently, however, community groups prevented rather than fostered improvements in educational practice, for most of them were essentially anti-intellectual and stubbornly conservative.

Educational development also continued in Britain and France. In England, however, a movement to raise the school-leaving age to 15, though partially successful, was seriously hindered in 1921 when Parliament cut school funds by a third. Nevertheless, a general reform of secondary education in the late 1920s was followed by a steady increase in enrollment. In 1926 only 10 percent of the children of secondary school age were actually attending classes; by 1938, the figure had risen to 20 percent.

In France the long battle for control of education had gradually subsided after the separation of church and state in 1905. Church schools still held a significant place in education, but they were firmly under state control, their students required to take a state examination for the baccalaureate degree at the end of their secondary education, and their teachers required to have state licenses. The trend toward uniformity of curriculum for boys and girls continued after the war until by 1940 the difference was unimportant. Secondary education was made tuition-free by 1933, and the two-track system of vocational-academic preparation was made more flexible so that students might switch from one to the other. Higher education remained the privilege of an elite, as it had been since Napoleon's day.

The modernizing democracies recognized education as vital to further development. Progress in learning techniques was limited during the interwar period, but the need for more education for more students in democratic, industrialized nations finally became a generally accepted article of faith.

POLITICS BETWEEN THE WARS

Great Britain

The United Kingdom suffered more in the 1920s than did other democratic nations, but it weathered the depression, bad as it was, better than most.

David Lloyd George's National Government, entrenched after a spectacular electoral victory in 1918, lasted until 1923. It produced no striking achievements, seeking instead to get the nation back on a peacetime footing with a minimum of strain. The lifting of wartime economic controls, completed by the end of 1920, aggravated the inflation brought on by the war. Labor unions responded by striking, largely in protest against high prices, the shortage of housing, and, beginning in 1921, unemployment. The government promptly persuaded Parliament to pass a bill that reinstituted most of its wartime powers. It also increased the amounts paid under the unemployment insurance program, but its other economic policies were orthodox — by cutting expenditures and thereby increasing unemployment, it actually made problems worse. Embarrassed by its failure to end the Irish rebellion as well as economic upsets, Lloyd George's government fell in October 1923. Succeeding governments followed policies hardly different from those of Lloyd George; even the Labour party, which held office from January to October 1924, was unable to introduce sharp innovations because it lacked a solid majority. From 1918 until the onset of the depression, governments sought what Andrew Bonar Law, Conservative party leader and prime minister in late 1923, called for in one of his electoral campaigns: "Tranquillity and freedom from adventures and commitments both at home and abroad."

The pursuit of tranquillity seemed to call for little government action, but British society continued to modernize sporadically. Neville Chamberlain (1869–1940), minister of health in the first postwar Conservative government, introduced a housing scheme intended to begin carrying through Lloyd George's election campaign promise of "homes fit for heroes." The weak Labour government headed by Ramsay MacDonald (1866–1937) expanded the program with the passage of the Housing Act of 1924. Partly because of the ensuing construction boom and partly because of the general improvement in world economic conditions, Britain's unemployment problem eased considerably around 1925. In the same year, however, the Conservative government headed by Stanley Baldwin (1867–1947) returned the nation to the gold standard, a move that overvalued the pound in terms of other nations' controlled currencies, thereby making British goods more expensive than others in the world market.

Despite some economic improvement, certain industries remained depressed throughout the 1920s. In 1925, the coal miners' threat to strike against a projected wage reduction led to a government inquiry. When the commission's report, issued in March, 1926, approved the cuts, the miners refused to accept its findings, and the mine owners brought the quarrel to a head by closing the shafts. Negotiations were so badly fumbled that on April 26 the Trades Unions Council called a selective general strike. The public understood the miners' grievances, but most Englishmen opposed the general strike. Baldwin's government had prepared for the emergency, and all sorts of people — students, clerks, executives — stepped in to operate stalled railroad trains, to load goods, and in general to keep the economy going. After ten days the T. U. C. called off the strike on the ground that the miners had refused reasonable government suggestions for a settlement. The miners stayed out another six months, when they finally capitulated without having stopped the wage cuts. Despite the ultimate failure of the miners, the general strike had temporarily united the workers in a common cause. But the public response showed that, in Britain at least, the dreaded general strike was not, as revolutionary syndicalists had long argued, a quick path to revolution.

The depression called forth another National Government, this one headed by Labour's Ramsay MacDonald but dominated by Conservatives. Like its predecessors it accomplished little. Because housing construction continued, and, perhaps, because Britain had not had as big an economic boom in the 1920s as other modernized nations had, the nation suffered somewhat less from the depression than did its neighbors. Still, unemployment rose to nearly four million in 1932, and the remedies tried by a lackluster government failed to bring improvement. As we have seen, however, Britain left the gold

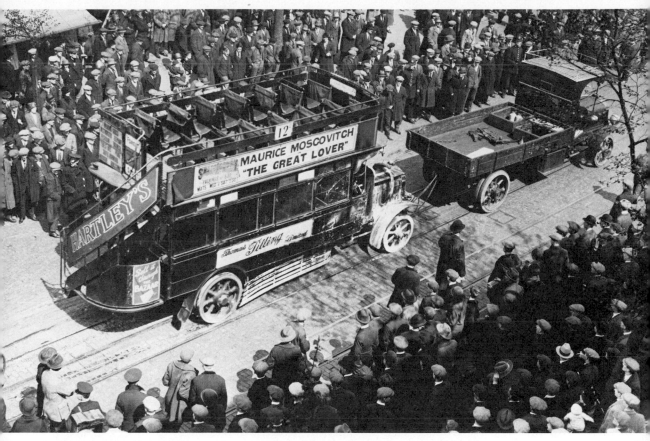

A bus being towed away after it was put out of action by demonstrators on the third day of England's general strike, April 29, 1926.

standard for good in 1931; and in that year the government finally instituted a comprehensive protective tariff.

As Hitler's aggressiveness brought war closer during the late 1930s the people of Britain did their best to ignore the danger signals. The decision of the new king, Edward VIII, to abdicate in December 1936 because of the establishment's objections to his marriage to a divorcee caused far more talk than Hitler's remilitarization of the Rhineland nine months earlier. Not until the Spanish Civil War, which began in July 1936, had dragged on for more than a year did the public — or the government — show much concern for rearmament. All in all, the British muddled through the interwar period in an unimpressive fashion, but they were to

prove in World War II that their traditional courage, ingenuity, and perseverance had not deserted them.

The British Commonwealth of Nations

Britain's major dominions came out of World War I well on their way to independence. They were populated largely by British emigrants who had brought with them attitudes already proven highly congenial to the building of a humane modern society. The war had vastly stimulated their economies, for all of them were largely agricultural, producing raw materials — particularly wheat and wool — needed everywhere. It also fostered a new national pride; not only had the dominions contributed men and material to Britain's war effort, but also their delegates to the Paris Peace Conference had signed the treaties as if they represented sovereign nations.

The dominions differed, however, in their attitudes toward the "mother country." Most Canadians had sentimental and commercial ties with Britain; but good relations with the United States were absolutely vital. A fifth of Canada's factory production came out of American-owned plants, and Americans bought a large share of Canada's farm and forest products. Defense against American attack was unthinkable. A further complication was the hostility of the French Canadians toward all Anglo-Saxons. Australia and New Zealand, on the other hand, were still in some sense outposts of empire. Both depended heavily on British markets for the sale of their products, and both depended on the British navy for protection against potential enemies, the most obvious of which was Japan. Their nationalism, however strong it might become, was by necessity muted. Thus it is not surprising that Canada's prime minister, Robert Borden, led the campaign for dominion representation in the Imperial War Cabinet and at the Paris Peace Conference, while the Australians and New Zealanders followed safely behind.

In the 1920s and 1930s the same pattern prevailed: at the 1926 Imperial Conference, Canada's demands produced an official statement that the dominions were:

. . . *autonomous Communities within the British Empire, equal in status, in no way subordinate one to another in any aspect of their domestic or external affairs, though united by a common allegiance to the Crown, and freely associated as members of the British Commonwealth of Nations.*

That definition was formalized in 1931 in the Statute of Westminster, which specified that legislation passed by the British Parliament would apply to a dominion only with the consent of that dominion. Canada ratified the new arrangement immediately, while Australia waited until 1942 and New Zealand until 1947 to adopt all its provisions.

All three of these British dominions were hit hard by the postwar depression, and, since they were primarily agricultural producers, none shared fully in the industrial boom of 1925 to 1929. When the Great Depression came they all suffered intensely—their markets collapsed, and they found themselves almost bankrupt overnight. Just as in Europe, labor unrest was widespread after the war. In Australia, particularly, socialist doctrines found ready acceptance among workers hit by the rapid succession of booms and busts. Consistent defeat at the polls tamed the Labour parties of Australia and New Zealand, and by the end of the 1920s they were obviously committed not to revolution but to peaceful reform. In Canada, on the other hand, the Labour party never developed into a serious political force. The French electorate—one third of the total—was violently anti-Conservative because the Conservatives were strongly pro-British. Hence it combined with the more progressive elements in Ontario to keep the Liberal party in office through the 1920s.

Yet in all three of these new nations, whether under conservative or liberal control, the long agricultural depression fostered the development of producers' cooperatives, foreign to proponents of laissez-faire. Wheat pools in Canada and export subsidies in Australia and New Zealand were instituted to protect the farmers whose products sustained all three economies. Moreover, industrialization proceeded, cities grew, and the many social services typical of modern urban living also grew in importance.

Centralization, suspect in both Australia and Canada since the days of federation, slowly gained at the expense of provincial autonomy. In Australia, Reform (conservative) Prime Minister Stanley M. Bruce arranged for the Commonwealth to take over state debts when credit became tight in 1928, and, by the Murray River Agreement, conservation and irrigation became partly the responsibility of the central government. With the coming of the depression, centralization also accelerated in Canada: the Dominion government took over much of the cost of unemployment relief in the provinces and established a Canadian Wheat Board to reorganize the bankrupt wheat pools. Just as in the United States, however, the tradition of "rugged individualism" was strong enough to keep centralization at a minimum.

Meanwhile, in Ireland political problems not only hindered modernization but kept the country in turmoil. Irish rebels ignored the Government of Ireland Act passed by the British Parliament in 1920, which gave southern Ireland virtual independence but tied the north to Britain. Not until July 1921 did the harsh repression carried out by the hated "Black and Tans" (special volunteer police so-called because of their khaki uniforms and black belts) produce a truce in the savage civil war. In December 1921 a preliminary treaty was barely approved by the Dial, the rebellious Irish parliament. In 1922 a new Irish Constitution gave the Catholic south dominion status as the Irish Free State, but it took a year of harsh repression by the new government there to put an end to the resistance of diehard republicans who refused to accept the separate existence of Ulster, the six Protestant-dominated northern provinces. The next years saw considerable economic progress, particularly in the building of hydroelectric power stations. In 1937, after years of conflict with Britain over the continuing partition of the island, Prime Minister Eamon de Valera successfully introduced a new constitution that severed almost every Irish connection with the British Commonwealth of Nations.

France

Few countries suffered more from World War I than France did. With almost a million and a half dead and much of their best industry destroyed, the French found themselves temporarily without allies after the United States and Britain reneged on their promises of postwar solidarity. Moreover, alleged Communist domination of the labor movement badly frightened the middle class. As a result, France went through the interwar years in the state of permanent irritability induced by deep feelings of insecurity. It was a mood not likely to foster remarkable progress, although the war damage prompted the building of some new plants.

Government compensation for war-damaged lands could be spent within a radius of 50 kilometers of the damaged area, so that many farmers seized the opportunity to spend their awards by resettling in towns. By 1925, however, the war-devastated agricultural lands of the north were back in production, and farms everywhere were operating more efficiently because the shortage of manpower forced farmers to use more machinery. Industry also was mostly rebuilt by 1925, and the builders of plants were able to use the most modern production techniques. With the return of Lorraine, France had control of the second largest iron-ore field in the world; its own steel industry grew rapidly, and it exported ore in large quantities. New industries, particularly aluminum, aircraft, and automobile production, became important. The harbors of Marseilles, Cherbourg, and other seaports were improved, as were the railroads, run either by the state or by subsidized private owners. Suburbs grew, but housing in the cities remained scarce, mainly because there was little incentive to build in the face of continuing wartime rent controls.

Wage earners and peasants found their lot improved after the war. Unemployment never went over 100,000 — a tiny part of the working force — during the 1920s. North Africans, Poles, and Italians flocked into the country to relieve the chronic labor shortage. Because the peasants who went to the cities usually were leaving farms of poor quality, the average income of the peasantry in general increased. Moreover, the general postwar prosperity extended to farmers in France, largely because the home market was both large and well-protected.

But recovery cost money, and the burning political problems of the 1920s generally boiled down to the question of who would pay for it. When, in December 1922, the Germans showed they were unwilling to pay in the form of reparations, the French reacted by invading the Ruhr Valley; they would take what the Germans refused to give. As we shall see later, the French occupation of the Ruhr cost more than it brought in forced payments in goods. When it failed, economic reality could not be ignored and the franc began to fall at an even faster rate. By July 1926 the problem of inflation had become acute.

The French Radical party had for years held the balance of power in domestic politics. Thoroughly republican, generally in favor of civil liberties and not unfavorable to labor, the Radicals, representatives of France's small shopkeepers and professional men, tended to support the left as long as the economy seemed stable. When their pocketbooks were endangered, however, they swung to the right. Such a swing to the right occurred in 1926 when they supported Raymond Poincaré (1860–1934), the embodiment of French financial orthodoxy, in his attempt to stabilize the franc. He raised taxes and cut government spending, including pensions. The operation succeeded: the franc stood solidly in 1928 at one-fifth of its prewar value. The cost to bondholders, pensioners, and others on fixed income was tremendous, but it was not pauperization, as it was for the same groups in Germany. (See p. 713.)

Poincaré's solution, however, was not a lasting one. Although the depression came slowly to prosperous France, by 1932 industrial production was only two-thirds as high as in 1929, and unemployment went from practically none in 1929 to 255,000 in 1931. These disasters produced hardships for people not so badly hurt by the earlier inflation, particularly wage earners. Political reactions were inevitable, particularly when the economic slump was combined with dangerous developments in foreign affairs—the signing of a nonaggression pact with Russia and the rise of Hitler—and big domestic financial scandals.

Fascist and more conventional rightwing nationalist groups had blossomed as unemployment grew. Incensed by the scandals and the rapprochement with the Soviet Union and heartened by Hitler's German triumph, these groups struck in January and February 1934 with violent riots in Paris. Communists and Socialists demonstrated in opposition. A new "national" government supported by the center appeared unable to stem the fascist tide. The Communists and Socialists, deadly enemies since the Communist party was founded by militant socialists in 1920, finally combined to form a Popular Front. With Radical support, they won the elections of 1936 and installed France's first Socialist premier, Léon Blum (1872–1950).

The Popular Front's slogan was "Bread, Peace, and Liberty." Blum reacted to a massive, nationwide sitdown strike by forcing France's employers to concede cuts in working hours, pay raises, and paid vacations. He also devalued the franc, hoping to stimulate trade, and he effectively controlled agricultural prices. Both the strikes and Blum's remedies frightened conservatives. The Radicals, willing enough to join Communists and Socialists in fighting fascism, quickly felt the danger to their pocketbooks as soon as the Republic seemed likely to weather the storm. Blum fell from office; his reforms, not strong enough to end unemployment or increase production appreciably, were quickly chipped away. Only the sudden need for rearmament seemed likely to solve France's problems.

The United States

In the United States, even more than in most of the other capitalist democracies, politicians in the 1920s were remarkable not for what they did but for what they failed to do. After the war most Americans preferred to return to their private concerns, convinced that political change was both unnecessary and undesirable. Once the immediate postwar depression ended, labor lost its militancy; union membership declined, and radical political parties lost most of their following. Despite government scandals, the rise of powerful criminal gangs, and the chronic problem of low farm incomes, the Democratic party found it impossible to make inroads upon the huge majorities run up by the incumbent Republicans. People seemed content to enjoy the nation's prosperity, spending their money on new cars, radios, movies, and bootleg whiskey. Popular evangelists stirred more passion than the few political figures who demanded reform. It seemed that the prewar progressive vein had been exhausted.

When Warren G. Harding (1865–1923), an amiable Ohio newspaper publisher, became president in 1921, his friends came into office with him. Before he died some of those friends had looted U.S. Navy oil reserves and made fortunes in kickbacks from illegally awarded government contracts.

Sacco and Vanzetti under guard, about to enter the courthouse at Dedham, Mass.

Moreover, the coming of Prohibition in 1919—a triumph for the old Protestant attitudes that were even then giving way under the onslaughts of modernization—opened unparalleled opportunities for the development of organized crime. Harding's vice-president, Calvin Coolidge (1872–1933), was far more competent and careful when he became president after Harding's death, but he was no reformer; his major actions were to cut the federal budget and to reduce taxes.

Meanwhile, the great fear of "communism" shared by the middle classes everywhere produced a steady passage of state statutes prohibiting "criminal syndicalism," variously defined but usually working to the detriment of any labor organization except the old, conservative craft unions in the conformist American Federation of Labor. American attitudes toward unorthodox political beliefs were strikingly demonstrated when two anarchists, Nicola Sacco and Bartholomeo Vanzetti, were executed in 1927 for armed robbery after a long series of highly prejudiced trials and appeals. The general distaste for anything out of the ordinary also produced in 1921 the passage of immigration "quota" legislation designed to maintain the ethnic mix in the population of the United States as it had been in 1890, before the great influx from Italy and Eastern Europe. These laws also totally excluded Orientals; they were passed by huge majorities with much racist oratory and little dissent.

By the end of Coolidge's administration, intelligent and informed observers like Herbert Hoover (1874–1964), the secretary of commerce, were becoming alarmed about the wild increase in stock speculation, but they were ignored. Shortly after Hoover became president—he took office in March, 1929—he had to face an economic debacle far worse than he or anyone else believed possible.

Devoted to financial orthodoxy, President

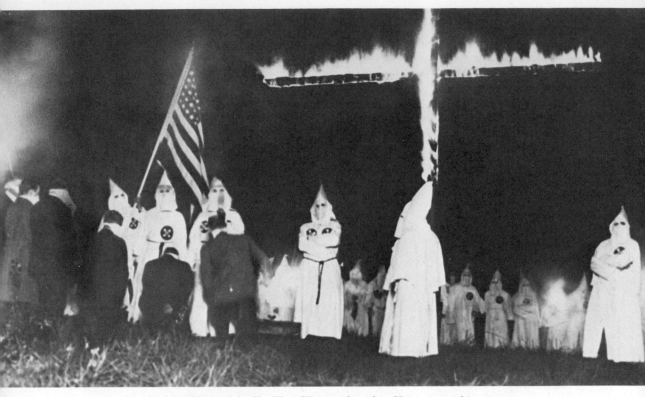

Twelve hundred members of the Ku Klux Klan gathered in Virginia, within view of the White House, to celebrate the Klan's 57th anniversary, April 1924.

Hoover did not welcome an unbalanced budget, but he did persuade the Federal Farm Board, established just before the stock market crash, to support farm prices by increasing loans to farmers and purchasing surplus produce. He also increased public works and urged with some success the maintenance of existing wage rates. During his last two years in office he finally approved the use of some federal funds for relief and with Congress established a new loan agency, the Reconstruction Finance Corporation, which lent significant sums of money to stricken railroads, banks, farmers, and industrialists. But Hoover's moves, certainly correct as far as they went, had little effect on the national welfare. When the crisis hit Europe in 1931 it deepened the depression in the United States. With millions unemployed, the election of the 1932 Democratic candidate, Franklin Delano Roosevelt (1882–1945), was easily predictable.

In February 1933, a month before Roosevelt took office, with the economic slump at its worst and unemployment over 12 million, banks began to close throughout the country. One worker in four was without a job. Roosevelt, whose engaging optimism and promise of a "New Deal" quickly caught the nation's favor, believed in taking vigorous action to solve problems as they came, but he based his actions on no particular doctrine. He had given no indication that he supported radical changes during his campaign, but once in office he immediately pushed through a series of emergency measures that won him the adulation of the masses and the hatred of much of the business community. First, he declared a nationwide bank holiday, thereby lifting the pressure that was forcing many banks out of business. Second, an Emergency Banking Act, passed by Congress at a special session on March 9, 1933, five days after Roosevelt took office, gave him the

Victims of depression and drought, "Okies" left their Dust Bowl homes to seek a living somewhere else, often without success.

power to control the banking crisis and reestablished public confidence to a remarkable degree. The Glass-Steagel Act of June 1933 established federal insurance on savings deposits and strengthened the power of the Federal Reserve System to control credit. In quick succession other bills passed by overwhelming margins. The Civilian Conservation Corps took 300,000 unemployed young men off the city streets and put them to work in the nation's forests. The Public Works Administration, and then the Federal Emergency Relief Administration, dwarfed Hoover's efforts to increase employment on public buildings. The Agricultural Adjustment Act gave the president wide controls which he used to force the destruction of a quarter of the year's cotton crop and the slaughter of six million pigs in order to bol-

ster farm prices. The act also reorganized rural credit banks and made possible the refinancing of farm mortgages.

Once the immediate emergencies were being met, more complex actions, meant for long-term application, followed. Probably the most controversial aspect of this so-called New Deal was the National Industrial Recovery Act of 1933, which provided for the creation of industrial codes that would set minimum wages and maximum hours by industrywide business groups, the codes to be approved and enforced by the government. For the first time in American history labor was guaranteed the right to collective bargaining. At first the N.I.R.A., promoted in carnival fashion by the National Recovery Administration, created new confidence, but small businessmen, hurt by codes drawn up

An N.R.A. rally in Manhattan.

by their large competitors, were quickly disenchanted. In 1935 the Supreme Court declared the N.I.R.A. unconstitutional.

The demise of the N.I.R.A. was not much mourned, for now other moves, less shocking to advocates of free enterprise, were beginning to restructure the American economy. The Tennessee Valley Authority, authorized to develop public electric power, became a model for operation of public utilities. Other laws weakened the influence of special interest groups promoting tariffs and of stock swindlers. Perhaps the most important legislation of the New Deal was the Social Security Act of 1935, which established the contributory old age insurance program. In the same year Congress passed, without much encouragement from the president, the Wagner National Labor Relations Act, which made collective bargaining mandatory in major industries, regulated union elections, listed a number of "unfair labor practices" and established a government board to judge violations of the law.

Despite the distaste of businessmen for some of his acts, Roosevelt was reelected by an unprecedented majority in 1936, carrying every state except Maine and Vermont. His second term was far less productive, at least partly because so much had been done during the first. When the Supreme Court began striking down his legislation—the

N.I.R.A. and the Agricultural Adjustment Act as well as other less significant laws — Roosevelt attempted to exert his power over the court by increasing its membership, but he was defeated in Congress. The Court's attitude toward Roosevelt's legislation eventually became more favorable, for the vacancies that arose through death and resignation allowed him to appoint justices willing to accept New Deal legislation. Congress quickly passed new laws to fill the gaps left by the Court's invalidations.

Although Roosevelt's work was impressive in many areas, it failed to solve the problem of unemployment. Early in 1938, after a moderate decline through the president's first term and a sudden rise that began late in 1937 when Roosevelt, fearing inflation, cut government spending, unemployment once more reached the staggering total of eleven million. Soon afterward, however, the need to prepare for war reactivated the sluggish economy, and unemployment became only a bleak but lasting memory.

Despite some failures, the New Deal partially changed the character of American life. Later administrations not only continued Social Security, federal controls over labor practices, and other innovations of this period; they also refined and extended them. "States' rights" sentiment and resentment against "big government" remained strong, but Roosevelt had laid the basis of the modern welfare state; "big government" had come to stay.

The Democracies of Northern Europe

During the period between the two world wars the nations of Scandinavia pioneered in those areas of modernization connected with social legislation. Sweden, in particular, aggressively sought radical solutions for economic and social problems. On the other hand, Switzerland, Belgium, and the Netherlands, following traditional policies, paralleled the course of the larger nations.

The Swedes were the first to learn that modernized nations need not allow economic slumps to turn into national disasters. During the 1920s Scandinavian trade unions were already forcing major economic gains for their members. When the depression came, the governments of all the Scandinavian countries, strongly influenced by socialist and peasant parties, moved rapidly to attack the problems it raised. The Swedish finance minister, Ernst Wigfors, set out to stabilize the nation's economy. Budgets need not be balanced every year, he said, if they balanced over a longer period; therefore governments should pump money into the economy, incurring deficits if necessary during depression periods, and pay back the money borrowed by cutting down on spending when the economy boomed. Adopting Wigfors' theories, the Swedish government systematically maintained wage levels by providing work for the unemployed at standard wages and subsidizing businesses or lending them money at low interest rates. Recovery began as soon as the program went into force. Although foreign trade was still one-third lower in 1938 than it had been ten years before, manufacturing had increased by nearly two-thirds, and unemployment was lower than it had been before the depression began. This Swedish success attracted attention everywhere.

Denmark suffered more during the depression than Sweden because it was more dependent on agricultural exports, but Danish policies showed equal disdain for orthodox economics. Shortly after the depression began, the Danish government placed strict controls on the marketing of agricultural goods. Careful accounting, accompanied by elaborate systems of price controls, resulted in production cuts that kept prices high and helped farmers weather the storm. Norway, mainly dependent on marine produce and shipping for foreign exchange, rode out the depression with little difficulty largely because demand for its goods and services remained high.

Belgium and the Netherlands, where trade unions were less powerful than in Scandinavia, followed France in adhering to orthodox economic principles despite the depression, and, like that of France, their recovery was slow. Neither of them came close to matching the Swedish record of quick recovery.

INTERNATIONAL RELATIONS

Neither victors nor vanquished were satisfied with the treaties made at Paris in 1919. France, in particular, was left without major allies when the United States and Britain failed to ratify their treaties of alliance with it. The French were ready to strike without mercy at the first sign of German resurgence. Britain, on the other hand, depended on trade; British statesmen were soon eager to see Germany, their best prewar customer, recover enough to take its old place in the European economic system. Thus while France sought to keep Germany weak and to find new allies against any potential German threat, Britain consistently put forward schemes designed to rehabilitate Germany as a trading partner. The United States by this time had again lost interest in European affairs, satisfied as long as payments continued to flow in from the nations that had borrowed from it during the war. Attempts to settle the thorny reparations issue merely drove the French and Germans farther apart; indeed, in 1922 the Germans signed a trade treaty with the Soviet Union, which was diplomatically isolated by the western Allies for having deserted them in the war.

France, meanwhile, began trying to replace the defunct Russian and British alliances. Belgium, as badly hurt by the war as France, joined it in a defensive alliance in 1920. Poland, grateful for French aid against the Red Army in 1920 and afraid that Germany might menace its newly won independence, signed a defense pact with France in 1921. By 1927 diplomats had forged a new eastern alliance system, the "Little Entente," which included Czechoslovakia, Rumania, and Yugoslavia, all allies of France. Once more France was attempting to assure its immunity against German attack by threatening Germany with a counterattack from the east.

As we have seen, Germany confirmed French fears in December 1922 by defaulting on its reparations payments. Over British objections, France and Belgium decided to extract the payments by force. They occupied the Ruhr Valley, the rich industrial area around Duisberg, Düsseldorf,

and Essen. The Germans reacted with passive resistance — officials and factory owners refused all cooperation with the occupying troops, workers went on strike, and the German government supported the resistance financially, thus tremendously accelerating the already rapid German inflation. The occupation lasted nearly two years. French troops were withdrawn only after French voters, many of them afraid the occupation foreshadowed a new war and others irritated at its cost, elected a parliament more willing to negotiate the issues involved. Aristide Briand (1862–1932), the new French premier, guided his country's foreign policy from 1924 to 1930; he favored a more conciliatory approach to Germany. At the same time Gustav Stresemann (1878–1929), a German nationalist equally disposed to negotiations, became the leading influence on German foreign policy. A new plan, drawn up by a commission under the chairmanship of an American, Charles G. Dawes, rescheduled reparations payments and made possible the withdrawal of French troops in November 1924. With this issue settled, a new, stable, mark replaced the old, worthless ones. (See p. 712.)

Tension declined rapidly after the acceptance of the Dawes Plan. Despite the failure of several earlier attempts to establish international machinery for enforcement of the peace treaties, a conference held at Locarno, Switzerland, in October 1925 produced a set of agreements that caused rejoicing throughout Western Europe. French fears of Germany were the overriding cause of international tension. At Locarno those fears were greatly lessened when Germany agreed to accept as fixed its border with France and Belgium. If troops crossed that border in either direction, the Council of the League of Nations was to determine the aggressor, after which Britain and Italy were to come to the aid of the victim. Questions concerning Germany's eastern border were to be settled by arbitration treaties.

The "Locarno spirit" that reigned in Europe was, however, deceptive, for Germany refused to accept its eastern border, and no international guarantee of that border could be arranged. Thus only Germany's willingness to honor its arbitration agree-

French soldiers camping in the headquarters of the Ruhr Coal Syndicate, January 1923.

ments protected Poland and Czechoslovakia. Events were to show that was not enough, particularly since the Soviet Union still was not included in the European concert. Meanwhile, however, war clouds receded, and hopes for permanent peace were high.

A year later the Locarno Pacts were strengthened by Germany's entrance into the League of Nations. In 1928 the Locarno spirit reached its height with the signing of the Kellogg-Briand Pact, under which most of the nations of the world renounced war as an instrument of national policy and agreed to settle their disputes "by pacific means." Such an agreement now seems unrealistic, but in 1928 most people saw it as the keystone of a peaceful world system. Its flaw was obvious: most of the signatories reserved for themselves the right of self-defense, and who would judge when that right was justly exercised? In fact, whatever their interest in signing general agreements, nations still relied on their own armaments and those of their allies as the ultimate guarantee of their security.

Disarmament, cited as a worldwide aim in

the Treaty of Versailles, never was seriously considered. The only arms limitation agreement made in the 1920s and 1930s, despite a succession of conferences that lasted until 1937, was drawn up at a conference in Washington in 1921. Under this pact the existing naval strength of the major powers was recognized and presumably perpetuated through a system of ratios. Great Britain, the United States, Japan, France, and Italy agreed to maintain a ratio of $5:5:3:1.67:1.67$ in numbers of battleships. Despite later Japanese demands for parity, the ratios held well into the 1930s. But the signatories made no agreements on cruiser and submarine strength, so competition in naval armaments continued below the battleship level.

The coming of the depression in 1930 quickly upset the precarious system of international relations established in the preceding five years. The European nations, except for Finland, stopped paying installments on their war debts to the United States, thus confirming American distrust of Europeans. When Hitler came to power in Germany in early 1933 he was committed to major revi-

NORWAY
Oslo ★
SWEDEN
★ Stockh
*Balt
Se*

North Sea
DENMARK
★ Copenhagen

EIRE

GREAT
BRITAIN

★ London
Dover

Amsterdam ★
NETHERLANDS

Danzig
"Polish Corridor"
EA
PRUSS

Elbe River

Berlin ★

Oder

Vistula

★ Warsaw

Cherbourg
Atlantic Ocean

Brussels ★
BELGIUM
LUX.

Seine

Rhine River

GERMANY

River

Versailles ★ Paris
SAAR
to Ger. 1935

Prague ★

CZECHOSLOVAKIA

Loire River

River

ALSACE

Danube River

Bay of Biscay

FRANCE

SWITZERLAND

★ Zurich

River

Vienna ★

Geneva ★

Locarno ★

AUSTRIA

Budapest ★

HUNGARY

Rhône River

ITALY

Po River

★ Trieste

Belgrade
★

PORTUGAL

Ebro River

ANDORRA

Marseilles ★

YUGOSLAVIA

Adriatic Sea

Sarajevo ●

Lisbon ●

★ Madrid

CORSICA
(Fr.)

SPAIN

BALEARIC ISLANDS
(Sp.)

SARDINIA
(It.)

Rome ●

Tirana ●

ALBANIA

Gibraltar (Br.)

SPANISH MOROCCO

SICILY

MOROCCO
(Fr.)

Mediterranean Sea

TUNISIA
(Fr. protec.)

ALGERIA
(Fr.)

LIBYA
(It.)

EUROPE BETWEEN THE WARS, 1922–1938

FINLAND

★ Helsinki

el ★

STONIA

· Novgorod

· Riga

TVIA

· Leningrad (Petrograd)

Volga River

THUANIA

ovno

· Minsk

· Smolensk

★ Moscow

LAND

· Kiev

Dnieper

River

UMANIA

· Odessa

★ Bucharest

Sea
of Azov

· Sevastopol

ULGARIA

ia

Black Sea

Istanbul

ECE

thens

ODECANESE
ISLANDS
(It.)

RETE

UNION OF SOVIET

SOCIALIST REPUBLICS

Don River

· Stalingrad

URAL MOUNTAINS

Aral
Sea

Caspian Sea

· Ankara

TURKEY

CYPRUS
(Br.)

SYRIA
(Fr. mandate)

PERSIA

IRAQ
Ind. 1932

PALESTINE
(Br. mandate)

TRANSJORDAN
(Br. mandate)

KUWAIT

Persian
Gulf

EGYPT

Nile

River

ARABIA

New nations

Red Sea

sions of the peace treaties of 1919. One of his earliest acts as dictator was to take Germany out of the League of Nations. Examined in retrospect the course of international relations after 1933 was a rapid degeneration into hostility and war. It can best be discussed in the next chapter in connection with origins of World War II.

The League of Nations

President Wilson had considered the foundation of a League of Nations so important that he made serious concessions on other matters involved in the 1919 treaties in order to obtain it, but the League failed to live up to Wilson's expectations. Established by a covenant included in each of the peace treaties, the League consisted of three bodies: an Assembly, in which each member nation had one vote; a Council made up of the great powers as permanent members and several members elected by the Assembly; and a Secretariat. The Assembly functioned as a parliament; the Council was a kind of executive committee. Various actions to be taken in case of war or the danger of war were outlined in the covenant, but the effectiveness of the League in preventing aggression was ruined by two limitations: it could not intervene in the internal affairs of member nations, and the Council had to order any action unanimously. In fact, internal affairs in many nations strongly affected the prospects for peace, and unanimity in the Council was never possible when great power interests were involved.

Despite its weakness the League did succeed occasionally in solving disputes among the weaker states, and it served effectively in other areas of life. It settled territorial disputes between Norway and Sweden and between Iraq and Turkey and, in 1925, actually stopped a war between Greece and Bulgaria. When the great powers were involved, however, it was unable to act. On the other hand, the League's agencies — its Health Committee, its Advisory Committee on Traffic in Opium, and its Refugee Organization, for example — performed useful tasks that individual nations were unable to attack. Those committees set precedents for the far more extensive social activities of the later United Nations.

President Harding's vision of "normalcy," Bonar Law's call for "tranquillity" — these were the authentic voices of the upper levels of society in the capitalist democracies after World War I. These men sounded, probably without realizing it, like the victorious allies meeting in Vienna in 1815, determined to restore the world as it had been before the French Revolution. In fact, nothing but an end to the process of modernization could have produced a return to the political conditions of 1914. But modernization continued, and crisis, not tranquillity, accompanied it.

During the 1920s traditional ruling elites maintained their positions. They used force to put down militant advocates of change, and they were supported by citizens whose fear of change was greater than their dislike of poverty or insecurity. An illusion of tranquillity returned when the initial stages of postwar readjustment were over and trade-unionist and radical clamors were quelled. The economic practices of the 1920s — unlimited speculation, unbridled competition, thoughtless dependence on the payment of reparations no government was prepared to collect by force — contributed to the illusion. When depression came, and the illusion was shattered, the masses sought relief. Informed by radio and newspapers of ineffectual government attempts to meet the crisis without giving up orthodox economic principles, they turned to the New Deal, the Popular Front, the National Government, each one promising, if nothing else, a change in attitudes. In fact, the hold of the old elites was still too strong to dislodge. Reforms were made, but they failed to solve the enormous problems of modern societies. Greater changes were necessary; indeed, the problems were only beginning to be understood.

The threat of a new war solved the problem of depression, at least temporarily. The pressure for social and economic reform was suddenly less. While it was quite apparent that the leaders of the capitalist democracies could not deal effectively with social and economic crises, they thought they knew how to deal with military threats. But the war would not last forever; the confrontation was merely postponed.

SUGGESTED READINGS

White, Morton, *The Age of Analysis: 20th Century Philosophers*. New York: New American Library, 1956. Paperback.
Selections from all the major philosophers, with commentaries by a major authority.

Aaron, Daniel, *Writers on the Left*. New York: Avon books, 1961. Paperback.
The impact of the idea of communism on American writers.

Galbraith, J. K., *The Great Crash: 1929*. Boston: Houghton-Mifflin, 1955. Sentry Paperback.
Vivid narrative, good analysis.

Childs, Marquis W., *Sweden: The Middle Way*. New Haven: Yale University Press, 1961. Paperback.

Wolfers, Arnold, *Britain and France Between Two Wars*. New York: W. W. Norton, 1940.
On politics and foreign policy.

Graves, Robert and Allan Hodge, *The Long Weekend: A Social History of Great Britain, 1918–1939*. New York: W. W. Norton, 1963. Paperback.
Amusing and penetrating social history.

Werth, Alexander, *The Twilight of France, 1933–1940*. New York: H. Fertig, 1966.

Colton, Joel, *Léon Blum*. New York: Knopf, 1966.

Allen, Frederick Lewis, *Only Yesterday: An Informal History of the 1920s*. New York: Harper and Row, 1931. Perennial Library Paperback.
Delightful analysis of the U.S. scene.

Burns, James M., *Roosevelt: The Lion and the Fox*. New York: Harcourt, Brace, and World, 1956. Harvest Paperback.
One of the best short biographies.

CHAPTER **23**

Totalitarian Alternatives to Capitalist Democracy

Mass participation in politics is one of the essential marks of modernization; democracy and capitalism are not. Thus nations eager to share in modernization may adopt any political and economic system they think will best achieve their aims. The two alternatives chosen most frequently in the twentieth century have been communism and fascism.

The conditions that gave rise to communism in Russia have already been discussed (see Chapter 21): an old, inefficient monarchy was laid low by modern war, and its successor, a Western-style democracy, lacked the strength or the will to take the drastic action necessary to preserve itself. Determined revolutionaries won power and kept it by promising an exasperated people solutions to immense problems. Fascists in Italy and Nazis in Germany did the same thing. Parliamentary government meant little to millions of Italians, especially peasants, whose lives had changed little since the nation was unified. World War I brought disaster to Italy; the war was followed by economic hardship and social disorder. Because only Mussolini seemed able to restore stability, Italians were willing to put their future in his hands. Germans were forced in defeat to accept a government in which most of them had little faith; modernization had begun in Germany without democracy, and many Germans had no real desire to see a change of regime. The Weimar government never won their loyalty, and its failure to cope with the depression ruined its chances of survival. Hitler succeeded largely because Germans believed that democracy had failed them.

Even in those nations where democracy and personal freedom were valued most highly, World War I and the depression tore the fabric of society. Where those values were less strongly held, people scrapped them quickly in return for promises of a better future. But as it turned out, totalitarianism—the attempt by governments to control everything—often produced greater hardship and injustice than capitalist democracy.

SOVIET RUSSIA, 1920–1939

Some 19 million people died in Russia between 1914 and 1920, and war, revolution, and civil war produced indescribable destruction. By the end of the civil war the economy was almost totally ruined. "War communism" (see p. 657) brought victory for the new regime, but even the doctrinaire Lenin realized that with the end of the fighting the masses would no longer tolerate the crushing burdens they had borne for years. By 1920 factory production had declined to 13 percent of its prewar volume, and less than a third of Russia's farm land was still under cultivation. The ruble had become worthless. Moreover, 1920 was a disastrous crop year in the nation's best agricultural areas: famine gripped the country by the spring of 1921. Rumblings of discontent came from peasants and workers alike. South of Moscow peasants rose in revolt against the depredations of government requisition teams early in 1921, and the sailors at Kronstadt, once the strongest supporters of the Bolsheviks, mutinied. Foreign relief organizations fed millions of Russians, but Lenin was convinced that radical action must be taken.

In March 1921, he issued the first of the decrees that led to the development of the New Economic Policy, a tactical retreat that put Russia on the road to a remarkable economic recovery. Requisitions were replaced by a grain tax, making it possible for peasants to know exactly what they would have left after their harvests and to sell their surplus on a free market. Trade between town and country was reopened. A state bank was founded and the ruble stabilized. The government controlled only what Lenin called "the commanding heights" of the economy, ignoring small factories and retail establishments. Within a short time thrifty, hard-working peasants were rebuilding their small fortunes and a new class of "NEPmen," petty merchants taking advantage of the new freedom to trade, came into existence. By 1927, after six years under the NEP, Russian production had climbed back to 1913 levels. The NEP was a retreat from the principles of communism, but it was effective.

In foreign policy the Russians engaged in a similar retreat. By 1920, when the Red Army met defeat in Poland, it was clear that world revolution was not as near as the Bolsheviks had originally thought. The Russians signed treaties with the Baltic states in 1920 and with Persia, Afghanistan, and Turkey in 1921. That same year the Russians overcame the distrust and fear the conservative democracies of the West felt toward the Soviet Union and managed, after long and bitter negotiations, to sign a trade treaty with Britain. In 1922 the Russians startled the world—and ruined a British plan for a European trade consortium—by signing with Germany a treaty that provided for diplomatic relations and trade between the two countries and for Russian renunciation of reparations. This treaty, signed in Rapallo, Italy, also marked the beginning of secret military agreements between the two nations.

Lenin lived long enough to initiate these new policies but not long enough to see their effects. His health began to deteriorate in 1922 and he died on January 21, 1924. Most observers had assumed that Trotsky was the logical heir, but they had not reckoned on Trotsky's tactical ineptitude or the cleverness of Joseph Stalin (1879–1953).

Trotsky opposed both the NEP and the retreat in foreign affairs, arguing that both represented victories for capitalism that Communists should never have permitted. Moreover, his great prominence had inevitably brought him enemies, particularly when it became clear that the question of Lenin's successor was soon to arise. Stalin, on the other hand, from his earliest days in the Bolshevik movement had agreed with Lenin and had remained in the background, a faithful lieutenant of the great man and an enemy to none of his comrades. Born near Tiflis, in Georgia, he had worked underground in tsarist Russia, fought for the Communist government in the civil war, and become commissar of nationalities under Lenin. In 1922 he became general secretary of the Communist party. He used his power carefully, putting his friends in key party posts and arranging the disgrace or transfer to lesser positions of men he distrusted. After Lenin's death the government and the party were managed by committees whose members agreed primarily on the necessity of preventing Trotsky's ascent to power. Condemning his commitment to the idea of "permanent revolution" as a deviation from Leninism, his rivals drove him from post to post, finally expelling him from the Politburo, the party's small executive committee, in 1926, and from the party itself in 1927. By 1929 Trotsky was in exile; he was eventually assassinated in Mexico in 1940 by a Stalinist agent. Meanwhile, Stalin played one rival against another until he was left, in 1929, supreme among the Communist leaders.

Stalin's doctrinal motto was the opposite of Trotsky's: he supported "Socialism in One Country," arguing that while the ideal communist society would inevitably triumph someday, it was the duty of the Soviet Union to perfect itself in the meantime. The NEP, necessary or not, was not socialism. For practical purposes Stalin adopted Trotsky's economic program (now that Trotsky was out of the way), putting an end to private trade and instituting a system of state planning far more efficient and an economy far more tightly controlled than anything done under War Communism.

Plans for electrification of the country, for collectivization of farms, for revitalization of education, and for scores of other modernization efforts had been drawn up during the years after the revolution, and a State Planning Commission was established in 1921, but none of these bore fruit until 1928, when the first Five-Year Plan was inaugurated. Marx had said little about the way the workers' state should be run, but Engels had likened it to a big factory: production plans should be made; needs in raw materials, capital, and labor ascertained; and the processes of production carefully coordinated for maximum efficiency. Thus the Five-Year Plans, though first instituted in 1928, were not without doctrinal precedent. Three Five-Year Plans were instituted between 1928 and 1941, when the third was suddenly cut off by German invasion. Under the Plans both agriculture and industry in the U.S.S.R. were revolutionized.

During the period of the NEP, agriculture, like industry, had recovered so thoroughly that production surpassed that of 1913. Further growth was not likely, however, since modern farming methods had not been introduced. Large estates had been broken up during the revolution, so that by 1928 the U.S.S.R. was a nation of small farms, most of them operated by men who lacked the capital or the incentive to buy machinery or to plan major improvements. The "kulaks"—peasant capitalists who employed labor—had prospered during the past decade, and Stalin looked on them with suspicion. The first Five-Year Plan called for the beginning of collectivization: about one-seventh of the nation's farmland would be collectivized by 1932. In 1929, however, crops failed badly, and Stalin suddenly ordered mass confiscation of farms, livestock, and equipment. The peasants resisted bitterly. Many of them slaughtered livestock to avoid turning it over to the collectives, while others burned crops requisitioned by the government. Retaliation was swift: some ten million peasants were exiled to Siberia or Central Asia, while millions of others died of starvation or were executed. In March 1930, Stalin accused subordinate officials of proceeding too harshly, but collectivization continued. By 1932 more than 60 percent of peasant households had been collectivized, and by 1936 more than 90 percent were included in collectives.

Peasants on each collective farm (*kolkhoz*) received their land rent-free from the government and chose their own board of managers. Each farmer received a share of the profits made by the *kolkhoz* based on the number of days he had worked. Eventually every peasant household was allowed a small private plot, the produce of which was heavily taxed. Because capital was in short supply, farms shared the use of machinery supplied by state-owned Machine Tractor Stations (until 1958, when the stations were abolished and each farm had its own machinery). In contrast, the State Farm (*sovkhoz*), also established in 1928, operated as a factory does, with a state-appointed manager and wage labor. In the early years the *kolkhoz* was the preferred type, but the *sovkhoz* increased in numbers and in size as time passed.

Collectivization failed in its objective. Peasant resistance reduced farm production

Starting for the fields from the Bejetsk Machine Tractor Station, Moscow Province.

markedly. The number of cattle, pigs, and sheep on Soviet farms declined from more than 200 million in 1929 to slightly less than half that figure in 1933, and production fell sharply, returning to 1913 levels only in 1937. Stalin told Winston Churchill during World War II that the drive for collectivization was worse than the war against the Nazis. Whether or not that was so, it was a disaster from which the Soviet Union has not yet fully recovered.

In industry the Five-Year Plans were far more successful. Quotas for every factory were set, and managers were held responsible for meeting them. The plans stressed heavy industry; production of consumer goods was kept low, and the masses lived with shortages of everything from clothes to kitchen knives and soap. But industry grew. New regions were industrialized and new cities built, the most important of them Mag-

nitogorsk, in the Urals, and Stalinsk (now Novokubnetzsk) in the Kuzbass coalfield of western Siberia. Iron and steel production quadrupled between 1928 and 1936, and coal did nearly as well. Railroads were carrying five times as much freight in 1938 as they had in 1913.

The Soviet System

Such rapid modernization in the economy could only have been carried out in a society modernizing in every sector. The driving force behind the modernization movement was the Communist party. The revolutionary slogan, "All power to the Soviets," guided the establishment of the formal system of government, but the real power remained in the hands of the Communists. The old empire was reorganized in 1922: the territories of Russia, Belorussia, the Ukraine, a Trans-

Caucasian Federation (consisting of Armenia, Azerbaijan, and Georgia), Turkmen, Uzbek, and Tajik were each organized as republics joined together in the Union of Soviet Socialist Republics. In accordance with the Constitution of 1918, every village and factory had its own soviet and each of these basic units elected representatives to a territorial soviet, which, in turn, elected delegates to the All-Union Congress of Soviets. The Congress, in which urban areas were heavily overrepresented, met at two-year intervals, at which time it elected its Central Executive Committee. That Committee had two divisions, the Soviet of the Union, which represented the total population, and the Soviet of Nationalities, which represented the national divisions of the Union. The 27-member Presidium of the Central Executive Committee, elected by the two Soviets, served as the executive authority, but it, too, had an executive committee, the Soviet of People's Commissars, which corresponded to the cabinet in a parliamentary system.

COMMUNISM

Since 1918, when the Russian Bolsheviks began to call themselves the "Communist party," the term communism has been used by noncommunists to describe the totalitarian socialist political system that exists in the U.S.S.R., China, and elsewhere. It is also used to describe doctrines that justify governmental practice in those states: Marxism-Leninism, Stalinism, Titoism, and Maoism. Communism always refers to a socialist system of production and distribution in which land and capital—the "means of production"—belong not to individuals but to the whole group of producers and consumers. The term has a long history, however, and its precise meaning depends on the context in which it is used.

Primitive communism involved the ownership of capital by a tribe or sect, and a system of distribution of goods divorced from any concept of earning. Each person received whatever he needed from the common hoard without regard to his part in production. Communism and socialism were long used interchangeably to describe any doctrine that aimed at the elimination of private property and the establishment of free distribution of articles for consumption. In this sense communism is theoretically compatible with any political system, whether democracy, oligarchy (control by an elite), or dictatorship.

Karl Marx believed that communism would be established by the "proletariat," the propertyless industrial workers, after a successful revolution against the capitalist system. The state would then "wither away." Lenin later insisted that the workers must be led to their triumph by a small, disciplined corps of professional revolutionaries. After the revolution, that small group, through the Communist party, would control the state until all the enemies of Communism were eliminated. Mao Tse-tung of the Chinese People's Republic has preached a new variation of communism. He holds that in lands lacking industry the Communists must lead not the workers but the peasants against the forces of capitalist imperialism. Also, Mao spurned the U.S.S.R.'s doctrine of peaceful coexistence and argued until recently that war between the capitalist and communist camps is inevitable.

The fact that the many delegates filling positions in these bodies were chosen by indirect election made it easy for the Communist party, not even mentioned in the Constitution, to control the government. Admission to the party was carefully restricted to persons who were willing to dedicate themselves wholeheartedly to party work. Party membership nonetheless rose from half a million members in 1921, to a million in

1929, to three and a half million in 1933. Members were scattered throughout society, one or two in each village or workshop, and they were expected to dominate the local soviets through hard work, study, and their control of government patronage. Enough of them were elected to territorial soviets to ensure party domination there and thus to ensure party control of higher political positions. In that manner the party controlled the state.

The party itself was organized, like the state, as a pyramid of groups covering increasingly large areas from the factory cell to the All-Union Congress. At every level—city or district, regional, provincial, and republican—an elected committee was to oversee the work of full-time secretaries who carried on the daily affairs of the party. At the top of the pyramid was the Secretariat chosen by the Political Bureau of the Central Committee of the Communist party. Its control over party policy, supposedly checked by the Central Committee, was almost absolute, for it could dispense patronage or punishment to enforce its domination. Stalin, as general secretary, controlled the Secretariat; through the party, the Secretariat controlled the state.

With all other parties proscribed, significant political activity in the Soviet Union was restricted to intraparty strife. Here party doctrine laid down clear limits. According to Lenin's definition of "democratic centralism," party members were urged to debate party policy at great length before a course of action was chosen, but once a decision had been made every party member had to accept it as his own. Any attempt to force reconsideration of points already decided, or refusal to carry out party decisions, was a breach of discipline leading directly to expulsion, except in the few cases in which the dissenter expressed a view so popular that it won support in the Politburo before the disciplinary machinery went into action. Factions were banned as contrary to the Communist system, and when they developed their leaders were expelled or forced to drop their opposition. When persuasion failed, the secret police, used as much against party members as against ordinary citizens, could and did swiftly put an end to recalcitrance. Control over the highest organs of the state gave the leaders of the party control over their fellow party members, so that only the tiny governing elite, numbering perhaps less than a hundred, had any actual control over affairs. When Stalin had finally ousted his rivals, he was himself the sole source of power. Through his network of loyal supporters he controlled the party; through the party he controlled the state. The state controlled not only the economy but every aspect of life in the Soviet Union.

Soviet Culture

Arts, letters, sports, and leisure activities were as much subject to state control as the economy. Lenin insisted that criticism of the Soviet system amounted to counterrevolution; Stalin tightened the controls on criticism even more. Writers might attack slovenly workers, inefficient bureaucrats, or anyone who showed "bourgeois" tendencies, but anything that was construed by the men in power as an attack on Communism was swiftly punished. Although such restrictions tended to limit creativity, during the first decade after the Revolution literary experiment flourished, and such authors as Boris Pilnyak (1894–1935?) and Isaak Babel (1894–1941) won international reputations. A few older writers, the most important being Maxim Gorki (1868–1936), also continued to produce distinguished work. In art and music the same situation existed; at the beginning of the Soviet period such painters as Wassily Kandinsky (1866–1944) and Marc Chagall (1887–   ) were briefly given state positions.

Around 1928, however, the intellectual climate changed when the party, no longer content to prohibit alleged counterrevolutionary writings, began to demand that literature be "constructive." Some writers simply ceased to write, while others turned out propaganda about heroic workers and collective farmers in the guise of novels, poetry, and drama. In 1932 party control became even stricter when literary groups were banned in favor of a single All-Union Congress of Soviet Writers. In 1934 the first meeting of that organization, under party domination, approved the doctrine of "socialist realism," which restricted litera-

Workers at the Krasny Bogatyr factory in Moscow take time off to study during a Communist literacy campaign in 1932.

ture to simple-minded praise of the working class, as the sole guide to literary effort. Few writers were able to rise above the level of lifeless propaganda that became the approved norm. Even painting and music were subjected to political control; Kandinsky and Chagall had already left the U.S.S.R. in the early 1920s, and soon afterward the avant-garde art they championed was denounced as useless in a proletarian state. Dimitri Shostakovich (1906–   ), the leading Soviet composer, was almost constantly denounced by the authorities from 1927 until 1936, when he modified his style to fit current requirements of the regime. While other Europeans experimented with new kinds of art, Soviet artists glorified the workers' state in old-fashioned forms.

In education the immediate post-Revolutionary period was marked by the abolition of the old class-dominated school structure, the nationalization of private schools, and the adoption of a democratic system with a great deal of pupil self-government. In 1923 the government scrapped its experiment in educational democracy, increasing teachers' authority and strengthening technical education and political indoctrination at the expense of general culture. In 1928 this trend was carried further when universities were dissolved into special institutes and university instruction in history and philosophy was abolished. The new methods produced an increase in the number of graduates, but the quality of education suffered so severely that the policy was reversed in 1933. The universities were reopened, political indoctrination was reduced and students in technical schools were required to study general cultural subjects.

Soviet schools at all levels were concerned primarily with instruction in immediately useful subjects, but the great expansion in education during the 1920s and 1930s, no matter what its quality, tremendously increased the intellectual resources of the na-

Part of the Leningrad contingent at a Moscow sports exhibition.

tion. It also prepared a new generation that was thoroughly indoctrinated with communist values and loyal to the new regime.

Like other activities, sports in the Soviet Union were put under the control of special agencies and were strongly influenced by politics. Before the Revolution, sports had been limited to the upper classes, who liked to hunt, row, race horses, and sail. During the Civil War, however, the Communists introduced a physical culture movement to improve the condition of Red Army recruits. Workers' groups and military units took up exercise programs on their own initiative. The Communists encouraged such activities from the beginning, but in 1929 they established a government department to oversee the entire field of physical culture and sports. In 1931 the Young Communist League (*Komsomol*) instituted a series of physical fitness tests under the slogan, "Ready for Labor and Defense." Contestants who scored high in the tests won medals and other prizes. The state also encouraged competition among teams from various factories and, as the popularity of sports increased, star athletes were granted increasingly desirable privileges such as good jobs, time off from work, and priority in housing. The state

recognized the propaganda value of international competition, and Soviet athletes—all "amateurs" by Soviet definition—were given advantages open to those of few other nations.

Sports have long been recognized as excellent training for future military recruits, not only because they enhance physical fitness but because they develop team spirit. Totalitarian states, including Soviet Russia, Nazi Germany, and Fascist Italy, found sporting organizations particularly useful as avenues for political indoctrination and as a means of encouraging discipline and regimenting youth.

The Purges

The danger of arbitrary arrest has long been a normal factor in Russian life. Just as the tsars had their secret police, the Bolsheviks instituted their Cheka (later OGPU, and, still later, NKVD). Lenin had no compunction about disposing of his opponents, and from the start Soviet justice was dominated by political considerations. Under Stalin, however, the use of terror for political ends reached heights previously unknown.

As noted earlier, the first Five-Year Plan

Members of a unit of the Moscow Garrison listen to a broadcast of the indictment of several members of the "Right-Trotskyist Block" during the purge trials of the 1930s. Sovfoto's caption says they expressed "the strongest condemnation and denunciation" of the accused.

ushered in a purge of millions of peasants who resisted collectivization. In industry, show trials of "saboteurs" intimidated workers, managers, and engineers into meeting the production quotas they were assigned. In 1934, however, Stalin began a series of purges that spread through all of Soviet society.

On December 1, 1934, assassins killed Serge Kirov, head of the Leningrad Communist party and Stalin's best-known protégé. It has been argued, but not proved, that Stalin himself engineered the murder in order to eliminate a possible rival. In any case, the dictator moved savagely after Kirov's death: more than a hundred political prisoners in Leningrad were shot immediately, and thousands of citizens of the city were sent to Siberia. Hundreds of foreigners were summarily shot. In January 1935, Gregory Zinoviev and Leo Kamenev, Bolsheviks of long standing, friends of Lenin, and former members of the ruling Politburo, were

charged with murdering Kirov. They were supposed to have had the help of the German Gestapo and also of a secret group of supporters of Trotsky. Both Zinoviev and Kamenev were sent to prison. Moreover, because they were suspected of conspiracy, many of their former associates were arrested. Zealous officials accused all sorts of people of conspiring against the state, and more arrests followed. Peasants and workers, scientists, writers, and party officials fell under suspicion and were jailed. By 1938 at least six million people had been arrested. Many were imprisoned or sent to labor camps in remote areas. Probably close to 900,000 were shot. The world marvelled as three large show trials were held. Zinoviev and Kamevev were retried and executed. Fifty-two other eminent party officials also were tried; they all confessed crimes against the state.

Much has been written about the Great Purge, but no explanation of the confessions has been completely accepted. It is widely agreed, however, that both Trotskyite and German conspirators were indeed active in Russia. How many of the accused were actual plotters is not so clear. Obviously, however, Stalin made use of the opportunity to rid himself of every potential rival for power. Among those purged were all the former leaders of the "left" and "right" opposition groups that had fought him in the past, along with most of the men who, with Stalin, had been Lenin's lieutenants in the Revolution; so were 98 out of the 139 members and candidates (alternates) elected to the Central Committee in 1934. Most of the six million arrested probably were innocent. Many of the victims of the purge trials have since been exonerated by the post-Stalin government.

The effects of the purges lingered on. When the purges ended in 1939, the Soviet Union had a new ruling class. Practically all the nation's functionaries and high party officials were under forty years of age; most of them had become Communists in the late 1920s. The old revolutionaries, men who could see that the Soviet Union of the 1930s was not the utopia for which they had fought, were gone. The men who took their places owed their careers to the dictator. They knew no other society, and they had vested interests in perpetuating Stalin's rule and policies. They were not necessarily the best men to rule the Soviet Union, for their one common characteristic was the ability to avoid irritating Stalin. The army, in particular, had been badly hurt by the removal of most of its higher officers. Finally, the cause of world communism undoubtedly suffered greatly when worldwide attention was focused on Stalin's atrocities.

The Comintern

Large sections of the world's socialist parties voted to join the Third International in 1919 and 1920, but many socialist leaders refused to become Communists. In a few years these leaders had regained much of their old following, for Lenin and Trotsky, prime figures in the International as well as in the Soviet Union, ruthlessly weeded out foreign Communists who refused to accept Moscow's

directions. By 1925 the Comintern was little more than a collection of puppet parties controlled by the Russians. The Soviet leaders used their power over the foreign parties to promote Russian interests. Western Communists propagandized against their own nations' anti-Soviet policies and noisily demanded proletarian revolution. Governments everywhere bitterly resented the Russian tactics, and Communist activities so frightened the middle classes that rightwing movements gained significant new support.

For the Communists, however, the greatest enemies were neither the capitalists nor members of rightwing organizations: they kept their greatest hatred for the Socialists, whom they accused of betraying the working class. Wherever Communists gained a significant following they split union movements, thus weakening support for labor reform legislation, while their hatred of Socialists, heartily reciprocated, generally hindered working-class organizational efforts. The consequences of the Socialist-Communist split were most momentous in Germany.

Hitler's rise to power was facilitated by the inability of Communists and Socialists to work together against him. But the triumph of Nazism made Germany potentially dangerous to the Soviet Union. Stalin tried to come to an agreement with Hitler in 1934 but failed—Hitler preferred to keep a free hand. Faced with the need for allies, Stalin then took the U.S.S.R. into the League of Nations. In 1935 he signed a treaty of mutual assistance with France. At the same time he announced a dramatic change in Communist tactics: thenceforward Communists were to work for "a broad people's front with those laboring masses who are still far from Communism, but who nevertheless can join us in the struggle against fascism." He also began denying that Communists had ever intended to overthrow the governments of capitalist powers. Socialists and liberals greeted these pronouncements with skepticism, but the danger of fascism was so great that within a year they began to cooperate politically with Communist parties in "popular fronts." The Comintern's support for the Spanish Republicans tended to bolster belief in the sincerity of the new Communist line, even though the purges in the Soviet Union tended to revive old distrust. Communist efforts were effective, however. For a few years communism won remarkable acceptance everywhere outside the fascist nations. The illusions of the leftwing were shattered only in August 1939 when Stalin signed a pact with Hitler. Millions of Socialists, liberals, and idealistic Communists reverted to bitter enmity against the Soviet Union and its satellite parties. Diehard Communists accepted Stalin's argument that the pact was justified because it gained new security for the Soviet Union, vanguard of the working class. The Comintern had once more demonstrated its total subservience to Stalin's rule.

FASCIST ITALY

Demoralized by both the war and the seemingly meager fruits of their victory, Italians in 1920 were deeply divided. Most of them saw little hope of bettering their lot through their ineffective parliamentary government. Returning veterans found themselves unemployed; idealistic students developed contempt for self-serving politicians. Strikers in the industrial north occupied the factories only to find that when their employers refused to offer generous settlements they could do nothing more to enforce their demands. Many peasants rioted or forcibly seized fields belonging to absentee landlords, but these acts did nothing to raise the price of farm produce. The fact that by the end of 1920 labor and peasant unrest had peaked did not lessen disgruntlement among wage earners or the fear of revolution among the middle classes.

To many Italians the only bright spot in the immediate postwar period was the seizure of Fiume by the poet and war hero Gabriele d'Annunzio (1863–1938). Fiume (now Rijeka) was a largely Italian town on the northeastern coast of the Adriatic Sea. Because it was surrounded by a Croatian hinterland the Allied statesmen at the peace conference had been unable to determine the city's fate. D'Annunzio, at the head of a "legion" of veterans, forced the issue in September 1919 by marching in, replacing the temporary Allied occupation troops, and creating his own government. He ruled the city for fifteen months, until a settlement was finally made and regular Italian troops entered the city. During his heyday at Fiume millions shared D'Annunzio's sentiments: "Me ne frego," he declared, "I don't give a damn."

By December 1920, when D'Annunzio and his legions were forced out of Fiume, the Fascist movement was beginning to spread. Composed largely of squads of angry young men in black shirts—called squadristi—the movement adopted D'Annunzio's motto and his extreme nationalism. These squadristi shared a contempt for liberal democracy and for the elites that made up the Italian establishment. They demonstrated their anger and impatience by breaking up labor meetings, terrorizing rural villages, and, on many occasions, battling rival gangs. Their violence was the base on which Fascism was built, but they could never have won their subsequent victory if other segments of society had felt any strong attachment to established institutions. Their victory was made easier by the able leadership of Benito Mussolini (1883–1945).

Mussolini, the son of a blacksmith, had been a well-known journalist and revolutionary Socialist before 1914; he had split with the Socialists by supporting Italy's intervention in the war, but when peace came he considered himself still a revolutionary and a man of the left. When he helped to form the first fascio di combattimiento (fighting group) in March 1919 at Milan, its program was antiparliamentary, anticapitalist, and antibourgeois—indeed, he seemed to be a nationalist Lenin. Most of his early supporters were nationalistic syndicalists; they opposed socialism and communism because they opposed class war, but they also detested the profit-oriented capitalists who controlled Italy. Many syndicalists thought that Mussolini would improve the status of labor, and some thoughtful supporters of modernization believed that he would create a new cultural and technical elite. But his movement gained popularity primarily because of the activities of the squadristi against the forces of the left. The squadristi ousted forcibly both socialist and liberal local governments. Methods such as forcing castor oil down the throats of their opponents or beating them brutally gained them control of large areas. Many of Mussolini's syndicalist supporters opposed the attacks made on Catholic or Socialist trade union meetings, but they hoped to profit by the other victories of the *squadristi*. The government, a shaky coalition, refused to intervene against the Fascist gangs.

Belatedly, in August 1922, the leftwing unions called a general strike to protest Fascist lawlessness, only to have their own "law-and order" slogan turned against them by the Fascists. The *squadristi* took on the role of vigilantes, warning the government that if it did not act immediately, they would enforce the law and keep the public services operating themselves. They gained special popularity by keeping the railroads and streetcars going. The strike was thus a dismal failure. The following month Mussolini clinched his popularity with many members of the establishment by abandoning his former anticlericalism and pledging fealty to the monarchy. This frank appeal to the right prepared the conditions for Mussolini's seizure of power.

Neither the king nor the current government was prepared to stop Mussolini's bid for power. One army leader offered to crush the Fascists, who were threatening a "March on Rome," but his help was refused, for members of the cabinet hoped to join Mussolini's new government. Late in October 1922 Fascist *squadristi* began converging on the capital; they were preceded

FASCISM

Fascism can refer to an ideology or attitude, an organized movement, or a political regime that a fascist movement has succeeded in establishing. Unlike communism, fascism was never an international movement with a coherent ideology, yet wherever it appeared it was ultranationalistic and antiliberal. Whereas communism appealed especially to industrial workers victimized by capitalism, fascism tended to appeal to lower and lower-middle-class people who saw themselves as losers in modern, technological society: small farmers, businessmen, and craftsmen; white-collar employees who felt the loss of economic independence; and people in those professions that opposed changing social values, including some soldiers and teachers. Along with counter-revolutionary backers of fascism from the upper classes, these people feared a communist revolution in the name of the proletariat. Fascist ideology was therefore militantly anticommunist. After World War I, organized fascist movements in Italy, Germany, and other European countries used gangs of demobilized soldiers, hotheaded university students, and other "military desperadoes" to terrorize their opponents and intimidate the established authorities. Every fascist movement also had its charismatic leader.

Mussolini's Italy and Hitler's Germany were the best-known and most durable fascist regimes in Europe, though there have been others in Latin America and, with important modifications, in contemporary Africa. Peron's Argentina came closer than any other fascist regime to improving the material condition of the lower classes. Once in power, Mussolini and Hitler were more interested in staying in power than in aiding any particular class. These dictators mobilized entire societies around the ideas of nationalism, militarism, and service to the state. They destroyed democratic government and due process of law, eliminated all rival organizations, including trade unions, and silenced all criticism with police terror and arbitrary imprisonment. Whereas communist regimes tended to favor international peace and domestic modernization, fascist regimes were usually eager for war and opposed to such aspects of modernization as urbanization, consumerism, and the emancipation of women.

Mussolini leads a Fascist march shortly before he took power in 1922.

by four of Mussolini's lieutenants, who, on October 28, demanded that the premier, Luigi Facta, resign. After some obvious wavering, Facta at last decided to declare martial law, but King Victor Emmanuel III (1900–1946), bowing to a number of influences at court and in the army, refused to sign the declaration. On October 30 Mussolini came to Rome at the king's invitation to become premier in a new rightwing coalition government.

Mussolini at first attempted to govern in a constitutional manner, but his cabinet colleagues were not prepared for Fascist tactics, and his coalition in parliament could dissolve on a moment's notice. In 1923 Mussolini forced the passage of a new electoral law that assured Fascist domination in the parliament. In April 1924 the Fascists, with the aid of government officials and the cooperation of some of the traditional parties, won 65 percent of the seats in the Chamber of Deputies. Even that victory was not total, however, for some deputies still defied Musso-

lini. One of the dissenters the Socialist deputy Giacomo Matteoti, was murdered in June 1924. The public outcry that followed almost led Mussolini to make concessions to the left, but pressure from some *squadristi* leaders persuaded him instead to strengthen his hold on the government and the nation. Within two years Italy had become a full-fledged Fascist dictatorship.

In January 1925, Mussolini declared that he was assuming dictatorial powers. For a year Fascist gangs roamed Italy intimidating the remaining opposition. Strict press censorship was instituted. Leading opposition deputies were imprisoned. Mussolini gained the allegiance of the state bureaucracy and the army. Now firmly in power he tamed the *squadristi* by enrolling them in the Fascist Militia and by providing them with jobs in the growing party bureaucracy.

Fascist doctrine developed only after the party had come to power. Mussolini's original programs were essentially simple appeals to nationalism and attacks on socialism combined with vague promises to better the conditions of the poor. Nevertheless, a doctrine did develop out of Mussolini's opportunistic actions, and it was far from negligible. In a 1927 Charter of Labor the basic attitude of Fascism was clearly expressed: "The Italian Nation is an organism endowed with a purpose, a life and means of action transcending those of the individuals or groups of individuals composing it." The slogan of the *squadristi* had been D'Annunzio's "I don't give a damn," but the new regime replaced it with "Everything in the state, nothing against the state, nothing outside the state."

To believe in the nation and its leader was the first duty of the Fascist, for nationalism was the emotional basis of the entire movement. *Il Duce*—the leader—was the personification of the state; his wishes were law and had to be obeyed. This doctrine, a perversion of Rousseau's idea of the general will, was powerful because it mitigated the evil of alienation so common in modern societies. No longer was the individual responsible for generating his own values, dependent on weakened traditions of Christianity or liberal humanism for his feelings of personal worth. Instead, he could see himself as part of a living nation, his efforts, no matter how insignificant, contributing to the glory of a nation that was more than a mere aggregate of individuals. This feeling of belonging was stimulated by constant propaganda in the press and in schools, by youth groups, and by a huge system of organized leisure time activities (*Dopolavoro*).

The regime also set up a system of corporations, groups including representatives of labor, employers, and the government, who were supposed to work together for the good of the state. This ideal, gleaned from the works of nineteenth-century thinkers who, in turn, had developed it out of a rosy view of medieval society, has been extremely influential, even though Mussolini corrupted it by systematically favoring employer groups at the expense of the workers.

In the 1930s and 1940s fascism shared with communism an immense attraction as an alternative to liberal democracy. Its glorification of militaristic virtues caught the imagination of many youths who led humdrum lives. Fascism's ridicule of bourgeois values, particularly the ideals of security and a quiet life, also appealed to the young. Fascist propagandists spoke of the need for a ruling elite while at the same time encouraging equality of opportunity for the lower classes. Thus they recognized real problems inherent in modern society and offered solutions for them, many of which had obvious appeal. The costs were high, however, because fascist solutions depended on the destruction of the major asset of liberalism—personal liberty. The regime also depended too much on the leadership of a superman, which Mussolini was not and no man was likely to be. Finally, fascist devotion to violence and to nationalism led to war, and war destroyed the system.

Mussolini's early efforts to restore stability and order won a great deal of praise. He reestablished confidence in the lira, and his bureaucracy tended to run the state monopolies, such as the railroads, more efficiently than that of his predecessors. He also carried through a limited number of public works programs such as the draining of the Pontine marshes, which won him worldwide regard (although later students of ecology might find such projects actually harmful in the long run). Like most nationalists, Mussolini tended to insist on *autarky*, that is, national economic self-sufficiency. The "Battle of Wheat," which increased Italy's production of its staple food by more than 50 percent, was almost successful in making the nation independent of foreign suppliers, but it also raised the price of wheat considerably and cut down production of important export items such as fruit and olive oil. When world depression hit, Italy's economy was already in difficulty.

Perhaps the shrewdest and most popular action taken by the Fascist regime was its reconciliation of church and state. Since 1870, when the armies of the new Kingdom of Italy had occupied Rome, the popes had considered themselves "prisoners" in the Vatican grounds and had refused to deal directly with the state that had put them in this position. Although many early Fascists were anticlerical, Mussolini saw that an accommodation with the church would give his regime much needed support and respectability among Italian Catholics. Thus, in early 1929, his government and the papacy signed the Lateran Accords, which ended the separation between church and state and restored much of the Catholic Church's influence in public life, especially in education.

By 1931 the main trends of the Fascist regime were set. The parliament was merely a rubber stamp for dictatorial rule. Local government was made wholly subordinate to Rome. The Grand Council of Fascism, a group of high party officers, was the only place in which policy was discussed freely. Unfortunately for the regime, the Duce so feared possible rivals that he surrounded himself with mediocre lieutenants who often lacked the courage to give him realistic appraisals of public affairs. During the depression the state had to subsidize some of Italy's major banks and industries, but Mussolini reacted to the slump largely by using orthodox remedies—he cut expenses and allowed unemployment to rise.

Italy's economic difficulties were made worse by Mussolini's adventurous foreign policy. Despite its bitter disappointment in the peace treaties, Italy remained basically friendly to the United States, France, and Britain during the 1920s. But aside from confirming Italy's possession of the Dodecanese Islands and establishing an informal protectorate over Albania, Mussolini tried to assert Italian influence in Austria and Hungary, two small states with much to gain from a revision of the peace settlement. He was not friendly toward German "revisionism" at first, and when Hitler tried to take over Austria in July 1934, Mussolini stepped in to defend his neighbor, going so far as to send troops to the Brenner Pass.

It was in Africa, not Europe, that Mussolini sought a new empire. Italy had maintained control of Tripolitania, Cyrenaica, and part of Somaliland since before World War I, and it won small concessions in Africa from Britain after the war. Relations with France in Africa were strained until January 1935, when France, pleased by Mussolini's stand in support of Austria against Hitler, ceded to Italy certain areas bordering the Italian colonies. Meanwhile, Italy had long intended to win influence in, if not control over, the Empire of Ethiopia. Mussolini assumed that France had given him a free hand in Ethiopia.

In October 1935, he sent in Italian troops without declaring war. The League of Nations, of which Ethiopia was a member, reacted by imposing trade restrictions against Italy, but French and British efforts prevented the impositions of sanctions on oil—the only restriction that could have stopped the Italians. By May 1936, Ethiopia had been conquered. The League then voted to do away with the sanctions.

France and England had only half-heartedly opposed Italy's conquest, but sanctions had been applied, and Italians were incensed. When German and Italian troops joined in supporting the Nationalist rebellion in Spain (see p. 720), the two dictatorships were thrown together, and opinion in the democratic countries hardened against Mussolini. On November 6, 1937, Italy, Germany, and Japan signed the Anti-Comintern Pact, and on May 22, 1939, Italy and Germany signed the "Pact of Steel," a military alliance. The stage was set for Italy's participation in World War II.

NAZI GERMANY

The Weimar Republic

By mid-1920, after its inauspicious beginnings in defeat, famine, and revolutionary and counterrevolutionary pressures, the new German Republic seemed securely established. It had been preserved in early 1919 by the army and the Free Corps (see p. 659) partly because of fear of a communist takeover and partly because the Army High Command knew that Germany's victorious enemies would not permit the restoration of the kaiser. Germany lacked a democratic tradition, and the middle and lower classes, who might have been expected to support democracy as they did in England and France, seemed almost as much inclined toward authoritarianism as were the old imperial bureaucrats, the generals, and the aristocrats. The Weimar Republic might have become more acceptable to the German masses in time, but there was not enough time.

The new German government was obsessed with one overwhelming aim: the revision of the Versailles treaty. Each political

Italian troops guarding a supply train on one of the roads they built during their invasion of Ethiopia.

party sought to advance its own special interest, but all—even the Communists—agreed that the treaty was completely unjust. The first item on Germany's agenda should have been to pay the costs of the war, most of which had been financed by buyers of government bonds. But to raise taxes would have been considered unpatriotic, for some of the money collected would have gone to Germany's former enemies as reparations payments. Thus an unbalanced budget was a

certainty, and inflation inevitable. The total sum to be collected by the victors was set in May 1921 at $32 billion. The value of the mark immediately began to drop. For more than a year the government paid as little as possible, and in December 1922 it failed to deliver a specified quantity of timber to the Allied authorities. Despite British efforts to settle the ensuing dispute, French and Belgian troops, in accordance with treaty provisions, marched into the Ruhr industrial

The German mark was worth so little on August 12, 1923, that clerks had to load baskets of money onto carts to meet a factory payroll.

district on January 11, 1923, to enforce payment.

Capitulation would have been fatal to any German government. Passive resistance, sure to produce inflation, was the obvious alternative. The Chancellor, Wilhelm Cuno, decided to fight back. Railroad, telegraph, and postal employees refused to accept French orders or to handle their communications, and the government supported them. Officials ignored the invaders. The French retaliated by setting up their own administration, jailing company officials who refused to cooperate with them, and fiercely repressing riots. Unable to collect taxes from the nation's richest industrial area, the German government simply created millions of marks in new money. Then inflation took gigantic leaps. Within a month the mark had dropped to 20,000 to the dollar; by the end of September 1923, when a new government under the leadership of Gustav Stresemann decided to give in, it stood at more than 5,000,000 to the dollar. It was finally stabilized, in November, at 25 billion to the dollar.

Stresemann's successor established the new *Rentenmark,* backed by a national mortgage on all German land, at a rate of one to a trillion old marks. He thereby put the seal on the pauperization of much of the German middle class. Workers suffered from the inflation because their wages always rose more slowly than prices, but few of them owned bonds, mortgages, or large sums of cash, all of which became worthless. The very rich, the bankers and industrialists, owned real property and corporation stocks, which were immune to the hazards of inflation. Many of them took the opportunity to buy up valuable businesses bankrupted when their accounts receivable became valueless. The losers were the thrifty: the holders of government or industrial bonds, the widows and pensioners living on fixed incomes, and the small businessmen who sold on credit or made small loans.

From the standpoint of the modernizers the inflation was clear gain. The national debt was wiped out, and the conservative small bondholders, who tended to reject grandiose schemes in favor of modest but less risky business as usual, were also wiped out. The industrialists who believed in consolidation and expansion not only survived but increased their wealth and power. The inflation was partially responsible for Germany's remarkable ability to take advantage of technological progress during the next few years.

Politically, however, the inflation was a disaster, for it ruined the one group of people that should have been most anxious to preserve the republic. When a worse economic disaster came in the early 1930s they were quick to turn to Hitler for salvation.

With the restoration of a stable currency and the end of the French occupation in 1924, the German political scene became relatively quiet. The war hero, General Paul von Hindenburg (1847–1934), was elected President of the Republic. Under the guidance of Stresemann, an old-time nationalist, the government turned from defiance to cooperation with Germany's old enemies. The Locarno pacts, by which the great powers of Europe pledged to maintain Germany's western frontier, were signed in December 1925; in April 1926, Germany and Russia signed a neutrality agreement, and in September of that year Germany was admitted to the League of Nations. Meanwhile, Stresemann, who was as much dedicated to revision of the Versailles treaty as any other German, quietly assisted in the rebuilding of the German army, which concentrated on making the small number of soldiers allowed to Germany under the treaty into the nucleus of a modern army that could be expanded rapidly.

The Rise of Nazism

Germany's authoritarian tradition of government did not dictate the form the next authoritarian German government would take. Many of the unique qualities of Nazism clearly derive from the personal touch of Adolf Hitler. Hitler was the son of a minor Austrian customs official. His early life, spent in Vienna and Munich, was a series of failures: he thought himself an artist, but could hardly make a living. After fighting honorably in the German army in World War I,

he returned to Munich and, like many other veterans unable to adjust to civilian life, he became a political extremist. He joined a fringe group known as the German Workers' party, quickly becoming one of its leaders. In 1920 the party added the words National Socialist to its name, and a year later launched its brown shirted organization of storm troopers, the SA (*Sturmabteilung*). In November 1923, amid the chaos that followed Stresemann's decision to end resistance in the Ruhr, Hitler succeeded in taking over the leadership of an attempted rightwing coup being planned in Munich. The police easily suppressed this so-called Beer Hall Putsch, and Hitler was jailed for eight months. He wrote his blueprint for Germany's future, *Mein Kampf* (*My Struggle*), in prison. After his release he continued his political activities, perfecting his phenomenal oratorical ability and building the Nazi party into the strongest extremist group in Germany.

Hitler's next opportunity to seize power came after the onset of the depression. The German economy prospered from 1924 to 1928, but that prosperity was built on an unsound base. As we have seen, German banks received short-term loans from foreigners, mostly Americans, in turn making long-term loans to German entrepreneurs, who used this new capital to rebuild the factories worn out by the war. Late in 1928, however, American stocks became so attractive that foreign lenders began calling in their funds, leaving German banks severely overextended. Investment in new plant facilities began to decline, and by the summer of 1929 German stock prices had fallen 25 percent. When the American stock market crashed in October, American bankers called in the rest of their loans in an attempt to meet the needs of American investors. Its funds exhausted, the European banking system collapsed in May 1931. By the end of 1932 almost every German bank was dependent on government funds for survival, and unemployment increased from two to six million between 1929 and 1933.

The National Socialists, or Nazis, numbered 178,000 party members in 1929. Faced with growing economic difficulty and a government that seemed powerless to deal with the situation, thousands of Germans began to pay attention to Hitler, whose violent speeches exuded confidence. Nazi doctrine, like that of Mussolini's Fascists, was incoherent and vague, but full of promise for citizens in distress. Hitler blamed Germany's problems on the Treaty of Versailles, the Jews, and the Communists. If the race could be purified, alien blood and alien philosophy rooted out, Germany could reassert its power and break the bonds that held it prostrate. By January 1933, Nazi membership reached one million.

Meanwhile, in 1932 a new chancellor, Heinrich Brüning, ruled by decree, trying to stem the tide of disaster without inconveniencing the great landowners of the east or the industrialists of the Rhineland. In the elections of September 1930, Hitler's party won a sixth of the vote. In the Reichstag the 107 Nazi deputies, wearing Nazi uniforms, delivered the familiar tirades against Jews, Communists, and Versailles. In April 1932, Hitler ran for the presidency against the venerable incumbent, Hindenburg. He was defeated, 19 million to 13 million, but the Nazis obviously had become a power to be reckoned with. Even socialists supported Hindenburg, a conservative and a nationalist, rather than the Communist leader Ernst Thälmann, who got less than 4 million votes. Brüning tried to weaken Hitler by outlawing the paramilitary Nazi storm troopers (SA). At the same time he offended President Hindenburg by moving to cut down the heavy subsidies regularly given to the Junker landowners, and he was summarily ousted from his post. His successor, Franz von Papen, a diplomat close to both the High Command and the industrial magnates, rescinded the decree against the SA. In the July 1932 elections the Nazis more than doubled their representation in the Reichstag, winning more than 37 percent of the vote and becoming the largest single parliamentary party. Further maneuvers by the old ruling classes were futile; industrialists and military leaders finally turned to Hitler, who was named chancellor on January 30, 1933.

Like his immediate predecessors, Hitler came into office with the power to rule by decree. In March 1933, the Nazis in the Reichstag combined with the Nationalists to pass an Enabling Act that made him dicta-tor. Within a year the process he called *Gleichschaltung* (equalizing) had changed the face of the nation. All parties except the Nazis were outlawed; the civil service and the universities were purged of recalcitrants; the Gestapo (*Geheimestaatspolizei*) was created; the Hitler youth programs were underway; trade unions were replaced by a Nazi-controlled Labor Front; the federal system was scrapped and full centralization instituted; and concentration camps were opened for the detention of political prisoners. Persecution of Jews began, and in 1935 the infamous Nuremberg laws, prohibiting marriage between Jews and non-Jews, were issued. Jews were systematically purged from the universities and government service, and most private corporations followed suit. As yet the atrocities of the war period—mass murders—had not begun, but Jews were made to suffer every possible economic loss and personal indignity, either by official decree or by the unofficial actions of Storm Troopers or their sympathizers.

Nazism, like Fascism in Italy, had included in its early programs vaguely socialistic elements that had attracted a number of radicals to the party. Hitler was no economist, however, and, like Mussolini, he had no interest in economic equality. His political aim—the reconstruction of German power—guided his economic decisions. When he purged the SA in June 1934 in order to satisfy the jealous generals of the regular army, he also had the leading advocates of social revolution still within the party murdered. After that he rapidly took control of the economy, forcing industrialists to do his bidding but leaving them their profits. Rationing of consumer goods, control of raw materials, allocation of labor to specific jobs, strict licensing of all businesses—these methods, most of them used by the belligerents of World War I as emergency procedures, became the rule in Nazi Germany.

Bureaucracy and terror gave Hitler what he wanted: an economy strong enough to prevent social unrest and to support the development of a modern war machine. Germany made rapid strides toward self-sufficiency under this regime. Hitler encouraged costly production of *ersatz* goods: substitutes for rubber, oil, and cotton. In

A Jewish prisoner, forced to wear a yellow Star of David, in a Nazi concentration camp.

1935 and 1936 military spending was more than doubled over the previous two-year period. Industrial investment increased by 71 percent between 1936 and 1938; productivity per worker went up 14 percent. To prevent inflation the government stabilized price levels late in 1936 and maintained strict control over prices from then until 1945. Thanks to technological progress, and to government encouragement in its practical application, German industry flourished under the Nazis. New housing was built, and, in some ways, Germans were better off than citizens of France and Britain. Most important for the regime's popularity, mass unemployment disappeared by 1937.

Hitler's real aims, however, were profoundly uneconomic. From the start he was determined to force a revision of the Versailles treaty, by war if necessary, and he expected Germany to be prepared for war by 1938. Most Germans, if not eager for total war, were eager for the benefits a short war might bring—the defeat of 1918 would be avenged. Hitler's propaganda and his use of terror guaranteed the stability of his regime, but, at bottom, his greatest asset rested in his giving his countrymen what they wanted.

"Youth greets the workers and the Fuehrer" at a rally in Berlin's Lustgarten in Nazi Germany.

GERMAN AND ITALIAN CULTURE

Like most of their fellow citizens, many German intellectuals had nothing but contempt for the parliamentary government that owed its existence to Germany's defeat. The liberal tradition was weak in Germany, and the new doctrines of despair and irrationalism that developed around the turn of the century found quick acceptance. The disasters of war and its aftermath reinforced the trend. The novelist Ernst Jünger (1895–) won immense popularity by glorifying primitive instincts and calling for a leader who would make Germany a nation of warriors. Spengler's *Decline of the West,* which predicted and seemed to approve the coming of a new age of barbarians, captivated a wide public. Other intellectuals, like Berthold Brecht (1898–1956), became disgusted by the failure of the revolution to regenerate German society and turned to communism. Even world-famous humanitarian authors like Thomas Mann (1875–1955) and Hermann Hesse (1877–1962) lacked any deep faith in political liberalism. They seemed merely to find parliamentary democracy less objectionable than totalitarian regimes. Weimar Germany produced great art and architecture—particularly the Bauhaus school of Walter Gropius (1883–1969). But few of the artists were any wiser politically than the common man.

Once in power, Hitler quickly suppressed freedom of expression and tried, with remarkable effectiveness, to stamp out every form of opposition to his regime. Like the Russian Communists and the Italian Fascists, the Nazis established highly regimented youth organizations designed to develop unthinking supporters for the regime. Churchmen, teachers, and professors were forced to accept Nazi principles; those who did not were imprisoned or killed. Books written by Hitler's opponents were burned at huge outdoor rallies, and music written by Jews was eliminated from concert programs. German science was impoverished because Nazi censors forced scientists to ignore the discoveries of Jews, including the relativity theory of Albert Einstein (1879–1955), which had revolutionized the world of physics. Newspapers were censored, and authors unwilling to glorify Nazism were not permitted to publish their works. Thomas Mann and many others fled the country. The Nazi regime rapidly destroyed the intellectual life in Germany and replaced it with a chorus of praise for Hitler.

Mussolini's dictatorship, harsh as it was, never was as destructive as Hitler's. In 1924 and 1925 the government passed new, strict press laws to keep the nation's newspapers in line. Gangs of *squadristi* persecuted writers who dared attack the regime. But Benedetto Croce (1866–1952), Italy's greatest philosopher, went unpunished when he issued an "anti-Fascist manifesto" in 1925. Croce, who had not opposed Mussolini's takeover in 1922, soon became a symbol of liberalism, continually attacking the regime in his works and inspiring younger intellectuals to keep hopes for freedom alive. Many poets, novelists, and playwrights continued to publish their works, but those who wished to attack Fascism openly in popular writings were imprisoned or exiled to remote sections of the country.

JAPAN

Japan fought little and won a great deal in World War I. Its prizes from the peace conference—Germany's Asian possessions—were less significant than the industrial growth that took place in the war years. Its competitors in foreign trade not only had to abandon their markets to Japan, they also ordered munitions and manufactured goods in large quantities. Prices went up, but wages climbed still more, so that the standard of living improved noticeably.

But all except one of the *genro,* the heroes of the Restoration who had advised the emperor since the 1870s, were dead by 1922. Business had grown, and labor at last was beginning to organize. The political stability of the last years of Meiji no longer existed. In the Diet the parties had become powerful enough to exercise a veto on legislation, but they still lacked internal unity, coherent policies, or popular following. Moreover, many Japanese were less than satisfied with the fruits of their war effort, for, if Japan was powerful, it was still not considered an equal by the great powers. The diplomats at Versailles had refused to include a statement asserting racial equality in the League Covenant, the United States refused citizenship to Orientals, and, by the Naval Agreement of 1921, Japan was forced to agree to accept inferiority to the United States and Britain in sea power.

The years immediately after the war were marked by labor strife. Workers struck for higher wages at first, then, when recession hit in the early 1920s, they faced unemployment. Unions grew rapidly, despite tight restrictions. Farmers suffered even more, for the price of rice fell almost to prewar levels while manufactured goods remained expensive. Rural riots became common. Attempts by conservative members of the business and government oligarchy to maintain complete control over the parties amid these tensions finally failed when Takaaki Katō (1860–1926) succeeded in building a coalition that won the elections of 1924. Katō successfully passed a universal manhood suffrage act in May 1924. raising the number of voters from 3 to 13 million overnight. He also cut the military budget and thinned the ranks of the bureaucracy. Although Katō also demonstrated his basic conservatism by agreeing to a new and strict *Peace Preservation Act*, his death, in January 1926, marked the end of serious reform. The governing parties soon were again using bribery and strong-arm methods to assure their majorities. In 1928, the Peace Preservation Act was amended to make agitation against private property a capital crime, thereby ensuring the destruction of any truly socialist party.

Katō's whittling of the military budgets confirmed the army in its opposition to party control of the government. Nationalist extremists like the agitator Kita Ikki (1883–1937) began to find sympathizers among the junior officers. This trend was strengthened by reforms made in 1924 and 1925 under which recruitment of officers from the lower-middle class began, because such men, often from families in economic distress, tended to be not only opposed to big business but also highly suspicious of democratic trends that threatened to benefit workers or farm laborers at the expense of their own families and friends. By 1928 it was clear that the army had become a serious threat to parliamentary government in Japan.

The army was eager to promote a more warlike foreign policy. In 1928 officers of the Kwantung army, guarding the Japanese-owned railway in southern Manchuria, hoped to commit the government to war by murdering a Chinese warlord, but policies did not change. Then, in September 1931, the same army began the conquest of Manchuria without orders. Government attempts to halt the action failed, and the army quickly overran the area. The government, faced with a *fait accompli,* established a puppet regime, calling the new state Manchukuo. League of Nations investigators called on Japan to evacuate the area, whereupon Japan left the League.

The Japanese could hardly be expected to object to their army's new conquest. They had gained greatly from wars against China, Russia, and Germany, and had paid little for their gains. The army once more seemed to have proved that Japan could ignore the superior airs of the western nations. The masses had little respect for the politicians and no serious democratic tradition. The depression had just destroyed the market for silk, and rice prices were falling to new lows. Only conquest, it seemed to many, could alleviate the nation's woes. Nationalism ran wild.

Some extremist army officers, the *Kodo* faction, wanted to establish an open military dictatorship, but the more sophisticated *Tosei* faction preferred to control the nation by building influence within the constitutional government. The *Kodo* group attempted a *coup* in February 1936, but the *Tosei* officers, by putting down the rebellion, won added influence in the government. Thus, in July 1937, when field officers in Manchuria once again widened the struggle with China without government permission, civilian authorities in Tokyo were in no position to bring them to heel. The government remained nominally civilian, but by 1937 military leaders controlled its foreign policy.

Though Japan in the late 1930s was often called a fascist state, its society and government resembled the European fascist nations only superficially. The army forced the merger of all parties into a single *Imperial Rule Assistance League* in 1940, and it placed controls on the economy, but it did not destroy a responsible parliamentary government, as Mussolini and Hitler had. Japanese parties had always been fluid, made up of factions based on various regions; they differed little in their policies, since all of them were essentially conservative; none of them ever had a large following. No really liberal or socialist group had ever become significant. The government remained an oligarchy, as it had been for centuries. Army rule was not so different from Meiji rule—the army, too, wished to enrich the nation and make it strong, and the Japanese masses had almost always favored a militant foreign policy. In a sense, Japanese development was the prototype for the "guided democracy" common among the developing nations of the 1960s. That it ended in war and disaster was hardly surprising, for neither the masses nor their leaders realized that Japan, whatever its past triumphs or the quality of its

Japanese soldiers in a walled military headquarters near Mukden, Manchuria.

army, simply lacked the power to defeat the mobilized industrial powers of the West.

EASTERN EUROPE

All the new nations carved out of enemy territory by the victors at Versailles or liberated from tsar's empire began as democracies. Only two remained democracies by the time war broke out again. This transformation was natural, for the land reforms and social revolutions that had laid the groundwork for modernization in Western Europe had never taken place in the east. Moreover, despite the efforts of the statesmen of Versailles, in almost every country large unreconciled ethnic minorities not only complicated the problems of government but steadily demanded reunification with some foreign homeland.

A good deal of the arable land in this predominantly agricultural area was still owned by aristocrats, some of them of minority ethnic stock. Land redistribution was therefore vital if modern political forms were to endure, but political, ethnic, and religious struggles complicated every effort at economic reform. Major reforms were undertaken in the Baltic states, Czechoslovakia, Rumania, and Bulgaria; in Austria and Yugoslavia such reforms were unnecessary; in Hungary and Poland, where they were needed most, attempts at land redistribution were frustrated by conservatives.

In Hungary, Poland, Yugoslavia, and Lithuania democratic forms perished in the 1920s as conservative nationalists asserted their power when multiparty systems failed to produce governments acceptable to peasants used to authoritarian regimes. The depression, along with the pressures generated by German resurgence, destroyed democracy in Austria, Rumania, Greece, Latvia, and Lithuania. Only Czechoslovakia, the most advanced industrial nation among the newly created states, remained democratic despite serious minority problems.

In essence, the independence of Eastern Europe was abnormal; either Russian, German, or Austrian power had prevailed there for centuries, and only the temporary weakness of Russia and Germany made the existence of the weak eastern states possible. Overpopulated, rural, divided by insurmountable ethnic conflict, most of these states lacked the material wealth, the educated population, or the military security necessary for the maintenance of democratic governments. For most of them, modernization would begin only when they became either part of or satellites of the Soviet Union. Meanwhile, nearly everywhere in Eastern Europe fledgling democracies were replaced by old-style royal or military dictatorships, some of them wearing the outer trappings of fascism, but all of them devoted to maintenance of rule by the old privileged classes.

THE SPANISH CIVIL WAR

Spain, like some of the Eastern European nations, was still primarily a land of poor peasants and workers ruled by an oligarchy of great landowners, wealthy businessmen, prelates, and military officers. From 1923 to 1930 its government was a military dictatorship led by General Miguel Primo de Rivera (1870–1930) and supported by King Alfonso XIII (1902–1931). Republicans won the elections following Primo de Rivera's fall from power, and the king was forced into exile. The government of the new Spanish Republic pursued an ambitious reform policy that included land redistribution and the separation of church and state, but rightwing parties won the elections of 1933 and put a stop to the reforms. In 1936 a Popular Front similar to that formed in France returned moderate democrats to power, but fear of revolution prompted the oligarchy to support an army rebellion by forces calling themselves Nationalists. At first the civil war was purely a Spanish affair, but Germany and Italy quickly began supplying arms and men to General Francisco Franco (1892–   ), the Nationalist leader. England, France, and the United States, eager to remain neutral

and frightened by the presence of Communists in the Madrid government, refused to aid the Republicans. The Soviet Union gave aid, but Stalin helped the Republicans just enough to prolong the war, not enough to give them victory.

Meanwhile, the Communists, Socialists, Anarchists, and liberal democrats fought among themselves. Franco took Madrid in March 1939 after a long and bloody struggle. His government was theoretically based on the Falangist party, a fascist organization, but in reality Spain had returned to the kind of military dictatorship it had seen before. Church, landed aristocracy, and upper class ruled through an army that saw no need for change.

In every case, the totalitarian states were those in which old elites long refused to allow any serious move toward political democracy. Their middle classes were weak and unable to force the ruling classes to share their power. Thus the old regimes rested on narrow bases. They accepted economic modernization as a necessary evil to assure their countries' military security. But with industrialization, widespread literacy, better communications, and all the other aspects of modernity, came mass agitation for political power.

In Russia, because the old regime collapsed, leaders who claimed to speak for the masses and to be able to modernize quickly were able to seize control. In Italy and Germany the old elites, having learned the lesson of Russia, chose to share their power with demagogues who knew how to play on the perennial insecurity of the lower middle classes. In Japan, the army took power because it was able to represent the same stratum of society. In each of these cases a numerous, relatively satisfied, and secure middle class was conspicuously lacking. In Russia, Italy, and Japan it had never developed; in Germany it was seriously demoralized by inflation and the depression that followed.

Finally, special circumstances played a part in each case. In Russia, the war killed off the old regime. In Italy, fear of social revolution, combined with economic uncertainty, made Mussolini's triumph easy. In Germany, the universal hatred of the Treaty of Versailles gave Hitler an enormous advantage. In Japan, past victories gave the army unrivalled prestige. Other, perhaps equally significant, factors also were at work in every case.

Once installed, the totalitarian governments had to make good their promises. Fascism, Nazism, and Japanese militarism were all based squarely on nationalist pride. Ultimately, they had to prove themselves in war. Until war came, they could boast that they had certainly performed as well as the capitalist democracies. They claimed to be more efficient, more considerate of the needs of their citizens, more responsive to the basic drives of human nature. Surely the democracies had produced a sorry record in the 1920s and 1930s. It remained to see whether they could rise to meet the challenge of war.

SUGGESTED READINGS

Nettl, John Peter, *The Soviet Achievement*. New York: Harcourt Brace and World, 1967. Paperback.
An excellent survey: balanced and sympathetic.

Conquest, Robert, *The Great Terror*. New York: Macmillan, 1968.
A devastating but apparently accurate account.

Warth, Robert D., *Stalin*. New York: Twayne, 1969.
A brief, up-to-date biography.

Meyer, Arthur G., *Communism*. New York: Random House, 1960. Paperback.
Short but good.

Bullock, Alan, *Hitler: A Study in Tyranny*. Revised edition. New York: Harper and Row, 1964. Paperback.
One of the great biographies of the twentieth century.

Bracher, Karl Dietrich, *The German Dictatorship*. New York: Frederick A. Praeger, 1970. Paperback.
The most authoritative study in any language.

Allen, William Sheridan, *The Nazi Seizure of Power: The Experience of a Single German Town*. Chicago: Quadrangle Books, 1967. Paperback.
A remarkable study of the rise of the Nazis at the grass roots.

Weiss, John, *The Fascist Tradition*. New York: Harper and Row, 1967. Paperback.
A good comparative study.

Tannenbaum, Edward R., *The Fascist Experience: Italian Society and Culture, 1922–1945*. New York: Basic Books, 1972.
A survey of life in Mussolini's Italy.

Jackson, Gabriel, *The Spanish Republic and Civil War*. Princeton, N.J.: Princeton University Press, 1965. Paperback.
The best analysis of Spain's troubled history in the 1930s.

Reischauer, Edwin O. *Japan, Past and Present*. New York: Knopf, 1953. Paperback.
Authoritative and well written.

CHAPTER **24**

Revolutionary Nationalism in Asia and the Middle East, 1919–1939

Throughout Asia the interwar years (1919–1939) were a time of intense political turmoil and upheaval. The motive force behind much of the unrest was a revolutionary form of nationalism, directed primarily against the entrenched European colonial powers but also against the new imperial pretensions of the Japanese and, especially in Southeast Asia, against dominant racial minorities within. The movements discussed in this chapter achieved varying degrees of success. They were led by a bewildering array of men: saints and terrorists, priests and secularists, kings and constitutionalists. Together they represented a resurgent Asia claiming ever more forcefully the right to determine its own destiny.

THE ARAB WORLD AND AFRICA DURING WORLD WAR I

Although the major nationalist movements among Africans and Arabs came after World War II and will be discussed in Chapter 29,

their origins in World War I will be noted here.

There was fighting in Africa and the Middle East as the warring nations sought to alter the colonial balance of power and deprive their enemies of strategic and economic assets there. Turkey attacked the Suez Canal, and the Allies battled throughout the Arab lands. Tropical Africa might have been insulated from World War I had it not been for the territorial ambitions and jealousies of the European powers. By 1918 South African troops had overrun German Southwest Africa, and the British had invaded the German colonial territories of East and West Africa. In the aftermath of the war the British, French, Belgians, and South Africans shared in the partition of the German African Empire, placing their new colonies under a mandate system of the League of Nations.

The war made many disruptive demands upon Africa and the Middle East. All available manpower, including that of the non-Western world, was exploited; thus military conscription ran at high levels in most colonies. The absence of able-bodied adult males from cities and rural areas of the colonies resulted in economic burdens being thrust upon women, children, and older men. African and Arab soldiers and auxiliaries were transported long distances to fight and die for an empire for which they felt only faint loyalty. For the first time Africans were armed by white men and instructed to kill white men. Many Africans and Arabs were also transported out of the continent to the front lines in Europe. This experience widened their horizons, deflated any images they had about European civilization, and gave them modern military training.

World War I caused economic dislocation in Africa as it did throughout the world. Because Europe consumed virtually everything it produced or imported in the war efforts, the traditional export trade with Africa and the Middle East was severely curtailed. The industrial products that these countries had imported from Europe were no longer available. In areas like Egypt, where food products had to be imported to feed a growing population, the war brought a steep rise in the price of essential foodstuffs and a general inflation that tended to benefit the well-to-do classes and to hurt the poor. Economic dislocation, like military recruitment, created bitterness against colonial authorities and fanned the flames of nationalism.

In their quest for military victory the Western powers employed their ideologies as well as their military and economic arsenals. Ideological pronouncements were used to justify the war to the citizenry and to weaken the determination of the opponents. Although ideological appeals were meant primarily for Western consumption, they had far-reaching repercussions throughout the non-Western world. President Woodrow Wilson was the most effective publicist of the Allied war effort in World War I. Through his Fourteen Points, in which he emphasized the goal of national self-determination, he hoped to win the subject nationalities of East Central Europe to the Allied side. But his appeals could not be shielded from the Allied countries' own colonial territories, where nationalist leaders began to demand the implementation of these principles. At the end of World War I, nationalists in Egypt demanded inclusion of an Egyptian nationalist delegation at the Paris Peace Conference. Nationalist sentiments also were felt in Tunisia and Syria, and in Syria these feelings led to a military confrontation between French troops and Syrian nationalists. Although African nationalism was not as well developed as Arab nationalism, in 1919 a Pan-African Congress was assembled in Paris, and a group of West African intellectuals created a British West African Congress. Neither group demanded the full autonomy of their homelands, but they were insisting, with the use of Wilsonian rhetoric, that African leaders be consulted on the disposition of the former German colonies.

REVOLUTIONARY NATIONALISM: INDIA

World War I marked a major turning point in the growth of the Indian nationalist movement. Nationalism, confined to a moderate English-educated elite group with a small radical terrorist wing before the war, became a mass movement after 1919 with both traditional and modern characteristics under the charismatic leadership of Mohandas K. Gandhi. The distinctive character of revolutionary nationalism in India was almost exclusively the work of this towering Mahatma, or "great soul," as he soon came to be known.

The hopes and disillusionments of the war years set the stage for Gandhi's rise to power. When war broke out in 1914, the Indian people, considering Britain's plight their own, rallied enthusiastically to the Allied cause. Over a million men joined the Indian army, and many distinguished themselves fighting in the Middle East. As the war dragged on, however, with victory no closer than at the start, a sense of uneasiness and a heightened sense of expectancy settled over the country. The Irish revolt of 1916, the collapse of tsarist Russia, and, above all, the proclamation of President Wilson's Fourteen Points, with its inclusion of the right of self-determination, undermined the old certainties and quickened the pace of Indian political life. In late 1916 the old radical Tilak, at last released from his long confinement, easily captured the Indian National Congress and in company with the colorful and eccentric English free-thinker, Mrs. Annie Besant, campaigned throughout the country on behalf of Home Rule.

Constitutional Reform

At this point the British government finally stirred. In August 1917, Edwin Montagu, the Indian Secretary, declared that the goal of India's constitutional advance would be responsible self-government within the British Empire on the model of Canada and Australia. This declaration was a radical departure in British imperial policy, for it finally laid to rest the notion that Britain intended to rule India forever. It was followed in 1919 by a far-reaching constitutional revision known from the names of its authors as the Montagu-Chelmsford Reforms. The underlying principle of the new constitution was realization of self-government by stages; its central feature was the novel concept of dyarchy. Under this dual rule the central government of India remained a British bastion, but substantial authority was given to the provinces, where it was shared by appointed officials and ministers responsible to the provincial legislatures. Responsibility for law and order and revenue was retained in British hands, but education, agriculture, and other so-called "nation-building" departments were transferred to Indian ministers. The new constitution also provided for an increase in the number of voters and large majorities of elected members in all the legislatures, central as well as provincial. The British Government committed itself to further reform at regular intervals.

Despite the great advance toward responsible government which it embodied, the Montagu-Chelmsford constitution was not universally hailed in India. Indeed, before it could even be inaugurated it was repudiated by the Congress party. Several factors combined to drive the government and the Congress apart at this critical juncture. For one, the new scheme did not meet the demand for Home Rule; in fact, it secured continued British supremacy. More important, however, was an unfortunate combination during 1919 of inflated expectations, fanned by the Paris Peace Conference, with the bitter realities of postwar economic dislocation. Economic problems were heightened by a panicky resort to repression on the part of the British government of India, never wholly reconciled to the reforms and fearful of an outbreak of violent anarchism in the unsettled postwar atmosphere.

British Repression

The first repressive measure of the Indian government, the Rowlatt Act, extended wartime powers of internment and trial without jury for political offenders. This new curtailment of civil liberties provoked at once an angry outcry against the government and a determination to resist. The resulting agitation propelled Gandhi, hitherto known only as the leader of a successful passive resistance campaign among the Indians of South Africa, to the leadership of the Indian National Congress and set the movement on the new path of *satyagraha,* or nonviolent civil disobedience. To protest the Rowlatt Act, Gandhi proposed *hartals,* or the closing of all businesses, in place of the usual public meetings. In the excited state of public opinion the *hartals* erupted in several places into violent rioting, which, in turn, provoked the government to severe retaliation. On April 13, 1919, General Dyer broke up a prohibited meeting in the Punjab city of Amritsar by firing on a crowd confined in a closed space called Jallianwalla Bagh; when the shooting ended, 379 were dead and over 1200 wounded. The brutal ferocity of this act, which the Punjab governor defended as necessary to head off a full-scale rebellion in the province, horrified the Indian public and added racial bitterness to the flames of discontent. The government of India's investigative body, the Hunter Committee, repudiated Dyer's action but its criticisms of the civil authorities in the Punjab were mild. On his return to England, Dyer himself won a favorable vote in the House of Lords and a heavily subscribed public fund in appreciation of his services.

Gandhi and the Noncooperation Movement

This resurgence of unrepentant imperialism in the wake of the "Amritsar massacre"

Gandhi as a prosperous young lawyer in South Africa (1895). At that time he had not abandoned Western dress or the goal of worldly success.

ended whatever hopes remained of Congress's participation in the new constitution. Gandhi, who considered Dyer's reception in England the last straw, now proclaimed that cooperation with the "satanic" British government was sinful and wicked. In August 1920, he launched a general non-cooperation movement. Its adherents agreed to resign from government office, withdraw from government schools and colleges, and boycott the forthcoming elections to the councils. Once their initial hesitations were overcome, the educated, particularly the youth, were rapidly caught up in the movement, which offered the satisfaction of dramatic and visible action without the danger and futility of terrorism. Many prominent moderates remained aloof, but their eminence was far greater than their numbers. Organized as the Liberal party, outside the Congress, they worked the machinery of the dyarchy constitution and often acted as mediators between the Congress and the British. The defection of the moderates, however, was more than compensated for by the adhesion of the Muslims, angered over the British treatment of the Turkish caliph, whom they regarded as the spiritual leader of all

Islam, and by the support of the rural peasantry, now drawn into the nationalist movement in most areas for the first time. The wider base of support had its drawbacks as well as its advantages, for the peasants were not so well-disciplined and hence their enthusiasm could easily boil over into violence. Indeed, the burning alive of 22 policemen by an enraged peasant mob in a remote area in February 1922 induced Gandhi to call a halt to the entire civil disobedience campaign. Only 8 years later, after further training in Gandhian techniques of self-discipline, were the masses again unleashed in a movement of civil disobedience.

At the heart of Gandhi's appeal and largely responsible for his striking success was a unique combination of ethical idealism and shrewd political sense. Although revered almost as a god incarnate, Gandhi was in no way a *swami* or *faqir* of the traditional Hindu sort. Born in a merchant caste on the remote west coast of Gujerat, Gandhi grew up amid the ascetic pacifism of the trading community of that area, heavily influenced by Jainism, the Indian sect most imbued with the ideals of nonviolence. From there he went to London where he qualified as a barrister-at-law. After a brief but thoroughgoing fling with Anglicization, during which he took up dancing and the violin, he drifted back to the ascetic, self-denying ethic of his youth. His English experience left its mark, however, in a familiarity with the Christian pacifism of Ruskin and Tolstoy. During his lengthy stay in South Africa, from 1893 to 1914, his ideas slowly matured and found initial political expression in fighting for the rights of the Indian community there.

Unlike most nationalist leaders, Gandhi insisted that means were as important as ends, that only ethically pure acts could bring about desirable results. For this reason he abhorred violence as an expression of unreason and hate. Instead, the opponent must be won over by the force of truth, with any suffering imposed not on him but upon oneself in the form of fasts and penance. Nor did Gandhi believe that political questions could be separated from moral or social ones. In his view, India would be truly free only when the inequities of the caste system and the exploitation of wage labor, as well as

foreign domination, had been abolished. He saw the India of the future as a society of self-reliant villages, based on hand spinning and peasant agriculture, and awarding an honored place to the untouchables, whom he called *harijans* or children of God.

Gandhi's political strength lay in his ability to capitalize upon the Hindu traditionalism of the peasant without at the same time antagonizing the English-educated elite. Although they cared little for asceticism and less for hand spinning, the educated Indians supported Gandhi because he brought them a following they could never have won by themselves. Moreover, he was a genius as a political tactician. Gandhi had a shrewd sense of timing and could dramatize issues with an unerring instinct. When others in 1930 walked out of the Assembly as a gesture of defiance, Gandhi walked 60 miles to the sea to make illicit salt. In all that he did Gandhi strove to throw the onus of guilt onto the British and to establish the moral supremacy of the Indian *satygrahi*. In this way he not only salved the wounded pride of a people who had long been suppressed by the West, but he also worked upon the British at the weakest point in their imperial armor, their liberal conscience.

Despite Gandhi's leadership the history of the independence struggle during the 1920s and 1930s was not one of steady progress. Instead, the struggle exhibited a markedly cyclical pattern. The cycle would begin with provocation by the British, such as the Rowlatt Act or the appointment in 1927 of the all-white Simon Commission to study constitutional reform. The resulting sense of grievance enabled Gandhi to unite the Congress behind him in a concerted program of mass action. There would then follow a period of intense political activity throughout India marked by processions, picketing, *hartals,* and occasional riots. After two or three years, however, the zeal and enthusiasm of the Congress workers would flag, mass arrests would deprive the movement of its leadership, and slowly the rank and file, demoralized, would drift back to their normal occupations. A prolonged period of quiescence would then ensue, during which Gandhi retired to spin and work among the untouchables while the Congress reverted to the

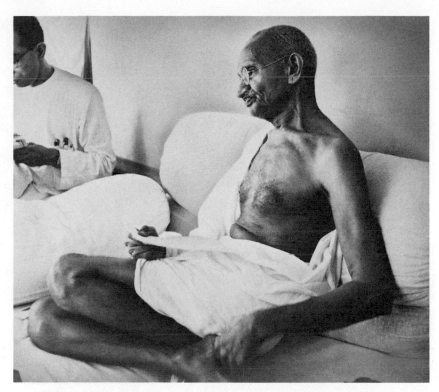

Gandhi in a pose characteristic of his later years as leader of the nationalist movement. An abstemious vegetarian, he wore only homespun (Khadi) cloth and commanded solely by the force of his personality.

status of a normal political party, contesting elections and at times even holding ministerial office. Gandhi, waiting patiently in the wings, never tempted by office or honors, would return only when the times were ripe for another mass movement.

The British reaction to the Congress movement during these years was one of watchful waiting combined with occasional severe repression. As long as Gandhi remained committed to nonviolence, however, the repression after 1919 was never brutal, for the British were themselves committed to ultimate Indian independence and had no wish to antagonize the moderates, both inside Congress and out, upon whom they depended for the working of the reformed constitution. Indeed, even during the heat of combat an aura of reasonableness and mutual courtesy marked the relations of the British and the Congress. Imprisoned nationalist leaders, for instance, were provided with superior jail accommodations, including books, visitors, and special food. The height of the spirit of cordiality came with the Gandhi-Irwin Pact of March 1931, concluded in the midst of the second noncooperation movement. The agreement was soon to collapse, for the positions of the British and the Congress were too far apart to make possible a lasting accommodation. Nevertheless, the discussions and the sympathy that the viceroy showed toward nationalist aspirations convinced Gandhi that the British would not go back on their promise of eventual self-government. Henceforth controversy centered solely on the rate of progress.

The Constitution of 1935

Finally, in 1935, a wholly new Indian constitution emerged out of the discussions begun by the Simon Commission in 1928 and continued in a series of Round Table Confer-

A scene at the Second Round Table Conference in London (1931), where British officials met Indian representatives, including Gandhi (right center), the sole spokesman of the Congress, to hammer out India's future constitution.

ences held in London between 1930 and 1932 without the participation of the Congress except on one occasion. The 1935 Act was in many ways a blueprint for independence, and opposed for just that reason by Winston Churchill and a few other diehard imperialists. It introduced the principle of federalism into Indian government, made provision for the incorporation of the princes into the system, replaced dyarchy with complete ministerial autonomy at the provincial level, and vastly extended the electorate to include 30 million voters, or one-sixth of the total adult population. The federal principle, which conceded larger powers to the provinces, was the heart of the scheme and the device by which the dissident princes and Muslims were to be reconciled to ultimate Congress rule. Unfortunately the princes were too shortsighted and the Muslims too fearful of Hindu domination to cooperate in the working of the new constitution. As a result, large parts of it never came into effect, and in the provinces, where the Congress swept the polls in 7 of the 11 states, the refusal of its victorious leaders to form coalition governments with the Muslim League further aroused Muslim distrust and led directly to the "two nation" Pakistan Resolution of 1940.

New Blocs within the Congress

By the late 1930s, as the prospect of power drew closer, the Congress found itself increasingly divided not only over questions of political tactics, but over the future shape of the Indian social order. On one side stood the industrialists and "old guard" conservatives such as Rajendra Prasad, who had contributed heavily to the Congress treasury and who sought freedom without disturbance of the existing order. Against them were set a group of young radicals led by Jawaharlal Nehru, a sensitive, Westernized intellectual imbued with ideals of reform socialism and anxious to do away with landlords, princes, and capitalists alike. The depression of the 1930s, in which agricultural prices fell further and more rapidly than rents, added the fuel of intense peasant discontent to Nehru's intellectual critique of the old order. Gandhi, the moral idealist in the middle, recoiled from class conflict and appealed for harmony and trust.

Other influential critics were to be found both farther to the right and to the left. The poet Rabindranath Tagore (1861–1941) rejected Gandhi's program as too narrowly nationalist and too backward looking. A cosmopolitan intellectual, he called for a universal culture compounded of Western material and political values with Eastern spiritualism. His stress on the spiritual primacy of Asia, and especially of India, did much to relieve the educated Hindu's sense of psychological inferiority. But his ideas were ignored by the bulk of the Congress and had very little influence.

At the other end of the political spectrum and equally restive under Gandhi's tutelage were the radical activists who were willing to risk violence to achieve a wholesale transformation of Indian society. Most prominent among this group were the sometime Communist M. N. Roy and the romantic Subhas Chandra Bose, whose bid to take over the Congress was turned aside by Gandhi in 1939. Embittered, he fled the country and organized the Indian National Army, which collaborated with the Japanese in Burma and Malaya during the Second World War.

War and the Coming of Independence

The coming of that war transformed the Indian political scene once again. At first uninvolved and then moved by sympathy for Britain's beleaguered position, the Congress nevertheless refused to offer the unqualified assistance it had given in 1914. Tested and self-confident, it demanded a substantial transfer of power as the price for cooperation in the war effort. The British, although willing to associate Indians with the government and

Rabindranath Tagore (1861–1941), Nobel prize winner in poetry and founder of the rural university of Shantiniketan, did much to revive India's traditional arts and crafts.

to promise independence after the war, insisted that effective power must remain in British hands as long as the fighting continued. Several unsuccessful attempts were made to bridge the gap, most notably Sir Stafford Cripps's mission of March 1942, on the heels of the Japanese invasion of Burma. Churchill proclaimed that he had not become prime minister (in May 1940) to preside over the liquidation of the British Empire, while Gandhi disdained Cripps's offer as a postdated check on a failing bank. The result was a new civil disobedience campaign, the "Quit India" movement, led by Gandhi and supported only with extreme reluctance by those like Nehru who sympathized with the Allied war effort. The movement erupted into serious violence in the countryside, including some sabotage, and ended only with the jailing of 60,000 people.

The Congress leaders, locked up even before the outbreak of violence, remained in prison for three years, until June 1945. In the political vacuum thus created the Muslim

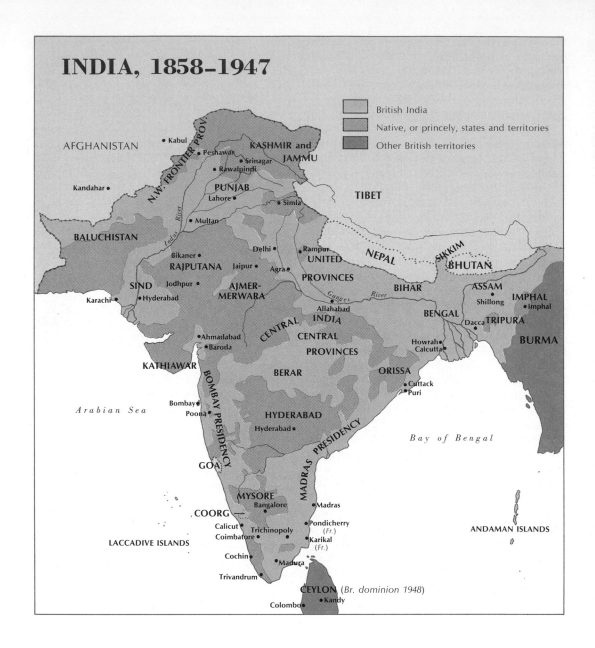

INDIA, 1858–1947

British India

Native, or princely, states and territories

Other British territories

AFGHANISTAN

• Kabul

N.W. FRONTIER PROV.

KASHMIR and JAMMU

Peshawar•
• Srinagar
• Rawalpindi

Kandahar•

PUNJAB
Lahore•
• Simla

TIBET

Multan•

BALUCHISTAN

Indus River

Bikaner•
RAJPUTANA   Jaipur•
Jodhpur•

Delhi•
Agra•

• Rampur
UNITED
PROVINCES

NEPAL

SIKKIM

BHUTAN

SIND

Karachi•
• Hyderabad

AJMER-
MERWARA

Ganges River

Allahabad•

BIHAR

ASSAM
• Shillong

BENGAL

IMPHAL
•Imphal

Ahmadabad•
•Baroda

CENTRAL INDIA

CENTRAL
PROVINCES

Dacca•

TRIPURA

Howrah•
Calcutta•

BURMA

KATHIAWAR

BERAR

ORISSA
• Cuttack
• Puri

Arabian Sea

BOMBAY PRESIDENCY

Bombay•
Poona•

HYDERABAD

Hyderabad•

MADRAS PRESIDENCY

Bay of Bengal

GOA

MYSORE
Bangalore•

• Madras

COORG

Calicut•
Coimbatore•

Trichinopoly•

Pondicherry
(Fr.)
Karikal
(Fr.)

ANDAMAN ISLANDS

LACCADIVE ISLANDS

Cochin•

•Madura

Trivandrum•

CEYLON (Br. dominion 1948)

Colombo• •Kandy

League under Muhammed Ali Jinnah had a free hand to campaign among the Muslims on behalf of the demand, enunciated in 1940, for the creation of a separate state of Pakistan. The extent of his success can be seen in the League's victories, fought on the sole issue of Pakistan, in all but one of the Muslim majority provinces during the elections, held in the winter of 1945, to the long-promised Constituent Assembly. The Congress, still committed to a united India,

swept to victory everywhere else. In April 1946, a top-level cabinet mission, sent out by the recently installed British Labour government, made a final attempt to resolve the constitutional tangle. They put forward an intricate scheme, based on a weak federation of provinces, which would preserve the unity of India while conceding the essence of the Pakistan demand. But, since neither the Congress nor the League was willing to compromise, the scheme failed. In August the

Muslims turned to direct action and thus touched off a slaughter that rapidly grew in intensity and terror and badly disfigured the coming of independence. Once the killing had started, the British, already fast losing interest in the burdens of empire, decided to leave India as soon as arrangements could be made for the transfer of power. The last British viceroy, the dashing war hero Lord Mountbatten, convinced the Congress, now led by Nehru, that partition was the only alternative to chaos and civil war. Independence then came quickly. On August 15, 1947, the two new dominions of India and Pakistan entered the community of nations.

REVOLUTIONARY NATIONALISM IN THE MUSLIM WORLD

Revolutionary nationalism grew rapidly in the Muslim world during the interwar years in several areas, most notably Turkey; it also began to rise in Iran, Indonesia, and among the Muslims of India. However, in much of the Middle East, the 1920s and 1930s were years of demoralization and decay, particularly in the Arab lands. This was so because the collapse of the Ottoman Empire in World War I and growing Western interest in the oil deposits of the region led to the imposition of British and French imperial control on the entire region from the Nile to the Euphrates through the League of Nations Mandate system. Only outside the Arab heartland was revolutionary nationalism able to gain a foothold, and it is with these areas that we now concern ourselves.

Turkey

By its support of the Central Powers during World War I, the Ottoman Empire, long the "sick man" of Europe, brought about its own final destruction. Beset by Allied armies and Arab revolts, by 1919 the empire had lost all its Arab provinces and was subjected to Allied occupation of the Turkish coast and the capital, Istanbul. The degradation involved was soon heightened by atrocities committed by the occupation army of the hated Greeks at Izmir (Smyrna) on the eastern Aegean coast. This final blow to Turkish pride provoked massive demonstrations in Istanbul and led to the mutiny of a major portion of the Ottoman army under Mustafa Kemal Pasha, the most successful Turkish general in the war. Retiring to the dry and thinly populated Anatolian Plateau, Kemal convened a National Assembly at Ankara in April 1920, and called for national resistance to the humiliation of foreign occupation and Ottoman subservience. From his new capital Kemal skillfully exploited dissensions among the occupying powers. After two years of hard fighting he pushed the European armies out of Anatolia and won agreement to the establishment of an independent Turkish state.

Renouncing all foreign ambitions and the imperial Pan-Islamic ideology of the Ottomans, Kemal turned to the creation of a modern secular state within ethnic Turkey. Since he regarded the Ottoman sultan as an anachronism, Kemal induced the National Assembly in October 1923 to proclaim a Turkish Republic and to vest itself with the powers of a parliament. At the same time elections were held in which Kemal's followers, called the Republican People's party, were victorious. Kemal himself was elected president and ruled as a virtual dictator in a one-party state for fifteen years until his death in 1938. But his rule was benevolent and almost completely free of the demagogy and repression that marked the contemporary dictatorships of Europe.

Kemal's political reforms were immediately followed by an attack on Islamic orthodoxy. A determined modernizer, Kemal believed that Islam's hold upon society retarded development and kept Turkey in a condition of oriental backwardness. He first attacked the caliphate, the institutional embodiment of Islamic theocracy, which awarded the Ottoman ruler spiritual preeminence over Muslims everywhere. In the face of strong conservative opposition the caliphate was abolished and all members of the Ottoman royal family sent into exile in 1924. Kemal next undermined the authority of the Muslim religious leaders (ulama) by closing the religious schools and the courts that administered sacred (shariat) law. They were replaced by a secular system of national education and by new courts administering codes of law based upon Western jurispru-

Mustafa Kemal, founder President of the Turkish Republic. He is known by the title Atatürk, or "father-Turk."

dence. Two final reforms were of great symbolic importance: the prohibition of the wearing of the fez, the traditional Islamic headgear, and the conversion of the Turkish language from Arabic to Roman script. By the end of the Kemalist era, Turkey had become thoroughly Westernized, at least at the level of the educated elite, while Turkish loyalties, torn loose from their broader Islamic and Ottoman moorings, were now focused exclusively upon the land and heritage of Anatolian Turkey.

Iran

Iran during the 1920s and 1930s experienced similar though less dramatic and far-reaching changes. Before and during World War I Britain and Russia, one coveting oil, the other a warm-water port, had contended for the mastery of the country and in 1907 had even divided it into spheres of influence. They succeeded, however, only in weakening the authority of the Teheran government and in stirring up hostility to themselves. In 1921, when the Russian and British troops at last withdrew, an ambitious, self-

made military officer, Reza Khan, led his men into Teheran and in a *coup d'etat* took over the government. Once in power, Reza Khan set out to modernize Iran along Turkish lines. The obstacles, however, were substantially greater. He had to spend much of his energy simply asserting the authority of the central government over rebellious nomadic tribes and distant provinces, while the conservative forces in society—the religious leaders and landed aristocracy—were far stronger than those in Turkey.

The Muslim religious divines, known as *mujtahids* in Iran, where the Shi'ite sect of Islam was predominant, had strengthened their independent position in the villages during the disorder of the nineteenth century and thus were able to oppose Reza Khan's attempt in 1924 to establish an Iranian republic. Reza Khan then took the crown himself, founding the Pahlevi dynasty, which still rules the country. Similarly, the entrenched landed aristocracy stood in the way of any real reform of Iran's backward peasant agriculture. Nevertheless much was accomplished during the 20 years of Reza Khan's rule. New state-run industries and a national bank and university were founded, a uniform civil code on the French model was introduced, communications were improved, most notably by the construction of the Trans-Iranian Railroad from the Persian Gulf to the Caspian Sea, and the privileged position of foreigners and of the Anglo-Iranian Oil Company in the country was gradually cut back. By 1941, when Reza Khan abdicated in favor of his son, Iran was not fully a modern national state, but the foundations had been laid. Further progress required only more vigorous leadership.

Pakistan

Nationalist sentiment among the Muslims of India was largely the product of their colonial subjugation and was given a distinctive shape by their status as a minority community in a land of Hindus. The earliest modernizing leaders such as Sayyid Ahmad Khan, more fearful of Hindu domination than of British rule, held aloof from the National Congress and looked to the British for support and sustenance. As the Congress wrung political concessions from the British, the

Muslims responded by demanding safeguards for themselves. These took the form of special or separate electorates that would insure the return of a certain number of Muslims to the reformed councils. Lord Minto's agreement to this demand in 1906 was followed by the formation of the Muslim League. This league, which soon became the major Muslim political party, was at the outset and for many years a loose and very conservative gathering of aristocratic notables.

Since the Indian Muslims lacked a recognizable territorial base around which to focus their loyalties, they sought refuge in the ideals of Pan-Islam and identified themselves with the traditional Islamic order in the Middle East, presided over by Ottoman caliph. Hence, when Britain attacked Turkey during World War I, the Indian Muslims found themselves drawn toward the Congress camp. An alliance was consummated in 1916 by Congress's recognition of separate electorates. After the war, British imposition of harsh peace terms on Turkey induced the Muslims to join Gandhi in his first noncooperation movement. But when Kemal Ataturk abolished the caliphate and established a secular national state, the Turks, secure in their new nationalism, no longer sought support from outside. Thus in 1924 the Indian Muslims, bereft of a cause, abandoned the Congress alliance and entered a period of leaderless demoralization. Their distrust of the Hindu-dominated Congress was soon renewed when in 1928 the Congress again renounced separate electorates. At the same time the Muslims were reluctant to return to the subordinate partnership with the British that had served them at the turn of the century, for they realized, especially after the 1935 reforms, that the transfer of power would not long be delayed.

At this time there emerged the idea of Pakistan — an Islamic national homeland within the Indian subcontinent. First put forward in 1930 by the poet-philosopher Muhammed Iqbal (1875–1938), the idea only slowly gathered adherents among the Western-educated elite until it was taken up and popularized by Muhammed Ali Jinnah. This elegant Westernized lawyer from Bombay had preached Hindu-Muslim cooperation as a youth, but by the late 1930s he had lost faith in the Congress movement. He argued instead that the Hindus and Muslims of India constituted two distinct communities and that when independence came each should have its own separate national state. Expertly playing upon the fears of the Muslim minority and taking advantage of the tactical errors of the Congress, Jinnah by 1946 had built the Muslim League into a powerful political organization committed to one demand — Pakistan. He then only had to stand firm to force the British and the Congress to concede.

The creation of Pakistan has been the subject of intense historical debate. Some observers argue that the British policy of divide and rule may have incited the Muslims to demand a separate state. Others feel that the austere figure of Jinnah, relentlessly ambitious, may have conjured up forces he could not control. Perhaps the idea of Pakistan was implicit in the deep-seated cultural separateness of the Indian Muslim community; many Pakistanis claim the creation of Pakistan was inevitable from the earliest days of Muslim settlement in the subcontinent. Although the British did not encourage the demand for Pakistan, they clearly repaid the support of the Muslims in the early nationalist era by preferential treatment. They remained committed to securing for the minority community a satisfactory place in the new India. The Muslims' distinct cultural heritage could no doubt have been subordinated to a secular nationalism as was the case in Turkey. And the Congress indeed claimed to be a secular organization, able and willing to represent the interests of the Muslims as of all other religious groups. Yet, because of the sheer predominance of Hindus in the population, the Congress to some extent took on a Hindu coloring; many of its leaders, among them Gandhi, appealed to the people in the traditional way, through religion. Even those who did not, such as Nehru, were often insensitive to Muslim feelings and thereby inadvertently antagonized Muslims, as, for example, in the refusal to form coalitions with the League after the 1937 elections. As a result, despite the mass migrations and massacres that it involved, the partition of the country ultimately seemed to most Indian

HINDUS AND MUSLIMS IN SOUTH ASIA

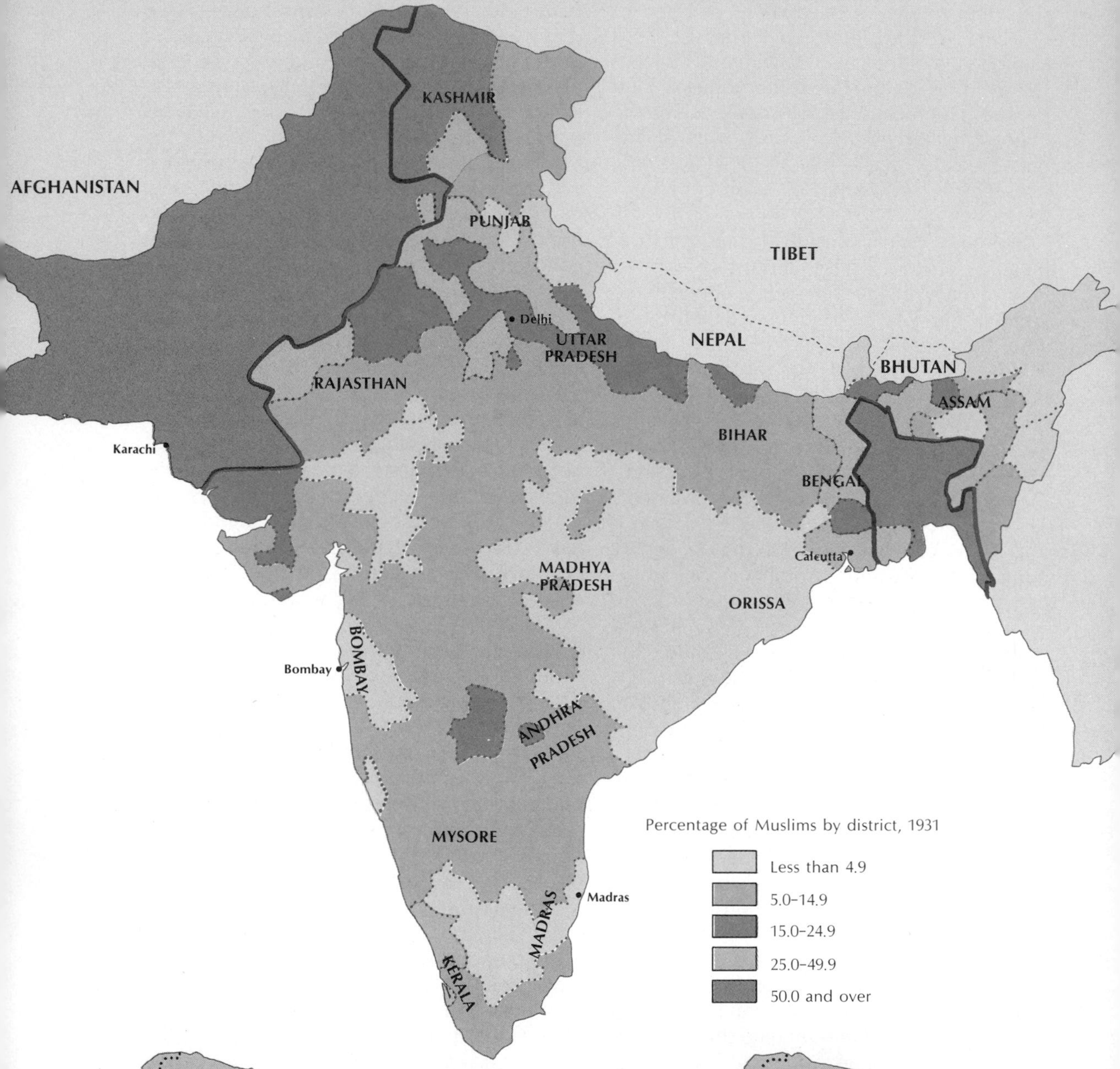

AFGHANISTAN

KASHMIR

PUNJAB

TIBET

• Delhi

UTTAR
PRADESH

NEPAL

BHUTAN

RAJASTHAN

ASSAM

Karachi •

BIHAR

BENGAL

Calcutta •

MADHYA
PRADESH

ORISSA

BOMBAY

Bombay •

ANDHRA
PRADESH

MYSORE

Percentage of Muslims by district, 1931

Less than 4.9

5.0–14.9

Madras •

15.0–24.9

MADRAS

25.0–49.9

KERALA

50.0 and over

MOVEMENT OF DISPLACED
PERSONS, 1947–1951

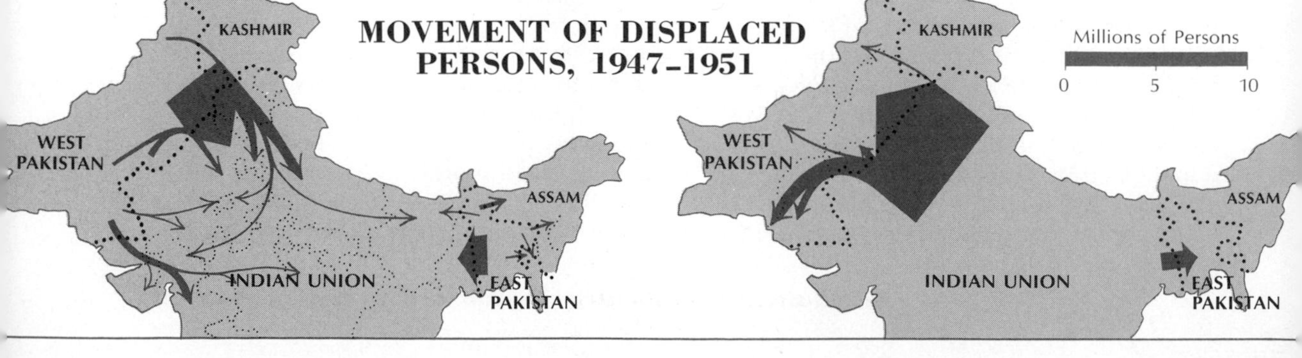

KASHMIR

KASHMIR

Millions of Persons

0   5   10

WEST
PAKISTAN

WEST
PAKISTAN

ASSAM

ASSAM

INDIAN UNION

EAST
PAKISTAN

INDIAN UNION

EAST
PAKISTAN

Muslims the only way of gaining security and self-esteem.

Indonesia

In Indonesia, as in India, revolutionary nationalism was a product of colonial rule. It emerged there, however, considerably later than in India, for the Dutch, preoccupied with commercial exploitation, did not provide any Western-style education or establish modern political institutions in the country until the twentieth century. In 1901, after the liberal leader Van Deventer argued that Holland owed the Indies a "debt of honor" in return for the wealth it had drained from them, the Dutch inaugurated the so-called Ethical Policy of benevolent paternalism. Under it, education, health, and agricultural extension services were developed, administrative responsibility was partly decentralized, and local representative assemblies were established. The capstone of the reform program was the creation in 1918 of a central advisory body, the *Volksraad* or People's Council.

Despite the confident optimism of the Dutch reformers, who looked forward to a Dutch-Indonesian partnership in an autonomous East Indies, the Ethical Policy was only fitfully and half-heartedly implemented; and, during the 1920s, it was in large part abandoned. From the start the cost was more than the Dutch Parliament was prepared to meet. Conservative European officials at the same time stubbornly resisted sharing power with representative councils and untutored subordinates, while the privileged position of the large Dutch commercial firms, which was never challenged, set sharp limits to what could even be attempted. Nevertheless, the new policy touched off a flood tide of social change which spilled over the limits set by the Dutch administrators and indeed after 1930 frightened them into trying to shore up their imperial position.

In the rural areas much of the beneficial effect of the Dutch welfare measures was wiped out by a phenomenal growth in the population, due partly to improved health and sanitation. At the same time deeper penetration of the government into rural society disrupted the social patterns of the village and heightened both the peasant's aspirations and his sense of frustration. The result was a growing agrarian unrest that crystallized first around the local Muslim religious leaders, the *ulama,* and then erupted in 1926–1927 in a large-scale revolt under Communist leadership on Java and Sumatra. The ruthless suppression of this revolt ended political mass action among the peasantry for many years.

Meanwhile, in the cities and towns of Indonesia the new Dutch schools were slowly creating a new, Western-educated elite. Although few in number compared to those in British India, the members of this intelligentsia were profoundly alienated from the traditional culture and yet unable to gain a footing in the new. Excluded from the better posts in government and commerce, and often without employment, they soon turned to politics. Like the Indian Muslims, they first embraced the cause of Pan-Islam and in 1912 founded the Sarekat Islam, a wide-ranging movement that gave expression to a variety of discontents. During the 1920s, however, the organization slowly foundered amidst its own internal divisions. In 1921 the radicals left to form the Communist party of Indonesia, which actively promoted worker and peasant revolution until its suppression after the 1926–1927 uprising. At the same time there grew up among the students and other young people a secular nationalism that rejected association with either Dutch or Islamic politics. This movement soon found a charismatic leader in Achmed Sukarno (1901–1970), who founded the Nationalist party in 1927. As his radical program of noncooperation soon ran afoul of the increasingly conservative Dutch government, Sukarno was arrested and his party banned in 1929. But he remained a powerful symbol of Indonesian nationalism throughout his long exile, which only ended with the coming of the Japanese in 1942.

Although Dutch repression effectively secured tranquillity and order during the 1930s, the resentment of the Indonesians led many of them to collaborate with the Japanese invaders in 1942. Both the secular nationalist and the Muslim modernist parties hoped by working with the Japanese to consolidate their position and widen popular support for the nationalist movement. The Japanese, in turn, encouraged the nationalist leaders as a device to rally the Indonesian people behind their war effort. At first the Japanese gave these leaders little power; only as their military position crumbled in late 1944 did they take practical steps for the establishment of an independent Indonesia. By the time the war ended in August 1945, an Indonesian Republic had been proclaimed, Sukarno was installed as president, and troops were poised to meet the returning forces of their former Dutch masters. The stage was set for the four-year struggle that was to follow.

NATIONALISM IN THE SMALLER COUNTRIES OF ASIA

The decisive event in eastern Asia was the fall of the Ch'ing in 1912, which created a situation among China's non-Chinese subjects and neighbors similar to that of Eastern Europe during the dissolution of Austria-Hungary after World War I. Distinct nationalities within the Chinese Empire demanded independence; by 1921, both western Tibet and Outer Mongolia had established sovereign governments. On the other hand, nationalism in independent Siam (renamed Thailand in 1939) focused on the abolition of the special privileges granted to foreigners and was sustained by antiforeign movements directed tragically against Chinese minorities within the country.

Most of the remainder of Asia was under direct colonial rule: Burma and Ceylon under the British; the Philippines under Spanish, and, after 1898, American, domination; Korea annexed by the Japanese in 1910. Thus national identity and purpose were usually found in movements directed against foreign rule. Typical in many respects of such anticolonial movements was the nationalist struggle in Vietnam, which went through three phases: gentry resistance to the French, popular nationalism, and finally underground revolutionary warfare.

French colonialists had already met with stiff resistance from Vietnam's intellectuals during the nineteenth century. Remembering earlier heroes who had fought off the Mongols and Chinese, some of the gentry had organized a fervent "scholars' revolt" against

the French army from 1889 to 1895. After it was defeated, one of the movement's leaders, Phan Boi Chau, fled to Japan and was encouraged by exiled Chinese nationalists there to found an overseas "Eastern Study" (Dong Du) group, which incited several abortive uprisings in Vietnam itself. Back home, another group of intellectuals looked to a scholar named Phan Chu Trinh for leadership. However, when his academy (the Dong King Nghia Thuc) became implicated in peasant revolts in 1908, the French were given whatever pretext they needed to imprison this entire generation of gentry-nationalists. The independence movement then entered a second stage. A more broadly based Nationalist party (Viet Nam Quoc Dan Dang) was formed. By 1930 the party had 1500 members and felt strong enough to incite a desperate revolt. Once again it brought French repression, driving the nationalists underground and into the arms of leaders better suited for underground revolutionary organization.

The best known of these new leaders was a scholar's son named Nguyen Ai Quoc. Nguyen had traveled to Europe as a seaman. During World War I, he lived in Paris with other revolutionary intellectuals and joined the French Communist party. Later he studied in Moscow, served with the Comintern in China, and eventually organized a Vietnamese Communist party in 1930. After forming a Popular Democratic Front with other revolutionary nationalists, Nguyen carefully established Communist cells throughout Vietnam. Therefore, when World War II broke out, he was ready to move across the border into South China and direct a resistance movement against the French and Japanese occupations of Vietnam. A new League of Vietnamese Independence (Viet Nam Doc Lap Dong Minh or as it was usually abbreviated, Viet Minh) was created; this organization provided the Chinese and Americans with intelligence in exchange for military supplies. Nguyen Ai Quoc repeatedly changed one alias for another to facilitate his crossing and recrossing of the Sino-Vietnamese border on secret missions. On one of these missions he was seized by the Chinese who mistook him for a Japanese spy. After other Communists helped secure his release, Nguyen adopted a more permanent name and under this *nom de guerre* — Ho Chi Minh — he continued to prepare for war's end in hopes of Vietnamese independence.

REVOLUTIONARY NATIONALISM: CHINA

The attack on the Manchus in 1911 (see pp. 599–601) was only a diversion from the three major questions facing China on the eve of World War I: imperialism, social injustice, and political disintegration. The issue of imperialism was foremost in men's minds because the titanic struggles at the Marne and Ypres soon demanded Europe's total attention, allowing the Japanese to occupy the German concessions in Shantung without diplomatic obstruction. Confident now that no Western power would intervene, Japan presented Twenty-One Demands to the Chinese. The Twenty-One Demands were designed to turn all of China into a protectorate of the Japanese, who wished to control everything from railways to police forces. But the demands had a great effect on public opinion: throughout the cities of China, merchants and students boycotted Japanese goods. The Chinese president, Yüan Shih-k'ai, was able to exploit this popular indignation to refuse some of Japan's demands. He continued, however, to make concessions to foreign governments in exchange for loans to finance his administration in Peking. His regime was therefore thought by many to be bargaining away precious national rights just to stay in power.

China's weak finances were part of a much larger problem of social instability. The modernization of one sector of the economy — port shipping, urban industry — created new disparities. Urban capitalists invested in rural land, inflicting a harsh system of absentee landlordism, including usury and the imposition of high rents, on the Chinese peasantry. Factory conditions matched the worst of nineteenth-century England's. Taxes soared as China labored under the many indemnities of the imperialist age. Moreover, no strong central government existed to sponsor reform. The government, lacking political legitimacy, found it impossible to exert effective civil control over warlords who now controlled the country. Sensing this, and believing that the populace still favored a monarchy, Yüan Shih-k'ai tried to make himself emperor. But he was rejected by his own military lieutenants and died in 1916. Then there was even an attempt to restore the last Ch'ing ruler, P'u-yi. When this, too, failed, the Chinese Republic at Peking became no more than the seat of a rotating presidency sought as a political prize by competing military cliques. The rest of the country was occupied by tyrannical warlords who fought among themselves to tax the peasants or control opium monopolies.

The May Fourth Movement

Many Chinese hoped that an Allied victory in World War I would somehow solve the problems of China, especially since the war was ostensibly fought in the name of national self-determination. When the Paris Peace Conference turned to the Shantung question, however, the liberal Wilson was dismayed to discover that, unknown even to the Chinese plenipotentiaries, the Peking regime had already signed a secret agreement with the Japanese recognizing their "rights" there. Wilson also discovered that the other major powers intended to honor secret treaties made in 1917 which gave the former German leasehold of Shantung to Japan. In order to keep Japanese cooperation in forming the League of Nations (which could then deal with the Shantung question) and to make peace quickly as a defense against Bolshevik disruption, Wilson agreed to award Shantung to Japan. When news of the arrangement was telegraphed to Peking, popular fury knew no bounds. Angry young students held impassioned meetings at Peking University in protest, scrawling patriotic slogans on the wall with their own blood. On May 4, 1919, 3000 students marched out of T'ien-an-men square to celebrate "National Humiliation Day." When the mob assaulted one of China's pro-Japanese officials, the government jailed 1150 students. In response, militant student unions were formed all over China to boycott Japanese goods and demand political reform.

The "May Fourth Movement" of 1919 marked the first time young Chinese radical

Marshal Feng Yü-hsiang, the "Christian General" whose private army controlled vast portions of North China until 1930. Far from typical, he still symbolized the twentieth-century warlord to many Chinese.

intellectuals became involved with the urban masses in joint political activity. Students, traditionally contemptuous of illiterate "coolies," actually took to the streets to organize urban workers into strike committees. From this moment, therefore, date the modern Chinese student and labor movements. The "May Fourth Movement" also speeded cultural "reform": the cause of China's weakness—argued the students—was intellectual conservatism; China was fettered to a stagnant past by an outdated ideology that kept old men and effeminate scholars in control under the paternalistic gaze of Confucius. "Give us our freedom," shouted the students to their fathers. "Let us be individuals, to do as we want and marry as we please. Stop stifling us. Throw Confucius out of the classroom and replace him with Spencer or Marx. New values—even a new language—have to be found. Why not write in the language of the people, in the vernacular *pai-hua*? We need new aesthetics, new morals, new vigor!"

Debate over the value of the traditional culture of China soon divided the May Fourth intellectuals. "Liberals" like Hu Shih argued for a limited pragmatic solution to China's problems, whereas more radical thinkers like Ch'en Tu-hsiu insisted that the entire system would have to be replaced with a new revolutionary one. His revolutionary example was close at hand. In 1918 his friend Li Ta-chao hailed the Bolshevik Revolution in Russia as the dawn of a new historical era. A revolutionary tide was sweeping the world, Li wrote, and China must participate. Communist Russia itself added force to this argument by disavowing tsarist concessions in China. Impressed, eager young intellectuals joined Ch'en Tu-hsiu to found a Chinese Communist party.

The Communist Party

The new Chinese Communist party soon came into contact with the leaders of the 1911 revolution. After turning over the presidency to Yüan Shih-k'ai, Sun Yat-sen returned to his overseas life in Japan. The May Fourth tumult drew him back to China to head the Kuomintang (National People's party). But Sun soon realized how difficult it was for a civilian political group to survive in an age dominated by warlords. Without his own army, without a tightly organized group of followers, he would always have to rely on militarists like Ch'en Chiung-ming at Canton. At best Sun could hope for foreign aid; and he even urged the United States to lend financial support to a democratic Kuomintang regime that would transform Canton into a revolutionary base for a northern expedition to destroy the warlords and reunify the country. America failed to respond, but another ally presented itself. In 1922 a Russian envoy, Adolphe Joffe, concluded an agreement with Sun Yat-sen for a "United Front" between Soviet and Chinese Communists and Sun's own Kuomintang. In addition to military aid and training facilities, the Soviet government sent an American schoolteacher-turned-revolutionary named Michael Borodin to provide organizational advice. Borodin easily persuaded Sun to reorganize the Kuomintang according to Leninist principles of tight party discipline and stressed the need to mobilize mass workers' and peasants' groups.

This coalition arrangement better served the Kuomintang than the much smaller Chinese Communist party. Ch'en Tu-hsiu, that party's leader, realized that Leninist reorganization of the Kuomintang would make it all the more difficult for Communist members to retain their own sense of tactical purpose; but he was helpless to resist Soviet pressure to subordinate independence to the United Front. The strongest source of this pressure was Stalin, who believed that a socialist revolution in China was possible only after the Chinese Communist party (CCP) had ridden to power on the coattails of a bourgeois-democratic nationalist like Sun. Stalin's conviction turned into dogma when his rival Trotsky argued insistently that Moscow was strengthening the Chinese bourgeoisie while betraying the revolutionaries. Therefore, the CCP's revolutionary tactics were in part decided by the outcome of the struggle between these two Russian leaders. Stalin's victory over Trotsky forced a tragically unrealistic policy onto Chinese Communists, who recovered from the consequences only by rejecting Soviet leadership.

The year 1924 was spent largely in reorganization of the Kuomintang (KMT) in Canton. A party hierarchy was rigidly defined. Mass organizations were created in the provinces. A young officer named Chiang Kai-shek was sent off to the Soviet Union to observe Soviet training methods. After his return, he helped establish a military school at Whampoa to train officers for the KMT army. Preparations were made for a northern expedition, but the task of defeating the warlord armies in the north seemed hopeless without massive popular support for the revolutionaries. The KMT's call for a national struggle against conservatives and imperialists was answered, however, after May 30, 1925, when British-officered police fired on Shanghai strike-demonstrators, killing thirteen of them. The anti-imperialist sentiment provoked by this and the similar Shameen incident of June 23 exceeded even the May Fourth Movement in intensity. The Shanghai strike spread to Hong Kong, and antiforeign agitation swept rapidly across central China.

Once again cries were heard for the expulsion of foreigners, for an end to the warlord system, for social equity and welfare. To foreigners, watching nervously from the treaty ports, China seemed a stirring volcano.

In the late spring of 1925, before he could take advantage of the "May Thirtieth Movement," Sun Yat-sen died, leaving his party prepared for an expedition but divided over who would lead it. There were several contenders for power, ranging from intellectuals on the far left to a military faction associated with Chiang Kai-shek. Chiang himself moved cautiously against his opponents until the spring of 1926, when he suddenly dismissed the Soviet advisers in Canton. Although these were clear signs of the impending breakup of the United Front, Stalin refused to heed them. Instead, he ordered the CCP members to continue to give as much help as they could to the KMT's long-awaited Northern Expedition, launched in July 1926.

The expedition divided into several columns. One marched toward the central Chinese cities of Wu-han where peasants and workers were already up in arms. Warlord armies along the route were either defeated or absorbed, as propagandists working in advance of the KMT column deprived the warlords of support. By the end of that year, the KMT (dominated by the "leftwing" and the Communists) had moved to Wu-han and established a government there. Another column headed for Shanghai, where labor unions had seized municipal power under the guise of a syndicalist commune. Fearful of military intervention by the powers, the Shanghai workers eagerly awaited the appearance of Chiang Kai-shek's armies to liberate the concessions occupied by foreigners since the nineteenth century. Chiang reached the outskirts of Shanghai in the winter of 1926–1927, but instead of moving directly to support the strike he set up headquarters at Nanchang while deliberating his next move. It was obvious that the Wu-han government was outside his control. Furthermore, since his major contribution to the Kuomintang-Communist alliance was military, the very success of the Northern Expedition might mean his political demise. On the other hand, foreign commercial interests and native bankers in Shanghai badly needed someone of nationalist repute to overcome the socially radical aspirations of the KMT. These commercial interests got into touch with Chiang, guaranteeing financial aid in exchange for his military support against the labor unions. An agreement was reached, and on April 12, 1927, Chiang Kai-shek's forces allied with Shanghai concession police and blackleg gangs to smash the workers' movement. Chiang then established his own KMT regime at Nanking and went on to create the first central government China had known for over a decade by continuing to destroy the power of the warlords and crush urban uprisings of the Communists.

The new republic in Nanking was placed under the "tutelage" of the Nationalist party (KMT), obedient in turn to a Standing Committee controlled by Chiang. In this respect, the "statist" Nanking regime combined Leninist party control and personal dictatorship, reinforced by a well-trained army of 300,000 men. The army was a government in its own right outside Nanking, since newly recovered provinces were left under military rule. The KMT organized a system of political commissars within the army to ensure party control over it, while Chiang made certain that the Military Affairs Commission was always staffed with officers loyal to him. These were usually graduates of the military academy that Chiang had supervised in Canton and hence came to be known as the "Whampoa Clique." In short, the Nationalist government was roughly divided into central-civil and provincial-military wings. This division affected the course of social reform.

Economic policies within the central government were determined by a new elite of Western-trained technocrats and social scientists sponsored by an equally new financial and party oligarchy. Members of these new elites sometimes were related by blood or marriage; for example, the minister of finance, T. V. Soong, was the brother of Madame Chiang, whose own brother-in-law—H. H. Koong—often represented Nationalist interests in the United States. It was T. V. Soong who sponsored a system of modern banks that helped finance the government. Soong also reformed tax laws, established state monopolies, and took advantage of China's recovery of tariff autonomy to develop a crucial source of revenue in customs' duties.

While important advances were thus made in the modern urban sector, rural China was largely left to itself. The worst of the warlords' taxes were abolished, public health precautions were introduced, some land was reclaimed, and modest amounts of credit were extended to the peasantry. But little was done to carry out the land reform promised earlier by Sun Yat-sen. In fact, Chiang Kai-shek's espousal of the "New Life Movement" (which acclaimed a crypto-Confucian philosophy of self-discipline and respect for authority) and his revival of traditional control and police systems (*pao-chia*) lent support to the established elites of the countryside. The coastal cities, not inland China, were to be the focus of economic development and social reforms that were eventually supposed to affect the countryside, allowing for gradual rather than revolutionary social change.

This strategy depended upon the strength and unity of Chiang's central government in Nanking. If he were to play Ataturk to China's ills, his control over the country would have to be enduring. Yet Chiang Kai-shek's own power was never free from threats. Within his own party, he faced challenges from both left (Wang Ching-wei) and right (Hu Han-min) and was forced to rule by balancing one clique against the other. Outside of Central China he was confronted by powerful warlords. Many were destroyed during a bitterly fought war in 1930, but most of the south and southwest remained under the rule of independent militarists throughout the entire Nanking period. Above all, soon to be the greatest internal threat to Chiang's regime were the Chinese Communists — destroyed in the cities perhaps, but active in the countryside.

Out of their defeat in 1927 emerged a new kind of Chinese Communist party, molded by a new leader named Mao Tse-tung. Unlike Chiang Kai-shek, Mao came from inland China. The son of a Hunanese landowner, Mao was a student activist who became a Communist after an early interest in European anarchism. During the United Front period, he became a specialist at organizing

Early portrait of Chiang Kai-shek, who rose to power in the Kuomintang in 1925.

farmers into rural associations. He was sent ahead of the Northern Expedition to travel through the Hunanese countryside, attending peasant meetings, agitating for lower rents, and urging opposition to local landlords. But Mao soon encountered difficulties within his own party. Stalin realized that many members of the Kuomintang were landlords themselves and feared that a radical attack on these elements would disturb the Communist-Kuomintang alliance. At this point, when the Communist party's central committee ordered rural agitators to avoid antagonizing landlords, Mao Tse-tung became disgusted with the party line and began to search for a new theory of socialist revolution. Orthodox Marxism attributed revolution to the class consciousness of the proletariat. Since Lenin had demonstrated that it was possible for Bolshevik intellectuals to arouse that class consciousness as a "vanguard of the proletariat," the Chinese Communists invested their major efforts in placing cadres among urban workers. At the most, though, there were only about two million industrial workers in China in 1927, while there were hundreds of millions of peasants. In the summer of 1927, therefore, Mao is-

Red Army soldiers toiling up Chiachin Mountain during the Long March of 1934–1935.

sued a report on the peasant movement in Hunan, urging his party to recognize that revolution would be won not by the proletariat but by the peasantry. "The rise of the present peasant movement is a colossal event. In a very short time, several hundred million peasants will rise like a tornado or tempest, a force so extraordinarily swift and violent that no power, however great, will be able to suppress it. . . . To reject them is to reject revolution!" Like Gandhi, Mao sensed the power of an aroused peasantry. Unlike Gandhi, though, he did not believe that means were as important as ends. A revolution, he wrote, was not a tea party. It was necessarily violent, murderous, destructive; but all of this was a small price to pay for that final end, a revolutionary and nationalist China.

Mao Tse-tung's populism was anathema to the urban wing of his party. Li Li-san (then head of the CCP) accused Mao of being no more than a peasant guerrilla who would debase the revolution. In order to keep the party pure, members would have to sponsor urban revolution. In practice this meant using Red Army units—carefully built up from a peasant base by precisely such men as Mao—to attack cities frontally in hopes of inspiring revolution within them. Urban attacks exposed the CCP's military units to crushing counterattacks by Chiang Kai-shek's forces, but Marxist orthodoxy rigidly insisted that sacrifices had to be made. The result of this "adventurism" (as Mao later condemned the attacks) was the systematic destruction of urban cells, leaving scattered pockets of rural revolutionaries who looked more and more to Mao Tse-tung for leadership. When the Russian "line" was

THE LONG MARCH, OCTOBER 1934 TO OCTOBER 1935

Legend:
— 1st front army
—·— 2nd front army
---- 3rd front army
▓ Communist-controlled territory

discredited, Mao retired to an isolated southern base camp, or "soviet," in the mountains of Kiangsi.

The Long March

By 1931 Chiang Kai-shek had driven the Communists out of the cities and became determined to destroy the last traces of them in the countryside. Between 1930 and 1934, Chiang launched five "encirclement" campaigns that successively battered the mountain soviets of South China. Time and time again Mao Tse-tung's forces fought free, but Chiang Kai-shek's superior military strength finally took its toll. On October 16, 1934, the Communists abandoned their camps in Kiangsi and desperately began to seek a safer military refuge westward. Pushing deep into southwestern China, Mao's 100,000-man army set out on the famous "Long March." First they moved across Hunan and then up the snow-covered mountains of Kweichow, where Mao wrote at Loushan Pass:

"Do you say that the pass is defended with iron.
This very day at one step we shall cross over it,
We shall cross over it.
The hills are blue like the sea,
And the dying sun is like blood."

The Red Army slogged into Szechwan, across the Tatu River, and north through the stinking black mud of the grasslands. Back on the coast, many thought Mao and his men had literally been swallowed up by barely explored lands. Yet 6000 miles and 370 days later, the Red Army emerged in northern Shensi. Of the original 100,000 only a third survived, but they were jubilant at their own endurance.

The Long March both confirmed the Com-

In the spring of 1938, Imperial Japanese troops completed their conquest of the Chinese coast. In the meantime the Nationalist Chinese moved inland to continue defending their country. Here Japanese soldiers take over Canton.

munists' sense of mission and profoundly influenced Mao's own theories of revolution. It had been such a stunning victory over both the enemy and nature itself that it inspired Mao to believe that men, if properly motivated, could overcome all obstacles to progress. A belief in the superhuman efficacy of the people's will recurs again and again in Mao's later writings and characterizes his view of the permanent revolution. The Long March also established Mao's leadership beyond challenge. Some commanders wished to strike out for the security of the Russian border, but Mao insisted that the Chinese Communists establish a new soviet in Shensi, closer to the central plain of Hopei, where he foresaw a war of national resistance against Japanese imperialism.

Japanese Intervention

Mao's prediction was to prove correct, as we shall see. After the occupation of Manchuria in 1931, the Japanese had set up a puppet regime in Peking. By 1937 the Japanese high command had come to feel that it was time for them to acquire control over all of China. An incident at Lu-kuo-ch'iao near Peking in July 1937, gave them the pretext they needed to move swiftly down the coast and occupy the central and southern parts of the country.

Although his armies were initially defeated by the Japanese, Chiang Kai-shek's Nationalist regime survived by retreating westward up through the Yangtze gorges to Szechuan, which was ringed with impenetrable mountains. But the withdrawal to Szechuan forced his government to rely upon that province's conservative landlord class for financial support, which, in turn, meant that the KMT dared not carry out a much-needed land reform. As peasant discontent with Nationalist tax collectors and army conscription increased, Chiang's own military forces grew corrupt and weak. Was it true—as many said—that he was unwilling to fight the Japanese because it would weaken the armies that he wanted to hold in reserve against the Communists? As early as 1935 Chinese student groups had begun agitating against the KMT's decision to suppress the Communists instead of reforging a second United Front against the common enemy, Japan. Chiang resisted these pressures, believing that his government would not be strong enough to drive out the Japanese unless the Communists were first defeated. Others on the Nationalist side felt differently, and one of his own commanders seized Chiang at Sian in 1936 and refused to release him until he agreed to a truce with the Chinese Communists.

Meanwhile at his base camp at Yenan, Shensi, Mao Tse-tung was also having difficulties persuading party members to support a United Front. Too many of them bitterly remembered the defeat of the first United Front. But Mao insisted that conditions had changed since then; China was no longer divided into disguised imperialist spheres of influence. Rather, it now faced military occupation by a single power, moving from a "semicolonial" to a "colonial" stage in its historical development. This meant that the bourgeoisie would now be forced to choose between actual collaboration or active resistance. Those who were nationalists could therefore be enlisted as temporary allies if the CCP momentarily subordinated its radical struggle against the upper classes to the demands of a grand alliance against fascism. Indeed, argued Mao, China had entered a period of "New Democracy" in which all but the most reactionary could cooperate at Yenan to create a self-governing headquarters for warfare against Japan.

Once again, Mao's diagnosis proved correct. Not only did Yenan attract middle-class patriots from all over China, but it also provided the Chinese Communists with a place in which to practice revolutionary recruitment and government among poor peasants. At the same time, guerrilla warfare against the Japanese helped the People's Liberation Army perfect bold new military tactics, while Japanese suppression of rural resistance drove ever greater numbers of peasants over to the Communists' side.

This reasoning convinced all but a few of the need for a United Front, and on September 22, 1937, an agreement was signed between the Communists and the Kuomintang. In spite of nationwide acclaim for the two parties' statesmanship, each entered the alliance with reservations. Mao, for example, had no intention of living up to the letter of the agreement by limiting the size of his forces to Chiang's low quotas or allowing KMT political commissars control over his own Communist troops. Conversely, KMT generals had little stomach for welcoming Communist organizational cadres into areas under their personal command. Minor skirmishes occurred frequently between these erstwhile allies. Thus, when the Nationalists openly destroyed most of the Communist New Fourth Army in January 1941, it came as no surprise to either regime, even though the Communists were able to win national sympathy by expressing great shock at the KMT's perfidy.

As an arrangement to face Japan the United Front lasted throughout World War II precisely because both Chiang and Mao realized that the appearance of patriotic good faith was important as far as their countrymen were concerned. The mantle of national leadership—of country over party—might be a crucial asset during the civil war that was certain to follow the defeat of Japan. In 1941, therefore, both Communists and Nationalists were already looking ahead to a final and bloody resolution of the harsh conflict that had kept them at each other's throats for a quarter of a century.

The nationalist revolutions of twentieth-century Asia were—and are—paradoxical combinations of external and internal factors. From the outside came such hopeful yet shattering events as the two world wars. Chinese dreams of Wilsonian democracy, which were dashed by the Paris Peace Conference, launched the May Fourth Movement, just as Indonesian nationalists were later stimulated by the Japanese expulsion of the Dutch. Similarly, external and supranational movements like Pan-Islam helped galvanize nationalist sentiment among Muslims in the Middle East and in India. On the other hand, these same revolutions turned within their own societies in search of native roots for revolutionary leaders soon found that movements for independence would not succeed unless the masses' aspirations coincided with their own.

Thus Asian nationalism often embodied another paradox as radical ideologies of social revolution were colored with traditional overtones. Gandhi's importance to the Indian nationalist movement was his ability to endow innovative aspiration with Hindu inspiration, just as Mao Tse-tung rose to power in the Chinese Communist party because he realized that Marxism-Leninism had to be adapted to the perennial conditions of Chinese peasant revolts. But whether the Salt March to the sea or the Long March to Yenan, these momentous convulsions were truly novel events. For the first time in the history of the East, the peasant became politically aroused to participate consciously in revolutions that have yet to end.

SUGGESTED READINGS

Marr, David G., *Vietnamese Anticolonialism, 1885–1925*. Berkeley: University of California Press, 1971.
> *One of the first studies that uses Vietnamese sources to get inside the early history of the nationalist movement.*

Wright, Mary C., ed., *China in Revolution: The First Phase, 1900–1913*. New Haven: Yale University Press, 1968.
> *A collection of essays that challenges the once-prevailing interpretation of the Revolution of 1911 as a conspiracy engineered by Sun Yat-sen. The essays present a variety of new theses explaining why and how the Ch'ing dynasty fell.*

Tse-tsung, Chow, *The May Fourth Movement: Intellectual Revolution in Modern China*. Cambridge: Harvard University Press. 1964.
> *A comprehensive survey of the intellectual currents and political events behind the May Fourth Movement.*

Johnson, Chalmers, *Peasant Nationalism and Communist Power: The Emergence of Revolutionary China, 1937–1945*. Stanford: Stanford University Press, 1962.
> *This important study argues that the rise of the Chinese Communist party was largely enabled by the Japanese invasion of China in 1937. As the Chinese peasant came to link his own survival with that of the nation, he was mobilized by the Communists to engage in revolution.*

Ch'en, Jerome, *Mao and the Chinese Revolution*. London: Oxford University Press, 1965.
> *A standard biography of the leader of the Chinese Communist party that provides an excellent background history of China itself during that period.*

Gandhi, M. K., *An Autobiography*. Boston: Beacon Press, 1957. Paperback.
> *Remarkable for its candor and openness. Carries the story up to 1920 only.*

Nehru, Jawharlal, *Toward Freedom*. Boston: Beacon Press, 1958. Paperback.
> *The story of his life and views on Indian politics up to 1940.*

Tandon, Prakash, *Punjabi Century, 1857–1947*. Berkeley: University of California Press, 1968. Paperback.

Life and society under the British illuminated through the history of one Indian family.

Moon, Penderel, *Divide and Quit.* London: Chatto & Windus, 1961.
A first-hand account by a British observer of the massacres and migrations that accompanied the coming of independence.

McLane, John R., *The Political Awakening in India.* Englewood Cliffs, N.J.: Prentice-Hall, 1970.
A collection of documents. Especially useful for Hindu-Muslim antagonism and the problem of untouchability.

Lewis, Bernard, *The Emergence of Modern Turkey.* New York: Oxford University Press, 1961.
Sensitive and sophisticated.

Avery, Peter, *Modern Iran.* New York: Frederick A. Praeger, 1965.

Kahin, George McT., *Nationalism and Revolution in Indonesia.* Ithaca: Cornell University Press, 1952.
A classic study.

CHAPTER **25**

World War II and the
Chinese Communist Revolution

The seeds of World War II were sown at Versailles in 1919 when the victorious Allies dictated a treaty that they were not willing to enforce. Only France and Belgium, Germany's near neighbors, combined enough fear and vindictiveness to try to collect reparations by force. Unsupported by their former allies, they finally lost that resolution. Their invasion of the Ruhr Valley further weakened the strife-torn Weimar government, whose signing of the peace terms German nationalists had never pardoned. Even if no Hitler had appeared, most Germans were committed to revision of the peace terms. But Hitler did appear, and he was willing to use force to revise the treaty where Stresemann had relied on diplomatic maneuvers.

In Japan, too, men bent on aggression came to power in the 1930s. They, too, owed their support partly to their nation's dissatisfaction with the outcome of World War I. Japan's assertion of power over China was voided by the Western nations, and those same Westerners maintained that Japan was their inferior not only in military force but in every sphere of action. The racist arrogance

of white Westerners was easily matched by that of the Japanese.

In the past, most wars, wasteful as they were, had promoted modernization. World War II was to have the same effect, but, as always, the price of modernization would be high, and the forms it took far from what most men expected.

THE IMMEDIATE ORIGINS OF THE WAR

Hitler's blueprint for conquest, *Mein Kampf*, showed that he did not want colonies for Germany but an extension of the homeland. France, the ally of Poland and Czechoslovakia, would stand in the way of German expansion toward the east: it must be crushed, for Hitler dreamed of expanding the new German Empire all the way into western Russia and the Ukraine. He even dreamed of enlisting Britain as an ally. But Hitler was an opportunist—he did not necessarily have to follow his blueprint in every detail.

Failing to get permission from the Western powers to rearm Germany, Hitler withdrew

DESTRUCTION OF CZECHOSLOVAK STATE, 1938–1939

GERMANY

SUDETENLAND

Elbe River

• Prague

• Pilsen

BOHEMIA

MORAVIA

CZECHOSLOVAKIA

POLAND

■ Ceded to Germany at Munich, Sept. 30, 1938

■ Seized by Poland, Oct. 2, 1938

■ Ceded to Hungary, Vienna Award, Nov. 2, 1938

■ Seized by Hungary, Mar. 15, 1939

SLOVAKIA
(*Ind. Mar. 18, 1939; under Ger. protec.*)

• Bratislava

RUTHENIA
(*Carpatho-Ukraine, ind. Mar. 18, 1939*)

AUSTRIA

HUNGARY

RUMANIA

from the League of Nations in October 1933. On March 7, 1936, he sent troops into the demilitarized zone of the Rhineland, thus violating both the Treaty of Versailles and the Locarno pacts. German strategists had expected French resistance, but French generals, unwilling to fight, argued that they could not prevent Hitler's move without aid from Britain, and that aid was not forthcoming. In the same year Hitler began testing his troops and weapons, in cooperation with Mussolini, by sending them into battle on behalf of General Franco. Quite as ominous was the diplomatic alliance taking shape among the three major revisionist powers: the Rome-Berlin Axis was formally announced on October 25, 1936, and Germany, Italy, and Japan joined in the Anti-Comintern Pact in 1937.

Britons and Frenchmen, unwilling to face a new war, could easily justify Hitler's "revision" of the Versailles treaty. He rearmed Germany, but other nations had failed to keep their promises to disarm. He stationed troops in the Rhineland, but the Rhineland

was after all a part of Germany. He also stood as a bulwark against communism. When he annexed Austria in March 1938, he was only granting the Austrians' expressed wish for union with Germany. When he announced his determination to annex the Czechoslovakian Sudetenland, an area most of which was inhabited by ethnic Germans, Prime Minister Neville Chamberlain of Britain could call it a quarrel in "a far away country between people of whom we know nothing."

On September 29, 1938, Chamberlain and Edouard Daladier (1884–1970), the French premier, flew to Munich to discuss the new demand with Hitler and Mussolini. Hitler assured the two chiefs of government that he had no further expansionist designs and agreed to sign a four-power guarantee of Czechoslovakia's sovereignty in return for cession of the Sudetenland. The Czech government had no alternative but to give in. Most Britons and Frenchmen were relieved that war had been avoided by the Munich Pact, even though France had broken a sol-

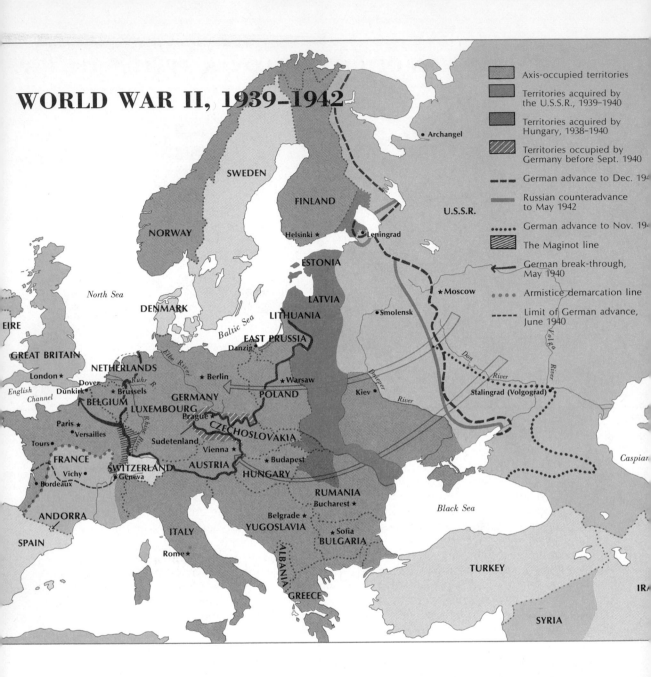

WORLD WAR II, 1939–1942

	Axis-occupied territories
	Territories acquired by the U.S.S.R., 1939–1940
	Territories acquired by Hungary, 1938–1940
	Territories occupied by Germany before Sept. 1940
− − −	German advance to Dec. 194
───	Russian counteradvance to May 1942
····	German advance to Nov. 19
	The Maginot line
←	German break-through, May 1940
······	Armistice demarcation line
− − −	Limit of German advance, June 1940

emn treaty engagement. They believed that the new agreement meant that they could expect, in Chamberlain's phrase, "Peace in our time." Six months later, in March 1939, Hitler's armies overran the remainder of Czechoslovakia. On April 7 Mussolini's legions occupied Albania. Slowly and reluctantly, France and Britain at last began to prepare for war.

Hitler made war almost certain on March 21, 1939, by informing the Polish government that he intended to annex the Free City of Danzig, on the Baltic Sea. France was already Poland's ally; Britain guaranteed Polish independence on March 31. Chamberlain and Daladier opened negotiations with the Soviet Union immediately, seeking a mutual guarantee for Poland and Rumania.

The Russian foreign minister, Maxim Litvinov, replied by asking for what amounted to a sphere of influence that would extend from Finland through Poland and the Balkan states. Negotiations dragged; the price was higher than Chamberlain was willing to pay. Hitler, however, did not hesitate when the Russians asked to deal with him on the same terms. On August 23, 1939, Germany and the Soviet Union signed the Moscow Pact of nonaggression with a secret protocol that would, in case of war, divide Poland between the two of them.

The controversy over the immediate origins of World War II probably will never be settled. Britain and France have been accused of not standing up to Hitler soon enough; the U.S.S.R. has been accused of giving Hitler a free hand in the West by signing the Moscow Pact; Nazi Germany has been accused of deliberately provoking a world conflict. The fact remains, however, that it was Hitler who invaded Poland on September 1, 1939, and that Britain and France honored their commitment to Poland by declaring war on Germany two days later.

THE WAR: THE BATTLE FRONTS

Hitler's tank divisions crushed Poland's armies within three weeks in the world's first *blitzkrieg* (lightning war). On September 17 the Russians occupied eastern Poland, which had been assigned to them under the terms of the Moscow Pact. Hitler, still convinced that France and Britain would not fight, offered them peace on the basis of the new situation on October 6, but his offer was spurned. Bad weather forced him to cancel his plan to attack France on November 12. Britain and France stepped up arms production and began to organize for war while French soldiers sat in their bunkers in the Maginot Line, their "impregnable fortress" system on the German border, playing cards and awaiting the attack that did not come.

Meanwhile, Stalin consolidated his gains by arranging military pacts with the Baltic nations. Finland, however, refused the Soviet demand that it cede a small strip of strategic border territory near Leningrad. French and British efforts to help the Finns against Soviet aggression were stymied when Norway and Sweden, protecting their neutrality, refused passage to the Allied troops. That failure unseated Premier Daladier, who was succeeded by Paul Reynaud. In March 1940, after three months of war, Finland surrendered more territory than the Russians had originally demanded.

The Fall of France

Hitler began preparations for his western offensive on April 9, 1940, by occupying Denmark and the coastal cities of Norway, thus preventing the British from controlling the North Sea. Chamberlain, unable to stop Hitler's maneuver, fell from office and was replaced by a National Government under the leadership of Winston Churchill. On May 10, 1940, just as Churchill took office, Hitler attacked Belgium and the Netherlands. Three days later German tanks thundered through the Ardennes forest—which French generals had believed impenetrable—and entered northern France. By May 22 the German tank divisions, led by a blitzkrieg expert named Heinz Guderian, reached the Atlantic coast. The Netherlands had surrendered on May 15, and Belgium stopped fighting on May 28. During the next eight days, at Dunkirk, British naval and civilian craft evacuated the 220,000 British and 120,000 French troops stranded in Belgium, while the Germans hurried the bulk of their armies into France itself.

In France, panic reigned. Italy attacked in the south on June 10, but the real threat was the German advance on Paris. On June 11 the French government left the capital and moved to Tours; a few days later it moved on to Bordeaux. On June 16 Premier Reynaud, who had argued for continuing the fight, resigned; he was replaced by Marshal Henri Philippe Pétain, the hero of Verdun, who advocated peace. On June 22 an armistice was arranged. Hitler occupied two-thirds of France, leaving the southeast under control of a French administration. Pétain and former premier Pierre Laval proceeded to establish an authoritarian state with its headquarters at Vichy, a health resort. Although the French army was destroyed, the navy and France's overseas possessions remained virtually intact under Vichy rule.

Hitler ready to make a May Day speech in Berlin, 1940. Foreign Minister Ribbentrop is on the right.

The blow to French morale was immense; recriminations over the defeat have never stopped. Vichy partisans blamed "moral degeneracy" for the defeat and accused the republican government of corruption. Corruption there was, but, as former Premier Léon Blum demonstrated when he was put on trial in 1941, the government had consistently given the generals all the equipment they asked for. Whatever the "moral" causes of the defeat, it is clear that the army, badly led by generals who still thought in the defensive terms of World War I, was quite unable to react effectively against the superior strategy of Hitler's tank divisions and dive bombers.

The Battle of Britain

In August and September 1940 Hitler's air force pounded the British Isles with high explosives in preparation for a German invasion across the Channel. But Air Marshal Hermann Goering (1893–1946) planned his attack badly. Instead of destroying the newly built radar stations that warned the Royal Air Force of the German approach, the Germans tried to destroy the air bases, and, at the same

Tens of thousands of cheerful Londoners spent every night in the Tube—the subway—for months as they took in stride the Nazi bombings of 1940.

time, to terrorize the British by bombing cities. Royal Air Force pilots fought back, bringing down almost twice as many planes as they lost themselves. On September 17 Hitler cancelled the invasion. The bombing continued, but a handful of brave Spitfire pilots had saved their country from invasion. For the next two years the British, strongly supported by forces from the Dominions, fought their main battles against the Germans in Libya and Egypt. In 1944 Hitler was to resume his air attack on England, but the Battle of Britain was won in 1940.

Germany Attacks the Soviet Union

Shortly after the defeat of France the Soviet Union began collecting its spoils in the Balkans, beginning a series of events that finally destroyed the Nazi-Soviet alliance. The Soviet Union annexed Latvia, Estonia, and Lithuania with German agreement, but on June 26, 1940, without notifying Hitler of his intention, Stalin forced Rumania to cede to Russia the border province of Bessarabia and part of neighboring Bukovina. Hitler replied by forcing Rumania to hand over Transylvania to Hungary; he thus won Hungary's solid allegiance and completely undermined the Rumanian government, which fell and was replaced by a dictatorship subservient to Germany. Nevertheless, the German *Fuehrer* viewed the presence of Russian troops so near the oil fields of Rumania, upon which his legions depended for fuel, as a threat he could not accept He immediately began planning an attack on the Soviet Union. An attempt to persuade Stalin to give him a free hand in the Balkans in return for German agreement to Soviet takeovers in India and Iran failed. In December 1940, Hitler set the date May 15, 1941, for his onslaught against Russia.

The situation in the Balkans spoiled his plans. On October 28, 1940, Mussolini sent his troops into Greece, but the attack bogged down in the face of strong Greek resistance, and, in February 1941, Britain agreed to send troops to reinforce the hard-pressed Greek armies. Hitler had to save the situation in Greece and secure his entire right flank in the Balkans before attacking Russia. In March he occupied Bulgaria; on April 6 he invaded Yugoslavia, which he overran in eleven days. A week later Greece surrendered, and by June 1 Germany had defeated Greek and British forces in Crete, thereby securing its communications in the Aegean area. Hitler's operations in the Balkans were brilliantly successful, but they delayed the invasion of Russia by six weeks.

The invasion finally came on June 22, 1941. Hitler, confident that his blitzkrieg tactics would work once more, expected to win in less than three months. By the middle of July he had taken Smolensk and a million prisoners. His northern army reached the outskirts of Leningrad and his southern thrust penetrated to the Black Sea by the end of August. By the end of September the Nazis held Kiev and had destroyed more than half of the Red Army's troops on the front, but Hitler had lost a quarter of his attack force. He then turned his armies once more toward Moscow. Just outside the city, the Russians, helped by a sudden onset of 30° below zero weather, counterattacked strongly. On December 8, 1941, Hitler put his army on the defensive for the first time.

When the Russian counterblow came Hitler was in a position of immense strength. He controlled most of Europe. Only Britain and Russia held out, and both were in dire straits. Italy was Germany's junior partner; the Balkans were occupied; Vichy France, though not a belligerent, was helping the Germans with men and materials; Spain and Portugal were neutral but cooperative. On December 7, 1941, however, Japan started another war by attacking the United States fleet at its Hawaiian base at Pearl Harbor.

The United States Enters the War in Europe and the Pacific

The outbreak of war in Europe found the United States neither ready nor willing to join the coalition against Hitler. During the 1920s, Washington had carefully limited participation in European affairs, and the onslaught of the depression had deepened American isolationism. When Japan invaded China in 1931, many Americans still hoped that China could become a great market for American goods or were concerned for the protection of American missionaries. The government was seriously alarmed, but it could do no more than state publicly that the United States would not recognize territorial changes brought about by Japanese aggression. As the danger of war in Europe increased, Congress hurried to throw up barriers to any possible American involvement. It passed a Neutrality Act prohibiting the export of arms in 1935, and in 1937 passed another law putting most American trade with belligerent nations on a cash-and-carry basis. As late as 1938, polls showed that two-thirds of the American people favored a proposed constitutional amendment that would have made any declaration of war subject to a national referendum.

Nevertheless, concern for national defense was growing inside the government. In 1937 Congress authorized a modest expansion of United States naval power, and in 1938 it approved a loan to the hard-pressed Chinese. President Roosevelt began pushing for higher defense expenditures in January 1939, and in August he denounced the 1911 treaty regulating American-Japanese trade. When war broke out in Europe, he won congressional permission to sell arms to Britain and France. Various steps toward greater aid culminated in September 1940 in a spectacular trade of 50 American destroyers for British permission to establish American bases on British possessions from Trinidad to Newfoundland. In that same month Congress passed the Selective Service Act, establishing America's first peacetime conscription system.

During the 1940 presidential election campaign Roosevelt strengthened the growing bipartisan consensus for aid to Britain by adding two important Republican leaders to his cabinet. The Republican convention rejected isolationism by nominating Wendell R. Willkie, a businessman who shared Roosevelt's views on the war, to oppose the president. In December 1940, two months after his election victory, Roosevelt proclaimed that America would become "the Arsenal of Democracy." In March 1941, Congress authorized a "Lend-Lease" program that provided war materials to the Allies through sale, transfer, exchange, or lease, ending the cash-and-carry policy. Roosevelt cautiously extended American air and naval patrols far into the Atlantic in order to protect the supplies crossing to Britain from German submarines. In September, when an American destroyer was attacked, he accused the Germans of piracy and ordered American ships to fire on any submarines they might find.

The reality of war had quickly shifted American sentiment away from isolationism. Nevertheless, most Americans still believed that the United States should carefully avoid the final step into belligerency. Roosevelt made a public show of American friendship with Britain in August 1941, by meeting with Prime Minister Churchill in Newfoundland to issue the Atlantic Charter, a declaration of solidarity among supporters of democracy. But that solidarity did not imply American entrance into the war, which Roosevelt could not promise.

Meanwhile, the Japanese pursued their plans for Asian empire. Soon after France fell, they occupied northern Indochina. In September 1940, they signed the Tripartite Pact with Germany and Italy. Each signatory pledged assistance to the others in case of an attack by a power not yet at war; the United States was obviously the only nation likely to bring the pact into play. Roosevelt reacted immediately with an embargo on the shipment of scrap iron to Japan, thereby seriously weakening Japan's ability to manufacture war materials. Further restrictions on strategic goods, including such significant supplies as copper and brass, soon followed. The Japanese then announced that the embargos made future relations between Japan and the United States "unpredictable."

Slowly, the American government hardened its position; in the spring of 1941 secret British and American military staff conferences produced an agreement on disposition of troops should the United States enter the war. But while military leaders prepared for war, Secretary of State Cordell Hull continued to seek peace in talks with a special Japanese envoy, Admiral Kichisaburo Nomura.

These negotiations never got past the basic point of disagreement: Japan was determined to dominate China, and the United States was determined to prevent it from doing so. In July 1941 the Japanese extended their occupation of Indochina to several major bases in the south, including Saigon and Camranh Bay. In retaliation the American government froze all Japanese assets within the United States. Trade with Japan stopped. The government of the Dutch East Indies, Japan's major source of oil, followed suit. Japan had oil reserves for only two years and no source for their replenishment; faced with a gradual decline in its power as its oil reserves dwindled, Japan began to prepare for war even as negotiations continued. The Japanese premier, Prince Fumumaro Konoye (1891–1945), still wanted to press for peace; army leaders ousted him and put in his place the minister of war, General Hideki Tojo (1885–1948), who was ready to undertake the desperate gamble involved in an attack on the United States. The Japanese knew that their chance for victory was slim, but the dream of empire was strong. It was certain that Japan's expansion would be halted if it did not fight. American leaders knew at the end of November that war was near, and the armed forces were alerted. The alert, how-

The U. S. battleship Arizona *sinking at Pearl Harbor, December 7, 1941.*

ever, was not taken seriously enough. As a result, most of the United States Pacific fleet was destroyed, and 2500 American soldiers and sailors died when Japanese carrier-based planes bombed Pearl Harbor, Hawaii, on the morning of Sunday, December 7, 1941. The United States and Britain declared war on Japan on December 8. Three days later Germany and Italy declared war on the United States.

America's involvement in the fighting meant that the war had to be fought on four major fronts: in the Atlantic, which the Allies had to secure in order to attack the Germans in Western Europe; in Russia; in the Pacific, where Japan quickly conquered the huge area from Southeast Asia through the Dutch Indies and the chain of islands stretching from the Aleutians to the Solomons; and in China. Despite the shock of Japan's attack, President Roosevelt confirmed an informal agreement made earlier with Britain that the defeat of Germany, in the heart of the Axis coalition, was to be the first Allied priority.

The Allied Victory in Western Europe

When it had become clear in July 1940 that Britain was not likely to surrender, Hitler had authorized a rapid increase in the manufacture of submarines. As a result of increased German undersea attacks, Britain had lost a third of its merchant shipping tonnage by December 1941; only 30 percent of the losses could be replaced. By the middle of 1942, although the submarine toll was still increasing, the United States and Canada were building ships faster than the Germans could sink them. Improved escort systems combined with Allied aircraft (using a new microwave radar to locate submarines) to cut the number of sinkings in half in April 1943; in May, Allied surface and aircraft sank a third of Germany's operational submarines. Germany was forced to cut back sharply on submarine warfare, and the Allies had won the Battle of the Atlantic.

Stalin began pressing for a second front in

WORLD WAR II, 1942–1945

EIRE

GREAT BRITAIN

SWEDEN

North Sea

DENMARK

LATVIA

★ Moscow

LITHUANIA

EAST PRUSSIA

*BATTLE LINE,
JAN. 1945*

NETHER:

London ★

*SURRENDER OF BERLIN,
MAY 8, 1945*

GERMANY

★ Berlin

POLAND

★ Warsaw

U.S.S.R.

Kharkov •

*NORMANDY INVASION,
JUNE 6, 1944*

BELG.

*THE
RUHR*

★ Torgau

Breslau •

• Kiev

Paris
★

LUX.

*REMAGEN
BRIDGE*

★ Prague

CZECHOSLOVAKIA

• Rostov

Pilsen •

FRANCE

Vichy •

SWITZ.

AUSTRIA

Vienna ★

HUNGARY

RUMANIA

CRIMEA

Yalta •

Milan •

ITALY

• Bologne

YUGOSLAVIA

• Bucharest

Black Sea

*Battle line,
Sept. 1944–
Apr. 1945*

BULGARIA

• Toulon

*ALLIED
INVASION,
AUG. 1944*

CORSICA

Rome ★

*Battle line,
June 1944*

• Sofia

• Skopjle

Istanbul •

• Ankara

SPAIN

•SARDINIA

ALBANIA

GREECE

TURKEY

SYRIA

Gibraltar
(Br.)

Algiers •

Tunis •

*ALLIED
INVASION,
JULY–SEPT.
1943*

SICILY

Athens •

CYPRUS
(Br.)

LEBANON

-ANISH MOROCCO

-sablanca •

*ANGLO-AMERICAN LANDINGS,
NOV. 8, 1942*

Kasserine •

TUNISIA

Mediterranean Sea

CRETE

PALESTINE

JORDAN

ALGERIA

Tripoli •

Tobruk •

• El Alamein
FINAL BRITISH DRIVE, OCT. 1942

EGYPT

SAUDI
ARABIA

*FREE FRENCH
from
EQUATORIAL AFRICA*

LIBYA

Allied powers

Axis powers

Neutral states

Axis powers overcome by Allies
Neutral powers overcome by Allies

---- Line of farthest German advance, Nov. 1942

—·— Front in May 1944

—··— Front in Jan. 1945

⟶ Allied-Russian advances and invasions

Europe soon after the United States entered the war, and the Western Allies sought to meet his demands. Early plans to invade France in 1942 had to be scrapped because neither the men nor the equipment was available. Instead, American and British troops landed in North Africa on November 8, 1942. The amphibious force quickly overcame early resistance by Vichy French forces in Morocco and Algeria, and by December the Allied force was poised on the Tunisian frontier. Meanwhile, British forces in Egypt, driven back to El Alamein earlier in the year, had broken through the front lines of the German and Italian troops. Led by General Sir Bernard Montgomery, they pushed the German and Italian armies all the way across Libya into Tunisia, where the Axis armies were trapped between two advancing forces. After five months of hard fighting the Allies forced the Axis powers out of Africa. As soon as the battle ended in May 1943, the Allies, still not ready for landings in France, began preparations for the invasion of Sicily. Once more triumph was swift: the Allies landed on July 9, and the island was secure in the middle of August.

As we shall see later, the defeat in Sicily

unseated Mussolini, who was arrested by order of King Victor Emmanuel and replaced by Marshal Pietro Badoglio. The new government dragged out its secret negotiations with the Allies for a month and a half, thus giving German troops ample time to be deployed throughout the country. When Italy's unconditional surrender to the Allies was made public on September 8, 1943, German troops occupied Rome and established control over most of the Italian mainland.

By that time plans for a major Allied landing on the French channel coast were almost complete. Only a limited force was available for an Italian campaign, but Italian airfields would be valuable for increasing the air offensive against Germany and for threatening German control of the Balkans. Therefore the invasion of Italy was carried out as planned. The first Allied troops landed on September 3, 1943, and began their advance northward. The Germans gave ground so slowly that only the collapse of their homeland in 1945 put an end to the war in Italy.

The buildup for the landings in northern France began at the end of 1943. On the eve of the invasion, which took place on June 6, 1944, the Allies had available in England 47 divisions, more than 5000 ships, and more than 10,000 planes, all under the command of General Dwight D. Eisenhower (1890–1969). Scattered throughout Western Europe were Hitler's 60 divisions, protected by their "Atlantic Wall," a string of fortifications extending from Norway to the Pyrenees. Careful planning gave the Allies the advantage of surprise. Spearheaded by ground forces under the command of General Montgomery, the invasion force secured its beachheads immediately. After six weeks of heavy fighting, during which troops and supplies flooded across the English Channel, the Allied forces broke through the German defenses in Normandy in mid-July and began the long journey across France and the Rhine to Berlin. On August 15 new armies landed on the southern French coast. Paris, liberated by its own citizens as the Allies advanced, was in the hands of General Jacques Leclerc's Free French 2nd Armored Division on August 25. Hitler's defeat had become practically inevitable, but his troops fought relentlessly. As the battles raged, new German

weapons—bombs carried by pilotless airplanes and supersonic rockets—rained on London and the British countryside. A German counterattack in the Ardennes region in December 1944 threatened momentarily to break through the Allied front, but American and British troops held firm to win the "Battle of the Bulge." The Allied advance resumed in March 1945, and American and Russian troops met on the Elbe in May while Hitler lay dead, a suicide, in the ruins of his bunker in Berlin. His successor, Admiral Karl Doenitz, surrendered formally on May 8, 1945.

The Russian Victory in Eastern Europe

Mutual distrust made coordination of the military efforts of the Russians with those of the Western Allies impossible, but the actions of each one were vital to the achievement of victory in Europe.

In December 1941 Hitler's armies, made up not only of Germans but of troops from Finland and the German satellites in the Balkans, stood on a line that went from Leningrad through Rostov into the Caucasus. Russian counterattacks in the winter of 1941–1942 failed to dislodge the Axis forces. Hitler renewed his offensive at the end of June 1942, and by the end of August his armies stood outside Stalingrad (now Volgograd). The Germans still menaced Moscow and Leningrad, but immense losses had sapped their morale, and their supply lines were very long. Through September and October they hammered at Stalingrad, but the city would not fall. On November 19, Soviet troops hit both flanks of the attacking German army. By November 23, the Germans were surrounded. Faced with disaster, Hitler ordered his southern army to pull back from the Caucasus, just in time to escape the Soviet pincers, but the 250,000 Axis troops surrounded at Stalingrad could not retreat. They capitulated on February 2, 1943. In March, Hitler pulled back his armies from the outskirts of Moscow. The Russian advance bogged down as the ground thawed, however, and the Germans stood in the spring of 1943 close to the Leningrad-Smolensk-Dnieper River line they had at-

British soldiers surrendering to their Japanese conquerors at Singapore, February 15, 1942.

tained in the first three months of the war.

Hitler planned one final offensive, but while his troops had dwindled in numbers, the Soviet forces, receiving American Lend-Lease supplies through Murmansk and Archangel, had grown stronger. When Hitler's armies attacked on July 5, Soviet troops held firm. The counterattack came on July 12, and it was the first blow in a steady advance that carried Soviet forces into the heart of Germany. By January 1944 they had driven the Germans across the Polish frontier; by the middle of July they were deep in northeastern Poland and Lithuania. In August they paused outside Warsaw, thus, purposely or accidentally, giving the Germans a chance to quell the rebellion sparked by the Polish "home army." But they were at that time stopped along the entire front; the Soviet armies, in their long advance, had outrun their supply forces. They recovered quickly, however, and moved rapidly through the

German-occupied Balkan nations. Rumania deserted the Axis late in August 1944; Belgrade was liberated on October 20; and Soviet troops passed through Rumania to occupy Bulgaria without opposition. Budapest withstood four months of siege, but it finally surrendered in February 1945. Early in 1945 Soviet troops entered East Prussia. Like the British, Canadians, French, Americans, and the other Western Allies, they faced strong opposition, but victory was in their grasp. They surrounded Berlin on April 25, and Russian generals joined those in the West in accepting Germany's surrender in May.

The War in the Pacific

Although Allied statesmen gave the war in Europe priority over the battle in the Pacific, they could not ignore Japan's aggression. The attempt to stem the Japanese advance began immediately after the attack on Pearl Harbor.

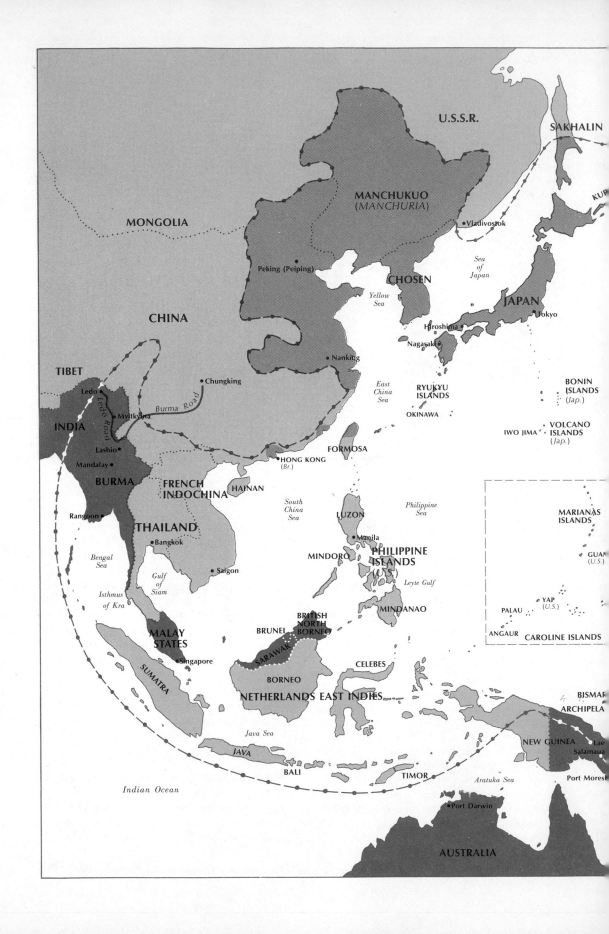

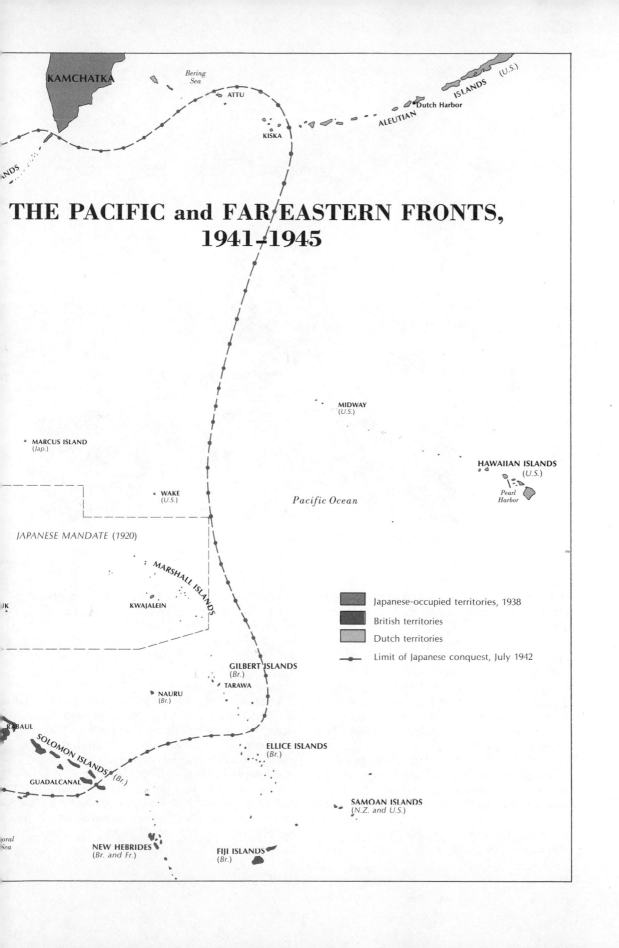

THE PACIFIC and FAR EASTERN FRONTS, 1941–1945

KAMCHATKA

Bering Sea

ATTU

ISLANDS (U.S.)

Dutch Harbor

ALEUTIAN

KISKA

NDS

MARCUS ISLAND
(Jap.)

MIDWAY
(U.S.)

WAKE
(U.S.)

HAWAIIAN ISLANDS
(U.S.)

Pearl
Harbor

Pacific Ocean

JAPANESE MANDATE (1920)

MARSHALL ISLANDS

UK

KWAJALEIN

GILBERT ISLANDS
(Br.)
TARAWA

NAURU
(Br.)

RABAUL

SOLOMON ISLANDS (Br.)

GUADALCANAL

ELLICE ISLANDS
(Br.)

SAMOAN ISLANDS
(N.Z. and U.S.)

oral
Sea

NEW HEBRIDES
(Br. and Fr.)

FIJI ISLANDS
(Br.)

▨	Japanese-occupied territories, 1938
▨	British territories
▨	Dutch territories
━●━	Limit of Japanese conquest, July 1942

American Marines raise the flag at Iwo Jima.

The Japanese sank or seriously damaged eight American battleships in their first attack, leaving the United States Pacific fleet severely crippled. Simultaneously, they opened attacks on Wake Island, Guam, the Philippines, and Hong Kong. Heroic defenders could not withstand the well-prepared Japanese onslaught: within a month all those bases had fallen. The attack continued throughout Southeast Asia. Singapore, Britain's most important base in the Far East, fell on February 15, 1942; Japanese troops, attacking from Malaya, easily penetrated the flimsy defenses on the island's landward side. On March 9 the Japanese finished their conquest of the Netherlands East Indies, thus assuring themselves the oil they had been denied by the Dutch and American govern-

ments. Burma, the depot for supplies going to China, fell at the end of April. Thailand had no choice but to collaborate with Japan. In less than six months the Japanese had built the Asian empire their military leaders had dreamed of. Whether they could hold it remained to be seen.

In March 1942, Japan began to round out its island conquests in order to protect the eastern perimeter of its new empire. In May, however, the small remaining United States aircraft carrier force succeeded in preventing the capture of Port Moresby, in Papua (Australian New Guinea). A month later, when the Japanese tried to conquer Midway, an American-controlled island uncomfortably close to Hawaii, U.S. Navy planes sank four Japanese carriers. The Battle of Midway was

Hiroshima after atomic attack, August 1945. View from a Red Cross hospital about one mile from the center of the explosion.

the turning point in the Pacific war: it stopped Japanese preparations for further conquests and did irreparable damage to the Imperial Navy.

Allied forces soon were preparing to recapture the chain of islands extending from near the shores of Australia directly to Japan. The Japanese landed troops on Guadalcanal (in the Solomon Islands) on July 6 and began to build an air base there. A month later, on August 7, the U.S. First Marine Division went ashore to begin the long task of reconquest. Both sides poured in reinforcements; the battle lasted six months. The Japanese managed to evacuate 12,000 troops early in February 1943, leaving the island to the Allies. Hindered by a chronic shortage of troops and equipment because of the agreement to give priority to the drive against Germany, American and Australian troops moved from island to island as Allied ships and planes gradually destroyed the remainder of the Japanese fleet. During 1942 and early 1943, the Japanese were forced out of Papua and eastern New Guinea; in 1944 the Marianas and Palau Islands fell to the Allies and

troops led by General Douglas MacArthur (1880–1964), who had been commander of the Philippine army defeated early in the war, retook Leyte. MacArthur had control of the rest of the Philippines by July 1944. In 1945 the inexorable advance washed over Iwo Jima and Okinawa after particularly bloody battles. Desperate Japanese pilots, dedicated to self-sacrifice in special religious ceremonies, damaged and sank dozens of Allied ships in *Kamikaze* suicide attacks. Japan had lost the war but refused to surrender.

Plans for the invasion of Japan were under way when an American plane dropped a new and awesome weapon, the first atomic bomb, on Hiroshima on August 6, 1945. On August 8 the Soviet Union declared war on Japan and moved into Manchuria and northern Korea. On that same day another atomic bomb was dropped on Nagasaki. On August 14 the Japanese, assured that they would be permitted to retain their emperor, surrendered. Their surrender was formally accepted on an American battleship in Tokyo Bay on September 2, 1945.

The China-Burma Theater

The Sino-Japanese War, in progress since 1931, was little affected by the outbreak of war in Europe, but when Japan attacked the United States in 1941 China's long resistance began to look less hopeless. The shaky alliance made at the end of 1936 between Chiang Kai-Shek and Mao Tse-tung temporarily put an end to fighting between the Kuomintang and the Communists, but it did not halt Japan's drive into China. Japanese troops took Shanghai in August 1937, after three months of heavy fighting, and in December they drove Chiang out of Nanking, his capital. By the end of 1938 the Kuomintang army had retreated all the way to Chungking, in Szechuan, far in the interior of China.

Chiang made little effort to counterattack, but the Communists, used to operating underground, moved into villages behind the Japanese lines in the early 1940s. There they began building a mass peasant organization based on the old Chinese tradition of mutual aid. In the past, mutual aid had been a family affair — relatives helped each other when help was needed. The Communists altered the system by recruiting young peasant leaders who could organize whole villages for cooperative endeavors. Simultaneously, they turned the work teams thus formed into military organizations, the villages into military bases. Meanwhile, instead of persecuting well-to-do peasants, as they had in Kiansi in the 1930s, they encouraged them to increase production. The Kuomintang, afraid that armed peasants would never return to docility, made no effort to compete with the Communists in guerrilla warfare. Peasants, who had lost most of their traditional leaders when the rich left the countryside during the period of warlord rule, reacted to Communist leadership with enthusiasm, particularly because the Communists were scrupulously fair in all their dealings. Many intellectuals, relieved to see the Communists drop their violent antilandlord campaigns and delighted with Communist success in disrupting Japanese supply lines, gradually lost their distrust of Mao and his followers.

Chiang's troops meanwhile fought to hold their Szechuan stronghold. Local farms kept the Kuomintang army supplied with food, while heavy military equipment, which the Chinese could not manufacture, came in over the Burma Road and the Yunnan-Indochina railway. Japanese military offensives in 1938 failed to dislodge Chiang. A diplomatic offensive designed to bring a negotiated peace on Japanese terms was equally unsuccessful. In 1940 France and Britain, trying to appease Japan as they earlier had tried to appease Germany, cut off the flow of supplies over China's two import routes, but Chiang still held out. Japan then moved to organize the coastal areas it occupied, setting up a Chinese puppet government and establishing new industries that could produce supplies for the greater war that was to come.

After Pearl Harbor, Chiang began to cooperate with American and British troops in hard-pressed Burma. In return, he received a trickle of vital aviation gasoline and equipment flown from India over the Himalayan "hump" and tactical air support, at first from American volunteers and later from a U.S. fighter squadron. Japan cut off the old Burma Road and the Indochina railway permanently in 1942, but by early 1944 British and American engineers had hacked out the Ledo Road, over which supplies could once more move by land from India to China. Meanwhile, Chiang's troops, contented merely to hold their base in the interior of China, fought little against the Japanese until the war was nearly over. Early in 1944, however, Chiang raised nine new divisions, which he used to open counteroffensives in northern Burma and western China. Working with U.S. troops, they captured the city of Myitkyina, Burma, with its airport, in August 1944, thereby tremendously easing Allied delivery of supplies to China. Within his own country Chiang's troops made similar advances as Japan's power steadily weakened. Most of western and southern China was in Chiang's hands when the Japanese surrender came in September 1945.

THE ALLIED HOME FRONTS

Britain, the Soviet Union, and the United States, unprepared when war came, simply held off their enemies until they could pro-

English housewives stood in queues like this one in London's East End to get their daily food rations throughout the war and for years afterward.

duce enough to supply their growing armies. They had learned the necessity for central planning in World War I, so they quickly organized to cut civilian production to the barest minimum and to produce ever-increasing quantities of war materiel. Meanwhile, normal political affairs had to be readjusted to fit the needs of war.

Britain

In Britain the threat of invasion brought about major upheavals. Chamberlain's government fell in May 1940 because the House of Commons wanted more vigorous leadership. Churchill, his successor, organized a National Government that included representatives of the Labour and Liberal parties as well as his own Conservative followers. Aware that Hitler's submarine blockade might force them into submission at any time, Britons accepted with good grace the strictest austerity. Meanwhile, the Lord President's Committee, chaired most of the time by Labour party leader Clement Attlee

(1883–1967), took total control of the economy. Gradually, increasing manpower coordination became complete in December 1941, with the passage of the National Service Act. The economist John Maynard Keynes, advising the Treasury, devised a system of war finance that minimized inflation: taxes were raised, bond drives were held, compulsory saving was instituted, and goods rationing covered every scarce resource. By 1944 Britain was paying 55 percent of its war costs with current taxes, and British production of tanks and aircraft was greater than that of Germany.

The war brought about new government intervention in daily life, laying the basis for the postwar welfare state. In November 1942, Sir William Beveridge issued a *Report on Social Insurance and Allied Services* that showed the government's quickening interest not only in preventing abject poverty but also in establishing protection for the entire population against sickness and unemployment. Some of Beveridge's recommendations became law before the end of the

Japanese-American civilians held in an evacuation camp at Manzanar, California, in 1942.

The United States

War was never a campaign issue in the United States: Congressional elections were held on schedule and President Roosevelt easily won a fourth term in 1944. Eminent Republicans served in the president's cabinet, and many businessmen who would normally have fought a Democratic administration not only dropped their opposition "for the duration" but served as "dollar-a-year men" in special wartime agencies. Labor unions promised not to strike during the war, and the promise was generally kept despite a flare-up of labor strife around the issue of miners' wages early in 1943. Pro-Nazi groups, some of which had won notoriety before the war, disappeared in the face of public abhorrence when the United States entered the war. Fears of sabotage led, however, to the forced evacuation of 110,000 Japanese-Americans from West Coast areas to internment camps in less strategic areas. The conduct of Hawaii's large population of Japanese descent, plus the brilliant performance of Nisei army units, showed that such fears were unjustified.

To gear production for war and to prevent inflation, price, wage, and manpower controls were imposed in the United States as they were in Britain. Housewives carefully counted cardboard coins that represented "red points" when they planned trips to the butcher shop; car pools were developed; and commuters schemed to get special windshield stickers that would entitle them to extra gallons of gasoline. Imported or scarce

war. The government pledged in 1944 that it would follow policies designed to promote full employment. But probably the most important change the war brought to England was a surge of egalitarian feeling: class lines seemed to lose much of their importance when the entire nation was fighting for its life.

raw materials were rationed carefully to producers by a War Production Board. Military conscription, with deferments for men in "essential" occupations, controlled the use of manpower. Though most of the special war agencies were scrapped in 1946, Americans had received another lesson in the advantages (and disadvantages) of state control of the economy.

Soviet Union

Stalin took advantage of the breathing space provided by his pact with Hitler in August 1939 to establish new industrial bases in Siberia and in other areas far from his western frontier. Hitler's early conquests cut Soviet industrial production in half, but the shift of more than 1200 entire factories to the east saved the Soviet Union from defeat. In Leningrad and other cities under siege, however, hundreds of thousands of people starved. But equipment made in the relocated factories, plus American Lend-Lease supplies of trucks, food, and clothing, kept the army supplied while the nation struggled to its feet once more.

Although the Soviet Union suffered far more during World War II than either Britain or the United States, Stalin had little need to alter his government in order to resist Hitler's attack, for state control was part of the Communist way of life. Yet the Nazi onslaught threatened at first to destroy the whole Communist system. In order to inspire the sacrifices necessary for victory, Stalin's propagandists began to glorify Russia's past military greatness and to play down Communist internationalism. The government, in a major reversal, reestablished the Russian Orthodox Church in 1943 and encouraged worship. It also reintroduced rank insignia and special uniforms for military officers. Toward the end of the war, however, government propaganda again stressed the role of the Communist party in the struggle for victory, preparing for the return of peace and a return to standard Stalinist doctrine.

Science in Wartime

Governments were intensely aware of the importance of scientists in World War II.

Special boards of scientific advisers were established in Britain and the United States to coordinate technological development. The British invention of radar came from a team backed by air ministry funds. The great atomic power establishments—Harwell in Britain, Los Alamos and Oak Ridge in the United States—were government owned and organized. Aircraft plants that built constantly improving planes, including jets toward the end of the war, worked on government contracts under close government supervision.

The great wartime inventions and the perfection of little known but highly useful older achievements like penicillin and DDT have had immense influence on the postwar world, but the new organization of science was even more important. Since World War II, government and science have been closely allied. During the war, the possible fruits of such collaboration became obvious. The possible disadvantages also were made clear when a group of leading scientists trying to prevent use of the first atomic bomb were not even able to get a message through to President Harry S. Truman, Roosevelt's successor.

HITLER'S EUROPE: "THE NEW ORDER"

Germany at War

During the first two years of the war Germany controlled most of Europe, and from Berlin Hitler exploited his conquests for Germany's benefit. Quick as he was to appreciate every military innovation, however, he miscalculated the cost of total war.

Instead of reorganizing the German economy to produce massive quantities of military supplies, Hitler planned to build stockpiles that would suffice only for each *blitzkrieg* as it came. In that way he could easily switch production from fighter planes to tanks, or from rifles to submarines, to prepare for whatever campaign he had in view. Moreover, he was able to fight the first two years of war without cutting into civilian production or expanding his munitions plants: all that was necessary was to bring Germany's production up to capacity. The system broke down, however, when the Soviet Union stalled the German drive toward Moscow at the end of 1941.

In February 1942, Hitler had to change his plans. He appointed a new munitions minister, Albert Speer, who dramatically increased war production despite serious obstacles. Rival planners in the air force and in the elite SS (*Schutzstaffel* — Security Service) army corps kept control of large areas of production. High Nazi officials disapproved of Speer's methods, and Hitler himself interfered with economic planning when Speer began to cut too deeply into civilian production. As a result, Germany's economy never really was geared for total war: production for purely civilian purposes remained high until late in 1944, and German armies suffered increasing shortages of supplies while Allied stockpiles were growing ever larger.

The Areas of German Occupation

Hitler followed no particular policy in dealing with the lands he conquered. He simply annexed large areas of Poland, while German administrators controlled most of the rest of occupied Europe, including whole nations such as the Netherlands, Belgium, and Czechoslovakia. Local Nazis, like the Norwegian Major Vidkun Quisling, or men prepared to collaborate with Hitler, like Marshal Henri Pétain of France, held office with German support in some areas. In every case, however, Hitler's demands had to be met.

Those demands were immense. Nazi administrators used legal forms for sophisticated plundering of the occupied nations. By inflating the taxes collected to pay for the occupation Hitler's henchmen were able to use local funds to buy control of important industries in France, Belgium, and Rumania. Nazi managers ran a million and a half acres of state farms in the Soviet Union, but they failed to bring the industries of the Don basin back into production. When the long war began to strain the German economy, foreign workers were brought in, at first as volunteers then by coercion. Some seven million slave laborers were at work in Germany by mid-1944. Early attempts at model occupation policies rapidly gave way to a system of brutal repression.

Marshal Pétain, the hero of Verdun, played a thankless role as chief of state in unoccupied France. Old and infirm, convinced that he could somehow pull his country out of the "degeneracy" that brought its defeat, he was actually the pawn of politicians like former premier Pierre Laval (1883–1945) and Admiral François Darlan (1881–1942), who served at different times as Pétain's chief minister. Ruling from the temporary capital at Vichy, Pétain established a reactionary government that increased church influence, installed a "corporative" economic organization, and tried to maintain a shred of independence in the face of Hitler's power. Laval, chief engineer of the parliamentary decision to give Pétain full power, later claimed that he had served France by sabotaging Hitler's demands for increasing aid; some scholars have accepted his argument. In any case, Hitler put an end to Vichy's independence by occupying the whole of France when the Allies invaded North Africa in November 1942. A little over two years later Laval was shot after a hurried trial after France was liberated; Pétain was imprisoned. To most Frenchmen, Vichy was a disgrace added to the disaster of defeat.

Hitler's Genocide

Hitler took advantage of his immense power to put into practice his racial theories. From his earliest days as chancellor he had jailed or murdered anyone who stood in his way. During the war he tried to build his new order by genocide. He described the Poles as "especially born for hard labor." Therefore he set out to exterminate wealthy and educated men who might lead Polish opposition to his plans. Half the Czechs he planned to "Germanize," the other half to exterminate. Hitler particularly hated intellectuals, and they were ruthlessly wiped out in occupied Europe.

Most of all, Hitler persecuted Jews. In the occupied areas Jews were jailed and forced to work under inhuman conditions until they died. Women, children, old people and others unable to do hard labor were killed immediately. At first they were shot; soon

Bodies of prisoners tortured to death by Nazi guards at Oswiecim, Poland.

Nazi technicians found ways to do the job more efficiently. Hitler's SS shipped millions of victims in cattle cars to five large extermination centers. Some captives were singled out to be subjected to "medical experiments"; various sadistic guards and camp commanders arranged to keep souvenirs such as lampshades made of human skin; inlays were stripped from the mouths of victims and added to the German gold reserves. At Auschwitz alone more than two million people, most of them Jews, were gassed and burned, and half a million more died of starvation and disease. Nazi-appointed Councils of Jewish elders were sometimes forced to choose victims for execution. When Jews resisted, as they did when the Germans destroyed the Warsaw ghetto in April 1943, they were slaughtered to the last man, woman, and child. Nearly five million Jews died in Hitler's gas chambers. Another million of Hitler's enemies suffered the same fate, and another million Jews were shot or beaten to death.

Mass killing was hardly new; the Japanese had killed thousands of Chinese, and Stalin had killed millions of Russians, during the 1930s. But Hitler was the first modern ruler to institute genocide as a national policy.

Italy's Role in the War

Marshal Badoglio's assumption of power marked the end of Italy's imperial ventures, but it did not end the sufferings brought on by Mussolini's dreams of glory. The conquest of Ethiopia had given the Italian dictator an unrealistic notion of his country's military capability. After Italian troops failed to subdue the Greeks and invade Egypt, Italy became little more than Hitler's client state. A major portion of Italy's meager food and factory output went to Germany in return for continually decreasing returns. Italian troops were badly armed, Italian civilians badly fed. When Sicily fell, Mussolini's prestige fell with it. He was removed by the Fascist Grand Council in July 25, 1943, and arrested by the king. No public outcry greeted this act, and other Fascist leaders temporarily disappeared.

The Allies allowed Badoglio to rule in the areas they liberated in the south and accepted Italy as an inactive cobelligerent largely in order to avoid difficulties behind the lines as they advanced slowly northward. Meanwhile, in September 1943, the Nazis rescued Mussolini from prison and installed him as head of a puppet Italian Social Republic in northern Italy. Gradually the Allies moved north, turning over administration to the Italians as they moved. Allied food and medicine served to begin the huge task of reconstruction. Once reinstalled in Rome in July 1944, Badoglio's caretaker government relinquished its power to a new coalition under Ivanoe Bonomi, a pre-Fascist premier, who began to grapple with the financial and material chaos of a nation torn by years of occupation and war. Finally, as German defeat drew near in April 1945, Italian partisans seized the former dictator, killed him, and strung his body up alongside that of his mistress in a public square in Milan.

The Resistance Movements

Few citizens in modernized nations welcomed occupation. After an initial period of pessimism that followed conquest, resistance groups grew in most occupied nations. In France, local groups tended to look for leadership either to General De Gaulle, who had begun building a Free French armed force in England immediately after the defeat, or to the well-organized Communists after the German invasion of the U.S.S.R. freed them from inactivity in July 1941. By August 1944, French resisters were so strong that they were able to play a significant part in the liberation of Paris. In Poland, resisters organized a powerful Home Army. They rose in arms as the Russians advanced toward Warsaw, but, as we have noted, the Russian army was either unable or unwilling to aid them: they were crushed by the Germans. As for Russia, Stalin credited resisters in the occupied areas with a major share in the rollback of German troops. Resisters in Italy worked with the Western Allies during the last year of the war, and Italian partisans executed Mussolini. Everywhere unreconciled patriots sacrificed themselves in acts of propaganda, sabotage, or outright assault against the conqueror. In the last stages of the war their efforts undoubtedly saved the lives of thousands of the invading liberators.

Communists in Europe had suffered a grievous political blow when Stalin signed the Moscow Pact with Hitler, but soon after the Germans invaded the Soviet Union they began to use their experience in underground work to organize resistance bands. Following the Soviet example, they soft-pedalled Leninist doctrine and stressed their patriotism. Stalin helped by officially disbanding the Comintern in 1943. By the end of the war, Communist organizations tended to overshadow other resistance groups in most of the occupied nations, and their heroism in the battle against the conquerors caused many Europeans to forgive their early passive acceptance of the Nazis. When the war ended, they had become politically powerful all over Europe, but especially in France, Italy, and Greece. In Yugoslavia, Communist partisans led by Marshal Tito (Josip Broz, 1892–   ) won control of most of the nation's extensive mountainous area despite the German, Italian, Hungarian, and Bulgarian occupation. Urging all Croats, Serbs, Macedonians, and other ethnic groups to put aside their old quarrels in order to fight the occupying powers, Tito's partisans built support that enabled them to defeat royalist resisters in open civil war while simultaneously fighting foreign enemies. In October 1944, they liberated Belgrade. When the war ended Tito's personal popularity was so great and his organization so strong that he was able to win full control of the country.

Even in Germany a small band of resisters was organized by 1944, but most of its members sought to unseat the dictator not because they were anti-Nazi but because Germany was losing the war. They attempted to assassinate Hitler by bombing a conference room in July 1944, but he escaped with only minor wounds and immediately carried out a widespread purge that disposed of most of the plotters.

JAPAN'S "CO-PROSPERITY SPHERE"

Meanwhile, Japan was committed to the building of its Greater East Asia Co-Prosperity Sphere. Because its aims and its philosophy differed from those of Hitler, it was constrained to treat conquered territories far more carefully than did the Nazis. Throughout East Asia, Japanese authorities taught the Japanese language, attempted to "reform" education to eradicate Western influences, and organized scholarly conferences. Puppet leaders under Japanese control were put into office in China and Burma, and the Philippines were declared independent in 1943. Malaya and the Dutch East Indies, sources of vital supplies, were governed by Japanese administrators until defeat became inevitable; the conquerors then encouraged the development of nationalist movements. Despite these basically positive policies, however, the Japanese occupation became increasingly unpopular in most areas, because Japanese administrators used torture and execution to maintain their control.

By replacing Western colonialists in positions of power the Japanese gave a strong psychological lift to Asian independence movements. Japanese troops, by driving out Western garrisons, not only showed the vanity of Western boasts that European powers could protect their colonial charges from invaders but also proved once again that yellow men could defeat whites in battles. They also opened to local administrators posts once reserved for Westerners, thus giving the occupied territories experience in self-government. In the Dutch East Indies, the nationalist agitator Achmed Sukarno (see p. 846) worked openly with the Japanese while other nationalists worked underground against them. Sukarno established an Indonesian government with Japanese aid in 1945 before British troops arrived to accept the Japanese surrender. In Indochina, Ho Chi Minh staged a coup after the surrender and established a Democratic Republic of Viet Nam that refused to recognize French authority over the country. No other nationalist leaders achieved success as spectacular as that of Sukarno and Ho, but all over Asia independence movements gained new prestige as a result of Japan's occupation.

Economically, the "Co Prosperity Sphere" was always a sham. Most of the occupied areas had been Western colonies and had traded heavily with their foreign rulers. Japan did not establish new industries or otherwise improve the economies of the lands it conquered. Instead, the Japanese simply substituted themselves for the Western exploiters, importing raw materials like tin from Malaya, rubber from Indochina, and oil from the East Indies, and paying for them with industrial products. As the war continued, Japan took more and returned less. But Japan demonstrated its power to replace the West as Asia's industrial supplier.

Like Germany, Japan had survived the early years of the war without difficulty, but by the end of 1944 imports on which it depended were cut drastically by American naval action. In late 1944 and 1945 ceaseless bombings disrupted daily life, killed thousands of civilians, and destroyed thousands of buildings. In April 1945, a new administration headed by Premier Kantaro Suzuki (1867–1948) began to try to negotiate peace, but the United States would accept only unconditional surrender. The catastrophe of the atomic bombs merely hastened a collapse already accepted as inevitable.

THE WAR AND MODERNIZATION

World War II may have been the vehicle for the most rapid modernization in world history. In the most modern nations—the great powers and the small states of northern Europe—the war tremendously spurred the development of integrated mass societies. In the United States, for example, the wartime production boom, with its great demand for factory labor, lured millions of blacks away from marginal farms in the south toward the big cities. Major race riots took place in Detroit, and black "ghettos" expanded in every major city. It was no longer possible for white America to ignore the plight of the blacks—the development of great black urban clusters set the stage for the struggles that are still in progress. In Britain, the shared horrors of war tended to break down class lines and to promote demands for a more general sharing of Britain's wealth. In France, the resistance became a battle for social revolution as well as an underground war against the conqueror.

In all those nations the demands of war tended to destroy vestiges of regionalism and to promote the growth of loyalty toward and dependence upon central governments. Regional and provincial governments lost much of their autonomy when conscription, rationing, and wage and price controls, established by national administrations, radically altered old ways of life. Meanwhile, millions of men left their homes and traveled widely, either in the military service or to work in war industries, often at the direct order or request of central governments. Looking to the national capital for direction became habitual.

In less developed nations, World War II had an even greater impact. In colonial areas, leaders of independence movements found the war working in their favor. They usually combined demands for modernizing reforms with their demands for national freedom. Colonial peoples who fought in imperial armies expected rewards. In conquered areas in both Europe and Asia, modernizing nationalists, some Communists and others not, led resistance movements. During the war, Ho Chi Minh, Sukarno, Mao Tsetung, and Tito all established the prestige that made their postwar achievements possible. In other areas, such as French North Africa, official propaganda promoted nationalism and modernization by promising postwar social reforms. Thus in almost every area touched by the war the forces of modernization were so greatly strengthened that nothing could prevail against them when peace returned.

WARTIME DIPLOMACY AND THE BALANCE SHEET OF VICTORY

From the earliest days of the war, national leaders not only had to decide among themselves how the battles would be fought but also had to consider what sort of world they wanted to construct when the fighting stopped. Moreover, diplomacy clothed in idealistic slogans was essential from the start if the masses were to make the sacrifices essential in total war. Just as in World War I, however, the necessity for demagoguery deeply influenced the nature of the decisions made. Because each nation had its own reasons for fighting, conflicts were bound to arise, and differences had to be settled or papered over.

Roosevelt, convinced that America would be endangered by a British defeat, wanted to aid Britain as much as possible even before the war began. Americans, however, would not react with solid enthusiasm to balance-of-power arguments. Roosevelt therefore gave them grander goals. In August 1941, he and Churchill signed the Atlantic Charter, in which they pledged their countries to create an international security system and to let boundaries be drawn and governments established by the people whose lives would be most affected by such decisions. Self-determination was still a mighty slogan; even Stalin, certain to keep control of the Baltic states and the Polish territory he had taken before the German attack on Russia, agreed to sign the Charter. He also went along in 1942 when Roosevelt proclaimed the existence of the United Nations, a grouping of powers fighting fascism and dedicated to the defense of "human rights and justice." These vague but stirring phrases were meant to move the masses; what they meant in practical terms was yet to be worked out.

At later meetings Churchill, Roosevelt, and Stalin made the decisions that laid out the course of the war and shaped the postwar period. Roosevelt agreed to British and Russian demands that the defeat of Hitler be given priority over the war in the Pacific. With Churchill's reluctant support, the President played on the emotional attitudes of Americans by issuing, in 1943, a demand for unconditional surrender of the Axis powers. Real difficulties began to arise, however, when victory drew near.

Churchill began to fear the power of the Soviet Union as soon as he was convinced that the German danger was past. At every opportunity he supported the demands of General De Gaulle, the Free French leader,

Churchill, Roosevelt, and Stalin at Yalta.

for actions that would enhance the power of France. He suggested an Anglo-American invasion of southeastern Europe, a plan that would put Western troops in the way of a Soviet advance deep into the center of the continent. Stalin, meanwhile, insisted that Russia's borders should be surrounded only by nations whose governments were "friendly"; what that meant was not clear, for in several areas of eastern Europe no freely elected government was likely to be friendly to Russia. Roosevelt relished the role of middleman, siding with either Churchill or Stalin depending on the item in dispute. He vetoed Churchill's eastern invasion plans, for example, but he helped France obtain a part in the occupation of Germany.

Yalta and Potsdam

Major decisions could no longer be evaded when the three leaders met at the Russian resort of Yalta, in the Crimea, in February 1945. There they settled six major questions. The nature of United Nations organization and procedures had to be decided. Most important was the question of the veto — it was decided that the great powers could veto only acts involving enforcement of decisions, not the holding of discussions on subjects that might come up. It was agreed that zones of occupation in Germany would be awarded to Britain, the Soviet Union, the United States, and France. The three leaders agreed on a basis for later discussion of reparations and declared that free elections would be held in liberated territories. Most important, they made decisions on the future of China and Poland.

The Soviet Union won major concessions in both countries. It was awarded a naval base at Port Arthur, given a share in control of two railroads in northern China and Manchuria, and its control of Outer Mongolia was affirmed. Roosevelt agreed to obtain approval of these decisions from the Chinese president, Chiang Kai-Shek. Poland's border was to be redrawn to let the U.S.S.R. retain the part of eastern Poland it had taken in 1939, while Poland would be granted an unspecified amount of German territory in compensation. Moreover, the Western powers agreed to recognize the Communist-controlled provisional government of Poland that the Soviet Union had installed when its troops drove out the Germans. Democratic leaders sponsored by the Western powers were to be added to that government.

Roosevelt's critics attacked him bitterly as soon as these decisions were announced. He was accused of "selling out" both Poland and China. His defenders argued that he had no choice. Soviet troops controlled Poland, and nothing short of a war would have dislodged the Communist government. As for China, the concessions Roosevelt made were the price of Russia's entry into the war against Japan; it was feared that the scheduled invasion of Japan's home islands would cost thousands of American lives if Russian aid was withheld.

Hitler's defeat made new negotiations necessary, but when the "Big Three" met at Potsdam, outside Berlin, in July 1945, circumstances had changed radically. Roosevelt had died suddenly on April 12, 1945, and had been succeeded by Vice-President Harry S. Truman, who had been kept ignorant of many facets of American diplomatic activity. In late July, British voters had ousted Churchill's government and the new Labour prime minister, Clement Atlee, replaced Churchill at the conference table. Meanwhile, relations between the powers grew noticeably cooler. Stalin, erroneously believing that the United States was trying to arrange a separate armistice with Germany, had carried out his obligation to add democratic representatives to the Communist government of Poland only after Truman sent a special envoy to Moscow to reassure him. The Russians had flouted earlier liberation agreements by installing a Communist regime in Rumania within a month after the Yalta conference. Negotiations on the founding of the United Nations Organization, held at San Francisco in June 1945, were slow and bitter. Visions of success in producing

the atomic bomb caused Truman to take a tougher position in his relations with the Soviet Union.

At Potsdam, therefore, agreement was difficult. Nevertheless, necessary agreements were made, particularly in regard to the occupation of Germany. Arrangements for disarmament, demilitarization, and "de-Nazification" of Germany were established, and plans were made for the trial of "war criminals." Boundaries were established for the four occupation zones. It was decided that Germany was to be treated as a single economic unit, that the U.S.S.R. would receive limited reparations, and that Germany would be left enough material goods to support itself at a minimal level. Poland's western "administrative boundary" was drawn temporarily at the Oder and western Neisse rivers, thus legitimizing Polish control of a large area of eastern Germany. Germans in Poland, Hungary, and Czechoslovakia were to be removed to Germany in an "orderly and humane manner." Finally, the conferees agreed to establish a Council of Foreign Ministers which would prepare peace treaties for the former German satellites.

The end of the war put an end to the cooperation among the three major victors. While fighting continued, they had to agree on military matters in order to assure their victory. Moreover, United States aid to Russian Communists had to be justified to the American public, so it was necessary to develop the illusion of friendship even where little friendship existed. Difficulties increased as the armies advanced. Westerners insisted that elections held in countries occupied by the Red Army were anything but free. Stalin replied that he had not complained when a new government was installed in Italy by the Anglo-American liberators without consultation with him, so why should his Allies complain when he acted in Eastern Europe as they had in the west? In the Allied Control Commissions set up in occupied countries disagreement was immediate and bitter. The issuing of idealistic statements and the appearance of harmony were part of the war effort. Like any other form of propaganda, such statements seemed a little naïve when the war was over. In fact, the basis for the "cold war" was laid long before Hitler, who forced the capitalist democracies and the Soviet Union into cooperation, was defeated.

Costs of the War

More than 15 million soldiers and sailors died in World War II; if civilians are included, the death figures have been estimated at around 30 million (see Table 25.1). Such figures, breathtaking as they may be, omit the other costs of the war: millions of men, women, and children maimed physically and mentally; untold destruction of homes, public buildings, the living countryside; and the waste of a great part of the world's effort for more than five years. Actual money costs are impossible to estimate, but the direct cost to the United States alone for military purposes and supplies sent to allies abroad was around $350 billion.

THE TRIUMPH OF COMMUNISM IN CHINA, 1945–1949

In 1945, when defeat by the Western powers forced Japan to evacuate China, Chiang's Nationalists held the western provinces and much of the south. Most of the rural areas of the north were under Communist control, however, and the peasantry everywhere preferred Communist land reforms to Chiang's support for the landlord class.

The Allied High Command was committed to the Kuomintang government both by international law and political preference. At Chiang's demand, American ships and planes delivered Kuomintang troops to the cities of the north, where they accepted the surrender of Japanese garrisons. The Russians, who had liberated Manchuria from Japanese occupation, also turned over control to Chiang, as they had agreed to do at Yalta. Civil war between Chiang's troops and those of the Communists became almost inevitable. Most northern Chinese, grateful for Communist successes during the war, considered American transportation of Chiang's troops a hostile move carried out for imperialist motives. The Communists used their control of the countryside to cut

TABLE 25.1
Major Belligerents' Military War Dead

COUNTRY	DEATHS	% OF POPULATION
U.S.S.R.	7,500,000	4.50
Germany	2,850,000	4.00
China*	2,200,000	0.50
Japan	1,506,000	2.17
United Kingdom	398,000	0.67
Italy	300,000	0.67
U.S.A.	292,000	0.22
France	211,000	0.50

* 1941–1945 only.

off Chiang's garrisons from all communication with the Kuomintang government.

The end of the war and the impending resumption of civil conflict led the Communists to establish new policies in the countryside. Early in 1946, they began encouraging their young peasant recruits to take control of the villages by ousting the old village chiefs. In September 1946, they issued a new land law whereby state-owned land and that owned by wealthy peasants was redistributed to the poor. Peasants began slaughtering landlords. Most Communist officials tried to prevent mass killings, but they generally failed, for peasant hatreds, once released, were impossible to control. A revolutionary terror was in progress.

In the Kuomintang-controlled areas of the south, Chiang's government failed completely to win the loyalty of the people. Corruption flourished among government officials. Secret police terrorized the universities with sudden arrests of suspected subversives; inflation was destroying the economy. Desperate men fled to Communist-controlled villages with vital information about Chiang's plans. The Kuomintang government crumbled from the inside, while the Generalissimo tried to extend its control over the entire nation.

The United States sent General George C. Marshall (1880–1959), its wartime chief of staff, to negotiate an agreement between

Chiang and Mao in 1946, but he failed, for neither side wished to compromise. Chiang, assured of American aid, thought he could destroy the Communists; Mao was sure he could destroy the Kuomintang. A Democratic League, composed of university professors and other intellectuals, was the only organized political body of any importance that sought a liberal solution. When Marshall indicated that he saw it as an alternative to the authoritarian Kuomintang government, Chiang reacted by suppressing the League. Wen I-to, the League's leader, was murdered in July 1946. Other eminent members of the League were assassinated or driven into exile. When Marshall left China in January 1947, the League no longer existed. In fact, the League never had a chance, for in postwar China no party could compete for control without military backing, and the League had no divisions. Chiang would not surrender his power without a fight, and only Mao was prepared for battle.

Chiang opened hostilities early in 1947, hoping to win full control of North China and Manchuria. The Communists, organizing their guerrilla bands into great armies equipped with surrendered Japanese arms, destroyed the attackers. Mao opened his own offensive in the summer of 1947 and quickly established new bases in the south. In October, Chiang made his last gamble, landing his best troops on the south Manchurian coast in a final attempt to establish contact with his isolated city garrisons. His forces, however, simply surrendered rather than fight the huge Communist armies that met them. In February 1949, the Communists took Peking. Futile negotiations stalled their progress momentarily, but their victory was assured. In December 1949, Chiang Kai-Shek and the remainder of his armies retreated to the island of Taiwan.

Chiang had lost his prestige with both peasants and intellectuals by his failure to stem the Japanese tide. Moreover, his failure to prevent inflation, and the corruption of his regime, cost him the loyalty of many of his early supporters. The Communists, on the other hand, performed relatively effectively against the Japanese and at the same time were laying the basis for control of the rural areas. Once the Japanese were gone, Chiang could not promise the Chinese people even law and order, much less serious reform. Communist propagandists everywhere spread tales of the harsh rule of Kuomintang generals and the massive extortion Chiang's men practiced against peasants under their control. They were believed because their stories were largely true. In battle, the peasants who made up Chiang's armies were neither well-trained nor eager to die for their commanders, while the capability and the morale of Mao's men was high. Communist agents easily persuaded Kuomintang soldiers to surrender and convinced peasants that they must rebel. By 1947, Chiang had almost no support left; his corrupt regime was detested. Mao, on the other hand, had won the loyalty of most of China's peasants. Many intellectuals still would have preferred a Western-style democracy, but that choice was not available. They had to choose between Chiang's corruption and Mao's dictatorship. The vast majority chose Mao.

The Allied triumph over Nazi and Japanese armies opened a new era in world politics. Europe was exhausted; the two giants, the United States and the Soviet Union, remained to face each other, full of mutual suspicion and hostility. For the present the balance of power principle was inoperative, for no third power existed to right the balance if one became too strong. Intelligent observers knew even before the war ended that the victory would bring only a precarious peace.

Moreover, the introduction of nuclear warfare promised to change the conditions of international rivalry beyond recognition. American scientists were certain that the secret of the bomb would soon be known by others. But politicians and generals still thought primarily in terms of territory to defend and armies to defend it.

One other factor in the international scene had changed. Throughout the underdeveloped world, the end of the war and the weakness of the imperialist nations was the signal for the beginning of a struggle for independence. Ho Chi Minh in Indochina, Mao Tse-tung in China, Sukarno in Indonesia—these were only a few of the leaders who were already planning to throw off the imperial yoke. The war gave new impetus to nationalism; its end brought new opportunities for revolution.

Finally, the war increased the demands of the masses who had borne its brunt for a greater share in the abundance they could produce in a peaceful world. In Britain, the strain of war led to new hope for a society less class-ridden; in France and elsewhere, members of resistance groups were determined to turn their struggle against Nazism into a battle against poverty and injustice. Everywhere expectations were high.

Technical progress, the spread and strengthening of nationalism, increased state control in every area of life, and more widespread distribution of wealth all are marks of modernization. Like World War I, World War II, broader in scope and even more destructive, quickened the pace of modernization and increased the clamor for its continuation.

SUGGESTED READINGS

Eubank, Keith, *The Origins of World War II*. New York: Thomas Y. Crowell, 1969. Paperback.
  A good introduction to the outstanding issues.

Taylor, A. J. P., *The Origins of World War II*. New York: Fawcett, 1961. Paperback.
  The most famous book on the subject, and the most controversial.

Langer, William L. and S. E. Gleason, *The Challenge to Isolation: The World Crisis of 1937–1940 and American Foreign Policy*. 2 Vols. New York: Harper and Row, 1952. Torchbook paperback.

Wright, Gordon, *The Ordeal of Total War, 1939–1945*. New York: Harper and Row, 1968. Torchbook Paperback.
  The best short but comprehensive view of the war in Europe.

Ryan, Cornelius, *The Longest Day*. New York: Pocket Books, 1967. Paperback.
  A stirring popular account of the Normandy invasion.

Hilberg, Raul, *The Destruction of the European Jews*. Chicago: Quadrangle Books, 1961. Paperback.
  The fullest account.

Feis, Herbert, *The China Tangle: The American Effort in China from Pearl Harbor to the Marshall Mission*. New York: Atheneum, 1953. Paperback.

Toland, John, *The Rising Sun: The Decline and Fall of the Japanese Empire, 1936–1945*. New York: Bantam Books, 1970. Paperback.
  The war from the Japanese viewpoint.

Feis, Herbert, *The Atomic Bomb and the End of World War II*. Princeton: Princeton University Press, 1970.
  Not uncritical, but basically a defense of American actions.

Alperowitz, Gar, *Atomic Diplomacy: Hiroshima and Potsdam*. New York: Random House, 1965. Vintage Paperback.
  A revisionist view, arguing that Truman used the atomic bomb against Japan as part of his anti-Soviet policy.

Fitzgerald, C. P., *The Birth of Communist China*. Revised edition. Baltimore: Penguin Books, 1964. Pelican Paperback.
  The best short treatment.

Mailer, Norman, *The Naked and the Dead*. New York: Signet Books, 1948. Paperback.
  The best American novel of the war.

S ince the end of World War II the masses everywhere have become the most important new force to be reckoned with—from the streets of New York and Cairo to the collective farms of China and Bulgaria. Most of the new developments of our century have been, at least in part, either causes or effects of the rise of the masses. Among the obvious causes are the technological advances that have allowed more people to live longer and better than ever before; these advances include not only higher productivity in industry and agriculture, but also improvements in health, education, and welfare. Without these advances another obvious cause, the population explosion, would have been—and may yet be—a catastrophe. The two world wars were both causes and effects of the rise of the masses: mass passions helped start these wars which, in turn, made the masses demand more power and influence because of their participation in them. Veterans, labor, and women benefited most in the advanced countries, but, as we have already seen, in Russia in 1917–1920 and China in 1946–1949 the hitherto "invisible" peasant masses also became leading participants in mighty revolutions. The People's Republic of China has mobilized its almost 800 million inhabitants more thoroughly than any other regime in history.

The nature of domestic politics in almost all countries has been transformed by the need of political leaders to cater to entire subdivisions—often polarized—of national populations. These subdivisions include other formerly "invisible" social groups like the untouchables in India and most blacks in the United States; even the dropouts are making themselves more visible and beginning to demand their rights in some places. The period since the end of World War II has produced more outstanding demagogues outside of Europe than Europe itself had ever known. In Latin America, Juan Peron openly imitated the fallen fascist dictators, whereas Fidel Castro created a new type of communist leadership. In the newer independent states demagogues like Achmed Sukarno, Kwame Nkrumah, and Abdel Gamal Nasser combined the roles of tribal demigod and modernizing miracle worker in their efforts to transform the masses of their poor, illiterate followers into integrated national communities.

The gap between the rich and poor countries has never been greater; they are really two different worlds. Modern technology and widespread education through diverse media have helped reduce population growth to manageable rates in Europe, North America, Japan, and the U.S.S.R. and should be able to eliminate poverty in these areas. But on much of the rest of our planet the number of people has continued to outstrip available resources. The resultant misery has become more apparent than ever because much of it has been transferred from rural to urban slums and because it has been highly publicized by television and picture magazines. These problems are especially acute in traditionally poor countries like Egypt and India, but even Brazil, despite its ultramodern cities and vast mineral wealth, has been unable to lift much of its burgeoning population out of abject poverty and ignorance. Latin America as a whole has a higher rate of population growth than any other section of the globe and is potentially the most explosive politically and socially.

So far, however, the main international tensions have involved other parts of the world. The "cold war" between the United States and the Soviet Union, with its threat of push-button nuclear warfare, seemed to put conventional military establishments in the background, but this was never true everywhere and has become less so in recent years. During the painful process of decolonization European military commanders on the spot sometimes helped provoke radical local leaders into wars of national liberation, particularly in Indochina and North Africa. And army officers have seized political power in many of the new nations of Africa and Asia as well as older ones in Latin America. Not only are there more military regimes in the world today than ever before, but even in the civilian regimes of the most modern countries military influence has triggered bellicose policies like the Cuban missile crisis and the Vietnam war. Ideologies—especially communism and nationalism—have also created international tensions between traditionally peaceful Jews and Arabs and among the communist countries themselves, which during the "cold war" were thought to have been all on the same side. In international affairs as in everything else the rate of change has accelerated so fast that even the most sophisticated game theories have become ineffective in predicting future developments on the basis of present trends.

CHAPTER **26**

Modernization in High Gear, Post World War II (North America, Europe, the USSR, and Japan)

Today more than ever before the world is divided between modern and backward societies: the official terminology of the United Nations Organization is "developed" and "developing"; in plainer language the words are rich and poor. Ideological and cultural differences still matter a great deal among both the rich and the poor nations, and the richest nation of all has millions of poor people of its own. Yet the basic contrast remains: the majority of people in the United States are *not* poor; the majority in India, Bolivia, and Nigeria are. The rich nations of the world have less than one-third of its population and over nine-tenths of its wealth. They have the highest life-expectancy rates and the highest literacy rates; they also have an almost complete monopoly over science, technology, and the most powerful weapons ever conceived. The key to their wealth and power is their degree of modernization.

As we have seen earlier, modernization occurred first in Western Europe and North America and has spread to other parts of the world during the past hundred years. In all cases it has involved the transformation of traditional institutions and values to meet new needs. Although latecomers have been able to combine and even skip some stages of modernization, historically the expansion of scientific and practical knowledge came first, followed by the rise of modernizing leaders in politics, war, and economic affairs—men like Napoleon Bonaparte, Helmut von Moltke, and Henry Ford. The next stage in the process of modernization was an economic and social transformation—the shift from agriculture to industry and from a predominantly rural to a predominantly urban society. Once this transformation became irreversible, people uprooted from their old ways of life had to be integrated into new, larger organizations, usually culminating in the nation-state. This integration of society at a new level was fostered by mass education and the mass media of communication and was accelerated by the two world wars and certain revolutionary regimes during the twentieth century.

As modernization has moved into high gear, new problems and new divisions have threatened integration where it was thought to have been achieved and hindered its achievement elsewhere. In a completely modern society all individuals and groups would be able to develop their potential to the fullest, free of the shackles of the past and limited only by the welfare of the community as a whole. No one would be held back on grounds of class, race, sex, or life style. On the one hand, nonfunctional institutions would be swept away; on the other hand, functional institutions would be protected from attack by irresponsible minorities. But no existing society has yet reached this stage. Meanwhile, in all but the most advanced countries social and cultural change continue to lag behind economic and technological change. Thus, those societies with the most rapidly changing economies are witnessing the greatest threats of social and cultural disintegration from groups that simply did "not count" in the eyes of the established elites.

Modernization in high gear has produced new ways of viewing and coping with the world. A traveler from Seattle, Toronto, or Stockholm would feel as lost on his own (away from the make-believe setting of Hilton hotels and American Express tours) in Indonesia or Egypt as Gulliver did in his travels among the Lilliputians and the Yahoos. If he stayed for any length of time, our visitor might "go native" in some respects. But, like that other eighteenth-century fictional traveler, Robinson Crusoe, he would undoubtedly try to teach the natives to use applied knowledge, to be efficient and punctual, and to make judgments based on reason rather than tradition. In most modern societies people who cannot remember a time when there were no jet airplanes and no television satellites think differently and feel differently even from their elders, let alone from Indonesians and Egyptians.

Although all modern nations have to cope with the worldwide "generation gap," those that consider themselves powers in the tradi-tional sense have also had to deal with the new international conflicts that replaced those World War II had settled. At first these conflicts were centered in Europe, with the Soviet Union and its allies on one side and the United States and its allies on the other side. As new conflicts arose in Africa, the Middle East, and Southeast Asia, these two alliance systems began to break up. The Russians had to deal with rebellions by their own satellites, the French began to go their own way, and the Americans resumed their role as policemen of the Caribbean and got bogged down in a demoralizing war in Vietnam. One sign of the lessening of cold war tensions between the United States and the Soviet Union was that the nuclear arms race of the 1950s gradually gave way in the 1960s to joint efforts to limit the testing and spread of nuclear weapons. But the 1970s are certain to bring new conflicts with new protagonists.

INTERNATIONAL RELATIONS: THE "COLD WAR"

World War II and its aftermath drastically altered the relations of the European states among themselves and their relative power in the world as a whole. Perhaps the most striking change was the polarization of power in the United States and the Soviet Union, apparently placing the countries west of the so-called "iron curtain" under the protection of the former and leaving those countries east of it at the mercy of the latter. By the 1950s the reintegration of Italy and most of Germany into Western Europe was a second major change; the "communization" of East Germany and the smaller countries of Central and Eastern Europe was a third. The emergence of dozens of new nations in the former colonial territories of Africa and Asia has complicated but not basically altered the new pattern of international relations. Even if they had not lost their colonies, Great Britain and France would no longer be able to compete with the two giants in the struggle for world power. Only the transformation of the ten-member European Economic Community (the Common Market) into a military and political power bloc could create a "third force" between the United States and the Soviet Union in Europe. In Asia, Japan has emerged as a new industrial giant, and China is challenging the ideological predominance of the Soviet Union everywhere, but in Europe itself the Soviet Union has no rival for its position as the number one power.

It seems pretty clear now that the "cold war" began as a struggle between the two largest and most powerful victors for control over Hitler's former empire in Europe. Unlike the situation in 1919, there was no peace treaty with the principal enemy after World War II. Hence, today the former Third Reich remains divided between West Germany— the Federal Republic—and East Germany— the German Democratic Republic. (In August 1970 the government of the Federal Republic recognized the existing frontier between East Germany and Poland, in effect renouncing all claims to former German territory east of the Oder-Neisse rivers.) In February 1947, in peace treaties with the former Axis satellites, the United States and Great Britain kept their wartime promise to let the Soviet Union retain the territories it had gained from Finland, Poland, and Rumania as well as the three Baltic states, the Czechoslovak province of Ruthenia, and the northern half of East Prussia. In all, the Soviet Union acquired about 200,000 square miles of territory and 22 million people and pushed its pre-1939 border almost 300 miles westward. But the United States and Great Britain feared that the Russians wanted more and accused them of seeking military bases at the Dardanelles and of encouraging Greek Communist guerrillas against the rightwing regime in Athens. One month after the signing of the peace treaties with the former Axis satellites, President Truman announced that the United States was sending military missions to Turkey and Greece and giving $400 million to the governments of those two countries; these measures inaugurated the "Truman Doctrine." The Russians, in turn, accused the "Anglo-Saxon powers" of plotting against them. Soon thereafter the consolidation of Soviet control over much of Eastern Europe

plus the launching of the Marshall Plan— named after the American general who sponsored it—in Western Europe confirmed the existence of a "cold war" between the former wartime allies.

In announcing that the United States would "support free peoples who are resisting attempted subjugation by armed minorities or by outside pressure," the Truman Doctrine launched the United States on a new career as policeman of the world. The moral and ideological justifications for this role have been debated ever since, but in the late 1940s it would have been extremely difficult for the United States government to ignore Stalin's imperialist ambitions. Even the Marshall Plan, originally conceived as a program of economic aid for *all* of Europe, became transformed into an instrument of the "cold war" once Stalin prevented his East European satellites from participating. The Americans felt that they had not liberated Europe from Nazi tyranny only to have it come under communist tyranny. The Russians, in turn, viewed every American effort to help Western Europe—and especially West Germany—as a capitalist-imperialist threat to them. Ideological preconceptions colored the views of each side, but the basic issue was power. Unfortunately for its public image it was usually the United States that did its policing with troops, while the Soviet Union—except in suppressing the Hungarian Revolution in 1956 and in halting the liberal trend in Czechoslovakia in 1968—managed to intervene in the affairs of other nations in less obvious ways.

The "cold war" took many forms. In Europe, the North Atlantic Treaty Organization, or NATO, was launched in April 1949 with the signing of an alliance for mutual defense by the United States, Canada, Great Britain, France, Belgium, the Netherlands, Luxembourg, Italy, Norway, Denmark, Iceland, and Portugal. Greece and Turkey joined NATO two years later. When West Germany was brought into NATO in 1955, the Soviet Union responded to the rearmament of its former enemy by forming a new alliance with Poland, Czechoslovakia, Hungary, Rumania, Bulgaria, and East Germany. This Warsaw Pact thus became a counterforce to

NATO military commanders in the late 1950s.

NATO. The United States and the Soviet Union used diplomatic pressure and economic aid to gain friends outside of their alliance systems all over the world. They also used the meetings of the United Nations Organization to further their own ends. At the outbreak of the Korean War (1950–1953), for example, the United States persuaded that body to participate in its "police action" to prevent North Korea from taking over South Korea. The Soviet Union used its veto power in the Security Council many times to block resolutions it opposed. The most ominous form of the "cold war" was the nuclear arms race, which threatened to destroy much of the world if an open military confrontation should ever occur between the two superpowers.

By the early 1960s the danger of such a confrontation had begun to recede. Except for periodic crises over the status of West Berlin, Europe ceased to be the main center of conflict in the "cold war." In 1962 the American and Soviet governments stood at the brink of nuclear war over the presence of Russian missiles in Cuba, but the Russians removed the missiles, and "the unthinkable"

was avoided. The Russians were no more willing to go to war with the United States over Vietnam than they had been over Cuba, despite their military aid to the Communists in both countries. The United States, in turn, began blaming China, rather than the Soviet Union, for sponsoring aggression in Southeast Asia. Under these conditions, the terms of the "cold war" were drastically changed.

The war in Vietnam, which was still going on in 1972, was an indirect legacy of the disintegration of the great European overseas empires since the end of World War II. In a very real sense the United States assumed the role of the French, who, between 1946 and 1954, had tried to prevent the Vietnamese Communists from taking over their colonies in Indochina. The effects of decolonization on emerging nations are discussed in later chapters; here we are concerned with the impact of the end of empire on Europe. Although the loss of colonies reduced the political and diplomatic influence of Great Britain and France, it had little effect on them economically. Even the Netherlands and Belgium, which had proportionately greater investments in their colonies, continued to prosper without them.

The most important effects of the end of empire in Europe have been noneconomic. At strategic bases from Dakar to Singapore, the tricolor and the union jack have been lowered forever. Each instance was a blow to the national pride of the French and the British as well as to their military and naval power. Although the British suffered no military humiliation comparable to that of the French in Vietnam in 1954, the cumulative psychological effect of the end of empire touched them more deeply than any other nation. Just as the former colonial peoples continued to bear the scars of inferiority and subjection thrust upon them by the colonizers, many Europeans remained unpersuaded in their hearts that they were not in fact superior to peoples of darker skins and were ready to prevent further inroads on what remained of their overseas holdings.

These tensions came out in the open in the Suez crisis of 1956. In July of that year President Abdel Gamal Nasser of Egypt announced the nationalization of the Suez Canal, which was owned and operated by a private Franco-British company. The British and French governments condemned the nationalization as illegal and determined on show of power. On October 31, British and French aircraft began bombing Egyptian airfields preparatory to landing operations in the Canal Zone. The Anglo-French task force was obviously capable of routing the Egyptians, but at the United Nations the Soviet Union and even the United States condemned the invasion. The task force then withdrew. In contrast, the Soviet Union continued to crush the Hungarian Revolution (see p. 804) with no apparent concern for the United Nations' condemnation. It took the French over five years more to give up Algeria, but to the British, the bitter setback at Suez marked the true end of the imperial era.

Along with the appearance of dozens of new nations in Asia and Africa and the continuing preponderance of the United States and the Soviet Union, the emergence of mainland China as an independent power further altered the framework of international relations and the place of both Western and Eastern Europe within it. The new China has already asserted its claims on disputed territories in India and Soviet Siberia. Coupled with its effort to outbid the Soviet Union for the leadership of world communism, these territorial claims seemed to turn the Russians' wrath more against China than against the West. At the same time China's bid for ideological leadership gave some of the communist countries of Eastern Europe more leeway in pursuing their own paths toward socialism and in following their own foreign policies. By 1960, Albania had already opted for China, and Yugoslavia was becoming more independent than before. In 1964, Rumania was trying to play the role of mediator between the Soviet Union and China and seeking economic and cultural contacts with Western Europe, particularly France. President de Gaulle was not alone in foreseeing the day when the "iron curtain" might lift and all the nations of Europe, including the Soviet Union, might be forced to cooperate against the new "yellow peril."

THE UNITED STATES

Many sensitive people in Europe and in other advanced parts of the world are even more wary of "Americanization" than they are of the "yellow peril." They fear the United States not as a conqueror but as a model of modernization in high gear. Usually they stress the most distasteful phenomena — crime in the streets, pollution of the environment, the dehumanization of work and interpersonal relations — rather than the long-range material and social improvements. Racism has brought special problems to the United States, but the other major developments have been paralleled in Canada, Australia, and New Zealand, and are rapidly taking over in Europe and Japan. These developments are: urbanization, automation, bureaucratization, the welfare state, and a mass society preoccupied with consuming more and more goods and services.

World War II brought the United States out of the depression and intensified the economic and social transformation of the country; it also seemed to hasten the integration of all citizens into the national society. In 1940, the least integrated Americans were

Supporters of civil rights march from Selma to Montgomery, Alabama, in March 1965.

poor blacks and whites in the rural south. Some of these people moved to the northern cities to work in war plants; others fought in the armed forces alongside their white compatriots. Soon after the war was over, many thoughtful Americans, both black and white, began to demand that these people be brought, at last, into the mainstream of American life.

Since the 1954 Supreme Court ruling on desegregation in the public schools the civil rights movement made notable gains in the fields of education, voter registration, job opportunities, and housing. By the mid-1960s the south was beginning to experience desegregation due to the efforts of courageous leaders like Dr. Martin Luther King, Jr., and the forces of the federal government. By then, however, the problem of hard-core poverty in a booming economy became increasingly visible as the poor continued to leave the rural south for the cities, especially in the north.

This problem of poverty in the midst of plenty is closely linked to racial discrimination and cultural deprivation, but it is also a by-product of continuing technological change and urbanization. The story is not a new one. Each country that has become industrialized has transformed part of its rural proletariat into an urban proletariat. The first example was the Irish who, in the 1820s, began flocking to Birmingham, Glasgow, and other British cities to work in the most menial and insecure occupations: the men did the digging, hauling and loading; the women became domestic servants. And the big cities of the world, from ancient Rome to eighteenth-century Naples to Cairo or Bombay today, have been havens for people of all ages "with no visible means of support." But, as everybody knows, automation has drastically reduced the number of unskilled jobs during the past twenty years, while the population of the American urban ghettos has climbed steadily. Add to this the hope for a better life instilled by the mass media and the resentment over having been treated as "invisible" for centuries and you have all the ingredients of the black, proletarian, urban riots of the late 1960s.

But all blacks are obviously not proletarian, and civil rights and violence in the ghettos are part of a broader black revolution. Some militant black leaders have rejected the goals of emancipation and integration in favor of "liberation" and "Black Power." Like so many "subject peoples" they have sought to arm themselves with a cultural heritage from the remote past (and in this case a remote continent) so that their "oppressors" will respect them and treat them as a separate "nation." The most extreme black nationalists draw comparisons with the struggles against imperialism in Southeast Asia, South Africa, Latin America, and the Middle East, but the name by which they want to be called—Afro-Americans—belies these comparisons. It is a perfectly suitable name, just as Italian-American, Japanese-American, and American Jew used to be. Many of these people wanted to have their own communities as a base from which to participate in the larger, national society. The present situation of most American Negroes (a white man's term) is different mainly in that they have come to it from two hundred years of slavery followed by one hundred years of second-class citizenship. It is this heritage that is responsible for both white and black racism which, in turn, have sparked the black revolution. The essence of this revolution seems to be that those blacks who support it want to deal with the whites on their own terms rather than on the whites' terms.

It remains to be seen whether or not this demand can be made a reality and, if it is, how long both "sides" will want to preserve it. No situation can be defined indefinitely in terms of black and white (either figuratively or literally) forever. The attitudes of both whites and blacks are divided according to their class, their age, their temperament, and where they live; and there is always a silent majority that would rather not get involved at all. The ruling moderates win over some of the disaffected with real and token concessions. The radicals fight among themselves.

Once their immediate goals are achieved, many radicals become more easy-going and even conservative. The children of revolutionaries and counterrevolutionaries sometimes wonder what all the fuss was about. These are the lessons of history; they will mean little to today's white and black racists, but they will hopefully help others to understand the world around them.

Meanwhile, we must turn to other developments involving urbanization: in addition to exploding ghettos, overcrowded schools, air pollution, and traffic jams, the cities have spawned suburbia. Interrupted by World War II—when gasoline was rationed and new automobiles and new homes were simply not built—the flight to the suburbs resumed with a vengeance in the late 1940s. By 1970, a slightly larger number of Americans lived in suburbs than in the central cities these surrounded. But life in colorless developments of prefabricated houses has not been as attractive as in Oyster Bay, Lake Forest, or Grosse Pointe. Although there is grass, and the schools are better than those in the central cities, middle- and lower-middle-class suburban living has produced millions of demoralized parents and rebellious children. Commuting, by whatever means, is time-consuming and hard on the nerves. The mass media encourage suburban teenagers to imitate urban delinquents without ever really meeting any. Continuity between generations has also broken down: grandma lives in Florida or in an old people's home; daddy is someone who pays the bills and whom one sees on Sunday when he is not playing golf, mowing the lawn, or watching the ball game on television; big brother is away at college or in the army. All that is left are the mothers and the children, each with their own homogenized subcultures.

These social and cultural developments have been fostered by unprecedented economic and technological changes. By 1960, automation made it possible for over half of the working population to be employed outside of agriculture and manufacturing: in commerce, government, banking, insurance, transportation and communication, education, and the other professions and service occupations. There are now more office clerks than farmers; there are more truck drivers than workers in the entire auto industry. Increasingly, the typical skilled worker tends machines rather than operating them. More and more people work for large organizations, processing, selling, and manipulating people and things they never see.

Bigness breeds bureaucrats. The more people and things there are to be "handled" in a given situation, the more elaborate the bureaucratic structure doing the "handling" becomes. This "law" applies to big business, big unions, big education, and, most of all, big government. Bureaucracies that carry out decisions of governments are not new; what is new is the growing tendency of high-level bureaucrats to take over the decision-making process itself. They do this partly because they feel that they alone understand the organizational means by which particular decisions can be executed and partly because the technical aspects of such matters as public finance, defense, and economic planning are too complex for the ordinary legislator to understand. The legislator will haggle over the cost of a parking lot but will allow fantastically expensive military proposals by technically trained bureaucrats to pass with a minimum of discussion.

During the past twenty-five years the power of the executive branch of the United States government has never stopped growing. Under each president some new power was added: Harry S. Truman (1945–1953) created new administrative agencies and made military and foreign policy decisions in peacetime that Roosevelt would have hesitated to make even in wartime; under Dwight D. Eisenhower (1953–1961) the state department, the armed forces, and the CIA became increasingly independent from outside control; John F. Kennedy (1961–1963) and Lyndon B. Johnson (1963–1969) expanded the activities of the executive branch in the fields of civil rights, education, and welfare, though, unfortunately for everyone concerned, they got stuck with an unwanted war in Vietnam. Richard M. Nixon (1969–   ) has not reversed any of these trends, except for "winding down" this war.

Congress has also made its influence felt, especially through some of its powerful com-mittees. In the late 1940s and early 1950s, the House Un-American Activities Committee and the Senate Internal Security subcommittee, led by Senator Joseph McCarthy, used inquisitorial methods to denounce alleged subversives among Hollywood actors and writers, government officials, teachers, and labor leaders. The "McCarthy Era" plus a morbid fear of "the bomb" produced the "silent generation" of students. In the late 1950s, another Senate investigating committee turned its attention to organized crime and its infiltration into certain labor unions and local governments. In the mid-1960s the Senate Foreign Relations Committee openly criticized the administration's handling of the Vietnam War. The "lesson" of these three examples is that Congress has been most effective when badgering powerless individuals, less effective when dealing with large private organizations (from the Mafia to General Electric), and least effective when bucking the President and the defense establishment. On the other hand, the powerful rules and finance committees, which hold no colorful hearings, have prevented much legislation from reaching the floor of the Senate or the House.

Despite its many imperfections, the American political process continued to satisfy the majority and to allow organized minorities to have their say. The placid 1950s gave way to the agitated 1960s for students, ghetto dwellers, labor unions, and dissident political groups. In the 1968 presidential election Richard M. Nixon defeated Hubert H. Humphrey by the narrowest of margins, while the white segregationist George M. Wallace polled 13 percent of the national vote. But aside from Wallace's bid, no new political grouping seriously challenged the two major parties. The Democrats, although they lost the presidency, still controlled Congress. Dissident minorities continued to challenge the administrators of their universities. For all their hostility to the "establishment," extremists usually did not aim their attacks at the big corporations, except on issues such as "complicity" in the Vietnam War, investments in South Africa, or discrimination in employment. It was certainly easier to heckle a mayor or a dean than to intimidate the board of directors of a bank, an oil

Former Governor George Wallace of Alabama during the 1968 presidential election campaign.

or automobile company, or a television network. Yet, this part of the "establishment" controls our lives at least as much as government officials. As long as most Americans accept the present political and economic system, no minority, no matter how militant, can hope to make a successful revolution. In fact, the majority, if its fears were sufficiently aroused, could easily support a counter-revolution.

The "confrontation politics" of recent times was a sign of deep divisions in American society: white versus black, suburbia versus the ghettos, women's liberation versus male supremacy, adolescents versus adult authorities of all kinds. As this society moved into the 1970s many thoughtful people asked if affluence was enough. This kind of question was new in the history of mankind. In traditional societies and, until recently, in most modern societies, people usually knew what their individual and national purposes were. The current generation has seemed to have neither goals nor identity. As a means of creating a new identity or image its instinct has sometimes plunged it into tragic violence. The challenge to "establishment"

liberals" is to find new ways of reconciling individuals and conflicting groups to the society to which they all belong. But their efforts could prove futile in the face of new social tensions and psychological and cultural discontents.

CANADA

Canada has changed even more rapidly than the United States since World War II. Starting from a level of modernization a generation behind that of its southern neighbor during the first 40 years of this century, it closed the gap in most respects by the 1960s. By 1961, as in the United States, 70 percent of its population was urban. By 1967, the average hourly wage in Canadian industry was $2.25, as compared to $2.75 in American industry, and Canada's gross national product of $62 billion for a population of a little over 20 million compared favorably with $650 billion in the United States for a population of close to 200 million. Since the 1950s Canada's man-made environment has undergone a revolution with the introduction of jet travel, superhighways, shopping plazas, television, computers, tranquillizers, medicare, and ultramodern centers for the performing arts.

Social and educational changes have lagged somewhat behind these economic, technological, and cultural transformations. In 1961, 44 percent of all males in the labor force had only an elementary-school education. Since then the proportion of children going on to secondary and higher education has increased, but the country has continued to rely heavily on immigrants for professional and technical personnel. The pace and scope of economic growth began to broaden the base from which the predominantly British-Canadian leadership groups were recruited. Nevertheless, except for some middle- and upper-middle-class French-Canadians in politics and the Catholic church, the remainder of the country's ethnic groups were scarcely represented in the top decision-making positions. The fault lay mainly in Canada's undemocratic system of higher education, the cost of which was far higher than in any other comparable industrial society, with little money available for subsidizing poorer students.

Unequal opportunities for education and social mobility held back the complete integration of Canadian society. Unlike the United States, Canada has had no unifying ideology based on a revolutionary declaration of independence; instead of adopting the ideal of a melting pot, Canada has tried to create a nation-state made up of many mutually exclusive subcultures that must find a way to live together within a larger society. Indeed, in its official documents, Canada does not even recognize itself as a nation in the sense that "Canadian" can be an ethnic origin. Among the 43 percent of British origin who have been Canadian for several generations, memories of old rivalries among the English, the Scots, and the Irish have been preserved, and the cue was given to all other groups to do the same thing. Aside from the French (30 percent) these include Germans, Ukrainians, Dutch, Italians, Poles, and native Indians and Eskimos.

Ethnic divisiveness has been reinforced by the political divisiveness of the federal system. Since the beginning of Confederation in 1867 there has been a tug of war for power between the federal government at Ottawa and the provincial governments. Canada's participation in the two world wars strengthened the federal government, but since the 1950s the provinces have demanded and recovered many of their powers. The case of Quebec vividly illustrates the relationship between ethnic differentiation and provincialism in politics. Neither the Conservative prime minister John Diefenbaker nor the Liberal Lester Pearson could stem the growing demand not only for autonomy but for outright separation in Quebec. In 1968, a younger, keenly perceptive, Liberal prime minister, Pierre Elliott Trudeau, began a new effort to keep the Confederation together on a bilingual basis while allowing the French to be their own masters in Quebec.

The conflict of interests between Quebec and the rest of Canada was expressed in nationalistic terms, but it also represented a revolt against the old culture, in which French-Canadian elites ruled in coalition with the dominant British. Since the late 1950s Quebec's modernizing leaders paradoxically claimed to be safeguarding their culture by in fact rejecting it. The traditional themes of French-Canadian culture were ruralism, large families, church-centered parochialism, authoritarianism in church and politics, and a rejection of worldly acquisition of skills and economic gain. Quebec's new leaders demanded changes based on the alien values of the French and American revolutions (neither of which had much influence on French Canada): political and educational democratization, equality of opportunity, and the reduction of the influence of the church in nonreligious activities. In addition, they championed rationalization and efficiency in economic life. During the 1960s they brought about a "quiet revolution" that transformed the face of the province and the values of its French-speaking majority. Millions of visitors to the 1967 world's fair in Montreal were amazed at the city's prosperity, modernity, and sophistication. The people of Quebec were not so much catching up with the rest of Canada as reassessing their whole way of life and their relations with the outside world.

While French- and English-speaking Canadians struggle with the problem of living with

Expo '67 Montreal. The United States pavilion.

each other they face the common perplexity of how to exist independently from their giant twin to the south. By 1960, half of Canada's manufacturing industry was American-controlled. Canada's economic dependence on the United States brings many advantages, just as joint defense arrangements give both countries added protection. But, having acquired a taste for self-assertion on the international scene—in the U.N., in NATO, and as mediators in numerous disputes—pan-Canadian nationalists tend to be systematically anti-American. Confederation came into being in defiance of the United States over a hundred years ago, and so it remains. Yet, nowhere in the world have two countries lived in greater harmony and cooperation than these two North American neighbors.

WESTERN EUROPE

Unlike the United States and Canada, the major European and Asian belligerents of World War II had the additional burden of physical reconstruction in their move toward further modernization. But the rapid recovery of Germany, the USSR, and Japan was inevitable because their economic systems carried within them the seeds of their own resurgence. Their capacity for producing material goods was based on their knowledge of the techniques for sustained growth. This knowledge, plus the survival of some machine tools under the rubble, allowed them to surpass prewar production figures within less than ten years and to move forward steadily ever since.

The most striking feature of Western Europe in recent years has been the universal desire for economic advancement, both collective and individual. Stimulated by the problems of postwar recovery, this desire soon became self-sustaining, creating an unprecedented openness to new ideas like managerial efficiency, state planning, and mass consumption. In the 1950s, the application of some or all of these ideas brought a

EUROPE, 1972

Legend:
- NATO (*North Atlantic Treaty Organization*)
- Common Market (*European Economic Community*)
  United Kingdom, Denmark, Norway, and Ireland accepted 1971, pending ratification by their respective parliaments
- Warsaw Pact and COMECON (*Council for Mutual Economic Aid*)

ICELAND — Reykjavik

NORWAY — Oslo
SWEDEN — Stockholm, Göteborg
DENMARK — Copenhagen

SCOTLAND — Glasgow, Edinburgh
NORTH IRELAND — Belfast
REPUBLIC OF IRELAND — Dublin
UNITED KINGDOM — Liverpool, Manchester, Birmingham, London, Southampton
WALES
ENGLAND

North Sea
Baltic Sea

NETHERLANDS — The Hague, Amsterdam, Rotterdam
Hamburg, Bremen
EAST GERMANY — Berlin, Leipzig, Dresden
R.S.F.S.R. — Gdansk (Danzig), Kaliningrad, Königsberg
POLAND — Warsaw, Wroclaw, Cracow
Vistula

BELGIUM — Antwerp, Brussels
Cologne, Bonn, Hanover
Frankfurt
LUX.
WEST GERMANY — Nuremberg, Munich
CZECHOSLOVAKIA — Prague, Brno
Elbe River, Oder River

Le Havre
Paris
FRANCE — Bordeaux, Lyons, Toulouse, Marseilles
Seine River
Rhone River
Rhine River

SWITZERLAND — Bern, Zürich, Geneva
LIECHTENSTEIN
AUSTRIA — Vienna
HUNGARY — Budapest
Danube
Milan, Turin, Venice, Trieste
Po River
Genoa, Bologna, Florence
YUGOSLAVIA (nonaligned) — Belgrade

Atlantic Ocean
Bay of Biscay
English Channel

PORTUGAL — Lisbon
SPAIN — Madrid, Barcelona, Valencia, Seville, Malaga
Bilbao
Ebro River
Gibraltar (Br.)

ANDORRA
MONACO
SAN MARINO
CORSICA (Fr.)
VATICAN CITY
ITALY — Rome, Naples
SARDINIA (It.)
BALEARIC ISLANDS
Adriatic Sea

ALBANIA (aligned with China) — Tirana
Salo
GREECE
SICILY — Palermo

Mediterranean Sea

MOROCCO
ALGERIA
TUNISIA

wave of growth and affluence to most of the already industrialized societies of Western Europe; by the 1960s, it was spreading to Austria, Spain, Portugal, and Greece. Contrasts between advanced and backward areas remain, but the inhabitants of the latter have become less resigned to their lot than in the past. French farmers, who were still one-third of the working population in 1945, were leaving their small, inefficient holdings for the city at the rate of 140,000 a year by the early 1960s; by 1970 they constituted less than 15 percent of the work force. Spanish agricultural workers were deserting the countryside for new jobs in Madrid and Barcelona or even Bordeaux and Düsseldorf.

Economic growth has been accompanied by social and political modernization, though at a slower pace. Ruling groups still exist, but they are recruited increasingly on the basis of ability rather than status or privilege. Furthermore, there have been more opportunities for talented and ambitious individuals to rise to the middle ranks of the power structure. Higher wages and an abundance of mass-produced consumer goods and services have permitted many skilled workers and employees to attain a bourgeois level of material comfort, if not social status. (For example, by the late 1960s the highways of Spain and Italy were jammed with the Volkswagens and Renaults of vacationing mechanics and office clerks from West Germany and France.) These developments, along with the growth of the welfare state, have lessened traditional class antagonisms.

Political ideologies based on traditional class interests began to decline by the beginning of the 1950s as the general desire for economic growth and government efficiency spread. This decline was then reinforced by economic improvement and increased social mobility. On the other hand, the ascendancy of bureaucrats and other kinds of "organization men" in all areas of modern life has reinforced a desire to preserve the new status quo, even among the supposedly leftist parties and labor unions. This trend in turn has given rise to new forms of protest, as we shall see presently.

Another major development has been the abandonment of national rivalries in favor of international cooperation, especially in economic affairs. Beginning with a common market for coal and steel in the early 1950s the efforts of France, West Germany, Italy, Belgium, the Netherlands, and Luxembourg toward economic integration led to their signing the Treaty of Rome in March 1957. This treaty set up a timetable for the full achievement of this goal in the European Economic Community (EEC), or Common Market. First, "the Six" agreed to a progressive elimination of all tariffs and other trade barriers among themselves within fifteen years. Second, they agreed to cooperate in their agricultural, transport, investment, and labor policies. Third, they agreed to present a common tariff to the outside world. An independent executive European Commission in Brussels has dominated the EEC on all but the highest policy matters, which are still decided by representatives of the national governments.

The most remarkable thing about the EEC has been the determination of the six member states to make it work. They have disagreed on specific policies, especially the equalization of agricultural prices, yet, despite these disagreements, the Rome treaty has been applied more rapidly than had originally been planned. Within six years after its signing the customs duties between the member states had been cut across the board by 40 percent; unconditional freedom of movement was granted to broad categories of investment capital; few restrictions remained on the free movement of labor from one country to another. By 1972, the full customs union and the full economic union were yet to be achieved, but the assumption that they will be is likely to be even more influential than the specific measures already taken.

Until 1971 one major difficulty was the reluctance of some members, particularly France, to allow other countries, especially Great Britain, to join the EEC; another has been what the French author Jean-Jacques Schreiber has described in *The American Challenge*, a book that sold over a million copies in Western Europe in 1968. This "challenge" lies in superior American financial and organizational practices. Using these practices, General Motors took over the Opel automobile company in Germany;

A mod clothing store in London in the mid-1960s.

IBM took over the Bull computer firm in France. The author of *The American Challenge* argues that, if this trend continues, not the Common Market countries, but the United States in Europe, will soon be the third major industrial power in the world, after the United States itself and the Soviet Union. His prescription for answering the "challenge" is for European big business to move faster in adopting American techniques.

Each country of Western Europe has had its own special problems, and it would be impossible even to mention all of them in a few pages.

Great Britain, shorn of its role as a world and imperial power, barred until 1971 from the EEC, and unable to find dynamic leadership, has experienced a growing sense of loss of purpose and direction since the mid-1950s. This has been so under both Conservative governments (1951–1964, 1970–   ) and the last Labour government (1964–1970). Class distinctions have remained more persistent than in other highly industrialized countries, despite growing affluence and the health, education, and welfare reforms of the first postwar Labour government (1945–1951). An unfavorable balance of payments, technological inefficiency, and labor unrest have handicapped Britain's competitive position in the world market and thus limited economic growth at home. The "generation gap," expressed itself earlier in Britain than elsewhere—in criticisms of "the Establishment" in the mid-1950s, in pop music and "mod" clothes in the early 1960s, and in a spate of films, plays, and jokes ridiculing the unity and heroism of the British people during World War II.

In West Germany most people have preferred to forget World War II for obvious reasons, and they have remained far more apathetic politically than the British. Since the beginning of the 1950s economic growth and parliamentary democracy have been taken for granted. But the German Socialists have become even less socialistic than the British Labour party: after eighteen years of impotent opposition to the ruling Christian Democrats they formed a "grand coalition" with them in 1967 and became the ruling party two years later. Despite the disruptive effects of two world wars, the Nazi regime, and the problem of absorbing over ten million refugees from the east, the social structure has retained more of its traditional rigidity than in other Western countries. Traditional values have also been reinforced by the education system, the churches, and the press. It remains to be seen whether or not exaggerated materialism and political stability alone will prove effective substitutes for true modernization, particularly for the younger generation.

Italy, like most of Western Europe, has also acquired the trappings of a modern, technological society. Faith in continued economic growth has become almost universal, and the prevailing materialism has brought a growing apathy toward public affairs. In Italy, however, the fact that 25 percent of the people consistently vote for the Communist party has dramatized the lack of integration in Italian society. Many of these voters were expressing their protest against the current government rather than a desire to overthrow the entire existing order. As in West Germany, the Christian Democrats have made as few institutional reforms as possible in Italy, with or without the collaboration of the Socialists. But the Italians tend to be suspicious of their national leaders and divided along regional and class lines. Economic and cultural differences between Milan and Sicily are comparable to those between New York City and Puerto Rico, and the Sicilians and other southerners who move to Milan in search of employment are treated almost as badly as Puerto Ricans in New York.

A good example of a modern society supposedly integrated at a new level was De Gaulle's France. That nation's humiliating defeat and occupation during World War II had jolted some Frenchmen out of their old ways, and by the mid-1950s the modern sector of the nation's economy was booming and its young people were becoming more numerous and more independent than ever before. But there was massive resistance to these changes, particularly among small shopkeepers and farmers, and this resistance, combined with that of the professional army and of French colonists in North Africa, led to the abandoning of France's overseas empire. The old-fashioned parliamentary coalitions of the Fourth Republic (1946–1958) became increasingly immobile in the face of the pressure groups representing these kinds of people. In May 1958, the European settlers in Algeria, backed by the army, captured the local government from the Paris authorities out of fear that they would abandon Algeria to the Muslim National Liberation Front. There were also rumors that the rebellious generals planned to set up their own government in Paris in order to avoid such a "betrayal." The day was saved by the coming to power of General Charles de Gaulle (1890–1970), hero of the wartime resistance and the head of France's first postwar government until his retirement in January 1946. Not only did he bring the settlers and generals in Algeria to heel, but he also framed a new constitution, that of the Fifth Republic, strengthening the office of president and reducing the functions of the legislature and the traditional parties in political life. It took De Gaulle almost four years to liquidate the Algerian War, with its acts of terrorism and counterterrorism in France as well as in Algeria and with the deep divisions it caused among Frenchmen. But by the summer of 1962, Algeria was independent, the majority of the Europeans were leaving, the army was once again a loyal instrument of the state, the government was stable and efficient, and the economy was growing faster than ever. Although some small farmers still demonstrated along the highways, others simply left the countryside for better jobs in the cities.

Yet, the upheaval of May–June 1968 showed the illusory character of the newly integrated Gaullist society and once again made France the barometer of new development in modern civilization. Beginning as a student revolt, it culminated in the biggest general strike in history. For three weeks, almost 10 million workers (out of a total population of 50 million) brought the nation's economic life to a standstill. Neither the trade-union leaders nor the Communist party could control the strikers. The government of President de Gaulle itself seemed on the verge of collapse, but even this was not the ultimate goal of "the movement." A large percentage of young Frenchmen were saying "no" to the technocratic, bureaucratic society of the modern world. More specifically, the rebels were protesting against the efforts of the new managerial elite to condition them, manipulate them, and integrate them into this society. Although no other country experienced a general strike, students in Italy, Germany, Czechoslovakia, Yugoslavia, Japan, Mexico, and the United States engaged in similar protests in 1968 and 1969.

Neither in France nor anywhere else did the students or workers develop an effective political organization for achieving their goals; in fact, their goals were not really the same. The young French workers who occupied their factories in May 1968 refused to have anything to do with the student rebels. They were not trying to "change society" but to gain a voice in managing their plants. The workers came from a lower social class than the students and viewed them as pampered bourgeois, much as American construction

President de Gaulle at a press conference in June 1968.

workers viewed American students protesting the war in Indochina in 1970. Similar class differences played almost as great a part as race in dividing militant blacks from white student radicals in the United States. Clearly, the new ruling elite in most modern countries is now technocratic rather than bourgeois. But class, race, and even language (as in Belgium and Canada) determine people's goals as much as hostility toward any established order. In France the government appeased the workers with higher wages and defused much student unrest by decentralizing the university system. It remains to be seen if Italy, West Germany, the United States, and other modern countries will follow a similar path to relieve tensions and maintain instability within bounds with similar apparent success. From the point of view of the would-be revolutionaries, of course, such an eventuality would be a disaster.

TECHNOLOGICAL SOCIETY

Technological society is a mass society organized on the basis of techniques, which are complexes of standardized means for attaining predetermined results. It has been brought into being not only by machine technology but also by improved techniques in food production, medicine, communication, warfare, and government. And it has been reinforced by manipulating masses of people with new techniques in education, propaganda, and public relations. In the past, men consciously used techniques as means to achieve traditional human ends and values. But as techniques became more elaborate, institutionalized, self-perpetuating, and pervasive, they seemed to suppress the ends they were originally designed to achieve and to become ends in themselves; a few obvious examples are bureaucratic management, army routine, and computers.

For over forty years, critics of technological society have lambasted "technocrats"—a label they applied to the technical experts who were allegedly becoming society's real rulers—and have conjured up dark visions of a future in which people are mindless consumer-creatures whose education and culture and even whose feelings are completely standardized. Yet it is difficult to imagine how a mass society could be organized on a nontechnological basis. Anyone who has experienced a power failure or a traffic jam has had a taste of what life would be like when even a part of our technology ceased to function effectively. There are already signs that automation can make possible greater diversity and choice in goods and services than earlier forms of technology. The real trouble with technological society may turn out to be too much novelty, diversity, and change, rather than numbing standardization.

THE SOVIET UNION

Utopias, by definition, are not of this world. The Soviet Union was the classic example of a society revolutionized in the name of Marxist principles. The Five-Year Plans of the 1930s generated mass enthusiasm of a kind unknown in tsarist days. For the first time in their history the Russian people felt that they were building a better future for themselves, but the first signs of the betrayal of Marxism had already appeared in the form of terror and dictatorship. Then came the rise of the new middle class of managerial and professional people, to whom efficiency, status, and comfort meant more than ideology. According to Marx, communism was a classless, stateless utopia based on the principle "to each according to his needs." In this sense, the revolution in the Soviet Union is unfinished and will undoubtedly remain so.

The victorious Soviet Union reverted to its prewar routine. In 1946, new political repression took the form of a purge of local party leaders, whose numbers had grown in the wartime effort to reestablish contact with the masses. The Fourth Five-Year Plan, also launched in 1946, was designed not only to rebuild the economy—at least one-fourth of whose total capital had been destroyed in the war—but also to "catch up with and overcome the West" in technological development. It called for renewed sacrifices on the part of the Soviet people, sacrifices both of consumer goods and housing, and of leisure time. Nowhere was the reversion to prewar practices clearer than in Stalin's personal dictatorship. The party as a policy-making organization practically ceased to exist. Like the state bureaucracy, it confined itself to the day-to-day functioning of the government machinery. Even the Politburo met irregularly.

Stalin also tried to use Russian nationalism, revived during the war, for his own repressive ends. National pride among the non-Russian peoples of the Soviet Union was condemned; "cosmopolitanism" was labelled a sin next to treason; anti-Semitism became almost an official policy. The forced identification of Russian nationalism with Communist orthodoxy was extended to all fields of culture. In 1946, for example, the poet Anna Akhmatova was expelled from the Union of Soviet Writers for having displayed an "unsocialist loneliness" and other "decadent Western vices."

The economic and social transformation of the Soviet Union resumed, but Stalin's harsh rule delayed the integration of Soviet society. More than two decades of collectivized farming had not succeeded in integrating the peasants into the new industrial society, and by the early 1950s Soviet agricultural output barely surpassed the precollectivization figures. Industrialization had created new aspirations among the growing number of professional people and technicians, but the resumption of prewar repressive policies thwarted their modest desire for a modicum of personal security and legality and for some minimal contact with the outside world.

Since Stalin's death in 1953, competing leaders have attempted to gain credit for liberalizing policies while trying to brand their opponents as diehard defenders of the old, bad order. Personal intrigue, deception, and occasional violence have remained part of the atmosphere of Soviet politics. Nevertheless, the main contenders for power have had to take a much greater account of public sentiment than at the time when one man stood so far above everything and everybody.

During the "thaw" following Stalin's death, his successors granted a number of concessions. They softened the edge of immediate economic grievances by improving living standards; they abolished secret trials by the political police and largely disbanded the forced-labor camps; they permitted a limited degree of intellectual freedom and contact with foreigners. Their "sane totalitarianism" reflected not only a response to social pressures but also a confidence in the ability of the regime to withstand an occasional outspoken novel or news about the number of washing machines in the United States. But the concessions of the "thaw" period did not constitute even a first step toward democracy. They were mainly the by-products of the struggle for Stalin's mantle.

Toward the end of 1954, Nikita Khrushchev (1896–1971) was sharing public honors with Georgi Malenkov, Stalin's immediate successor as prime minister, but it took him almost four years of political maneuvering to establish his supremacy. Khrushchev's rule, though it restored the authority of the party, was less stable than Stalin's (except during the height of the terror in the late 1930s). The basic dilemmas — agriculture, the aspirations of the new middle class, and the use of ideology to justify totalitarianism in a highly industrialized society — remained. The growing conflict with the Chinese Communists posed an additional danger to the ideological structure by showing at least some of the younger party members that the interests of the Soviet Union and those of world communism were beginning to diverge.

Russia's current rulers cannot admit even to themselves that their monopoly of power, the interests of the nation, and the cause of world communism might not coincide. They use the repressive instruments of totalitarianism more sparingly than Stalin, while basing their policies of the moment on their ability to prove to Soviet citizens that communism is a superior way of life: How illusory are obsolete democratic and liberal ideas compared with Russian achievements in the harnessing of nuclear energy and space exploration! Was not the fact that the Russians were the first to put a satellite into orbit (1958), to launch a rocket to the moon (1959), and to send a man around the world in a space ship (1961) necessarily connected with the totalitarian rule exercised by the Communist party?

In the late fifties and early sixties the limited liberalization of Soviet life, sometimes called "de-Stalinization," gave Khrushchev's government a greater measure of popularity and acceptance than any of its predecessors. The West should not take the rebellion of a poet or restlessness among a group of intellectuals or students as a widespread desire for democracy as we understand it. The hopes of most Soviet citizens probably do not go beyond an improvement in their standard of living and a final obliteration of

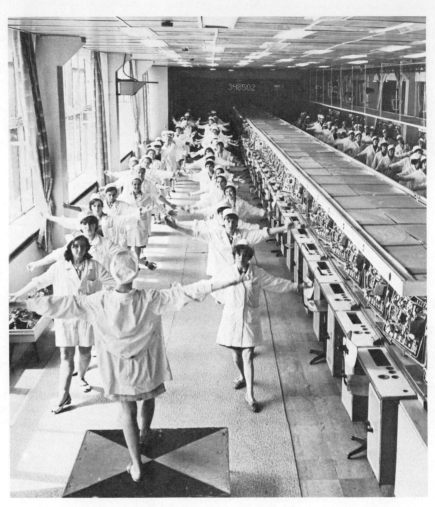

Physical fitness exercises in a Soviet TV factory.

Stalinism—that is, a regime that will grow more humane and tolerant, while remaining totalitarian.

Still, the desire for a freer life has not been entirely stifled in the Soviet Union, nor is there universal contentment with a regime that can arbitrarily order a thaw or a period of renewed vigilance. The policy of "de-Stalinization" itself was a clever attempt to persuade the Soviet people that the cause of their past sufferings was the criminal personality of one man rather than the system under which they still lived. Furthermore, current acceptance of that system may give way to future aspirations for a freer society as material improvement continues at home and as

efforts toward liberalization in other communist countries continue to gain publicity.

More important than future discontent is the perennial problem of political in-fighting in a one-party dictatorship. Khrushchev himself finally fell victim to it in October 1964, when he was ousted by the party Presidium (the new name of the Politburo after 1953). Leonid Brezhnev took over his post as first secretary of the party, Alexei Kosygin his post as prime minister. At the time of this writing, these two men were still in power, but they were already being challenged by younger, less ideologically oriented party officials.

Even more than liberalism and nationalism

in the West, Marxism has retained its aura of sanctity in the Soviet Union long after it had served its purpose in destroying the country's traditional leadership and carrying through the subsequent phases of modernization. The leaders of the post-Stalin generation, like their contemporaries in other countries, tend to be more pragmatic than their elders in dealing with current problems. In the mid-1960s, for example, a Soviet economist named Evsei Lieberman proposed a limited free market for agricultural products and consumer goods as a means of stimulating the farmers to produce more and of improving the quality of goods and services in the retail trade. Despite its resemblance to capitalist free enterprise, Liebermanism was a pragmatic answer to an immediate need, and it seems to be working. As elsewhere, however, it is much more difficult to initiate ideological deviations in foreign policy, for, since the French Revolution, "the nation in danger" is the ultimate slogan that entrenched rulers have had for rallying the people behind them.

EASTERN EUROPE

Like Western Europe, Eastern Europe has changed considerably during the past 25 years. Of the 8 communist countries there, only 4 — East Germany, Hungary, Bulgaria, and Poland — could still be considered loyal satellites of the Soviet Union by the end of the 1960s. Under the leadership of Marshal Tito, Yugoslavia has managed to maintain its independence since 1948, and Albania switched its allegiance to China in 1960. Rumania's leaders began following their own foreign policy in the mid-1960s, seeking contacts with the West and adopting a neutral position on the Sino-Soviet rift, although they have not yet relaxed their totalitarian rule at home. In 1968 a new group of Communist leaders in Czechoslovakia adopted a sweeping program of liberalization: they abolished censorship, permitted the public expression of non-Communist political views, and began to make Czech life a little more democratic at all levels. Although military intervention by the Soviet Union forced them out of office, their effort at reform expressed the longings of other East Europeans for more freedom and more independence from the Warsaw Pact.

The problem of what the Soviet Union called "national deviationism" involved both patriotic and economic motives. Beginning in the early 1950s, the Kremlin insisted that the satellite regimes follow the Russian example in government and in everything else; the Russian language was made compulsory in the schools, and Western cultural influences were eliminated. The Soviet Union also forced the satellite countries to concentrate their production on heavy industry, coal, and oil — products that would serve its own military and economic needs. Impressive results were achieved by 1954 when Poland, Czechoslovakia, Hungary, Rumania, and Bulgaria produced a total of 10 million tons of steel. This was one-fourth of the production of the Soviet Union and equal to it on a per capita basis. Still, the standard of living in the satellites showed no improvement until the beginning of the 1960s. These were examples of the kinds of exploitation that led to the Polish Revolt of June 1956, and the Hungarian Revolution of October 1956.

The Polish Revolt began as an anti-Russian uprising by the workers in the city of Poznan. Although the Polish government crushed this revolt, it recognized the uprising as a symptom of widespread unrest and tried to appease the people by raising wages and promising to improve living conditions. When these concessions failed, the Polish Communist party decided that it could keep the allegiance of the people only by giving them a change of leadership and some sense of independence. Thus, in October they installed Wladyslaw Gomulka — who had been arrested in 1951 as a "national deviationist" — as the new head of the party. The Soviet leaders tried to stop Gomulka's appointment, but they finally accepted it in return for his promise to retain close relations with them and to allow Russian troops to remain in Poland, ostensibly to protect its frontier with East Germany. Since 1956 there has been further unrest in Poland by workers, students, and intellectuals. In 1970 economic unrest finally drove Gomulka out of power, but despite his "national deviationist" leanings, he had not openly challenged Soviet policy.

Protest demonstration against Soviet occupation of Prague, Czechoslovakia, August 1968.

The brutal crushing of the Hungarian Revolution had taught him his lesson.

The Hungarian Revolution was the most serious threat to Soviet domination in Eastern Europe. It began in late October 1956, as a "national deviationist" protest demonstration against Hungary's Stalinist leadership, but it quickly turned into a mass upheaval when Russian troops came in to restore order. Non-Communists joined the Communist insurgents in demands for political and civil liberty, free and secret elections, free competition among political parties, par-

liamentary democracy, independent trade unions, the right of workers to run the factories, the abolition of compulsory membership in collective farms, and the abolition of the secret police—all, however, within the framework of socialism. The situation really came to a head when the new premier, Imre Nagy, withdrew Hungary from the Warsaw Pact. On November 4, fifteen Russian divisions, with six thousand tanks, began an all-out attack on Budapest and other towns. Tens of thousands were killed in the fighting, which continued into December. Thereafter,

Partisans and their prisoner at the beginning of the Hungarian Revolution, October 1956.

200,000 Hungarians fled the country. The Russians replaced Nagy with János Kádár, who has remained loyal to them ever since, and they maintained large numbers of Russian troops in the country. The presence of these troops plus the permanent loss of most of the people who were willing to resist, precluded any further "national deviationist" activities for the foreseeable future.

But in all the communist countries of Eastern Europe, including Hungary, even the staunchest Communists want modernization for its own sake rather than for the convenience of the Soviet Union. Within the Soviet bloc, Czechoslovakia, which from the start had been the most modernized of these countries, tried to go the furthest in following its own course, as we have seen. Because the hold of the Communist parties in all these countries is more recent and hence less secure than in the Soviet Union, the ideological justification for totalitarianism is so unconvincing to most educated people that the party leaders are virtually forced to allow more intellectual and professional freedom

than in Russia. It was, after all, a Yugoslav writer, Milovan Djilas, who first publicized the growth of the "new class." In Yugoslavia, as in the remaining Soviet satellites, this "new class" of modernizing professional people and technicians is likely to become increasingly resentful of both Soviet interference and what it considers unwarranted rigidity on the part of its own leaders. Even in communist countries, modernization raises not only hopes for a better material existence but also protests against all rules and institutions based on "mere" authority, no matter how recently installed.

JAPAN

Like West Germany, Japan was forced to adopt a democratic constitution in the late 1940s, but under the command of General Douglas MacArthur the American Occupation imposed a revolution in other areas of Japanese life as well. The 1947 constitution made Japan into a truly parliamentary state. It also guaranteed "minimum standards of wholesome and cultural living" and the right of workers to bargain collectively. Emperor Hirohito became a purely constitutional monarch; all political parties participated in free elections; the influence of the militarists was destroyed. The Occupation also instigated a major land reform by redistributing the estates of absentee landlords to their tenants. In so doing it created a mass of small, independent farmers and ended their social and political subordination to their "feudal" masters. Educational reforms made the schools more open at all levels, increased the number of years of compulsory attendance to nine, and created hundreds of new junior colleges and universities. Economic recovery was helped by American aid and by the fact that Japan did not have to maintain a large military establishment. In 1951 a peace treaty was signed, the American occupation forces withdrew (except from a few naval bases), and Japan took its place as a full-fledged member of the community of nations.

In no other country does the phrase "modernization in high gear" seem more appropriate than in Japan. For two decades after 1950 its average yearly rate of economic growth was the highest in the world. Its gross national product rose from $15.1 billion in 1951 to $51.9 billion in 1962 and continued to increase by more than 10 percent each year. Gone was the Asian pattern of near-subsistence living, still visible until World War II. By 1970 life expectancy had risen to 65 for men and 70 for women. As in all modern countries, young people continue to desert the countryside, and the traditional pattern of rural life is collapsing. Yet, with a population of 100 million living in an area slightly smaller than that of California (and almost as mountainous), Japan is now self-sufficient in agriculture. Increased productivity has made this possible, just as it has allowed Japanese industry to compete successfully in the world market in fields hitherto the preserve of Great Britain, Germany, and the United States: shipbuilding, optical instruments, electronics, and automobiles. Japan's remarkable economic growth has also made possible its success in parliamentary government and the gradual democratization of society.

Modernization has brought sweeping social changes to Japan. It was the first non-Western nation to limit population growth to the point where it no longer outstripped economic growth. In 1948 the government passed a Eugenics Protection Law legalizing abortion for economic as well as medical reasons, and since then public and private campaigns have made birth control practices popular. Japan's garish and bustling cities have also transformed the nation's social life. By the early 1960s Tokyo's public transportation system was so overcrowded that students were hired as "pushers" and "pullers" to help pack passengers into subway trains and to detain those whose attempted entry prevented the car doors from closing. Perhaps the most important social change has been the growth of the white-collar and professional classes, without roots in the traditional social and political structures. Their middle-class level of living has become the ideal to which less-favored Japanese aspire, while they themselves, and especially their children, are already beginning to feel their own unimportance and powerlessness, despite their consumer comforts, opportunities to travel, and educational advantages. It is the new middle-class salaried employees in government offices and large corporations who hold the key to Japan's political future, since perhaps half of them vote Socialist.

Until the early 1960s the conservative legacy of the prewar period and the popularity of Marxism in the immediate postwar years dominated Japanese party politics. The ideological split between the two leading parties — Socialists and Liberal-Democrats (conservatives) — deprived the nation of a political consensus, which gave a base of popular support for government in other modern countries. This split reflected differences in thinking between middle-aged union leaders and late-middle-aged businessmen and conservative politicians who found the 1947 constitution too democratic. But recently, as in other modern democracies, the two parties have sought to appeal to all classes, thus blurring their ideological differences to some extent. As the middle class grows, its vote becomes crucial. And whether a member of this class votes Socialist or conservative depends upon his feeling

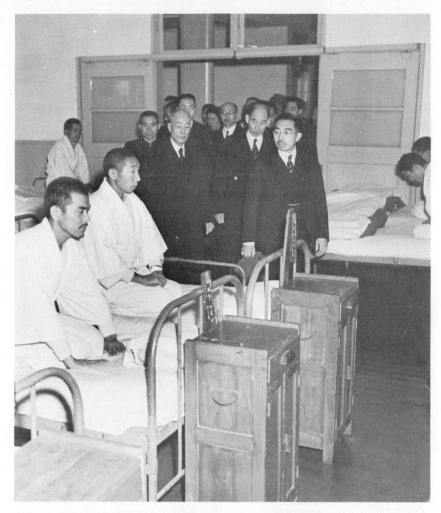

Emperor Hirohito of Japan visits an army hospital in his new role as a "democratic" monarch during the late 1940s.

of personal frustration or contentment rather than his social status. Most people vote conservative because they are satisfied with the steadily rising prosperity of the past two decades. Most people who vote Socialist are voting not for socialism but for democracy and against the established order.

In power continuously since the late 1940s, the ruling conservative party forms part of Japan's "establishment," along with the bureaucrats and big businessmen. Civil servants who have reached the top level of the bureaucracy frequently become Liberal-Democratic members of Parliament. Government agencies concerned with the nation's economy cooperate closely with Japan's industrial and banking leaders. Thus not only workers but also many middle-class people feel left out of the decision-making process. The most "alienated" group in Japan is its almost one million college students. Until the early 1960s many of them expressed their hostility toward the "establishment" and its pro-American orientation in highly organized demonstrations and strikes. Since then important segments of the student movement have clung to Soviet or Chinese versions of Marxism, but, except in them and in a handful of unions, the Communist party has little effect on Japanese life. In order to compete with the Socialists for the middle-class vote the Liberal-Democrats have begun to champion a conservative welfare state. The Socialists, though still Marxists in their goals, have dropped "violent revolution" in favor of "structural reform."

Despite all the obvious similarities with the modern nations of the West, the influence of Japan's recent non-Western past remains. The horror of Hiroshima and the dismantling of Japan's armed forces undoubtedly helped to change the Japanese from fanatical warrior-nationalists into peace-loving internationalists. But this sudden transformation can also be viewed as a shift from the militaristic to the tranquil side of the Japanese cultural tradition—from the sword to the chrysanthemum. Even as they attain greater logical precision, the most mentally adventurous would like to live by their aesthetic sensitivities. Whereas many postwar Japanese intellectuals cultivated American or Soviet ideals, the most widespread new movement was the Soka Gakkai (Value Creating Association), a traditional, "organic" social organization based on Buddhist beliefs. By the mid-1960s perhaps one out of every fifteen Japanese was a member of the Soka Gakkai. Although class lines have become blurred and there is a growing range of choices open to individuals, Japanese society remains more family oriented than that of the West, and the desire to maintain a sense of group intimacy persists. The older generation laments the more relaxed, frank, less polite, and selfish behavior of young people, but Japanese manners and mores have not changed as fast as those of Western nations that have experienced comparable rates of economic and social transformation during the past twenty years. Social obligations are taken only slightly less seriously than before World War II. Japanese women have gained the right to vote and many freedoms from old restraints, but their social circles still remain separate from those of their husbands.

THE CURRENT CRISIS

Since World War II modernization has produced a rate and quality of change unprecedented in the history of the world. Jet air-planes and television satellites continuously circling the planet have turned it into a kind of "global village" in which everyone can instantaneously know and be affected by events taking place anywhere. The rapid spread of agricultural and medical techniques has so reduced the need for population increase that women's future and the future rearing of children is being profoundly altered. In recent years, however, the population explosion, particularly in the great metropolitan areas, has created apparently unmanageable problems of pollution, transportation, social disorganization, and even elemental security of life and property. Along with the population explosion, the rapid growth of a mass-consumption economy in more and more places, with its disposable products and industrial waste, threatens to upset the ecology of the entire planet.

Integrated societies have yet to become true communities. In an integrated society the individual is torn from his traditional community moorings—local, regional, ethnic—and left to find his way along among the bureaucratized mass organizations that govern him, draft him, employ him, manipulate him, and provide him with a multitude of social services from the cradle to the grave. Most of his contacts with other people become mere encounters rather than meaningful relationships. Increasingly, his contacts with large organizations take place through computers rather than persons. On the one hand, tens of millions of people can feel a common bond while watching an international sporting event on television; each one sides with his own national team, but all accept the rules of the game and admire the prowess of foreign athletes. On the other hand, within the most modern nations self-conscious ethnic and social groups demand the revival of traditional forms of political and cultural autonomy in opposition to the bureaucratized institutions that dominate their lives: local control of public schools, student control of universities, attempts to preserve or revive languages other than the official national language (French in Canada, Catalan and Basque in Spain, Flemish in Belgium, Ukrainian in the Soviet Union).

Pressure to adapt prevailing values, norms, and institutions to new conditions has arisen in many areas: the civil rights movement and the black revolution in the United States, demands for educational reforms in almost all modern countries; even the churches have tried to become up-to-date. In France in the late 1940s a group of young Roman Catholic priests tried to reach the religiously indifferent industrial workers by working and living with them. The Vatican soon condemned this practice. But beginning with Pope John XXIII (1958–1963) the Vatican itself sponsored a more "ecumenical" attitude toward the other Christian churches and a more "participatory" role for the bishops in matters of high policy. Although the Vatican Councils of the early 1960s also recognized the need to reexamine the church's views on birth control in the face of the population explosion, in 1968 Pope Paul VI (1963–   ) maintained the ban on all forms of artificial contraception. On matters of social and racial justice, however, many Catholic, Protestant, and Jewish clergymen have championed the most advanced views. A few Protestant theologians have even taken the position that "God is dead." Aside from denying the very meaning of the word theologian, this position evokes the fundamental dilemma of organized religion in a fully modern civilization.

The assertion that "God is dead," by implicitly rejecting the old conception of God as the infallible autocrat, reflects other forms of protest against authority in the name of equality. This "equality revolution" spares no entrenched authorities, from popes and deans to party leaders, government executives, and office managers. The forms it takes vary according to one's present status. Members of oppressed minority groups, whatever rhetoric they use, are mainly demanding equality, pure and simple: I am as good as you are and I insist on being allowed to do all the things you do without interference from you. Workers, students, and ordinary citizens press for more democracy, for greater participation in decisions affecting their work and their lives, and for greater responsiveness to their demands from the existing authorities. Upper-middle-class youths with no responsibilities and older persons who reject theirs ask for more autonomy, for the freedom to be what they want to be and to choose how they will spend their short time on this earth.

Protests against bureaucratization, atomization, and massification have even challenged those ideologies that have fostered modernization: liberalism, nationalism, socialism, communism. The events in France in the spring of 1968 dramatized this challenge. Both the Socialist and Communist parties seemed to share the students' and workers' opposition to De Gaulle. But the young activists accused these parties of being "integrated" into France's modern institutions and hence no longer capable of "liberating" people from a newly felt bondage. That young people in Communist countries should accuse their party leaders of putting their ideology in the service of a new "establishment" is understandable; that a Communist party in a capitalist country should be so charged illustrates the growing alienation of many young people from older political leaders whatever their ideology.

It seems unlikely, however, that protest and alienation alone will change the basic character of modern society. In France, as elsewhere, the ruling "establishment" has been able to retain the loyalty of the majority by playing on its fears of instability and to fragment the protesters with the technique of the carrot and the stick. Integration need not mean homogenization; there is room in modern society for minority-group subcultures and individual self-expression. But some form of integration is essential in order to hold everybody together. Modern civilization is man's triumph over the "state of nature." We cannot go back to that "state" without most of us perishing.

SUGGESTED READINGS

Sampson, Anthony, *Anatomy of Europe.* New York: Harper and Row, 1970. Paperback.
A recent survey of all aspects of contemporary life in Western Europe, including the student revolts of 1968.

_____*The New Anatomy of Britain.* New York: Stein and Day, 1972.
  An up-to-date analysis.

Grosser, Alfred, *Germany in Our Time.* New York: Frederick A. Prayer, 1971. Paperback.
  A political history of the postwar years.

Ardagh, John, *The New French Revolution.* New York: Harper and Row, 1969.
  Carries the changes through the 1960s.

Carlyle, Margaret, *Modern Italy.* New York: Frederick A. Praeger, 1968. Paperback.

Tatu, Michel, *Power in the Kremlin: From Khrushchev to Kosygin.* New York: Viking, 1969.
  A penetrating account by an outstanding French journalist.

Crozier, Michel, *The Bureaucratic Phenomenon.* Chicago: University of Chicago Press, 1964. Paperback.

Ellul, Jacques, *The Technological Society.* New York: A. Knopf, 1964. Paperback.
  Pushes the logic of the triumph of technique to its extreme.

Curtis, Michael, *Western European Integration.* New York: Harper and Row, n.d. Paperback.
  A good history of the subject.

Reischauer, Edwin O., *The United States and Japan.* New York: Viking, n.d. Paperback.
  See especially for recent developments.

Byrnes, Robert F., ed., *The United States and Eastern Europe.* Englewood Cliffs, N.J.: Prentice-Hall, 1967. Paperback.
  A topical approach.

Seton-Watson, Hugh, *The East European Revolution.* 3rd ed. New York: Frederick A. Praeger, 1956. Paperback.
  Especially good on the "communization" and "satellization" of Eastern Europe.

Harrington, Michael, *The Accidental Century.* New York: Macmillan, 1965. Paperback.
  An astute commentary on the American scene.

O'Neill, William, *Coming Apart. An Informal History of America in the 1960s.* Chicago: Quadrangle Books, 1971.
  An excellent, popularly written survey.

CHAPTER 27

Latin America in Recent Times

Twentieth-century Latin America has participated in most of the advances known to the rest of civilization and has suffered many of the problems. Although the two world wars and the protracted periods of tensions and lesser conflicts have not directly touched Latin America, they have greatly affected it. World War I created expanded trade opportunities for Latin America. Since that time, economic development has been spectacular in some sections, retarded in others. The automobile, airplane, radio, motion pictures, popular press, television, and enlargement of electrical power sources have changed the face of Latin America while substituting new values and habits for its society. In every country the middle sectors have expanded and the lower classes have begun to emerge from their traditional poverty and despair. Demands for political institutions to bring material benefits to the masses have changed the character of government. Recent dictators as well as democratic leaders have had to deliver such benefits, particularly in the way of economic growth and the welfare state. Partly because of the difficulty of achieving these ends, governments have continued to be unstable.

Women have been emancipated nearly everywhere. Oppression and segregation of colored races have been breaking down. Domestic immigration has brought the rural poor, often Indians or blacks, into the cities, making runaway urbanization a familiar problem. Strident nationalism has led to defiance of foreign countries that had often been the sources of capital and technology as well as good customers; nationalists began depicting foreigners as imperialistic exploiters, sometimes with sound reason. Foreign systems—democratic capitalism or socialism, fascism, and communism—have had strong influence but have also caused revulsion as Latin Americans seek their own way.

Relations with the United States, especially, have been uneasy. In power and wealth the Yankee giant has grown far beyond Latin America. American preoccupation with struggles against rivals in the northern hemisphere has created envy and a sense of neglect in Latin America. Yet, Latin America sharply condemned the massive intrusion of the United States into the Caribbean in 1898 and after, even while copying many aspects of American business and pop-

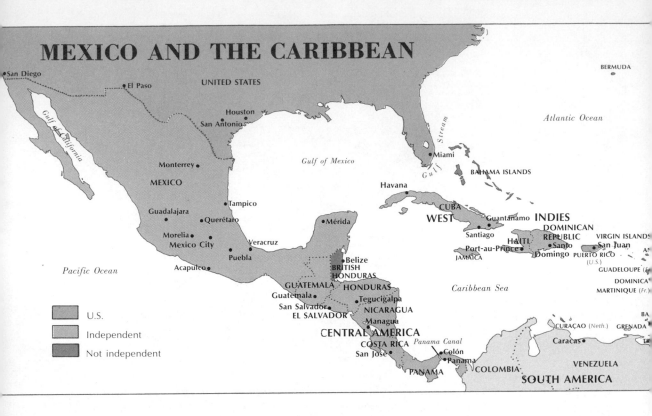

MEXICO AND THE CARIBBEAN

U.S.

Independent

Not independent

ular culture and seeking to stimulate investment and trade. Protectorates and "dollar
diplomacy" caused much genuine alarm, as
did American interference in Mexico. The
Good Neighbor policy of the 1930s brought
about better relations, only to be followed by
a long period of American indifference. The
likelihood of communism in the Caribbean
caused the United States to revert to inter-
ventionist policies, direct or covert, in the
1950s and 1960s. It also stimulated the massive program of aid, conditional on Latin
American social reform and self-help, known
as the Alliance for Progress. The Organization of American States, established in 1948
as a successor to the previous Pan-American
or Inter-American system, has offered a
somewhat fragile institutional basis for the
community of western hemisphere nations.
Meanwhile, Latin Americans have been responsive to both economic and cultural advances from powers outside that community
as they grope for their own destiny in their
own ways.

MEXICO

This great mestizo republic, the largest
Spanish-speaking land in the world, has institutionalized one of the major revolutions of
this century. It began in 1910 as an effort to
overthrow the dictatorship of Porfirio Díaz,
who had brought domestic peace and great
material progress to Mexico. He fell in 1911
because he and his henchmen had grown old
and because Mexicans had come to regard
the government as too tyrannical, the church
as too powerful, the foreigner as too favored,
and the division of wealth so unfair that most
people were worse off than they had been in
colonial times. Francisco I. Madero was the
leader of this revolution. Idealistic but inept,
Madero was overthrown and murdered in
1913 by elements abetted by the U.S. ambassador, who favored a restoration of the *Díaz-
potismo* without Don Porfirio. There followed a tragic period in which Victoriano
Huerta occupied the capital and center of the

Diego Rivera mural of the Mexican Revolution.

country, governing in gangster style from various taverns. Meanwhile, the folk leader Emiliano Zapata revolutionized the southern farmlands while the bandit-cowboy Pancho Villa dominated much of the ranchlands or desert of the north. Because of these challenges and pressure from the United States, which involved the occupation of Veracruz, Huerta fled.

Late in 1915, a regime headed by a reformed Díaz supporter, Venustiano Carranza, won control of the country. Carranza remained in power until 1920, restoring some measure of internal peace to Mexico, with Zapata being killed and Villa curbed. The most enduring achievement of the times, however, was the constitution of 1917, hurriedly put together by radical reformers with lukewarm approval by Carranza. This document enunciated, even before the Russian Revolution of that year, the doctrine of state control of resources as well as subordination of individual rights to the will of the nation. It also called for the severe downgrading of the Catholic church, the expulsion of foreign owners, and redistribution of the large landholdings. The constitution of 1917 has been widely copied, although it only gradually went into effect in Mexico itself. Carranza failed to seat his heir in 1920 and was murdered as he fled. He has been the last ruler of Mexico to suffer this fate, and the rebellion of 1920 has been the last to succeed.

Ten years after the overthrow of Díaz it seemed that, materially speaking, Mexico was worse off than ever. It was Álvaro Obregón, whose military skills had brought Carranza to power in 1915 and thwarted his plans for 1920, who saved the revolution. President from 1920 to 1924, Obregón assembled a new power structure that has since ruled Mexico. He relied on leaders of the agrarians, the revolutionary army and its new chieftains, and freshly unionized urban proletarians to pacify the country. This new elite began to fulfill the promises of the constitution of 1917. Obregón's heir, Plutarco Elías Calles, carried forward these programs and initiated a severe persecution of the church and of religion itself. Calles reached an agreement with the United States concerning the expropriation of foreign-owned lands, and the two neighbors ended their prolonged hostility. Calles divided some land among small farmers but came to voice doubts as to the wisdom of rapid agrarian reform. He tightened the official revolutionary structure by creating a single, dominant party. In all, he achieved some aims of the revolution, but his regime was corrupt and undemocratic enough to cause critics to refer to it as "gilded socialism." President from 1924 to 1928, Calles was virtual dictator ruling through three puppet presidents from 1928 to 1934.

Calles' choice for the presidential term of 1934–1940, Lázaro Cárdenas, was to become the most beloved of all Mexican presidents save Benito Juárez. Cárdenas broke with Calles, whom he considered too reactionary, and refired the revolution. Massive land divisions, often in the form of communal *ejidos,* and vast irrigation projects relieved agrarian pressures. Cárdenas democratized the army by favoring the enlisted man over the pampered generals. The labor unions were regrouped in a new national organization with Marxist leadership. In 1938 Cárdenas thrilled many Latin Americans by expropriating the huge British and American oil industry in Mexico. He quietly abandoned the most extreme forms of antichurch persecutions. Despite his professions of socialism, free enterprise flourished, and Mexico saw the establishment of great numbers of small factories and businesses to make and distribute consumer articles. Cárdenas, an Indian himself, dramatized the role of the Indian in Mexican history, making Indianism a cult that reached into every layer of society. The number of schools multiplied; many of the new schools were conventional but others were itinerant or mobile units that went from village to village. Overwhelmingly popular, Cárdenas stepped down when his term ended and made way for the nominee of the revolutionary party, virtually the only political organization in Mexico.

Under Manuel Ávila Camacho (1940–1946) and Miguel Alemán (1946–1952), the revolution cooled, for World War II and its aftermath brought great prosperity and close ties with the United States. And the mood changed, with anticlericalism losing its force and the profit motive becoming respectable. Not ideological matters, but economic growth, was the national preoccupation. Foreign capital was again welcome. Mexican capitalism flourished, with a large new class of rich men and a greatly widened middle class. Even the proletarians were captivated by the values of middle-class society, although they continued to ritualistically invoke socialist slogans. Moreover, the land division program had to be slowed, for it had decreased national food supplies. Small farmers raised food for themselves but did not put it on the market. Furthermore, the program encouraged peasants (peons) to move to the cities. The ruling party remained monolithic and self-satisfied, undemocratic in practice but permitting considerable freedom of expression. Its corruption was accepted as inevitable by a people who had seldom known anything else.

Adolfo Ruiz Cortines (1952–1958) temporarily unnerved the party by threatening to curb graft and corruption, but he achieved little reform. During his presidency and that of Adolfo López Mateos (1958–1964) Mexico's economic development was spectacular. Construction and improvements in communications were widespread. Its industry was sufficient to make Mexico almost self-reliant in consumer goods and some heavier items. Mining made some progress, and the nationalized oil industry slowly recovered from the effects of the 1938 expropriations. Agriculture and livestock production increased enough to supply most Mexicans with sufficient food. By 1965 the Mexican Revolution was regarded as so triumphant that its success was creating new dilemmas.

Of the new and dangerous problems in Mexico, the worst was the population explosion, which was a threat to all of the food

President Lázaro Cárdenas of Mexico.

production, school construction, sanitation, public services, and urban programs. Another problem was shortage of land: when López Mateos tried to redistribute land, he found little left to distribute. Rural restlessness and renewed assertiveness by the labor unions were the chief problems facing Gustavo Díaz Ordaz, elected president by the ruling party in 1964. In adopting a hard stance against disorders, he represented the determination of an older generation of revolutionaries, who had won all they wanted, to withstand challenges from a younger generation claiming a renewed revolutionary spirit. The major challenge by the young rebels came in the protracted and bloody student riots of 1968. Most of these rebels came from well-to-do families, but they were rightly alarmed at the prospect that Mexico's population, perhaps 50 million in 1970, could not live comfortably on the nation's resources. Luis Echevarría Álvarez, a hard-liner like Díaz Ordaz, was elected president in 1970.

CENTRAL AMERICA

Guatemala

Until 1944 Guatemala seemed dormant under the familiar pattern of dictatorship sponsored by a landed, largely white oligarchy ruling Indian masses who were mainly unassimilated to Western ways. Coffee plantations in the highlands and mammoth banana-producing forests in the lowlands supported the economy. Welfare capitalism in the banana industry, owned by foreigners, chiefly the United Fruit Company, had brought many benefits of health and education, but the alien donors were resented. Juan José Arévalo, a socialist, became president after a revolution in 1944 and introduced ideas of reform that stirred the masses. He later wrote *The Shark and the Sardines,* which indicated by its title his attitude toward the United States.

In 1950 Jacobo Arbenz Guzmán was

elected president and the ferment of Arévalo's years grew. Guatemala was soon full of leftists who swarmed in from many countries and assumed direction of its government. Liberty was extinguished and only Marxism was acceptable. Confiscations or threats to seize landed properties alarmed the oligarchy and the foreign owners. Neighboring countries were also fearful of what seemed a communist foothold, for they feared that communism was a monolithic worldwide aggressive movement ruled by Moscow. In 1954, Guatemalan dissidents armed and aided by United States intelligence services and by other Central Americans invaded their homeland. Arbenz appeared to have no supporters willing to fight for him, and he fell. Afterward, the United States poured lavish economic and technical aid into the little country. For some years, Guatemala had the highest economic growth rate in Latin America, and some social injustices were righted. More remained, however, and repression of suspected Communists was severe. The continuing instability of Guatemala's presidents and wide-scale popular violence are ominous signs of deeply rooted troubles.

Nicaragua

Nicaragua, a land of white, black, and Indian peoples, seemed so likely to provoke European intervention through nonpayment of debts that U.S. Marines landed in 1912 to support a supposedly responsible regime. Not until 1933 were they withdrawn. This military "occupation" insured payment of debts, but ferocious opposition arose in much of Latin America against Yankee interference. Anti-American feeling found a focus in Augusto César Sandino, who for several years led guerrilla bands which harassed the marine contingents, seldom numbering more than a hundred. After the marines departed and Sandino was murdered by a Nicaraguan, Anastasio Somoza rose to the presidency. He maintained a classic dictatorship from 1936 until his assassination in 1956. The republic enjoyed order, received significant foreign investment, and underwent steep economic growth. Most of the benefits, however, went to Somoza and his family. Although the

dynasty has continued since his death, it has liberalized political life in some respects and is attempting to distribute wealth and income more equitably.

Panama

Panama became an independent republic in 1903 when President Theodore Roosevelt recognized a minor rebellion against Colombia as a national liberation movement. The United States immediately negotiated a permanent treaty with the new nation that transferred the rights of a bankrupt French company that had started a trans-isthmian canal and a 10-mile zone across Panama to the Americans. In the zone, the United States was to have perpetual rights "as if it were sovereign." Under the direction of Colonel George W. Goethals the Panama Canal was completed in 1914. During its construction malaria and yellow fever were eliminated under the leadership of Dr. William C. Gorgas. By 1918 the United States relinquished direct political control of Panama, though it remained a protectorate until 1939. The government was really a plaything of a few wealthy families, who resorted to violence and corruption as they competed with one another for control. The canal itself was a great success, with the ship transits bringing in large tolls and with passengers buying Panamanian goods and spending money as tourists. Americans who operated the canal and those stationed in the area to protect it also brought income to Panama. And Panama earned additional funds by registering ships that ignored the safety or labor union regulations of their home ports; thus Panama had, on paper, one of the largest merchant marines in the world.

In spite of the advantages the canal brought, Panama was a troubled nation. Racism flared against the Asians and the West Indian blacks who had been brought in to work on the canal. The United States, too, was resented by Panamanians. The American colony in Panama, administering the Canal Zone, was regarded as an arrogant, isolated ruling class. Panama objected to its status of a virtual protectorate and to its receiving only a small share of the canal tolls. In 1939 the United States made

The Panama Canal.

Panama an ally rather than a protectorate and on several occasions raised its share of the toll income. A comparatively placid period in U.S.-Panamanian relations followed; there was no serious trouble during World War II and the Korean War. Panamanian resentment surfaced after the Suez crisis of 1956 (see p. 787), the outcome of which encouraged Panamanians to try to take over the canal. In 1959 and 1964 there were dangerous incidents involving popular invasions of the Zone. As a result of these tensions, the United States and Panama renegotiated the treaty governing the situation but so far have not ratified it.

Although the Panama Canal has been successful, it will probably prove inadequate in the future. The volume of traffic through the canal is steadily growing. Moreover, it is strategically desirable to have another canal in the area should war or changing alliances make the present canal unusable. The political situation created by an American-owned canal in Latin America also presents problems. Latin Americans consider this an affront, and, on the other hand, Americans fear that Panama may use the canal for political leverage. For all of these reasons, con-

struction of additional canals in other countries seems desirable. In 1968 a virulent anti-Yankee, Arnulfo Arias, was fairly elected president. He was soon ousted and a military regime that proved to be populist, nationalistic, and repressive took over the country.

Smaller Nations

El Salvador, a tiny, rugged republic with an economy dependent on coffee exports, attempted to modernize but was hampered by militarism. Honduras remains what it has been for a century and a half: one of the two or three most turbulent and backward lands in the Americas. Costa Rica, long admired as a democracy with wide distribution of wealth and a strong educational system, began to suffer by mid-century because it could not support an elaborate welfare-state establishment. Moreover, volcanic eruptions polluted the air and poisoned the soil. Historically aloof from its neighbors, Costa Rica finally joined the Central American common market, which, in the 1960s, showed some signs of increasing commerce and economic development in this region. A severe setback to Central American amity occurred in 1969, when violence at a soccer game between the teams of Honduras and El Salvador led to an attempt by Honduras to expel the thousands of Salvadoreans who had moved into that country as farmers or squatters. The Organization of American States soon ended the war but not the ill feelings.

THE CARIBBEAN ISLAND NATIONS

Cuba

By the end of World War I it was clear that Cuba's republic, so hopefully founded under American auspices in 1902, failed to provide effective administration, liberty, or order. Corruption saturated all levels; public and private immorality characterized the island. American interventions or threats to intervene under the so-called Platt Amendment of 1901 had not induced responsibility among Cuban politicians. Instead, they tried to invoke American power to ruin their enemies. Moreover, World War I and the immediate postwar economic boom boosted the price of sugar, with the consequence that the island devoted itself to producing this crop to the neglect of others. The slump of 1920 led to the sudden sale of many farms to plantation owners, often American companies. Thus numerous Cuban farmers became mere day laborers in the sugar fields and the mills. The sugar industry, however, could only provide work for three to six months of the year with the result that rural unemployment or underemployment became a chronic situation. Much of the population became accustomed not only to leisure but to destitution.

From 1924 to 1933 Cuba was governed by Gerardo Machado, who was freely elected president but who gradually established a cruel dictatorship. During the first years of his rule, the country was outwardly prosperous. Sugar was exported at adequate prices, mostly to the United States. American investments poured into Cuba to build public utilities and small industries. And American tourists, servicemen, and rum-runners found it a paradise during the Prohibition era. The crash of 1929 quickly revealed the unhealthy character of the island's system. Although there was no historic landed aristocracy,

individuals and foreign companies monopolized the best farmlands for sugar. When the outside world reduced its sugar purchases, all of Cuba suffered, for the country was not diversified enough to grow its own food or export crops. Conditions became unbearable in the early 1930s under Machado, whose tyranny tightened as protests grew. In 1933 the United States intervened to remove Machado from office.

Power soon devolved on Sergeant Fulgencio Batista, who promptly made himself a colonel and chief of staff of the army although he awarded the presidency to someone else. For a few months it appeared that a socialist revolution would take place under Grau San Martín, the official president. The United States government, however, disapproved of Grau and prompted Batista to oust him. Batista was in control of Cuba, and he appointed and dismissed presidents until 1944. The Americans showed their goodwill by repealing the Platt Amendment and other tutelary treaties. Preference to Cuban sugar in American markets, which had been given since 1902, continued in a different form, and the United States government replaced private banks as financiers for Cuba. Economic conditions slowly improved. Batista's power, exhibited mainly behind the scenes, did not greatly restrict liberty, and elections were comparatively honest. Although he was no idealist, Batista was a man of the people who understood the need for strong welfare measures. These were passed readily and included in a constitution of 1940, which made Cuba one of the most advanced nations in the world in social legislation, at least on paper. In that year Batista took the office of president and served for four years. He was a cooperative ally of the United States during World War II. The free election of 1944 brought to the presidency Batista's long-time enemy, Grau San Martín.

World War II gave the Cuban economy a strong boost in terms of sugar exports and mining development. Many fortunes were made and often spent in vulgar display. Grau San Martín's one-time socialist commitment was lost in this so-called "dance of the millions." Yet there remained much rural poverty and urban dissatisfaction. Many Cuban intellectuals, disenchanted over repeated failures of their country to become a sound society, turned to Marxism-Leninism. Communists took over much of the organized labor force. For reasons not always logical, the United States was coming to be depicted not as Cuba's protector and best customer, but as the root cause of its lopsided economy. Yet the economy was rapidly becoming less lopsided in the 1940s and 1950s, and Cuban nationals were acquiring a great majority of the sugar industry. As expectations among the masses rose, so did revolutionary fever.

In 1952 Batista seized control of the government. Rival politicians enjoyed so little respect that the people showed scant opposition to the coup. For much of the next six-and-a-half years Batista permitted constitutional practices and liberties. Cuba was outwardly prosperous, with little inflation, rising production, and considerable diversification of the economy. By the mid-1950s Cuban society was more urban than rural: indeed, a growing number of people considered themselves middle class. There was no traditional class of landed aristocrats. The church was notably understaffed and weak in influence. Batista pampered his army and police, aided only very modestly by American war surplus supplies, but these forces, like everything else in Cuba, were corrupt and ineffective. There was no resistance to dedicated and skilled revolutionaries, and no moral authority in the existing establishment.

An attack on some barracks near Santiago on July 26, 1953 led by the brothers Fidel and Raúl Castro was a fiasco, but it acquired heroic fame among those who detested the regime of Batista and his coterie, which enjoyed the fruits of office and, in contrast to his earlier regime, neglected social problems. Late in 1956 the Castro brothers, who had been released from prison, and an Argentine Communist, Ernesto "Che" Guevara, landed in eastern Cuba and established headquarters in the Sierra Maestra mountains. There they circulated anti-Batista propaganda and organized guerrilla units to terrorize the island. Both within and without Cuba, the Movement of the 26th of July attracted idealists and dedicated revolutionaries. In two years Fidel Castro undermined the regime and captured the sympathy of much of the world. Batista, his system dissolving almost without a fight, fled on New Year's Day, 1959.

Fidel Castro was thirty-one, a big and athletic man of Spanish ancestry who combined an intellectual air with a cult of informality that attracted many, especially the young. His immense personal charm and his skill as a speaker, together with his boldness and acumen, made an enormous impact on world opinion. Some, of course, regarded him as comical or sinister. His initial appearance as an international figure brought much praise from those who felt that a revolution in Cuba was long overdue. Castro, however, began his rule by severely punishing those Batista henchmen he could catch and then moving on to punish moderates and liberals of long standing. Although the United States made tentative offers to aid Cuba, Castro soon began to abuse that country and to court the Soviet Union. Perhaps he was the first Cuban ruler to realize that he had an alternative to being a dependent of Uncle Sam. In 1960 the Cuban government nationalized all banks and principal businesses, which had been mainly U.S. owned. Castro planned to industrialize Cuba with great speed and with the aid of the Communist bloc. This goal would involve reducing sugar production and changing the entire character of the economy. Meanwhile, the flow of refugees became a flood. Within ten years one-twelfth of the population left, and an equal number were on lists to emigrate. A U.S. government effort to arm and transport almost 1200 Cubans to liberate the island resulted in ignominious failure at the Bay of Pigs in April 1961. After publicly proclaiming himself a Marxist-Leninist, Castro in 1962 allowed the Soviet Union to install missiles capable of striking most American cities. In the memorable confrontation of October 1962, however, President Kennedy compelled the Russians to remove these weapons and most of the troops they had sent to the island. All the Latin American nations but Mexico eventually broke with Cuba, their governments objecting to the guerrilla warfare units and terrorists that Castro was exporting to such danger spots as Central America, Venezuela, the Brazilian northeast, and the Andean backlands.

Fidel Castro speaking to crowd in Havana, 1966.

Castro and Guevara publicly admitted that their economic program had failed and that Cuba must revert to producing sugar, more than ever. Indeed, there was much poverty in the island, with food (even sugar) being rationed, and with machines breaking down and clothing wearing out. Yet, morale seemed high and Castro beloved by many. For the first time, honesty prevailed in government. Women, blacks, and the young had been advanced in status. Foreigners were still much in evidence, but they were Russians, Communist Chinese, or East Europeans rather than Yankees. University education and scholarship were debased; on the other hand, technical and elementary education were widespread for the first time. Probably a majority of the skilled and professional population had emigrated, but a new revolutionary generation was expected to replace them. If Castro had failed to export his revolution successfully, he had scared most

of the Americas into meeting social problems in the hope of preventing violent solutions. Most noncommunist governments abhorred the Castro regime. Fidel, however, has remained a hero and mentor to many dissatisfied persons throughout the world.

Haiti

Haiti was the second country in the New World to become independent, but it has long ranked last in civilization. After years of riotous politics, it was occupied by American armed forces in 1915 and reduced to a protectorate, a status it held until 1934. Puppet presidents and officials, closely supervised by U.S. fiscal and military authorities, presided over comparative internal peace. There was some economic development, particularly in the coffee industry and in tourism. After the Americans departed, an educated, French-speaking class of mulattoes usually dominated, though they occasionally used black military men as fronts. Haiti underwent some modernization and health improvements, and it remained a land of small, free farmers. It was not necessary for most of the population to work hard. Simple pleasures, popular art, and colorful religious practices often associated with witchcraft or voodoo occupied much of their time.

Haiti had long spurned foreign contacts, but modern machines and French culture had broken down much of its xenophobia. After 1957 it turned inward again. In that year François Duvalier, a voodoo practitioner and physician known as "Papa Doc," became president. Inconspicuous in appearance and no longer young, he possessed an uncanny ability to detect potential enemies. Soon he replaced the army with an unofficial force of his own. The mulattoes were driven out or degraded with great cruelty. Foreign ties were broken, and aliens sent away. Duvalier deported many Catholic clergymen as enemies of the state. Somehow the populace responded with awe to the supposedly magical powers of the tyrant. In 1964 he declared himself elected president for life and talked of taking a crown. No one was able to openly defy either Duvalier while he lived or his son, who succeeded him in 1971. Refugees who seek to liberate their homeland have so far been tortured and killed. Haiti drew away from Western civilization and from its neighbors under "Papa Doc," but is renewing ties under "Bébe Doc."

The Dominican Republic

The Dominican Republic, most of whose people are Spanish-speaking mulattoes, has long lived in fear of reconquest by the black Haitians. Its government was so disorderly that payment of foreign debts was jeopardized, with the result that President Woodrow Wilson took over the country in 1916. For eight years it was ruled by navy and marine officers, most of them unqualified and unwilling. The Dominicans were disarmed and compelled to refrain from civil war. Roads, sanitation, and elementary schools were benefits brought by the Americans. Injured pride and outrage in much of Latin America were effects of another character. When the Americans departed, the Dominican Republic had the basis for economic development and constitutional government.

In 1930 a U.S. Marine-trained Dominican, Rafael Leonidas Trujillo, seized the government and declared himself president. Until he was assassinated in 1961, Trujillo ruled as a dictator, sometimes allowing others to serve in the office of president. It was a period of severely policed order and tremendous economic growth. Trujillo, who liked to be called the "Benefactor," introduced modern agricultural methods that greatly increased sugar and food production, built small factories, constructed roads, docks, and airports, and otherwise improved the economy. If the educational system glorified him outrageously, it also expanded enormously and brought literacy to the masses. Vocational training improved the skills of the population, and some features of the welfare state provided protection for the working classes. For years Trujillo seemed to be adored by the population. Foreigners usually praised him as a miracleworker and a genius.

Only gradually did it become known how brutally he kept order and stimulated adulation. Mysterious "suicides" and "accidents" ended the careers of his enemies; torture was common. The men surrounding the Benefactor had to sacrifice their self-respect to remain in his good graces. And Trujillo himself and his family accumulated wealth far beyond that allowed even by the admittedly loose standards of Latin American rulers. By interfering in the gangster politics of the Caribbean, Trujillo revealed himself the worst disrupter of them all. The Organization of American States condemned him for attempting to kill the president of Venezuela, and there were other accusations of this nature. So great was his hold, however, that his death inspired a nationwide exhibition of mourning and swift punishment for the personal enemies who had gunned him down.

By the end of 1962 this small country had finally been "de-Trujilloized," as the process was phrased, and a writer named Juan Bosch was elected president. Seven months later he was ousted by the military for encouraging runaway radicalism. Conditions remained very shaky, with subsequent regimes unable to govern and with the economy so bad that one-third of the working force was unemployed. After a revolt in April 1965, President Lyndon B. Johnson, believing that the Communists were about to take control, sent the U.S. Marines to occupy the capital city, Santo Domingo. A few Latin American nations soon sent units to join this force. After an uneasy year, in which the United States was widely criticized for its intervention, an election resulted in victory for Joaquín Balaguer over Juan Bosch. Balaguer, a long-time puppet of Trujillo, had largely removed this stigma and in 1966 began the uphill task of restoring the economy of the Dominican Republic. Only optimists could seriously hope that the long-abused Dominican people could rule themselves democratically; by 1969 even the archdemocrat Bosch began calling for a "popular dictatorship." In the presidential election of 1970 Balaguer won an overwhelming victory over Bosch.

Puerto Rico

A Spanish colony since 1508, the island of Puerto Rico was stagnant and undeveloped in the nineteenth century. Its population was a mixture of Europeans, Africans, and Indians. A rebellion for independence, begun at Lares in 1868, was severely repressed, as was a movement in 1887 to achieve autonomy within the Spanish monarchy. The United States overran and annexed Puerto Rico after the war with Spain in 1898. It was then ruled by an appointed American governor who shared little authority with the inhabitants. In 1917, however, self-government on the lower levels was conceded, and Puerto Ricans became United States citizens. Not since 1898 have there been duties on commerce between the island and the mainland, and Puerto Ricans pay no federal taxes.

During the first 40 years of American rule Puerto Rico's economy came to be based increasingly on sugar production and export. This situation intensified its dependency on the United States, the underemployment of its population, and the concentration of its fertile lands, especially in the hands of a few mainland companies. Health and sanitation measures in those years resulted in an enormous increase in the population. Hundreds of thousands migrated to the United States until 1953, when a decline in the flow began.

By the time of World War II Puerto Rico was in a very depressed state economically and socially. Most of its population was rural and often undernourished. A turning point came in the 1940s during the governorship of the New Dealer Rexford Guy Tugwell and the ascendancy in island politics of Luis Muñoz Marín. A reform and developmental program known as "Operation Bootstrap" caused a spectacular transformation. Massive American investment, encouraged by tax exemption and low labor costs, brought about so much industrialization that agriculture, itself much expanded, dropped to second place in its share of the gross output in the mid-1950s. The total product itself grew five or six times between 1940 and 1970. Agrarian reform and crop diversification improved the condition of the rural sector. Social legislation and unionization benefited the working classes in general. A middle class increased rapidly. Yet unemployment has continued high in spite of the much-admired "Operation Bootstrap," and poor people from the depressed rural areas continue to seek work on the mainland.

In 1948 the Puerto Ricans elected their first governor, Muñoz Marín, who served four terms. In a plebiscite of 1952 they overwhelmingly approved the change in status of the island from a territory to a commonwealth associated with the United States, self-governing and in control of its affairs except for foreign relations. Even though nationalists agitated for outright independence, sometimes violently, and other elements sought statehood, 60 percent of the voters in another plebiscite in 1967 ratified the commonwealth.

Spanish influence lingers but has greatly declined before the American impact. Protestantism now claims about one-fourth of the population. Women have gone far toward achieving equality. Puerto Rico has had a distinctive cultural renascence, associated in part with the movement for political independence. It also attracts great hordes of tourists and American immigrants. Enjoying civil liberties and self-government, Puerto Rico stands foremost in the tropical world in standard of living, health, education, and democracy.

THE ANDEAN COUNTRIES

Venezuela

Venezuela's history during this century has been conditioned by the long (1908–1935) dictatorship of Juan Vicente Gómez. Gómez, a coarse, venal, and cruel rustic warrior, maintained strict order through a large army. He encouraged foreign investment and economic development, and after 1918 profits from oil exports were so great that the government enjoyed abundant revenue. Under Gómez most of the money went to himself and his associates and to maintain the large, showy army and police force. Most of the population lived in poverty and were illiterate. The petroleum itself was extracted mainly by foreigners and processed in Dutch or British islands off Venezuela's coast or shipped by tankers to distant localities.

Gómez's death in 1935 caused an explosion of joy, but the regime that followed was only somewhat less repressive. In 1945 a group of young army officers and intellectuals of a party called *Acción Democrática* seized the government and proposed to spread the benefits of the oil income throughout all sectors of society. They increased Venezuela's share of the income to one-half, still leaving the foreign companies with considerable profits. Talk of socialism and land division created opposition among the historic conservative groups, which overthrew *Acción Democrática* in 1948.

For most of the 1950s Venezuela was under the dictatorship of Marcos Pérez Jiménez, who was supported by a pampered army and police. Spectacular highways, airports, and public buildings were constructed. Caracas became one of the most modern cities in Latin America. Like the country, it contained opulence and poverty, sophistication and ignorance. Some improvement in agriculture and ranching resulted from the dictatorship's policies, and steel production was begun near iron-ore deposits that may be the largest in the world. Yet the rule of Pérez Jiménez was harsh, and most of the oil royalties went to small groups he favored.

In 1958 Pérez Jiménez fell. Later that year Romulo Betancourt of *Acción Democrática* was elected president. Setting a precedent, he served out a full five-year term and turned his office over to another member of his party who had also been freely elected. There was much terrorism, however, some of it inspired by Trujillo of the Dominican Republic, some by Fidel Castro of Cuba, and some by extremists of other types. Economic growth was sharp in some respects, sluggish in others. The oil income was distributed far more widely than it had ever been before, and some of the ancient social problems began to yield in a liberal atmosphere. Late in 1968 the candidate of a Christian Democratic coalition, Rafael Caldera, won an honest election, giving rise to hopes that Venezuela, after three constitutionally conducted tests at the polls, was attaining political maturity.

Colombia

Colombia was so humiliated by the loss of Panama in 1903 that its leaders ended a long period of civil war. Chief among these leaders was Rafael Reyes, president from 1904 to 1909, a Conservative who set up a regime that continued the clerical, centralist policies of the constitution of 1886 but permitted the Liberals some share in the government. From the time he left the presidency until 1930, the so-called Reyes system continued to operate under the Conservatives. Colombia was peaceful and orderly. Its coffee and banana exports grew to such a volume that many finished goods could be imported, and light industries were established and communications improved. Aviation was particularly important to this mountainous land, where roads are difficult to construct and railways can be nothing more than short lines. The discovery of large oil pools on the Caribbean coastlands also brought in revenue, and production of Colombia's historic treasures — gold, lead, emeralds, and platinum — increased. The cultured classes of Bogotá were among the most alert and informed of the Americas. Schooling was widespread by Latin American standards.

By 1930 the Conservative oligarchy was in decline and the masses were demanding a

Panama Canal

Barranquilla

★Panama

PANAMA

Buenaventura

Cali •

COLOMBIA

Quito ★

ECUADOR

Guayaquil •

Talara •

Caribbean Sea

Valencia •   Caracas

★ Bogotá

Cauca River

Magdalena River

Orinoco River

VENEZUELA

GUIANA

Ciudad Bolívar •

GUYANA

★Georgetown

SURINAM

(Neth. Guiana)

★Paramaribo

★Cayenne

FRENCH GUIANA

HIGHLANDS

Manaus •   Amazon River

Belém •

A   N   D   E   S

PERU

Callao • ★ Lima

• Cuzco

Arequipa •

Lake Titicaca

★ La Paz

Oruro •

BOLIVIA

• Sucre

BRAZIL

Recife •

São Francisco

★Brasília

Salvador •

M   O   U   N   T   A   I   N   S

Pacific Ocean

Antofagasta •

CHILE

PARAGUAY

★Asunción

• Tucumán

Paraná River

Uruguay River

São Paulo •

• Río de Janeiro

Atlantic Ocean

Valparaíso •

★

Santiago

Concepción •

Córdoba •

• Mendoza

Rosario •

ARGENTINA

Santa Fe •

Porto Alegre •

URUGUAY

Buenos Aires ★

• Punta del Este

★ Montevideo

Río de la Plata

Puerto Montt •

FALKLAND ISLANDS (Br.)

Strait of Magellan

SOUTH AMERICA

Oil production in Lake Maracaibo, Venezuela.

larger share of the national wealth. The election of a Liberal president and his peaceful assumption of office suggested that Colombia was a mature republic. A number of measures were enacted by the Liberals to broaden the suffrage, weaken the power of the established church, and facilitate social welfare and labor unionization. The constitution issued in 1936 seemed to indicate that Colombia would become a social as well as a political democracy. The nation was one of the most admired in Latin America.

During World War II, however, uneven prosperity and economic dislocations, as well as floods of ideological propaganda, caused many urban workingmen to turn to a type of labor-union authoritarianism advocated by a theatrical demagogue, Jorge Eliécer Gaitán. His candidacy in 1946 split the Liberal vote, allowing a Conservative to win the presidency. In 1948, while the Ninth Inter-American Conference was meeting in Bogotá, Gaitán was murdered. Popular riots,

some stimulated by foreign revolutionaries like the young Fidel Castro, brought death to many persons and wrecked much of the capital. Soon Colombia reverted to its nineteenth-century tradition of chronic civil war. *La Violencia,* which was waged in every department of the country, pitted Liberals against Conservatives, towns against towns, and families against families. Much of it degenerated into mere rural lawlessness and urban terrorism, but often real issues caused men to kill. Estimates place the deaths due to *La Violencia* prior to 1960 at more than 100,000.

The Conservatives were so repressive that, in 1953, the army ousted them and installed Gustavo Rojas Pinilla as dictator. For a time he seemed popular, and the country began to boom again. Industrialization, output of mines, oilfields, and plantations, and construction of all kinds burgeoned. But Rojas was vain and tyrannical, and in 1957 the army removed him. A pact between Liberals and Conservatives of that year, ratified by a plebiscite, stipulated that until 1974 the two parties would combine in a National Front and share all public offices equally with the presidency alternating. The system worked reasonably well, and internal peace returned. Yet the politicians continued to be fractious and the public quick to criticize. The country seemed full of aggressions in search of targets. Economic conditions were unstable, with growth very sharp in the western plateaus and sluggish in other areas. Although much had been done to improve housing and schooling, Colombia's facilities were in danger of being swamped by rapid population growth. In 1970 the National Front candidate, the Conservative Misael Borrero Pastrana, barely defeated former dictator Rojas Pinilla, running as a populist.

Ecuador

Ecuador, the Republic of the Equator, has remained underdeveloped in spite of the richness of its soil and forests. Almost nine-tenths of its people live in primitive conditions and know little of the outside world. Moreover, those who are politically alert maintain the traditional division between conservatives at Quito, the capital, and liberals at Guayaquil, the port. The extreme clerical character given the little nation by García Moreno in the 1860s changed under the liberal leader, Eloy Alfaro, in the early twentieth century. The export of cacao pods and Panama hats gave the country enough income to purchase a few machines and to build a railroad from Quito to Guayaquil. Yet Ecuador remained appallingly backward. Its government was nearly always dominated by the army, which often had fascist sympathies. A boundary settlement, forced on Ecuador by the other American nations in 1942, gave almost half of its claimed territory to Peru, thus breeding resentments and border violence that have continued.

A modernizer was elected president in 1948: Galo Plaza Lasso, a liberal much admired abroad, who later became, in the early 1970s, secretary general of the Organization of American States. Favoring civilian control and personal liberty, he urged that Ecuador increase production drastically as a basis for eventual social reforms. Although he was successful in fostering the growth of the banana industry into a major source of income, he was unable to dominate the country after his term ended. Ecuador has been exceedingly unstable since the end of Lasso's administration in 1952. Its brushes with current technology and thought, as well as massive doses of American aid and recent discoveries of great oil pools, have produced considerable ferment to bring about better conditions for the masses.

Peru

Peru's rigid social structure has changed little in the twentieth century. During the dictatorship of Augusto Leguía (1919–1930), the traditionally conservative landed oligarchy lost no power even though it was forced to include businessmen who became prominent during those years of steep economic growth. Prosperity arose from sales of petroleum, copper, lead, cotton, and sugar and the stimulation of automobile and airplane transportation. North American bankers and investors loaned Peru much money during those years but did not make the country an economic colony. Instead, Peru defaulted on its bonds and defrauded most of the investors. Leguía did something to benefit the long-oppressed lower classes and to awaken the Indians, so many of whom had lived in sullen isolation for centuries. He also recovered, through diplomacy, the province of Tacna, which Chile had occupied since the War of the Pacific in 1879–1883.

In 1930 Leguía's government fell as a consequence of the world depression. There emerged a movement known as APRA (American Popular Revolutionary Alliance), the creation of Víctor Raúl Haya de la Torre, which promised a socialistic, Christian, Indo-American state. Popular as it was, APRA was prevented by the army from winning elections, and successive governments between 1930 and 1945 sought to deflect its appeal by permitting some freedom and by offering welfare benefits to the Indian and *cholo* (mestizo) masses. After another period of economic growth stimulated by good business and American aid during World War II, a free election was held in 1945. APRA appeared to win a dominant position. Yet it was unable to profit from it. Ridiculed by the Communists and frustrated by the traditionalists, it resorted to violence and failed. By 1948 APRA was outlawed and Haya was a forlorn refugee in the Colombian legation, where he stayed for five years.

General Manuel Odría ruled dictatorially from 1948 to 1956. He improved public education and social security and opened Peru to foreign businessmen and its greatest period of economic growth. Production in nearly every line increased. Assembly plants and distribution establishments went up rapidly. For a few years the fishmeal industry was the source of Peru's greatest income. Odría's successor was also a strong ruler, but by 1962 the formula of enlightened conservatism had played itself out. Business conditions declined, the fish disappeared, and the flow of rural Indians into Lima signified a new alignment of classes. Stirred at last, the masses were no longer content to await the creation of wealth by capitalism and technology but demanded a share at once. Haya won the election of 1962 but was not allowed by the army to take office.

In 1963 he ran again but lost to Fernando Belaúnde Terry, who had the support of the Christian Democratic movement then on the upsurge in Latin America. Belaúnde seemed an admirable leader, much praised abroad. He planned to divide much of the land among the peasants, to widen democratic practices, and to create an interior highway to make use of the rich, neglected hinterland. Although he was slow to become alarmed at guerrilla warfare in the provinces, he eventually quashed it. Nationalists found him slow also in attacking alien ownership of Peruvian property. And many powerful people covertly opposed his program of land reform. Suddenly, in October 1968, he was deposed by the army. Since then the country has remained tense, and the military government has adopted a truculent, even hostile, attitude toward the United States and foreign owners of property. No longer the tool of the traditional oligarchy, the army is taking the lead in promoting social welfare, labor unions, and division of land—a trend that seems to be spreading in Latin America and the Middle East.

Bolivia

Bolivia had farther to go than Peru in bringing its huge Indian population into modern life, and it has succeeded better. Although this chilled, bleak highland republic, where most of the people live in basins between ridges of the Andes, is a nominal democracy, landowners, mine operators, and military men have long fought for control of the government. Unfavorable boundary settlements, including loss of their coastline after the war with Chile in 1879–1883, developed in Bolivians an acute sense of persecution. Strides into modern life began in the twentieth century with the tin-mining industry, which was developed mainly by the British. Imports could then be financed and a fairly good network of railways completed. During the 1920s, many Americans bought Bolivian bonds, thus enabling the country to purchase machines and other samples of current technology. Yet most of the people were Indians who did not speak Spanish and continued to live in isolation.

Between 1928 and 1938 a major war with Paraguay, perhaps the worst ever fought in Latin America, began the dissolution of this stratified Bolivian society. At issue was control of the torrid and almost worthless Chaco Boreal region. During this struggle, a quarter of a million Bolivians were drafted for service at the front, and 52,000 died in action. Bolivia lost the war, and most of the disputed Chaco Boreal, to Paraguay. Afterward, it was receptive to reformers, often returned soldiers who had socialistic ideas. In 1943 the MNR (National Revolutionary Movement) came into power through rebellion. Overthrown in 1946, it made a comeback in 1952 under Víctor Paz Estenssoro, who nationalized the tin mines, supplanted the army with a peasants' and workers' militia, and encouraged the Indians to occupy the large landed estates. Although Paz was hostile to foreigners and took over much of their property, the United States decided to encourage his movement as a wholesome effort to restructure Bolivian society. Many American technicians and advisers were sent to Bolivia, and for some years it received more aid from the United States than any other Latin American country. Schools were established in great numbers, and illiteracy rapidly declined. The tin industry was operated by the labor unions, and many farm machines, implements, and new methods were introduced.

Paz held the presidency from 1952 to 1956 and from 1960 to 1964, with an ally serving in the interval. Although popular and effective, he was not altogether successful. The tin workers drew their pay but performed little work. Inflation was acute. The rural population engaged in almost chronic warfare over the land. And hatred of aliens was so strong that many well-meaning advisers had to flee. Much of the American aid program had, in fact, been mismanaged. Furthermore, food production declined, as did tin production. In 1964 Paz was removed by his vice-president, General René Barrientos, who charged that he had failed to carry out the MNR program. Barrientos thereupon dismantled the MNR organization and replaced it with a military group that professed similar ideals. The tin mines were placed under a government monopoly and, with the workers being disciplined, began to produce again. Rural disorders diminished despite the efforts of "Che" Guevara, the French journalist Régis Debray, and other foreign revolutionaries to stimulate guerrilla insurgency among the farmers. Debray was captured and Guevara killed. The Barrientos government was also able to slow down the rate of inflation, with the result that business in general improved. The changes brought about in Bolivian society since 1952 were so fundamental that no one, it appeared, could undo them. After Barrientos was killed in a helicopter crash in 1969, a more leftist element in the military took control and refueled the revolution along ultranationalistic lines. But in 1971 other elements in the military staged a counterrevolution, the 186th change of government in Bolivia's history, and displayed a less radical orientation.

Chile

In Chile, where the population is largely concentrated in a mountain-ringed central valley, conservatism was dominant from 1830 to 1920. A land-owning oligarchy con-trolled the farmlands, which were worked by peons or migratory laborers. A few men of commerce in the cities were wealthy, and so were those who operated the nitrate excavations in the northern deserts. Racially, the people were largely mestizo. After 1891 the Chilean government was the only one in Latin America to be dominated by the congress and not the president. The parliamentary leaders represented a closed society in directing political affairs, restricting the vote, and imposing only a few taxes. Civil liberties prevailed, however, and education was available to most of the people.

An economic crisis at the end of World War I fundamentally disturbed this order. Nitrate sales for war purposes abruptly ended, bringing to a close easy financing familiar for generations; socialist doctrines then attracted the long-deprived working classes. In 1920 Arturo Alessandri was elected president with a program to strengthen the executive, separate church and state, and provide universal suffrage. Long frustrated by a recalcitrant parliament, he saw his projects passed in a single day in 1924 when a group of young military men forced the legislators to act. Alessandri departed in protest over the methods employed for this purpose, but he returned long enough in 1925 to sponsor a new constitution, and then he left again. Now it was possible for social welfare laws to be passed and for labor unions to organize on a large scale. Chile also became prosperous for a short time, thanks to vast copper output, most of which was mined by American companies and sold in the United States.

The depression of 1929 returned the country to poverty and disorders. After a series of short-lived governments in 1931 and 1932, the voters restored Arturo Alessandri to the presidency. In this term, extending from 1932 to 1938, he stressed order over reform, in contrast to his previous incumbency. Nonetheless, a rapid drift to the left occurred; in 1938 the Popular Front won, and Liberals ruled until 1952. The Popular Front was a leftwing group, usually supported by the Communists. During this period, Chile instituted the most extensive social legislation known in any Latin American country. Economic development was striking, especially because of wartime pro-

Copper mine in Chile.

duction of nitrates and copper. Deposits of iron and oil were found, and the inferior coal of the south was exploited. The war boom made it possible to modernize the mining industry, the public utilities, and the transportation system. Chile's income enabled it to create many assembly plants and mills producing "import substitution" articles and thus to diversify the economy. Yet, the landed oligarchy remained powerful in rural areas, a constant threat to the radicals and innovators. Furthermore, government policies initiated an inflationary spiral that continued through the 1960s, one that has made Chile a classic case for study of this condition.

The Popular Front lost in 1952, when an elderly general and former president, Carlos Ibáñez, became president again. By then it was apparent that, although much had been done to bring social justice to the country, the rural sector remained underproductive and unreformed. Whenever copper prices fell abroad, Chile experienced sharp reces-

sions. The nation could not afford the welfare program that had been enacted for the urban masses. With an educated public and articulate intellectuals, Chile was restless and uncomfortable in the modern world and often inclined to blame the United States. In the term of Jorge Alessandri (1958–1964) austerity measures and massive infusion of American aid perhaps staved off economic collapse and even civil war.

A genuine change for the better came with the election of 1964. By that time the historic parties had all but perished and a new grouping had taken place: Christian Democrats and their moderate allies versus a radical combination known as the FRAP, whose candidate was the Marxist Salvador Allende. Eduardo Frei of the Christian Democrats won an overwhelming victory, the largest in modern Chilean history. Promising "revolution within liberty and law," he began the reform of an agrarian system in which 3% of the people held 75% of the productive lands.

Bowing to nationalists who wanted to confiscate the American copper holdings, Frei devised a compromise by which the government would become a partner of the alien firms. He hoped that Chile would eventually become self-sufficient in food, as theoretically it should be despite the steep population growth, and that it would realize its great potential. The nation's tradition of liberty made Frei's program difficult to achieve by democratic methods, and he was only partially successful.

In the elections of 1970 Salvador Allende won a slight plurality of popular votes. Like Fidel Castro, his efforts to create a socialist economy brought shortages and dislocation of resources. But unlike Castro, Allende did not make his country a satellite of the Soviet Union, and he preserved democratic processes. Consequently, his opposition could work openly to discredit him, though whether or not it would succeed was an open question at the time of this writing.

PARAGUAY AND URUGUAY

Paraguay, largely destroyed by the war of 1865–1870, recovered so slowly that it remained one of the most retarded nations in Latin America. Its population, mostly Guaraní or mixed-blooded, seldom honored the institution of marriage. There was no need to work hard in the pleasant climate. Although Paraguayans have shown themselves to be fierce soldiers, they are notably passive before homegrown oppressors. If life is easy, it is rarely long, for the people tend to be sickly and to die young. Apart from subsistence agriculture, Paraguay's economic life has been dominated by enterprising foreigners who export sugar, cotton, rubber, and timber. The steamboat and a stunted railway were long its only touches of modernity. Until recently its school system has been pitifully small.

The war with Bolivia over the Chaco Boreal region (1928–1938) cost Paraguay 36,000 men, but it won the war and most of the Chaco and survived the censure of the League of Nations as the aggressor in the struggle. Since then, the military has ruled the country, the heads of state usually being heroes of that war. General Alfredo Stroessner

has been dictator since 1954. An old-style *caudillo,* he has ruled oppressively but has sponsored increases in production and commerce. Some social welfare benefits are available to the working classes, and sanitation and education have improved. Both Brazil and Argentina have been eager to stimulate Paraguay's economy and attach it to their own.

Uruguay has long seemed the antithesis of Paraguay. A racially uniform nation oriented toward Europe, so democratic that its government can scarcely govern, and virtually classless, it has long been held up as a model Latin American republic. During the 1950s the outside world suddenly no longer needed Uruguay's wool and beef, at least to the extent of paying good prices for them. The resulting depression enabled the conservative Blanco party to come to power in 1958, defeating the rival Colorado liberals for the first time in 93 years. Conditions failed to improve, and the Colorados returned in 1966. Uruguay almost ceased to function as a modern society. The elaborate welfare system, begun early in the century, degenerated into a racket, with people retiring on full salary in early middle age. There was no incentive to modernize the ranching and agricultural industries or to create manufacturing establishments in a land where private enterprise was penalized and collectivization could not work because of lack of popular discipline. Almost continuous strikes, inflation, and breakdown of services caused immense irritation and economic stagnation. Uruguayan leaders and foreign observers alike often charged that the entire population wished to live like the idle rich. Uruguay's severe moral and psychological crisis continues, and terrorism has recently blemished its long reputation for internal peace. Yet, the past successes of the country provide a basis for hope that it may recover its prosperity and sense of direction.

ARGENTINA

There was much rejoicing in Argentina when the Radical party assumed power in 1916 with Hipólito Yrigoyen as president. At last the urban masses, most of them foreign-born or first-generation Argentines, had come into their own with a liberal program. Yrigoyen's first administration, extending to 1922, did not deliver many specific benefits, but its mood was such that labor unionization on a large scale began, and the common people felt that the government was sympathetic. Argentina prospered during World War I by selling meat and grain to the Allies, though Yrigoyen was isolationist or even pro-German. Light industries started to produce articles that could not be imported because of the war. The country was also culturally active. Its educational establishment flourished, and its university reform of 1918 was copied over most of Latin America, democratizing higher education and making many concessions to demands for student power. Although Yrigoyen put down a general strike and used a "red scare" to his own advantage, he was almost deified by the masses. During the term of his chosen successor, Marcelo Alvear (1922–1928), the country reverted to its usual internal peace and profitable export of raw materials in exchange for finished goods and for capital. European immigrants arrived in great numbers.

Yrigoyen, who was nearing eighty in 1928, ran for president again to spite Alvear, who had broken with him. The old man was easily elected. Adored though he was, he proved unable to cope with the depression of 1929, which cut Argentina's exports in half and ended its supply of foreign capital. In 1930 a military coup ousted Yrigoyen, who by now was senile. It was the first action of this type to succeed in Argentina for seventy years. The precedent was fateful, for in 1943, 1944, 1955, 1962, 1966, and 1970, the army again deposed presidents.

The period from 1930 to 1943 represented something of a restoration of the domination of the old *Régimen* of cattle barons and capitalistic wheat farmers who had run the country prior to 1916. Argentina was not an obvious dictatorship for most of this period, although Radicals were not allowed to win elections. And the country was more cooperative with other western hemisphere nations during the 1930s than it had ever been before. Yet its ruling group failed to detect that Argentina was changing fundamentally, that its industry and distribution businesses were surpassing ranching and agriculture. Moreover, European immigrants were stopped at the source, mainly by European governments who wanted more soldiers, and Argentine rustics were now thronging into the cities. These migrants tended to be ultranationalistic. Yet the government repeatedly offended national pride by tightening the historic ties with Britain and by giving more concessions to European owners of railways, slaughterhouses, public utilities, and flour mills. To Argentines it seemed that their country was an economic colony in contrast to other western hemisphere nations which were breaking Old World ties. And reformers could easily denounce the social imbalance of their nation. Landowners and exporters seemed to be favored while little was offered the working classes.

In the worst days of World War II, in 1940, Vice-President Ramón Castillo became acting president. Suddenly he sent congress home and imposed censorship. Soon he made it clear that he regarded an Axis victory as both inevitable and desirable. The military deposed him in 1943 but revealed that, if anything, it was even more pro-Hitler than Castillo. In 1944 another army coup brought "the colonels" into power. This group was openly fascist in temper and, despite the way the war was going, pro-Axis. Nonetheless, Argentina enriched itself greatly during World War II by selling meat, wool, and grain to the Allied nations.

The most important figure among "the colonels" was Juan Domingo Perón, who had studied Mussolini, Hitler, and Franco at first hand during a tour of duty in Europe. Skillfully establishing control of key officers, he also catered to Argentine labor by unionizing it and by delivering rapid wage increases. His social program was overdue and highly popular. Perón was a magnetic, virile man who, like Fidel Castro, combined the gifts of an intellectual with those of an athlete and was a hypnotic public speaker. His charisma attracted the lower income groups, Argentine nationalists, and women. Those he repelled were mainly moderate liberals and the upper classes, whom he derided as snobs. Such groups he terrorized by creating an unofficial force composed of urban manual laborers

President Juan Perón at second inauguration, 1952. His wife Eva, shown here, died a few months later.

known as *descamisados* (shirtless). In 1946 he was elected President in a fair election, and in 1952, in a test at the polls that was less free, he was reelected. An invaluable ally was his beautiful wife, Eva, a former actress who became a shrewd organizer and propagandist. To the Argentine poor she seemed an angel of mercy, for she distributed charity on an unprecedented scale. To working girls she personified glamor and held out hope that they too might come to enjoy the jewels, clothing, and furs that she flaunted. The *descamisados* adored her as a humanitarian and a strident scourge of the "best people." After her death from cancer in 1952 Perón's hold on women and the lower income groups conspicuously declined. No other woman in Latin America had ever been so popular or influential.

Although he ruled dictatorially, Perón put through a social welfare and economic development program that made him a demigod to the masses. He catered to the working class more than most dictators in Latin America. He forced foreigners, mainly the British, to sell their holdings to the Argentine government. His policies avoided redivision of the land, most of which was held by a small number of people; he, however, deliberately downgraded the livestock and grain industries that had so long supported the country. Perón used the wartime surpluses in foreign banks wisely in purchasing heavy machinery that would make Argentina self-sufficient as an industrial power. He increased the supply of electricity through massive hydroelectric dam systems and he encouraged the exploration for oil and other minerals, with good results. He improved such industries as fishing, forestry, and shipping. Under Perón's policies Argentine production rose sharply in most respects, especially manufacturing.

Perón's program was in danger of collapse by the mid-1950s because he had sought to transform the country too rapidly. In addition, inflation, corruption, and mismanagement prevailed. While dislocations

Buenos Aires, Argentina.

and unrest were spreading, Perón made a costly political mistake: he attacked the Catholic church, which had long been quiescent or even friendly to him. Possibly Perón was concerned about the growth of a Christian Socialist movement, which he regarded as a threat to his plans. His sudden assault on the church aggravated his other problems, and the military, which had never been entirely in his power, decided to overthrow him. The coup was accomplished with almost no bloodshed in 1955.

Since 1955 Argentina has been notably unstable and economically depressed. Peronism without Perón has continued as the strongest single political force in the country. Both in 1962 and 1966 the army ousted elected presidents because they seemed unable to govern. Furthermore, the military has been critical of the efforts of civilian politicians to bring the Peronists back into the national family. General Carlos Onganía,

who became dictator in 1966, dismissed the congress, the courts, and most of the officials. Universities have been severely restricted, even purged, and censorship has been restored. Onganía became so unpopular that his brother officers ousted him in 1970. They promised a skeptical country that Argentina would eventually become democratic again. A country of great natural riches and more than 20 million people, mostly of European descent and unusually skilled for Latin America, Argentina seems to have compromised its destiny.

BRAZIL

Under the republic the political history of Brazil had been largely placid and nonviolent. Yet the government had been comparatively ineffective—an easygoing and corrupt fair-weather regime. The people were free but unable to influence their rulers

President-dictator Getúlio Vargas of Brazil.

because of the hold of political machines. All literate males, about one-fifth of the population, were eligible to vote in the 1920s, but only 1 percent of them did, for the bosses counted the ballots and decided on the winners. Long-mounting cynicism concerning the republic turned into a revolutionary mood in the depression year of 1930, when the outgoing administration, as usual, named its successor in a rigged election. The loser, Getúlio Vargas, challenged the count and organized various disaffected elements.

The rather good-natured revolution of 1930 was easily victorious. Little violence accompanied the collapse of the old regime and the installation of Vargas, who brought into power politicians from the far south, junior army officers, and reformers. He was to remain in office for 15 years.

The revolution of 1930 was a major turning point. Temporarily, at least, it signified the demotion of Brazil's most dynamic state, São Paulo, and a willingness to experiment with totalitarian methods then coming into vogue in Europe. Vargas seemed an unlikely dictator. A small, colorless person from the ranching country of the southern-most province, he appeared suave and genial. Yet his hold deepened, and he was able to throw his opponents off balance and acquire their weapons. In 1932 he defeated a revolt by the state of São Paulo. In 1935 he suppressed small but dangerous Communist uprisings in the military. In 1937 he destroyed what was left of constitutional government and openly declared himself a dictator. After almost being captured by Nazi-oriented Green Shirts in 1938, he shattered their organization. Not until 1945 did his enemies combine against him and force him to resign. As in Emperor Pedro's deposition in 1889, the army was responsible for his overthrow. Vargas remained popular after his fall, and in 1950 he was chosen president in a free election.

Despite their anticlimactic end, the Vargas years changed the face of Brazil. Extensive social legislation gave the workers every benefit except the right to strike. Vargas's enduring popularity, like that of Perón in Argentina, stems mainly from his services to the laboring classes. He also sponsored the modernization of every aspect of Brazil's formerly languid economy. Coffee, the chief export by far, was burned until world prices rose. Demand became voracious again during World War II and it has continued. Sugar, cotton, and other crops were improved by the new methods of agricultural science. Cattle breeding made Brazil's ranching establishment the best in South America, surpassing even that of Argentina. Vast iron deposits began to be exploited, and steel mills were constructed. Forest products continued to sell well, as they had since the early sixteenth century.

During the Vargas period, factory production of consumer articles rose to the level where most of the nation's demand could be supplied domestically; many items were even exported to the Spanish-speaking countries. Construction was a great industry in itself: lost-cost housing, highways, airports, public buildings, carefully planned new cities built by the government, and luxury apartment houses and palatial villas put up by the private sector. Brazil's urban planning

and futuristic experimental architecture attracted worldwide admiration. Though Vargas catered to nationalists by denouncing foreign investors and to radicals by condemning free enterprise, he covertly sought foreign capital. Capitalism flourished: many individuals made fortunes, and many more who had lived under primitive conditions entered the national economic structure. Furthermore, the regime provided electricity to operate the booming economy and water for the farmlands by an imaginative program of building dams and rerouting rivers. And Brazil's long-neglected educational system received a strong impetus. Illiteracy declined, and universities were started. Modern methods of sanitation and public hygiene greatly reduced disease — and helped begin a population explosion.

The boom continued after Vargas fell, due partly to surpluses accumulated in foreign banks during World War II. (Brazil was the only Latin American country to participate in World War II to the extent of sending an army overseas.) Prosperity, however, brought new problems. Wild inflation and extravagant spending on imported luxuries encouraged corruption in a government that was weak and ineffective after the years of Vargas's dictatorship. The economy appeared to be in a chronic state of hysteria as speculation, price increases, strikes, and threats of bankruptcy intensified. Vargas himself, as constitutional president from 1951 to 1954, was unable to chasten or control the country, and he committed suicide. Juscelino Kubitschek, president from 1956 to 1961, encouraged spending and inflation along with mammoth developmental projects and began building the costly new capital in the interior, Brasília, an architectural marvel that has to some extent justified the hope that its presence would enable the central part of the country to become productive.

The voters were in a sober mood in 1960, when they elected the frugal and honest Jânio Quadros president. But soon after he took office in 1961, he exhibited erratic traits, including alcoholism, and stunned the nation by resigning. Probably he hoped to be recalled with more powers, but the public did not respond. The army would not allow

The Brazilian congress building, Brasília.

the vice-president, Joao Goulart, to take over until the presidential office was weakened. This arrangement did not function well, and in 1963 Goulart succeeded in restoring the power of the presidency. A radical and admirer of Argentina's Peron, Goulart apparently sought to disorganize the government so badly that he could set up a dictatorship. Instead, the military deposed him in 1964, charging that runaway radicalism, inflation, and lack of discipline were ruining the country.

Since then the military, which exercises the "moderating power" once employed by the emperors of Brazil, has ruled with considerable arrogance. Censorship, denial of civil rights, and undemocratic methods of passing laws and selecting officials prevail. Despite much evidence of its unpopularity, the regime has curbed inflation and restored economic growth, especially that of heavy industry and petrochemicals. American aid and foreign investments have helped to steady the economy. Brazil now has more than 80 million people. It is the foremost multiracial society and the leading tropical civilization in the world. Despite much turbulence on the surface, it is making genuine progress in its thrust toward greatness.

At the beginning of the 1970s it is difficult to assess the seriousness of Latin America's troubles or judge the effectiveness of existing regimes in dealing with them. Some observers warn that the population explosion is nullifying any gains from economic growth and generating a mass revolt of the poor. Others argue that, with enough capital and enterprise, Latin America can use its vast resources and manpower to achieve a better life. Both of these points of view assume that material needs are foremost and that the surface turbulence in Latin American politics feeds on "mere" psychic needs. Yet, in a demagogic age, the poor and downtrodden masses can be just as easily aroused by expressions of aggressive, antiforeign, egotistical nationalism as by demands for more land and higher wages. Indeed, the most popular regimes seem to be those that self-consciously cater to both sets of needs: the Communist dictatorship in Cuba and the military dictatorship in Peru. The most unpopular, though hardly the most ineffective, regimes are the more conservative military dictatorships in Argentina and Brazil, whereas the least effective regime of all is that of Uruguay, the most economically advanced and politically democratic country in Latin America.

One thing is certain, the greatest single demand in Latin America is for change. The Cuban example has shown that traditional military dictatorships ignoring the needs of the masses do not last indefinitely. Hence many younger army officers, even in more conservative regimes, seek to bring about changes and governments that think and act like the Castro government, but in the name of anticommunism. Within the Catholic church there are also many radical priests and professors who talk about "communitarianism" and who work with independent Marxists and the younger, revolutionary army officers. Many middle-class students have also asserted their ideological commitment to social justice for the masses.

It could be argued that all these demands for change are merely new forms of traditional Latin American rhetoric. The army, the church, and the universities have had their would-be reformers in the past, and no other part of the world has had so many varied revolutions without really changing very much. Yankee-baiting has been a perennial pastime for almost a century — nothing new about this either. As a reminder of the petty nationalism of the traditional type, in the summer of 1969 El Salvador and Honduras broke off diplomatic relations over a dispute between the fans of their rival soccer teams.

Whether Latin America is headed toward peaceful or violent change remains to be seen. In any case, modernization has brought a host of new problems and new demands that will test the statesmanship of its leaders.

SUGGESTED READINGS

Cumberland, Charles C., *Mexico: The Struggle for Modernity*. New York: Oxford University Press, 1968. Paperback.

Wilkie, James W. and Michaels, Albert L. (eds.), *Revolution in Mexico: Years of Upheaval, 1910–1940*. New York: Alfred A. Knopf, 1969. Paperback. *Excellent selections illustrating the revolution.*

Parkes, Henry Bamford, *A History of Mexico*. Revised. Boston: Houghton Mifflin, 1970. Paperback.

Rodriguez, Mario, *Central America*. Englewood Cliffs, N.J.: Prentice-Hall, Inc., 1965. Paperback.

Thomas, Hugh, *Cuba: The Pursuit of Freedom*. New York: Harper & Row, 1971. *Lengthy and detailed. Outstanding on the Castro years.*

Fagg, John Edwin, *Cuba, Haiti, and the Dominican Republic*. Englewood Cliffs, N.J.: Prentice-Hall, Inc., 1965. Paperback.

Bernstein, Harry, *Venezuela and Colombia*. Englewood Cliffs, N.J.: Prentice-Hall, Inc., 1964. Paperback.

Poppino, Rollie E., *Brazil: the Land and People*. New York: Oxford University Press, 1968. Paperback.

Covers Brazil's entire history but stresses the recent period. Economic and social emphasis.

Burns, E. Bradford, *A History of Brazil*. New York: Columbia University Press, 1970.

A comprehensive treatment.

Skidmore, Thomas E., *Politics in Brazil, 1930–1964*. New York: Oxford University Press, 1967.

Very useful for the Vargas period and its aftermath.

Whitaker, Arthur P., *Argentina*. Englewood Cliffs, N.J.: Prentice-Hall, Inc., 1964. Paperback.

Emphasizes the Perón period. Mostly political history.

Scobie, James R., *Argentina: A City and a Nation*. New York: Oxford University Press, 1964. Paperback.

Treats the entire history of Argentina with social and economic stress.

Pike, Fredrick B., *The Modern History of Peru*. New York: Frederick A. Praeger, 1967

CHAPTER 28

Contemporary China, India, and Southeast Asia

The building of a modern nation-state depends on many things—a stable political leadership, a reasonable prospect of economic advance, an effective governmental administration, and, above all, on a mobilized or politically involved citizenry. Only a people actively committed to its success can hope to bring about political or economic development. Yet the individual citizen is most easily aroused in defense of his own nationality. Hence the process of nation-building in Asia has been accompanied by frequent outbreaks of hostilities among and even within the various Asian states. This warfare, and the consequent diversion of funds to armaments, has substantially hindered the slow climb of the Asian peoples out of poverty; it has also offered opportunities for interference by outside powers, especially the United States—the predominant power in the Pacific basin—but also the Soviet Union.

THE ERA OF NATION-BUILDING

India and Pakistan

When the two new states of India and Pakistan emerged onto the world stage in August 1947, they found themselves at once confronted with immense problems of consolidation, indeed even of survival. The coming of independence was the signal for an outburst of mass rioting and massacre, as Muslims in India sought the refuge of Pakistan while Hindu refugees fled into India. Over five million traveled each way across the new India-Pakistan border in the Punjab alone, while another half million were killed before they could reach the frontier. Both governments were helpless in the face of this pent-up hostility. Only Gandhi was able to quiet the rage, and he ultimately gave his life to the cause; he was assassinated at his prayers in January 1948 by a Hindu fanatic

839

opposed to conciliation of the Muslims. This shocking act finally induced a grief-stricken India and Pakistan to turn to more constructive tasks.

First on the agenda was the problem of assimilating some 450 princely states, ranging in size from mammoth Hyderabad to tiny principalities of a few square miles. Diehard supporters of British supremacy, the princes had by 1947 become hopelessly out of date, and all except three were soon forced into joining the Indian Union. There they were pensioned off, and their states merged into the surrounding territories. Of the three hold-outs, two (Hyderabad and Junagadh) were deep within India and quickly brought to their knees by armed invasion. Kashmir, however, bordered both India and Pakistan, and its maharaja, a Hindu, ruled an overwhelmingly Muslim population. When Pathan tribesmen from Pakistan moved on the capital in October 1947, the maharaja belatedly acceded to India, whose troops then rescued him and held off the Pathans, who were supported by Pakistani regulars, until a cease fire could be arranged in late 1948. Since that time India, holding the major towns and the populous Vale of Kashmir, has stood firmly on the legal validity of the maharaja's accession, and has refused to consider a plebiscite or other means of testing popular opinion. Infuriated, Pakistan tried unsuccessfully first through the United Nations, and then in 1965 for a second time on the field of battle, to oust the Indians. This unresolved conflict still embitters relations between the two countries, each of which regards the possession of Kashmir as essential to its national purpose: for Pakistan, that of Muslim homeland; for India, that of a secular democracy.

An unwieldy country put together out of portions of several British Indian provinces, and divided by 900 miles of unfriendly territory, Pakistan barely survived the first years of its existence. A makeshift government had to be thrown together overnight, since the bulk of the administrative and commercial middle class had disappeared with the Hindu refugees. In the west the headwaters of the Indus canals were now in Indian hands, while the export crops of the east were cut off from their normal trading outlets along the Hoogly near Calcutta. The political scene was equally bleak, for the Muslim League had exhausted its purpose in the creation of Pakistan, and soon fell prey to squabbling factions. An attempt was made to set up a parliamentary style government on the British pattern, but Jinnah's untimely death in September 1948 and that of his trusted lieutenant Liaqat Ali Khan two years later left the country bereft of leadership. Ministry followed ministry in an atmosphere of deepening crisis, marked by cynical opportunism and occasional popular violence, until finally, in October 1958, President Iskander Mirza abrogated the constitution, which had never been tested before the electorate, and instituted martial law. Thus ended Pakistan's experiment with parliamentary democracy.

Throughout this agonizing decade only the determination of its people and their shared Islamic faith saved Pakistan from disintegration. Yet even these basic ties were severely tested by the antagonism between east and west, and between fundamentalist and modernist Muslims. The Pakistanis in the east, though a majority of the population, were an impoverished peasantry dominated, if not exploited, by the politically active and more educated Punjabis of the west. The resentments this situation produced led directly to the initial eruption of the military into politics in the mid-1950s. Despite occasional gestures of reconciliation, such as the recognition of Bengali as an official language of the nation, western dominance persisted throughout the 1960s, leaving the underdeveloped east a restive partner in the enterprise of Pakistan. Similarly, although Pakistan was established on religious grounds, the westernized political elite refused to hand the government over to the orthodox *ulama,* who clamored for the enforcement of strict Koranic law and persecution of the remaining minorities. Yet Pakistan could not become a fully secular state without losing its reason for existence. This dilemma, which has never been resolved, keeps Pakistan one of the most conservative of Muslim countries.

From the start India was determined to establish a democratic system of government. The constitutional framework was worked

Peasant voters lined up outside the polls for an Indian election. Despite widespread illiteracy, India (the world's largest democracy) has held free and open elections regularly since independence.

out smoothly by the existing Constituent Assembly and brought into force in 1950. The first of a series of general elections under universal suffrage, which have been held at regular intervals ever since, followed in 1951–1952. Central to the new constitution was a federal system giving substantial powers to the states, each with its own elected legislative assembly and responsible ministers. At the same time extensive powers were reserved to the federal government, including even the right to take over the administration of a state whenever a stable ministry could not be formed. The constitutional preeminence of the center was reinforced in the actual working of the government by the commanding presence of Jawaharlal Nehru at the head of the Congress party.

As prime minister, Nehru—Gandhi's chosen heir—brought to the task of nation-building much of the master's universal appeal. His magnetic personality, intellectual brilliance, and eloquent patriotism won him the devotion of the Indian people and make it possible to speak of the first fifteen years of independence almost as the "age of Nehru." Behind Nehru was the Congress party. Riding on its record in the freedom struggle and exploiting the magic name of Nehru, the Congress everywhere swept to victory at the polls. Pushed to the far left and far right of the political spectrum by Congress dominance of the center, the opposition parties were unable to combine, and thus were reduced to the role of demoralized spectators of the political drama.

The goals of the Indian government under Nehru can be described as the pursuit of secularism, socialism, and neutralism. The first was close to the heart of the atheistic Nehru, who disliked even his own Hindu title of Pandit. The constitution proclaimed the freedom of religious belief, and Muslims have risen to high office in the state, including the important but largely ceremonial

The government-owned Rourkela Steel Mill. Factory chimneys are now a common sight in India as industrialization under both government and private auspices extends to an ever-widening range of products.

position of president. Yet orthodox Hindus have always provided much of the support for the Congress, occasional religious rioting has taken place, and the position of the large Muslim community in India has never become completely secure.

The pursuit of social justice involved, first of all, an attack upon the immense concentrations of private wealth on the land and in industry. In the early 1950s the great *zamindari,* or landlord, estates in northern India were broken up, and ownership vested in the peasant cultivators. The *zamindars,* however, received ample compensation while their former tenants obtained title only to the land they had previously cultivated, and the landless farm laborers got nothing at all. Similarly, in commerce and industry, despite Nehru's radical talk, Indian socialism in fact meant little more than heavy taxation and close government regulation of private business, combined with the creation of a separate public sector in the economy. Most of

the new heavy industrial plant was placed in this sector, but private and even foreign enterprise continue to prosper. This moderation in Indian socialism was not all Nehru's doing. It reflects rather the inherently conservative nature of the Congress as a coalition of interests dominated by the well-to-do peasantry and the urban bourgeoisie. Throughout his tenure of office, Nehru was continually forced to slow his pace so as not to get too far ahead of his followers.

Social justice was accompanied by economic development and modernization. The goal here was to raise India's appallingly low standard of living, and the method chosen was constructive use of the power of government channeled through comprehensive planning. The first plan, inaugurated in 1951, concentrated upon agricultural production and achieved a stunning success, with production increasing by 25 percent over a 5-year period. Much of the credit for this must go to the community development program, which spread a variety of agricultural extension services throughout the countryside. In 1956 a second and more ambitious plan was launched in which the emphasis was on large-scale industrialization. India's capital resources, however proved inadequate for so large a task. Hence Nehru sought, and to a large extent obtained, foreign aid on a massive scale, particularly from the United States. Although the ambitious goals of the planners were not achieved, India had by 1961 come a long way in a very short time. The new industrial plant brought the country to the verge of self-sufficiency in iron and steel and many light consumer goods and enabled it even to develop export markets for certain items. Overall national income rose over the decade 1951–1961 by some 42 percent. Although an explosive population increase of some 2 percent a year (which government birth control clinics did little to halt) undercut much of this economic advance, there was still a net per capita gain of 20 percent in average income over the 10-year period.

Nehru's attitude toward the world outside India, apart from the special case of Pakistan, was determined by the ideals of neutralism or nonalignment. In a manner not unlike that of the United States in the early years of its existence, the Indian government was sensitive to imagined threats to its own independence and suspicious of the former imperialist powers. Thus Nehru vigorously opposed the Dutch in Indonesia and the French in Indochina, he was more severe with Britain at Suez than with Russia over Hungary in 1956, and he finally resorted to force in 1961 when the Portuguese refused to vacate their Indian enclave at Goa. But Nehru's distrust of the European colonial powers did not induce him to ally with either the United States or the Soviet Union. He believed that the stark confrontation of two hostile power blocs, each armed with nuclear weapons, posed a grave threat to world peace. Therefore the more uncommitted states like India there were, the more the great powers would be forced to moderate their hostility. Besides, Nehru saw that the diversion of resources involved in any major war would cripple India's vital development efforts.

Nor was neutralism, in Nehru's view, an entirely negative policy. He tried on several occasions, though usually with little success, to mediate great power conflicts and he did his best to organize the like-minded nations of Asia and Africa into a "Third World" or neutralist bloc. The keystone of this policy was friendship with China. Historically, despite their long common border in the Himalayas, India and China had never been antagonists; united behind the *Panch Shila*, or Five Principles of Co-existence, they could be a powerful force for world peace. This amity reached its height in the Bandung (Indonesia) Conference of 1955 attended by the leaders of 29 Asian and African states. Nothing substantive emerged from this conference, however, and it soon became apparent that China had other aims in view than courting Nehru's goodwill.

Consolidation of the Revolution in Communist China

On October 1, 1949, the Communist party established a government in Peking, and with surprising speed consolidated its control over China's vast territory. As peace was restored to the country, a People's Democratic Dictatorship was organized according to Soviet principles of democratic centralism. Elected People's Congresses chose local executive committees while the central government was theoretically ruled by a People's Government Council accountable to a nationwide "Political Consultative Conference" – the source of legitimacy. The source of authority, however, was the Communist party and Young Communist League, whose membership grew to represent about 5 percent of the population. These party members, governed by strict rules of party discipline, answered to a Central Committee, which, in turn, selected a Politburo. The seven members of the Politburo's Standing Committee in turn actually ruled the country under the chairmanship of Mao Tse-tung himself. At first this central authority was not entirely secure. During its early years of political consolidation the new government had been forced to let a great deal of power slip into the hands of local military commanders, but the threat of regionalism (which had hamstrung so many rulers in Chinese history) was removed after 1954

Jawaharlal Nehru and his trusted lieutenant V. K. Krishna Menon at the United Nations. During the cold war era Nehru often used the world body as a platform from which to preach international amity and neutralism to the great powers.

when the party secretary and virtual overlord of Manchuria, Kao Kang, was purged.

The foremost concern of the new government was the extension of political control into the countryside. For over a millennium Chinese rulers had found it necessary to rely upon the local gentry as intermediaries between the central government and the populace. The Chinese Communists were determined not to repeat that experience and as early as 1946 realized that radical land reform would both benefit the bulk of the peasantry and destroy the economic foundations of the rural gentry. In 1951 and 1952 a zealous mass campaign against "counterrevolutionary" landlords was led by party cadres throughout the country. Hundreds of thousands were disgraced, others killed, and once and for all the position of the old gentry was destroyed. To replace these traditional "brokers of power" the central

government created a new administrative unit: the *hsiang* (village), a population grouping of two to three thousand people which elected delegates to local government committees.

The *hsiang* was also an economic unit that urged farmers to form mutual aid teams for the cooperative cultivation and harvesting of crops. By 1952, 40 percent of the peasantry had been organized into such teams, though individual farmers continued to own the land given them during the land reform. The next step toward socialism was to collectivize this property. In some cases this meant taking back newly distributed land — a process that had met with fierce resistance several decades earlier in the Soviet Union. Nevertheless, Mao declared in 1955 that the party had little choice in the matter because "autonomous capitalistic forces" had already reappeared in the villages. Even though the "feudal gentry" had been destroyed, a new class of "capitalist peasants" was busily amassing land, just as the traditional rural elite had done before them. Party cadres were therefore ordered to direct the peasants to turn all but a small private plot over to "Higher-Level Agricultural Producers' Cooperatives." This transfer was so skillfully carried out that by July 1957, 97 percent of the peasant households of China were organized into cooperative groups that farmed their amalgamated property.

This rural revolution was supposed to help increase agricultural productivity in order to permit rapid industrial development. By 1952 the new government had already increased the quantity of 33 major industrial products 26 percent above prewar levels. Consequently, a five-year plan along Soviet lines was set for 1953–1958 in the hope of doubling output. But whereas this goal was exceeded, agricultural production did not seem to be growing quickly enough to generate the surplus needed for more capital investment. Furthermore, China was experiencing a demographic explosion. According to the 1953 census figures—which were underestimated—China had 583 million people. By 1957 this figure had been corrected to 695 million. The fear that economic growth might fall behind population expansion eventually led to the "Great Leap Forward," which is described in a later part of this chapter.

In the view of the Politburo the success of these early efforts to transform China from a weak to a strong country appeared to depend upon the government's ability to organize human labor by means of mass mobilization campaigns. The first of these had been the antilandlord campaign of 1951–1952, which had taught the party that it was possible to incite class conflict by having cadres lead normally apolitical peasants in denouncing landlords who had once been respected members of the community. The second great movement was the "Five-Anti" and "Three-Anti" campaigns during the Korean War period (see the following section), which played upon Chinese fears of foreign aggression to encourage the people to believe in the invincibility of the "mass mind." Such campaigns succeeded because they were coordinated by mass organizations that were established under party control in all sectors of society. By 1953, for example, the average citizen belonged to at least one of these associations (the All-China Federation of Labor, the All-China Democratic Women's Federation, the Peasants' Association, and so forth) which were organized into small weekly "study groups" that discussed current issues and assessed the political attitudes of each of their members. A unique method of "self-criticism" was perfected. Each person had to account for his social "deviations" to the group, which constantly examined the ideological purity of its members' motives.

While the individual thus found himself subjected to the constraints of orthodoxy and sacrificed personal desires to collective goals, he could console himself with the new meaning to be found in common effort. The hundreds of thousands who paraded through T'ien-an-men Square in Peking during the Five-Anti Campaign were not marched at the point of a gun. Like the poet, Mu Jen, they thrived on the exhilaration of self-denial for the sake of the whole society.

I would like to be a tiny screw
So that they can put me where they want
*   and screw me in tightly*
Whether on the arm of a powerful crane
Or in the simplest wheel.

Put me in place and screw me in tightly
There I shall stay firmly put, my heart at rest.
Perhaps people will not know that I exist
But I know that vibrating to the throbbing of
*   a great machine is the life of a tiny*
*   screw.*

I would like to be a tiny screw,
So that they can put me where they want
*   and screw me in tightly.*
I shall be happy, and in the choir of heroes
I shall tremble to hear my own passionate
*   voice.*

Indonesia and Malaya

After four years of struggle Indonesia gained its independence in 1949. A unitary republic was established with a parliamentary cabinet form of government. Sukarno, the old nationalist leader, was named head of the state.

Sukarno, flamboyant president of Indonesia from independence to the abortive Communist coup of 1965. His successor, army general Suharto, is the current president.

From the first, however, the government was beset with troubles. One problem was the multiplicity of parties, which enforced coalition rule along with a search for the widest possible area of agreement even at the cost of action. The most prominent parties were the Nationalists, the Communists (who with a membership of over two million constituted the largest Communist party in Asia outside China), and two Muslim parties, one modernist and one conservative. The state was further weakened by persisting antagonism between populous long-dominant Java and the more conservative outer islands, such as Sumatra and Celebes, which contributed the bulk of the country's foreign exchange earnings. During 1956–1958, restive under central control and alarmed by the growing strength of the Communist movement on Java, army chiefs on various outer islands rose in rebellion. The rebellions were crushed, but in revealing the weakness of the central government they opened the way for the seizure of full power by the popular President Sukarno.

Skillfully exploiting his appeal to the masses, Sukarno built up his own preeminence through the device of "guided democracy." Under this system consultative assemblies based on consensus took the place of the party-dominated parliament, and Sukarno led the country on a quest for national solidarity and revolutionary purpose. Economic development, bureaucratic efficiency—indeed all domestic problems—were subordinated to an agitational style of politics in which slogans and symbols, and an adventurist foreign policy, predominated. Attacks on outside enemies (first the Dutch for their continued possession of West New Guinea, and then, when that dispute was satisfactorily resolved, on the neighboring Federation of Malaysia) kept Indonesian nationalism tuned to a fever pitch and diverted attention from domestic shortcomings. This emphasis on national integration also served to strengthen Sukarno's own position, which despite appearances was never that of personal dictator. He was in fact precariously balanced between the Communists, whom he often favored in order to widen the national consensus, and the army, whose support was essential to his rule.

Sukarno's balanced system was dramatically upset on September 30, 1965, when the Communists made their own bid for power and were turned back by the army, which proceeded to consolidate its victory by massacring thousands of Communists along with their supporters and then by stripping Sukarno of all his power. The army has continued to rule ever since, in alliance with the conservative Muslim parties, and it has made valiant efforts to check the rampant inflation and corruption left behind by Sukarno. The new regime has likewise repudiated the leftist foreign policy of its predecessor and sought friendship with Malaysia as well as the United States. But Indonesia remains an overpopulated and impoverished country whose social divisions are not likely to be easily healed.

Unlike Indonesia, Malaya did not have to fight for independence from its colonial master, and it has remained firmly wedded to liberal democratic forms since the departure of the British in 1957. Nor has the country had to face severe economic difficulties, for

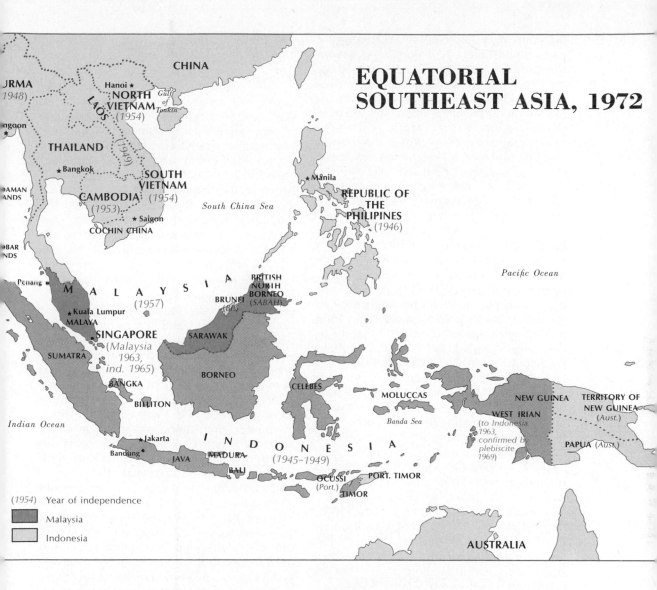

EQUATORIAL SOUTHEAST ASIA, 1972

CHINA

North Vietnam (1954) — Hanoi ★
Gulf of Tonkin
LAOS (1949)
JRMA (1948)
ngoon
THAILAND
★ Bangkok
SOUTH VIETNAM (1954)
CAMBODIA (1953)
★ Saigon
COCHIN CHINA
AMAN NDS
BAR NDS
South China Sea
★ Manila
REPUBLIC OF THE PHILIPPINES (1946)
Pacific Ocean

Penang
MALAYSIA (1957)
★ Kuala Lumpur
MALAYA
SINGAPORE (Malaysia 1963, ind. 1965)
SUMATRA
BANGKA
BILLITON
BRITISH NORTH BORNEO (SABAH)
BRUNEI (Br.)
SARAWAK
BORNEO
CELEBES
MOLUCCAS
Banda Sea
NEW GUINEA
WEST IRIAN (to Indonesia 1963, confirmed by plebiscite 1969)
TERRITORY OF NEW GUINEA (Aust.)
PAPUA (Aust.)

Indian Ocean
★ Jakarta
Bandung
JAVA
MADURA
BALI
INDONESIA (1945–1949)
OCUSSI (Port.)
PORT. TIMOR
TIMOR

(1954) Year of independence
■ Malaysia
■ Indonesia

AUSTRALIA

it has long possessed valuable export crops and has continued to welcome foreign investment. The major political problems first centered around the Communist guerrilla uprising of 1948, which was only suppressed after twelve years of intense jungle fighting, and then around the position of Singapore, a natural part of Malaya but a city whose Chinese population would overwhelm the native Malays in any merger with the mainland. In 1963 federation was achieved by including the British Borneo territories as well. After two years, Singapore chose independence as a city-state instead, but relations between it and the Malaysian Federa-

tion have remained cordial. There remains, however, the lasting problem of relations between the Malays and the large Indian and Chinese minorities. Enterprising and prosperous, the latter have never been reconciled to their position of political and social subordination, while the Malays have resented the economic power of the Indians and Chinese. Consequently, bloody rioting broke out in 1969 between these racial groups.

Thailand and the Philippines

In contrast, the Chinese in Thailand (Siam) were much more assimilated, even serving as high-ranking military officers. That same military establishment had dominated government since 1932, even though Thailand was nominally a constitutional monarchy ruled by King Phuniphom. Powerful officers like the premier, Marshal Thanon, and the minister of interior, General Praphas, did support a democratic reform in 1968. But the legislature that emerged in 1969 consisted largely of their appointees or political allies. Indeed, after 1972 all civil liberties were curtailed and military government reinstated. For, even though economic growth had been impressive under the generals, insurgency increasingly became a political problem during the 1960s. Most rebellions were in the northeastern portion of the country, where a mixed population of Thais, Meo tribesmen, and Vietnamese grew restive under the central government's police control. After 1964, a Communist-dominated "Thailand Independence Movement" became a major political force in that area, although it was hard to estimate how much popular support it enjoyed. The United States naturally helped the government combat these revolutionaries by providing financial aid and military advice, especially since there were so many American bases in Thailand.

The Philippines also faced the problem of rural insurgency during these same years, but its Huk rebels were as much gangsters as revolutionaries. The original Hukbalahap revolt had lasted from 1948 to 1954, drawing upon the discontent of a peasantry that often had to pay over 80 percent of its harvests to a small and wealthy landlord class. After the revolt was suppressed by Ramon Magsaysay, efforts were made to reduce tenantry and increase rural income. The most dramatic success was the development in Manila in the 1960s of a new type of rice seed that tripled production in regions where it was introduced. Basic land reform met with much less success. Successive presidents (Diosdado Macapagal, 1961–1965, and Ferdinand E. Marcos, 1965–1972) increased the power of village government and sought to limit rents while turning the lands over to the tillers. But they were so frustrated by the legislative power of the great landlords that very little land reform actually occurred. Beset by high urban crime rates and exten-

sive political corruption, the Philippines had many problems left to solve in the 1970s.

Burma

Burma, like the Philippines, had to deal with civil unrest for almost the entire first decade of its independent existence after 1948. Communist rebels, retreating Kuomintang troops from China, and Shan, Karen, and other hill tribes not reconciled to the dominance of the lowland Burmans, all harried the government of U Nu and delayed the rebuilding of the Burmese economy after the devastation of the war years. Although a popularly elected chief executive, U Nu was not an efficient or vigorous administrator. He preferred instead to devote himself to Buddhist religious activities, including the convening of a spectacular General Buddhist Council in 1954–1956. U Nu's failure to discipline the politically ambitious younger monks, or to integrate the ethnic minority tribes with the dominant Burmans, led Burma first to the brink of civil war and then to an army takeover in 1962. The government of General Ne Win, which remained in power thereafter, embarked at once on a program of revolutionary socialism imposed by force of arms. All private trading was abolished, the large Indian business community was expelled, and peasant agriculture encouraged. In its international relations the Ne Win regime, suspicious of all foreign contacts (except for its powerful Chinese neighbor), pulled Burma into a shell of isolation. Burma thus remained relatively unaffected by the turmoil in the rest of Southeast Asia during the 1960s, while its development programs, if slowed by the lack of foreign aid, at least distributed the available wealth equitably.

WAR AND DIPLOMACY IN THE 1950s

The Korean War (1950–1951) and U.S. Support of Nationalist China

The United States had aided the Kuomintang (Nationalist) forces of Chiang Kai-shek during the civil war, but it had withdrawn its support after his regime was driven off the

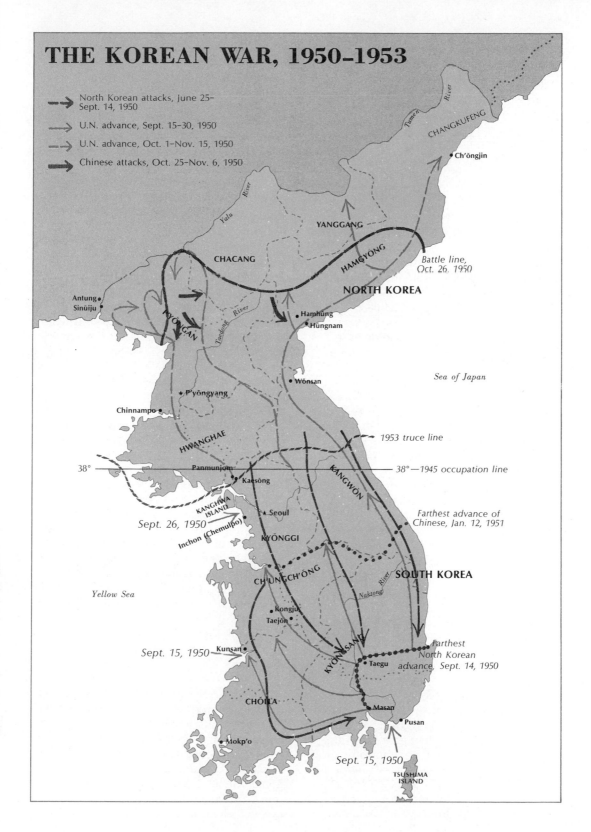

THE KOREAN WAR, 1950–1953

→ North Korean attacks, June 25–
Sept. 14, 1950

→ U.N. advance, Sept. 15–30, 1950

⇢ U.N. advance, Oct. 1–Nov. 15, 1950

⇒ Chinese attacks, Oct. 25–Nov. 6, 1950

CHANGKUFENG

• Ch'ŏngjin

Tumen River

Yalu River

YANGGANG

CHACANG

HAMGYONG

Battle line,
Oct. 26, 1950

Antung •
Sinŭiju •

NORTH KOREA

PYONGAN

Taedong River

• Hamhŭng
• Hŭngnam

Sea of Japan

• Wŏnsan

+ P'yŏngyang

Chinnampo •

HWANGHAE

1953 truce line

38° ——————— Panmunjom

38°—1945 occupation line

• Kaesŏng

KANGWŎN

KANGHWA
ISLAND

Sept. 26, 1950

▲ Seoul

Inchon (Chemulpo)

KYŎNGGI

Farthest advance of
Chinese, Jan. 12, 1951

Yellow Sea

CH'UNGCH'ŎNG

Naktong River

SOUTH KOREA

• Kongju

• Taejŏn

KYŎNGSANG

Sept. 15, 1950 — Kunsan •

Farthest
North Korean
advance, Sept. 14, 1950

• Taegu

CHŎLLA

• Masan

• Pusan

• Mokp'o

Sept. 15, 1950

TSUSHIMA
ISLAND

mainland into exile on Taiwan. The Korean War altered this policy. Korea, ruled by Japan since 1910, had been guaranteed its independence by the great powers at the Cairo Conference (December 1943). During the autumn of 1945, Soviet and American troops entered Korea and divided it along the thirty-eighth parallel into two occupation zones, which quickly became sovereign nations. In the north, a Soviet-trained Communist named Kim Il Sung became chairman of a Democratic Republic of North Korea, while in the South an American-educated Christian nationalist, Syngman Rhee (Yi Sung Man) was elected president in August 1948. Relations between the two republics worsened, until North Koreans invaded the south in June of 1950. The attack was immediately condemned by the United Nations' Security Council as President Truman committed American forces to the defense of its ally. At the same time, Truman hardened his attitude toward Communist China, and declared that an invasion of Taiwan would threaten the United States' security. On the military front the American Seventh Fleet began to patrol the Formosan straits, while Washington's diplomats insisted that the Communists had usurped power from Chiang Kai-shek, and therefore did not constitute the legitimate government of China.

Taiwan (Formosa) itself lies 100 miles off the Chinese coast, and at that time had a population of 8 million Taiwanese (descended from seventeenth-century immigrants from China) and 2 million exiled Mainlanders. Under Japanese colonial rule (1895–1945), the island had developed oil and sugar refineries, cement plants, and banana plantations. China recovered Taiwan as part of the postwar settlement, but Kuomintang officials promptly antagonized many Taiwanese by mulcting the island of much of its industrial equipment and by placing their own functionaries in positions of overweening importance. A revolt broke out in 1947 which the governor met with mass executions. Afterwards, though, the Kuomintang attempted to transform the island into a "model province," introducing many of the reforms it had neglected to carry out on the mainland. In 1949 a land reform reduced tenancy from 41 to 16 percent of farm acreage; and thanks to one billion dollars in U.S. aid between 1950 and 1956, Taiwan appeared to be one of the unqualified successes of American foreign aid programs. This growth continues on its own to the present time, though it barely keeps up with a soaring population increase (3.5 percent per year) and is hindered by a burdensome military budget that supports a huge army of 600,000 men held in reserve for the supposed recovery of the mainland.

The Communist government of the People's Republic of China on the mainland viewed American military support of the Kuomintang regime on Taiwan just as seriously as it regarded Truman's "police action" in Korea: both appeared preludes to invasion of China. The response of the United States to the Communist North Korean invasion of South Korea in 1950 was to send a large expeditionary force under General MacArthur, who recovered Seoul and drove the North Koreans back to the thirty-eighth parallel. In order to win the war and reunify Korea under an anticommunist regime, the American troops then crossed the demarcation line and began to push north toward China's border at the Yalu River. Peking grew alarmed at the prospect of losing a friendly buffer state along its Manchurian border and warned the United States that it would resist this "provocation." As American troops continued their advance, 300,000 Chinese "volunteers" crossed the Yalu to aid their North Korean allies by attacking MacArthur's flanks. At first they forced him to lead his armies back to Seoul in a disastrous retreat, but U.S. air and artillery power imposed a military stalemate on the Chinese and North Koreans, who agreed to a cease-fire in July 1951. Although an armistice was signed two years later, Korea still remains divided into two hostile parts.

The French-Indochinese War

Another source of tension between China and the United States was the crisis that broke out in Vietnam after World War II. As Japan was being defeated in the Pacific, Ho Chi Minh's Communist (Viet Minh) forces under General Vo Nguyen Giap captured much of the north and proclaimed a Democratic Republic of Vietnam in Hanoi on September 2, 1945. But Vietnamese independence was more apparent than real since Free French (Gaullist) soldiers and administrators had quickly reoccupied the south (Cochin-China) while 185,000 of Chiang Kai-shek's troops were garrisoned in the north. Nor were the Vietnamese themselves united. Some supported the emperor, Bao Dai, who had governed a united front under Japanese rule. Others joined politico-religious sects like the Cao Dai, which enrolled over one million followers into private armies controlling entire provinces. In the cities, racketeers fought among themselves to control municipal administrations. Finally, the Viet Minh themselves revolted because France would not fully support their Democratic Republic. In late November 1946, the French commander, Admiral D'Argenlieu, took matters into his own hands by bombarding the port of Haiphong. A Viet Minh counterattack on the French in Hanoi on December 19, 1945, failed; the Communists then took to the hills for the final stage of the war against French colonialism.

During the next three years the French tried to restore effective civil government to Indochina. Bao Dai was made head of the new state of Vietnam, which along with Laos and Cambodia was given limited independence within the French Empire. By 1950, though, Viet Minh guerrilla warfare was becoming a serious threat to government control in the north. The French commander-in-chief, Marshal De Lattre de Tassigny, built an elaborate network of pillboxes, watch towers and patrolled check points to restrict the guerrillas' mobility across the countryside. An "oil spot" (*tache d'huile*) strategy was adopted: great effort was devoted to pacifying single key districts from which civil order would supposedly radiate as a spot of oil expands across the surface of a pond. Ultimately, this strategy failed to destroy the complex political infrastructure patiently erected by the Viet Minh since the 1930s. Utilizing the same principles of village organization as Mao Tse-tung had used against the Japanese in World War II, the Vietnamese Communists had placed cadres in every northern hamlet. By 1953 the French realized that the "oil" simply was not spreading, and decided on a major military attempt to turn the tide. Hoping for a "set-piece" battle where French armor and air power could defeat the enemy once and for all, the French commander (General Navarre) made an enormous tactical blunder by electing to make a stand at the isolated valley of Dien Bien Phu, which could easily be cut off from logistic support. In March 1954, Vo Nguyen Giap's forces beseiged this fortress and, after inflicting enormous casualties on the French, forced the 16,000 survivors to surrender on May 7.

By this time, both Russia and China were shifting their own diplomatic positions. Stalin himself had declared in 1952 that "peaceful coexistence" was possible between communist and capitalist nations, and as the Korean War was resolved, he helped China urge the Viet Minh to negotiate a settlement. A meeting was convened at Geneva in 1954 to discuss Vietnam. There, the coincidence of Dien Bien Phu, of a Socialist electoral victory in France, and of Chou En-lai's pressure on the Viet Minh to accept a Korean-like division of their country, made diplomatic accords possible. In July 1954, a cease-fire agreement was signed between the French and Ho Chi Minh's government, and a further declaration (the Geneva Accords) temporarily divided Vietnam along the seventeenth parallel, leaving the Viet Minh in control of the north and Bao Dai temporarily in charge in the south. Provisions were made for an International Control Commission to prevent military infiltration by either side, and for national elections to be held in 1956 to reunify the country. The United States pledged to "refrain from the threat or use of force to disturb" the accords.

Chinese Foreign Relations (1954–1960)

The Geneva Conference had been only one of a series of personal triumphs for Peking's foreign minister, Chou En-lai, who best symbolized China's peaceful "people's diplomacy" for the other countries of Asia. He was especially successful with Nehru, who signed an agreement in April 1954, recognizing Chinese sovereignty over Tibet and declaring Sino-Indian relations to be conducted according to principles of mutual respect, nonaggression, noninterference, equality, and peaceful coexistence. The climax of "peoples' diplomacy" was the Asian-African Conference held at Bandung in 1955, which has already been mentioned.

Maintenance of such relative international order in Asia depended in some degree on the stability of relations between Moscow and Peking. Indeed, Stalin's death in 1954 was followed by a brief period of warmest amity. The alliance was somewhat shaken by Khrushchev's denunciation of Stalin in February 1956, perhaps because Mao feared that he might someday also be accused of fostering a "cult of personality." The Polish and Hungarian crises later that year (see pp. 803–805 provoked more uncertainties among ambivalent Chinese leaders. China could not approve of the liberalization of communist regimes, but it did favor "polycentrism" in which national communist regimes were no longer dominated by Moscow's "great nation chauvinism." On the other hand, China could find comfort in the thought of Soviet military support in the event of war with the United States. In fact, Russian development of an intercontinental ballistic missile and the launching of Sputnik inspired Mao Tsetung to state in November 1957, that "the east wind prevails over the west wind." Paradoxically, the Chinese belief that the world balance of power had suddenly shifted in favor of the Communist bloc marred Sino-Soviet relations because China was prepared to go much further than the U.S.S.R. in abandoning "peaceful coexistence" for a policy of aggression. In 1958, for example, the Chinese attacked the Kuomintang installations on the offshore islands of Quemoy and Matsu. One year later the Soviet Union, concerned that this "adventurism" would lead to war with the United States, abandoned its nuclear sharing agreement with China. Peking, in turn, worried that Moscow would come to terms with America at China's expense. Furthermore, the Russians were openly introducing "capitalist" incentives in Soviet factories and seemed to be liberalizing their government. These were all grounds for the Chinese publicly to pin the Marxist epithet of "revisionist" on the Russians in the spring of 1960. Such insults led the Soviet Union to withdraw its technical advisers that fall, thus delivering a heavy blow to China's industrial development plans. Relations between the Chinese Communists and the Soviet Union had not been at such a nadir since Stalin had forced the Communists into their uneasy alliance with the Kuomintang during the 1920s.

Relations with other neighbors worsened as well. India especially suffered from the change in Chinese foreign policy, which in this case was partly the result of Peking's own difficulties in ruling Tibet. Tibet had been occupied by Communist troops early in the 1950s, but owing to Tibetan resistance to the appointment of Chinese officials, Peking promised in 1957 to withdraw many of its cadres and postpone "democratic reform" of Tibetan landlords and the great monastic orders until 1962. Nevertheless, tensions continued to mount as the Chinese continued their campaign against the theocracy, and the Tibetans finally revolted with clandestine American and Kuomintang assistance in March of 1959 against Chinese Communist rule. After fierce fighting and massacres which were at the time condemned as genocide, the Chinese crushed the rebellion and forced the ruler of Tibet, the Dalai Lama, to flee to India with 13,000 of his followers. When India granted sanctuary, and as well sent army patrols into disputed border territories, it provoked a crisis that put an end to "peaceful coexistence" in Asia for the time being.

INDIA AND PAKISTAN SINCE 1960: NEW DIRECTIONS AND NEW PROBLEMS

In October 1962, China invaded India across the Himalayas, successfully gaining the plains of Assam before voluntarily withdrawing. Just over 18 months later a tired Jawaharlal Nehru died in office. These two events transformed the Indian scene and opened up an era of change and uncertainty that is still with us. Despite Nehru's reluctance to admit it, the conflict with China had been brewing on the high plateau of Tibet since the mid-1950s and reflected a resurgent China's determination to assert itself as the leading power of Asia. Aroused by the subjugation of Tibet and the flight in 1959 of the Dalai Lama, India tried to oppose the further Chinese expansion into the barren wastelands of eastern Ladakh, where the Sino-Indian border had never been properly demarcated. When Nehru sent patrols to make good India's claim to the territory, the Chinese retaliated with the punitive and humiliating strike into Assam. This war left Nehru's neutralist policy in ruins and forced the country increasingly to divert its scarce resources from developmental to military purposes. After 1962 India's foreign policy was directed to a frantic search for allies against China, as well as against its old antagonist Pakistan. This quest in the mid-1960s brought the country quite close to the United States, and in 1971 led it to conclude an alliance with the Soviet Union. On the whole, however, India has been left isolated, ringed with unfriendly neighbors, and bereft of that reputation for superior moral virtue in international relations that Gandhi had bequeathed it.

Similarly, Nehru's death, although not precipitating an immediate political crisis (for his successors Lal Bahadur Shastri and Indira Gandhi were able and worthy leaders), still marked a watershed in Indian politics. Without his presence, the Congress could no longer so easily command the loyalty of the Indian masses, nor could it ignore the clamorous demands of local linguistic, caste, and religious groups for greater autonomy and a greater voice in government. Indeed, Nehru himself was forced to take the first step in 1955 when he gave a reluctant assent to the reorganization of the Indian states along linguistic lines. This act testifies to the enduring strength of regional ties, and of language as a source of cultural identity in the face of the centralizing tendencies of British rule and the freedom struggle. Since reorganization, the states have increasingly become the locus of political power in India. Despite pessimistic predictions to the contrary, however, this growth of regional loyalties has not been at the expense of national unity. Indeed, most concessions to regional linguistic demands, by removing deeply felt grievances against the central government, have had the effect of strengthening the Indian nation. Even in the Tamil-speaking areas of the far south, where there was a demand for independence, the issue was dropped after the

Chinese invasion, and the once separatist Dravida Munnetra Kazhagam party has worked amicably with the center since coming to power in 1967.

The other disturbing linguistic issue was the attempt to impose Hindi, the language of the northern 40 percent of the Indian people, upon the rest of the country. Although motivated by a desire to find a national language other than that of the old imperial master, the campaign smacked of Hindi imperialism to many and roused violent antagonism in the south, culminating in a series of riots in Madras in January 1965. The controversy was temporarily put to rest when the government amended the constitution to give the southern states a veto over the use of Hindi in the south.

The growth of regionalism has been accompanied by a steady rise in the importance of caste in Indian politics. In the process, caste itself is being transformed. No longer simply rural occupational and marriage groupings, castes are joining together in statewide associations to mobilize political influence. This they then use to secure the election of friendly candidates for office and to extract for themselves from the government more of the benefits of development, such as schools and irrigation canals. Although this "caste-ism" and the associated decay of political idealism are universally deplored by the educated elite, they are, if anything, the mark of a healthy and functioning democracy. Moreover, these caste associations, together with the new *Panchayati Raj* local self-government institutions, provide useful training in modern techniques of organization and enable the large but traditionally disadvantaged lower castes to better their economic and ritual position. So far the chief beneficiaries of this process have been the peasant cultivators, but the untouchables—the largest as well as the most depressed class in India—are rapidly learning to manipulate democratic politics to their advantage.

The growth of competitive interest-group politics spurred the revival of the formerly moribund opposition parties. The fastest growing parties during the later 1960s were the rightist Hindu Jan Sangh on the northern plains, and the Communists, now divided

Indira Gandhi, Nehru's daughter and prime minister of India since Shastri's death in 1966.

into hostile Moscow- and Peking-oriented factions, among the impoverished but literate masses of West Bengal and Kerala. At the same time the Congress itself, fat and complacent after so many years in office, had become corrupt and rent by factional disputes. As a result, though still able to command a majority in the central Parliament, the Congress lost its dominant position in the state legislatures in the 1967 elections. Two years later it split into two antagonistic groups, one led by the prime minister, Indira Gandhi, the other by the old bosses of the "syndicate." Despite the opportunities presented by the decline of the Congress, the old opposition parties remained as disunited as before. Rarely were they able to put together coalitions sufficiently stable to carry on the government of any state for more than a few months. Hence when parliamentary elections were held in March 1971, Mrs. Gandhi's party, which presented to the voters a radical image and promise of aggressive leadership, swept easily to victory.

Economically, the 1960s were marked both by despair and by hope. The wars with China and Pakistan, followed by two devas-

tating droughts in successive years, checked the growth of the previous decade and discredited the ambitious schemes of the planners. At the same time the cost of maintaining the new industrial plant built by Nehru drained all of India's scarce foreign exchange earnings and drove the country deeply into debt. By the end of the decade, however, a spirit of innovation, aided by new seeds and fertilizers, was beginning to take hold in Indian agriculture, now as always the keystone of the country's prosperity. Borne on the flood tide of record food production, India's national income rose 9 percent in the single year 1967–1968. The benefits of this "green revolution" were, however, in large part dissipated by a continuing rapid growth in the Indian population, which rose by 24 percent over the decade of the 1960s and stood at 550 million in 1971. This meant that in just one decade India had added to its already congested land more than the total population of Japan. For the first time birth control was being energetically encouraged by the government with American aid. But it remains an open question whether population growth can be checked in this way, for the peasantry, spread through some half million villages, are so numerous and so impoverished that it is difficult even to provide them with birth control devices, let alone convince them of the need for their use. Yet only by a dramatic fall in the birth rate can the individual Indian ever hope to get a decent job and enough food to break the cycle of poverty.

In Pakistan, where democracy had never truly taken hold, the political turmoil of the mid-1950s was ended by the rise to power of a military dictator, the British-trained General Muhammed Ayub Khan. Ayub ruthlessly stamped out the endemic corruption of the old regime and gave the country a much-needed period of political stability. He tried to create a facade of popular support for his regime by promulgating a new constitution in 1962 under which 80,000 "basic democrats" selected the president by a process of indirect election. Handpicked for their loyalty and conservatism, these men were, like the Pakistani press and the enfeebled National Assembly, effectively under Ayub's control. His foreign policy, while retaining at

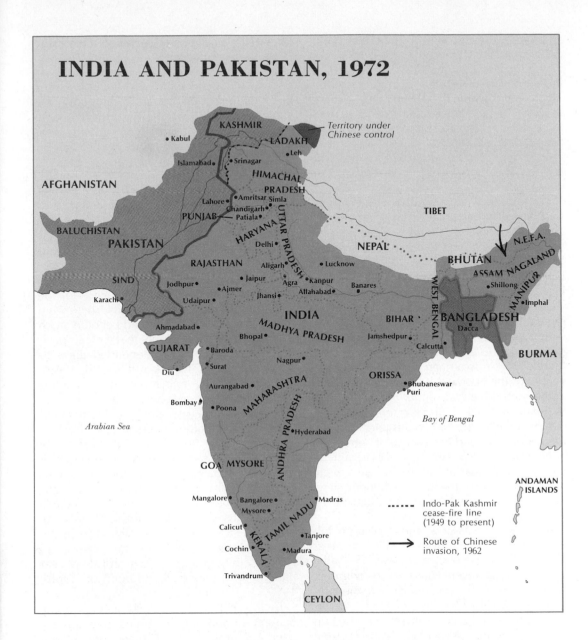

INDIA AND PAKISTAN, 1972

KASHMIR
• Kabul
LADAKH
• Leh
Islamabad • • Srinagar
HIMACHAL
PRADESH
AFGHANISTAN
• Amritsar Simla
Lahore • Chandigarh • Simla
PUNJAB • Patiala
TIBET
BALUCHISTAN
PAKISTAN
HARYANA
• Delhi
NEPAL
Territory under
Chinese control

N.E.F.A.
BHUTAN
RAJASTHAN
Aligarh •
ASSAM NAGALAND
SIND
• Jaipur • Lucknow
Jodhpur • Agra • Kanpur
• Shillong
MANIPUR
• Ajmer
Banares
• Imphal
Karachi •
Udaipur •
Jhansi • Allahabad •

INDIA
WEST BENGAL
Ahmadabad •
MADHYA PRADESH
BIHAR • BANGLADESH
Bhopal •
Jamshedpur • Dacca
BURMA
GUJARAT
• Baroda
Calcutta •
Diu •
• Surat
Nagpur •
ORISSA
Aurangabad •
MAHARASHTRA
• Bhubaneswar
• Puri
Bombay •
• Poona
ANDHRA PRADESH
Arabian Sea
Bay of Bengal
• Hyderabad

GOA MYSORE
ANDAMAN
ISLANDS
Mangalore • Bangalore •
• Madras
Mysore •
Calicut •
----- Indo-Pak Kashmir
cease-fire line
(1949 to present)
KERALA
TAMIL NADU
• Tanjore
Cochin • • Madura
→ Route of Chinese
invasion, 1962
Trivandrum •

CEYLON

its core the traditional hostility to India, was surprisingly flexible and successful. Without abandoning his ties to the West, including the military alliance with the United States which his predecessors had contracted in the hope of getting aid against India, Ayub steadily maneuvered toward a more neutral position by befriending China and seeking closer ties with the Soviet Union.

Ayub's greatest achievement, however, was the modernization of Pakistan's long-stagnant economy. Ruling out showy projects, Ayub concentrated upon encouraging private enterprise by the provision of subsidies and tax incentives, especially in such critical areas as fertilizers, irrigation, and light industry. Testimony to his success is the 45 percent rise in Pakistan's gross national income over the decade 1958–1968. The benefits of this development, however, were very unevenly distributed, the bulk going to the west and to the well-to-do industrialists and landlords who were Ayub's chief political supporters. The resulting dislocation and frustration, especially after the debacle of the 1965 war with India, opened up all the old divisions within the country, and enabled the students and intellectuals (who yearned for a return to parliamentary government) to mobilize widespread support in the east and in the cities for an attack on the Ayub regime. This movement forced Ayub to step down in 1969.

His successor, General Yahya Khan, promised to restore parliamentary democracy, and in December 1970 held elections based on universal suffrage to elect members of a National Assembly. In the east the Awami League, a regional party dedicated to achieving greater autonomy for Bengal, swept to victory everywhere, while in the west the radical People's party of Zulfikar Ali Bhutto won a majority of the seats. The two parties proved unable to work together, so in early March 1971 Yahya Khan postponed the convening of the National Assembly. The sullen and resentful Bengalis under Sheikh Mujibur Rahman, sensing in this act an attempt to deprive them of the fruits of this electoral victory, at once turned to a course of nonviolent noncooperation with the central government. On March 25, fearful that the Bengalis might break away to form an independent state, Yahaya Khan jailed Mujib and loosed the army on the populace.

An orgy of massacre and spoliation followed, during which over 9 million refugees fled to India for safety, and upwards of half a million Bengalis were killed. As the common people remained unreconciled to the predominance of the west, armed bands of guerrillas harrassed the government at every turn until finally the desperate Pakistanis sent troops to root them out of their sanctuaries across the Indian border. The Indians retaliated in early December 1971 by launching a full-scale invasion of East Pakistan. After two weeks of fighting the Pakistani forces surrendered, and the independent Republic of Bangladesh was established. Sheikh Mujib, released from prison in January 1972, returned to lead the new state, which remained closely allied with its liberator, India. In West Pakistan the disastrous defeat in the war brought about the collapse of the Yahya Khan regime, and its replacement by a civilian government under Z. A. Bhutto. The restoration of full Parliamentary democracy was once again promised for 1972, but Pakistan has remained a restive and profoundly discontented land.

CHINA AND THE PERMANENT REVOLUTION

By 1955 the government of Mao Tse-tung had clearly demonstrated its commitment to a program of intensive economic and social development designed to give China its rightful place as a world power. This commitment accompanied a revolutionary conviction that "feudal remnants" of China's traditional society would have to be destroyed along the way. Finally, there were hints of an attitude that would become much more explicit later, namely that China's position as a world power depended upon its leadership of a "Third World" of Asian, African, and Latin American societies struggling to modernize themselves. After only five years of Communist party rule this determination had already expressed itself in three characteristics: first, state intervention in rural society; second, mass campaigns to mobilize China's population for public work projects; and third, a faith that almost any goal could be reached as long as the people could be inspired to strive for it. These same characteristics can also be observed in the history of the communes, the Great Leap Forward in 1957 and 1958 and the Great Proletarian Cultural Revolution of 1966–1969.

By the middle of 1957, 97 percent of the peasant households in China had already been organized into socialized Agricultural Producers' Cooperatives. That winter some of these cooperatives were joined into larger and more complex communistic organizations. This increase in the tempo of radical social change was the result of three different factors. First was a campaign against "rightists," which meant that millions of people were sent into the countryside (hsia-fang) to be "reformed through labor" (lao-tung kai-tsao). This repression of dissidence followed a brief period of liberalization in 1957, when Mao Tse-tung had declared that

Workers, in from the fields for their noon meal, at a commune in eastern China. This photo was released by the Chinese to illustrate the "happiness of three generations of women liberated from kitchen drudgery."

there were necessary and healthy "contradictions" among the people which should not be confused with counterrevolutionary "poisonous weeds," but should be resolved by public discussion. In May of that year, therefore, the populace was invited to criticize the government under the slogan, "Let a hundred flowers bloom together, let a hundred schools of thought contend." The "Hundred Flowers" period lasted two months. At first timidly, then quite openly, thousands of people—primarily intellectuals and factory managers—scathingly criticized the dictatorship of the Communist party. Apparently not having foreseen how much discontent existed, Mao reacted to this shocking attack

by permitting the party to conduct an "antirightist campaign" against the most outspoken critics. Fifty members were expelled from the National People's Congress, while many second-level party leaders were purged and over one million bureaucrats transferred to labor in the villages. They were to provide both manpower and organizational skills for the ensuing commune movement.

A second factor leading to communes was the way in which the collectivization campaign of 1955–1957 created an atmosphere conducive to "high-speed" irrigation development which in turn required labor crews exceeding the size of a regular cooperative.

The Chinese caption to this photograph reads: "Chairman Mao, the most, most beloved leader of the Chinese people and his close comrade-in-arms, Comrade Lin Piao, review the great army of the cultural revolution." Lin, on the Chairman's left, holds a copy of the "Little Red Book" of Mao's quotations.

Until this time peasant production teams had worked within their own villages; now large groups of peasants were moved about the country to dig canals or build dams. This state labor system began transforming the organization of work in the countryside, so that basic village and kinship ties were replaced by districtwide work units that resembled military squadrons. Furthermore, there was now a shortage of people for simple cultivation. Peasant women had to be relieved from household duties to work in the fields. That in turn required joint nurseries and kitchens to replace the "inefficient" single household by a communal living unit. Therefore, the revolution in work activities radically altered the nature of the family, the nucleus of traditional peasant society.

A third factor was the victory in September 1957, of Mao's clique within the Politburo. One group of party leaders, headed by Ch'en Yun, had argued that balanced economic development required material incentives. But Chairman Mao had convinced the others

that intensive social mobilization was the best means of achieving rapid economic growth. The "natural" communes arising from waterworks projects were thus taken as the model for national agricultural development, and in August 1958, the entire country was ordered to communize. By the end of the year, China's 700,000 collective farms had been amalgamated into 26,000 communes which averaged 25,000 people apiece. This was the most daring step taken so far toward the creation of that Marxist dream, a society without a state; but it hardly represented a "withering away" of political organization. More than anything else, the communes were like army units. The peasant was consciously identified as a soldier in the battle against famine. As the party journal, *Red Flag (Hung-ch'i)* put it: "The people's commune which combined the industrial, agricultural, commercial, educational, and military sectors at a time when there are no attacks from external enemies is an advancing army fighting against nature, fighting for the industrialization of the village, the organization of the village, and for the happy future of Communism in all the villages."

This same crusading fervor—the rhetoric of an army on the march—permeated the simultaneous Great Leap Forward. At the Eighth Party Congress (May 1958), President Liu Shao-ch'i argued that balanced economic growth was an illusion. Instead, industrial output would increase by leaps and bounds in an uneven rhythm. The time had arrived for such a "great leap," which would be successful if peasants aided industrialization by building backyard smelting furnaces, and if the entire population drove itself to meet unprecedented industrial and agricultural goals. In response to Liu's suggestion, the government set extremely high quotas for local party units which, in turn, zealously increased them to even higher levels. The subsequent statistical confusion made the accomplishments of the Great Leap Forward seem greater than they were. Still, despite the amplification of growth figures there was no doubt that amazing progress occurred in some sectors, even though at the price of economic imbalance. It has been suggested, for example, that the enormous irrigation projects (which helped bring 30 percent more land under cultivation) inadvertently caused good soil to become excessively alkaline. Such problems may have combined with the drought of 1960 to cause a severe famine. Consequently, the Central Committee decided to reduce the size of each commune, curb the zeal of party cadres, and permit peasants to own small private plots (a "material incentive") once again in order to produce more food for the starving cities.

This step backward from radical Communism seemed proof enough to foreign observers that China's leaders had recognized how necessary "sensible" economic policies were for a country that depended so vitally on a steady rise in production. In 1966, though, another great social convulsion shook China, revealing how crucial Mao Tse-tung's ideological convictions were to the development of Chinese Communism. Unlike Marx, Mao did not believe that history ends when socialism is realized. He argued instead that "nonantagonistic contra-dictions" within a socialist society will cause continuing historical change: revolution is perpetually ongoing, or "permanent."

In practice this theory of permanent revolution meant that Mao feared that the People's Republic might lose its youthful vigor as once-zealous party cadres fell prey to the same "bureaucratism" (kuan-liao chu-i) that had made Confucian China so stagnant and the Soviet Union so "revisionist." Perhaps it was inevitable that the ardent young cadres who survived the Long March would grow into grayhaired office workers dreaming of a personal car or a house in the country; but Mao was prepared to argue that this inevitability could be forestalled. One way of doing this was to make the party itself aware of these dangers through "inner party struggle." In November 1957, Mao announced: "In the future we aim to conduct a rectification campaign every year or every other year—a very short campaign—as one of the main methods of resolving various social contradictions in our country during the whole period of transition (to socialism and communism)." If these tendencies toward bureaucratization went too far, though, it might be necessary to rely on elements outside the regular party structure. Closest at hand was the People's Liberation Army, which had played such a major role in the organization of communes and of rural militia in 1958. While Marshal Lin Piao was elevated within the Politburo ranks after 1962, a "socialist education campaign" was launched to glorify military heroes as examples of conduct for the Chinese masses. The most famous was Lei Feng, whose diary, reprinted thousands of times, reads: "A man's life is limited, but service to the people knows no bounds. I must devote my life to the boundless service of the people."

Heroes like Lei Feng helped inspire a revolutionary society mobilized on a scale unique in history. Literacy spread rapidly; public health improved dramatically; particular loyalties to kin and self were replaced by a universal wish to promote the common good. This public spirit was still enlisted by the Communist party, however, which began to create its own status quo. Increasingly, students at the better schools and universities were largely the sons and daughters of im-

During the Cultural Revolution, the Chinese Communist government emphasized cooperation among party, army, and people. Here, at Tachai in Shansi, the People's Liberation Army helped the local production brigade and party cadres (one of whom is gesturing as he leads the parade) build a reservoir.

portant cadres. Higher posts were monopolized by a selected elite. In short, the revolution's own officers were being transformed into civil bureaucrats, as entangled in red tape as had been their imperial predecessors.

Mao Tse-tung was dismayed by this betrayal of the revolution's original intent. Furthermore, his own personal control over the party was slipping. Both to save his own position and to reinvigorate the revolutionary momentum of the nation, he decided to call on forces outside the party. After losing a crucial vote at the eleventh plenum of the Central Committee (August 1–12, 1966), Mao unprecedentedly introduced radical young student leaders into the meeting to support him. Seven days later a mass campaign was initiated to organize paramilitary units in high schools and colleges. These "Red Guards" descended by the millions on the capital to carry out a "Great Proletarian Cultural Revolution" against "feudal remnants" and to "defend Mao Tse-tung" against prominent party functionaries like the mayor of Peking. Then the conflict spread from higher to lower levels of the party, and by September 1966, local Communist cadres all over the country were being physically assaulted by Red Guard units. Retaliating, party leaders in the cities urged factory workers to form armed committees and fight back. In all of this, no one seemed to know which side Mao himself favored. In fact, Red Guard units sometimes fought between themselves, as in Kwangtung; while army units in western China refused to obey central orders and insisted that a group of extremists was using Mao's name to further "infantile" theories of revolution.

In short, China entered another period of

social disorder prompted by revolutionary zeal. Many factories shut down until 1968, when Mao finally declared that the youthful guardsmen should cease their attacks and participate in new local revolutionary committees, composed of workers, students, party members, and soldiers alike. By 1971 these committees, dominated by the army (which would itself soon be curbed by the demise of Marshal Lin Piao), had been established in every province and industrial development had returned to normal. Yet what, after all, represented "normalcy" for Communist China? If Mao's theories of permanent revolution continued to determine policy in the future, there might be fresh attacks on bureaucratic authority by calling upon adolescents once again to inject revolutionary vigor into the government. Could patterned disorder, some new *yin-yang* rhythm of nonrule, become a novel form of revolutionary order? Such a state of affairs may appear contradictory, but who could say where Mao's vision might lead China?

For Russian Communists the answer to that question was quite simple: Mao would lead China into anarchy. Hence the Red Guards and the Great Proletarian Cultural Revolution did nothing to ameliorate Sino-Soviet relations, already jeopardized by China's claim of international leadership of "wars of national liberation" among countries of the "Third World." Although rightist coups in Africa, the destruction of the Indonesian Communist party, and Fidel Castro's decision to side with Moscow all represented foreign policy defeats for Mao and Marshal Lin Piao, the Chinese continued to insist that "the whole cause of world revolution hinges on the revolutionary struggles of the Asian, African, and Latin American peoples who make up the overwhelming majority of the world's population. Socialist countries should regard it as their internationalist duty to support the people's revolutionary struggles in Asia, Africa and Latin America." In addition to this attempt to wrest Marxist doctrinal supremacy from the Soviet Union, Chinese border troops clashed with Soviet army units on March 2, 1969, along the Ussuri River and in Sinkiang. For, as the Russians wish to settle these reaches of their own "Far East" so do the Chinese hope to recover these same lands ceded to the tsar in the nineteenth century. These incidents have been cause for alarm on both sides of the Sino-Soviet border. As Moscow grew even more worried by China's development of atomic weapons and ballistic missiles, Peking came to fear the possibility of Soviet marshals' persuading their presidium to authorize a preemptive attack on China. The result was the opening of negotiations over the border issue which dragged on without substantial results.

Peking's vocal promotion of "people's revolutionary struggles" also hardened American policy towards Communist China over the Vietnam question. This complicated conflict in Southeast Asia was originally regarded by the United States government as a simple test of its capacity to defeat "wars of national liberation" and contain Communism in Asia. As Secretary of State Dean Rusk declared in April, 1966: "We must take care to do nothing which encourages Peking . . . to believe that it can reap gains from its aggressive actions and designs. It is just as essential to 'contain' Communist aggression in Asia as it was, and is, to 'contain' Communist aggression in Europe." In short, the Vietnamese civil war was misrepresented by Washington as a symbolic struggle against Chinese Communism.

THE TRAGEDY OF VIETNAM

Within a very short period after the 1954 Geneva Conference, the "temporary" demarcation line along Indochina's seventeenth parallel had become a political border between two separate countries belonging to inimical international blocs: the Democratic Republic of Vietnam in the north, fully supported by the Soviet Union and the People's Republic of China; and the Republic of Vietnam in the south, backed up by an American-inspired alliance called the Southeast Asia Treaty Organization (SEATO).

Consolidation of the Revolution in the North

The Democratic Republic of Vietnam, which possessed more industrial resources than the agricultural south, was governed by

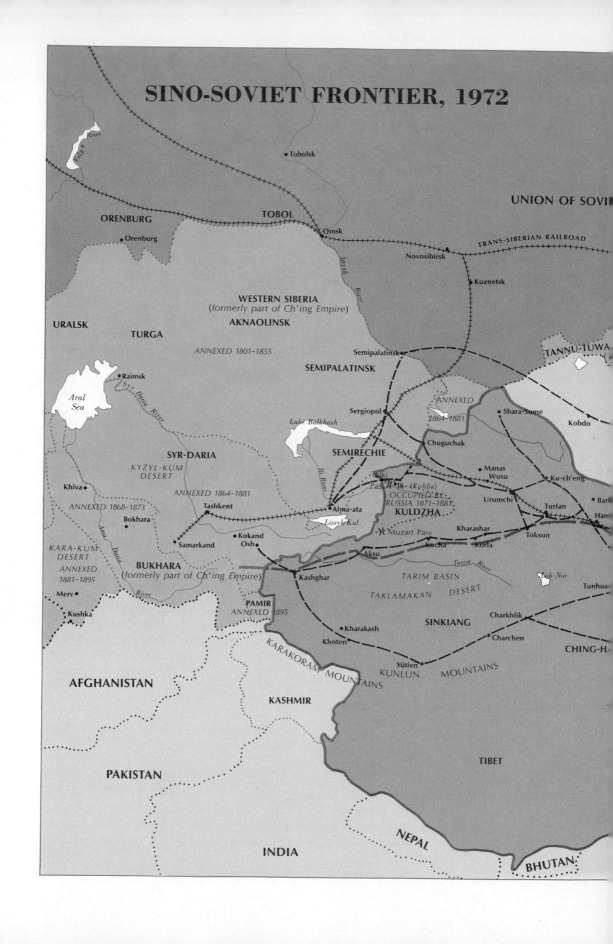

SINO-SOVIET FRONTIER, 1972

Yenisey River

Tobolsk

UNION OF SOVI

ORENBURG

TOBOL

Orenburg

Omsk

TRANS-SIBERIAN RAILROAD

Irtysh River

Novosibirsk

WESTERN SIBERIA
(formerly part of Ch'ing Empire)

Kuznetsk

URALSK

AKNAOLINSK

TANNU-TUWA

TURGA

ANNEXED 1801–1855

Semipalatinsk

Raimsk

Syr Darya River

SEMIPALATINSK

*ANNEXED
1864–1881*

Shara-Sume

Kobdo

*Aral
Sea*

Sergiopol

Lake Balkhash

Chuguchak

SYR-DARIA

*KYZYL-KUM
DESERT*

SEMIRECHIE

Manas
Wusu

Ku-ch'eng

Khiva

ANNEXED 1864–1881

Ili River

Talki
Pass

Ili (Kuldja)

Urumchi

Turfan

Barl

ANNEXED 1868–1873

Tashkent

Alma-ata

OCCUPIED BY
RUSSIA 1871–1881

Ham

Bokhara

Lissyk-Kul

KULDZHA

Kharashar

Toksun

Kokand
Osh

Amu Darya River

Samarkand

Muzart Pass

Kucha

Korla

*KARA-KUM
DESERT
ANNEXED
1881–1895*

BUKHARA
(formerly part of Ch'ing Empire)

Aksu

Tarim River

Lob Nor

Merv

River

Kashghar

TARIM BASIN

Tunhua

PAMIR
ANNEXED 1895

TAKLAMAKAN   DESERT

Charkhlik

Kushka

Kharakash

SINKIANG

Charchen

AFGHANISTAN

KARAKORAM MOUNTAINS

Khoten

CHING-HA

KASHMIR

Yütien

KUNLUN   MOUNTAINS

PAKISTAN

TIBET

INDIA

NEPAL

BHUTAN

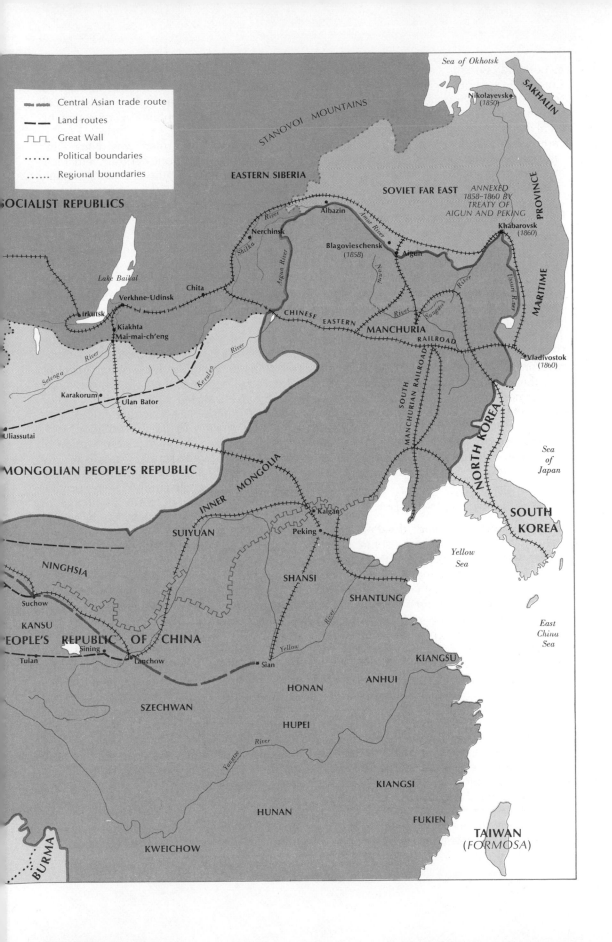

Legend:
- Central Asian trade route
- Land routes
- Great Wall
- Political boundaries
- Regional boundaries

Sea of Okhotsk

SAKHALIN

STANOVOI MOUNTAINS

EASTERN SIBERIA

SOVIET FAR EAST *ANNEXED 1858–1860 BY TREATY OF AIGUN AND PEKING*

MARITIME PROVINCE

Nikolayevsk (1850)

Albazin

Nerchinsk

Blagovieschensk (1858)

Aigun

Khabarovsk (1860)

Shilka River

Argun River

Nonni River

Amur River

Ussuri River

Sungari River

Lake Baikal

Chita

Verkhne-Udinsk

Irkutsk

Kiakhta
Mai-mai-ch'eng

CHINESE EASTERN RAILROAD

MANCHURIA

Vladivostok (1860)

SOCIALIST REPUBLICS

Selenga River

Kerulen River

Karakorum

Ulan Bator

Uliassutai

SOUTH MANCHURIAN RAILROAD

NORTH KOREA

Sea of Japan

MONGOLIAN PEOPLE'S REPUBLIC

INNER MONGOLIA

SOUTH KOREA

SUIYUAN

Kalgan

Peking

SHANSI

SHANTUNG

Yellow Sea

East China Sea

NINGHSIA

Suchow

KANSU

PEOPLE'S REPUBLIC OF CHINA

Sining

Lanchow

Tulan

Sian

Yellow River

HONAN

ANHUI

KIANGSU

SZECHWAN

HUPEI

Yangtze River

KIANGSI

FUKIEN

HUNAN

TAIWAN (FORMOSA)

KWEICHOW

BURMA

a political system similar to Communist China's. In fact, its socialist programme closely followed its northern neighbor's: land reform from 1954 to 1956, destroying the local gentry's power; local resistance and cadre extremism, producing in reaction a "mistakes rectification" campaign similar to the Hundred Flowers movement; collectivization through cooperatives by 1958; and a five-year plan (1961–1965) for industries later crippled by American bombing. In 1960 Ho Chi Minh was elected president of the republic; while Phan Van Dong was appointed premier and foreign minister, and Vo Nguyen Giap was made minister of defense.

Hanoi has never acknowledged that it rules only the north. Instead, it called for implementation of the Geneva proposal to unify the country through elections; and after 1960 urged armed revolution against the government of the south. A National Front for the Liberation of South Vietnam was formed to unite South Vietnamese of all classes under a new People's Revolutionary party—identified by the North Vietnamese as an extension of the Communist Worker's party (Lao Dong)—to organize guerrilla warfare below the seventeenth parallel.

Civil War in the South

The target of this warfare, the Republic of Vietnam in the south, bore some resemblances to Nationalist China in the 1930s. In both cases a strong-minded ruler stepped forth under chaotic social conditions, played one opposing group against the other in an effort to consolidate his control, created a personalistic government, and received ambivalent aid from Western allies. The last resemblance is most marked. American aid to Chiang Kai-shek had been partly predicated upon the belief that his regime would reform itself in order to save China from social revolution led by the Communists. Yet the United States could not publicly force these reforms on Chiang for fear that he would be regarded by Chinese patriots as an American puppet. Nor could Chiang be quietly threatened with the loss of American aid, since he himself knew he held the trump card by representing the only viable alternative to a socialist revolution, which capitalist

America deeply feared. The same was true for South Vietnam's ruler after 1955 in all but one respect: the United States finally did call this particular leader's bluff by approving his overthrow.

South Vietnam's ruler was Ngo Dinh Diem, scion of a patriotic central Vietnamese mandarin family of Catholic belief. To many Americans Diem seemed a perfect conservative nationalist leader capable of turning back the Communist movement in Vietnam. This hope appeared justified after June 1954, when Diem skillfully moved against the sects, gangsters, and generals, restoring order to the country with a powerful political machine of his own. A popular hero, Diem was soon elected chief of state, ousting Emperor Bao Dai. He then secured the diplomatic recognition of the United States, which approved his decision not to hold the national elections dictated by the Geneva Accords. Diem's political machine—which combined ward organization, mass parties, police informers, and a state doctrine called "Personalism"—failed to quell revolution. One reason may have been the identification of "Personalism" with simple "familism." By 1961 South Vietnam had become a state dominated by a single family: Diem's brother and sister-in-law (the Nhus) in charge of political parties, his brother, Canh, virtual governor of all central Vietnam, and a third brother, Thuc, head of Vietnam's Catholic church. Furthermore, "Personalism" seemed to most Vietnamese merely another version of traditional Confucian appeals to personal responsibility and collective duty. Like Chiang Kai-shek's "New Life Movement," or England's "Moral Rearmament," "Personalism" insisted on individual moral solutions to social problems. Usually such a doctrine only appears worthy of belief if it stimulates genuine reform. There was no question of the need for such radical social change in South Vietnam. Fifty percent of the cultivated land in the Mekong delta was held by only three percent of the landowners, so that over 600,000 tenants turned over half of their rice crops in rents to the local gentry. In order to ease the harshness of this tenantry system, Diem set rent and acreage ceilings, ordering that some land be distributed to poorer peasants. The reform failed, largely because the

A Viet Cong (South Vietnam Liberation Army) unit poses before launching an attack on American positions in the Dong Thap Muoi area (1966).

price of the distributed land was too high, and acreage laws were not enforced by government officials who were usually landowners themselves.

This failure, however, almost went unnoticed in Western capitals, because terrorism by the Viet Cong military arm of the National Liberation Front increased markedly after 1955. The Front's plan was to destroy administrative links between rural villages and urban government by attacking local police stations and executing local officials. After 1958, regular Republic of Vietnam army units were engaged in battle. At this point the arguments began over infiltration —over whether the revolution was "native" or "exported" from the north—which became so central to American justifications for intervention. Most experts agree that there was no large-scale invasion by North Vietnamese units until the United States increased its forces to 22,000 men at the end of 1964. What is also clear is that earlier Ameri-

can military aid was misdirected. American advisers prepared the 150,000-man South Vietnamese army only to resist a conventional invasion on the Korean model, leaving "counterinsurgency" to Diem himself. Diem in turn, impressed by the British defeat of guerrilla insurgency in Malaya, relied on moving the peasants first into newly built and heavily defended rural "cities" (*agrovilles*), then into "strategic hamlets" so that the guerrillas would be denied intelligence, recruits, and supplies. Tens of thousands of refugees were created, as peasants were forced to move from their ancestral hamlets into spiritless refugee centers, thus shattering the continuity of rural life.

As the crescendo of disorder increased in the countryside, Diem's support in the cities weakened. Individual political opponents could be jailed, but dissent soon spread to mass organizations: Buddhist sects and student groups, united by anti-Catholicism and a common search for "neutral" solutions to the civil war. After riots and demonstrations (including personal immolations) in 1963, the government sent commandos into Buddhist sancturies. This brutal repression finally aroused American opposition to the Diem regime. Washington suspended financial subsidies, and on November 1, 1963, a coalition of South Vietnamese officers under General Duong Van Minh took over Saigon. In the fracas Diem and Nhu were both murdered. After a period of continuous civil-military and Buddhist-Catholic bickering, two young officers, General Nhuyen Van Thieu and Air Commodore Nguyen Cao Ky, took power in June 1965. But in the meantime the Viet Cong had been moving much closer to Saigon and rapidly accelerating the tempo of revolt. It was obvious that the countryside was being lost, and that without a massive American intervention, the Saigon regime would perish in the midst of its own squabbles.

United States Intervention in Indochina

The United States government hesitated over this difficult decision. On the one hand, powerful voices in the national security bureaucracy insisted that Saigon's defeat would permit the Communists to overrun the rest of Southeast Asia. But others pointed out that at least 500,000 troops would be required to pacify the country, and that the United States should never become involved in a land war of human attrition on the populous Asian mainland. The debate was resolved in August 1964, by the Tonkin Bay incident, in which North Vietnamese torpedo boats allegedly attacked two United States destroyers. Despite later doubts, at the time most citizens agreed with President Johnson that "aggression" should be met with "firmness": bombing North Vietnamese naval bases and passing a Congressional resolution to give Johnson a free hand for further military action.

To the Communist bloc, the war that followed was a perfect example of the fight between revolutionary consciousness and superior military technology. As Marshal Lin Piao once wrote: "A people's army . . . . does not rely purely on its technique.

It relies mainly on politics, on the proletarian revolutionary consciousness, on the courage of its commanders and fighters, on the support and backing of the masses." American strategists, on the other hand, shuffled repeatedly through an arsenal of tactics and devices in search of a key to military success in the south without being forced to invade the north. Three techniques were most prominent. One emphasized Diem's old program of "strategic hamlets," defended by rural militia, and financed by American aid projects. A second was the deployment of "search and destroy" units, which were moved at amazing speed by fleets of helicopters across the jungles and mountainous terrain. Third was the bombing of both North and South Vietnam. Small planes selectively dropped concussion or napalm bombs. Larger B-52's flew in from Guam or Thailand to indiscriminately "saturate" target areas. By the fall of 1971 more than 5 million tons of bombs had been dropped on the 37 million people of North and South Vietnam — 270 pounds of napalm and TNT for every man, woman, and child.

The tactical use of these weapons made the war an expensive venture for the United States: at the beginning of 1969 over 5 thousand American aircraft had been lost, helping run up annual bills of 30 billion dollars. However, Americans felt it was better to lose equipment than men. Sensing this, and wishing to increase American casualties above the average 200 per week, the Viet Cong decided to abandon conservative guerrilla tactics for head-on offensives. Marshal Giap announced that the Front had to be willing to suffer high losses in order to "bloody the enemy," believing that the war would be won, not in Vietnam, but rather in the hearts of Americans grown sick of a costly "colonialist venture." As the United States escalated the war, so did the Viet Minh. By December 1965, 165,000 American troops had been shipped to South Vietnam. Early the next year, the Viet Cong numbered 200,000 soldiers and North Vietnamese regulars increased from 400 to 15,000. Within two more years there were indeed half a million American soldiers in Vietnam.

As early as 1964, U Thant, secretary gen-

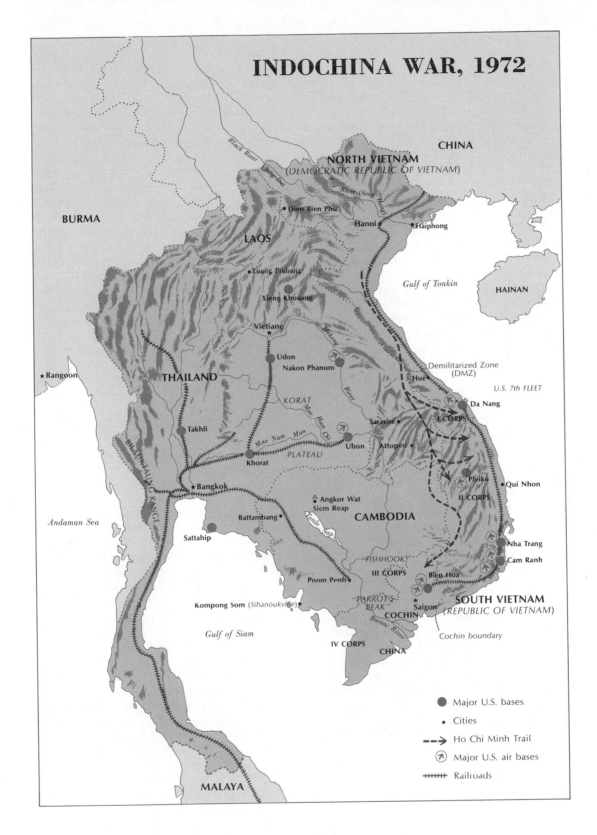

INDOCHINA WAR, 1972

CHINA

NORTH VIETNAM
(DEMOCRATIC REPUBLIC OF VIETNAM)

Black River (Song Da)

BURMA

• Dien Bien Phu

Red River (Song Hong)

Hanoi • Haiphong

LAOS

Gulf of Tonkin

HAINAN

• Luong Prabang

Xieng Khouang

Vietiane ★

Demilitarized Zone (DMZ)

U.S. 7th FLEET

Udon •
Nakon Phanom

THAILAND

Hué •

★ Rangoon

KORAT

Mae Khong River

Saravne •

I CORPS

Da Nang

Takhli •

Mae Nam Mun

Ubon

Attopeu •

Khorat •

PLATEAU

Pleiku •
Qui Nhon •

BILAUKTAUNG RANGE

★ Bangkok

II CORPS

Andaman Sea

Angkor Wat
Siem Reap •

Tonle Sap

Battambang •

CAMBODIA

Nha Trang

Sattahip •

Cam Ranh

FISHHOOK

III CORPS

Bien Hoa

Pnom Penh ★

SOUTH VIETNAM
(REPUBLIC OF VIETNAM)

PARROT'S BEAK

Kompong Som *(Sihanoukville)* •

Saigon •

COCHIN

Bassac River

Gulf of Siam

IV CORPS

CHINA

Cochin boundary

MALAYA

● Major U.S. bases

• Cities

- - -→ Ho Chi Minh Trail

⊘ Major U.S. air bases

++++++ Railroads

eral of the United Nations, attempted to mediate the conflict. He later bitterly claimed that Washington had offhandedly rejected North Vietnamese offers. Other peace attempts were instigated by neutral diplomats, American journalists, and the prime minister of England; but Washington and Hanoi continued to suspect each other of duplicity. As popular discontent mounted in the United States, President Johnson declared on March 31, 1968, that he would not run for reelection and that he was going to suspend all bombing above the twentieth parallel. Shortly afterwards Hanoi agreed to open negotiations. Four-and-a-half years later, the talks desultorily continued in Paris without a cease-fire in sight.

Before and after his election to the presidency in 1968 Richard Nixon repeatedly promised to end the war. Although the President was in principle willing to permit Communist participation in free elections in South Vietnam once a cease-fire was arranged, he in fact extended a kind of veto power over the details of such a cease-fire to South Vietnamese President Thieu. The constitution of Thieu's republic did not permit Communists to run for office. Also, the 1967 election laws that were used to administer the elections legitimizing the regime stipulated that no one could be a candidate who had "directly or indirectly worked for communism or pro-communist neutralism or worked in the interests of communism." Under these conditions Communist support for a cease-fire was unlikely. Besides, Thieu so rigged his reelection in October 1971, as to run for office unopposed. In the meantime, President Nixon moved to "Vietnamize" the war by gradually withdrawing American combat troops, leaving behind noncombatant military personnel to support the Army of the Republic of Vietnam. In 1969 there had been 543,400 American troops in Vietnam; by the spring of 1972 the number had been reduced to 65,000.

Reactions to the "Vietnamization" program were mixed. Many felt that the administration was moving as quickly as it safely could, in the absence of a political settlement, to "wind down the war" in Vietnam. Detractors argued that this with-drawal of combat troops by no means signified the end, or even a substantial curtailment, of warfare in the area. For example, once B-52 airplanes stopped flying over North Vietnam, the United States increased its heavy bomb payloads fourfold over Communist-controlled areas of neighboring Laos, monthly dropping a tonnage of TNT equal to that of three Hiroshima atomic explosions. On April 30, 1970, the words of these doubters seemed shockingly verified. That day United States and South Vietnamese armed forces invaded Cambodia. Though this was a limited incursion designed to destroy the sanctuaries of North Vietnamese troops just across the border and therefore aimed to speed up "Vietnamization," the United States seemed to be extending the war to all of Indochina. Since the occasion for this invasion was provided by a pro-American coup in Cambodia led by General Lon Nol, who had overthrown Prince Sihanouk, the neutralist chief-of-state, was the United States not once again backing an unpopular rightwing regime? President Nixon did fulfill his promise to withdraw American expeditionary forces from Cambodia by the end of June 1970, and he insisted that the invasion did speed up "Vietnamization," but a large number of American citizens remained skeptical of his stated intentions in Southeast Asia.

These doubts were revived in April 1972, when North Vietnamese troops crossed the seventeenth parallel, causing the United Stated government to resume air raids in the North. As Nixon disengaged American ground troops, the only alternative to defeat of the Thieu regime seemed to be massive United States bombing attacks.

Much more dramatic than events in Indochina, however, were the contacts between the United States and Communist China. Fearing Soviet forces on its borders as well as the prospect of a remilitarized Japan, Peking decided to explore the possibility of high-level diplomatic negotiations with Washington. Following preparatory visits by his national security coordinator, President Nixon spent a week in China during February 1972. A joint communiqué promised to explore the possibility of future peaceful relations. This rapprochement was welcomed by most of the other nations of the world. The General Assembly of the United Nations had already expelled Nationalist China from its midst and, on October 25, 1971, formally had given the People's Republic of China Taiwan's permanent seat in the Security Council.

Despite its recent overwhelming importance for the United States, the Vietnam war pales in significance beside the larger question of the future of China and India. It is fashionable to contrast the communist and democratic paths these two Asian giants have chosen, but they also share many characteristics. Both are peasant lands of deep and persistent poverty. Despite Soviet aid to China in the late 1950s and substantial American (and Soviet) programs of assistance for India, both countries have set out to modernize without the large capital inputs that made rapid industrialization possible in Western Europe, Japan, and the United States. Both also face constraints of population growth and social inertia which set sharp limits on what can be achieved. At the same time, both countries are attempting to eradicate age-old social injustices while having to deal with continuing problems of political instability. Hence it is not surprising that growth has been erratic and uneven. In sum, although India and China are national competitors, they are also protagonists in the same "Asian Dilemma," for whom the process of development will stretch far into the future.

The smaller countries of Asia—from a Pakistan rent by civil war to the rice-rich but socially heterogeneous lands of tropical Southeast Asia—share many of the problems of their two large neighbors. A few like Burma, though impoverished, are at least free from the pressures of population that hold back so many Asian countries. Several others, most notably Malaysia and Taiwan, together with the city-states of Hong Kong and Singapore, blessed with ample foreign aid, valuable resources, and an enterprising Chinese mercantile community, have made rapid economic progress. For almost all Southeast Asian countries, however, the problems of poverty have been exacerbated by ethnic rivalries, rioting, and warfare. These have made economic development almost impossible in the states of Indochina, and have encouraged a resort to authoritarian rule throughout much of the area. But such military dictatorships, though they have sometimes made possible more rapid economic growth, have almost always brought about the concentration of wealth in the hands of a few families close to the seat of power, and so carry within them the seeds of their own destruction. The smaller nations of Asia face an even more uncertain and difficult future than the potentially great powers, India and China.

SUGGESTED READINGS

Hinton, William, *Fanshen: A Documentary of Revolution in a Chinese Village*. New York: Vintage Books, 1966. Paperback.
Based upon the experiences of the author, who personally witnessed the development of land reform in a Communist-held area during 1946, this account presents a particularly exciting and favorable perspective on the Chinese Communist revolution.

Schurmann, Franz, *Ideology and Organization in Communist China*. Second edition. Berkeley: University of California Press, 1969. Paperback.
Perhaps the most important single work on Communist China, this is not an easy book to read. Nevertheless, anyone wishing to understand how the People's Republic is governed must study this work, which dialectically traces the constantly changing interplay between ideology and organization in state and society.

Schram, Stuart, *The Political Thought of Mao Tse-tung*. Revised and enlarged edition. New York: Frederick A. Praeger, 1969.

Containing key annotated texts from Mao's writings (many of them unavailable elsewhere), the volume also includes a lengthy essay by a scholar recognized by many to be the West's leading authority on Mao's thought.

Baum, Richard, ed., *China in Ferment: Perspectives on the Cultural Revolution*. Englewood Cliffs, N.J.: Prentice-Hall, 1971.

A collection of essays and articles representing the latest scholarly opinions about the origins and development of the Cultural Revolution.

Shaplen, Robert, *Time out of Hand: Revolution and Reaction in Southeast Asia*. New York: Harper Colophon Books, 1970. Paperback.

A journalist's report on the recent political history of Southeast Asia.

Kothari, Rajni, *Politics in India*. Boston: Little, Brown & Co., 1970. Paperback.

Comprehensive account of the origins and working of the Indian political system.

Srinivas, M. N., *Social Change in Modern India*. Berkeley: University of California Press, 1966. Paperback.

The changing role of caste and religion in Indian society.

Rudolph, Lloyd I. and Susanne H., *The Modernity of Tradition*. Chicago: University of Chicago Press, 1967. Paperback.

Discusses the persistence of traditional institutions and attitudes in modern Indian society.

Wiser, William and Charlotte, *Behind Mud Walls, 1930–1960*. Berkeley: University of California Press, 1963. Paperback.

Sensitive account of changing village life in India.

Brecher, Michael, *Nehru: A Political Biography*. New York: Oxford University Press, 1959. Paperback abridgement.

Not only Nehru's life but a history of India from the 1930s to the 1950s.

Geertz, Clifford, *The Religion of Java*. Glencoe, Ill.: Free Press, 1964.

CHAPTER 29

Africa and the Middle East since the 1930s

Kwame Nkrumah (1909–1972), the man who led Ghana to independence, said: "Seek ye first the political kingdom." This slogan sets the tone for the major historical events in twentieth-century Africa and the Middle East. Political concerns overrode all others; leaders of this period were preoccupied with the growth of nationalism, decolonization, and nation building. Trends that began at the end of World War I were accelerated by the effects of World War II and culminated in the independence movements still going on in this area today.

EFFECTS OF WORLD WAR II

World War II affected Africa much as World War I had. (See p. 723.) Just as Wilson's Fourteen Points had called for self-determination, the Atlantic Charter, promulgated by President Franklin Roosevelt and Prime Minister Churchill in 1941, called for the restoration of sovereign rights and self-government to all who had been forcibly deprived of them, further stirring nationalist hopes in the colonial world.

Both world wars upset European assumptions of cultural superiority and European certainty that colonialism benefited the colonies more than the colonials. How could countries that had slaughtered millions in two world wars and produced as amoral a political leader as Adolph Hitler affirm, without doubt, the right to export their civilization to the rest of the world? This sense of pessimism and uncertainty about the virtues of European civilization influenced decolonization decisions. World War II left the two great colonial powers, Britain and France, economically exhausted. France had been invaded and defeated by Germany. Britain had averted defeat, but it too lacked the resources to control its empire in the face of rising nationalist activity. The British and French lost their preeminent world position to two superpowers, the United States and the Soviet Union, whose record on colonialism was mixed but who were both willing to countenance the dismantling of the old European empires. The Soviet Union pursued such a policy openly, using the United Nations as a propaganda forum whenever feasible. Because of the American alliance with Britain and France, the Americans had to be more circumspect in supporting nationalist movements.

In response to these changing circumstances the British and French began to formulate new plans for their colonies. The British policy had been to guide their colonies toward some degree of autonomy while they still remained within the larger British imperial community. Before World War II most British administrators believed that the colonies would move toward autonomy only far in the future; in most respects their policies had not been influenced by pressures to prepare their colonies for independence. By 1945, however, it was clear to all but the most confirmed imperialists that independence could no longer be postponed indefinitely. Hence swift efforts were made to provide colonies with the necessary political experience and economic well-being to stand on their own. A Colonial Welfare Fund, created just before the war, was reactivated to provide vigorous programs of economic development. The British formula for decolonization in the late 1940s was to expand the functions and size of legislative bodies where they existed and to foster an alliance between traditional leaders — through whom the indirect rule system had been channeled — and the emerging educated elite.

The Burns Constitution in the Gold Coast in 1946 sought to build on such an alliance. The Legislative Council was composed of elected representatives and delegates appointed by the government. The British still thought that there was considerable time to develop political expertise, and most administrators could not believe that the Gold Coast would become independent in 1957. In any case, the alliance between the well-educated and the traditional leaders did not work well. The educated elite and the chiefs did not cooperate, while, at the same time, new political parties were drawing on a wider base of popular support and calling for a faster timetable of independence.

The French also recognized the need for reform. In the economic sphere they created a special organ, the Investment Fund for the Economic and Social Development of the Overseas Territories, which provided considerable French subsidies for these purposes. In the political sphere they retained their assimilationist philosophy. They rejected the British goal of ultimate independence and called instead for closer integration between France and the empire, renamed the French Community. The first such steps were taken at the Brazzaville Conference in 1944 where, under the leadership of General Charles de Gaulle, the French promised to alter much of the legislation discriminating against colonial peoples. The changes envisioned were the abolition of the *indigenat** and subject status, the granting of vaguely defined citizenship rights to all members of the French community, and franchise rights for elections to the French National Assembly. The reforms enacted by the French in 1946 were not entirely satisfactory to the colonial peoples and fell short of what had been promised; but the changes did abolish the hated *indigenat* and subject status and gave electoral powers to the colonial territories. The French struggled to maintain their assimilationist formulas, but the growth of nationalism undermined these goals.

NATIONALISM

Nationalism in the colonial world is a phenomenon difficult to define. The broadest definition would encompass all forms of political or even quasi-political protest against the colonial power. But such a broad definition would include many movements of protest that did not point in the direction of creating independent nation-states. A much narrower and perhaps more precise definition would restrict the term to movements consciously striving for the creation of independent nation-states. If this criterion is applied, however, much of the political activity in Africa before World War II could not be called nationalistic because it strove for a different distribution of political power between the imperial power and the colonial peoples rather than full-fledged independence. Although the precise definition would focus discussion on political action directed

* Arbitrary powers given to French administrators. (See p. 628.)

toward establishing nation-states, it would be a mistake to ignore other forms of political protest, such as early resistance movements and religious revolts that helped to mold the more fully developed nationalism of later years.

Early Political Protest

The first stage of opposition to European colonialism involved resistance movements, which appeared in most areas under European control. In general, the goal was to force intruders out and restore the traditional society, but some of the resistance activities introduced forward-looking elements. The Maji-Maji rebellion in German East Africa at the beginning of the twentieth century mobilized a number of disparate tribes previously unaccustomed to acting in unison. In the Middle East and North Africa, Islam served as an immediate rallying force for resisting European encroachment and promoting unity. Yet, at the same time, Muslim intellectuals were also exhorting their people to embrace the technology and economic strength of the West.

Although the early resisters were defeated, they paved the way for later developments. They revealed the weaknesses of the traditional society in the face of overwhelming European military superiority. They showed the need to understand European civilization and thus they ushered in an age when Africans sought to acquire new knowledge. The failure of the resistance movements also demonstrated the need to mobilize more support than local and tribal organizations possessed. A more quiescent period followed in which Africans set about adapting their institutions for economic and educational changes.

Education has been one of the keystones of nationalist activity. Particularly in British West Africa, where political criticism was tolerated by the colonial authorities, a second stage of political protest began to take shape as colonial peoples acquired European education. A very small educated elite came into existence: lawyers, doctors, teachers, and government officials who felt some disaffection with the imperial system. Their education trained them for nontraditional oc-cupations and tended to set them off from the rest of the population. Their political goals were usually rather modest; they were in favor of a better distribution of powers between the home government and the colonial peoples. Their political organizations were weakly articulated, and their propaganda was directed more frequently at European audiences. They practiced what might be termed the politics of persuasion; that is, they sought by means of reasoned arguments—and not by means of the strength and widespread influence of political organizations—to persuade European authorities to make alterations in the colonial system. The colonial administrators, however, disregarded them, claiming that they were not representative of the mass of the population. Nevertheless, this new intelligentsia played an important role in helping to define political goals, launching discussions on nationalism, and grappling with the meaning of the concept "nation-state."

British West Africa provides a typical example of the rise of a nationalist-minded intelligentsia. The conditions that enabled the intellectuals to flourish were missionary- and government-supported Western education, a reasonably liberal colonial administration, high levels of economic development, and urbanization. Already at the end of the nineteenth century the educated elite had cooperated with chiefs in the Gold Coast, for example, in creating the Aborigines Protection Society in order to protect the rights of Africans against the British colonial system. This movement was subsequently supplanted by a British West African Congress under the leadership of a West African, J. Casely Hayford, who sought to align intellectuals from all the British West African territories (the Gold Coast, Nigeria, Sierra Leone, and Gambia) in order to demand more autonomy and better education. In the 1920s the intellectuals of the area moved freely from one colony to another and had yet to develop fully a sense of Gold Coast or Nigerian nationalism. In the 1930s Nnamdi Azikiwe (1904–   ), later the most dynamic Nigerian nationalist, settled in the Gold Coast, where he began publishing a newspaper, the *African Morning Post*. As the nationalist movements matured after World War II, these men sought to put down roots in their own territories and build stronger political organizations. They were forced to do this because of their failure to alter the colonial system. While the nationalist intellectuals recognized their need for a broader base of support, peoples outside the major cities were becoming politically conscious, making criticisms of the colonial system and demanding political representation, better and more numerous schools, and better economic opportunities.

One of the most important institutions for developing political consciousness was the voluntary association. When Africans left their village communities and went to the cities, they were cut off from the economic and emotional supports that the local community provided so well. As a substitute they created new organizations in the city which strove to provide the same feeling of security. These organizations assumed many forms: graduates of the same primary or secondary schools would form alumni clubs; people from the same rural areas formed regional associations; and people from the same tribe formed tribal unions. All these associations provided social facilities, financial support when needed, and in general were agencies for helping new city immigrants fit smoothly into their new environment. Inevitably, since they were so deeply concerned with education, taxation, and local economic development, they became politicized. As their political horizons broadened from local to national politics, they put themselves in touch with national politicians. In Nigeria, for example, the first important political party was the Nigerian National Democratic party, founded in 1923. But its sphere of activity was confined to Lagos. In 1944 a new party was founded, The National Council of Nigeria and the Cameroons (NCNC), under the leadership of Azikiwe who had returned to his home country in the late 1930s. The NCNC was made up of 87 member units of which 60 were tribal unions or associations; it had appeal all over southern Nigeria rather than merely in Lagos. The NCNC espoused the feelings of nationalist discontent among the newly politicized groups outside as well as inside the major cities.

In areas governed more autocratically the intelligentsia were not able to create political parties. They did, however, form many non-political clubs and societies, such as tribal associations, literary societies, and alumni clubs, in which political issues were often debated and which became the springboards for political parties as soon as these were legally permitted.

Religious Opposition

Religious revolt was another important aspect of early resistance to European influence. Revolts were especially prevalent among Christian converts. Missionaries' activities were often resented because they undermined traditional African practices and because missionary organizations were reluctant to accord African Christians positions of authority within church organizations. Some of the religious rebellions were simply endeavors to create independent African churches, patterned after the parent organizations in all ways except for an autonomous church polity and an African clergy. In some colonies these churches represented the only important modern institutions run by Africans. Religious revolt was carried further in many African churches and incorporated many African customs as part of the creed. The translation of portions of the Bible into vernacular languages was a decisive event in stimulating religious independence, for it convinced religious leaders that the missionary injunctions against polygamy, circumcision, prophetic healing, ecstatic states, and visions — to mention but a few issues — were not grounded in the Scriptures.

The European form of Christianity was obviously at variance with traditional African religious views, and many of the African religious revolts were basically an effort to make Christianity more compatible with these beliefs. In very general terms there were three major areas of disagreement between European Christianity and African traditional religion. First, European Christianity argued that suffering would be compensated in an afterlife, whereas traditional religion affirmed that suffering could be alleviated here and now through religious powers possessed by diviner-healers. Secondly, missionaries stressed that man was

Aerial view of the harbor and city of Lagos, one of the busiest commercial centers of West Africa and the capital of Nigeria.

responsible for his own actions and failings whereas traditional religion believed that witches and evil spirits thwarted man's good intentions. Finally, Christianity taught that there was only one God and that his grace alone brought salvation, whereas in traditional religion there were many gods, approachable through one another and serving different kinds of needs. Thus many African movements of religious independence stressed such themes as healing and curing, protection against witches, and the recognition of lesser divinities as a help in reaching the Christian God.

It was primarily in the radical, millenarian churches that religious independence took on political overtones. These churches arose especially in repressive colonial areas, such as the Congo and South Africa, and the people believed that a day of reckoning would soon come when a messianic figure would oust the European oppressors and restore

African freedom. In some of these churches the Messiah or Christ figure was portrayed as black and the devil as white.

One of the best documented histories of an African millenarian movement is that of Simon Kimbangu in the Belgian Congo. A member of the Bakongo tribe of the lower Congo River basin, Kimbangu had visions exhorting him to go forth and preach Christianity to his fellow Africans and to heal the sick. His claims to have prophetic and healing powers disturbed the European missionaries and administrators, although in most other respects his teachings were quite orthodox. As his following increased, the colonial administrators became alarmed and arrested and imprisoned him in the early 1920s. Although he remained in prison until his death, his followers continued to glorify his memory and develop his religious organization. In time they came to regard Kimbangu as a messianic figure who at some future date would return to the Congo and expel the Belgian administrators and missionaries.

Islam, too, was bound up with many movements of political protest. Secular nationalists tried to emphasize the nonreligious symbols of loyalty, but often they resorted to Islam as a more certain means of energizing the masses. Reform movements within Islam itself had a considerable political content. One of the most dynamic Middle Eastern political leaders of the nineteenth century, Jamal al-Din al-Afghani, had preached Pan-Islamic unity in order to stave off the threatening partition of the Muslim world. Before World War I some of his ideas were taken up by a group of Muslim reformers, the *Salafis*, especially prevalent in Egypt and North Africa, who believed that the Muslim world could reclaim its former greatness only by returning to a purified Islam. The Salafi reformers in Morocco and Algeria constituted one of the early strands of North African nationalism. The most active of the Muslim protest movements was the Muslim Brotherhood, with its headquarters in Egypt and branches throughout the Arab countries. Founded in 1929 by Hasan al-Banna, an Egyptian schoolteacher and a spellbinding orator, it was a paramilitary body based on a powerful politico-religious organization in Egypt. The Muslim Brotherhood exhorted its followers to repudiate evil Western practices, to embrace the teachings of Muhammad and the Koran, and through their new-found strength to rid their countries of foreign oppressors. For a considerable period of time the Muslim Brotherhood was a force to be reckoned with in Egyptian politics. It practiced political assassination and contributed to the climate of Egyptian political instability which eventually led to the overthrow of the monarchy in 1952 by a military coup d'état.

New Political Parties

Neither the religious leaders nor the parties of persuasion founded by the educated elite made much headway toward independence for their countries. Instead, newly organized political parties with a broader base of support came to the fore in the 1930s in Arab lands and in the 1940s and 1950s in Black Africa. Whereas the earlier political parties had directed much of their appeal at influential European politicians, the new parties sought to mobilize new groups in the population for political action: primary and secondary school graduates, the urban proletariat and unemployed, and wherever possible the rural masses. These parties drew their strength primarily from the cities, where the educated and partially educated tended to be located and where people could be organized for demonstrations. Two of the new nationalists, Nkrumah in the Gold Coast and Azikiwe in Nigeria, had studied in the United States, where they learned the techniques of radical journalism and the belief that only through disciplined political action could they bring an end to colonialism.

Although the new parties such as Nkrumah's Convention People's Party (CPP), Azikiwe's National Council of Nigeria and the Cameroons (NCNC) and Felix Houphouet-Boigny's *Parti Démocratique de la Côte d'Ivoire* (PDCI) are sometimes characterized as mass parties, their appeal was only slightly less limited than that of the old parties. They arose in opposition to earlier so-called patron parties that were dominated either by traditional chiefs or a small educated elite. The new parties were better organized and disciplined, and they adopted a more radical, equalitarian social and political ideology, thus appealing to a broader spectrum of the population than the older, elite parties. Yet a close examination of election statistics in the preindependence period reveals that in addition to the considerable numbers voting for opposition parties there were many nonvoters. In the first election in the Gold Coast (1951), Nkrumah's CPP won a stunning victory, capturing 34 of the 38 popularly contested seats, even while Nkrumah was in prison. In the hotly contested election of 1956, just one year before independence, the CPP achieved another impressive victory, winning 71 out of the total 104 seats. But they were able to win only 57 percent of the total votes cast, only 28.5 percent of registered voters, and only 15 percent of the estimated adult population. As one scholar has observed: "Although nearly six out of ten adults who voted in . . . [the] election cast their lot with the CPP—which thus did a little better than its opponents could do—the party, after many years of effort and in spite of [many] advantages . . . could mobilize, to the extent of having them register and vote, only about one out of six or seven adult Ghanaians."

These new parties were not the well-disciplined, centrally controlled organizations their propaganda suggested. Local candidates often ran on local issues, and although they bore a party label, their political philosophy was quite different from that of the party leadership. Indeed, party control of outlying regions could never be taken for granted. The party's relationship with a distant area always posed a problem. The idea of mass parties, tightly controlled and disciplined, stemmed from the writings of African politicians but represented far more what they were striving for than what they had attained.

Although the educated elite provided nationalist leadership, Africans in most other groups had grievances against colonialism and were potential nationalists. The educated resented racial discrimination, pay differentials between Europeans and Africans, and occupational discrimination, and came to the conclusion that these grievances would be eradicated if political subordination came to an end. The less educated—primary and sometimes secondary school graduates—often were unable to obtain the kind of employment they regarded as worthy of their educational attainments. They were easily mobilized by the new political parties. Wealthy farmers, like the cocoa growers in West Africa, were angered by the pricing policies of large European export firms to which they were forced to sell their produce. Ordinary peasant farmers felt that taxes bore heavily; communal work obligations in the villages and on roads were onerous. At all levels of society resentments waited to be channeled into political action.

For the most part the political parties mobilized the educated and urban population. Rural people were more difficult to reach, and the programs of the parties did not have widespread appeal to them. Their experiences and grievances were different from those of the educated elite. Unlike their rural compatriots, many intellectuals adopted European standards; they aspired to equality of status and resented any discrimination. Education had set them off and given them a privileged position. Many had not felt the labor obligations and communal tasks of rural colonial Africa. They had grown up at boarding schools, gone for secondary education to the cities, and sought advanced education overseas. Thus their view of priorities for an independent Africa were different from those of people in the villages and the bush.

The recent history of Tunisia serves as an excellent case study of nationalist development. Occupied by the French in 1881, Tunisia formed no significant political movement against French rule until the beginning of the twentieth century. At that time two forces emerged: a traditionally trained religious elite that appealed to Islam in danger, and a new Western-educated group whose ideology was based on the ideals of a secular nation-state. World War I, particularly the impact of Wilsonian national self-determination, helped to forge an alliance between these two elements. They made representations to the Allied powers at the Paris Peace Conference and created a new political party, the *Destour* (meaning constitution in Arabic), which argued for the introduction of more representative and constitutional government in Tunisia.

The Destour, which was the leading organ of political protest throughout the 1920s, was like many other early colonial political parties. It was restricted to a small, religious and Western-educated elite and lacked organizational intensity. Most of the secular nationalists were, in fact, drawn from the capital city of Tunis.

By the 1930s a new generation of political leaders appeared; its members were drawn from many different regions of Tunisia and consequently had a larger following than the old Destour. Their educational attainments were impressive, but they also came from lower social strata. Their most dynamic figure was Habib Bourguiba (1903–   ), a French-trained lawyer from a modest family in the Sahelian town of Monastir, who had returned to Tunisia after his education and founded a political newspaper. In 1934 the new leadership coalesced and formed a new political party called the Neo-Destour, which had a broader base of support and a more vigorous program of political opposition to French colonialism. Under the tactful direction of Bourguiba the party was able to build support throughout the country and undercut other competitors for power. The Neo-Destour's struggle against the French eventually culminated in the French decision to grant independence to Tunisia in 1956, along with its other North African protectorate, Morocco.*

DECOLONIZATION

The growth of nationalism coupled with changing European attitudes toward empire created the preconditions for decolonization in the 1950s and 1960s. The term "decolonization" is widely used to describe the process by which colonial nations have obtained political independence. Yet decolonization has not brought complete independence. African nations remain economically weak and often divided against each other. Their economic weakness compels them to seek foreign assistance and compromises their political autonomy. In fact, certain people, including Nkrumah, President of Ghana from 1957 until 1966, have said that Africa is in a neocolonial situation, its political and economic institutions subordinate to foreign powers and huge Western business organizations. For Nkrumah, the only recourse was African unity, but little progress has been made in this direction.

In considering the process of decolonization a basic distinction can be made between areas with European settlers and those without them. Settlement colonies experienced greater violence during decolonization as European populations resisted efforts to confer independence on the African majority. On the other hand, in most colo-

nies without settlers the march toward political independence was accomplished without much violence. To be sure, there were imprisonments, riots, and demonstrations but no warfare like that in Algeria, Kenya, or the Portuguese colonies.

The British led the way in granting independence. They had not been committed to the French goal of assimilating their colonies to the mother country. Once the keystone colony, India, had been granted independence in 1947 it was only a matter of time before the others followed. In 1954 the British signed an accord with the new Egyptian military government granting it independence. In 1956 the Sudan became self-governing.

Ghana

The first tropical African state to gain its freedom was the Gold Coast (renamed Ghana), in 1957. It led the way for a number of reasons. The Ghanaians had been in contact with Europeans longer than most African states. Missionary education began as early as the nineteenth century and helped to create a powerful and sophisticated educated elite. The large-scale cultivation of cocoa for export beginning at the turn of the twentieth century had benefited the country economically. Particularly noteworthy was the leadership of Kwame Nkrumah. As we have seen, he had been educated in the United States in 1949 and had organized the Convention Peoples Party (CPP), which won three national elections in the 1950s before independence was granted. Nkrumah had great personal charm and was a gifted orator. During the quest for independence, he built up a large following among the young, urban dwellers, market women, and disgruntled primary school graduates.

During the postindependence period, Nkrumah became a firm advocate of the one-party state and centralized economic planning. Under his increasingly autocratic rule the leaders of other parties were harassed and their party activities obstructed. Nkrumah argued that national unity could be realized only by a national party supplanting tribal loyalties with national symbols. As an avid proponent of Pan-Africanism, he fa-

---

* Other Arab countries gained their independence in the following years:

Jordan	1946
Lebanon	1946
Syria	1946
Iraq	1948
Libya	1951

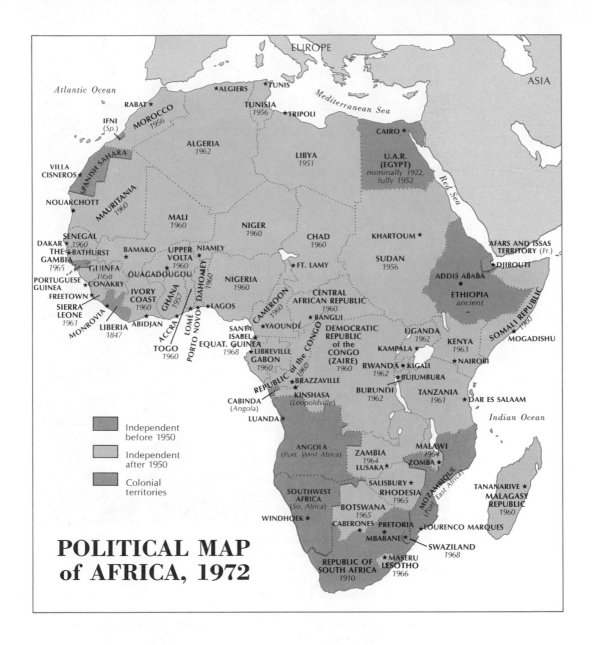

POLITICAL MAP
of AFRICA, 1972

Independent before 1950

Independent after 1950

Colonial territories

vored closer political integration of African states, but his foreign policy sometimes impeded even ordinary cooperation. By means of economic planning he sought to promote Ghanaian industrialization while still providing social welfare benefits, such as education and health services. He bent most institutions to his goals: the universities, the judiciary, the parliament, and the military. His rule was resented by many Ghanaians, as made clear by the exuberant demonstrations when he was overthrown in 1966. Nevertheless, Nkrumah held a preeminent position on the African continent as the leader of the first independent tropical African country and the most vigorous proponent of Pan-Africanism, economic planning, neutralism in foreign affairs, and socialism at home.

The success of Ghana in attaining independence was contagious. The French had hoped to associate their West and Equatorial African colonies more closely with them. But

Kwame Nkrumah, Africa's leading nationalist in the struggle against colonialism and the first prime minister of Ghana. He governed from 1957 to 1966 when he was overthrown by a military coup.

this goal was doomed by separatist nationalisms. In 1958 Guinea under Sekou Touré voted to withdraw from the newly formed French Union and claim complete independence. The other states inevitably followed Guinea's lead, and in 1960 the former colonies in French West and Equatorial Africa had obtained full independence.

Nigeria

Nigeria's march toward independence was more difficult than that of the Gold Coast. Nigeria is an enormous country with a large

(55 million) and ethnically diverse population. Moreover, its various peoples had experienced colonial rule differently and were at different levels of development. The people of the western region of Nigeria, mainly Yorubas, were well educated and wealthy because of the lucrative cocoa trade. In the east the Ibos had embraced Western education avidly, and a large number of Ibos had migrated into other regions in search of work. The north, dominated by the Hausa-Fulani ruling elite, was educationally more backward and fearfully viewed political union with the better educated and wealthier

Scene from the bitter Nigerian civil war from 1967 to 1970.

Yorubas and Ibos. The explosive tribal situation was further exacerbated by the presence of numerous minority peoples in the three major regions.

Because of the country's political and ethnic diversity a dominant party like the Ghanaian CPP could not emerge. The party that came closest to this ideal was the NCNC, under Nnamdi Azikiwe, an Ibo. Founded in 1944, it claimed to be a national party but was regarded by northerners and westerners as pro-Ibo. In response, Obafemi Awolowo, an English-educated Yoruba lawyer, created a predominantly Yoruba party, called the Action party, and the Hausa-Fulani elite established the Northern Peoples' Congress. As independence approached, controversy revolved around the questions of whether Nigeria should be a unitary or federal state, how many provinces should be established, and the distribution of powers between the provinces and the central government. The final constitutional arrangements, which gave Nigeria its independence in 1960, called for the division

of the former colony into four regions (North, East, West, and the enclave of Lagos), a federal bicameral legislature, and regional administrations and legislatures with considerable powers. Many observers viewed Nigeria as potentially the best example of stable democracy in Africa because of its multiparty coalition government, but the coalition proved a tenuous one. Antagonisms continued to ferment and led to a military coup in 1966 and then a civil war as the Ibos unsuccessfully attempted to secede from the federation by creating an independent state, called Biafra.

The task of administering Nigeria now seems in hindsight an impossible one, and the civil war an inevitability. The country did not have the territorial or ethnic compactness of Ghana. Its size worked against political integration. The British had merely welded together the disparate regions permitting them to develop on their own. Nigeria was an administrative creation of the British rulers, held together in a loose federation by only a small staff of foreigners during the colonial period. In the north among the Hausa-Fulani peoples a system of indirect rule was established. Missionaries were kept out of Muslim areas with the result that education there lagged behind the south. In haste the British had sought to foster national loyalty as they saw Nigeria moving toward independence at the end of World War II. Their efforts had been too little and too late.

Congo

The country that probably received the most international publicity during decolonization was the Belgian Congo. The Congo is, of course, a huge and rich country. Its preparations for independence were minimal prior to 1950, for the Belgians were even more indifferent than the British and French toward preparing Africa for self-rule. The state of unpreparedness was made strikingly clear by the agonizing problems of attaining political stability after independence in 1960. Yet in the light of Nkrumah's overthrow and the Nigerian civil war can one be sure any longer that the British prepared their colonies any more effectively than the Belgians?

Nowhere did independence come so abruptly as in the Belgian Congo. Nowhere did it produce such fundamental changes; as one scholar has pointed out, within two years the Congo went from "tropical Africa's most completely European dominated power structure to a degree of Africanization that only Guinea could match." The Congo had been insulated from the currents of nationalism and decolonization because of disinterest in Belgium, the unity of the European groups in the Congo, and an autocratic, paternalistic, and at times repressive colonial administration. The three major European agencies in the Congo—the administrators, the missionaries, and the business firms—were in substantial agreement over the continuation of Belgian rule. The colonial administration was larger than most others and was entirely staffed at the top levels by Belgian officials.

Nevertheless, the monolithic structure began to crumble in the 1950s. A new government in Belgium came to power in 1954 and began to attack the educational system of the missionaries in the Congo. In 1955, a Belgian scholar, Van Bilsen, stunned the Belgian public by formulating a proposal for conferring independence on the Congo within 30 years. The changing political climate prompted the Belgian government to promise municipal elections in a few of the major Congolese cities. As the colonial system was made more liberal, the Congolese responded, in the customary fashion, by creating political parties. The first, created in 1951, was the Abako party, a political organ of the Bakongo people in the Lower Congo region. By 1959 there were 53 different political groups officially registered, and in the few months before independence the number had grown to 120. Most were ethnically based parties or regional parties. Only two truly aspired to be national.

In 1958 the Belgians still thought they had considerable time to prepare for independence. But in January 1959, there were bloody riots in Leopoldville, and for the first time the Belgians gained a full appreciation of the intensity of Congolese feeling against their rule. The riots made clear that Belgian control of the Congo could be maintained only through the use of considerable coercion—a policy that few were willing to endorse. Thus the Belgian government agreed to grant the Congo its independence in 1960.

During its first year of independence, the Congo was beset by severe problems. There was competition for power among the political leaders. One of these leaders was Patrice Lumumba whose party garnered the most seats to the National Assembly in the 1960 election. Lumumba became prime minister but was not able to solidify his power. His opponents looked to the Western world for support while Lumumba turned to the Soviets. Lumumba was dismissed from his office, imprisoned, and then killed while attempting to flee from his captors. His death shocked the world, and for many Lumumba became a martyr to Africa's struggle for genuine economic and political independence against the neocolonial West. During this turmoil there was trouble in the army, which had been under the control of the Belgians and had not developed an African identity. The Congolese army mutinied, many Belgian technicians fled, and Katanga, the richest province in the Congo, seceded from the central government. The flight of European technicians left the Congo with few professional people or trained administrators because Africans had not been educated for these roles. United Nations forces eventually helped to bring Katanga back into the state, but civilian government was ultimately replaced by military rule.

Settlement Areas: South Africa and Rhodesia

Decolonization either has not been attained or has come with greater difficulty and more bloodshed in areas dominated by European settlers. These areas included Algeria, Kenya, South Africa, Rhodesia, and the Portuguese colonies of Angola, Mozambique, and Portuguese Guinea. Settlers regarded their political interests as paramount, and their presence in a country as indispensable for its economic and political well-being. They were fearful of domination by an African majority and thus had their own formula for political change. In the English-speaking areas they urged the gradual transfer of political authority into their own hands. Their models were the earlier settlement areas of Australia, New Zealand, and Canada, where the British government had progressively turned political power over to the white immigrant community. Disregarding the overwhelming majority of nonwhites, the settlers claimed that parliamentary bodies should be dominated by the white population and should become increasingly autonomous of the mother country. Despite their numerical inferiority to the blacks, mulattoes, and Asians, their efforts were remarkably successful. South Africa, with a population of 4 million whites to over 17 million nonwhites, crowned its political independence from the British Empire when it withdrew from the Commonwealth in 1961. Rhodesia (250,000 whites to 4 million blacks) followed the same course, unilaterally declaring its independence from Britain in 1965. The Rhodesian whites have likened their independence struggle to the American War of Independence, thus again calling forth the image of early white settlement areas.

In the independent white colonies of South Africa and Rhodesia the politically dominant European population has tried to protect its privileged position by maintaining racial separation. The white and nonwhite populations have unequal access to economic and educational opportunities and political power. Also the black and white populations have been assigned different agricultural areas. The European population, even the European working class, enjoys a standard of living far higher than that of the black majority. On the whole, the blacks fill the subordinate positions in the modern economic sector. When Africans are able to obtain more skilled jobs, their rate of pay is lower than that of whites doing the same work.

The policy of racial separation has been carried to its greatest extremes in the *apartheid* system of South Africa. The entire twentieth-century history of South Africa has moved in the direction of increased racial separation and white dominance over blacks, but the election of 1948 was an important turning point. This election was won by the Nationalist party, which drew its strength from the strongly white racist Afrikaner segment of the European population. In power until today the Nationalists have implemented their political philosophy of apartheid, which is supposed to mean separate development of the races but which has solidified white supremacy. Apartheid has been enshrined in laws such as railway segregation, prohibition against marriage and sexual intercourse among the races, a Group Areas Act, which restricted each race to areas it already occupied, and a law requiring all people to carry a certificate of racial identity. The Nationalist government has crushed resistance within the country from Africans, Asians, and a sizable minority of European liberals. Although the party commands support among the white population, it clearly rules through coercion. It relies heavily on a powerful army and police force to protect it from internal and external enemies.

In the non-English-speaking settler colonies of Africa—particularly Algeria and the Portuguese territories—the Europeans tried to maintain their power through close association with the mother country. Both the settlers and the "home government" maintained the fiction that these areas were not

OORGANG ALLEENLIK OOR DIE BRUG.

CROSS THE LINE BY THE BRIDGE ONLY.

NGUMLA ISIPOLO NGEBLORO KUPELA.

The separate walkways for whites and nonwhites dramatizes the aims of apartheid South Africa—separate facilities and goals for the different races.

colonies but overseas provinces. At its height the European population in Algeria was over one million, and today the Portuguese government is encouraging a steady migration of whites to Angola and Mozambique. As in other settler areas, Europeans had better standards of living, dominated the economic resources, such as land, labor, and minerals, and controlled the political system. Africans remained on the outside, only a small number qualifying for political rights through education.

In the 1950s nationalist movements arose to challenge white supremacy in Portugal's African "provinces": Angola, Mozambique, and Portuguese Guinea. At first these movements operated underground, but in the 1960s open rebellion occurred. The Portuguese have endeavored to suppress the outbreaks through massive military intervention, but armed resistance and political warfare were still going on at the time of this writing.

Algeria

In two settlement areas—Algeria and Kenya—European settler dominance was overthrown but only with much bloodshed. In Algeria, the Europeans were determined to retain their predominant position, and the French army, smarting from the humiliations of World War II and Indochina, was committed to keeping Algeria French. By this they meant keeping the Muslim Arabs and Berbers "in their place" as a politically impotent and economically marginal majority existing on French suffrance. At the end of World War II, European-educated Arab leaders began to demand political independence. But these moderate nationalists were unable to make headway, and in 1954, some younger, radical nationalists, under the lead of Mohammed Ben Bella, established a new political party, the FLN (National Liberation Front), and created a secret military organization with which to combat the French. Fighting broke out in 1954 and lasted until independence was granted to Algeria in 1962.

The fighting was carried out with great ferocity by both sides. The French army was convinced that it had acquired the skill for dealing with insurgent nationalist movements through its experiences in Indochina and was prepared to set aside civilian law and even to employ torture against its opponents. The French government at home was deeply torn over the dispute, worn out by its economic burdens, and morally revolted by the nature of the warfare. Yet the French were incapable of making the decision for independence until General de Gaulle, who returned to power in 1958, finally forced it on France and Algeria four years later. (See p. 797.) The last stages of Algeria's decolonization struggle were marred by even more violence as segments of the settler community established their own terrorist societies and carried out bombings and assassinations against all opponents of a French Algeria. Last-minute hopes for future European-Arab cooperation in Algeria were severely hindered by these events, and most of the European population left Algeria once it became independent.

Kenya

The European population of Kenya was much smaller than that of Algeria, approximately 60,000 at its peak, but here also Europeans were anxious to retain their privileged position. The British settlers' colonialism toward the African population resulted in violence—the Mau Mau rebellion beginning in 1952. Mau Mau, the meaning of which is not definitely known, was a movement of protest by a segment of the Kikuyu people. Located in the highlands of Kenya, quite close to the centers of European settlement, the Kikuyu traditional society was much disrupted by social change. Some land was taken from its people by the European settlers—a bitterly resented grievance because of the Kikuyu veneration of their land. The Kikuyu were recruited in large numbers, sometimes by force, to work on European plantations. Many able-bodied men had also served in both world wars, and some served in Southeast Asia. The community's relationship with the European missionaries was an awkward and ambigious one at best. On the one hand, many Kikuyu were extremely receptive to mission-sponsored education and Christianity. However, they resisted efforts to compel them to renounce many of their most cherished social customs. In the late 1920s a dispute had flared up between the Kikuyu and the missionaries over the issue of female circumcision. Integral to the Kikuyu social system was the practice of circumcising young males and females as a symbol of the end of childhood and the beginning of adult life. The missionaries were repelled by the practice of female circumcision (removal of the clitoris), which they believed had harmful consequences on the health of girls. Their efforts to exact a promise from Kikuyu Christians not to permit the circumcising of their daughters resulted in a split in the church and the creation of independent churches and schools.

Social change led inevitably to political action, and in this area the Kikuyu encountered stern European resistance. When the political situation did not improve after World War II, a young militant segment of the Kikuyu community began to urge more violent action. This group drew its support from the urban proletariat and unemployed (mainly in Nairobi), the landless Kikuyu peasantry, and peasants forced off European estates in the highlands. These fighters hated the landed and wealthy Kikuyu gentry as much as they hated the European settlers.

Oath-taking began to develop as a means for promoting unity and secrecy within the group.

Mau Mau goals are difficult to discern with precision. The movement was probably fragmented and had different sources of leadership. At first it restricted its violence to physical beatings and even killings of conservative, pro-settler Kikuyu, confining its attacks against the Europeans to damaging their property and crippling their livestock. Nevertheless, there were rumors that the Mau Mau insurgents were planning a general onslaught against the settlers. In a climate of virtual hysteria the Kenya government proclaimed a state of emergency in 1952 and called in troops and planes from the Suez Canal base, still in British hands at that time.

The real struggle between the British and the radical Mau Mau began only with the proclamation of the 1952 emergency. The Mau Mau freedom fighters, as they were called, withdrew into the mountainous forest regions of Mt. Kenya and the Aberdare Mountains. The numbers involved have been estimated at 10,000 to 15,000—but they were supported by a large passive Mau Mau wing in Nairobi and the countryside. The British eventually defeated the Mau Mau by insulating its armed forces from its passive wing outside the forests. The military operations cost the British £55,000,000 and required a large army of Kikuyu and other African forces in support of the British troops. During this period, 32 European settlers were killed, whereas more than 10,000 Kikuyu died, mostly as a result of the clash of armies. The Mau Mau movement was primarily a Kikuyu civil war, and its strong anti-European thrust came only after the emergency proclamation.

Although the Kikuyu insurgents were defeated, the Mau Mau galvanized English thinking on Kenya. The settlers' Legislative Council was opened to greater African representation. The elections of 1961 and 1963 showed that the people supported the Kenya African National Union (KANU), under the leadership of Jomo Kenyatta, a long-standing leader of the nationalist movement. In 1963 Kenya was given its independence with a ruling black majority.

PALESTINE

The most important area involving European settlement in the Middle East was Palestine, part of which became Israel in 1948. The Palestinian-Israeli problem is a complex one, and to understand it one must unravel a great deal of history. Three forces interacted with each other: Zionism, Arab nationalism, and British imperialism. The Zionist movement emerged as a political force of consequence in the late nineteenth century under the leadership of the Austrian Jew Theodore Herzl. In 1896 Herzl published a political pamphlet, *The Jewish State,* and helped to found the World Zionist Organization. He believed that the assimilation of the Jews into European societies could not be made to work and called upon Jews to form a state of their own. Zionist ideology appeared at this time partly as the culmination of nationalist aspirations long held by members of the Jewish community and partly as a response to European anti-Semitism. Russian anti-Semitic pogroms alarmed the Jewish people, and even in the more liberal regimes of Western Europe many Jews were disappointed at continuing prejudice and discrimination. The Dreyfus affair in France (see p. 466) at the end of the nineteenth century revealed strong anti-Semitic feelings in that nation and further heightened the fears of the Western European Jews. At the same time, some Jews held important political and economic positions in Europe and the United States and could use their influence, if they chose, to support Zionist aspirations.

At first the Zionist leadership was not united in its determination to return to Palestine. Its leaders even considered a British proposal to settle in Kenya! But the attraction of Palestine—the return to the homeland—was too strong, and it became the symbol and dream of Zionist hopes. World War I proved to be a turning point for Zionism. Partly out of sympathy for oppressed Jewish peoples and partly to win the support of influential Jews for the war effort, Lord Balfour, the British Foreign Secretary, issued the following declaration in 1917: "His Majesty's Government view with favor the establishment in Palestine of a national home

Jomo Kenyatta, lifelong nationalist leader and prime minister of independent Kenya, addresses a mass rally in Nyanza region.

for the Jewish people, and will use their best endeavors to facilitate the achievement of this object, it being clearly understood that nothing shall be done which may prejudice the civil and religious rights of existing non-Jewish communities in Palestine, or the rights and political status enjoyed by Jews in any other country." When the Balfour declaration was issued the Jewish population of Palestine was approximately 80,000; the Arab population was close to 700,000.

Jewish immigration grew during the 1920s but not at the pace that many Zionists had hoped. It was Hitler's campaign against European Jews which increased the population movement from a trickle to a groundswell. Between 1933 and 1939 almost 225,000 Jews entered Palestine. The Jewish population was further increased at the end of World War II as displaced Eastern European Jews left refugee camps to find new lives in Palestine, then again after the two Arab-Israeli wars of 1948 and 1956 when Asian and African Jews, primarily from the Arab countries, either were expelled or chose to live in the safer Israeli political climate. By 1960 the population of Israel exceeded two million. Although the Jewish population of European ancestry provided the political leadership, had higher standards of living, and were better educated, the Asian and African Jewish population constituted about half the total.

Whereas the Balfour declaration had merely promised a homeland for Jews with safeguards for the Arab population, some Jewish leaders had long favored the establishment of an independent state under

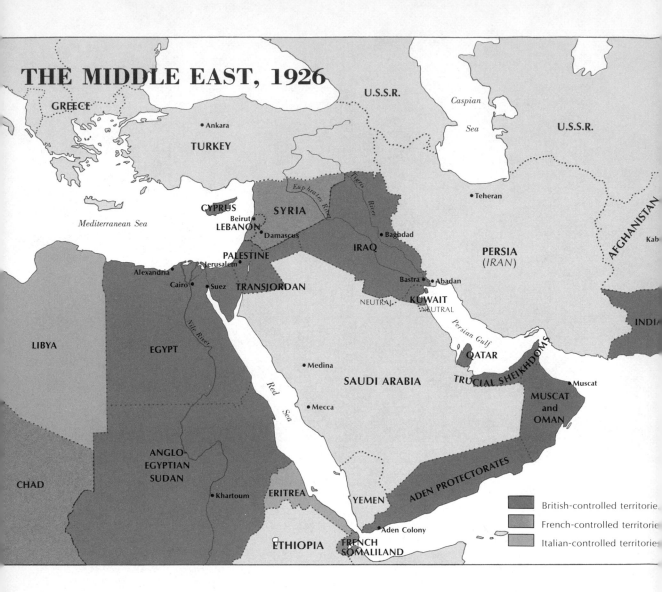

THE MIDDLE EAST, 1926

GREECE

U.S.S.R.

Caspian Sea

U.S.S.R.

• Ankara

TURKEY

• Teheran

AFGHANISTAN

Kab

CYPRUS

SYRIA

Beirut •
LEBANON
• Damascus

Mediterranean Sea

Euphrates River

Tigris River

• Baghdad

IRAQ

PERSIA
(IRAN)

PALESTINE
Jerusalem •

Alexandria •

Cairo • • Suez

TRANSJORDAN

Bastra • • Abadan

NEUTRAL

KUWAIT
NEUTRAL

Persian Gulf

INDIA

LIBYA

EGYPT

Nile River

Red Sea

• Medina

SAUDI ARABIA

QATAR

TRUCIAL SHEIKHDOMS

• Muscat

MUSCAT
and
OMAN

• Mecca

CHAD

ANGLO-
EGYPTIAN
SUDAN

• Khartoum

ERITREA

YEMEN

ADEN PROTECTORATES

British-controlled territorie

French-controlled territorie

Italian-controlled territories

ETHIOPIA

FRENCH
SOMALILAND

• Aden Colony

Jewish domination. Moderates supported an accommodation with the Arabs, but Arab opposition to the establishment of a Jewish state frustrated such accommodation. As we saw in Chapter 24, the British ruled Palestine as a League of Nations Mandate. As the Palestinian Mandate developed, Zionist demands for their own state hardened, along with Arab opposition to these demands.

As Zionism grew, Arab nationalism, which had been strengthened during World War I, also grew. Arab nationalists, both inside and outside Palestine, remained antagonistic to Zionism. Arab moderates who favored

accommodation with Jewish politicians were rarely heeded. Faisal, the leader of the Syrian Arab nationalists at the end of World War I, agreed conditionally to the Balfour declaration while negotiating in Paris, but he withdrew his agreement later. No Palestinian Arab leader emerged willing to work with the Zionists. The dominant figure in the Arab opposition was the Mufti (religious head) of Jerusalem, who was opposed to any concessions to the Palestinian Jews.

From the outset the British experienced enormous difficulties in governing Palestine. The most controversial issues revolved around the amount of Jewish immigration to allow, the sale of land by Arabs to Jews, and proposals for the future political development and eventual autonomy of Palestine. Under Zionist pressures the British would open the gates of immigration wide, but when responding to the demands of the Arab community they would restrict immigration and land sales. At the end of World War II the political climate in Palestine had become exceedingly tense. The Arab and Jewish communities were arming, and each had secret paramilitary organizations. In 1947 the issue was placed before the United Nations, and a special committee on Palestine, drawn entirely from small states, recommended a partition, which the United Nations supported. The Arabs opposed the plan while the Jews were more receptive but cautious. The United States attempted to make the British responsible for order during the period of transition to independence, but the British announced that they would withdraw in May 1948 and would not enforce the United Nations decision against either Arabs or Jews.

Palestinian Arabs and Jews armed for the inevitable struggle while the armies of the neighboring Arab countries stood poised for action. On May 14, 1948, the new state of Israel under the premiership of David Ben Gurion proclaimed its independence. It was recognized almost immediately by the United States and somewhat later by the Soviet Union. Fighting ensued throughout the area as armies of neighboring Arab states invaded Israel. Israel's chances were not regarded as good in a struggle with the much larger armies of Egypt, Syria, Iraq, Lebanon, and Transjordan. But the Israelis had stronger determination and a better organized military. The Arab forces were not united. From the outbreak of the war in May 1948 until a tenuous truce was established in 1949, the Israelis repulsed the Arab armies and added substantially to their territories.

The new state of Israel stretched from the Gulf of Aqaba north to the Lebanese and Syrian border. The city of Jerusalem was divided between Jordan and Israel. The Israelis felt themselves under seige, surrounded by hostile Arab nations. Internally, however, the Israelis were far more unified than their defeated Arab neighbors. Their parliamentary democracy was dominated by the man who had brought the country to independence, David Ben Gurion, and his political party, the *Mapai*. The country underwent economic development despite its lack of natural resources and the small size of the country and its population. Israeli economic achievement owed much to the resourcefulness and educational attainments of its population and also to a considerable influx of capital. For a long time the German government paid reparations to the new state. The United States government also provided a great deal of assistance, but the most important source of capital came from private donors, especially Jewish groups in the United States. This dependence on outside capital worried Israeli economic planners, who consequently tried to develop the economy to the point where it would no longer require regular and large capital inflows for continued growth.

The loss of the 1948 war radicalized Arab politics by undermining the legitimacy of the leaders of the Arab countries and preparing the way for new rulers—usually more nationalist, more anti-Western, and more anti-Israeli. In Egypt, Prime Minister Nuqrashi was assassinated in 1948, and Egyptian politics became so chaotic that the army felt impelled to intervene in 1952. Jordan's King Abdullah was assassinated in 1951 and eventually replaced by his grandson, Husayn. The question of Israel became so explosive and emotion-ridden that it was difficult for any Arab official to adopt a moderate position.

The real losers of the 1948 Arab-Israeli war, however, were the Arab refugees. It is estimated that 600,000 to 800,000 Arabs fled Israel either before or during the fighting. Some left in response to Arab propaganda and in the firm belief that they would be able to return behind the victorious Arab armies. Radio broadcasts from neighboring Arab states led Palestinian Arabs to believe that Arab armies would soon be victorious. They left their towns and villages confident that they would return with the victorious armies. And Israeli terrorism caused many more Arabs to flee. By the end of the war there were only about 200,000 Arabs left in the territory held by Israel. Most of the refugees were located in hastily established camps in the neighboring Arab states, awaiting their return to Palestine and supported primarily by United Nations contributions. But the Arabs and Israelis were unable to settle the refugee problem. The Arabs insisted on the right of repatriation or resettlement at the expense of Israel, while the Israelis argued that the refugee question could be settled only after the Arab states formally recognized Israel and ended their state of war against it.

NATION-BUILDING AND MODERNIZATION

Political independence has intensified the search for modernization and national unity. The newly independent African and Arab states have experimented with many methods of economic development, but two approaches have prevailed: the gradualist and forced methods. The gradualist approach has been adopted in the Ivory Coast and Kenya, to cite but two examples. Its proponents have argued that economic growth should not entail radical new departures but should emphasize those aspects of the economy already growing and should rely on private initiative wherever possible. In both societies agricultural development has been emphasized as the key to general development. Major plans of industrialization await the generation of substantial surpluses in the agricultural sector and the increase of consumer demands. Both societies have recognized their need for capital and have sought to make economic and political conditions attractive for foreign investors. In Kenya, in fact, although land was appropriated from some European settlers, many of the European farmers were encouraged to remain in the country because of their important contributions to the economy.

The forced approach to economic development has emphasized state control of the economy, forced savings, rapid industrialization, skepticism about foreign investment because of fears of neocolonialism, and in some cases provision of considerable social benefits to the mass of the population.

Two good examples of this approach are Egypt under Nasser and Ghana under Nkrumah.

Egypt

From the British occupation (1882), Egypt was a hotbed of anticolonial nationalism. The exiling of the nationalist leader, Ahmad Urabi, did not extinguish these feelings. The full force of this nationalist feeling was experienced at the conclusion of World War I. The war had made heavy demands on Egypt. Peasants and their livestock were requisitioned to serve in the Syrian campaigns against the Turks. Inflation enraged urban dwellers whose incomes did not keep pace with rising costs. By the conclusion of the war the country was seething with discontent against the British. And when the British rejected nationalist demands and exiled the nationalist leader, Saad Zaghlul, in 1919, they ignited a spark of open rebellion. Spreading outward from the cities to the countryside, the revolt involved students, civil servants, professionals, the urban proletariat, and the peasantry. Railroad and telegraph lines were torn up as people in the countryside attempted to cut their physical connections with the cities where British power was concentrated. In a few villages peasants and intellectuals proclaimed short-lived republics. From 1919 until 1924 the country was under seige. The British were finally able to restore order only by promulgating a new parliamentary constitution and conferring nominal independence on the country. But independence was encumbered with so many restrictions on Egypt's freedom of action that it was a sham.

From 1924 until Nasser's military coup d'état in 1952 the most popular political party in the country was the Wafd, which had been founded by Saad Zaghlul. In open elections it always won an impressive majority of the votes. But Britain and Egypt's theoretically constitutional monarch conspired to deny power to the Wafd. The country was usually ruled by minority parties supported by British arms. Still the failure of the Wafd to make headway discredited parliamentary democracy. New parties came into existence pledged to overthrow democratic govern-

Gamal Abdul Nasser, president of the United Arab Republic until his unexpected death in 1970. On his left is Abdul Hakim Amer, commander of the Armed Forces until his dismissal and death following the Arab-Israeli War, and Anwar Sadat, Nasser's successor.

ment. The Muslim Brotherhood created para-military organizations and fostered a climate of political violence. In this climate of political instability the military carried out a coup d'état in 1952. Its leaders deposed King Faruq, a symbol of all that was corrupt and regressive in Egypt, set aside the old constitution, and dissolved political parties. Although they promised to restore civilian and parliamentary government, they remain in power today.

The guiding force behind the coup d'état was a young Colonel, Gamal Abdel Nasser. As a youth his patriotic fervor had been fired by reading nationalist histories written by Egyptian historians. Egypt was humiliated, he felt, by continuing British colonial rule and by its defeat at the hands of the Israeli army in 1948. With other young officers he vowed to expunge corruption and set the country on a modernizing pathway. But these reforms proved more elusive than the new military leaders at first realized. The country had a half-century backlog of economic and social deficiencies. Its economy depended on a single cash crop export, cotton. The amount of land planted in cotton could only be increased through massive and expensive hydraulic works on the Nile. The Egyptian population, which had been estimated at under 3 million in 1800, was over 20 million by 1950 and continuing to grow at an alarming rate. Population densities in agricultural Egypt were heavier than in the industrialized European countries.

Nasser's efforts to cope with these obstacles drove the government into increased control of the economy. By 1961 the Egyptian state was deeply involved in nearly all sectors of the economy. The holdings of major foreign capitalists had been expropriated after the Anglo-French-Israeli invasion of 1956. The Egyptian bourgeoisie had itself been dismantled between 1958 and 1961 by a series of nationalization laws. Earlier, in 1952 the Egyptian government had intervened in the agricultural sphere and carried out a land redistribution scheme at the expense of the large landholders and in favor of the smaller peasantry. Thus in the 1960s the keys to Egyptian economic growth were central planning and an increasing emphasis on industrialization, which the Egyptian leaders believed was the only means to improve standards of living for a rapidly growing population.

Late in 1970 the world was shocked at the news of Gamal Abdel Nasser's death from a heart attack. His reign of power undoubtedly exhausted his energies. His doctors had advised him to reduce his schedule, but he had thrown himself into rebuilding the Egyptian army following its disastrous defeat in 1967. Although his latter years of rule had been tarnished by a wearying war in the Yemen, defeat by the Israelis, and a sluggish economy, the Egyptian people showed their deep affection during the funeral ceremonies. Thousands turned out to pay their respects to the man who had brought the dignity of political independence to Egypt and who had not feared to stand up against the great powers.

Nasser's successor, Anwar Sadat, had also helped bring about the coup d'état of 1952. Although he was not expected to play so dynamic a role as his predecessor, he withstood a major challenge to his authority (May 1971) and imprisoned his opponents, some of them high ranking cabinet members. Sadat still faced the problems that Nasser could not resolve: Israel, Palestinian refugees, Arab unity, and economic development.

Ghana

In Ghana, Nkrumah allowed more leeway for foreign capital, as evidenced by American financial support for the Volta River dam project. Nevertheless, he too was in favor of forcing the pace of economic change by means of active state intervention. There was a strong emphasis on industrialization. Savings were generated through the Ghana marketing boards, which operated as purchasing agencies for export commodities such as cocoa and attempted to sell the exports on the world market at higher prices than they paid to the Ghanaian farmers. In keeping with Nkrumah's philosophy of socialism, the state also sought to provide substantial welfare benefits to the people in the form of mass education and medical services.

But Nkrumah's economic system did not realize its goals. Marketing boards created deep resentment among the cocoa farmers, who felt that they were being excessively taxed for the benefit of the rest of the population. There were questionable state expenditures on foreign policy ventures, supposedly motivated by Nkrumah's commitment to Pan-African goals. The social services and the emphasis on rapid industrialization were a heavy burden on Ghana's limited resources. As world cocoa prices began to decline in the 1960s, inflation set in, and the people became discontented. The failures of Ghana's economic system were an important factor in Nkrumah's overthrow in 1966.

Modernization and Socialism

Despite their different approaches to economic change, nearly all the independent states of Africa and the Arab world have espoused socialism. Indeed, even countries with as diverse economic systems as Kenya and Ghana claimed to be socialistic. Nationalist leaders sought to broaden the base of their movements by employing socialist rhetoric and arguing that independence would bring important economic and political benefits to all segments of the population. In Africa nationalists have contended that the

The frustration and defeat sustained by the Arabs in the 1967 war with Israel brought forth a new force in Arab politics—the guerrillas—interfering in domestic Arab politics and championing the cause of the Palestinian Arabs.

sions and civil wars provided ample scope for "cold war" maneuvering. The United States practiced limited intervention during various stages of the Congo crisis, but preferred to rely on the United Nations. In the Nigerian civil war of the late 1960s the Soviet Union and Great Britain supplied the federal Nigerian government with armaments. Looming large on the horizon was the problem of the white-dominated governments of southern Africa: South Africa, Rhodesia, Southwest Africa, Mozambique, and Angola. These states were intolerable to the independent states of black Africa, many of which were prepared actively to assist liberation movements in these territories. Political instability and nationalist movements in the states of southern Africa will surely have critical repercussions on the continuation of Western influence in Africa.

SUGGESTED READINGS

Crowder, Michael, *Senegal: A Study in French Assimilation Policy.* London: 1967. Methuen Paperback.
   The best study in English of French colonialism in Africa.

Austin, Dennis, *Politics in Ghana, 1946–1960.* Oxford: 1964.
   An authoritative study of the rise of Nkrumah.

Rosberg, Carl and Nottingham, John, *The Myth of Mau Mau: Nationalism in Kenya.* New York: 1967. Praeger Paperback.

communal nature of traditional African societies, with their emphasis upon the sharing of wealth, makes them particularly receptive to a socialist way of life. Nevertheless, African and Arab socialism has remained sufficiently vague and flexible to permit many different programs of economic development.

Although the Soviet Union has served as a powerful model for economic growth, African political and economic realities are quite different from those of the Soviet Union. African states do not have highly centralized and disciplined parties with which to manipulate economic resources. Their economies are thus far poorly integrated. Because surpluses cannot be generated easily from within the economy, African states must continue to look to foreign capital. The agricultural sector remains the key to economic change because it alone is capable of producing substantial surpluses.

From Tribalism to National Integration

In addition to promoting economic growth, the political elites of independent African and Arab states grappled with the complex problems of national integration. Numerous factors divide these societies; one of the most important, especially in tropical Africa, is ethnic loyalty. Individuals regard themselves primarily as members of a tribe rather than citizens of the new states. Their first allegiance is to the Yoruba, Ibo, or Kikuyu tribes, and in the competition for political power and economic gain they struggle for their tribe rather than for the nation. In addition, the new states are troubled by urban-rural tensions, the wealthy versus the poor, the educated versus the uneducated, and the Christian versus the Muslim communities. All of these tensions are heightened by the limited economic resources of the new societies and the rivalry to control them.

There are many, of course, who are committed advocates of the new nation-states and are working to substitute national loyalties for other allegiances. Their activities still have limited appeal because the territorial units of Africa and the Middle East were largely the creation of European colonialism

and have had an existence for only a short period of time. It is not surprising that politicians fall back on other, more secure sources of unity. In the Middle East and parts of Africa, Islam is still powerful and invoked to promote unity. Even tribalism can be seen as a new stage of unity because traditionally many tribes were not politically unified. The Ibos, for instance, were fragmented into numerous small, rather autonomous political communities. The sense of "Iboness" that has prevailed in recent times is a new phenomenon and entails wider allegiances than the Ibo knew in the past. Thus tribalism could become a bridge between traditional loyalties and commitment to the nation-state. Some African and Arab spokesmen have sought to leap over the building of national unities and have called for Pan-African and Pan-Arab unity. So far, however, these appeals have fallen on deaf ears, and most of the leadership has been committed to forging national identities.

For a brief period following independence the single-party state was felt to be the solution to the manifold problems of political integration. The single party, it was argued, could promote the new symbols of national unity and undermine tribalism. There are many who still adhere to this orientation, as for instance Julius Nyerere of Tanzania, but the experience of the first decade of independence has not been a happy one in most single-party states. Far from promoting unity, the single party seemed to favor certain segments of the population at the expense of others, especially the urban dwellers, the educated, and a few powerful tribes. Other groups felt themselves to be outside the political system and consequently turned against it.

In country after country civilian government was overthrown by military regimes. The military seemed to be the only group capable of maintaining unity, although the Nigerian civil war demonstrated that the military was not free from the same factors of disunity that disrupted the rest of the country. Most African governments lack widespread popular support even now; thus frequent changes of government, coups, violence, and even civil war will probably continue for some time.

The Six-Day Arab-Israeli War of 1967 was dominated by quick military thrusts and advanced weaponry. With their tanks and planes the Israelis swept across Sinai to the Suez Canal overrunning and destroying Egyptian equipment.

CONTINUING CONFLICT IN THE MIDDLE EAST

The new nations of tropical Africa have been inward looking, for they have been concerned with the problems of nation-building. As a result, tropical Africa has been remarkably free of military conflicts between nations. The same cannot be said for the Middle East, where tension has erupted in two Arab-Israeli wars since the creation of the state of Israel in 1948. The Arabs have not recognized Israel, and at best an uneasy truce existed between these two protagonists to be shattered by two military conflicts.

Egyptian-Israeli relations have been the key to war in the Middle East because no other Arab state would undertake large-scale military operations against Israel without support from the Egyptian army, the largest in the Arab world. The 1956 war—a combined British, French, Israeli invasion of Egypt—followed President Nasser's nationalization of the Suez Canal Company, until that time a private French Company. The 1967 war came after military buildups on the Egyptian-Israeli border. In both wars the Egyptian army was decisively defeated, but in 1956 international pressures forced the Israelis, British, and French to give up their military conquests. In the second conflict the Israeli army overran a huge amount of land belonging to Egypt, Syria, and Jordan.

The 1967 war radically changed the Middle Eastern political situation. The Israelis occupied extensive territories with a large Arab population, and a new refugee group had been created. What the Israelis in-

tended to do with these territories was unclear, but if they hoped to trade them for concessions, such as the end of belligerency, recognition of Israel, and navigational rights through the Suez Canal and the Gulf of Aqaba, no Arab leaders came forward for the negotiations. In fact, the Israeli government was divided over the occupied Arab territories, for there were important advantages and disadvantages involved in holding them. Their retention gave Israel more defensible frontiers, but their occupation entailed the governing of a large and potentially hostile Arab population, particularly on the left bank of the Jordan River.

The defeat in 1967 created confusion in the Arab world and another step toward political radicalization. The popularity of Nasser and King Husayn of Jordan was weakened. Vigorous guerrilla organizations, the best known being *al-Fatah*, became powerful as a result of the war and endeavored to use terrorism and the support of the friendly Arab peoples in the occupied territories against the Israelis. The guerrillas acquired extraordinary popularity among the Arab peoples, and within Jordan they became virtually a state within a state. Although the Israeli army either destroyed or captured a great deal of Arab military equipment, the Soviet Union rearmed its two chief allies—Egypt and Syria. The Israelis and Arabs faced each other again, suspicious and heavily armed just below the nuclear weapons level.

The Soviet Union has exploited anti-Western and anti-Israeli feeling to make considerable diplomatic gains with the Arabs. Egypt sells most of its cotton crop to Soviet-bloc countries, and its army is equipped with Soviet weaponry. Syria and Iraq look to the Russians for military assistance. In Jordan, King Husayn has tried to maintain his pro-Western orientation, but in the face of much criticism.

The Arab-Israeli situation was a bleak one. Time seemed to be running out. The Arab peoples and their rulers regarded Israel as an imperialist state, and the new guerrilla groups and radical political leaders vowed to overturn Israel and restore the old Palestinian entity. It was increasingly difficult for moderate Arab leaders to negotiate a compromise treaty with Israel in the face of these

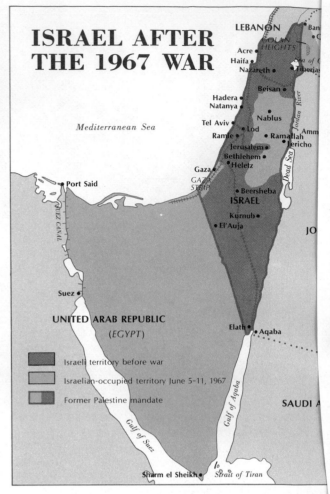

ISRAEL AFTER THE 1967 WAR

LEBANON
Acre
Haifa
Nazareth
GOLAN HEIGHTS
Hadera
Natanya
Tel Aviv
Ramle
Lod
Nablus
Jerusalem
Bethlehem
Heletz
Ramallah
Jericho
Gaza
GAZA STRIP
Beersheba
ISRAEL
Kurnub
El'Auja
Mediterranean Sea
Port Said
Suez
UNITED ARAB REPUBLIC (EGYPT)
Elath
Aqaba
SAUDI A
Sharm el Sheikh
Strait of Tiran
Gulf of Suez
Gulf of Aqaba

Israeli territory before war
Israelian-occupied territory June 5-11, 1967
Former Palestine mandate

radical elements and the existence of refugee groups. Israeli leaders were also growing concerned about the value of negotiated settlements with unstable governments. They were suspicious of international guarantees of their territorial integrity. Many felt that they must rely on their own military might and questioned the value of returning any territory to the Arabs for paper concessions. At the same time Arabs and Israelis continued to arm themselves with the latest equipment provided by the United States and the Soviet Union.

Tropical Africa had been somewhat more insulated than the Arab world from "cold war" tensions. Nevertheless, internal divi-

Although the title suggests that the book is about Mau Mau, in reality it is a perceptive account of the rise of Kenya nationalism culminating in the Mau Mau revolt.

Gallagher, Charles F., *The United States and North Africa: Morocco, Algeria, and Tunisia*. Cambridge, Mass.: 1963.
Most of the best literature on North Africa is in French, but this book is a handy introduction.

Young, W. Crawford, *Politics in the Congo: Decolonization and Independence*. Princeton: 1965. Princeton Paperback.
A masterful analysis of one of the most complex decolonization stories in Africa.

Coleman, James S., *Nigeria: Background to Nationalism*. Berkeley: 1963.
One of the first studies of the growth of nationalism in Africa, and in many ways one of the best.

Hodgkin, Thomas, *Nationalism in Colonial Africa*. New York: New York University Press, n d. Paperback
The major themes and movements in African nationalism are examined.

Little, Kenneth, *West African Urbanization: A Study of Voluntary Associations in Social Change*. Cambridge: 1965. Cambridge Paperback.
Clear exposition of the problems that face the new urban dwellers and their efforts to solve these problems.

Lacouture, Jean and Simone, *Egypt in Transition*. New York: 1958.
Although this was one of the first books on Nasser's Egypt, few others have had the sympathetic grasp of modern Egyptian history.

The reader is also referred to the bibliography at the end of Chapter 20 where the standard area histories are listed.

ILLUSTRATION CREDITS

CHAPTER 1 From J. Augusta and Z. Burian, *Prehistoric Man.* Courtesy Paul Hamlyn (Holdings) Ltd. 10 Musee de L'Homme, Paris 11 Department of Antiquities, Ashmolean Museum 14 (Left) Department of Antiquities, Ashmolean Museum 14 (Right) British Museum 19 New York Public Library 22 Marburg/Art Reference Bureau 27 (Left) Marburg/Art Reference Bureau 27 (Right) Art Reference Bureau 33 British Museum 36 Courtesy of the Oriental Institute, University of Chicago 39

CHAPTER 2 National Museum of Pakistan, Karachi 47 National Museum, New Delhi 48 From E. O. Reischauer and J. K. Fairbank, *A History of East Asian Civilization,* Vol. I. Courtesy Houghton Mifflin Co. 55 British Museum 57 Collection of the National Palace Museum, Taipei, Taiwan, Republic of China 60 Marc and Evelyne Bernheim/Rapho Guillumette 67 Saunders/Monkmeyer 68

CHAPTER 3 Raghubir Singh/Nancy Palmer Agency 76 Giraudon 77 Burt Glinn/Magnum 78 Japan Airlines 79 New York Public Library 80 Collection of William Rockhill Nelson Gallery of Art, Kansas City, Mo. 86 Rene Burri/Magnum 90 Royal Ontario Museum, Toronto 95

CHAPTER 4 Marburg/Art Reference Bureau 105 British Museum 117 Staatliche Museen, Berlin 123 Camera Press/Pix 129 Alinari/Art Reference Bureau 130 Marburg/Art Reference Bureau 131 Alinari/Art Reference Bureau 132 Marburg/Art Reference Bureau 133 Metropolitan Museum of Art, Rogers Fund, 1909 135

CHAPTER 5 Alinari/Art Reference Bureau 142 Alinari/Art Reference Bureau 145 Alinari/Art Reference Bureau 147 Anderson/Art Reference Bureau 149 Vatican Museum 151 Alinari/Art Reference Bureau 152 Anderson/Art Reference Bureau 153 Alinari/Art Reference Bureau 158 Art Reference Bureau 161 Alinari/Art Reference Bureau 167

CHAPTER 6 Marburg/Art Reference Bureau 187 (Left) Anderson/Art Reference Bureau 187 (Right) Alinari/Art Reference Bureau 188 New York Public Library 196 The Metropolitan Museum of Art, Rogers Fund, 1933. 197 Anderson/Art Reference Bureau 198

Roger Viollet 199 Bibliotheque Nationale, Paris 203 Marburg/Art Reference Bureau 204 Alinari/Art Reference Bureau 205 Kunsthistorische Museum 212

CHAPTER 7 Indian Government Tourist Office 220 Indian Government Tourist Office 222 Leonard Von Matt/Rapho Guillumette 229 Eastfoto 232 J. Allan Cash/Rapho Guillumette 233 Consulate General of Japan, New York 235 Sesshu/National Museum, Tokyo 239

CHAPTER 8 Staatsbibliothek, Munich 253 French Embassy Press & Information Division 261 Metropolitan Museum of Art 262 (Left) New York Public Library 262 (Right) Alinari/Art Reference Bureau 264 Alinari/Art Reference Bureau 265 Marburg/Art Reference Bureau 266 (Left) Marburg/Art Reference Bureau 266 (Right) Bibliotheque Nationale, Paris 267 Alinari/Art Reference Bureau 269 Brogi/Art Reference Bureau 270 (Left) Brogi/Art Reference Bureau 270 (Right)

CHAPTER 9 Pix 284 Bibliotheque Nationale, Paris 290 (Bottom right) Marburg/Art Reference Bureau 290 (Top left) Marburg/Art Reference Bureau 290 (Bottom left) Marburg/Art Reference Bureau 291 (Top left) The Cleveland Museum of Art, from J. H. Wade Fund, Bequest of Leonard C. Hanna Jr. 291 (Top right) Alinari/Art Reference Bureau 291 (Bottom) The Metropolitan Museum of Art, Gift of J. Pierpont Morgan, 1917 293 Bibliotheque Nationale, Paris 294 (Top) Bibliotheque Nationale, Paris 294 (Bottom)

CHAPTER 10 Alinari 304 Staatliche Kunstsammlungen, Dresden 305 Radio Times Hulton Picture Library 307 Bibliotheque Nationale, Paris 308 Bibliotheque Nationale, Paris 310 British Museum 318 Photo Ullstein 320 National Museum, Stockholm 325 Courtesy of The Hispanic Society of America, New York 327 Museum des Beaux Arts, Lausanne 330

CHAPTER 11 New York Public Library 336 National Maritime Museum 340 New York Public Library 342 The Granger Collection 343 New York Public Library 344 Culver Pictures 346 Culver Pictures 348 New York Public Library 356 Culver Pictures 359 Historical Pictures Service, Chicago 361

CHAPTER 29 Marc & Evelyn Bernheim/Rapho

Guillumette 875 Camera Press/Pix 880 Gilles
Caron-Gamma/Pix 881 Camera Press/Pix 884
Camera Press/Pix 887 Bill Vaughn/Black Star 891
Charles Harbutt/Magnum 894 Bruno Barbey/
Magnum 896

Cambodia, U.S. invasion of, 868
Cambyses, 38, 39
Canaanite civilization, 3, 7
Canada, French settlement of, 341–343; French and Indian War and, 343–345; before World War II (1815–1914), 506; and British Commonwealth, before World War II, 682; postwar political trends in, 791–793; and French-speaking populace, 792
Canadian Pacific Railroad, 508
Canning, Lord, in India, 577
Cape Mycale, Battle of, 115
Capet, Hugh, 208
Capetian kings, 259–262
Capitalism, 2, 321; rise of (thirteenth to sixteenth century), 320–322; in Marxist theory, 441
Cárdenas, Lázaro, Mexican president, 814, 815
Caribs (Indians), 69–70
Carlsbad Decrees (1819), 432
Carnegie, Andrew, 495
Carnot, Marie François Sadi, 460
Carolingian age, 202–206, 208, 209, 210; rise of Charlemagne and, 202–203; technological innovations in, 203–205; culture of, 205–206; partition of empire in, 206, 207, 211
Carranza, Venustiano, Mexican ruler, 813
Cartels, growth of, in Western Europe, 455
Cartesian philosophy, 371–374, 377, 381
Carthage, 141, 193; in Punic Wars, 145, 146, 605–606
Cartwright, Edmund, inventor, 433
Cassiodorus, 173
Cassius, 150
Castiglione, Baldassare di, 306, 307
Castile, conquest of Moors by, 247; union of, with Aragon, 281
Castillo, Ramón, Argentine leader, 529, 831
Castro, Cipriano, 527
Castro, Fidel, 780, 819–820, 823, 825, 830, 831, 837
Castro, Raúl, 819
Catherine of Aragon, 312
Catherine the Great (of Russia), 354, 357–358, 360, 361, 403
Catholicism, Luther and (indulgence controversy), 310–311; Counter-Reformation and, 314–315; and Hapsburg Austrian monarchy, 351; in eighteenth-century China, 557; in Bismarck's Germany, 463; in French Third Republic, 466; in colonial Latin America, 514–516; in nineteenth-century Latin America, 536; Mussolini and, 709–710; in postwar era, 809. See also Inquisition; Papacy
Cato, 146
Caudillos, in Latin America, 524–530
Cavaliers (England), 392
Cavour, Camillo Benso di, 447
Central America, in twentieth century, 815–818
Central Europe, under Old Regime, 348–362; War of the Austrian Succession, and 358; Seven Years' War and, 359–360; Napoleonic wars and, 417–419; nationalistic movements in (in nineteenth century), 446–447; modernization and population growth in (after 1850), 454; World War I and, 471–476, 638–641, 653–654; see also Austria
Central Powers (Germany and Austria), in World War I, 640, 651
Centuriate Assembly (Rome), 143, 144
Cervantes, Miguel de, 309
Ceylon, 75, 76
Chaeronea, Battle of, 119
Chagall, Marc, 701, 702

Chakravartin (Universal Emperor), 74, 75
Chamberlain, Houston Stewart, propagandist, 461
Chamberlain, Neville, 680; and Munich conference, 749–751
Champlain, Samuel de, 315
Ch'an Buddhism, 97–98, 234; in Japan, 238–239
Chandragupta II, 77
Chandragupta Maurya, 74
Chang Chih-tung, 575
Charlemagne, 181, 202–206, 209, 212, 264; see also Carolingian age
Charles (Dauphin of France), 279
Charles, Emperor (Hapsburg), 645
Charles I (England), 393
Charles II (England), 392, 393
Charles II (Spain), 338
Charles V (France), 279–280
Charles V (Holy Roman Emperor), 311, 511
Charles VI (Holy Roman Emperor), 351
Charles VI, the Mad (France), 280
Charles VII (France), 278, 280, 285
Charles X (France), 443
Charles XII (Sweden), 356
Chartist movement, 442
Chateaubriand, François René de, 428
Chaucer, Geoffrey, 292
Cheka, 657
Chemistry, in late nineteenth century, 460–461
Cheng Ho, 232, 233
Ch'en Yun, 858
Chiang Kai-shek, 774, 851; early rivalry of, with Communists, 739–743; in United Front, during Japanese aggression, 744–745, 764; in postwar era, 775–776; and Taiwan, 848, 850, 864
Ch'ien-lung, Emperor, 557, 558, 559
Chikamatsu, 568
Chile, 528; independence of, from Spain, 521; failure of self-rule in, 523; era of stability in (1830–1900), 532; in twentieth century, 828–830; Allende Marxist government of, 829–830
China, 2, 3, 6, 7, 71, 88–89, 178, 308; in Stone Age (Yang Shao and Lung Shan cultures), 54–55; Hsia dynasty, 55; Shang dynasty, 55–57; Chou dynasty, 57–64; Eastern Chou period, 58–60; Ch'in empire, 64, 89–90, 224; early Confucianism in, 88–89, 91–93, 95–97; Han dynasties, 3, 91–95, 224; Hsin (New) dynasty, 94; later Han dynasty, 95; Buddhism in 96–98, 224, 226; period of disunity in (A.D. 220–589), 95–96; influences of, in Asia (to 700 A.D.), 98, 100; Sui dynasty, 224; T'ang dynasty, 224–226, 227, 228; Sung dynasty and north-south split, 226–229; Mongol domination of, 178, 230–231; Yuan dynasty (Mongol), 230; Ming dynasty and centralized power, 231–234; Manchu dynasty (Ch'ing), 234, 555–558, 573–576; eighteenth-century European contacts with, 557, 558; European trade with, 558–563; Opium Wars and, 560–563, 564; Taiping rebellion in, 563–564, 573–574; T'ung-chih restoration (Self-Strengthening Movement, 1863–1874), 573–576; French competition with, in Vietnam (1884–1885), 592–593; imperialism of, in Vietnam, 593; Sino-Japanese War and (1894–1895), 594–595; European and U.S. interventions in, 595–599; Boxer Rebellion in, 597–598; democratic reforms in (1905–1910), 599; Revolution of 1911 and founding of Republic, 599–601; World War I and, 655, 737; Japanese aggression in, 737; May Fourth Movement in (1919), 737–739; Kuomintang and, in 1920s,

Convention People's Party (CPP), Ghana, 876–877, 878
Coolidge, Calvin, 685
Copernicus, Nicholas, 368; see also Scientific revolution
"Copperheads," 492
Cordova, 198; caliphate of, 247, 248
Corinth, 117
Corn Laws, England, 441
Cornwallis, General Charles, 397, 550
Corpus Juris Civilis (Justinian's civil law), 185
Cortés, Hernando, 65, 66, 315
Cortines, Adolfo Ruiz, 814
Cossacks, 356
Costa Rica, in nineteenth century, 525; in twentieth century, 817, 818
Counter-Reformation, 314–315; Jesuits and, 314; Council of Trent and, 314–315
Court of the Star Chamber, 326
Cranmer, Thomas, 312
Crassus, 149
Crecy, Battle of, 279
Cretan civilization, see Minoan civilization
Crimean War, 449, 450, 458, 621
Croce, Benedetto, 717
Croesus (of Lydia), 37–38
Cro-Magnon man, 10, 11, 14
Crompton, Samuel, inventor, 433
Cromwell, Oliver, 375, 391; and Puritan revolution, 392
Cromwell, Richard, 392
Cromwell, Thomas, 312, 326
Crusader States (Near East, thirteenth century), 248, 249
Crusades, 247–248, 251, 263
Cuba, 500, 501, 526; and Spanish-American War, 526–527; to World War II, 818–819; Batista regime in, 819; under Castro, 819–820
Cuban missile crisis, 786, 819
Cultural Revolution (1966–1969), China, 860–861
Culture System (Dutch economic policy, in Indonesia), 549, 590
Cuneiform writing, 15, 34, 40
Cuno, Wilhelm, 712
Curzon, Lord, 585
Cynics (Greek philosophers), 136, 137
Cyril, Byzantine cleric, 189
Cyrus the Great, 37, 38, 39, 114
Czechoslovakia, 275, 660; emergence of, after World War I, 653, 654, 661; and Munich Pact, 749–750; and World War II, 768; under Soviet domination, 803, 805
Czernin, Count Ottokar, 651

Daladier, Edouard, and Munich conference, 749–751
Dalai Lama, 852
d'Alembert, Jean le Rond, 381
Dalhousie, Lord (in India), 553, 554
Dalton, John (scientist), 461
D'Annunzio, Gabriele, 706, 709
Dante, Alighieri, 265–266, 270
Danton, Georges Jacques, 408
Dara, Shukoh, 544
D'Argenlieu, Admiral, 851
Darius I, 38–40, 74; and Persian Empire, 39–40, 114; and Persian Wars, 115
Darwin, Charles, 121, 461
Darwinism, 461, 536
David, 41
da Vinci, Leonardo, 306
Davis, Jefferson, 494
Debray, Régis, 828
Declaration of Independence, 377, 387, 388, 396, 479

Declaration of the Rights of Man and the Citizen (French Revolution), 407
Defoe, Daniel, 365
De Gaulle, Charles, General, 787, 809; in resistance, 770; and Allied war settlements, 772–773; in Fifth Republic, 798–799; and colonies, 872, 885
de Gribeauval, Jean-Baptiste Vaquette, 365
Delacroix, Eugène de, 428
de las Casas, Bartolomé, 512
de Lattre de Tassigny, Marshal, 851
Delcassé, Théophile (French minister), 472
Delhi sultanate, 217–218, 223
Delian League, 116
Delos, 116
Demeter, 104, 107, 121, 136
Democratic party, 485, 490, 499, 504
Democratic Republic of North Korea, 850, 851
Democratic Republic of Vietnam (North Vietnam), founding of (in World War II), 771; United States war and, 861, 864
Democritus, 122
de Molina, Tirso, 374
Denmark, 469; ninth-century invasions by, 207, 208; social legislation of in 1930s, 689
Depression (1929), see Great Depression
Descartes, René, 370–374, 375; see also Cartesian philosophy
Dessalines, Jean-Jacques, 522
Destour (early independence movement in Tunisia), 877–878
Dewey, Admiral, 597
Dewey, John, 679
Dharma (Hinduism), 82, 83, 84, 87
Diáz, Porfirio, 534–535, 812
Diáz Ordaz, Gustaro (Mexican president), 815
Diderot, Denis, 381, 388
Diefenbaker, John, 792
Diem, Ngo Dinh, 864, 865, 866
Dien Bien Phu, 851
Dingiswayo (African leader), 613
Din Illahi, 220
Diocletian, 163, 167, 171, 184; reforms of, 165–166
Diogenes, 136
Dionysus, 107, 121, 127, 136
Directory (post-Revolutionary French government), 411–412, 414
Disraeli, Benjamin, 442, 463
Djoser, 30
Doctors of Latin Church, 168–170, 172
"Dollar diplomacy," 812
Dolliver, Jonathan, 504
Domesday Book (1086), 257
Dominican order, 263, 268
Dominican Republic, under Trujillo, 821; United States intervention in (1965), 822
Donatello, 304
Dong, Phan Van, 864
Dorian Greeks, 105, 106, 111
Douglas, Stephen, 489, 490
Drake, Francis, 320, 516
Dravida Munnetra, Kazhagam (Indian political party), 853
Drew, Daniel, 495
Dreyfus affair, 457. 466
Dual Monarchy (Austria), 645, 653
Duong Van Minh, General, 866
Dupleix, Joseph François, 347
Dupont de Nemours, Pierre-Samuel, 384n
Durham, Lord, 507
Dutch East India Company, 367, 549, 617

Dutch Reformed Church, and South Africa, 617
Dutch War (1672–1678), 338
Duvalier, Francois, 821
Dyaus-piter, 49

Eastern Europe, under Old Regime, 348–362;
    modernization and population increase of (after
    1850), 454; World War I and, 638–641, 653–654;
    postwar economic slump of, 670–673; failure of
    postwar democracies in, 719–720; in World War II,
    758–759; postwar diplomatic settlements regarding,
    774; and Soviet satellites, 785, 803–805. See also
    Russia; Poland; and other countries
Eastern Roman Empire, see Byzantine Empire
East India Company, 347
East Indies, under Dutch rule (eleventh and nineteeth
    centuries), 548–549
Ebert, Friedrich, 659
Echevarría Alvarez, Luis, 815
Eckhart, Meister, 274
Economics, liberalism and, 438–439; free trade and,
    384–385, 454, 455
Ecuador, 524; independence of from Spain, 521; under
    dictators, 527–528; in twentieth century, 826
Edict of Nantes, 330–331; revoking of, 337
Education, public (in modern Western nations),
    678–679
Edward I (England), 257, 259, 274, 277
Edward II (England), 277
Edward III (England), 278
Edward IV (England), 279
Egypt, 3, 6, 13, 35, 40, 43; Old Kingdom, 29–31;
    Middle Kingdom, 31–32; New Kingdom, 32–33;
    Saite Dynasty, 33, 36; religions of, 27–29, 32–33;
    Islamic conquests in, 192, 193, 197; under Mamluk
    Turkish rule, 251, 605, 617; under Muhammad Ali
    (1805–1848), 617–619; decline under Ismael
    (1863–1879), 619–620; British occupation of, 620,
    622–624; nationalism of in World War I, 722, 890;
    unstable period of (1924–1952), 890–891; under
    Nasser, 891–892
Einstein, Albert, 461–462, 717
Eisenhower, Dwight D., in World War II, 758;
    Presidency of, 790
Electoral college, 484
Elector of the Palatinate, 313
Eleusinian Mysteries, 107
El Greco, 374
Eliot, T. S., 678
Elizabeth, Empress of Russia (1741–1762), 358, 359
Elizabeth I (England), 312, 326, 329, 390
El Salvador, 525, 817, 818
Emancipation Proclamation, 492, 493
Empiricism, 289, 373–374
Encyclopedia (philosophes), 379, 381
Engels, Friedrich, 440, 441, 460
England, Christian conversion of, 202, 207; Alfred and
    Danish invaders, 207–208, 209; Norman conquest
    and growing consolidation of, 257; loss of French
    territory (Angevin Empire) by, 257, 261; Magna Carta
    and rise of Parliament (thirteenth century), 257–259;
    prominence in of House of Commons (fourteenth
    century), 277; in Hundred Years' War, 277–278;
    Wars of the Roses in, 278–279; Reformation in
    (under Henry VIII), 312; New World exploration by,
    319–320; under rule of Henry VIII, 326, 390–391;
    under Elizabeth I, 329; and Spanish Armada, 329;
    Stuarts, 391, 392–394; civil war and Cromwellian
    revolution, 391–392; Restoration, 392–393;

"Glorious Revolution" (1688), 393–394; New World
    colonies of, 339–343, 344–346; conquests in French
    and Indian War, 343–345; War of Austrian
    Succession and, 358; Seven Years' War and,
    358–360; and American Revolution, 395–397; and
    Napoleonic wars, 416–417; and Congress System
    (alliances, 1815–1828), 430; Industrial Revolution
    in, 433–434; social and political reforms in
    (1830–1867), 441–442, 462–463; Education Act of
    1870 and spread of literacy in, 455–456, Panic of
    1873 (resulting in cartels and tariffs), 454–455; under
    Disraeli, 462; and World War I, 472–476, 635–645,
    650–655; political events between the wars,
    679–681; Munich Pact and, 748–751; and World
    War II, 751–758, 765–770; Battle of Britain
    (1939–1940), 752–753; domestic wartime events in,
    765–766; and diplomatic war settlement, 772–775;
    and Cold War, 784–787; postwar political and social
    developments of, 797–798; see also British Empire
English East India Company, 347, 367, 396, 549, 550,
    550, 553, 558, 559, 576, 591, 627; and Opium
    Wars, 560–563
English Peasants' Revolt (1381), 287
Enlightened despots, in Central and Eastern Europe,
    402–403; in France, 403
Enlightenment, 377–385, 388, 402, 438, 455; social
    and cultural background of, 378–381; the
    philosophes and, 381–385
Entente Cordiale (France, England), 472–473, 476
Entrepreneur system (in Western Europe), 323
Epicureanism, 137
Erasmus, 274
Eratosthenes, 138
Erie Canal, 483
Estates General, 279; French Revolution and, 403, 405
Ethiopia, Italian conquest of (1935–1936), 710
Etruscans, 142; fall of, 144
Euclid, 138
Eugene of Savoy, Prince, 350
Euripides, 127, 128
Europe, see Western Europe
European Economic Community (Common Market),
    784–785, 796
Eusebius, 168
Evans, Sir Arthur, 103
Evolution, theory of, 461; see also Darwinism

Fabian Society, 463
Fa-hsien, 77, 78, 97
Faisal, 888
Farmers' Alliance, 499
Farouk, King, 891
Fascism, 707; under Mussolini, 706–710, 716–717;
    and Nazi Germany, 713–717
Fatimid dynasty, 193, 197
Federal German Republic (West Germany), 785, 798
Federalists, 479, 485
Federal Reserve System, 503, 687
Federal Trade Commission Act, 503
Ferdinand I (Austrian Emperor), 445, 446
Ferdinand II, Emperor, 333
Ferdinand III, Emperor, 332
Ferdinand VII (Spain), 519, 520, 521
Ferdinand (of Aragon), 281, 326, 327, 331
Ferry, Jules, 466, 592
Feudalism, 2, 210, 246; rise of in France, 208–211; in
    Japan, 210, 237; in England, 257–259; end of, 287
Fichte, Johann Gottlieb, 432
Ficino, Marsilio, 289
Fielding, Henry, 379

late Middle Ages, 282; and Lutheran reformation, 309–312; Thirty Years' War, division of German realm, and, 331–333; after Congress of Vienna (1815), 419; unification movement in (late nineteenth century), 446, 447–449; Franco-Prussian War and, 448–449; Panic of 1873, growth of cartels and tariffs, and, 454–455; under Bismarck, 458–459, 463–464, 471–472; social reforms in, under Kaiser William II, 464–465, 472; prewar developments in, 471–476; African colonies of, 622–624, 626–627, 629; in World War I, 635–645, 650–654; postwar leftist movements in, 659–660; Weimar Republic, 659, 710–713; treaty with Soviet Russia (1922), 697; under Nazism, 713–717; Munich Pact and, 748–751; World War II and, 751–758, 765–770; wartime occupation and annexation by, in Europe, 768; wartime atrocities by, 768–769; Allied occupation of, 773; postwar partition of, 785; *see also* Federal German Republic; German Democratic Republic

Gerson, John, 289
Ghana, as colony (Gold Coast), 611, 872, 873; independence movement of, 871, 876–877; decolonization of, 878–880; nationhood of, 892
Ghent, Treaty of, 399
Giap, Vo Nguyen, 850, 851, 864, 866
Gibbon, Edward, 383
Gilgamesh, 17, 20–21
Giolitti, Giovanni, 661
Girondists, 410, 411
Glorious Revolution (England), 393–394
Gneisenau, Neithardt von, 417
Gnostics (Christian heresy), 161, 184
Goa, Nehru's seizure of, 843
Goering, Hermann, 752
Goethals, George W., 816
Goethe, Johann Wolfgang von, 379, 428
Gokhale, G. K., 585
Gold Coast, *see* Ghana
Golden Bull (1356), 282
Gomez, Vicente, 527, 823
Gomulka, Wladyslaw, 803
Good Neighbor Policy, 812
Gordon, Charles George, 564, 626
Gorgas, Dr. William C., 816
Gorki, Maxim, 701
Gothic art and architecture, 266–268; late forms (Flamboyant), 290–291, 293–294
Goulart, João, Brazilian leader, 836
Gould, Jay, 495
Gracchus, Tiberius and Gaius, 147–148
Grace, Michael and W. R., 529
Granada, Muslim state of, 280, 281
Grange, the, 499
Grant, Ulysses S., 491, 492, 494
Great Britain, *see* British Empire; England
Great Depression, 675–676, 682, 684, 686, 694; Germany and, 713
Greater East Asia Co-Prosperity Sphere (Japanese-occupied Pacific in World War II), 771
Great Khan (Khubilai), 230, 231, 251
Great Leap Forward (1957–1958), China, 856–859
Great Ordinance, 279
Great Purge, Soviet Union (1934–1939), 703–705
Greece, independence struggle of (nineteenth century), 430, 432, 474; World War I and, 661; World War II and, 754; Communism, civil war, and, 785
Greek civilization, 103–139; Minoan civilization and, 104–105; Mycenaeans and, 105–106; Dorian era,

106; Homeric era, 106–107; polis (city-state) and, 107–108; colonization by (750–550 B.C.), 108–109, 141–142; age of Tyrants (650–550 B.C.), 109–111; Athenian ascendancy and, 112–114, 144; Persian Wars and, 114–116; Athenian Empire, 116–118; Peloponnesian War, 117–118; decline of polis, 119–120; Ionian culture and, 120–121; Pythagorean School and, 121–122, 125, 126; classical philosophy and, 122–126; Periclean age and culture, 126–130, 157; Hellenistic age, 131–139; conquests of Alexander and, 131–133; Successor States and, 133–135; Roman conquest and, 145, 146
Gregory (the Great), Pope, 202
Gregory VII, Pope, 254, 256, 263
Gregory XI, Pope, 275
Grey, Lord Charles, 441
Groot, Gerard, 274
Gropius, Walter, 717
Grosseteste, Robert, 270, 289
Guarani (Indians), 69
Guarino, Battista, 304
Guatemala, dictatorships in (1838–1920), 525; postwar leftist regime and foreign intervention in, 815–816
Guevara, Ernest "Che," 819, 820, 828
Guinea, decolonization of, 880
Gunpowder, 365
Gupta Empire, India, 73, 77–79
Gustav III (Sweden), 402
Guzmán Blanco, Antonio, 527

Hadrian, 153, 154, 156
Haiti, liberation and early attempts at self-rule of, 522–523, 525; as U.S. protectorate, 526; in twentieth century, 820–821
Hamilton, Alexander, 399, 402, 483
Hammurabi, 22, 46; Code of, 22–24
Han dynasties, 3, 91–95, 224; Confucianism and, 91–93; under Liu Pang, 91–92; under Wu Ti, 93; under Wang Mang, 93–95; Later Han Dynasty, 95
Han-fei-tzu, 64
Hannibal, 145, 606
Hanovers, 394
Hanseatic League, 245, 250
Hapsburgs, 314, 328, 331, 338, 645; Austrian monarchy and (eighteenth century), 350–351
Hardenberg, Karl August, 418
Hardie, Keir, Scottish union leader, 463
Harding, Warren G., 684–685, 694
Harris, Townsend, 584
Harsha (Indian ruler), 78, 215
Harun-al-Rashid, 196, 197, 198
Hasan al-Banna, 876
Hastings, Lord Warren, 550, 552
Hastings, Battle of, 257
Hausa people, Africa, 613
Hawaii, 501
Hawkins, John, 320
Haya de la Torre, Victor Raul, Peruvian leader, 826, 827
Hayes, Rutherford B., 494
Hayford, J. Casely, West African leader, 873
Hebrews, 7, 34, 40–43; beginnings of, 40–41; settlement of, 41–42; religion of, 41–42; in captivity, 42. *See also* Jews: Judaism
Hegel, Georg W. F., 440
Hegira, 191
Hellenistic age, 131–139, 146, 147; cosmopolitanism of, 134–135; religion and philosophy in, 135–137; science in, 137–138; Rome and, 146–147; Christianity and, 159–162

Monk, George, 392
Monophysites (Egyptian sect), 184, 186, 192
Monotheism, 33, 42, 43, 126, 191
Monroe, James, 483
Monroe Doctrine, 501, 519
Montagu, Edwin, 724
Montaigne, Michel de, 309
Montcalm, Marquis of, 343, 344
Montesquieu, 381, 383, 387
Monteverdi, 374
Montezuma II, 66
Montgomery, General Sir Bernard, 757, 758
Moors, defeat of, in Spain (thirteenth century), 247
Morazán, Francisco, 522
Morelos, José Maria, 520
Moreno, Garcia, Ecuadoran leader, 826
Morgan, Henry, 516
Morgan, J. P., 496
Morocco, European imperialism and (to 1914), 474,
   605–606
Moscow Pact (Hitler-Stalin nonaggression treaty), 705,
   706, 750, 751
Moses, 41
Moshweshwe, African leader, 614
Mo-tzu, 61–62, 63, 64
"Muckraking," 503
Mughal Empire, 216, 219–223, 346, 543–548; Akbar
   and successors, 220–221, 543; culture of, 221;
   Sikhism and, 221–223; seventeenth-century Islamic
   resurgence and, 543–544; southern conquests by
   Aurangzeb, 544–546; disintegration of, 546–548
Muhammad Ali, Egyptian ruler, 617–619, 620, 621
Muhammad Shah, 546
Muhammed of Ghur, 217
Mu Jen, Chinese poet, 845
Munich Pact (1938), 749–750
Muñoz Marín, Luis, Puerto Rican leader, 822
Murad, Ottoman ruler, 605
Murasaki, Lady, Japanese novelist, 236
Muslim League, 729–730, 733
Muslims, see Islamic civilization
Mussolini, 670, 696, 714, 831; rule of, 706–710;
   culture under regime of, 717; World War II and, 749,
   750, 754, 758; defeat and death of, 769–770
Mycenaean Greeks, 105–106
Mysticism, 289; in Hellenistic world, 158; in Roman
   Empire, 158; Christianity and, 162; in Byzantine
   religion, 186
Myths, 16; Egyptian, 29; Chinese, 55

Nabodinus (of Babylonia), 37, 38
Nagy, Imre, 804, 805
Napier, John, 369
Napoleon, 390, 408, 412, 413, 427, 429, 455, 458;
   Napoleonic era and, 414–417, 431–432, 445; defeat
   of, 428, 429, 431, 441, 443, 449; Spain and,
   519–520; Egypt and, 617
Napoleon III, 591; Second Empire under, 443–444,
   448, 449, 458, 459, 534
Napoleonic Civil Code, 415–416, 417
Narmer, King (Egypt), 27
Nasser, Abdel Gamal, 780, 787, 890; reign of, 891–892
Nationalism, in nineteenth century, 424, 425, 431, 432;
   origins of, 431–432; Revolutions of 1848 and,
   458–459, 461; World War I and, 476; African
   colonial independence and, 872–878
National Liberation Front (Vietnam), 864, 865
Natural rights (doctrine of), 377
Nazism, rise of Hitler and, 713–714; economic and

industrial programs under, 714–715; culture of,
   716–717
Neanderthal man, 9, 10–11
Near East, see Middle East
Nebuchadnezzar II, 36
Nehru, Jawaharlal, 728, 844, 854; as Indian prime
   minister, 841–843; neutralism of, 843; war with
   China and, 851, 852–853
Neo-Babylonian Empire, 36–37
Neo-Confucianism, 97, 228–229
Neolithic Age, 12–13; agriculture in, 12–13; peasant
   societies in, 13
Neo-Platonism, 162, 169, 197; in late Middle Ages,
   289, 292
Nero, 153, 156, 163
Nerva, Roman emperor, 153
Nestorian Christianity, 224, 226
Netherlands, revolt against Spain by (sixteenth century),
   328–329; mercantilism and (seventeenth and
   eighteenth centuries), 340–341; founded by
   Congress of Vienna, 419; conquest and rule of East
   Indies (Indonesia) by, 548–549, 590; in Great
   Depression, 689; Indonesian independence
   movement and, 735–736; World War II and, 751
Nevsky, Alexander, 251, 252
New Deal, 686–689
New Economic Policy (Soviet Union, 1921), 697–698
Ne Win, General, Burmese leader, 848
Newspapers, growth of, in late-nineteenth-century
   Europe, 456–457; intellectuals and, 457
Newton, Sir Isaac, 372–374, 380, 381, 388, 460, 461
New World explorations, 315–319; by Spain and
   Portugal, 281, 282, 317–319
New Zealand, British Commonwealth and, 682
Ngo Dinh Diem, 864, 865, 866
Nguni peoples, Africa, 613
Nguyen Ai Quoc (Ho Chi Minh), 735–736
Nhu, family of Ngo Dinh Diem, 864, 866
Nicaea, Council of, 167, 168
Nicaragua, in nineteenth century, 525; in twentieth
   century, 816
Nichiren, 238
Nicholas I, Tsar, 449, 595
Nicholas II, Tsar, 467, 468, 645
Nicholas of Cusa, 276, 289, 292
Nietzsche, Friedrich, 462
Nigeria, 615, 622; early history of, 606–607, 610, 611;
   decolonization of, 874, 880–881; Ibos in, civil war
   and, 881–882
Nirvana, 54, 81, 96
Nitti, Francesco Saverio, 661
Nixon, Richard M., 790; Vietnam and, 868; China and,
   868–869
Nizam-ul-Mulk, 546
Nkrumah, Kwame, 780, 881, 890; Ghanaian
   independence and, 871, 876, 878–880, 892
Nobunaga, Oda, 241
Normandy invasion, World War II, 758
Normans, settlement of, in France, 208, 247; conquest
   of Sicily and southern Italy by, 247
North Africa, see Maghreb
North America, British and French colonies in,
   341–343; French and Indian War, 343–345; British
   rule of, 346
North Atlantic Treaty Organization (NATO), 785
Northwest Ordinance, 399
Norway, ninth-century natives of, 207; split from
   Sweden (1905), 469; in Great Depression, 689
Núñez, Rafael, 527
Nuqrashi, Egyptian prime minister, 889

Philip IV, the Fair (France), 261–262, 274, 275, 277, 278
Philip V (France), 278, 338
Philippines, 501; in post-World War II era, 848
Philips, Wendell, 487
Philistines, 41
Philo Judaeus, 160
Philosophes (Enlightenment), 381–385, 428
Phoenicians, 34, 43, 141, 605
Phuniphom, Thai king, 848
Physics, in late nineteenth century, 460
Physiocrats, 384
Picot, M. Georges, 641
Piedmont-Sardinia, kingdom of, 419, 445, 447
Piérola, Nicolás, 529
Pilnyak, Boris, 701
Pilsudski, Josef, 656, 661
Pisa, Council of, 276
Pisastratus, 113, 114, 127
Pitt, William, 397
Pius II, Pope, 288
Pius VI, Pope, 409
Pius, IX, Pope, 466
Plassey, Battle of, 347, 364, 549
Plataea, Battle of, 115, 116
Plato, 123, 124–125, 199; in Christian theology, 160–161, 162, 169, 170, 173, 270, 289
Platt Amendment (1901), 818
Plebeians, 142–144
Pleistocene epoch, 9
Plekhanov, George, 468
Plotinus, 162, 163, 289
Plutarch, 156
Po-Chu-i, poet, 228
Poincaré, Raymond, 684
Poitier, Battle of, 279
Poland, 202; German domination of, in Middle Ages, 249–250; Polish-Lithuanian state (from 1386), 283; partitions of (eighteenth century), 360–361, 362; "Congress Poland" (1815), 419; nineteenth-century revolts in, 432; reconstruction of, after World War I, 653, 661; World War II and, 750, 751, 759, 768; resistance movement, 770; postwar settlement and, 774; revolt against USSR (1956), 803–804
Polis (Greek city-state), 107–108, 119–120, 122–127, 132, 135–136, 138
Pompey, 149, 150
Popes, *see* Papacy
Popular Front (France), 684
Population, world, growth of, 13–14; European (to 1650), 322; French (eighteenth century), 404; Latin America (nineteenth century), 536; China (to nineteenth century), 555; twentieth-century, in western industrial nations, 676; China (twentieth century), 845; India (in 1960s), 854
Populism (U.S.), 499, 500, 503
Portáles, Diego, 532
Portugal, 280, 282; early trade of, with India, 219, 548; contact of, with Japan (sixteenth century), 240; exploration by (sixteenth century), 318; South American conquests by, 69; union with Spain, 327; colonies in South America, political rule of, 511–514; colonial economics, 516–518; colonial independence and, 519–521; China trade of, 558; African decolonization and, 883–884
Poseidon, 106, 122
Positivism, philosophy of, 533
Potsdam Conference, 774
Pragmatic Sanction, 351, 358

Praphas, General (Thai leader), 848
Prehistory, 9–14
Presbyterianism, 313
Primo de Rivera, General Miguel, 720
Printing, development of, 308; in China, 228; in Enlightenment, 365; newspaper mass printing (late nineteenth century), 456–457
Progressivism (U.S.), 503–504
Protective tariffs, nineteenth-century Europe and, 438, 455
Protectorates, 536, 812
Protestantism, early doctrine of, 170; ethic of, in U.S., 481–482
Protestant movement, *see* Calvinism; Lutheranism; Reformation
Proudhon, Pierre-Joseph, 439, 440, 460
Provisional Government (Russia), 647, 650
Prussia, rise of (under Great Elector), 351–353; under Frederick William I, 353–354; under Frederick the Great, 354, 403; during Napoleonic era, 417–419; German reunification struggle and, 446, 448; under Bismarck, 458–459, 463–464; *see also* Germany
Ptolemaic dynasty, 133, 134, 137
Ptolemy (ruler of Egypt), 133
Ptolemy (astronomer), 138, 156, 199, 368, 369
Pueblos (Indians), 65
Puerto Rico, 501; in twentieth century, 822–823
Pugachev, Emilian, 358, 360
Punic Wars, 145
Pure Land sects (Buddhism), 238
Puritans, in England, 312, 313, 375; revolution of, under Cromwell, 391, 392
Pushkin, Alexander, 428
Pythagoras, 121
Pythagorean school, 121–122, 125, 126
Pythermus, 109

Quadros, Jâmo, Brazilian president, 835
Quadruple Alliance (Britain, Russia, Prussia, Austria), 430
Quebec Act (1774), 346, 395
Quetzalcoatl (Aztec deity), 66, 67, 68
Quito (Indians), 69

Ra, 28
Rabelais, François, 307, 309
Race, U.S. civil rights movement and, 787–789; racism, 461
Racine, Jean, 337
Radicalism, 420, 457
"Radicals" (in U.S. Civil War), 492, 493–494
Raffles, Sir Stamford, 591
Rahman, Sheikh Mujibir, Pakistani leader, 856
Railroads, 435, 483, 493, 508
Rajput (northern Indian) states, Islamic invasions of, 215–217
Raleigh, Sir Walter, 315
Ramakrishna, Shri, 583
Ramayana, 51
Ram Mohan Roy, 582, 584
Raphael, 305, 306
Rasputin, Gregory, 645
Rathenau, Walter, 642
Razin, Stenka, 356
Reed, John, 649, 650n
Reformation, 275, 301, 309–315; Lutheranism in Germany, 309–312; in England, under Henry VIII, 312; Calvinism, 312–313; Presbyterians (John Knox), 313; Puritans, 312, 313; Anabaptists, 313–314;

Counter-Reformation (Catholic) and, 314–315
Rembrandt, 307, 374
Renaissance, 287, 288–289, 301–309, 391; humanism
    and, 302–304, 306, 307; art and architecture in,
    304–306; new political thought in, 306–307;
    printing and, 307–309
Republican party (U.S.), 490, 493, 499
Republic of Vietnam (South Vietnam), war and,
    864–865
Restoration, England, 392–393
Revels, Hiram, 494
Revolution of 1905 (Russia), 468
Revolutions of 1848, 459; in France, 443, 445; in
    Austria and Prussia, 445–447
Reyes, Rafael, 527, 823
Reynaud, Paul, 751
Reza Khan, Iranian ruler, 732
Rhee, Syngman, 850
Rhodes, Cecil, 470, 624
Rhodesia, 613; independence of, and white rule, 883
Ricardo, David, 438–439
Ricci, Matteo, 233
Richard II (England), 277, 278
Richards, Frank, 638
Richard the Lion-Hearted, 248
Richelieu, Cardinal, 336
Riel, Louis, 507
Rigveda, 49, 50
Ripon, Lord, in India, 582, 583
Rivadavia, Bernardino, 523
Robespierre, Maximilien, 409, 410, 411
Rockefeller, John D., 496
Roger the Great (Norman), 247
Rojas Pinilla, Gustavo, 825, 826
Roman civilization, 303, 305; political organization in,
    141, 143, 144; beginnings of, 142; republic,
    142–149; legal system of, 143, 147, 157, 185; rise of
    Plebeians (to 287 B.C.), 142–144; conquests,
    144–145; Punic Wars, 145, 146; Hellenistic
    influences on, 146–147; equestrian class and, 147,
    148; violent revolutionary era (133–30 B.C.),
    147–149; under Julius Caesar, 149–150; Augustan
    age, 151–153; Silver Age (to 180 A.D.), 153–156;
    religion in, 157–158, 183–184; Christianity and,
    162–163, 167–168; chaotic period (third century
    A.D.), 163–165, 171; Diocletian reforms, 165–166;
    under Constantine, 166–168; decline of (to 476
    A.D.), 170–173; barbarian invasions, 164, 165,
    172–173; Germanic rulers of, 173–174, 200–201
Roman Empire, under Augustus, 151–153; height of (31
    B.C. to A.D. 180), 153–156; imperial succession
    problem and, 154, 163; chaotic era (third century),
    163–165; Diocletian and division of Empire,
    165–166; Constantine and Christian ascendancy,
    166–168; barbarian invasions of, 164, 165,
    172–173; decline of, 170-173; Germanic rule of,
    173–174, 200–201; *see also* Roman civilization
Romanov dynasty, 354
"Roman Peace," 151, 155, 158
Romanticism, in Europe, 427–429
Rome, sack of, 387 B.C., 144; 410 A.D., 172
Roosevelt, Franklin D., 790; World War II and,
    754–756, 766, 772, 871; Allied diplomacy and,
    772–774
Roosevelt, Theodore, 503–504; Latin America and,
    525, 816
Rosas, Juan Manuel de, 529, 530, 535
Roundheads, 392

Rousseau, Jean-Jacques, 385–387, 388, 428, 709
Rudolph of Hapsburg, 256
Rumania, 660, 661, 787
Rusk, Dean, 861
Russia, 3, 250; Kievan period and Byzantine Empire,
    189; Mongol domination of, 251–252; Muscovite
    Principality during Tatar domination (fifteenth
    century), 283–284; backward condition (during
    seventeenth century), 354–355; under Peter the
    Great, 355–357; under Catherine the Great, 357–358;
    Seven Years' War and Russian Empire, 360–362;
    Napoleonic wars and, 416–417, 419; modernization
    and serf emancipation (Alexander II), 449–451;
    Crimean Wars and, 449, 450; Russo-Japanese War,
    598–599; political repression under Alexander II and
    Alexander III, 466–467; Nicholas II and
    revolutionary parties, 467–468; World War I and,
    472–476, 638–641, 645, 651–652; Revolution of
    1917, 646–650. *See also* Russian Revolution of 1917;
    Soviet Union
Russian Orthodox Church, 355, 357
Russian Revolution of 1917, 646–650; background of,
    467–468, 645–646; Provisional Government under
    Kerensky, 647–650; Bolshevik triumph, 649–650;
    aftermath (1917–1920), 655–657, 659
Russian serfs, 355–356
Russo-Japanese War, 598–599

Sabuktegin, 216
Sacco and Vanzetti, case of, 685
Sadat, Anwar, Egyptian ruler, 892
Said, Egyptian ruler, 619
Saigo, Takamori, 586, 588
Saikaku, 568
Saint-Simon, Duke de, 337, 439, 440
Saladin, 251
Salafis, North African religious movement, 876
Salamis, Battle of, 115, 116
Salisbury, Lord, 623
Sallust, 146
Salutati, Coluccio, 303
Samoa, 501
Samsara, 51
Samuel, 41
Samurai, 237, 240, 586, 588; urbanization of, in
    Tokugawa regime, 565, 568–569
Sangh, Jan, Indian leader, 853
San Martín, José de, 521
Santa Anna, Antonio López de, 524, 535
Santander, Francisco de Paula, 521, 527
Sappho, 120–121
Saracens, invasions by, 206–207
Saraswati, Dayanand, 583
Sargon, 21–22, 43
Sarmiento, Domingo F., 531
Sassanid dynasty (Persian Empire), 164, 181
Saul, 41
Saxons, 203
Sayyid Ahmad Khan, 583
Scharnhorst, Gerhard von, 417
Schleswig-Holstein, 447
Schlieffen, Alfred von, 635
Schliemann, Heinrich, 103
Schmalkaldic League, 311
Schreiber, Jean-Jacques, 796
Science, late-nineteenth-century developments,
    460–462
Scientific revolution, during Enlightenment, 368–374;